The Palgrave Handbook of Service Management

Bo Edvardsson • Bård Tronvoll
Editors

The Palgrave Handbook of Service Management

palgrave
macmillan

Editors
Bo Edvardsson
CTF, Service Research Center
Karlstad University
Karlstad, Sweden

Bård Tronvoll
CTF, Service Research Center
Karlstad University
Karlstad, Sweden

Inland Norway University of Applied Sciences
Elverum, Norway

ISBN 978-3-030-91827-9   ISBN 978-3-030-91828-6   (eBook)
https://doi.org/10.1007/978-3-030-91828-6

© The Editor(s) (if applicable) and The Author(s), under exclusive licence to Springer Nature Switzerland AG 2022
This work is subject to copyright. All rights are solely and exclusively licensed by the Publisher, whether the whole or part of the material is concerned, specifically the rights of translation, reprinting, reuse of illustrations, recitation, broadcasting, reproduction on microfilms or in any other physical way, and transmission or information storage and retrieval, electronic adaptation, computer software, or by similar or dissimilar methodology now known or hereafter developed.
The use of general descriptive names, registered names, trademarks, service marks, etc. in this publication does not imply, even in the absence of a specific statement, that such names are exempt from the relevant protective laws and regulations and therefore free for general use.
The publisher, the authors and the editors are safe to assume that the advice and information in this book are believed to be true and accurate at the date of publication. Neither the publisher nor the authors or the editors give a warranty, expressed or implied, with respect to the material contained herein or for any errors or omissions that may have been made. The publisher remains neutral with regard to jurisdictional claims in published maps and institutional affiliations.

This Palgrave Macmillan imprint is published by the registered company Springer Nature Switzerland AG.
The registered company address is: Gewerbestrasse 11, 6330 Cham, Switzerland

Acknowledgements

We are immensely grateful to all the authors contributing to the Handbook of Service Management. Without their research, knowledge, and insights on specific topics, this handbook with a state-of-the art overview would not exist.

We also want to express our gratitude to CTF – Service Research Center at Karlstad University for supporting the work and publication of this handbook. We are especially grateful for the support from Britt-Marie Shandrew at CTF. Her professional support and work on coordinating the work and contacts with authors have been vital for us during initiating and finalizing the handbook.

Finally but not least, we would like to thank the staff at Palgrave Macmillan for their guidance, suggestions, and hands-on help in making this handbook possible.

Karlstad in May 2022

Bo Edvardsson
Bård Tronvoll

Praise for *The Palgrave Handbook of Service Management*

"The Handbook of Service Management is a comprehensive collection of state-of-the-art knowledge from the vast field of service management. Bo Edvardsson and Bård Tronvoll have done a huge job to knit together important aspects of the field covering everything from strategic issues, service quality and value creation to innovation and design, technology and digitalization. This handbook offers valuable reading for persons new to the field and equally much to person who want to familiarize themselves with any of its subfields. The handbook nicely reflects current research. It can be recommended as both an introduction to service management and source of inspiration for further research."

—Christian Grönroos, Professor Emeritus, *Hanken School of Economics, Helsinki Finland*

"We read some books but then never return to them. We buy other books but never get around to reading them. The Handbook of Service Management is a book that academics who study service management and managers who work in service management will use again and again and again. It is a "KEEPER" book, an impressive compilation of virtually all topics relevant to service management today, from customer experience with human providers to customer experience with robots, from service design to service recovery. Service scholars from throughout the world review existing literatures while introducing many new ideas in this ultimate reference volume. Whether you seek an introduction to a specific topic—or a refresh—the Handbook of Service Management should be on your book shelf, ready for you when you need it."

—Leonard Berry, *University Distinguished Professor of Marketing and M.B. Zale Chair in Retailing and Marketing Leadership, Regents Professor Mays Business School, Texas A&M University, USA*

"The Service Management Handbook edited by Edvardsson and Tronvoll promises to be an important base of service knowledge for scholars and managers in services going forward. It is a comprehensive and up-to-date volume covering important topics in service management, organized into six highly relevant and current themes. The authors of the forty-eight chapters are respected experts in service research representing all relevant disciplines and a diversity of countries and cultures. The Service Management Handbook should be required reading and an essential reference for all serious scholars and progressive managers in the service field. Bravo!"

—Mary Jo Bitner, *Emeritus Professor of Marketing and former Director of the Center for Services Leadership, W. P. Carey School of Business, Arizona State University, USA*

"I greatly enjoyed reading the Handbook of Service Management. It made me see the field of service management from a fresh perspective, and truly excited me about the future of this rapidly advancing field. Is there a golden age of service coming? Let's all hope so—and the seeds of the theories required are well surveyed in this timely book. In a rapidly changing and interconnected world of service systems that we all depend on for our lives and livelihoods, especially in these pandemic times, Edvardsson and Tronvoll have masterfully orchestrated the top interdisciplinary thought-leaders across industries and cultures to share their deep insights about the global service ecosystem and the competencies that leaders should invest in learning to create successful outcomes. I also recommend this book as an outstanding introduction for those starting their service journey—whether they are coming from a management, engineering, technology, social sciences, design and arts, or public policy perspective. For industry and societal leaders as well as experienced service researchers and newcomers to the field, the Handbook of Service Management is a highly recommended read about a fast changing field where the most valued outcomes are on the verge of becoming our co-created reality."

—Jim Spohrer, PhD and Director, *Cognitive Opentech Group (COG),*
IBM Research Almaden, USA

"This book symbolizes the maturity of Service Management and its unifying role in the field of business. A unique treasure, this book provides a holistic perspective of the latest knowledge in service research and practice from a variety of scholars and leaders across the globe. While presenting readers with a bird's—eye view of the field, it simultaneously offers an in-depth examination of nascent knowledge in 'service'. Given the unifying role of 'service' in the marketplace, this book should be a must read for all scholars in the field of business."

—Jay Kandampully, *Professor of Service Management in the*
Department of Human Sciences and Editor in chief Journal of
Service Management, Ohio State University, USA

"Bo Edvardsson was one of the pioneers of service research, and his Center at Karlstad University has played a central role in the field's development. The new Handbook of Service Management (co-edited with Nordic colleague Bård Tronvoll), provides a grand tour of some of the main areas of service research, with the help of a stellar author list, including such well-known service researchers as David Bowen, Rod Brodie, Ben Schneider, Steve Vargo and Jochen Wirtz."

—Roland T. Rust, *Distinguished University Professor and David Bruce Smith*
Chair in Marketing, Executive Director, University of Maryland's
Center for Excellence in Service, USA

"A must-have book for those who want to gain a deeper understanding of the fundamentals of service management and its recent evolution and application. The authors have involved the world's best researchers, offering a comprehensive, extraordinary and innovative systematization of the discipline, with a modern, interdisciplinary and intercultural interpretation. The reading is also enriched by the discussion of very stimulating cases and best practices. Thank you, Bo and Bard, for this enjoyable, effective and extremely useful work!."

—Alberto Pastore, *Professor of Management, Sapienza Università di Roma. Founder and former President of the Italian Society of Management (SIMA), Italy*

"The business environment is an increasingly complex system of stakeholders, technologies, and institutions, and all these elements are changing rapidly. The key to success in such an environment is to generate deep understanding of how each stakeholder generates value-in-use in their life-or workflow. The Handbook of Service Management is an excellent guide for this, as it allows leading scholars globally to cover various aspects of this new reality. By taking a multi-disciplinary approach, building on a wide theoretical base, it provides a "smorgasbord" of perspectives that also builds bridges between theory and practice"

—Kaj Storbacka, Hanken Foundation Professor, *Hanken School of Economics, Helsinki Finland*

"The world needs to understand that service management is not just managing a set of activities and tasks, nor just managing an ecosystem of actors, structures and behaviours, but managing the logic that makes a system exist and continues to be viable. That logic encompasses many facets and Professors Edvardsson and Tronvoll have accomplished the challenging task of bringing together world leading scholars to advance that logic in a coherent way for scholars and practitioners. Thank you and Congratulations!"

—Irene Ng, *Professor of Marketing and Service Systems and the Director of the International Institute for Product and Service Innovation at WMG, University of Warwick, UK*

"There is currently much discussion about the contribution of services to value creation and employment in the future. Without a doubt, services are already the economic backbone in many countries in terms of added value and employment. And if we think of our societal and ecological challenges ahead, as well as the potential of digitization, completely new service-oriented or interactive models of value creation will be developed in the future.

What service research can contribute to service-oriented value creation becomes impressively clear in the new "Handbook of Service Management" by Bo Edvardsson and Bård Tronvoll. In their new manual, current research results on 6 central service topics are presented in 48 articles, which in particular show the exciting further development of these topics.

In summary, it can be said that the new manual has put together contributions from many high-ranking experts who present new research results and practices on service management from different disciplinary perspectives. A very inspiring read."

—Walter Ganz, Managing Director, *Fraunhofer Institute for Industrial Engineering IAO, Stuttgart Germany*

Contents

Part I	**Perspectives on Service Management**	1

Overview of the Book   3
Bo Edvardsson and Bård Tronvoll

Defining and Framing Service Management   19
Bård Tronvoll and Bo Edvardsson

Service Management: Evolution, Current Challenges, and Opportunities   35
Bo Edvardsson and Bård Tronvoll

Service Management: Scope, Challenges, and Future Developments   53
Michael Kleinaltenkamp

Is Service Management Experiencing a Change of Era?   71
Jaqueline Pels and Cristina Mele

Service-Dominant Logic and Service Management 4.0   85
Julia A. Fehrer and Stephen L. Vargo

Adapting Service Management for the Sharing Economy   107
Sabine Benoit

xii   Contents

Part II   Service Strategy   127

Service Management Strategic Mindsets: That Create Positive Customer and Employee Experiences   129
David E. Bowen and Benjamin Schneider

Service Strategizing—Shaping Service in Dynamic Contexts   151
Tore Strandvik, Maria Holmlund-Rytkönen, and Ilkka Lähteenmäki

Servitization: A State-of-the-Art Overview and Future Directions   169
Wolfgang Ulaga and Christian Kowalkowski

Servitization and the Necessity of Becoming Ambidextrous: A 12-Year Longitudinal Study   201
Peter R. Magnusson and JanErik Odhe

How Contemporary Scholarship Addresses Service Management Practices   223
Robert C. Ford and David Solnet

Contract Innovation: Driving Scale and Scope of Nonownership Value Propositions—Chapter Description   247
Michael Ehret and Jochen Wirtz

Managing the Exclusivity of Luxury Service Experiences   263
Jonas Holmqvist, Jochen Wirtz, and Martin P. Fritze

The Transformative Role of Resource Integration in Shaping a New Service Ecosystem   277
Maria Colurcio, Angela Caridà, and Monia Melia

Behavior Change: Five Ways to Facilitate Co-creation of Service for a Better World   303
Per Kristensson, Jonas Hjalmar Blom, and Erik Wästlund

Contents   xiii

Part III   Service Leadership and Transition   315

Self-Leadership and Empowerment: Lessons from Service Firms   317
Soumaya Ben Letaifa and Jean-Yves Mercier

Organizational Communication in Service Management   335
Larry Davis Browning, Jan-Oddvar Sørnes, and Peer Jacob Svenkerud

Culture-Powered Service Excellence and Leadership: Chinese Characteristics   353
Xiucheng Fan, Tianran Wang, and Shiyi Lu

Toward Socially Responsible Business: A Typology of Value Postures in Nested Service Ecosystems   371
Jonathan J. Baker, Vicki J. Little, and Roderick J. Brodie

Customer-Centric Service Ecosystem for Emerging Markets   393
Varsha Jain, Anupama Ambika, and Jagdish N. Sheth

Service Management for Sustainable Business Transformation   411
Bo Enquist and Samuel Petros Sebhatu

Transformative Service Research: Where We Are and Moving Forward at the Collective Level   437
Laurel Anderson and Ying Xue

Service Design for Systemic Change in Legacy Organizations: A Bottom-Up Approach to Redesign   457
Ingo O. Karpen, Josina Vink, and Jakob Trischler

Part IV   Service Design and Innovation   481

Service Design: Innovation for Complex Systems   483
Birgit Mager and Nick de Leon

The Multiple Identities of Service Design in Organizations and Innovation Projects   497
Daniela Sangiorgi, Stefan Holmlid, and Lia Patricio

xiv Contents

Tracing the Systems Turn in Service Design and Innovation: Convergence Toward Service System Transformation 531
Kaisa Koskela-Huotari and Josina Vink

Service Innovation in Networks: Co-creating a Network Business Model 555
Kars Mennens, Dominik Mahr, Paul C. van Fenema, Tom Schiefer, and Adriana Saraceni

Beyond the Line of Visibility: Toward Sustainable Service Innovation 577
Lars Witell, Per Carlborg, and Hannah Snyder

Managing Employee Empowerment and Engagement to Foster Service Innovation 595
Jon Sundbo and Lars Fuglsang

Understanding Key Market Challenges Through Service Innovation 613
Bo Edvardsson, Bård Tronvoll, and Lars Witell

Customer-to-Customer Interactions in Service 629
Kristina Heinonen and Richard Nicholls

Understanding and Managing Customer Experiences 655
Elina Jaakkola, Larissa Becker, and Ekaterina Panina

How Customers' Resources Influence Their Co-creation Experience 677
Helena Alves and Cátia Jesus

Measuring and Managing Customer Experience (CX): What Works and What Doesn't 729
Janet R. McColl-Kennedy and Mohamed Zaki

Improving Service Quality Through Individuals' Satisfaction. Evidence from the Healthcare Sector 745
Roberta Guglielmetti Mugion, Maria Francesca Renzi, and Laura Di Pietro

Contents   **xv**

Service Productivities' Next Top-Models   773
Christiane Hipp and Silvia Gliem

Effective Service Operations Management: Aligning Priorities in Healthcare Operations with Customer Preferences   801
Lu Kong, Hessam Sadatsafavi, and Rohit Verma

Service Failure and Complaints Management: An Overview   823
Chiara Orsingher, Arne De Keyser, Dorottya Varga, and Yves Van Vaerenbergh

Part V   Service Interaction, Quality and Operation   847

Expanding the Scope of Service Recovery   849
Bård Tronvoll

Technology in Service   869
Anastasia Nanni and Andrea Ordanini

Smart Technologies in Service Provision and Experience   887
Cristina Mele, Tiziana Russo Spena, and Valtteri Kaartemo

Rapport-Building Opportunities and Challenges in Technology-Infused Service Encounters   907
Sijun Wang and Dwayne D. Gremler

Part VI   Service Technology   925

Artificial Intelligence and Decision-Making: Human–Machine Interactions for Successful Value Co-creation   927
Francesco Polese, Sergio Barile, and Debora Sarno

Managing Artificial Intelligence Systems for Value Co-creation: The Case of Conversational Agents and Natural Language Assistants   945
Tom Lewandowski, Christian Grotherr, and Tilo Böhmann

xvi Contents

Servitization and Digitalization as "Siamese Twins": Concepts and Research Priorities 967
Gerhard Satzger, Carina Benz, Tilo Böhmann, and Angela Roth

Toward a New Service Reality: Human–Robot Collaboration at the Service Frontline 991
Werner H. Kunz, Stefanie Paluch, and Jochen Wirtz

Index 1009

Notes on Contributors

Helena Alves is Associate Professor of Marketing in the Business and Economics Department and researcher at NECE, University of Beira Interior, Portugal. Her areas of expertise include customer satisfaction, services marketing, tourism marketing, and public and nonprofit marketing. She has authored and co-authored several articles and book chapters on these themes. For some years she was coordinator of the marketing degree and later of the Masters degree. She is the editor of the *International Review on Public and Nonprofit Marketing*, and is also on the editorial review boards of several journals.

Anupama Ambika is an FPM (Fellow Program in Management) scholar at the MICA, Ahmedabad (India). Her research interests are at the intersection of technology and consumer behavior, with publications in leading journals like the *European Journal of Marketing* and *Journal of Consumer Behavior*. Anupama is a Project Management Institute-certified project manager with a management degree specializing in Marketing. She has more than ten years of industry experience in marketing and management with leading organizations, including IBM and Capgemini.

Laurel Anderson is an associate professor of Marketing at Arizona State University and Research Faculty at ASU's Center for Services Leadership. Her expertise is in cultures, service, and wellbeing. She introduced the area of Transformative Service Research (TSR), which focuses on individual, collective, and societal wellbeing. Her research has appeared in the *Journal of Consumer Research*, the *Journal of Service Research*, the *Journal of Public Policy and Marketing*, and the *Journal of Business Research*, among others. She is an associate editor and Special Issue editor for the *Journal of Service Research* and on the Editorial Review Board of the *Journal of Public Policy and Marketing*.

xvii

Notes on Contributors

Jonathan J. Baker is a senior lecturer in the Department of International Business, Strategy & Entrepreneurship at Auckland University of Technology, New Zealand. His primary expertise is in market-shaping, informed by interdisciplinary research interests in marketing, strategy, and social impact. His research is published in *Industrial Marketing Management*, the *Journal of Business Research*, the *Journal of Business & Industrial Marketing*, the *Journal of Service Management*, and *Marketing Theory*.

Sergio Barile is a full professor of Management at Sapienza University of Rome, where he leads the Management Department and is the coordinator of the PhD on Management, Banking and Commodities Science. His main research fields are the Viable Systems Approach, complex systems, strategic management, management of innovation, and knowledge management. He is the author of many international and national scientific publications and he is principal investigator of several public and privately funded projects.

Larissa Becker is a postdoctoral research fellow in Marketing at Tampere University (Finland) and an assistant professor in the Postgraduate Program of Management at IMED (Brazil). She received a doctoral degree from the University of Turku (Finland) in 2020. Her main research interests are customer experience, customer journeys, consumer journeys, service-dominant logic, and practice theory. She has published in journals such as the *Journal of the Academy of Marketing Science*, the *Journal of Service Management*, and *Qualitative Market Research: An International Journal*.

Sabine Benoit is a professor of Marketing in the Department of Marketing and Retail Management at Surrey Business School (SBS) at the College of Business & Economics (CBE) at Australian National University (ANU) in Canberra. Her main research fields are service and retail marketing, in particular convenience retailing and the sharing economy. Her work has been published in leading international journals such as the *Journal of Marketing*, the *Journal of Service Research*, the *Journal of Operations Management*, and *Psychology & Marketing*. She has received various best paper awards for her research and is on the editorial review boards of all major service journals.

Carina Benz is a research associate at the Karlsruhe Service Research Institute (KSRI) and the Institute of Information Systems and Marketing (IISM) at the Karlsruhe Institute of Technology (KIT). Her research investigates the design of digital ecosystems and co-creation platforms emphasizing a human-centric perspective. Before joining the KSRI, she graduated from KIT with a Masters degree in Industrial Engineering and Management.

Jonas Hjalmar Blom is a licensed psychologist and PhD student in psychology at Service Research Center, CTF, at Karlstad University. His research focuses on long-term behavior change with the help of digital services.

Tilo Böhmann is head of the IT Management and Consulting research group at the University of Hamburg. His research areas include service systems engineering and IT management as well as innovative, digital services and their service business models. In 2010, he was a visiting professor at the Service Research Center (CTF) at the University of Karlstad (Sweden).

David E. Bowen is Faculty Emeritus and Former Chief Academic Officer, Thunderbird School of Global Management, and a member of the Distinguished Global Faculty Network, Center for Services Leadership, Arizona State University. His service research has focused on employee and organizational behavior issues in services management. He has received the Christopher Lovelock Career Contributions to the Services Discipline Award; an Article of the Year Award from the *Journal of Service Research*; and the *Academy of Management Review* "Decade Award Article". His books include the *Advances in Services Marketing and Management* series and *Winning the Service Game.*

Roderick J. Brodie is Professor Emeritus at The University of Auckland Business School. He is a leading international scholar in the areas of Service Relationships, Branding, and Customer Engagement. He has authored over 120 articles, many of which have appeared in leading international journals including the *Journal of Marketing*, the *Journal of Marketing Research*, *International Journal of Research in Marketing*, *Management Science*, and the *Journal of Service Research*. He is an associate editor of the *Journal of Service Research* and former associate editor of *Marketing Theory.*

Larry Davis Browning, PhD, The Ohio State University, Professor Emeritus, William P. Hobby Centennial Professor of Communication, Department of Communication Studies, University of Texas at Austin, Moody College of Communication and Adjunct Professor of Management, Nord University Business School, Bodø, Norway.

Angela Caridà is Assistant Professor of Business Management at the University Magna Græcia of Catanzaro, Italy. She is a member of several international research networks. Her research interests are in service management and focus specifically on the area of value creation through service and service-dominant logic, service innovation, social innovation, and digital transformation. She has published on these topics in several leading journals including *Marketing Theory*. She received the Outstanding Paper Award 2013 from the Emerald Literati Network.

xx Notes on Contributors

Per Carlborg is an assistant professor at Örebro University School of Business. His research interests cover service innovation, sustainability, and circular economy. He also conducts research on business model innovation in business markets. Per has published in journals such as the *Journal of Business and Industrial Marketing*, *Service Industries Journal*, and *Industrial Marketing Management*.

Maria Colurcio, PhD, is a full professor of Business Management at University Magna Græcia of Catanzaro, Italy, where she coordinates the research group of Service Management. Her area of expertise is innovation and in recent years she has focused on value co-creation with an emphasis on RI. She is Principal Investigator for many international research projects on innovation.Maria is an associate editor of SIJM and a board member of the Pearson book series. She is the author of more than 150 publications, many of them in high-impact journals, and has received many international awards for her research work.

Bo Edvardsson is a professor and founder of CTF, Service Research Center at Karlstad University, Sweden, and a visiting professor at Inland Norway University of Applied Sciences. Bo is the former editor of the *Journal of Service Management*. His research includes the logic of service, new service development and innovation, customer experience, complaint management, service ecosystems, and transition from product to service in manufacturing. Bo is on the review board for several scholarly journals including the *Journal of Service Research*, the *Journal of Service Management*, and *International Journal of Research in Marketing*. He is often invited to give keynote presentations research conferences and participate in leadership development programs. His research impact in August 2021 shows 20,800 Google Scholar citations. In 2008, he received the European Association for REsearch on SERvices (RESER) Award "Commendation for lifetime achievement to scholarship" by The European Association for Service Research and in 2004 The AMA Career Contributions to the Services Discipline Award. In 2013 Bo was appointed Honorary Distinguished Professor of Service Management, EGADE Business School, Monterrey Tech, Mexico. In 2011 Bo was appointed International Fellow, Centre for Service Management at Loughborough University in the UK. In the same year he was also appointed Guest Professor of Service Management, EMBA Center, Nankai University China. Bo has been a visiting professor to several universities, such as Cornell University and Roma Tree University in 2019 and University of Hawaii in 2020. In 2009 Bo was awarded an Honarary Doctorate from the Swedish School of Economics and Business Administration, Hanken. In 2008 he was awarded for public service with a medal from the City of Karlstad. He is a member of the editorial staff of the following journals: *International Journal of Service Industry Management, Managing Service Quality, International Journal of Internet Marketing and Advertising, International Journal of Research in Marketing,* and the *Journal of Service Research.*

Michael Ehret is Professor of Marketing and Digitalization, University of Graz.His research focus is on service governance and contract innovation, and business model innovation, in particular in business markets and service systems.Previously, he held positions as Reader in Technology Management in the Division of Marketing at Nottingham Business School, Assistant Professor at Freie Universität Berlin, and Visiting Professor at Technical University Munich and Universität Rostock, Germany.. Michael publishes regularly in leading international journals, such as the *Journal of Marketing, Industrial Marketing Management,* and the *Journal of Business Research.* He is a member of editorial review boards of leading international journals such as the *Journal of Business Research, Industrial Marketing Management,* and *Service Science.* Michael also has experience in applied research and consultancy work with companies such as Mercedes Benz, BioCity Nottingham, Roland Berger Strategy Consultants, and Springer Publishing.

Bo Enquist, PhD, has been Professor of Business Administration since 2010 and a research fellow at the Service Research Centre (CTF) at Karlstad University. He has worked since April 2017 for missions on implementing PRME at Karlstad Business School. He was a member of the executive team and the Deputy Director of the Vinn Excellent Center, Service and Market Oriented Transport Research Group (SAMOT) between 2006 and 2017. He worked for more than 20 years in different businesses at management and executive levels.His research interests are focused on value-based service, business based on service logic, and social and environmental challenges to transformation. He is working on Transformation (Transformative Change) and Innovation in relation to multi-stakeholder dialogue and Agenda2030 – Sustainable Developmental Goals (SDGs).

Xiucheng Fan is Professor of Marketing and the Director of the Center for Service Marketing and Management at School of Management, Fudan University, Shanghai, China. His research interests include service marketing, relationship marketing, and brand management. His work has appeared in the *Journal of Consumer Research,* the *Journal of the Academy of Marketing Science,* the *Journal of Service Research,* the *Journal of Service Management,* and the *Journal of Business Research,* among others. He is the editor-in-chief of the *Journal of Contemporary Marketing Science.*

xxii   Notes on Contributors

Julia A. Fehrer is a Senior Lecturer in Digital Marketing at The University of Auckland Business School (New Zealand) and Research Fellow at the University of Bayreuth (Germany). Her research is positioned at the interface of digital marketing, service management, and innovation and includes digital business models, customer and peer-to-peer engagement, market shaping, and systems innovation. Her research has been published in journals such as the *Journal of Service Research, Industrial Marketing Management*, the *Journal of Business Research*, and the *Journal of Service Management*. She has 12 years of professional experience with senior positions in strategic marketing in the insurance industry.

Paul C. van Fenema (PhD Rotterdam School of Management) is a professor of Military Logistics at Netherlands Defence Academy. His research focuses on practice-institutional change, dynamics of practice-value concepts, network value creation, and digital transformation. His research projects focus on military assets/logistics and public–private value chains. He has published in journals such as the *International Journal of Physical Distribution & Logistics Management, Industrial Marketing Management*, the *Scandinavian Journal of Management*, the *Journal of Organization Design*, the *International Journal of Management Reviews, Organization Science, MIS Quarterly*, and *Joint Forces Quarterly*. Previously he worked at Rotterdam School of Management and Florida International University.

Robert C. Ford, PhD, is Professor of Management Emeritus at the University of Central Florida. His teaching and research focus is on the management of hospitality and service organizations. Besides co-authoring several books, he has published over 100 refereed publications in both top research and practitioner journals. Bob has served the Academy of Management (AOM) as editor of The Academy of Management Executive and chaired two divisions of the Ethics Adjudication Committee. He has been active in the Southern Management Association (SMA) where he was president, awarded SMA's Distinguished Service Award, and elected a fellow.

Martin P. Fritze is Assistant Professor of Trade Fair Management and Marketing (endowed by Koelnmesse-Stiftung) at the University of Cologne, Germany.His research focuses on consumer behavior, services, and digital transformation. His work has been published in journals such as *International Journal of Research in Marketing* and the *Journal of Service Research*.

Lars Fuglsang is a professor at Roskilde University, Denmark. His research is on how institutional and organizational frameworks are created to deal with the impact of innovation, technology, and other forms of change on business, the public sector, and society. His research focuses on a practice-based understanding of the innovation process, that is, innovation seen as closely connected with practices and routines.

Silvia Gliem graduated in Business Administration and pursued her interest in service science as a research associate at the Chair of General Business Administration, Organization, and Corporate Governance at the Brandenburg University of Technology Cottbus-Senftenberg, Germany. She is finishing her PhD project in which she focuses on frontline employees' role in improving service productivity.

Dwayne D. Gremler, PhD, Arizona State University, holds the title of Distinguished Teaching Professor (of Marketing) at the Schmidthorst College of Business at Bowling Green State University. He has published in the *Journal of Marketing*, the *Journal of Service Research*, the *Journal of the Academy of Marketing Science*, the *Journal of Retailing*, and the *Journal of Service Management*. In 2014 he received the Christopher Lovelock Career Contributions Award from SERVSIG. Dwayne is a co-author (with Valarie Zeithaml and Mary Jo Bitner) of one of the leading service textbooks in the field, entitled *Services Marketing: Integrating Customer Focus Across the Firm*.

Christian Grotherr was a research associate in the Department of IT Management and Consulting until 2021. His research focuses on the design of service systems that are characterized by openness and learning. In various application domains, Christian has studied how these digital service systems, characterized by a high degree of engagement of external actors, can be designed and piloted and how scaling can be achieved.

Kristina Heinonen is Professor of Service and Relationship Marketing at Hanken School of Economics, Helsinki, Finland, and the director of the Centre for Relationship Marketing and Service Management (CERS) at Hanken. Her research expertise spanning over 20 years is in service marketing and management and particularly service innovation, business transformation, digitalization, value creation, and customer experience. She contributes extensively in various roles to the service research community and has authored more than 50 scientific articles and book chapters.

Christiane Hipp, Prof. Dr., became Full Professor for Organization and Corporate Governance in 2005 at the Brandenburg Technical University. She was acting president, vice president, and dean. Christiane received a diploma in industrial engineering and a PhD in economics. From 1995 until 1999

xxiv   Notes on Contributors

Christiane was research associate at the Fraunhofer Institute for Systems and Innovation Research, and from 1999 until 2005 she worked as a senior technology manager. She was a visiting scholar at the University of Manchester's Centre for Research on Innovation and Competition. Her areas of interest include service innovation and innovation strategies.

Stefan Holmlid is professor of Design at Linköping University. Since the early 2000s his research has resided in the meeting between design and service, as practices and research traditions. His contributions are founded in situated and distributed cognition, mediated action in complex adaptive systems, and contemporary developments in design research. He works with design as a transformational capability in heterogenic service organizations, such as municipalities and cross-sector healthcare networks. He also has a background in industry, as an entrepreneur, and as an cross-sectorial design consultant, and has a wide range of publications across design and service journals and conferences.

Maria Holmlund-Rytkönen is a professor of Marketing at Hanken School of Economics, Finland. Her research interests include service and customer-oriented management in business-to-business and business-to-consumer markets. She is an associate editor (service research) of the *Journal of Business Research*. Her publications have appeared in, for example, the *Journal of Business Research, Industrial Marketing Management*, the *Journal of Service Management, Business Horizons*, and *Marketing Theory*. More information on her can be found here: https://harisportal.hanken.fi/en/persons/maria-holmlund-rytk%C3%B6nen.

Jonas Holmqvist is Associate Professor of Luxury and Service Marketing, Kedge Business School, France. He holds a PhD in services marketing from Hanken School of Economics. His research focuses on consumer experiences and perceptions at the intersection of luxury and services, as well as on the influence of language and culture on service experiences. His work has been published in journals such as *International Journal of Research in Marketing*, the *Journal of Retailing*, and the *Journal of Service Research*.

Elina Jaakkola is a professor of Marketing at Turku School of Economics, University of Turku. Elina's research passion relates to value creation through service to create insights that enable service providers to become more customer-centric. Her projects focus on, for example, customer/actor engagement, customer experience and journeys, and service ecosystems. Her research has been published in the *Journal of the Academy of Marketing Science*, the *Journal of Product Innovation Management*, the *Journal of Service Research*,

Industrial Marketing Management, and the *Journal of Service Management*. She serves as an associate editor or editorial review board member at seven prominent journals and has received many awards for her scholarly activities.

Varsha Jain, PhD, is a professor of Integrated Marketing Communications and the Doctoral Program and research co-chairperson at the MICA, India. She has authored over 100 publications, including the *European Journal of Marketing, International Journal of Information Management,* and so on. Varsha is the recipient of more than 21 national and international awards and gold medals in scholarship. The recent awards include JCB Reviewer of the Year Award 2020, the *Journal of Consumer Behavior*, USA. In her research career, she is Visiting Guest at Emory Business School, Atlanta, USA, and Visiting Scholar and Guest at The Medill School, Northwestern University, USA.

Cátia Jesus is Guest Assistant and PhD student in Management in the Business and Economics Department, University of Beira Interior, Portugal.She has developed several studies in tourism and services marketing. Her main interests are customer satisfaction and customer behavior, especially in terms of their experience and co-creation of value.

Valtteri Kaartemo (DSc) is a postdoctoral researcher at Turku School of Economics, University of Turku, Finland. He is a co-author of several books, book chapters, conference papers, and peer-reviewed articles. His research interests include market shaping, service research, technology, innovation management, network dynamics, international entrepreneurship, business models, value co-creation, and various processes within and linking these phenomena. His research has been published in the *Journal of Business Research, Industrial Marketing Management* and the *Journal of Service Management*, among others.

Ingo O. Karpen is a full professor of Business and Design at CTF, Service Research Center, at Karlstad University, Sweden, and at Adelaide Business School, University of Adelaide, Australia. Ingo's interdisciplinary research revolves around designerly ways of thinking, working, and being, and how this enables organizations to better serve people and their (eco)systems. His research and education have been internationally awarded, and his publications have appeared in the *Journal of Service Research*, the *Journal of Product Innovation Management*, the *Journal of Travel Research*, the *Journal of Retailing*, and the *Journal of Business Research*, among others. Ingo has won prestigious grants for his ongoing work on service innovation and advancing societal wellbeing.

Arne De Keyser is Associate Professor of Marketing at EDHEC Business School (France). His research focuses on customer experience, service recovery, and frontline service technology. Arne has published articles in the *Journal of Service Research*, *International Journal of Research in Marketing*, the *Journal of Business Research*, and the *Journal of Service Management*, among others. He has won numerous research and teaching awards, including the SERVSIG Best Dissertation Award and the 2019 *Journal of Service Research* Best Paper Award. Arne serves on the editorial boards of the *Journal of Service Research*, the *Journal of Business Research*, and the *Journal of Service Management*.

Michael Kleinaltenkamp is a professor emeritus in the Marketing Department of Freie Universität Berlin (Germany) where he held the position as Professor of Business and Services Marketing from 1992 to 2020. In November 2013 he was awarded an honorary doctorate of the University of Rostock (Germany). His work focuses on business-to-business marketing, services marketing, and marketing theory. He has published in leading marketing journals like the *Journal of Marketing*, *Industrial Marketing Management*, the *Journal of Service Research*, the *Journal of Business Research*, *Marketing Theory*, the *Journal of Business and Industrial Marketing*, the *Journal of Service Management*, and the *Journal of Service Theory and Practice*.

Lu Kong is an assistant professor at the Muma College of Business at the University of South Florida. She received a PhD in operations management and a Masters degree in hospitality administration from Cornell University. She received a bachelor's degree in management from Tianjin University of Finance and Economics. Her research interests reside broadly in service operations. More specifically, Kong's research focuses on healthcare operations management, nursing home-related topics, and the interface of healthcare and hospitality.

Kaisa Koskela-Huotari is an assistant professor at Stockholm School of Economics. Kaisa's research interests lie at the intersection of service-dominant logic, institutional theory, and systems thinking. In her work, she uses these perspectives to learn more about change in social systems and inform the understandings of innovation, design, and market evolution. Her often conceptual work is published in the *Journal of Service Research*, the *Journal of Business Research*, and the *Journal of Service Management*, among others. Kaisa also serves as the assistant editor of the *AMS Review*, the only marketing journal that focuses exclusively on conceptual(-only) articles.

Christian Kowalkowski is a professor of Industrial Marketing at Linköping University and is affiliated with the Centre for Relationship Marketing and Service Management at Hanken School of Economics in Helsinki. Christian's research interests include service growth strategies, service innovation, and subscription business models. His work has been published in *Industrial Marketing Management*, the *Journal of Business Research*, and the *Journal of Service Research*, among others. He is the servitization editor for the *Journal of Service Management*, associate editor of the *Journal of Services Marketing*, advisory board member of *Industrial Marketing Management*, and editorial board member at the *Journal of Service Research* and the *Journal of Business Research*.

Per Kristensson is Professor of Psychology with a special interest in consumer psychology and innovation. He is also the director of Service Research Center, CTF, at Karlstad University. His research focuses on consumer behavior, service management, and the interface between users and organizations.

Werner H. Kunz is Professor of Marketing and Director of the digital media lab at the University of Massachusetts Boston. His research interests are in digital and social media, AI and service robots, innovation, and service marketing. His work has been published in the *Journal of Retailing*, *Tourism Management*, *International Journal of Research in Marketing*, *British Journal of Management*, the *Journal of Medical Internet Research*, the *Journal of Business Research*, the *Journal of Service Management*, and *Computational Statistics*, among others, and has been awarded multiple times. He is a board member of the Service Research Special Interest Group (SERVSIG) of the American Marketing Association (AMA), the primary professional association of service researchers with over 2000 community members worldwide.

Ilkka Lähteenmäki is a research fellow/adjunct professor at Aalto University, Department of Industrial Engineering and Management, Finland. He has long corporate experience in R&D of financial services. His research interests include financial business development, fintech evolution, data economy, and ESG. His publications have appeared in, for example, *Management & Organizational History*, the *Journal of Service Theory and Practice*, *International Journal of Bank Marketing*, and *Business Horizons*. More information on him can be found here: https://www.linkedin.com/in/ilkkalahteenmaki/.

Nick de Leon is Head of Knowledge Exchange and Partnerships at the Royal College of Art. He founded the Service Design Department at the Royal College of Art, which he led from 2012. The department is now recognized as the leading postgraduate program for Service Design in Europe with over 160

xxviii   Notes on Contributors

students undertaking Masters and PhD programs. He is a visiting professor at Liverpool Hope University, and is on the staff of London Business School. He has a PhD in Complex City Systems, a Masters degree from the Royal College of Art, and a BSc in Mechanical Engineering from Imperial College.

Soumaya Ben Letaifa has been an associate professor of Strategy at University of Quebec at Montreal (UQAM) since 2009. She has been teaching graduate and undergraduate courses in the fields of strategy, innovation, and international management in the Department of Strategy. Her research and teaching focus on emergent paradigms (strategic ecosystems, open innovation, service-dominant logic). She takes a special interest in grasping the complexity of contexts and closing the gap between research and practice. Thus, she works on connecting the macro, the meso, and the micro levels of the ecosystem perspective. CEO, Innova Conseil Director of Self-Leadership program in Africa and Canada.

Tom Lewandowski is a research associate in the Department of Informatics in the research group IT Management and Consulting at the University of Hamburg. His research focuses on the design and management of artificial intelligence systems in knowledge-intensive service systems.

Vicki J. Little is Senior Lecturer and Programme Manager Engagement at RMIT University Vietnam. She has also worked in Malaysia and New Zealand. Her research interests are marketing strategy, entrepreneurial marketing, sustainability, and innovation. She is a qualitative researcher, working in the life science and industrial contexts, with a particular interest in agri-food. More recently, she has responded to the climate emergency by embarking on a collegial program of reflective inquiry focusing on marketing education. Her work has appeared in journals including the *Journal of Macromarketing* and the *Journal of Business & Industrial Marketing*.

Shiyi Lu is a doctoral student at the School of Management, Fudan University, Shanghai, China. Her research interests include online marketing and sharing economy.

Birgit Mager, Professor of Service Design, TH-Köln, KISD, President, Service Design Network gGmbH, is Co-Founder and President of the International Service Design Network and editor-in-chief of *Touchpoint, the Journal of Service Design.*Since 1995 Birgit Mager has held the first European professorship on Service Design at the University of Applied Sciences Cologne, Germany, and has developed the field of Service Design constantly in theory, methodology, and practice. Her numerous lectures, publications, and projects have strongly supported the implementation of a new understanding of the economical, ecological, and social function of design in the domain of services.She received the Sir Misha Black Award 2020 for distinguished services to design education.

Peter R. Magnusson is a professor at Karlstad Business School, Karlstad University, Sweden. He is also affiliated to the CTF, Service Research Center at Karlstad University. He holds an MSc in electrical engineering from Chalmers University, and a PhD from the Stockholm School of Economics. Peter has 20 years' practical experience in R&D in the computing and telecommunications industries. His research focuses on innovation management and servitization. Peter has received several nominations and rewards for his research. His research has been published in leading refereed journals, including the *Journal of Product Innovation Management*, the *Journal of Service Research*, and the *Journal of the Academy of Marketing Science*.

Dominik Mahr is Professor of Digital Innovation and Marketing, Head of the Marketing and Supply Chain Management Department, and Scientific Director of the Service Science Factory at Maastricht University, The Netherlands. His research focuses on the human side of digitalization, and thus the implications of digital data, devices, and technologies for customers, organizations, and society, and has been published in journals including the *Journal of Marketing*, the *Journal of Consumer Research*, the *Journal of Service Research*, *MIS Quarterly*, and the *Journal of Product Innovation Management*. Prior to his academic career, he worked as a consultant in the automotive and high-tech industry.

Janet R. McColl-Kennedy, PhD, is Professor of Marketing and Director of Research at the UQ Business School, the University of Queensland, Brisbane, Australia, and a visiting professor, ongoing, at the University of Cambridge, UK. She is a distinguished Fellow of the Australian and New Zealand Marketing Academy and is recognized internationally as a leading researcher in Service Science. Her research interests include service recovery, customer complaining behavior, customer emotions, customer rage, customer experience, customer value co-creation, and digital transformation of services. Janet has a particular interest in healthcare. She leads several international research teams and has published articles in the *Journal of Retailing*, the *Journal of the Academy of Marketing Science*, *Leadership Quarterly*, the *Journal of Service Research*, *Harvard Business Review*, the *European Journal of Marketing*, *California Management Review*, *Psychology & Marketing*, the *Journal of Business Research*, *Marketing Theory*, the *Journal of Service Management*, the *Journal of*

xxx   Notes on Contributors

Marketing Management, and *Industrial Marketing Management*. Janet has been awarded several large competitive research grants, including prestigious Australian Research Council Discovery and Linkage Projects.

Cristina Mele (PhD) is Full Professor of Service Innovation and the coordinator of the PhD in Management in the Department of Economics, Management and Institutions, University of Naples Federico II. She is a delegate of Innovation and Third Mission at University. Her main research interests are innovation and smart technologies, value creation, markets, and service ecosystems. She has more than 220 publications. Her articles have appeared in the *Journal of the Academy of Marketing Science, Marketing Theory, Industrial Marketing Management*, the *Journal of Business Research*, the *Journal of Service Management*, and the *Journal of Service Theory and Practice*. Cristina is one of the co-chairs of The Naples Forum on Service.

Monia Melia is Adjunct Professor of Marketing and is a member of the research group Business Management, at the University Magna Græcia of Catanzaro, Italy. She is a member of several international research projects. She has published articles in several international journals such as *International Journal of Retail & Distribution Management* and the *Journal of Business Ethics*. She received the Outstanding Paper Award 2013 from the Emerald Literati Network. Her research interests are in marketing, service management, social innovation, and cultural heritage.

Kars Mennens is a postdoctoral researcher at the Brightlands Institute for Supply Chain Innovation and in the Department of Marketing and Supply Chain Management at Maastricht University, The Netherlands. His research focuses on inter-organizational innovation in the triple helix (industry, government and academia) and the role of the employee in the innovation process. Prior to his postdoctoral position, he worked as a trainee in the telecommunications industry.

Jean-Yves Mercier is Director for Pedagogical Innovation, Geneva School of Economics and Management, University of Geneva; CEO, Self-Leadership Lab; Professor of Self-Leadership and Change Management for different schools and universities (CH, F, E, AUS); Senior Consultant for Boards; coach for top executives; former Corporate Human Resource Manager for the Bahlsen Group; and President of the Self-Leadership Foundation.

Roberta Guglielmetti Mugion is an assistant professor at Roma Tre University, Department of Business Studies. She is interested in quality management and sustainability in services, quality in healthcare, quality and innovation, sharing mobility, and cultural heritage management. In particular, she focuses on audience satisfaction. She is part of many research projects related to the TQM diffusion and cultural heritage management system. She is part of the Italian Academy of Commodity Science.

Anastasia Nanni is a PhD candidate in Marketing at Bocconi University, Milan (Italy). Her main research interests focus on the area of service marketing, in particular on the effect of AI solutions on customers, employees, and firms in different service encounters. She is also interested in the topic of managerial/strategic decision-making. Anastasia implements field experiments with companies as the main methodology in her projects.

Richard Nicholls is Senior Lecturer in Marketing at Worcester Business School, University of Worcester, UK, where he also leads the Customer Interactions research team. He has taught and researched service management for over 30 years. His main area of scientific interest is customer-to-customer interaction. He has written three books and over 80 articles and chapters.

JanErik Odhe is a PhD candidate and teacher at Karlstad University, Sweden. He graduated in 1992 from Linköping University with an MSc in Mechanical Engineering. JanErik is a practitioner with more than 20 years of experience from management positions in different manufacturing sectors like automotive, mining, and paper machinery. His research focus is servitization in manufacturing companies.Acknowledgement. The authors would like to thank Thomas Gustafsson, Head of Product Verification Engineering at GKN Aerospace, for his invaluable assistance in validating the facts in the manuscript.

Andrea Ordanini is a full professor in the Department of Marketing at Bocconi University, Milan (Italy). He also holds the BNP Paribas endowed Chair in Marketing and Service Analytics. He has been a Visiting Professor at the University of California at Irvine, and a Visiting researcher at the London School of Economics and Political Sciences. His research interests range from services marketing to service innovation and consumption of cultural goods.

Chiara Orsingher is Associate Professor of Marketing at the University of Bologna. Her research interests include customer experience, customer satisfaction and complaining behavior, referral-reward programs, and meta-analysis and frontline service technology. She has published articles in the *Journal of the Academy of Marketing Science*, the *Journal of Service Research*, *Academy of Management Perspectives*, *International Journal of Research in Marketing*, *Psychology & Marketing*, the *Journal of Business Research*, and

xxxii   Notes on Contributors

the *Journal of Service Management*, among others, and has received several research awards from service journals.

Stefanie Paluch is Professor of Service and Technology Marketing, in the TIME Research Area, School of Business and Economics, at RWTH Aachen University. Her research is concerned with digital transformation, particularly the acceptance and management of smart services and related innovative technology-based services in the consumer and organizational context. Stefanie publishes her research in leading outlets such as the *Journal of Service Research*, the *Journal of Business Research*, and the *Journal of Service Management*.

Ekaterina Panina, MSc, is a doctoral candidate in Marketing at the Turku School of Economics, University of Turku. Her research project focuses on customer experience management activities and practices at business-to-business service firms, with an emphasis on examining the strategic use of target experiences as part of customer experience management. She is also interested in understanding the dynamics of customer journeys in a variety of service contexts.

Lia Patricio is Associate Professor at the University of Porto, where she is the Director of the Master in Service Engineering and Management. Her research focuses on service design, service system transformation, and customer experience, particularly in technology enabled services and service ecosystems. She coordinated the project with the Portuguese Ministry of Health for the design of the Portuguese Electronic Health Record and she was Principal Investigator of the Service Design for Innovation, Marie Curie Innovative Training Network. She is also working on citizen engagement with sustainable transitions. Lia is associate editor of the *Journal of Service Research* and the *Journal of Services Marketing*. She is Global Faculty Member of the Center for Services Leadership, Arizona State University, and Academic Scholar at the Cornell Institute for Healthy Futures. Her research has been published in the *Journal of Service Research*, the *Journal of Service Management*, *Design Studies*, the *Journal of Business Research*, and the *Journal of Cleaner Production*, among others.

Jaqueline Pels is Full Professor of Marketing at the University Torcuato Di Tella Business School, Buenos Aires, Argentina. She is Director of the Inclusive Business Think Tank (ENI-DiTella). Her research interest is in the areas of inclusive business, emerging economies, international business, marketing theory, relationship and networking marketing, as well as service-dominant logic. Her publications have appeared in leading international journals including the *Journal of the Academy of Marketing Science*, *Marketing Theory*, the *Journal of Business Research*, the *Journal of Business and Industrial Marketing*,

European Journal of Marketing, and the *Journal of Relationship Marketing*, among others. She has served on the Editorial Boards of the *Journal of Marketing*, *Marketing Theory*, and the *Journal of Business and Industrial Marketing*, amongst others.

Laura Di Pietro is an assistant professor at Roma Tre University, Department of Business Studies. She has a PhD in Commodity Science and Quality Management. She is interested in commodity science, TQM, service innovation, sustainability and CSR topics applied in a transversal way to different sectors (e.g., cultural heritage and tourism, education, public administration, healthcare, transport). She is involved in many research projects in the public and private sectors. She is a member of the Italian Academy of Commodity Science.

Francesco Polese is a full professor of Business Management at the University of Salerno, Italy. He is founder and Director of SIMAS (Laboratory of Systems for Innovation and Healthcare Management). He is the author of books, books chapters, and articles in international journals on topics such as the Viable Systems Approach, Service Science, service, and networks. He is co-chair of the Naples Forum on Service: Service-Dominant Logic, Service Science and Network Theory, an event that every two years since 2009 gathers 'service research' top scholars from all continents. He is the winner of the 2019 Service Dominant Logic Award.

Maria Francesca Renzi is Full Professor at Roma Tre University, Department of Business Studies. She teaches Quality Management, Corporate Social Responsibility, and Operations Management. Her main areas of interest concern various aspects of quality: quality management in the public and private sector, quality of the food sector, quality and environment management systems, corporate social responsibility, and cultural heritage management. She is director and co-ordinator of many research projects and is involved in several institutional engagements.

Angela Roth is a professor at the Institute of Information Systems at the Friedrich-Alexander University Erlangen-Nuremberg and works at the Chair of Information Systems – Innovation and Value Creation. She leads the Open Service Lab (OSL) https://openservicelab.org/ and is researching, consulting, and teaching in the fields of service innovation, service systems in digital contexts, and organizational competencies for service innovation. She is also conducting research on interactive service innovation in living labs (e.g., JOSEPHS®). In the context of organizational competencies and change, also future of work play a crucial role. Angela is works closely with non-university research institutes and industry partners.

xxxiv   Notes on Contributors

Hessam Sadatsafavi is a senior healthcare data analyst at Sentara Healthcare. He received a PhD in construction engineering and management from Texas A&M University and a Master of Arts degree and a bachelor's degree from University of Tehran. Hessam is a skilled business intelligence developer using SQL, R, Python, SPSS, and SAS and a certified Epic data modeler.

Daniela Sangiorgi, PhD in Design, is Associate Professor in the Design Department of Politecnico di Milano. She was one of the first scholars to investigate the area of Service Design. She worked for eight years at the research group Imagination at Lancaster University (UK). Her research theme is the role of design in the development of services, with a particular focus on public sector innovation. She has recently investigated the role of design for the transformation of mental healthcare systems in Italy. She has been publishing in international design and service research journals such as *International Journal of Design, The Design Journal, Design Studies*, the *Journal of Service Science*, and the *Journal of Service Research*.

Adriana Saraceni, PhD in Industrial Engineering, is a postdoctoral researcher at the School of Business and Economics, Marketing and Supply Chain Management Department at Maastricht University, The Netherlands. Her research focuses on complex industrial systems sustainability, network inter-relations, models to support decision-making, with expertise in the Sustainable Development Goals (SDGs), sustainability, and automation for logistic. Highlights of her research career include publications and award of a patent process for the development of a method approaching network inter-relations and environmental impacts of fostering Industrial Symbiosis (IS) implementation. In prior work, she led an IS implementation project in Langford area, Ireland.

Debora Sarno is an associate professor of Business Management at the Parthenope University of Naples, Italy. Her research interests are service management and marketing within the scientific frameworks of Service-Dominant Logic and the Viable Systems Approach. She is a project management professional certified by the Project Management Institute (USA) and has supervised several research and start-up projects in tourism and facility management.

Gerhard Satzger is Director of the Karlsruhe Service Research Institute (KSRI), an "industry-on-campus" initiative focused on innovation via digital services, and a professor at the Institute of Information Systems and Marketing (IISM) at KIT. His research interests include the use of data and artificial intelligence to develop and transform service business models. Gerhard draws on multi-year industry experience with IBM and drives innovation with a variety of industry partners. He holds a habilitation degree from the University of Augsburg, a PhD from the University of Giessen, an MBA from Oregon State University, and a diploma in Industrial Engineering and Management from KIT.

Tom Schiefer MSc, is a PhD candidate at the Brightlands Institute for Supply Chain Innovation and in the Department of Marketing and Supply Chain Management at Maastricht University, The Netherlands. The focus of his research is on inter-organizational collaboration for data-driven innovation, smart packaging, and obsolescence management.

Benjamin Schneider is Professor Emeritus of Psychology at the University of Maryland and a research affiliate at the Center for Effective Organizations, Marshall School of Business, USC. Ben is widely published, including 13 books and more than 125 peer-reviewed journal articles and book chapters, and has won numerous awards for his research contributions from major professional societies. He writes about and consults with organizational clients on employee engagement, service quality, organizational climate and culture, staffing, and the role of personality in organizational life. More details about Ben and his work can be found at www.DrBenSchneider.com.

Samuel Petros Sebhatu PhD, is Assistant Professor of Business Administration at Karlstad Business School and a researcher at the Service Research Center (CTF), Karlstad University, Sweden. His research focuses on management, corporate governance, corporate social responsibility, business models, and sustainability in different contexts of service research in both private and public sectors. Samuel has also studied sustainability in the city context from the service ecosystem perspective. He has conducted extensive studies of cities ecosystems. He is working on Transformation (Transformative Change) and Innovation in relation to multi-stakeholder dialogue and Agenda2030 – Sustainable Developmental Goals (SDGs). Samuel is PRME coordinator at Karlstad Business School.

Jagdish N. Sheth holds the Charles H. Kellstadt Chair in Marketing at Emory University, Georgia, USA. He has published more than 300 research papers and 30 books across consumer behavior, multivariate methods, competitive strategy, relationship marketing, and emerging markets. His book *The Theory of Buyer Behavior* (1969) with John A. Howard is a marketing classic. Jagdish is a fellow of the American Psychological Association, American Marketing Association (AMA), and Academy of Marketing Science. He was President of the Association for Consumer Research. Jagdish is the recipient of all the top four academic awards bestowed by the AMA.

Hannah Snyder is an associate professor in the Department of Marketing, BI Norwegian Business School, Oslo, Norway. Her research interests relate to service innovation, customer creativity, business model innovation, and service encounters. She has published in the *Journal of Service Research*, the *Journal of Business Research*, the *Journal of Service Management*, and the *European Journal of Marketing*.

David Solnet, PhD, is an associate professor of Service and Hospitality Management at University of Queensland Business School. He serves as lead academic for the new fully online Master of Leadership in Service Innovation offered through the prestigious edX platform. He comes from a restaurant background, with 18 years of experience including senior management roles in the USA and Australia, and is also recognized internationally for his research, teaching, and consulting, all focused on managing and leading service organizations. David has published over 40 peer-reviewed academic journal articles, with over 4500 citations, a textbook, and book chapters, and has led numerous funded research and consulting projects.

Jan-Oddvar Sørnes received his PhD from Norwegian University of Science and Technology in Organizational Communication. He is a professor at Nord University Business School. Jan-Oddvar is also Adjunct Professor at Inland University of Applied Sciences, Norway.

Tiziana Russo Spena is an associate professor of Management. She obtained her PhD in management and economics in 2002. Her main areas of interest are innovation management, service innovation, and digital marketing. She has attended several international conferences and co-authored over 100 refereed articles in journals and six books on innovation topics. She has written many articles and books and published in Italian and international journals, including *Industrial Marketing Management*, the *Journal of Business Ethics*, and the *Journal of Service Management*. She is a member of RESER, The European Association for REsearch on SERvices.

Tore Strandvik is an emeritus professor of Marketing at Hanken School of Economics, Finland. His research interests include customer-dominant logic, service research, managerial sensemaking, and branding. His publications have appeared in, for example, the *Journal of Service Management*, the *Journal of Services Marketing*, the *Journal of Business and Industrial Marketing*, *Industrial Marketing Management*, and *European Management Journal*. More information on him can be found here: https://harisportal.hanken.fi/en/persons/tore-strandvik.

Jon Sundbo is Professor of Business Administration and Innovation at Roskilde University, Denmark. His research field is innovation, service, and the experience economy. He has published over 200 articles, books, and book chapters, primarily on innovation, service business, experience, and tourism. He has been advisor to the EU, the Danish government, and several firms and trade organizations within service and tourism.

Peer Jacob Svenkerud received his PhD from Ohio University and is Professor and Rector at Inland Norway University of Applied Sciences, Norway.

Jakob Trischler is an assistant professor with the CTF, Service Research Center in Karlstad, Sweden. His research focuses on service design and studying the consequences of user involvement in innovation processes. Additional research interests include user innovation, innovation ecosystems, and sustainability oriented innovations. His recent publications appear in the *Journal of Business Research*, *Public Management Review*, the *Journal of Service Research*, and the *Journal of Public Policy and Marketing*.

Bård Tronvoll is a professor of marketing at the Business School at Inland Norway University of Applied Sciences and a professor of Business Administration at CTF, Service Research Center at Karlstad University, Sweden. He has been a senior guest researcher/visiting professor at Hanken, the Swedish School of Economics in Helsinki, Finland. Bård is a member of the editorial advisory board at the *Journal of Service Management*. Bård established and was responsible for the Masters program in Business Management at the Inland Norway University of Applied Science and is now director of CREDS – Center for Research on Digitalization and Sustainability. He is an active researcher with many publications in international research journals and books and has presented research work at many international scientific conferences. Bård's research interests are in dynamic customer relations focusing on theory in service, value co-creation, service innovation, digitalization, complaining behavior, and service recovery. He has worked with international trade and has been rector at Oslo School of Marketing (now Kristiania University College). Bård sits on several boards of executives in Norwegian companies.

Wolfgang Ulaga is Senior Affiliate Professor of Marketing, INSEAD in Fontainebleau, France. He serves as a director of INSEAD's Research & Practice Center on Marketing & Sales Excellence (MSEI). Wolfgang's research interests focus on service growth strategies, service innovation, service pricing (free-to-fee), subscription-based recurring revenue models, service sales transformation, solutions selling, and customer success management. His work has been published in the *Journal of Marketing*, the *Journal of the Academy of*

xxxviii   Notes on Contributors

Marketing Science, the *Journal of Service Research*, the *Journal of Business Research*, *Industrial Marketing Management*, *Harvard Business Review*, and *Sloan Management Review*, among others. He serves as editorial board member at the *Journal of Service Research* and *Industrial Marketing Management*.

Yves Van Vaerenbergh is an associate professor of Marketing at KU Leuven (Belgium). His research focuses on service and customer experience management and seeks to better understand customer experience innovations, customer loyalty drivers, customer experience measurement, and customer dissatisfaction management. His publications have appeared in the *Journal of the Academy of Marketing Science*, the *Journal of Service Research*, and the *Journal of Retailing*, among others. He has received numerous best reviewer awards, best paper awards, and best teacher awards. He is also the co-founder of The Kalepa Group, a university spin-off mostly focused on helping organizations to become more customer oriented.

Dorottya Varga is a postdoctoral researcher in the Department of Marketing at KU Leuven (Belgium). Her research mainly focuses on service failures, service recovery, and customer mistreatment. Her work has appeared in the *Journal of Service Research*. She has won the 2019 Liam Glynn Service Research Scholarship Award from AMA SERVSIG and Arizona State University's Center for Services Leadership, and the 2019 *Journal of Service Research* Best Paper Award.

Stephen L. Vargo, PhD, is a Shidler Distinguished Professor and Professor of Marketing at the University of Hawai'i at Manoa. He has articles published in the *Journal of Marketing*, the *Journal of the Academy of Marketing Science*, the *Journal of Service Research*, *MIS Quarterly*, and other top-ranked journals, in addition to three books. He serves as editor-in-chief of the *AMS Review* and on the editorial/advisory boards of 17 other journals. Stephen has been awarded the Shelby D. Hunt/Harold H. Maynard Award (twice) and the AMA/Sheth Foundation Award for his contributions to marketing theory, among other awards. The Web of Science Group has named him to its *Highly Cited Researchers* list (top 1%) in economics and business, worldwide, for each of the last seven years.

Rohit Verma is a professor in the Operations Technology and Information Management area at Johnson College of Business of Cornell University. He is on leave from Cornell University serving as the Founding Provost of VinUniversity, Hanoi. Rohit holds his PhD (Business Administration) and MS (Engineering) from University of Utah and his bachelor of technology from Indian Institute of Technology, Kanpur. He has published over 75 articles in prestigious academic journals and has also written numerous reports for the industry audience. His research interests reside broadly in service operations management, hospitality and service design, and healthcare, wellness, and senior living and care.

Josina Vink is an associate professor of Service Design at the Oslo School of Architecture and Design (AHO) and Design Lead within the Center for Connected Care (C3) in Norway. Josina has over 10 years of experience as a service designer working in international healthcare contexts, including in Canada, the USA, and Sweden. Josina has developed new services, supported policy change, facilitated shifts in practices across sectors, and led social lab processes. Josina's research aims to contribute to building more systemic service design theories and approaches, as well as understanding health systems transformation.

Sijun Wang, PhD, University of Alabama, is Professor of Marketing and Director of the MS in Business Analytics at Loyola Marymount University (LMU). Her research focuses on customer relationship management and service employee–client interfaces. Her work has been published in the *Journal of Marketing*, *Organization Science*, the *Journal of Service Research*, the *Journal of Business Ethics*, and the *European Journal of Marketing*, among others.

Tianran Wang sis a doctoral student at the School of Management, Fudan University, Shanghai, China. His research interests include online WOM and consumer experiences in service encounters.

Erik Wästlund is an associate professor of Psychology and is affiliated with Service Research Center, CTF, at Karlstad University. Erik's research revolves around the intersection between users and technology and how users' decision-making processes regarding health and privacy can be understood and influenced.

Jochen Wirtz is Vice Dean MBA Programmes and Professor of Marketing, National University of Singapore. He holds a PhD in services marketing from the London Business School and has published over 200 academic articles, book chapters, and industry reports. His over 20 books include *Services Marketing: People, Technology, Strategy* (9th edition, 2022), *Essentials of Services Marketing* (4th edition, 2022), and *Intelligent Automation: Learn How to Harness Artificial Intelligence to Boost Business & Make Our World More Human (2021)*. His recent work can be downloaded from JochenWirtz.com.

Lars Witell is a professor at the CTF, Service Research Center at Karlstad University, Sweden. He also holds a position as Professor of Business

xl   Notes on Contributors

Administration at Linköping University, Sweden. He conducts research on service innovation, customer co-creation, and service infusion in manufacturing firms. He has published in the *Journal of Retailing*, the *Journal of Service Research*, the *Journal of Business Research*, and *Industrial Marketing Management*.

Ying Xue is a doctoral student at Arizona State University focusing on service research. She did her undergraduate work at Nanjing University in China and her marketing research Masters degree at Clemson University in the USA. Her research interests include technology and service and the impact of female presence in TMTs on service strategy.

Mohamed Zaki, PhD, is the Deputy Director of the Cambridge Service Alliance at the University of Cambridge, a research center that brings together the world's leading firms and academics to address service challenges. Mohamed's research interests lie in the field of machine learning and its application in digital manufacturing and services. He uses an interdisciplinary approach of data science techniques to address a range of real organizations' problems such as measuring and managing customer experience and customer loyalty. His other research interests include digital service transformation strategy and data-driven business models. Mohamed's research has been published in highly ranked journals such as the *Journal of Service Research*, *Harvard Business Review*, *Expert Systems with Applications*, the *Journal of Service Management*, *the Journal of Business Research*, *the International Journal of Operations and Production Management*, *PloS ONE*, *the Journal of Production Planning & Control*, and the *Journal of Services Marketing*, and has published an edited book, book chapters, and many conference articles. Mohamed raised over £10 million from the research council and industry to fund his research. He is a recipient of many international awards for customer experience management.

List of Figures

Overview of the Book

Fig. 1 Overview of the field of service management 4

Service Management: Evolution, Current Challenges, and Opportunities

Fig. 1 Service platform (based on Tronvoll and Edvardsson's (2020) innovation platform) 46

Service-Dominant Logic and Service Management 4.0

Fig. 1 Service Management 4.0 and its penetration in S-D logic research 97

Adapting Service Management for the Sharing Economy

Fig. 1 The sharing economy pentagon 111
Fig. 2 Positioning in the sharing economy 114
Fig. 3 Pricing in the sharing economy 116
Fig. 4 People management in the sharing economy 118
Fig. 5 The traditional service blueprint and the sharing economy blueprint 119
Fig. 6 Example application of the sharing economy blueprint 121

Service Management Strategic Mindsets: That Create Positive Customer and Employee Experiences

Fig. 1 Slightly adapted service climate framework from Bowen and Schneider (2014). © David E. Bowen and Benjamin Schneider; used and adapted by permission 131

xlii   List of Figures

Fig. 2   The three-tiered view of service organizations. From Schneider and
           Bowen (1995). © Benjamin Schneider and David E. Bowen; used
           by permission   132

Service Strategizing—Shaping Service in Dynamic Contexts

Fig. 1   How dynamics in the market links to strategizing   155
Fig. 2   Different mindsets on service   159
Fig. 3   Service strategizing based on an individual manager's constant
           reflection in a dynamic setting   162

Servitization: A State-of-the-Art Overview and Future Directions

Fig. 1   Key service concepts   173
Fig. 2   Service growth and reduction processes: two continua
           (Kowalkowski et al., 2017)   174
Fig. 3   Key drivers of servitization (adapted from Kowalkowski
           & Ulaga, 2017, p. 7)   177
Fig. 4   Industrial service classification framework (adapted from
           Ulaga & Reinartz, 2011, p. 17)   181
Fig. 5   CS, CS Management, and CS Managers in the value creation
           spheres framework (Eggert et al., 2020; Ulaga et al., 2020)   191

Servitization and the Necessity of Becoming Ambidextrous: A 12-Year Longitudinal Study

Fig. 1   AIR's transition from MTP to DPS   212
Fig. 2   The six transition challenges   218

Contract Innovation: Driving Scale and Scope of Nonownership Value Propositions—Chapter Descriptiony

Fig. 1   The architecture of contract innovations   251

The Transformative Role of Resource Integration in Shaping a New Service Ecosystem

Fig. 1   The RI process: Matching, resourcing and valuing.
           (Adapted from Caridà et al., 2019c)   285
Fig. 2   The transformative RI within a service ecosystem.
           (Adapted from Anderson et al., 2013)   293

Self-Leadership and Empowerment: Lessons from Service Firms

Fig. 1   Self-leadership as a resource-integration process   325

List of Figures   xliii

Culture-Powered Service Excellence and Leadership: Chinese Characteristics

| Fig. 1 | The links in the service profit chain | 354 |
| Fig. 2 | The relationship between culture and manager decision | 361 |

Customer-Centric Service Ecosystem for Emerging Markets

| Fig. 1 | Customer-centric ecosystem | 395 |

Service Management for Sustainable Business Transformation

| Fig. 1 | Service management ecosystem model for sustainable business transformation | 429 |

Service Design for Systemic Change in Legacy Organizations: A Bottom-Up Approach to Redesign

Fig. 1	Metaphors for Helsehjelpen (Designers: Maria Våge Traasdahl, Ameesha Timbadia and Greta Hohmann)	465
Fig. 2	Test called TogetherApart with healthcare staff. (Designer: Angel Lamar, Photo: Mette Landsverk)	467
Fig. 3	Illustrative canvas to play with metrics that matter. (Illustration by Ingo Karpen)	469
Fig. 4	Perspectives workshop. (Photo by Thiago Freitas)	470
Figs. 5–7	Illustrative examples of staff creating visual representations of their organizational structure and culture. (Images by Ingo Karpen)	471

Service Design: Innovation for Complex Systems

| Fig. 1 | Adapted from the Double Diamond, UK Design Council 2005 | 489 |
| Fig. 2 | Mager, B., 2004, unpublished | 489 |

Tracing the Systems Turn in Service Design and Innovation: Convergence Toward Service System Transformation

| Fig. 1 | Divergence and convergence of service design and service innovation discourses | 542 |

Service Innovation in Networks: Co-creating a Network Business Model

| Fig. 1 | Overview of the early-stage alignment process for network service innovation | 563 |

xliv   List of Figures

Beyond the Line of Visibility: Toward Sustainable Service Innovation

| Fig. 1 | The line of visibility | 582 |

Managing Employee Empowerment and Engagement to Foster Service Innovation

| Fig. 1 | The innovation process. (Drawn after Sundbo, 1996, p. 407) | 600 |
| Fig. 2 | Model for empowerment and engagement of employees in service innovation processes | 602 |

Understanding Key Market Challenges Through Service Innovation

| Fig. 1 | Conceptualizing the structuration of service innovation | 618 |

Customer-to-Customer Interactions in Service

| Fig. 1 | Conceptual framework of CCI | 637 |

Understanding and Managing Customer Experiences

| Fig. 1 | Illustration of a consumer's goal hierarchy | 663 |
| Fig. 2 | A goal-oriented view of customer journeys (Becker et al., 2020) | 664 |

How Customers' Resources Influence Their Co-creation Experience

Fig. 1	Conceptual model	691
Fig. 2	Proposed model only with first-order constructs. (Source: Output SmartPLS 3.3)	695
Fig. 3	Proposed model with reflective and formative constructs. (Source: Output SmartPLS 3.3)	701
Fig. 4	Schematized summary of assessment of the proposed model. (Source: Output SmartPLS 3.3)	706

Measuring and Managing Customer Experience (CX): What Works and What Doesn't

| Fig. 1 | Step-by-step guide for practitioners to apply AI to measure CX | 738 |

Improving Service Quality Through Individuals' Satisfaction. Evidence from the Healthcare Sector

Fig. 1	GAP model. (Source: Parasuraman et al., 1991)	749
Fig. 2	Valdani and Busacca's model. (Source: Valdani & Busacca, 1992)	752
Fig. 3	The Service Profit Chain. (Source: Heskett et al., 1994)	755

| | List of Figures | xlv |

Fig. 4	Baldridge award framework. (Source: Foundation for the Malcolm Baldrige Award, 2015. Criteria for Performance Excellence, 2015)	756
Fig. 5	European Foundation for Quality Management framework. (Source: EFQM, 2019)	756
Fig. 6	Service excellence chain in healthcare. (Source: Guglielmetti et al., 2020)	757
Fig. 7	The SB for the emergency delivery process of an Italian hospital. (Source: Own elaboration)	761
Fig. 8	IPMA for employee satisfaction model (Ward 1 = Maternity; Ward 2 = Cardiology)	764
Fig. 9	IPMA for patient satisfaction model (Ward 1 = Maternity; Ward 2 = Cardiology)	765
Fig. 10	IEGSI measure in the cardiology unit	767
Fig. 11	OOBN scenario for IEGSI measure in the cardiology unit, acting on leadership	767
Fig. 12	OOBN scenario for IEGSI measure in the cardiology unit, acting both on leadership and patients' contact	768

Service Productivities' Next Top-Models

Fig. 1	The triple P-model (Tangen, 2005, Figure 2)	776
Fig. 2	Service productivity model of Grönroos and Ojasalo. (Source: Grönroos & Ojasalo, 2004, p. 418)	779
Fig. 3	Service productivity model by Johnston and Jones. (Source: Johnston et al., 2012, p. 7)	783
Fig. 4	Relationship between service quality and service productivity. (Source: Parasuraman, 2002, p. 8)	784
Fig. 5	Two-stage service productivity model. (Source: Corsten, 1994, p. 61)	785

Effective Service Operations Management: Aligning Priorities in Healthcare Operations with Customer Preferences

Fig. 1	Frequency of healthcare operations management literature thrusts	805
Fig. 2	Frequency analysis of perceived customer healthcare concerns. *High Costs of Care (All) includes: High Costs in General, High Costs of Insurance, and High Costs of Medication	815

Service Failure and Complaints Management: An Overview

Fig. 1	Organizational and customer service failure-recovery journey	824

xlvi   List of Figures

Expanding the Scope of Service Recovery

| Fig. 1 | The service recovery diamond | 855 |

Technology in Service

Fig. 1	The pyramid model (Parasuraman & Grewal, 2000)	871
Fig. 2	Evolution of technology in Services Marketing Literature	873
Fig. 3	Configurational approach	879

Smart Technologies in Service Provision and Experience

| Fig. 1 | Smart service practices | 899 |

Rapport-Building Opportunities and Challenges in Technology-Infused Service Encounters

| Fig. 1 | Rapport building with service robots/employees | 917 |

Artificial Intelligence and Decision-Making: Human–Machine Interactions for Successful Value Co-creation

| Fig. 1 | The vSa/S-D logic framework for human–machine interactions for DM | 933 |

Managing Artificial Intelligence Systems for Value Co-creation: The Case of Conversational Agents and Natural Language Assistants

| Fig. 1 | Multilevel design framework for service systems. (Based on Grotherr et al., 2018) | 952 |

Servitization and Digitalization as "Siamese Twins": Concepts and Research Priorities

Fig. 1	Product-service dimensions and examples, based on Meffert et al. (2018, p. 18)	971
Fig. 2	"III" value proposition continuum	972
Fig. 3	Scheme of a service system	974
Fig. 4	Intertopic distance map (left) and term frequency for an exemplary topic "service quality" (right)	976
Fig. 5	Example for topic modeling results: Growth of selected topic clusters (left) and geographical development of total service publication output (right)	977
Fig. 6	"High-tech meets high-touch", based on Böhmann et al. (2021, p. 4)	978
Fig. 7	Research agenda "high-tech meets high-touch", based on Böhmann et al. (2021, p. 11)	980

List of Tables

Service Management: Evolution, Current Challenges, and Opportunities

Table 1	Different definitions of service over the years	39

Is Service Management Experiencing a Change of Era?

Table 1	Era of changes and change of era	73

Service-Dominant Logic and Service Management 4.0

Table 1	S-D logic informed strategies and methods for contemporary service management	94

Adapting Service Management for the Sharing Economy

Table 1	Key service concepts	173

Servitization: A State-of-the-Art Overview and Future Directions

Table 1	Summary of topics	225

The Transformative Role of Resource Integration in Shaping a New Service Ecosystem

Table 1	Main objectives of the IVP by Airbnb	282

Organizational Communication in Service Management

Table 1	Communication about service	350

xlviii   List of Tables

Culture-Powered Service Excellence and Leadership: Chinese Characteristics

Table 1	Scores of 17 countries in the six dimensions of Hofstede model	359
Table 2	Comparation of Haidilao and Qingdao Seaview Garden Hotel	367

Toward Socially Responsible Business: A Typology of Value Postures in Nested Service Ecosystems

Table 1	Five value postures	377

Customer-Centric Service Ecosystem for Emerging Markets

Table 1	Overview of CSE factors	405

Service Management for Sustainable Business Transformation

Table 1	Key labels and concepts of service management for sustainable business transformation framework	421
Table 2	Overview of IKEA's ambitions and commitments of the key focus areas for implementing Agenda 2030	425

The Multiple Identities of Service Design in Organizations and Innovation Projects

Table 1	Sample design	506
Table 2	Individual and collective service design identities	508
Table 3	Evolving service design identities	517

Tracing the Systems Turn in Service Design and Innovation: Convergence Toward Service System Transformation

Table 1	Systemic conceptualizations of service design and service innovation	543
Table 2	Perspective differences between service design and service innovation	544

Service Innovation in Networks: Co-creating a Network Business Model

Table 1	Network-level generative script (script 1 of 3)	565
Table 2	Organizational-level generative script (script 2 of 3)	566
Table 3	Relationship-level generative script (script 3 of 3)	567

Beyond the Line of Visibility: Toward Sustainable Service Innovation

Table 1	Summarizing the research on service innovation	579
Table 2	Research agenda	586

Managing Employee Empowerment and Engagement to Foster Service Innovation

Table 1	Comparison of the three cases	608
Table 2	Recommendations for management to create an efficient employee-base innovation system	609

Understanding Key Market Challenges Through Service Innovation

Table 1	An overview of the existing service innovation frameworks	615
Table 2	Conceptualizing structuration of service innovation	618

Customer-to-Customer Interactions in Service

Table 1	Key terms used for CCI	635
Table 2	The range of CCI research methods	636
Table 3	Strategies for managing CCI	641
Table 4	Key issues for future research	644

Understanding and Managing Customer Experiences

Table 1	Overview of the research background of customer experience (cf. Becker & Jaakkola, 2020)	659
Table 2	Future research avenues on customer experience	671

How Customers' Resources Influence Their Co-creation Experience

Table 1	Resources and co-creation processes over the three phases of purchase	685
Table 2	Constructs, scales, and main authors with ordinal scales	693
Table 3	Indicators' simple correlations	696
Table 4	Discriminant validity of the constructs through the Fornell-Larcker criterion	698
Table 5	Discriminant validity of the constructs through cross-loadings	699
Table 6	Assessment of individual reliability, internal consistency, and convergent validity	702
Table 7	Assessment of discriminant validity: Fornell-Larcker and cross-loadings	702
Table 8	Analysis of multicollinearity	704

| List of Tables

| Table 9 | Weights and levels of significance of the formative indicators | 705 |
| Table 10 | Effects on the endogenous/dependent variables | 705 |

Measuring and Managing Customer Experience (CX): What Works and What Doesn't

| Table 1 | Illustrative examples of conceptualizations of customer experience (CX) | 731 |

Improving Service Quality Through Individuals' Satisfaction. Evidence from the Healthcare Sector

Table 1	Emergency department quality dimensions adapted by the GAP model	760
Table 2	Qualitative surveys for measuring internal and external perceptions of an Italian emergency department	762
Table 3	The questionnaire construct	763
Table 4	The sample	766
Table 5	The sample	766

Effective Service Operations Management: Aligning Priorities in Healthcare Operations with Customer Preferences

Table 1	List of interview questions and response choices used in our study	810
Table 2	Archival data: variables, sources, and descriptive analysis	812
Table 3	List of topics (categories) of perceived customer healthcare issues	813

Service Failure and Complaints Management: An Overview

| Table 1 | Summary of the organizational responses throughout the service recovery journey | 837 |
| Table 2 | Dimensions of a sustainable service recovery system | 839 |

Smart Technologies in Service Provision and Experience

| Table 1 | Definition and features of smart technologies | 891 |

List of Exhibits

Exhibit 1	Contrasting service robots with traditional self-service technologies	995
Exhibit 2	Contrasting frontline employees with service robots	997
Exhibit 3	The Service Robot Deployment Model. (Adapted from Jochen Wirtz, Paul Patterson, Werner Kunz, Thorsten Gruber, Vinh Nhat Lu, Stefanie Paluch, and Antje Martins (2018), "Brave New World: Service Robots in the Frontline," Journal of Service Management, Vol. 29, No. 5, pp. 907–931, https://doi.org/10.1108/JOSM-04-2018-0119)	998
Exhibit 4	Future research directions in robotic service encounters. (Note: Adapted from Lu, Vinh Nhat, Jochen Wirtz, Werner Kunz, Stefanie Paluch, Thorsten Gruber, Antje Martins, and Paul Patterson (2020), "Service Robots, Customers, and Service Employees: What Can We Learn from the Academic Literature and Where are the Gaps?" Journal of Service Theory and Practice, Vol. 30 No. 3, pp. 361–391)	1003

Part I

Perspectives on Service Management

Overview of the Book

Bo Edvardsson and Bård Tronvoll

The *Handbook of Service Management* has a broad scope and includes the latest research and findings, including service management best practices. The book covers different perspectives of the diverse and complex service management field and is structured in five, to some extent overlapping parts. We have included contributions for different academic disciplines such as marketing, management, human resources, service operations management, informatics, and computer science to secure different perspectives. With this blend of academic disciplines comes a number of complementing theories such as resource-based theory, consumer behavior theory, theory on innovation, and value theory, together with more general management theories. Furthermore, findings from empirical studies, cases, and conceptual frameworks from Europe, the US, Latin America, Australia, India, and Asia secure a global scope, different cultural perspectives, and a wide range of management practices. We do not claim that all aspects are dealt with but that the important topics are presented, at least to some extent.

B. Edvardsson (✉)
CTF, Service Research Center, Karlstad University, Karlstad, Sweden
e-mail: bo.edvardsson@kau.se

B. Tronvoll
CTF, Service Research Center, Karlstad University, Karlstad, Sweden

Inland Norway University of Applied Sciences, Elverum, Norway
e-mail: bard.tronvoll@inn.no

© The Author(s), under exclusive license to Springer Nature Switzerland AG 2022
B. Edvardsson, B. Tronvoll (eds.), *The Palgrave Handbook of Service Management*,
https://doi.org/10.1007/978-3-030-91828-6_1

The *Handbook of Service Management* provides an overview of the field grounded in service research. More than 100 service scholars from around the world have contributed with a total of 47 chapters. The content of this book is presented in the form of six broad parts: service management, service strategy, service leadership and transition, service design and innovation, and technology in service. See Fig. 1 for an overview.

The right part of the figure, the service management processes and outcomes, put forward that service management is about organizing activities and interactions among collaborating actors. Thus, carrying out meaningful and vital tasks, solving problems, and realizing outcomes of value for engaged actors (e.g., customers, employees, firms, society) are the cores of service management. Outcomes refer to meeting needs and expectations, creating favorable expectations, and avoiding service failures or, more to the point, intended value-in-context (the use-value of the actors' specific and current context). This, of course, includes individual, business, and societal values. Service management processes and outcomes are organized in ecosystems and shaped by available resources, norms, rules, and habits. These processes are sometimes referred to as service structures or institutional arrangements.

During the development of service management as a field of knowledge, the service encounter or moments of truths were focused on (Carlzon, 1989), both as processes and as outcomes. This approach was limited to a dyad or the interactions between a customer and a firm or rather a frontline employee and in particular the service encounter (e.g., Bitner, 1990). Important contributions to service management were developed that informed, for example, service quality (e.g., Parasuraman et al., 1985), complaints management (e.g., Tax et al., 1998), service recovery (e.g., Hart et al., 1990), as well as the role

Fig. 1 Overview of the field of service management

of employee competence, attitude (Grönroos, 1984), and behaviors when interacting with customers. Also, implications for service marketing in general, particularly how to manage expectations, develop and design service offerings and service productivity. This research developed a broader view on processes to include multiple collaborating actors and coordinating their activities and interactions (Vargo & Lusch, 2018). Early development of this view also resulted in the service blueprinting method (Bitner et al., 2008), now widely used in service management practice.

The focus in this stream of dyad-centric service management research focused on outcomes in terms of perceived service quality, customer satisfaction, loyalty, and profitability, and later on, customer experience. However, we may argue that the firm-customer dyad approach was too narrow to understand the full potential of service and how to manage service organizations. This is because service processes are not isolated entities but embedded in and dependent on system support, often including a number of systems providing access to resources but also come with norms, rules, and established routines—the role of the service game (North, 2005; Vargo & Lusch, 2016). With the development of service logic and service-dominant logic, the scope has broadened. Multiple intertwined processes are paid attention to, and actors collaborate to realize service processes and secure intended outcomes, not only for the customer, a focal firm but allows for all other collaborators in the ecosystem (Grönroos & Voima, 2013; Vargo & Lusch, 2004). This has later resulted in a view that service management is a perspective on co-creating value for all engaged actors in a service ecosystem, and outcomes refer to value-in-use of the actor's business or life context. This has major implications for managing service, service businesses, and all types of value-creating organizations. This handbook covers many of these "new" challenges and opportunities, also for manufacturing companies. Thus, we may argue that processes and outcomes are about managing value creation processes that result in intended value outcomes for engaged actors and also for how to renew value creation over time through, for example, innovation or by managing different self-adjustments in the service ecosystems. Based on this understanding, we have defined service management as "a set of competencies available for actors in the ecosystem, enabling and realizing value creation through service" (see chapter "Framing and Defining Service Management").

The Handbook has an impressive number of well-known researchers representing different areas of expertise and a long-standing research and publication record. Some of the best universities and business schools are included, and the Handbook has many links to service management practice, examples, and brief descriptions of cases to present best and even next practice.

1 Part I: Perspectives on Service Management

Altogether, this is a unique, up-to-date "smorgasbord" for anyone who wants to learn about the field of service management, especially those who are new to the field.

1 Part I: Perspectives on Service Management

Edvardsson and Tronvoll provide in *Overview of the Book* an introduction to the field of service management and the book's content. The chapter briefly discusses how theory and concepts from different academic disciplines have informed the field. The view also includes how service management has developed from mainly focusing on the firm-customer dyad to become more systemic and include multiple collaborating actors in co-creating value. In the chapter *Framing and Defining Service Management*, Tronvoll and Edvardsson define service management as an academic field and use service as a perspective on value creation and define service management as "a set of competencies available for actors in the ecosystem, enabling and realizing value creation through service".

In the chapter *Service Management: Evolution, Current Challenges, and Opportunities*, Edvardsson and Tronvoll give a brief overview of the evolution of service research and how to manage service in practice. The first section describes the development of service from being understood as unproductive labor to service as a perspective on the value creation. The chapter continues with a brief overview of current challenges and opportunities. Next, service as a perspective on value creation in service ecosystems is discussed by drawing on service-dominant (S-D) logic. Finally, we draw on our own, ongoing research on platforms as part of the ecosystem. Platforms offer multiple actors new opportunities to manage service and value cocreation.

Kleinaltenkamp continues to discuss the development within service management in the chapter *Service Management: Scope, Challenges, and Future Developments*. He argues that depending on the understanding of the term service, service management encompasses very different aspects. He identifies and discusses four perspectives on service that build the foundation for corresponding views of service management. He argues that the common core of the various perspectives is that the coordination of service activities and the actors involved forms their focal aspect. To increase the efficiency of the resulting coordination tasks, a number of efforts are being made, particularly in the field of information technologies.

Next, Pels and Mele in *Is Service Management Experiencing a Change of Era?* describe how service management has undergone different stages and how new perspectives continue to emerge. They pose that these changes are part of a broader shift taking place in the management discipline and society at large.

Fehrer and Vargo, in their chapter *Service-Dominant Logic and Service Management 4.0*, discuss how the contemporary service environments characterized by advanced technologies are augmenting customer-frontline interactions, presenting significant changes in the working environment of service managers. This chapter explicates how complex contemporary service environments can be better understood when applying service-dominant (S-D) logic informed strategies and methodologies that promote value co-creation processes and the engagement of broad sets of actors. Finally, in this part, Benoit shows how to *Adapting Service Management for the Sharing Economy*. A triangle of actors usually co-creates services in the sharing economy: platform providers, customers, and often non- or semi-professional peer providers. Because of this nature, it is necessary for many models in service management to be adapted, and five existing models have adapted models in (1) strategy, (2) positioning and competitive advantage, (3) pricing and capacity management, (4) people management, and (5) process management.

2   Part II: Service Strategy

Bowen and Schneider describe *Service Management Strategic Mindsets That Create Positive Customer and Employee Experiences*. Four "strategic mindsets" that can build an effective service organization capable of creating positive customer and employee experiences (CXs and EXs) are presented. First, "service is still all about people" mindset as the basis of competitive advantage? The following two mindsets ("service climate" and "coordination") create an organizational context in which service excellence is facilitated, and the fourth mindset is "high performing customers" as co-producers and co-creators of value. Strandvik, Holmlund-Rytkönen, and Lähteenmäki continue with mindsets in *Service Management Strategic Mindsets That Create Positive Customer and Employee Experiences*. They elaborate on the idea that individual actor's mental models in use are significant and need to be recognized in service management theorizing and practice. In increasingly dynamic business contexts, mental models of service value creation are challenged, and the capability to update them becomes critical. A conceptual framework is outlined depicting continuous strategy work in dynamic contexts, labeled service strategizing, where doing, observing, and thinking represent embodiments of mental models.

Kowalkowski and Ulaga in *Servitization: A State-of-the-Art Overview and Future Directions* argue that servitization over the past two decades has emerged as a major growth engine in many markets for firms looking beyond their traditional product core. Following a brief account of the history of servitization, the authors discuss the conceptual foundations and main drivers of the strategic move toward service transition. This literature review provides an up-to-date account of the state of the art of servitization research and key insights from this research domain. Servitization is also discussed by Magnusson and Odhe in *Servitization and the Necessity of Becoming Ambidextrous—A 12-Year Longitudinal Study*. They report the findings from a longitudinal study spanning 12 years, describing how servitization actually happens and affects the organization. The focal company AIR was a B2B manufacturing company in the aviation business, specializing in manufacturing jet engines. The case describes and analyzes how a unit at AIR made the successful transition from a pure make-to-print actor (product/production logic) to offering overall solutions (service logic) where they focus on the challenges that AIR encountered.

Ford and Solnet highlight service management practices. In *How Contemporary Scholarship Addresses Service Management Practices*, they are zooming in on current managerial challenges and showcase how contemporary scholarship can be of value in addressing these challenges. The chapter weaves contemporary scholarship with informed speculation about what service management practices will be in a post-COVID world. The authors select four topics linked to humanizing the service experience; contingent (gig) work and workers; the evolution from customer service to customer experience; and finally, managing diverse customer resources in the co-production of a service experience. Next, Michael Ehret and Wirtz, in *Contract Innovation: Driving Scale and Scope of Non-ownership Value Propositions*, argue that non-ownership value is one fundamental value proposition of services. This chapter systemizes contract innovation and its potential to enhance the scope and scale of services, evident in the growth of the sharing economy, industrial servitization, and service automation. Contract innovation entails three areas: (1) contract design innovation and client-driven learning, like systematic learning for improved service specifications; (2) contract technologies enhancing human capacity to control physical resources through enhanced physical connectivity, service interfaces, and legal technology, for example, digital contracts, payments, and registries; and (3) contracting infrastructures for orchestrating service ecosystems through physical networks, software interfaces, and service ecosystems.

The last chapter in this part is written by Holmqvist, Wirtz, and Fritze and focuses on *Managing the Exclusivity of Luxury Service Experiences*. They argue that luxury services offer consumers hedonic, extraordinary experiences. However, even the extraordinary experience risks becoming ordinary if consumed regularly (hedonic adaptation), undermining the appeal of the service. The authors argue for the importance of exclusivity combined with hedonic escapism to retain the uniqueness and desirability of the luxury service experience and distinguish between four manifestations of exclusivity (monetary, social, hedonic, and constructed). For managers, the chapter offers several practical insights on managing exclusivity in the service and incorporating hedonic escapism to appeal to consumers.

3 Part III: Service Leadership and Transition

This part begins with a chapter by Colurcio, Caridà, and Melia on *The Transformative Role of Resource Integration in Shaping a New Service Ecosystem*. The authors discuss the dynamics of value co-creation by adopting the principles of Transformative Service Research (TSR). The chapter provides a framework that emphasizes the transformative power that can lead to changing social relations and collective well-being, and therefore to changes in institutions and the institutional arrangements of the service ecosystem. The next chapter by Kristensson, Blom, and Wästlund on *Behavior Change—Five Ways to Facilitate Co-creation of Service for a Better World* also focuses on behavior change. For new services to be successful, users (customers, patients, citizens, etc.) must embrace and sometimes engage in new and difficult behaviors. As research has emphasized the importance of being user-centric, it is hard to understand why the behavior change that often is required for the user has not been problematized more. The authors present five evidence-based ways to describe and explain how behavior change can enable important services such as sustainability, education, and health services to make the world a better place.

The following chapter by Ben Letaifa and Mercier is zooming in on *Self-Leadership and Empowerment: Lessons from Service Firms* by exploring how managers and leaders need to develop self-leadership. High levels of self-awareness enable managers to be impactful, as they are aware of their behaviors, can focus on their motivations, and know how to leverage social and emotional resources to implement action plans. Unleashing every aspect of individual potential will result in more capacity for initiative and innovation, confidence, serenity, and better management of personal energy and will lead to collective resilience and agility. The authors draw on a case study of an airline to highlight how, in a context of unprecedented crisis, self-leadership leverages resources at the individual level and then creates collective loops of agility and resilience. Insights from practitioners are also put forward in the following chapter by Davis, Sørnes, and Svenkerud in *Organizational Communication in Service Management*. The chapter integrates the concept of organizational communication with the writing on service management by first demonstrating the relationship between the two, then offering six stories of communication in service management to provide examples of their integration. The results show that key features of defining stories, when the story begins and when it ends, are helpful in understanding service management. Service can begin as early as the planning stages for infrastructure, and it can end once a problem with service has been resolved.

Fan, Wang, and Lu, in *Culture-Powered Service Excellence and Leadership-Chinese Characteristics*, explain how and why service excellence practices are culturally specific. Based on the service profit chain framework, the authors discuss the impacts of national culture and organizational culture on human resource management. With two exemplar cases of service excellence in the Chinese context, the authors show how Chinese culture, more specifically guanxi, family sense, and parental leadership style, shape the way of pursuing service excellence for firms operating in China.

Baker, Little, and Brodie argue in *Toward Socially Responsible Business: A Typology of Value Postures in Nested Service Ecosystems* that the need to share value with multiple stakeholders has become a business imperative. A service ecosystem perspective gives insight into how this might be achieved. The authors propose five interrelated and interdependent "value postures" that system actors adopt—systemic, strategic, relational, operational, and individual. A value posture is the way actors think about and practice creating and delivering value to others. Each posture reflects unique combinations of stakeholders, stakeholder goals, resources, and institutional arrangements.

Jain, Ambika, and Sheth discuss *Customer-Centric Service Ecosystem for Emerging Markets* and argue that customer service is gaining importance as a vital component for competitive advantage. However, companies are grappling with a multitude of challenges in their journey toward superior customer support services. The challenges are more profound in emerging markets due to the heterogeneity, unique socio-economic-political factors, and infrastructural inadequacies. Hence, based on the insights from leading industry practitioners, the authors present an emerging market-focused, customer-centric service ecosystem (CSE), featuring the factors that influence customer service.

Social responsibility is also discussed by Enquist and Sebhatu in *Service Management for Sustainable Business Transformation*. They explain how transformation in complex environments requires the engagement of multiple stakeholders from different organizations and domains to impact the whole service ecosystem. Service management is not only for micro and meso processes but must respond to global challenges of complexity and wicked problems. The authors go back to the roots of service management with a societal aspect, to serve someone with the insight that business and ethics are intertwined.

Anderson and Xue in *Transformative Service Research: Where We Are and Moving Forward at the Collective Level* summarize the most recent research in the field of Transformative Service Research (TSR). They identify the continual building of parts of co-creation and well-being along with vulnerable consumers and inclusion in services. Newer trends in TSR research include a multidisciplinary approach to TSR, more collective-level well-being emphasis, services bridging transformation to society, transformation and organizations, sustainability of the natural environment, and crises and well-being. The chapter suggests that the most crucial gap in TSR research is examining more at collective levels. Mutuality is suggested as a concept to further investigate, especially in light of the issues that came to the surface during the pandemic.

4   Part IV: Service Design and Innovation

Karpen, Vink, and Trischler in *Service Design for Systemic Change in Legacy Organizations: A Bottom-Up Approach to Redesign* explain how service design can realize a change in legacy service organizations. They link service design research with literature on legacy organizations characterized by highly regulated and well-established constellations of actors, resources, and structures. Illustrative examples of service design approaches from healthcare and legal services show that tapping into the agency at the individual level is important to enable and drive collective change. In this context, the role of service design is to establish an open and safe environment for actors to unpack underlying assumptions and experiment with new ways of working that can catalyze large-scale change. Mager and de Leon are also focusing on service design challenges. In the chapter *Service Design: Innovation for Complex Systems*, the authors describe how service design, as a systematic process and a mindset, brings continuous innovation into the complex systems of service creation and delivery. Design is a key component of today's service management. It no longer means management by administrating and controlling but instead involving other key stakeholders and enabling systems to continuously adapt to changes in user's requirements, the environment, and context of use. The authors explain how design is contextualized in a contemporary framework that has moved beyond styling and beautification. This includes the ability to reframe problems, discover opportunities, and co-create scenarios of solutions that do not yet exist, prototyping, testing, and implementation. Another perspective on service design is presented by Sangiorgi, Holmlid, and Patricio. Their chapter on *The Multiple Identities of Service Design in Organizations and Innovation Projects* uses the theoretical construct of professional identity to study this evolution through a qualitative study with key experts and practitioners. Results highlight the professional development of service designers in organizations from more operational and tactical roles to more strategic and leadership positions, the ongoing hybridization of service design practice and potential future scenarios, the transversal and vertical trajectories, and strategies to develop design capabilities in organizations.

Koskela-Huotari and Vink argue for a system turn in *Tracing the Systems Turn in Service Design and Innovation: Convergence Toward Service System Transformation*. They show how service design and service innovation scholars are embracing a more systemic understanding of the outcomes and processes underpinning design and innovation in the service context. The authors provide an overview of this ongoing "systems turn" and show how service design and service innovation discourses are converging toward informing a common phenomenon: service system transformation. The two discourses provide distinct yet complementary perspectives in understanding how transformation within service systems unfolds. The chapter sheds light on the nature of intentional design and innovation interventions and how these intentional efforts bring forth change as part of the broader institutional processes at play within service systems.

Mennens, Mahr, van Fenema, Schiefer, and Saraceni connect design with innovation and explain how digitalization increasingly requires collective innovation for joint value creation. Their chapter *Service Innovation in Networks: Co-creating a Network Business Model* argues for a service design approach for achieving early-stage alignment for network service innovation. This chapter is grounded in the authors' action research, involving a service logistics network responsible for maintaining maritime equipment for a Navy organization. Generative scripts are used to capture essential elements of the network business model at organizational and network levels. The result offers practitioners a methodology for achieving early-stage alignment on elements of a network business model. Another perspective on service innovation is presented by Witell, Carlborg, and Snyder in *Beyond the Line of Visibility: Toward Sustainable Service Innovation*. They discuss research on service innovation, covering what service innovation is and what sustainable service innovation is. A key insight is that service research has taken a customer perspective on service innovation, and we ask if this is enough for service innovation research to stay relevant. Research on service innovation needs to address transparency and open the line of visibilities toward value creation, the environment, social, financial, and privacy to further our understanding and increase managerial relevance. The book chapter ends by suggesting research on service innovation in a sustainable direction.

Sundbo and Fuglsang continue the part on service innovation in *Managing Employee Empowerment and Engagement to Foster Service Innovation* by discussing employees' engagement in service innovation based on empirical research and a conceptual model. The chapter summarizes what the literature reports about employees' role in innovation processes. Then, the authors present a model illuminating the balanced innovation where employees are empowered to engage in intrapreneurship and innovation activities, but management controls this process. Three cases are used to illustrate different versions of balanced innovation with different results. Management should emphasize different roles that employees can play in innovation processes. The final chapter in this part by Edvardsson, Tronvoll, and Witell on *Understanding Key Market Challenges Through Service Innovation* argues that service innovation is a crucial source of competitive advantage across firms and markets has become critical to firm growth and profitability. Firms face market challenges when both designing and introducing new service offerings to the market. Service innovation can be used as a lens to understand how firms can overcome market challenges to improve their performance. This chapter provides an integrating framework to explain three key market challenges: novelty, diffusion, and value capture from the perspective of engaged actors. The chapter shows how the framework can be applied and finishes with some theoretical implications and managerial guidelines.

5 Part V: Service Interaction, Quality, and Operation

Heinonen and Nicholls, in *Customer-to-Customer Interactions in Service*, provide an excellent introduction to Part V and highlight that customers are constantly interacting with different actors and resources in the marketplace. This chapter explores how customers can be influenced by other customers present in the service setting. While research has devoted considerable attention to interactions between customers and employees, far less attention has been paid to interactions among customers. Generally known as customer-to-customer interaction (CCI), these positive or negative interactions represent a significant potential for service organizations. A conceptual framework is developed to outline the range of CCI, and it is used to direct managerial attention to strategies for supporting CCI. The following chapter by Jaakkola, Becker, and Panina on *Understanding and Managing Customer Experiences* offers a state-of-the-art overview of customer experience, how it emerges, and how it can be managed in service contexts. The chapter outlines the research background and alternative conceptualizations of customer experience, discussed from two perspectives: first, how experiences emerge from the customer's perspective, along with a range of journeys that they take with a network of providers in pursuit of lower- and higher-order goals, and second, how service firms can seek to design and manage these journeys to create intended experiences for customers.

Alves and Jesus show *How Customers' Resources Influence Their Co-Creation Experience* by zooming in on which resources are most used by the consumer in an event context and their influence on the outcome of the experience. Based on qualitative and quantitative studies, they aimed to identify the resources used by consumers in an event context and test the relationship between event consumers' resources on the outcomes of their co-creation experience. The authors found that physical, cultural, and social resources all positively and significantly influence consumer satisfaction and behavioral intentions. McColl-Kennedy and Zaki continue to discuss customer experience in *Measuring and Managing Customer Experience (CX): What Works and What Doesn't*. The chapter outlines key conceptualizations of customer experience (CX), pointing out the limitations of commonly used methods and metrics. Customer satisfaction measures and the net promotor score (NPS) have been used extensively to measure CX; however, the authors show that these measures can be very misleading, with organizations believing their customers are happy when they are not. They outline the latest thinking on CX measures highlighting the importance of combining both qualitative and quantitative measures. Finally, the authors demonstrate how AI can provide deep insights into what customers think and feel to assist organizations in facilitating great customer experiences.

Service quality and satisfaction have been key concepts in service management for many years. Mugion, Renzi, and Di Pietro in *Improving Service Quality Through Individuals' Satisfaction. Evidence from the Healthcare Sector* discuss how we today can understand and use service quality, analyzing service measurement, customer and employee satisfaction. They use the healthcare field as their empirical context. The health sector is crucial as care and assistance services for potential and intrinsic characteristics are considered engines for a broader and more general transformation of modern society. An integrated perspective between internal and external satisfaction is described regarding service quality focusing on the critical relationships between internal and external satisfaction that contribute to the continuous improvement of delivered service quality. Service quality and satisfaction make a bridge in the following chapter by Hipp and Gliem on *Service Productivities' Next Top-Models*. Quality and satisfaction are both important foundations for service productivity. This chapter provides an overview for scholars and practitioners about service productivity models that center or, at least, incorporate frontline employees. Models are sorted into schools of thought and evaluated in terms of the necessities for the holistic analysis of service productivity. The chapter ends with a synopsis displaying the evolution of the considered models.

Productivity is key to effective service operations, discussed by Kong, Sadatsafavi, and Verma. Their topic is *Effective Service Operations Management: Aligning Priorities in Healthcare Operations with Customer Preferences*. Three questions related to healthcare operations are discussed: (1) what are the most concerning issues in the US healthcare system from its customers' perspective? (2) What factors account for these perceptions? (3) Is there alignment between customer perceptions and healthcare operations research? A multi-year study shows that customers are concerned with (1) cost of care, (2) access and coverage, and (3) quality and efficiency. These concerns are found to be associated with health policies and sociodemographic characteristics. The authors compare these concerns with published healthcare operations research and respectfully suggest future healthcare operations research directions. The next chapter is zooming in on customer complaints and service recovery. Orsingher, De Keyser, Varga, and Van Vaerenbergh in *Service Failure and Complaints Management: An Overview* synthesizes existing service failure and complaint management knowledge. Building on a recovery journey perspective, the chapter discusses how different organizational responses at various points of the recovery process can help organizations overcome disruption in customers' experience. It concludes with a series of general recommendations on establishing recovery and complaint management as a core part of the organization. With this effort, the chapter supports practitioners in dealing with failure and setting up appropriate service recovery systems. Finally, in this part, Tronvoll argues in *Expanding the Scope of Service Recovery* that service recovery becomes vital for the competitiveness and survival of both firms and their network partners in complex service ecosystems. Current service recovery literature highlights three types of recovery outcomes: customer, procedural, and employee. The chapter expands the scope to argue for a fourth recovery component, the network recovery. The introduction of network recovery moves service recovery beyond its traditional customer context to include business-to-business settings. Network recovery is portrayed according to network characteristics, network structure, network relationships, and network dynamics. The proposed description of varied service recovery outcomes thus emphasizes both network recovery and a service recovery strategy.

6 Part VI: Service Technology

The part on service technology is introduced by Nanni and Ordanini, providing an overview on *Technology in Service Systems*. The chapter delineates the role of technology, considered as one of the core elements of any service system. Such a role is first described using historical streams of literature of technology in services (e.g., self-service, digital services) and then envisioned based on new technological trajectories (i.e., AI). The chapter proposes a configurational view of technology in services, according to which it is the alignment of technology with the other elements of the service system that ensures success. The chapter combines theoretical insights with empirical evidence taken from short cases/incidents. The following chapter by Mele, Spena, and Kaartemo on *Smart Technologies in Service Provision and Experience* also focuses on technology. The authors argue that service technologies have evolved rapidly in the last 20 years, concretely affecting service practices. The spread of smartphones, tablets, and smart objects has contributed to the exponential increase in connectivity. The growing number of connected smart devices configures complex ecosystems in which objects interact and communicate through the exchange of data and access to a multiplicity of previously shared information. In this context, technologies open new horizons and scenarios that are not always imaginable and highlight the need to rethink service practices and methods of organizing service relations radically. This chapter addresses how smart technologies (e.g., artificial intelligence, wearables, chatbots, service/social robots, blockchain) can affect service practices by making service provision smart and fostering a smart service experience.

Wang and Gremler, in *Rapport-Building Opportunities and Challenges in Technology-Infused Service Encounters*, continue with discussing opportunities with technology in service organizations and argue that service robots increasingly find their way into service encounters. To lay a foundation for understanding customer rapport with service robots (CRR), the chapter reviews the customer-employee rapport literature and the *virtual rapport* literature. The authors then elaborate on the distinct nature of CRR compared to how rapport has been conceptualized in other disciplines and the opportunities and challenges of CRR. Another aspect of service technology is discussed by Polese, Barile, and Sarno. Their chapter *Artificial Intelligence and Decision Making: Human-Machine Interactions for Successful Value Co-Creation* elaborates on the question what elements should be taken into account for successful value co-creation due to human-machine interactions in decision-making? In particular, by integrating service-dominant logic with the viable systems approach, the chapter proposes a framework of four elements: (i) knowledge process in decision-making—the knowledge curve; (ii) characteristics of the decision-maker(s)—the knowledge endowment; (iii) context—the service ecosystem; and (iv) outcomes of the interaction—value co-creation (and intelligence augmentation). The role of artificial intelligence in service management is also emphasized by Lewandowski, Grotherr, and Böhmann. In *Managing Artificial Intelligence Systems for Value Co-Creation. The Case of Conversational Agents and Natural Language Assistants*, they explain how conversational agents (CAs) are a form of artificial intelligence that is increasingly used to support and automate service encounters. CAs are cost-effective service actors which enable new forms of service provisioning and value co-creation scenarios. Despite their potential, organizations struggle to leverage the potential of CAs in real-life settings. They analyze the nascent literature and provide insights from a DSR project on the implementation of CAs in a service setting to identify challenges in the design, implementation, and operation of CAs in service systems. Using the lens of a multilevel framework for service systems, the authors present insights on how CAs can be designed and managed for value co-creation.

Digitalization plays a key role in enabling servitization. This is elaborated in the chapter *Servitization and Digitalization as "Siamese Twins": Concepts and Research Priorities* by Satzger, Benz, Böhmann, and Roth. The authors discuss trends and the need to change business models in favor of service offerings ("servitization") as well as trends to apply digital technologies for value creation ("digitalization"). First, a conceptual analysis is presented to explain their interdependence. Second, the authors combine a topic modeling literature study and a qualitative expert interview approach to identify key research fields for the service and information system research communities. The work deepens the understanding of service concepts to inform the purposeful design and application of digital technologies for service innovation along with the identified research roadmap—as "high-tech meets high-touch".

The final chapter in this part and in the book is zooming service robots. Kunz, Paluch, and Wirtz, in *Toward a New Service Reality: Human-Robot*

Collaboration at the Service Frontline, argue that the digital service revolution will significantly change the way we do business. A big part of this revolution is service robots in various forms and shapes. In this article, we illustrate the implication of service robots for the service industry. They compare service robots with traditional self-service technologies as well as human service personnel and identify opportunities and challenges. In the Service Robot Deployment Model (SRD Model), the authors highlight promising areas for human-robot collaboration and derive managerial implications for the service frontline in this new reality with service robots.

References

Bitner, M. J. (1990). Evaluating service encounters: The effects of physical surroundings and employee responses. *Journal of Marketing, 54*(2), 69–83.

Bitner, M. J., Ostrom, A. L., & Morgan, F. N. (2008). Service blueprinting: A practical technique for service innovation. *California Management Review, 50*(3), 66–94.

Carlzon, J. (1989). *Moments of truth*. Harper Collins Publishers.

Grönroos, C. (1984). A service quality model and its marketing implications. *European Journal of Marketing, 18*(4), 36–44.

Grönroos, C., & Voima, P. (2013). Critical service logic: Making sense of value creation and co-creation. *Journal of the Academy of Marketing Science, 41*(2), 133–150. https://doi.org/10.1007/s11747-012-0308-3

Hart, C. W. L., Heskett, J. L., & Sasser, W. E. (1990). The profitable art of service recovery. *Harvard Business Review, 68*(4), 148–156.

North, D. C. (2005). *Understanding the process of economic change*. Princeton University Press.

Parasuraman, A., Zeithaml, V. A., & Berry, L. L. (1985). A conceptual model of service quality and its implications for future research. *Journal of Marketing, 49*(4), 41–50.

Tax, S. S., Brown, S. W., & Chandrashekaran, M. (1998). Customer evaluations of service complaint experiences: Implications for relationship marketing. *Journal of Marketing, 62*(2), 60–76.

Vargo, S. L., & Lusch, R. F. (2004). Evolving to a new dominant logic for marketing. *Journal of Marketing, 68*(1), 1–17.

Vargo, S. L., & Lusch, R. F. (2016). Institutions and axioms: An extension and update of service-dominant logic. *Journal of the Academy of Marketing Science, 44*(1), 5–23. https://doi.org/10.1007/s11747-015-0456-3

Vargo, S. L., & Lusch, R. F. (2018). *The Sage handbook of service-dominant logic*. SAGE.

Defining and Framing Service Management

Bård Tronvoll and Bo Edvardsson

1 Introduction

Service management is a dynamic field grounded in a wide range of theories, concepts, and managerial models. Therefore, there is a need to define and discuss how service management can be understood, both as a management practice and as an academic discipline. This chapter describes ways of defining and framing service management as a relatively new academic discipline in a developing mode within service research.

In its broadest sense, service management has traditionally existed through centuries of a wide variety of activities: taking care of elderly people, providing transportation and healthcare services, and running restaurants, shops, and accommodation services. On the other hand, service management as an academic discipline is relatively new, with little consensus regarding its scope, theoretical underpinnings, and key concepts. This lack of a widely accepted definition of service has consequences for defining and understanding service management implications. This has limited the advancement of a discipline-specific research agenda and teaching practices, thus affecting the

---

B. Tronvoll (✉)
CTF, Service Research Center, Karlstad University, Karlstad, Sweden

Inland Norway University of Applied Sciences, Elverum, Norway
e-mail: bard.tronvoll@inn.no

B. Edvardsson
CTF, Service Research Center, Karlstad University, Karlstad, Sweden
e-mail: bo.edvardsson@kau.se

© The Author(s), under exclusive license to Springer Nature Switzerland AG 2022
B. Edvardsson, B. Tronvoll (eds.), *The Palgrave Handbook of Service Management*,
https://doi.org/10.1007/978-3-030-91828-6_2

development of a scholarly approach to service management. Despite this limitation, service management can be described as a dynamic field that develops responses to important societal and organizational challenges. The reason for this dynamism is that the importance of service in all sectors of modern economies is increasing, including service provided by manufacturing firms. The service perspective also informs general management literature, models, and practices.

Service management can be viewed as an academic discipline, a concept, and a practice, making it even more critical to define and illustrate. Service management as an academic discipline has, in a broad sense, tended to focus on value creation with a specific emphasis on meeting customers' expectations, the interactions between customers and front-line employees, the necessary supporting processes and structures in the service organization. In this way, the practice of service management has developed and renewed the provision of service to enhance customer-oriented experiences and fulfill organizational goals.

Defining, developing, and using concepts, models, and theories is an integral part of rigorous scholarly practice. Defining concepts is part of a broad academic discussion that provides the prerequisites and foundation for analyzing and communicating about an academic discipline. A concept describes an abstract idea that scholars use in academic dialogues to make sense of the world. Each academic discipline has its own theoretical concepts, which are used to describe, explain, and analyze phenomena of the discipline and investigate a phenomenon, contexts, and issues for the purpose of generating responses or solutions. Thus, each discipline, such as service management, has its disciplinary language (specialist terms), and learning and defining these concepts is essential for successful academic development. Proper operationalization and use of the concepts reveal the relevance of understanding and explaining the phenomena under study. As such, the discipline of service management has developed with contributions from marketing, operations management, and human resources, as well as theories from areas such as communication theory, resource advantage theory, systems theory, social construction theory, value theory, and innovation theory.

It is no easy task to position service management as an academic discipline because it has multidisciplinary roots that are intertwined in various research traditions. Furthermore, many concepts have theoretical roots in management studies that focused on manufacturing firms that were later adjusted to service organizations. However, service management research has also developed based on theorizing on the logic of service, often with close links to service management practice (see, e.g., Shostack, 1977; Vargo & Lusch,

Defining and Framing Service Management **21**

2004). The logic of service, emphasizing value creation, and drawing on value theory have also influenced scholars in other areas, not least healthcare (see, e.g., Porter & Teisberg, 2006).

In response to this brief and multifaceted framing of a dynamic and growing discipline, we present various ways of understanding service management in terms of theoretical underpinnings, concepts, models, and management implications. The nature of service and its implications for management have long occupied service researchers. Their focus has been on service encounters, customer relationships, and quality perception in the firm/customer dyad. More recently, service management has embraced a broader scope, including multiple collaborating actors and the challenges and opportunities present in service ecosystems. This broader scope, beyond the customer/firm dyad and narrow organizational framing, has widened the view of service management during the last 20 years toward a service ecosystem view. This chapter aims to frame service management in terms of this ecosystem view as a discipline by highlighting the three parallel shifts that have shaped the development of the field. First, the academic field is framed and defined. Next, different portrayals and theoretical underpinnings are presented, and, third, three shifts in service management research are discussed.

2 Framing Service Management

Framing the Discipline

Framing a discipline or defining a concept is typically challenging because it might have different ontological and epistemological underpinnings. We have had many discussions with scholars and reflected on how service management as a discipline is presented in the literature. These discussions on framing the discipline have particularly focused on key concepts, important models, frameworks, and empirical studies and results as a basis for portraying service management. However, we have not been able to summarize these reflections in one agreed-upon understanding. One portrait is not enough. Instead, we suggest that service management as a research discipline can be described as intrinsically diverse and lacking a singular foundational theory or agreed-upon definition. We may also conclude that the discipline has developed over recent decades, starting with the article by Shostack (1977) more than 40 years ago (see Chapter "Service Management: Evolution, Current Challenges, and Opportunities" in Tronvoll and Edvardsson). During that time, service management has borrowed from many related disciplines, such as marketing, economics, human resources, strategy, systems thinking, and organization theory.

Furthermore, the discipline has been informed by management practices in a wide range of service organizations in many industries. Service management has both influenced and learnt from many sectors of the economy, including manufacturing firms, government organizations, and other public service providers. Thus, the dynamic development of service management over 50 years or more has influenced specific sectors such as healthcare, hospitality, and information communication technology (ICT), including software development and platform-based organizations. A search for the term "service management" reveals more than 530,000 search results in Google Scholar and more than 15,000 articles in the academic database EBSCO when the search is limited to business and academic areas (as of July 2021).

An essential component of the development of the discipline of service management has been the *Journal of Service Management* (*JoSM*), which is currently in its 32nd year of publication and has become a highly appreciated and valuable journal. As the *JoSM* website states, "As economies across the world have become more service oriented, the importance of studying and understanding all aspects of managing service has increased. This presents new opportunities to undertake cutting-edge research within various industry sectors. … All require new knowledge, skills, and abilities to meet the changing marketplace." Nonetheless, *JoSM* is not the only academic journal in the service management field. Many journals have been established over the years to address service management issues, including the *Journal of Service Research* (*JSR*), *The Service Industries Journal*, *Journal of Service Marketing*, *Service Science*, and *Journal of Service Theory and Practice*.

In a widely cited book, Normann (1984) provided a service management framework that stressed a streamlined service management system that focuses on strategic service management practice. The critical components of his framework are market segment, service concept, service delivery system, image, culture, growth strategies, and the nature of innovation. Normann emphasized using image and culture as management instruments as well as compelling and persuasive communications. For their part, Sasser et al. (1991) presented a wide range of case studies that focused on "breakthrough" service providers that dramatically transformed the industry. They argued that these firms had transcended the established rules of service by consistently meeting or exceeding their customers' needs and expectations. These breakthroughs fostered growth, productivity, and profitability, and these service providers became role models for many other service organizations.

A few years later, Christian Grönroos (1994), also using real-world examples from both service and manufacturing firms, focused on the fact that most firms face service competition. Hence, managing services becomes of strategic importance for service firms and manufacturers of goods alike. Schneider and Bowen (1995) argued that companies that master the rules of the service game can outperform the competition. The key to winning, according to them, is understanding that the customer experience is the foundation for how an organization is managed, extending to how employees are treated and the condition of the physical facilities. They emphasized that people (i.e., customers, employees, and managers) are a prominent key to success in service and that this should be fully recognized in the increasingly technical sophistication of service science (Ehrhart et al., 2011). These scholars also argued that service management requires an understanding of the cocreation of value by and for people. This occurs when an appropriate psychosocial context is created for people to produce, deliver, and experience a service process. Thus, service management requires understanding the complexities of people as cocreators of service in often complex and interdependent systems. We can therefore conclude that these early, influential scholars often had a management interest and emphasized people, processes, and systems. Case studies and management practice influenced their work, while in-depth theorizing was less emphasized.

The field of service management concerns what are traditionally known as "service organizations" and constitutes a future paradigm for organizations in general (Gummesson, 1994). The division of goods and services, in its traditional sense, was outdated: "it represents a myopic production view, while the service economy is an expression for customer-oriented and citizen-oriented, value-enhancing offering" (Gummesson, 1994). Johnston and Clark (2005) offered a similar view in their article on service operations management by suggesting a window of opportunity for operations academics to engage in the service arena. Service scholars can apply their knowledge and skills to answer fundamental questions in the areas of quality, productivity, and efficiency, and thus exercise their expertise in business services as well as the voluntary sectors. These opportunities have been explored and exploited in service management research by responding to emerging societal and organizational management challenges.

Christian Grönroos (2015), in *Service Management and Marketing*, examined management in the arena of service competition. He drew on decades of experience to explain how to manage any organization as a service business and move closer to current and future customers. He argued that service management is all about customer-focused, outside-in management and that

24   B. Tronvoll and B. Edvardsson

current academic research and business practice can be used to make organizations more successful in the service-based economy. Although the discipline has taken a giant leap since the late 1970s, we are just beginning to see a new era of service management that will become the basis for value creation and economic survival.

Framing the Concept

A useful definition could prevent the reader from misunderstanding the term "service management" or aid understanding of it in the case of unfamiliarity. One way to define "service management" is to individually define the two words "service" and "management." However, it is often not enough to define the separate words because combining the two words results in more than the sum of its parts. Many scholars have defined both of these terms in recent decades, but no definition has achieved dominance.

Christian Grönroos (2007) defined "service" as a process consisting of a series of more or less intangible activities that normally, but not necessarily always, take place in interactions between the customer and service employee and/or physical resources or goods and/or systems of the service provider, which are provided as solutions to customer problems. Meanwhile, Kotler et al. (2009) defined "service" as any act or performance one party can offer to another that is essentially intangible and does not result in the ownership of anything. On the other hand, several researchers, textbook authors, and English language dictionaries have defined "services" as acts, deeds, performances, efforts, or processes (Hoffman & Bateson, 2006; Rathmell, 1966; Wilson et al., 2012). This definition of service implies that acts are performed after customers and firms finalize a deal, that sellers or agents perform acts, and that acts are physical. At its core, the definition regards economic activity as more accurately conceptualized in terms of service-for-service exchange, with "service" defined as using one's resources to benefit oneself or others (Vargo & Lusch, 2004).

"Management," on the other hand, has been defined even more broadly, with different intentions and from different theoretical perspectives. When "management" is described in academic literature, it often refers to the skills, habits, motives, knowledge, and attitudes necessary to manage people and resources successfully. When developed, management competencies promote improved leadership and contribute to business success. Moreover, an organizational goal is always related to creating value for actors engaged in the service ecosystem, such as shareholders, employees, customers, partners, suppliers, and society. A shift in attention toward the notion of a service eco-system, defined as a "relatively self-contained, self-adjusting system of resource-integrating actors connected by shared institutional arrangements and mutual value creation through service exchange" (Vargo & Lusch, 2016, pp. 10–11), is also influencing the conceptualization of service management.

Some definitions of management are very focused and may denote the optimal way to accomplish tasks and achieve goals (see, e.g., DuBrin, 2009; Kurtz, 2011). A similar view is suggested when defining management as an act of engaging with an organization's human talent and its resources to accomplish desired goals (Sen, 2019). Although the concept of "service man-agement" could give the impression of being rooted in the management field, management and organization theories have had relatively little influence on the development of the term, assuming that "management" is understood as the coordination and administration of tasks to achieve a goal. Such activities, often grounded in organization theory, include setting the organization's strategy, linking activities in processes, and coordinating the efforts of staff to accomplish these objectives through the application of available resources, control, and follow-up activities.

Traditionally, management has been defined by focusing on the planning perspective, which defines management as the effective and efficient utiliza-tion of resources to attain the set objectives through planning, organizing, directing, and controlling organizational resources (Michalisin et al., 1997). In contrast, Koontz and Weihrich (1990) focused on the process perspective and defined "management" as the process of designing and maintaining an environment in which individuals, working together in groups, efficiently accomplish selected tasks. Other scholars have emphasized the strategic per-spective by defining "management" as the bundle of tactics and strategies that actors devise to articulate this power, to resist power, to act in conflicting situ-ations, or to cope with uncertainty (Crozier, 1964), or by using a practice perspective, as Drucker (1954) did when he defined "management" as the commonly understood practice of organizing an organization's resources to achieve agreed-upon objectives and overall purpose.

Other management scholars have emphasized the key role of competencies or core competence (see, e.g., Prahalad & Ramaswamy, 2000). For instance, Bogner and Thomas (1994) elaborated on value creation and exchange value in relation to competencies and management. They focused on value creation that resulted in use-value, exchange value, and value capture. Use-value denotes customers' perceptions of the usefulness of a product, service, or other offering. Exchange value refers to the amount paid by the buyer to the seller for the use-value. Value capture relates to the realization of exchange value by economic actors (firms, customers, resource suppliers, or employees). We use this as a way to connect management, competencies, and service, with service being understood as a perspective on value creation (see, e.g., Edvardsson et al., 2005; Vargo & Lusch, 2004) and not only service as intangible offerings. We also assert that management has always focused on value creation and specifically on customers, owners, employees, and other stakeholders. Furthermore, service management is not only about possessing or having access to resources but also how these resources are integrated and used by engaged actors in relation to their intended individual and collective goals. Therefore, service management focuses on value creation in the context of service ecosystems, in which the engaged actors' competencies or sets of competencies play a crucial role.

Thus, the core of service management is carrying out meaningful and vital tasks, solving problems, and realizing outcomes of value for customers, firms, and other engaged actors. Outcomes refer to creating favorable experiences, avoiding service failures to secure intended value-in-context for customers and other engaged actors. Service management is focused on actor-driven processes and outcomes, organized in ecosystems and shaped by available resources, norms, rules, and habits. We may argue that actors need to possess or have access to different competencies when managing service activities, interactions, and collaboration between actors to form and realize value-creating processes and outcomes. Thus service management is about managing value creation processes that result in intended value outcomes for engaged actors. Based on this understanding, we have defined service management as "a set of competencies available for actors in the ecosystem, enabling and realizing value creation through service." This definition emphasizes the crucial role of actors—individuals and firms as well as other organizations—and their competencies for service provision, including creating value for themselves and others. Furthermore, value is created and assessed in ecosystems and results from the collaborations of actors. Thus, service denotes a perspective on value creation rather than a specific market offering, which is different from managing the production and delivery of physical products or goods. With the above view on service management, we emphasize the creation of value for customers and other engaged actors. In brief, service management is about "getting things done": the focus is on realizing value outcomes by managing the necessary supporting prerequisites, structures, competencies, and resources.

3 Shifts in the Service Management Perspective

Independent of how "service" and "management" are defined, we argue that service management has developed from a customer/firm-centric and dyadic understanding to a multi-actor and systemic perspective. Service organizations today are part of or embedded in many other systems and structures, including digital infrastructures. In addition, the extensive collaborations with external partners have changed the focus of service management to include the topics and research questions that service management scholars emphasize. Organizations as legal entities are a too narrow scope and limit the understanding and manage value creation, and thus for understanding service management. Digitization, service robots, smart technology, and platformization have begun driving transformations in many service industries in recent years. This development not only enables the shift from a narrow focus on the service encounter or a standalone organization or firm, but it also makes it necessary to embrace and manage access to resources and collaborations in ecosystems (Tronvoll, 2017). We suggest, however, that collaboration in service ecosystems requires managing specific sets of competencies for value cocreation and value capture. This can include and integrate customer competence (Prahalad & Ramaswamy, 2000).

We also assert that three parallel shifts have changed the focus and understanding of service management away from the traditional management approach. These shifts are as follows:

* A shift from a narrow focus with an inside-out perspective (departure from the need of the firm selling its products, including service offerings) to an embracing of the outside-in perspective (departure from the customer's needs, preferences, and relationships). This means that the scope of service management has been extended from focusing on the firm's effectiveness to emphasize customer satisfaction, loyalty, and experiences, and, over time, to promote long-term relationships in which the customers are at the center. The centrality of the customer does not imply a passive role or focus but rather an actively engaged and orchestrated role in mobilizing the customer's competencies and providing support that enables value cocreation to its full potential. Moreover, value creation is not limited to being embedded in units of output, such as services. Managing service delivery is broadened to encompass value creation, thus including the customer's

competencies, other resources, and collaborations with multiple actors in the customer's service ecosystem.

* A shift from a focus on the product, resources, and structure (static view) to a focus on activities, interactions, processes, and experiences (dynamic view). This shift implies that focusing on the dyad of the product/service (offering) and structure are insufficient for managing service. Service management must also include often-interdependent, parallel, and sequential processes, multiple outcomes, and a wide range of individualized customer experiences. Furthermore, these processes do not always result in intended value-creating outcomes and favorable customer experiences. Service management, therefore, must also include complaints management (Knox & van Oest, 2014) and service recovery (Van Vaerenbergh & Orsingher, 2016; Xu et al., 2014). However, studies have shown that, often, the same service failures recur, are inbuilt, and require service management attention and collaborative approaches (Arsenovic et al., 2019) to resolve them and avoid value codestruction (Echeverri & Skålén, 2011)

* A shift from focusing on the direct relationships between customers, frontline employees, and other touchpoints linked to a firm to a systemic approach to understanding service and service management. The systemic approach emphasizes multiple processes, activities, and interactions within direct and indirect relationships among all involved in the service ecosystem. Many actors (e.g., focal firm, suppliers, government bodies, and organizations) can play a critical role in creating value with the customer. Businesses and other organizations, including public service providers and governmental organizations, form loosely coupled and self-adjusting systems centered on value cocreation among multiple actors (Meynhardt et al., 2016). The overall focus is on mutual value creation, and the ecosystem strives for long-term viability (Barile et al., 2016; Vargo & Lusch, 2016). However, various actors within the service ecosystem might have different purposes (Meynhardt et al., 2016). At the same time, they are both individually and collectively able to adapt when confronted with change while maintaining their uniqueness and distinctiveness (Lusch & Nambisan, 2015). This can result in service management breaking free from the firm/customer dyad and the organization as the unit to be managed, to a focus on routines for resource integration and management of multi-actor collaborations in service ecosystems (Tuominen et al., 2020). Moreover, value cocreation is often enabled by digitization and smart technology (Mele et al., 2021).

Thus, the field of service management has moved toward a system perspective on value creation, in which engaged actors integrate resources and benefit from collaboration. This requires a system-informed management mindset and service logic focus that differs from applying conventional manufacturing-oriented management theories and models (Christian Grönroos, 2015; Vargo & Lusch, 2004). Service management emphasizes the importance of humans and the differences among collaborating actors with complementary competencies to address ecosystem complexities. More specifically, managing specific challenges and tasks in service provision to shelter the customer experience and the viability of the service ecosystem becomes important (Gummesson et al., 2019). Furthermore, a service management perspective requires that a firm knows its customers, both as individual actors and as groups or communities, to fulfill their specific needs and support their individualized value creation.

The ecosystem perspective on service management also embraces the opportunities provided by digitization, digital service platforms, and enablers such as sensors, streaming technology, and various interactive solutions. These opportunities open up the global marketplace, both for firms and for customers. As such, service management has become more technology-driven, which implies that adopting and managing smart sensing technology, service robots, and artificial intelligence (AI)-enabled management practices is becoming more common. However, we believe this automation will never replace the importance of the personal service encounter and the human touch. Rather, the task becomes balancing technology and the human touch ("high tech and high touch") to successfully develop service management. Thus, the central requirement of management in service competition is to adopt and embrace the systemic service perspective as a strategic approach to service technology and the digital workplace.

The ability to work anywhere, anytime is no longer something that is simply "nice to have." Enabling work-from-anywhere has become an essential tool in service management. For example, service providers that lacked digital workplace solutions prior to the outbreak of the COVID-19 pandemic experienced serious challenges. New solutions were developed very quickly to mobilize their workforces and allow them to connect to the workplace and customers from any location as well as to work efficiently with little or no reduction in productivity. Service management developed the sets of employee competencies and supporting toolsets to provide service with the same level of quality (functionality, speed, and accessibility) when it is desirable to work remotely or impossible to work in the traditional workplace. To succeed in this endeavor, service technologies must be fully integrated with all digital customer and partner systems. Changes in behaviors make this imperative as physical interactions decrease, engagement via alternative digital channels rises, and the Internet of Things (IoT) scales automation. In a world of service, in which refrigerators automatically order goods when needed and television suggests new programs based on previous viewing behaviors, service management solutions must now manage the scale of resources and new opportunities, including the service touchpoints that are present in trillions of devices.

The current changes in service ecosystems toward digital service management necessitate transformation of how service processes and service provision are carried out. Artificial intelligence (AI) and machine learning proactively support digital service provision. Customers no longer have to wait for someone to notice a service degradation. Instead, technology can identify and remedy a situation before it influences customers. At the same time, customers increasingly interact with social robots, chatbots, and virtual agents, which free employees to work on issues that are more complex as well as to explore innovation opportunities. Issues that cannot be resolved automatically are detected and automatically diverted to the most appropriate human resource for resolution.

In these ways, service management will increasingly embrace digital transformation as practitioners cocreate value with and for customers, employees, and all other engaged actors. A cultural shift into a digital mindset is under way to facilitate the widespread adoption of new and more efficient practices. We therefore conclude this chapter by illustrating the shift in service management toward a digital service mindset with the transformation in the financial industry. Since modern banks were first established, all customer services were conducted by a teller at a brick-and-mortar location. Over time, the proliferation of bank branches and the management of many employees have become expensive. Thus, bank operators began to ask themselves, "how can we better service our customers and reduce overall costs?" This question gave birth to online banking and, eventually, mobile banking, in which customers can access their bank information, pay their bills, buy shares, and receive many other services anywhere and at any time with just one or a few clicks.

We can conclude that service management is still at a point where dynamic technology fosters new opportunities, but the initial focus on servicing customers remains a core task. Service management currently focuses on improving customer and employee engagement by creating more personalized service. This is done using self-service and self-help technologies, which can boost value for customers as well as employee productivity. However, transforming the provision of service also requires a more sustainable value cocreation that emphasizes the 3Ps (people, planet, and profit), which we believe will be a priority for all service managers in the future. Therefore, we argue that defining service management as "a set of competencies available for actors in the ecosystem, enabling and realizing value creation through service" will be a useful compass when managing the challenges of tomorrow.

References

Arsenovic, J., Edvardsson, B., & Tronvoll, B. (2019). Moving toward collaborative service recovery: A multiactor orientation. *Service Science, 11*(3), 201–212. https://doi.org/10.1287/serv.2019.0241

Barile, S., Lusch, R., Reynoso, J., Saviano, M., & Spohrer, J. (2016). Systems, networks, and ecosystems in service research. *Journal of Service Management, 27*(4), 652–674. https://doi.org/10.1108/JOSM-09-2015-0268

Bogner, W. C., & Thomas, H. (1994). Core competence and competitive advantage: A model and illustrative evidence from the pharmaceutical industry'. In G. Hamel & A. Heene (Eds.), *Competence-based competition* (pp. 111–144). Wiley.

Crozier, M. (1964). *The bureaucratic phenomenon*. University of Chicago Press.

Drucker, P. F. (1954). *The practice of management*. Harper and Row.

DuBrin, A. J. (2009). *Essentials of management* (8th ed.). Thomson/South-Western.

Echeverri, P., & Skålén, P. (2011). Co-creation and co-destruction: A practice-theory based study of interactive value formation. *Marketing Theory, 11*(3), 351–373.

Edvardsson, B., Gustafsson, A., & Roos, I. (2005). Service portraits in service research—a critical review through the lens of the customer. *International Journal of Service Industry Management, 1*(16), 107–121.

Ehrhart, K. H., Witt, L. A., Schneider, B., & Perry, S. J. (2011). Service employees give as they get: Internal service as a moderator of the service climate-service outcomes link. *The Journal of Applied Psychology, 96*(2), 423–431. https://doi.org/10.1037/a0022071

Grönroos, C. (1994). From scientific management to service management. *International Journal of Service Industry Management, 5*(1), 5. https://search.ebscohost.com/login.aspx?direct=true&db=buh&AN=3981182&site=ehost-live

Grönroos, C. (2007). *In search of a new logic for marketing: Foundations of contemporary theory*. Wiley.

Grönroos, C. (2015). *Service management and marketing: Managing the service profit logic* (4th ed.). Wiley.

Gummesson, E. (1994). Broadening and specifying relationship marketing. *Asia-Australia Marketing Journal, 2*(August), 31–43.

Gummesson, E., Mele, C., & Polese, F. (2019). Complexity and viability in service ecosystems. *Marketing Theory, 19*(1), 3–7. https://doi.org/10.1177/1470593118774201

Hoffman, K. D., & Bateson, J. E. G. (2006). *Services marketing: Concepts, strategies & cases* (3rd edn., international student ed.). Thomson/South-Western.

Johnston, R., & Clark, G. (2005). *Service operations management* (2nd ed.). Financial Times/Prentice Hall.

Knox, G., & van Oest, R. (2014). Customer complaints and recovery effectiveness: A customer base approach. *Journal of Marketing, 78*(5), 42–57. https://doi.org/10.1509/jm.12.0317

Koontz, H., & Weihrich, H. (1990). *Essentials of management* (5th ed.). McGraw-Hill.

Kotler, P., Hansen, T., Brady, M., Goodman, M., & Keller, K. L. (2009). *Marketing management* (European edn.). Pearson/Prentice Hall.

Kurtz, D. L. (2011). *Contemporary business* (14th edn., Internat. student vers. ed.). Wiley.

Lusch, R. F., & Nambisan, S. (2015). Service innovation: A service-dominant logic perspective. *MIS Quarterly, 39*(1), 155–176.

Mele, C., Russo Spena, T., Kaartemo, V., & Marzullo, M. L. (2021). Smart nudging: How cognitive technologies enable choice architectures for value co-creation. *Journal of Business Research, 129,* 949–960. https://doi.org/10.1016/j.jbusres.2020.09.004

Meynhardt, T., Chandler, J. D., & Strathoff, P. (2016). Systemic principles of value co-creation: Synergetics of value and service ecosystems. *Journal of Business Research, 69*(8), 2981–2989. https://doi.org/10.1016/j.jbusres.2016.02.031

Michalisin, M. D., Smith, R. D., & Kline, D. M. (1997). In search of strategic assets. *International Journal of Organizational Analysis (1993–2002), 5*(4), 360. https://doi.org/10.1108/eb028874

Normann, R. (1984). *Service management: Strategy and leadership in service business.* John Wiley & Sons.

Porter, M. E., & Teisberg, E. O. (2006). *Redefining health care: Creating value-based competition on results.* Harvard Business Review Press.

Prahalad, C. K., & Ramaswamy, V. (2000). Co-opting customer competence. *Harvard Business Review, 78*(1), 79–87. http://search.ebscohost.com/login.aspx?direct=true&AuthType=ip,url,uid,cookie&db=buh&AN=2628909&loginpage=Login.asp&site=ehost-live&scope=site

Rathmell, J. M. (1966). What is meant by services? *Journal of Marketing, 30*(4), 32–36. https://doi.org/10.2307/1249496

Sasser, W. E., Hart, C. W., & Heskett, J. L. (1991). *The service management course: Cases and readings.* Press [u.a.].

Schneider, B., & Bowen, D. E. (1995). *Winning the service game.* Harvard Business School Press.

Sen, S. (2019). *Talent management.* Society Publishing.

Shostack, G. L. (1977). Breaking free from product marketing. *Journal of Marketing, 41*(2), 73–80.

Tronvoll, B. (2017). The Actor: The key determinator in service ecosystems. *Systems, 5*(2), 38.

Tuominen, T., Edvardsson, B., & Reynoso, J. (2020). Institutional change and routine dynamics in service ecosystems. *Journal of Services Marketing, 34*(4), 575–586. https://doi.org/10.1108/JSM-06-2019-0243

Van Vaerenbergh, Y., & Orsingher, C. (2016). Service recovery: An integrative framework and research agenda. *Academy of Management Perspectives, 30*(3), 328–346. https://doi.org/10.5465/amp.2014.0143

Vargo, S. L., & Lusch, R. F. (2004). Evolving to a new dominant logic for marketing. *Journal of Marketing, 68*(1), 1–17.

Vargo, S. L., & Lusch, R. F. (2016). Institutions and axioms: An extension and update of service-dominant logic. *Journal of the Academy of Marketing Science, 44*(1), 5–23. https://doi.org/10.1007/s11747-015-0456-3

Wilson, A., Zeithaml, V., Bitner, M. J., & Gremler, D. (2012). *Services marketing: Integrating customer focus across the firm*. McGraw-Hill UK Higher Ed.

Xu, Y., Marshall, R., Edvardsson, B., & Tronvoll, B. (2014). Show you care: Initiating co-creation in service recovery. *Journal of Service Management*, 369–387. https://doi.org/10.1108/JOSM-11-2012-0253

Service Management: Evolution, Current Challenges, and Opportunities

Bo Edvardsson and Bård Tronvoll

1 Introduction

As a research field, service management is interdisciplinary, with contributions emerging from a wide range of theoretical backgrounds, including marketing, operations management, human resources, strategy, and information technology. Furthermore, management practices have responded to the growing importance of services in modern economies, and service management has developed as a professional field in different service sectors. These sectors include healthcare, hospitality, tourism, IT, and managing the transition from product to service in manufacturing. Thus, service management has many facets, and quite a few will be focused on in the different sections and chapters in this handbook. However, in this chapter, we provide a brief historical

---

Edvardsson, B., & Tronvoll, B. (2022). Service management: Evolution, current challenges, and opportunities. In B. Edvardsson & B. Tronvoll (Eds.), *The Palgrave handbook of service management* (pp. xx–xx). Cham: Palgrave Macmillan. Forthcoming.

B. Edvardsson (✉)
CTF, Service Research Center, Karlstad University, Karlstad, Sweden
e-mail: bo.edvardsson@kau.se

B. Tronvoll
CTF, Service Research Center, Karlstad University, Karlstad, Sweden

Inland Norway University of Applied Sciences, Elverum, Norway
e-mail: bard.tronvoll@inn.no

© The Author(s), under exclusive license to Springer Nature Switzerland AG 2022
B. Edvardsson, B. Tronvoll (eds.), *The Palgrave Handbook of Service Management*,
https://doi.org/10.1007/978-3-030-91828-6_3

35

overview of the evolution of service management, including those aspects related to the current challenges and opportunities for the future in service management.

The rest of the chapter consists of four sections. The first section provides an overview of the evolution of service management research and practice; it includes the development of a service from being understood as unproductive labor to a service as a perspective on the value creation. The chapter continues with a brief discussion of the current challenges and opportunities, including a summary of service research priorities. Then, we discuss service as a perspective on value creation in service ecosystems by drawing on service-dominant (S-D) logic. S-D logic directs attention to the processes, patterns, and benefits of service-for-service exchange, where the focus is on the outcomes rather than the units of output. S-D logic also suggests that value creation takes place in ecosystems and is shaped by institutional arrangements, where digitalization and platforms play a crucial role today. Finally, we draw on the ongoing research on platforms as part of the service ecosystem. Platforms and digitalization offer new opportunities to manage service and value cocreation among multiple stakeholders. We argue that the essential enabler for value cocreation in service ecosystems is the service platform and platformization.

2 Evolution of Service Management

The concept of service is not new as a management topic because it has been researched for decades. The service concept can be traced back to the Scottish liberal economist and philosopher Adam Smith (often referred to as the father of capitalism and economic science). He is probably the most well-known scholar to focus on the role of services in the economy. In his seminal work, *The Wealth of Nations*, Smith ([1776] 1969) distinguished between the outputs of what he termed "productive" and "unproductive" labor. Productive labor is the production of goods that could be stored after production and subsequently exchanged for money or other resources of value. On the other hand, unproductive labor creates services that perished at the time of production and, therefore, do not contribute to wealth. These ideas were later rejected by several scholars, such as Jean-Baptiste Say, a liberal French economist and businessman, who argued in favor of competition, free trade, and lifting the restraints on business. Say ([1803] 2001) noted that production and consumption were inseparable in services, coining the term "immaterial products."

A significant step in service management thinking was developed by the French scholar Fredric Bastiat ([1848] 1964, p. 162), who claimed, "Services are exchanged for services. ... It is trivial, very commonplace; it is, nonetheless, the beginning, the middle, and the end of economic science." Frederic Bastiat (1860, p. 40) argued that individuals have "wants" and seek "satisfactions," which are the foundation of economics. Later on, John Stuart Mill (1849) argued that services are "utilities not fixed or embodied in any object, but consisting of a mere service rendered ... without leaving a permanent acquisition." He believed that "the value of production was not in the objects themselves, but in their usefulness" (p. 46).

A century later, when service management emerged as a separate field of study, it was mainly as a protest against the prevailing product-centric views. In 1960, the US economy changed forever, and for the first time in a major trading nation, more people were employed in the service sector than in manufacturing industries. Other developed nations soon shifted to become service-based economies. Services were understood as being important in their own right rather than as some residual category leftover after the goods were taken into account. This recognition triggered a change in the way services were defined. Scholars began defining services in terms of their unique characteristics rather than comparing products and management implications (see, e.g., Sasser et al., 1978).

As an essential phenomenon in society, services were discussed with a focus on not only defining and classifying services but also comparing them with goods. The old theories and models were not useful for managing services; hence, there has been rapid development in service research starting from the 1950s (Furrer & Sollberger, 2007). Shostack (1977) argued for "breaking free from product marketing," and Hill (1977) suggested a shift in understanding services as offerings to denote changes in the condition of a person or something in possession of the customer. The focus on service offerings has been replaced by considering services to be activities, deeds or processes, and interactions (Lovelock, 1991; Solomon et al., 1985).

Gradually, more of the discussion has focused on managing service organizations and infusing services into manufacturing firms (Grönroos, 1982). Using an evolutionary metaphor as a framework, Fisk et al. (1993) traced the evolution of service research from its embryonic beginnings in 1953 to its maturity in 1993. They identified three stages in this evolution: crawling out (1953–1979), scurrying about (1980–1985), and walking erect (1986–1993). During the crawling out stage, the first service scholars focused on how and why services were different from goods, identifying the characteristics of services, such as intangibility, heterogeneity, inseparability, and perishability, that eventually became the intangible, heterogeneous, inseparable, and perishable (IHIP) dominant characteristics.

In the scurrying about stage, attention shifted from "Are services different from goods?" to "What are the implications of these differences?" Lovelock (1983, p. 115) noticed that services marketing research put "too much emphasis on drawing distinctions between goods and services and not enough on developing good insights for practices in the service sector." To solve this issue, he proposed several classifications of services, with each type of service requiring a different marketing and management treatment. This stage also saw the first papers in new areas, such as service design and service mapping (Shostack, 1984) and service encounters (Czepiel et al., 1985), which flourished in the next period.

During the walking erect stage, publications matured on topics like managing quality given the heterogeneity of the service experience; designing and controlling intangible processes; managing supply and demand in capacity-constrained services; and organizational issues resulting from the overlap in marketing and operations functions (Fisk et al., 1993). The debate about the pros and cons of alternative methodologies to measure and manage service quality began (Brown & Peterson, 1993; Cronin & Taylor, 1992; Parasuraman et al., 1993; Parasuraman et al., 1988). Service quality and customer satisfaction were two of the most studied themes between 1993 and 2003. Even if they had started to decline, these themes can be considered the main centers of interest in the service marketing field in the 1990s (Furrer & Sollberger, 2007). Some themes such as "design and delivery," "modeling and measurement," and "service recovery" emerged as the main research streams. Furthermore, topics such as "service encounters," "relationship," "new service development," "servitization," "complaints management," and "technology infusion in service" became appearing, being supported by developments in and with the expansion of information and communication technology. Moreover, in an editorial, Rust (1998, p. 107) asked the following: What is the domain of service research? He stressed that service research should not be "a niche field characterized by arcane points of difference with the dominant goods' management field."

Gustafsson and Johnson (2003, p. 29) suggested that the service organization should "create a seamless system of linked activities that solves customer problems or provides unique experiences." Also, Vargo and Lusch (2004) called for a new dominant logic for marketing, one in which service—rather than goods—is fundamental to economic exchange. In their literature review and results from expert interviews, Edvardsson et al. (2005) suggested that service is a perspective on value creation and that value creation is best understood from the lens of the customer and is based on the value in use. Throughout the history of "service," the understanding and scope of the term have changed. In Table 1, some definitions of service can describe the development over time.

Service Management: Evolution, Current Challenges...

Table 1 Different definitions of service over the years

References	Definition of service
Bastiat (1848)	The great economic law is this: services are exchanged for services…it is trivial, very commonplace; it is nonetheless, the beginning, the middle, and the end of economic science.
Alderson (1937); Alderson (1957)	What is needed is not an interpretation of the utility created by marketing, but a marketing interpretation of the whole process of creating utility.
Rathmell (1966)	Goods are produced: services are performed.
Kotler and Connor Jr. (1977)	The importance of physical products lies not so much in owning them as obtaining the services they render.
Lehtinen (1983)	A service is an activity or a series of activities which take place in interactions with a contact person or a physical machine and which provides consumer satisfaction.
Lovelock (1991)	A service is a process or performance rather than a thing.
Bateson (1992)	The heart of the service product is the experience of the consumer, which takes place in real time … it is the interactive process itself that creates the benefits desired by the consumer.
Gummesson (1995)	Consumers do not buy goods or services, but rather purchase offerings that render services, which create value.
Zeithaml and Bitner (1996)	Services are deeds, processes, and performances.
Grönroos (2000)	Service is a process consisting of a series of more or less intangible activities that normally, but not necessarily always, take place in interactions between the customer and service employee and/or physical resources or goods and/or systems of the service provider, which are provided as solutions to customer problems.
Vargo and Lusch (2004)	Service is the application of specialized competences (knowledge and skills) through deeds, processes, and performances for the benefit of another entity or the entity itself.
Edvardsson, Gustafsson, and Roos (2005)	Service is a perspective on value creation rather than a category of market offerings. Cocreation of value with customers is key and the interactive, processual, experiential, and relational nature forms the basis for characterizing service.
Lovelock and Wirtz (2007)	Services are processes (economic activities) that provide time, place, form, problem-solving, or experiential value to the recipient.
Vargo and Lusch (2016)	Service is a perspective on value and value is always cocreated, often involving multiple actors who integrate resources in service ecosystems. Institutional arrangements shape value cocreation.

3 Service Management Challenges and Opportunities

For the past few decades, service research, including service management, has been growing in content and scope. Ostrom et al. (2015) examined the future needs in service research and identified several interesting topics for further research and development. They argued that the context in which service is created and experienced has, in many respects, fundamentally changed. For instance, advances in technology, especially information technology, have led to a proliferation of revolutionary services and changed how customers serve themselves before, during, and after purchase. To understand the changing landscape of the service context, an interdisciplinary research effort is needed to identify the research priorities that can advance the service field and benefit customers, organizations, and society. These service priorities can be understood as important service management challenges and opportunities. Ostrom et al.'s (2015) findings resulted in the following 12 service research priorities:

1. Stimulating service innovation;
2. Facilitating servitization, service infusion, and solutions;
3. Understanding organization and employee issues relevant to successful service;
4. Developing service networks and systems;
5. Leveraging service design;
6. Using big data to advance service;
7. Understanding value creation;
8. Enhancing the service experience;
9. Improving well-being through transformative service;
10. Measuring and optimizing service performance and impact;
11. Understanding service in a global context; and
12. Leveraging technology to advance service.

For each priority, crucial service topics and related research questions were identified. Although all the priorities and related topics were deemed essential, value creation for engaged actors was found to be a fundamental goal of service management. This is also emphasized in a review article on service management research in the *Journal of Management* by Subramony and Pugh (2015); they argued that the micro-foundation research in service management is still in its infancy and of great importance for a sound theoretical grounding of service-related constructs. Furthermore, they argued "that a study of individual actors and their impact on firm-level outcomes has both theoretical and empirical value. Such research might include qualitative studies of how leaders adopt customer-oriented strategies, how these strategies are interpreted by Human Resources (HR) Managers and then translated into HRM systems, and the role of change agents in creating customer orientation throughout the unit" (Subramony & Pugh, 2015, p. 363). The article also showed opportunities in quantitative studies to examine the effects of a wide range of micro-level actors or phenomena, such as the organizational or team leader characteristics associated with performance and profitability. The authors also discussed the challenges related to the "turnover of high performing individual employees, and acquisition of new 'high-potential' employees, on service outcomes" (p. 364). Here, we refer to service outcomes as value-in-context resulting from resource integration and value cocreation processes.

Service management challenges and opportunities have been analyzed in different areas, such as healthcare and operations management. Aksoy et al. (2019) discussed disruption and opportunity in hospitality and tourism; their views and suggestions were based on input from 50 scholars from the service marketing, management, tourism, and hospitality domains who came together in 2018 to ponder the evolution in service management. They identified various challenges and opportunities where technology-informed thinking, new business platforms (such as peer-to-peer business models and smart service provision to enhance customer experience), and big data implications in the customer value creation process are central. Furthermore, the human side of service, such as service experience, service innovation, and cocreation, was identified to still be of great importance but "through a twenty-first-century lens, emphasizing the need for traditional thinking to evolve in a new paradigm" (Aksoy et al., 2019, p. 449). Also, significant themes were recognized: "peer to peer platform business models; service systems value creation/destruction; service experience stakeholder management; technological disruptions in service; smart service experience; big data and customer value; social innovation in service; hospitable service and human touch; and innovation and authenticity" (Aksoy et al., 2019, p. 449). We believe that these challenges and opportunities inform service management in general by fostering forward thinking and the quest to ensure its evolution is sustainable.

The discussion on these challenges and opportunities shows that service management is characterized by substantial complexity involving a wide range of issues, including leveraging technology and platforms, smart service experience and provision, new business platforms, how leaders adopt service management strategies, and leveraging service design and innovation. We can conclude that these issues are all related to value creation. Thus, enhancing the knowledge of value creation continues to be a critical area of research and management. In addition, services are increasingly designed, created, and experienced in network or system constellations involving multiple actors and digital platforms. These constellations enable interlinked structures that create new ways of collaborating. Therefore, the key challenges should be addressed with an ecosystem's lens and should focus on managing value creation for the engaged actors in a sustainable way. This calls for scholars from different academic disciplines to collaborate and join forces with reflective practitioners to move service management to the next level. To move service management forward, a fruitful method is to elaborate on service as a perspective on value creation in service ecosystems. This includes how platforms become vital institutionalized arrangements for the engaged actors and their resource integration and value cocreation efforts. These concepts are discussed in the following sections.

4 Service as a Perspective on Value Creation in Ecosystems

Service is often referred to as a special category of offerings to the market, such as financial services, education, or transportation services. Service can also denote a perspective on value creation and is further discussed in this section.

In their seminal work introducing the S-D logic, Vargo and Lusch (2004) viewed service as a perspective on value creation in service ecosystems. At the core of S-D logic is the idea that all exchanges can be viewed in terms of a service-for-service exchange, the reciprocal application of resources for oneself or others' benefit (Vargo & Lusch, 2004). According to the authors, a good (physical product) is without value until it is integrated with the customer's own resources. A smartphone has no or at least very little value without a subscription to a telecom service provider, enabling access to the Internet. Furthermore, the user needs to know how to use the smartphone, including downloading apps, using the email system, or taking and storing photos—to mention only some of the knowledge and skills needed—to enable a customer (or user) to create the intended value. This example also shows that value is cocreated, and the cocreation is driven by the customers' access to a wide range of resources in different systems or an ecosystem.

S-D logic uses the singular term *service*, focusing on the process of doing something beneficial for and in conjunction with some entity (e.g., using a smartphone), rather than the units of output as implied by the plural *services* (Vargo & Lusch, 2008). S-D logic steers attention to the process, patterns, and benefits of exchange rather than the output (e.g., goods) and how access to and integration of resources in ecosystems become crucial for value in use. Introducing value in a social context, Edvardsson et al. (2011) noted that value in use must be considered in the broader setting. This powered the debate into a broader systemic view, where value creation occurs in service ecosystems as resources are exchanged among multiple actors and are more accurately conceptualized as value cocreation (Vargo & Lusch, 2008; Vargo et al., 2008). The core ideas of S-D logic are formulated into five axioms of S-D logic (Vargo & Lusch, 2016): (1) service is the fundamental basis of exchange; (2) value is cocreated by multiple actors; (3) all actors, including the beneficiary, are resource integrators; (4) value is always uniquely and phenomenologically determined by the beneficiary; and (5) value cocreation is coordinated through actor-generated institutions and institutional arrangements.

These axioms provide a broad understanding of service as a perspective on value cocreation. The perspective emphasizes that actors are both inhibited and enabled by institutional arrangements when integrating resources to cocreate value for themselves and others. This understanding of service is, how we see it, the conceptual foundation for service management.

S-D logic argues that services, rather than goods, are always what actors exchange as they attempt to become better off, thus informing how actors are managing a service. Thus, service management engages multiple actors in value cocreation, suggesting that value is always cocreated through actors' interactions, either directly or indirectly (e.g., through goods). Hence, value creation is seen as unfolding over time because of continuing social and economic exchanges. Value creation is also best understood and managed from a system view and cannot be fully managed at the dyadic level (Chandler & Vargo, 2011).

A fundamental understanding of S-D logic is that all actors are resource integrators. This highlights that all actors fundamentally provide services by integrating and using (or operating on) resources (Vargo & Lusch, 2011; Wieland et al., 2016). Resource integration requires reciprocal service exchange, reinforcing that value is assessed by individual actors in their use context. Therefore, value is understood as always being uniquely and phenomenologically determined and experienced by each engaged actor, and it is understood in terms of the holistic combination of resources in the actor's context (Chandler & Vargo, 2011). Thus, value is always unique to a single actor—the use situation—and can only be determined by that actor or the actor as the central referent.

S-D logic describes resource integration and value cocreation as coordinated through shared institutions (Lusch & Vargo, 2014; Vargo & Lusch, 2016). Institutions are humanly devised rules, norms, and beliefs that enable and constrain action and make social life predictable and meaningful (North, 1990; Scott, 2001). Institutions and institutional arrangements—a set of interrelated institutions—enable or inhibit actors from accomplishing resource integration and value cocreation in service ecosystems (Vargo & Lusch, 2016). The service ecosystems' perspective implies that all actors can influence the institutional arrangements, hence guiding value cocreation (Wieland et al., 2016). In essence, actors are continuously shaping institutional arrangements through their actions, and when they do so intentionally, they are involved in the processes of managing the service ecosystem. The service ecosystems' perspective further infers that the shaping of service ecosystems involves collective, collaborating processes (Vargo & Akaka, 2012). These resource integrating and value creation processes are increasingly enabled by different digital enabling technologies and platforms that are acting as institutional arrangements and resources in service ecosystems. Therefore, in the section below, we discuss new opportunities to manage service through value cocreation platforms.

5 Platforms as Part of the Ecosystem: New Opportunities to Manage Service

Service platforms are where a service exchange is performed, here underlying resource integration and the actor's implicit role (Lusch & Nambisan, 2015). Thus, the service platform is an essential enabler for value cocreation and utilizes the flow of resources that can serve actors in their exchange efforts. Among management scholars, Wheelwright and Clark (1992, p. 73) invoked the concept of a *platform* to describe products that meet the needs of a core group of customers but can be modified through the addition, substitution, or removal of features. McGrath (1995) argued that platforms are collections of common elements (often technological) implemented across various products. Meyer and DeTore (1999) defined a platform as a set of subsystems and interfaces forming a typical structure from which a stream of products can be developed. Gawer and Cusumano (2014) recommend that managers should move from "portfolio thinking" to "platform thinking," which they defined as understanding the commonalities that tie a firm's offerings, markets, and processes together, arguing that these should be exploited to create leveraged growth and variety. Krishnan and Gupta (2001) used the term product platforms to refer to the subsystems and interfaces forming a typical structure that enables a firm to efficiently develop and manufacture a family of products. Parker et al. (2017) used the term "platform ecosystem," showing how, for example, Apple, Google, and Microsoft are using external ecosystems and how the locus of value creation moves from inside the firm to outside, enabled by platforms in ecosystems.

Perks et al. (2017) argue that the traditional firm- and product-centric view of platforms is changing as the lead firm within a network of collaborating actors develops platforms. These actors orchestrate dynamic and purposive inter- or intradependent networks in which the actors cocreate value (Autio & Thomas, 2014). Gawer and Cusumano (2008) argued that a platform must (1) perform a *function* that is essential to a broader technological system and (2) solve a *business* problem for multiple firms and users in the industry. A platform provides a technological foundation for interfaces used by complementary interoperating subsystems (Tiwana et al., 2010).

A characteristic of the platform approach is that it is neither a firm (which has specific boundaries) nor a marketplace (with more permeable boundaries). Instead, the platform is "a foundation created by a firm that lets other firms build products and services upon it as in a marketplace" (Kelly, 2016, p. 122). Therefore, a platform owner must consider the system design that will solve the challenges of integrating the activities that stimulate the cocreation of value, such as in a "marketplace" (Gawer & Cusumano, 2014). This highlights the critical roles that platform-based value cocreation plays in supporting collaboration between multiple actors and, thus, resource integration.

This chapter notes that service platforms, with their activities (agency) and space (structure), are designed to support and direct value cocreation efforts. A service platform builds on existing resources and relations with engaged actors to accomplish and coordinate multiactor collaboration and facilitate value propositions. As part of the value cocreation efforts, the key actors invite other collaborating actors with complementary resources to play various supporting roles. Carida et al. (2019) discussed this in terms of the embedded processes of matching, resourcing, and valuing, shedding light on how key actors use service platforms to orchestrate these processes. The integrative and exchange spaces and activities coordinate and facilitate multiactor collaboration to improve the service ecosystem's viability (Normann, 2001).

Building on Tronvoll and Edvardsson's (2020) idea of an innovation platform, we define a service platform as *a space with structures designed for engaged actors' collaborative activities to enable value cocreation in the service ecosystem.* The activities performed on the platform rely on a constellation of actors and their purposeful value cocreation efforts. Cocreation activities need the support, coordination, and control provided by the architecture of value cocreation, a space that is guided by institutional arrangements embedded in structures. Moreover, the value cocreation space is an open and fuzzy supportive structure (Fetterhoff & Voelkel, 2006). For example, a value cocreation space may include a physical location or virtual communities that can help in developing and supporting the value proposition. The combination of value cocreation space and activities constitutes the service platform.

The service platform is also a strategic response to changes among actors and the market to enable value cocreation. This must be in line with the engaged actors' value propositions and the firm's business model. The platform's built-in structure with norms and values links the proposing actor's (firm's) business model and strategy statements to value cocreation activities. The key actor's orchestration of value cocreated activities forms the basis for the service platform at the intersection of agency-driven (integrative and exchange activities) and structure-driven (integrative and exchange space) concepts, as shown in Fig. 1.

In this view, integrative and exchange *activities* are carried out by actors with agency or, rather, a constellation of collaborating actors with the needed knowledge and skills and who have access to a wide range of resources. The activities are intended to result in new and useful value propositions that fit

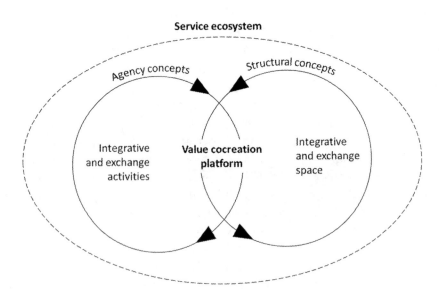

Fig. 1 Service platform (based on Tronvoll and Edvardsson's (2020) innovation platform)

the firm's business model and contribute to developing the ongoing business and viability of the service ecosystem. The outcomes of integrative and exchange activities are manifested in the renewal of existing or new value propositions. The interdependencies between value propositions and resources and actors should provide the basis for the agency needed for these activities to arrive at a stream of intended value cocreation. An integrative and exchange *space* refers to an institutionalized practice generated inside and outside the ongoing business at the service platform. The space can be designed in various ways, involving different sets of resources and constellations of actors. The space includes governance, legal, and technological structures.

Constituted by shared structures, including norms, standards, and rules, together with value cocreation logics, the service platform functions as the institutionalized site of resource integration and value cocreation processes. Platforms are becoming increasingly critical in managing service and scaling a service business on global markets. Making it possible to manage service platforms to enhance value cocreation and innovation in ecosystems is provoking service leaders into creating new challenges and opportunities.

Digitalization, robotization, and developments in visualization and Artificial Intelligence (AI) are among the developments that will continue to create both pressures and opportunities for the renewal of value cocreation, which can be enabled by platforms in service ecosystem. Platforms will also stimulate service innovation, and innovation will become increasingly systemic, involving networks of actors facilitated by a wide range of platforms. We believe that in the future, service management will develop more innovative ways of cocreating value in service ecosystems than we can imagine today. We are just beginning the service revolution and service as a business, propelled by new technology and digitalization. In addition to private firms, government, public service, and service in nonprofit organizations will benefit from adopting and using existing service platforms and designing and developing new and more powerful ones.

References

Aksoy, L., King, C., & Chun, H. H. (2019). Evolving service thinking: Disruption and opportunity in hospitality and tourism. *Journal of Service Management, 30*(4), 449–451. https://doi.org/10.1108/JOSM-07-2019-413

Alderson, W. (1937). A marketing view of competition, editorial. *Journal of Marketing*, 189–190. https://proxy.hihm.no/ebsco/

Alderson, W. (1957). *Marketing behavior and executive action: A functionalist approach to marketing theory.* Irwin.

Autio, E., & Thomas, L. (2014). Innovation ecosystems. In *The Oxford handbook of innovation management* (pp. 204–288). Oxford University Press.

Bastiat, F. ([1848] 1964). Selected essays on political economy. In S. Cain & G. B. d. Huszar (Eds.), Van Nordstrand.

Bastiat, F. (1860). *Harmonies of political economy*. John Murray.

Bateson, J. (1992). *Managing services marketing: Text, cases & readings*. Dryden.

Brown, S. P., & Peterson, R. A. (1993). Antecedents and consequences of salesperson job satisfaction: Meta-analysis and assessment of causal effects. *Journal of Marketing Research (JMR), 30*(1), 63–77. http://search.ebscohost.com/login.aspx?direct=true&AuthType=ip,url,uid,cookie&db=buh&AN=9511203699&loginpage=Login.asp&site=ehost-live&scope=site

Carida, A., Edvardsson, B., & Colurcio, M. (2019). Conceptualizing resource integration as an embedded process: Matching, resourcing and valuing. *Marketing Theory, 19*(1), 65–84. https://doi.org/10.1177/1470593118772215, pp. 1–20.

Chandler, J. D., & Vargo, S. L. (2011). Contextualization and value-in-context: How context frames exchange. *Marketing Theory, 11*(1), 35–49. https://doi.org/10.1177/1470593110393713

Cronin, J. J. J., & Taylor, S. A. (1992). Measuring service quality – A reexamination and extension. *Journal of Marketing, 56*(3), 55–68. <Go to ISI>://A1992JD96100004.

Czepiel, J. A., Solomon, M. R., & Surprenant, C. F. (1985). *The service encounter: Managing employee/customer interaction in service businesses*. Lexington Books.

Edvardsson, B., Gustafsson, A., & Roos, I. (2005). Service portraits in service research – A critical review through the lens of the customer. *International Journal of Service Industry Management, 1*(16), 107–121.

Edvardsson, B., Tronvoll, B., & Gruber, T. (2011). Expanding understanding of service exchange and value co creation. *Journal of the Academy of Marketing Science, 39*(2), 327–339.

Fetterhoff, T. J., & Voelkel, D. (2006). Managing open innovation in biotechnology. *Research-Technology Management, 49*(3), 14–18. https://doi.org/10.1080/08956308.2006.11657373

Fisk, R. P., Brown, S. W., & Bitner, M. J. (1993). Tracking the evolution of services marketing literature. *Journal of Retailing, 69*(1), 61–103.

Furrer, O., & Sollberger, P. (2007). The dynamics and evolution of the service marketing: Literature 1993–2003. *Service Business, 1*, 93–117.

Gawer, A., & Cusumano, M. A. (2008). How companies become platform leaders (cover story). *MIT Sloan Management Review, 49*(2), 28–35. http://search.ebscohost.com/login.aspx?direct=true&db=buh&AN=28452300&site=ehost-live

Gawer, A., & Cusumano, M. A. (2014). Industry platforms and ecosystem innovation. *Journal of Product Innovation Management, 31*(3), 417–433. https://doi.org/10.1111/jpim.12105

Grönroos, C. (1982). *Strategic management and marketing in the service sector*. Helsingfors.

Grönroos, C. (2000). *Service management and marketing: A customer relationship management approach*. John Wiley & Sons, Ltd.

Gummesson, E. (1995). Relationship marketing: Its role in the service economy. In W. J. Glynn & J. G. Barnes (Eds.), *Understanding services management* (pp. 244–268). John Wiley & Sons.

Gustafsson, A., & Johnson, M. D. (2003). *Competing in a service economy: How to create a competitive advantage through service development and innovation* (1st ed.). Jossey-Bass.

Hill, T. P. (1977). On goods and services. *Review of Income & Wealth, 23*(4), 315–338. https://doi.org/10.1111/j.1475-4991.1977.tb00021.x

Kelly, K. (2016). *The inevitable: Understanding the 12 technological forces that will shape our future*. Penguin Publishing Group.

Kotler, P., & Connor, R. A., Jr. (1977). Marketing professional services. *Journal of Marketing, 41*(1), 71–76.

Krishnan, V., & Gupta, S. (2001). Appropriateness and impact of platform-based product development. *Management Science, 47*(1), 52. http://search.ebscohost.com/login.aspx?direct=true&db=buh&AN=4114169&site=ehost-live

Lehtinen, J. (1983). On defining service. Paper presented at the *XIIIth Annual Conference of the European Marketing Academy*. Bruekelen.

Lovelock, C. H. (1983). Classifying services to gain strategic marketing insights. *Journal of Marketing, 47*(3), 9–20.

Lovelock, C. H. (1991). *Services marketing*. Prentice Hall.

Lovelock, C. H., & Wirtz, J. (2007). *Services marketing: People, technology, strategy* (6th ed.). Pearson/Prentice Hall.

Lusch, R. F., & Nambisan, S. (2015). Service innovation: A service-dominant logic perspective. *MIS Quarterly, 39*(1), 155–176.

Lusch, R. F., & Vargo, S. L. (2014). *Service-dominant logic: Premises, perspectives, possibilities*. Cambridge University Press.

McGrath, M. E. (1995). *Product strategy for high-technology companies: How to achieve growth, competitive advantage and increased profits*. Irwin Professional Publishing.

Meyer, M. H., & DeTore, A. (1999). Creating platform-based approaches to new services development. *Journal of Product Innovation Management, 18*(2), 188–204.

Mill, J. S. (1849). *Principles of political economy: With some of their applications to social philosophy* (Vol. 2, 2nd ed.). John W. Parker.

Normann, R. (2001). *Reframing business: When the map changes the landscape*. Wiley.

North, D. C. (1990). *Institutions, institutional change and economic performance*. Cambridge University Press.

Ostrom, A. L., Parasuraman, A., Bowen, D. E., Patrício, L., & Voss, C. A. (2015). Service research priorities in a rapidly changing context. *Journal of Service Research, 18*(2), 127–159. https://doi.org/10.1177/1094670515576315

Parasuraman, A., Berry, L. L., & Zeithaml, V. A. (1993). More on improving service quality measurement. *Journal of Retailing, 69*(1), 140–147. <Go to ISI>://A1993LQ73600006.

Parasuraman, A., Zeithaml, V. A., & Berry, L. L. (1988). SERVQUAL: A multiple-item scale for measuring consumer perceptions of service quality. *Journal of Retailing, 64*(1), 12–40.

Parker, G., Van Alstyne, M., & Jiang, X. (2017). Platforms ecosystems: How developers invert the firm. *MIS Quarterly, 41*(1), 255–A254. http://search.ebscohost.com/login.aspx?direct=true&db=buh&AN=121204231&site=ehost-live

Perks, H., Kowalkowski, C., Witell, L., & Gustafsson, A. (2017). Network orchestration for value platform development. *Industrial Marketing Management, 67*, 106–121. https://doi.org/10.1016/j.indmarman.2017.08.002

Rathmell, J. M. (1966). What is meant by services? *Journal of Marketing, 30*(4), 32–36. https://doi.org/10.2307/1249496

Rust, R. (1998). What is the domain of service research? *Journal of Service Research, 1*(2), 107–107. https://doi.org/10.1177/109467059800100201

Sasser, W. E., Oslen, R. P., & Wyckoff, D. D. (1978). *Management of service operations: Text, cases, and readings.* Allyn and Bacon.

Say, J.-B. ([1803] 2001). *A treatise on political economy.* Transaction Publishers.

Scott, W. R. (2001). *Institutions and organizations.* Sage.

Shostack, G. L. (1977). Breaking free from product marketing. *Journal of Marketing, 41*(2), 73–80.

Shostack, G. L. (1984). Designing services that deliver. *Harvard Business Review, 62*(1), 133–139.

Smith, A. ([1776] 1969). *The wealth of nations, books I-III, with an introduction by A. Skinner.* Penguin Books.

Solomon, M. R., Surprenant, C., Czepiel, J. A., & Gutman, E. G. (1985). A role theory perspective on dyadic interactions: The service encounter. *Journal of Marketing, 49*, 819–856.

Subramony, M., & Pugh, S. D. (2015). Services management research: Review, integration, and future directions. *Journal of Management, 41*(1), 349–373. https://doi.org/10.1177/0149206314557158

Tiwana, A., Konsynski, B., & Bush, A. A. (2010). Platform evolution: Coevolution of platform architecture, governance, and environmental dynamics. *Information Systems Research, 21*(4), 675–687. https://doi.org/10.1287/isre.1100.0323

Tronvoll, B., & Edvardsson, B. (2020). *Explaining how platforms foster innovation in service ecosystems.* http://hdl.handle.net/10125/63937

Vargo, S. L., & Akaka, M. A. (2012). Value cocreation and service systems (re) formation: A service ecosystems view. *Service Science, 4*(3), 207–217.

Vargo, S. L., & Lusch, R. F. (2004). Evolving to a new dominant logic for marketing. *Journal of Marketing, 68*(1), 1–17.

Vargo, S. L., & Lusch, R. F. (2008). From goods to service(s): Divergences and convergences of logics. *Industrial Marketing Management, 37*(3), 254–259. https://doi.org/10.1016/j.indmarman.2007.07.004. http://search.ebscohost.com/login.aspx?direct=true&AuthType=ip,url,uid,cookie&db=buh&AN=31679617&loginpage=Login.asp&site=ehost-live&scope=site

Vargo, S. L., & Lusch, R. F. (2011). It's all B2B…and beyond: Toward a systems perspective of the market. *Industrial Marketing Management, 40*(2), 181–187. https://doi.org/10.1016/j.indmarman.2010.06.026

Vargo, S. L., & Lusch, R. F. (2016). Institutions and axioms: An extension and update of service-dominant logic. *Journal of the Academy of Marketing Science, 44*(1), 5–23. https://doi.org/10.1007/s11747-015-0456-3

Vargo, S. L., Maglio, P. P., & Akaka, M. A. (2008). On value and value co-creation: A service systems and service logic perspective. *European Management Journal, 26*(3), 145–152. https://doi.org/10.1016/j.emj.2008.04.003. http://search.ebscohost.com/login.aspx?direct=true&AuthType=ip,url,uid,cookie&db=buh&AN=32645250&loginpage=Login.asp&site=ehost-live&scope=site

Wheelwright, S. C., & Clark, K. B. (1992). Creating project plans to focus product development. *Harvard Business Review, 70*(2), 70–82. http://search.ebscohost.com/login.aspx?direct=true&db=buh&AN=9206292188&site=ehost-live

Wieland, H., Koskela-Huotari, K., & Vargo, S. L. (2016). Extending actor participation in value creation: An institutional view. *Journal of Strategic Marketing, 24*(3/4), 210–226. https://doi.org/10.1080/0965254X.2015.1095225

Zeithaml, V. A., & Bitner, M. J. (1996). *Services marketing*. McGraw Hill.

Service Management: Scope, Challenges, and Future Developments

Michael Kleinaltenkamp

1 Introduction

The term "service" is dazzling and multifaceted, and consequently so is the term "service management"—depending on the understanding of service that is or needs to be managed. Essentially, there are four such perspectives, which are outlined in the following chapter. They see service management as managing (1) service outputs, (2) service processes, (3) resource access, or (4) resource integration to enable and realize value through service. However, despite all differences, the various perspectives are characterized by a common feature, which is that the coordination of service activities as well as of the actors involved forms their focal aspect. Because this coordination incurs costs, a number of efforts are being made, particularly in the field of information technologies, to improve the efficiency of service provisioning and usage. Consequently and concluding, this paper argues that the respective endeavors to reduce the coordination costs within service enactment are challenges and opportunities alike for the future development of service management.

M. Kleinaltenkamp (✉)
Marketing Department, School of Business & Economics, Freie Universität Berlin, Berlin, Germany
e-mail: Michael.Kleinaltenkamp@fu-berlin.de

© The Author(s), under exclusive license to Springer Nature Switzerland AG 2022
B. Edvardsson, B. Tronvoll (eds.), *The Palgrave Handbook of Service Management*,
https://doi.org/10.1007/978-3-030-91828-6_4

2 The Various Perspectives of Service and Service Management

Service Management as Creating Outputs of Service Industries

In everyday language, services (noun plural!) are often understood as the counterpart to goods. This understanding corresponds to the industry-related view of services that sees services as outputs or products that can be exchanged on markets or in other forms between individuals and/or organizations. This is especially reflected in the various service industries as they are covered by official statistics and that together represent the "tertiary sector" (Fisher, 1952; Fourastié, 1952). Here, the following industries (in alphabetical order) are typically distinguished: (1) business services, (2) craft services, (3) cultural services, (4) educational services, (5) environmental services, (6) financial services, (7) healthcare services, (8) information technology services, (9) institutional and advocacy services, (10) logistics and transport services, (11) professional services, (12) real estate business services, (13) research and development services, (14) social services, (15) sports and recreational services, (16) technical services, (17) testing, certification, and conformity assessment services, (18) tourism services, and (19) trade services. In the developed economies, these service industries typically account for 70% to 80% of a country's total economic output as well as employment (OECD, 2005). In this sense, service management stands for the management of the operations of a service business, which includes the following aspects, among others.

First, the services offered and delivered by these service industries refer to different reference objects, which are either people or objects, with the objects themselves in turn being owned by individuals or organizations (e.g., Wirtz & Lovelock, 2018). Here, people processing services can further be divided into individual services like hairdressing or healthcare services and collective services like public transport or sports events where a multitude of people use the same service simultaneously. All other services are processing either tangible objects like a car or an aircraft engine being repaired or intangible objects like data or information that is collected, processed, transformed, or transmitted.

Often, various types of such services are also combined to service bundles or solutions. For example, the service of attending a football match includes not only the experience of the match itself but also information services regarding when and how best to get to the stadium, the results of other matches running in parallel and so on, restaurant or hospitality services as well as the possibility of exchanging information and emotions with other visitors at the event. The example also shows that such services are often not delivered by one provider alone but rather by a number of commercial and/or private actors. This is well illustrated by the example of airports. All services provided here, such as car parking, check-in process, loading and unloading of baggage, refueling of aircraft, and so on, are usually operated by separate service providers that are contracted by the airports and with whom the end-customers of the service themselves do not have a direct business relationship.

Second, the various examples also illustrate that all sorts of services are exchanged between different groups of providers and customers or users, which is reflected in the terms "business-to-consumer" (B2C), "business-to-business" (B2B), "business-to-government" (B2G), "consumer-to-consumer" (C2C), "government-to-consumer" (G2C), or "government-to-business" (G2B). The fact that the behavior of the various groups of actors, whether as providers or recipients of services, is very different for a variety of reasons is one of the causes for the diversity and heterogeneity of the service sector.

Third, the elements of the various types of service offerings are often separated into core and supplementary services (Lovelock, 1995). Here, core services represent the solutions for the basic needs customers or users seek to be satisfied and for which they typically provide something in return, for example, in the form of a payment. Supplementary services are typically offered as beneficial tools or enhancements to create interest, develop awareness (among service recipients), or make the acquisition, delivery, or usage of a service more convenient. Service management related to the outputs of service industries has thus do deal with all tasks that are necessary to effectively and efficiently create these various service outputs in their heterogeneity.

Service Management as Designing and Steering Service Processes

Despite the manifold differences of service outputs described in the previous section, one overarching commonality of services is that customers or users always participate in their enactment. The provision of services thus always requires at least a minimum of customer or user participation that comprises the degree of an actor's effort and involvement, either physical, mental, or emotional relating to the definition, production, and delivery of a service (e.g., Cermak et al., 1994; Silpakit & Fisk, 1985). Consequently, a different view on service and thus on service management focuses on the processes in which an individual or an object is served (verb!). The service recipients as individuals themselves or as owners of the respective objects as well as their objects are thus always part of the service processes. Depending on the degree of standardization of the respective service design, the service recipients thus influence the processes of service provision and their outcomes through their participation and contributions to a greater or lesser extent (Bendapudi & Leone, 2003).

Service management in this sense thus needs to describe the method and sequence in which a service operating system works and to steer and control the respective procedures. For such purposes, a number of tools like flow-charting or service blueprinting (Fließ & Kleinaltenkamp, 2004; Shostak, 1985) have been developed. They display and structure the succession of the different steps involved in the processes and how the various participants interact within. Moreover, in order to improve the quality and productivity of service processes, measures of service process redesign need to be carried out. Such activities aim at reducing the number of service failures and the cycle time from the initiation of a service process to its completion or at increasing the quality of the service and thus the satisfaction of its recipient. These measures thus comprise, for example, an examination of the service process with key stakeholders, an elimination of non-value-adding steps, an identification of bottlenecks, and a possible shift to a self-service design.

Service Management as Getting Access to Resources

The process view of service and service management also reveals that such processes are characterized by an interplay of provider resources on the one side and customer or user resources on the other. However, for a service to be performed, it is not necessary to acquire ownership of the respective resources of the other party (e.g., Lovelock & Gummesson, 2004; Wittkowski et al., 2013). In contrast, for a service to be provided, both the provider and the user "only" need to get access to each other's tangible or intangible resources. Service transactions are thus associated with an exchange of property rights that always leads to an attenuation of property rights that are attributed to the parties involved (Haase & Kleinaltenkamp, 2011). Hence, during the period of service provision, service providers transfer certain rights of using their resources to the service recipients—for example, when a car rental company rents a car to a customer or a sports event organizer allows the public to access an arena for a sporting event. To deliver their services, providers must thus grant service recipients temporary rights of access and use that limit their own property rights, at least temporarily. At the same time, users must participate personally

Service Management: Scope, Challenges, and Future Developments **57**

or through "their" objects in the creation of the services. In turn, this limits the users' property rights and/or their free disposal of time as well—at least in part. Consequently, every offer and creation of service always include the need to ensure access to and exchange of relevant rights among involved actors and to avoid possible negative consequences of the fact that several actors have rights to a resource like in public transportation or in a sports arena.

As, in many cases, service providers themselves are not the owners of the resources used to enact a service, these contractual relationships are regularly complicated, often more so than they commonly appear from the outside and as they are perceived by service users. Air travel may serve as an illustrative example. About one-third of all aircraft are purchased by leasing companies and leased to the airlines in question (Spero & Rennison, 2019). Hence, in these cases, passengers fly on aircrafts that are not owned by the companies that issued the ticket. In addition, often in the form of so-called wet leasing, both aircraft and the personnel who work on board are leased from other airlines. In these cases, therefore, there is not even a direct employment relationship between the airline and the human resources involved in the service provision. When purchasing a ticket, passengers thus acquire a number of rights that allow and enable them to access, for a limited period of time, the resources of the companies, which are directly or indirectly involved in the creation of the numerous service processes. In turn, airlines cannot deliver their service, if customers do not allow that they themselves or their cargo is being transported.

This access to resources thus needs to be coordinated and harmonized spatially, temporally, and legally. This means that an exchange of information must take place to clarify who or what will or must be located when and where, and who may use the resources in question and in what form. The respective information is exchanged between the various partners involved in a wide variety of ways: through personal conversations, written communication, telephone calls, e-mails, advertisements, and so on. Service management in this sense thus means to coordinate the access and the integration of the various resources that are necessary and need to be brought into play in order to deliver a service.

Service Management as Enabling and Realizing Value Creation Through Service

The notion of resource integration that is occurring in the course of service processes leads to the fourth understanding of service and service management. It is based on the purpose that a service provides or is intended to provide: to create value for its recipient. This idea has been driven primarily by the service-dominant logic (S-D logic). According to this view, all social and economic actors are resource integrators, who cocreate value through their resource-integrating activities together with other actors (Vargo & Lusch, 2016). This cocreation of value is based on "service-for-service" exchange as all resources involved "serve" (verb!) the respective actors in order to cocreate value. Hence, following such value creation perspective on service leads to an understanding of service management as "a set of competencies available for actors in the ecosystem, enabling and realizing value creation through service" (Edvardsson & Tronvoll, *this book*, Chap. 1).

An important prerequisite for this type of service management is obviously to have a clear understanding of what value is in the first place. In S-D logic, value is framed as an "experiential outcome" (Vargo & Lusch, 2017, p. 54). Consequently, the concept of value cocreation "is developing into [a narrative] of resource-integrating, reciprocal-service-providing actors cocreating value through holistic, meaning-laden *experiences* in nested and overlapping service ecosystems, governed and evaluated through their institutional arrangements" (Vargo & Lusch, 2016, p. 7; emphasis by the authors). Accordingly, service management in this sense has to focus on shaping the actors' experiences (Helkkula et al., 2012) in order to create value for them.

For this purpose, the theory of goal-directed behavior (Bagozzi & Dholakia, 1999; Perugini & Bagozzi, 2001) helps to clarify how value is assessed. According to this perspective, value results from the extent of goal achievement an actor perceives (Woodruff, 1997). Here, a goal is defined as "a mental image or other end point representation associated with affect toward which action may be directed" (Pervin, 1989, p. 474). Each goal is typically embedded in a hierarchy of superordinate and subordinate goals. While superordinate goals explain *why* an actor wants to achieve for which (s)he strives, subordinate goals describe *how* an actor can achieve for which (s)he strives (Bagozzi & Dholakia, 1999). Accordingly, actors identify attractive options for service-for-service exchange that are expected to contribute to their goal achievement, choose between competing options to attain their goals, and assess the extent of goal achievement that is experienced during resource integration.

Moreover, for this type of service management, it is also crucial to have a clear understanding of who are those "other actors" who are part of the value cocreating processes that are enabled by service. Here, a narrower and a broader view have been developed in literature. The first one is represented by the so-called service logic that emphasizes that actors cocreate value "only" when they interact directly with each other. This understanding is reflected in the three "spheres" that are distinguished in this regard. In the "provider sphere" and the "customer sphere", providers "only" act as a "value facilitators" who produce resources that are used in customers' value creation either independently or in interactive processes. In contrast, within the "joint sphere", customers and providers cocreate value "in interaction" as both customers and providers are engaged in the respective co-productive value creating processes (Grönroos & Voima, 2013). In contrast, S-D logic sees all actors that are also indirectly connected to resource-integrating activities as members of a service ecosystem in which value is jointly created. Accordingly, a service ecosystem is defined as a "relatively self-contained, self-adjusting system of resource-integrating actors connected by shared institutional arrangements and mutual value creation through service exchange" (Vargo & Lusch, 2016, pp. 10f.). Consequently, depending on the perspective taken, service management has to focus on a smaller or larger number of actors as its addressees.

3 Coordination of Actors and Activities as the Core of Service Management

Following the previous characterizations, managing service outputs, service processes, resource access, as well as resource integration to enable and realize value through service obviously always go hand in hand with coordination. Consequently, regardless of the underlying understanding of service, service management can be seen as the *coordination of service-related activities and their actors*, which is the "management of interdependence between tasks but also between the people who perform those tasks" (Gittel, 2011, p. 400). Hence, the more actors and activities are involved in service exchange, delivery, or provision, the higher is the degree of interdependence. This leads to a higher complexity of the relevant coordination processes and thus rising coordination costs resulting from them. As coordination relies on the exchange of information to a large extent, it is not surprising that, striving to reduce the relevant costs, all sorts of coordination tasks have been increasingly simplified, shortened in time, and ultimately made more convenient and efficient through the use of modern information technologies over the last decades. A striking example is car- and bike-sharing services that are currently gaining more and more importance. They could not have been realized effectively and efficiently without the digitization of the relevant booking, reservation, and payment processes. Similarly, in the future, as "Industry 4.0" or "Internet of Things" (IoT) applications become more widespread, equipment such as machines, robots, but also work-pieces and tools will communicate with each other via a global information infrastructure across functional boundaries (e.g., procurement, supply chain management, operations, and sales), corporate boundaries (e.g., manufacturers, wholesalers, retailers, service providers, and end users), and geographical boundaries. This will also dramatically simplify the coordination of the service provision, thus making it more cost-efficient at the same time. Moreover, it is also foreseeable that the increasing spread of platform technologies will make it even easier in the future to link providers and users of resources of all kinds with each other cost-efficient and conveniently at the same time. This will offer a wide range of opportunities for the creation of new service offerings or the transformation of existing ones, not least in the C2C sector (Fehrer et al., 2018). In the following section, future opportunities and challenges of such simplified and cost-efficient coordination of service are discussed.

4 Opportunities and Challenges of Simplified and Cost-Efficient Coordination of Service

Effects on Resource Utilization

The reductions in coordination costs caused by an increasing application of IT will firstly enable a more efficient use of resources. At the same time, the resulting new business models will allow more people to consume while satisfying their needs, values, and lifestyles through "sharing" and "access" rather than "ownership". Therefore, many people see such practices of resource sharing, especially when they are non-commercial in nature, as a way to express community-building and social values and to strengthen their respective self-image—although, in some cases, such forms of sharing economy only repackage old consumerist behaviors into a more appealing message. Nevertheless, ownership loses its importance as an identity-building element (Fritze et al., 2020). In turn, we are increasingly seeing manifestations of "psychological ownership" (e.g., Pierce et al., 2001) that refers to the resources of a provider that are necessary to deliver a service, such as the car of a car-sharing provider. Users thus develop or have the feeling that they own the respective objects— or parts of them—although they are not their legal owners at all. Since such "psychological ownership" has a positive impact on the value of a service used and subsequently on customer satisfaction as well as on behavioral intensions in terms of loyalty and willingness to recommend (Kleinaltenkamp et al.,

2018), service providers need to focus on increasing the psychological ownership of their customers the more access-based service offerings become more widespread.

At the same time, the differentiation of the market system that accompanies the spread of platform technologies also leads, especially within commercially oriented business models, to a more speculative investment behavior regarding assets such as real estate, cars, motorcycles, bicycles, and so on. In addition, the provision of such services increasingly involves small entrepreneurs who manage these assets. Hence, uncertainty about future demands and market developments, as well as the logic of platform business models according to which "the winner takes it all", tends to promote the emergence of overcapacity in this context. This impressively exemplified by the "bike share graveyards" that frequently encountered in China, for example. This is typically accompanied by a greater resource exploitation, which could reduce the ecological sustainability of the service economy. The sustainable design of value creation processes is therefore not (any longer) just a problem the manufacturing industry is facing, but also poses a challenge for service management. This has been made evident, for example, in the discussions about the impact of air travel on climate change or the use of disposable tableware and cutlery in fast food and coffee shop chains.

Alternatives of Future Structures of Resource Ownership

In addition to the issues of a resource-friendly design of future service offerings, the question of who ultimately owns the resources to which access is granted in the course of service provisioning also represents an important future challenge for service management. After all, only because access to resources is simplified, ownership of the resources in question does not become completely obsolete. Various scenarios are conceivable.

First, there could be a concentration of resources in the hands of a few individual owners in certain areas, who could thus gain a corresponding position of power, which they could in turn try to exploit to their advantage. Large housing companies active in the real estate sector and initiatives to cap rents or even expropriate companies can serve as examples of such developments. In these fields, therefore, there are at least tendencies to place resources that are regarded as critical more strongly in the hands of the state.

A second solution lies in the greater emergence of cooperatives, in which various individuals join together for the purpose of sharing resources and which are widespread in many service sectors, such as wholesale and retail trade, banking, housing, energy supply, education, and health care. From the perspective of ownership of the resources in question, this not only prevents excessive concentration. At the same time, common ownership and the exclusion of people who do not participate in a cooperative prevent the "tragedy of commons" (Hardin, 1968). This typically occurs when, in the case of a commons good, no one can be excluded from its use, but at the same time there is rivalry in consumption, that is, in access to the resource in question.

A third variant can be observed in platform businesses such as AirBnB, Uber, or Lyft, where the ownership of the resources through which the respective services are provided (apartments, cars, etc.) remains with the large multitude of service providers, while the platform operators "merely" have to enable and coordinate access to the resources and provide the necessary technical infrastructure. Thus, the predominant risks of ownership are left with the relatively small providers of the services, while the platform operators themselves only have to make comparatively small investments but can appropriate the benefits from coordinating access to resources.

Opportunities and Challenges of New Forms of Rights Assurance and Rights Transfer

But it is not only the coordination of access to the required provider resources in the context of service provision that is being simplified and made more cost-efficient by digitization. This also applies to the securing of the transfer of rights that take place in this context. This is particularly evident in the example of blockchain technology. Blockchain represents a distributed ledger technology that aims to reduce the cost of establishing and maintaining trust between actors (Nakamoto, 2008), such as those who interact in various types of service transactions. Based on so-called smart contracts that consist of codes comprising a set of rules through which the negotiation and execution of an agreement or transaction is enabled or facilitated, verified, and enforced (Mattereum., 2018), blockchain opens up new and efficient solutions for peer-to-peer transactions of all kinds. In this way, the role and importance of intermediaries and platforms that today ensure the security of such transactions is reduced, if not eliminated. Consequently, blockchain has the potential to transform and fundamentally challenge all types of formal or informal governance through which service transactions in all service sectors are currently steered and controlled by governments, markets, communities, or other social institutions.

By its very nature, blockchain thus challenges many concepts that deal with the management and control of processes in business, politics, and society, and in the service sector in particular. From a service management perspective, the technology opens up a wide range of opportunities for developing new service offerings or transforming existing ones. For example, blockchain can be used to improve customer engagement in service organizations, just as the technology can be used within service organizations to improve business efficiency. In addition, blockchain will make it possible for completely new business models to emerge for the provision of services, whereby in many cases an increase in efficiency will be achieved simply by the fact that companies previously acting as intermediaries, such as banks, lawyers and notaries, auditors, and so on, will be leapfrogged and thus become superfluous, at least in part. In addition, it is to be expected that, with the aid of blockchain technology, new forms of management of intra- as well as inter-organizational cooperation will emerge in the service sector, which in turn will contribute to increasing the efficiency of service provision. The future challenge for service management is therefore to explore the options that blockchain and similar technologies provide for the design of service offerings and to manage the transition to a redesign of business models in which such applications may form essential components.

Opportunities and Challenges of Reducing (Personnel) Costs Through the Use of New Technologies

Increasing digitization will not only simplify communication between service providers and customers, it will also fundamentally change it. Up to now, the production of services has been more labor-intensive than the production of tangible goods, which is particularly true for many consumer and personal services (e.g., nursing services). This results not only in the service sector's lower share of value added compared to employment but also in the fact that the services in question often are or can be only automated to a lesser extent. The lower productivity resulting from the lower capital intensity in turn creates a continuing incentive to develop new technologies or further develop existing ones, with the help of which personnel costs can be reduced. Accordingly, as digitization progresses and as a result of general technological progress, services provided by people will increasingly be replaced in whole or in part by technology-based solutions. This applies not only to more standardized services, such as those provided by ATMs, ticket machines, or vending machines, but also increasingly to individualized and personalized services due to the further development of technologies in areas such as sensor technology, robotics, optics, and machine learning. Such developments can already be observed today in the many forms of self-service technologies, voice assistance systems, and so on.

However, further development of technologies does not necessarily mean that certain service creation processes will be completely taken over by machines, robots, or other technical systems. Rather, services that are still ultimately performed by humans can be simplified, shortened in time, or even performed more precisely (Wirtz et al., 2021). For example, service technicians are already being provided with information on tablets or via data glasses while carrying out repair and maintenance work on site, which they can then use directly to perform their services. Likewise, they can send corresponding information via the aforementioned channels, which can then in turn be analyzed elsewhere to improve their services.

This can even mean that providers no longer perform all the activities involved in a service themselves, but instead equip their customers with appropriate technology and process knowledge so that they are enabled to perform certain tasks themselves. In this way, employees of customer companies already interact with back-office specialists from manufacturers when carrying out repair and maintenance work, for example, whereby the use of augmented reality makes it possible for devices or systems to be examined in parallel without actually having to inspect them on site.

For service management, this gives rise to numerous questions, such as in which sub-areas and processes of service offerings customers or users accept that they are not provided personally, but by machines or technical systems. The question also arises as to how the acceptance of such machine-based services can be increased, if necessary, and how man-machine interfaces can be designed in such a way that the greatest possible user benefit is achieved for the customer and operating errors can be effectively prevented.

Opportunities and Challenges of New Service Offerings Through Data Usage

All of the aforementioned developments are also leading to an increase in the scope and extent of connectivity between people, between people and the devices they use, and between the devices in question (e.g., Kumar et al., 2017). Thus, data is increasingly being generated that can be used to develop new services and new digital business models that can both increase the value of certain service offerings to customers and reduce the cost of creating services. A generic process view of human life (Leyer et al., 2016) provides a good starting point for this. It assumes that individuals—similar to the view developed by Porter for value creation processes of companies (2004)—perform both primary and supporting processes to shape their lives. Here, primary processes refer to physical health, education, work, leisure, and locomotion, while supporting processes include activities that involve individual organization, acquisition of resources of all kinds, information gathering, self-expression, and housework.

Any of these processes can be simplified, improved, or made more cost-effective by using data obtained from and with customers or users. In addition, entirely new service offerings can be created in this way, which ultimately offer the people who use them—just as with "traditional" service offerings—a time saving or a pastime. At present—and presumably also in the near future—the improvement of the individual work-life balance is increasingly becoming the focus of interest among service users.

This development may lead to create future autonomous service systems that include homes and buildings, transportation and logistics services, areas of agriculture, or the healthcare system (Lim & Maglio, 2018). An autonomous home, for example, is characterized by automating various property-related activities (e.g., lighting, cooking, temperature control, etc.) for the homeowners by collecting data, using algorithms, and performing communication and control operations. Accordingly, such an autonomous home can significantly simplify the lives of homeowners by performing the various activities not only autonomously but also, based on the preferences of the respective users, in an individualized manner.

However, these fundamentally positive aspects are offset by possible negative consequences in terms of data protection, which means that people who have concerns in this regard do not make their data available for these purposes and therefore do not become users of such offerings. Such resistance can only be overcome by finding new ways of reconciling business interests on the one hand and data protection on the other (e.g., Chandler et al., 2019).

Opportunities and Challenges of Future Service Offerings Linked to Data Usage

If, ultimately, in the course of providing both "traditional" and data-based services, data is increasingly transferred, stored, and made available in a timely manner, it is obvious that services will also have to be provided to an ever greater extent which, in turn, support precisely the provision of these services, simplify them, make them more cost-efficient, or make them more convenient for the users. This can currently be seen in the dramatic growth of the cloud business where more and more firms are using the services of companies like Amazon Web Services (AWS), Microsoft, or Google to network factories and supply chains, to store and analyze data from measuring devices of all kinds, or to transfer audio and video files. However, the services offered by cloud providers now go far beyond the mere storage of data in corresponding data centers. AWS, for example, is planning to use satellites to transmit data to and from its customers, and often from their customers as well, for example, for weather forecasts or data-based services for agriculture. By integrating these services into the AWS value chain, customers can send the relevant data directly to the data centers, store it, analyze it, and process it further.

Moreover, from a purely technical perspective, basically all of a company's IT tasks could be moved to the cloud. Hence, it can be expected that in the coming decades an increasing number of companies will no longer operate their own data centers. This means that the relevant activities will be performed within the framework of corresponding cloud solutions and only those tasks where the proximity between the location of data generation and use on the one hand and data storage on the other is of particular importance, such as in a manufacturing factory, will still be performed on site in the future. It is therefore not surprising that cloud providers are increasingly offering various services around the purely data-related business. These range from the design and development of the projects concerned to the training of employees. Thus, value creation structures based on the division of labor are increasingly emerging in the provision of IT-related services, as was characteristic of the manufacturing sector in the course of industrialization in the twentieth century and is still the case today.

5 Conclusion

Service and thus also service management appear in the most diverse forms. In literature, four basic views have been developed in this regard. They see service management as managing (1) service outputs, (2) service processes, (3) resource access, or (4) resource integration to enable and realize value through service. However, regardless of these different perspectives, the commonality of the various forms of service management is that it comprises the *coordination of service-related activities and their actors*. Consequently, also the future challenges and opportunities of service management are mainly thrusted by the relevant coordination tasks as well as the costs associated with them. Based on this assumption, six areas are identified representing opportunities and challenges for the future development of service management. They relate to (1) the efficiency of resource utilization, (2) the future structures of resource ownership, (3) the forms of rights assurance and rights transfer, (4) cost reductions through the use of new technologies, and the development of (5) service offerings through data usage as well as (6) service offerings linked to data usage. Those being responsible for service management should thus be aware of and cope these challenges to take advantage of the respective opportunities they offer to enable and realize value through service for customers, suppliers, and all other actors engaged in service enactment.

References

Bagozzi, R. P., & Dholakia, U. (1999). Goal setting and goal striving in consumer behavior. *Journal of Marketing, 63*(4), 19–32.

Bendapudi, N., & Leone, R. P. (2003). Psychological implications of customer participation in co-production. *Journal of Marketing, 67*(1), 14–28.

Cermak, D. S. P., File, K. M., & Prince, R. A. (1994). Customer participation in service specification and delivery. *Journal of Applied Business Research, 10*(3), 90–100.

Chandler, J. D., Danatzis, I., Wernicke, C., Akaka, M. A., & Reynolds, D. (2019). How does innovation emerge in a service ecosystem? *Journal of Service Research, 22*(1), 75–89.

Fehrer, J. A., Benoit, S., Aksoy, L., Baker, T. L., Bell, S. J., Brodie, R. J., & Marimuthu, M. (2018). Future scenarios of the collaborative economy: Centrally orchestrated, social bubbles or decentralized autonomous? *Journal of Service Management, 29*(5), 859–882.

Fisher, A. G. B. (1952). A note on tertiary production. *Economic Journal, 62*, S. 820–S. 834.

Fließ, S., & Kleinaltenkamp, M. (2004). Blueprinting the service company: Managing service processes efficiently and effectively. *Journal of Business Research, 57*, 392–404.

Fourastié, J. (1952). *Le grand espoir du XXème siècle*. Presses Universitaires de France.

Fritze, M. P., Marchand, A., Eisingerich, A. B., & Benkenstein, M. (2020). Access-based services as substitutes for material possessions: The role of psychological ownership. *Journal of Service Research, 23*(3), 368–385.

Gittel, J. H. (2011). New directions for relational coordination theory. In K. S. Cameron & G. M. Spreitzer (Eds.), *The Oxford handbook of positive organizational scholarship* (pp. 74–94). Oxford University Press.

Grönroos, C., & Voima, P. (2013). Critical service logic: Making sense of value creation and co-creation. *Journal of the Academy of Marketing Science, 41*, 133–150.

Haase, M., & Kleinaltenkamp, M. (2011). Property rights design and market process: Implications for market theory, marketing theory and S-D logic. *Journal of Macromarketing, 31*(2), 148–159.

Hardin, G. (1968). The tragedy of the commons. *Science, 162*(3859), 1243–1248.

Helkkula, A., Kelleher, C., & Pihlström, M. (2012). Characterizing value as an experience: Implications for service researchers and managers. *Journal of Service Research, 15*(1), 59–75.

Kleinaltenkamp, M., Storck, F., Gumprecht, P., & Li, J. (2018). The impact of psychological ownership on value in use and relational outcomes. *SMR – Journal of Service Management Research, 2*(2), 50–66.

Kumar, V., Lahiri, A., & Dogan, O. B. (2017). A strategic framework for a profitable business model in the sharing economy. *Industrial Marketing Management, 69*, 147–160.

Leyer, M., Kronsbein, D., & Rosemann, M. (2016). Individual process management: A first step towards the conceptualisation of individual activities. *International Journal of Business Environment, 8*(2), 105–120.

Lim, C., & Maglio, P. P. (2018). Clarifying the concept of smart service system. In P. P. Maglio, C. A. Kieliszewski, J. C. Spohrer, K. Lyons, L. Patrício, & Y. Sawatani (Eds.), *Handbook of service science, Volume II* (pp. 349–376). Springer.

Lovelock, C., & Gummesson, E. (2004). Whither services marketing? In search of a new paradigm and fresh perspectives. *Journal of Service Research, 7*(1), 20–41.

Lovelock, C. H. (1995). Competing on service: Technology and teamwork in supplementary services. *Strategy & Leadership, 23*(4), 32–47.

Mattereum. (2018). *Smart contracts. Real property.* Retrieved July 15, 2019, from https://www.mattereum.com/upload/iblock/af8/mattereum_workingpaper.pdf

Nakamoto, S. (2008). Bitcoin: A peer-to-peer electronic cash system. Zugriff am 15. Juli 2019, von. https://bitcoin.org/bitcoin.pdf

OECD. (2005). Growth in services – Fostering employment, productivity and innovation, meeting of the OECD council at ministerial level, Paris.

Perugini, M., & Bagozzi, R. P. (2001). The role of desires and anticipated emotions in goal-directed behaviours: Broadening and deepening the theory of planned behavior. *British Journal of Social Psychology, 40*(1), 79–98.

Pervin, L. A. (1989). Goal concepts: Themes, issues, and questions. In L. A. Pervin (Ed.), *Goal concepts in personality and social psychology* (pp. 473–479). Lawrence Erlbaum Associates.

Pierce, J. L., Kostova, T., & Dirks, K. T. (2001). Toward a theory of psychological ownership in organizations. *Academy of Management Review, 26*(2), 298–310.

Porter, M. (2004). *Competitive advantage* (11th ed.). The Free Press.

Shostak, G. L. (1985). Planning the service encounter. In A. Czepiel, R. Solomon, & F. Surprenat (Eds.), *The service encounter* (pp. 243–254). Lexington.

Silpakit, P., & Fisk, R. P. (1985). Participating the service encounter: A theoretical framework. In T. M. Block, G. D. Upah, & V. A. Zeithaml (Eds.), *Service marketing in a changing environment* (pp. 117–121). American Marketing Association.

Spero, J., & Rennison, J. (2019, May 13). Boeing crisis puts aircraft leasing in the spotlight. *Financial Times*. Retrieved July 15, 2019, from https://www.ft.com/content/c6cd02b2-6d86-11e9-80c7-60ee53e6681d

Vargo, S. L., & Lusch, R. F. (2016). Institutions and axioms: An extension and update of service-dominant logic. *Journal of the Academy of Marketing Science, 44*(1), 5–23.

Vargo, S. L., & Lusch, R. F. (2017). Service-dominant logic 2025. *International Journal of Research in Marketing, 34*, 46–67.

Wirtz, J., Kunz, W., & Paluch, S. (2021). The service revolution, intelligent automation and service robots. *The European Business Review, 2021*, 38–44.

Wirtz, J., & Lovelock, C. (2018). *Essentials of services marketing* (3rd ed.). Pearson.

Wittkowski, K., Moeller, S., & Wirtz, J. (2013). Firms' intentions to use non-ownership services. *Journal of Service Research, 16*(2), 171–185.

Woodruff, R. B. (1997). Customer value: The next source for competitive advantage. *Journal of the Academy of Marketing Science, 25*(2), 139–153.

Is Service Management Experiencing a Change of Era?

Jaqueline Pels and Cristina Mele

Withstanding the specific topics/themes the different service management meta-analysis have elicited (e.g., Furrer et al., 2020; Gummesson, 2012), the concept of change is ever present. This dynamic situation raises a series of questions: how radical are these changes? Why are dichotomous positions adopted? Are these changes part of a broader shift that involves not only service management, but also management at large? Do the changes go beyond management? In other words, are the changes identified within the service field a reflection of broader socio-economic-political changes that society, at large, is experiencing?

According to Gummesson (2012), a paradigm "consists of principles, assumptions and axioms which we take for granted and on which we base our research and practice often even without knowing it. They are often not proven; they may be the best we have for the time being but they may also be just myths. They form the stage for the marketing opera" (p. 6). Gummesson (2012) identifies three service paradigms: pre-1970s, services are not recognized, all is goods and manufacturing; 1970s–2000s, the era of goods-service differences; and post-2000s, the era of commonalities, interdependencies and

---

J. Pels (✉)
Universidad Torcuato Di Tella, Buenos Aires, Argentina
e-mail: jpels@utdt.edu

C. Mele
Department of Economics, Management and Institutions, University of Naples Federico II, Naples, Italy
e-mail: Cristina.mele@unina.it

© The Author(s), under exclusive license to Springer Nature Switzerland AG 2022
B. Edvardsson, B. Tronvoll (eds.), *The Palgrave Handbook of Service Management*,
https://doi.org/10.1007/978-3-030-91828-6_5

a systemic approach. The last one is still developing, promoting a fresh view of service and value as outcomes of value propositions and resource integration from many actors in complex service ecosystems (Gummesson et al., 2010).

Recently, Furrer et al. (2020) conducted a content analysis on more than 3000 articles published in ten major service and marketing research journals over the last three decades. Their work offers an overview of key service research themes and their developments over time. Moreover, they look at prior service literature reviews adopting different types of methods: expert-based surveys (Fisk et al., 2000; Ostrom et al., 2010, 2015), citation studies (Kunz & Hogreve, 2011; Wilden et al., 2017), and content analyses of published research (Fisk et al., 1993; Furrer & Sollberger, 2007; Nel et al., 2011). Thus, it can be argued that they provide the reader with a clear positioning of the field. Furrer et al. (2020, p. 311) conclude that service research can be depicted as a "dynamic research domain".

While Gummesson's (2012) work identifies three periods in which the overall outlook shifts, Furrer et al.'s (2020) work allows to infer that service management topics seem to be undergoing a series of shifts: (a) from being highly focused on the customer (consumer behavior, customer satisfaction) and/or on the organization (quality, strategy, performance) to being more diffused (relationship marketing, technology/e-service, emotions, environmental context, innovation, leadership, ethics), (b) from very monolithic and service-centric toward a higher interdisciplinary dialogue (e.g., with psychology, in the human resource management (HRM) issues of climate and employees, or with the operations literature in the topics of distribution, price/value, usage/purchase and communication) and (c) from a good-dominant logic to a service-dominant logic. These findings are aligned with the different views presented in this book. For example, Enquist and Sebhatu (Chap. 22, this volume) highlight the shift from firm-centric to a broader sustainable stakeholder view and societal perspective for Business Societal Transformation. Shifts are often presented adopting a dichotomous view. For instance, Kleinaltenkamp (Chap. 4, this volume) analyses different forms of service management (e.g., business to customer [B2C] vs. business to business [B2B], person-related vs. object-related, individual vs. collective, analog vs. virtual), while Vargo and Fehrer (Chap. 6, this volume) review good-dominant/service-dominant logic approaches and Enquist and Sebhatu look at before and after COVID-19 pandemic distinction.

Many of the changes are not a service management specific phenomenon, for example, the importance of sustainability issues, the irruption of technological innovations and the digital transformation (i.e., robots, artificial intelligence, blockchain technology, the Internet of Things) or the understanding that customer engagement and co-creation process occur in extended ecosystems that include various stakeholders (rather than dyadic affairs between an organization and its customers).

In this chapter, we will support the argument that the changes, within the service field, reflect a broader change. To this end, we will clarify the differences between an Era of Changes and a Change of Era. Relatedly, we will reflect on the way we think, analyze options and provide solutions. Particularly, we will explore our tendency to think in a dichotomous way and, consequently, create axis of tensions. Finally, we will look at the role of COVID-19 in this process and suggest possible future paths for the discipline.

1   Change of Era or Era of Changes?

This subtitle sounds as a play of words, but it uncovers a profound distinction (Pels, 2020). It allows understanding the magnitude of different types of changes. An illustrative way to visualize these differences is by looking at history.

If we told a feudal lord that, in the future, kings would not be the most important political figures, that his servants would have the right to vote (just like him) for authorities (named presidents or prime ministers), that agriculture would not be the center of the economy, that cities would house the majority of the population, that the horses would not be the means of transportation, that pigeons would no longer be the means of communication, surely, he would have laughed assuming we were jesters in his court. Today we are experiencing a Change of Era of the same magnitude. These are exceptional moments, humanity has gone through just a few of them. In the western world, we can list Prehistory, Classical, Middle Ages, Early Modern and the Modern Era. Living through one of these is a privilege but, also, a mystery. So, what distinguishes an Era of Changes from a Change of Era? Drawing on Raskin et al. (2002), as well as decades studying history, allows identifying four characteristics (see Table 1).

Table 1 Era of changes and change of era

	Era of changes	Change of era
Type of change	Incremental and fast	Radical modifying the intrinsic logic
Impact of change	Easy to predict	Unpredictable
Influence of the change	Compartmentalized	Transversal
Timespan of the change	Human (decades)	Historic (century)

In an *Era of Changes*, first, transformations accelerate but they do not change the intrinsic logic of the time. For example, throughout the twentieth century, cars have become technologically more sophisticated, but the means of transportation did not change. Second, it is relatively easy to predict the impact of change; the introduction of Skype directly affected the incumbent business of long-distance calls. Third, changes are compartmentalized, what happens in one field does not affect others. For example, the rise of dotcoms affected industries but did not change the political or economic system. Finally, due to its intense rhythm, in the course of a person's lifetime, we can see its birth, development and maturity, for example, the emergence and development of television.

> When applied to the service management literature, we can argue that research associated to breaking free from product focus (Shostack, 1977) and the introduction of the importance of service quality (Parasuraman, Berry, & Zeithmal, 1991) both fit this definition.

Alternatively, in a *Change of Era*, the four abovementioned characteristics no longer hold. First, changes are radical. As we saw in the example of the shift between medieval times and modernity, the nature of transportation was revolutionized—from horses to automobiles. Second, it is easy to see what "no longer is", but, we do not know, what "shall be". Does it make sense to compare current changes with the industrial revolution of the nineteenth century? Is it necessary to change the education system (not just the delivery, but the content)? If we tried to define it, surely, we would be right for a short period, but wrong about the final result. Let us return to the example of tele-communications. Solutions that seemed new, such as Skype, were quickly replaced by others like WhatsApp and Zoom. Today, we *know* that there will be further developments in interpersonal communications. Third, processes are transversal. As all Eras of Change, the twentieth century was focused on specialization; this leads to lose sight of the set of forces that are presented in interrelated mode, where a change impacts and amplifies the others. In the twenty-first century, changes will transcend technological innovations (e.g., the Internet of Things, artificial intelligence, blockchain); they will involve interrelated changes: in communication (e.g., social networks, fake news), in economics (e.g., the future of work, blockchain/bitcoin), in geopolitics (e.g., Brexit, the rise of China, the fall of the USA-Russia axis), in philosophy (e.g., post-modernity, the post-scientific truth), in the collective objectives (e.g., United Nations' sustainable development goals), in art (e.g., digital art), in education (e.g., continuous training), among others. Finally, timespan is long;

Is Service Management Experiencing a Change of Era? 75

changes are measured in centuries. Though Raskin's report shows that periods have shortened and we have gone from cycles from 100,000 years to 10,000 years to 1000 years to approximately 100 years, they all exceed human lifetime. If we take the case of the French Revolution of 1789, usually, history places it as the end of totalitarian monarchies and as the historical fact that lays the foundations of modern democracy. However, in the 80 years following the French Revolution, France went through seven political regimes: three constitutional monarchies, two ephemeral republics and two empires (including Napoleon). We can say that a Parisian who participated in the seizure of the Bastille surely felt confused: he knew that they had beheaded the King Louis XVI, but were they moving forward? Backward? Sideways?

When applied to the service management literature, we can argue that research associated to the service-dominant logic (note the adoption of the words *logic* and *dominant*) could be associated to manifestations of this type of change. We assist to a profound change in the tenets and axioms of service research (Vargo & Lusch, 2004, 2008). Some of suggested shifts are: from the traditional producer and consumers divide to the generic actor to actor mutual service provision; from focus on the dyad to contemplating the entire service ecosystem; and from the service as output to the service provision as resource integration. These changes do not simply witness a movement from static entity (noun) to dynamic process (verb) (Mele et al., 2015) but prompt the framing of a new thinking (Lusch & Vargo, 2014). Other examples, from the service literature, are the recent research on smart services (Wuenderlich et al., 2015) and studies based on the application of cognitive technologies (Mele et al., 2021a). As Mele et al. (Chap. 42) address, smart technologies are affecting service provision and service experience not simply through automation or augmentation of process and capabilities but engaging the customer in emerging ways not always designed by providers. Thus, the smartness of service technology does not lie in the wider use of a more advanced technology but in finding new ways of value co-creation.

Similarly, in service management practice, the sharing economy depicts a new peer-to-peer economic model, overcoming the traditional producer/customer view. Everyone can become a service provider, renting his/her house or care or other stuff through the web. The profound change is from the ownership to the rental or the access to goods and services, often facilitated by a community-based online platform, as in the cases of Airbnb, Uber, or TripAdvisor. As a result, a different kind of capitalism emerges, labeled crowd-based capitalism: the capitalism based on crowds indicates how the organization of economic activities is moving from the entrepreneur to the "crowds" or how entrepreneurship is distributed among the population. Another example of the profound change in service business is the development of the digital platform economy, with digital service business models such as Amazon or Netflix. When Netflix was launched in 1997, Blockbuster was the undisputed champion of the video rental industry. Between 1985 and 1992, the brick-and-mortar rental chain grew from its first location (in Dallas, Texas) to more than 2800 locations around the world. Back then, before the Internet became integrated into nearly every facet of our lives, it was hard to imagine brick-and-mortar Blockbuster stores disappearing. However, though technology changed, Blockbuster's innovation stagnated. It was unable to understand where the danger might come from and this happened because they did not know how to correctly define how the market was changing. Netflix rode such a change. By exploiting big data, cloud, algorithms, new companies open the way for radical changes in how people work, socialize and co-create value.

As a result of the nature of a Change of Era, we need to befriend ourselves with four situations we are, usually, uncomfortable with. We need to accept that a new overall rationale will emerge. Recognize that we are in a state of "being", that as a result of interrelationships, trying to predict its final form, is *just* an exercise. We need to beware that it is risky to think that "we have arrived" because it creates false certainties. Given that processes are transversal, one should be aware that partial readings will probably be wrong. Moreover, from this perspective, technological advances, while very important, are only a symptom and it is important to acknowledge that changes occur at the legal, political, economic, social and individual level. Thus, it is important to take a holistic and systemic approach. Finally, the twentieth century taught us how to live with changes; now, we must learn to live with uncertainty, and we have to develop patience and resilience.

2   The Role of Axis of Tensions, in the Evolution of Humanity

We have highlighted some shifts within the service management field: from being focused on the product versus service dichotomy to looking at resource integration; from focus on the customer and/or on the organization to adopting a broader perspective; from very monolithic and service-centric toward a higher interdisciplinary dialogue and from a good-dominant logic to a service-dominant logic. The from/to manner in which we present the options shows that we are inclined to exacerbate dichotomies and tensions. Such tensions are dilemmas scholars try to solve. For example, O'Discoll (2008, p. 95) argues that "a trade-off is considered between two forces, one remains in the ascendant and the overall outcome is a win–lose proposition". When discussing axis of tension, normally, an invitation is made to overcome simple binary choice in order to comprehend "the complexity, diversity, and ambiguity of business and organizational life ... [and] examining the impacts of plurality and change, helping understanding of divergent perspectives, and coping with disruptive experiences" (O'Driscoll, 2008, p. 95). In such a view, solutions are a synthesis. They seek to harmonize, to integrate and suggest how to overcome the tension; however, these solutions are always within the suggested axis of tension. Why do we tend to think in terms of opposite pairs and confrontations and try to find synthesis? To answer this question, let us make an example from a different arena.

Many years ago, one of the authors coached a sports team, in the junior category. Like every team, they aimed to win. In Argentina, after the game was over, both teams met, shared cocoa and developed camaraderie. At that moment, differences were put aside, the result of the match no longer mattered (that much); love of sports and communion arose. The trainers knew that the spirit of this after-game get together was as (if not more) important as the game itself. So, why have a competition rather than a friendly match? One possible answer is that confrontation made the sport, as a whole, better. It improved because everyone aimed at doing their best and it was an encouragement to create new moves; finally, a good match was, above all, beautiful, harmonious and surprising. In short, in any field, tensions have the role of driving innovation and creativity. However, there are also frustrating matches, when the teams aim to overrun the opponent and the effect is devastating. So, the question we would like to explore is why have we exacerbated tensions in recent years?

Before answering this question, it would be interesting to see whether there have always been tensions. Once again, history is a good ally. It seems that tensions have been with us for a long time. In the twentieth century, between communism and capitalism; further back in time; in the sixteenth century, between Protestants and Catholics; further back still, in the twelfth century, between Guelph and Ghibellines; and the list goes on. So, if tensions have always accompanied us, it is worth asking if, in essence, they're all one and the same.

The answer seems to be affirmative. To understand their similarity, it is necessary to shift focus from the specific topic and look at the structure of tensions. When we take this approach, tensions can be seen as socially constructed dichotomies—opposite ends of a continuum. It is easy to visualize the tension between communism and capitalism as extremes of an axis that represents alternative types of political and economic models: planned or free market. Similarly, the tension between Protestants and Catholics can be seen as opposing extremes of an axis that represents contrasting ways of seeing the dialogue with God: direct or mediated by the Pope. In our third example, the tension between Guelph and Ghibellines represents extremes of the axis of power: divine (represented by the pontiff) or earthly (represented by the emperor of the Holy Roman Empire).

Why is this axis-thinking exercise helpful? Thinking in terms of axis (rather than the specific topic) implies adopting a higher level of abstraction and it enables us to look at the process. Ultimately, from this perspective, we will be able to analyze tensions from a different rationale. The examples will allow seeing that when the tension occurs within an axis, "it is good". It is functional to generate debate, dialogue and acts as a stimulus to development. Returning to the sports metaphor, it improves the match. Without this kind of tension, possibly, there would have been no progress and we would still be living in caves. More importantly, to answer the question we posed, seeing tensions in terms of pairs of dialectical extremes of a given axis helps understand that, when we have explored all the possibilities offered by that axis (all the moves within a specific game), we are at the verge of a radical change—what we have labeled as a Change of Era. Moments, when a *new* axis needs to emerge.

Our historical examples help illustrate this point. The debate within the Guelph-Ghibellines axis discussed who held power (pontiff or emperor), but it did not question the idea that power was centralized. It was the new Protestantism-Catholicism axis that introduces the idea of decentralization. Similarly, the Protestantism-Catholicism axis did not question the Bible as the revealed truth; it is modernity and the rise of scientific truth that introduce the possibility of man as the source of knowledge. Trying to identify the right combination of both extremes does not seem to be the solution either. We would like to argue that our axis has been exhausted, we (humans) need to search for a change of axis; in other words, a Change of Era.

Some exercises in this direction can be found in the service management literature. For example, in 2004 two awarded articles published in *Journal of Service Research* (Lovelock & Gummesson, 2004) and *Journal of Marketing* (Vargo & Lusch, 2004) conceived a disruption. Lovelock and Gummesson (2004) challenge the validity and usefulness of one of the service marketing core criteria to differentiate goods and services: the IHIP (intangible, heterogeneous, inseparable and perishable). Alternatively, they propose a novel view that overcomes the tenet of ownership to introduce the idea of temporary possession. Their view about non-ownership is aligned with the new types of business exploiting digital platforms (i.e., Spotify, Coursera). Aligned with prior changes mentioned above, Vargo and Lusch (2004) propose dropping the product-service distinction and introduce a new idea: that service (i.e., the application of competences for the benefit of another) is the fundamental basis of value creation through exchange. That is, service is exchanged for service (i.e., by service systems) and goods, when involved, are service-provision vehicles. From this seminal article, a new language and lexicon for service management started to develop (Gummesson et al., 2010).

In the service management practice, the case of Tweeter exemplifies the emergence of a new rationale. The news was no longer provided by a certified expert, such as a reporter, but by "regular" citizen. Additionally, social media such as Instagram, Facebook, YouTube and TikTok spur a radical change in the language used by actors, from the written forms to photos, videos, hashtags and emoticons. New words enter daily communication and the linguistic change is inevitable: to google, tag, link, post, chat, tweet, screenshots and new sentences: "WhatsApp me the photo you IG (Instagram) so I post it on FB (Facebook)?" Furthermore, the "like" phenomenon enacts a reward learning. Seeking and receiving feedback from others can help build new social relationships and strengthen existing bonds.

3   Is COVID-19 the Cause of this Change of Era?

Let us, now, address our last point. Why in these last few years, and with the COVID-19 it becomes more evident, are tensions being exacerbated? At this stage, the answer is self-evident; we are living the birth to a new axis. As stated in Changes of Era, processes are transversal, we start realizing that the way things were "will no longer be" and it is difficult to foresee the outcome. From a geopolitical perspective, we can position the beginning of this process (though history will surely find another date/fact) with the fall of the Berlin Wall and Fukuyama's (1989) article the *End of History*, where he argues that with the dissolution of the Soviet Union, democracy and capitalism have won the Cold War. At the time, Fukuyama did not see that both extremes were interrelated and that they held a dialectical tension. From an economic perspective, a strong signal of the changes in act was the collapse of Lehman Brothers, in September 2008, and the subsequent rescue of financial sector by governments (note that the subprime market was one of the least regulated). In the same year, also indicating winds of change, Nakamoto coined the bitcoin and, more recently, Facebook's Libra[1] was announced (it does not matter that it did not prosper). It is interesting to note that these "currencies" are not within the decision range of the central banks. From a political point of view, Brexit, as well as the election, in G20 countries, of presidents who did not hold long standing political carriers, was also a signal that conventional political parties were reaching saturation point. From a philosophical standpoint, post-modernism and the central role of discourse (over Truth) and, societally, the ecological versus growth movements can also be considered as part of the interrelated systemic trend.

Zygmunt Bauman (2013) brilliantly synthesized all these trends into the expression liquid modernity. For example, he signals ephemeral social relationships (in antithesis of stable ones), the rise of narratives (above data), the speed at which companies changes and/or disappears (the average life of a company in the twentieth century was 60 years; today is 18 years, less than a third), decentralization (which involves loss of control), new forms of management such as lean management, fail fast, canvas (vs. long-term planning or corporate structures), among others. Bauman, being a twentieth-century philosopher, sees "what it no longer is". Alternatively, we can comprehend them as characterizing a phase transition.

From this historic perspective, COVID-19 and its effects can be seen as a catalyzer, an accelerator of a process that was already in motion; it is not a coincidence that Harari's (2014, 2016) books became a best seller. Without doubt, COVID-19 is making visible all the unaddressed tensions globalization/protectionism, human intelligence/artificial intelligence, governments/companies, virtual/real and ecology/growth. As stated, we are in a process of "being" so it is impossible to make predictions; however, it is very likely that the current situation will become the tipping point (Fuchs, 2007). The twentieth-century axis has reached its saturation in *all* its dimensions. At this stage, we can revisit the dynamism found in the field of service management (Furrer et al., 2020) as part of this broader Change of Era. A stage of experimentation is opening in front of us; which will be the new axis?

> COVID-19 also has opened debate with the service management literature. For example, Mele et al. (2021b) recognize that the coronavirus has had a tremendous impact on companies worldwide and that researchers have no clear idea of the key issues requiring their attention. They offer a fresh view on research priorities addressing essential service provision, bricolage service innovation, responsible shopping practices and market shaping amid crisis. These priorities

---

[1] https://libra.org/en-US/white-paper.

have an overarching focus on innovation and responsibility to bridge theory and practice "by building knowledge that is useful to businesses, individuals, communities, institutions, society and the bio-environment" (Bolton, 2020, p. 279).

4   Future Path

From this standpoint, we differ from Furrer et al.'s (2020) conclusion. They identify the future as a result of the past and the present and state "service research may evolve in two broad, complementary directions: expansion and diversification; and refocusing and revisiting" (p. 311). Alternatively, we suggest the future is open. We would argue that we will be seeing a set of explorative approaches, highly interdisciplinary trying to contribute and learn from other disciplines, not necessarily akin as HRM or operations. We argued that our rationale is, still, intrinsically tied to the past, that we are in the process of "being" and that there is a risk in believing that partial solutions will become institutionalized. With this warning, we can explore a few questions:

* Modernity introduced the notion of nation-states, in the future; will governments still define economic frontiers, if not, how will it affect service management?
* The digital world taught us it is difficult to tax companies that do not need to be physically anchored; will this expand to non-digital exchanges?
* Several economies are based on in situ experience (e.g., tourism); will experience go virtual?
* Concern with ecology is growing and it seems in conflict with a growth model based on consumption; will ecology be a component in the nascent axis?
* Competition has been the mantra for innovation, growth and profit; will cooperation, community focus, co-creation, collaborative intelligence, connectivity become the new mantras?
* Research has focused most on profitable customers; will studies concentrate to people in vulnerable positions in a post-coronavirus world?
* Complexity approaches have been marginal to service research; will scholars adopt more co-evolutive and emergent framework?

In short, a Change of Era is the period between two peaks. For example, we described the characteristics of the heyday of the Middle Ages. The height of the Modern Age was characterized, among other things, by the predominance of science over religion, technological changes and the emergence of nation-states. The transit between one and the other was not easy; neither will it be for the current Change of Era. It is natural to feel uncertainty and disorientation. However, if we are tied to the tensions represented by the axis of the past, we will not allow the future "to become". The challenge lies in innovation, in new moves that have not been tried before. Why? Simply because the previous ones did not lead us to a world that is either just or harmonious. We may have to accept the exercise of exhausting the current axes, these labor pains, before we can enjoy a period of inclusion. The challenge is, what role will service management play?

Service research could provide a more robust conceptualization for understanding how, in turbulent times, actors innovate as complex adaptive systems. Some insights have been suggested. They become sensitive to certain dramatic changes (Heinonen & Strandvik, 2021). Moreover, they exhibit resilience, effectively adapting to a wide range of environmental change. Koskela-Huotari et al. (2016) argue that service innovation can perform a key role in this endeavor. Service innovation emerges in a non-linear path involving non-linear dynamics with multiple actors and new shared and co-constructive practices (Russo-Spena et al., 2017). The Change of Era perspective invites the question: how will multiple socio-material connections arise at the cross-points of actors' interactions and resource integration, revealing a broader picture that can depict emerging phenomena more accurately?

References

Bauman, Z. (2013). *Liquid modernity*. John Wiley & Sons.

Bolton, R. N. (2020). Commentary: Future directions of the service discipline. *Journal of Services Marketing, 34*(3), 279–289.

Enquist, B., & Sebhatu, S. P. (this volume). Service management for business societal transformation. In B. Edvardsson & B. Tronvoll (Eds.), *Handbook of service management* (pp. XXX–XXX). Palgrave.

Fisk, R. P., Brown, S. W., & Bitner, M. J. (1993). Tracking the evolution of the services marketing literature. *Journal of Retailing, 69*(1), 61–103.

Fisk, R. P., Grove, S. J., & John, J. (2000). Services marketing self–portraits: Introspections. In *Reflections, and glimpses from the experts*. American Marketing Association.

Fuchs, C. (2007). Self-organizing system. In M. Bevir (Ed.), *Encyclopedia of governance* (pp. 863–864). Sage.

Fukuyama, F. (1989). The end of history? *The National Interest, 16*, 3–18.

Furrer, O., Kerguignas, J. Y., Delcourt, C., & Gremler, D. D. (2020). Twenty-seven years of service research: A literature review and research agenda. *Journal of Services Marketing, 34*(3), 299–316.

Furrer, O., & Sollberger, P. (2007). The dynamics and evolution of the service marketing literature: 1993–2003. *Service Business, 1*(2), 93–117.

Gummesson, E. (2012). The three service marketing paradigms: Which one are you guided by? *Mercati e Competitività, 1*, 5–13.

Gummesson, E., Lusch, R. F., & Vargo, S. L. (2010). Transitioning from service management to service-dominant logic: Observations and recommendations. *International Journal of Quality and Service Sciences, 2*(1), 8–22.

Harari, Y. N. (2014). *Sapiens: A brief history of humankind*. Random House.

Harari, Y. N. (2016). *Homo Deus: A brief history of tomorrow*. Random House.

Heinonen, K., & Strandvik, T. (2021). Reframing service innovation: COVID-19 as a catalyst for imposed service innovation. *Journal of Service Management, 32*(1), 101–112.

Kleinaltenkamp, M. (this volume). Service Management–Scope, challenges, and future developments. In B. Edvardsson & B. Tronvoll (Eds.), *Handbook of service management* (pp. XXX–XXX). Palgrave.

Koskela-Huotari, K., Edvardsson, B., Jonas, J. M., Sörhammar, D., & Witell, L. (2016). Innovation in service ecosystems – Breaking, making, and maintaining institutionalized rules of resource integration. *Journal of Business Research, 69*(8), 2964–2971.

Kunz, W. H., & Hogreve, J. (2011). Toward a deeper understanding of service marketing: The past, the present, and the future. *International Journal of Research in Marketing, 28*(3), 231–247.

Lovelock, C., & Gummesson, E. (2004). Whither services marketing? In search of a new paradigm and fresh perspectives. *Journal of Service Research, 7*(1), 20–41.

Lusch, R. F., & Vargo, S. L. (2014). *Service-dominant logic: Premises, perspectives, possibilities*. Cambridge University Press.

Mele, C., Pels, J., & Storbacka, K. (2015). A holistic market conceptualization. *Journal of the Academy of Marketing Science, 43*(1), 100–114.

Mele, C., Russo-Spena, T., & Kaartemo, V. (2021a). Smart technologies in service provision and experience. In B. Edvardsson & B. Tronvoll (Eds.), *Handbook of service management* (pp. XXX–XXX). Palgrave.

Mele, C., Russo-Spena, T., & Kaartemo, V. (2021b). The impact of coronavirus on business: Developing service research agenda for apost-coronavirus world. *Journal of Service Theory and Practice, 31*(2), 184–202.

Mele, C., Russo-Spena, T., Kaartemo, V., & Marzullo, M. L. (2021). Smart nudging: How cognitive technologies enable choice architectures for value co-creation. *Journal of Business Research, 129*, 949–960.

Nakamoto, S. (2008). Re: Bitcoin P2P e-cash paper. *The Cryptography Mailing List*.

Nel, D., Van Heerden, G., Chan, A., Ghazisaeedi, M., Halvorson, W., & Steyn, P. (2011). Eleven years of scholarly research in the Journal of Services Marketing. *Journal of Services Marketing, 25*(1), 4–13.

O'Driscoll, A. (2008). Exploring paradox in marketing: Managing ambiguity, towards synthesis. *Journal of Business & Industrial Marketing, 23*(2), 95–104.

Ostrom, A. L., Bitner, M. J., Brown, S. W., Burkhard, K. A., Goul, M., Smith-Daniels, V., Demirkan, H., & Rabinovich, E. (2010). Moving forward and making a difference: Research priorities for the science of service. *Journal of Service Research, 13*(1), 4–36.

Ostrom, A. L., Parasuraman, A., Bowen, D. E., Patricio, L., & Voss, C. A. (2015). Service research priorities in a rapidly changing context. *Journal of Service Research, 18*(2), 127–159.

Parasuraman, A., Berry, L. L., & Zeithaml, V. A. (1991). Understanding customer expectations of service. *Sloan Management Review, 32*(3), 39–48.

Pels, J. (2020). Change of era or era of changes. In M. A. Marinov & S. T. Marinova (Eds.), *Covid-19 and international business: Change of era* (pp. 19–25). Routledge.

Raskin, P., Banuri, T., Gallopín, G., Gutman, P., Hammond, A., Kates, R., & Swart, R. (2002). *Great transition: The promise and lure of the times ahead* (pp. 1–111). Global Scenario Group, Stockholm Environment Institute – Boston.

Russo-Spena, T., Mele, C., & Nuutinen, M. (2017). *Innovating in practice.* Springer International Publishing.

Shostack, G. L. (1977). Breaking free from product marketing. *Journal of Marketing, 42*(2), 73–80.

Vargo, S. L., & Fehrer, J. A. (this volume). Service-dominant logic: Foundations and service management applications. In B. Edvardsson & B. Tronvoll (Eds.), *Handbook of service management* (pp. XXX–XXX). Palgrave.

Vargo, S. L., & Lusch, R. F. (2004). A new dominant logic. Evolving to a new dominant logic for marketing. *Journal of Marketing, 68*(1), 1–17.

Vargo, S. L., & Lusch, R. F. (2008). Service-dominant logic: Continuing the evolution. *Journal of the Academy of marketing Science, 36*(1), 1–10.

Wilden, R., Akaka, M. A., Karpen, I. O., & Hohberger, J. (2017). The evolution and prospects of service–dominant logic: An investigation of past, present, and future research. *Journal of Service Research, 20*(4), 345–361.

Wuenderlich, N. V., Heinonen, K., Ostrom, A. L., Patricio, L., Sousa, R., Voss, C., & Lemmink, J. G. A. M. (2015). "Futurizing" smart service: Implications for service researchers and managers. *Journal of Services Marketing, 29*(6/7), 442–447.

Service-Dominant Logic and Service Management 4.0

Julia A. Fehrer and Stephen L. Vargo

1   Introduction

The Agenda 21 of the World Economic Forum was set up around the themes: healthy futures, ways forward toward fairer economies and better business, global cooperation for social justice, strategies to save the planet and technological breakthroughs of the Fourth Industrial Revolution that merge the physical, digital and biological worlds (World Economic Forum, 2021a). These themes are similarly represented on the top of many agendas of leading service organizations. PayPal Chief Risk Officer, Aaron Karczmer, for example, refers to the need for rethinking the way how organizations work together. He points to the unprecedented challenges of COVID-19 that require innovative solutions ranging from promoting physical health and mental well-being, to catalyzing economic recovery and empowerment, and even refortifying cyber safety and security in the accelerating digital world. Carolina Klint, Managing Director at Marsh, calls for partnerships between public and private sectors to upskill workers for an exploding digital economy and collaboration across society that incentivizes sustainable recovery efforts, green

---

J. A. Fehrer (✉)
The University of Auckland Business School, Auckland, New Zealand
e-mail: j.fehrer@auckland.ac.nz

S. L. Vargo
Shidler College of Business, University of Hawai'i at Mānoa, Honolulu, HI, USA
e-mail: svargo@hawaii.edu

© The Author(s), under exclusive license to Springer Nature Switzerland AG 2022
B. Edvardsson, B. Tronvoll (eds.), *The Palgrave Handbook of Service Management*,
https://doi.org/10.1007/978-3-030-91828-6_6

infrastructure and clean energy projects (World Economic Forum, 2021b). These themes pose significant changes to the way service professionals operate and may require service leaders to work more closely together for a more inclusive, cohesive and sustainable future (World Economic Forum, 2021a).

Service-dominant (S-D) logic offers a holistic framework of value cocreation and guidance to navigate change in complex service ecosystems (Vargo & Lusch, 2008, 2016) and is therefore particularly useful to support service leaders in their strategic decision making in today's versatile, uncertain, complex and ambiguous environments. The seminal S-D logic article 'Evolving to a New Dominant Logic for Marketing' (Vargo & Lusch, 2004) is one of the most-cited service-based articles in the last 30+ years. Several citation analyses show how its influence spread from the field of marketing and service research to computer sciences, social sciences, economics, engineering, environmental science, the arts and humanities (Pohlmann & Kaartemo, 2017; Tregua et al., 2021; Wilden et al., 2017). This indicates that a logic of value cocreation not only resonates with service and marketing scholars but also attracts an ever-growing array of other disciplines (Benoit et al., 2017). Service management in practice similarly increasingly acknowledges the importance of cocreating, co-executing and co-operating dynamically among business partners, customers and other actors to move forward in today's challenging times (BCG, 2019; IBM, 2020).

The purpose of this chapter is to explicate how S-D logic applies to the new era of service management defined by the pressures of COVID-19, advanced technologies and the wicked challenges and opportunities of environmental, social and economic sustainability. We further point toward S-D logic informed strategies and methodologies that promote value cocreation processes, the engagement of broad sets of actors and recent work related to designing service ecosystems (Vink et al., 2021). These strategies can support service leaders in their efforts to shape the increasingly complex service ecosystems of which they are part (Vink et al., 2021; Nenonen & Storbacka, 2020). We provide further a set of methods as a tool kit for service managers and designers to visualize the complexity of service ecosystems and to engage various actors in cocreative processes to nudge them.

Arguably, S-D logic allows for responding more systemically to intertwined economic, environmental, social and technological challenges of our complex, interdependent world. By synthesizing the Agenda 21 of the World Economic Forum (World Economic Forum, 2021a) with recent calls for service research (e.g., Bolton, 2020; Furrer et al., 2020), we arrive at four overarching themes that we consider as important for the next era of service management—an era that we call Service Management 4.0. These four themes include (1) advancing human-centered technologies in service, (2) navigating smart (cyber-physical) service ecosystems, (3) fostering inclusive service for inclusive growth and (4) nurturing nature-positive service. We present nascent contributions of S-D logic informed research related to these themes and close the chapter with reflections on applications for service management and future S-D logic informed research.

2 S-D Logic—An Evolving Perspective for Service Management

The Customer Is Always a Cocreator of Value

One of Vargo and Lusch's motivations for developing S-D logic was to provide an integrative perspective on divergent strands of thought that had been occurring in the marketing discipline since the 1980s, including market orientation (Kohli & Jaworski, 1990; Narver & Slater, 1990), services and relationship marketing (Grönroos, 1994; Gummesson, 1994) and quality management (Parasuraman et al., 1988). The seminal publication 'Evolving to a New Dominant Logic for Marketing' (Vargo & Lusch, 2004) reconceptualized service with important implications for service research and service management. Instead of viewing service as an additional output or special type of a product (i.e., intangible product), Vargo and Lusch (2004) define service as a *process of using one's resources (such as, knowledge and skills) for the benefit of another entity*. This brings service to the core of any economic and social exchange. It also means that both parties, the service provider and the customer, are active participants (i.e., actors) in the service process, and hence, the customer is always a cocreator of value.

The idea of *value cocreation* challenges many of the traditional strategy frameworks (e.g., Porter's value chain; Porter, 1985), because it does not assume that one actor (i.e., the firm) creates value in order to deliver this value—usually embedded in tangible goods—to another actor (i.e., the customer). Instead, it promotes a view of all actors involved in service-for-service exchange creating value collectively for mutual benefit. Take the example of the food delivery service, UberEats: a customer orders food from the UberEats app, the restaurant prepares and packages the meal, a driver picks it up and delivers it to the customer, however without the customer actively integrating the delivered food into their own lives through, for example, setting the table, eating the food, having conversations with family members, no value would be created and, arguably, no service would be provided. This example shows that no one single actor can create value, *value is always cocreated* (Vargo & Lusch, 2004).

This fundamental shift in thinking about service and value cocreation resonated particularly well with the Zeitgeist of digital economies and the Web 2.0 as they were on the rise in the early 2000s. It provides a way for service management to redefine the role of customers and their actions on social media and other digital platforms of the sharing economy and more generally lays the foundation for strategies that acknowledge the 'active customer' in the service process.

Value Is Always Experiential

Since its introduction, the development of S-D logic has continued first by extending value cocreation processes from those centered on service-for-service exchange to broader resource integration processes acknowledging that all actors (customers, firms, suppliers, the government, etc.) are resource integrators (Vargo & Lusch, 2008). Second, Vargo and Lusch (2008) suggest that value should be viewed as *experiential*, always determined by the beneficiary. The food delivery example from above shows that the perception of value can vary depending on the time, space and actors involved in the value cocreation process (Chandler & Lusch, 2015). A pizza delivered may create a different value for a family depending on them eating it together at the kitchen table or in front of the TV. Further, value may be perceived differently by different family members depending on their degree of hunger, their diet, their available time and so on. This is what S-D logic describes as value-in-context (Chandler & Vargo, 2011). In other words, value is not only always cocreated, but also always determined by the situation and actors' experiences attached to this situation (Vargo & Lusch, 2008). This is an important extension to understand value cocreation, because it means that for any value proposition of an actor, there may be varying views of its phenomenological value (Vargo & Lusch, 2016).

For service management that means that value cocreation with customers and other actors requires knowledge of the situational (e.g., space and time), social (e.g., social networks) and broader socio-cultural (e.g., social norms) context of service encounters (Chandler & Vargo, 2011). It points toward understanding customers' and other actors' experiences and experience journeys instead of single service interactions (Becker & Jaakkola, 2020).

Institutions and Institutional Arrangements Coordinate Value Cocreation

The most recent extension to the S-D logic narrative is the inclusion of *institutions and institutional arrangements* (such as rules, structures, norms, meanings, values, symbols and similar heuristics) as coordination mechanism for value cocreation (Vargo & Lusch, 2016). Let's go back to the food delivery example. It demonstrates that value cocreation processes expand beyond the immediate customer-firm relationship. The food needs to be delivered by a driver; thus mobility systems are required, including vehicles, streets, traffic lights and many more institutions. The customer needs to pay for the food, usually using a credit card service and the Internet is required to connect all actors in this service process. Going beyond the immediate food delivery service process, broader peripheral structures, such as tax laws, food quality regulations and social security systems, enable and constrain resource integration processes among actors. That is, value cocreation depends on and is coordinated through institutions and institutional arrangements (i.e., assemblages of interrelated institutions). These institutional arrangements, however, are not given, they are shaped collectively by actors (Vargo & Lusch, 2016). For example, the tax laws, food quality regulations and other more informal conventions (e.g., social norms) that guide food delivery services are developed and adopted by the society using these food delivery services.

S-D logic emphasizes that value cocreation can only be truly understood when contexts and 'external' environments are internalized and institutional arrangements are considered. It promotes a *service ecosystems perspective* that explains how shared and enduring institutional arrangements—interrelated rules, roles, norms and beliefs—guide resource integration and service exchange (Vargo & Lusch, 2016). As Vink et al. (2021) point out, the service ecosystem perspective not only provides a more systemic and holistic understanding of value cocreation, but also offers important insights into how actors are able to influence value cocreation through designing the service ecosystems of which they are part. Like biological ecosystems, service ecosystems exhibit the quality of *emergence* (Polese et al., 2021) and are therefore beyond the control of any individual actor (Chandler et al., 2019). However, actors are able to intentionally influence (i.e., design), at least partially, how service ecosystems evolve (Mele et al., 2018). This is usually done through reconfiguring the institutional arrangements that are guiding value cocreation within service ecosystems (Koskela-Huotari & Vargo, 2016; Vargo et al., 2015).

Service ecosystems, by their nature, evolve over time through complex processes of individuals, organizations and societies continually adapting to changing contextual requirements, while simultaneously creating this change (Levin, 1998). S-D logic therefore explains innovation in service ecosystems as a *combinatorial evolution* process (Akaka & Vargo, 2014; Vargo et al., 2020). Arthur (2009, p. 167) describes combinatorial evolution as the process in which "new elements are constructed from ones that already exist, and these offer themselves as possible building-block elements for the construction of still further elements". He further explains that any technological advancement is embedded in dynamic social systems and thus institutions and technologies cannot be viewed in isolation from each other. In fact, technology needs to be viewed as "an assemblage of practices and components" and "a means to fulfil a human purpose" (2009, p. 28).

This holistic perspective of service ecosystems broadens the scope of service management from designing and innovating service offerings, managing service processes and running service organizations to orchestrating, navigating and shaping service ecosystems. It means that not only the value cocreation processes between customers and firms, but also those of broad sets of actors, such as customers' social networks, business networks, investors and even policy makers need to be on service leaders' radars. It also means that broader sociotechnical structures (i.e., institutional arrangements) need to be taken into consideration for service management and service innovation. Contemporary service environments make this complex entanglement of technology and institutions salient. For example, service exchange on UberEats only works because of its technical infrastructure (i.e., digital platform) that connects actors (restaurants, drivers and customers) and the social structure that allows service providers and customers rating and reviewing one another.

In sum, S-D logic provides service managers with an alternative lens to think about and make sense of contemporary service environments. In the next section, we will comment on S-D logic informed midrange theories that have been developed alongside with S-D logic's conception. Put simply, midrange theories connect ways of thinking about the world (e.g., a new S-D logic) with the empirical world (e.g., new service management practice) (see, Brodie et al., 2011). It is important to acknowledge that there is a growing body of S-D logic informed midrange theory and by no means is our overview in the next section complete. We focus on midrange theories that promote value cocreation processes, the engagement of broad sets of actors and collective service ecosystem design to foreground how systemic, as opposed to firm-centric, strategies can address some of the challenges of volatile, uncertain, complex and ambiguous environments.

3 S-D Logic Informed Strategies and Methods for Contemporary Service Management

Cocreation and Engagement Strategies

The fundamental shift in thinking about value creation as a cocreative and collaborative process between firms, customers and other actors inspired many service scholars to develop new strategic frameworks for service management. For example, Karpen et al. (2012), in an effort to bridge S-D logic and strategy research, propose a framework of S-D orientation comprising a portfolio of six strategic cocreation capabilities that organizations can develop to create value together with rather than for their customers. McColl-Kennedy et al. (2012) propose a typology of five cocreation practice styles that healthcare service managers can draw from to increase their customer's quality of life. Frow and Payne (2011) explicate how service managers can create and negotiate value propositions in reciprocal ways to facilitate the alignment of cocreation practices among multiple actors.

This and related work on value cocreation uses the guiding principles of S-D logic to further explore how, often complex, value cocreation processes involving broad sets of actors can be influenced, aligned and navigated. Similarly, work on customer engagement, highlighting the blurring boundaries of firms and customers, provides guidance for service managers to stimulate and coordinate customer's resource investments in the service process, especially those that go beyond pure purchase transactions (e.g., Brodie et al., 2011; Hollebeek et al., 2019; Jaakkola & Alexander, 2014).

Going one step further, more recent work on actor engagement—informed by S-D logic—offers strategies to encourage and coordinate resource investments of broad sets of actors to collectively cocreate value (Brodie et al., 2019). Such midrange theories provide pathways forward to facilitate (not manage!) value cocreation. The idea of facilitating, navigating and orchestrating service processes rather than managing them is important for service managers to consider, because it highlights that service processes are out of the control of one single actor. Many business models in the sharing economy, for example, are built on the idea of facilitating the engagement of actors. They provide platforms for users to connect and exchange service; however, they neither manage nor control the service provisions of their users, instead they trust self-governance through, as previously mentioned, rating and review mechanisms.

Service Ecosystem Design and Innovation Strategies

S-D logic's systemic perspective led further to the development of midrange theories related to service design and service innovation. Vink et al. (2021), for example, reconceptualize service design to embrace the complexity of service ecosystems and their emergent nature. Their work paves the way for service designers to rethink their 'unit of design' from developing service offerings to facilitating the emergence of desired forms of value cocreation and change in service ecosystems. It promotes collective design processes involving broad sets of actors, and, instead of touchpoints and interfaces, it focuses on institutional arrangements as the 'design material'. Similarly, Wieland et al. (2017) question traditional strategic thinking by reconceptualizing business model design from a firm-centric activity that promotes owning key resources and altering sets of decision variables to one that highlights the facilitation of broad institutional change processes. The authors develop a new systemic business model framework.

To reiterate, S-D logic states that service processes and value cocreation are coordinated by institutional arrangements (Vargo & Lusch, 2016). That is, service innovation can only be truly understood, when institutions and institutional change are considered. To advance the study of innovation in complex adaptive service ecosystems, Chandler et al. (2019) develop midrange theory to nurture systemic innovation. They suggest, rather than focusing too narrowly on the innovation process, service and innovation managers should also revise norms, rules and beliefs that support new ideas. Furthermore, these efforts should not only be directed toward potential customers but also toward other private, public and market-facing actors. Similarly, Jonas et al. (2018) suggest that in order to cover the complexity of inter-organizational innovation in service ecosystems, it is important to understand stakeholders' engagement in innovation processes on the individual as well as on the organizational level.

Methods for Service Design

S-D logic informed frameworks and strategies require methods and tools that facilitate systemic design and innovation processes. Recently introduced methods from design science research (Hevner, 2007) and action design research (Sein et al., 2011) to the field of service research can support service managers to fuel, catalyze and navigate service innovation (Grenha Teixeira et al., 2017; Sudbury-Riley et al., 2020). Sudbury-Riley et al. (2020), for example, use design science research to develop a new method, the Trajectory Touchpoint Technique that aids understanding customer experiences throughout the service process, while also taking multiple (micro-, meso- and macro-) service ecosystem levels into account to fuel service innovation.

Further, as Fehrer and Wieland (2021) point out, ecosystem design methods need to reflect complexity and ongoing, iterative processes of learning and change on various system levels. The authors reviewed a set of methods, initially developed in the field of sustainability research, that address systemic complexity. These methods include, for example, Backcasting and Eco-design (e.g., Heyes et al., 2018) as ways of incorporating environmental considerations into product and service design. Furthermore, the Systems of Practices approach with tools, such as Business Origami (Hobson et al., 2018), allows for collectively mapping and modeling complex systems by explicitly emphasizing the interplay between elements that occur over time and the context they occur in. Similarly, Giga-Mapping facilitates the creation of system maps across multiple layers and scales, supported through various visual artifacts (Sevaldson, 2017). These and other systems design methods support service managers and service designers with a tool kit not only to visualize the complexity of service ecosystems, but also to engage various sets of actors in the design process.

To summarize, we have shown that S-D logic provides an alternative lens to think about service and value cocreation and have pointed toward some selected S-D logic informed strategies, methodologies and conceptual frameworks to transfer this service logic into service management practice. Table 1 provides an overview of S-D logic informed strategies and related service design methods that can support service leaders in their efforts to respond to increasingly complex service environments and shape the service ecosystems of which they are part (Vink et al., 2021; Nenonen & Storbacka, 2020).

In the next section, we will provide an outlook for the service management—what we refer to as 'Service Management 4.0'. We will show how nascent S-D logic informed work is starting to provide a more systemic foundation to make sense of technological breakthroughs, social issues and environmental challenges of complex contemporary service environments. We will also outline where we see potential for future service research and service management applications.

Table 1 S-D logic informed strategies and methods for contemporary service management

S-D logic informed strategies	Related service design methods	
Cocreation and engagement strategies	* Create value together with rather than for customers and other actors (e.g., Karpen et al., 2012) * Understand customers' and other actors' experiences and experience journeys (Becker & Jaakkola, 2020) * Negotiate value propositions in reciprocal ways with other actors (Frow & Payne, 2011) * Motivate, empower and measure customers' and other actors' voluntary resource investments that go beyond the core, economic transaction (e.g., influencing, co-developing, augmenting, referring, etc.) (Brodie et al., 2019; Hollebeek et al., 2019; Jaakkola & Alexander, 2014)	*Value Mapping* (Bocken et al., 2013; Breuer & Lüdeke-Freud, 2017)	Process of developing shared value propositions for diverse stakeholders, such as customers, suppliers and governments. By taking a network rather than a company-centric perspective, the value-mapping tool offers a way to integrate the perceptions of multiple stakeholders
		Value Shaping (Oskam et al., 2018)	A mutually constitutive engagement process between stakeholders in which networking helps to refine and improve the business model and vice versa the business model spurs the expansion of the network
		Stakeholder Preference Mapping Technique (Lou et al., 2021)	Method to identify stakeholders' preferences and the influence of these preferences on their decisions so that organizations can facilitate stakeholder engagement in ways that meet their strategic goals
		Trajectory Touchpoint Technique (Sudbury-Riley et al., 2020)	Service design methodology that harnesses customer experiences for enriched understanding of value throughout multilevel service components to ultimately increase innovativeness
		MINDS Method (Grenha Teixeira et al., 2017)	Three-level service design approach including (1) designing the service concept (e.g., value the service provides to support a given customer activity); (2) designing the service system (e.g., defines how people, frontstage and backstage processes, technology support and other elements will be orchestrated to support the service concept) and (3) designing the service encounter (e.g., frontstage and backstage processes that support specific customer actions in specific service interfaces)

| Service ecosystem design and innovation strategies | ◦ Embrace the complexity of service ecosystems and their emergent nature (Vink et al., 2021; Chandler et al., 2019)
 ◦ Rethink the 'unit of service design' from developing service offerings and managing service processes to orchestrating, navigating and shaping viable service ecosystems (Nenonen & Storbacka, 2020)
 ◦ Promote collective design processes involving broad sets of actors and, instead of touchpoints and interfaces, focus on institutional arrangements as the 'design material' (Vink et al., 2021) | *Systems of Practices Design/Business Origami* (Hobson et al., 2018)

 Backcasting and Eco-design (Heyes et al., 2018)

 Giga-Mapping (Sevaldson, 2017)

 Business Patterns (Beynon-Davies, 2018) | Practice of collective mapping and modeling complex systems by explicitly emphasizing the interplay between elements that occur over time and the context they occur in

 The practice of developing scenarios aimed at exploring the feasibility and implications of achieving a certain desired end-point in the future, while systematically incorporating environmental considerations into the business innovation process
 A systems-oriented design practice, mapping systems across multiple layers and scales drawing on soft systems methodology, critical systems thinking and systems architecting
 Drawing on design science, this design method describes ways of visualizing existing and envisaged business patterns through the visual artifact of a comic. It allows for creating discourse between multiple actors in complex supplier-buyer retail relations |

4 S-D Logic Informed Service Management 4.0

From Industry 4.0 to Service Management 4.0

The Fourth Industrial Revolution describes a new era that 'industrialized nations' are entering, characterized by simultaneous waves of technological breakthroughs, merging the physical (e.g., Internet of Things [IoT], autonomous driving, smart materials), digital (e.g., AI, 5G, Blockchain) and biological (biomimetic robots, bio- and nanotechnologies) worlds (Schwab, 2016; World Economic Forum, 2021a). While the Fourth Industrial Revolution is often reduced to greater automation and digitalization of industrial processes (i.e., Industry 4.0), its original vision is much broader. The World Economic Forum (the platform that initially coined the term in 2016) discusses the Fourth Industrial Revolution as part of a broader agenda that is set up around: healthy futures, ways forward toward fairer economies and better business, global cooperation for social justice, strategies to save the planet and technology for good (World Economic Forum, 2021a). The forum connects technological progress with the requirement for solving today's grand challenges of climate change and social inequalities.

This agenda aligns with recent research agendas for future service research (Bolton, 2020; Furrer et al., 2020) and agendas of leading service organizations (e.g., IBM, 2019; McKinsey & Company, 2021). Bolton (2020) encourages service scholars to shape the future of the service discipline by building knowledge that is useful to businesses, individuals, communities, policy makers, society and the bio-environment. She explicitly refers to future service challenges arising from socioeconomic, demographic, technological, environmental and social changes and advocates for more study of sustainability in service ecosystems, automation, the nature and future of service work, inclusion, equality and well-being of service workers, service in subsistence markets and the societal implications of new technologies. She points toward the great potential for the service discipline to directly influence the generation and adoption of new ideas that can create a better world. Similarly, Furrer et al. (2020) refer to the important role of service ecosystem research and the integration of multiple stakeholders in co-designing and cocreating sustainable solutions. The authors further emphasize service robots, blockchain technology, the IoT, smart and access-based service as important areas for future research.

From mapping calls for future service research (Bolton, 2020; Furrer et al., 2020) and topics on the agenda of the World Economic Forum (World Economic Forum, 2021a), we arrived at four overarching themes that, arguably, begin to form a new era of service management—one that we define (in

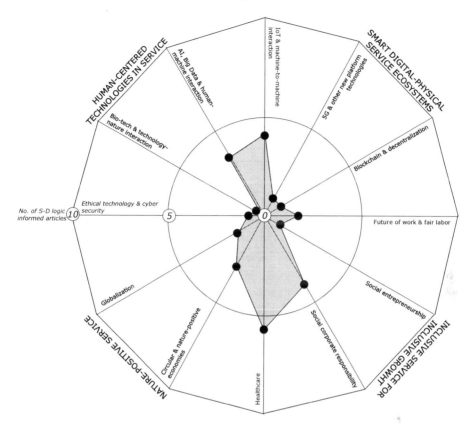

Fig. 1 Service Management 4.0 and its penetration in S-D logic research

reference to Industry 4.0) as Service Management 4.0. These four themes include (1) human-centered technologies, (2) smart (cyber-physical) service ecosystems, (3) inclusive service for inclusive growth and (4) nature-positive service. In the remainder, we will present nascent contributions of S-D logic informed research related to these themes and point toward implications for the future of service management. Figure 1 provides an overview of the themes and subthemes of Service Management 4.0 and illustrates (schematically) the penetration of emerging S-D logic informed research related to these themes.

Human-Centered Technologies in Service

Technologies, including automation, robotics and AI, are profoundly expanding the variety of service interfaces and therefore the possible ways for customers, firms and other actors to interact across their experience journeys and create an unprecedented amount of data (Akter et al., 2020; Roy et al., 2019). Urbinati et al. (2019) point out that Big Data has recently emerged as a new digital paradigm, one that service organizations need to adopt in order to both transform existing business models and nurture their innovation activities. Understanding digital technologies and how they can enhance service experience is a budding theme in service research. However, most studies focus on the way companies can create and capture value from Big Data. There is a lack of complete understanding how companies and users can cocreate value through Big Data. We argue that a more holistic and integrated view of data providing firms, data providing customers and other actors can support service managers and scholars to develop solutions for mutual benefit.

Related to this are ethical considerations of Big Data management. Breidbach and Maglio (2020) offer new insights into how using machine learning, AI and Big Data sets can lead to unethical implications and list 13 ethical challenges related to data-driven business models. The authors call for future research to use advanced Big Data analytics more effectively and ethically. Our review shows that ethical discussions related to Big Data and cyber security are underdeveloped in service research and service management. Hence, we encourage scholars and practitioners to further drive this debate. S-D logic can provide potentially interesting frameworks to discuss ethical challenges more systemically and from an institutional perspective.

Further, Mikalef et al. (2020) suggest using complexity theory (one of S-D logic's foundational theoretical frameworks) to cover the systemic and interrelated challenges of implementing Big Data in business processes. The authors apply a fuzzy-set qualitative comparative analysis (fsQCA) to grasp the complexity of Big Data analytics. We see much potential in using this and other mix-method approaches to draw a more complete picture of the wicked issues related to fast-paced technological change. Similarly, service managers may want to consider different data sources (e.g., unstructured text and image analysis, netno- and ethnographic analysis, focus groups, etc.) that complement insights from dashboards like Google Analytics to develop a holistic picture for what customers and other actors in their network need.

Smart (Cyber-Physical) Service Ecosystems

The convergence of the physical and digital sphere has the potential to redefine a wide range of industry sectors (Langley et al., 2021) and is another important field for service research and service management to consider. Technological disruptions such as the IoT, autonomous devices and rich media (virtual and augmented reality) are creating smart environments that are transforming industry structures, processes and service (Buhalis et al., 2019). Buhalis et al. (2019) predict that the emergence of smart environments will redefine how customers and other actors experience their environment. Fundamentally, IoT and smart technologies allow everyday things to 'think, interact and connect' through sensor-enabled materials, such as smart clothes and smart surfaces (Ng & Wakenshaw, 2017).

This has important implications for both industrial and customer-focused service management. As the complexity and intensity of connections increase through smart devices, there is a need to understand smart service ecosystems from a holistic and integrated perspective. Langley et al. (2021) develop a layered framework and show how the IoT influences organizations on micro, meso and macro levels. Gupta et al. (2020) examine how authorities on a macro level orchestrate smart city data ecosystems through openness, diffusion and a shared vision. This recent work points to the importance of understanding technological developments and connectivity embedded within broader social and institutional structures. We see great potential for future service research extending the 'social' component in cyber-physical systems. For service managers, we recommend considering the social structures within and beyond their service organizations when evaluating and implementing new technologies.

Inclusive Service for Inclusive Growth

Inclusive growth means economic growth that is distributed fairly across society and creates opportunities for all. In many OECD countries, inequalities are at their highest levels in 30 years and are widening and further rising due to the COVID-19 crisis (OECD, 2021). Current challenging times require service managers to design service for inclusion that provides customers and other actors in the service ecosystem with fair access to service, fair treatment during the service process and fair opportunities to exit service (Fisk et al., 2018). Service inclusion means understanding service ecosystems and the fundamental role of service in human well-being (Bolton, 2020; Fisk et al., 2018).

While highly important, much of the discussion related to human well-being to date is related to healthcare service (e.g., Brodie et al., 2021; Peltier et al., 2020), while other social and service inclusion discussions seem to be mainly in the context of CSR (Iglesias et al., 2020; Simpson et al., 2020). In practice, social responsibility and inclusion are often reduced to communication efforts of the social media departments (Okazaki et al., 2020). Drawing on Fisk et al. (2018), we argue that service inclusion is a systemic challenge that involves all value cocreation activities of a service organization. Hence, we promote future research related to the complex challenges of service inclusion on all levels of the service ecosystem.

Further, we see much potential in service research related to social entrepreneurship and social entrepreneurial ecosystems. While recent research on social entrepreneurship advocates for a holistic and systemic perspective (Weerawardena et al., 2019), social entrepreneurship has—with a few notable exceptions (e.g., Sigala, 2019)—not been discussed in the field of marketing and service research. The intersection between social entrepreneurship and S-D logic has the potential to produce frameworks, strategies and methods for more inclusive socially driven value cocreation and service design.

Nature-Positive Service Ecosystems

Environmental sustainability, similar to social inequality, represents a key challenge facing humanity. Issues such as climate change, pollution, destruction of biodiversity, (food) waste, water scarcity and natural resource depletion are viewed as pressing environmental issues that pose significant threats to societies around the globe (Fehrer & Wieland, 2021). This brings sustainability to the top of many strategic agendas of corporate and industry boards and to the heart of Service Management 4.0. As Gallo et al. (2018) point out, environmental challenges are so vast that a real transition toward nature-positive business demands joint efforts. The authors argue that sustainability efforts of a single organization can barely lead to success.

That is, for service organizations to succeed in their sustainability actions, they need to engage 'allies' to collectively drive change. Furthermore, as we have explicated in the previous sections, sustainable service innovation requires efforts related to revising and shaping the norms, rules, beliefs and measurement instruments that define business and economic success. We encourage service managers and service scholars to further explore design frameworks, methods and measurement tools related to service ecosystems and value cocreation in the context of sustainability and the circular economy.

Guyader et al. (2019) point to the problem that sustainable service often means reducing the negative environmental impact of existing services. However, to fully grasp the idea of nature-positive service, it is important to understand the resourceness of natural resources, that is, the active part that natural resources play in the service process (Vargo, 2018). Guyader et al.

(2019) promote a view of nature-positive (green) service that includes resource integration processes through recreation and renewing of the natural resources to increase their resourceness. Nature-positive and sustainable service research is still in its infancy and provides huge potential to apply and further develop ecosystemic frameworks for service design and service innovation.

5 Conclusion

This chapter provides a review of and outlook for S-D logic informed service research and service management. It shows how complex contemporary service environments can be better understood, when taking a systemic perspective that promotes value cocreation processes of broad sets of actors. It offers a set of strategies and methods for service managers to draw from to operate successfully in complex service ecosystems. It highlights strategies for service managers to move forward in today's challenging times. S-D logic offers an alternative lens to discuss, rethink and navigate complex and intertwined issues spanning a possible new era of Service Management 4.0. We encourage service researchers and service managers to apply and further develop S-D logic informed frameworks, strategies and methods related to this new era, including human-centered and ethical technology in service, smart (cyber-physical) service ecosystems as well as inclusive and nature-positive service.

References

Akaka, M. A., & Vargo, S. L. (2014). Technology as an operant resource in service (eco) systems. *Information Systems and E-Business Management, 12*(3), 367–384.

Akter, S., Motamarri, S., Hani, U., Shams, R., Fernando, M., Babu, M. M., & Shen, K. N. (2020). Building dynamic service analytics capabilities for the digital marketplace. *Journal of Business Research, 118*, 177–188.

Arthur, W. B. (2009). *The nature of technology: What it is and how it evolves*. New York: Free Press.

BCG. (2019). Transforming the urban innovation ecosystem. https://www.bcg.com/en-au/publications/2019/transforming-urban-innovation-ecosystem

Becker, L., & Jaakkola, E. (2020). Customer experience: Fundamental premises and implications for research. *Journal of the Academy of Marketing Science, 48*(4), 630–648.

Benoit, S., Scherschel, K., Ates, Z., Nasr, L., & Kandampully, J. (2017). Showcasing the diversity of service research. *Journal of Service Management, 28*(5), 810–836. https://doi.org/10.1108/JOSM-05-2017-0102

Beynon-Davies, P. (2018). Characterizing business models for digital business through patterns. *International Journal of Electronic Commerce, 22*(1), 98–124.

Bocken, N., Short, S., Rana, P., & Evans, S. (2013). A value mapping tool for sustainable business modelling. *Corporate Governance: The International Journal of Business in Society, 13*(5), 482–497. https://doi.org/10.1108/CG-06-2013-0078

Bolton, R. N. (2020). Commentary: Future directions of the service discipline. *Journal of Services Marketing, 34*(3), 279–289.

Breidbach, C. F., & Maglio, P. (2020). Accountable algorithms? The ethical implications of data-driven business models. *Journal of Service Management, 31*, 163–185.

Breuer, H., & Lüdeke-Freud, F. (2017). Value-based network and business model innovation. *International Journal of Innovation Management, 21*(3), 1750028. https://doi.org/10.1142/S1363919617500281

Brodie, R. J., Fehrer, J. A., Jaakkola, E., & Conduit, J. (2019). Actor engagement in networks: Defining the conceptual domain. *Journal of Service Research, 22*(2), 173–188.

Brodie, R. J., Hollebeek, L. D., Juric, B., & Ilic, A. (2011). Customer engagement: Conceptual domain, fundamental propositions, and implications for research. *Journal of Service Research, 14*(3), 252–271. https://doi.org/10.1177/1094670511411703

Brodie, R. J., Ranjan, K. R., Verreynne, M.-L., Jiang, Y., & Previte, J. (2021). Coronavirus crisis and health care: Learning from a service ecosystem perspective. *Journal of Service Theory and Practice, 31*(2), 225–246.

Brodie, R. J., Saren, M., & Pels, J. (2011). Theorizing about the service dominant logic: The bridging role of middle range theory. *Marketing Theory, 11*(1), 75–91. https://doi.org/10.1177/1470593110393714

Buhalis, D., Harwood, T., Bogicevic, V., Viglia, G., Beldona, S., & Hofacker, C. (2019). Technological disruptions in services: Lessons from tourism and hospitality. *Journal of Service Management, 30*, 484–506.

Chandler, J. D., Danatzis, I., Wernicke, C., Akaka, M. A., & Reynolds, D. (2019). How does innovation emerge in a service ecosystem? *Journal of Service Research, 22*(1), 75–89.

Chandler, J. D., & Lusch, R. F. (2015). Service systems: A broadened framework and research agenda on value propositions, engagement, and service experience. *Journal of Service Research, 18*(1), 6–22. https://doi.org/10.1177/1094670514537709

Chandler, J. D., & Vargo, S. L. (2011). Contextualization and value-in-context: How context frames exchange. *Marketing Theory, 11*(1), 35–49. https://doi.org/10.1177/1470593110393713

Fehrer, J. A., & Wieland, H. (2021). A systemic logic for circular business models. *Journal of Business Research*, 609–620. https://doi.org/10.1016/j.jbusres.2020.02.010

Fisk, R. P., Dean, A. M., Alkire, L., Joubert, A., Previte, J., Robertson, N., & Rosenbaum, M. S. (2018). Design for service inclusion: Creating inclusive service systems by 2050. *Journal of Service Management.* https://doi.org/10.1108/JOSM-05-2018-0121

Frow, P., & Payne, A. (2011). A stakeholder perspective of the value proposition concept. *European Journal of Marketing, 45*(1/2), 223–240. https://doi.org/10.1108/03090561111095676

Furrer, O., Kerguignas, J. Y., Delcourt, C., & Gremler, D. D. (2020). Twenty-seven years of service research: A literature review and research agenda. *Journal of Services Marketing, 34*, 299–316.

Gallo, P. J., Antolin-Lopez, R., & Montiel, I. (2018). Associative sustainable business models… in the bean-to-bar chocolate industry. *Journal of Cleaner Production, 174*, 905–916.

Grenha Teixeira, J., Patrício, L., Huang, K.-H., Fisk, R. P., Nóbrega, L., & Constantine, L. (2017). The MINDS method: Integrating management and interaction design perspectives for service design. *Journal of Service Research, 20*(3), 240–258.

Grönroos, C. (1994). Quo vadis, marketing? Toward a relationship marketing paradigm. *Journal of Marketing Management, 10*(5), 347–360.

Gummesson, E. (1994). Making relationship marketing operational. *International Journal of Service Industry Management, 5*, 5–20.

Gupta, A., Panagiotopoulos, P., & Bowen, F. (2020). An orchestration approach to smart city data ecosystems. *Technological Forecasting and Social Change, 153*, 119929.

Guyader, H., Ottosson, M., Frankelius, P., & Witell, L. (2019). Identifying the resource integration processes of green service. *Journal of Service Management, 31*, 21.

Hevner, A. R. (2007). A three cycle view of design science research. *Scandinavian Journal of Information Systems, 19*(2), 4.

Heyes, G., Sharmina, M., Mendoza, J. M. F., Gallego-Schmid, A., & Azapagic, A. (2018). Developing and implementing circular economy business models in service-oriented technology companies. *Journal of Cleaner Production, 177*, 621–632. https://doi.org/10.1016/j.jclepro.2017.12.168

Hobson, K., Lynch, N., Lilley, D., & Smalley, G. (2018). Systems of practice and the circular economy: Transforming mobile phone product service systems. *Environmental Innovation and Societal Transitions, 26*, 147–157. https://doi.org/10.1016/j.eist.2017.04.002

Hollebeek, L. D., Srivastava, R. K., & Chen, T. (2019). SD logic–informed customer engagement: Integrative framework, revised fundamental propositions, and application to CRM. *Journal of the Academy of Marketing Science, 47*(1), 161–185.

IBM. (2019). IBM at Davos: Business Leadership in the Fourth Industrial Revolution. https://www.ibm.com/blogs/ibm-training/ibm-at-davos-business-leadership-in-the-fourth-industrial-revolution/

IBM. (2020). Dynamic service delivery—Defining the future of service delivery. https://www.ibm.com/blogs/services/2020/07/15/dynamic-service-delivery-defining-the-future-of-service-delivery/

Iglesias, O., Markovic, S., Bagherzadeh, M., & Singh, J. J. (2020). Co-creation: A key link between corporate social responsibility, customer trust, and customer loyalty. *Journal of Business Ethics, 163*(1), 151–166.

Jaakkola, E., & Alexander, M. (2014). The role of customer engagement behavior in value co-creation: A service system perspective. *Journal of Service Research, 17*(3), 247–261. https://doi.org/10.1177/1094670514529187

Jonas, J. M., Boha, J., Sörhammar, D., & Moeslein, K. M. (2018). Stakeholder engagement in intra-and inter-organizational innovation. *Journal of Service Management, 29*(3), 399–421.

Karpen, I. O., Bove, L. L., & Lukas, B. A. (2012). Linking service-dominant logic and strategic business practice: A conceptual model of a service-dominant orientation. *Journal of service research, 15*(1), 21–38.

Kohli, A. K., & Jaworski, B. J. (1990). Market orientation: The construct, research propositions, and managerial implications. *Journal of Marketing, 54*(2), 1–18.

Koskela-Huotari, K., & Vargo, S. L. (2016). Institutions as resource context. *Journal of Service Theory and Practice, 26*(2), 163–178. https://doi.org/10.1108/JSTP-09-2014-0190

Langley, D. J., van Doorn, J., Ng, I. C. L., Stieglitz, S., Lazovik, A., & Boonstra, A. (2021). The Internet of everything: Smart things and their impact on business models. *Journal of Business Research, 122*, 853–863.

Levin, S. A. (1998). Ecosystems and the biosphere as complex adaptive systems. *Ecosystems, 1*(5), 431–436.

Lou, E. C. W., Lee, A., & Lim, Y. M. (2021). Stakeholder preference mapping: The case for built heritage of Georgetown, Malaysia. *Journal of Cultural Heritage Management and Sustainable Development.* https://doi.org/10.1108/JCHMSD-08-2020-0114

McColl-Kennedy, J. R., Vargo, S. L., Dagger, T. S., Sweeney, J. C., & van Kasteren, Y. (2012). Health care customer value cocreation practice styles. *Journal of Service Research, 15*(4), 370–389.

McKinsey & Company (2021). The next normal arrives: Trends that will define 2021—And beyond. https://www.mckinsey.com/featured-insights/leadership/the-next-normal-arrives-trends-that-will-define-2021-and-beyond

Mele, C., Nenonen, S., Pels, J., Storbacka, K., Nariswari, A., & Kaartemo, V. (2018). Shaping service ecosystems: Exploring the dark side of agency. *Journal of Service Management, 29*, 521–545.

Mikalef, P., Krogstie, J., Pappas, I. O., & Pavlou, P. (2020). Exploring the relationship between big data analytics capability and competitive performance: The mediating roles of dynamic and operational capabilities. *Information & Management, 57*(2), 103169.

Narver, J. C., & Slater, S. F. (1990). The effect of a market orientation on business profitability. *Journal of Marketing, 54*(4), 20–35.

Nenonen, S., & Storbacka, K. (2020). Don't adapt, shape! Use the crisis to shape your minimum viable system—And the wider market. *Industrial Marketing Management, 88*, 265–271.

Ng, I. C. L., & Wakenshaw, S. Y. L. (2017). The Internet-of-Things: Review and research directions. *International Journal of Research in Marketing, 34*(1), 3–21.

OECD. (2021). Inclusive growth. https://www.oecd.org/inclusive-growth/#introduction

Okazaki, S., Plangger, K., West, D., & Menéndez, H. D. (2020). Exploring digital corporate social responsibility communications on Twitter. *Journal of Business Research, 117*, 675–682.

Oskam, I., Bossink, B., & Man, A.-P. de. (2018). The interaction between network ties an...of sustainability-oriented innovations. *Journal of Cleaner Production, 177*, 555–566.

Parasuraman, A., Zeithaml, V. A., & Berry, L. (1988). SERVQUAL: A multiple-item scale for measuring consumer perceptions of service quality. *Journal of Retailing, 64*(1), 12–40.

Peltier, J. W., Dahl, A. J., & Swan, E. L. (2020). Digital information flows across a B2C/C2C continuum and technological innovations in service ecosystems: A service-dominant logic perspective. *Journal of Business Research, 121*, 724–734.

Pohlmann, A., & Kaartemo, V. (2017). Research trajectories of Service-Dominant Logic: Emergent themes of a unifying paradigm in business and management. *Industrial Marketing Management, 63*, 53–68.

Polese, F., Payne, A., Frow, P., Sarno, D., & Nenonen, S. (2021). Emergence and phase transitions in service ecosystems. *Journal of Business Research, 127*, 25–34.

Porter, M. E. (1985). *Competitive advantage: Creating and sustaining superior performance*. Free Press.

Roy, S. K., Singh, G., Hope, M., Nguyen, B., & Harrigan, P. (2019). The rise of smart consumers: Role of smart service scape and smart consumer experience co-creation. *Journal of Marketing Management, 35*(15–16), 1480–1513.

Schwab, K. (2016). The Fourth Industrial Revolution: What it means, how to respond. https://www.weforum.org/agenda/2016/01/the-fourth-industrial-revolution-what-it-means-and-how-to-respond/

Sein, M. K., Henfridsson, O., Purao, S., Rossi, M., & Lindgren, R. (2011). Action design research. *MIS Quarterly, 35*, 37–56.

Sevaldson, B. (2017). Redesigning systems thinking. *FormAkademisk, 10*(1). https://doi.org/10.7577/formakademisk.1755

Sigala, M. (2019). A market approach to social value co-creation: Findings and implications from "Mageires" the social restaurant. *Marketing Theory, 19*(1), 27–45.

Simpson, B., Robertson, J. L., & White, K. (2020). How co-creation increases employee corporate social responsibility and organizational engagement: The moderating role of self-construal. *Journal of Business Ethics, 166*(2), 331–350.

Sudbury-Riley, L., Hunter-Jones, P., Al-Abdin, A., Lewin, D., & Naraine, M. V. (2020). The trajectory touchpoint technique: A deep dive methodology for service innovation. *Journal of Service Research, 23*(2), 229–251.

Tregua, M., Brozovic, D., & D'Auria, A. (2021). 15 years of service-dominant logic: Analyzing citation practices of Vargo and Lusch (2004). *Journal of Service Theory and Practice*. https://doi.org/10.1108/JSTP-08-2019-0174

Urbinati, A., Bogers, M., Chiesa, V., & Frattini, F. (2019). Creating and capturing value from Big Data: A multiple-case study analysis of provider companies. *Technovation, 84*, 21–36.

Vargo, S. L., Akaka, M. A., & Wieland, H. (2020). Rethinking the role of diffusion in innovation: A service-ecosystems and institutional perspective. *Journal of Business Research* (forthcoming). https://doi.org/10.1016/j.jbusres.2020.01.038

Vargo, S. L., & Lusch, R. F. (2004). Evolving to a new dominant logic for marketing. *Journal of Marketing, 68*(1), 1–17.

Vargo, S. L. (2018). Situating humans, technology and materiality in value cocreation. *Journal of Creating Value, 4*(2), 202–204.

Vargo, S. L., & Lusch, R. F. (2008). Service-dominant logic: Continuing the evolution. *Journal of the Academy of Marketing Science, 36*(1), 1–10. https://doi.org/10.1007/s11747-007-0069-6

Vargo, S. L., & Lusch, R. F. (2016). Institutions and axioms: An extension and update of service-dominant logic. *Journal of the Academy of Marketing Science, 44*(1), 5–23. https://doi.org/10.1007/s11747-015-0456-3

Vargo, S. L., Wieland, H., & Akaka, M. A. (2015). Innovation through institutionalization: A service ecosystems perspective. *Industrial Marketing Management, 44*, 63–72. https://doi.org/10.1016/j.indmarman.2014.10.008

Vink, J., Koskela-Huotari, K., Tronvoll, B., Edvardsson, B., & Wetter-Edman, K. (2021). Service ecosystem design: Propositions, process model, and future research agenda. *Journal of Service Research, 24*(2), 168–186.

Weerawardena, J., Salunke, S., Haigh, N., & Mort, G. S. (2019). Business model innovation in social purpose organizations: Conceptualizing dual social-economic value creation. *Journal of Business Research, 125*, 762–771.

Wieland, H., Hartmann, N. N., & Vargo, S. L. (2017). Business models as service strategy. *Journal of the Academy of Marketing Science, 45*(6), 925–943.

Wilden, R., Akaka, M. A., Karpen, I. O., & Hohberger, J. (2017). The evolution and prospects of service-dominant logic: An investigation of past, present, and future research. *Journal of Service Research, 20*(4), 345–361.

World Economic Forum. (2021a). The Davos Agenda 2021. https://www.weforum.org/events/the-davos-agenda-2021

World Economic Forum. (2021b). What changes to economic systems will 2021 bring? Here's what business leaders say. https://www.weforum.org/agenda/2021/01/davos-agenda-2021-fairer-economies-economic-systems-business-leaders-strategic-partners/

Adapting Service Management for the Sharing Economy

Sabine Benoit

1 Introduction

When Shostack in the 1970s (1977, p. 73) called for "service marketing to break free from product marketing", the main reason was that existing marketing models for product marketing could not be applied to services, due to services having a number of characteristics that differed to products. My claim is similar in nature, arguing that service management for the sharing economy needs to break free from service management for "traditional" services. Eckhardt et al. (2019, p. 6) make a similar observation for the marketing discipline "by examining sharing economy's disruptive potential for marketing's traditional beliefs and practices" and following on from this "encourage scholars to move beyond current assumptions and frameworks". This chapter encourages service scholars to do so, because some of the most prominent models in service management need to be adapted to be usefully applied to sharing economy services.

Services in the sharing economy are distinct (Van Alstyne et al., 2016) in that they are co-created by (at least) a triangle of actors, comprising a platform provider, a customer and an actor, that is often a non- or semi-professional peer provider (Benoit et al., 2017). The core value proposition of sharing

---

S. Benoit (✉)
Surrey Business School, University of Surrey, Surrey, UK

Australian National University (ANU), Canberra, ACT, Australia
e-mail: s.benoit@surrey.ac.uk

© The Author(s), under exclusive license to Springer Nature Switzerland AG 2022
B. Edvardsson, B. Tronvoll (eds.), *The Palgrave Handbook of Service Management*,
https://doi.org/10.1007/978-3-030-91828-6_7

economy services, in the way understood here, deal with capacity-constrained, that is, physical, non-digitisable assets, such as cars or accommodation (Wirtz et al., 2019). Because it is the peer provider who gives customers access to his or her tangible assets with no exchange of ownership, for large parts of the service experience, platform providers rely on these non- or semi-professional peer providers (Benoit et al., 2017) or, as Belk (2021) calls them, "amateur providers". A customer might have a (not so) great experience with the platform brand (e.g. Airbnb), with the platform provider having limited influence over the contact points of the peer provider with the customer. Hence, the brand and the customer experience in sharing economy settings are more difficult to manage (Eckhardt et al., 2019). "Traditional" transactions, however, are co-created within a dyad under more controlled circumstances, usually by more or less carefully chosen and trained employees or designed technology. By traditional services we mean services that rely on a business model of one customer-facing focal firm (dyad) that has been called a pipeline businesses or M-model, comprising a linear series of company insourced activities (Van Alstyne et al., 2016; Andreassen et al., 2018). In contrast, services in the sharing economy rely on platforms or T-models which have multiple customer-facing actors with more horizontal communication (Van Alstyne et al., 2016; Andreassen et al., 2018).

This chapter aims to contribute to the discussion on how models and theories in service management can be adapted to be applicable to sharing economy services. This contribution is relevant to academia, because we need fit-for-purpose models and theories to guide our thinking and empirical endeavours. This is in line with literature that has called for theory building for the sharing economy (Parente et al., 2018; Hazée et al., 2020). This is relevant for the managerial world since sharing and traditional, non-sharing economy business models are converging, with competitors moving into each other's spaces, so that it becomes relevant to understand each other's business models, for instance, Airbnb offering their own room capacity and Marriot offering peer-to-peer accommodation (Wirtz et al., 2019). Similarly, Brown (2016) states that many firms consider "opening up" their pipeline model to become more like a platform. This should be decided carefully since many such endeavours fail (Täuscher & Kietzmann, 2017) and peer providers and customers are hesitant to participate in the sharing economy (Hazée et al., 2020). At the same time, predictions are clear that many more sectors than just accommodation and transportation will be disrupted by the sharing economy (Andreassen et al., 2018; Fehrer et al., 2018b).

Taken together, the sharing economy bears enormous potential *and* risk to many service firms. This chapter aims to create awareness of the uniqueness of

Adapting Service Management for the Sharing Economy   **109**

services in the sharing economy, trying to contribute to a discussion on how and what adaptations are needed to make some established models in service management relevant for the sharing economy. For this, we will first take a resource perspective in dyads versus triads (Sect. 2). In Sect. 3, we will propose an adaptation of some well-established service management models to a sharing economy context in five areas: (1) strategy, (2) positioning and competitive advantage, (3) pricing and capacity management, (4) people management and (5) process management. From there, further areas of research are suggested; however, this is not the core aim of this chapter since others have done this very effectively (e.g. Barnes & Mattsson, 2016; Andreassen et al., 2018; Parente et al., 2018). This chapter ends with a conclusion.

2 Resources and Co-creation in Dyads Versus Triads

Services are associated with challenges for marketeers, and it has been argued that customer participation or integration is the key reason for these challenges (Fließ & Kleinaltenkamp, 2004; Moeller, 2008, 2010). One of these challenges is that not only the process (e.g. capacity management) but also the outcome of the service (e.g. service quality) depends on customer resource contributions (Fließ & Kleinaltenkamp, 2004). Based on the notion of customers contributing resources, Moeller (2010) revisits the traditional IHIP characteristics of services and deduces that service providers (1) sell intangible (I) performance promises, (2) have to deal with heterogeneous (H) customer resources, (3) that customer resources are inseparable (I) from the co-creation process and (4) face the challenge that capacity perishes (P) when customer resources are not available in time.

The above also applies to services in the sharing economy, with the extension that resources are needed from both customers *and* peer providers. First, the platform provider enables a peer provider to sell an *intangible performance promise* on the platform involving offering access to the tangible, non-digitisable asset. This is in line with Täuscher and Kietzmann (2017, p. 257) stating that "sharing economy firms are often not physically involved in delivering the service to customers". It is also in line with Breidbach and Brodie (2017) stating that the main resources exchanged between the platform and peer provider, as well as the platform and customers, are money and information.

Second, the platform provider deals with *heterogeneous peer provider and customer resources*. The core of sharing economy services is that peer providers give customers access to their heterogeneous physical assets (Benoit et al., 2017). Information, property rights and money can be digitised and, more importantly, often standardised, so that the platform provider mainly deals with heterogeneity of peer provider resources for reputation and quality management, but not operationally. For instance, the content of the photos of the properties on Airbnb might be heterogenous, but the format can be standardised to the requirements of the platform provider, also enabling better scalability (Täuscher & Kietzmann, 2017). In contrast, the peer providers and customers are the actors in the triangle that deal with heterogeneous, non-digitisable human and tangible resources, such as a passenger getting into an Uber or someone collecting a drill from the neighbour. Since these resources cannot be digitised or fully standardised, the peer providers and customers rather than the platform provider need to deal with the heterogeneity of assets (Andreassen et al., 2018), which is what is said to make these services more authentic, also leading to a higher tolerance for imperfection (Bucher et al., 2018; Shuqair et al., 2019), but which has also led to complaints (Kumar et al., 2018). Essentially, the platform provider has limited control over many resources involved in the co-creation, so is more "orchestrating" the different resources (Van Alstyne et al., 2016; Fehrer et al., 2018b), amongst which are the tasks to provide information and set the right expectations about these heterogeneous physical assets from peer providers (Breidbach & Brodie, 2017).

Third, both the customer resources and the resources of the peer provider are inseparable from the co-creation process which, fourth, results in the platform provider facing the challenge that peer provider capacity perishes when customer resources are not available in time and, vice versa, that demand perishes if there is no peer provider resources available. Hence, aligning resources from both peer providers and customers, that is, "matchmaking" is one of the main tasks of the platform provider (Benoit et al., 2017). Hence, it is mainly the peer provider who is confronted with the challenge that capacity perishes when there is no customer demand.

Overall, the platform provider is in charge of digitisable, intangible resources and the peer provider is in charge of often heterogeneous, physical assets core to the service co-creation process. This subdivision of which actor deals with which kind of resources explains why the sharing economy platforms can scale up so quickly (Täuscher & Kietzmann, 2017). This resource perspective is important in understanding what changes for service management and why and how traditional models need to be adapted.

3 Service Management Models for the Sharing Economy

Strategy: The Sharing Economy Pentagon

One of the most fundamental models for strategy is what is called the strategic (Ohmae, 1982) or value triangle (Brodie et al., 2006). The underlying idea visualised in Fig. 1 is that for a good strategy, three key players need to be taken into account: corporations, customers and competitors (Ohmae, 1982), where strategy is defined as "endeavour by a corporation to differentiate itself positively from its competitors, using its relative corporate strengths to better satisfy customer needs" (Ohmae, 1982, p. 38). This also means that the value of a service will be seen in the light of this triangle of the competitors (Brodie et al., 2006), whereas Ohmae (1982) warns that price-based competition is a consequence when customers cannot differentiate between the value propositions of corporations.

Contrasting traditional product-focused marketing, and to emphasise the importance of the service encounter between customer and employees as part of the service co-creation (Bitner et al., 1990), early service marketing literature suggested a different triangle. This so-called service marketing triangle includes companies, customers and employees as the three focal actors. The sharing economy literature similarly wanted to emphasise the particularity by

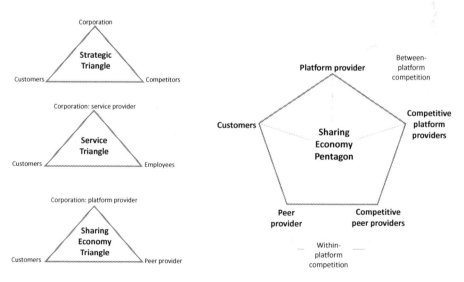

Fig. 1 The sharing economy pentagon

defining that services in the sharing economy are co-created by yet another triangle and that is the platform provider, the peer service provider and the customer (Benoit et al., 2017). One could argue that peer providers in the sharing economy triangle are replacing the customer contact employees in the service marketing triangle. However, despite current court rulings in the UK suggesting the opposite (BBC, 2021), in most parts of the world, peer providers offering their services in the sharing economy are currently seen as independent providers over which control is limited, and not as employees. Albeit possible in customer-oriented companies, we also assume there should be less direct competition between employees, which is built into the sharing economy setting. This distinction is important as it has implications for marketing-related concepts such as branding, value propositions, pricing, customer experience, loyalty and many more.

Merging the ideas from these three triangle models, I suggest that for *strategy* we adapt the sharing economy triangle, which still captures the individual transaction (Benoit et al., 2017), to a sharing economy pentagon (see Fig. 1). This perspective will support strategising and competitive positioning in the sharing economy. This is in line with Fehrer et al. (2018a) stating that most business models take a business-to-consumer and firm-centred perspective, whereas given the increasing connectivity, an actor-to-actor and platform logic seems more appropriate. The sharing economy pentagon clarifies that customers are essentially exposed to two value propositions from two different, albeit connected, actors that are seen in the light of two different types of competitors. Customers usually make two choices: the choice for a platform and, often, a choice for a peer provider.

One of the core questions within the sharing economy triangle is the subdivision and coordination of tasks in the service co-creation. Adding the competitive side puts emphasis on the fact that platform providers need to consider and deal with two layers of competition. There is an internal, "within-layer", that is, competition between the different peer providers on the platform, and there is an external, "between-layer", that is, competition from one platform competing against the other. Hence, the sharing economy triangle supports the operational side of service co-creation. For forming a competitive strategy, the sharing economy pentagon—also considering the competitive environment of this co-creation—is more recommendable.

Network Effects, Positioning and Competitive Advantages in the Sharing Economy

Traditionally, it is recommended to service providers to make choices of certain customer segments and then choose their respective positioning (see, e.g. Wirtz & Lovelock, 2016). Unless for some government services, which might be forced to do so, it is not recommended to serve too many segments or an entire market under one brand (Wirtz & Lovelock, 2016). For platform businesses, however, positioning and segment-specific competitive advantages follow a different logic, since in the sharing economy, competitive advantages are mainly based on network effects (Breidbach & Brodie, 2017). Network effects, according to Gawer and Cusumano (2014), mean users benefit from other users joining the network, that is, the more users adopt a platform the more valuable it becomes. Network effects can be understood as economies of scale on the demand side (Van Alstyne et al., 2016). The value of the platform for these asset-light platform providers (Parente et al., 2018) grows with more and more peer providers offering their assets and more and more customers demanding them. This is one of the reasons for the platform providers' ability to scale up quickly (Täuscher & Kietzmann, 2017).

In two- or multi-sided markets, such as platforms in the sharing economy, network effects can occur on the same side or across the sides of the market (Gawer & Cusumano, 2014). On sharing economy platforms, network effects occur across sides, meaning between customers and peer providers: the more peer providers offer their assets, the more valuable it will be for customers and vice versa. However, Gawer and Cusumano (2014) warn that too much competition on either side (within-platform competition in Fig. 1) may discourage additional actors from making the investment to join the platform. However, after a critical mass of peer providers has been reached to make the platform attractive, growing this number of peer providers further does not create positive network effects for the peer provider. For them, the value of the platform falls with more competition since aggressive competition on the peer provider side leads to low margins (Verboven & Vanherck, 2016; Andreassen et al., 2018). Critical voices have therefore raised issues relating to the fairness amongst actors calling it the "taking economy" rather than the "sharing economy" (Calo & Rosenblat, 2017). These critical voices relate not only to who benefits from network effects, but also to the abuse of the information generated fulfilling this intermediary, matchmaking position of the platform provider (Calo & Rosenblat, 2017).

The core assets of the platform provider are the networks on either side and, by using the information relating to the actors, the ability to carefully manage these resources, that is, the main positioning is that of being able to effectively "orchestrate" the platform actors and resources and *manage resources* (Van Alstyne et al., 2016; Fehrer et al., 2018b). This said, while the platform providers positioning is along the dimension of resource management, the positioning of the peer provider remains in the traditional realm of offering the right *price-benefit position* (D'Aveni, 2007) to be attractive to consumers and peer providers. Figure 2 illustrates this.

Pricing and Managing Capacity in the Sharing Economy

In line with the triadic structure of sharing economy services, three prices are relevant and required (Eisenmann et al., 2006; Benoit et al., 2017). First, the price the peer providers have to pay for being able to offer their performance promise on the platform (*peer provider fee*), (2) the price the customer pays to the platform for being matched (*customer fee*) and (3) the price the customer pays to get access to the asset of the peer provider (*access price*). From the perspective of the customer, this three-dimensional price can seem like one, but for the management of pricing services in the sharing economy, it is useful to subdivide these prices.

Fig. 2 Positioning in the sharing economy

The peer provider fee (1) is often a fee per transaction or based on the transaction value (Wirtz, 2021); it is essential to get an exchange value for the matchmaking. This is similar to the customer fee (2), if there is any. If there is, this fee is often hidden in the overall price and not visible to the customer. Lastly, the access price (3) can be either chosen by the platform provider (e.g. Uber) or chosen by the peer provider (e.g. Airbnb). The essential question here is whether the platform provider gets involved in choosing the price for the access (see Andreassen et al., 2018).

That the platform provider chooses the price is most likely when the asset is homogeneous or easy to evaluate (e.g. car model for transportation, peer-to-peer EV charging or peer-to-peer Wi-Fi), making it easier for the platform provider to choose the price from a virtual distance. Having multiple beneficiaries (peer providers and customers) enables the platform provider to consider a willingness to pay on either side of the triangle. Sometimes there is one side (partly) subsiding the other side (Eisenmann et al., 2006), whereas this can be useful to balance out not only short-term demand and supply as done by Uber with its algorithms and surge pricing (e.g. Andreassen et al., 2018), but also more in the long term in creating a fee structure upon market entry that makes it attractive for peer providers to start listing their offerings. Either side can also be subsidised from the outside, for example, governments aiming to incentivise certain behaviour as has been done with non-peer-to-peer bike-sharing concepts (Cohen & Kietzmann, 2014).

Pricing and capacity management become very much interlinked when the platform providers choose the price, since over time, their business model allows them to have very deep knowledge about price demand functions of the actors used for optimisation. That said, prior research suggests that peer providers over time get dissatisfied when they are not enabled to choose their prices (Kumar et al., 2018). The more attractive the platform for customers, the more likely there will be aggressive competition on the peer provider side so that their margins will likely be low (Verboven & Vanherck, 2016; Andreassen et al., 2018). At the same time, previous research has shown that even though many sharing economy platforms use up-front pricing—meaning that the price is clear and transparent before customers make the purchase decision—customers dislike, for example, surge pricing being used as a capacity smoothing instrument (Calo & Rosenblat, 2017).

It has sometimes been seen as a core of sharing economy platforms that peer providers are the ones who choose the access price customers have to pay (Querbes, 2018). However, so far, there has been little research on supporting peer providers on choosing the optimal prices (Klarin & Suseno, 2021, and the cited literature, e.g. Gibbs et al., 2018). This is even more important since

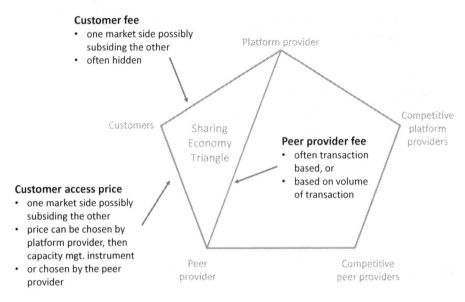

Fig. 3 Pricing in the sharing economy

the access price varies over time depending on the rating of the peer provider (Köbis et al., 2021). The above is summarised in Fig. 3.

People Management in the Sharing Economy

Two types of actors are involved in sharing economy services: customers and peer providers (Benoit et al., 2017). Since the peer provider is the actor who performs the interactions with customers around accessing the assets, the platform provider is essentially losing control over large parts of the service encounter and experience (Andreassen et al., 2018). Even though the platform provider specifies certain rules (e.g. Airbnb's hosting standards), the above "losing control" puts a lot of emphasis on platform governance (Wirtz et al., 2019). The risk of this loss of control is accelerated by the fact that these peer provider-customer interactions can become quite close (Bucher et al., 2018). Hence, platform providers usually try—within their means—to ensure the quality of those service encounters. However, not just the selection but also the management of peer providers is limited and restricted.

Selection. Just as with customers, there is limited control by the platform provider over who signs up as a peer service provider. Platform providers can try to select peer providers by creating barriers for platform providers such as certain quality levels for the assets, certifying the photos of the assets or other

Adapting Service Management for the Sharing Economy 117

quality checks related to the person, such as ID checks. That said, a current common practice is to trust the market to regulate itself through the rating system (Andreassen et al., 2018). Customers know that unrated peer providers are associated with higher risk (Lanzolla & Frankort, 2016), and peer providers know that they will need to enter the platform with sometimes extremely low prices until they gain reputation (Hong & Pavlou, 2017).

Over time, this poses a very important challenge for platform providers. Because of the difficulty for new peer providers with no credentials to gain market access, the platform provider needs to support these new peer providers to avoid "ageing" of the platform (Hong & Pavlou, 2017). At the same time, Andreassen et al. (2018) state that many sharing economy platforms have a problem with peer provider churn, since they tend to have low levels of loyalty to the platform. This poses another threat that if peer providers move platforms and the loyalty is on the customer-peer provider level, then the platform provider might need to ensure the bond does not get too close and communication is not taken off the platform. This is why one-off, very contextual transactions (such as transportation and accommodation) are particularly suited. Repeated transactions amongst geographically close actors, such as accessing a lawnmower or a babysitter, are less suitable for sharing economy platforms since the risk for the actors taking the transaction off the platform after the first couple of transactions to avoid the transaction fees is substantial.

Management. The sharing economy relies on peer providers performing well and satisfying customer expectations. Higher ratings mean a customer is more likely to come back, it increases trust in the platform and transaction (Parente et al., 2018) and they relate to higher earnings for peer providers (Köbis et al., 2021). Airbnb, for instance, offers live webinars and one-to-ones for new hosts and also offers a community centre and local Facebook groups, so that hosts can exchange experiences and tips (Airbnb, 2021). That said, unlike pipeline-based service businesses that can manage their employees, platform providers are limited in managing peer providers, due to two main reasons. First, peer providers are independent entities and therefore will have different assets and act differently. As mentioned above, when there is too much standardisation, management and training (Täuscher & Kietzmann, 2017), this independence is challenged, leading to substantial legal, tax and operational consequences (BBC, 2021). Second, training peer providers like employees and aiming for standardisation are essential in contrast to the positioning of many sharing economy platforms. For instance, more heterogeneous (aka potentially authentic) accommodation or experiences on sharing economy platforms are exactly their envisioned competitive advantage

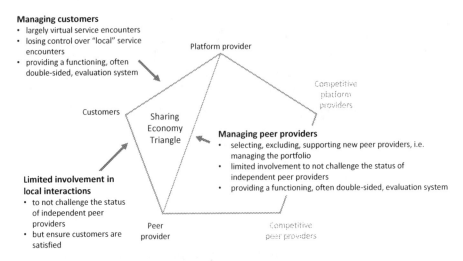

Fig. 4 People management in the sharing economy

(Bucher et al., 2018; Shuqair et al., 2019). Overall, managing the peer provider portfolio includes selecting, excluding, but also supporting new peer providers; this can partly be done through limited means of training, through the rating system, but also through the way or the order in which the platform is displaying individual listings. Figure 4 summarises these tasks.

Process Management in the Sharing Economy

Scholars have emphasised the procedural nature of services (e.g. Hill, 1977) "unfolding over a period of time through a sequence or constellation of events and steps" (Bitner et al., 2008, p. 68). Because customers are often part of this process, the process should be coordinated and managed (Bitner et al., 2008). To do so, methods to map service processes have been suggested, with the most prominent model being the service blueprint (Shostack, 1984; Fließ & Kleinaltenkamp, 2004; Bitner et al., 2008). It has gained much attention in service management because it enables an "integrated view of customer contributions and service provider activities" and can show not only points of interaction, but also what information or other resources are needed and when (Fließ & Kleinaltenkamp, 2019).

Service blueprinting is a method that requires the service process to be subdivided into steps undertaken by the actors involved and then mapped onto a two-dimensional space with the horizontal axis representing time and the vertical axis representing sections that differ in terms of, for example, the visibility of firm activities by customers (Shostack, 1984), what positions the actors have in the process, that is, support service versus contact employees (Bitner et al., 2008), or whether or not the activities have been induced by customers (Fließ & Kleinaltenkamp, 2004). Traditional service blueprints differentiate the following activities from each other (see Fig. 5): the *line of interaction* separates customer activities from employee activities, the *line of visibility* separates visible contact employee activities from invisible contact employee activities and the *line of internal interaction* separates customer contact employee activities from support employee activities that have no customer contact (Kingman-Brundage et al., 1995; Bitner et al., 2008).

We propose a slightly different blueprint to represent the triadic structure of services in the sharing economy. It also incorporates, as deduced above, that the peer provider mainly deals with physical resources, whereas the platform provider mainly deals with digitisable resources from customers and peer provider. The change suggested is that rather than putting emphasis on the visibility, as is done in traditional offline settings, based on the foundation of Sect. 2 it is suggested that emphasis be put on the virtuality in the sharing economy context related to the question of whether resources can be digitised or not. The *line of virtuality* demarcates the local (offline) activities between peer provider and customer in some local, 'physical sphere' from anything happening via a virtual interface controlled by the platform provider (virtual sphere). As explained above, the limited control over peer providers makes this line of virtuality from the customer perspective to be a line of transparency and hence control from the platform provider perspective. Taking the limited control of the platform provider about the service encounter into account, it makes sense to differentiate between local (offline) and virtual peer

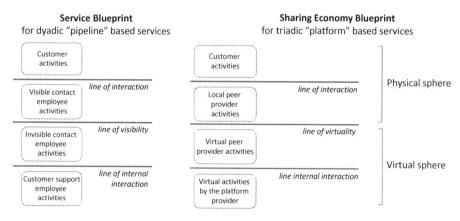

Fig. 5 The traditional service blueprint and the sharing economy blueprint

provider activities that happen in the virtual sphere of the platform provider. Over and above this, the differentiation between which of the two providers is in charge of which process step also needs to be clearly defined. Hence, it makes sense to visualise this by including the *line of internal interaction* initially proposed in the service blueprint. It not only separates for which process steps the peer provider is responsible and for which process steps the platform provider is responsible, but it might also be used to define and clarify the "handover" of the process from one to the other for it to be designed as frictionless as possible. This suggested adaptation of the blueprint to a sharing economy blueprint is aimed at supporting providers in optimising and designing their processes.

The following example of a simplified process of a Stashbee transaction exemplifies the above. Stashbee.com is a platform matching owners and seekers of storage space. As a first step, it is on the peer provider to list the storage space, whereas the platform provider checks, approves and then lists it. When a query or booking from a customer comes in, it is first received by the platform provider. Under usual circumstances, this will directly and automatically be forwarded to the respective peer provider, but it is important to note that it is first received by the platform provider. If an owner of storage space does not live up to the standards of the platform, for example, the storage space being wet, items getting lost or he/she is not available to meet the customer, then the platform provider can cut the space owner out, usually with a few clicks. In the next step, and since storage availability might have changed, the query is checked and approved by the peer provider. To avoid frustration by customers, platform providers should regularly check with their storage owners whether their listings are up to date. These activities all happen around the *line of internal interaction*. In the next step, the process is then taken off the platform, it moves beyond the *line of virtuality* and customer and peer provider meet, usually in person, to deal with the items needing storage. For these steps in the physical sphere, the platform provider loses its ability to monitor interactions. Hence, guidelines and training of peer providers should particularly focus on these process steps to ensure a good customer experience. Since monetary resources can again be digitised, the process moves across the line of virtuality and the platform provider is back "in the loop", meaning the process steps take place in the virtual sphere and the platform provider has full transparency and control (Fig. 6).

Adapting Service Management for the Sharing Economy 121

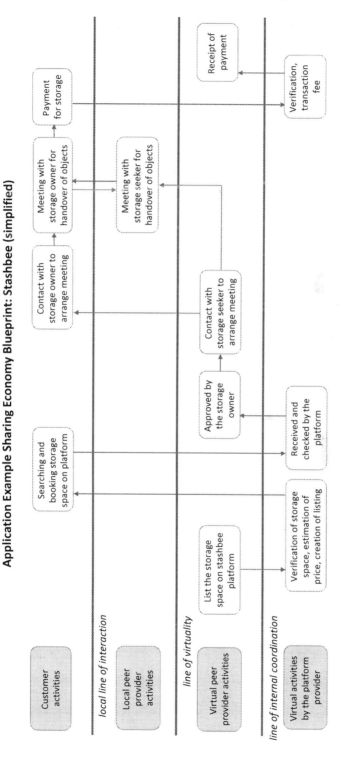

Fig. 6 Example application of the sharing economy blueprint

4   Conclusion: Sharing Economy and Other Service Sectors

This chapter had a modest aim to create awareness of the uniqueness of services in the sharing economy and encourage a discussion on adapting service management models to this context. Hence, it makes the claim that service management for the sharing economy needs to break free from service management for "traditional", dyadic, pipeline-based services. This is because the most prominent existing models in service management need to be adapted before they can be usefully applied to a sharing economy setting. A resource and actor perspective served as a theoretical foundation (Sect. 2, dyads versus triads) before a proposal was made that is up for discussion on how some well-established models relating to (1) strategy, (2) positioning and competitive advantages, (3) pricing and capacity management, (4) people management and (5) process management in service management can be adapted (Sect. 3). Even though the core aim of this chapter was not a research agenda (see, e.g. Barnes & Mattsson, 2016; Andreassen et al., 2018; Parente et al., 2018), the author still hopes that these proposed adapted models will inspire further research in empirically testing and/or applying them.

References

Airbnb. (2021). *How to start hosting with confidence.* Retrieved July 4, 2021, from www.airbnb.co.uk/resources/hosting-homes/a/how-to-start-hosting-with-confidence-359

Andreassen, T., Lervik-Olsen, L., Snyder, H., Van Riel, A. C. R., Sweeney, J. C., & Van Vaerenbergh, Y. (2018). Business model innovation and value-creation: The triadic way. *Journal of Service Management, 29*(5), 883–906.

Barnes, S. J., & Mattsson, J. (2016). Understanding current and future issues in collaborative consumption: A four-stage Delphi study. *Technological Forecasting & Social Change, 104*, 200–211.

BBC. (2021). *Uber drivers are workers not self-employed, Supreme Court rules.* Retrieved April 9, 2021, from https://www.bbc.co.uk/news/business-56123668

Belk, R. (2021). Commodifying service in the sharing economy. In M. P. Fritze, M. Benkenstein, R. Belk, J. Peck, J. Wirtz, & B. Claus (Eds.). Commentaries on the sharing economy: Advancing new perspectives. *Journal of Service Management Research, 5*(1), 3–19.

Benoit, S., Baker, T., Bolton, R., Gruber, T., & Kandampully, J. (2017). A triadic framework for collaborative consumption: Motives, roles and resources. *Journal of Business Research, 79*, 219–227.

Bitner, M. J., Booms, B. H., & Tetreault, M. S. (1990). The service encounter: Diagnosing favorable and unfavorable incidents. *Journal of Marketing, 54*(1), 71–84.

Bitner, M. J., Ostrom, A. L., & Morgan, F. N. (2008). Service blueprinting: A practical technique for service innovation. *California Management Review, 50*(3), 66–94.

Breidbach, C. F., & Brodie, R. J. (2017). Engagement platforms in the sharing economy: Conceptual foundations and research directions. *Journal of Service Theory and Practice, 27*(4), 761–777.

Brown, C. (2016). 3 questions to ask before adopting a platform business model. *Harvard Business Review.* Retrieved April 4, 2021, from https://hbr.org/2016/04/3-questions-to-ask-before-adopting-a-platform-business-model

Brodie, R. J., Glynn, M. S. and Little, V. (2006). 'The service brand and the service-dominant logic: missing fundamental premise or the need for stronger theory?', Marketing Theory, 6(3), pp. 363–379.

Bucher, E., Fieseler, C., Fleck, M., & Lutz, C. (2018). Authenticity and the sharing economy. *Academy of Management Discoveries, 4*(3), 294–313.

Calo, R., & Rosenblat, A. (2017). The taking economy: Uber, information, and power. *Columbia Law Review, 117*(6), 1623–1690.

Cohen, B., & Kietzmann, J. (2014). Ride on! Mobility business models for the sharing economy. *Organization & Environment, 27*(3), 279–296.

D'Aveni, R. (2007, November). Mapping your competitive position. *Harvard Business Review*, 110–120.

Eckhardt, G. M., Houston, M. B., Jiang, B., Lamberton, C., Rindfleisch, A., & Zervas, G. (2019). Marketing in the sharing economy. *Journal of Marketing, 83*(5), 5–27.

Eisenmann, T., Parker, G., & Van Alstyne, M. W. (2006). Strategies for two-sided markets. *Harvard Business Review, 84*(10), 92–101.

Fehrer, J. A., Woratschek, H., & Brodie, R. J. (2018a). A systemic logic for platform business models. *Journal of Service Management, 29*(4), 546–568.

Fehrer, J. A., Benoit, S., Aksoy, L., Baker, T. L., Bell, S. J., Brodie, R. J., & Marimuthu, M. (2018b). Future scenarios of the collaborative economy: Centrally orchestrated, social bubbles, or decentralized autonomous? *Journal of Service Management, 29*(5), 859–882.

Fließ, S., & Kleinaltenkamp, M. (2004). Blueprinting the service company: Managing service processes efficiently. *Journal of Business Research, 57*(4), 392–404.

Fließ, S., & Kleinaltenkamp, M. (2019). Commentary essay on "blueprinting the service company – Managing service processes efficiently". *Journal of Global Scholars of Marketing Science, 29*(3), 281–292.

Gawer, A., & Cusumano, M. A. (2014). Industry platforms and ecosystem innovation. *Journal of Product Innovation Management, 31*(3), 417–433.

Gibbs, C., Guttentag, D., Gretzel, U., Morton, J., & Goodwill, A. (2018). Pricing in the sharing economy: A hedonic pricing model applied to Airbnb listings. *Journal of Travel and Tourism Marketing, 35*(1), 46–56.

Hazée, S., Zwienenberg, T. J., Van Vaerenbergh, Y., Faseur, T., Vandenberghe, A., & Keutgens, O. (2020). Why customers and peer service providers do not participate in collaborative consumption. *Journal of Service Management, 31*(3), 397–419.

Hill, T. P. (1977). On goods and services. *Review of Income and Wealth, 23*(4), 315–338.

Hong, Y., & Pavlou, P. A. (2017). On buyer selection of service providers in online outsourcing platforms for IT services. *Information Systems Research, 28*(3), 547–562.

Kingman-Brundage, J., George, W. R., & Bowen, D. E. (1995). Service logic: Achieving system integration. *International Journal of Service Industry Management, 6*(4), 20–39.

Klarin, A., & Suseno, Y. (2021). A state-of-the-art review of the sharing economy: Scientometric mapping of the scholarship. *Journal of Business Research, 126*(1), 250–262.

Köbis, N., Soraperra, I., & Shalvi, S. (2021). The consequences of participating in the sharing economy: A transparency-based sharing framework. *Journal of Management, 47*(1), 317–343.

Kumar, V., Lahiri, A., & Dogan, O. B. (2018). A strategic framework for a profitable business model in the sharing economy. *Industrial Marketing Management, 67*, 147–160.

Lanzolla, G., & Frankort, H. T. (2016). The online shadow of offline signals: Which sellers get contacted in online B2B marketplaces? *Academy of Management Journal, 59*(1), 207–231.

Moeller, S. (2008). Customer integration – A key to an implementation perspective of service provision. *Journal of Service Research, 11*(2), 197–210.

Moeller, S. (2010). Characteristics of services – A customer integration perspective uncovers their value. *Journal of Services Marketing, 24*(5), 359–368.

Ohmae, K. (1982). The strategic triangle: A new perspective on business unit strategy. *European Management Journal, 1*(1), 38–48.

Parente, R., Geleilate, J.-M., & Rong, K. (2018). The sharing economy globalization phenomenon: A research agenda. *Journal of International Management, 24*(1), 52–64.

Querbes, A. (2018). Banned from the sharing economy: An agent-based model of a peer-to-peer marketplace for consumer goods and services. *Journal of Evolutionary Economics, 28*, 633–665.

Shostack, G. L. (1977). Breaking free from product marketing. *The Journal of Marketing, 41*(2), 73–80.

Shostack, G. L. (1984). How to design a service. *European Journal of Marketing, 16*(1), 49–63.

Shuqair, S., Pinto, D. C., & Mattila, A. S. (2019). Benefits of authenticity: Post-failure loyalty in the sharing economy. *Annals of Tourism Research, 78*, 102741.

Täuscher, K., & Kietzmann, J. (2017). Learning from failures in the sharing economy. *MIS Quarterly Executive, 16*(4), 253–264.

Van Alstyne, M., Parker, G., & Choudary, S. (2016, April). Pipelines, platforms, and the new rules of strategy. *Harvard Business Review*, 54–62.

Verboven, H., & Vanherck, L. (2016). The sustainability paradox of the sharing economy. *UWF Umwelt Wirtschaftsforum, 24*(4), 303–314.

Wirtz, J. (2021). P2P sharing platforms will beat pipeline providers, or will they? In M. P. Fritze, M. Benkenstein, R. Belk, J. Peck, J. Wirtz, B. Claus (Eds.). Commentaries on the sharing economy: Advancing new perspectives. *Journal of Service Management Research, 5*(1), 3–19.

Wirtz, J., & Lovelock, C. (2016). *Services marketing: People, technology, strategy* (8th ed.). World Scientific Publishing Company.

Wirtz, J., So, K. K. F., Mody, M., Chun, E. H., Liu, S., & Chun, H. (2019). Platforms in the peer-to-peer sharing economy. *Journal of Service Management, 30*(4), 452–483.

Part II

Service Strategy

Service Management Strategic Mindsets: That Create Positive Customer and Employee Experiences

David E. Bowen and Benjamin Schneider

Some 25 years ago, we wrote "Wining the Service Game" (1995) which opened with "service organizations can outperform the competition if they master what we offer as the rules of the *service* game." Fifty-three rules were proposed for shaping the roles of managers, employees, and customers, and the interactions among them, to win in the marketplace. The rules were based on our combined 30 years of research, teaching, and consulting about the management of service organizations. Now, 25 years later and based on some combined 80 years of thinking about and studying and writing about service management, we propose four strategic mindsets—ways of thinking—that can help position service organizations to create positive customer and employee experiences (CXs and EXs) and forge sustainable competitive advantage, overall.

In what follows, we first provide an overview of our four strategic mindsets and how they fit with a focus on both employee and customer experiences. Then we elaborate on each strategic mindset and conclude with thoughts on the continued importance of focusing both on employees and on customers for service organizations to be maximally effective.

D. E. Bowen (✉)
Thunderbird School of Global Management (Emeritus), Phoenix, AZ, USA
e-mail: david.bowen@global.thunderbird.edu

B. Schneider
University of Maryland (Emeritus), College Park, MD, USA

© The Author(s), under exclusive license to Springer Nature Switzerland AG 2022
B. Edvardsson, B. Tronvoll (eds.), *The Palgrave Handbook of Service Management*,
https://doi.org/10.1007/978-3-030-91828-6_8

1 Overview of the Four Mindsets

A "Service Is Still All About People" Mindset

Our guiding belief is that, as Schneider (1987) put it: "[P]eople, not the nature of the external environment, organizational technology, or organizational structure are the fundamental determinants of organizational behavior (p. 437). ... The people make the place" (p. 451). Also, at the end of the day, you bet on people, not on strategies (Bossidy et al., 2002). The challenge is to think of people as a foundation on which to build *organizational* capability— a synergistic mix of people throughout the company and the practices that guide, support, and engage them (Ulrich & Lake, 1990). This people-based synergistic mix is difficult for others to copy making it strategically meaningful. The challenge is to meld individual talents into collective organizational capability (Ulrich in forward to Lawler, 2008). The three additional strategic mindsets provide direction on how to accomplish this.

A "Service Climate" Mindset

Climate for service is a strategic organizational climate (Schneider, 2020a); it is a climate for a key organizational priority such as innovation, safety, or service. This mindset is the imperative for the creation of a strong and positive organizational service climate. As shown in Fig. 8.1 (Bowen & Schneider, 2014), this climate weaves together leadership, systems support from Operations, Marketing, IT, and so on, and a pervasive emphasis on HRM practices, with the climate built on a foundation of employee engagement that yields desired customer experiences and organizational performance (Bowen, 2020; Bowen & Schneider, 2014; Schneider, 1973; Schneider et al., 2009). Service climate research typically emphasizes the relationship between internal organizational functioning and external effectiveness, such as customer experiences and various indicators of individual and organizational performance (e.g., Hong et al., 2013). Figure 8.1 also includes a feedback arrow from customer experiences back to the antecedents of service climate, for example, HRM practices, reflecting how customer experience outcomes return to shape the ongoing design of the service climate.

A service climate mindset is solidly based on programmatic research by numerous researchers, including ourselves, over decades (e.g., Bowen, 2020; Bowen & Schneider, 2014; Hong et al., 2013, for syntheses of replicated findings). The logic behind this research and its mindset is that what employees

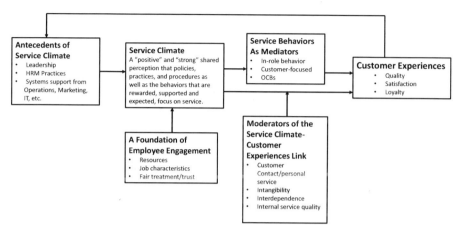

Fig. 1 Slightly adapted service climate framework from Bowen and Schneider (2014). © David E. Bowen and Benjamin Schneider; used and adapted by permission

experience internally is reflected also in what the external customer experiences. In sum, the case for a service climate mindset is strongly evidence-based and theoretically grounded.

A "Coordination" Mindset

"The way we work together" is the true basis of organizational success and competitive advantage (O'Toole & Lawler III, 2007). The interdependent attributes and practices comprising a service climate (see Fig. 8.1) are more effectively managed in organizations with cultures that emphasize "coordination" as a strong, shared value. Indeed, as displayed in the "Three-Tiered View of Service Organizations" (Fig. 8.2; Schneider & Bowen, 1995), we proposed that management's most compelling task is not to exercise formal top-down, one-way control but to create a culture of coordination that helps weave together all the human and non-human actors essential for a seamless service system. In turn, the Boundary Tier is composed of all points of customer contact, both customer-contact employees and customer-contact technology (equivalent to the "organizational frontline" concept in Singh et al., 2017), and the Customer Tier with customers acting both as consumers, per se, and also often as co-producers of their service. Note that customers are included as part of the organization, not viewed as external to it; they are shown as the foundation of the service organization. Dashed lines indicate that interactions and information flows move both downward and upward across the three tiers.

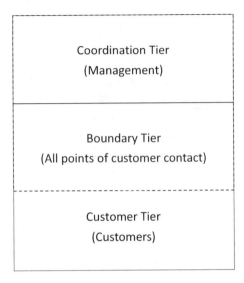

Fig. 2 The three-tiered view of service organizations. From Schneider and Bowen (1995). © Benjamin Schneider and David E. Bowen; used by permission

A "portfolio of coordination mechanisms" (Larsson & Bowen, 1989) is necessary for managing these many interdependencies. The portfolio for our strategic mindsets perspective includes organizational culture, the foundation on which the visible surface layer of organizational climate rests (Schneider, 2020b); employee involvement/empowerment versus employees being controlled (Bowen & Lawler, 1992, 1995); and a socio-technology perspective to help weave together people and technology (Baxter & Sommerville, 2011; Emery & Trist, 1965). Note that this coordination mindset does not emphasize tangible mechanisms such as formal structure but instead emphasizes less visible and less tangible coordination mechanisms which are not as easily copied by competitors. These less tangible sources of information about employee behavioral norms can also guide employees in dealing with the often higher customer-induced input uncertainty in services such as when customers want to play an active role in co-producing their service (Larsson & Bowen, 1989), which reinforces the case for our fourth strategic mindset.

A "High-Performing Customers as Competitive Advantage" Mindset

Whereas the service climate mindset identifies how to manage the customer experience as a key outcome, this mindset specifies how to manage customer *performance* in co-production, as well as how organizations enable value co-creation by customers (Bettencourt et al., 2014; Greer et al., 2015; Vargo & Lusch, 2004). In a co-production role, Bowen (1986) refers to customers as human resources and Mills et al. (1983) called them "partial employees." The organization must have two interrelated sets of practices, one for the customer experience (e.g., satisfaction) and another for customer performance, the latter of which may add or subtract from a positive customer experience depending on the level of the customer's performance. This mindset is challenging for management to implement, given the less control over customer behaviors than employee behaviors, but if done well can be a competitive edge.

The Goal of the Four Mindsets: Positive Customer and Employee Experiences

These four mindsets, well-envisioned and enacted, can create positive customer and employee experiences. In the following elaboration of the four mindsets, we include some illustrative pieces of evidence that demonstrate these experiences indeed follow from companies operationalizing the different mindsets. For example, enacting the organizational practices of the "service climate" mindset is empirically linked to improved customer experiences such as customer service quality, satisfaction, and loyalty (Bowen & Schneider, 2014). After specifying all four mindsets, we will highlight in closing how the four mindsets also provide entrée into exploring the frequently overlooked but established *reciprocal* effects between employee and customer experiences (Bowen, forthcoming; Schneider et al., 1998; Shepherd et al., 2020) as well as how customer experience outcomes then come back to the organization to influence how the four mindsets are enacted in, hopefully, an ongoing cycle of success.

These four overlapping, mutually reinforcing mindsets have much bandwidth, and we concentrate primarily on the people management and HRM practices highly relevant to the four mindsets and the positive impact they can have on employee and customer experiences. Specifically, our people management focus is twofold (Schneider, 2020a). First, we provide an answer to the central question of how the management of people inside the organization gets reflected in how successful organizations are in their marketplace. Second, we provide an answer to the question concerning the consequences of people management practices for the people in those organizations. Our answers to these two interrelated questions can guide managers toward, providing positive experiences for both customers and employees and strategic effectiveness for organizations.

2 Elaborating the Four Strategic Mindsets

We turn now to the more complete specification of the four mindsets. The first (service is still all about people) is an overall guiding philosophy, and the following two mindsets (service climate and coordination) share a focus on creating an organizational *context* in which the delivery of service excellence is facilitated. The fourth (high-performing customers) proposes building organizational capability by extending the organizational boundary to include customers as co-producers and co-creators of value.

A "Service Is Still All About People" Mindset

People have always ultimately determined what organizations choose to do, how they do it, and how well they do it. This is still certainly true of service organizations, despite a service research literature increasingly dominated with technology infusion with AI, service robots, and so on. Even with the rise of AI, technology, and the like, people guide organizational design, still develop service strategy, still design service processes, and still design and place any new service technologies (Schneider & Bowen, 2019).

Putting this into a strategy perspective, people are the ultimate advantage (Lawler, 1992, 2008). Lawler even encourages referring to employees or workers as "talent" to appropriately label their status and contribution. In common strategy thinking, a source of *sustainable* competitive advantage must be (a) valuable to the customer; (b) unique in that it is rarely to be found from competitors; and (c) *inimitable* in that it cannot be copied by competitors, thus making it a sustainable competitive advantage (Porter, 1998). Lower prices than competitors, enhanced product features, and new technologies are more easily copied than having the best people. Ulrich and Lake (1990), in regard to employees, state competitive advantage resides in "organizational capability—competing from the inside out" which at first blush sounds contrary to the external services marketing focus. However, they note, for example, a company philosophy to be the "employer of choice" makes the most value-adding sense if the organization is the employer of choice of employees their customers would choose.

Unfortunately, organizations often select and manage people with less care and sophistication than they use in selecting new service technologies. For example, hiring new employees with precious little investment in the details, time and care required for a valid decision is quite usual according to Schneider (2020b, based on Capelli, 2019) who notes that "It is almost as if senior management feels people are completely interchangeable—like batteries in a flashlight." Senior management, viewing technology as an investment (people after all are costs), expends more time and money evaluating potential new technologies to be implemented at the customer interface than in the people on the frontlines using those technologies. It is quite startling to us how little management knows about the revenues to be generated and the costs to be reduced through careful hiring practices (Scott & Cascio, 2017) let alone careful general human resources management practices (Snow & Snell, 2011).

Additionally, here are four value-adding, largely non-substitutable roles which employees, particularly frontline employees, can increasingly fill to contribute to this new era of service often highlighting the role of technology more so than employees (Bowen, 2016).

1. *Innovator*—human capital still is a powerful source of creativity and innovation not fully substitutable by technology. Research has shown that the more employees are involved in the service innovation process, the greater the innovation volume and innovation radicalness (Ordanini & Parasuraman, 2011)
2. *Differentiator*—Human touch and interaction can still provide a customer-valued source of differentiation in markets where offerings are increasingly similar in design and delivery. The human touch can help avoid the commoditization of very often undifferentiated services (Bolton et al., 2014).
3. *Enabler*—Employees must often help enable both customers and technology to perform their roles in service delivery. Many customers may not be fully "technology ready" and helpful employees offer non-substitutable value at challenging, technology-frustrating moments in the customer experience. This will be especially true when new technology is introduced at the frontlines.
4. *Coordinator*—Service delivery and consumption increasingly is via a network of providers with a mix of technology and human delivery. This challenges customers to have a postive experience as they try to weave together the necessary webof service providers; think medical care, for example. Employees trained to help consumers navigate will promote the consumer experience.

Employees are an empirically validated source of intelligence about how customers view the quality of service provided by the organization and the organizational practices that deliver it. Both Schneider et al. (1980) and Schneider and Bowen (1985) replication found a strong, significant correlation between employees' and customers' rating of overall service quality of their bank branch—0.67 in the original and 0.63 in the replication. Actually, the employee item asked what they thought customers' attitudes are about the quality of service. So, senior management can spend much time and expense on consultants to conduct organizational diagnoses of what their employees think about internal practices—*or* managers could directly listen to their employees, particularly those on the frontlines—who would feel valued to be consulted about the organization's quality and practices and turn out to be accurate in their views of such matters.

Finally, consider *all* employees and all they can contribute. The service management literature should more fully take into account *all* the people in the service organization or overall service delivery system and stop focusing almost entirely on the frontline. Research, for example, reveals that the internal service quality frontline people say they receive from the so-called back room is also reflected in customer satisfaction (Ehrhart et al., 2011). In addition to the aforementioned employees both behind and "above" the frontline, more attention is due to contract and gig workers supplementing "regular" employees (Subramony & Groth, 2021). Companies will increasingly use and find value in such workers, but since they are not employees, but rather independent workers, the management of them can pose challenges.

A "Service Climate" Mindset

Service climate is "employees'" shared sense of the service quality-focused policies, practices, and procedures they experience and the service quality emphasis they observe in behaviors that are rewarded, supported, and expected (Schneider et al., 1998). Service climate is a "strategic" climate—a climate for a key organizational priority/desired strategic outcome such as innovation, safety, or, indeed, service (Schneider, 2020a). Also, in the measurement of service climate, survey items are descriptive of how things are in the organization, not evaluative as in job satisfaction, for example, so the survey data can guide organizational change toward a given organizational priority. True to the spirit of Gestalt psychology, a strategic climate focuses on and measures a bundle of issues and the priority given to them vis a vis the given strategic focus (Schneider, 2020). Worth noting is that there is evidence that service climate is a stronger correlate of customer experiences and customer satisfaction than is job satisfaction (Schneider et al., 1980; Way et al., 2010).

In Fig. 8.1 (Bowen & Schneider, 2014), service climate is positioned at the "center" of internal organizational dynamics such as leadership and HRM practices and the external world of customer experiences. It displays how to create a strong and positive service climate, supported by employee engagement, that gets reflected in desired customer experiences (quality, satisfaction, and loyalty). A service climate mindset is created in companies when HR, Marketing, and Operations all work together to ensure that the people, the products/services, and the technology of a company all focus on producing a positive customer experience.

A strong service climate is one in which there is little variance in how employees experience the service climate, that is, employees agree on their view of the organization's climate for service. It must also be a positive service climate in which there is a high/positive overall mean on employees' survey responses to the essential facets of a service climate and the aggregation thereof. Research reveals that there is good reason to believe that climate strength is a boundary condition on the relationship between service climate and favorable customer outcomes (Schneider et al., 2002).

Linking HRM Practices to Customer Experiences. Service climate research as a central focus validates HRM practices against customer outcomes such as their perceptions of service quality, not just internal employee outcomes such as their job performance. This has been clearly demonstrated in HRM linkage research (Bowen & Pugh, 2009; Schneider & Bowen, 1985). In HRM linkage research, employee perceptions of the company's HRM practices are surveyed (e.g., new employee training, supervision as to feedback and reward contingencies, and the image employees believe the organization has in the eyes of outsiders), and these employee data are correlated/linked with customer survey data on their experiences (e.g., staff courtesy/competence and overall quality). These kinds of linkage data are of course not only conceptually interesting but also practically useful. So, these linkage data again reveal how useful employee data are for understanding customer experiences and the data can be used as guides for management in ensuring that HRM practices are maximally attended to that link to these customer outcomes.

The Strength of the Entire HRM System Impacts Service Climate. It is particularly interesting to think about HRM practices not as individual practices but in the aggregate—the package or bundle of HRM practices. For example, to focus on "bundles" of HRM practices which can create an organizational climate with a particular strategic focus such as a high performance work system or service. There is very excellent research across companies which reveal that when the bundle or package of HRM practices is strong and positive, then positive consequences for customers also emerge (Snow & Snell, 2011). Indeed, it has been found that HRM bundles have significantly greater effects on outcomes than do their individual practices, separately

(Subramony, 2009). And the shared strategic focus is a key. For example, bundles of service-oriented HRM practices had stronger relationships with service climate than generic, high performance practices did (Bowen & Schneider, 2014).

This "bundles" perspective, then, encourages management to focus on the "strength" of the HRM system *as a whole*, not just the properties of individual practices, separately. A "strong HRM system" in which the practices, as a set, are high in visibility, internal consistency, validity, and relevance can, in turn, create a positive and strong organizational climate with a particular strategic focus (Bowen & Ostroff, 2004)—such as service.

Employee Engagement as a Foundation for Service Climate. A foundation for service climate (Fig. 8.1) refers to the conditions under which a service climate is more likely to exist (Salanova et al., 2005). Employee engagement is a function of the feelings of vigor, dedication, and absorption that employees have about their work and work context and the energetic behaviors they display in the work role for the good of the company (e.g., Schneider et al., 2009). A service climate is more easily built on a foundation of engaged employees (Schneider et al., 2009). Employee engagement is a key employee experience, deeper than job satisfaction, on which to build a service climate; it is not an outcome of service climate.

We would be remiss if we did not add a caveat to this discussion with regard to B2B businesses. That is, the research reviewed here on the service climate mindset has been conducted primarily in the B2C world but we have no doubts based on logic and field work in companies (e.g., on the service-profit chain; Heskett et al., 2015) that these same linkages between employee experiences of service climate as developed in strong HRM systems apply there as well to customer experiences.

A "Coordination" Mindset

The goal here is to create a seamless service system by designing a "portfolio of coordination mechanisms" (Larsson & Bowen, 1989) to weave together the interdependencies among employees and between employees and customers. This includes coordinating front-office employees with back-office employees who remain essentially missing persons in service theory and research. Larsson and Bowen (1989) described how customer-induced input uncertainty, ranging from low to high based on increasing degrees of customer diversity of demand and customer disposition to participate in co-production, creates different interdependence patterns which, in turn, require different portfolios of coordination mechanisms. The objective is coordination across all employees, front and back office, who must work together to satisfy both customers' unique desired service outcomes and preferred amount of co-production. In what follows, we describe a portfolio of coordination mechanisms well fitted to management, employee, customer, and technology interdependencies and interactions which can help enact our strategic mindsets and positively affect customer and employee experiences.

Organizational culture may be the ultimate coordination mechanism for "the way we work together" and prescribing "how we do things around here." To be clear on constructs, climate, described above, is employees' sense of where their energies and competencies should be focused and culture is their sense of how their organization functions and what it values in a more macro sense (Ehrhart et al., 2014). A strong culture is one in which espoused values, such as the importance of coordination and cooperation, indeed are also the behaviorally enacted values. Ulrich and Lake (1990) refer to culture as a "shared mindset" among managers, employees, customers, and even investors. The absence of such a shared mindset was evidenced in Schneider et al. (1980) and Schneider and Bowen (1985) which found moderate to strong evidence of a "service orientation discrepancy" with employees holding an "enthusiast" orientation toward service but believing management held a "bureaucrat" orientation toward service; coordination is difficult when central parties to service are not in agreement about how to do it, and if the culture is not shared, then there will be cracks in the seamlessness desired.

One way to instill a coordination culture is through employee involvement. Also termed employee empowerment (Bowen & Lawler, 1992, 1995), employee involvement refers to sharing with employees, particularly frontline employees, four key organizational ingredients: (1) information about organizational performance, (2) rewards based on the organization's performance, (3) knowledge/skills that enable employees to understand and contribute to organizational performance, and (4) power to make decisions that influence organization direction and performance. Sharing, on the one hand, and possession, on the other hand, of these four ingredients create an empowering, self-managing shared "state of mind" that stands in sharp contrast to the very common control-oriented, top-down approach to coordination. The employee involvement approach delivers positive experiences not just to the empowered employee but also to customers in the form of speedier, real-time responses to customer needs during service delivery, as well as during service recovery. Continuing examination of the effects of management sharing of information, knowledge, rewards, and power shows a pattern of significant relationships to a composite measure combining customer satisfaction, quality, speed, and productivity (Lawler III et al., 2001). A caveat is that the implementation of employee involvement/empowerment must match certain strategic contingencies. For example, it is better matched to a basic business strategy of differentiation, customization, and personalization, whereas the control-oriented coordination may be better matched to low-cost, high-volume circumstances.

As to coordinating people and technology, a socio-technical systems perspective is necessary. Socio-technical systems understand that there is no such thing as technology that stands alone. Socio-technical systems theory (e.g., Baxter & Sommerville, 2011; Emery & Trist, 1965) views organizational systems as involving complex interactions between humans, technology, internal subsystems, and the external environment including customers. As Schneider and Bowen (2019) highlight, socio-technical theory points out that system designs that are driven by technology may fail to adequately support the complexity of the real work of the organization due to not sufficiently considering the role of people (both employees and customers) in them (Baxter & Sommerville, 2011). A socio-technical mindset, properly enacted, ensures that those who design and implement technology have those who use it (employees) and those who are served by it (customers) as their focus and not just efficiency or cost as their guiding principles.

A "High-Performing Customers as Competitive Advantage" Mindset

Customers of all kinds (in banks, in hospitals, and so forth) often help co-produce their service and always co-create value. High-performing customers can confer a strategic competitive advantage to the organization; poor performing customers can muck up the works.

A framework for managing customer performance (Bowen, 1986) is based upon a long-established, well-accepted OB/HRM theoretical framework (Vroom, 1964) for what individual attributes employees must possess to perform their jobs as expected. These expectations include (1) role clarity: do they understand how they are expected to perform?; (2) ability: are they able to perform as expected?; and (3) motivation: are there valued consequences for performing as expected?

Customers, too, require role clarity, ability, and motivation to perform their self-service and co-production roles well. Thus, for role clarity, does the firm provide a clear description to the customer of what is expected of them or do they experience ambiguity about what to do and how to do it? Is this clarity provided best face-to-face or online? For ability, does the firm ensure customers have the knowledge and skills necessary to perform as expected by targeting specific customer segments likely to possess the ability necessary and/or invest heavily in training a wider segment of customers in how to perform their roles well? For motivation, is a customer segment intrinsically motivated drawn to a love of "doing it themselves" through self-service? Or are they motivated to co-produce by extrinsic rewards such as price reductions for performing significant self-service and having co-production roles. Finally, the organization must track how well customers perform, as they do with their employees to guide possible customer job redesign and/or better training of the customer. If executed well, high-performing customers can contribute to a sustainable competitive advantage for the service firm by lowering costs, providing more customized services, attracting the growing number of customers who like doing it themselves as well as the sense of control it provides them.

This HRM/OB-based view of customers as partial employees and human resources has been expanded with much more sophisticated conceptualization and marketing insight over many years with (1) the co-creation of value and S-D Logic (Bettencourt et al., 2014; Greer et al., 2015; Vargo & Lusch, 2004); (2) the idea of the co-creation of experiences (Prahalad & Ramaswamy, 2004); and (3) the idea of customer engagement behavior (van Doorn et al., 2010). While these conceptual and marketing insights are provocative, what is attractive about the HRM/OB model is that it is specific about to what companies must pay attention (customer role clarity, ability, and motivation) when they desire customer performance as part of their delivery matrix.

From a socio-technical perspective, another specification of how high-performing customers can add value is found in "Service Encounter 2.0: An investigation into the roles of technology, employees and customers" (Lariviere et al., 2017). This framework conceptually synthesizes the changing interdependent roles of employees, customers, and technology. Lariviere et al. note that technology either augments or substitutes for service employees and also can foster network connections. It then uses the Bowen (2016) framework, above, of four non-substitutable, value-adding roles for employees and describes how these same four roles can also specify how *customers* can add value in service encounter 2.0. Customer as innovator, acting as free consultants in development and delivery of new services; differentiator, greater control over the service encounter process and outcome, particularly when technology enables customers to self- or co-produce, allows them to differentiate service for themselves; enabler, customers supporting employees and/or technology in the service encounter; and coordinator, acting as a resource integrator bringing together communities of customers with similar needs such as in healthcare.

The four mindsets we have presented obviously do not stand alone; they are all part of the interrelated ways service systems function both internally and vis a vis their external customers. The people mindset is primarily internal; the service climate mindset is all about crossing boundaries; the coordination mindset is focused on "the way we work together" rather than on control; and the high performance customer mindset focuses on the central role of customers in their own service delivery and how important it is for organizations to know they have a role in helping these customers be productive and to enable value co-creation. We bounce back and forth between internal employees and external customers because our vantage point on service organizations is all about the connections and the interrelationships between what happens internally and what happens externally. And, in that very focus, we always address both the ways in which employees experience this relationship and the ways customers experience this relationship; we turn now to these interrelated EXs-CXs in a bit more detail.

3 Positive Employee and Customer Experiences

The focus here is on customer experiences (CXs), not the singular customer experience (CX) concept as in Lemon and Verhoef (2016) and the TCQ model of the customer experience (De Keyser et al., 2020). As to employee experiences (EXs), the services management literature does little to identify these and also does not specify an EX concept; these are examples of how the services literature focuses far more on the role of the customer than on the role of the employee (Bowen, forthcoming; Kraak & Holmqvist, 2017; Subramony et al., 2017). In HRM and OB, of course, it is all about EXs and our goal in this chapter was to show how the two, CXs and EXs, are inextricably linked in theory and practice.

We have earlier noted ways in which EXs and CXs are interconnected, such as linkage research establishing that service climate—and EXs within it—is consistently and significantly linked to these interrelated customer experiences of quality, customer satisfaction, and loyalty (see Fig. 8.1). Service climate has also been linked to financial and market performance at the organizational level of analysis as well as the American Customer Satisfaction Index (ACSI; Schneider et al., 2009). Also, the greater the difference between what employees and branch management in banks think is important for the ways in which service should be delivered, the "service orientation discrepancy" noted earlier, the greater were the negative EXs for employees, including frustration, turnover intentions, role conflict and ambiguity, as well as poor views of the service quality they delivered—which was significantly related to CXs (Schneider & Bowen, 1985). Naturally, there is also EXs and CXs research and insight beyond our chapter overview here, certainly including the Service-Profits Chain (SPC; Heskett et al., 1994), as documented in the meta-analysis of the SPC links (Hoegreve et al., 2017).

EXs-CXs Reciprocal Effects and the Success Spiral with People

We have often mentioned the relationships between EXs and CXs throughout this chapter because the evidence indicates the two sets of human experiences are correlated (see Bowen, forthcoming, on the relationship between human experience/HX, and EX and CX). One of course can question which comes first: positive EXs or positive CXs? That is, do employees who experience a positive service climate impact the customers or does having positive customers impact the EXs—or both?

The earliest studies of service climate (Schneider, 1980; Schneider & Bowen, 1985) were based on the foundational idea that how employees experienced the service climate in their work settings somehow got transferred to the customers they served. Subsequent research (Schneider et al., 1998) revealed that there was a reciprocal relationship between employees' service climate perceptions and customer satisfaction. That is, Schneider et al. assessed both EXs (e.g., service climate) and CXs (e.g., customer service quality) at two points in time so they were able, through panel analysis, to explore which comes first, EXs or CXs—and the conclusion is that they have mutual effects over time.

Other examples worthy of brief mention include reciprocal effects between customer attitudes and employee turnover intentions, and employee attitudes and customer turnover intentions (Schneider & Bowen, 1985), turnover intentions certainly being one indicator of employee and customer experiences. Results indicated that the relationship between customer attitudes and employee turnover intentions was the stronger of the two. Now, some 35 years later, Shepherd et al. (2020) studied reciprocal effects between employee and customer experiences. One finding was that collective customer perceptions of service quality produced a stronger effect on collective employee job satisfaction and service climate than vice versa. One explanation for this pattern of stronger influence from customer to employee experiences is "employees are constrained by supervision, performance appraisals, and so forth from revealing their attitudes to customers" (Schneider & Bowen, 1985, p. 430).

Finally, another lens on reciprocal effects is how an organization's positive customer experience outcomes can yield future ongoing success with past successes returning resources and confidence to the organization going forward, As mentioned earlier, positive customer experiences cycle back, as shown by the feedback arrow in Fig. 8.1, to reinforce the ongoing effective design of the antecedents of service climate (such as the HRM practices and employee engagement) that created positive employee experiences, representing what Schneider (2020b) termed "the success spiral with people." Yet the reverse may also be true in which negative customer experiences can start to create a stressed organization in which EXs suffer which then can adversely affect CXs even further; see Schlesinger and Heskett (1991), "Breaking the Cycle of Failure in Services."

A Closing Reflection: Strategic Mindsets as an Organizational Effectiveness Perspective

In sum, the four strategic mindsets ("Service Is Still All About People"; "Service Climate"; "Coordination"; and "High Performance Customers as Competitive Advantage") are proposed to be shared mindsets at the organizational level. As our organizational behavior, colleagues (e.g., Ulrich & Lake, 1990; Lawler, 1992, 2008) cited earlier emphasize a daunting challenge for organizations is to meld individual talent into a collective organizational capability energized and guided by a shared mindset. Indeed, our organizational-level strategic mindsets perspective will continue to require more integration of the organizational behavior literature into the service management literature.

The overall mindset is to (1) create a special type of organization that is both employee- and customer-focused, (2) view employees not just as human resources to help implement a corporate strategy, but to view employees essentially *as the strategy*—talent is a valuable, unique, tough to copy competitive advantage; (3) immerse that talent in an organizational context of a strong and positive service climate; (4) install coordination mechanisms for constructively shaping how people work together; and (5) have a view of customers as partners in the co-creation of value. When these exist, coupled with management attention to all their complex, reciprocal interrelationships, then we can predict positive EXs and CXs. The rules for winning the service game are never simple but they are facilitated by the right mindsets.

References

Baxter, G., & Sommerville, I. (2011). Socio-technical systems: From design methods to systems engineering. *Interacting with Computers, 23*(10), 4–17. https://doi.org/10.1016/j.intcom.2010.07.003

Bettencourt, L. A., Lusch, R. F., & Vargo, S. L. (2014). A service lens on value creation: Marketing's role in achieving strategic advantage. *California Management Review, 57*(1), 44–66. https://doi.org/10.1525/cmr.2014.57.1.44

Bolton, R. N., Gustafsson, A., McColl-Kennedy, J., Sirianni, N. J., & Tse, D. K. (2014). Small details that make a big difference. A radical approach to consumption experience as a firm's differentiation strategy. *Journal of Service Management, 25*(2), 253–274. https://doi.org/10.1108/JOSM-01-2014-0034

Bossidy, L., Charan, R., & Burck, C. (2002). *Execution: The discipline of getting things done.* Penguin Random House.

Bowen, D. E. (1986). Managing customers as human resources in service organizations. *Human Resource Management, 25*(3), 371–383. https://doi.org/10.1002/hrm.3930250304

Bowen, D. E. (2016). The changing role of employees in service theory and practice: An interdisciplinary view. *Human Resource Management Review, 26*(1), 4–13. https://doi.org/10.1016/j.hrmr.2015.09.002

Bowen, D. E. (2020). Lessons for all when service scholarship and management practice come together. *Organizational Dynamics, 49*(3), 1–10. https://doi.org/10.1016/j.orgdyn.2019.04.003

Bowen, D. E. (forthcoming). A human experience (HX) perspective on emotional labor and service: Building a service climate on a foundation of authenticity and justice. *Journal of Service Management Research, 5,* 229–240.

Bowen, D. E., & III Lawler, E. E. (1992). The empowerment of service workers; What, why, how and when. *Sloan Management Review, 33*(3), 31–39.

Bowen, D. E., & III Lawler, E. E. (1995). Empowering service employees. *Sloan Management Review, 36,* 73–84.

Bowen, D. E., & Ostroff, C. (2004). Understanding HRM-Firm performance linkages: The role of the "strength" of the HRM system. *Academy of Management Review, 29,* 209–221. https://doi.org/10.5465/amr.2004.12736076

Bowen, D. E., & Pugh, D. (2009). Linking human resource management and customer outcomes. In J. Storey, P. M. Wright, & D. Ulrich (Eds.), *Routledge companion to strategic human resource management* (pp. 502–518). Routledge.

Bowen, D. E., & Schneider, B. (2014). A service climate synthesis and future research agenda. *Journal of Service Research, 17*(1), 5–22. https://doi.org/10.1177/1094670513491633

Capelli, P. (2019, May–June). Your approach to hiring is all wrong: Algorithms and out-sourcing won't get you the people you need. *Harvard Business Review,* pp. 47–56.

De Keyser, A., Verleye, K., Lemon, K., Keiningham, T. L., & Klaus, P. (2020). Moving the field forward: Introducing the touchpoints, context, qualities (TCQ) nomenclature. *Journal of Service Research, 23,* 433–455. https://doi.org/10.1177/1094670520928390

Ehrhart, K. H., Witt, L. A., Schneider, B., & Perry, S. J. (2011). Service employees give as they get: Internal service as a moderator of the service climate-service outcomes link. *Journal of Applied Psychology, 96,* 423–431. https://doi.org/10.1037/a0022071

Ehrhart, M. G., Schneider, B., & Macey, W. H. (2014). *Organizational climate and culture: An introduction to theory, research and practice.* Routledge.

Emery, F., & Trist, E. L. (1965). The causal texture of organizational environments. *Human Relations, 18,* 21–32. https://doi.org/10.1177/001872676501800103

Greer, C. R., Lusch, R. F., & Vargo, S. L. (2015). A service perspective: Key managerial insights from service-dominant logic. *Organizational Dynamics, 12,* 28–38. https://doi.org/10.1016/j.orgdyn.2015.12.004

Heskett, J. L., Jones, T. O., Loveman, G. W., Sasser, W. E., & Schlesinger, L. A. (1994, March–April). Putting the service profit chain to work. *Harvard Business Review,* pp. 164–174.

Heskett, J. L., Sasser, E. W., Jr., & Schlesinger, L. A. (2015). *What great service leaders know and do.* Berrett-Koehler.

Hoegreve, J., Iseke, A., Derfuss, K., & Eller, T. (2017). The service profit chain: A meta-analytic test of a comprehensive theoretical framework. *Journal of Marketing, 81,* 41–61. https://doi.org/10.1509/jm.15.0395

Hong, Y., Liao, H., Hu, J., & Jiang, K. (2013). Missing link in the service profit chain: A meta-analytic review of the antecedents, consequences, and moderators of service climate. *Journal of Applied Psychology, 98*(2), 237–267. https://doi.org/10.1037/a0031666

Kraak, J. M., & Holmqvist, J. (2017). The authentic service employee: Service employees' langage use for authentic service experiences. *Journal of Business Research, 72,* 199-209. https://doi.https://doi.org/10.1016/j.jbusres.2016.04.182

Lariviere, B., Bowen, D., Andreassen, T. W., Kunz, W., Siranni, N. J., Voss, C., Wunderlich, N. V., & De Keyser, A. (2017). "Service Encounter 2.0": An investigation into the roles of technology, employees, and customers. *Journal of Business Research, 79,* 238–246. https://doi.org/10.1016/j.jbusres.2017.03.008

Larsson, R., & Bowen, D. E. (1989). Organization and customer: Managing design and coordination of services. *Academy of Management Review, 14*(2), 213–233. https://doi.org/10.5465/amr.1989.4282099

III Lawler, E. E. (1992). *The ultimate advantage: Creating the high-involvement organization*. Jossey-Bass.

Lawler, E. E., III. (2008). *Talent management: Making people your competitive advantage*. Jossey-Bass.

Lawler, E. E., III, Mohrman, S. A., & Benson, G. (2001). *Organizing for high performance: Employee involvement, TQM, and knowledge management in the fortune 1000*. Center for Effective Organizations, University of Southern California.

Lemon, K. N., & Verhoef, P. C. (2016). Understanding customer experience throughout the customer service journey. *Journal of Marketing, 80*(6), 69–96. https://doi.org/10.1509/jm.15.0420

Mills, P. K., Chase, R. B., & Margulies, N. (1983). Motivating the client/employee system as a service production strategy. *Academy of Management Review, 8*(2), 301–310. https://doi.org/10.5465/amr.1983.4284740

O'Toole, J., & Lawler, E. E., III. (2007). *The new American workplace*. St. Martins Griffin.

Ordanini, A., & Parasuraman, A. (2011). Service innovation viewed through a service-dominant logic lens: A conceptual framework and analysis. *Journal of Service Research, 18*(2), 127–159. https://doi.org/10.1177/1094670510385332

Porter, M. E. (1998). *Competitive advantage: Creating and sustaining superior performance*. Free Press.

Prahalad, C. K., & Ramaswamy, V. (2004). Co-creation experiences: The next practice in value creation. *Journal of Interactive Marketing, 18*(3), 5–14. https://doi.org/10.1002/dir.20015

Salanova, M., Agat, S., & Peiro, J. M. (2005). Linking organizational resources and work engagement to employee performance and customer loyalty: The mediation of service climate. *Journal of Applied Psychology, 90*(6), 1217–1227. https://doi.org/10.1037/0021-9010.90.6.1217

Schlesinger, L. A., & Heskett, J. L. (1991). Breaking the cycle of failure in services. *Sloan Management Review, 32*(3), 17–28.

Schneider, B. (1973). The perception of organizational climate: The customer's view. *Journal of Applied Psychology, 57*, 248–256.

Schneider, B. (1980). The service organization: Climate is crucial. *Organizational Dynamics, Autumn*, 52–65.

Schneider, B. (1987). The people make the place. *Personnel Psychology, 40*(3), 437–453. https://doi.org/10.1111/j.1744-6570.1987.tb00609.x

Schneider, B. (2020a). Strategic climate research: How what we know should influence what we do. In W. H. Macey & A. A. Fink (Eds.), *Employee surveys and sensing: Challenges and opportunities* (pp. 121–134). Oxford University Press.

Schneider, B. (2020b). People management in work organizations: Fifty years of learnings. *Organizational Dynamics*. https://doi.org/10.1016/j.orgdyn.2020.100789

Schneider, B., & Bowen, D. E. (1985). Employee and customers perceptions of service in banks: Replication and extension. *Journal of Applied Psychology, 70*(3), 423–433. https://doi.org/10.1037/0021-9010.70.3.423

Schneider, B., & Bowen, D. E. (1995). *Winning the service game.* Harvard Business School Press.

Schneider, B., & Bowen, D. E. (2019). Perspectives on the organizational context of frontlines: A commentary. *Journal of Service Research, 22*(1), 3–7. https://doi.org/10.1177/1094670518816160

Schneider, B., Ehrhart, M. W., Saltz, J., Mayer, D. E., & Niles-Jolly, K. A. (2005). Understanding organization-customer links in service settings. *Academy of Management Journal, 48*(6), 1017–1032. https://doi.org/10.5465/amj.2005.19573107

Schneider, B., Macey, W. H., Lee, W. C., & Young, S. A. (2009). Organizational service climate drivers of the American Customer Satisfaction Index (ACSI) and financial and market performance. *Journal of Service Research, 12*, 3–14. https://doi.org/10.1177/1094670509336743

Schneider, B., Parkington, J. J., & Buxton, V. M. (1980). Employee and customer perceptions of service in banks. *Administrative Science Quarterly, 25*(2), 252–267. https://doi.org/10.1037/0021-9010.70.3.423

Schneider, B., Salvaggio, A. N., & Subirats, M. (2002). Climate strength: A new direction for climate research. *Journal of Applied Psychology, 87*, 220–229. https://doi.org/10.1037/0021-9010.87.2.220

Schneider, B., White, S. S., & Paul, M. C. (1998). Linking service climate and customer perceptions of service quality. Test of a causal model. *Journal of Applied Psychology, 83*(2), 150–163. https://doi.org/e10.1037/0021-9010.83.2.150

Scott, J. C., & Cascio, W. F. (2017). The business value of employee selection. In J. L. Farr & N. T. Tippins (Eds.), *Handbook of employee selection* (2nd ed., pp. 226–248). Routledge.

Shepherd, W. J., Ployhart, R. E., & Kautz, J. (2020). The neglected role of collective customer perceptions in shaping collective employee satisfaction, service climate, voluntary turnover, and involuntary turnover: A cautionary tale. *Journal of Applied Psychology, 105*(11), 1327–1337. https://doi.org/10.1037/apl0000480

Singh, J., Brady, M., Arnold, T., & Brown, T. (2017). The emergent field of organizational frontlines. *Journal of Service Research, 20*(1), 3–11. https://doi.org/10.1177/1094670516681513

Snow, C. C., & Snell, S. A. (2011). Strategic human resource management. In S. W. J. Kozlowski (Ed.), *The Oxford handbook of industrial and organizational psychology* (pp. 993–1011). Oxford University Press.

Subramony, M. (2009). A meta-analytic investigation of the relationship between HRM bundles and firm performance. *Human Resource Management Review, 48*(5), 745–768. https://doi.org/10.1002/hrm.20315

Subramony, M., Ehrhart, K., Holtom, B. C., van Jaarsveld, D. D., Yagil, D., Darabi, T., Walker, D., … Wirtz, J. (2017). Accelerating employee-related scholarship in service management. *Journal of Service Management, 28*(5), 837–865. https://doi.org/10.1108/JOSM-02-2017-0055

Subramony, M., & Groth, M. (2021). Enacting service work in a changing world: Time for a dialogue. *Journal of Service Research0.* https://doi.org/10.1177/1094670521989452

Ulrich, D., & Lake, D. (1990). *Organizational capability: Competing from the inside out.* Wiley.

van Doorn, J., Lemon, K. N., Mittal, V., Nass, S., Pick, D., Pirner, P., & Verhoef, P. C. (2010). Customer engagement behavior: Theoretical foundations and research directions. *Journal of Service Research, 13*(3), 253–266. https://doi.org/10.1177/1094670510375599

Vargo, S. L., & Lusch, R. F. (2004). Evolving to a new dominant logic for marketing. *Journal of Marketing, 68*(1), 1–17. https://doi.org/10.1509/jmkg.68.1.1.24036

Vroom, V. (1964). *Work and motivation.* Wiley.

Way, S. A., Sturman, M. C., & Rabb, C. (2010). What matters more? Contrasting the effects of job satisfaction and service climate on hotel food and beverage managers' job performance. *Cornell Hotel Quarterly, 52*(3), 379–397. https://doi.org/10.1177/1938965510363783

Service Strategizing—Shaping Service in Dynamic Contexts

Tore Strandvik, Maria Holmlund-Rytkönen, and Ilkka Lähteenmäki

1 Introduction

To set the scene for this chapter: we envision a successful *individual decision maker* as a representative of an organization *in a dynamic business context*. This person can be a start-up entrepreneur or a manager in a larger company, both of which aim to make the organization successful. We intend to show that the name of the game is not to follow the rules but rather to break or make them. The rules are equivalent to the *mindsets or mental models of business* that both explicitly and implicitly orchestrate business activities. So, we emphasize the need to change *mental models as the key to responding to increased dynamics* in the business environment. Mental models refer to a comprehension of concepts and relationships along with underlying assumptions about them within a specific domain (Fiol & Huff, 1992; Rydén et al., 2015), in this case service value creation. We argue that *challenging the mental model and its underlying assumptions by reflection* is essential when operating in a dynamic business setting. Mental models guide decision making and materialize in concepts and frameworks used to depict the service business. We will discuss how service

---

T. Strandvik (✉) • M. Holmlund-Rytkönen
Department of Marketing, Hanken School of Economics, Helsinki, Finland
e-mail: tore.strandvik@hanken.fi; maria.holmlund-rytkonen@hanken.fi

I. Lähteenmäki
Department of Industrial Engineering and Management, Aalto University, Helsinki, Finland
e-mail: ilkka.lahteenmaki@aalto.fi

© The Author(s), under exclusive license to Springer Nature Switzerland AG 2022
B. Edvardsson, B. Tronvoll (eds.), *The Palgrave Handbook of Service Management*,
https://doi.org/10.1007/978-3-030-91828-6_9

research and practice can benefit from focusing on dynamics in the business context instead of the relative stability that is traditionally assumed in service theorizing and practice. The chapter title refers to this perspective, that is, *service strategizing*, which denotes how a company operating in a changing business context aims to continuously envision the value-creating capacity of its service and thereby shape it.

In this chapter, service strategizing is primarily seen from an individual human actor's (manager's) point of view. This means that the focal unit of interest is not the company or organization as in most service management theorizing, but a manager who has power or individual influence over the company. There are several reasons for applying this individual-centered perspective. We believe single individuals play a larger role than what has been recognized in the literature. In smaller companies, which the majority of companies are, the entrepreneur as an individual often plays a dominant role. This is even more the case in start-up companies founded around one person or a few individuals that retain their influence as the company grows. In larger companies, it is not uncommon for individual (top) managers to have a disproportionate influence on company decisions. Seemingly shared meaning might in fact be a manifestation of the presently dominant mental model held by significant actors in a constant power struggle (Normann, 1975). This situation may be in constant flux because of manager turnover and changes in business situations and may change when individuals arrive or leave, or as new mental models emerge. So, rather than assuming a company has or even could achieve and maintain a shared meaning concerning their business, we believe single individuals in the organization have different extents of influence on the constellation of meanings in the company. This leads us to apply a micro perspective and what has been called the micro-foundations of strategizing in the strategic management literature. Hence, we focus on individual managers' sensemaking and mental models.

There are a couple of caveats related to our exploration of service management from a managerial point of view in changing business environments. Although we use terms relating to business and commercial settings, the argumentation does not exclude non-commercial service settings, such as public administration or ideological organizations. We use company to denote a service provider in a generic sense for any kind of service-oriented organization. *Managerial is* not meant to imply formal top or middle management roles in organizations but rather *the function of acting on behalf of the company or organization*. We aim to introduce and advance the notion of service strategizing as a concept rather than conduct and review a stream of literature. We draw on different strands of the strategic management and service literature to build our service strategizing framework. This paper is about mental models of individuals rather than mental models on the team level, organizational level, or a more aggregate level. It furthermore addresses sensemaking issues, not strategy implementation issues, and the interest is in service value creation centered around customers, offerings, and markets, while leaving organizational, production, and profitability issues aside. We have in mind primarily micro-, small-, and medium sized enterprises rather than large and multinational companies.

In the following, we outline issues in the emerging future of service management and offer some conceptual tools for tackling increasingly dynamic business contexts. We start by briefly discussing some drivers and types of change and continue by outlining how dynamics brings about strategizing to cope. We then compare different service theorizing perspectives in a map depicting the evolution over time and propose a new dynamics scope. Against this background, we next discuss service strategizing focusing on manager mindsets and reflective capabilities using a generic *DOT-model* (Doing, Observing, Thinking). We end with the new service strategizing conceptualization and emerging service management issues in increasingly dynamic business contexts.

2 Business Dynamism Impacting the Company

Firms may adopt a reactive approach and adapt to changing circumstances, but they may also actively exploit them in their present markets and in what they see as their potential markets. One kind of dynamics is captured by the concept of disruption, denoting more abrupt and unexpected changes in the business context, for example, as a result of the COVID-19 pandemic. Kilkki et al. (2018) characterize disruption as an event in which an agent must redesign its strategy to survive a change in the environment. Forces in the business environment that drive service management into constant re-evaluation are mostly grounded in societal changes that alter the logics and way of operating, not only for industries but also for society. In stable markets, companies aim to stand out from known competitors, but now the goal is to constantly discover emerging viable positions in markets where understanding customers and their changing priorities and behavior is the main challenge. This has been characterized as managing in a VUCA world, meaning that it is volatile, uncertain, complex, and ambiguous (Sinha & Sinha, 2020).

Regulation, technologies, digitalization, sustainability, and changes in the usability of resources such as data are additional examples of sources of dynamism and reasons for a VUCA business environment. For example, data's role and usability have changed radically lately as digitalization forms new kinds of platforms and (eco)systems between firms. These changes are quite often threatening, especially to incumbent business, but for others and reflective firms, they offer the possibility to create totally new business opportunities.

While it is challenging to evaluate the impacts of different sources of disruption, the change of analogical processes into digital processes in various social and business contexts is undoubtedly one typical consequence. Gartner (https://www.gartner.com/en/information-technology/glossary/digitalization) defines digitalization as the change of business models with digital technologies to provide new revenue- and value-producing opportunities. For businesses that rely strongly on personal interactions with customers (such as banking), digitalization has had profound effects and changed the whole understanding about interaction and ways to form value, from both the firm and the customer perspective. Moreover, there is an additional cluster of technologies such as artificial intelligence (AI), mobile technologies, blockchain, and open interfaces that accelerate this change.

In addition to digitalization, the way in which data is used is another source of dynamics. The use of data in digital form has created a new sphere of economy called the data economy, namely, an ecosystem of organizations for whom data is the main source or object of their business. The data economy is affecting firm boundaries as these change from proprietary resources to shared structures. The value of data increases as its use expands; the use is implemented by joint development, which creates and changes business models, co-creation, and customer interaction. Innovations in the data economy take place both in firms and inside the ecosystem, where partners form platforms for open and systemic innovation, creating and needing new roles of firms and specialists. These platforms may be seen as a consequence of the data economy, forming a parallel economy that is a concrete business model of the data economy. Figure 1 illustrates how dynamics links to strategizing in such an innovation setting.

Sources of dynamics are many—some of them can be predicted, whereas others are surprising. There are different dimensions of dynamics, as some sources are more predictable than others, some develop quickly and others evolve gradually; some are more encompassing in scope than others, affecting more aspects of business life than others. The dynamics result in impact with different levels of pressure to respond and strategize. Some companies may take a proactive approach, whereas others may choose to adapt, that is, a reactive approach. In the former situation, the dynamics may generate

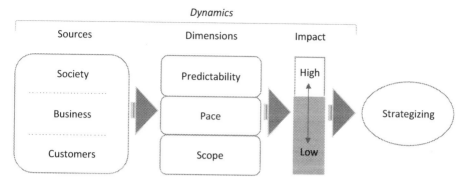

Fig. 1 How dynamics in the market links to strategizing

opportunities and new possibilities for growth; in the latter they can become a question of survival. How well the company succeeds can depend on how well it strategizes.

3 Strategic Theorizing in Practice

Strategic theorizing in practice refers to managers' sensemaking as strategists, using and reflecting on their *theories-in-use* about their company's performance, customers, offerings, and the market. Managers' theories-in-use (also called mental models, belief structures, mindsets, logics) have been portrayed in several streams of the management literature as driving and directing the company's activities (Argyris, 2003; Weick et al., 2005). A step further is the suggestion that managers can be seen as theorists (Felin & Zenger, 2009; Felin & Zenger, 2017). *Managerial theorizing* suggests a dynamic perspective on mental models being potentially constantly formed and reformed.

In the strategic management literature, the concept *dominant logic* (Prahalad & Bettis, 1986) refers to managers' mindsets of the business directing decisions to achieve company goals. This stream of research has evolved to suggest that the dominant logic is not only invisible in the minds of managers as concepts, linkages between them, and underlying assumptions, but also visible as embedded in practices and organizational structures (Engelmann et al., 2020). The dominant logic at play represents on the organizational level the mental model that is used to make decisions. Individual managers may have different mental models but adhere to the dominant logic in their roles. Normann (1975) and Kaplan (2008) suggest that there is constant competition between logics to become dominant. In the scholarly marketing and service literature, the "dominant logic" notion has been adopted to represent different theoretical perspectives on service and service management, service-dominant logic (Vargo & Lusch, 2004), service logic (Grönroos, 2006), customer-dominant logic (Heinonen et al., 2010), and public service logic (Osborne, 2018).

Another related conceptualization is *strategic agility* (Doz & Kosonen, 2008), referring to behaviors and skills of a company in taking and implementing strategic actions. Strategic agility consists of three capabilities: strategic sensitivity, resource fluidity, and collective commitment (Doz, 2020). Strategic sensitivity, which is the most relevant for this paper, refers to "the sharpness of perception and the intensity of awareness and attention to strategic situations as they develop" (Doz, 2020, p. 2). The challenge for senior executives in developing strategic agility is to be able to shed old mindsets and practices and develop new ones. Strategic agility is mainly seen as an organizational capability but rooted in individual managers' activities.

Dynamic capabilities is a concept in the strategic management literature to capture the organization's ability to adapt to changes (Teece et al., 1997). Teece (2020, p. 10) specifies the character of dynamic capabilities compared to ordinary capabilities: "by contrast, require entrepreneurial styles that contribute to the orchestration of a company's resources in alignment with the changing demands of customers, the evolving possibilities opened up by new technology, and the need to respond to emerging threats." Dynamic capabilities are considered mainly on the organizational level, but also on a top management team level (Teece, 2020) and an individual level (Felin & Foss, 2005; Felin & Powell, 2016). The dynamic capabilities concept highlights the capacity of managers to create strategic change (Helfat & Martin, 2015). Teece (2007) suggested three dynamic capabilities: sensing, seizing, and transforming as generic descriptors, which are essential in responding to strategic challenges. For our purpose, sensing, implying managerial sensemaking of opportunities, is relevant and related to strategic sensitivity in the strategic agility framework. Within the dynamic capabilities field of research, it has been suggested that increased attention should be paid to the role of dynamic capabilities in shaping markets and ecosystems and how dynamic managerial capabilities affect organizational dynamic capabilities (Schilke et al., 2018).

Strategy is commonly seen as a plan with goals and steps that aim to give an enterprise a competitive advantage. *Strategizing* is derived from strategy and denotes the detailed process and practices that constitute the daily activities in a company and relate to strategic outcomes. Bolland (2020, p. 3-4) defines strategizing as "the continuous thinking and acting based on the past, present, and future of the organization and its environment resulting in a clearly defined path towards a desired organizational state involving analysis of internal and external factors with opportunity for participation by all members of the organization." Bolland (2020) contends that strategizing has some common features in continuous attention to change, challenging assumptions, introducing opposite assumptions, and actively engaging in thinking about the future: "Strategy is important because it bridges the present with the future" (Bolland, 2020, p. 9).

Weaving these theoretical threads together to construct our approach, we focus on individual actors (managers) serving as representatives of their organization in their role and capacity as influencers of the organization's strategy. We take the stance that their mental models drive their attention, decisions, and actions. We consider the domain of the mental model to be the organization's service value creation capacity. The dominant logic concept refers to the dominant mental model in use in the company, which may or may not be embraced by all managers. We therefore see individual managers as embedded in a mindset landscape on group, organization, industry, and higher levels. We assume the individual can influence the dominant logic in the organization by possessing individual dynamic capabilities, power, and personal influence. Dynamic capabilities capture the ability to either respond to emerging challenges or proactively create change. Strategizing is an approach for continuously performing strategic actions where dynamic capabilities are put into use according to the dominant logic. Strategic agility represents a perspective specifying requirements for adequate strategizing. In this way, different approaches to capturing managerial cognition are related to each other. However, the main point is not only how mental models are related to strategic action, and how individuals are related to higher level aggregates, *but how mental models change to either reactively adapt to changes in the environment or to proactively create change*. Here we return to the idea that managers can be seen as *active theorists, continuously theorizing and reflecting about value creation strategies.*

4 Framing the Dynamics of Service Management—A Service Dynamics Mindset

The scope and application field of service thinking have expanded. When service marketing and management emerged in the early 1980s, it was mainly applied to situations involving person-to-person interactions in retailing and hospitality settings and focused on service quality (e.g., Fisk et al., 1993). Since then, a considerable evolution in terms of scope and focus on service thinking has taken place and resulted in a multitude of perspectives on service (as shown in our earlier analysis). Much of this is due to an increased focus on processes, which started with the early service theorizing on (person-to-person) interactions in a confined setting, the service episode, or service encounter (Grönroos, 1984; Parasuraman et al., 1985). This focus was gradually expanded to service processes over time as relationships (Liljander & Strandvik, 1995; Ravald & Grönroos, 1996) and more complex connections between processes in systems (Vargo et al., 2008; Vargo & Lusch, 2011).

These perspectives and their managerial implications that reflect streams of research in service management have been elaborated in Heinonen and Strandvik et al. (2018) and Strandvik et al. (2018). Different focuses have been applied to service—for example, that of the seller, an interaction, and the customer—indicating that service has different facets depending on the perspective from which it is viewed. Another aspect is the scope or breadth of the company's service offering, corresponding to the question: what are we actually selling? The nature of a service as an element in value creation has been seen as a transaction/episode, as a relationship (containing multiple episodes over time), or as a system (containing a collection of service elements and providers, with multiple episodes over time). Many sources of change, for example, digitalization enabling new collaboration constellations, contribute to a gained interest in the system views.

Such views can be used in service management to inform managers of options to understand service and consider in their practice, and simultaneously they form the basis for the mental model. They do not, however, adequately consider change and dynamics, so we suggest that dynamics is a platform for a new and different view on service theorizing and service management. Adding dynamics as a new *extended scope* unlocks a new managerial mindset to understand service and service management. This is justified in order to meet the need to capture more of the dynamism that is gaining increasing relevance. Deliberately focusing on dynamics rather than stability will shift the attention to new issues and emphasize underlying mental model alternatives. In Fig. 2, we include this extension of scope into the map of mindsets on service from Strandvik et al. (2018).

A *service dynamics mindset* would shift attention from what is to what has been, what will be, what could be, and what should be. It would also imply continuous issues for management: what has changed, what can be changed, and what will probably change in our business and context. Taken together, these questions represent a completely different perspective compared to the traditional assumption of a fairly stable environment. We propose that shifting the focus to dynamics and change will significantly shape the mental model of business and redirect attention, observations, decisions, and actions.

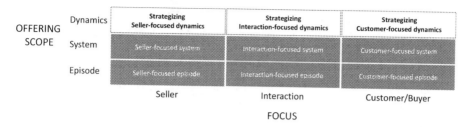

Fig. 2 Different mindsets on service

Disruptions in business environments and society create challenges and opportunities. Applying a dynamics perspective instead of a stability perspective would shift the attention from *strategy* as a noun to *strategizing* as a continuous activity. Instead of focusing on service offerings as designed entities, attention would need to be paid to the dynamics and changes of service offerings, in terms of both intentional shaping and contextual changes.

Concerning interactions between providers and customers, more attention would be paid to *how interactions change* rather than the structure of interactions, for example, due to digitalization. Most research on value creation is based on theorizing about participants, dimensions, processes, and outcomes of value creation (see, e.g., Vargo et al., 2008; Heinonen et al., 2010; Vargo & Lusch, 2011; Grönroos & Voima, 2013; Heinonen & Strandvik, 2018).

Scholarly knowledge and practitioner knowledge represent two different but related facets of knowledge about service and service management (Sandberg & Tsoukas, 2011; Wierenga, 2002; Zeithaml et al., 2020). It can, however, be argued that in both realms a change in mindsets requires reflection (Alvesson & Sköldberg, 2009; Rydén et al., 2015).

A service dynamics mindset focusing on change rather than assuming stability will shift the attention to issues such as disruption, pace, rhythm, trends, waves, and evolution of value creation, creating a new perspective for service research and practice. Problematization of current underlying assumptions (Alvesson & Sandberg, 2011) in theory and practice enables reflection in order to break free from and renew current mental models. From a managerial point of view, this implies *service strategizing* as an approach.

5 Service Strategizing

This paper emphasizes the ability to reflect, which all humans have, some more than others. *Reflection* in its simplest form means "To think carefully, especially about possibilities and opinions" (https://dictionary.cambridge.

org/dictionary/english/reflection). It is essentially about individuals' cognitive processes, such as becoming conscious of, analyzing, evaluating, questioning, and criticizing experiences, assumptions, beliefs, or emotion (Hilden & Tikkamäki, 2013). It is a triggered process during which new beliefs about possibilities emerge, when new possibilities are created and potential consequences of actions and behaviors are assessed. The notion of reflection fits very well with strategizing, defined as continuous thinking and acting based on the past, present, and future of the organization and its environment (Bolland, 2020).

Reflection, similarly to theorizing in general or among entrepreneurs, emerges from experience and perception and contains triggering fragments, the imagination of possibilities, and the process of reasoning and justification (Felin & Zenger, 2009). The experiences and perceptions, as they induce contemplating and what-if questioning, may trigger the process of reflecting. In practice, this implies reasoning about alternative possibilities as well as conceiving and considering new possibilities and impossibilities for actions. Further reflection with reasoning and justifying means carefully evaluating and cognitively testing the ideas and actions further. Although not the focus of this paper, reflection tends to involve social processes, for example, when seeking input from others and when potential consequences are broad.

Another main element in the strategizing process is the *mental model* of the manager. A mental model is a belief structure, an individual's comprehension of concepts and relationships together with underlying assumptions about them within a specific domain. Specifically, for service the relevant mental model is the comprehension of service value creation capacity. A manager is driven by this mental model and it is reflected in how s/he reasons and reacts, what s/he pays attention to and observes, and what s/he decides to do. For the manager, the mental model functions as the underlying belief structure that steers attention and forms priorities and benchmarks. The mental model may or may not change as a result of reflection. Some managers' mental models are more rigid and thus more reluctant to change than others; the mental model's adaptability depends on how reflective the manager is.

As described in the previous section, the idiosyncratic mental model determines how the manager sees customers, offerings, and markets, and it underlies the manager's priorities when it comes to service value creation and how the company should shape the service.

The third set of essential strategizing elements comprises ongoing *doing, observing, and thinking* that the manager encounters in the organization. We group these different processes into what we label DOT. DOT distinguishes different elements in a continuous flow of activity, insights and thought processes that embed the manager. Each of these elements captures broad complementary areas that are essential for managing service value creation, and they relate to customers, offerings, or the market. These doing, observing, and thinking processes are the triggers for the manager's reflection. Doing corresponds to actions, that is, what is done or what occurs, and it refers to any and all such activities the manager encounters and reflects on. Observing denotes not only all kinds of data and information, but also other impulses and signals a manager comes across that are linked to customers, offerings, and the market. Thinking implies interpreting experiences about customers, offerings, and the market but doing so without a critical assessment. This type of interpreting would be on a lower level of thinking than the reflection it subsequently can but does not need to induce (Alvesson & Sköldberg, 2009; Ringberg & Reihlen, 2008). Thinking alone does not necessarily lead to any further action but is needed for reflection. Reflection is conceptually distinguished from thinking and represents a higher order cognitive process similar to the distinction between double-loop learning and single-loop learning (Argyris, 1976) and reflective thinking and categorical thinking (Rydén et al., 2015). Reflecting is a kind of second-order dynamic capability that allows the organization's fundamental capabilities and resources to change (Collis, 1994).

Reflecting functions as a lens through which the manager evaluates the continuous flow of doing, observing, and thinking, and it assesses whether there is a trigger to start reasoning and eventually a need or opportunity to make changes to strategies or the mental model. When a manager is able to reflect on his or her thought processes, it sets the stage for a potential disruption of the existing mental model. If nothing catches the attention of the manager and nothing extraordinary is detected, there is no cause to reflect. On the other hand, if something stands out and a surprise is found, a tension or a misalignment, then reflecting may be started by the manager. For example, a manager may realize that current customer insights are becoming less useful for shaping service, as customer behavior and priorities are undergoing rapid changes. This recognition triggers efforts to think about alternative ways of gathering customer insights, finding out about different options, and enquiring about what they would imply. Eventually this would lead to revisions that will affect new ways of doing, observing, and thinking. Figure 3 illustrates service strategizing and its key elements.

Service strategizing highlighting an individual's ability to reflect is particularly relevant in a dynamic setting. It is a way for service organizations to shape the service continuously, where being responsive can determine the company's destiny. Reflecting rather than planning becomes important. In a stable situation, these DOT elements tend to streamline with each other to

162 T. Strandvik et al.

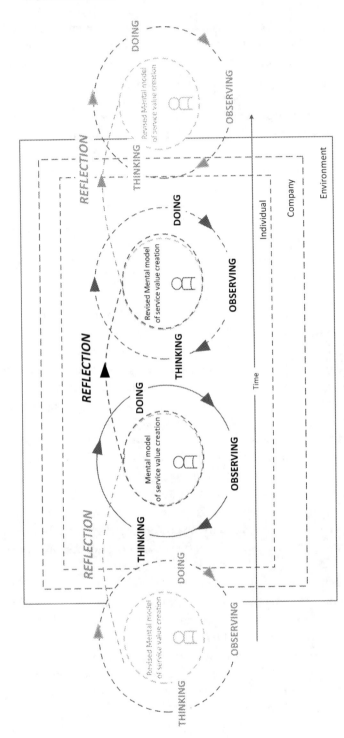

Fig. 3 Service strategizing based on an individual manager's constant reflection in a dynamic setting

the point that they cause inertia. When change occurs in the environment, it becomes difficult for the individual and the company to match the change since each of the elements can lag or change out of sync with each other. For example, in the banking sector, marketing appears to have changed dramatically and some adjustments have occurred, but there are still gaps in how to make sense of the new situation. Many assumptions from the past bank business logic still seem to exist and constitute an institutional logic. All in all, there is limited knowledge about what the changing business setting implies.

6 The Emerging Future of Service Management

This chapter highlights emerging service management issues in increasingly dynamic business contexts. We argue that managers' mental models play a central role and need to be explicitly recognized as the underpinnings of strategies and action and as the foundation for responding to emerging challenges. In fact, differing mental models about what value to prioritize and the meaning of customers, offerings, and markets drive companies' decisions and operations, and therefore, they are fundamental for understanding strategy. We furthermore argue that emphasis should be put on individuals as potential change makers and propose that change in sensemaking in an organization starts from an individual. Many ideas in strategic management related to sensemaking in dynamic contexts, like strategic agility, dynamic capabilities, dominant logics and strategizing, are assumed to be organizational characteristics disguising the processes of how these come about. By focusing on individuals and how they change their sensemaking and mental models, organizational-level changes can be understood. We claim that reflection is the key process to change mental models and that strategizing represents a service management approach taking a dynamics perspective, thereby corresponding to continuously changing business environments and society.

The logic is the following. The significant decision maker's mental model is embodied in three types of interconnected continuous processes—doing, observing, and thinking. The mental model can only be developed by reflection, which implies challenging the assumptions that the mental model is based on and creating new beliefs about possibilities and assessing potential consequences of actions. Strategizing denotes how these elements are involved in managing service organizations in dynamic contexts, where there is a need to be constantly prepared to make changes. Strategizing represents the service provider's intentional activities to influence the outcome of its service understanding. Service shaping denotes the service provider's continuous attempts through strategizing to adapt the service to changing value creation potentials. Many times, the process may be more straightforward than expected, for example, when a new CEO is given the mandate to change the company in a crisis, or in smaller companies with an effective owner/manager.

Applying a dynamic perspective enables the future to be considered as continuously emerging. It becomes relevant to think about an evolving future without any specified time horizon, and it is informative to reflect on changes that challenge our assumptions from the past and the present and their possible implications. We argue that service strategizing highlights a novel service dynamics mindset that challenges current and past management thinking by stressing continuous attention to positioning and repositioning an organization in a dynamic context.

The proposed perspective spurs three issues for further consideration among service researchers and service management practitioners.

How Does a Manager's Mental Model of Service Value Creation Change?

In our framework, we outline what should be done (reflection, theorizing) to update mental models. Mental models are assumed to be a source of achieving competitive advantages for the organization. In practice, updating is difficult. Reflection does not happen or happens only too late. Metaphorically, this represents the situation where the map gradually becomes less adequate, but still is used as if it were valid.

Topics for researchers: What do practitioners' mental models of service value creation look like? How does an individual manager's mental model influence the dominant logic in the organization and service system?

Topics for practitioners: How can the manager become aware of the mental model their own mental model? Which reflection techniques can be used to change the mental model?

The diversity of mental models of service value creation

Our framework highlights the potential of a diversity of mental models within the organization. Rather than assuming shared meaning, the approach suggests that there naturally is non-shared meaning among individuals within the organization but, through different continuous processes, a dominant logic on the organization level is emerging. Over time, the dominant logic is dynamic. This diversity of mental models represents an interesting field for service research and a challenge for service practitioners. Metaphorically, this represents the situation that each member of the organization has different maps of the terrain—but they do not know it and assume that others have the same map.

Topics for researchers: How do practitioners' mental models differ from the pure theoretical perspectives and models proposed in the scientific literature? Why do practitioners have such mental models?

Topics for practitioners: How can colleagues' mental models be identified? Why are they different—what underlying assumptions are critically different? Which are those assumptions that are affected by changes in the business environment and are open for reassessment?

The Relevance and Adequacy of the Mental Model of Service Value Creation

The mental model is a representation of the relevant reality with the intention to serve a purpose—to guide service management. Considering the framework proposed is generic, it can be used to understand other actors in the business environments: customers, competitors, and other stakeholders, in a similar way. Each actor is involved in "strategizing" and reflection and, consequently, in a dynamic business environment, potentially changing their mental models that guide their actions. Metaphorically, this means that these actors as elements on the manager's map might change character and position, endangering the adequacy and usefulness of the map.

Topics for researchers: What is the value creation logic (mental model) of different actors: diversity in mental models among customers, diversity among competitors, and diversity among other stakeholders? Do service providers' assumptions of other actors' logics correspond to these actors' own logics? How are all actors' logics changing in dynamic business contexts?

Topics for practitioners: How can we understand the mental models (logics) of customers and changes in them? Which factors in the dynamic business environment will cause changes in other actors' mental models, at what pace, and with what consequences? How do colleagues in the company interpret these changes in the business environment?

References

Alvesson, M., & Sandberg, J. (2011). Generating research questions through problematization. *Academy of Management Review, 36*(2), 247–271.

Alvesson, M., & Sköldberg, K. (2009). *Reflexive methodology: New vistas for qualitative research* (2nd ed.). Sage.

Argyris, C. (1976). Single-loop and double-loop models in research on decision making. *Administrative Science Quarterly, 21*(3), 363–375.

Argyris, C. (2003). A life full of learning. *Organization Studies, 24*(7), 1178–1192.

Bolland, E. J. (2020). *Strategizing: New thinking about strategy, planning, and management.* Emerald Group Publishing.

Cambridge dictionary. https://dictionary.cambridge.org/dictionary/english/reflection

Collis, D. J. (1994). Research note: How valuable are organizational capabilities? *Strategic Management Journal, 15*(S1), 143–152.

Doz, Y. (2020). Fostering strategic agility: How individual executives and human resource practices contribute. *Human Resource Management Review, 30*(1), 1–14.

Doz, Y., & Kosonen, M. (2008). The dynamics of strategic agility: Nokia's rollercoaster experience. *California Management Review, 50*(3), 95–118.

Engelmann, A., Kump, B., & Schweiger, C. (2020). Clarifying the Dominant Logic Construct by Disentangling and Reassembling its Dimensions. *International Journal of Management Reviews, 22*(4), 323–355.

Felin, T., & Foss, N. J. (2005). Strategic organization: A field in search of microfoundations. *Strategic Organization, 3*(4), 441–455.

Felin, T., & Zenger, T. R. (2009). Entrepreneurs as theorists: On the origins of collective beliefs and novel strategies. *Strategic Entrepreneurship Journal, 3*(2), 127–146.

Felin, T., & Powell, T. C. (2016). Designing organizations for dynamic capabilities. *California Management Review, 58*(4), 78–96.

Felin, T., & Zenger, T. R. (2017). The theory-based view: Economic actors as theorists. *Strategy Science, 2*(4), 258–271.

Fisk, R. P., Brown, S. W., & Bitner, M. J. (1993). Tracking the evolution of the services marketing literature. *Journal of Retailing, 69*(1), 61–103.

Fiol, C. M., & Huff, A. S. (1992). Maps for managers: Where are we? Where do we go from here? *Journal of Management Studies, 29*(3), 267–285.

Gartner. https://www.gartner.com/en/information-technology/glossary/digitalization

Grönroos, C. (1984). A service quality model and its marketing implications. *European Journal of Marketing, 18*(4), 36–44.

Grönroos, C. (2006). Adopting a service logic for marketing. *Marketing Theory, 6*(3), 317–333.

Grönroos, C., & Voima, P. (2013). Critical service logic: Making sense of value creation and co-creation. *Journal of the Academy of Marketing Science, 41*(2), 133–150.

Heinonen, K., Strandvik, T., Mickelsson, K. J., Edvardsson, B., Sundström, E., & Andersson, P. (2010). A customer-dominant logic of service. *Journal of Service Management, 21*(4), 531–548.

Heinonen, K., & Strandvik, T. (2018). Reflections on customers' primary role in markets. *European Management Journal, 36*(1), 1–11.

Helfat, C. E., & Martin, J. A. (2015). Dynamic managerial capabilities: Review and assessment of managerial impact on strategic change. *Journal of Management, 41*(5), 1281–1312.

Hilden, S., & Tikkamäki, K. (2013). Reflective practice as a fuel for organizational learning. *Administrative Sciences, 3*(3), 76–95.

Kaplan, S. (2008). Framing contests: Strategy making under uncertainty. *Organization Science, 19*(5), 729–752.

Kilkki, K., Mäntylä, M., Karhu, K., Hämmäinen, H., & Ailisto, H. (2018). A disruption framework. *Technological Forecasting and Social Change, 129*, 275–284.

Liljander, V., & Strandvik, T. (1995). The nature of customer relationships in services. *Advances in Services Marketing and Management, 4*(141), 141–167.

Normann, R. (1975). *Skapande företagsledning.* Bonniers.

Osborne, S. P. (2018). From public service-dominant logic to public service logic: Are public service organizations capable of co-production and value co-creation? *Public Management Review, 20*(2), 225–231.

Parasuraman, A., Zeithaml, V. A., & Berry, L. L. (1985). A conceptual model of service quality and its implications for future research. *Journal of Marketing, 49*(4), 41–50.

Prahalad, C. K., & Bettis, R. A. (1986). The dominant logic: A new linkage between diversity and performance. *Strategic Management Journal, 7*(6), 485–501.

Ravald, A., & Grönroos, C. (1996). The value concept and relationship marketing. *European Journal of Marketing, 30*(2), 19–30.

Ringberg, T., & Reihlen, M. (2008). Towards a socio-cognitive approach to knowledge transfer. *Journal of Management Studies, 45*(5), 912–935.

Rydén, P., Ringberg, T., & Wilke, R. (2015). How managers' shared mental models of business–customer interactions create different sensemaking of social media. *Journal of Interactive Marketing, 31*, 1–16.

Sandberg, J., & Tsoukas, H. (2011). Grasping the logic of practice: Theorizing through practical rationality. *Academy of Management Review, 36*(2), 338–360.

Schilke, O., Hu, S., & Helfat, C. E. (2018). Quo vadis, dynamic capabilities? A content-analytic review of the current state of knowledge and recommendations for future research. *Academy of Management Annals, 12*(1), 390–439.

Sinha, D., & Sinha, S. (2020). Managing in a VUCA world: Possibilities and pitfalls. *Journal of Technology Management for Growing Economies, 11*(1), 17–21.

Strandvik, T., Holmlund, M., & Lähteenmäki, I. (2018). "One of these days, things are going to change!" How do you make sense of market disruption? *Business Horizons, 61*(3), 477–486.

Teece, D. J., Pisano, G., & Shuen, A. (1997). Dynamic capabilities and strategic management. *Strategic Management Journal, 18*(7), 537–533.

Teece, D. J. (2007). Explicating dynamic capabilities: the nature and microfoundations of (sustainable) enterprise performance. *Strategic Management Journal, 28*(13), 1319–1350.

Teece, D. J. (2020). Fundamental issues in strategy: Time to reassess. *Strategic Management Review, 1*(1), 103–144.

Vargo, S. L., & Lusch, R. F. (2004). Evolving to a new dominant logic for marketing. *Journal of Marketing, 68*(1), 1–17.

Vargo, S. L., & Lusch, R. F. (2011). It's all B2B… and beyond: Toward a systems perspective of the market. *Industrial Marketing Management, 40*(2), 181–187.

Vargo, S. L., Maglio, P. P., & Akaka, M. A. (2008). On value and value co-creation: A service systems and service logic perspective. *European Management Journal, 26*(3), 145–152.

Weick, K. E., Sutcliffe, K. M., & Obstfeld, D. (2005). Organizing and the process of sensemaking. *Organization Science, 16*(4), 409–421.

Wierenga, B. (2002). On academic marketing knowledge and marketing knowledge that marketing managers use for decision-making. *Marketing Theory, 2*(4), 355–362.

Zeithaml, V. A., Jaworski, B. J., Kohli, A. K., Tuli, K. R., Ulaga, W., & Zaltman, G. (2020). A theories-in-use approach to building marketing theory. *Journal of Marketing, 84*(1), 32–51.

Servitization: A State-of-the-Art Overview and Future Directions

Wolfgang Ulaga and Christian Kowalkowski

1 Introduction

Servitization has emerged as a powerful engine for firms looking to grow beyond their traditional product core. The concept refers to the transformational shift from a product-centric to a service-centric business model and logic (Kowalkowski et al., 2017). Across industry sectors, firms increasingly pursue servitization strategies, including traditional manufacturers bundling services with their core product offerings and software firms moving to cloud-based subscription models rather than selling software products. The concept of servitization was coined by Vandermerwe and Rada (1988) to describe a market strategy based on the integration of products and services into innovative offerings, with services in the lead role. This phenomenon is by no means new; for example, Schmenner (2009) showed that the antecedents of servitization stretch back more than 150 years. However, digital technologies afford new opportunities for value creation and revenue generation that have further accelerated service growth.

W. Ulaga (✉)
INSEAD Europe, Fontainebleau, France
e-mail: wolfgang.ulaga@insead.edu

C. Kowalkowski
CBMI – Centre for Business Model Innovation, Department of Management and Engineering, Linköping University, Linköping, Sweden
e-mail: christian.kowalkowski@liu.se

© The Author(s), under exclusive license to Springer Nature Switzerland AG 2022
B. Edvardsson, B. Tronvoll (eds.), *The Palgrave Handbook of Service Management*,
https://doi.org/10.1007/978-3-030-91828-6_10

Servitization is now among the most active domains in service research, attracting interest from multiple disciplines that include marketing, operations, engineering management, service management, and general management. This trend is evidenced by a sharp accompanying rise in publications, special issues, and dedicated conferences and conference tracks over the last decade (Kowalkowski et al., 2017). However, this growing interest in servitization as a theoretical construct and empirical phenomenon points to issues of conceptual ambiguity (Kowalkowski et al., 2017; Raddats et al., 2019) and limited knowledge diffusion across diverse research communities (Rabetino et al., 2018).

Against this backdrop, the purpose of the chapter is threefold. First, we provide a historic account of servitization as empirical phenomenon and theoretical construct, discuss the conceptual underpinnings of service strategies, and review the main drivers. We then provide an overview of the servitization literature and discuss key insights from this prolific research domain. Finally, we discuss key trends that will accelerate servitization in years to come and suggest avenues for promising future research in this domain.

2 A Brief History of Servitization

Servitization has been a powerful growth engine in most industries. Its antecedents date back to the mid-to-late 1800s, when the completion of nationwide transportation and communications networks in the US (railroads and the telegraph system, respectively) accelerated the trend of combining manufacturing and service activities within the same organization (Schmenner, 2009). Faster and more reliable networks enabled the extensive geographic spread of marketing, sales, repair, financing, and purchasing activities controlled by supply chain innovators such as Singer, the sewing machine manufacturer. Schmenner (2009) argues that the reasons for servitization were essentially the same then as now: to grow and maintain profits and to erect barriers to market entry by tying the customer to the firm in new and more effective ways. By engaging in this type of vertical integration to control their supply chains and to bundle goods and services—including new services like product demonstrations, in-field repairs by factory mechanics, and financing—many manufacturers would come to dominate their industries for decades.

During the Great Depression in the 1930s, many service business models like leasing and rental of products ranging from railroad cars to household floor waxes proved more resilient than traditional models based on product sales (McNeil, 1944). In 1932, for example, US automotive manufacturers faced by low passenger car sales offered their cars on a rental basis to the taxi industry. Making the case for leasing as a marketing tool, McNeil (1944) contended that these servitization models benefited manufacturers by enabling them to target customers who could not commit to large-scale capital expenditure. In times of uncertainty, these service models also allowed the customer to hedge business risk. In 1932, for example, well over half of IBM's income derived from leasing electromechanical tabulating machines and other equipment, earning almost as much as in 1929, when the US stock market collapsed. According to Spohrer (2017), services were an integral part of IBM's business long before the recent sales of its hardware divisions and the move into cognitive computing and cloud-based services: "IBM's hardware became so advanced so rapidly, that without field service engineers, the business managers and employees would not be able to effectively use IBM hardware to save time, labor, and money."

As another case in point, Xerox's rapid growth in the 1960s was founded on its disruptive service business model for the 914 office copier. Instead of selling the equipment, Xerox offered customers a lease costing $95 per month, including all required service and support. This business model imposed most of the risk on the small vendor, as the customer would pay 4¢ per copy only beyond the first 2000 copies each month. Despite the skepticism of competitors and industry analysts, it proved to be a smart bet; demand was intense, as users averaged 2000 copies *per day*, generating revenues beyond even the most optimistic expectations. The new business model powered compound growth, turning the $30-million firm into a global enterprise with $2.5 billion in revenues by 1972 (Chesbrough & Rosenbloom, 2002).

Despite these early examples of successful servitization initiatives, research in this area is relatively recent, dating back to the mid-1980s and only really taking off in the 2000s. Kowalkowski et al. (2017) identified two distinct phases in the evolution of servitization research. The first phase addressed the boundaries—*why* product firms should focus on service growth—while the second phase (from the early 2000s onward) has focused more on *how* service growth is actually achieved. Influential early research emphasized that services were more than a "necessary evil" (Lele, 1997) or a basic add-on to products. Instead, service provision came to be seen as a means of sustaining competitive advantage (Matthyssens & Vandenbempt, 1998) and as a pivotal part of the buyer-seller relationship (e.g., Martin & Horne, 1992). Bowen et al. (1989) suggested that an emphasis on service-oriented goals such as customer responsiveness and high customer contact would require manufacturers to introduce organizational and resource allocation arrangements appropriate to a service-oriented manufacturing configuration as described in the service literature.

Servitization is by now almost synonymous with service growth in product firms (e.g., Baines et al., 2017; Fliess & Lexutt, 2019; Tukker, 2004). However, when introducing the term *servitization of business*, Vandermerwe and Rada (1988) envisaged it as a competitive tool for firms in every industry. According to Levitt (1972), "Everybody is in service. Often the less there seems, the more there is" (p. 42). Echoing this idea, Vandermerwe and Rada argued that the traditional, simplistic distinction between goods and services was outdated: "Most firms today, are to a lesser or greater extent, in both. Much of this is due to managers looking at their customers' needs as a whole, moving from the old and outdated focus on goods or services to integrated 'bundles' or systems, as they are sometimes referred to, with services in the lead role" (p. 314).

Servitization research can also be traced back to the early literature on "systems selling" (Kowalkowski et al., 2015). According to Mattsson (1973, p. 108), systems selling is "a fulfilment of a more extensive customer need" that extends beyond product sales to bundled products and services. Hannaford (1976) argued that firms should design such product-service combinations to perform "a complete function for a buyer" (p. 139). At that time, emphasis was placed on the importance of balancing the standardization of product and service components with the development of tailor-made systems rather than on the transition from one type of business (product) to another (service) (Kowalkowski et al., 2015). Building on the work of Mattsson and Hannaford, Page and Siemplenski (1983) discussed "systems marketing," arguing that product firms "are turning to the marketing of systems to satisfy the more extended and complex needs of their customers" (p. 89). While these concerns are echoed in more recent studies, the discussion has moved beyond solving customers' operational problems to include more strategic forms of marketing based on "solution selling" (Davies et al., 2007; Helander & Möller, 2008; Ulaga & Kohli, 2018).

3 Key Concepts and Dimensions

Decades of research on service growth in product firms and a growing body of related literature have generated a plethora of terms, and the central concept of servitization has been variously interpreted and defined. In this regard, Kowalkowski et al. (2017a) noted that "the servitization community seems to lack a common lexicon and analytical tools that might structure scholarly or

Servitization: A State-of-the-Art Overview and Future Directions

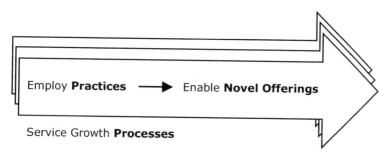

Fig. 1 Key service concepts

Table 1 Key service concepts

Facet of service growth	Key concepts and references
Process	Servitization (Baines et al., 2009; Neely, 2009; Vandermerwe & Rada, 1988) Service infusion (Brax, 2005; Kowalkowski et al., 2012) Service transition (Fang et al., 2008; Gebauer & Friedli, 2005; Oliva & Kallenberg, 2003) Servicizing (Agrawal & Bellos, 2017; Plepys et al., 2015; Toffel, 2008)
Offering	Product-service systems (PSS) (Mont, 2002; Tukker, 2004) Industrial product-service systems (IPS²) (Meier et al., 2010) Solutions (Davies, 2004; Sawhney, 2006; Tuli et al., 2007) Hybrid offerings (Shankar et al., 2009; Ulaga & Reinartz, 2011) Advanced services (Baines & Lightfoot, 2014; Bigdeli et al., 2018)
Practice	Systems selling (Hannaford, 1976; Mattsson, 1973) Solutions selling (Doster & Roegner, 2000; Ulaga & Kohli, 2018) Systems integration (Hobday et al., 2005; Prencipe et al., 2003) Service (business) development (Fischer et al., 2010; Kindström & Kowalkowski, 2009) Service innovation (Eggert et al., 2015; Kindström & Kowalkowski, 2014)

practice-led debate" (p. 6). As Fig. 1 and Table 1 show, these diverse service concepts refer essentially to processes, offerings, or practices.

Several of these concepts denote the *processes* of service growth. While the operations- and systems-led concept of *servitization* tends to focus on business models, structural transformation processes, and supporting digital technologies, the marketing-led concept of *service infusion* emphasizes how a firm's offering can be extended by adding services (Ostrom et al., 2015). *Service transition* again describes the deliberate shift from products to services, and *servicizing* emphasizes the sustainability of "green" business models that sell a product's functionality or use rather than the product itself.

A second cluster of concepts describes innovative combined *offerings* of goods and services. Within engineering management, *product-service systems* and *industrial product-service systems* are the most commonly used terms. Complex offerings that combine supplier and customer resources to create value-in-use are frequently referred to in the marketing and management literatures as *integrated, business*, or *customer solutions* or as *hybrid offerings*. More recently, the operations-led concept of *advanced services* has been used to denote a firm's most sophisticated offerings in the move to servitization.

Firms are also discussed in terms of the *practices* they employ to grow their service business. In particular, where service or solution offerings are based on high-technology and high-value goods or on complex product systems (CoPS) (Davies & Brady, 2000), success in the marketplace is seen to depend on *systems selling* and *solutions selling* practices. *Systems integration* is also seen as a core activity for high-technology firms, where system design and integration and management of supplier networks enable selective movement up- and downstream in the marketplace through vertical integration or disintegration (Hobday et al., 2005). Finally, *service business development* and *service innovation* are seen as key activities in bringing competitive offerings to market.

In general, the extant literature discusses servitization mainly as an outcome. In practice, however, many firms continuously pursue both service addition and reduction initiatives, as demonstrated by the evolution of the computer industry (Cusumano et al., 2015). According to Kowalkowski et al. (2017), these processes can be described on two continua that reflect a firm's strategy and modus operandi, where *servitization* and *service infusion* refer to service growth dynamics, and *deservitization* and *service dilution* refer to service reduction. This framework is shown in Fig. 2.

While the concepts of *servitization* and *service infusion* are often used interchangeably to denote service growth strategies and processes (e.g., Eloranta & Turunen, 2015), the above framework draws a distinction between them in the interests of conceptual clarity. As defined by Kowalkowski et al. (2017), service infusion is "the process whereby the relative importance of service

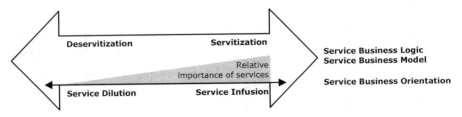

Fig. 2 Service growth and reduction processes: two continua (Kowalkowski et al., 2017)

offerings to a company or business unit increases, so augmenting its service business orientation (SBO)" (p. 7). In line with Homburg et al. (2002), they operationalize SBO as a three-dimensional construct comprising *number of services offered, number of customers to whom services are offered,* and *relative emphasis on services.* All three dimensions are positively associated with service infusion and relate to Shostack's (1977) product-service continuum, in which a firm's service orientation increases as more intangible service elements become central to its offering. While service infusion is generally characterized as an incremental process (Kowalkowski et al., 2012), either as part of a deliberate strategy or in more emergent form (Brax & Visintin, 2017), a firm may also expand its service business through major acquisitions. Furthermore, while firms are generally seen to move from basic, product-oriented services toward more complex process-oriented services and solutions (e.g., Oliva & Kallenberg, 2003; Raddats & Easingwood, 2010; Ulaga & Reinartz, 2011), they may in some cases increase their SBO by shifting the emphasis from more advanced to more standardized service offerings (Finne et al., 2013; Kowalkowski et al., 2015).

As an overarching concept, servitization encompasses the transformational processes involved in the shift from a product-centric to a service-centric business model and logic beyond service infusion (Kowalkowski et al., 2017). To varying degrees, servitization involves the reconfiguration of a firm's resources, capabilities, and organizational structures (Baines et al., 2009), including the development of a service culture and redefinition of the firm's mission (Kowalkowski & Ulaga, 2017). In the first place, a service-centric business model differs from a product-centric, transaction-based model by assuming greater responsibility for the customer's overall value-creating process (Kowalkowski et al., 2017). In this context, success is not dependent on the number of products, spare parts, or billable hours sold but on the outputs of the value-creating process—for example, guaranteeing a specified level of availability or achieving an expected level of performance.

Second, this service logic encompasses the firm's *raison d'être* and managers' mental models (or theories-in-use). Whereas the role of service in a product-centric firm is to protect and consolidate the core product business, service-centricity requires a change of mentality and approach, from reactive order-taking to proactive service management, including where necessary a willingness to cannibalize product sales (Kowalkowski & Ulaga, 2017). It is worth noting that, in line with Vandermerwe and Rada's (1988) account of servitization, pure service firms may also maintain a product-centric mindset and business logic. For example, many financial services firms still retain a product logic (e.g., maximizing the sale of standard "financial products") while employing automation and digitization to create a distance from their customers. Similarly, as Grönroos (2006) observed, a manufacturing firm may adopt a service logic that focuses not on products but on the processes in which those products are integrated, where customer value is created. In short, a predominantly service-based firm with high SBO may pursue a product-centric logic, and vice versa (Kowalkowski et al., 2017).

While research to date has focused almost entirely on servitization as a beneficial or necessary process or strategy, less has been said about deservitization and service dilution, which Valtakoski (2017) characterized as a special case of industry evolution. As the opposites of servitization and service infusion, these refer to deliberate or emergent processes that increase product-centricity; for example, a firm may decide to curtail service provision if it proves unprofitable. The dynamics of servitization and deservitization are not confined to upstream or downstream service flows from one actor to another but may also depend on such factors as innovation, maturity, and competence (Kowalkowski et al., 2017). Here again, Xerox serves as a case in point. Hailed by many as a posterchild for servitization, Xerox pursued wide-ranging service transformation in the early 2000s. However, although the chairman and CEO told investors in 2013 that the shift to a services-led growth portfolio was paying off, the firm decided less than three years later to separate its service business. A lack of positive spillover effects between the hardware and service businesses forced the firm to take "further affirmative steps to drive shareholder value" by sharpening the management focus and differentiating value propositions for customers and investors (Kowalkowski & Ulaga, 2017).

4   Key Drivers of Servitization

Why should product-centric firms pursue service growth? Essentially, there are two fundamental reasons for extending the product business to include related services: to maintain or gain competitive advantage. The more common strategy is to pursue servitization as a defensive stance—that is, to protect or enhance an existing core product business. The second strategy is to acquire new customers and build a service business that exists in its own right (Kowalkowski & Ulaga, 2017). While market and differentiation potential may be enhanced by focusing on services as the primary value driver, this strategy can also diminish positive product-service spillover effects or create additional tensions between the two businesses, impacting negatively on product sales. For example, when Xerox moved into business process outsourcing, it found that its industrial clients purchased fewer products.

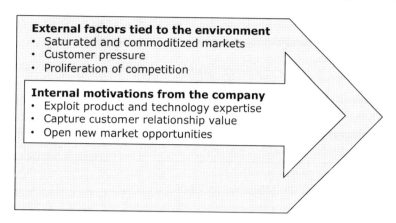

Fig. 3 Key drivers of servitization (adapted from Kowalkowski & Ulaga, 2017, p. 7)

According to Kowalkowski and Ulaga (2017), these moves are fueled by external environmental factors as well as company motivations (see Fig. 3). First, as a growing number of product markets become saturated or commoditized, profit margins are eroded, and there are limited opportunities for growth in the product domain. Services may then be seen as a means of escaping the product commoditization trap (Rangan & Bowman, 1992). In the elevator industry, for example, Otis has achieved higher growth and significantly higher margins in the service business; while 57% of the firm's sales relate to maintenance and other services, these account for 80% of its operating profit. Similarly, margins on new equipment are about 7%, but Otis' service business enjoys margins of more than 21% (Otis, 2020).

A second external driver of servitization is that as customers become more professional, they commonly reduce their supplier base and expect their remaining suppliers to offer a more complete product-service portfolio. Many also prefer to pay for performance rather than for product and service components. A third external factor that challenges product companies is the proliferation of competition, not only from other industry incumbents but from emerging markets, pure service companies, and software firms that operate beyond traditional industry boundaries. For example, Amazon's cloud arm AWS looks to boost its presence in the industrial sector by offering machine learning-based services.

Fourth, servitization enables companies to capture more customer relationship value, as services like long-term preventive maintenance contracts facilitate closer and potentially more strategic relationships throughout the product life cycle. In addition, services may provide a more stable source of income, as they are more resistant to economic cycles that affect product investment and to disruptive events such as the global recession of 2009 or the COVID-19 pandemic (Rapaccini et al., 2020). Fifth, by exploiting their unique engineering and technology expertise, firms can offer novel services for restoring or enhancing product functionality. Based on product usage and customer process data, firms can create a virtuous cycle with feedback loops to both product development and service operations. Finally, servitization affords opportunities for new and potentially disruptive "anything-as-a-service" business models. For example, the earthmover manufacturer Caterpillar aims to transform the construction industry by supplying smart machines and subscription-based connectivity services.

5 Overview of Servitization Research

Since the early 2000s, a second phase of servitization research has focused on how companies can exploit opportunities for profitable service growth. Research trends have evolved significantly in recent years and have become increasingly diverse, centering on five main themes: (1) service offerings; (2) strategy and structure; (3) motivations and performance; (4) resources and capabilities; and (5) service development, sales, and delivery (Raddats et al., 2019).

Service Offerings

In marketing research, there is a long tradition of developing frameworks to define and classify services (e.g., Lovelock, 1983; Rathmell, 1966; Zeithaml et al., 1985). While this research stream addresses how and why services differ from physical goods, servitization scholars have focused more on the relationship between the two domains (Raddats et al., 2019). In a servitization context, services are most commonly characterized as product complements that facilitate the sale and use of physical goods (services supporting the product/SSPs) or as process-oriented offerings that are not linked to specific products (services supporting the customer's process/SSCs) (Mathieu, 2001). Typical SSPs include maintenance, repair, and provision of spare parts; examples of SSCs include process optimization, energy-efficiency auditing, and R&D services. Mathieu's (2001) study is conceptual, but its relevance has been empirically validated in subsequent research (e.g., Antioco et al., 2008).

Taking the SSP-SSC dichotomy as one dimension, Ulaga and Reinartz (2011) developed a taxonomy of industrial services. A second dimension captured the extent to which a service is grounded in a promise to perform some action (i.e., input-based) or to achieve a certain performance (i.e., output-based). Combining these two dimensions produces four distinct combined offerings of goods and services, each affording different growth opportunities (see Fig. 4). *Product life cycle services* are product-oriented, input-based services that facilitate access to a product and ensure proper functioning throughout its life cycle. Often regarded as "must-haves," these services provide a platform for more advanced services. *Asset productivity services* are output-based offerings that help customers to achieve improved gains by turning investments into assets. While these too are product-oriented services, their purpose is to achieve a specified level of availability or performance. *Process optimization services* help customers to improve their own business processes (e.g., manufacturing operations, and transportation).

Finally, process-oriented, output-based *customer solutions* perform specified activities on behalf of the customer. This most complex type of offering is highly customized to meet customer-specific needs and requires operational integration beyond the sum of the solution's individual components to deliver enhanced outcomes (Sawhney, 2006). Effective implementation of these solutions depends on high levels of customer involvement throughout the relationship (Tuli et al., 2007) and strong alignment of interests between the parties (Kowalkowski & Ulaga, 2017). Solutions frequently involve complex gain-sharing agreements that require the supplier to assume some or all of the outcome risk (Ulaga & Reinartz, 2011), including issues related to knowledge transfer, intellectual property, data management, and outcome guarantees of various kinds (Nordin et al., 2011).

The engineering management literature typically refers to different combinations of goods and services as product-service systems (PSS). Tukker's (2004) widely used taxonomy of PSS specifies three main categories: *product-oriented* PSS, which are generally standardized, transactional, and input-oriented; *use-oriented* PSS, which focus on ensuring equipment availability (e.g., uptime), with an output-based revenue model (Ulaga & Reinartz, 2011); and *result-oriented* PSS, which are the most complex offerings or solutions and require the closest customer-supplier relationships. The existing body of research serves to highlight the great heterogeneity of services and the consequent diversity of business models. While some firms focus on providing one type of service or solution, different offerings and business models may also coexist, especially in larger firms, and must be managed in parallel (Kowalkowski et al., 2015).

Strategy and Structure

Servitization is frequently discussed in terms of a transition from products to services (e.g., Oliva & Kallenberg, 2003), and the evolution of service strategy can be likened to a process of maturation as manufacturers' increasing emphasis on services alters their offerings, capabilities, and processes (Raddats et al., 2019). However, servitization and a service-centric business orientation may arrive by different paths. First, this change may occur gradually or in more sudden leaps. Although most research to date has focused on organic growth opportunities (Kowalkowski et al., 2017), mergers and acquisitions (M&As) play a key role in service growth for many firms (e.g., as in the case of Xerox). Second, while some firms transition *from* products *to* services (e.g., IBM), servitization more often involves service expansion, extending the firm's offering rather than moving definitively from product to service sales. For example, companies like Apple have built an extensive service business alongside traditional hardware sales.

For a firm that seeks to become a solution provider, the unidirectional incremental view of servitization would imply a strategic change of emphasis from life cycle services (see Fig. 4) to process optimization and/or asset productivity services, leading ultimately to the broader role of solution provider. While most of the extant research supports this assumption (e.g., Ulaga & Reinartz, 2011), some studies have reported evidence of other service growth trajectories, including standardization and downscaling of customized solutions to promote repeatability in pursuit of a potentially larger customer base (Kowalkowski et al., 2015). It is also commonly assumed that firms choose to provide advanced services and solutions only in response to industry maturity or product commoditization. However, Araujo and Spring (2006) and Cusumano et al. (2015) have noted that opportunities for service growth may also arise from product innovations that create a gap between producer and user capabilities.

When pursuing servitization, a firm must also design an appropriate strategy-structure configuration (Raddats & Burton, 2011). In this regard, one key decision is whether to integrate or separate product and service strategic business units (SBUs). In order to focus more effectively on their service business, many firms create a separate service unit with responsibility for profits and losses. This can have a positive effect on financial performance by ensuring greater accountability and facilitating the development of services that are independent of the company's products (Oliva et al., 2012). On the other hand, integration can enhance cooperation between product and service units (Neu & Brown, 2005). Studies of organizational change patterns in the manufacturing sector suggest that separation may be a necessary first step in building

Fig. 4 Table Content

3. Asset Productivity
Services to achieve productivity gains from assets invested by customers

Examples:
- Remote monitoring of a high-voltage circuit breaker
- On-site preventative maintenance on a ball bearing
- Online software retrofitting of a banknote printing system
- Uptime guarantee on a pump in a nuclear power plant

4. Customer Solutions
Services to perform processes on behalf of the customers

Examples:
- Tire fleet management for a global logistics and supply chain expert
- Operating of paint shop in a car manufacturing plant
- Total gas and chemicals supply sourcing for a semiconductor plant
- Fly-by-the-hour agreement for commercial jet engines

1. Product Life Cycle
Services to facilitate access to and proper functioning of a product throughout the lifecycle

Examples:
- Delivery of industrial cables
- Calibration of a gas chromatograph
- Inspection of an ATM
- Installation of a power transformer
- Regrooving of a truck tire

2. Process Optimization
Services to assist customers in improving their own business processes

Examples:
- Diagnostics of a welding process
- Energy-efficiency audit of a store
- Warehouse material flow assessment
- Training on new safety regulations
- Consulting to achieve cost reductions

Promise to Achieve Performance ("Outcome")

Promise to Perform an Activity ("Input")

Nature of the Value Proposition

Supplier Product — Customer Process

Focal Object of Offering

Fig. 4 Industrial service classification framework (adapted from Ulaga & Reinartz, 2011, p. 17)

the commitment and managerial focus needed for service-led growth. However, to avoid the risk of confining expertise to organizational silos and undermining coordination between product and service units serving the same customer, firms may need to create a customer-focused structure (Gebauer & Kowalkowski, 2012). This is especially important for solutions provision (Davies et al., 2006) and should include the establishment of a centralized strategic unit to coordinate back- and front-office activities (Gulati, 2007).

Motivations and Performance

While early servitization research discussed drivers, more recent studies have focused more on performance and the strategies and structures that best support profitable growth. The various measures of service performance include revenue (Antioco et al., 2008), profitability (Eggert et al., 2015), and firm value (Fang et al., 2008). However, single measures may provide an incomplete picture; for example, a firm may increase revenue by adding services without necessarily improving profitability (Eggert et al., 2011; Suarez et al., 2013). A range of firm- and industry-level contingency factors also influence financial performance, including how closely a firm's goods and service offering are linked (Fang et al., 2008; Josephson et al., 2016). Solutions are more profitable than other types of service, but this positive effect depends on factors such as the supplier's sales capabilities and the buyer's relative strength (Worm et al., 2017). Research on probability of bankruptcy indicates that a higher service ratio (i.e., the ratio of service revenue to total sales revenue) reduces the likelihood of survival for new manufacturing ventures (Patel et al., 2019); on the other hand, offering more product-related services (SSPs) reduces bankruptcy likelihood for firms with a sufficiently diversified product business (Benedettini et al., 2017).

Service performance is more likely to be weak in the early stages of servitization (Benedettini et al., 2015), and new resources, capabilities, organizational structures, and a service culture must be developed to reap the benefits of the process (Kowalkowski & Ulaga, 2017). To ensure a positive impact on firm performance, firms may need to reach a critical service ratio (Kohtamäki et al., 2013). For example, Fang et al. (2008) found that the impact of servitization on firm value is slightly negative until the firm reaches a service ratio of 20–30%, after which there is an accelerating positive effect. However, it is less clear whether investing in product-oriented (SSP) or process-oriented services (SSC) is more likely to improve profitability (Raddats et al., 2019). Eggert et al. (2014) reported that firms can maximize performance by first investing in SSP as necessary groundwork before developing an SSC portfolio to address a wider range of customer needs. In contrast, Antioco et al. (2008) argued that firms should develop SSC first to leverage product sales before deploying SSP to increase service volume. According to Kowalkowski and Ulaga (2017), basic product-oriented services are generally the "low-hanging fruit" that should be picked first before moving on to more complex offerings. In addition, firms can improve their profitability by making the most of existing services—for instance, by capturing more value through better pricing practices—rather than focusing exclusively on service portfolio growth.

Resources and Capabilities

In general, firms can achieve competitive advantage by developing and deploying unique resources and distinctive capabilities. According to Ulaga and Reinartz (2011), "Resources are productive assets the firm owns; capabilities are what the firm can do. Resources per se do not confer competitive advantage but must be transformed into capabilities to do so" (p. 6). Among several extensive studies of the key resources or capabilities for successful servitization, Ulaga and Reinartz's (2011) framework is one of the most influential and comprehensive, showing how four overarching resources can be leveraged to build five distinctive capabilities that in turn produce competitive advantage. Turning first to their account of resources, the installed base of product sold represents a unique asset for manufacturing firms, and access to *installed base product usage and process data* affords a significant advantage over both direct competitors and third-party service providers. Second, by exploiting synergies between manufacturing and services, firms can leverage their *product development and manufacturing assets* to develop innovative product-service combinations. Third, *the product salesforce and distribution network* is another resource that firms can leverage to expand their service business. Finally, an in-house *field service organization* is both a key resource for cost-effective SSP provision and facilitates initiatives related to more complex solutions offerings.

As well as acquiring unique resources, firms must be able to develop distinctive capabilities by assembling those resources into specific configurations that can transform inputs into more valuable outputs (Amit & Schoemaker, 1993). First, firms need *service-related data processing and interpretation capability*, using advanced technologies to translate those data into new offerings and more efficient service provision. A second key requirement is *execution risk assessment and mitigation capability*, especially when moving into more extensive long-term service agreements involving various forms of outcome guarantee. This includes the capacity to evaluate uncertainty and to implement the necessary safeguarding mechanisms. Third, a servitizing firm needs *design-to-service capability* to ensure operational integration (Sawhney, 2006), allowing tangible and intangible elements of its offering to interact synergistically. Fourth, *service sales capability* is needed to reach key decision makers in the customer organization, to coordinate key contacts in the customer and supplier firms, to engage in value-based selling, and to align the salesforce with both the field service organization and channel partners. Finally, firms need *service deployment capability* in order to standardize back-office service processes while simultaneously implementing front-office customization (Ulaga & Reinartz, 2011).

Among other studies, Storbacka's (2011) extensive solutions capabilities framework addresses the resources and capabilities needed for offerings of a particular type. According to Matthyssens and Vandenbempt (2008), firms may not be able to develop all of the requisite capabilities internally and must therefore build relationships with other actors. In this regard, relationships with customers (Tuli et al., 2007) and other actors such as channel partners (Kowalkowski & Ulaga, 2017) are key resources. Finally, Story et al. (2017) highlighted the need to align the service capabilities of customer and manufacturer.

Service Development, Sales, and Delivery

Service development, sales, and delivery are critical processes for the successful implementation of servitization initiatives (Kindström & Kowalkowski, 2014). While product and service innovation often compete for limited resources within the same firm, manufacturers can generally outperform their competitors by combining product and service innovation (Eggert et al., 2015). Several authors have argued that manufacturers should adopt a structured and formalized New Service Development (NSD) approach similar to New Product Development (NPD). However, Kindström and Kowalkowski (2009) caution against off-the-shelf NPD models that fail to capture unique service characteristics and the specific conditions for service development in a product-centric setting.

While NPD projects are generally back-heavy (in terms of time and other resources spent on R&D, prototyping, etc.), NSD projects are front-heavy, allocating more time and resources to pilot testing and the infrastructures and capabilities needed for rollout. This challenge becomes especially clear where a firm relies on channel partners for sales and delivery, as the commitment and competence of these external actors must also be ensured before launching the service (Kowalkowski & Ulaga, 2017). Additionally, while product development is likely to be managed centrally and driven by technology, service development often occurs locally through interaction with key customers (Kindström & Kowalkowski, 2014). These factors must be taken into account when designing NSD projects, along with support for cross-functional collaboration and an iterative and flexible process. As service innovation is more often ad hoc (Gallouj & Weinstein, 1997), it may be difficult for central management (especially in large firms) to gain a comprehensive view of all local service activities. This renders many services "invisible," in the sense that they are neither formalized nor measured (Kindström & Kowalkowski, 2009). The ability to formalize and standardize services while exploiting what Davies and Brady (2000) called "economies of repetition" is a key aspect of successful NSD (Kindström & Kowalkowski, 2014).

A further major hurdle, especially for product-centric firms, is selling novel services. A study of more than 500 NSD projects reported that the rate of new services brought to market and then withdrawn because of low sales was as high as 43% (Edvardsson et al., 2013). To promote service sales and to change the behavior of a product-centric salesforce, firms must align incentive systems with strategic service objectives (Reinartz & Ulaga, 2008). In this regard, many traditional industrial salespeople do not fit the required competence profile; as a general rule of thumb, only a third transition easily from selling products to selling complex services and solutions while a further third need significant management support to master the service sales process, only the remaining third switch easily to selling both services and products (Ulaga & Reinartz, 2011).

As services become more important, the salesperson must take on a clearer role as a customer resource and problem solver, working closely with the customer (Kindström et al., 2015). Value-based pricing and selling become critical competencies, requiring interrelated knowledge of marketing, sales, and field service units (Raja et al., 2020). To be successful, salespeople must develop a deep understanding of their customers' business models and key performance metrics. While the sales process is not necessarily more complex, it is longer and involves more interactions with decision makers at different levels in the customer organization. In addition, it becomes more important to be able to manage customer expectations, ensure success, and demonstrate tangible value outcomes (Ulaga & Loveland, 2014).

A field service network is a final prerequisite for successful servitization. In many cases, this includes both internal service units and external service partners. To ensure the profitability of service operations, firms should adopt a lean service production approach (Kowalkowski & Ulaga, 2017), which includes understanding (and influencing) customer expectations in terms of the desired quality and value potential. As recruiting and maintaining skilled employees can prove challenging, especially in remote locations (Kindström & Kowalkowski, 2014), firms must exploit digital opportunities as well as investing in human resources to reduce costs and enhance performance. To optimize service delivery, firms can also influence customer behavior. Because many services involve frequent (or ongoing) interactions and active value co-creation, cost-cutting initiatives should target non-value-added activities, including processes that can be automated or eliminated. Capacity utilization and demand fluctuations can be managed by designing effective internal-external arrangements for service operations—for example, by relying on external partners during peak periods or in regions with low service demand (Kowalkowski & Ulaga, 2017).

6 Servitization in a Digital Economy: Future Directions

Digital transformation will continue to affect industries and accelerate servitization for years to come. Against this backdrop, four major trends will fuel the servitization movement in the future: the growing role of platform-based business models across many service industries; the fast-paced adoption of innovative recurring revenue models; the shift from frontline-heavy field service to back office-heavy software-based services; and the growing emphasis on embedding sustainability goals into corporate strategies, accelerating growth through circular business models, and fostering the sharing economy. Taken together, these four trends will also lead to major organizational changes in the way companies engage with customers, including new customer-facing functions, such as customer success management.

Platform-Based Business Models Driving Service Growth

For more than two decades now, disruptive platform-based business models have accelerated servitization even further. Consider the example of Salesforce.com. More than 20 years ago, the company's founder, Chairman, and CEO Marc Benioff became an early proponent of the *Software-as-a-service (SaaS)* model in an industry dominated by software sales and licensing. With a market capitalization of more than $ 216 billion in the first quarter of 2021,[1] Salesforce.com today relies on an impressive platform and ecosystem of partners that serves as a powerful competitive advantage in its industry.

Likewise, innovative platform-based business models have also gained traction in traditional service industries. For example, in the United States, Arizona-based Vixxo disrupted the facility management industry with an innovative business model built around data and analytics (Ulaga et al., 2020). The company initially created a two-sided platform model connecting over 150 Fortune 500 customers with distributed real estate portfolios in the retail, supermarket, convenience store, and restaurant sectors with local service providers deploying over 150,000 technicians across the US and Canada, in addition to its own field organization. Vixxo provides a "one-stop shop" solution for over 100 services, including electricity, heating, ventilation, and air conditioning (HVAC), lighting, plumbing, refrigeration, and waste management,

---

[1] Financial Data accessed on 22 March 2021 at https://finance.yahoo.com/quote/CRM?p=CRM&.tsrc=fin-srch.

among many others, and maintains over 1.1 million dispersed revenue-generating critical assets across over 65,000 sites, representing over $1 billion in facility management spend. The company also works in close cooperation with service providers, that is, often small, privately owned local businesses, to improve performance and gain more revenues. Over time, Vixxo grew its model into a three-sided platform, including equipment manufacturers in the equation, and bringing all parties together for unleashing new value creation opportunities. Taken together, the two illustrations of Salesforce.com and Vixxo exemplify how the growing role of platform-based business models fuels many of the trends discussed next.

Fast-Paced Growth of Recurring Service Revenue Models

Along with the trend toward new platform-based business models, a growing number of companies explore new recurring revenue models which further accelerate the servitization movement. For example, subscription models have been described by many as the next "business tsunami" (Mehta et al., 2016). Consider Netflix, the subscription-based streaming platform and service provider. The company added 15.8 million subscribers during the first quarter of 2020 to its customer base. Likewise, videoconferencing service provider Zoom's revenue grew 169% year-over-year in Q1 2020 (Ulaga & Mansard, 2020). Interestingly, subscription models have proven resilience in difficult economic times. During the COVID-19 pandemic, half of the US subscription businesses, continuously monitored by global subscription platform provider Zuora, were still growing and had not seen a significant impact to their subscriber acquisition rates in May 2020. Thirty-five percent of companies experienced growth, and only 14% of companies were contracting.

Subscription models represent a formidable lever for motivating firms to grow beyond their goods-centric core and move deeper into services. McCarthy et al. (2017, p. 17) define subscription-based business models as "businesses whose customers pay a periodically recurring fee for access to a product or service." While subscription-based pricing has long dominated selected industries, such as newspapers, magazines, or telecommunications, this trend now gains traction among new business ventures, start-ups in the digital economy, and long-standing industry leaders (e.g., Microsoft Office 365). Hence, subscription-based models are adopted not only in Business-to-Consumer domains but also in traditional Business-to-Business domains. For example, in addition to selling point-of-sale hardware and software to small restaurants, retailers, or business owners, enterprise technology provider NCR now also promotes a 36-month subscription package, including hardware, software, concierge services, upgrades, training, and device warranties, for an all-inclusive monthly fee.[2]

Shift from Frontline-Heavy Field Service to Back Office-Heavy Software-Based Services

The faced-paced adoption of digital technologies and rapidly progressing recurring revenue models in service industries also shift firms' focus from frontline-heavy field service to back office-heavy automation and software-based services. This evolution affects all industries, and especially those traditionally relying to a large extent on frontline interactions.

Consider the example of InsurTech start-up Lemonade's disruptive new business model aimed at creating and delivering a "shockingly great user experience" around a "lovable brand," in a service industry plagued by low customer satisfaction (Heeley et al., 2020). The digital disruptor leverages principles of behavioral economics to address conflicts of interest and mistrust which prevail in the existing industry. It uses digital technologies to automate, accelerate, and manage an impressive amount of work—with few employees—thereby reducing customer effort and increasing customer satisfaction to achieve cost-effective service excellence through automation of customer interaction and internal processes. The effortless experience is aggressively priced and relies on an innovative and flexible subscription-based pricing model. Artificial intelligence (AI), data, and machine learning are key in the race to achieving data parity with incumbents in the insurance industry.

Focus on Sustainability, Circular Economy Business Models, and Sharing Economy

Digitalization and software-based services also provide major opportunities for firms to improve their environmental impact. Consider the example of Schneider-Electric, the global provider of energy distribution and industrial automation offerings. On a global basis, a tremendous amount of energy is lost due to inefficient energy distribution infrastructures and resources. As the company's clients seek support in achieving their own environmental and social sustainability goals, Schneider has substantially grown its portfolio of offerings combining energy technologies, real-time automation, software, and

---

[2] See NCR Silver; accessed on 3 June 2021 at: https://www.ncr.com/silver.

Servitization: A State-of-the-Art Overview and Future Directions **189**

services. Changes to traditional field service activities can also have a substantial environmental impact. During 2020, as travel restrictions were imposed due to the COVID-19 pandemic, climate systems provider Munters launched remote assist—a service which gives customers on-demand access to service expertise through mobile phone or tablet. Not only can Munters provide instant diagnosis and resolution, while increasing the utilization rate of its expert technicians; the service also lessens the environmental impact due to the elimination of travel. Overall, servitization provides several entrepreneurial opportunities for both increased economic and environmental performance.

While a linear "take-make-dispose" model of production and consumption has been dominant since the early days of industrialization, increased environmental and climate concerns have spurred the development of service business models based on circular economy principles. A circular economy "is one that is restorative by design, and which aims to keep products, components and materials at their highest utility and value at all times" (Webster, 2017). As sustainability has become a more mainstream corporate concern, the aims and practices of the economically inspired notion of servitization and the ecologically inspired circular economy are rapidly converging. Hence, firms and circular economy networks that can guarantee supply in reverse cycles of reuse, remanufacturing, and recycling can gain a competitive advantage over those who are less able to seize these opportunities (Spring & Araujo, 2017). Signify's circular lighting service is a case in point; instead of buying the luminaire, customers such as Schiphol airport in the Netherlands pay for the light. Signify ensures agreed-upon energy improvements and reuse or recycle the luminaires at the end of their lifespan, helping the airport on its mission to become the most sustainable airport in the world.

The emergence of the sharing economy has provided additional opportunities for servitization, such as peer-to-peer lending and mobility-as-a-service. Sharing economy offerings, such as BlaBlaCar's long-distance carpooling, have five definitional characteristics: they are temporarily accessed rather than permanently owned; this access involves economic transactions or quid-pro-quo exchanges; the offerings rely on a (digital) matching platform; the customer role is enhanced; and supply is being crowdsourced (Eckhardt et al., 2019). However, not all such servitization models are environmentally superior; for example, they may lead to larger production quantity or drive increased usage (Agrawal & Bellos, 2017). Overall, manufacturers may have to think about how to manage and organize for the combination of sustainability initiatives, manufacturing, software development, service delivery network, and data capture and use (Spring & Araujo, 2017).

Servitization and Organizational Change: The Growing Role of Customer Success

Collectively, the above-mentioned trends explain major organizational changes firms implement today with respect to customer-facing roles and responsibilities. For example, a growing number of companies today establish dedicated customer success structures, processes, and job function in their organizations. In line with the heightened interest in customer success, emerging professional organizations attempt to provide content and shape to a nascent organizational function and its roles and responsibilities (see, e.g., the Customer Success Association, claiming over 36,000 members worldwide since 2012). End of August 2020, on the professional social network LinkedIn alone, almost 100,000 professionals described themselves as working in a Customer Success function (Hochstein et al., 2021).

What is Customer Success? Initially confined to the software industry, the concept today increasingly gains momentum elsewhere, especially as information ubiquity and digital transformation affect a wide cross-section of industries and markets. Nonetheless, academic research on Customer Success is still at an early stage. Ulaga et al. (2020) and Eggert et al. (2020) provide a more fine-grained perspective based on an explorative analysis of more than 300 job descriptions of Customer Success Managers of a social professional network. Drawing on Grönroos and Voima's (2013) value sphere concept, the authors distinguish between Customer Success (CS), the organizational process of Customer Success Management (CSM), and the job function of Customer Success Managers (CSMR). First, they conceptualize CS as a subjective, customer-perceived construct that resides in the customers' and the joint value creation sphere; it is the customer-perceived achievement of desired outcomes by using the supplier's offering (Ulaga et al., 2020). Second, they define CSM as a joint management process that spans the customers' and the suppliers' value creation spheres, comprising all of the firms' activities aiming at aligning their goal achievement. Finally, Ulaga et al. (2020) refer to CSMR as an organizational function operating in the suppliers' and the joint value creation sphere. As a supplier-based position, Customer Success Managers orchestrate CSM activities and integrate tasks from marketing, sales, training, and support during the customer acquisition, retention, and expansion phases (see Fig. 5).

The nascent domain of customer success research opens promising opportunities for future research. For example, Hochstein et al. (2020) identify

Fig. 5 CS, CS Management, and CS Managers in the value creation spheres framework (Eggert et al., 2020; Ulaga et al., 2020)

three main research priorities, that is, (1) organizational leadership, (2) customer health scores, and (3) performance benefits of Customer Success. Similarly, Ulaga et al. (2020) highlight three particularly promising research directions.

First, from a firm strategy perspective, platform-based businesses and recurring revenue models deeply rely on effectively minimizing churn among all parties involved, and especially customers. Hence, customer success increasingly emerges as a critical success factor for creating and maintaining competitive advantage in these business models (Ulaga et al., 2020). Yet, growing new capabilities in customer success management requires considerable investments that may come to the detriment of other resources. Executives need to know whether, when, and how investment in customer success structures, processes, and people can (and will) achieve a return on investment. Therefore, there is a need to investigate the relationship between customer success initiatives and firm performance. Further, there is a need to understand key moderators and mediators of this relationship. Second, from an organizational perspective, more knowledge is needed to understand how the customer success function relates other functions, such as customer experience management, key account management, service operations, or sales. While servitization research has started to acknowledge the importance of customer experience management—across functions, touchpoints, and the customer's journey (Witell et al., 2020)—research should investigate the interplay between the different customer-facing functions. We also need to understand where and how this recent function is best located in the organization, under what conditions, and how it interacts best with other functions that touch customers. Finally, from an individual employee-level perspective, we are only at the beginning of understanding how to set up this new function for success and help those who take on its role and responsibilities excel in their position.

Bright Future? Servitization in a Post-COVID-19 World

The recent coronavirus pandemic shed new light on servitization challenges and opportunities. Around the globe, firms struggled to protect employees, prevent supply chain disruptions, maintain operations and cash flows, and continue to serve customers. Customer solutions providers were particularly impacted. Consider the example of British aero-engine group Rolls-Royce. The firm pioneered service contracts in the aircraft industry and trademarked "power-by-the-hour" contracts. The concept was invented in 1962, and after signing a long-term contract with American Airlines in 1997, it transformed the aircraft engine services landscape. With a payment mechanism under which it is paid for the number of hours its engines fly, risks are transferred back to Rolls-Royce, and reliability becomes a profit driver for both the manufacturer and its customers (Macdonald et al., 2016). However, the unprecedented halt in flying because of the COVID-19 pandemic meant most of its income dried up, and the firm reported a major loss for 2020.

Clearly, while outcome-based contracting and performance-based solutions have been touted as the next service growth engine, such strategies can seriously backfire in times of crises when customer operations stand idle.

Against this backdrop, Bond et al. (2020) discuss six major downsides of customer solutions that the recent pandemic brought to the forefront. First, the interdependence among solution components greatly magnified supply chain disruptions as the COVID-19 pandemic evolved. Second, customers were unable to quickly acquire solutions from alternative sources, and providers were unable to swiftly redeploy offerings tailored to individual customers in one area to customers in other areas. Third, the COVID-19 crisis often left suppliers with excessive risks, costs, and sharply lower revenues. Fourth, solution agreements lacked the flexibility and responsiveness needed in a crisis to adequately respond to fast-changing customer needs during the pandemic. Fifth, it became apparent that providers and customers at times lost sight of their mutual goals and objectives and relapsed into a self-interest focus driven by as "us-versus-them" mindset. Sixth, the COVID-19 pandemic prevented in-person meetings and interactions which greatly hindered coordination and co-creation by providers and customers. Finally, the crisis also dramatically exposed the negative consequences of lacking or inadequate solution governance structures, processes, and people.

Mirroring the seven downsides noted above, Bond et al. (2020) identify seven promising research directions. A first research avenue refers to questions evolving around the design of customer solutions with an emphasis on how to build greater agility and flexibility into such offerings. A second research direction relates to balancing the benefits of customization against the costs of non-retrievable investments. A third research avenue discusses how solution providers and customers might better mitigate risk in the aftermath of an unforeseeable widespread shock. Fourth, Bond et al. (2020) discuss the need for envisioning new performance metrics, evaluation processes, and gain-sharing mechanisms that allow parties involved to adapt to rapidly changing customer requirements in a timely manner. A fifth research direction refers to developing a better understanding of how exactly customers' (and providers') goals evolve during a crisis, especially when such changes occur in a very short time window and force parties to swiftly re-assess and realign goals and objectives. Sixth, Bond et al. (2020) invite researchers to investigate how the deployment of remote technology in the solution process—from identifying new solution sales opportunities to automated identification of deviations from targets and post-deployment support processes—can restore and redirect co-creation processes. Finally, a seventh research direction relates to governance structures, processes, and people for a better understanding of how to foster coordination among providers and customers in order to gain greater flexibility and responsiveness in case of unforeseeable widespread shocks.

In conclusion, the above-mentioned trends, and the related organizational changes, collectively illustrate that scholarly inquiry of servitization continues to remain a promising research domain. We hope that this chapter contributes to motivate scholars to explore the avenues discussed and continue the lively debate.

References

Agrawal, V. V., & Bellos, I. (2017). The potential of servicizing as a green business model. *Management Science, 63*(5), 1545–1562.

Amit, R., & Schoemaker, P. J. (1993). Strategic assets and organizational rent. *Strategic Management Journal, 14*(1), 33–46.

Antioco, M., Moenaert, R. K., Lindgreen, A., & Wetzels, M. G. M. (2008). Organizational antecedents to and consequences of service business orientations in manufacturing companies. *Journal of the Academy of Marketing Science, 36*, 337–358.

Araujo, L., & Spring, M. (2006). Services, products, and the institutional structure of production. *Industrial Marketing Management, 35*(7), 797–805.

Baines, T., Bigdeli, A. Z., Bustinza, O. F., Shi, V. G., Baldwin, J., & Ridgway, K. (2017). Servitization: Revisiting the state-of-the-art and research priorities. *International Journal of Operations & Production Management, 37*, 256–278.

Baines, T., & Lightfoot, H. W. (2014). Servitization of the manufacturing firm. *International Journal of Operations & Production Management, 34*(1), 2–35.

Baines, T. S., Lightfoot, H. W., Benedettini, O., & Kay, J. M. (2009). The servitization of manufacturing: A review of literature and reflection on future challenges. *Journal of Manufacturing Technology Management, 20*(5), 547–567.

Benedettini, O., Neely, A., & Swink, M. (2015). Why do servitized firms fail? A risk-based explanation. *International Journal of Operations & Production Management, 35*, 946–979.

Benedettini, O., Swink, M., & Neely, A. (2017). Examining the influence of service additions on manufacturing firms' bankruptcy likelihood. *Industrial Marketing Management, 60*, 112–125.

Bigdeli, A. Z., Baines, T., Schroeder, A., Brown, S., Musson, E., Guang Shi, V., & Calabrese, A. (2018). Measuring servitization progress and outcome: The case of 'advanced services'. *Production Planning & Control, 29*(4), 315–332.

Bond, E., de Jong, A., Eggert, A., Houston, M. B., Kleinaltenkamp, M., Kohli, A. K., Ritter, T., & Ulaga, W. (2020). The future of B2B customer solutions in a post-COVID-19 economy: Managerial issues and an agenda for academic inquiry. *Journal of Service Research, 23*(4), 401–408.

Bowen, D. E., Siehl, C., & Schneider, B. (1989). A framework for analyzing customer service orientations in manufacturing. *Academy of Management Review, 14*(1), 75–95.

Brax, S. (2005). A manufacturer becoming service provider – Challenges and a paradox. *Managing Service Quality, 15*(2), 142–155.

Brax, S. A., & Visintin, F. (2017). Meta-model of servitization: The integrative profiling approach. *Industrial Marketing Management, 60*, 17–32.

Chesbrough, H., & Rosenbloom, R. S. (2002). The role of the business model in capturing value from innovation: Evidence from Xerox Corporation's technology spin-off companies. *Industrial and Corporate Change, 11*(3), 529–555.

Cusumano, M. A., Kahl, S. J., & Suarez, F. F. (2015). Services, industry evolution, and the competitive strategies of product firms. *Strategic Management Journal, 36*(4), 559–575.

Davies, A. (2004). Moving base into high-value integrated solutions: A value stream approach. *Industrial and Corporate Change, 13*(5), 727–756.

Davies, A., & Brady, T. (2000). Organisational capabilities and learning in complex product systems: Towards repeatable solutions. *Research Policy, 29*(7–8), 931–953.

Davies, A., Brady, T., & Hobday, M. (2006). Charting a path toward integrated solutions. *Sloan Management Review, 47*(3), 39–48.

Davies, A., Brady, T., & Hobday, M. (2007). Organizing for solutions: Systems seller vs. systems integrator. *Industrial Marketing Management, 36*(2), 183–193.

Doster, D., & Roegner, E. (2000). Setting the pace with solutions. *Marketing Management, 9*(1), 51–54.

Eckhardt, G. M., Houston, M. B., Jiang, B., Lamberton, C., Rindfleisch, A., & Zervas, G. (2019). Marketing in the sharing economy. *Journal of Marketing, 83*(5), 5–27.

Edvardsson, B., Meiren, T., Schäfer, A., & Witell, L. (2013). Having a strategy for new service development – Does it really matter? *Journal of Service Management, 24*, 25–44.

Eggert, A., Hogreve, J., Ulaga, W., & Muenkhoff, E. (2011). Industrial services, product innovations, and firm profitability: A multiple-group latent growth curve analysis. *Industrial Marketing Management, 40*(5), 661–670.

Eggert, A., Hogreve, J., Ulaga, W., & Muenkhoff, E. (2014). Revenue and profit implications of industrial service strategies. *Journal of Service Research, 17*(1), 23–39.

Eggert, A., Thiesbrummel, C., & Deutscher, C. (2015). Heading for new shores: Do service and hybrid innovations outperform product innovations in industrial companies? *Industrial Marketing Management, 45*, 173–183.

Eggert, A., Ulaga, W., & Gehring, A. (2020). Managing customer success in business markets: Conceptual foundation and practical application. *Journal of Service Management Research, 4*(2–3), 121–132.

Eloranta, V., & Turunen, T. (2015). Seeking competitive advantage with service infusion: A systematic literature review. *Journal of Service Management, 26*(3), 394–425.

Fang, E., Palmatier, R. W., & Steenkamp, J. B. E. M. (2008). Effect of service transition strategies on firm value. *Journal of Marketing, 72*(5), 1–14.

Finne, M., Brax, S., & Holmström, J. (2013). Reversed servitization paths: A case analysis of two manufacturers. *Service Business, 7*(4), 513–537.

Fischer, T., Gebauer, H., Gregory, M., Ren, G., & Fleisch, E. (2010). Exploitation or exploration in service business development?: Insights from a dynamic capabilities perspective. *Journal of Service Management, 21*(5), 591–624.

Fliess, S., & Lexutt, E. (2019). How to be successful with servitization – Guidelines for research and management. *Industrial Marketing Management, 78*, 58–75.

Gallouj, F., & Weinstein, O. (1997). Innovation in services. *Research Policy, 26*(4/5), 537–556.

Gebauer, H., & Friedli, T. (2005). Behavioral implications of the transition process from products to services. *Journal of Business & Industrial Marketing, 20*(2), 70–78.

Gebauer, H., & Kowalkowski, C. (2012). Customer-focused and service-focused orientation in organizational structures. *Journal of Business and Industrial Marketing, 27*(7), 527–537.

Grönroos, C. (2006). Adopting a service logic for marketing. *Marketing Theory, 6*(3), 317–333.

Grönroos, C., & Voima, P. (2013). Critical service logic: Making sense of value creation and co-creation. *Journal of the Academy of Marketing Science, 41*(2), 133–150.

Gulati, R. (2007). Silo busting: How to execute on the promise of customer focus. *Harvard Business Review, 85*(5), 98–108.

Hannaford, W. J. (1976). Systems Selling: Problems and Benefits for Buyers and Sellers. *Industrial Marketing Management, 5*, 139–145.

Heeley, L., Ulaga, W., & Carmon, Z. (2020). Lemonade: Delighting insurance customers with AI and behavioural economics. A disruptive InsurTech business model for outstanding customer experience and cost-effective service excellence. *INSEAD Case Study* 06/2020-6597.

Helander, A., & Möller, K. (2008). How to Become Solution Provider: System Supplier's Strategic bell. *Journal of Business-to-Business Marketing, 15*(3), 247–289.

Hobday, M., Davies, A., & Prencipe, A. (2005). Systems integration: A core capability of the modern corporation. *Industrial and Corporate Change, 14*(6), 1109–1143.

Hochstein, B., Rangarajan, D., Mehta, N., & Kocher, D. (2020). An industry/academic perspective on customer success management. *Journal of Service Research, 23*(1), 3–7.

Hochstein, B., Ulaga, W., Gehring, A., & Eggert, A. (2021). Customer success management: What it is and why it is important to B2B marketing? Proceedings *AMA Winter Academic Conference*, Online, February 17–19.

Homburg, C., Hoyer, W. D., & Fassnacht, M. (2002). Service orientation of a retailer's business strategy: Dimensions, antecedents, and performance outcomes. *Journal of Marketing, 66*(4), 86–101.

Josephson, B. W., Johnson, J. L., Mariadoss, B. J., & Cullen, J. (2016). Service transition strategies in manufacturing: Implications for firm risk. *Journal of Service Research, 19*(2), 142–157.

Kindström, D., & Kowalkowski, C. (2009). Development of industrial service offerings – A process framework. *Journal of Service Management, 20*(2), 156–172.

Kindström, D., & Kowalkowski, C. (2014). Service innovation in product-centric firms: A multidimensional business model perspective. *Journal of Business & Industrial Marketing, 29*(2), 96–111.

Kindström, D., Kowalkowski, C., & Alejandro, T. B. (2015). Adding services to product-based portfolios: An exploration of the implications for the sales function. *Journal of Service Management, 26*(3), 372–393.

Kohtamäki, M., Partanen, J., Parida, V., & Wincent, J. (2013). Non-linear relationship between industrial service offering and sales growth: The moderating role of network capabilities. *Industrial Marketing Management, 42*(8), 1374–1385.

Kowalkowski, C., Gebauer, H., Kamp, B., & Parry, G. (2017). Servitization and deservitization: Overview, concepts, and definitions. *Industrial Marketing Management, 60*, 4–10.

Kowalkowski, C., Gebauer, H., & Oliva, R. (2017). Service growth in product firms: Past, present, and future. *Industrial Marketing Management, 60*, 82–88.

Kowalkowski, C., Kindström, D., Alejandro, T. B., Brege, S., & Biggemann, S. (2012). Service infusion as agile incrementalism in action. *Journal of Business Research, 65*(6), 765–772.

Kowalkowski, C., & Ulaga, W. (2017). *Service strategy in action: A practical guide for growing your B2B service and solution business*. Service Strategy Press.

Kowalkowski, C., Windahl, C., Kindström, D., & Gebauer, H. (2015). What service transition? Rethinking established assumptions about manufacturers' service-led growth strategies. *Industrial Marketing Management, 45*(2), 59–69.

Lele, M. M. (1997). After-sales service – Necessary evil or strategic opportunity? *Managing Service Quality, 7*(3), 141–145.

Levitt, T. (1972). Production-line approach to service. *Harvard Business Review, 50*(5), 41–52.

Lovelock, C. (1983). Classifying services to gain strategic marketing insights. *Journal of Marketing, 47*(3), 9–20.

Macdonald, E. K., Kleinaltenkamp, M., & Wilson, H. N. (2016). How business customers judge solutions: Solution quality and value in use. *Journal of Marketing, 80*(3), 96–120.

Martin, C. R., Jr., & Horne, D. A. (1992). Restructuring towards a service orientation: The strategic challenges. *International Journal of Service Industry Management, 3*(1), 25–38.

Mathieu, V. (2001). Product services: From a service supporting the product to a service supporting the client. *Journal of Business & Industrial Marketing, 16*(1), 39–61.

Matthyssens, P., & Vandenbempt, K. (1998). Creating competitive advantage in industrial services. *Journal of Business & Industrial Marketing, 13*(4/5), 339–355.

Matthyssens, P., & Vandenbempt, K. (2008). Moving from basic offerings to value-added solutions: Strategies, barriers and alignment. *Industrial Marketing Management, 37*(3), 316–328.

Mattsson, L.-G. (1973). Systems selling as a strategy on industrial markets. *Industrial Marketing Management, 3*, 107–120.

McCarthy, D., Fader, P. S., & Hardie, B. G. S. (2017). Valuing subscription-based businesses using publicly disclosed customer data. *Journal of Marketing, 81*(January), 17–35.

McNeil, R. B. (1944). The lease as a strategic tool. *Harvard Business Review, 22*, 415–430.

Mehta, N., Steinman, D., & Murphy, L. (2016). *Customer success: How innovative companies are reducing churn and growing recurring revenue.* John Wiley and Sons.

Meier, H., Roy, R., & Seliger, G. (2010). Industrial product-service systems – IPS 2. *CIRP Annals-Manufacturing Technology, 59*(2), 607–627.

Mont, O. K. (2002). Clarifying the concept of product–service system. *Journal of Cleaner Production, 10*(3), 237–245.

Neely, A. (2009). Exploring the financial consequences of the servitization of manufacturing. *Operations Management Research, 1*(2), 103–118.

Neu, W. A., & Brown, S. W. (2005). Forming successful business-to-business services in goods-dominant firms. *Journal of Service Research, 8*(1), 3–17.

Nordin, F., Kindström, D., Kowalkowski, C., & Rehme, J. (2011). The risks of providing services: Differential risk effects of the service-development strategies of customisation, bundling, and range. *Journal of Service Management, 22*(3), 390–408.

Oliva, R., Gebauer, H., & Brann, J. M. (2012). Separate or integrate? Assessing the impact of separation between product and service business on service performance in product manufacturing firms. *Journal of Business-to-Business Marketing, 19*(4), 309–334.

Oliva, R., & Kallenberg, R. (2003). Managing the transition from products to services. *International Journal of Service Industry Management, 14*(2), 160–172.

Ostrom, A. L., Parasuraman, A., Bowen, D. E., Patrício, L., Voss, C. A., & Lemon, K. (2015). Service research priorities in a rapidly changing context. *Journal of Service Research, 18*(2), 127–159.

Otis. (2020). Annual Report.

Page, A. L., & Siemplenski, M. (1983). Product systems marketing. *Industrial Marketing Management, 12*(2), 89–99.

Patel, P. C., Pearce, J. A., & Guedes, M. J. (2019). The survival benefits of service intensity for new manufacturing ventures: A resource-advantage theory perspective. *Journal of Service Research, 22*(4), 352–370.

Plepys, A., Heiskanen, E., & Mont, O. (2015). European policy approaches to promote servicizing. *Journal of Cleaner Production, 97*, 117–123.

Prencipe, A., Davies, A., & Hobday, M. (2003). *The business of systems integration.* Oxford University Press.

Rabetino, R., Harmsen, W., Kohtamäki, M., & Sihvonen, J. (2018). Structuring servitization-related research. *International Journal of Operations & Production Management, 38*, 350–371.

Raddats, C., & Burton, J. (2011). Strategy and structure configurations for services within product-centric businesses. *Journal of Service Management, 22*(4), 522–539.

Raddats, C., & Easingwood, C. (2010). Services growth options for B2B product-centric businesses. *Industrial Marketing Management, 39*(8), 1334–1345.

Raddats, C., Kowalkowski, C., Benedettini, O., Burton, J., & Gebauer, H. (2019). Servitization: A contemporary thematic review of four major research streams. *Industrial Marketing Management, 83*, 207–223.

Raja, J. Z., Frandsen, T., Kowalkowski, C., & Jarmatz, M. (2020). Learning to discover value: Value-based pricing and selling capabilities for services and solutions. *Journal of Business Research, 114*, 142–159.

Rangan, V. K., & Bowman, G. T. (1992). Beating the commodity magnet. *Industrial Marketing Management, 21*(3), 215–224.

Rapaccini, M., Saccani, N., Kowalkowski, C., Paiola, M., & Adrodegari, F. (2020). Navigating disruptive crises through service-led growth: The impact of COVID-19 on Italian manufacturing firms. *Industrial Marketing Management, 88*, 225–237.

Rathmell, J. M. (1966). What is meant by services? *Journal of Marketing, 30*(October), 32–36.

Reinartz, W., & Ulaga, W. (2008). How to sell services MORE profitably. *Harvard Business Review, 86*(5), 90–96.

Sawhney, M. (2006). Going beyond the product: Defining, designing, and delivering customer solutions. In R. F. Lusch & S. L. Vargo (Eds.), *The service-dominant logic of marketing: Dialog, debate, and directions* (1st ed., pp. 365–380). M. E. Shape.

Schmenner, R. W. (2009). Manufacturing, service, and their integration: Some history and theory. *International Journal of Operations & Production Management, 29*(5), 431–443.

Shankar, V., Berry, L. L., & Dotzel, T. (2009). A practical guide to combining products and services. *Harvard Business Review, 87*(11), 94–99.

Shostack, G. L. (1977). Breaking free from product marketing. *Journal of Marketing, 41*(April), 73–80.

Spohrer, J. (2017). IBM's service journey: A summary sketch. *Industrial Marketing Management, 60*, 167–172.

Spring, M., & Araujo, L. (2017). Product biographies in servitization and the circular economy. *Industrial Marketing Management, 60*, 126–137.

Storbacka, K. (2011). A solution business model: Capabilities and management practices for integrated solutions. *Industrial Marketing Management, 40*(1), 699–711.

Story, V. M., Raddats, C., Burton, J., Zolkiewski, J., & Baines, T. (2017). Capabilities for advanced services: A multi-actor perspective. *Industrial Marketing Management, 60*, 54–68.

Suarez, F. F., Cusumano, M. A., & Kahl, S. J. (2013). Services and the business models of product firms: An empirical analysis of the software industry. *Management Science, 59*(2), 420–435.

Toffel, M. W. (2008). Contracting for servicizing. *Harvard Business School Technology & Operations Mgt. Unit Research Paper* (08-063).

Tukker, A. (2004). Eight types of product–service system: Eight ways to sustainability? Experiences from SusProNet. *Business Strategy and the Environment, 13*(4), 246–260.

Tuli, K. R., Kohli, A. K., & Bharadwaj, S. G. (2007). Rethinking customer solutions: From product bundles to relational processes. *Journal of Marketing, 71*(July), 1–17.

Ulaga, W., & Kohli, A. K. (2018). The role of a solutions salesperson: Reducing uncertainty and fostering adaptiveness. *Industrial Marketing Management, 69*, 161–168.

Ulaga, W., & Loveland, J. M. (2014). Transitioning from product to service-led growth in manufacturing firms: Emergent challenges in selecting and managing the industrial sales force. *Industrial Marketing Management, 43*(1), 113–125.

Ulaga, W., & Mansard, M. (2020). Future-proof your business with the subscription business model. *ZUORA Whitepaper*. Retrieved March 22, 2021, from https://www.zuora.com/resource/subscription-resiliency-future-proof-your-business/

Ulaga, W., & Reinartz, W. (2011). Hybrid offerings: How manufacturing firms combine goods and services successfully. *Journal of Marketing, 75*(November), 5–23.

Ulaga, W., Eggert, A., & Gehring, A. (2020). Customer success – The next frontier in business markets? In M. Bruhn, C. Burmann, & M. Kirchgeorg (Eds.), *Marketing Weiterdenken, Zukunftspfade für eine marktorientierte Unternehmensführung* (2nd ed., pp. 357–373). October, Springer-Gabler.

Valtakoski, A. (2017). Explaining servitization failure and deservitization: A knowledge-based perspective. *Industrial Marketing Management, 60*, 138–150.

Vandermerwe, S., & Rada, J. (1988). Servitization of business: Adding value by adding services. *European Management Journal, 6*(4), 314–324.

Webster, K. (2017). *The circular economy: A wealth of flows.* Ellen MacArthur Foundation Publishing.

Witell, L., Kowalkowski, C., Perks, H., Raddats, C., Schwabe, M., Benedettini, O., & Burton, J. (2020). Characterizing customer experience management in business markets. *Journal of Business Research, 116*, 420–430.

Worm, S., Bharadwaj, S. G., Ulaga, W., & Reinartz, W. J. (2017). When and why do customer solutions pay off in business markets? *Journal of the Academy of Marketing Science, 45*(4), 490–512.

Zeithaml, V. A., Parasuraman, A., & Berry, L. L. (1985). Problems and strategies in services marketing. *Journal of Marketing, 49*(Spring), 33–46.

Servitization and the Necessity of Becoming Ambidextrous: A 12-Year Longitudinal Study

Peter R. Magnusson and JanErik Odhe

1 Introduction

The concept of servitization was introduced by Vandermerwe and Rada (1989) and has, ever since, been the subject of numerous studies. Servitization can be described as gradually transiting a spectrum with the starting point of offering purely physical products that are clinically free from services to the other endpoint, the servitization nirvana, where all offerings are considered to be services or solutions. Commonly, servitization is described as a process composed of different stages, whereby the company gradually slides from one stage to another (e.g., Oliva & Kallenberg, 2003). It is more or less implicitly assumed that the underlying wish to deliberately become more servitized is what drives the servitization process. Servitization efforts have often been reported as being unsuccessful (Brax, 2005; Neely, 2008). The difficulties of accomplishing successful servitization have even been named as the service paradox (Gebauer et al., 2005). Challenges are many; in a review, Alghisi and Saccani (2015) identified no less than 17 servitization challenges, spanning many different areas. However, more has to be understood regarding how to successfully tackle these challenges. The relevance of this was stressed by Ostrom et al. (2015), who identified "facilitating servitization, service infusion, and solutions" as one of 12 research priorities in service research.

P. R. Magnusson (✉) • J. Odhe
CTF, Service Research Center, Karlstad University, Karlstad, Sweden
e-mail: peter.magnusson@kau.se; janerik.odhe@kau.se

© The Author(s), under exclusive license to Springer Nature Switzerland AG 2022
B. Edvardsson, B. Tronvoll (eds.), *The Palgrave Handbook of Service Management*,
https://doi.org/10.1007/978-3-030-91828-6_11

Drawing on Kastalli and Van Looy (2013) they stated that challenges regarding servitization research focus on "understanding the development of new business models, the organizational and structural transformation processes required, and the technologies (e.g., sensors and digital interfaces) to support them". One of the issues was "understanding the impact of servitization and solutions on companies, industries, and service systems" better. They conclude that, "Overall, there is a need to move on from mere rhetoric that service infusion and servitization are the basis of service-led growth and focus more on investigating *how* to make this happen successfully" (p. 134).

This chapter contributes to an improved understanding of *how* servitization actually happens, and, more specifically, how it affects the servicizing organization. We base our insights on a longitudinal case study spanning 12 years. The focal company, AIR, was more or less forced into a servitization process due to the surrounding business ECO system; ECO system is understood here to be a network of companies with a great deal of autonomy that focus on combined customer offerings. These offerings are usually based on modularity, whereby the actors complement each other (Jacobides et al., 2018). The chapter describes and analyzes how a unit at AIR made the successful transition from a pure make-to-print actor to offering overall solutions where we focus on the challenges that AIR encountered. This transition corresponds quite well to the transition from the "Prototypic Manufacturing Characteristics Configuration" to the "Service-Oriented Manufacturing Configuration", as defined by Bowen et al. (1989).

Most, if not all, of the challenges and drivers identified in the case have been reported over the years. However, research in this field—as emphasized by Ostrom et al. (2015)—is often based on aggregated data that does not enable an in-depth understanding of the actual issues. Therefore, the longitudinal dimension and in-depth nature of the present study contribute to a deeper and better understanding of what to expect and *how* to manage the type of servitization captured in the AIR case. The aim is, thus, to contribute research-based actionable knowledge regarding the challenges and drivers of leading a servitization transition.

2   Method

The study is longitudinal, spanning the years 1996–2007. The data is based on both archive material and interviews with 24 key personnel from the focal company, AIR. The archive data was mainly captured from AIR's printed in-house magazine (in the text, abbreviated as IHM), published internally for the employees between 1996 and 2007. The IHM was thus targeted at the employees of the company to provide them with updated information on what was happening at the company, functioning as a company Intranet would today. In each issue, someone from top management, often the CEO, wrote a leader column providing top managements' view of different topics. Furthermore, articles described important projects and contracts, for instance. The IHM thus captures many of the strategic intentions and changes that took place at the company during this 12-year period. A company survey carried out in 1998 showed that 71% of AIR employees read the IHM and, in particular, the "information from top management column". The editor of the IHM was on the top management team.

All issues of the IHM between 1996 and 2007 were read, focusing on articles that in some way related to AIR's efforts to increase its service business and to become a solution provider. Articles found to be of interest were scanned into the PDF format, resulting in a file 176 pages long. This PDF file was then converted using OCR software into searchable text in order to facilitate analysis of this extensive material. Furthermore, AIR's official annual report (AR) for the years 1996 to 2011 has been collected and analyzed.

Between October 2005 and November 2007, 28 interviews were conducted on-site with 24 key personnel at AIR, from different departments. All the interviews were recorded and transcribed. The interviews enabled further in-depth information and triangulation of the archive data. In parallel with the interviews, direct observations were made of the design and production facilities.

Between January and March 2021, three follow-up interviews were conducted with people employed at AIR during the period included in the case. The manuscript has also been factually checked by an expert from the aircraft industry with more than 20 years' experience.

3 The Focal Company "AIR" and the Aviation Sector

AIR was a B2B manufacturing company in the aviation business, specializing in manufacturing jet engines. It started in the 1930s. At the beginning, its focus was military aviation, more or less. In that field, it both designed and produced all the parts of its engines. In the 1970s, AIR's military division accounted for 90% of its revenues. After that, its share of the military market became smaller, accounting only for about 33% at the start of the 1990s. In

1996, the CEO of AIR declared that its future strategic focus would be the *commercial aircraft* market (AR, 1996). He also declared that the company would specialize as a "gas turbine company" (IHM, no. 5, 1996). The purpose of specialization was to enable access, in future development programs, to commercial aircraft. These programs have a main Original Equipment Manufacturer (OEM) who is responsible for the whole aircraft, like Boeing or Airbus. Aircraft are composed of different *sub-systems,* with engines being one. Normally, one, or two, of the three main jet engine manufacturers—Rolls-Royce, GE, and Pratt & Whitney—is assigned as responsible to the head OEM for the engine. The engine is composed of several *modules* and *components*. The responsibility for developing, producing, and supporting these sub-systems and components is assigned to different companies, which then become a part of the program contractually. To conclude, the engine design is, thus, more or less standardized into different modules whereby different companies specialize in order to assume full responsibility—including development, production, and support—for certain components. A component usually consists of "double digit" quantity of item numbers.

The development of a new commercial aircraft can thus be described as an ECO system (Jacobides et al., 2018) that includes many different companies, whereby products, components, services, and knowledge are linked together to provide the customer with a solution. An established industry concept supporting this is the Risk Sharing Partnership (RSP; Figueiredo et al., 2008). This accomplishes not only the gathering of specialized competencies but also the financial risk and revenue sharing of the whole project over time. It also helps to clearly identify the actors of the ECO system. In an article in the IHM (no. 13, 1996), the president of Commercial Engines at AIR lists the four most important issues as regards being accepted as a member of the major aircraft development programs: financial capability, risk willingness, technical competence, and development and production skills. The common goal of the strategic partnership is supporting the ECO system in order to bring the customer added value. For instance, the RSP is shown to decrease lead times during the development process since key competencies are involved earlier on in the project, and the long-term relationships between the OEM and the key suppliers are secured (Halvorsen et al., 2020). Entering the ECO system, AIR had done its strategic homework. One task was mapping the system and connecting up the dots between allied organizations and finding potential market gaps to fill in the case of a new entrant like AIR.

The following is a brief chronological description of AIR's journey from almost being a pure component manufacturer to developing and offering solutions within an ECO system. We have identified the different periods and milestones that had a huge impact on the company. Our analysis is restricted to the servitization efforts regarding the *component production of the commercial aircraft division of the company.*

Specialization: Three Components (1996–1997)

As previously mentioned, a strategic decision was taken in 1996, that is, that AIR would become a "gas turbine company" and would specialize in three different components. At this time, the commercial division of AIR consisted of hardware production and engine maintenance, each approximately the same size. The hardware production division was known as *make-to-print (MTP)*, meaning that the input was a blueprint of the component the customer wanted to have produced. The deal was fulfilled when the hardware component was delivered. AIR also had a department for servicing and maintaining jet engines. This had, however, been hived off as an in-house business unit that served different airlines on a contractual basis.

Specializing in a limited number of components provided AIR with both backward (design) and forward vertical integration (product support). To become members of the major development programs, actors were expected to assume responsibility for all stages—design, production, and support (DPS)—of the components they had signed up for.

The ambition to enter the development programs gave results. At the beginning of 1997, AIR's Deputy CEO declared that the company had signed up for its first participation in one of the major development programs (IHM, no. 2, 1997).

Understanding Customer Value (1997–2001)

It became more evident that technology skills alone would not be enough if AIR was to succeed in the long run. Understanding what is valuable to the customer became essential. Proof of this came in June 1997, when the in-house magazine reported on a milestone. One of the employees had received a prize of 13,000 Euros for a suggestion that would lead to reduced short-term revenues for AIR but, more importantly, better *customer value*. One of the managers stated that this was a new mindset at AIR. Focusing on customer value would be important in the future.

Ten years ago, a suggestion that would bring AIR reduced revenues would not have found any favor. Today it's different. (IHM, no. 10, 1997)

The importance of taking the *customer perspective* was further emphasized by the CEO. In the September issue of IHM the same year, he stated that endeavors in support and maintenance had brought the company closer to understanding the customer.

> *Our efforts in maintenance and support have brought us closer to the end customer. This has been a strategic effort and a natural development of our company. (IHM, no. 14, 1997)*

The CEO continued highlighting the customer focus, in the no. 5 issue in 1998, declaring: "*Historically, marketing was not a necessary skill at our company, now it is!*"

During this period, the company linked services to its physical products (services supporting the product). It also started developing services that can support the customer post-delivery, that is, services supporting the customer's processes (Mathieu, 2001). The importance of understanding what is valuable to the customer was emphasized. It was evident that AIR was unable to rely merely on technical skills—understanding the customer was becoming equally important. In 1999, during a customer audit, customer representatives got the opportunity to put important issues regarding customer value to all the managers at AIR. When AIR surveyed employee satisfaction and employee knowledge regarding its corporate vision and strategies, the results showed that a high level of knowledge and understanding contributed toward a high level of job satisfaction. This intensified the work of deploying knowledge of these issues to all employees via multiple communication channels, for example, printed materials, departmental meetings, "CEO meetings", and, evidently, the in-house magazine.

At the end of 1999, the IHM (IHM, no. 13, 1999) reported on an internal project aimed at standardizing AIR's business development. One of the strategists was interviewed and defined AIR's product as being composed of a combination of both physical products and services.

> *By product, we mean both hardware and software, that is, both components and service. A product doesn't need to be a totally new idea, it can also be a new product offering. You can, for instance, launch new services in terms of financing and leasing linked to existing hardware.*

This essentially broadened what was defined as AIR's "business". Physical products (components) can also be linked to supporting services. In issue no. 12, of the IHM of the same year, a project was presented aimed at building an

Servitization and the Necessity of Becoming Ambidextrous... **207**

IT-based "service platform" based on something called 4th generation product support (4GPS).

4GPS products are offered separately, but they can also be integrated into a system consisting of 1) the ADS, "Advanced Diagnostic System", a troubleshooting system, 2) Maintenix, an operating and maintenance system, and 3) MainTool, a tool including vibration gauging.

In the article, it was explained that the development of 4GPS has been transferred to a new unit, Advanced Product Support (APS).

These are new and existing areas that will give us opportunities to offer our customers flexibility and cost savings. (CTO)

This was also a milestone as services were previously isolated from component production. The 4GPS tools could now enable AIR to build totally new and advanced maintenance systems to support the components delivered to customers. This goes beyond merely transferring a physical product to a customer. This was the first sign that the company was also aiming to contribute value to its customers during product use. What we observe here is essentially the genesis of a transformation from a pure production logic to a logic where delivering customer value is the most essential thing.

The emphasis on the importance of understanding the customer is further described in the IHM, no. 13, 2000. A new senior manager was hired to work at the company. He is described as an extrovert leader that focuses on marketing and sales. This indicates how the company's future managers should be, that is, understanding the customer side will be essential in the future. It indicated a "new era" when it is no longer enough just to be technically skilled; we also have to understand our customers. The value of nurturing customer relations is something that emerged during many of the interviews.

A new business logic is also indicated in issue no. 12, 2001. One of the project champions indicates a paradigm shift—from product focus to something new where the "process is the product" (IHM, no. 12, 2001). This should be interpreted as different types of services.

The product, or hardware, can't be developed that much more technically, and thus we have to offer the customer supplementary services like repairs, maintenance, spare parts, technical support and information systems.

Shock and Survival (September 11, 2001)

The terrorist attack on September 11, 2001, did, of course, hit the whole aerospace business extremely hard, including AIR's operations. First there was a shock and then came a struggle for survival. In the IHM, senior management's message to the employees focused on financial issues, such as increased cash flow and cost reductions. It took the industry until 2004 to start recovering from the effects of 9/11.

Overall Solutions: Develop, Produce, and Support (DPS) (2004)

When the airline business slowly started to recover, the CTO announced the new route for the future (IHM, no. 1, 2004). The whole article is a statement about where AIR was coming from and where it was heading. He emphasized the technological knowledge the company had accumulated and which would be decisive as regards being competitive in the future. The prime message for the future was that AIR had to continue to strive for specialization in some limited parts of the jet engine to become an attractive partner in *development, production, and product support* (DPS). Moving from word to deed, AIR made an organizational change, merging three divisions into one. This made the advanced design and engineering knowledge of the former Space and Military Divisions available across the entire organization. In addition, a strategic acquisition was made to broaden the component portfolio. By excelling in the fields of design, production, and support, AIR could become an attractive partner providing overall solutions to its partners. This was, thus, the vision that had been announced more than seven years earlier. During the previous stage, as a pure MTP, AIR had to excel in costs, quality, and volumes; now, it also needed to emphasize the customer relations perspective in order to meet a broader range of expectations.

Partnership with customers is further emphasized in other articles during the year. The importance of this is further emphasized by referring to quotes from the three most important jet engine OEMs, that is, potential partners for AIR (IHM, no. 5, 2005). The unifying message from them is that their partners must be competent in both design and production.

The Beginning of a New Era: GEnx (2005–)

In December 2004, AIR signed a contract with GE, one of the major jet engine OEMs. This was the largest engine component contract in the history of AIR and the first to include product design/development, manufacturing, and product support for all three components. A new project, GEnx, was started on the basis of this new contract.

With the GEnx contract, the need to further develop AIR's design competence became clear. An internal project, "A designing organization", was initiated that aimed to build up and consolidate AIR's design competence. Reference was made to this competence being based on the principle of "learning by doing".

> *We use GEnx to build up our ability as a designing organization with lifecycle responsibility. It's important to have real customers for this work.* (IHM, no. 5, 2005)

The importance of having real customers to learn from when developing overall solutions was thus emphasized. The GEnx project has been referred to in articles in almost every issue of the IHM. It was described as a role model for the future way of organizing work at AIR. It became obvious that taking on the role of DPS entailed new demands on internal cross-functional collaboration. The key to success was working in *cross-functional* teams on the project. It was a challenge finding new ways of carrying out processes and communicating internally. If the production facility was informed about the design too late, this would result in a reworking of the engineering specifications and drawings, causing extra costs and delays.

> *This work challenged us a lot, and we had to make changes, but a major challenge also makes people grow and perform.*
> *(Former Manager of Technology & Services)*

It seems that the GEnx project became a vehicle for *learning* new ways of organizing work at the company, but also for learning from each other. "*The GEnx project has contributed to tearing down walls and transferring knowledge between the divisions*": the IHM, no. 6, 2005. The same year, in issue no. 7 of the IHM, the Head of Procurement appraised the GEnx project thus:

> *With GEnx, it has been very obvious how dependent we are on each other [different divisions of AIR]. … GEnx is a good example of how, with joint efforts, we can accomplish good results for AIR.*

Reporting about GEnx became a tool for providing the employees with a holistic understanding of AIR's organization; AIR's identity was thus transformed by both the GEnx project and by the articles in IHM.

Issue no. 6 in 2005 reported on a cross-functional "Reflection summit" for 120 employees participating in the GEnx project. This summit created the opportunity to reflect upon the project and discuss improvements to the processes. This "lessons learned process" was adopted by the organization. After some modification, it was used in all future major projects.

To coordinate the interplay between development, production, and support, a formal organizational unit was formed, named *product management* (IHM, no. 3, 2006). It was understood that this would be an essential unit at the company for handling the challenges that come with assuming total responsibility and offering solutions instead of products.

To move on in order to underline the importance of customer relationships, a liaison officer was appointed at the customer site. This appointee could attend meetings with the customer at very short notice, acting as a clear hub for communication between AIR and the customer. This way of working was established for future projects.

The positive synergy effects of cross-functional collaboration were dealt with in a two-page issue of the IHM, no. 2, 2007. The title was "The new AIR demands collaboration". Collaboration was advocated as the company's key for handling the overall commitments necessary to make an attractive partner.

We've moved from being a manufacturing company to a company that develops and manufactures [...] it's a competence platform of people, methods, materials, and technology. (IHM, no. 2, 2007)

The message to the reader was that the AIR of the future would demand that several divisions of the company collaborate. Besides the internal collaborative efforts made, AIR also made a strategic acquisition (AR, 2007) in order to develop its technology knowledge in materials and lightweight design. This was to meet the contemporary trend in the aviation industry, where climate issues were high on the agenda. A lighter aircraft consumes less fuel and thus emissions will decrease.

The organizational change, moving away from divisions toward one single company, the new project model, and the new demands of the GEnx project and the acquisitions all challenged AIR and its employees a great deal. Competencies and skills had to be developed during a learning-by-doing process. It could be said that the times were dynamic. However, annual employee satisfaction surveys showed positive trends regarding job satisfaction, motivation, and trust in management. Staff churn was also kept on a very low level.

The longitudinal study, started in 1996, discerned several strategic decisions which had made AIR a vital partner in the ECO system. This was an example of a successful transition from a make-to-print supplier to a company specializing in just a few components and being responsible for design, production, and support. The OEMs are the major aircraft builders of the world and AIR's strategy has put them in the position where they have a stable financial situation.

4 Analysis

Over the years, the commercial aircraft industry has evolved into a complex ECO system consisting of a number of actors. Today, no single company can assume the overall responsibility for building new aircraft. The design architecture of aircraft consists of systems, sub-systems, modules, and components, with rather well-defined interfaces. Different actors sign up and assume the overall responsibility for (design, production, and support) the different parts. The result was what Neely (2008) defines as a "product oriented product service system", whereby the tangible product is transferred to the customer, but with the provision of additional services directly related to the product, for example, design and development services, installation, maintenance, and support.

The focal case company, AIR, had a long history of producing engine parts for aircraft. In the mid-1990s, it was still purely a manufacturer, known as MTP. By this time, senior management had realized that for the company's long-term survival, it had to become a member of the major development consortiums. AIR decided to specialize in some key engine components, in order to be able to assume the overall responsibility for these. From a servitization perspective, this is essentially an example of a company transiting from being a product manufacturer to offering solutions. The transition from MTP to DPS is illustrated in Fig. 1.

As an MTP, input consisted of a ready-made blueprint from the customer specifying the component to be produced. AIR's work effort was to produce the component in accordance with the specification and to then deliver it. As a DPS partner, the work process became much more complex, as illustrated in Fig. 1.

The input for a DPS job is a requirements specification, which needs to be translated into a design specification. To ensure that the requirements were correctly interpreted, AIR's designers had to interact with their customers. Furthermore, AIR also had to be responsible for and ensure that all regulations and legislations were complied with.

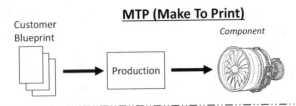

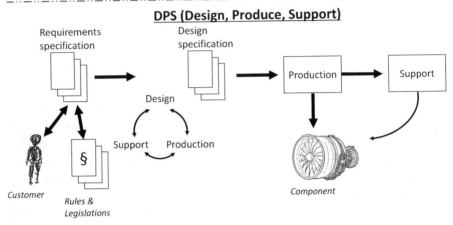

Fig. 1 AIR's transition from MTP to DPS

In the new support process, AIR's main responsibility was to provide support in the form of knowledge and expertise during engine assembly. This could be done on or off site, depending on the issue. The same procedures were applied when maintenance work was carried out.

The longitudinal case study provides good opportunities for analyzing and revealing the challenges that servitization can entail. We analyze the case from two managerial perspectives—*challenges for organizing* and *challenges for business*—as both of these dramatically changed during the transition, which took about 15 years.

Challenges for Organizing

From the case, we have identified some major organizational challenges occurring when transiting from product to solution. The new position entailed handling *creative and innovative* activities. It further entailed a new, deeper understanding of the customer side of the product. Having the overall responsibility entailed intra-collaboration across formal organizational boundaries.

The Need to Become Creative and Innovative

A new offering (e.g., a product or a service) can be described, on the conceptual level, as a "solution to a relevant problem", thus consisting of two sides (c.f., Sukhov et al., 2019). In the role of MTP, the solution (i.e., the blueprint for the component) was provided by the customer. The problem was not, in fact, even relevant to producing the component; conformity with the blueprint was everything. There was virtually no creative work involved in the process.

In the role of DPS, the scene was dramatically different. Here, the input was a requirements specification, essentially a draft of the problem to be solved using a design. However, the problem needed to be clarified by means of interacting with the customer, as well as ensuring conformity with the applicable legislations and regulations. The design was essentially a *creative process*—a problem-solving activity, that is, finding the best solution for the problem defined, something that Neely (2008) noted too.

Finding 1 (F_1): The transition from product to solution (MTP to DPS) demands new creative and innovative skills in the organization.

The Need to Obtain New Knowledge

In recurring articles in the IHM, senior management advocated the importance of competence development. The head of jet engine components wrote (IHM, Sep, 2001):

We're developing our design competence with the aim of becoming an effective partner that can assume overall product responsibility.

The importance of knowledge was reinforced during the interviews. AIR had a strategy of developing its competence in collaboration with universities and by means of making strategic acquisitions. It was often emphasized that knowledge was a vehicle for the company.

It is evident that the transition from MTP to DPS (offering solutions) demanded extensive knowledge development. Two essential and complementary types of knowledge are needed for successful innovative work, namely *technology knowledge* and *use knowledge* (von Hippel, 1994). Technology knowledge is mainly used for the solution part, that is, problem-solving and implementation, while use knowledge is required in order to understand the problem side, that is, what the problem is and why it exists.

As noted, with MTP, there was virtually no need to understand the customer's actual needs and demands other than the price and delivery schedule. Conformity with the customer's blueprint was the only guidance regarding what to do. Becoming a DPS actor brought totally new terms and challenges. The process became more complex with a requirements specification that had to be translated into a technical design. Many of the requirements emanated from the end-customer, for example, *low fuel consumption* and *low noise*. Tackling reduced fuel consumption enabled AIR to gain design knowledge in lightweight materials. This was partly accomplished internally, on the military side, but also by means of the dedicated project ("A designing organization"). However, it was also accomplished through the acquisition of a company specializing in lightweight materials. The challenge of understanding the customer has also been identified in other research (e.g., Brax, 2005; Martinez et al., 2010; Neely, 2008). During the GEnx project, AIR started the concept of stationing a liaison officer at the customer's premises, in order to improve and simplify customer communications.

But for AIR, it was not enough to understand the customer. The aim of becoming effective also included teaching suppliers about AIR's requirements. For the purposes of knowledge transfer, one of AIR's experts was stationed at the premises of one important supplier for one and a half years (IHM, no. 5, 2002). This arrangement was reported as a mutual learning experience for both parties, and one that strengthened the bonds between the two companies. Internal knowledge transfer benefitted from the organizational change, when three business units were transformed into one organization.

The transition to DPS forced AIR to adopt new knowledge. Previously, operations had only required a production logic, that is, delivering a specified volume at a given quality at minimum cost and on schedule. Handling solutions demanded a thorough understanding of both the customer and how to use the technology—use knowledge. Also, new technology knowledge was necessary in order to translate the requirements into technical solutions.

Finding 2 (F_2): The transition from product to solution (MTP to DPS) will demand more use as well as technology knowledge.

Intra-collaboration and Coordination

The new design work not only had to follow the requirements specification, it also had to include producing and supporting it in an efficient way. Design, production, and support were not mutually exclusive; on the contrary, they were deeply intertwined. This became evident during the GEnx project, starting in 2005. The project also became a learning ground for how to coordinate the three processes. This was also heavily communicated in the IHM as a role model for work processes in the future at AIR. The GEnx project became a learning project for the new way of organizing work when adopting the role of DPS. The result was, thus, an organizational transition away from working in "functional pipes" toward cross-functional teams. Later, the cross-functionality was institutionalized in terms of organizational unit product management.

As pointed out in a follow-up interview recently, at start-up, the GEnx project was struggling with a dilemma. As noted, it was too expensive, and risky, to amass the necessary resources before the contract had been signed. When these types of contracts are signed, the organization "knows" that it will need to learn new things in order to deliver. It was indeed learning-by-doing, or rather "learning-while-doing".

Finding 3 (F_3): The transition from product to solution (MTP to DPS) will demand new intra-collaboration and concurrent learning.

Changes in the Business Mindset

The transition from providing products to offering solutions will also enable management to handle multiple business/management logics. Furthermore, the transition will also put the focus on knowledge as a prime asset within the organization, in turn affecting how IP (Intellectual Property) is managed.

Multiple Business Logics

The transition from MTP to DPS had an impact on the business models of AIR. As an MTP, revenues were payments for manufacturing activities. The main *asset was production skills*, that is, efficiently processing incoming raw materials into an engine component, according to specification. Returns were decided by how efficiently AIR could produce a specific volume at a given quality, on time at minimum cost.

In the role of DPS, *knowledge* became an important asset. Under the revenue share program, AIR was expected to contribute a total solution. The competitive edge for AIR was the accumulated knowledge resulting from more than 70 years' experience in the business. Knowledge could now be embedded in the design of the physical products (components) and the support services delivered. Knowledge became an asset that could be turned into a revenue.

Even if knowledge became an important asset for AIR, as a DPS, productions skills were just as important as before. This was also emphasized externally in the annual financial reports; one of the 4–5 most important goals for the next year was recurringly *productivity, shortened lead times,* and *cost control*.

Internally, other focus areas were also mentioned in terms of being important when transiting toward DPS. *Customer value* became a catchword. The aim was to understand and deliver customer value; also noted as a challenge by, for instance, Neely (2008). This was emphasized in many different ways in the case. One example of this was the reward for increasing customer value despite this reduced AIR's revenues; another being the CEO signaling maintenance as a means of getting closer to, and better understanding, customer value. In other words, the aim was to adopt a service logic (Grönroos, 2011).

DPS will thus need to handle at least two partly contradictory logics simultaneously: a production logic and a service logic. This is also known as ambidexterity (Hodgkinson et al., 2014; Tushman & O'Reilly III, 1996).

Finding 4 (F_4): The transition from product to solution (MTP to DPS) will need to handle ambidexterity.

New Logic for Intellectual Property Rights (IPR)

Immaterial assets had been important even before the transition from MTP to DPS. Patents had, for instance, enjoyed a long history at AIR, mainly on the military side. During the transition to DPS, patents were still important, but much knowledge could not be formally protected by, for example, patents or copyright. The avoidance of unintentional knowledge spillover has been attended to in the literature (e.g., Hipp & Grupp, 2005). At AIR, it was, however, tricky to avoid and was mentioned in several interviews. "Technology is very important, as well as our skills and knowledge, as is not sharing it with anyone", as the Head of Innovation put it.

A problem during the transition was convincing the employees that knowledge was a major asset for the "new AIR". Previously, the engineers had often helped the customers with many issues for free, but this was now to be charged for. It had been assumed, more or less, that this help would be included in the price of the hardware. The paradox here was that the transition to offering solutions, and in doing so adopting a service perspective, in fact meant that the customer would get less help than before, unless he paid for it. However, charging for expert knowledge was a challenge. Many of the engineers "leaked" information to the customer. One frustrated project leader considered this a cultural problem: *"We [AIR] have a climate where it's virtually impossible to get any help from our engineers if you call them as a co-worker. But if a customer calls, they'll do anything."* She meant a cultural change was needed in order to overcome this mentality, something that would take time. In a sense, becoming a knowledge company that provides solutions requires a new corporate culture, which is a challenge noted in many studies (Alghisi & Saccani, 2015; Gebauer & Friedli, 2005; Neely, 2008)

Finding 5 (F_5): The transition from product to solution (MTP to DPS) demands a cultural change in order to fully exploit IP assets.

Technology Implications of Service Perspective

As previously discussed, the transition to offering solutions and adopting a service logic entails the company having to better understand the customer's needs and what is valuable, that is, gaining more use knowledge. However, it was notable that, in understanding the customer better, the company also proactively came to realize the need to develop its technology knowledge. In its design activities, AIR had to understand the requirements of both the customers and the authorities. It could, for example, foresee the need to develop its knowledge of lightweight materials and designs. As an MTP actor, this new requirement would probably have been realized too late. It was thus important for the transition to be proactive and at the forefront of how the aircraft market was developing. This finding can be seen as a challenge, but it was probably more of an opportunity for the company to understand which future technology would be relevant as regards delivering customer value.

Finding 6 (F_6): Adopting a service perspective will demand an even deeper understanding of future technology knowledge.

The findings are summarized in Fig. 2.

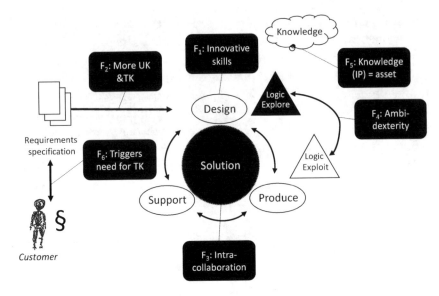

Fig. 2 The six transition challenges

5   Concluding Discussion

The contribution made by this chapter is a deeper understanding of how successful servitization actually happens, in-line with the request from Ostrom et al. (2015). More specifically, the AIR case provides insights into a successful servitization transition whereby this company went from producing components, based on customer blueprints (MTP), to being an attractive partner in the ECO system of developing, producing, and supporting aircraft.

Servitization as a Fundamental Process of Change, Learning, and Gambling

AIR's transition from MTP to DPS was essentially a transition from a product logic to a service logic. Linked to this, previous research has emphasized that this requires a better understanding of the customer—known as use knowledge—in order to understand customer value. Interestingly, these processes also brought about the need to further develop organizational technology knowledge in order to understand which solutions would be most suitable in the future.

The new role of assuming full responsibility (develop-produce-support) for certain components of an ECO system further caused AIR to develop creative and innovative skills, but also internal collaboration across traditional functional units, for example, development and manufacturing. It is important to emphasize that the transition took more than a decade to complete. These endeavors need persistence in order to be successful; it is not a quick fix.

The case also illustrates the often-delicate balance of being able to develop new abilities within a competitive industry. AIR could not risk amassing the necessary competence to handle DPS until a deal had been signed. Signing the first contract was consequently a gamble since not all the necessary competence and resources were in place. The transition was indeed a process of "learning-while-doing". It was thus a decision about either taking a financial risk or running the risk of not tackling the new situation at all. This is probably a decision-making dilemma that is common to these types of situations. Future research should look into this balance and how to handle it.

The Necessity of Ambidexterity

From the case study, it became evident that ambidexterity was an essential ingredient of successful servitization. The former MTP business demanded either strict *production* or *exploitative logic*—that is, focusing on cost reductions and high quality. For a manufacturing company, this is a must in order to survive. Even when AIR transformed into its new DPS role, it was still important to keep the production logic. At the same time, a fundamentally different logic, an *explorative logic,* was essential when it came to, for instance, understanding how to develop value for the customer, how to create new business models, and how to tackle design challenges.

In the literature, servitization is normally perceived, by a manufacturing company, as an activity whereby an organization departs from a goods/production logic and transforms itself so that it can adopt a service logic. In practice, at least in this context, this is not entirely the case. Both logics are fundamental and must coexist. The link between servitization and ambidextrous leadership has not been elaborated upon in previous research, but should be in the future.

Is Servitization Important?

From a scholarly theoretical perspective, the story of AIR can be interpreted as a servitization process, that is, a company moving away from manufacturing in order to offer solutions is a classic example of a transition away from a goods logic toward a service logic. However, for AIR, the whole journey was not about servitization per se—it was a necessity for staying in business. The company had to adapt to a changing business landscape where the development and production of aircraft had grown so complex that it could not be handled by one company alone: It was now an ECO system of different manufacturers. To become a part of this ECO system, AIR had to change. It was no longer enough simply to produce components from a blueprint. The members of the ECO system had to assume full responsibility—development, production, and support—for the dedicated components. In retrospect, this transformation can be described as a servitization process. But, servitization, or the service logic, was never explicitly mentioned in any of the annual reports, nor in the IHM. Of the 22 interviewees, only 3 discussed servitization.

It is evident from the AIR case that servitization is becoming a matter of perspective. The question is whether or not it is important for a company to use the rhetoric of servitization. Based on this, and other cases we have studied over the years, the answer is *no*. Manufacturing companies striving to offer solutions as well will indeed need more knowledge of the customer's operation and usage. Also, will they need to develop generative capabilities in order to develop solutions for the customer, these often being totally new areas for the organization. Knowledge becomes a prime asset that needs to be developed. At these hi-tech, knowledge-intensive companies, service operations are often considered to be of low status, due to being associated, for instance, with cleaning and repairs. Even if scholars differentiate between different types of services, the concept of "service" seems to be more generic among practitioners—with the label of service frequently also being misinterpreted as routinized and mundane work processes. Knowledge, however, have by all means high status in these organizations. If management speaks of adopting a service perspective, this might instead result in a backlash. Thus, maybe the AIR case was not (just) an example of a transition from product to solution, but also an illustration of a company's transition to a knowledge company.

Perhaps, therefore, it may be better to listen to one of interviewees when he declared: "We are NOT a service company … we are a knowledge company!"

References

Alghisi, A., & Saccani, N. (2015). Internal and external alignment in the servitization journey—overcoming the challenges. *Production Planning & Control, 26*(14-15), 1219–1232.

Bowen, D. E., Siehl, C., & Schneider, B. (1989). A framework for analyzing customer service orientations in manufacturing [article]. *Academy of Management Review, 14*(1), 75–95.

Brax, S. (2005). A manufacturer becoming service provider—challenges and a paradox. *Managing Service Quality: An International Journal, 15*(2), 142–155.

Figueiredo, P., Silveira, G., & Sbragia, R. (2008). Risk sharing partnerships with suppliers: The case of EMBRAER. *Journal of Technology Management & Innovation, 3*(1), 27–37.

Gebauer, H., Fleisch, E., & Friedli, T. (2005). Overcoming the Service Paradox in Manufacturing Companies. *European Management Journal, 23*(1), 14–26.

Gebauer, H., & Friedli, T. (2005). Behavioral implications of the transition process from products to services. *Journal of Business & Industrial Marketing, 20*(2), 70–78.

Grönroos, C. (2011). A service perspective on business relationships: The value creation, interaction and marketing interface. *Industrial Marketing Management, 40*(2), 240–247.

Halvorsen, T. K., Hannås, G., & Hellström, M. M. (2020). Adaptation of Risk Sharing Partnerships (RSP) to New Industries. The 10th International Conference on Engineering, Project, and Production Management, Singapore.

Hipp, C., & Grupp, H. (2005). Innovation in the service sector: The demand for service-specific innovation measurement concepts and typologies. *Research Policy, 34*(4), 517–535.

Hodgkinson, I. R., Ravishankar, M. N., & Aitken-Fischer, M. (2014). A resource-advantage perspective on the orchestration of ambidexterity. *The Service Industries Journal, 34*(15), 1234–1252.

Jacobides, M. G., Cennamo, C., & Gawer, A. (2018). Towards a theory of ecosystems. *Strategic Management Journal, 39*(8), 2255–2276. https://doi.org/10.1002/smj.2904

Kastalli, I. V., & Van Looy, B. (2013). Servitization: Disentangling the impact of service business model innovation on manufacturing firm performance. *Journal of Operations Management, 31*(4), 169–180.

Martinez, V., Bastl, M., Kingston, J., & Evans, S. (2010). Challenges in transforming manufacturing organisations into product-service providers. *Journal of Manufacturing Technology Management, 21*(4), 449–469.

Mathieu, V. (2001). Service strategies within the manufacturing sector: Benefits, costs and partnership. *International Journal of Service Industry Management, 12*(5), 451–475.

Neely, A. (2008). Exploring the financial consequences of the servitization of manufacturing. *Operations management research, 1*(2), 103–118.

Oliva, R., & Kallenberg, R. (2003). Managing the transition from products to services. *International Journal of Service Industry Management, 14*(2), 160–172.

Ostrom, A. L., Parasuraman, A., Bowen, D. E., Patricio, L., & Voss, C. A. (2015). Service research priorities in a rapidly changing context. *Journal of Service Research, 18*(2), 127–159.

Sukhov, A., Magnusson, P. R., & Netz, J. (2019). What is an idea for innovation? In P. Kristensson, P. R. Magnusson, & L. Witell (Eds.), *Service innovation for sustainable business—Stimulating, realizing and capturing the value from service innovation* (pp. 29–47). World Scientific.

Tushman, M. L., & O'Reilly III, C. A. (1996). Ambidextrous organizations: Managing evolutionary and revolutionary change. *California Management Review,* *38*(4), 8–30.

Vandermerwe, S., & Rada, J. (1989). Servitization of business: Adding value by adding services. *European Management Journal, 6*(4), 314–324.

von Hippel, E. (1994). "Sticky Information" and the locus of problem solving: Implications for innovation. *Management Science, 40*(4), 429–439.

How Contemporary Scholarship Addresses Service Management Practices

Robert C. Ford and David Solnet

1 Introduction

As this chapter is written, Coronavirus has created consequential changes in the global economy, with major elements of the service sector heavily impacted. While we anticipate the changes this pandemic has caused will lessen in their impact as the world's population becomes vaccinated, some changes will inevitably become permanent in the "new normal". The writing of this chapter, consequently, is even more speculative than we originally anticipated as contemporary scholarship has generally followed a path of researching existing services to extrapolate findings to describe how customers respond in an increasingly globalized world of trade and travel. To the extent that this path has become disrupted as a dominant predictor of excellent service management practices and behaviors, this chapter aims to weave together contemporary scholarship with informed speculation as to what service management practices will be in a post-COVID world.

R. C. Ford (✉)
Department of Management, College of Business Administration, University of Central Florida, Orlando, FL, USA
e-mail: rford@bus.ucf.edu

D. Solnet
University of Queensland Business School, Brisbane, QLD, Australia
e-mail: David.solnet@uq.edu.au

© The Author(s), under exclusive license to Springer Nature Switzerland AG 2022
B. Edvardsson, B. Tronvoll (eds.), *The Palgrave Handbook of Service Management*,
https://doi.org/10.1007/978-3-030-91828-6_12

While we could identify several dozen topic areas to focus on, given the limited space we have to present our thinking, we have chosen four that we think merit the most attention in a Handbook used by future scholars and practitioners. These four are (1) humanizing the service experience; (2) contingent (gig) work and workers; (3) further evolution from customer service to customer experience; and (4) managing diverse customer resources in the co-production of a service experience.

The chapter is divided into four sections in which we (a) identify a significant service issue and its importance to managers and (b) present a summary of contemporary scholarship related to this issue that can help inform future practice. Table 1 offers a brief overview of each topic, the core concepts, and insights from researchers.

2 Humanizing the Service Experience

What Is the Topic and Why Is it Important to Managers?

Consider this scenario. A customer enters a hotel and finds no front-desk agents to greet him or her, no concierge to provide information on local destinations, and no full-service restaurant. Instead, there are self-check-in terminals and signage directing guests to smartphone apps to check-in or access whatever information or service is needed during the stay. This is not the future—it is now! This technology currently exists and is being accelerated by the adoption of robots on the frontline (Wirtz et al., 2018), creating a real dilemma for service organizations seeking the optimal balance between meeting customers' expectations for human touch with their desire for speed, price, and efficiency offered by technology (Solnet et al., 2019). This topic explores the role of human touch as a vital component of value creation in service organizations and presents a sampling of scholarly work on finding the optimum balance between tech and touch.

Technology-driven changes to the service process are shifting the balance of responsibility from employees to customers and are rapidly becoming the norm in many industries. By substituting standardized technology for differential human touch is creating high levels of commoditization through digitization (Bolton et al., 2014). This movement away from human-generated service or "touch" is particularly stark in the realm of hospitality and related sectors relying on person-to-person interactions. Where well-trained and guest focused human interaction was once regarded as a source of competitive

How Contemporary Scholarship Addresses Service Management...   225

Table 1 Summary of topics

Topic	Key concepts	Clues from scholars
Humanizing the service experience	Customers' expectations of human touch in service experiences Finding the best balance between tech and touch to meet customer expectations Contexts create complexity	The study of hospitableness and its impact on customers Authenticity and emotional connection Changing role of service employees Social exchange theory
Contingent work and workers	Growing segment of the workforce Emerging challenges to workers and employers Recognizing and responding to the different needs of different types of contingent workers	Investment strategies Emerging work ecosystems Recruitment/inducements Inclusivity/culture to integrate contingent workers with full-time worker teams
Evolution from customer service to customer experience	Management theory historically based on product orientation Growth of the experience economy requires rethinking the definition of a "product" Social media/ease of sharing good or bad stories creates profound and immediate word of mouth	How to transform to be fully customer centered Merging physical, digital, and social realms Customer journey mapping Emotions and critical touchpoints
Managing diverse customer resources in the co-production of a service experience	Managerial challenges of co-producing customers Firms must design the role of the quasi employee customer as part in their service offering	Expanding co-production and value co-creation opportunities in experience design How to understand and utilize customer's resources and capabilities Training and motivating customers to successfully co-produce

advantage, technology solutions are rapidly eroding the roles of front-desk staff, airline check-in agents, service advisors, and many other frontline service roles. These changes are being viewed as mutually beneficial for both the organization (a strategy to reduce labor costs and human errors) and customers (by improving the efficiency of service delivery, reducing wait times and prices). This trend was accelerated by the COVID-19 imperative to physically separate customer-facing service personnel from customers and is likely to continue expanding significantly to change customer expectations in their service experience.

What Are Some Key Contributions from Scholarship?

While decreased human interaction in service may increase efficiency and lower costs, it may come at the expense of customer needs for social contact, warmth, and authenticity that can differentiate a service within a highly competitive environment. The trade-off between technology and human-driven service delivery has been effectively captured in several recent models (Bowen, 2016; Mody et al., 2019; Solnet et al., 2019). In general, these models point at the importance of both "touch" and "tech" in enhancing customer experiences, with each complementing or substituting for the other depending upon the simplicity/richness of the service-interface, customer expectations for interaction versus efficiency, organizational strategy or value-propositions, and human resource management (HRM) principles and practices aligned with the aims of balancing the trade-off of a simple economic transaction versus building long-term customer relationships with an organization's employees.

For over two decades, researchers (e.g., Brotherton, 1999; King, 1995) have been noting the importance of the *human exchange* in a service experience and how it translates into the sense of caring and building strong human relationships in providing hospitable behavior by customers or what is now termed "hospitableness". Defining hospitableness has led to research on how customers perceive this in a service interaction. Studies have been done on the importance of authentic smiles (Grandey et al., 2005), authentic caring behavior straight from the heart (Ariffin & Maghzi, 2012) as well as identifying specific behavioral aspects of what it means for employees to display hospitableness in the service experience. These include cultural sensitivity and non-discriminatory behavior (Ariffin & Maghzi, 2012; Ford & Heaton, 2001; Teng, 2011), nuances of verbal tone (Guerrier & Adib, 2000), warmth and courtesy (King, 1995), attentiveness and politeness (Prayag & Ryan, 2012), offering the generous feelings of friendship (Lashley, 2007), and employee authenticity (Yagil & Medler-Liraz, 2013).

Several researchers have sought to capture the concept by proposing measures of hospitableness. For example, Pijls et al.'s (2017) "Experience of Hospitality Scale" includes three factors that measure the customer's perception of the degree of hospitality provided by a service organization: inviting (open, inviting, freedom), care (servitude, empathy, and acknowledgment), and comfort (feeling at ease, relaxed, and comfortable). Solnet et al. (2019) developed a model to define four distinct service configurations describing the different ways technology and people can interact to create the human touch that co-creates value for guests and service organizations. Their model proposes a 2 X 2 with two axes—*a customer's preference for how the service is delivered* (i.e., human touch vs. technology)—and the type of organizational structure and strategy a firm might have (i.e., price and transaction vs. a relational orientation). This model and various other proposed configurations can help organizations' leaders and researchers to better understand how, when, and how much the human element should be included in the service experience versus technology.

Addressing the workforce changes in a world driven by technology and automation, Bowen (2016) proposed four changing roles for service employees, essentially arguing that service employees remain vital but that their roles will change as technology changes service delivery processes. Bowen's proposed new or enhanced roles for customer-facing service employees are "Innovators"; "Differentiators"; "Enablers"; and/or "Coordinators". Service employees are "innovators" because machines are still generally unable to do many tasks innately human (creative writing, interpreting readings, and exhibiting emotions). Service employees can be "differentiators" (and reduce commoditization of service) when their human interactions create "nonsubstitutable points of differentiation" (Bowen, 2016, p. 9). Employees can be "enablers" when their tasks include sensing customer difficulties in co-producing their service experiences and then intervening to help customers have the experience they expect and avoid or correct a service failure. Finally, employees can be a "coordinator" when someone needs to synchronize or organize the elements of complex service ecosystems by listening and responding to a customer who needs help in figuring out the best resolution for a co-production dilemma or a service delivery problem. While all of these roles may include technology, employees are still required to add the human touch as technology is not yet able to accommodate the unique variations in customer wants and behavior caused by the unique variations in individual customers. Until the technology evolves an employee must fill those gaps or risk the negative outcomes from a dissatisfied customer. Ultimately, technology is still unable to fully replace human workers, especially in contexts which are highly dependent on what only humans can offer—the human touch in the form of hospitable behaviors. Other researchers have entered the conversation about changing roles of service employees in a technology context. For example, Wünderlich et al. (2012), assessed user perceptions of smart technologies through smart interactive services (microchips, sensors, wearables) and highlighted the importance of the "service counterpart" (employee) in implementing technology solutions. Their work employed expert panels to assess likely trends, concluding that service organizations can benefit by emphasizing interpersonal and social aspects of the service experience by using human interactions to raise a social presence and enhance human trust.

Technology as a substitute or augmenter of the human touch in service will only continue to increase. The key question we seek to highlight in this chapter is how organizations determine the degree and intensity of human touch that meets their customers' expectation in the design of the service experience and to allocate co-producing tasks and resources accordingly. By better understanding the ways humans connect with each other, when and where customers expect that connection, the changing nature of the service employees' co-production tasks and responsibilities, and the competitive advantage that can be obtained through hospitable service, managers can identify ways to balance their customers' expectation for human touch with the advantages offered by the substitution of technology to capture that human touch derived competitive advantage in a growing market of technology-driven standardization.

The COVID-19 pandemic caused adaptations to customer expectations of human touch are likely to impact this balance into the future as customers have become accustomed to the increased substitution of technology for touch in the roles they play in co-producing their experiences. Customers have become accustomed to touchless transactions, the separation of employees behind plastic barriers, and curbside delivery. We predict that these new patterns of co-production will have a lasting impact on the types of human interactions customers expect and will speed up the substitution of technology for human touch. It is not so far-fetched to think of how a robot with emotional display capabilities will redefine the definition and delivery of hospitableness.

3 Contingent Work and Workers

What Is the Topic and Why Is it Important to Managers?

Contingent workers can be found in a variety of employment relationships and represent people with a wide variety of motivations for accepting part-time or contingent work (Feldman & Doerpinghaus, 1992). Connelly and

Gallagher (2004) define four categories of contingent workers by their organizational relationship. These are agency (those who work for an organization that provides workers to temporary jobs), direct hires (those who are hired for temporary work), contract (those who work under contract for a defined time), and seasonal (those who work for short periods of time). Since these four may not be mutually exclusive we instead categorize contingent workers on the basis of their reasons to be contingent. Thus, we suggest defining contingent workers into those that "must", "may", or "can" work on a contingent basis and review these further below with some implications for managers relevant to each. Those who "must" include those who have no other choice generally include two types of workers. The first includes those who perform low-skill jobs for which training cost and time are nominal (e.g., retail clerks and fast-food workers). Workers who do these jobs are generally young, unskilled, inexperienced, and otherwise unemployable but who are willing to trade low wages and temporary work for the opportunity to gain some income, training, and experience that will qualify them to enter into the world of work. The second type of "must" contingent workers are those who are looking for a permanent job because they must have income and seek contingent work until they find it (Bosmans et al., 2016).

The second category of contingent workers are those who "may" work but do not have an imperative to do so. These may include older, experienced, and often skilled people who choose to trade free time, usually in retirement, for the personal satisfaction (fun) of doing something with their time, the opportunity for having social interactions, and, frequently, extra income. Unpaid volunteers also fall into this category as does the high school student whose parents (or they themselves) think a job (like a grocery bagger or seasonal field hand) would be a good way to use their time for development and extra money.

The workers who are categorized into the "can" group are those who generally are in such high demand that they can forego permanent employment and are able to choose where, when, and on what they work. These include professionals and non-agency consultants who are ready, willing, and able to affiliate with an organization for a defined period of time to do a specific assignment that fits their expertise, on their own terms. Often web designers, IT professionals, accountants, trainers, consultants on specific topic areas, or other professionals who are in demand can elect to sell their services as contingent employees.

Organizations need to understand the motives behind their contingent employees to ensure they offer the array of inducements sought by the non-permanent part of their organization. Unless employing organizations offer the kinds of inducements contingent workers value, they risk failing to attract the number and quality of contingent employees required to deliver the quality service customers expect. Moreover, unless employing organizations also take the time and effort to integrate these contingent workers into the organization's culture, their ability to effectively collaborate and cooperate in any team efforts to represent the values defined by the service mission alongside permanent employees will be diminished.

What Are Some Key Contributions from Scholarship?

Companies need contingent employees for several reasons including accessing specific talents and kills, reducing costs incurred when hiring permanent employees (Boudreau et al., 2015; Cascio & Boudreau, 2015), and flexible staffing (e.g., staffing for temporary surges in demand). However, in contrast to the extensive literature on managing permanent employees, there is limited research on attracting, assimilating, motivating, and rewarding contingent workers and especially in regard to their varying motives for employment as contingent workers. We do point to two recent publications on this topic that provide insights into worker motivation (Subramony & Groth, n.d.; Subramony et al., 2018).

In regard to the first category of contingent workers, those that must work as contingent employees, there is little research from which to draw conclusions. While some study has been done on employing young, unskilled, inexperienced, and first time employees, the extent to which researchers have identified the best ways to manage, motivate, and reward these workers is limited (e.g., Jaworski et al., 2018). The general assumption by management, with rare exceptions, seems to be that these workers will not be around long enough to recover any money spent on job design, training, or career development. However, some organizations might offer prospective employees contingent work to evaluate fit before making a long-term commitment that would be harder to sever than it is for a part-time employee (Dahling et al., 2013). Likewise, the second group, those who "may" work on a contingent basis, has also not received much in the way of research investigations (e.g., Gascoigne & Kelliher, 2018). Generally, most assume that for those who may be enticed to apply their Knowledge, Skills, Abilities (KSAs) to an organization for a limited time, the willingness to work will be some combination of economic and psychic income that the employing organization must discover.

Research on the third category of those who "can" choose to work as contingent workers, especially as professionals, is more extensive than the first two groupings. This literature has identified rewards and incentives that are not only attractive for all employees but may be especially important for contingent professionals who are in such high demand that they can choose when, where, and on what to work. These include offering programs that enable talent mobility (Collings, 2014), work-life balance (Deery, 2008), onboarding and supervisory support (Kuvaas et al., 2014; Selden & Sowa, 2015), participating in talent pools (Seopa et al., 2015; Swailes & Blackburn, 2016) and the availability to participate in a learning culture (Kontoghiorghes, 2015). Herbert (2016), as an example, argues that organizations should enable contingent workers to explore work opportunities in different divisions or locations as an inducement to both join and stay by offering them opportunities to learn new capabilities. A related inducement that appears to be critical to retaining skilled contingent professionals is personalizing the conditions of employment (Deery & Jago, 2015; Dizaho et al., 2017). Providing breaks for childcare, stipends for carpoolers, choice of work laptop are a few examples of desirable inducements for both permanent and contingent professionals. The level of supervisor support for the contingent worker is very important in establishing a meaningful connection with the organization (Gentry et al., 2007).

Finally, as is also true for permanent employees, contingent workers seek to work in challenging jobs with talented workers as peers (Wilkin, 2013). Radford and Chapman (2015) found in their study that an organized and thoughtful onboarding process when supplemented by continuing supervisory support for career growth and development added to recognition for job accomplishments of contingent workers enhances their retention. Other strategies include creating talent pools that lead to a feeling of exclusivity by the contingent workers (Swailes & Blackburn, 2016) and giving contingent workers opportunities to learn and improve their skills (Schlechter et al., 2015).

Contingent professionals expect a higher quality of life resulting from the autonomy to decide how to do the job, freedom to choose their assignments and to work virtually from any location, and the flexibility to schedule their working hours and pace (King and Zaino, 2015). These findings support earlier findings that identified that inducements like training and development opportunities, competitive salary, and a supportive organizational environment are essential as part of a management strategy for contingent professionals (Wilkin, 2013). More recently, in a summary of his research study's findings Shabiyi (2019) suggests that the best inducements to offer contingent professionals to work for client-organizations are rewards with an emphasis on compensation and benefits, a recognition of work-life balance policies to allow autonomy and job flexibility, and organizational support for personal and career development.

Bringing contingent workers into a team of permanent employees does have challenges for the organization and its managers. The biggest downside for managers is to find ways to include the contingent professional in the organization's culture as much as possible. In many situations the full-time employees will be somewhat antagonistic to or jealous of the typically higher paid and less restrained "hired gun slingers" who bring extra talent and capacity to the workplace (Ashford et al., 2007; George & Chattopadhyay, 2017). Thus, managing contingent employees requires a greater sensitivity to concerns of both full-time and contingent employees and how they view each other. This downside can be especially challenging when the contingent workers are customer facing as these service delivery workers are the face of the organization to customers and unless extra effort is made to integrate these contingent employees into the service culture, there will be potential for a customer experience that fails to meet service standards. Getting buy in to the organization's brand promise by those who are not permanent representatives of the brand is a significant managerial challenge.

4 From Customer Service to Customer Experience

What Is the Topic and Why Is it Important to Managers?

In the late part of the twentieth century, writers argued that we had entered the next phase of economic evolution, termed the experience economy (Meyer & Schwager, 2007; Pine & Gilmore, 1998). In the experience economy rather than buying a birthday cake from the local bakery or making a cake at home using premixed ingredients, consumers now sought a full "birthday experience" at either a restaurant or a "fun creation" business (a fun park, themed restaurant, even at a McDonald's private room and playground). Thinking of providing customers with experiences means that nearly everything, in degrees, offered as a service should be viewed through an experiential lens by companies and organizations seeking to satisfy an ever greater level of customer expectations of an experience in their service transactions. To satisfy the growing expectations of increasingly informed customers requires radical thinking about and new understanding of how value is co-created.

In the experience economy, value is created through memories co-created during the full range of interactions across a customer's experience journey. Readers of this handbook will be familiar with the dozens of exemplar organizations who have prospered through their successful management of the customer experience. Ikea has transformed the idea of buying furniture into an experience, Apple's intuitive operation has created an experience that transformed the concept of a phone and generated nearly irrational loyalty by its users, Amazon's ease of online shopping and intelligent use of customer data transformed the retail business model, and Nespresso created a cult for home coffee drinking with its unique design and marketing strategy. While there are recurring debates about whether these firms have adopted an entirely new approach to their business model or rather just an advancement on earlier ideas such as overcoming Levitt's "marketing myopia" (Levitt, 1975) where he claimed that too many firms were guilty of looking inward at their products, rather than outward at their customer needs, there has been an unarguable explosion of academic and industry literature on radically new managerial practices necessary to put their customers' experiences and their end-to-end journey at the center of all decisions.

We predict experiences are likely to be even more important to the next generations of consumers, who will be less interested in "owning and collecting things" but more interested in investing in satisfying and memorable intangible experiences—such as live performances, travel, river rafting, sport, theater, educational opportunities—things which create meaning (and a selfie photo opportunity) and memories. While the continuing rise in disposable income across the world is an important driver of this change in customer expectations (what do you buy when you have all the "things" you want?), social media has accelerated it. People value posting or documenting their emotion-driven memories of joyful experiences when they share their accomplishments, mastery of learning or discovering, and something new about themselves or their world with friends. The move to offer or add "experiences" as the service product can be attributed to fundamental changes in how customers view transactions with organizations:

1. Customers no longer view a product or service as a free standing "thing" but as some integrated part of their ongoing life experiences.
2. As disposable income levels increase across the world, the next generation of consumers will expand their search for satisfaction beyond functional uses of their purchases to experiences that yield emotional connections.
3. Technology will continue to lower the barriers of time, capability, and cost between organization and customers—and between customer and customers—all of whom can communicate in "real time" as they co-produce experiences

4. The more "touchpoints" between an organization and its customers in the customer journey, the more opportunities to expand differentiating the service experience by focusing on unique resources to create competitive advantage.

Therefore, organizations must recast their view of the experience they offer to their customers, and the implications for every part of the organization, and realize that they create value from a comprehensive view of how customers think, feel, and act through an extended set of interactions, each of which can be of critical importance.

What Are Some Key Contributions from Scholarship?

Customer centricity—easy to say, hard to do. Customer centricity is a total organizational approach that focuses on the needs, wants, and resources of customers as the starting point of all organizational activities (Lamberti, 2013). Drucker (1954) predicted (correctly) that the balance of power in business would evolve from suppliers and manufacturers to the customer, driven by exponentially greater access of information and direct communications to consumers. Unfortunately, proclaiming customer-centered practices and actually doing so are two very different concepts, with continued research findings showing that few firms practice genuine customer centricity and those that do benefit from it (Inversini et al., 2020; Solnet & Kandampully, 2008). Shah and colleagues (Shah et al., 2006) developed a most instructive set of barriers to customer-centered practices as well as a set of pathways to overcome these barriers. These barriers include changing organizational culture so that leadership behaviors convey choices about how to spend time and other scarce resources (e.g., spending time with customers rather than reviewing financial reports); changing organizational structure to ensure that organizing by old style "product categories" does not prevent effective cross-department customer-centered collaborations; and changes in performance metrics to ensure that customer-centered elements are measured, rewarded, and given the right importance over more traditional metrics driven by financial returns and cost efficiencies. Perhaps the most extensive efforts to develop customer-centric organizations can be seen in the hospitality literature where Disney's "Guestology" is frequently mentioned as the basis for managing this exemplar of a customer-centric organization (Ford & Sturman, 2020). The implementation of customer centricity is often linked to the employee's belief and participation in an organization's culture and the hospitality literature offers strategies and practices that lead to customer-centric cultures (e.g., Ford et al., 2008).

Complexity and managerial implications of the customer experience approach. Customer experience has been conceptualized as a "multidimensional construct focusing on a customer's cognitive, emotional, behavioral, sensorial, and social responses to a firm's offerings during the customer's entire purchase journey" (Lemon & Verhoef, 2016, p. 71). Most definitions emphasize the importance of a customer's experience taking place across many points of contact and interactions, with growing explanations and complexities added to this relatively older field of study and practice. For example, Bolton et al. (2014) proposed specific challenges and even contrasts in their discussion of a customer journey by integrating digital, physical, and social realms that can lead to opposing strategic options that organizations must reconcile in order to assess customer journeys in different contexts and different conditions. Their research introduces growing technology-enabled services such as automated intelligence, automated social presence, and social robots in developing new thinking about customer experience. Customer experience reaches far beyond only marketing concerns. Homburg et al. (2015) emphasized firm-wide managerial implications of customer experience and the vital need to change culture, mindsets, strategic directions and innovations within firm capabilities.

Mapping the customer journey. Initially conceptualized from a marketing and operations perspective "blueprinting" (Shostack, 1984: Bitner et al., 2008;) is a close relative to the more commonly used customer journey map process (Følstad & Kvale, 2018; Lemon & Verhoef, 2016). Because services were often viewed as transactions, an experiential perspective requires much deeper and broader thinking about how the customer interacts with a service organization. Accordingly, the term touchpoints was developed and typically depicted horizontally on customer journey maps in accordance with a customer experience. These maps are often depicted into at least three separate periods, sometimes more—pre-service (calling, researching online), service (the service period refers to touchpoints that customers experience during an actual service [entering a parking lot, signage, engaging with employees, interacting with kiosks]), and post-service (posting to social media, an email incentive to return). Most firms today engage in some form of journey mapping and many use these maps as a foundation for decision-making within many areas of the business (strategy, operations, human resources, branding, etc.), and there are numerous reputable practical and scholarly guides to support the development of well-constructed customer journey maps (Edelman & Singer, 2015; Lemon & Verhoef, 2016; Rosenbaum et al., 2017)

5 Managing Diverse Customer Resources in the Co-production of a Service Experience

What Is the Topic and Why Is it Important to Managers?

Perhaps no topic is more discussed in discussions of present and future management practices than this one as organizations seek ways to substitute lower cost technology aided customer participation for employee interfaces in co-producing service experiences. Successfully doing this requires a careful balancing of customer expectations for employee involvement with the degree to which technology offers a viable substitute in service experiences (Solnet et al., 2019). These discussions range from the value of using simple telephone trees that direct callers to find their own desired party as substitutes for operators to the more complex AI applications that guide customers through financial transactions like investment management programs which substitute for an investment advisor (Paluch & Wirtz, 2020).

What Are Some Key Contributions from Scholarship?

Increasingly the trend has been to have customers, often with technological assistance, do for themselves what employees used to do for them to meet their service expectations (De Keyser et al., 2019: Xiao & Kumar, 2021; Wirtz, 2019). As the service dominant logic posits, both customers and companies co-create the value of a service by co-producing it (Ford et al., 2012; Prahalad & Ramaswamy, 2004). Both must bring tangible and intangible resources and capabilities to that experience in some quantity and quality for the co-creation of value to be successful (Lusch & Vargo, 2014). Some co-production experiences may require many customer and few company resources and some are just the opposite (Ford & McColl-Kennedy, 2015).

One important way in which customers can co-produce is to possess the required resources and capabilities designed into the expected role required of the customers while performing their part of the co-production experience and to be ready, willing, and able to use them (McColl-Kennedy et al., 2015: Jaakkola et al., 2015). This role can be simple or complex but the important thing here is that the service provider has designed the service with an expected role performance by the customer in the service co-production that applies that customer's resources in a predetermined way (Hilton et al., 2013).

Thus, organizations have two issues of concern. One is to design the service in a way that can properly align resource requirements between the company and the targeted customer. The issue is focused on the degree to which customers can and will perform their roles in co-production equal to what the organization has designed the experience to have them do (Bettencourt, 1997; Bowen, 1986; Ford & Bowen, 2004). The second issue is how can companies ensure the success of the service by preparing for variance in customers' willingness and capabilities to apply their own resources to perform the designed co-production roles (Ford & McColl-Kennedy, 2015).

This second issue requires the company to view the service as a totaled result of the combined resources of it and the customer (McColl-Kennedy et al., 2015). This view results from analyzing the possibility of a can/will-do versus the must-do gap in the performance of all the tasks required in delivering a service to a customer (Ford & McColl-Kennedy, 2015). If, for example, an online portal is designed to require a customer to fill out a form and follow directions then there must be some fail-safe process created to ensure that those customers who either can't or won't fill out the form might still get the service expected (Heidenreich et al., 2015). TurboTax, a self-service tax preparation service, has multiple fail safes built into it to ensure that the customers using it are double checked, provided additional information to clarify questions, or given access to a live person to avoid clicking out when encountering problems in the experience. Likewise, Disney World offers strollers, wheel chairs, and lockers to its arriving customers who forgot or didn't anticipate needing them until they saw how big the parks are. Organizations in this era of social media have become increasingly attentive to not only their targeted customers but even those outside the standard experience design as their complaining voices are increasingly echoed in the social media and the press (Maecker et al., 2016).

How to deal with this potential co-production gap can take one of two paths. The first is an experience design path where the organization simulates various ways customers can arrive unprepared in the co-production process to identify and prepare to fill those gaps before they happen (e.g., Chen et al., 2015). They can do this by studying customers, making a careful review of complaints and service failures to identify design flaws, researching best practices in both trade and academic journals, or creating an actual simulation of the experience. Disney simulated Epcot before it opened to plan its food service capacity and locations and discovered that its designers had not accurately predicted what guests would actually do when seeking food outlets (Ford & Dickson, 2009), By careful study of customers' actual behaviors, organizations can learn when they come unprepared, unequipped, unable, or untrained to perform their expected roles in co-production (Bateson, 2002). Thus, the organization can erect signage to guide them, offer equipment to supply whatever is missing, redesign the experience to correct problem areas, post employees at potential fail points, or offer a customer training process to ensure they know what they are supposed to do (Ford & Sturman, 2020).

The second path is to focus on customer willingness to apply their resources and capabilities to the co-production role (Handrich & Heidenreich, 2013). By studying customers the company can identify what motivates them to do what they need to do to ensure successful co-production. This path incorporates promoting customer self-efficacy, clarifying the co-production role, providing rewards that motivate role-related behaviors, and goal-setting.

There are several ways to induce customer willingness. One way for a company to get a customer to perform a required role in co-production is to build self-efficacy (Ford & Dickson, 2012). Some customers don't believe they can perform what is required of them, that their resources are adequate or their capabilities sufficient. Promoting customers' self-efficacy will, consequently, increase the likelihood that customers will perform the requisite co-production role. Self-efficacy is a person's belief in his or her ability to succeed in a particular situation and that belief will either motivate the customer to perform or not. There are strategies a company can employ to promote self-efficacy such as enactive mastery (e.g., setting a goal of improving on past successes, employee encouragement, self-talk imagery, success levels in gaming), vicarious experience (e.g., modeling success by others), verbal persuasion (e.g., friends and peers encouragement, self-talk encouragement, computer generated feedback), and physiological arousal (e.g., cheering, rousing music). These can include training employees to be encouraging when seeing a customer showing doubt, providing video screens that show other customers enjoying the experience, or displaying inspiring slogans and getting other customers to cheer. All these strategies are designed to boost the customer's confidence in successfully performing the tasks required in co-producing the experience (Ford & Dickson, 2012).

A second way to induce customer willingness is to assure the customers that if they perform the requisite co-production roles appropriately, then the experience will match their expectations (Bendapudi & Leone, 2003). Since the customer had a reason to seek out a service provider, then organizations can make it clear that if the customer performs the co-production role successfully, the customer will get whatever it was that was sought. The more important the reason or the greater the benefit, the more willing the customer should be to exert effort. Fulfilling a need or achieving a goal is motivating. Some customers are motivated to participate because of the benefits in time and money saved for taking on larger roles in co-production. Self-check in at hotels, buying take out at restaurants, or carrying their own bags saves customers time and money (Meuter et al., 2000). Others are motivated by their personalities or their familiarity with the experience being offered, or they are simply looking for something to do while waiting for the other parts of the customer experience to take place. Some people also think they are able to do a better job of producing the desired service than an employee. Distinguishing when, where, and how much the customer should or should not be involved in any specific part of the overall customer experience depends on a customer-driven factors that management should identify and address as they vary by customers' capabilities and motivations.

The company also has to assess its costs and benefits as it designs the roles it expects customers to play in co-production along with identifying the resources and capabilities required to perform those roles (Ford & Sturman, 2020; Lovelock & Young, 1979; Mustak et al., 2016). Co-production is in the organization's interest when it can save money, increase production efficiency, or differentiate its service from that of competitors in a key way.

Organizations that see mutual benefits to co-production and try to encourage it must always have a backup plan to accommodate the fact that some customers will and some customers won't want to (or are unable to) participate. Those organizations that find ways of enabling customers to participate as much as possible in co-producing their own experiences will, however, decrease their costs and increase the value and quality of the service for those customers.

6 Conclusion to Chapter

If you asked any two scholars to identify the most important future trends in service management, you will get many options. We started with 22 and after much debate settled on the four which we included in this short space. We readily acknowledge that there are many others that have equal claim on inclusion. The issues of sustainability, over tourism, and transformative service for example are major discussions in the literature. The areas covered in this chapter and those which were not all contain countless questions and the need for future research. For example, the merger of human resource management and service management must collectively enhance our understanding of face the emerging dilemma of how to find entry level workers for increasingly sophisticated entry jobs. Similarly, the challenge of preparing people to ascend a corporate ladder that requires mastery of jobs that are increasingly computer assisted means a whole new level of training and selection requirements that most companies and employees are unprepared to meet. On the customer side, the post-COVID era may see customers seeking facilities that have more space between customers than most currently available locations offer. Also, will customers now used to videoconferencing seek to avoid distant travel to meetings and conventions or even local travel to offices and shopping malls. Our point is simple. There will be more changes for both service organizations and their customers and an endless need for further research into these vital questions.

References

Ariffin, A. A. M., & Maghzi, A. (2012). A preliminary study on customer expectations of hotel hospitality: Influences of personal and hotel factors. *International Journal of Hospitality Management, 31*(1), 191–198.

Ashford, S. J., George, E., & Blatt, R. (2007). 2 old assumptions, new work: The opportunities and challenges of research on nonstandard employment. *Academy of Management Annals., 1*(1), 65–117.

Bateson, J. (2002). Are your customers good enough for your service business? *Academy of Management Perspectives., 16*(4), 110–120.

Bendapudi, N., & Leone, R. P. (2003). Psychological implications of customer participation in co-production. *Journal of Marketing, 67*(1), 14–28.

Bettencourt, L. A. (1997). Customer voluntary performance: Customers as partners in service delivery. *Journal of Retailing, 73*, 383–406.

Bitner, M. J., Ostrom, A. L., & Morgan, F. N. (2008). Service blueprinting: A practical technique for service innovation. *California Management Review, 50*(3), 66–94.

Bolton, R. N., Gustafsson, A., McColl-Kennedy, J., Sirianni, N. J., & Tse, D. K. (2014). Small details that make big differences: A radical approach to consumption experience as a firm's differentiating strategy. *Journal of Service Management, 25*(2), 253–274.

Bosmans, K., Hardonk, S., De Cuyper, N., & Vanroelen, C. (2016). Explaining the relation between precarious employment and mental well-being. A qualitative study among temporary agency workers. work. 249-264.

Boudreau, J. W., Creelman, D., & Jesuthasan, R. (2015). *Lead the work: Navigating a world beyond employment*. John Wiley & Sons.

Bowen, D. E. (1986). Managing customers as human resources in service organizations. *Human Resource Management, 25*, 371–383.

Bowen, D. E. (2016). The changing role of employees in service theory and practice: An interdisciplinary view. *Human Resource Management Review, 26*(1), 4–13.

Brotherton, B. (1999). Towards a definitive view of the nature of hospitality and hospitality management. *International Journal of Contemporary Hospitality Management., 11*(4), 165–173.

Cascio, W. F., & Boudreau, J. (2015). *Talent management of nonstandard employees.* Center for Effective Organizations.

Chen, S. C., Raab, C., & Tanford, S. (2015). Antecedents of mandatory customer participation in service encounters: An empirical study. *International Journal of Hospitality Management, 46*, 65–75.

Collings, D. G. (2014). Toward mature talent management: Beyond shareholder value. *Human Resource Development Quarterly, 25*, 301–319.

Connelly, C. E., & Gallagher, D. G. (2004). Emerging trends in contingent work research. *Journal of Management., 30*(6), 959–983.

Dahling, J. J., Winik, L., Schoepfer, R., & Chau, S. (2013). Evaluating contingent workers as a recruitment source for full-time positions. *International Journal of Selection and Assessment, 21*(2), 222–225.

De Keyser, A., Köcher, S., Alkire, L., Verbeeck, C., & Kandampully, J. (2019). Frontline service technology infusion: Conceptual archetypes and future research directions. *Journal of Service Management, 30*(1), 156–183.

Deery, M., & Jago, L. (2015). Revisiting talent management, work-life balance and retention strategies. *International Journal of Contemporary Hospitality Management, 27*(3), 453–472.

Deery, M. (2008). Talent management, work-life balance and retention strategies. *International Journal of Contemporary Hospitality Management, 20*, 792–806.

Dizaho, E. K., Salleh, R., & Abdullah, A. (2017). Achieving work-life balance through flexible work schedules and arrangements. *Global Business & Management Research, 9*(1), 455–465.

Drucker, P. F. (1954). *The practice of management.* HarperCollins.

Edelman, D. C., & Singer, M. (2015). Competing on customer journeys. *Harvard Business Review, 2015*(November), 1.

Feldman, D. C., & Doerpinghaus, H. I. (1992). Patterns of part-time employment. *Journal of Vocational Behavior, 41*(3), 282–294.

Følstad, A., & Kvale, K. (2018). Customer journeys: A systematic literature review. *Journal of Service Theory and Practice., 28*(2), 196–227.

Ford, R. C., & Bowen, J. T. (2004). Getting guests to work for you. *Journal of Foodservice Business Research, 6*(3), 37–53.

Ford, R. C., Edvardsson, B., Dickson, D., & Enquist, B. (2012). Managing the innovation co-creation challenge. *Organizational Dynamics, 4*(41), 281–290.

Ford, R. C., Wilderom, C. P. M., & Caparella, J. (2008). Strategically crafting a customer-focused culture: An inductive case study. *Journal of Strategy and Management, 1*(2), 143–167.

Ford, R. C., & Dickson, D. R. (2009). The father of guestology: An interview with Bruce Laval. *Journal of Applied Management & Entrepreneurship, 12*(2), 80–99.

Ford, R. C., & Dickson, D. R. (2012). Enhancing customer self-efficacy in co-producing service experiences. *Business Horizons, 55*(2), 179–188.

Ford, R. C., & Heaton, C. P. (2001). Lessons from hospitality that can serve anyone. *Organizational Dynamics, 30*(1), 30–47.

Ford, R. C., & McColl-Kennedy, J. R. (2015). Organizational strategies for filling the customer can-do/must-do gap. *Business Horizons, 58,* 499–468.

Ford, R. C., & Sturman, M. C. (2020). *Managing Hospitality Organizations* (2nd ed.). Sage.

Gascoigne, C., & Kelliher, C. (2018). The transition to part-time: How professionals negotiate 'reduced time and workload' i-deals and craft their jobs. *Human Relations, 71*(1), 103–125.

Gentry, W. A., Kuhnert, K. W., Mondore, S. P., & Page, E. E. (2007). The influence of supervisory-support climate and unemployment rate on part-time employee retention: A multilevel analysis. *Journal of Management Development, 26*(10), 1005–1022.

George, E., & Chattopadhyay, P. (2017). *Understanding nonstandard work arrangements: Using research to inform practice. SHRM-SIOP Science of HR Series.* University of Auckland.

Grandey, A. A., Fisk, G. M., Mattila, A. S., Jansen, K. J., & Sideman, L. A. (2005). Is 'service with a smile' enough? Authenticity of positive displays during service encounters. *Organizational Behavior and Human Decision Processes., 96*(1), 38–55.

Guerrier, Y., & Adib, A. S. (2000). 'No, we don't provide that service': The harassment of hotel employees by customers. *Work, Employment and Society, 4*(14), 689–705.

Handrich, M., & Heidenreich, S. (2013). The willingness of a customer to co-create innovative, technology-based services: Conceptualisation and measurement. *International Journal of Innovation Management, 17*(04), 1350011.

Heidenreich, S., Wittkowski, K., Handrich, M., & Falk, T. (2015). The dark side of customer co-creation: Exploring the consequences of failed co-created services. *Journal of the Academy of Marketing Science., 43*(3), 279–296.

Herbert, B. (2016). Moving employee talent: Key to competitive edge. *Strategic HR Review, 15*(2), 65–69.

Hilton, T., Hughes, T., Little, E., & Marandi, E. (2013). Adopting self-service technology to do more with less. *Journal of Services Marketing, 27*(1), 3–12.

Homburg, C., Jozić, D., & Kuehnl, C. (2015). Customer experience management: Toward implementing an evolving marketing concept. *Journal of the Academy of Marketing Science, 45,* 377–401.

Inversini, A., De Carlo, M., & Masiero, L. (2020). The effects of customer-centricity in hospitality. *International Journal of Hospitality Management, 86,* 102436.

Jaakkola, E., Helkkula, A., Aarikka-Stenroos, L., & Verleye, K. (2015). The co-creation experience from the customer perspective: Its measurement and determinants. *Journal of Service Management., 26*(2), 321–342.

Jaworski, C., Ravichandran, S., Karpinski, A. C., & Singh, S. (2018). The effects of training satisfaction, employee benefits, and incentives on part-time employees' commitment. *International Journal of Hospitality Management, 74,* 1–12.

King, C. A. (1995). What is hospitality? *International Journal of Hospitality Management, 14*(3), 219–234.

Kontoghiorghes, C. (2015). Linking high performance organizational culture and talent management: Satisfaction/motivation and organizational commitment as mediators. *The International Journal of Human Resource Management, 27*, 1–21.

Kuvaas, B., Dysvik, A., & Buch, R. (2014). Antecedents and employee outcomes of line managers' perceptions of enabling HR practices. *Journal of Management Studies, 51*(6), 845–868.

Lamberti, L. (2013). Customer centricity: The construct and the operational antecedents. *Journal of Strategic Marketing, 21*(7), 588–612.

Lashley, C. (2007). Studying hospitality: Beyond the envelope. *International Journal of Culture, Tourism and Hospitality Research, 1*(3), 185–188.

Lemon, K. N., & Verhoef, P. C. (2016). Understanding customer experience throughout the customer journey. *Journal of Marketing, 80*(6), 69–96.

Levitt, T. (1975). Marketing myopia. *Harvard Business Review, 53*(5), 26–183.

Lovelock, C. H., & Young, R. F. (1979). Look to consumers to increase productivity. *Harvard Business Review, 57*(3), 168–178.

Lusch, R. L., & Vargo, S. L. (2014). *The service-dominant logic of marketing: Dialog, debate, and directions.* Routledge.

Maecker, O., Barrot, C., & Becker, J. U. (2016). The effect of social media interactions on customer relationship management. *Business Research, 9*(1), 133–155.

Meuter, M. L., Ostrom, A. L., Roundtree, R. I., & Bitner, M. J. (2000). Self-service technologies: Understanding customer satisfaction with technology-based service encounters. *Journal of Marketing, 64*(3), 50–64.

Meyer, C., & Schwager, A. (2007). Understanding customer experience. Harvard Business Review (February), 117-126.

Mody, M., Suess, C., & Lehto, X. (2019). Going back to its roots: Can hospitableness provide hotels competitive advantage over the sharing economy? *International Journal of Hospitality Management, 76*(Part A), 286–298.

Mustak, M., Jaakkola, E., Halinen, A., & Kaartemo, V. (2016). Customer participation management: Developing a comprehensive framework and a research agenda. *Journal of Service Management, 27*(3), 250–275.

Paluch, S., & Wirtz, J. (2020). Artificial intelligence and robots in the service encounter. *Journal of Service Management Research, 4*(1), 3–8.

Pijls, R., Groen, B. H., Galetzka, M., & Pruyn, A. T. H. (2017). Measuring the experience of hospitality: Scale development and validation. *International Journal of Hospitality Management, 67*, 125–133.

Pine, B., & Gilmore, J. (1998). Welcome to the experience economy. Harvard Business Review, July-August: 97-106.

Prahalad, C. K., & Ramaswamy, V. (2004). Co-creation experiences: The next practice in value creation. *Journal of Interactive Marketing, 18*(13), 5–14.

Prayag, G., & Ryan, C. (2012). Visitor interactions with hotel employees: The role of nationality. *International Journal of Culture, Tourism and Hospitality Research., 6*(2), 173–185.

Radford, K., & Chapman, G. (2015). Are all workers influenced to stay by similar factors or should different retention strategies be implemented? Comparing younger and older aged-care workers in Australia. *Australian Bulletin of Labour, 41*(1), 58–81.

Rosenbaum, M. S., Otalora, M. L., & Ramírez, G. C. (2017). How to create a realistic customer journey map. *Business Horizons, 60*(1), 143–150. https://doi.org/10.1016/j.bushor.2016.09.010

Schlechter, A., Thompson, N. C., & Bussin, M. (2015). Attractiveness of non-financial rewards for prospective knowledge workers: An experimental investigation. *Employee Relations., 37*(3), 274–295.

Selden, S., & Sowa, J. (2015). Voluntary turnover in nonprofit human service organizations: The impact of high performance work practices. *Human Service Organizations Management, Leadership & Governance, 39*, 1–26.

Seopa, N., Wocke, A., & Leeds, C. (2015). The Impact on the psychological contract of differentiating employees into talent pools. *Career Development International, 20*(7), 717–732.

Shabiyi, A. O. (2019). Retaining Contingent Professionals: Identifying the Inducements that Fulfill Psychological Contract Expectations. Unpublished Doctoral Dissertation. Winter Park FL: Rollins College.

Shah, D., Rust, R., Parasuraman, A., Staelin, R., & Day, G. (2006). The path to customer centricity. *Journal of Service Research, 9*(2), 113–124.

Shostack, G. L. (1984). Designing services that deliver. *Harvard Business Review, 62*(1), 133–139.

Solnet, D., & Kandampully, J. (2008). How some service firms have become part of "service excellence" folklore: An exploratory study. *Managing Service Quality, 18*(2), 179–193.

Solnet, D., Subramony, M., Ford, R. C., Golubovskaya, M., Kang, H. J. A., & Hancer, M. (2019). Leveraging human touch in service interactions: Lessons from hospitality. *Journal of Service Management., 30*(3), 392–409.

Subramony, M., & Groth, M. (n.d.). Enacting service work in a changing world: Time for a dialogue. *Journal of Service Research, 0*(0), 1094670521989452. https://doi.org/10.1177/1094670521989452

Subramony, M., Solnet, D., Groth, M., Yagil, D., Hartley, N., Beomcheol Kim, P., & Golubovskaya, M. (2018). Service work in 2050: Toward a work ecosystems perspective. *Journal of Service Management, 29*(4), 956–974.

Swailes, S., & Blackburn, M. (2016). Employee reactions to talent pool membership. *Employee Relations, 38*(1), 112–128.

Teng, C.-C. (2011). Commercial hospitality in restaurants and tourist accommodation: perspectives. *International Journal of Hospitality Management, 30*(4), 866–874.

Wilkin, C. L. (2013). I can't get no job satisfaction: Meta-analysis comparing permanent and contingent workers. *Journal of Organizational Behavior, 34*(1), 47–64.

Wirtz, J. (2019). Organizational ambidexterity: Cost-effective service excellence, service robots, and artificial intelligence. *Organizational Dynamics, 49*(3), 1–9.

Wirtz, J., Patterson, P. G., Kunz, W. H., Gruber, T., Lu, V. N., Paluch, S., & Martins, A. (2018). Brave new world: Service robots in the frontline. *Journal of Service Management, 29*(5), 907–931.

Wünderlich, N. V., Wangenheim, F. v., & Bitner, M. J. (2012). High tech and high touch. *Journal of Service Research, 16*(1), 3–20. https://doi.org/10.1177/1094670512448413

Xiao, L., & Kumar, V. (2021). Robotics for customer service: A useful complement or an ultimate substitute? *Journal of Service Research, 24*(1), 9–29.

Yagil, D., & Medler-Liraz, H. (2013). Moments of truth: Examining transient authenticity and identity in service encounters. *Academy of Management Journal, 56*(2), 473–497.

Contract Innovation: Driving Scale and Scope of Nonownership Value Propositions—Chapter Description

Michael Ehret and Jochen Wirtz

1 Chapter Description

Nonownership value, delivering benefits without transferring the burdens of ownership, is a key pillar of service value propositions. To date, service research and management have put their attention primarily on the value that emerges when clients substitute ownership of assets, like vehicles, facilities or factories, with nonownership services, like rides, accommodation bookings or manufacturing orders. Currently scale and scope of nonownership services is growing at a breathtaking scale, connecting potentially any device or resource to the global information infrastructure. Once an asset is connected to global information infrastructures, it is transformed into a platform for service delivery, like renting, sharing or even performance outcomes. Not least, public communication infrastructure removes traditional barriers to scales of service contracts. In this chapter we argue that contract innovation provides the key to the extension of scale and scope of services. We hold that contracting competency, defined as the capabilities to translate customer needs into service specifications for governing effective service demand, define the current

---

M. Ehret (✉)
University of Graz, Graz, Austria
e-mail: michael.ehret@uni-graz.at

J. Wirtz
NUS Business School, National University of Singapore, Kent Ridge, Singapore
e-mail: jochen@nus.edu.sg

© The Author(s), under exclusive license to Springer Nature Switzerland AG 2022
B. Edvardsson, B. Tronvoll (eds.), *The Palgrave Handbook of Service Management*,
https://doi.org/10.1007/978-3-030-91828-6_13

frontiers of service growth. We identify three key dimensions of contracting capabilities: Contract design capabilities reside on the ability of service actors to translate client needs into specifications of effective service demand. Contract design capabilities entail identifying the potential of existing technology for improving service specifications, such as rental terms, problem definitions or pricing capabilities. Contract innovations have been opening up novel dimensions for service demand in virtually any industry, pioneered by internet advertising, and continuously removing barriers and costs delimiting scope and scale of service contracting. Over time, service providers have employed these technologies for client-driven learning, enabling their capabilities to configure attractive and effective service contracts. Second, we offer a systematic overview of fundamental technological innovations enabling contract innovations. In particular, hardware innovations connect human and physical resources to information infrastructures, facilitating both the specification of contracts on resource use and their seamless integration into effective service processes for contract fulfillment. Hardware innovations connect a growing range of devices, facilities and equipment to service systems, facilitating the specification of asset-based services. The software dimension entails the user-interface to service systems. With almost ubiquitous access to mobile networks, mobile applications constitute general information interfaces and provide genuine interfaces for orchestrating service contracting with operations for fulfillment. Not least, innovations in infrastructures have worked as disruptive forces furnishing service growth, opening industries like financial services, industrial manufacturing or agriculture for novel forms of disruptive services. We offer a primer on research opportunities and management implications on the path to unlock service growth with enhanced contracting capabilities. We conclude stating that service firms thrive as contract innovators furnishing service productivity, transforming industrial forms of capitalism into service capitalism.

2 Introduction: The Role of Contract Innovation in Driving the Growth of Service Businesses

Nonownership value, delivering benefits without transferring the burdens of ownership, is a key pillar of service value propositions. Service management and theory have put their attention on substituting ownership with services (Chesbrough, 2011; Ehret & Wirtz, 2010; Lovelock & Gummesson, 2004):

A taxi hire contract offers partial relieve from a perceived need to own and operate a car, at least for the duration of that particular trip. In recent years, nonownership options in transportation and virtually any service industry have been proliferating. Besides taxi hires, clients find a growing range of contracts including rental agreements, car sharing booking, free-floating car hires, ride-haling, robo-taxi hire, taxi-pooling services, mileage-billed car-shares and many more (see Chesbrough, 2011).

This is no coincidence. The diffusion of the internet, the prospect of almost ubiquitous Information and Communication Technology (ICT) connectivity of service resources along with institutional and organizational innovations collapses into a stream of contracting innovations (Varian, 2010; Zuboff, 2019). Without internet connections and remote controls for unlocking cars, contract innovations like free-floating car hires or ride-hailing would be prohibitive expensive if not impossible. With the global diffusion of the internet and vibrant innovation in components like sensors or actuators, almost any potential resource, such as vehicles, facilities or manufacturing equipment, can be transformed into a bundle of service contracts, such as transportation trips, accommodation or manufacturing orders, on an almost global scale (Ehret & Wirtz, 2017). Contracting innovations push the boundaries of service economies, extending the range of services available to clients and offering opportunities for those companies who design, implement and realize contracting innovations.

While almost any industry offers opportunities for contract innovations, companies make mixed experiences. In the case of transportation, mobility platforms like Uber or Didi, or office sharing platform WeWork still struggle to turn innovations on ride-contracts toward financial viability (Economist, 2019). However, in the B2B transportation services, contract innovations have been proven and matured in business markets. For example, Mercedes-Benz service subsidiary "Charterway" offers almost any imaginable contract for truck-related services, including managing entire fleets of trucks, operating a particular transportation trip by using a truck and a hired driver, and leasing or financial services associated for companies who aim at the status of truck owners or proprietors (Semple, 2004). Not least, contract innovations have extended service markets way beyond the transformation of assets into nonownership services. The most significant examples are mobile super-apps like WeChat that offer an almost universal mobile service interface for Chinese service users, thereby increasing ease of contracting and service delivery (Economist, 2016).

In this chapter we elaborate a framework, with the aim to stimulate systematic research and management approaches for contract innovation. We build on the economic function of the service contract, by translating client requirements into key specifications of a service and an agreement of the rights responsibilities of providers and clients in service cocreation (Hodgson, 2015, pp. 111–115; Varian, 2010). Virtually any commercially offered service builds at least on an implicit contractual agreement on service terms. With technology advances connecting a growing range of resources and people by communication networks on a global scale, technological capabilities for specifying service contracts have been proliferating. We start our investigation with the key role of contracts in translating customers' demand into service specifications and the role of information technology of extending contracting capabilities and capacities of service actors. Service contracting is a core competency of virtually any service provider that conditions the capability of a provider to translate customer needs into effective service demand and meet contractual promises with sufficient quality and profitable. Under any given technological regime, service companies progress by extending their capabilities to translate service demand into contracts for effective service delivery. However, identifying and realizing the contract innovation potential of existing technologies is far from trivial, usually resulting from experimentation and business failures. Thus, we begin our investigation by looking at pioneering innovations that unveiled the potential by digital contracting. Against this background, we take a closer look at the technological development that is currently extending the frontier of contracting capabilities. Not least, innovations in information infrastructures, software and social networking constitute service ecosystems offer a context that facilitates contract innovations. Building on our contract innovation framework, we discuss major implications for management and research for capturing the opportunities of contract innovations.

3 The Drivers of Contract Innovations

The Architecture of Contract Innovations

Economic theory and service research hold that service companies create nonownership value by relieving their clients from the burden ownership. In the case of asset-based services, a nonownership contract transforms an asset, such as a vehicle, a facility or an industrial factory, into a bundle of services, such as rides, accommodation bookings or manufacturing orders (Chesbrough, 2011; Ehret & Wirtz, 2010; Zuboff, 2019). Thus, virtually any service business builds on the capability to identify customer needs and translate these into specification of services (see Fig. 1). Regardless of the state of

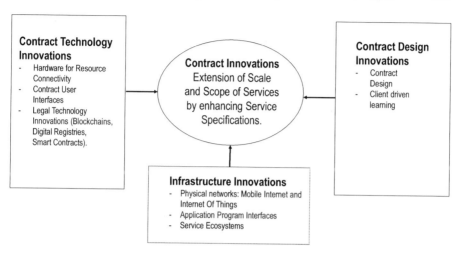

Fig. 1 The architecture of contract innovations

technologies, service businesses need to identify the most effective and profitable services that meet their clients' needs. Recent history shows that contract innovations reside on user-driven innovations, where companies employ existing technologies for enhancing their contracting capabilities (Zuboff, 2019). Regardless of the state of technology, contracting resides on the effective use of existing legal frameworks and technical tools. The case of Google, the pioneer of digital contracts, shows that contracting innovation resides on exploration with technologies that have been existing for considerable time (Varian, 2010; Zuboff, 2019). Over time, the use of contract innovations proves through its effectiveness in specifying services. That not withholding, technological innovation in contracting is thriving and pushes the boundaries of service contracting. Not least, innovations in infrastructure, such as communication networks, Application Program Interfaces (APIs) and the emergence of service ecosystems, furnish contracting capabilities. We take a closer look at innovation in contract design, contract technology and contract infrastructures in the following sub-sections.

Contract Design Innovations and Client-Driven Learning

While current contract innovations build on a technology push from advancements in ICT, contracting inventions tend to build on technologies that have been existing for considerate time. The pioneering act that paved the ways for digital contract innovation was Google's move to offer advertising placements on internet search (Varian, 2010; Wirtz, 2016; Zuboff, 2019). In conventional media businesses, publishers aim to attract advertisers with segmenting macro-profiles of prospective media-audiences, hoping to justify advertising prices by expected media-consumption and eventual buying behavior of recipients. Regardless of attractiveness of media and ingenuity of advertising design, advertising companies remained left wondering which half of their budget was wasted. Google's advertising business turns the conventional advertising business on its head, starting the contracting process for advertisements with evident user behavior. Google's Adsense service auctions advertising space around user search entries. Thus, advertisers judge and buy advertisement space based on evident user behavior (Wirtz, 2016).

Google's advertising business revealed the path to a far more significant business impact than the change of an individual business model: By moving from mere search behavior to "User Profile Information", Google paved the way for data-driven learning on customer behavior, empowering the company to understand and eventually predict user behavior. Key pillars of data-driven customer learning are the systematic capturing of behavioral data, such as internet queries, electronic transactions and any other accessible trace of user behavior, in order to connect this with contextual data and analytical methods. Google's analytics of behavioral user-data paved the way for the adoption of machine-learning approaches for constructing internet business models. The halo-moment of Google's analytical team was the discovery of what pushed the query "Carol Brady's maiden name" to the top of its search rankings. It turned out that the broadcast "Who wants to be a Millionaire" pushed the queries (Zuboff, 2019: 1365): Subsequent waves of related internet searchers followed exactly the path of the broadcasting schedule along the US timezones, revealing the potential of internet-user data to furnish behavioral predictions (Zuboff, 2019: 1365).

With the exponential growth of internet usage and its extension to geo-information systems, connected devices and machines, data are becoming the raw material for digital contracts. Furnished by ease of access to behavioral data, companies get improved insights into user behavior empowering to customize contracts based on evident specification and pricing information (Agrawal et al., 2018).

Data-driven learning is transforming the conditions of service contracting in virtually any service industry. Capacity restricted service businesses like transportation or accommodation are particular pertinent service domains for contract innovation (Lovelock & Wirtz, 2016). Like in advertising space on media, service capacity providers navigate a thin line between idle capacity due to low demand or crowding out of profitable clients by over use of capacity and potential ill-adjustment to the financial value of services. In fact, long before the advent of commercial internet use, some industries like aviation acted as contract innovators. The SABRE booking system pioneered the use of IT for service contracting by empowering airlines to build up revenue management capabilities, for example, furnishing aggressive pricing for low-demand situations and reserving capacity for high-value clients in high-demand situations (Wirtz & Lovelock, 2016). The advent of the internet technologies opened a new dimension, as global connectivity and open IT standards opened novel gateways for customer-driven contracting. Combining customer information with an ever-growing range of contextual data and analytical capabilities has been empowering the contracting capabilities of companies in transportation-related industries.

Building on internet connectivity, sharing businesses have opened a new dimension of contracting innovation by attracting and orchestrating service capacity with service demand. Sharing companies, like airbnb, Uber, DiDi or WeWork, innovate service contracting configuring business opportunities for owners of service capacity and match them with potential clients (Iansiti & Lakhani, 2020). While internet technologies provide the technical platform, the contract innovation of matching latent client needs with idle capacity has put the potential to effective use. As a result, contract innovators have been activating idle capacity and met new dimensions of latent service demand.

Contract Technology Innovation

ITC constitute the basic technology underlying contract innovation. With growing scale and scope of ITC, costs of specifying service contracts drop exogenously, enhancing the capabilities of service providers to translate latent customer needs into effective service demand. Contracting technology entails three decisive dimensions: Hardware capabilities that furnish the service system to capture, store, analyze and share data for the specification of service contracts. On the software dimension, providers use data and code to automate service contracting and subsequent service operations management. Last but not least, contracting has become a genuine domain of innovation, with systematic development of technologies for smart contracting and blockchains.

1. Hardware Capabilities of Contracting. Technology incorporates capacities and capabilities for contract processing. Internet clouds constitute a significant technology base, building a data-repository for the global capture, sharing and use of data for specifying service contracts and managing of service operations. Amazon Web Services (AWS) pioneered the link of

cloud-storage of internet-user data and its link to machine learning and Artificial Intelligence, enhancing the capacity and capabilities of data-driven learning (Iansiti & Lakhani, pp. 89–96), as described in the contract design section. Cloud-computing, connected by global communication networks, provides the physical platform capturing, analyzing and sharing data on a global scale. In the case of Amazon, the key motivation resulted from the increased complexity the electronic retailer experienced with the gradual broadening of its assortment, which started with books and gradually included virtually any tradable retail item. At the user-end enhanced sharing of data empowers the capability to customize contracts, based on user profiles and recommendation systems, furnished by the use of machine learning and Artificial Intelligence. Upstream, joint use of cloud-computing eases the use of contract-data with Amazon-connected suppliers and delivery complementors. Not least, cloud-computing works as the physical backbone for Artificial Intelligence use by AWS customers like NASA and Pinterest.

2. Contracting Software and Payment Innovations. With the almost global diffusion of mobile internet services, mobile software applications have become the standard information interface for virtually any service, ranging from retailing, banking to transportation, health, legal, public services, business services and many more. The most significant development is the rise of super-apps like WeChat (Economist, 2016). WeChat connects a mobile payment service with a messaging app. In its Chinese homeland, WeChat has become the contracting-conduit for virtually any tradable service, ranging from retailing, transportation to business services. Mobile payments and their implementation in apps work as disruptive contracting innovations, moving the interface of contracting to the fingertips of clients. Mobile payments and their integration in super-apps like WeChat, Alipay or MercadoLibre find fertile ground in emerging economies, where conventional infrastructures for financial services are under-developed if not entirely missing. Mobile payment services enable to "bank the unbanked" and offer links for long-time disconnected populations to banking and an ever-growing range of services connected to mobile payments. As methods and terms of payment are key components of virtually any service, mobile apps and payment systems show disruptive innovation potential for service contracting.

3. Genuine Contract System Innovations: Blockchains and Smart Contracts. Contracting has been evolving into a genuine innovation domain on its own, witness the rise of blockchain and smart contracting approaches (Pistor, 2019). Blockchains mark the most radical idea. Cyber-Utopians

answer the question "whether digital code has the capacity to replace law" (Pistor, 2019: 3355) bluntly stating that digital "code is law" (Lessig, 2008). One particular cyber-libertarian scenario builds of distributed "Blockchain" databases that record and track the fulfillment of contractual commitments and thereby may eventually replace social institutions like the state, legal courts and business. In this extreme Cybertopia version, digital code would not only replace legal contracts but also B2B corporations by connecting people directly with resource markets. Now, B2B companies start to invest into blockchains, for example, Maersk and IBM with their TradeLens joint venture that uses blockchain technology to eliminate paperwork from supply chains (Economist, 2019). Experience with TradeLens illustrates both the bright and dark sides of technological contract innovation. TradeLens enables to control the fulfillment of shipping order seamless along the supply, thus cutting time and red-tape for suppliers, customers and the various companies involved in the shipping operation. The dark side emerged when Maersk became the target of the NotPetya Cyberattack that brought the entire shipping system of Maersk to a halt for three days (Greenberg, 2018). Eventually, the only way for recovery was to use a Maersk computer-server in Nigeria, which by coincidence was disconnected by the time of the attack and helped the recovery team to restore databases of shipping orders along a network of around 4000 servers and 45,000 client computers and around 2500 software programs.

Data offer also source of genuine contract innovations as apparent of companies that manage to build up valuable data pools and eventually find means to commercialize them. The Biopharma company Myriad is an example for the smart use of legal instruments (Pistor, 2019: 2084 ff.): Initially, Myriad used its patent protection for a cancer test to build up a database of genetic sequences by charging licensing fees on its method. Anticipating the expiry of its patent in 2013, the company built a database on the genetic sequencing tests. While patent protection has a limited lifeline, US trade-secrecy law knows no such limits. Myriad used the patent protection phase to build up an information service protected by the US law of trade secrets (Pistor, 2019: 2341 ff.). In a world of growing data-traffic, trade-secrecy laws offer the legal backbone for a growth of innovation services. Experiences with corrupted contracting technologies and dynamic innovation in the legal profession show that the future of legal contracting innovations resides on complementing legal competencies and digital technologies rather than substituting legal code with digital code (Ehret, 2021)

Contracting Infrastructure Innovations

The Evolution of the Global Communication Infrastructure Building on the Internet

The internet is the defining infrastructure innovation, opening the prospect of ubiquitous computing, connecting people and equipment around the globe. Internet technologies continue to evolve (Ehret & Wirtz, 2017). Fourth generation standards of mobile communication have facilitated the sharing of mobile data. Mobile data transform contracting capabilities by enhancing access to shared innovation. Perhaps one of the most significant transformations is the rise of mobile money, in particular in rural areas of emerging economies. Lacking any infrastructure associated with established banking, emerging economies use mobile infrastructures as backbone for payment and financial services. Considering that payments constitute virtually any commercial service contract, mobile payment infrastructures constitute the backbone for disruptive contracting innovations.

The other substantial transformation builds on standards for connecting physical devices and assets by the internet of things (Ehret & Wirtz, 2017; Geisberger & Broy, 2015). Servitization of industrial, urban or agricultural assets by the use of communication technologies was limited to proprietary networks until recently (Ehret & Wirtz, 2017). Fifth generation (5G) mobile communication standards offer a global network enabling prospective service providers to generate bundles of services from virtually any physical asset. Infrastructure innovations continue to evolve, for example, by global geolocation services or meteorological services that furnish contracting in a wide array of logistics, hospitality or transportation services.

Information Interfaces Furnishing Contract Innovation: The Example of Application Program Interfaces

Effective use of contracting infrastructures resides on standards for shared processing of data. Application Program Interfaces (APIs) constitute a blueprint for sharing information for contract innovations across organizational boundaries. Microsoft pioneered APIs as the conduit between its own operating systems and the network of application programmers aiming to tap into Microsoft systems. Within the company, APIs mandate a consistent use of company-wide information, forcing service companies to maintain standardized information processes. Amazon CEO Jeff Bezos infamously voiced the mandate for internal data consistency, announcing anybody not complying with the company-wide information rules will be fired (Iansiti & Lakhani, 2020).

However, the company-wide standardization empowers the connectivity, and inter-operability of company data thus works as the technological platform for service ecosystems building on networked suppliers, partners and various types of stakeholders. APIs constitute the software dimension of the technical glue of such ecosystems. But the social and institutional dimension becomes ever more apparent. The most visible testimonies are developer communities of the big platform providers, with Apple, Amazon, Google and Microsoft as the dominant orchestrators of such ecosystems. Besides joint technologies, operating systems and development infrastructures, platform providers invest into the social cultivation of developer community, hoping to sustain the viability of their service ecosystems.

The Social Dimension of Infrastructure Innovations: Service Ecosystems

The growth of communication hard-and software infrastructures has been facilitating the formation of service ecosystems, where various types of platform companies, partners, suppliers, resource owners, complementors and many more collaborate with users and clients in interactive modes of value creation (Iansiti & Lakhani, 2020, pp. 129–130). For example, the pharmaceutical industry has been moving from vertically integrated commercialization of internal R&D toward ecosystems where basic university researchers, Biotech companies, medical practitioners, insurers, suppliers and many more cocreate for progress in health. While performance of Biopharma ecosystems was a question mark 15 years ago, product pipelines have been filling up and innovation circles have been accelerating (Ernst & Young, 2017), as apparent in the recent quick discovery of COVID-19 vaccines.

Contracting innovation integrates the technological and the institutional pillar for service cocreating ecosystems. Looking at the ecosystem management of the leading platform companies, the social dimension of interaction across organizational boundaries is the key to realize the opportunities evolving from legal and ITC innovations.

4 Discussion

Implications for Research: The Case for a Service-Systems Perspective

Contract innovations extend scale and scope of the service economies by facilitating clients, providers and stakeholders in translating latent needs into effective service demand. Having identified the potential of nonownership value, service research is still in the early stages of a systematic understanding on the drivers and the impact of contracting capabilities. In the face of the mixed outcomes, and both bright and dark sides associated with contract innovations, service research needs to support decision makers in business and society in unlocking the full potential of contracting. As our tour d'horizon shows, effective contracting resides on technologies that facilitate sharing and use of information, social interaction between contracting parties and their stakeholders and institutional solutions for maintaining trust and resolving conflicts in contracting systems. Thus, service research needs to move beyond narrow engineering and lofty constructivist approaches and open the perspective for the study and design of the systematic interplay of technologies, social interaction and institutional rules at work in contracting processes. Systems approaches like Searle's (1995) communication-driven theory of institutions, Edvardsson et al.'s (2011) social construction approach, or the adoption of evolutionary or cyber-systems theories (Barile et al., 2016; Ng & Vargo, 2018) as the foundation for service-systems approaches pave the way for integrating social and technological dimensions at work in contract innovations and their impact in extending scope and scale of service business.

On a more narrow scale, the financial dimension of contracting is as prevalent as understudied. Moving the commercialization of an asset from selling ownership to offer nonownership contracts shares some properties with the move from trading financial assets to that of financial options. Thus, service research needs to improve the basic understanding of the financial implications of information abundance for valuing and pricing service contracts. While data are becoming abundant, capabilities to transform abundant data into valuable knowledge is in short supply. Service Research has advanced in furnishing revenue management approaches (Wirtz & Lovelock, 2016). Contract innovations call for the implementation of Real Option approaches that build on the insights of finance research (Wei & Tang, 2015)

Implications for Management

ITC innovation is continuously transforming conditions and tools of service contracting. In contrast to Cybertopian visions to substitute legal code with computer code, exploiting the potential of technological innovation into improved service performance is far from trivial. Effective contract innovation resides on crafting and orchestration of emergent technological potential with legal and social dimensions of service business. Service managers take the pole position in driving the contract innovation process, connecting novel technologies with legal instruments to customer-driven learning processes.

5 Conclusion

Contract innovations define the frontiers of service growth. While evolution of ICT provides a continuous technology push, capabilities of companies to use contract technologies for translating demand into effective service contracts has been proving the limiting factor of service growth. In business, contracting competencies, the capabilities to translate latent demand into effective service demand, are vital for future service growth. Service research faces the challenge to develop a systematic understanding of the conditions of contracting competencies and their impact on service design, operations and governance. While in industrial capitalism firms took the role as architects of manufacturing productivity (Micklethwait, 2005), service firms thrive by orchestrating technology, social interaction and legal institutions for pushing the boundaries of contracting productivity, opening up novel domains for service business and stimulating scale of service markets.

References

Agrawal, A., Gans, J., & Goldfarb, A. (2018). *Prediction machines: The simple economics of artificial intelligence.* Harvard Business Review Press.

Barile, S., Lusch, R., Reynoso, J., Saviano, M., & Spohrer, J. (2016). Systems, networks, and ecosystems in service research. *Journal of Service Management, 27*(4), 652–674.

Chesbrough, H. W. (2011). *Open services innovation: Rethinking your business to grow and compete in a new era.* Jossey-Bass.

Economist. (2016). WeChat's World. The Economist, online edition, August 6th 2016. Retrieved April 3, 2019, from https://www.economist.com/business/2016/08/06/wechats-world.

Economist. (2019). Why WeWork Doesn't work yet. Economist online edition, September 17, 2019. Retrieved April 3, 2019, from https://www.economist.com/graphic-detail/2019/09/17/why-wework-doesnt-work-yet.

Edvardsson, B., Tronvoll, B., & Gruber, T. (2011). Expanding understanding of service exchange and value co-creation: A social construction approach. *Journal of the Academy of Marketing Science, 2011*(39), 327–339.

Ehret, M. (2021). Book-Review of Katharina Pistor (2019): The code of capital: How the law creates wealth and inequality. Princeton: Princeton University Press (Kindle edition), 2019. *Industrial Marketing Management, 93*(2021), 187–190.

Ehret, M., & Wirtz, J. (2010). Division of labor between firms: Business services, non-ownership-value and the rise of the service economy. *Service Science, 2*(3), 136–145. https://doi.org/10.1287/serv.2.3.136

Ehret, M., & Wirtz, J. (2017). Unlocking value from machines: Business models and the industrial internet of things. *Journal of Marketing Management, 33*(1), 111–130.

Ernst & Young. (2017). Beyond Borders. Staying the Course. Biotechnology Report 2017.

Geisberger, E., & Broy, M. (2015). *Living in a networked world. Integrated research agenda cyberphysical systems (agendaCPS).* Herbert Utz Verlag.

Greenberg, A. (2018). The Untold Story of NotPetya, the Most Devastating CyberAttack in History. Wired Magazine, August 8th 2018. Retrieved April 3, 2018, from https://www.wired.com/story/notpetya-cyberattack-ukraine-russia-code-crashed-the-world/.

Hodgson, G. M. (2015). *Conceptualizing capitalism: Institutions, evolution, future.* The University of Chicago Press.

Iansiti, M., & Lakhani, K. R. (2020). *Competing in the Age of AI. Strategy and Leadership when Algorithms and Networks Run the World.* Harvard Business Review Press.

Lessig, L. (2008). *Code and other laws of cyberspace, Version 2.0.* Basic Books.

Lovelock, C., & Gummesson, E. (2004). Whither services marketing? In search of a new paradigm and fresh perspectives. *Journal of Service Research, 7*(1), 20–41.

Lovelock, C. H., & Wirtz, J. (2016). *Services marketing: People, technology, strategy* (p. 2016). World Scientific.

Micklethwait, J. (2005). *The company: A short history of a revolutionary idea.* Phoenix.

Ng, I. C. L., & Vargo, S. L. (2018). Service-dominant (S-D) logic, service ecosystems and institutions: Bridging theory and practice. *Journal of Service Management, 29*(4), 518–520.

Semple, J. (2004). Charterway comes to fore 12 years on. Motor Transport. 9/2/2004

Varian, H. R. (2010). Computer mediated transactions. *American Economic Review, 100*(2), 1–10.

Wei, S., & Tang, O. (2015). Real option approach to evaluate cores for remanufacturing in service markets. *International Journal of Production Research, 53*(8), 2306–2320. https://doi.org/10.1080/00207543.2014.939243

Wirtz, B. (2016). *Business Model Management: Design Process Instruments* (2nd ed.). German University of Administrative Science.

Zuboff, S. (2019). *The age of surveillance capitalism: The fight for the human future at the new frontier of power*. Profile.

Managing the Exclusivity of Luxury Service Experiences

Jonas Holmqvist, Jochen Wirtz, and Martin P. Fritze

1 Introduction

Global sales of luxury services are growing fast, faster than for luxury goods (Müller-Stewens & Berghaus, 2014). However, there is a lack of research and guidance for managers on how to create, market, and deliver luxury service experiences, which motivated us to write this chapter. In particular, this chapter offers contributions to both luxury theory and practice by exploring a critical characteristic of luxury services, that is, exclusivity. Exclusivity is commonly recognized as a key element of classic product luxury in the existing literature (Kapferer & Bastien, 2009; Ko et al., 2019). In this chapter, we show how applying exclusivity to the service field is more complex, and we adapt the manifestations of exclusivity to service research to customer value in social contexts (Edvardsson et al., 2011; Holmqvist, Visconti, et al., 2020a).

J. Holmqvist (✉)
Kedge Business School, Bordeaux, Talence, France
e-mail: jonas.holmqvist@kedgebs.com

J. Wirtz
NUS Business School, National University of Singapore, Kent Ridge, Singapore
e-mail: jochen@nus.edu.sg

M. P. Fritze
University of Cologne, Cologne, Germany
e-mail: fritze@wiso.uni-koeln.de

© The Author(s), under exclusive license to Springer Nature Switzerland AG 2022
B. Edvardsson, B. Tronvoll (eds.), *The Palgrave Handbook of Service Management*,
https://doi.org/10.1007/978-3-030-91828-6_14

Luxury services are distinct from both luxury products and from ordinary services (Wirtz et al., 2020). In this chapter, we will not dwell on the differences between luxury products and luxury services given that, from a service perspective, many of these differences mirror known service characteristics. These characteristics include the intangibility, heterogeneity, inseparability (i.e., the simultaneous production and consumption), and perishability (also called 'IHIP') that set most services apart from most products (Lovelock & Gummesson, 2004; Parasuraman et al., 1985). For a discussion of the differences between luxury products and luxury services that are unique to the luxury sector, we refer the reader to Wirtz et al.'s (2020) detailed discussion.

For the service field, we believe that the distinction of how luxury services differ from ordinary services is more relevant and so we devote this chapter to discussing this distinction. Below, we first define luxury services and then move on to develop how key luxury characteristics set them apart from many other services and what the managerial implications of these differences are.

2 What Do We Mean by Luxury Services?

Why do service researchers and managers need to know about luxury services, can we not just apply our understanding of services in general to the luxury sector? Unfortunately, no. Not only is luxury often different from other sectors, it is in fact frequently the opposite of ordinary goods (Kapferer & Bastien, 2012). In this chapter, we adopt the following definition of luxury services from Wirtz et al. (2020), underlining both the key roles of a multifaceted exclusivity and service characteristics:

> *Luxury services are **extraordinary hedonic experiences** that are **exclusive**. Exclusivity can be **monetary, social** and **hedonic** in nature. Luxuriousness is jointly determined by **objective service features** and **subjective customer perceptions**. Together, these characteristics place a service on a **continuum**, ranging from **everyday luxury** (i.e., with low levels of exclusivity and extraordinariness) to **elite luxury** (i.e., with high levels of exclusivity and extraordinariness). (Wirtz et al., 2020 p. 668)*

In line with the definition of Wirtz et al. (2020) of luxury services being hedonic and exclusive experiences, we explore the relationship of hedonic experiences and exclusivity in more depth. For hedonism, we extent how the concept of escapism can serve to strengthen the hedonic and extraordinary nature of the luxury service and also discuss the risk of the extraordinary reverting to the ordinary if experienced too often, a concept called hedonic adaptation. Hedonic adaptation goes back to the seminal study by Brickman and Campbell (1971) which examines the long-term impact of both extreme positive events such as winning the lottery and extreme negative events such as an accident resulting in paraplegia. The study found that even such extreme events led to people neither feeling happier nor feeling less happy in the long run. The authors explained these findings through adaptation, that is, people adapting to their circumstances. Wiesing (2015) used the concept of hedonic adaptation to describe the sensory saturation that luxury consumers can come to feel, while Wirtz et al. (2020) introduced hedonic adaptation to luxury services as a key reason for why luxury services need to contain as escapist element. We build on this literature to argue that one way to reduce the risk of hedonic adaption is through keeping the luxury service exclusive. Specifically, we develop the importance of exclusivity for service experiences to be perceived as luxurious and conceptualize four different manifestations of exclusivity for luxury services.

3 Why Is the Hedonic Escapism of Luxury Services so Important?

One key element of all forms of luxury is their hedonic nature (Holmqvist, Diaz, & Peñaloza, 2020c; Kapferer & Bastien, 2012; Thomsen et al., 2020), meaning that luxury should be fun and enjoyable. While many luxury experiences are hedonic, hedonic escapism further enhances the experience to allow the consumer to become immersed in the luxury experience, engage fully in it, and even 'escape' reality through the experience (Holmqvist, Diaz, & Peñaloza, 2020c). Luxury experiences often draw on an escapist element in order to accomplish this hedonism (Atwal & Williams, 2009). The concept of escapism is often used to understand consumer experiences (see Cova et al., 2018 for a review of escapism in consumer studies). Escapism relates to Turner's (1969, 1974) description of a liminal state and may refer to any extraordinary experience, ranging from the immensely enjoyable to the war-like, painful experience (Cova et al., 2018).

Adapting escapism to conceptualize pleasurable consumer experiences, Holbrook and Hirschman (1982) introduce hedonism as well as escape from reality (Hirschman & Holbrook, 1982) as parts of the consumption experience. Similarly, extant consumer research often frames extraordinary experiences as an 'escape from structure' (Tumbat & Belk, 2011, p. 46) to emphasize how consumers are able to escape daily routines for a short interlude. Consumers may achieve this escape from routines by engaging in extraordinary experiences such as river rafting (Arnould & Price, 1993), skydiving (Celsi et al., 1993), salsa festivals (Holmqvist, Wirtz, & Fritze, 2020b), or obstacle courses (Scott et al., 2017).

The concept of escapism also features in Pine and Gilmore's (1998, 1999) conceptualization of consumer experiences as the most immersive and active of the experiential realms. This understanding of escapism as an intense and engaging experience has been adapted to luxury settings to emphasize the importance of the experience for luxury consumers (Atwal & Williams, 2009). More recently, luxury research increasingly identifies the concept of hedonic escapism as a cornerstone of the customer's luxury experience (Holmqvist, Wirtz, & Fritze, 2020b; Klaus, 2021). Holmqvist, Diaz, and Peñaloza (2020c) conceptualize Tumbat and Belk's (2011) description of escape from structure with escapism to develop the 'moment of luxury' as a short, liminal moment offering the customer a temporary break from everyday routines. Holmqvist, Visconti, et al. (2020a) further develop the role of escapism as a driver of customer value in luxury services by showing how it helps the luxury service provider to accomplish a figurative, hedonic transportation that helps the service provider facilitate customers' value creation process. This hedonic consumer escapism can combine escaping from reality and escaping from structure. For example, Holmqvist, Diaz, and Peñaloza (2020c) explore how consumers use moments of luxury both to negotiate and briefly transform their identities ('escape from reality') as well as to set aside normal roles in society ('escape from structure').

Hedonic Adaptation

While hedonism is important to luxury experiences, Wirtz et al. (2020) extend the understanding of hedonism in luxury services by building on the concept of hedonic adaptation (Brickman & Campbell, 1971): the human tendency to grow accustomed to even the extraordinary over time. Most individuals have a tendency to gradually come to consider even the most extraordinary experience as ordinary if they are exposed to it regularly. This represents a real problem for luxury as luxury should be extraordinary, even escapist in nature (Holmqvist, Visconti, et al., 2020a). Even though this is a problem for all forms of luxury to some extent, the implications are even more serious for luxury services. The thrill of a Lamborghini, a bespoke suit, and a diamond necklace will wane over time as the consumer gets used to owning them

(Wiesing, 2015), but their practical use and monetary value remain. For luxury services, the experience is the essence of the service, and as services are produced and consumed at the same time (Grönroos, 1978; Parasuraman et al., 1985), there is no monetary value left after the service is over. For service managers in the luxury sector, this represents a problem. Many guests at luxury hotels, luxury restaurants, and luxury spas tend to be frequent visitors, meaning that even the most elaborate servicescape and experience may grow to become mundane and hence lose its appeal.

As the discussion above shows, hedonism and hedonic escapism are important to turn luxury services into enjoyable, extraordinary experiences (Holmqvist, Wirtz, & Fritze, 2020b; Wirtz et al., 2020), but hedonic adaptation can undermine the feeling of extraordinary as customers adapt to even luxurious services over time. We argue that one way to reduce this risk is through the exclusivity of luxury services, as exclusivity serves not only to keep luxury services extraordinary, but also makes customers appreciate them more. We next develop the role of exclusivity and its different manifestations in luxury services.

4   Exclusivity in Luxury Services

Exclusivity is a key element of luxury, both for luxury products (Kapferer & Bastien, 2009, 2012) and for luxury services (Wirtz et al., 2020). Many researchers define exclusivity as one of the core aspects of luxury. Reviewing the extant luxury brand literature, Ko et al. (2019) found exclusivity to be common to most luxury definitions. Kapferer and Bastien (2009) make a case for exclusivity being *the* core concept of luxury while Wirtz et al. (2020) argue that exclusivity is a key part of what set luxury services apart from ordinary services.

In this chapter, we argue that the exclusivity of luxury services presents a more complex picture than for luxury products. Exclusivity for luxury products is primarily established through a high price, contributing to limiting the number of potential customers willing and able to buy the luxury product as well as by constructed exclusivity in the form of intentionally keeping supply low (see Kapferer & Bastien, 2009). For luxury services, price and constructed exclusivity can also play a role, yet managers of luxury services have additional tools at their disposal to create an exclusive service. In line with this, Wirtz et al.'s (2020) define exclusivity in luxury services as consisting of three main forms: monetary exclusivity, social exclusivity, and hedonic exclusivity. In this chapter, based on conversations with luxury managers, we recognize and extend these three expressions of exclusivity with an additional but less common form of exclusivity for luxury products that may also apply to luxury services: the practice of intentionally limiting the available supply of desired luxury offerings, either goods or services, a form of artificially constructed exclusivity.

Monetary Exclusivity

Monetary exclusivity reflects the classic understanding of the product luxury literature, in which a high price means that the product remains out of reach for most consumers and can only be purchased by those with the means to afford it (Kapferer & Bastien, 2009, 2012). This is the kind of exclusivity that the extant luxury literature treats in conspicuous consumption and social signifiers: luxury items that only few customers can afford, the use of which signals the prestige and status of the user (Han et al., 2010). Monetary exclusivity is relative; while always sold at a price premium (Kapferer & Laurent, 2016), it can range from a few hundred euros for a Dior sweater, passing through a Savile Row bespoke suit at above 5000€, a Lamborghini Aventador at around 400,000€, or a Baltic Yacht at over 40 million euros. Common to all of these cases is that the luxury good sells at a considerable price premium compared to non-luxury goods (Kapferer & Laurent, 2016).

While many manifestations of exclusivity are different between luxury services and luxury goods, monetary exclusivity for luxury services seems similar. It can range from a drink at around 20€ at a luxury bar, a treatment at high-end spa for a few hundred euros, and a dinner at above 500€ at luxury restaurants, while the suite at Le Royal Monceau Raffles in Paris comes at over 15.000€ per night. Monetary exclusivity is thus as common in luxury services as it is in luxury products. However, whereas it is together with artificially constructed exclusivity the main aspect of exclusivity for most luxury goods, luxury services feature several other forms of exclusivity as well.

Social Exclusivity

Social exclusivity refers to a form of exclusivity that is mandated by the social context rather than money (Wirtz et al., 2020). Contrary to monetary exclusivity, social exclusivity is more typical of luxury service settings than for luxury goods, and controlling access represents a relatively common practice for managing prestigious settings to increase their prestige even further. One of the more typical service contexts featuring social exclusivity is the case of high-end nightclubs. In many cities, upscale clubs face a stronger demand than they can accommodate, allowing management to select customers. In such clubs, doormen are frequently instructed to prioritize attractive and well-dressed guests, and also bestow VIP status such customers. This practice is not uncontroversial; for example, some upscale clubs around Stureplan in Stockholm have faced media accusations of racism in their customer selection. Even if the clubs deny racism, they are open about the practice of selecting their patrons. In Paris, a luxury bar faced criticism in French media after employees revealed that some ethnic visitors were turned away while 'old and ugly people' were seated out of sight as management wanted attractive customers to sit at the most visible tables (Poingt, 2018).

These examples show that social exclusivity is common in luxury services, but also reveal that the application of social exclusivity can be controversial. Managers of luxury services need to consider both the applicability and the implications of social exclusivity selection criteria. Several luxury fashion brands, while mainly operating monetary exclusivity, also practice social exclusivity in their boutiques in the way service employees interact in service encounters with customers (Dion & Borraz, 2017). In these cases, the social exclusivity is more subtle; no customers are turned away, yet service employees adjust their level of attention to align with their perception of whether the visitors to the boutique are real potential customers or 'lurkers' (Leban et al., 2020) who come into the store to browse and perhaps receive some complimentary drink but without any intention to buy (Wirtz et al., 2020).

Another well-known example of social exclusivity concerns high-end social clubs. These clubs often function by invitation only, and prospective members must be approved by other members, thus guaranteeing a form of social exclusivity. See Box 1 for an example.

Box 1 The Exclusivity of Hunting with a King

The Royal Hunting Club of Sweden (H.M. Konungens Jaktklubb) provides an illustration of social exclusivity. The Royal Hunting Club was founded by King Charles XV in 1863 and has ever since remained a highly prestigious society with very limited membership. The current King of Sweden remains an active member himself and membership in the club remains a desired social signifier, yet it is not possible to pay to be invited into the club. Unlike luxury services, such as hotels or restaurants for which customers do pay a high price, exclusivity is maintained by invitation. Enjoying this kind of luxury services is in line with Kapferer and Bastien's (2009) argument that exclusivity rather than price drives luxury.

Hedonic Exclusivity

Hedonic exclusivity is a concept developed by Wirtz et al. (2020) to acknowledge that many luxury services may require a certain level of initiation on behalf of the customers. Unlike social exclusivity, this does not mean that customers cannot participate, but rather that it may be difficult for them to appreciate the finer nuances of many luxury services. A common example concerns wine tasting; most experts agree that knowledge of fine wine is a learnt art, hence a customer well acquainted with the subtleties of great wines may appreciate a testing with some premier grand crus more than uninitiated guests.

Opera represents another example of a service in which hedonic exclusivity is at play as expertise develops over time. Describing attending the opera as a collective, co-created service experience, Carù and Cova (2015) show how the less initiated visitors to the famous La Scale opera in Milan wait for the reaction of the *loggionisti*, the most experienced and knowledgeable opera lovers, before they react themselves. This example shows that expertise of key service elements may be needed to fully appreciate a luxury experience.

In many luxury service contexts consumers need to learn and gain access to the appreciation of hedonic value in order to fully enjoy the experience. The process of becoming an expert for luxury enjoyment is also known as 'hedonic learning' (Latour & Deighton, 2019). A hedonic learning experience can be (a) a service centered on luxury goods, (b) a stand-alone service, or (c) a supportive service for a luxury service, depending on how the hedonic learning experience is marketed. For example, a wine tasting event can be arranged by a wine producer to acknowledge the value offered by a certain produce in order to sell it. It can be arranged as an event that is supposed to enrich the customer's taste expertise skills and appreciation of future consumption. Finally, it can be arranged to generally increase the enjoyment as wine pairing of a luxury dining experience. In all three cases, customers are guided and educated by the service provider in order to gain access to a hedonic enjoyment that otherwise might remain an ambiguous if not elusive experience.

While hedonic exclusivity may act as a barrier to the uninitiated (Holmqvist, Wirtz, & Fritze, 2020b), there are many things service managers can do to help less experienced customers navigate complex luxury service settings. For example, a skilled sommelier may guide customers, suggesting where to start and offer explanations about the wine customers are about to drink, and later suggest another, more complex wine to help customers develop their knowledge as they experience the differences. Box 2 provides an example for how luxury service providers can guide novice customers and educate them to appreciate the full experience.

Box 2 Expertise for Enjoyment

It is possible that customers rely on the expertise of service providers and enjoy experiences by having 'hedonic trust' in their expertise. For instance, the London based wine and spirits merchant Berry Bros & Rudd offers customers a cellar plan. The family-owned company has been selling wine since the late seventeenth century (founded in 1698) and gained a world-class reputation for exceptional wines and spirits. For the cellar plan, there is no management fee. Customers simply pay a minimum amount of 100 GBP each month. Depending on the money invested, expert buyers will select the wines and store them at the company's wine cellars. The cellar plan is a good example how providers can support customer learning instead of making hedonic learning a pre-requisite for consumption enjoyment.

Artificially Constructed Exclusivity

In addition to the above manifestations of exclusivity, we propose that constructed exclusivity constitutes a fourth form. Artificially constructed exclusivity means that the company deliberately limits its supply to sell less than it actually could sell. This practice represents another sharp contrast between the luxury sector and most other businesses, which instead tend to increase the supply to meet demand. For luxury brands, however, it is important not to have too many customers (Kapferer & Bastien, 2009, 2012). As Patrick Thomas, former CEO of French luxury giant Hermès, framed it:

> *The luxury industry is built on a paradox: the more desirable the brand becomes, the more it sells, but the more it sells, the less desirable it becomes.*

In luxury fashion, constructed exclusivity is rather common. As Holmqvist, Wirtz, and Fritze (2020b); Holmqvist et al. (2022) outline, many luxury brands want to keep the traditional exclusivity of the sumptuous boutique servicescape even in online settings. This represents a challenge given that most digital services are instantly available to everyone, everywhere. Several top luxury brands such as Hermès and Dior manufacture exclusivity both in-store and online. In boutiques, many luxury brands have a limit on how many items of each product they sell each month. If this quota is reached, they will not sell more even if they have the product available, instead telling customers that it is currently out of stock. Similarly, Dior closely monitors its digital sales to see whether certain iconic products sell a lot; if that happens, the product will be temporarily removed from the online store in order to keep it from becoming too widely sold (Holmqvist et al., 2022). For an example on how luxury brands can construct exclusivity, see Box 3.

Box 3 Constructed Exclusivity at Hermès

Hermès is one of the most famous luxury brands, particularly well known for its bags and scarfs as well as for its elaborate servicescapes incorporating artifacts. Perhaps the most iconic Hermès product is the Birkin bag. The bag is named after English actress Jane Birkin who once sat next to legendary Hermès CEO Jean-Louis Dumas at a flight and who subsequently designed the bag for her. Not only is the Birkin bag expensive (monetary exclusivity) at around 10.000€—200.000€ depending on the model, but it is also impossible to buy from Hermès online or by just walking into a store. Customers can ask to be added to a waiting list and may have to wait several months for their bag. Curiously, the Birkin Bag represents both a product in itself and a service as it can be given to highly exclusive VIP customers as a gift. In this way, Hermès extends the monetary exclusivity with artificially constructed exclusivity, keeping its most iconic products scarce.

Extending this concept to luxury services, we argue that artificially constructed exclusivity is not limited to digital services and in-store services of luxury brands. For example, many famous luxury restaurants have very few tables. This helps them to create an appealing servicescape where customers have their space and receive attentive service as each table has its own waiter— yet it also helps the luxury restaurant to manufacture exclusivity, as they receive less customers than other, non-luxury restaurants would be able to fit into the same space.

5   Summary and Discussion

This chapter extends the emerging literature on luxury services (Holmqvist, Wirtz, & Fritze, 2020b; Wirtz et al., 2020) by developing the key concepts of hedonic escapism as well as multifaceted exclusivity. We first developed the role of hedonic escapism in rendering luxury services enjoyable and extraordinary. This represents a key implication for managers of luxury services: customers engaging in a luxury service usually have high expectations and demands that the service needs to satisfy. Even though the service quality may be very high, this may not be enough in itself and would rather fall into the 'good service' category. While this may often be enough for most services, it is less likely to meet the demands of customers expecting an extraordinary experience. This challenge to deliver the extraordinary, even to customers who become used to the very best service quality, represents a crucial challenge for managers in luxury services.

Managing the Exclusivity of Luxury Service Experiences   273

In addition to hedonic escapism, we also contribute to research on luxury services by extending the role of exclusivity and detail four different manifestations of exclusivity in luxury service contexts. For practitioners in luxury services, we believe that appeal of exclusivity and the role of exclusivity in keeping luxury services attractive are best understood through the lens of customer value in social contexts (Edvardsson et al., 2011). Building on this value in social context, we find conspicuous consumption and exclusivity of particular importance for luxury service managers. First, managers should explore how they can manage exclusivity to increase the appeal of the service for conspicuous consumers. Given the risk of hedonic adaptation reducing the appeal of luxury over time (Wiesing, 2015), we believe that service managers could employ all the four forms of exclusivity in order to keep the service feeling special for the customers. For example, conspicuous consumption can be enhanced by tangible cues, such as branded souvenirs and giveaways, and materialized through stories and photos. Special attention should be placed on social media which can help enhancing conspicuousness of services. Customers can 'post' and 'share' luxury experiences, for example, related to dining and the arts, and signal their affluence and sophistication. Service firms should encourage this, for example, by offering 'instagrammable' cues (Wirtz et al., 2020).

Not every luxury customers is interested in conspicuous consumption. As luxury services are consumed and experienced at the same time, luxury service providers have to proactively manage conspicuousness. For example, a celebrity dining out may want to sit at a quiet table in order *not* to be disturbed by fans. Many top-end travelers value privacy and Singapore Airlines therefore has private first-class check-in lounges in Singapore that even comes with a private link directly to immigration, after which passengers can proceed to Singapore Airlines' first-class lounges. Even on board, privacy is provided in its suites with a sliding door that screens the outside world away (Wirtz et al., 2020)

Second, managers should explore using the gamut of the different types of exclusivity to enhance the luxury experience. Monetary exclusivity is obvious and simply means luxury service firms need to be extremely careful with price promotions. Social exclusivity combines with the constructed exclusivity of luxury goods to allow service providers to limit and to control access to the service in order to enhance its appeal. Upscale clubs screen at the entrance, exclusive social events can be made 'by-invitation-only,' and luxury services-capes can even be designed to intimidate non-target consumers (Dion & Borraz, 2017). Hedonic exclusivity can be used to target a service only at the initiated whereby a certain degree of expertise serves as a barrier for the less initiated to fully appreciating a service.

In closing, we believe that luxury services are important and deserve research attention. This chapter further shows that luxury services need to be studied in their own right rather than being subsumed in the much more developed luxury goods literature. We hope that this chapter will inspire more research in the field of luxury services.

References

Arnould, E. J., & Price, L. L. (1993). River magic: Extraordinary experience and the extended service encounter. *Journal of Consumer Research, 20*(1), 24–45.

Atwal, G., & Williams, A. (2009). Luxury brand marketing–the experience is everything! *Journal of Brand Management, 16*(5-6), 338–346.

Brickman, P., & Campbell, D. T. (1971). Hedonic relativism and planning the good society. In M. H. Appley (Ed.), *Adaptation level theory: A symposium*. Academic Press.

Carù, A., & Cova, B. (2015). Co-creating the collective service experience. *Journal of Service Management, 26*(2), 276–294.

Celsi, R. L., Rose, R. L., & Leigh, T. W. (1993). An exploration of high-risk leisure consumption through skydiving. *Journal of Consumer Research, 20*(1), 1–23.

Cova, B., Carù, A., & Cayla, J. (2018). Re-conceptualizing escape in consumer research. *Qualitative Market Research: An International Journal, 21*(4), 445–464.

Dion, D., & Borraz, S. (2017). Managing status: How luxury brands shape class subjectivities in the service encounter. *Journal of Marketing, 81*(5), 67–85.

Edvardsson, B., Tronvoll, B., & Gruber, T. (2011). Expanding understanding of service exchange and value co-creation: A social construction approach. *Journal of the Academy of Marketing Science, 39*(2), 327–339.

Grönroos, C. (1978). A service-orientated approach to marketing of services. *European Journal of Marketing, 12*(8), 588–601.

Han, Y. L., Nunez, J. C., & Drèze, X. (2010). Signalling status with luxury goods: The role of brand prominence. *Journal of Marketing, 74*(4), 15–30.

Hirschman, E. C., & Holbrook, M. B. (1982). Hedonic consumption: Emerging concepts, methods and propositions. *Journal of Marketing, 46*(3), 92–101.

Holbrook, M. B., & Hirschman, E. C. (1982). The experiential aspects of consumption: Consumer fantasies, feelings, and fun. *Journal of Consumer Research, 9*(2), 132–140.

Holmqvist, J., Visconti, L. M., Grönroos, C., Guais, B., & Kessous, A. (2020a). Understanding the value process: Value creation in a luxury service context. *Journal of Business Research, 120*, 114–126.

Holmqvist, J., Wirtz, J., & Fritze, M. P. (2020b). Luxury in the digital age: A multi-actor service encounter perspective. *Journal of Business Research, 121*, 747–756.

Holmqvist, J., Diaz, R. C., & Peñaloza, L. (2020c). Moments of luxury: Hedonic escapism as a luxury experience. *Journal of Business Research, 116*, 503–513.

Holmqvist, J., Wirtz, J., & Fritze, M. P. (2022). Digital luxury services: Tradition versus innovation in luxury fashion. In J. Wirtz & C. Lovelock (Eds.), *Services Marketing: People, Technology, Strategy* (9th ed.). World Scientific.

Kapferer, J. N., & Bastien, V. (2009). The specificity of luxury management: Turning marketing upside down. *Journal of Brand Management, 16*(5-6), 311–322.

Kapferer, J. N., & Bastien, V. (2012). *The luxury strategy: Break the rules of marketing to build luxury brands* (2nd ed.). Kogan Page.

Kapferer, J. N., & Laurent, G. (2016). Where do consumers think luxury begins? A study of perceived minimum price for 21 luxury goods in 7 countries. *Journal of Business Research, 69*(1), 332–340.

Klaus, P. (2021). What matters most to ultra-high-net-worth individuals? Exploring the UHNWI luxury customer experience (ULCX). *Journal of Product and Brand Management.*

Ko, E., Costello, J. P., & Taylor, C. R. (2019). What is a luxury brand? A new definition and review of the literature. *Journal of Business Research, 99*, 405–413.

Latour, K. A., & Deighton, J. A. (2019). Learning to become a taste expert. *Journal of Consumer Research, 46*(1), 1–19.

Leban, M., Seo, Y., & Voyer, B. G. (2020). Transformational effects of social media lurking practices on luxury consumption. *Journal of Business Research, 116*, 514–521.

Lovelock, C., & Gummesson, E. (2004). Whither services marketing? In search of a new paradigm and fresh perspectives. *Journal of Service Research, 7*(1), 20–41.

Müller-Stewens, G., & Berghaus, B. (2014). The market and business of luxury: An introduction. In B. Berghaus, G. Müller-Stewens, & S. Reinecke (Eds.), *Management of luxury: A practitioner's handbook.* Kogan Page Publishers.

Parasuraman, A., Zeithaml, V. A., & Berry, L. L. (1985). A conceptual model of service quality and its implications for future research. *Journal of Marketing, 49*(4), 41–50.

Pine, J. B., & Gilmore, J. H. (1998). Welcome to the experience economy. *Harvard Business Review, 76*(4), 97–106.

Pine, J. B., & Gilmore, J. H. (1999). *The experience economy: Work is theatre and every business a stage.* Harvard Business Press.

Poingt, G. (2018). À Paris, un restaurant chic accusé de discriminer « les arabes, les moches et les vieux ». *Le Figaro,* 18/05/2018 https://www.lefigaro.fr/actualite-fra nce/2018/05/18/01016-20180518ARTFIG00135%2D%2Dparis-un-restaurant-chic-accuse-de-discriminer-les-arabes-les-moches-et-les-vieux.php

Scott, R., Cayla, J., & Cova, B. (2017). Selling pain to the saturated self. *Journal of Consumer Research, 44*(1), 22–43.

Thomsen, T., Holmqvist, J., von Wallpach, S., Hemetsberger, A., & Belk, R. (2020). Conceptualizing unconventional luxury. *Journal of Business Research, 116*, 441–445.

Tumbat, G., & Belk, R. W. (2011). Marketplace tensions in extraordinary experiences. *Journal of Consumer Research, 38*(1), 42–61.

Turner, V. W. (1969). *The ritual process*. Aldine.

Turner, V. W. (1974). *Dramas, fields, and metaphors*. Cornell University Press.

Wiesing, L. (2015). *Luxus*. Suhrkamp Verlag.

Wirtz, J., Holmqvist, J., & Fritze, M. P. (2020). Luxury services. *Journal of Service Management, 31*(4), 665–691.

The Transformative Role of Resource Integration in Shaping a New Service Ecosystem

Maria Colurcio, Angela Caridà, and Monia Melia

1 Introduction

The social and environmental relevance of value creation processes are now ranked high on the institutional agenda of policy makers and are priorities when setting corporate strategies.

The 17 Sustainable Development Goals of the United Nations Agenda 2030 emphasize the need for a decisive reversal of the mode of production and wealth destruction toward resource conservation and environmental and social sustainability, in a broad sense of those terms.

Corporate management cannot ignore such imperatives and is challenged to align business models and marketing strategies with a broader perspective in which the concept of value is multidimensional and includes both social and environmental value. In a socio-economic context heavily affected by the global COVID-19 pandemic, priorities related to collective well-being and health have become even more important. Specifically, the profound impact of the pandemic on the service sector requires a Transformative Service approach (Anderson & Ostrom, 2015; Anderson et al., 2013) that considers the well-being and sustainability of all stakeholders in the ecosystem according to a social-collective perspective. "The stakeholders must collaborate to

---

M. Colurcio (✉) • A. Caridà • M. Melia
Department of Law, Economics and Sociology, University Magna Græcia of Catanzaro, Catanzaro, Italy
e-mail: maria.colurcio@unicz.it; angela.carida@unicz.it; monia.melia@unicz.it

© The Author(s), under exclusive license to Springer Nature Switzerland AG 2022
B. Edvardsson, B. Tronvoll (eds.), *The Palgrave Handbook of Service Management*,
https://doi.org/10.1007/978-3-030-91828-6_15

combat the pandemic, not only to achieve synergy for business growth, but also enhancing human wellbeing and a functional ecosystem" (Prentice et al., 2021, p. 7).

This chapter starts from the above premises and debates the dynamics of value co-creation in the broad perspective of the service ecosystem by adopting the principles of Transformative Service Research, which addresses *"how the interaction between service and consumer entities and the macroenvironment in which these interactions occur affect well-being outcomes"* (Anderson et al., 2013, p. 1209). It provides a framework, based on the potential and becoming value of resources, that emphasizes the transformative power that can lead to a process of changing social relations and collective well-being, and therefore to epochal changes in institutions and in the institutional arrangements of the service ecosystem, that is, social innovation (Pel et al., 2020).

The chapter explains these concepts with the help of a number of examples and empirical illustrations. It is divided into three sections. The first section frames the problem of value co-creation from a service perspective; the concept is defined in its multidimensionality, and the social and economic actors are identified. The next section describes the resource integration (RI) process through the three-phase Matching-Resourcing-Valuing framework. The last section is devoted to the discussion of RI in the service ecosystem. Here, special attention is paid to the issue of the transformative approach to RI and value-in-context.

2 Value Co-creation from the Service Perspective

Traditionally, the value-in-exchange concept has dominated the management and marketing literature. This means that value is embedded in goods and reflects the fixed set of characteristics and attributes that firms add to products through standardized and closed production processes.

Business scholars and practitioners are aware that the goods-dominant (G-D) logic perspective and the value-in-exchange concept, to which we referred above, are anachronistic today. Over the last 20 years, interactions among multiple actors have emerged as the new locus of value creation, and it has become increasingly apparent that there is no value until an offering is used (Vargo & Lusch, 2008).

For example, a smartphone creates value when customers use apps to access different mobile service platforms after downloading and configuring those apps on their own devices. People use their smartphones to (1) share their personal lives on Facebook, Instagram, and so on for online business or social networking; (2) create, listen to, and share their own playlists with friends or the entire community on Spotify; and/or (3) use mobile payment systems to make secure and reliable payment transactions. These examples show that rather than adopting a particular product, customers are co-creating their own smartphone by choosing apps with which they pursue a variety of goals.

Customers decide what the smartphone represents to them through their engagement with it; they decide why, when, and how to mix and match the smartphone's features with their own lifestyles to pursue different goals and capture different values. In other words, value (i.e., value in use) emerges during the actual usage process or service application (Lemke et al., 2011) and is created when customers integrate and operate on resources with the intention to co-create value for themselves and for others (Edvardsson et al., 2011).

This thinking is consistent with the key concept of service-dominant (S-D) logic that *"enterprises can offer their applied resources for value creation and collaboratively (interactively) create value following acceptance of value propositions, but cannot create/deliver value independently"* (Vargo & Lusch, 2008, p. 6).

Considering again the smartphone business, the value proposition (VP) offered by companies such as Apple, Samsung, Huawei, and Xiaomi has an inherent potential value: the VP enables customers to access the product/service and create value.

The tenets of S-D logic posit that VP is a representation of potential value (Vargo, 2020) and that the key role for firms is to instruct customers how to operate on the VP to facilitate and enable the mutual co-creation of value (Vargo & Lusch, 2008). In this regard, Vargo (2020) pointed out that *"customers do not use firms' offerings in the way firms intend and anticipate but rather adapt them to their own purposes in their own context"* (p. 310). In turn, the company's strategic focus is on how to help customers get more out of service activities to improve their daily routines, processes, and experiences (Karpen et al., 2012).

The supporting and facilitating role (Grönroos, 2011) of companies can also influence the value fulfillment and future buying behavior of customers and is therefore the basis for the future and successful strategies of the company.

The VP is the core of any company's business strategy. It can be defined from different perspectives, and beyond the close dyadic relationship between customer and company, as a promise (Grönroos & Voima, 2013), a proposal (Holttinen, 2014), and/or an invitation (Chandler & Lusch, 2015; Tronvoll & Edvardsson, 2020; Vargo et al., 2015).

Despite the divergence in the understanding of the definition of a VP, the service management literature states that offering attractive VPs is the *conditio sine qua non* for companies to engage customers and potentially other actors in joint value creation. "Live like a local" by Airbnb is a good example of an attractive VP (Caridà et al., 2020). The Airbnb platform provides a user-friendly interface that helps guests to search for and book short-term accommodation by comparing options from different listings around the world. The Airbnb platform allows locals (i.e., the hosts) to showcase and rent out their underutilized spaces to a global audience in a mass-customized way. The hosts create lasting connections between guests and the local context; for example, in Italy, making pasta based on an old family recipe and eating it in a private garden in front of the Colosseum. The hosts allow tourists to share special knowledge with local experts and to access local places and communities that guests would not find on their own.

That is, both guests and hosts combine and integrate their own resources into and through Airbnb and other VPs to collectively create an enjoyable, memorable experience and treasured memories.

In summary, it is only when actors integrate, operate, and recombine resources in direct interaction that co-creation of value occurs. Thus, the Airbnb example demonstrates that superior value co-creation is replacing the prevailing notion of superior VP as the cornerstone of business strategy, and that the value co-creation process can involve many different actors beyond customers and firms (Karpen et al., 2012). This brief example also shows that "*the firm's role should be understood as one of significant participation in, rather than provider of, its value proposition*" (Vargo, 2020, p. 310). As Vargo (2020) recently stated, to accomplish this role, firms must consider the systemic, co-creative nature of value and its phenomenological relationship with beneficiaries.

This latter point is discussed in the next section on value co-creation in the context of service ecosystems.

Value as a Multidimensional Concept

A central implication of S-D logic is that the concept of value is understood as a phenomenological experience (Holbrook, 2006) that is assessed from the perspective of the service beneficiary and is not limited to economic or financial aspects. Rather, value is a multidimensional construct that includes various interrelated dimensions that can be referred to as environmental, social, and cultural spheres.

The Transformative Role of Resource Integration in Shaping a New... **281**

That is, social actors interact and jointly integrate and operate on their own available resources to co-create and experience different types of value in the social context (Caridà et al., 2019a).

For example, Airbnb launched the Italian Village Project (IVP) to promote the development of sustainable tourism practices in 40 small Italian towns that are off the beaten track and at risk of disappearing. Following the Italian Ministry of Cultural Heritage and the Year of Villages Action Program, Airbnb coordinated public and private stakeholders and leveraged its service ecosystem to promote small villages internationally through a dedicated website and social media campaign and to support the restoration and economic valorization of some of the historic and significant public buildings in small villages. The project contributed to the self-sustainability of small village communities by improving home-sharing practices and services that support their local economies and the creation of new resources, as well as their long-term investments in social and cultural projects (Caridà et al., 2019a, 2020).

To provide a better understanding of value as a multidimensional construct, Table 1 presents a brief overview of the different types of value that the IVP generates for the small communities involved.

Different types of value—economic, sustainability/environmental, social, and cultural—can be interwoven. The Airbnb's IVP is a good example of this; it serves to illustrate how cultural, social, and sustainability value converge to create economic value for Airbnb, hosts, local businesses, and the community at large, as well as to remind us that value is the outcome of (often) multiple actors' activities, interactions, and collaboration, and that it is "*always uniquely and phenomenologically determined by the service beneficiary*" (Vargo & Lusch, 2008, p. 213).

To summarize, value is multidimensional, inherently personal, and context dependent. Different beneficiaries (i.e., economic and social actors) potentially value the same VP differently, and the same actor can also value the same VP differently at different times and in different contexts.

For example, consider dinner at a restaurant with family and friends; think about that experience before and after the COVID-19 pandemic; think about how you perceive and value it now.

This is consistent with Edvardsson et al. (2011), who claimed that the perception and determination of value/outcomes are influenced by a variety of factors that are interwoven in the broader social context. Furthermore, Caridà et al. (2019c) stated that the determination of positive value/outcomes (i.e., valuing) reflects the broader RI process and results from positive resource matching and resourcing. It is discussed in detail in Sect. 3.

M. Colurcio et al.

Table 1 Main objectives of the IVP by Airbnb

Type of value	Outcome/Value-in-context
Economic	New economic investment in the hospitality industry.
	New tourist niche in the Italian rural tourism market.
	New and valuable micro-entrepreneurship opportunities: hosts in rural areas have an additional income of 1600 euros per year (Airbnb, 2017); local businesses that do not normally benefit from tourism spending increase their turnover by taking advantage of the new connection with tourists from all over the world.
	Reduction in unemployment.
Sustainability environmental	Develop new service and quality standards in small villages to better distribute visitor flows and manage over-tourism in well-known destinations.
	Develop responsible home-sharing to improve community well-being: environmentally friendly practices.
Social	Develop new public–private business relationships and new collaborative practices to fund restoration/maintenance of historic properties and other cultural and social projects.
	Develop new tourism models (rural tourism) that encourage tourists and visitors to have an immersive experience with and in the local community: over 540,000 guest arrivals choose to stay in rural Italy over typical tourist hotspots (Airbnb, 2017).
Cultural	Develop a new idea of hospitality.
	Enhance territorial heritage by linking tourists with products and services from local cultural and creative industries.
	Develop long-term investment in festivals, cultural and social events, and urban regeneration.

Adapted from Caridà et al. (2019a)

Social and Economic Actors: Who Co-creates Value?

Actors are social and economic entities (companies, customers, public organizations, citizens, etc.) embedded in a larger social context. They are in an exchange relationship and serve as resource integrators by taking on the role of both resource provider and value beneficiary (Vargo & Lusch, 2008). For example, the customer becomes a service provider when he/she provides feedback to the company on how its processes could be improved, while the company becomes a service beneficiary.

Actors can integrate human resources (e.g., creativity, knowledge, skills, time, and effort) and non-human resources (e.g., technological infrastructure) and can take on specific social roles depending on their personal interests and the collective interest of the service ecosystem as a whole.

For example, the focal firm can play the role of orchestrator in the actors' value creation process (Hurmelinna-Laukkanen & Nätti, 2018; Pikkarainen et al., 2017) by acting as an inspirer, facilitator, and attendant within the value creation process (Gidhagen et al., 2011). Using again Airbnb's IVP as an example, the company plays the role of facilitator/orchestrator to drive the process of value co-creation and capture. The role of the platform goes beyond orchestrating transactions between property owners and accommodation seekers; it drives and coordinates the value co-creation process by mobilizing and leveraging resources from interdependent and engaged actors (Alexander et al., 2018; Hollebeek et al., 2019), such as property owners, citizens, institutions, designers, companies, and platform users. Property owners (e.g., rural hosts) act as partners and connectors; they connect tourists from all over the world with locals, creating the conditions that enable tourists and visitors to have an immersive and unique experience. This fundamentally strengthens the role of tourists as viral ambassadors, increasing positive word of mouth for the small village worldwide (Caridà et al., 2019a, 2020).

Social roles (i.e., orchestrator, partner, and connector) are a set of practices through which actors implement their intended activities into practice. Social roles link actors to perform RI and value co-creation activities; thus, they are neither static nor mutually exclusive.

According to the S-D logic, RI is the core process of value co-creation that takes place in the social context and is orchestrated by actor-generated institutions and institutional arrangements. The RI process is discussed in detail in the next section.

3 The RI Process

RI is the antecedent of the service provision/exchange (FP1) and of the value co-creation process (FP9) (Peters et al., 2014; Vargo & Lusch, 2008).

It is the process by which customers and other actors deploy resources when they undertake bundles of activities that create value directly or facilitate subsequent consumption/use from which they derive value (Hibbert et al., 2012).

Successful RI requires resourceness (i.e., the actors' awareness of the potential resources available to them: Koskela-Huotari & Vargo, 2016) and the continuous interaction and collaboration between the actors (Mele et al., 2010). Both the resourceness and interaction enable actors to access additional and potential resources to transform them into valuable resources through integration.

This is consistent with the dynamic nature of resources (Edvardsson et al., 2014; Zimmermann, 1951) for which resources (things, people, machines, money, institutions, or concepts) have only potential value until they are put to use.

Take natural resources as an example: the resourceness of wind becomes available to people only after the knowledge and skills have been developed to use it for specific purposes (e.g., for the production of renewable energy for the agricultural and industrial sectors). Therefore, potential resources become valuable when they are used through integration with other potential resources, in this case the wind energy system. This brief example serves to better conceptualize the transformative power of RI, which states that "*the usefulness of any particular potential resource from one source is moderated by the availability of other potential resources from the other sources, the removal of resistance to resource utilization, and the beneficiary's ability to integrate them*" (Vargo & Lusch, 2011, p. 184).

To explain clearly how resource transformation through integration can occur in practice, we conceptualize RI as an embedded process that results from a sequence of three phases—matching, resourcing, and valuing (Fig. 1)—that are interdependent and strongly influence each other (Caridà et al., 2019c). During the first two phases, the resources of actors match and come into being. These phases involve the transformation of basic operant resources (e.g., wind) into composite operant resources (e.g., wind energy) and interconnected operant resources (e.g., renewable energy for agriculture and industry) (Madhavaram & Hunt, 2008; Paredes et al., 2014). Finally, during valuing, the actors interpret the social context and determine the value outcomes they co-create within and through the social context.

RI Phases

Matching

The matching phase refers to the fit of existing resources that mobilizes and enables the successful transfer and activation of the actors' resources into the value creation process of other actors. It is the guiding principle of RI (Gummesson & Mele, 2010). It is also the preliminary phase of the RI process, which mainly concerns the interaction between actors.

Resource matching occurs through actor dialogue—the fundamental structure of interaction that enables the exchange of ideas, knowledge, and experiences (Gummesson & Mele, 2010). It is mediated by the social context and institutions that coordinate interaction and collaboration (Edvardsson et al., 2014; Koskela-Huotari & Vargo, 2016; Vargo & Lusch, 2011).

The Transformative Role of Resource Integration in Shaping a New...

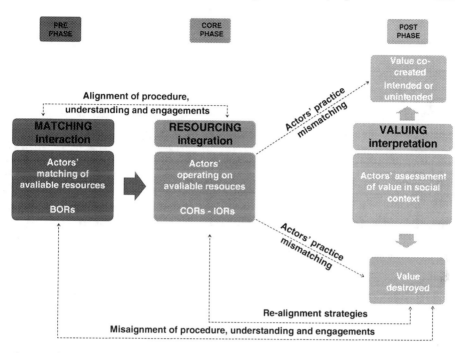

Fig. 1 The RI process: Matching, resourcing and valuing. (Adapted from Caridà et al., 2019c)

It is evident to us that RI is increasingly practiced in a digitalized and networked social context enabled by technological platforms (Tronvoll & Edvardsson, 2020). Digital platforms provide actors with new opportunities for interaction and dialogue, giving them access to additional resources that can optimize their limited abilities to create value together. However, although digital platforms promote interaction and dialogue between firms and customers, they do not ensure that the resourcing and congruent practices for positive value creation are made available. Indeed, the transition from matching to resourcing requires the alignment of procedures, understanding, and engagements (Schau et al., 2009; Skålén et al., 2015) to ensure the mutual alignment of relevant practices between actors through which they contribute to the well-being of the social context.

The SPAR Bag Design Contest (Caridà et al., 2019c; Gebauer et al., 2013) aptly explains this concept. The retail chain SPAR Austria engaged actors with different backgrounds, skills, interests, and scopes (e.g., professional designers, SPAR brand enthusiasts, and design students) to submit creative and original designs for shopping bags. The SPAR contest platform enabled a variety of features (e.g., voting, commenting, and texting other participants) and provided a range of resources (e.g., an easy-to-use online bag configurator) to enhance co-creation of values, but it was not enough. Negative outcomes and values were perceived and evaluated by many participants. Community members' complaints resulted from the lack of clear information and transparency about the contest rules and procedures (the selection of the winner was based on wordplay rather than esthetic factors), the lack of shared heritage and meaning among participants (the pun could not be understood by non-German-speaking participants), the lack of recognition of the participants' role within the community (brand indifference; the community's preferences were not considered in the jury's final decision), and the exclusion of the participants and lack of responses to their questions, which led to destructive interaction between the participants and the brand (Caridà et al., 2019c).

Therefore, the failure to achieve an expected outcome due to a lack of dialogue and constructive interaction (i.e., misalignment of procedures, understanding, and engagements: Schau et al., 2009; Skålén et al., 2015) between the community and the brand led to dissatisfaction and misbehavior that stalled the RI process in the resource matching phase (Caridà et al., 2019c). This led to emotions such as anger, frustration, and irritation (Gebauer et al., 2013), which reduced the well-being of community members.

Resourcing

Resourcing refers to the actors' operation on available resources to mutually reinforce and transform them for a common purpose and shared meanings (i.e., value creation). It is a social and cultural process that enables an actor to become a member of a network (Caridà et al., 2019c).

Resourcing is about resource formation, integration (e.g., mutual reinforcement of resources), and the removal of resistance (Lusch et al., 2008) to transform a potential resource into a specific benefit (i.e., resources become; Edvardsson et al., 2014; Vargo & Lusch, 2011; Zimmermann, 1951). This phase emerges through knowledge, skills, and institutional arrangements that act as a coordination mechanism (Vargo & Lusch, 2016) in service ecosystems.

During the resourcing phase, resources shift from basic to complex, and to interconnected (Madhavaram & Hunt, 2008; Paredes et al., 2014). This phase ensures the service exchange and contributes to the formation of the social context from which actors can derive positive or negative value.

The RomAltruista Digital Volunteering Network (DVN) (Melia & Caridà, 2020) aptly explains this concept. RomAltruista is an Italian non-profit organization (NPO) whose inspiring vision is that everyone can do good deeds for

The Transformative Role of Resource Integration in Shaping a New...

the benefit of those in need, despite the scarcity of time and the limits imposed by our busy lifestyles. RomAltruista matches the demand for volunteers from NPOs and third sector organizations with non-professional and occasional volunteers available in Rome. To this end, it promotes the idea of flexible and easy (e.g., smart) volunteering via the use of a digital platform:

> Our idea is to provide an interactive and user-friendly space to attract people more easily to volunteer activities. [...] When I found RomAltruista on the Internet, I was very impressed by its smart and efficient working scheme: with one click you can be a volunteer even if you don't have much time! I booked my first volunteer experience through the site. I was thrilled! Today, I am proud to be a part of it. (Paolo, RomAltruista board member. Facebook online streaming meeting. December 2020. https://www.facebook.com/113234605428337/videos/1305784826453134)

The platform acts as a transactional platform (Gawer, 2020), and it represents the first engagement mechanism that encourages and enables volunteers (e.g., ordinary people who lack time and expertise in dealing with social problems) to easily access volunteer activities. From the NPOs' point of view, the platform provides many opportunities to present social activities to a wider audience and to make the search for volunteers easier and more effective, as seen in the quotes below.

> I was very scared of the idea of volunteering because it is a time-consuming activity and has a strong psychological impact. A friend introduced me to RomAltruista; with a simple click I could choose when, for whom, and how I wanted to offer my time. It's very easy to choose and book the activities listed on the platform, I love it! (Gisella, RomAltruista and NPO stable volunteer. Facebook online streaming meeting. December 2020. https://www.facebook.com/113234605428337/videos/1305784826453134)

> In the beginning I had many doubts, I felt inadequate, and I was not sure if I could do the different activities. After my first experience, I understood that no special skills or abilities are needed, only motivation and enthusiasm. (Valerio, RomAltruista volunteer. Facebook online streaming meeting. February 2021. https://www.facebook.com/113234605428337/videos/166039601692975)

Over time, the RomAltruista platform and the concept of flexible volunteering inspire and drive resourcing. They enable potential volunteers to overcome a range of barriers—practical (e.g., lack of time and availability), psychological (e.g., feelings of inadequacy, lack of technical skills and knowledge, intense emotional experiences), and institutional (e.g., volunteer training, formal and fixed involvement in NPOs)—to becoming successfully active in their community. Resourcing potential resources (e.g., potential volunteers) has led to the new and valuable practice of occasional civic volunteering.

The resourcing phase reflects the strong alignment of actors (volunteers, NPOs, etc.) with the procedure, understanding, and engagement mechanisms (e.g., user-friendly platform interface, and ease and flexibility of volunteering) that characterize DVN's new social and cultural system (Melia & Caridà, 2020).

Valuing

Finally, the valuing phase refers to the actors' assessment of the value in the social context—the interpretation and determination of the positive or negative value that the actors derive from the resourcing. As described in the previous paragraphs, value is the result of the co-created experience and relates to the types of outcomes that the actors perceive. Therefore, it reflects the actors' ability to interact and integrate resources (Akaka et al., 2012), as well as his/her awareness of the effects of the alignment/misalignment of procedures, understanding, and engagements (i.e., matching or mismatching) on their practice. Intended and unintended values/outcomes may emerge from the alignment of the actors' practice. Thinking again about the RomAltruista DVN, the following quote supports such a statement. It allowed us to reflect on the concept of value as an inherently personal and contextual variable.

> When I arrived at the meeting point, I felt excited and anxious because I didn't know anyone and I didn't know how to handle the responsibility of being a volunteer. But meeting the other volunteers who welcomed and provided me clear and easy instructions to do activities was enough to dispel all my fears and doubts. (Diana, RomAltruista volunteer. Facebook online streaming meeting. December 2020. https://www.facebook.com/113234605428337/videos/1305784826453134)

RI Enabler: Institutions and Institutional Arrangements

RI is not an automatic sequence of phases; rather, it is a process with interdependent phases that require adaptation to institutions and institutional arrangements.

Institutions and institutional arrangements facilitate or impede RI. They serve as the rules, norms, and values that define the rules of the game (Frow et al., 2019) and guide the actions and interactions of the actors for service exchange and value determination (Edvardsson et al., 2011).

Institutions are deeply rooted in the social system and social structures, express social norms, and function as a basic infrastructure to coordinate cooperation and make the social context understandable and meaningful (Edvardsson et al., 2014; Koskela-Huotari & Vargo, 2016; Vargo & Lusch, 2016).

In the SPAR case, a lack of shared institutions and institutional arrangements inhibited successful resourcing and the ability of the actors to interact with each other and adapt their own resources to additional resources. These mismatches drove negative responses and led to the co-creation of a negative experience and the evaluation/determination of negative outcomes.

In contrast, adherence to a shared institutional logic (Vargo & Akaka, 2012) supports the conditions for creating and sharing value with and for the entire ecosystem. The Airbnb IVP example mentioned earlier illustrates this proposition. The key role of institutions and institutional arrangements, as well as the social context in steering and aligning the interaction/integration process toward the goal of value creation, is further explained in the next section.

4 Value Co-creation in a Service Ecosystem

To conceptualize the configurations of the actors involved in value co-creation, the service ecosystem concept was introduced in S-D logic (Lusch & Vargo, 2014; Vargo & Lusch, 2011). Ecosystem is not new as a concept and did not originate in the management field. Many scholars and scientists from different disciplines (geography, anthropology, economics, and mathematics) have worked on the link between ecosystem research and human well-being. Specifically for the field of business, a definition of business ecosystem has existed since early 1996 (Moore, 1996, p. 26): "*an economic community supported by a foundation of interacting organizations and individuals—the organisms of the business world.*" In marketing science, Vargo and Lusch's ecosystem approach synthesizes the importance of systems thinking in S-D logic "*for dealing with the, often massive, direct and indirect service exchange that occurs in economy and society*" (Vargo et al., 2017, p. 262).

The service ecosystem perspective is a systemic view on value co-creation in which the activities of the resource-integrating actors, preceding a specific instance of value determination by an actor, are seen as part of the value co-creation process. It allows for a movement toward a more unified basis for theorizing about markets (Vargo et al., 2017)

Thus, the service ecosystem perspective emphasizes that value creation does not just take place through the activities of a single actor (e.g., the customer) or between a firm and its customers; instead, that value unfolds over time among many actors.

A service ecosystem is *"a relatively self-contained, self-adjusting system of resource-integrating actors connected by shared institutional arrangements and mutual value creation through service exchange"* (Vargo & Lusch, 2016, pp. 10–11). It is characterized by dynamism and self-adjusting properties (Vargo et al., 2015; Vargo & Akaka, 2012) and is centered on the combinatorial evolution of four interdependent concepts previously described: VP, actors, resources, and institutional arrangements.

The systemic lens of an ecosystem is particularly useful for interpreting and conceptualizing complex systems of human and business relations (Jacobides et al., 2018; Vargo, 2011). The adoption of this logic implies the recognition of the importance of the role of institutions and institutional arrangements within the service ecosystem (Edvardsson et al., 2014; Koskela-Huotari & Vargo, 2016). Institutions characterize the coordination of RI among actors at each level in service ecosystems (Edvardsson et al., 2014).

The service ecosystem comprises three levels of aggregation: (1) micro-aggregation level; (2) macro-aggregation level; and (3) meso-aggregation level (the crucial link between the micro level and the macro level) (Chandler & Vargo, 2011; Frow et al., 2019).

The micro level concerns the individual actor-to-actor aggregation level and allows for a deep and detailed analysis of the specific interaction/RI process. The macro level refers to a broader level where institutions and policies can have a greater impact on the aggregation of the interactions. The meso level is a crucial level of aggregation because it acts as a connecting level between the micro and macro levels; it is an intra-organizational level and concerns the interaction/RI process of many actors involved in the context.

Transformative Process of RI: The Food for Soul Service Ecosystem

In the previous sections, we described, with the help of examples, the process of the interaction and integration of the actors' resources as a natural antecedent of value co-creation mainly at the micro-aggregation level. In this section, we address value co-creation at the meso-aggregation level of the service ecosystem. Indeed, understanding RI at the meso level is highly relevant to understanding value co-creation across the ecosystem, as it allows us to examine how management actions that address macro-level changes emerge at the meso level and how these actions influence the micro-level actors (Frow et al., 2019).

Food for Soul (FS) is an NPO founded in 2016 by Massimo Bottura, the chef patron of a three-Michelin-star Italian restaurant, with the mission to build culture as a tool of resilience, provide new opportunities for social mobility, and promote a healthy and equitable food system through the transformation of people, places, and foods. The project aims to do more than provide meals by revaluing discarded food and reinventing neglected spaces to enable social inclusion.

The heart of FS is the Refettorio concept, a way to fight against food waste through social inclusion and the engagement of diverse actors in the food value chain. The Refettorio Ambrosiano in Milan is the first effort; it was founded in collaboration with the Italian NGO Caritas Ambrosiana when, inspired by the 2015 Milan Expo, Massimo Bottura decided to tackle the double problem of food waste and social vulnerability in a new way. Bottura's idea was to reinterpret the monks' refectory and transform it into a welcoming place where the city's most vulnerable population could find a moment of restoration and beauty. Every day, guests are served nutritious meals prepared from surplus food (that would otherwise go to waste) by volunteer chefs.

The Refettorio Ambrosiano has involved many actors who share the value system behind the project and support the activities financially, morally, and practically. Thus, companies operating at different levels of the food value chain (e.g., Lavazza, Parmigiano Reggiano, Coop, Pastificio di Martino, Pastificio Mancini, Eataly, and Secret Supper) and companies specialized in food equipment and cookware (e.g., Grundig, Pentole Agnelli, and Giblor's), architects, artists, chefs, and volunteers participate in the project.

As Massimo Bottura affirms in a video on YouTube:

You can use a resource to transform it and, how do we do that, it's to connect in different notes so one of these dots is chefs. We invite chefs to collaborate on our projects, to come one day and cook together with our staff different products in order to create new recipes, new ways of addressing these ingredients and of seeing them.

I think the most important message of this project is involving the chef, their creativity, their time, and their knowledge because finding waste you need experience, you need people, chefs. They are like taking these ordinary ingredients and create extraordinary meal.

We go and speak with designers and architects and artists that transform the spaces to be functional but also beautiful and we don't think this is something shallow, but through all our projects, we have experienced how this can have a big impact in people's life and the value that they see that the society are given to them: A warm and comfortable place for the homeless and good design is incredibly smart and one that we were definitely keen to be involved with. First and foremost, we wanted to make a place where people would feel comfortable and cared for. Volunteers serve at a table; we believe that the value of hospitality can change also the way we relate to the others and a lot of it is with people in need, so instead of having a wall or a glass and serving someone through that, we go to the tables, volunteers serve other tables and say to someone hi, how was your day and you may recognize it by name. [...] We say welcome come here so that's how we rebuild the dignity of the people. (https://www.youtube.com/watch?v=ANQ6tuK9dHA, June 2021)

As seen in Fig. 2, according to this transformative perspective, the RI process addresses changes at the macro-aggregation level and can create new institutional rules and norms (Taillard et al., 2016; Vargo & Lusch, 2016).

By transforming people, places and food, we build a culture of valuing the potential in all things. When we give value to culture, we build the foundation for systemic change.

The example of Le Curve di Pasta Lunga (long noodle curves) can help to better understand the concept of transformative RI and scaling from the meso-aggregation level to the macro level. It is a form of pasta obtained from the part that is normally discarded during the production process (e.g., the drying process) of some of the most popular long pasta varieties, such as spaghetti or linguine. The project was developed by Chef Bottura and Pastificio Agricolo Mancini with the purpose of avoiding waste in the production of long pasta with high environmental and social impacts (waste of resources, raw materials, and food). To this end, for every package of Food for Soul-branded Le Curve sold (online and at Eataly), Mancini donates 1 euro to FS, helping the organization turn awareness into concrete action. This can be seen as an example of the circular economy (Aminoff et al., 2016); thus, it is a new practice of value co-creation that concerns the macro-aggregation level and was triggered by a transformative RI process. The new rules, norms, and institutional arrangements that emerge from such a transformative RI process shape new practices of value co-creation that embrace the broad and cultural

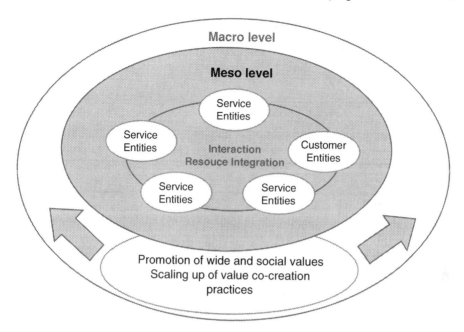

Fig. 2 The transformative RI within a service ecosystem. (Adapted from Anderson et al., 2013)

perspectives of collective well-being and can lead to the emergence of a new kind of service ecosystem.

The transformative power of the RI process we observe at FS depends heavily on the resourcing and valuing phases and on the alignment of actors' intentions, values, and practices. By integrating resources (both tangible, such as surplus food, equipment, and space, and intangible, such as technical skills, creativity, love, emotion, time, and passion) according to a shared schema of values and practices (alignment), the actors involved in the FS project fulfill a transformative role for both resources and people.

FS has saved 500 tons of food to date by actively sourcing imperfect and surplus ingredients and implementing best practices that reduce environmental impact and improve long-term sustainability. The activity of Refettorio Ambrosiano has included more than 785,000 meals, more than 1 million food deliveries, and approximately 850,000 guests since its inception. Refettorio welcomes people in vulnerable situations (isolated people, homeless people, refugees, and people facing marginalization) and provides a place of belonging to share the power of beauty with social inclusion.

More than 100 chefs, culinary apprentices, and volunteers involved in the project testify to the importance of purposeful passion, compassion, and empathy in creating social change—an open call to action that allows everyone to lend their expertise, time, and services to the resilience of humanity.

Obviously, FS aims to meet basic human needs, as Refettorios provide hot meals to homeless and struggling people, but they do much more: increasing well-being and accelerating opportunities for social mobility and economic growth through partnerships, programming, and professional development courses.

Through various initiatives, FS has built strategic alliances with operating partners and, by transforming resources, has created a socio-cultural system that enables communities to respond to the social, cultural, environmental, and economic changes they face. During the 2016 Olympic Games in Rio de Janeiro, the first international project of FS took place, RefettoRio Gastromotiva, which was realized thanks to the support of Grundig. RefettoRio Gastromotiva was part of the Sustainable Food initiative of the Committee of the Rio 2016 Olympic Games, and it was equipped with innovative products from Grundig to optimize the longevity of the food and to provide the highest level of culinary support. The partnership between Grundig and FS, as shown in the quote below from the 2017 press release issued by Grundig, triggered a new sustainable and human-based strategy:

Grundig technology assumes an authentic ethical role. As a premium global brand with a strong eco-conscience, Grundig champions the cause of reducing the world's food waste: an average of 1.3 billion tonnes of edible food is thrown away every year. Renowned for its "Respect Food" philosophy, Grundig believes people should enjoy good food—and respect it. The importance of sustainability therefore drives the company to design innovative product features that ensure food remains fresher for longer, whilst consuming less energy. (https://www.grundig.com/it-it/respectfood, June 2021)

All actors (businesses, volunteers, chefs, artists, and guests) play a transformative role as they make guests part of a community through their contribution to building and maintaining a system space that harnesses the potential of surplus food. Their transformative role is to inspire social progress and enable food solidarity and resilience, as in the case of Fatou Dineg, a refugee from Senegal who, finding herself homeless in Milan, heard about Refettorio Ambrosiano and soon became a guest. She is currently attending a computer course to find a suitable job (she is disabled and therefore can only work sitting down). She is now very happy about living in Italy:

The Transformative Role of Resource Integration in Shaping a New...

I now call this my country, more than Senegal is, because all the things I didn't have before, I got them here. (https://youtu.be/U6gJn4a3Rmw, June 2021)

Another interesting example of the transformative role of stakeholders through the Refettorio project is offered by the experience of the first culinary training workshop for guests of the Refettorio at St. Cuthbert's Centre in 2018. The course, led by chefs Gregg Brown and Simon Boyle and sponsored by St. Cuthbert's Centre to mitigate social exclusion and vulnerability, aimed to provide participants with professional kitchen experience and improve their employability. The course consisted of a 7-week program teaching 13 homeless people experiencing long-term unemployment how to cook nutritious recipes using surplus ingredients and how to serve at the door. The ultimate goal of the project was to motivate participants in gaining a positive work attitude and building self-confidence and to provide them with useful professional skills and a certificate and accreditation in food safety.

Transformativity also emerges from the words of chefs and volunteers, showing how the impact of the project is broader and deeper than goals related to charity and solidarity.

I believe that Refettorios are wonderful things: on one hand they allow you to serve those who are less fortunate, and on the other they teach us the importance of imposing and enforcing rules, especially from a social point of view. For example if a guest arrives late, it should be noted and they should be urged to be punctual the next time. The Refettorios can be a powerful social vehicle, especially if you identify fixed rules to be respected by all. There must be a unity of purpose, and only then is it possible to create a model. It is as if by establishing Refettorios, Food for Soul planted a seed. The desire to make people feel at home affects not only guests who benefit from it but, indirectly, also all those who revolve around it. Just think of the huge number of volunteers. This is the real strength of this project and I think it is enough to consider it a great victory. (Andrea, 22-year-old assistant chef, Fondazione Auxilium. https://www.foodforsoul.it/about-us/news-stories/news/the-power-of-participation/, June 2021)

FS is "not a charity," as Cristina Reni, FS Project Manager, affirms (https://www.youtube.com/watch?v=ANQ6tuK9dHA&t=2s); it is "a cultural project because we want to change the mindset of people not only regarding food ways and what food waste is."

Indeed, the transformative power of resources ensures that the individual contributions of the actors (volunteers, chefs, artists, businesses, and retailers) create culture as a tool for resilience, open up new opportunities for social mobility, and promote a fair and sustainable food system through the interpretation of shared and leading values. Moreover, this collaborative practice defines new rules and institutional arrangements at the macro-aggregation level, for example, the definition of a new social policy, tax benefits for actors who engage in such a context, and the emergence of new logistical operators for the emerging value system (Caridà et al., 2019b).

The meso-aggregation level of the service ecosystem provides space for a transformative process of RI (Cheung & McColl-Kennedy, 2015), which is a process through which the interaction between service entities (organizations, sectors, employees, companies, processes, and offerings) and consumer entities (individuals, social groups, collectives, and communities) influences collective well-being (Anderson & Ostrom, 2015) from both a social perspective (social inclusion) and an environmental perspective (sustainability).

Scaling Up and Post-COVID Pandemic Perspectives

In this chapter, we have attempted to give an interpretation of value co-creation using the TSR approach, which privileges the relational perspective. From this perspective, we have considered value co-creation within the ecosystem. In particular, we have insisted on the transformative role of RI in fostering a culture of change that aims to create value in a broad sense, including social and environmental dimensions. The brief case history of FS illustrates the shift of RI from the micro-aggregation to the meso-aggregation level. The actors are engaged in a comprehensive process of RI in which they match, resource, and value different types of resources (Caridà et al., 2019c) and collectively create a type of value that goes beyond value for the customer and for the organization, triggering new forms and practices of shared value co-creation that affect the macro-aggregation level.

In particular, by introducing the attribute of transformativity into the RI process, we add a broader than usual perspective to existing discourses on value co-creation, including social, cultural, and environmental dimensions. We explore the antecedents and consequences of value co-creation that addresses social and environmental needs, according to a view of true sustainability for people and the planet. We believe that value co-creation that incorporates social and environmental intent is more likely to occur under conditions of shared values and practices, and thus the role of institutional arrangements emerges as primary to the alignment of procedures, practices, and actors' engagement in RI.

By extending our frame of reference to social innovation studies (Schubert, 2018), the application of the transformativity concept to RI enables the activation of a social innovation. According to Pel et al. (2020, p. 3), social innovation is *"a process of changing social relations. Social innovation is a qualitative property of ideas, objects, activities or (groups of) persons, who can be considered to be socially innovative to the extent that they contribute to changing social relations."* Considering this, we can claim, especially with regard to the FS project, that the development of transformative RI enables the creation of social innovation.

"The severe impact of the COVID-19 pandemic on the service sector entails Transformative Service Research to addressing the wellbeing and sustainability of key stakeholders of this community, which include customers and employees on the micro-level, service organisations on the meso-level, the relevant industries [...] on the macro-level" (Prentice et al., 2021, p. 6). Therefore, we believe that the application of the transformative approach to RI, according to a shared and cultural project between the actors involved in the process, could offer interesting and valuable insights for the design of service and service management practices in the new normal after the pandemic.

> *We must never forget, even for a moment, that the economy is a tool created by us humans. Therefore, we must design and reconfigure it until it makes everyone happy. It is a tool designed to achieve the greatest possible collective happiness.* (Yunus, 2020)

References

Airbnb Newsroom. (2017). *Italy rural report: Sharing rural Italy a community overview.* https://s3.amazonaws.com/airbnbcitizenmedia/2017/10/Sharing_Rural_Italy_2017.pdf

Akaka, M. A., Vargo, S. L., & Lusch, R. F. (2012). An exploration of networks in value cocreation: A service-ecosystems view. *Review of Marketing Research, 9*, 13–50.

Alexander, M. J., Jaakkola, E., & Hollebeek, L. D. (2018). Zooming out: Actor engagement beyond the dyadic. *Journal of Service Management, 29*(3), 333–351.

Aminoff, A., Valkokari, K., & Kettunen, O. (2016). Mapping multidimensional value(s) for co-creation networks in a circular economy. In H. Afsarmanesh, L. M. Camarinha-Matos, & A. L. Soares (Eds.), *Collaboration in a hyperconnected world: 17th IFP WG 5.5 working conference on virtual enterprises, PRO-VE 2016, Porto, October 3–5, 2016 proceedings* (pp. 629–638). Springer.

Anderson, L., & Ostrom, A. L. (2015). Transformative service research: Advancing our knowledge about service and well-being. *Journal of Service Research, 18*(3), 243–249.

Anderson, L., Ostrom, A. L., Corus, C., Fisk, R. P., Gallan, A. S., Giraldo, M., Mende, M., Mulder, M., Rayburn, S. W., Rosenbaum, M. S., Shirahada, K., & Williams, J. D. (2013). Transformative service research: An agenda for the future. *Journal of Business Research, 66*(8), 1203–1210.

Caridà, A., Colurcio, M., Edvardsson, B., Pastore, A., & Melia, M. (2019a). Exploring the role of service platforms in shaping new service ecosystems. In C. Mele, F. Polese, & E. Gummesson (Eds.), *Naples forum on service: The 10th year. Book of abstracts: Service dominant logic, network & systems theory and service science. Integrating three perspectives for a new service agenda.* Naples Forum on Service.

Caridà, A., Colurcio, M., Spena, T. R., & Kandampully, J. (2019b). Service innovation in emerging economies: An inclusive perspective. *Sinergie Italian Journal of Management, 37*(3), 11–38.

Caridà, A., Edvardsson, B., & Colurcio, M. (2019c). Conceptualizing resource integration as an embedded process: Matching, resourcing and valuing. *Marketing Theory, 19*(1), 65–84.

Caridà, A., Colurcio, M., Edvardsson, B., & Pastore, A. (2020). Orchestrating multi-actor collaboration in service ecosystem. In *21st international CINet conference: Practicing continuous innovation in digital ecosystem* (pp. 158–166). Continuous Innovation Network.

Chandler, J. D., & Lusch, R. F. (2015). Service systems: A broadened framework and research agenda on value propositions, engagement, and service experience. *Journal of Service Research, 18*(1), 6–22.

Chandler, J. D., & Vargo, S. L. (2011). Contextualization and value-in-context: How context frames exchange. *Marketing Theory, 11*(1), 35–49.

Cheung, L., & McColl-Kennedy, J. R. (2015). Resource integration in liminal periods: Transitioning to transformative service. *Journal of Services Marketing, 29*(6/7), 485–497.

Edvardsson, B., Tronvoll, B., & Gruber, T. (2011). Expanding understanding of service exchange and value co-creation: A social construction approach. *Journal of the Academy of Marketing Science, 39*(2), 327–339.

Edvardsson, B., Kleinaltenkamp, M., Tronvoll, B., et al. (2014). Institutional logics matter when coordinating resource integration. *Marketing Theory, 14*(3), 291–309.

Frow, P., McColl-Kennedy, J. R., Payne, A., & Govind, R. (2019). Service ecosystem well-being: Conceptualization and implications for theory and practice. *European Journal of Marketing, 53*(12), 2657–2691.

Gawer, A. (2020). Digital platforms' boundaries: The interplay of firm scope, platform sides, and digital interfaces. *Long Range Planning, 102045.*

Gebauer, J., Füller, J., & Pezzei, R. (2013). The dark and the bright side of co-creation: Triggers of member behavior in online innovation communities. *Journal of Business Research, 66*(9), 1516–1527.

Gidhagen, M., Persson Ridell, O., & Sörhammar, D. (2011). The orchestrating firm: Value creation in the video game industry. *Managing Service Quality: An International Journal, 21*(4), 392–409.

Grönroos, C. (2011). Value co-creation in service logic: A critical analysis. *Marketing Theory, 11*(3), 279–301.

Grönroos, C., & Voima, P. (2013). Critical service logic: Making sense of value creation and co-creation. *Journal of the Academy of Marketing Science, 41*(2), 133–150.

Gummesson, E., & Mele, C. (2010). Marketing as value co-creation through network interaction and resource integration. *Journal of Business Market Management, 4*(4), 181–198.

Hibbert, S., Winklhofer, H., & Temerak, M. S. (2012). Customers as resource integrators: Toward a model of customer learning. *Journal of Service Research, 15*(3), 247–261.

Holbrook, M. B. (2006). Consumption experience, customer value, and subjective personal introspection: An illustrative photographic essay. *Journal of Business Research, 59*(6), 714–725.

Hollebeek, L. D., Sprott, D. E., Andreassen, T. W., Costley, C., Klaus, P., Kuppelwieser, V., Karahasanovic, A., Taguchi, T., Ul Islam, J., & Rather, R. A. (2019). Customer engagement in evolving technological environments: Synopsis and guiding propositions. *European Journal of Marketing, 53*(9), 2018–2023.

Holttinen, H. (2014). Contextualizing value propositions: Examining how consumers experience value propositions in their practices. *Australasian Marketing Journal (AMJ), 22*(2), 103–110.

Hurmelinna-Laukkanen, P., & Nätti, S. (2018). Orchestrator types, roles and capabilities: A framework for innovation networks. *Industrial Marketing Management, 74*, 65–78.

Jacobides, M. G., Cennamo, C., & Gawer, A. (2018). Towards a theory of ecosystems. *Strategic Management Journal, 39*(8), 2255–2276.

Karpen, I. O., Bove, L. L., & Lukas, B. A. (2012). Linking service-dominant logic and strategic business practice: A conceptual model of a service-dominant orientation. *Journal of Service Research, 15*(1), 21–38.

Koskela-Huotari, K., & Vargo, S. L. (2016). Institutions as resource context. *Journal of Service Theory and Practice, 26*(2), 163–178.

Lemke, F., Clark, M., & Wilson, H. (2011). Customer experience quality: An exploration in business and consumer contexts using repertory grid technique. *Journal of the Academy of Marketing Science, 39*(6), 846–869.

Lusch, R. F., & Vargo, S. L. (2014). *The service-dominant logic of marketing: Dialog, debate, and directions.* Routledge.

Lusch, R. F., Vargo, S. L., & Wessels, G. (2008). Toward a conceptual foundation for service science: Contributions from service-dominant logic. *IBM Systems Journal, 47*(1), 5–14.

Madhavaram, S., & Hunt, S. D. (2008). The service-dominant logic and a hierarchy of operant resources: Developing masterful operant resources and implications for marketing strategy. *Journal of the Academy of Marketing Science, 36*(1), 67–82.

Mele, C., Russo Spena, T., & Colurcio, M. (2010). Co-creating value innovation through resource integration. *International Journal of Quality and Service Sciences, 2*(1), 60–78.

Melia, M., & Caridà, A. (2020). Technological tools for social innovation: The digital voluntary ecosystem. In *21st international CINet conference: Practicing continuous innovation in digital ecosystem* (pp. 493–504). Continuous Innovation Network.

Moore, J. F. (1996). *The death of competition: Leadership & strategy in the age of business ecosystems.* Harper Business.

Paredes, M. R., Barrutia, J. M., & Echebarria, C. (2014). Resources for value co-creation in e-commerce: A review. *Electronic Commerce Research, 14*(2), 111–136.

Pel, B., Haxeltine, A., Avelino, F., Dumitru, A., Kemp, R., Bauler, T., Kunze, I., Dorland, J., Wittmayer, J., & Jørgensen, M. S. (2020). Towards a theory of transformative social innovation: A relational framework and 12 propositions. *Research Policy, 49*(8), 1–13.

Peters, L. D., Löbler, H., Brodie, R. J., Breidbach, C. F., Hollebeek, L. D., Smith, S. D., Sörhammar, D., & Varey, R. J. (2014). Theorizing about resource integration through service-dominant logic. *Marketing Theory, 14*(3), 249–268.

Pikkarainen, M., Ervasti, M., Hurmelinna-Laukkanen, P., & Nätti, S. (2017). Orchestration roles to facilitate networked innovation in a healthcare ecosystem. *Technology Innovation Management Review, 7*(9), 30–43.

Prentice, C., Altinay, L., & Woodside, A. G. (2021). Transformative service research and COVID-19. *The Service Industries Journal, 41*(1/2), 1–8.

Schau, H. J., Muñiz, A. M., Jr., & Arnould, E. J. (2009). How brand community practices create value. *Journal of Marketing, 73*(5), 30–51.

Schubert, C. (2018). Social innovation. In W. Rammert, A. Windeler, H. Knoblauch, & M. Hutter (Eds.), *Innovation society today* (pp. 371–391). Springer.

Skålén, P., Pace, S., & Cova, B. (2015). Firm-brand community value co-creation as alignment of practices. *European Journal of Marketing, 49*(3/4), 596–620.

Taillard, M., Peters, L. D., Pels, J., & Mele, C. (2016). The role of shared intentions in the emergence of service ecosystems. *Journal of Business Research, 69*(8), 2972–2980.

Tronvoll, B., & Edvardsson, B. (2020). Explaining how platforms foster innovation in service ecosystems. In T. X. Bui (Ed.), *Proceedings of the 53rd Hawaii international conference on system sciences* (pp. 1608–1617). HICSS.

Vargo, S. L. (2011). Market systems, stakeholders and value propositions: Toward a service-dominant logic-based theory of the market. *European Journal of Marketing, 45*(1/2), 217–222.

Vargo, S. L. (2020). From promise to perspective: Reconsidering value propositions from a service-dominant logic orientation. *Industrial Marketing Management, 87*, 309–311.

Vargo, S. L., & Akaka, M. A. (2012). Value cocreation and service systems (re) formation: A service ecosystems view. *Service Science, 4*(3), 207–217.

Vargo, S. L., & Lusch, R. F. (2008). Service-dominant logic: Continuing the evolution. *Journal of the Academy of Marketing Science, 36*(1), 1–10.

Vargo, S. L., & Lusch, R. F. (2011). It's all B2B ... and beyond: Toward a systems perspective of the market. *Industrial Marketing Management, 40*(2), 181–187.

Vargo, S. L., & Lusch, R. F. (2016). Institutions and axioms: An extension and update of service-dominant logic. *Journal of the Academy of Marketing Science, 44*(1), 5–23.

Vargo, S. L., Wieland, H., & Akaka, M. A. (2015). Innovation through institutionalization: A service ecosystems perspective. *Industrial Marketing Management, 44*(1), 63–72.

Vargo, S. L., Akaka, M. A., & Vaughan, C. M. (2017). Conceptualizing value: A service-ecosystem view. *Journal of Creating Value, 3*(2), 117–124.

Yunus, M. (2020, April 18). Coronavirus, Yunus: "Non torniamo al mondo di prima." *La Repubblica.* https://www.repubblica.it/economia/2020/04/18/news/coronavirus_yunus_non_torniamo_al_mondo_di_prima_-254319011/

Zimmermann, E. W. (1951). *World resources and industries: A functional appraisal of the availability of agricultural and industrial materials.* Harper and Row.

Behavior Change: Five Ways to Facilitate Co-creation of Service for a Better World

Per Kristensson, Jonas Hjalmar Blom, and Erik Wästlund

1 Introduction

Research into how new services are innovated has undergone many phases. The idea that new services happen simply due to *intuition, flair,* and *luck* was coined by Eric Langeard and co-authors (in Menor & Roth, 2007). This was a long-accepted truth about how new service offerings came to market, back when service was thought of as offering demarcated from goods-products (Vargo & Lusch, 2004b). Over time, however, service has evolved from a type of offering, present in specific sectors, to a mindset where service is viewed as the use of one's knowledge and skill to the benefit (i.e. serving) of other actors (Vargo & Lusch, 2004a; Vargo & Lusch, 2017). These actors are usually beneficiaries, referred to as customers, patients, citizens, visitors, users, or similar. While this latter theoretical idea is likely to resonate better with how businesses act in our world today, it still simplifies how these beneficiaries create value. Even though knowledge and skills are applied to serve the beneficiary, what the beneficiary has to do is typically referred to with a simple term: co-creation. Unfortunately, co-creation is often something that requires both effort and constraints and does not always follow the easy and predictable path that organizations sketch up.

P. Kristensson (✉) • J. H. Blom • E. Wästlund
CTF, Service Research Center, Karlstad University, Karlstad, Sweden
e-mail: Per.kristensson@kau.se; Jonashjalmar.blom@kau.se; erik.wastlund@kau.se

© The Author(s), under exclusive license to Springer Nature Switzerland AG 2022
B. Edvardsson, B. Tronvoll (eds.), *The Palgrave Handbook of Service Management,*
https://doi.org/10.1007/978-3-030-91828-6_16

The term *co-creation* embraces the fact that the beneficiary must be active in order for value to be created. For marketing scholars, simply referring to co-creation seems to do the job. However, users must deal with many hassles in order to experience the value they are interested in. In fact, in a society that has become increasingly complex, customers might often experience several kinds of limitations and not know how to co-create the value that can be important for themselves or maybe the society. This situation indicates that marketing focuses more on what happens in the organization, or the firm, than on what takes place for the beneficiary. Therefore, the beneficiary itself must work out what to do.

When users (whether they are customers, consumers, patients, citizens, guests, etc.) co-create, they turn the provided knowledge and skills from organizations into a valuable asset. Thus, produced spaghetti will probably only be of value if the user cooks it in boiling water for around 9–10 minutes. Unless the user has the competence to do that, all the knowledge and skills that employees at the providing company have served us with will be of little value. Co-creating easier tasks like making spaghetti might work for most users, but how are complex sustainable or health-promoting behaviors for the future co-created? Many of the behaviors that we have in front of us (i.e. sustainability, health, to name but a few) require changing harsh and complex behaviors in order for citizens to save our planet. Understanding behavior change is an important area that service research has largely overlooked.

Service development and service innovation are both areas that service researchers have studied extensively. Subsequent research areas have dealt with how customers can be involved in the innovation process, and more recently, service design techniques have been in focus, in terms of both applied methodologies and philosophy. Several recent articles have circled in on transformation and how to orchestrate the service ecosystem, a frequently used phrase. However, the perspective that has not been addressed in service research regards knowledge around how to manage behavior change. The co-creating activities that the user needs to be involved in may appear easy to apply; however, as soon as they entail even the smallest amount of behavior change they become a challenge that is seldom acknowledged, either by research or by practice.

In this chapter, we describe five ways in which behavior change methods can assist and guide users to change their behavior and thereby co-create the experience of value and help to save our planet. For each of the five ways, illustrative descriptions and research evidence are added.

2   Social Norm to Aid Energy Savings

The first transformative approach I would like to draw attention to is social norms. Social norms imply that the way other people behave will inform an individual about her/his upcoming behavior.

There are two types of social norms: descriptive norms depict what happens, while injunctive norms describe what should happen (Cialdini et al., 2006). Cialdini et al. (1991) defined a descriptive norm as people's perceptions of how most people behave in specific situations; it signifies what most people do without assigning judgment. For instance, if many people charge hybrid cars outside a company building, that can transmit the descriptive norm that people employed at that company value the environment. In contrast, an injunctive norm informs how people think about a certain behavior and instruct others to follow that behavior. For example, a person who watches another person wash their hands and use a face mask may pick up on the injunctive norm that he or she ought to take action to avoid spreading a virus as their upcoming behavior.

This approach to changing people's behavior implies sharing information about other people in a similar situation and then letting that information decide what actions to take.

With the emergence of climate change as a pressing challenge for societies to tackle, several issues, including energy consumption saving, are essential to face. Traditionally, politicians, policymakers, and—maybe above all—economists have been looking to employ rational price incentives to drive the change for consumers to implement various kinds of energy-saving programs. Typically neglected, but perhaps equally effective (Kristensson et al., 2017), social psychologists have shown that social norms can change people's behavior at the same rate as other more costly policy regulations, but at a lower cost.

In one of his most famous studies, Cialdini and his team went door to door, handing out information signs about energy conservation. One of the signs informed people that their neighbors had started a program to implement energy saving. (This was true, as some of the neighbors in the area were indeed adopting such behaviors, albeit on a small scale.) After a month, Cialdini and his researchers visited the same homes and asked to see the electricity meter of each house and how the residents had done in terms of energy consumption. The residents who had received information about what their neighbor had done had made significant behavioral changes. The most important aspect of this research is not that people do change, but that people generally think of themselves as independent and unaffected by what people around them do.

In another informative study, Kristensson and colleagues conducted a similar experiment in a retail store. They compared how price incentives, social norms, and various types of signals affected people's choices in a supermarket store. The social norms and the signals work similarly; social norms implied that consumers received information on how others had purchased (such as making pro-environmental choices), and the signals implied the reverse—that others would see what they had purchased. The price incentive implied that the store had reduced the price for environmentally labeled products. The results showed that social norms, whether one is picking up on them or sending them, are an equally effective means of changing people's behavior and often cheaper as they do not involve monetary incentives.

The importance of social norms and service configurations is also evident regarding plant-based food consumption (Beverland, 2014). From being a rather strict choice between vegetarian and non-vegetarian diets, the rise of the flexitarian has seen customers' decision-making processes change from pre-conceived to impromptu. The inclusion of plant-based alternatives on the menus of traditionally meat-centric global fast-food chains has contributed to the mainstreaming of plant-based foods. This change in the service offering makes it easy for customers to make pro-environmental choices while maintaining the value creating aspects of fast-food consumption.

3   Story Prompting to Keep Children in School

The second smart way of changing people's behavior toward a better world is story prompting (Wilson, 2011). It functions like a switch, whereby a person is redirected to a more positive track (Kristensson, 2021). The easiest way to do this is to simply assign a label to a person representing the behavior you want them to apply in the future. For example, you can label a person "math-clever" and encourage them to internalize a mindset about themselves as pro-math or pro-hard-working in school, which later affects their behavior in an intended way. The goal of story prompting is to guide people toward a certain etiquette (such as math clever) that enhances the likelihood that using that etiquette will attribute what their future behavior should be. For instance, for encouraging children to stay in school and learn, story prompting would imply reframing achievement more positively.

One of the premier research results regarding story prompting, focusing on pupils achieving good grades in school, comes from Dweck's (2006) research on the growth and fixed mindsets. A growth mindset is one where students expect better results if they practice a lot, whereas a fixed mindset is where individuals believe the truth of their performance is stable over time and, regardless of training, is not something that the pupil can improve.

Another example of this approach is found in Tybout and Yalch's (1980) classic research, in which they introduced the term *labeling*. Labeling entails classifying—or, more precisely, giving someone a describing characteristic— with the purpose that the individual's actions will be consistent with that classification or characterization. As with the example above, the classification may be considered an etiquette that prompts people to use a particular behavior. Using labeling as a behavior change method implies boosting the self-perception of a specific type of behavior, enhancing the likelihood that label-consistent behavior will be displayed later. Research shows that activation of cognitive and perceptual representations often leads to corresponding overt behavior (Dijksterhuis & Van Knippenberg, 1998). In a classic study, Dijksterhuis and Van Knippenberg (1998) found that activating the mental representation of a certain social group (such as hooligans) led to behaviors that corresponded with specific attributes of that social group (such as violent behavior) being displayed. Tybout and Yalch (1980) found that citizens labeled as having an "above-average probability of voting" were more likely to vote in an election than those citizens labeled as having an "average probability of voting." To sum up, assigning people with a certain way of thinking facilitates those people putting that behavior into action in the future.

4 Reduced Affective Forecasting to Help the Environment by Facilitating People's Commuting

In general, public transportation provides citizens with a convenient transportation mode to reach their destination more cheaply than via a private car, and often more quickly, as they can avoid traffic jams. However, most people disagree with this description because they have negative perceptions of public transportation. Thus, despite the availability of a smooth service that yields several customer benefits and also contributes to a greener society, users avoid adopting this service and prefer to travel by more expensive methods, typically their car.

Research has explored why users are slow to adopt public transportation, despite its numerous benefits. Factors that explain the reluctance relate to a lack of freedom of choice (Steg et al., 2001), overall psychological resistance to changing habits (Verplanken et al., 1994), and the status that having a car may bring (Beirão & Cabral, 2007). Another variable that needs to be taken into account concerns affective forecasting. Affective forecasting regards the misprediction of future satisfaction that an individual might make. This means that a car user may underestimate the potential satisfaction that public transport service might give them (Pedersen et al., 2011). The misprediction results in a persistent negative attitude toward public transport and an inaccurate positive attitude toward car use (Fujii & Gärling, 2003). From the viewpoint of sustainable development and a well-being perspective for the individual, these psychological mispredictions are undesirable.

How can affective forecasting be reduced? Research has shown that using a defocusing technique may reduce the inaccurate predictions that affective forecasting leads to. As an example of how defocusing might work, Wilson et al. (2000) asked American students to predict how happy they would be when their favorite football team had won an important game. The defocusing asked the students to consider different situations during each day of the week following the win. As a result of the defocusing technique, the students made less extreme—and, consequently, more accurate—predictions about the duration of the affect that they forecasted would take place knowing the results from the game. Instead of generalizing their feelings to all kinds of events, the defocusing led the students to consider many different activities specifically; thus, participants realized that the happiness they felt from the win might not affect their feelings while raking leaves in the backyard on a rainy day, for example.

Pedersen et al. (2012) investigated whether defocusing would increase car users' predicted satisfaction with public transport. One of their experiments applied a self-relevant defocusing technique. A self-relevant defocusing technique means that participants were asked to list up to 10 typical daily activities that they usually engage in and, with that knowledge at hand, predict their satisfaction with public transport. The defocusing technique was expected to normalize the user's prediction of public transport by making the user realize that public transportation is just one of a number of activities that an average person performs every day. The study showed that successful defocusing made car users take into account activities in life that would remain unchanged if they were to use public transport for their daily travel. Thereby, the study showed that users could make more accurate predictions of their future satisfaction with public transport. As these predictions were typically less positive from the beginning, the defocusing made users more realistic—more positive—toward public transportation.

Taken together, the extant research shows that in addition to reducing barriers such as travel planning and fare payment, public transport service providers should aim to minimize prospective customers' affective forecasting.

5 Future Self-continuity to Encourage People to Exercise More and Take Care of Their Health

As noted in the previous paragraph, people often make decisions with consequences that are pleasant in the present (such as driving their car), but harmful in the future. Many public health challenges can be construed in this way, as problems of prioritizing present over future benefits (the academic literature typically refers to this as temporal discounting). How can we help people overcome such prioritization errors?

An interesting idea that has gained support in earlier research involves zooming in on participants' tendency to reflect how their present behavior will affect their future selves. Research has related an increased focus on what life will be like in the future, with an overall reduced risk-taking and more protective behaviors, such as smoking (Adams & Nettle, 2009) and healthy dieting (Gellert et al., 2012).

In line with this, Rutchick et al. (2018) presented and examined an interesting idea that encourages people to think of their future selves to promote healthy behaviors. In short, their idea involves stimulating people to think of their future when they make present choices. Imagine you are at a restaurant and about to order a cheesecake for dessert; however, you start thinking about how you want to accomplish an upcoming 10-km run challenge and you consequently decide just to have a cup of coffee. Naturally, this is not accomplished as easily as it is described here. An intervention must occur to change the decision toward a present sacrifice and future benefit. Rutchick et al. (2018) suggested that *future self-continuity* represents the explanation that makes an intervention work in the desired direction. Future self-continuity regards a sense of identification and assimilation that connects one's present self with their future self.

There have been several similar interventions. For instance, Hall and Fong (2003) successfully promoted increased physical activity by having undergraduates undergo a series of learning sessions and activities meant to help them better understand the long-term consequences of their present actions.

Rutchick et al. (2018) stimulated conducive health behavior by inducing people to think about how their present actions will impact their lives in the future. They did this by letting participants write a letter to themselves. Hershfield et al. (2011) found that writing a letter or presenting vivid visual depictions of the future self increased the continuity between the present and the future self. In Rutchick et al. (2018), participants were instructed to write a letter to themselves in 20 years and, at the same time, consider what type of person they were at the current moment. By doing so, participants were induced to connect their present self with their future self. To sum up, helping people avoid decisions with immediate gratification can help them reach long-term values involving a healthy future.

6 Metaphoric Framing to Help People Reduce Food Waste

A final and fifth method for transforming people to perform the value-creation they likely want and need, but have difficulty achieving, regards *metaphoric framing*. The underlying idea, confirmed by research, is that the metaphors we use to describe straining and complicated processes influence how we tend to think about them later. To illustrate, Thibodeau and Boroditsky (2013) showed that when people read about criminal behavior being referred to as either a virus or a beast, it affected the way they believed society should deal with it. People who read about crime being described metaphorically as a beast viewed law enforcement and punishment as adaptive solutions significantly more than those who read about crime using the metaphor of a virus. Thus, the metaphors we use in our language shape our thinking and affect our subsequent choices.

Analogously, Lee and Schwarz (2014) showed that portraying a relationship through the metaphor of a single unit can result in feelings of threat when interpersonal conflicts arise, in contrast to thinking metaphorically about the relationship in terms of a journey that naturally has its ups and downs. Landau et al. (2014) confirmed this, showing that metaphor use enhances identity-based motivation, which resulted in positive academic engagement among young adults attending college.

To understand how metaphors shape thought, it is crucial to consider the conceptual structure that the metaphor has on the target area (Thibodeau & Boroditsky, 2015). Metaphors structure long-term conceptualizations and memories of abstract semantic knowledge (Boroditsky, 2000) and online processing of complex issues by highlighting certain aspects of a target domain and deemphasizing others. Thibodeau (2017) explained this using the metaphor of an anthill. You may receive mental pictures of ants building an anthill collectively. For example, the ant is a metaphor for being everywhere, working in large teams, being necessary for others' existence, working hard in teams, never giving up, and small things leading to something big. The metaphor of an ant might be helpful for a group of people, such as a school class, working on strenuous tasks.

Put into the context of Agenda 2030 and reducing food waste, one's performance can be described using the metaphor of a chef of a renowned Michelin-starred restaurant. This metaphor implies handling food resources in the most precious way, using raw materials without wasting any food, or using previously cooked meals as the input to the next meal. The metaphor of a Michelin-starred chef implies making great food and understanding how to use resources with knowledge of the circular life-cycle. Therefore, the positive mindset of using food as the essential resource for your next meal would imply the effect of such a metaphor. Alternatively, using the metaphor of a gold-seeking forty-niner, who views all the food resources given to him/her as potential gold, could imply a similar behavior of reducing food waste.

Given that the reduction of food waste is a key to the successful transformation of food-production and consumption, there is ample opportunity for service innovation. By creating novel services, such as metaphoric framing, services providers can help customers minimize food waste at the same time as maximizing the value of produce that has already been purchased.

7   Summary

This chapter has argued that customers, citizens, patients, and other user groups need to change their behavior in order to make our planet more sustainable. Behavior change is the final means of achieving successful new services and implies putting the beneficiary's perspective in focus (compared with the traditional organizational focus that characterizes much of marketing today). Today, although many new services have been developed, the role of users remains unacknowledged when it comes to research on sustainability and service. In this chapter, I have argued that the change processes that users need to undergo are a hidden resource for making our society greener.

The historical purpose of marketing, viewed from a helicopter perspective, has been to get people to buy things. However, complex goals such as long-term sustainability are unlikely to be reached unless we help users to change

P. Kristensson et al.

their behaviors. By understanding behavior change in a more proper way, new services can facilitate a sustainable future. This chapter has described five different ways that behavior change can happen. More knowledge can be found and applied in this area, but then researchers in service and sustainability must leave their traditional boundaries and apply scientific discoveries that have emerged outside their field.

References

Adams, J., & Nettle, D. (2009). Time perspective, personality and smoking, body mass, and physical activity: An empirical study. *British Journal of Health Psychology, 14*(1), 83–105.

Beirão, G., & Cabral, J. S. (2007). Understanding attitudes towards public transport and private car: A qualitative study. *Transport Policy, 14*(6), 478–489.

Beverland, M. B. (2014). Sustainable eating: mainstreaming plant-based diets in developed economies. *Journal of Macromarketing, 34*(3), 369–382.

Boroditsky, L. (2000). Metaphoric structuring: Understanding time through spatial metaphors. *Cognition, 75*(1), 1–28.

Cialdini, R. B., Kallgren, C. A., & Reno, R. R. (1991). A focus theory of normative conduct: A theoretical refinement and reevaluation of the role of norms in human behavior. In *Advances in Experimental Social Psychology* (Vol. 24, pp. 201–234). Academic Press.

Cialdini, R. B., Demaine, L. J., Sagarin, B. J., Barrett, D. W., Rhoads, K., & Winter, P. L. (2006). Managing social norms for persuasive impact. *Social Influence, 1*(1), 3–15.

Dijksterhuis, A., & Van Knippenberg, A. (1998). The relation between perception and behavior, or how to win a game of Trivial Pursuit. *Journal of Personality and Social Psychology, 74*(4), 865.

Dweck, C. S. (2006). *Mindset: The New Psychology of Success*. Random House.

Fujii, S., & Gärling, T. (2003). Development of script-based travel mode choice after forced change. *Transportation Research Part F: Traffic Psychology and Behaviour, 6*(2), 117–124.

Gellert, P., Ziegelmann, J. P., Lippke, S., & Schwarzer, R. (2012). Future time perspective and health behaviors: Temporal framing of self-regulatory processes in physical exercise and dietary behaviors. *Annals of Behavioral Medicine, 43*(2), 208–218.

Hall, P. A., & Fong, G. T. (2003). The effects of a brief time perspective intervention for increasing physical activity among young adults. *Psychology and Health, 18*(6), 685–706.

Hershfield, H. E., Goldstein, D. G., Sharpe, W. F., Fox, J., Yeykelis, L., Carstensen, L. L., & Bailenson, J. N. (2011). Increasing saving behavior through age-progressed renderings of the future self. *Journal of Marketing Research, 48*, S23–S37.

Kristensson, P. (2021). Behavior change—the final piece to service our world. In B. Enquist & S. Pethros (Eds.), *Business Transformation for a Sustainable Future*. Routledge.

Kristensson, P., Wästlund, E., & Söderlund, M. (2017). Influencing consumers to choose environment friendly offerings: Evidence from field experiments. *Journal of Business Research, 76*, 89–97.

Landau, M. J., Oyserman, D., Keefer, L. A., & Smith, G. C. (2014). The college journey and academic engagement: How metaphor use enhances identity-based motivation. *Journal of Personality and Social Psychology, 106*(5), 679.

Lee, S. W., & Schwarz, N. (2014). Metaphor in judgment and decision making. In M. J. Landau, M. D. Robinson, & B. P. Meier (Eds.), *The Power of Metaphor: Examining Its Influence on Social Life* (pp. 85–108). American Psychological Association.

Menor, L. J., & Roth, A. V. (2007). New service development competence in retail banking: Construct development and measurement validation. *Journal of Operations Management, 25*(4), 825–846.

Pedersen, T., Friman, M., & Kristensson, P. (2011). Affective forecasting: Predicting and experiencing satisfaction with public transportation 1. *Journal of Applied Social Psychology, 41*(8), 1926–1946.

Pedersen, T., Kristensson, P., & Friman, M. (2012). Counteracting the focusing illusion: Effects of defocusing on car users' predicted satisfaction with public transport. *Journal of Environmental Psychology, 32*(1), 30–36.

Rutchick, A. M., Slepian, M. L., Reyes, M. O., Pleskus, L. N., & Hershfield, H. E. (2018). Future self-continuity is associated with improved health and increases exercise behavior. *Journal of Experimental Psychology: Applied, 24*(1), 72.

Steg, L., Vlek, C., & Slotegraaf, G. (2001). Instrumental-reasoned and symbolic-affective motives for using a motor car. *Transportation Research Part F: Traffic Psychology and Behaviour, 4*(3), 151–169.

Thibodeau, P. (2017). The function of metaphor framing, deliberate or otherwise, in a social world. *Metaphor and the Social World, 7*(2), 270–290.

Thibodeau, P. H., & Boroditsky, L. (2013). Natural language metaphors covertly influence reasoning. *PLOS One, 8*(1), e52961.

Thibodeau, P. H., & Boroditsky, L. (2015). Measuring effects of metaphor in a dynamic opinion landscape. *PLOS One, 10*(7), e0133939.

Tybout, A. M., & Yalch, R. F. (1980). The effect of experience: A matter of salience? *Journal of Consumer Research, 6*(4), 406–413.

Vargo, S. L., & Lusch, R. F. (2004a). Evolving to a new dominant logic for marketing. *Journal of Marketing, 68*(1), 1–17.

Vargo, S. L., & Lusch, R. F. (2004b). The four service marketing myths: Remnants of a goods-based, manufacturing model. *Journal of Service Research, 6*(4), 324–335.

Vargo, S. L., & Lusch, R. F. (2017). Service-dominant logic 2025. *International Journal of Research in Marketing, 34*(1), 46–67.

Verplanken, B., Aarts, H., Van Knippenberg, A., & Van Knippenberg, C. (1994). Attitude versus general habit: Antecedents of travel mode choice 1. *Journal of Applied Social Psychology, 24*(4), 285–300.

Wilson, T. D. (2011). *Redirect: The surprising new science of psychological change.* Penguin UK.

Wilson, T. D., Wheatley, T., Meyers, J. M., Gilbert, D. T., & Axsom, D. (2000). Focalism: A source of durability bias in affective forecasting. *Journal of Personality and Social Psychology, 78*(5), 821.

Part III

Service Leadership and Transition

Self-Leadership and Empowerment: Lessons from Service Firms

Soumaya Ben Letaifa and Jean-Yves Mercier

1 Introduction

There is no reference case for the ongoing COVID crisis. In March 2021, the executive director of the International Air Transport Association noted that carriers will lose about $48 billion in 2021 and that "this crisis is longer and deeper than anyone could have expected. ... Losses will be reduced from 2020, but the pain of the crisis increases."[1] The airline sector has collapsed: revenues have shrunk due to travel bans and restrictions arising from outbreaks in major aviation markets such as India and Brazil. The roadmap out of the crisis has never been so unclear. In this context, airline carriers need to rely on new organizational and leadership capabilities.

---

[1] IATA, Reduced losses but continued pain in 2021, April 22, 2021, https://newsroom.aviator.aero/iata-reduced-losses-but-continued-pain-in-2021/.

S. Ben Letaifa (✉)
ESG-UQAM, Montreal, QC, Canada

Self Leadership Program, University of Geneva, Geneva, Switzerland
e-mail: ben_letaifa.soumaya@uqam.ca

J.-Y. Mercier
Self Leadership Program, University of Geneva, Geneva, Switzerland

Geneva School of Economics and Management, University of Geneva, Geneva, Switzerland
e-mail: Jean-Yves.Mercier@unige.ch

© The Author(s), under exclusive license to Springer Nature Switzerland AG 2022
B. Edvardsson, B. Tronvoll (eds.), *The Palgrave Handbook of Service Management*,
https://doi.org/10.1007/978-3-030-91828-6_17

The coronavirus pandemic has disrupted how businesses and governments operate. There is a profound change in the way leaders and managers think, behave, and deal with uncertainty. This is not the kind of turmoil that can be confronted through classic risk and crisis management. The complexity and duration of the situation have led to a single certainty: there is no simple way back to the former situation (Ritter & Pedersen, 2020).

Navigating by sight, monitoring the local and global evolution, assessing complex situations, envisioning and designing different scenarios for each alternative, and speedily adapting to daily data require new management competencies. This crisis is a roller coaster for every decision maker, and it calls for a turnaround in business models and mindsets.

In a way, the COVID crisis has made clear for everyone what a VUCA world means (Bennett & Lemoine, 2014). Facts and figures are no more than interpretations of the unknown. There is a common hope for a better future, but no shared vision of what it is. The crisis has shown that no leader has neither the knowledge nor the legitimacy to create trust in the long run. Each try is connected with a specific place and moment; there is no long-term solution to the *problem*. There is even no shared definition of what the "problem" is. In our health, businesses, societies, or paradigms, there is no answer available to rely on for deciding what the next step should be.

Self-leadership thus matters more than ever. A shift toward greater agility and resilience involves more self-awareness and empowerment. Managers need to unleash their full potential to cope with such complexity. Both businesses and governments have to be creative in the way they lead in these unique times. Therefore, we need to explore a new agile and resilient mindset: self-leadership. This chapter builds on a case study to highlight how self-leadership and empowerment can make a difference in a leading African Airline.

2 Theoretical Framing: Self-Leadership and Empowerment as Resources

Empowerment

"I will either find a way, or make one." This statement by Hannibal in 218 BCE summarizes how bold leaders cope with complexity and uncertainty. The crossing of the Alps was the most celebrated achievement of any military force in ancient warfare. Acting in the face of exceptional circumstances requires a blend of resourcefulness and courage. Complex situations can be unexpectedly enlightening experiences and triggers for innovation and success. Yet, they require decision makers to feel empowered in order to confront uncertainty through and beyond the crisis.

In times of uncertainty, successful leaders and managers have to embrace a creative framework in order to mobilize their troops. According to Freire (1974), an actor who is empowered becomes "politically conscious." "Developing critical consciousness" makes it possible to move from understanding to acting, from being a passive observer to being a confident and leading decision maker. In other words, "today it's imperative that people become self-leaders—individuals capable of setting priorities, taking initiative, and solving problems independently" (Blanchard et al., 2017).

Is it a way to delegate the process of decision making? Not exactly. It is much more about focusing the scope of *decisions*. Some authors define self-leadership as the ability to align with one's goals, that is, "the practice of intentionally influencing your thinking, feeling and actions towards your objective/s" (Bryant & Kazan, 2013). Others refer to "endogenous" and "self-focused" development (Tommasoli, 2004). Endogenous and self-focused development allow actors to become fully aware of their resources. They can thus activate and integrate their potential self-leadership competencies. Self-leadership appears as an iterative professional development process, through which a person:

* Becomes aware of his/her opportunities to interact differently with his/her environment
* Identifies scenarios that would allow him/her to solve a problem based on his/her competencies and inner drivers
* Assesses his/her readiness for the different scenarios
* Initiates a change

Decision making doesn't mean anymore "setting a direction," but experiencing a different way to interact. It is much more linked with learning, resilience, emotional intelligence, agility, and flexibility. It also leads the organization to consider the upper management level not as the one where the "knowledge about the future" should be, but as a catalysator for linking the trends of the market with the multiple micro-changes that will have been experienced within the company.

Self-Leadership as a Resource-Integration Process

Self-leadership starts with understanding the roles that people play in their environment, how they interact with it, and why they follow certain paths rather than others. Everyone contains an ecosystem of resources that can be leveraged with self-awareness and empowerment. The individual can be seen as a unique resource (Löbler, 2013) that can be augmented through interaction with others. An actor can be labeled as a macro-resource that can interact with other macro-resources. Each macro-resource is also an ecosystem of micro-resources in continuous learning and development. Therefore, self-leadership is a multiple-level process of resource integration: it confronts all actors with their latent (micro) resources and then considers them as a potential value for other actors in order to form networks of interdependent (macro) resources in an organization. It therefore combines and shapes two levels of resource integration: that within actors and that between actors. Empowerment is the lever of such self-transcendence.

From a managerial perspective, multiple interactions among actors generate a multilevel platform of resource integration. Through individual and collective reflection, iteration, and experimentation, individual introspection, and 360-degree feedback, managers reposition themselves in the complexity of their environment, become aware of their behaviors, focus on their motivations, and have the courage to define and implement action plans. In a nutshell, self-leadership allows managers to consciously follow the steps of Theory U in a systemic way by uncovering their intent, listening deeply to the entire system, connecting their sense of purpose, prototyping new possibilities through scenarios, and co-evolving with their environment (Scharmer, 2009). It helps those who have responsibilities to develop potential and new micro-resources and to become more effective and impactful with their teams and networks.

Today, managers need to become resilient and agile. Resilience is the ability to successfully cope with significant change—to transform the COVID-19 crisis into an opportunity, and to seize opportunities to contribute and rebound (Ben Letaifa & Mercier, 2020). The current uncertainty calls for cognitive and behavioral resilience, at the individual and organizational levels. These competencies are leveraged within self-leadership activities: small groups that collaborate in scenario formulation, peer confrontation, and introspection, which challenge and broaden everyone's perspective. At the end of the journey, the world or the crisis may not be less hostile, but actors will be more potent: they think, feel, and act differently individually and in their network. They develop agility and resilience competencies. These resources allow them to find a new equilibrium through social skills, good coping skills, and supportive relationships (Ben Letaifa & Mercier, 2020).

Value Co-creation Through Resource-Integration Activities: Subjective and Objective Outcomes of Resources

Actors co-create value as soon as they perform activities or tasks that integrate resources (Vargo & Lusch, 2016; Edvardsson et al., 2014). Resources in service industries are mainly knowledge and skills, often referred to as competencies. When actors combine their competencies, they generate new resources (Findsrud et al., 2018). New resources are outcomes of value co-creation that can be subjective (such as feelings and emotions) or objective (such as ideas and projects) or both. In fact, the emotional value (how people feel during and after the process of resource integration) and the tangible outcome (what they achieve as a group) of the process form new competencies at the individual and organizational levels. These new competencies nurture self-leadership and promote more co-creation activities.

The case study highlights how, despite a very harsh socioeconomic context (COVID-19 airline crisis), resource-integration activities unleash more individual and collective resources, thanks to the empowerment of self-leadership.

3 Case Study: Self-Leadership Applied to the Airline Industry

The case study sample (an African airline applying self-leadership) is critical, emergent, and opportunistic (Patton, 2002, p. 239). Critical single-case sampling is encouraged to reveal fine-grained data (Langley, 1999; Yin, 1994). The self-leadership program has been successful for more than a decade. The relevance and specificity of our case is related to the uniqueness of the crisis context.

As of April 2021, more than two thousand managers and leaders in Geneva, Paris, Sydney, Beijing, Casablanca, Dakar, and Tunis have benefited from the self-leadership journey.[2] Programs integrating collective intelligence, innovation, governance overhaul, and self-leadership projects have been developed to benefit many companies. By empowering managers, self-leadership is a strategy-execution accelerator. It reduces the gap between strategy and execution by committing the actors to the change they want to see, which unleashes individual and collective potential. The learning-by-doing approach leverages self-motivation and reveals the potential resources within each actor. Moreover, self-driven initiative may take place by replacing the classic psychological contract between managers and organizations with a field of opportunities for co-creation (Mercier, 1995). Leading by mutual objectives has thus less impact and importance than building scenarios and leading by co-learning.

Our case study focuses on a self-leadership program applied by a leading African airline to accompany the organizational transformation and create momentum for a new culture of agility and innovation in a context of major risk and crisis. The self-leadership agenda was customized to the specific needs and challenges of the airline business. Continuously changing travel restrictions and border shutdowns, shrinking revenue, and uncertain market forecasts and data required bold strategizing and decision making.

Yet, the suspension of many international flights due to continued lockdowns and new COVID-19 variants freed up many managers in different countries. Their availability provided an opportunity for the organization to step back and mobilize its collective intelligence by engaging a global taskforce. Because of the context, all of these people could be involved in a profound re-engineering of the company. The managers had the privilege and the responsibility of contributing to the global transformation not only to save their jobs but also to innovate. Strategies and data were uncertain and changing, so they had to take risks and take their place as leaders in an empowered, decentralized, and self-aware virtual taskforce network.

Building Taskforces

Building and functioning in taskforces was quite an innovation for this airline. It had simply never happened before. The organizational culture is vertical in the highly standardized global airline industry. Yet, top management agreed that the COVID-19 context required a disruptive way of thinking and doing business. Agile, proactive virtual teams were needed to enable endogenous innovation. The methodology relied on four critical steps: (1) consensus

---

[2] Jean Yves Mercier and Emmanuel Josserand pioneered this program in 2008 at HEC Geneva. See https://self-leadership-lab.org.

among top management on the current diagnosis of the airline situation and prioritization of key organizational challenges to be addressed by each taskforce; (2) the enrolling of each taskforce in a dedicated project to co-create an action plan; (3) the validation of each taskforce's work in a virtual global two-day workshop; and (4) the implementation of each roadmap by extended taskforces. For confidentiality reasons, the objectives of the taskforces will not be described. The authors had the privilege of being engaged as self-leadership coaches. External self-leadership coaching has accompanied all these steps to monitor teamwork progress and provide either challenge or validation.

First, top management agreed on the main strategic and organizational challenges to be prioritized. Then, a taskforce was designated to tackle each strategic challenge. All taskforces were composed of virtual global teams that fulfilled cultural and business diversity criteria (gender, seniority, core business, background, and so on). Top management also casted a net for high potentials from different core businesses and designated a senior leader and a strategic sponsor for each team. All taskforces had the same deadline for presenting their business plan and were guided by a self-leadership coach during the project-definition stage. The self-leadership coaches had three roles: first, to mentor and challenge each taskforce on a weekly basis in order to allow them to thrive; second, to guarantee the consistency and alignment of each taskforce's work with the global mission; and, third, to foster collaboration and cross-fertilization among the taskforces. After three months of coaching, a global virtual seminar was organized to share different roadmaps and aggregate them into a single comprehensive plan. Finally, each taskforce had to begin implementation of the roadmap by growing, recruiting new members in order to perform the new tasks, and collaborating with other taskforces to share real-time input and data.

4   Findings and Contributions

It should be recalled that between April and December 2020, the airline industry announced massive layoffs; major players were simply downsizing their workforce. Facing serious financial difficulties, all airlines were rationalizing their organizations. When the taskforces at our sample airline were launched, managers were anxious and stressed regarding not only their job security but also the airline's recovery. In this extremely anxiogenic context, the taskforce project was launched with a communication about the urgent need for resilience and disruptive innovation.

The Journey: A Tremendous Outcome in Itself

After six months of hard work, the organization succeeded in creating a new collaborative, communicative, and innovative ecosystem. The task-force challenge was no less than a cultural turnaround. Not only did the taskforces meet their objectives and deadlines, but they also enjoyed the journey. In fact, the journey itself was a resource-integration process that bolstered a variety of subjective experiential outcomes and objective organizational outputs.

We examine the journey instead of the results, as the journey is a longitudinal process that zooms in and reveals how potential resources can be augmented and integrated to create new ones. We focus on micro-resources (actors' skills and knowledge) and macro-resources (actors in a network of actors).

Micro-resource Integration: Experiential Outcomes at the Individual Level

The dimension of value co-creation is often perceived through subjective experiences (Findsrud et al., 2018) that reflect how individuals enjoy and assess the co-creation process. Indeed, value co-creating activities involving teamwork and collaboration generate positive energy. Professional social activities such as workshops, seminars, and taskforces are nourished by intrinsic and extrinsic motivation (Ben Letaifa et al., 2016) and fueled by gamification. Previous studies have highlighted how, thanks to intrinsic motivation, even small groups of actors can leverage heterogeneous resources to scale up limited social projects into nation-wide socioeconomic success stories (Ben Letaifa et al., 2016). When actors are involved in activities in which they gather to solve problems, innovate, and help their organization survive or move forward, they become driven by powerful emotions and feelings (energy as a resource for better resource integration). They feel empowered, strong, and bold. They gain confidence, optimism, and motivation, especially in contexts of stress and uncertainty. Every quick win and success in the value co-creation process will lead to more micro-resources, and more resource integration in teamwork will lead to more success. This process generates virtual loops of individual and organizational agility and resilience that bolster new self-leadership experiences. Figure 1 illustrates how self-leadership fuels empowerment, which bolsters additional micro- and macro-resources. New micro-resources result in individual agility and resilience, whereas new

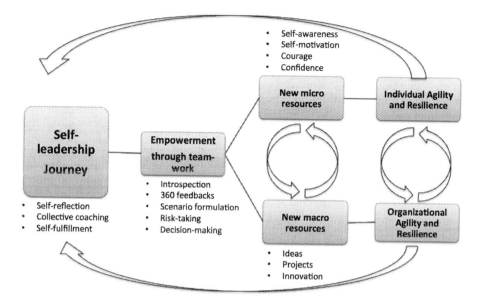

Fig. 1 Self-leadership as a resource-integration process

macro-resources lead to more organizational agility and resilience. Moreover, the micro and macro levels interplay and reinforce each other.

Macro-resource Integration: Organizational Outputs

The actors involved in the taskforces used and shared the same language, the same roadmap, target, and agenda, and real-time data. They learned to work transparently and developed ownership in a context in which the airline sector was paralyzed. Indeed, resource integration generates new potential resources that will involve additional co-creation processes (Vargo & Lusch, 2011), even during a crisis.

Self-leadership leads to individual and collective thriving. For managers, the experience crafted a real difference by leveraging awareness and retreatability, capacity for initiative and innovation, confidence, serenity, better management of personal energy, and mobility and professional development. They needed to think, step back, take a deep breath, engage their team, assess situations on a daily basis, and be confident as data and policies changed constantly. There was the pain of choosing to be resilient, and there was the gut wisdom of taking risks.

Creating synergies of energies. Today's complexity demands that all actors in a company play their role with all their personality. At least, this is the case for businesses and markets in which knowledge is the key resource. One can force an individual to follow a production process but not to innovate or find solutions to recurrent new situations. The airline ecosystem requires such a shift in management. Exploration and exploitation are key activities to innovation and organizational survival (Wilden et al., 2018). For airlines, these activities allowed the implementation of collective intelligence, supporting change during the COVID-19 crisis by mobilizing networks and communities of practice and teams around their leaders in the taskforces.

From Siloes to Networked or Ecosystemic Organizations

Resource integration takes place only if the collective activities mentioned above—workshops and taskforces—bring together managers who are fully involved and empowered. That is why these activities are supported by development programs that allow managers to develop their personal self-leadership. Such programs are designed not to "train" managers but to lead them in a kind of discovery journey that enables them to explore how they can deal with new opportunities in a way that fosters their self-fulfillment. In other words, they alternate between guided self-reflection and collective coaching for designing the kind of environment they need in order to contribute in a way through which they can learn and that is meaningful for them. Therefore, they don't look for sticking to a job or project description; rather, they better co-design the environment with their colleagues and leaders to follow their needs. They discover new potential resources in themselves, and the organization discovers new ways of solving problems. The result is development of a start-up mindset and emphasis on collective intelligence. To embark on a path that is not well marked and to co-develop it is simply the necessary paradigm for developing agile, self-organized, and resilient organizations (Noubel, 2004).

Taskforces provide space and time for management to gather, communicate, collaborate, take their rightful place, and co-create. Indeed, self-leadership activities allow synergy of energies.

Finally, in a complex crisis with no predetermined solutions, value consists no longer in implementing new business models but in knowing and understanding how to quickly embrace new mindsets and new scenarios. Managers must know themselves, which will help them to create the right answers to the various situations that they are going to encounter.

5　Discussion and Contribution

Level 1 of Resource Integration: How Micro-resources Interplay

All individuals adapt to their environment in unique ways. Behavior develops through challenges encountered, but people always refer back to patterns developed throughout their life. There is a tendency to think that people react to their environment in the same way, but actually different people facing a single situation are likely to react in different ways (Ben Letaifa, 2019). Each individual has preferred behaviors. Understanding, feeling, and knowing help individuals focus on their added value—the best situations and challenges for them to face, for which they can bring the most to their environment. They make it possible for people to choose the most suitable environments for themselves, and ultimately for them to interact with others. "If I know how you behave and you know how I behave, then we can probably better collaborate, solve conflicts, and create synergies" (Ben Letaifa, 2019). Furthermore, individuals are likely to choose and focus on the roles that suit their uniqueness. This is simply because these behaviors and interactions impact people's energy and efficiency at work (Csikszentmihalyi et al., 2014).

Having the resilience and agility to face challenges is not about willpower or denying emotions. When emotions are overly controlled, the result can be psychological damage and an inability to listen to the environment. To successfully cope with change, people need to get in touch with their emotional intelligence. The psychologists David and Congleton (2013) observe that people can be agile only through "emotional agility." This means "being flexible with our thoughts and feelings so that we can respond optimally to everyday situations."

But it is not always possible to do what we like and feel knowledgeable at. In fact, we cannot be in a flow state all the time. Growth can come in two ways (Ben Letaifa, 2019). First, we can gain skills in missions that we like but have not mastered or find more challenging environments and projects in which we use tasks at which we are expert but no longer enjoy (Csikszentmihalyi et al., 2014). Second, we can reduce how much time we spend on certain tasks. We understand that we can target specific tasks and rely on the team's resources to fulfill all of the needed activities. This is called collective intelligence, and it is an aspect of self-leadership.

From Accuracy of Competencies to Full Self-Leadership

Gaining knowledge and awareness on these dimensions helps to define the frame of what we can do if we wish to perform. But performance is more a widespread organizational need than something that human beings would automatically consider to be their target. The self-leadership discovery process is considered to be professional development more than pure personal development. It reveals the options that one can choose to foster one's own impact on one company. But empowerment needs more than personal accuracy of competencies and accuracy of the competencies required for the mission or the job description. It requires that "acting makes sense." This is the basis for a kind of contract between the self-leader and the organization.

In a complex and uncertain world, management for the whole company can no longer define "why one acts." Vision and mission statements are still useful. They describe the direction to take collectively at a particular moment. They will be modified and adapted to environmental changes. Organizational resilience means movement. The inner meaning of acting needs to be consciously revealed and identified by each person that one wishes to empower. This meaning is the only solid basis for full trust by each individual. It means nurturing self-motivation and encouraging all individuals to fulfill their specific and personal drivers in the collective journey.

Several dimensions may be considered. Schein and Van Maanen (2013), for example, has shown that we follow decision criteria, which he calls career anchors, throughout our career. Biographic interviews help managers to identify their own career anchors. But this dimension is not something that can be considered a personal trait. It is composed of a mixture of influences and choices that may be discussed again and again. Here, awareness makes it possible to identify not "who I am" but "which path I wish to follow." Age also plays a role. A single career anchor, such as looking for security or for challenges, involves different positionings at age thirty and at age fifty.

Self-leadership is thus based on awareness but finally requires a choice. The strategic choice is a decision that each of us has to make. Based on Ken Wilber's (1997) four quadrants, one can develop a personal compass synthesizing the main criteria needed to interact with one's environment: professional identity, contribution to society, the immediate work circle, and self-fulfillment. Tactically, one can then develop scenarios that may reflect this personal compass when evolving with and growing into the organization or the job market.

From Individual to Organizational Resilience and Agility Capabilities

There are times when one cannot simply wait or call for change and flexibility to occur. Confronted with paradoxes, people—and managers—tend to fall back on automatic and protective responses to their environment (Ben Letaifa, 2019). This provides neither resilience nor agility. Managers have to become aware of how to add value and how they can lead people through changes. In this perspective, self-leadership is a catalyst for change from inside. It starts with individuals and spreads to organizations.

Being aware of and relying on their own added value is the first key issue for managers. We all have tasks to do, some of which do not suit us well and can even be energy consuming (Ben Letaifa, 2019). Yet, if too much of our time is dedicated to such un-preferred tasks, which sap our energy, then we are hooked by negative emotions and feelings (such as boredom, stress, anxiety, apathy) and become unable to leverage self-motivation, to perform, and to fulfill ourselves. According to David and Congleton (2013), "The prevailing wisdom says that difficult thoughts and feelings have no place at the office: Executives, and particularly leaders, should be either stoic or cheerful; they must project confidence and damp down any negativity bubbling up inside them." It is necessary for managers to increase their focus on the tasks that are in their flow—that is, for which they are skilled and in which they feel a positive challenge.

Self-leadership will be critical to the recovery of African aviation. In other words, self-fulfillment nurtures resilience capabilities. Through self-reflection, collective coaching, and teamwork, managers will develop emotional agility and resilience. In a context in which it is crucial to be able to reduce the speed to market and the pace of change, managers need to bolster creativity, proactivity, and gut wisdom.

While navigating by sight, airline industry managers have to rely on their own convictions, to become aware of their behaviors, to focus on their motivations, and to have the courage to implement an action plan (Ben Letaifa, 2019). It is through being self-aware and self-confident that they can lead others. In an increasingly demanding and constantly evolving aviation industry and elsewhere, self-leadership helps those with responsibilities to become more effective and impactful.

Unleashing the airline industry's potential means unlocking individual potential and enabling collective intelligence to thrive within each company (Ben Letaifa & Mercier, 2020). To do this, companies are challenged to develop four axes:

* Empowering people through democratized innovation tasks and processes
* Designating sponsors and leaders for each team
* Providing coaching to support strategic alignment of taskforces or project teams
* Functioning in networks and communities of practice

These managerial practices require a new culture of co-creation, collaboration, and communication, which will foster new leadership competencies and values: self-awareness and self-motivation, transparency, ownership, capacity for initiative and innovation, confidence, better management of personal energy, courage, and more.

In a lot of change management processes, the so-called micro and macro levels are considered side by side, but not in a systemic way. Workshops are organized for the organizational issues, while trainings are provided to middle and field managers. Considering self-leadership as a resource-integration process means that within the change process, individuals benefit from specific coaching activities. These activities are necessary for them to define their own needs and value; as well as to decide for their own how they'd wish to contribute to the collective challenges.

Such leadership competencies and values are micro-resources that provide positive energy. Energy—like trust, courage, and confidence—allow us to act purposefully and in a way that aligns with our intrinsic drivers. Although leading others has still to be trained, self-leadership has, over the last decade, become the new way to help leaders take the driver's seat with their full set of resources (Ben Letaifa & Mercier, 2020).

Finally, the essence of transformative growth among aviation companies relies on empowering managers and leaders to enable them to take their rightful place. The future of the airline industry will require unleashing the full potential of people. In the current complex and rapidly changing ecosystems, we need to shape tomorrow's leadership through self-leadership training programs.

6 Limitations and Future Research

The conclusions seem limited by the single-case data. Yet, extreme case studies are insightful and relevant, as the outcomes are also true for less critical cases. Such changes have been led through dozens of organizations since 2010, mixing organizational co-design of the future and self-leadership explorations for the managers.

A study led by Kasagi (2017) shows that 92% of the participants in such iterative self-leadership programs ultimately developed new opportunities, either in their organization or by moving to another organization. The goal of any organization in launching such a program is to successfully face changes with people who are fully committed and engaged. Natural departures from the organization are part of professional life, but they have to be limited to a reasonable number (March, 1991). Self-leadership either deepens manager's sense of ownership of and membership in their organization or speeds up the decision to leave by those who do not fit into the culture, as empowerment allows them to make bold moves. This is a win-win situation, as organizations are then able to retain only motivated people. It happens only if collective activities, such as taskforces and workshops, are open to second-order learning, and not only to continuous improvement. Top management has to be willing to reopen discussion of the organization's culture and goals (Argyris, 1990).

Some observations show that this can happen only if top managers are themselves going through a self-leadership discovery program, so that they develop a vision for themselves while embracing change. In a way, this means transforming change management from a top-down approach—some leaders knowing the goal to achieve and some managers adapting to it—to a co-designed journey through uncertainty. Future studies could focus on how self-leadership programs for top managers could thus foster second-order learning within the organization, which probably means redefining the role of leaders in setting the collective vision.

References

Argyris, C. (1990). *Overcoming organizational defenses: Facilitating organizational learning*. Allyn & Bacon.

Ben Letaifa, S. (2019, February). Self leadership – Essential element for transformation & growth. *Wings Magazine*.

Ben Letaifa, S., & Mercier, J.-Y. (2020, March). Self leadership in aviation: A new innovation management agenda. *African Skies, 48*.

Ben Letaifa, S., Edvardsson, B. Å., & Tronvoll, B. (2016). The role of social platforms in transforming service ecosystems. *Journal of Business Research, 69*(5), 1933–1938.

Bennett, N., & Lemoine, G. J. (2014, January–February). What VUCA really means for you. *Harvard Business Review, 92*.

Blanchard, K., Fowler, S., & Hawkins, L. (2017). *Self-leadership and the one minute manager*. William Morrow.

Bryant, A., & Kazan, S. (2013). *Self-Leadership*. McGraw-Hill.

Csikszentmihalyi, M., Abuhamdeh, S., & Nakamura, J. (2014). Flow. In *Flow and the foundations of positive psychology* (pp. 227–238). Springer.

David, S., & Congleton, C. (2013). Emotional agility. *Harvard Business Review*. https://hbr.org/2013/11/emotional-agility

Edvardsson, B., Kleinaltenkamp, M., Tronvoll, B., McHugh, P., & Windahl, C. (2014). Institutional logics matter when coordinating resource integration. *Marketing Theory, 14*(3), 291–309.

Findsrud, R., Tronvoll, B., & Edvardsson, B. (2018). Motivation: The missing driver for theorizing about resource integration. *Marketing Theory, 18*(4), 493–519.

Freire, P. (1974). *Pédagogie des opprimés suivi de Conscientisation et révolution*. François Maspero.

Kasagi, A. (2017). *Self-leadership: Outcomes and results*. University of Geneva. Self-leadership survey by a market research project manager.

Langley, A. (1999). Strategies for theorizing from process data. *Academy of Management Review, 24*(4), 691.

Löbler, H. (2013). Service-dominant networks: An evolution from the service-dominant logic perspective. *Journal of Service Management, 24*(4), 420–434.

March, J. G. (1991). Exploration and exploitation in organizational learning. *Organization Science, 2*(1), 71–87.

Mercier, J.-Y. (1995). *Etude de l'influence des structures de pouvoir sur la dynamique d'apprentissage de l'entreprise*. Unpublished doctoral dissertation, Université de Genève, Geneva.

Noubel, J. F. (2004, November). Intelligence collective, la révolution invisible. *The Transitioner, 23*.

Patton, M. Q. (2002). *Qualitative research and evaluation methods*. Sage Publishing.

Ritter, T., & Pedersen, C. L. (2020). Analyzing the impact of the coronavirus crisis on business models. *Industrial Marketing Management, 88*, 214–224.

Scharmer, C. O. (2009). *Theory U: Learning from the future as it emerges*. Berrett-Koehler Publishers.

Schein, E. H., & Van Maanen, J. (2013). *Career anchors*. John Wiley & Sons.

Tommasoli, M. (2004). *Le développement participatif. Analyse sociale et logiques de planification*. Karthala.

Vargo, S. L., & Lusch, R. F. (2011). It's all B2B ... and beyond: Toward a systems perspective of the market. *Industrial Marketing Management, 40*(2), 181–187.

Vargo, S. L., & Lusch, R. F. (2016). Institutions and axioms: An extension and update of service-dominant logic. *Journal of the Academy of Marketing Science, 44*(1), 5–23.

Wilber, K. (1997). An integral theory of consciousness. *Journal of Consciousness Studies, 4*(1), 71–92.

Wilden, R., Hohberger, J., Devinney, T., & Lavie, D. (2018). Revisiting James March (1991): Whither exploration and exploitation? *Strategic Organization, 16*(3), 352–369.

Yin, R. (1994). *Case study research: Design and methods* (1st ed.). Sage Publishing.

Organizational Communication in Service Management

Larry Davis Browning, Jan-Oddvar Sørnes, and Peer Jacob Svenkerud

1 Introduction

We begin with this book's editors' statement: "We define 'service' as a perspective on value creation, and 'service management' as 'a set of organizational competencies for enabling and realizing value creation through service'" (Fisher, 1985). Value co-creation will always involve a constructive partnership between a provider and their consumer (Jaakkola & Alexander, 2014). Our analysis in this chapter will view *competencies* as communication practices, and will view *service* as a narrative outcome—the dénouement of a story. We'll start with an overview of organizational communication as a *process*. We'll then showcase six instances of communication and service that produced good narrative outcomes.

L. D. Browning (✉)
University of Texas at Austin, Austin, TX, USA

Nord University Business School, Bodø, Norway
e-mail: lbrowning@austin.utexas.edu

J.-O. Sørnes
Nord University Business School, Bodø, Norway
e-mail: jan-oddvar.sornes@nord.no

P. J. Svenkerud
Inland Norway University of Applied Sciences, Hamar, Norway
e-mail: peer.svenkerud@inn.no

© The Author(s), under exclusive license to Springer Nature Switzerland AG 2022
B. Edvardsson, B. Tronvoll (eds.), *The Palgrave Handbook of Service Management*,
https://doi.org/10.1007/978-3-030-91828-6_18

2 Organizational Communication

Organizational communication is a hybrid field that studies examples of communication (some better, some worse) as they affect organizations. These examples invariably involve both a sender and a receiver, the two of them communicating a message within a context of over-and-underlying processes. In processes, cycles of communication overlap to enact power and influence to constitute the organization (Deetz & Eger, 2014). An essential premise of organizations—that they are co-constructed via communication (Putnam & Mumby, 2014)—lets us employ varied considerations to our understanding of organizational communication and service. The importance of context and dénouement in communication invites an analysis of the communicative actions that enable and realize the creation of service. What is service if not communication?

Our view of the organizational communication model draws on Scott and Lewis's (2017) masterful four-volume encyclopedia of organizational communication. One feature that normally sets organizations apart from other kinds of collectivities is the presence of an understood purpose—an awareness of goals that the organization hopes to achieve. Of course, many kinds of collectivities can have goals with different degrees of focus on those goals (Carmon, 2017). A family, for instance, can have goals; so, too, an office group that meets periodically for drinks after work. The extent to which such groups focus on goals—everyone in the family having a fair chance, all members of the after-work group agreeing to meet at a new tavern—groups are organized and are likely to be aware of the role of communication in realizing those goals.

In organizational communication, an organization's purposes and goals contribute to its structure (Simpson & Holdsworth, 2017). There are all kinds of lesser structures—for example, job descriptions, evaluations, quarterly meetings, emails, and reports. These, in combination with the communication itself, constitute the organizational structure. Structures will vary in potency; they may change or remain stable; they may represent the values of the organization by placing resources behind different kinds of commitments; or they might find the resources-to-values alignment badly askew. Some organizations, such as accounting and investment firms, are loaded with structures; others make a point of retaining low structure—such as the after-work group that informally meets for drinks on Friday evenings.

The costs and benefits of structures are often at the forefront of people's minds. What gets measured are generally the things that get accomplished—the good news. Yet excessive structure can stifle creativity and innovation, causing some people to feel like mere cogs in a machine, while too little structure can cause managers to feel like they're herding alley cats. Thus, creating the proper amount of structure—the sweet spot of structure—inevitably brings communication to the forefront by increasing or decreasing insistence on communicating details (Rains & Bonito, 2017).

3 Organizational Communication and Service Narratives

What is the role of communication in service? We view "service" as a narrative with a dénouement—an ending that allows for an interpretation, an appraisal. When discussing narratives, we commonly use the term "in the beginning" (Fisher, 1985; Van der Merwe et al., 2019). Similarly, at the birth of any organization, someone or some committee no doubt initially had said: "We need to organize, and we need to put such-and-such structures into place." Some such speech act typically commands an organization into being. Such calls for organizing can be prompted by a problem needing solving, or a requirement, or an opportunity, or a vision. Often the communication in an organization will reflect the style of the founders' service orientation. In other instances, we'll see expressed a serene faith in the process—"trust the process"—rather than in an individual. Research on volition shows that organizations are difficult to start but resistant to extinction (Ghoshal & Bruch, 2003). In other words, once they come into being, organizations tend to be resilient (Doerfel & Harris, 2017).

A key precept of organization theory, especially with respect to theories of *organizing*, is that organizations rarely stay "made." Instead, they require continual reaccomplishment and regular attention (Weick, 2017). Despite grand organizational strategies and attempts at good management, organizations are in a constant state of entropy and disassemblage. Their propensity for falling apart is important, as it underscores the need to better understand how communication affects them. With the practice of reflexivity, we communicate first to establish organizations and then to adapt to any changes in the structures we've put in place. This continual reaccomplishment is achieved primarily through *communication*. Communication makes up for the fault lines in organizational structures and fills in the cracks with what we say to each other to keep things moving. Communication achieves this through adaptability (Rains & Bonito, 2017).

A key to our understanding of the sender-receiver model of communication is the *feedback loop*, which means that in the communication process, positionality is continually flipped between sender and receiver. The moment the receiver responds to the sender, the two exchange roles. These moments of trading places continue to play out as *double-interacts*, which means that properly understanding organizational communication requires our grappling with communication back-and-forth among players (Kramer, 2017). This is especially important in service contexts, where the chance for uncertainty is significant (Johlke & Duhan, 2000).

How does organizational communication apply to service? If we understand that the term "service" as it applies to service leadership, organizational scorecards, or client service in quality-improvement programs, "service" is invariably other-oriented. It refers to focusing on the needs and requirements of *others*, because doing so improves their individual performance—and thus the organization's too. Smart leaders subscribe to service leadership because they find that creating good conditions for performance improves organizational outcomes as well. A service orientation typically signals that members believe in the talent of their own organization. Similarly, service to the client is central in continuous improvement programs because it presumes that honoring the preferences of the receiver of the product or service constitutes the ultimate evaluation (Heuett, 2017), the ultimate compliment to their value.

4 Organizational Communication and the Co-creation of Value

Following are six examples, or stories, of organizational communication and the co-creation of value, all of which were researched or personally experienced by us, the writers of this chapter. To present them as stories, we took to heart five sensible narrative and co-creation prescriptions. First, a story, to hold our attention, must be about some actual *topic* located in time and space (Browning & Morris, 2012). What, in other words, is the example *about*? Second, a story will typically focus on some *problem* (Taylor, 2009). What problem were the protagonists hoping to solve? Third, how did users become part of planning the service? In other words, how was value created through interaction with them (Galvagno & Dalli, 2014)? Fourth, what in the story illustrates a moment of truth or breakthrough? Fifth, what was the narrative outcome, the ultimate effect (Browning & Morris, 2012)? We trust that our stories here are told in sufficient detail to clarify the communication service context.

5 Planning Discussions for Constructing Velodromes

Norway's first indoor velodrome was built for the 1993 UCI (*Union Cycliste Internationale*) World Road and Track Championships in Oslo. It was a temporary structure, designed to fit inside the Viking ship speed-skating stadium located at Hamar, Norway, for the 17th Winter Olympic Games in 1994. After hosting those UCI championships, the velodrome was dismantled and stored, awaiting permanent installation at some other location, not yet determined. But the installation never happened. Yet almost 20 years later, at the Norwegian cycling congress in 2012, a motion was passed to build *three* new velodromes. So what stalled the temporary one's permanent installation?

While an indoor soccer stadium or a ski-jumping hill turns out to be comparatively easy to plan, finance, and construct, given their traditional mass sports appeal in Norway, a velodrome has no government-defined price tag. So it took forever to figure out how much support the velodrome stadium might get from the government, and that in turn created uncertainty about its financing. The Norwegian government, administered by the Ministry of Culture, traditionally plays a major role in financing sports infrastructure and stadiums in that country, so when it stalled, the stored velodrome remained an orphan. Another reason for the delay was an endless quarrel about the best location for it. Norwegian culture typically experiences lengthy disagreements about the location of hospitals, airports, universities, and so on, and now the velodrome suffered from the same wrangling. The location problem was finally solved by the cycling congress in 2014. But Norway's government then faced the awkwardness of possibly crowning Norwegian champions in Poland or Denmark, as the cycling federation had to rent an arena in a foreign country in order to conduct the championship. A final problem was related to athletic performance, specifically the lack of in-country track riders—all because Norway had no home venue for track cycling and thus no strong base and culture for it.

Now that these issues have finally been solved, Norway counts three distinctive velodrome projects. The first of them, built at Sola, outside Stavanger, was financed and planned by four collaborating municipalities, with partial financing by the Ministry of Culture. The Asker project, outside Oslo, while also receiving a substantial government stimulus, enjoyed a much bigger commercial involvement for support, so only one municipality got involved. The third project, the big outdoor concrete velodrome at Levanger, outside Trondheim, is fully financed by the Levanger city municipality. Though costly, it proved an easier project to plan, finance, and construct than the others. All three projects were constructed from bottom-up participation, but they were driven by different actors, funding models, and organizational structures.

The 27 years between 1993 and 2020, when the Sola arena was completed, constitute the "Dark Ages" for indoor Norwegian track cycling, even while Norwegian *outdoor* cycling thrived in many other disciplines, including Road, Mountain bike, BMX, downhill, Trail, Endre, and CX.

The effects of the velodromes remain unknown, as they're offering a product and service never before available to Norwegian cyclists. The long-term outcome, how the product will fare, remains even more uncertain. Another outcome is that opposing sides within Norwegian cycling have buried the velodrome-hatchet and can now focus on developing track cycling as a co-creation for the benefit of all. With three velodromes soon to be opened, it will likely be a great boost for other parts of Norway to follow suit. Two lessons from the velodrome story: you cannot have service without infrastructure. Persistence must override planning conflicts for service to happen.

6   Standardizing Microchip Manufacturing at SEMATECH

SEMATECH, an acronym for SEMiconductor MAnufacturing TECHnology, was originally developed as an American manufacturing consortium. It was financed in part with contributions by the US government, especially its Department of Defense, because semiconductors (aka "chips") are a critical component of the electronics of weapon systems. SEMATECH was additionally supported by the major American chip manufacturers, because in the late 1980s, several Pacific Rim countries, like Japan, had consistently gained in production growth and the US deemed it necessary to form a consortium to redress the loss in market share. Over the last two decades, SEMATECH has evolved from a US-only consortium into a world-wide organization named *SEMATECH International*, ironically including the very Asian countries that it originally set out to defeat.

It became clear early on that SEMATECH needed to emphasize service, for if the member corporations were to solve the problem of declining market share, they would need to standardize their manufacturing process in order both to improve chip quality and to keep manufacturing costs low. Though the American manufacturers had formerly been fierce competitors, even referring to each other as "blood enemies," internal discussions at the consortium revealed that while they had their own names for different processes, some 80% of the production steps were actually common to all of them. The breakthrough on commonality occurred in a meeting when one of the leaders exclaimed, "Can't you see we are all talking about the same thing?!" Following this realization, SEMATECH sought to standardize that common 80% and agreed to compete only on the remaining 20%. The strategy allowed chip manufacturers both to cooperate as an industry and to pursue competitive business with traditional vigor.

A major part of the service realization that developed at SEMATECH involved the supply system essential to chip production. The 250 or so intricate processes required to produce a chip involve ceramics, metals, heat, photography, oxygen—all in clean rooms where workers wear "bunny suits" to avoid even a mote of damaging dust. The realization at SEMATECH that the relationship with the suppliers of these different manufacturing components was in shambles led to their directing most of their resources to servicing that same supply industry by sharing more information about needs, greater forecasting of future service requirements, and, most of all, greater planning integration. SEMATECH's effectiveness largely stemmed from the remarkable agreement and goal clarity it managed to achieve right down the line—from the chair of the board of directors, to the CEO, on through two levels of management, and down to the technical project teams that did the actual work. Agreement about a service orientation up and down the hierarchy meant that internal confusion and ambiguity about direction had been resolved. The SEMATECH story on service illustrates service change powered by a survival. Indeed, the IBM executive who toured the US promoting the founding of SEMATECH opened his slide presentation with an image of a gallows—a platform for hanging criminals—because he believed the US chip-manufacturing industry would be dead if it failed to make a prompt service adaption.

7 Providing Engine-Control Microchips at Elecoparts

Elecoparts (a pseudonym) is a global producer of electronics that range from retail customer products to components meant for others' products. The example we'll discuss here involves Elecoparts' role as supplier of the controller chip inserted into each of the automotive engines made by Bigmich (another pseudonym), one of America's major auto manufacturers. Because Bigmich is a particularly important customer and revenue producer, Elecoparts' top management had made it a priority, it thought, to keep that firm happy. But what was felt by Elecoparts to be a smooth relationship fell apart when Bigmich surprised Elecoparts with a one-page document listing no fewer than 19 problems it had encountered with the latter's engine chips. It ended with a devastating summary statement warning that these problems had to be resolved in nine months or else Ecoparts would be "de-sourced" and Bigmich would find itself another supplier. Ouch!

The Elecoparts leadership team was astounded, proclaiming to one another that this surely could not be true. But as they searched through their own production records, they discovered that Bigmich's complaint letter was fully justified. The handwringing about what to do next ended when some particularly pragmatic, creative leader turned Bigmich's 19-item problem statement into a strategy, saying, "Look, they have told us the specifics of everything that is wrong. All we need do is turn these 19 things into solutions and we'll have their commitment."

Ah, but could they do it in just nine months?

This leader's strategy was to establish a cross-functional team where each of the 19 problems was reviewed at a monthly meeting. Two weeks after the first meeting were used to follow up and solve problems identified at that meeting; two weeks before the next meeting were used to specify and nail down other problems that needed addressing. Because Elecoparts has production facilities in two major cities in the American Southwest, the monthly meetings rotated between the two plants so as to share the hosting and traveling costs.

The meetings themselves reminded one of a low-tech classroom: grand discussions centered on transparencies—transparencies!—displayed via an overhead projector with grease-pencil markings often listing the data that showed that month's problems. Displaying one, the leader might then ask, "Who knows why the bar code on the boxes is sending the chips to the wrong auto-production site?" A norm was soon established whereby anyone who volunteered to answer the leader's question had automatically committed himself or

Organizational Communication in Service Management **343**

herself to also resolving that same problem. Interestingly, these monthly cross-functional team meetings even included some of Bigmich's own employees. In fact, those outsiders numbered between a quarter to a third of all the attendees! Before each meeting, they'd make a point of touring the parking lot to see if the Elecoparts team members were driving Bigmich vehicles—*If you want us to buy your chips, you'd better drive our cars!*—and then they'd weigh in on the technical solutions proposed by Elecoparts' engineers. Bigmich participants helped ensure that Elecoparts' engine-chip problems were solved well before its chips entered the Bigmich automotive production line.

The Elecoparts story demonstrates the interchangeability of service provider and customer roles, plus the emphasis on reciprocity between them: "OK, we'll buy the cars that use the very microchips that you buy from us to insert in those same cars."

8 Communicating Diversity Through the Artic Dialogue

The "Arctic Dialogue," created in 2005, is an information-exchange forum meant to foster dialogue between a wild assortment of Arctic stakeholders—for example, environmental non-governmental organizations (ENGOs), indigenous communities, local/state/provincial/national governments, Arctic heads of state, major industry leaders, whaling captains, fishing communities, academics, and oil-and-gas companies, among others. Essentially, it provides learning opportunities for citizens all across the Arctic High North, including Alaska, Canada, Norway, and Russia. The main initiator? The US Geological Survey (2000 USGS) world-wide assessment had estimated that up to 20% of undiscovered oil-and-gas resources lie in the circumpolar Arctic. While this estimate was later challenged, it spurred massive stakeholder engagement initiated by oil-and-gas companies themselves, but also through the participation of local communities and national governments. The big idea behind the Arctic Dialogue was to foster communication—to create and increase information-sharing between stakeholders in the Arctic—and then to put this information into practice for both energy exploration and development.

Over the years from 2005 to the present, a series of seminars sprung up in Nordland, Tromsø, and Finmark in Norway, in North Aleutians Alaska, even in the Gulf of Mexico in the US and Sakhalin in Russia, all aiming to foster useful dialogue on sustainable development and sound environmental practices, as well as to share regional experiences among these countries' participants.

344   L. D. Browning et al.

A major challenge with such dialogues before 2005 was that the programs were initiated by the oil-and-gas companies themselves, creating a more lopsided approach, which resulted in some stakeholders choosing to skip the table altogether, put off by its corporate parochialism. The solution to that was a university-facilitated communication process that balanced the dialogue forum, ensuring that all sides of the energy-production issue received a hearing. Additionally, graduate students from these same Arctic countries would participate in the dialogue, promoting information exchange and research planning on socio-economic issues, environmental considerations, and the costs and benefits of oil and natural gas development in the Arctic. Strategically and symbolically, including these graduate students made for a wider vision, which in turn provided a major breakthrough, for all stakeholder presentations now changed to a more balanced focus for student learning beyond just the narrow interests of traditional stakeholders. Another moment of truth was utilizing the Norwegian approach to reaching agreement through consensus-driven dialogue. Participants from Russia, Canada, and the US commented that the model actually inspired the participants to participate and grab a spot at the table, where before they had felt unwelcome, or saw little value coming from the discussions. So the consensus-oriented Arctic Dialogue model dramatically changed their attitudes and behavior.

The Arctic Dialogue is also notable for taking the edge off resource dominance, emphasizing instead a broader set of issues that were attentive to service across the arc of time. For beginners, it has focused on supporting graduate students entering the industry. It has also emphasized ecological effects of petroleum extraction across generations.

9   Balancing Objectives at the Norwegian National Lottery

In 2006, Norway's government authorized Norsk Tipping (NT), the Norwegian National Lottery, to take over the country's market for slot machines and become its sole gaming operator. When previously operated by private vendors, that same market had created a pandemic of gaming addicts, making for lots of social problems. A study carried out by the Norwegian research organization SINTEF in 2007 indicated that 25,500 people in the Norwegian adult population present gambling problems, whereas 62,000 people had lifetime gambling problems and that problem gamblers most often played slot machines (Øren & Bakken, 2007).

Organizational Communication in Service Management 345

But even before the gambling-addiction problem arose, NT had already been practicing a delicate balancing act as the sole operator of standard lottery games in Norway. Its lofty goal was to channel surplus gaming revenue into popular sports and cultural organizations, yet it was also obliged to regulate gaming so as to minimize the negative effects of gaming activities. Indeed, curbing the troublesome social dynamics of gambling was the sole reason for its enjoying a monopoly. When the Norwegian parliament decided that the company was to take over the slot-machine market, NT was in charge of a new market of slot machines that had games notorious for causing still more addictions. (It's manifestly more addictive to pull a slot handle and get immediate results than it is to make a lottery bet and wait maybe days for results.) Even though NT's games were designed to be less aggressive than in the past, thus reducing players' gaming dependency on them, the company was criticized for pushing their games aggressively, and in fact had for some years been at the very top in advertising spending among Norwegian companies.

NT was convinced it would succeed in regulating this new market, and believed the public viewed it as a responsible operator. But surveys of external target groups failed to confirm that rosy perception. Meanwhile, internal surveys showed that NT's own employees viewed its operations positively. The contradiction puzzled NT management. But the differences in perception were unmistakable, and the public's distrust could not be talked away.

One item from opinion groups, affirmed by customers, showed that the company needed to get dead serious about addressing the issue of gaming dependency. Indeed, if NT were to succeed in operating the slot-machine market, it had to solve that problem, or else it would lose its license to operate.

Together with customers, gaming addicts, and a gaming-dependency specialist, NT set out to create what it labeled a "friendly" slot-machine market by setting several restrictions in place. In order to operate a slot machine, the customer was required to use a specially designed and restricted cash card. Players were only allowed to "lose" a predefined sum of money. The customer had to select their own restrictions as to how much money they allowed themselves to loose, before they automatically, through their restricted cash card, were excluded from further gambling (for a set period of time). Beyond these self-constraints, there remained an upper limit of losses that one could not exceed per week and month. If a customer wanted to change their own limits, they had to wait a 24-hour cooling-off period before they could return to play. The slot games themselves were also designed to operate at a less manic pace, produce less manic "noise," and to slam on predefined brakes after a certain time. According to gaming-dependency experts and gaming addicts, these constraints would offset triggers for aggressive gaming.

NT also realized that it had to refocus external communications and sharpen its own internal culture to be more focused on the negative effects of gaming. To those ends, it established relationships with gaming-addiction organizations, installed a gamblers' "help line," and launched information campaigns in cooperation with gaming-addict organizations with which they partnered.

The new concept for slot machines, based on monitors and developed in cooperation with gaming experts, addicts, and customers, proved a success. Now, after years of operations, the problems connected to slot machines and gaming dependency have been significantly reduced. In 2008, after one year of operating the new slot machines, the number of problem gamblers had been reduced. Investigations showed that out of three problem gamblers, now two could be classified as "normal-gamblers" (Rygh, 2017).

Further, NT's cooperation with external groups, such as gaming experts and addict-organizations along with customer input, strengthened NT's own understanding of gaming dependency. Being responsible became an existential bottom-line for company operations—a "make or break" for NT's very survival. The NT story, finally, is about how to reduce the product's addicts. Its unconventional, possibly unique corporate goal was not about how to generate more use of its product, but less of it.

10   The Renaissance of the Elverum Male Choir

The Elverum Male Choir, established in 1897, in the small rural town of Elverum in North East Central Norway, had, by 2001, been struggling for better than a century. It lacked direction, and its place in the local community seemed invisible. They lacked visible supporters in the community, and their audience was mainly other male-choirs attending the same events. The obstacles it faced centered on two issues: an aging choir (the average age was nearly 70) and a lack of future direction. The choir had become more of an oddity and an artifact than a compelling attraction for audiences.

Around 2010 the opportunity for recovery changed when new leadership came on board, made up of mostly new members. They immediately implemented an action plan to engage their fellow members in a joint turnaround operation.

They began by initiating a campaign to recruit new and younger members, highlighting humor and an untraditional repertoire. Member recruitment was strategic. They targeted opinion-leaders in various unfamiliar local networks, and these people themselves recruited key individuals from still other

Organizational Communication in Service Management

networks. They also created a carefully crafted website in cooperation with local media experts, rebranding the choir as the "Burgundy Jackets" (emphasizing the striking color of their new performance wardrobe), and actively communicating their new vision of "the borderless choir," meaning they were ready to perform Extra-Norwegian.

The results were stunning. Membership grew rapidly, and the novel activities caught the public's eye. Commercial support for the choir soared. The choir hired a new conductor to ramp up performance energy, ran innovative pedagogical workshops with external experts to sharpen performance, and raised funding to produce a CD, titled "Burgundy Vol. 1," to promote the Burgundy Jackets product. The CD was marketed as a "must have" Christmas gift in Norway.

The choir surfed on a wave of positivity. But the biggest challenge and opportunity lay still ahead. In 2016, the famous Norwegian film director Erik Poppe premiered a film, set during the Second World War, portraying the defiance of the King of Norway when he refused to hand over power to the German invading force. The German army chased him throughout the country, and in Elverum, he made his official stand to the Germans, refusing to surrender. The choir wanted to promote Poppe's film with an unusual event. They started planning an opera portraying the King's stance and other dramatic war stories involving Norwegian royalty. The choir's show, like the film, was labeled the "King's Choice." The program even appropriated the movie's chief star to serve as the charismatic toastmaster for its "King's Choice" performance.

The "Burgundy Jackets" prepared the opera for months, it being such a novel challenge for them. To prepare, the choir formed a partnership with the Oslo Opera and had on-site visits and workshops with professional opera singers. High-profile guest conductors were also contracted to guide them in various phases of opera, and several members of the Oslo Opera itself were showcased in the musical performance.

The concert was promoted to garner nationwide attention. Sponsor interest in the event was high, and the concert, which even included a three-course dinner (!), sold out. The show was also designed to promote Elverum, the choir's regional home, as a particularly special place, which allowed other local organizations and companies to piggyback on the event.

The choir actively engaged the community to renew itself by working with unfamiliar networks that strategically added creativity, thus repositioning what was once an aging and predictable choir. The added value created in the relationship with the Oslo opera and the development of a unique common performance positioned the choir as a distinctive, daring choir that broke traditional barriers.

The lasting effects on the choir and the local community were huge. The Burgundy Jackets are no longer an oddity, but instead regarded as an unusually entertaining organization that symbolizes creativity, humor, and singing skills. Needless to say, recruitment is no longer an issue. Tryouts have become the new practice!

The story of the men's choir beautifully illustrates a generativity script (McAdams & de St Aubin, 1992): an organization that performed at one plane elevates itself to novel performances by singing an opera with new vocalists in concert with a film. The skill sets that generated the change were familiar: network, renew the personnel, practice, pay attention to style, and be strategic about marketing.

11 Discussion

In presenting these stories, our research goal was to link specific service events with the communication that surrounded them. The overlap proved notable. Communication is altogether a process, a tool, and a technique through which co-creation occurs, especially when co-creation is defined as "the joint, collaborative, concurrent, peer-like process of producing new value, both materially and symbolically" (Galvagno & Dalli, 2014, p. 644). "Service" can be marked off as communication events that can be corrected or celebrated. In placing such corrective or applauding emphasis on them, "the symbolic and cultural meanings that consumers co-create are the very reason for their attractiveness" (Galvagno & Dalli, 2014, p. 645). The interactions that produce the dénouement, the assessment, are handled via informal communication channels as exemplified in the stream of service that emphasizes "positive word-of-mouth communications about the service provider" (Hennig-Thurau et al., 2002, p. 93).

These ideas about integration set the stage for four summary points.

First, our six examples are illuminating because they concretize service and organizational communication. Given the expansiveness of both concepts, service and communication can be applied to widely differing circumstances (van Hulst & Ybema, 2020). Our examples of service illustrate these differences and show the sheer variety of forms it can take. We've seen it reining in compulsive gamblers, both cooperating and competing in the world-wide microchip manufacturing industry, installing infrastructure via an indoor bicycle track, responding to a customer's ultimatum, trying to reach multi-national consensus about Arctic oil-and-gas exploration, and resurrecting a fossilized choral group. These efforts all used communication in pursuit of a service goal.

Second, the six examples exemplify cooperation (Lockwood et al., 2019). And while the idea of cooperation overlaps with organizational communication service, it's useful to bracket cooperation as both a process and an outcome. Such conditions allow for experimentation and innovation (Kaartemo et al., 2018). The term "co-creation of value" points our attention to how communication is used and also what steps add to co-created value.

Third, casting organizational communication service examples as stories makes them portable; that is, like a song, they can be picked up and examined for direct and implied meaning (Ricks, 2011; Green & Sergeeva, 2019). They can also be examined for mimicry or for opposition. Stories are more memorable than bare statistics and can be used for organizational learning because they are attention-getters in lectures.

Fourth, the six examples illustrate the complexity of the circumstances and purposes that occur when communicating about service (Johlke & Duhan, 2000). In these examples, communication is employed to protect a client, to develop suppliers, to renew a voluntary organization, and to keep an organization from being "desourced"—all by designing and emphasizing service programs. These examples invite an analysis of the context in which the service occurred and the central actions necessary to make the service happen (see Table 1). In Table 1, the context and the communication/service theme allow the following conclusions. What does the context of the six stories share? They are all driven to some large extent by failure—failure to renew, failure to adapt, failure to expand, failure to listen, or failure to understand. What is the meaning of these failures when applied to the co-creation of service? The lessons are familiar. Keep failures small so they don't swamp you. Learn from failures. Conceive of leadership as a response to failure (Sitkin, 1992). In understanding the communication/service theme in Table 1, note that each of them allows for a dramatic and provocative narrative. It is not difficult to imagine a story that goes with each key word. For *persistence*, there is determination—nothing comes easy. For *generativity*, there are generational hand-offs. Are tired, senescent ways renewed, or do young whippersnappers drive it in the ditch? For *realization*, the light bulb goes off. There exists an epiphany, a moment of clarity, a sudden realization that allows for a change in direction. In *responsiveness* to a threat, a show-down is avoided; instead, the threat is mollified and turned into a solution. In response to domination, a new model is employed, one that is multi-voiced and *inclusive*. For *restriction* in response to addiction, what is out of control is reigned in control.

Table 1 Communication about service

Story	Context	Communication service theme
1. Velodromes	Conflict	Persistence
2. Burgundy Jackets	Senescent	Generativity
3. SEMATECH	Identity	Realization
4. Elecoparts	Threat	Responsiveness
5. Arctic Tour	Domination	Expansion
6. Norsk Tipping	Addiction	Restriction

In summary, we apply organizational communication to service by clarifying the context of the client, by identifying the dramatic service theme, by being alert to service outcomes and to the kinds of communication necessary for establishing and maintaining a quality relationship.

References

Browning, L. D., & Morris, G. H. (2012). *Stories of life in the workplace: An open architecture for organizational narratology.* Routledge.

Carmon, A. F. (2017). Mission statements. In C. Scott & L. Lewis (Eds.), *The international encyclopedia of organizational communication, 4 volume set* (pp. 1620–1624). John Wiley & Sons.

Deetz, S. A., & Eger, E. K. (2014). Developing a metatheoretical perspective for organizational communication studies. In *The SAGE handbook of organizational communication: Advances in theory, research, and methods* (pp. 27–48).

Doerfel, M. L., & Harris, J. H. (2017). Resilience processes. In C. Scott & L. Lewis (Eds.), *The international encyclopedia of organizational communication, 4 volume set* (pp. 2058–2063). John Wiley & Sons.

Fisher, W. R. (1985). The narrative paradigm: In the beginning. *Journal of communication, 35*(4), 74–89.

Galvagno, M., & Dalli, D. (2014). Theory of value co-creation: A systematic literature review. *Managing Service Quality, 24*(6), 643–683.

Ghoshal, S., & Bruch, H. (2003). Going beyond motivation to the power of volition. *MIT Sloan Management Review, 44*(3), 51–58.

Green, S. D., & Sergeeva, N. (2019). Value creation in projects: Towards a narrative perspective. *International Journal of Project Management, 37*(5), 636–651.

Hennig-Thurau, T., Gwinner, K. P., & Gremler, D. D. (2002). Understanding relationship marketing outcomes: An integration of relational benefits and relationship quality. *Journal of Service Research, 4*(3), 230–247.

Heuett, K. B. (2017). Customer service. In C. Scott & L. Lewis (Eds.), *The international encyclopedia of organizational communication, 4 volume set* (pp. 618–623). John Wiley & Sons.

van Hulst, M., & Ybema, S. (2020). From what to where: A setting-sensitive approach to organizational storytelling. *Organization Studies, 41*(3), 365–391.

Jaakkola, E., & Alexander, M. (2014). The role of customer engagement behavior in value co-creation: A service system perspective. *Journal of Service Research, 17*(3), 247–261.

Johlke, M. C., & Duhan, D. F. (2000). Supervisor communication practices and service employee job outcomes. *Journal of Service Research, 3*, 154–165.

Kaartemo, V., Kowalkowski, C., & Edvardsson, B. (2018). Enhancing the understanding of processes and outcomes of innovation: The contribution of effectuation to SD logic. In *SAGE handbook of service-dominant logic* (pp. 522–535).

Kramer, M. (2017). Sensemaking. In C. Scott & L. Lewis (Eds.), *The international encyclopedia of organizational communication, 4 volume set* (pp. 2126–2135). John Wiley & Sons.

Lockwood, C., Giorgi, S., & Glynn, M. A. (2019). "How to do things with words": Mechanisms bridging language and action in management research. *Journal of Management, 45*(1), 7–34.

McAdams, D. P., & de St Aubin, E. D. (1992). A theory of generativity and its assessment through self-report, behavioral acts, and narrative themes in autobiography. *Journal of Personality and Social Psychology, 62*(6), 1003–1115.

Øren, A., & Bakken, I. J. (2007). Pengespill og pengespillproblemer i Norge. SINTEF 2007 (ISBN 9788214042528) 90 s. SINTEF Rapport(A3961).

Putnam, L. L., & Mumby, D. K. (Eds.). (2014). *The SAGE handbook of organizational communication: Advances in theory, research, and methods.* Sage Publications.

Rains, S. A., & Bonito, J. A. (2017). Adaptive structuration theory. In C. Scott & L. Lewis (Eds.), *The international encyclopedia of organizational communication, 4 volume set* (pp. 32–40). John Wiley & Sons.

Ricks, C. (2011). *Dylan's visions of sin.* Canongate Books.

Rygh, O. (2017). Ti år siden automatforbudet. *VG (june 30, 2017, online version).*

Scott, C., & Lewis, L. (Eds.). (2017). *The international encyclopedia of organizational communication, 4 volume set.* John Wiley & Sons.

Simpson, M. L., & Holdsworth, R. E. (2017). Structure. In C. Scott & L. Lewis (Eds.), *The international encyclopedia of organizational communication, 4 volume set* (pp. 2296–2316). John Wiley & Sons.

Sitkin, S. B. (1992). Learning through failure: The strategy of small losses. *Research in Organizational Behavior, 14*, 231–266.

Taylor, J. R. (2009). Organizing from the bottom up: Reflections on the constitution of organization in communication. In A. Nicotera, L. Putnam, & R. McPhee (Eds.), *Building theories of organization: The constitutive role of communication* (pp. 153–186). Routledge.

Van der Merwe, S. E., Biggs, R., Preiser, R., Cunningham, C., Snowden, D. J., O'Brien, K., & Goh, Z. (2019). Making sense of complexity: Using sensemaker as a research tool. *Systems, 7*(2), 1–19.

Weick, K. E. (2017). Perspective construction in organizational behavior. *Annual Review of Organizational Psychology and Organizational Behavior, 4*, 1–17.

Culture-Powered Service Excellence and Leadership: Chinese Characteristics

Xiucheng Fan, Tianran Wang, and Shiyi Lu

1 Introduction

How can enterprisers create more profit and achieve revenue growth? Heskett et al. (1994) provided the answer for this question in the service profit chain theory (SPC). The antecedents of profit and revenue growth are consumer satisfaction and loyalty. Consumers are satisfied and loyal to an enterprise because it provides them with service excellence. Services are provided by employees, so it is important for enterprises to create suitable internal environment and provide satisfied internal service for employees.

In this chapter, we argue that employees' perceived quality of the internal environment and the internal service depends on the local culture. Furthermore, we will show an internal management style based on Chinese cultural context and its application in two successful enterprises.

In Sect. 2, based on SPC, we provide a theoretical explanation of how internal service, such as leadership style, ultimately affects the revenue growth and profit of enterprises. In Sect. 3, we will give a brief introduction about national culture and organizational culture, and then elaborate how the national culture influences enterprises' leadership style through the

---

X. Fan (✉) • T. Wang • S. Lu
School of Management, Fudan University,
Shanghai, China
e-mail: xcfan@fudan.edu.cn; 20110690034@fudan.edu.cn;
20110690027@fudan.edu.cn

© The Author(s), under exclusive license to Springer Nature Switzerland AG 2022
B. Edvardsson, B. Tronvoll (eds.), *The Palgrave Handbook of Service Management*,
https://doi.org/10.1007/978-3-030-91828-6_19

organizational culture. In Sect. 4, after introducing two characteristics ("guanxi" and "family culture") of the Chinese culture, we will introduce a leadership style (paternalistic leadership) based on these two characteristics. In Sect. 5, with two cases of Chinese enterprises, we will introduce how this kind of leadership style is used in China.

2 Service Profit Chain Revisited

When we talk about an organization that has excelled in marketing, we usually focus on the revenue growth and profits of the business, which are often attributed to highly loyal, satisfied customers. The service profit chain theory holds that these external marketing factors are cultivated by satisfied employees (Heskett et al., 1994). In order to create satisfied employees, enterprises should attach importance to internal service quality.

Since first proposed by Heskett et al. (1994), the SPC has provided a path for service enterprises to guide external service value from internal service quality and ultimately improve their business performance including revenue growth and profitability. The adjustment model divided by internal, service, and external is shown in Fig. 1. To be more specific, on the internal side, better internal service quality will help companies create more satisfied employees, in turn bring out higher employee retention and employee productivity, which will later bring impacts on the quality of external services. As Heskett et al. (1994) mentioned, "leaders who understand the service-profit chain

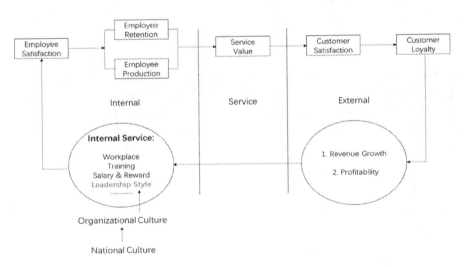

Fig. 1 The links in the service profit chain

develop and maintain a corporate culture centered on service to customers and fellow employees." On the external side, external service value win more satisfied customers, and then keep customers loyal by delivering better service results to them. Finally, high customer retention rate, repeated business transactions, and word-of-mouth recommendation will bring long-term profit to these enterprises.

Although there are still some details to be refined to discuss and clarify, such as the framework of the integration of complementary path, and whether maximizing employee satisfaction and external service quality could always optimize the long-term performance of enterprise performance, the positive and significant mean correlations for all core factors of the SPC are found (Hogreve et al., 2017). In addition, some scholars found that employee identification with the company is associated with a stronger customer–company identification, which later increases the customers' willingness to pay, thus improving financial performance as the commercial result, based on a large-scale triadic data set (Homburg et al., 2009). SPC provides a good perspective on understanding the relationship between internal organizational management and external value capture, which could also exist in a business-to-business context. According to the research made by Theoharakis et al. (2009), satisfied and loyal employees are usually more responsible and responsive, helping companies build healthy relationships with customers and strategic partners. In order to apply this concept to practical business operations, Kamakura et al. (2002) proposed a model that could be applied to a multi-branch service enterprise. This model can evaluate its own problems by collating, identifying, and applying data from enterprise stakeholders. At the same time, the model will also help enterprises to use the key data of employees and customers in the enterprise strategy formulation and operational analysis.

Some discussions on customer ownership and employee ownership are also worthy of attention. Heskett et al. (2008) described "Ownership Quotient" (OQ), which reveals how can an enterprise create customer-owners by stimulating employee ownership and thus delivering exceptional performance. They argued that customer-owners will relate their stories to others, persuade others to purchase, and provide constructive criticism and new product ideas. The authors also introduced the mirror effect, that is said, satisfied and loyal employees who have a sense of ownership will put the same attitude on the customer, and vice versa. To start such a positive cycle, business owners need to develop employees with high OQ, which is called the creation of a cycle of capability. The method includes the following work: carefully select employees and customers through attitude, clear enterprise value orientation, provide training and personal development opportunities to employees, and so on.

These discussions above point to a common proposition: In order to build a high-performing company, we need to develop more loyal customers, and the formation of loyal customers depends on the development of excellent, loyal, and satisfied employees.

In practice, many enterprises take improving employee satisfaction as the focus of improving performance. In terms of the impact of internal service quality on employee satisfaction, there are many examples showing that providing employees with better workplace design, job content design, and training opportunities will help to improve employee satisfaction. In human resource management, these designs are also referred to as part of employee welfare and are used to attract and retain employees. Tencent, a technology company and an excellent employer brand from China, trains its employees at different stages with different focuses.[1] At the same time, Tencent also encourages employees to start new businesses within the company, providing them with abundant resources and guidance to support their innovative ideas. By understanding employees' needs, Tencent has continuously improved their welfare system. Tencent, for example, has increased the amount of interest-free housing loans available to employees in first-tier cities to reduce their financial pressure. According to the internal tracking interview of Tencent, the talent turnover rate of employees applying for this welfare policy was basically lower than one-third of Tencent's average turnover rate, which shows the effectiveness of the policy.[2] These measures not only help to improve employee satisfaction, but also improve the work efficiency of employees, and help Tencent to continuously launch star products and have a good market performance. A case about employee retention from China Life Insurance also illustrates the relationship between employee retention and market performance. As a sales-oriented enterprise, the cultivation and retention of sales talents are the lifeblood of China Life Insurance. Liu Qiyan, the general manager of their human resources department, once said, "Sales managers need to have the ability to organize 700,000 sales staff, who serve customers in the front line of the market. They are our core competencies." Through a five-year talent cultivation plan, China Life Insurance has recruited and retained more than 8400 new young employees in grassroots management positions by 2015, helping the company to quickly respond to market changes, especially to meet the ever-changing needs of consumers.[3]

---

[1] Source: https://www.hbrchina.org/2018-1102/6874.html
[2] Source: https://www.hbrchina.org/2018-1030/6770.html
[3] Source: https://www.hbrchina.org/2018-1101/6836.html

According to the SPC, we suggest that managers need to provide internal service with high quality to improve the satisfaction of employees, thereby promoting employees to create service excellence for customers and making revenue growth and profit. Through a meta-analysis, Hong et al. (2013) found that leadership style is an important component of internal service quality. In addition, their research shows that service atmosphere plays a mediating role in the impact of human resource practices and leadership on employee attitude and service performance, which are further positively correlated with customer satisfaction and financial results. We argue that depending on the culture, managers need to implement appropriate leadership style as a part of internal service. In Sect. 3, we will introduce national culture, organizational culture, and the correlation between them. In Sect. 4, we will introduce paternalistic leadership, a leadership style based on Chinese culture, and in Sect. 5 we will present two cases about Chinese enterprises in using this leadership style and achieving excellent performance.

3   National Culture and Organizational Culture

In this section, we will introduce the national culture and the organizational culture. Then we propose that national culture of the host country will impact the organizational culture of the enterprise in that country.

Culture is everywhere in our life, and it influences our daily behavior all the time. Sweder and Levine (1984) defines culture as a meaning system shared by a certain group of people. Guiso et al. (2006) suggest that people from different social groups might have different beliefs and values from each other. Due to the different beliefs and values, employees from different countries might perceive different satisfaction from the same internal service. Therefore, we argue that it is necessary for manager to implement different leadership styles depending on the culture to provide satisfied internal service for employees.

In 3.5.3.1, according to the Hofstede model, we will explain the meaning of national culture and the elements it contains. In 3.5.3.2, we will illustrate the meaning of organizational culture and its components based on the Schein model. In 3.5.3.3, we propose that organizational culture depends on the national culture of the host country, so managers should choose appropriate leadership style, an important part of organizational culture, according to the national culture.

National Culture

Based on the definition of culture mentioned above, when the "certain group" is a country, the shared meaning system including beliefs and values is national culture. When it comes to the national culture, the Hofstede framework is one of the most famous theories. Based on large-scale surveys of employees around the world, Hofstede summarizes six dimensions of culture (Hofsted, 1980, Hofsted, 1991; Hofstede et al., 2010).

1. **Individualism versus collectivism**. It is an orientation reflecting how people deal with the relationship between the individual and the collective. People from an individualism (collectivism) culture prioritize the benefits of themselves (collective) and tend to work on themselves (with others).
2. **Power distance**. It is an aspect about the justice in interpersonal interactions. In a country with high (low) power distance, power is mainly controlled by top leaders (fairly distributed in the range of all people).
3. **Uncertainty avoidance**. It reflects people's attitudes to uncertainty. In a country with a high (low) uncertainty avoidance, people prefer to predictable (uncertain) alternatives, and are (are not) willing to reduce expected benefits to gain certainty.
4. **Masculinity versus femininity**. This aspect is focused on how people interact with others. People from a culture with high masculinity (femininity) are more competitive and arbitrary (humble and willing to help others).
5. **Long-term versus short-term orientation**. It is an aspect about how people make trade-off between recent and future benefits. People from a country with long-term (short-term) orientation pay more attention to future (recent) interests.
6. **Indulgence versus restraint**. It is the degree of tolerance of a certain society to people's hedonic desire. A society with indulgence (restraint) orientation allows (constraints) hedonic and indulgent behaviors of people.

These six dimensions of culture affect management practices in different ways. In a country with short-term orientation culture, for instance, employees are motivated to do tasks in which their effort can be paid in short-term (Venaik & Brewer, 2013).

According to the latest survey conducted by the team of Hofstede, the scores of 17 countries in these six dimensions are shown in Table 1.[4] Readers

---

[4] Source: https://geerthofstede.com/research-and-vsm/dimension-data-matrix/

Culture-Powered Service Excellence and Leadership: Chinese... 359

Table 1 Scores of 17 countries in the six dimensions of Hofstede model

	pdi	idv	mas	uai	lto	ind
Australia	38	90	61	51	21	71
Brazil	69	38	49	76	44	59
Canada	39	80	52	48	36	68
China	80	20	66	30	87	24
France	68	71	43	86	63	48
Germany	35	67	66	65	83	40
Great Britain	35	89	66	35	51	69
India	77	48	56	40	51	26
Italy	50	76	70	75	61	30
Japan	54	46	95	92	88	42
Korea South	60	18	39	85	100	29
Netherlands	38	80	14	53	67	68
New Zealand	22	79	58	49	33	75
Russia	93	39	36	95	81	20
Spain	57	51	42	86	48	44
Turkey	66	37	45	85	46	49
USA	40	91	62	46	26	68

pdi = power distance; idv = individualism; mas = masculinity; uai = uncertainty avoidance; lto = Long-term orientation; ind = indulgence.

can learn scores of more countries in these dimensions from the official website Hofstede.

Apart from Hofstede, other scholars also propose some meaningful dimensions of culture, such as high context versus low context, and tight culture versus loose culture (Gelfand, 2011; Hall, 1996). Readers can learn more about these theories from the references listed at the end of this chapter.

Organizational Culture

Schein (1992) points out that organizational culture is a series of assumptions that the organization has proved to be correct when dealing with external adaptability and internal integration. The organization develops and passes these assumptions to its new employees, and employees use these assumptions to understand, think, and feel related issues in their work. These assumptions can be divided into three levels (Schein, 1992).

(1) **Artifact.** It is the most detailed and observable level. It includes that all components can be seen, heard, or perceived by employees. Office decorations, clothing styles, ceremonies, stories, and heroes are all components of this level.

(2) **Value**. It is a potential belief about what an organization member should or not to do, and what should or not gained by a person. It cannot be directly observed, and people need to analyze behaviors of organization members and social word-of-mouth about the organization to realize values of the organization.

(3) **Basic assumption**. It is the most unobservable level, even not be directly realized by employees. These assumptions distinguish employees of an organization from those of other organizations, and no employee is allowed to deviate these assumptions. To be specific, these assumptions are answers of such questions about what is the essence of nature and relationship.

The Correlation Between National Culture and Organizational Culture

In this part, we argue that national culture of the host country has a significant influence on the organizational culture, and this influence is mainly formed through two mechanisms.

First, the national culture of the host country can directly affect the organizational culture. Zhang and Yang (1998) find that Western organizations mainly consider reason when making award allocation decisions, while Chinese organizations consider both reason and effect. Wei and Zhang (2010) find that if the national culture's power distance is high, these middle-level managers will have negative expectations of the prohibitive voice. As a result, even though they disagree with their superiors, or even if they find obvious problems in their current work, they will still choose to be silent.

Second, the national culture of the host country can indirectly impact the organizational culture by influencing the characteristics of the leader of the organization. Tsui et al. (2006) point out that the leadership style of the CEO has a significant effect on the organizational culture. CEOs of many companies were born and grew up in the host country where the company is located. In the process of their growth, education, and work, the national culture of the host country will deeply influence their values, beliefs, personalities, and leadership styles. Therefore, we argue that the national culture of the host country will indirectly influence the organizational culture of the company through the leadership of the CEO.

Based on above-mentioned analysis, the organizational culture of an enterprise depends on the national culture of the country where it is located, and the appropriate leadership style depends on the enterprise's organizational culture. Figure 2 is adapted from Hollensen (2017), and this figure shows the

Fig. 2 The relationship between culture and manager decision

relationship of national culture, organizational culture, and manager decision. Therefore, we argue that managers should choose the appropriate leadership style depending on the culture, so as to provide employees with satisfied internal service, thereby motivating employees to create service excellence for customers.

The leadership style of Haidilao, a Chinese hot-pot restaurant, is based on the Chinese culture and have achieved great success in the market in China. However, when it goes abroad, it needs to adjust its management mode and service mode in time to deal with the cross-cultural consumers. Haidilao, for example, needs to offer American consumers more one-person cooking POTS to fit their eating habits, while reducing some personalized pre-meal services such as manicures.[5] Little Sheep, another catering company from China, chose to introduce foreign-funded YUM for management in order to better cope with the cross-cultural team management problems.[6] From these examples, we can see that the culture of the host country where an enterprise is located has a significant impact on the effect of its manager decision and may later affect its external service.

In 3.4, the next section, focusing on the Chinese market, we will introduce "guanxi" and "family culture," two unique Chinese cultures, and introduce a paternalistic leadership, a leadership style based on the Chinese culture.

---

[5] Source: https://stock.qq.com/a/20160719/005316.htm
[6] Source: http://q.chinasspp.com/1-20911.html

4 Leadership with Chinese Characteristics

The "Guanxi" in Chinese Culture

Guanxi is an important concept in the Chinese culture (Hwang, 2008), and it refers to the "intimacy" and "dependence" between one and the other (Greenberg & Cohen, 1982). Hwang (1987) proposes the "face and favor" model to divide guanxi into three categories called instrumental guanxi, mixed guanxi, and emotional guanxi respectively. In order to achieve a current goal, people might establish a short-term connection with strangers, and this kind of connection is named instrumental guanxi. Emotional guanxi refers to the long-term connection between people and very close people such as their families. The mixed guanxi is somewhere between the above-mentioned two kinds of guanxi. In an instrumental guanxi, people decide whether to accept others' requests based on the comparison of the current benefit and cost. In an emotional guanxi, to maintain the long-term connection, people might act in favor of others even if the current cost is higher than benefit (Hwang, 2008). In the West, these three kinds of guanxi are not easy to transform into each other because there are psychological boundaries between them. In the East, however, people can transform the current kind of guanxi into a kind with higher "intimacy" by guanxi-enhancement behaviors. In practice, some managers in China support, help, and take care of their employees, thereby establishing emotional guanxi with these employees. In the emotional guanxi, managers sincerely provide high-quality internal services to increase the well-being of employees, while employees try their best to create service excellence for customers to bring profits to their organizations (Tian et al., 2015; Xie, 2017).

The "Family Culture" of China

Xie (2017) argues that the family is very important in the lives and relationships of Chinese people, which is more obvious when we compare Chinese and Westerners. Therefore, Chinese people's behaviors are more susceptible to family influences.

Liang (2011) proposes two reasons about the importance of family in China. First, Chinese people are more advanced in emotion, while Westerners are more advanced in cognition. Therefore, Chinese people attach great importance to *guanxi* when dealing with interpersonal relationships. Second, Chinese people lack activities in social groups. Therefore, they usually seek help from their families when encountering difficulties. These two reasons determine the importance of family in Chinese culture. Chinese people use the term "family culture" to indicate the way they treat their families

With the change of society, the "family culture" expands to the society outside the family, which is the familization of the society (Xie, 2017). The manifestation of familization is that people use "family culture" to deal with the interpersonal relationship in companies or organizations. Tian et al. (2015) state that companies with "family culture" regard employees as family members and try to provide excellent internal environment for them. Employees of such a company are cultivated and loved, so they develop well and create service excellence for customers.

Paternalistic Leadership

Because different host countries have different cultures, if companies in China directly apply successful management experience that is widely accepted in the West, these companies may not be able to achieve good results as they expect, so based on the culture of China, a group of scholars propose some management theories with oriental characteristics (Xie, 2017). Paternalistic leadership is a kind of leadership style based on Chinese "family culture."

Paternalistic leadership means that managers treat their employees like parents treat their children, which is characterized by three kinds of behavior: authoritarian behavior, benevolent behavior, and moral behavior (Redding, 1990; Silin, 1976; Westwood, 1997; Zheng, 1999; Zheng et al., 2000; Zheng & Lin, 1998). Zeng (2011) summarizes features of these three kinds of behaviors. Authoritarian behavior means that paternalistic leader strictly manages his or her subordinates and requires them to totally obey his or her decisions. Benevolent behavior means that paternalistic leader provides customized, comprehensive, and long-term care for the well-being of his or her subordinates. Moral behavior means that paternalistic leader shows high morality and self-cultivation in order to win the admiration of his or her subordinates, so that they will follow him or her.

These three aspects of paternalistic leader have different effects on employee behavior and organizational performance, so a group of Chinese scholars have studied the impact of these three kinds of behaviors of paternalistic leaders (Jin et al., 2016; Tian & Huang, 2014; Wang, 2015; Wu et al., 2020). Zhang et al. (2009) studied the leadership behavior of 108 management teams and found that authoritarian behaviors of leaders do not have an effect on team performance, while benevolent behaviors and moral behaviors of leaders have significantly positive effect on team performance. Zeng (2011) conducted a survey of 692 employees and found that benevolent behaviors and moral behaviors of leaders can reduce the possibility of employees to meet career plateau, while leaders' authoritarian behaviors will make it more likely for employees to meet career plateau. Lin and Yang (2014) found that benevolent behaviors and moral behaviors of leaders can promote employees to spontaneously conduct more organizational citizenship behaviors, while authoritarian behaviors of leaders have a negative effect on the organizational citizenship behaviors of employees.

Many managers in business practice are inspired by this leadership style and apply it in management practice. In the next part of this chapter, we will introduce in detail two cases about Chinese companies. The two companies wisely use this leadership style in their business and achieved ideal results.

5 Two Cases: Haidilao Hot-Pot Restaurant and Qingdao Seaview Garden Hotel

As we have reviewed above, "family culture," as a unique corporate culture in China, let the relationship between superior and subordinate in Chinese enterprises become full of human interest. In this part, two cases will be discussed, showing how family culture enables enterprises to maintain their relationship with employees and even customers, and ultimately bring excellent performance. We will begin with a brief overview of the two cases and later summarize the key Chinese cultural characteristics in tabular form.

Haidilao Hot-Pot Restaurant

As a catering company, Haidilao has enjoyed a good reputation among Chinese consumers for its considerate and even surprising service since its establishment. The particularity of the catering industry lies in that people always come to the restaurant at concentrated time, which makes it inevitable for consumers to wait. Haidilao has seized the opportunity to attract waiting customers by offering them extra services such as manicures and chess games. In the process of dining, the waiters of Haidilao also pay close attention to the needs of every customer with a warm smile and provide thoughtful service. Such warm service was supported by the family-style corporate culture of the Haidilao.

Mentoring is a key part of the "family culture" of Haidilao. Every new employee will be assigned to an old employee as a mentor when they enter the company, and the mentoring relationship between them is very close. On the one hand, only when the master brings out excellent apprentices can the master be promoted; on the other hand, if the apprentice becomes the manager of a new store, then the master can also share the profits of the new store. In this way, the master will spend energy to train his own apprentices, and Haidilao will have a more stable talent training echelon.

Haidilao's family culture is also reflected in its warmth to employees. Since most of their employees come from less affluent areas, Haidilao not only give them high wages in the industry, but also pay attention to the psychological care of their employees. They give their employees decent work clothes, encourage husbands and wives to join the job together, set up schools in the employees' hometowns to solve the education problems of their children, and provide subsidies to the employees' elders. Haidilao also looks different in the way it treats resigned employees. If the resigned employee is Haidilao's store manager and above, regardless of whether the reason for the resignation was poached by a competitor, Haidilao will give the employee a "dowry" to thank his/her contribution. These measures provide a warm sense of family for employees, improving their satisfaction to enterprise's internal environment and motivating them to create service excellence for customers to bring revenue growth and profit for Haidilao.

Qingdao Seaview Garden Hotel

Qingdao Seaview Garden Hotel (QSG) first opened in January 1995 and was awarded as a five-star hotel in 2001. The hotel was once rated by *Forbes Magazine* as one of the 50 best business hotels in China and was recorded by a case of Harvard Business School. Approximately 20,000 practitioners come to visit the hotel every year to learn its successful experience. QSG creates a service brand of "family love" in order to "create surprise and touch for customers."

On the home page of its website, QSG says its staff will bring "stories worth telling" to their guests. The manager of the hotel adheres to such a pursuit of customer praise business philosophy: "if the service does not leave the consumer a story worth telling, then the service is zero service." As a hotel with outstanding reputation among customers, QSG has a strong customer orientation. In their values, the customer is always right, and the hotel should never say no to the customer. In QSG's management philosophy, they regard employees as representatives of both the hotel and the customers. On the one hand, employees represent the hotel when providing services; on the other hand, employees should also understand and strive to achieve the wishes of customers. To achieve their high requirements for the service, QSG needs to rely on the efforts of every employee of the hotel, that is, in order to motivate employees to serve customers like home, QSG need to provide employees with a family culture as well.

In terms of staff training, QSG is committed to providing staff with the same care as family love and cultivating employees just like how parents cultivate their own children. They train their employees to be honest, ethical, mannered, and responsible. They also strongly want their employees to be grateful, and here the scope of gratitude goes beyond what they need to be exposed to on a day-to-day basis. They are taught to be grateful to their parents for raising them, to their teachers for educating them, to QSG for nurturing them, and to their customers for providing them with the opportunity to work. In order to motivate the employees, QSG actively commends the excellent employees and punish the improper behaviors resolutely, and these punishments must be imposed, whether they are on the staff or managers. Thus, at QSG, it's not surprising that most managers have experienced demotions and basic pay cuts. Through the unique values and incentive means with clear reward and punishment, QSG not only shows the standardized operation quality, but also conveys the Chinese culture of love and care to their customers. Due to these measures, QSG create a family-like internal environment where its employees feel satisfied to the enterprise and will try their best to provide customers with excellent service which will bring sustainable revenue growth and profit for QSG (Table 2).

6 Summary

In this chapter, we first reviewed the SPC theory and sorted out how to create satisfied customers by creating satisfied employees from the internal organization, and then obtain good profits. Employees provide quality services to consumers, and at the same time, enterprises need to create a suitable internal environment for them. The judgment of "suitable" is often based on the local culture. Next, we learn how a country's organizational culture influences the corporate culture and, ultimately, the behavior of its employees. At last, we use two unique cases from China to discuss the special influence of Chinese "family culture." In these two typical cases of Chinese service enterprises,

Culture-Powered Service Excellence and Leadership: Chinese... 367

Table 2 Comparison of Haidilao and Qingdao Seaview Garden Hotel

Chinese characteristics	Specific practice in two cases
Collectivism	**Haidilao**: Every new employee will be assigned to an old employee as a mentor when they enter the company. On the one hand, only when the master brings out excellent apprentices can the master be promoted; on the other hand, if the apprentice becomes the manager of a new store, then the master can also share the profits of the new store.
	QSG: Requires employees to have the spirit of sacrifice and dedication. It is better for the department and the company to lose than for the customer.
"Guanxi"	**Haidilao**: Encourages husbands and wives to join the job together, set up schools in the employees' hometowns to solve the education problems of their children, and provide subsidies to the employees' elders.
	QSG: The management staff not only meticulously do practical things for employees, but also mobilize their family members (non-QS employees) to help them do practical things, so that employees feel that "they depend on their parents for everything at home, and they have relatives everywhere in QSG."
Paternalistic leadership	**QSG**: The aim of QSG is to cultivate every employee into a useful person for the society, and hope that they know how to be grateful. In this process, they take the form of heavy rewards and heavy punishment, and give them parental education and care.

these enterprises start from improving the welfare of employees and finally create high-quality service, which reflects the theoretical essence of service profit chain.

References

Gelfand, J. (2011). Differences between tight and loose cultures: A 33-nation study. *Science, 332*(6033), 1100–1104.

Greenberg, J., & Cohen, L. (1982). Why justice? Normative and instrumental interpretations. In J. Greenberg & R. Cohen (Eds.), *Equity and justice in social behavior* (pp. 437–467). Academic Press.

Guiso, L., Sapienza, P., & Zingales, L. (2006). Does culture affect economic outcomes? *Journal of Economic Perspectives, 20*, 23–48.

Hall, T. (1996). *The hidden dimension*. Doubleday.

Heskett, J., Jones, T., Loveman, G., Earl Sasser, W., Jr., & Schlesinger, L. (1994). Putting the service-profit chain to work. *Harvard Business Review, 72*(2), 164–170.

Heskett, J., Wheeler, J., & Earl Sasser, W., Jr. (2008). *The ownership quotient: Putting the service profit chain to work for unbeatable competitive advantage*. Harvard Business School Press.

Hofstede, G. (1980). *Culture's consequences: International differences in work-related values*. Sage.

Hofstede, G. (1991). *Cultures and organizations: Software of the mind*. McGraw-Hill.

Hofstede, G., Hofstede, J., & Minkov, M. (2010). *Cultures and organizations: Software of the mind* (3rd ed.). McGraw-Hill.

Hogreve, J., Iseke, A., Derfuss, K., & Eller, T. (2017). The service-profit chain: A meta-analytic test of a comprehensive theoretical framework. *Journal of Marketing, 81*(3), 41–61.

Hollensen, S. (2017). *Global Marketing* (7th ed.). Pearson Education.

Homburg, C., Wieseke, J., & Hoyer, W. (2009). Social identity and the service–profit chain. *Journal of Marketing, 73*(2), 38–54.

Hong, Y., Liao, H., Hu, J., & Jiang, K. (2013). Missing link in the service profit chain: A meta-analytic review of the antecedents, consequences, and moderators of service climate. *Journal of Applied Psychology, 98*(2), 237–267.

Hwang, K. (1987). Face and favor: The Chinese power game. *American Journal of Sociology, 92*(4), 944–974. (In Chinese).

Hwang, K. (2008). The theoretical construction of the guanxi of Chinese. In G. Yang, K. Hwang, & F. Yang (Eds.), *Indigenous psychology of Chinese* (pp. 210–240). Chongqing University Press. (In Chinese).

Jin, L., Chen, Y., & Xi, Q. (2016). A multi-level research on the effect of paternalistic leadership on scientific research team's innovation performance. *Science Research Management, 37*(7), 107–116. (In Chinese).

Kamakura, W., Mittal, V., De Rosa, F., & Mazzon, J. (2002). Assessing the service-profit chain. *Marketing Science, 21*(3), 294–317.

Liang, S. (2011). *Essentials of Chinese Culture*. Shanghai People Press. (In Chinese).

Lin, S., & Yang, B. (2014). A comparative study about the influence of paternalistic leadership on organizational support and organizational citizenship behavior in China and South Korea. *Management World, 2014*(3), 182–183. (In Chinese).

Redding, S. G. (1990). *The spirit of Chinese capitalism*. Walter De Gruyter.

Schein, H. (1992). *Organizational culture and leadership* (2nd ed.). Jossey-Bass.

Silin, R. H. (1976). *Leadership and values: The organization of large-scale Taiwanese enterprises*. Harvard University Press.

Sweder, R., & Levine, R. (1984). *Culture theory: essays on mind, self, and emotion*. Cambridge University Press.

Tian, Z., & Huang, P. (2014). Researches on the effects of paternalistic leadership on voice behavior from the self-cognitive perspective. *Science Research Management, 35*(10), 150–160. (In Chinese).

Tian, J., Xie, S., Fan, X., Su, C., & Zhou, N. (2015). Chinese standard for high-star hotels: A case on service management mode of See View Garden Hotel. *China Management Studies, 10*(3), 59–74. (In Chinese).

Tsui, A., Zhang, Z., Wang, H., Xin, R., & Wu, B. (2006). Unpacking the relationship between CEO leadership behavior and organizational culture. *Leadership Quarterly, 17*, 113–137.

Venaik, S., & Brewer, P. (2013). Critical issues in the Hofstede and GLOBE national culture models. *International Marketing Review, 30*(5), 469–482.

Wang, S. (2015). A study on the relationship between paternalistic leadership and individual innovative behaviors in Chinese firms. *Science Research Management, 36*(7), 105–112. (In Chinese).

Wei, X., & Zhang, Z. (2010). Why is there a lack of prohibitive voice in organizations? *Management World (in Chinese), 2010*(10), 99–109.

Westwood, R. (1997). Harmony and patriarchy: the cultural basis for "paternalistic headship" among the overseas Chinese. *Organization studies, 18*(3), 445–480.

Wu, S., Sun, Z., Liu, X., & Zhou, Z. (2020). Does parental leadership contribute to employees' altruistic behavior? multiple mediating effects based on Chinese context. *Management Review, 32*(2), 205–217. (In Chinese).

Xie. (2017). Research on hotel service management from a perspective of family-like culture. Dissertation for the degree of Doctor of Business Administration (DBA) of City University of Hongkong.

Zeng, C. (2011). Patriarchal leadership and subordinate career plateau: The mediating role of the leader-member relationship. *Management World, 2011*(5), 109–126. (In Chinese).

Zhang, Z., & Yang, C. (1998). Beyond distributive justice: The reasonableness norm in Chinese reward allocation. *Asian Journal of Social Psychology, 1*, 253–269.

Zhang, X., He, H., & Gu, F. (2009). The influence of paternalistic leadership on team performance: The mediating role of team conflict management. *Management World, 2009*(3), 121–133. (In Chinese).

Zheng, B. (1999). The trust between superiors and subordinates in the corporate organization. *Sociological Studies, 1999*(2), 22–37. (In Chinese).

Zheng, B., & Lin, J. (1998). The hierarchical structure and Chinese organizational behavior: A preliminary study based on large private enterprises in Taiwan of China. *Journal of the Institution of Ethnology of the "Central Research Institution", 1998*(86), 29–72. (In Chinese).

Zheng, B., Zhou, L., & Fan, J. (2000). A measurement of patriarchal leadership: Construction and measurement of the ternary model. *Indigenous Psychology Research, 2000*(14), 3–64. (In Chinese).

Toward Socially Responsible Business: A Typology of Value Postures in Nested Service Ecosystems

Jonathan J. Baker, Vicki J. Little, and Roderick J. Brodie

1 Introduction

The US Business Roundtable recently issued a pointed rebuke of the American corporation's primary focus on increasing shareholder value (Benoit, 2019). One hundred and eighty-one CEOs from some of the country's major corporations pledged to share value not only with firm owners, but also with wider stakeholder groups including workers, suppliers, and communities (Business Roundtable, 2019). The changing corporate responsibility narrative highlights that creating and delivering value for networks of stakeholders and wider society have become more of a priority for business today. However, an intention to share value beyond traditional recipients begs the question: *How can value sharing within and between networks of distributed actors be accomplished in practice?*

J. J. Baker (✉)
University of Adelaide, Adelaide, Australia
e-mail: j.baker@adelaide.edu.au

V. J. Little
Monash University Malaysia, Selangor, Malaysia
e-mail: Vicki.Little@monash.edu

R. J. Brodie
The University of Auckland Business School, Auckland, New Zealand
e-mail: r.brodie@auckland.ac.nz

© The Author(s), under exclusive license to Springer Nature Switzerland AG 2022
B. Edvardsson, B. Tronvoll (eds.), *The Palgrave Handbook of Service Management*,
https://doi.org/10.1007/978-3-030-91828-6_20

A service ecosystem perspective offers answers, as it expressly focuses on the creation and delivery of value within dynamic, complex, layered service systems. This fresh thinking derives from a network view of actor interactions that overturns the traditional two-way or dyadic model of social interaction. Put differently, rather than seeing firms as the producers or creators of value and customers as the consumers or destroyers of value, a service perspective argues that *all* actors in service systems are engaged in value co-creation (Vargo & Lusch, 2016). Both producers and consumers are seen as actors embedded in service systems, within which value co-creation processes unfold. The service systems in which value co-creation processes unfold are nested (Koskela-Huotari et al., 2016), where the largest is the global economy and the smallest is two individuals interacting with one another (Maglio & Spohrer, 2008). A service perspective therefore implies a multi-level view that includes macro- (e.g., global and national economies), meso- (e.g., markets and industries), and micro-level (e.g., organizational and individual) elements, thereby acknowledging the wider impact of business practices on all levels of society (Fisk, 2006; Layton, 2007).

Drawing on the service ecosystem perspective, this chapter seeks to unpack the inherent complexity of value creation processes that unfold within and between nested service systems. We integrate the social emergence perspective (Sawyer, 2005) and institutional theory (Scott, 1987; Thornton & Ocasio, 1999) within the service-dominant logic paradigm (Lusch & Vargo, 2014; Vargo & Lusch, 2004, 2016). Methodologically, we engage in typology development by identifying distinct conceptual variants related to value creation approaches (Jaakkola, 2020; Miles & Snow, 1978) and illustrate these variants through case examples. A typology is an analytical technique portraying the key attributes of a particular phenomenon. Consequently, our typology explains how organizational actors (firm owners, managers, and employees) can think about value co-creation processes that can lead to more responsible business. We also assist scholars in conceptualizing the ways and contexts in which value is created.

Inspired by traditional typologies of business "strategic postures" (e.g., Ansoff, 1984; Miles & Snow, 1978; Porter, 1980), we propose five "value posture" types: *systemic, strategic, relational, operational,* and *individual*. We define a value posture as *the way in which focal actors think about and practice value creation and delivery with other actors or stakeholders*. Rather than adopting the traditional neoclassical focus on competition, our value postures framework begins to uncover how coordination and cooperation can support value creation and co-creation by and for stakeholders in firms, markets, and more broadly, society. We identify the linkages within and between each value posture, identifying the ways and means by which actors create, co-create, deliver, and co-deliver value for themselves and other service system stakeholders. We also note the potential for tension between actors that may adopt more than one value posture. Thus, in complex nested systems conflict can arise between contrasting value postures adopted by the same actor at different system levels. To contextualize our arguments, we offer illustrative examples from the New Zealand (NZ) wine industry, drawing on case studies, media articles, and website data. We assert that by engaging in value-related processes consistently and harmoniously, business might move closer to being truly socially responsible.

This chapter proceeds by expanding on the service ecosystem perspective and discussing the general nature of value co-creation processes. Next, we consider the issue of strategic orientation and the notion of "value postures." We identify five distinct value posture types and present a conceptual framework integrating these value postures into service ecosystems nested at different levels. Finally, we consider how the theoretical framework might support managerial practice and research; highlighting the pluralistic and socially important nature of the service practices deployed in creating and delivering value.

2 Service Systems and Value Creation Processes

Almost six decades ago Alderson (1965) advocated a wider perspective of marketing systems, embracing both business and society (Hunt, 1981). However, a wider conception of business and markets as ecosystems did not materialize until the 1990s. In management, Moore's (1993) ecology-inspired "ecosystem" conceptualization of business contexts emerged, echoing relationship marketers' notion of a "value constellation" (Juttner & Wehrli, 1994; Normann & Ramirez, 1993). Subsequently, the notion of a business ecosystem became more widely accepted, capturing the systemic and holistic effects of marketing activities, and their embeddedness in communities and society. Recent work adopting the business ecosystem as the focus of enquiry has explored numerous contexts including innovation, technology, platform, entrepreneurial, and knowledge ecosystems (Autio & Thomas, 2020; Brodie et al., 2021), reflecting a growing systems sensibility in scholarship. By adopting a systems perspective, a considerably more holistic view of the business environment can be achieved, enabling consideration of major real-world phenomena like digitalization, globalization, and perhaps most critically, environmental issues (Möller et al., 2020).

In marketing, the service-dominant (S-D) logic asserts the service ecosystem as the context in which resource integration and value co-creation processes unfold (Vargo & Lusch, 2004). Service ecosystems are *"relatively self-contained, self-adjusting systems of resource-integrating actors that are connected by shared institutional logics and mutual value creation"* (Vargo & Lusch, 2016, pp. 10-11). Within service ecosystems, actors co-create value by integrating resources through service-for-service exchange. In other words, like-minded actors create value with and for each other. "Actors" can be individuals, organizations, or social collectives. The types of resources that might be integrated are limitless: public or private, *"tangible or intangible, internal or external, operand or operant that the actor can draw on for increased viability"* (Lusch & Vargo, 2014, p. 121).

As a meta-theoretic view, S-D logic provides a foil for the instrumental and functional perspectives prevalent in science, technology, engineering, and medicine by focusing on value co-creation as a unique, phenomenological experience for each actor (Autio & Thomas, 2020). In other words, value, like beauty, is personal and subjective rather than objective. Drawing on this more humanistic and relativistic approach, recent studies adopting the service ecosystem perspective focus on contexts as diverse as healthcare (Brodie et al., 2021; McColl-Kennedy et al., 2017), social services (Finsterwalder & Kuppelwieser, 2020; Finsterwalder et al., 2017), digital servitization (Sklyar et al., 2019), and the diffusion of sustainability innovations (Trischler et al., 2020).

Within S-D logic, the institutional perspective is helpful in unpacking these somewhat complicated ideas. Institutional theory supports a dynamic and holistic conception of value co-creation processes as it highlights the impact of these governing mechanisms on actor expectations and practices (e.g., Lusch & Vargo, 2014; Vargo & Lusch, 2016). The term "institutions" refers to the formal and informal rules, schemas, practices, assumptions, and behaviors that are taken-for-granted and guide people's daily lives (Scott, 2001). Institutions provide actors with a shared sense of experience, meaning and purpose, represented by a cohesive set of belief systems and accepted practices (Baker et al., 2019; Reay & Hinings, 2009). While institutions vary in different cultures and contexts, in Western countries they typically include formal institutions like property rights, democratic government and the rule of law, and informal institutions like how people greet one another.

Thus, institutional arrangements—"interdependent assemblages of institutions" (Vargo & Lusch, 2016, p. 6)—are the mechanism that both enable and constrain the coordination of value co-creation activities (Wieland et al., 2016) and structure and drive practice (Dolbec & Fischer, 2015; Ertimur &

Coskuner-Balli, 2015). However, Frow et al. (2019, p. 2665) highlight the impact of interactions on institutional arrangements in the context of the healthcare service ecosystem: *"Although institutional rules and norms guide interactions at each level of the ecosystem, at higher levels of aggregation the practices tend to create other institutional rules and norms, such that they fluctuate less and define how actors at lower levels interact, supporting its structure."* Hence, institutional arrangements occur as the behaviors, practices, and interactions of system actors generate higher-level institutional arrangements, while at the same time, institutional arrangements guide the behaviors, practices, assumptions, and expectations of embedded actors. Thus, institutional theory facilitates fresh thinking and theory development about service systems in general, and the dynamic and iterative nature of resource integration and value co-creation processes within service ecosystems (Brodie et al., 2011; Brodie & Peters, 2020).

Overall, S-D logic provides a meta-narrative of value co-creation processes involving multiple actors or stakeholders within nested service ecosystems. Next, we draw on this meta-narrative to unpack the complexity of value creation processes that unfold within, across, and between these complex service systems.

3 Characteristics of Service Ecosystems: Complexity and Emergence

As we have argued, service ecosystems feature assemblages of actors or stakeholders that can be united in common cause—sustaining business and society. However, this goal is far from easy to achieve as the business landscape is volatile, uncertain, complex, and ambiguous (VUCA) (Bennett & Lemoine, 2014). Under these conditions, traditional theory is not helpful as models based on neoclassical economics and traditional thinking about competitive business strategy are based on assumptions of a static and mechanistic context (Diaz Ruiz et al., 2020). Therefore, the notion of a service ecosystem more properly reflects the realities of contemporary markets, and the relationships and processes that unfold within and between them (Vargo et al., 2017).

However, both social contexts and service ecosystems are complex systems, that is, *"made up of a large number of parts that interact in a nonsimple way"* (Simon, 1962, p. 468). In addition to multiple moving parts (multiple actors, multiple layers) we must add interactions between actors and between layers to the dynamic, iterative process of value co-creation. Thus, service ecosystems present us with a further complex property—emergence. A system with emergent properties features capabilities and properties that are not present in its constituent elements (Elder-Vass, 2010). In other words, the system is more than the sum of its parts (Simon, 1962). Sawyer (2005) highlights emergent properties are an outcome of synergy, that is, the manifestation of complex interactions that result in greater outcomes than could be achieved by system elements in isolation. Hence, both individual actors and the interactions between actors imbue systems with emergent properties. Elder-Vass (2010, p. 194) puts it like this, *"Human beings…are entities with emergent causal powers …*[but] *do not have the power uniquely and totally to determine subsequent events. Rather, social events are always the outcome of many interacting factors, of which our input is only one."* Emergence is thus an important attribute of service ecosystems, and one that should drive theorization.

Reflecting the importance of emergence in service ecosystems, we draw on Sawyer's (2005) social emergence perspective to support our conceptualization of value postures (Table 1). Social emergence has previously been used in marketing research to explore dynamic change in social systems. For example, Baker and Nenonen (2020) explore the impact of competitor collaboration in the NZ wine industry on global markets, while Taillard et al. (2016) investigate the role played by individual and collective agency in service ecosystem formation. Social emergence holds that phenomena emerge from unplanned individual interactions in five mutually constituted ontological levels or "frames" of analysis: individual level, interaction level, ephemeral emergents, stable emergents, and social structure (Sawyer, 2005). Within and between these levels of analysis, the roles of actors, their attitudes and practices related to value creation, and the consequences of their value creation processes might overlap and conflict. We have applied these frames of analysis to derive five value postures that a focal actor may assume. Each posture features discrete characteristics, based on combinations of strategic foci, practices, necessary assets, and institutional arrangements related to value creation processes. Moreover, the postures are context-dependent, meaning different combinations of stakeholders, and stakeholder goals characterize each posture. Next, we provide a discussion of "strategic postures," originally featured in the strategic management literature, before elaborating further on value postures and presenting our conceptual framework.

4 Strategic Orientations and Value Postures

In the 1970s, strategic management scholars started to focus on the strategic orientation, or strategic posture, of firms (e.g., Ansoff, 1984). Strategic postures fundamentally define the intents and practices of a firm relative to

Table 1 Five value postures

	Value postures	Context	Strategic focus	Dominant stakeholders	Stakeholder goals	Assets employed	Institutional arrangements
MACRO	Systemic	Society / communities / biosphere	Economic growth, Social license to operate, Social and environmental sustainability	Policymakers, communities, NGOs / pressure groups, Natural environment	UN sustainable development goals[a], Ethical outcomes	Social & environmental commons	Regulatory institutions, Social expectations & norms
MESO	Strategic	Industry / markets	Competitive and/or cooperative, Industry networks & alliances, Longevity, Business model	Industry leaders, Senior managers (CEO, C-suite, Board), Shareholders, Media	Business / market / industry growth, PR, Financial performance	Strategic positioning, Inter-firm relationships / alliances, Brands, Capabilities; Public assets (e.g., roads, universities, etc.)	Contracts, Business ecosystems, Industry standards / expectations, Cognitive & normative institutions
	Relational	External-facing	Creation/co-creation of value; Value propositions, Technologies, Relationships, Sales growth, Profitability	Customer- / supplier-facing staff, Middle managers (e.g., project managers, product managers, marketing managers)	Customized solutions, Least cost of ownership / access, Value-in-use	Enterprise assets, Sales & external-relationship assets, Business development	Shared intentions, norms, rules, routines, Shared practices, contracts

(*continued*)

Table 1 (continued)

	Value postures	Context	Strategic focus	Dominant stakeholders	Stakeholder goals	Assets employed	Institutional arrangements
MICRO	Operational	Within-firm	Customer solution delivery (products, features, operations), business operational efficiency	Lower-level employees (clerical/administrative/user support)	Least cost and effort of acquisition, productive / fulfilling, livelihood	Internal business systems & tangible / intangible resources (e.g., technologies, intra-firm relationships, IP)	Roles, topics, preferences, formal; Collective conversations, negotiations, meetings
	Individual	Self	Phenomenological interpretation of value	Kinship networks, immediate contacts	Least cost / effort for greatest value / purpose / satisfaction	Knowledge, skills & personal resources (money, time, etc.) Human, emotional & social capital	Individual intentions, attitudes, cognitive processes, value perceptions, determination

Adapted from Baker and Nenonen (2020); Little et al. (2006)

[a]UNSDGs: 1 No poverty; 2 Zero hunger; 3 Good health & wellbeing; 4 Quality education; 5 Gender equality; 6 Clean water & sanitation; 7 Affordable & clean energy; 8 Decent work & economic growth; 9 Industry, innovation & infrastructure; 10 Reduced inequalities; 11 Sustainable cities & communities; 12 Responsible production & consumption; 13 Climate action; 14 Life below water; 15 Life on land; 16 Peace, justice & strong institutions; 17 Partnership for the goals (United Nations, 2021)

industry standards and expectations, ranging from, for example, entrepreneurial innovators to conservative defenders (Courtney et al., 1997; Covin & Slevin, 1990). Numerous posture frameworks continue to be taught in many business schools and may be familiar to readers. For example, Porter's (1980) four generic strategies derived from *cost leadership/differentiation* and *broad/ focused* postures, and Miles and Snow's (1978) *prospectors, analyzers, defenders,* and *reactors.*[1]

The generic strategic posture adopted by a firm has numerous implications including *"scope, resource deployment, and competitive advantages; and the direction in which these components are shifting over time"* (Galbraith & Schendel, 1983, p. 156). In short, the entire business model of the firm and its strategic business units (SBUs) is driven by the strategic postures adopted by its managers (Ammar & Chereau, 2018). Hence, for large corporates, multiple strategic postures might be present within the organization across different SBUs and the geographies and product categories in which they operate. Adopting a view of service ecosystems as nested phenomena, we argue SBU-level strategic postures and corporate-level strategies play out within service ecosystems at different levels. Therefore, we draw on this notion of "strategic postures" to explore the nature and characteristics of value creation processes within service ecosystems. We use the term "value postures" to capture the different contexts, approaches, stakeholders, mindsets, and activities of value creation processes enacted by a focal actor. We identify five different value postures adopted by focal actors within the wider service ecosystem. Importantly, while the illustrative examples we present here (the NZ wine industry) reflect value postures adopted by firms as focal actors, we argue value postures are equally present in all generic actors embedded within service ecosystems (e.g., consumers, non-profits, governments, regulators, etc.).

5 Five Strategic Value Postures

We posit a value posture is the way a focal actor thinks about and practices value creation and delivery with other actors or stakeholders. Thus, a particular value posture is both constituted and characterized by the different elements which focal actors consider when engaging in value co-creation processes with other actors or stakeholders. A focal actor may adopt different

---

[1] Prospectors shape industries through innovation and new market development; defenders protect stable product niches; analyzers are typically smart followers, and reactors respond, frequently poorly, to the changing environment.

postures depending on the context in which they are operating at a given time and may adopt more than one posture leading to pluralism. For example, in the NZ wine industry, a winemaker may assume one value posture when engaging in value co-creation processes with a supermarket category manager, another when engaged in value co-creation processes with a wine consumer, and another posture again toward vineyard employees. Based on social emergence theory, we derive five value postures (Table 1).

The five value postures manifest at three different levels of aggregation within service ecosystem(s)—at micro-level: (1) *individual* and (2) *operational* value postures; at meso-level: (3) *relational* and (4) *strategic* value postures; and at macro-level: *systemic* value posture. The five value postures can be differentiated by six supplementary, defining criteria. First is the *context* of the value posture, which is to say, the setting in which value co-creation processes unfold. Second is the *strategic focus of the focal actor* who has adopted the value posture. Third are the *dominant stakeholders* who the focal actor must be cognizant of, or responsive to, when engaging in value creation processes; and fourth, those stakeholders' goals. Fifth are the *assets* that might be employed by the focal actor when engaging in value creation processes and attempting to satisfy stakeholder goals; and finally, sixth are the *institutional arrangements* that govern, and in turn are generated by, the actors involved in value co-creation processes.

Value Posture 1: Individual—Lower-Micro-Level, Self-Focused Perspective

An *individual* value posture describes the approaches encountered at the lower micro-level. Here, individuals, governed by their own attitudes and values, cognitive processes, and value perceptions, seek out personal satisfaction and a sense of purpose within the context of their immediate contacts and network. As *"value is always uniquely and phenomenologically determined by the beneficiary"* (Vargo & Lusch, 2016, p. 8), value perceptions are not uniform across groups, but instead, reflect diverse goals and judgements. For example, wine consumers' value perceptions are as diverse as the number of wine drinkers. While one wine consumer may judge a wine in simple terms such as "nice" or "smooth," others are more fulsome in their assessments. For example, one of the co-authors of this chapter drew on the description provided by a winemaker of an expensive Pinot noir and described their experience as *"like being led through a forested glade with wildflowers, mingled with violets and wild raspberries!"*

An individual value posture is equally present in all actors involved in resource integration, for example, customers, functional-level employees, senior managers, and CEOs. Drawing on the NZ wine industry again, mindsets and practices can be inferred from the expressed intentions and actions of winemakers, winery founders, grape growers, and their immediate stakeholders: *"No great wine ever came from a spreadsheet. Winemaking is an art, not a numbers game"* (George Fistonich, founder of Villa Maria—Quinn, 2018, para. 18); *"It's very much a labour of love … about running small vineyards and managing them very hands on"* (Helen Masters, Ata Rangi, winemaker of the year (NZ Wine, 2019)). The mutually constitutive nature of value in complex systems is evident here—the attitudes and practices of key individuals such as these winemakers both influence and are influenced by wider institutions within the industry.

Value Posture 2: Operational—Upper-Micro-Level, Within-Firm Perspective

An *operational* value posture describes approaches encountered within a firm or organization. Here, actor interactions occur through conversations, meetings, and negotiations, with the focus being primarily on meeting immediate organizational expectations. These interactions influence roles and preferences, and impact system properties. An operational value posture is assumed within the smallest of all service ecosystems (Maglio & Spohrer, 2008) and employees of all levels are engaged in delivering to internal value propositions. Their goals include those applicable at individual level together with the social need to be productive and fulfilled in their interactions with their colleagues. The resources drawn on to deliver this value posture include business systems and intra-firm relationships. For example, Yealands Wines CEO Jason Judkins says *"[…] we have developed a strong culture where people enjoy coming to work and they do well. As a result, we get good people wanting to work for us which means the company does better […] I would rather have a good team than a group of individual rock stars"* (Pavlovich et al., 2017, p. 733). Front-line staff are supported by systems and processes that provide a rewarding working environment and sustainable growth (ibid). The inter-relations and interactions within and between individuals highlight the phenomenon of social emergence where the whole is greater than the sum of the parts.

Value Posture 3: Relational—Lower-Meso-Level, Externally Focused Perspective

A *relational* value posture has (B2C and B2B) customers and suppliers as its predominant stakeholders. It focuses on value-in-exchange and value-in-use, derived from price (value for money), functionality, reliability, and individual interpretations of what constitutes value. The value is delivered by front-line, external-facing employees who draw on enterprise assets (including relationship-specific assets) to interact with a broad range of primary stakeholders, both internal and external. For example, when speaking of consumer satisfaction, one national brand owner said, *"What I love about the business is that we are taking very basic agricultural produce from the land and turning it into something quite magical that enhances people's dining experiences and makes them happy"* (Bon Coeur Fine Wines, 2021, para. 7). To achieve that goal, wineries must negotiate relationships with suppliers (grape juice) and distributors (importers, supermarkets, and other major retailers). Hence, governing institutional arrangements include shared intentions, practices, and norms, partnered with formal contracts and rules.

The wine category is large, valuable, and intensely competitive—exacerbated by the emergence of store brands and private brands. As customer relationships become proximal, competitive intensity increases. Indeed, *"the competitive advantage of using unique resources … is lost, as the buyers cannot distinguish between the focal firm and the competitor"* (Bengtsson & Kock, 2000, p. 424). In the wine market, competition—or more correctly coopetition—between supermarket-own wine brands and national brands has intensified to the point where consumers find it difficult to distinguish one from the other (Little et al., 2018): *"The supermarkets are supersaturated … Even having a medal isn't enough to get on the shelves. I build relationships and I get loyalty and that secures my shelf space. If you can sell the wines for them by having a good image and reputation, then that's what they want"* (Winery General Manager, Coriolis Research, 2006, p. 120); and with contract growers: *"We don't have problems securing grapes … We look after our growers very well, we pay them well and promote it as a win-win. Our growers tell other growers that we are good to grow for. Some large companies screw people and don't have good relationships … We are never short of fruit those other companies are"* (Winery Managing Director, Coriolis Research, 2006, p. 133).

Benson-Rea et al.'s (2013) multi-case study of NZ wine producer business models likewise emphasized that, while some contract suppliers (e.g., grape growers, packaging companies) are hired simply to provide expertise, for critical capabilities (e.g., wine making, consumer-facing distribution) the wineries prioritized long-term, reciprocal relationships with likeminded organizations. Relationships, formal contracts, and informal shared intentions deliver reciprocal value for all actors. A skilled supplier leverages customer and end-user knowledge, comparing gaps or mismatches with knowledge about what can be supplied. Therefore, antecedents to value creation are supplier ability to leverage knowledge, mutual disclosure and correct interpretation of customer or supplier goals, and negotiation of mutually acceptable outcomes. As we can see from these examples, the ability to build long-term, trusting, reciprocal relationships with likeminded organizations is crucial.

Knowledge becomes the order winner within a relational value posture—enabling lower cost of ownership through customized solutions tailored to customers' specific needs. For such solutions, the customer may be prepared to pay a premium (ceteris paribus). The different wineries analyzed by Benson-Rea et al. (2013) offered multiple value propositions to their retail customers, ranging from exclusive, boutique wines crafted by family-owned wineries to unlabeled bulk wines offered by large commercial wineries to major transnational supermarket chains. Hence, a relational value posture focuses on stakeholder goals and phenomenological interpretations of value, for example, tailored solutions and perceptions of value-in-use. Due to the primacy of inter-organizational relational assets, the ability to partner and form strategic relationships is critical. Such agreements foster pluralism and enable mutual business growth, predicated on reciprocal understanding and shared goals.

Value Posture 4: Strategic—Upper-Meso-Level, Industry and Market Perspective

A *strategic* value posture is assumed by an organization's top management, senior leadership team, and board. Concerns include financing the business, enhancing long-term cash flows, sources of risk and key business drivers, with the goal being organizational longevity and survival. Rather than an internal or inter-organizational focus, the scope widens to the industry and to financial markets, particularly for publicly listed firms. Ability to deliver direct and immediate value to customers (e.g., through service-level agreements) is assumed to be present; however, it is not the focus.

As a strategic value posture unfolds within industries and market systems, primary stakeholders include industry leaders, investors, investment analysts, industry observers, and media commentators. Here, corporate-level strategies unfold within the wider market ecosystem, in turn driving competitive, or

SBU-level strategies operationalized by lower-level managers. The organizational assets drawn on at this level include competitive positioning (drawing on brand and reputational value), strategic competencies and capabilities, and brand capital of single or multiple businesses. Inter-organizational assets (e.g., alliances, business ecosystems, networks, etc.) and publicly owned assets (e.g., roads and utilities) are critical to enabling overall firm and wider industry goals of continued growth and longevity.

Clusters, alliances, and industry associations are an expression of a strategic value posture. As the New World wine sector is fragmented and dominated by small-medium enterprises, inter-organizational alliances featuring multilateral relationships abound (Nelgen & Anderson, 2011). The NZ wine industry is renowned for a high degree of coopetitive (i.e., both cooperative and competitive) activity in the interests of developing markets and creating a more robust industry. For example, a relatively recent but fast-growing wine region in NZ's South Island, Waipara, features a formal cluster with the goal of distinguishing the region from others and establishing it as "super premium" (Dana et al., 2013). The cluster includes growers and producers of various sizes, governed by a formal structure, informal norms, and shared expectations. The cluster enjoys positive relationships with universities, government agencies, and tourism operators. Cluster members engage in a wide range of sharing, including IP related to sales, growing and production techniques, and the cluster promotes the region domestically. One cluster member puts it simply: *"the only way we are going to be able to compete is through learning from one another"* (Dana et al., 2013, p. 47).

Likewise, in an attempt at protecting a region's reputation, Marlborough—the home of NZ's renowned Sauvignon blanc wines—created an appellation system called Appellation Marlborough Wine (AMW) in 2018. The group claims that with the global popularity of Marlborough Sauvignon blanc *"comes the proliferation of players and a range of quality expectations, which can put this hard-earned reputation at risk. AMW has been established to safeguard Marlborough wine and provide assurance to consumers who seek wines of provenance, authenticity and integrity"* (AMW, 2021, para. 2). Through collective effort, actors in an industry behave strategically to protect their own interests, and that of the industry. Institutional level work creates and protects industry brand values, and general actor behaviors, and institutional governance is achieved through formal contracts coupled with accepted industry standards and norms.

Value Posture 5: Systemic—Macro-Level, Intra- and Inter-society Perspective

A *systemic* value posture reflects the nature of an actor's approach to society and the natural environment. A firms' ability to create systemic value is governed through regulatory mechanisms and social expectations. Maintaining industry longevity and social license to operate (i.e., maintaining legitimacy and permission to conduct necessary business activities) can be supported through appropriate environmental and social sustainability initiatives. To achieve this outcome requires awareness of dominant stakeholders including policymakers, communities, and interested observers such as pressure groups and NGOs. Pro-social stakeholder goals are resident in the 17 UN Sustainable Development Goals, including good health and wellbeing, clean water and energy, decent work, equality, responsible production and consumption, and climate action (United Nations, 2021).

While many businesses have failed to adopt a sustainable systemic value posture, the NZ wine industry has taken a more proactive approach. "Brand NZ" is supported by multiple actors (e.g., government agencies, tourism operators, the media, and travel operators), orchestrating and exploiting a "clean and green" image; a systemic value posture at country level that either implicitly or explicitly aims for shared outcomes. Likewise, the NZ wine industry has adopted pro-environmental measures congruent with that image. Wine producers have positioned themselves strongly as "green," a position that lower-cost direct competitors like Chile and Argentina find difficult to mimic (Brodie & Benson-Rea, 2016). Industry actors (e.g., producers, retailers, and growers) share intent, adopting the tagline "Pure discovery," and an accompanying value proposition promising "excitement and clarity of flavor" (Brodie & Benson-Rea, 2016). Supporting these outcomes, the industry administers a world-first best practice model and certification program, whereby independent auditors certify growers and producers as sustainable, organic, or biodynamic (NZ Wine, 2020). For example, Jason Flowerday, an award-winning organic viticulturalist in the Marlborough region of NZ, uses biodynamic and organic principles to improve soil health and structure in his own family-owned vineyard and convenes workshops for other organic farmers in his region to share and promote these practices (Campbell, 2020). Although the program is voluntary, almost every wine producer and grower in the country is certified at least sustainable, a feat unmatched by any other wine-producing nation (Taylor, 2017). Thus, a systemic value posture translates to mutually constituted practices within and between service ecosystem

386 J. J. Baker et al.

stakeholders, supported by expectations and shared intentions, a property of emergence that translates to value co-creation for both the wine industry and NZ.

6 Conclusion

This chapter set out to explore the five different value postures that an organization might adopt in service ecosystems at different levels of aggregation. A service perspective embraces both "macro" and "micro" marketing, acknowledging the wider impact of business practice on society (Fisk, 2006; Layton, 2007). Within this perspective, the service ecosystem is a holistic conceptualization, drawing together assemblages of actors or stakeholders engaged in value co-creation processes through resource integration.

We propose five value postures that might be assumed by service ecosystem actors: systemic, strategic, relational, operational, and individual. We further assert these value postures can be either aligned or in conflict. As ecosystems are nested, a functional team within an organization, the organization and its immediate stakeholders, an organization and its broader industry or market, and an organization and its encompassing society and natural environment are all examples of ecosystems at different "levels." Within, between, and across those levels, through processes of emergence, different value postures do not necessarily deliver benefits that are consistent or aligned. For example, the value created for the benefit of shareholders or customers (at the meso-level) may indeed negatively impact value co-creation processes involving staff (at the micro-level) or the wider natural environment (at the macro-level). Hence, managers are encouraged to explore, realize, and align value postures across different levels by ensuring organizational culture, practices, relationships, and goals are consistent from top to bottom. This process begins with managers becoming aware of their own, and their colleagues', value postures. Additionally, across different SBUs, pluralism in value postures will naturally generate conflicting goals and intentions. Instead, aligning value postures both vertically (between and across system levels) and horizontally (within systems) with overall goals around purpose, and economic and social sustainability, could create truly responsible business.

Using examples from the NZ wine industry, we have illustrated how these value postures manifest. The value postures assumed in NZ wine demonstrate strong alignment and (largely) responsible business practices. Individual value postures reflect dedicated, purposeful industry players and within organizations, operational value postures include an emphasis on teams, collaboration, and best practice. Similarly, collaboration and reciprocal benefit are at the forefront of a relational value posture toward an organization's primary stakeholders such as customers and suppliers. Strategic value postures in the NZ wine industry reflect cooperation for mutual growth and industry success, and systemic value postures demonstrate a sense of responsibility for sustainable practices under the broader "Brand NZ wine" umbrella. Empirical research drawing on the value postures conceptualization in other industrial, market, and social contexts should be undertaken in the future. Specifically, horizontal and vertical alignment of value postures by organizations (i.e., for-profit, non-profit, and governmental) is worthy of further scholarly attention.

References

Alderson, W. (1965). *Dynamic marketing behavior*. Richard D. Irwin.

Ammar, O., & Chereau, P. (2018). Business model innovation from the strategic posture perspective: An exploration in manufacturing SMEs. *European Business Review, 30*(1), 38–65.

AMW. (2021). *Appellation Marlborough wine*. appellationmarlboroughwine.co.nz/

Ansoff, I. (1984). *Implanting strategic management*. Prentice-Hall.

Autio, E., & Thomas, L. D. (2020). Value co-creation in ecosystems: Insights and research promise from three disciplinary perspectives. In S. Nambisan, K. Lyytinen, & Y. Yoo (Eds.), *Handbook of digital innovation*. Edward Elgar Publishing.

Baker, J. J., & Nenonen, S. (2020). Collaborating to shape markets: Emergent collective market work. *Industrial Marketing Management, 85*, 240–253.

Baker, J. J., Storbacka, K., & Brodie, R. J. (2019). Markets changing, changing markets: Institutional work as market shaping. *Marketing Theory, 19*(3), 301–328.

Bengtsson, M., & Kock, S. (2000). "Coopetition" in business networks - To cooperate and compete simultaneously. *Industrial Marketing Management, 29*(5), 411–426.

Bennett, N., & Lemoine, G. J. (2014). What a difference a word makes: Understanding threats to performance in a VUCA world. *Business Horizons, 57*(3), 311–317.

Benoit, D. (2019, August 19). *Move over, shareholders: Top CEOs say companies have obligations to society*. *Wall Street Journal*. https://www.wsj.com/articles/business-roundtable-steps-back-from-milton-friedman-theory-11566205200

Benson-Rea, M., Brodie, R. J., & Sima, H. (2013). The plurality of co-existing business models: Investigating the complexity of value drivers. *Industrial Marketing Management, 42*, 717–729.

Bon Coeur Fine Wines. (2021). Michael Brajkovich MW, Kumeu River. https://www.bcfw.co.uk/information/meet-the-winemaker/winemaker-michael-brajkovich

Brodie, R., Saren, M., & Pels, J. P. (2011). Theorizing about the service dominant logic: The bridging role of middle range theory. *Marketing Theory, 11*(1), 75–91.

Brodie, R. J., & Benson-Rea, M. (2016). Country of origin branding: An integrative perspective. *Journal of Product & Brand Management, 25*(4), 322–336.

Brodie, R. J., & Peters, L. D. (2020). New directions for service research: Refreshing the process of theorizing to increase contribution. *Journal of Services Marketing, 34*(3), 415–428.

Brodie, R. J., Ranjan, K. R., Verreynne, M.-L., Jiang, Y., & Previte, J. (2021). Coronavirus crisis and health care: Learning from a service ecosystem perspective. *Journal of Service Theory and Practice, 31*(2), 225–246.

Business Roundtable. (2019). *Statement on the purpose of a corporation.* https://system.businessroundtable.org/app/uploads/sites/5/2021/02/BRT-Statement-on-the-Purpose-of-a-Corporation-Feburary-2021-compressed.pdf

Campbell, B. (2020). Jason Flowerday Te Whare Ra Wines: Viticulturist New Zealand winemaker of the year awards 2020. http://gourmettravellerwine.com/nz-winemaker-of-the-year-2020/viticulturist-award.html

Coriolis Research. (2006). *An overview of the New Zealand Wine industry.* https://coriolisresearch.com/pdfs/coriolis_overview_new_zealand_wine_industry_may2006.pdf

Courtney, H., Kirkland, J., & Viguerie, P. (1997). Strategy under uncertainty. *Harvard Business Review, 75*(6), 66–79.

Covin, J. G., & Slevin, D. P. (1990). New venture strategic posture, structure, and performance: An industry life cycle analysis. *Journal of Business Venturing, 5*(2), 123–135.

Dana, L.-P., Granata, J., Lasch, F., & Carnaby, A. (2013). The evolution of co-opetition in the Waipara wine cluster of New Zealand. *Wine Economics and Policy, 2*(1), 42–49.

Diaz Ruiz, C. A., Baker, J. J., Mason, K., & Tierney, K. (2020). Market-scanning and market-shaping: Why are firms blindsided by market-shaping acts? *Journal of Business & Industrial Marketing, 35*(9), 1389–1401.

Dolbec, P., & Fischer, E. (2015). Refashioning a field? Connected consumers and institutional dynamics in markets. *Journal of Consumer Research, 41*(6), 1447–1468.

Elder-Vass, D. (2010). *The causal power of social structures: Emergence, structure and agency.* Cambridge University Press.

Ertimur, B., & Coskuner-Balli, G. (2015). Navigating the institutional logics of markets: Implications for strategic brand management. *Journal of Marketing, 79*(2), 40–61.

Finsterwalder, J., Foote, J., Nicholas, G., Taylor, A., Hepi, M., Baker, V., & Dayal, N. (2017). Conceptual underpinnings for transformative research in a service ecosystems context to resolve social issues – Framework foundations and extensions. *Service Industries Journal, 37*(11–12), 766–782.

Finsterwalder, J., & Kuppelwieser, V. G. (2020). Intentionality and transformative services: Wellbeing co-creation and spill-over effects. *Journal of Retailing and Consumer Services, 52*(January), 1–10.

Fisk, G. (2006). Envisioning a future for macromarketing. *Journal of Macromarketing, 26*(2), 214–218.

Frow, P., McColl-Kennedy, J. R., Payne, A., & Govind, R. (2019). Service ecosystem well-being: Conceptualization and implications for theory and practice. *European Journal of Marketing, 53*(12), 2657–2691.

Galbraith, C., & Schendel, D. (1983). An empirical analysis of strategy types. *Strategic Management Journal, 4*, 153–173.

Hunt, S. D. (1981). Macromarketing as a multidimensional concept. *Journal of Macromarketing, 1*(1), 7–8.

Jaakkola, E. (2020). Designing conceptual articles: Four approaches. *AMS Review, 10*, 18–26.

Juttner, U., & Wehrli, H. P. (1994). Relationship marketing from a value system perspective. *International Journal of Service Industry Management, 5*(5), 54–73.

Koskela-Huotari, K., Edvardsson, B., Jonas, J. M., Sörhammar, D., & Witell, L. (2016). Innovation in service ecosystems: Breaking, making, and maintaining institutionalized rules of resource integration. *Journal of Business Research, 69*(8), 2964–2971.

Layton, R. A. (2007). Marketing systems – A core macromarketing concept. *Journal of Macromarketing, 27*(3), 227–242. https://doi.org/10.1177/0276146707302836

Little, V. J., Brookes, R. A., Smith, S. D., & Starr, R. G. (2018). *Coopetitive processes and complex brand strategy: The case of Marlborough Sauvignon blanc.* University of Auckland, unpublished working paper.

Little, V. J., Motion, J., & Brodie, R. J. (2006). *Discovering different perspectives of customer value: Implications for marketing theory and practice.* Paper presented at the Australian and NZ Marketing Academy (ANZMAC) Conference, University of Queensland, Brisbane, Australia.

Lusch, R. F., & Vargo, S. L. (2014). *Service-dominant logic: Premises, perspectives, possibilities.* Cambridge University Press.

Maglio, P. P., & Spohrer, J. (2008). Fundamentals of service science. *Journal of the Academy of Marketing Science, 36*(1), 18–20.

McColl-Kennedy, J. R., Hogan, S. J., Witell, L., & Snyder, H. (2017). Cocreative customer practices: Effects of health care customer value co-creation practices on well-being. *Journal of Business Research, 70*, 55–66.

Miles, R., & Snow, C. (1978). *Organizational Strategy, structure, and process.* McGraw-Hill.

Möller, K., Nenonen, S., & Storbacka, K. (2020). Networks, ecosystems, fields, market systems? Making sense of the business environment. *Industrial Marketing Management, 90*(2020), 380–399.

Moore, J. F. (1993). Predators and prey: a new ecology of competition. *Harvard Business Review, 71*(3), 75–86.

Nelgen, S., & Anderson, K. (2011). *Global wine markets, 1961 to 2009: A statistical compendium*. University of Adelaide Press.

Normann, R., & Ramirez, R. (1993). From value chain to value constellation: Designing interactive strategy. *Harvard Business Review, 71*(4), 65–78.

NZ Wine. (2019). *Helen masters: Winemaker of the year*. https://www.nzwine.com/en/media/our-people/helen-masters/

NZ Wine. (2020). *Sustainable winegrowing NZ*. https://www.nzwine.com/en/sustainability/swnz

Pavlovich, K., Connolly, H., Gibb, J., & Collins, E. (2017). Yealands wine group holdings: A case study. *Journal of Management & Organization, 23*(5), 728–740.

Porter, M. (1980). *Competitive strategy: Techniques for analysing industries and competitors*. Free Press.

Quinn, S. (2018). *NZ's most awarded winery*. https://sraquinn.org/2018/12/01/nzs-most-awarded-winery/

Reay, T., & Hinings, C. R. (2009). Managing the rivalry of competing institutional logics. *Organization Studies, 30*(6), 629–652.

Sawyer, R. K. (2005). *Social emergence: Societies as complex systems*. Cambridge University Press.

Scott, W. R. (1987). The adolescence of institutional theory. *Administrative Science Quarterly, 32*(4), 493–511.

Scott, W. R. (2001). *Institutions and organizations. Ideas, interests and identities*. SAGE Publications.

Simon, H. (1962). The architecture of complexity. *Proceedings of the American Philosophical Society, 106*(6), 467–482.

Sklyar, A., Kowalkowski, C., Tronvoll, B., & Sörhammar, D. (2019). Organizing for digital servitization: A service ecosystem perspective. *Journal of Business Research, 104*, 450–460.

Taillard, M., Peters, L. D., Pels, J., & Mele, C. (2016). The role of shared intentions in the emergence of service ecosystems. *Journal of Business Research, 69*, 2972–2980.

Taylor, S. (2017). *New Zealand wine: Pure discovery*. https://discoversustainablewine.com/new-zealand-wine-pure-discovery/

Thornton, P. H., & Ocasio, W. (1999). Institutional logics and the historical contingency of power in organizations: Executive succession in the higher education publishing industry, 1958–1990. *American Journal of Sociology, 105*(3), 801–843.

Trischler, J., Johnson, M., & Kristensson, P. (2020). A service ecosystem perspective on the diffusion of sustainability-oriented user innovations. *Journal of Business Research, 116*, 552–560.

United Nations. (2021). *Take action for the sustainable development goals*. https://www.un.org/sustainabledevelopment/sustainable-development-goals/

Vargo, S. L., Koskela-Huotari, K., Baron, S., Edvardsson, B., Reynoso, J., & Colurcio, M. (2017). A systems perspective on markets: Toward a research agenda. *Journal of Business Research, 79*, 260–268.

Vargo, S. L., & Lusch, R. F. (2004). Evolving to a new dominant logic for marketing. *Journal of Marketing, 68*(1), 1–17.

Vargo, S. L., & Lusch, R. F. (2016). Institutions and axioms: An extension and update of service-dominant logic. *Journal of the Academy of Marketing Science, 44*(1), 5–23.

Wieland, H., Koskela-Huotari, K., & Vargo, S. L. (2016). Extending actor participation in value creation: An institutional view. *Journal of Strategic Marketing, 24*(3–4), 210–226.

Customer-Centric Service Ecosystem for Emerging Markets

Varsha Jain, Anupama Ambika, and Jagdish N. Sheth

This chapter aims to explain the customer-centric service ecosystem for effective customer service from emerging markets. In recent years, the emerging markets (e.g., BRICS countries) have significantly increased their involvement in the global commerce scenario, achieving sustained growth (Ghauri & Cateora, 2014). As the sphere of economic activities shifts to the emerging markets, organizations and researchers are increasingly focusing on understanding the drivers for growth and competitive advantage (O'Cass & Carlson, 2019). Moreover, such rapid development of emerging markets has led to the rise of the new consumer with increased spending power and evolving needs, encountering wider choice of channels and products (McKinsey, 2017). However, in the present competitive market-sphere, where processes and technology can replicate quickly, winning in emerging markets is not easy (BCG, 2018). Under such circumstances, customer service can become a strategic differentiator for organizations (Singh, 2014). According to the American Express customer service barometer, customers are prepared to bear more than 20% additional cost to exchange superior customer service (American

---

V. Jain (⊠) • A. Ambika
MICA, Ahmedabad, India
e-mail: varsha.jain@micamail.in; anupama_fpm18@micamail.in

J. N. Sheth
Charles H. Kellstadt, Goizueta Business School of Emory University,
Atlanta, GA, USA
e-mail: jsheth@emory.edu

© The Author(s), under exclusive license to Springer Nature Switzerland AG 2022
B. Edvardsson, B. Tronvoll (eds.), *The Palgrave Handbook of Service Management*,
https://doi.org/10.1007/978-3-030-91828-6_21

393

Express, 2017). Though most companies claim that customers are indeed the central point of everything they do, the customers' service experience annihilates this theory (Snow & Yanovitch, 2009). There exists much disapproval about the prevalent customer service approaches and the resultant experiences (McGovern, 2017). Unhappy customers are not hesitant to express their worries in the digital space, and negative reviews can affect the brand image and revenue. However, organizations face multiple challenges in designing customer service to satisfy and wow customers. These impediments are higher in emerging markets due to unique challenges and opportunities (Sheth, 2011).

The infrastructural insufficiencies, cultural diversities, customer heterogeneity, higher-income disparities in the emerging markets pose complex challenges to organizations at different levels. However, active digitization and digital adoption are opening new pathways to serve customers. For instance, in some African regions, poor commutation infrastructure makes product delivery and physical support difficult. Still, more than 75% of customers can use mobile phones to access advanced networks and use mobile apps that may not exist in the West (Molino et al., 2015). Moreover, the customers' service demands and requirements from emerging markets are different from the mature markets. Hence, to wow the customers from the emerging markets through service, companies need to adopt a customer-focused service model. In the past, studies have focused on areas such as service recovery (Borah et al., 2020), customer relationships (Berndt et al., 2005; Gaur et al., 2019), service quality (Hoang et al., 2010), innovation (Baron et al., 2018; Koskela-Huotari et al., 2016), and technology adoption (Alavi, 2016). However, there is a scarcity of literature focusing on emerging nations from the perspective of customer service. Many widely employed frameworks in this domain originated in the developed economies, even though the emerging markets do not entirely confirm according to the market dynamics of the West (Roy et al., 2019). Hence, this chapter focuses on developing the customer-centric service ecosystem (CSE) for customer service in emerging markets. Here, we employ a theory in use approach (Zeithaml et al., 2020) where mental models and practitioners are harnessed to develop a new model. To create the CSE model we interviewed 52 leading practitioners focusing on various realms of customer service.

We define CSE as a model entailing a web of human and technology components that influence the customer service standards and customer service experience in the emerging markets. The key features of CSE include the microelements of the company and the macro components of the larger environment. The following sections would detail the key interconnected micro and macro features of a customer-centric service ecosystem.

1 Customer-Centric Service Ecosystem

A customer-centric service model comprises multiple stakeholders and processes within an organization. An organization can attain superior customer service levels with a service ecosystem centered on customer-centricity principles. The ecosystem consists of the micro-environment comprising the brand, employees, technology, and data. The CSE includes the more significant macro-environmental components, including measurement and metrics, culture, socio-political factors and socio-economic factors, investors, government, and infrastructure. Figure 1 presents a model of a customer-centric service ecosystem. A service ecosystem focuses on integrated resources connected by standard institutional systems and value creation (Vargo & Lusch, 2016).

The past studies have focused on these components independently in service contexts. Shah et al. (2006) advocate customer-centricity in service, supported by leadership commitment, revised organizational alignments, appropriate technology and processes, and customer-centric measurement metrics. Further, several scholars argue the role of employee training and empowerment for a customer-centric approach and better service performance (Lee et al., 2006; Rafaeli et al., 2008). According to Domegan (1996), technology becomes a facilitator by improving efficiency and effectiveness. From the perspective of emerging markets, Sinha and Sheth (2018) point out that the emerging markets' organizational challenges include heterogeneous consumers and market conditions, socio-political governance, unbranded competition, extreme resource limitations, and infrastructural inadequacies. However, through this study, we are bringing them together in an integrated

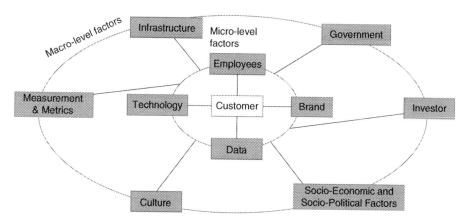

Fig. 1 Customer-centric ecosystem

framework, focusing on emerging economies and the context of customer service; the below sections elaborate on the various components of the framework.

Macro-environmental Factors

The macro-level factors include culture, socio-political factors and socio-economic factors, investors, government, infrastructure, and measurement and metrics. These factors significantly include the customer service ecosystem.

Culture

The emerging markets are home to diverse cultural platina. According to Hofstede (1980), culture relates to the economic drivers and the societal value system. These elements will further reflect in the conduct of employees and the customers, which may skew the ecosystem in diverse ways. For example, the people of Brazil follow "Jeitinho Brasileiro," a unique way of problem-solving, during Chinese focus on Guanxi, a form of networking. Such cultural elements affect every person in multiple ways. Past studies indicate that customers from different cultural backgrounds and orientations have varied expectations and service evaluations (Laroche et al., 2004). For instance, according to Guesalaga et al. (2016), Chile's service levels are considered slow and less professional than global standards. While the locals are accustomed to this, however, foreigners take time to adjust to the same.

Similarly, when an organization tries to imbibe a customer-centric culture, employees' ability to adapt to the same also becomes significant. Here, the independent and interdependent cultures also come to play. Many emerging markets have a predominantly interdependent culture. Hence the business environment of emerging markets is also heavily influenced by relationships, unlike the developed markets. For instance, the Chinese follow the principle of "Guanxi" for a business that amounts to relationships grounded on the reciprocity of favors through business and social networks based on one-on-one relationships (Paul, 2019). Such cultural nuances form critical components influencing the ecosystem, as it determines the behavior and expectations of customers and the stakeholders (Sarma, 2018). Hence, in the service context, a firm should develop relationships with all stakeholders bearing in mind the cultural facets and standards in the emerging market, and alter the models and frameworks developed for advanced economies (Paul, 2019).

Socio-economic and Socio-political Factors

The socio-economic and political factors exert massive influence on the components of the customer-centric ecosystem. The market, as well as the customer, is highly heterogenic. The income, education, and digital divide are high, leading to skills gaps and differential expectations. These variations connect with religious beliefs and languages. There are also differences in the politico-legal structures, which demand deliberation of several contextual factors. These dimensions are considered within the service strategies and processes (Sinha & Sheth, 2017).

Moreover, bureaucratic fights and "mafia-ism" are managed in many emerging markets, making and carrying out several decisions from setting up to daily operations (Williams, 2011). Further, the market functions and the service standards are determined by the government, business groups, religious sects, and so on. According to Elg et al. (2008), the success of the furniture retailer IKEA's entry into emerging markets such as China can be attributed to the networks with local interest groups, political actors, and the media.

Similarly, the market competition is also determined by the trade policies and market reforms within the emerging nations. In some of the emerging markets, there exist higher levels of government control on organizations. For instance, in Russia, the political and social capital are highly significant for companies to thrive (Rao-Nicholson et al., 2018). As elaborated by Sheth (2011), many emerging markets, such as those in the Gulf region, follow faith-based political systems and governance. The religious scripts advocate higher government participation in all aspects of business for the better interest of society. They also operate several government-owned, undertaking commercial companies, which leads to asymmetry of power in the market (Marinov, 2006). All the factors critically determine how the service ecosystem is designed.

Investor

Investors play a significant role in influencing the decisions and strategic directions (Fox & Lorsch, 2012). The resources, workforce, and opportunities presented by the emerging markets make them attractive investment destinations, stock options, or direct investments. The liberalizations of needs, increasing political steadiness, legal transformations, and supportive economic policies help increase foreign and domestic investments (Cavusgil et al., 2021; Marinov, 2006). Investors' role is critical in the design, maintenance, and functioning of the customer service ecosystem. If the investors believe in stellar customer service, then the same will reflect top management, trickling down to all organization levels (Newlands, 2014).

Further, foreign investors can support capital diversification, skill, technology updates, and managerial know-how, which can significantly upgrade the firm's service capabilities. Investors' say in the matters related to customer service will depend on the allowable controls as per the local government rules (Goncalves et al., 2014). Thus, the nation's ability to attract the right investors facilitates the effective transfer of knowledge and technology know-how, and productive engagement with the investor community influences the ecosystem.

Government

Government policies and regulations significantly influence all facets of business, including the customer service ecosystem. According to the institutional theory, official and informal rules and regulations govern the forms of organizational structures (North, 2005). Governments' influence will be through regulative measures such as taxation and investment norms for serving customers (Scott, 1995). For example, the current e-commerce policy of the Indian government directs aggregators to indicate the sellers' actual address, contact number for support, and feedback for every product listed (Economic Times, 2020). Moreover, the government policies also present several relative advantages. In China, the export-focused policies and specifically designed economic intensives and working zones have been significant in business growth (Sheth, 2011). Such interventions will necessitate substantial provisions on the customer service ecosystem as well.

However, some emerging nations have rampant corruption and "red-tapism" within the government hierarchy, posing difficulties to the business environment in general. Moreover, providing a level playing field for all companies and the influence of local lobbies on the government also influence the organization's decisions and processes (Pacek & Thorniley, 2007). Hence, the government's trustworthiness, stability, and flexibility are vital considerations while designing the service ecosystem.

Infrastructure

Emerging market countries continue to face massive infrastructure challenges, affecting transportation, storage, technology, and communication systems

(Sinha & Sheth, 2017). The challenges are not only limited to physical infrastructure but also extend to financial infrastructure. These challenges increase the cost and difficulty of reaching, serving, and communicating with new and potential customers (Chakravarthy & Coughlan, 2011). Governments in the emerging markets will have to develop robust regulatory environments to support public-private partnerships (PPP) to build the needed infrastructural support. For instance, in Brazil, PPP plans have been activated to build digital support systems. The infrastructural challenges and opportunities can hugely influence the customer-centric service ecosystem.

Even though the fixed infrastructure is still significantly underdeveloped, a considerable population still lives under mobile access areas. For instance, regions in the Middle East and countries like India are already spearheading 5G mobile facilities (WEF, n.d). Hence, customer support technologies will have to leverage mobile and digital channels to overcome infrastructural limitations on other fronts.

Metrics and Measurement

Scholars have indicated that metrics and measurements influence organizations' future actions, strategies, and decisions. Today, even while organizations declare themselves as customer-centric, their measurement systems emphasize company-centric metrics. The use of outdated or inappropriate metrics can be counter-productive and detrimental to the customer service ecosystem (Hauser & Katz, 1998). If employee performance is measured strictly against business KPIs, they might even sacrifice customer interests to achieve the business goals, like sales based on false service promises. However, when the employees are answerable to customer-oriented metrics, they inspire customer value, achieving shared success (Cornfield, 2020). Hence, the customer-centric approach necessitates changes in the performance metrics and measurement (Shah et al., 2006). Moreover, as the emerging markets are different from the West, as explained through the macro factors above, organizations should develop customized measurement methods other than the developed region's strategies (Khanna et al., 2005).

When an organization focuses on measuring customer service outcomes, they get rewards with higher returns in their business-relevant metrics. For instance, Net Promoter Score (NPS) is a popular measure, indicating customer readiness to recommend the brand. By timely NPS measurements followed by relevant improvement strategies, the optical store chain, Titan EyePlus, becomes a benchmark for customer service, winning awards at national and international levels (Titan Annual Report, 2019). The new entrant in this category is the Customer Effort Score (CES) that measures the ease at which a customer can connect and solve their needs and issues with the company (Bryan, 2020). Customer-oriented measures like first call resolution (the problem resolution at the first contact) and self-service usage levels can also reveal significant insights and improvement measures on customer service (Gani, 2020). Different organizations need to ensure that metrics such as Customer Lifetime Value (CLV) that measure customer spend over the lifetime of the relationship with the brand get due consideration on the segmentation and service levels.

The metrics should premise on the nature of service that customers desire from the organization. However, it is also vital to measure the potential association of the customer-centric metrics toward organizational KPIs (Cornfield, 2020) and the other micro factors in the service ecosystem.

The macro factors interact with the micro-environments together to form the customer service ecosystem for the emerging markets. The following section describes the micro-environmental elements.

Micro-environmental Factors

The micro-environmental factors include brand, employees, technologies, and data.

Brand

The brand's vision, mission, values, and communication are aligned to customer-centricity principles. This alignment means that organizations need to blend brand-centricity and customer-centricity seamlessly. Also, this alignment has to be reflected in the processes, guidelines, and decision-making (Palmatier et al., 2019). Keller (1993) defines a key measure, customer-based brand equity, as the "differential effect of brand knowledge on consumer response" (p. 1). When applied to customer service, we can consider what the consumer learns about the brand and reacts based on the service experience, which we define as customer-service-based brand equity. This customer orientation necessitates setting the right expectations by being transparent, ensuring that the service experience meets or exceeds the expectations, resulting in value. This process requires a long-term commitment from the senior management, which further propagates across the empowered employees (Palmatier et al., 2019).

Employees

Customer-centricity necessitates all employees to productively engage with customers and create meaningful relationships, resulting in value creation for customers and the organization (Kumar & Reinartz, 2016; Lamberti, 2013). The organizational identification with customer-centricity and communication of the same to the entire organization is inevitable to ensure that employees regularly demonstrate customer-centric behavior (Lamberti, 2013). However, organizations should focus on employees' training, development, and well-being to provide continuous high-level support to customers (Sheth et al., 2020). Hence, employees need to be equipped with constant training and supporting technology, tools, performance rewards, and pleasant working conditions to effectively understand and perform their roles (Dixon, 2018). According to Oshri et al. (2015), firms need to focus on human capital by investing in employee skill development in emerging markets.

Further, employees should also be trained to be empathetic to customer issues and respond appropriately. One of the most outstanding examples of excellent customer service in emerging markets comes from the famous tiffin delivery services, Dabbawallas, Mumbai, India. By hiring, cultivating humane values, and enhancing the links among the varied actors, the Dabbawallas have achieved superior customer service and a 99.9% accuracy rate (Ganapathy, 2017). Finally, trained employees with access to the right tools should be empowered to make decisions that serve customers' best interests. For example, Brazil-based Arcos Dorados, which operates McDonald's franchisees, is highly regarded by the customers for the excellent service culture. The company empowers employees to make instant decisions to offer personalized customer support. The following sections will look at the enabling technology for effective customer service.

Technology

Technology is a vital enabler and for customer-centricity. Here technology refers to information and communication technologies, which functions as a business tool to impart efficiency and competitive advantage if employed correctly (Domegan, 1996). Technical support is inevitable throughout the customer journey to access the required solutions with minimal cost and time efforts. There are three types of technologies that work. Customer enabling technologies (which facilitate customer contact and communication with the company for service requirements), employee enabling technologies (which help employees to know customers and serve them better), and other enterprise-wide technologies (which perform operational and administrative functions). The right combination of technologies at all levels is inevitable for exemplary service to customers. In this perspective, the digitization of emerging countries is advancing to the level of developed nations. Hence, 16 countries among the top 30 nations with the highest digital services revenue are emerging countries due to the rapid introduction and new technologies (Sharma, 2021).

However, before introducing a new technology to replace face-to-face/telephonic service/or early age technologies, it is vital to ensure that the new technology adds value and convenience. Going by the basic technology adoption model (Davis, 1989), customer-oriented technologies should be helpful and easy to use for successful adoption. Hence, firms' technology adoption should not be based only on cost savings but on customer convenience and value. The simple transactional tasks can be managed through the right tools for value-added, self-service, and automation, while the human agents can deal with complex issues. This process is particularly relevant for emerging markets where digital tools and adoption increase, with customer requirements for an Omnichannel approach for service. Organizations in the emerging markets have been leveraging upon digital technologies and tools for accelerated growth. For instance, a global study by Avaya (Ward, 2018) indicated that customers from emerging markets have much higher propensity to use social media-based customer service, than the customer from developed countries. Thus, a technology-enabled Omnichannel approach facilitates customers to reach the brand based on their convenience. The hospitality management brand Rotana (Middle East and Africa) has an all-inclusive mobile app with audio- and video-enabled customer care services and social media integration along with other regular functionalities. The option to video call provides personalized service perception to customers (Customer ME, 2012).

However, organizations need to consider the demographic factors and digital inequalities while developing suitable interfaces. Besides, the employees who work with customers around the clock should have access to enabling technologies that can quickly help get a 360-degree view of customers, bid database recommendations, signals for proactive support, opportunities for upselling, cross-sell, and so on. Importantly, organizations should adopt CRM systems and ensure technology integration across departments to develop one view of process and customer data.

Data

Data generation's rapidity from various sources and business operations opens up new opportunities and challenges for organizations (Sivarajah et al., 2017). With the wide range of modern tools and technologies, big data analytics can assimilate data from numerous channels and help organizations better understand customer, their needs, and the context of problems to ensure the correct responses (Lee, 2017). The data should be collected and analyzed and made accessible to the employees in a suitable format. The data can deliver personalized customer service, like the airports in China that employ face recognition to provide personalized flight details to the passengers (Patrawala, 2019).

However, organizations can adopt a transactional mindset in a data-fueled world, where customers are merely treated as numbers. This mindset is dangerous, as the brand will fail to connect with customers' fundamental aspects (Palmatier et al., 2019). Moreover, the customer service function can generate valuable data that can be vital inputs to the organization's power, quality improvement, innovation initiatives, and co-creation (Sheth et al., 2020). One outstanding example of the optimum usage of data for customer service comes from Maruti, a leading automobile manufacturer in India. Maruti utilized the data from social media platforms to gain insights into customer preferences, reviews, and feedback fed back to the product and service teams. The company is considered one of the most customer-centric organizations in India (Jha, 2015). However, sophisticated data tracking tools and technologies can make consumers apprehensive of their privacy. Hence organizations should also be transparent and socially responsible for informing customers on what data is collected and how it is utilized to serve them better (Sirich, 2020). Moreover, due to the rapid technology adoption, consumers in the emerging markets are not highly aware of the technology loopholes, making them more vulnerable to exploitation (Brougham, 2018).

Thus the micro factors should align with each other with an unwavering focus on customer-centricity. Further, all the elements are aligned with the customer.

Customer

Customer-centricity is an enterprise-wide approach that considers customers as the business epicenter (Shah et al., 2006). Customer-centricity's relevance has been advocated for decades, starting with Drucker (1954) and Levitt (1960). Customer-centricity is more relevant now in the emerging markets because studies have indicated that hyper customer sensitivity is vital in the emerging markets, as emerging market consumers are different from their counterparts in developed countries in many ways (KPMG, 2016). According to Smirnova et al. (2018), a customer-centric strategy helps firms serve their customers better, resulting in better market growth and profitability.

The path toward customer-centric service in an organization starts with "who is our customer?" Because the term "customer" is one of the most flexible definitions within the realms of management. Customer may be "people or entities that buy your products and services and supply your revenue" (Simons, 2014). However, the service perspective states that the customer gets in touch with the brand through any channel in the digital age. Bharti Airtel, a leading telecom brand in India, has developed the service design based on customer segmentation as per the revenue per customer. The platinum subscribers paying a higher tariff can access dedicated and priority customer service (Pandey, 2019). However, for the customer-centric service ecosystem to function, support from the immediate micro-environment consisting of brand, employees, data, and technology is inevitable.

2   Discussion and Conclusion

Emerging markets offer a queer mix of opportunities and challenges to organizations. The Organization of Economic Cooperation and Development predicts that middle-class consumers from emerging economies account for 70% of the consumption by 2030 (OECD, 2020). Hence, the emerging markets are on the priority radar of all businesses. However, to take advantage of the wealth of opportunities, companies have to offer superior customer service experience at all levels. This chapter provides a framework for a customer-centric service ecosystem, highlighting the macro and micro factors contributing to the design and delivery of superior service experiences. Table 1 represents a snapshot of the critical factors.

As the organization considers the macro-environmental components, such as culture, socio-political factors, and socio-economic factors, investors, the government would align their mission, vision, and customer-centric practices contextualized to the emerging markets. Along with these factors, they understand the unique infrastructural challenges, where digital technology is booming while the rest are lagging. Finally, the metrics and measurements for employees and organizations should be designed to reflect customer-centricity while considering the possibilities and limitations of the rest of the macro factors. These factors, in turn, influence micro-environmental factors, which

Table 1 Overview of CSE factors

Type	Factors	Description
Macro	Culture	Culture influences the economic drivers and the societal value system. The emerging markets have distinct cultural elements (e.g., Jeitinho Brasileiro in Brazil, Guanxi in China), which reflects in the conduct of employees and the customers
Macro	Socio-economic and socio-political factors	The emerging market and the customer are highly heterogenic w.r.t. income, education, digital divide, religious beliefs, and languages. There are also differences in the politico-legal structures. Such dimensions are considered within the service strategies and processes
Macro	Investors	Investors' role is vital in the design, maintenance, and functioning of the customer service ecosystem. If the investors believe in stellar customer service, then the same will reflect top management, trickling down to all organization levels
Macro	Government	The policies and regulations of the government considerably impact all facets of business, including the customer service ecosystem
Macro	Infrastructure	The emerging market countries face substantial infrastructure challenges, affecting transportation, storage, and specific technology systems, making it difficult to reach, serve, and communicate with the customers
Macro	Measurement and metrics	The emerging markets are different from the West; as explained through the macro factors above, organizations should develop customized measurement methods other than the developed region's strategies
Micro	Brand	The brand's vision, mission, values, and communication are aligned to customer-centricity principles
Micro	Employees	Organizations should focus on employees' training, development, and well-being to provide continuous high-level support to customers. Employee-centricity is vital for customer-centricity
Micro	Technology	The information and communication technologies that function as a business tool to impart efficiency and competitive advantage have to be aligned well with the ecosystem
Micro	Data	The data generated from multiple sources should be collected and analyzed, and accessible to the employees in a suitable format. The data can be utilized ethically to deliver personalized customer service
	Customer	A customer-centric strategy helps firms serve their customers better, resulting in better market growth and profitability. Hence, the customer should be the central focus, around which the macro and micro factors should be organized

include brand, employees, technology, and data. By aligning brands, people, technology, and data around customers, the organizations can deliver superior services to the customers.

Academic researchers can deepen the research on these factors utilizing quantitative testing and the inclusion of suitable moderating and mediating factors. Further, the factors explained in the ecosystem may be customized for each emerging country. Practitioners can expand their knowledge of the customer-centric service ecosystem's more refined components and adopt the relevant principles while moving to the emerging market. Developing the strategy and design aligned with the macro and micro factors explained in the framework, centered around the customer, will facilitate greater customer satisfaction in the emerging markets.

References

Alavi, S. (2016). New paradigm of digital marketing in emerging markets: From social media to social customer relationship management. *International Journal of Management Practice, 9*(1), 56–73.

American Express. (2017). *American Express global customer service barometer 2017 | Thought leadership | Trends & insights for smarter business* | American Express Singapore. American Express. https://business.americanexpress.com/sg/business-trends-insights/thought-leadership/american-express-global-customer-barometer-2017

Baron, S., Patterson, A., Maull, R., & Warnaby, G. (2018). Feed people first: A service ecosystem perspective on innovative food waste reduction. *Journal of Service Research, 21*(1), 135–150.

BCG. (2018, March 15). *Why MNCs are winning big in emerging markets*. India—EN. https://www.bcg.com/en-in/publications/2018/mncs-still-winning-big-emerging-markets

Berndt, A., Herbst, F., & Roux, L. (2005). Implementing a customer relationship management programme in an emerging market. *Journal of global business and technology, 1*(2), 81–89.

Borah, S. B., Prakhya, S., & Sharma, A. (2020). Leveraging service recovery strategies to reduce customer churn in an emerging market. *Journal of the Academy of Marketing Science, 48*(5), 848–868.

Brougham, I. (2018, September 19). Is data privacy in emerging markets feasible? *Medium.* https://medium.com/accion/is-data-privacy-in-emerging-markets-feasible-8421c7bdb8cb

Bryan, J. (2020, February 11). *What's your customer effort score?* Gartner. https://www.gartner.com/smarterwithgartner/unveiling-the-new-and-improved-customer-effort-score/

Cavusgil, S. T., Ghauri, P. N., & Liu, L. A. (2021). Doing business in emerging markets. *Sage Publications.*

Chakravarthy, B., & Coughlan, S. (2011). Emerging market strategy: Innovating both products and delivery systems. *Strategy & Leadership, 40*(1), 27–32.

Cornfield, G. (2020, April 30). *The most important metrics you're not tracking (Yet).* Harvard Business Review. https://hbr.org/2020/04/the-most-important-metrics-youre-not-tracking-yet?registration=success

Customer ME. (2012, October 10). *Keeping guests connected—Rotana group chooses Avaya to enhance customer service experience—Customer Middle East.* Customer Middle East. https://www.customer-me.com/keeping-guests-connected-rotana-group-chooses-avaya-to-enhance-customer-service-experience/

Davis, F. D. (1989). Perceived usefulness, perceived ease of use and user acceptance of information technology. *MIS Quarterly, 13*(3), 319–339.

Dixon, M. (2018). Reinventing customer service. *Harvard Business Review, 96*(6), 82–90.

Domegan, C. T. (1996). The adoption of information technology in customer service. *European Journal of Marketing., 30*(16), 52–69.

Drucker, P. (1954). *The practice of management.* HarperCollins.

Economic Times. (2020). *Government notifies new rules for e-Commerce entities.* ETRetail.com. https://retail.economictimes.indiatimes.com/news/e-commerce/e-tailing/government-notifies-new-rules-for-e-commerce-entities/77161830

Elg, U., Ghauri, P. N., & Tarnovskaya, V. (2008). The role of networks and matching in market entry to emerging retail markets. *International Marketing Review., 25*(6), 674–699.

Fox, J., & Lorsch, J. W. (2012). What good are shareholders? *Harvard Business Review, 90*(7/8), 48–57.

Ganapathy, C. (2017), Mumbai Dabbawalas: Social entrepreneurs who make India proud. https://www.grin.com/document/370831

Gani, F. (2020, July 14). 18 key customer service metrics + how to use them | blog | Hiverâ?¢. Hiver. https://hiverhq.com/blog/customer-service-metrics

Gaur, S. S., Kingshott, R. P., & Sharma, P. (2019). Managing customer relationships in emerging markets. *Journal of Service Theory and Practice., 29*(6), 598–608.

Ghauri, P., & Cateora, P. R. (2014). *International Marketing* (Auflage: 4. Auflage). McGraw-Hill Publ. Comp.

Goncalves, M., Alves, J., & Arcot, R. (2014). *Doing business in emerging markets: Roadmap for success.* Business Expert Press.

Guesalaga, R., Pierce, M., & Scaraboto, D. (2016). Cultural influences on expectations and evaluations of service quality in emerging markets. *International Marketing Review, 33*(1), 88–111.

Hauser, J., & Katz, G. (1998). Metrics: You are what you measure! *European Management Journal, 16*(5), 517–528.

Hoang, H. T., Hill, S. R., & Lu, V. N. (2010, November). The influence of service culture on customer service quality: Local vs. Foreign service firms in emerging markets. In *Proc. ANZMAC 2010 Conf* (pp. 1–9).

Hofstede, G. (1980). Culture and organizations. *International studies of management & organization, 10*(4), 15–41.

Jha. (2015, April 18). *Analytics helps Maruti Suzuki become the most customer centric auto manufacturer in India.* ETCIO.com. https://cio.economictimes.indiatimes.com/news/business-analytics/analytics-helps-maruti-suzuki-become-the-most-customer-centric-auto-manufacturer-in-india/46982787

Keller, K. L. (1993). Conceptualizing, measuring, and managing customer-based brand equity. *Journal of Marketing, 57*(1), 1–22.

Khanna, T., Palepu, K. G., & Sinha, J. (2005). Strategies that fit emerging markets. *Harvard Business Review, 83*(6), 4–19.

Koskela-Huotari, K., Edvardsson, B., Jonas, J. M., Sörhammar, D., & Witell, L. (2016). Innovation in service ecosystems—Breaking, making, and maintaining institutionalized rules of resource integration. *Journal of Business Research, 69*(8), 2964–2971.

KPMG. (2016). *Seeking customer centricity.* KPMG https://assets.kpmg/content/dam/kpmg/pdf/2016/06/seeking-customer-centricity-the-omni-business-model.pdf.

Kumar, V., & Reinartz, W. (2016). Creating enduring customer value. *Journal of Marketing, 80*(6), 36–68.

Lamberti, L. (2013). Customer centricity: The construct and the operational antecedents. *Journal of Strategic Marketing, 21*(7), 588–612.

Laroche, M., Ueltschy, L. C., Abe, S., Cleveland, M., & Yannopoulos, P. P. (2004). Service quality perceptions and customer satisfaction: Evaluating the role of culture. *Journal of International Marketing, 12*(3), 58–85.

Lee, I. (2017). Big data: Dimensions, evolution, impacts, and challenges. *Business Horizons, 60*(3), 293–303.

Lee, Y. K., Nam, J. H., Park, D. H., & Lee, K. A. (2006). What factors influence customer-oriented prosocial behavior of customer-contact employees? *Journal of Services Marketing.*

Levitt, T. (1960). Marketing myopia. *Harvard Business Review, 38*(4), 24–47.

Marinov, M. (2006). *Marketing in the emerging markets of Islamic countries.* Springer.

McGovern. (2017, November 27). *Customer experience continues to get worse.* CMSWire.com. https://www.cmswire.com/customer-experience/customer-experience-continues-to-get-worse/.

McKinsey. (2017, September 1). *Building brands in emerging markets.* McKinsey & Company. https://www.mckinsey.com/business-functions/marketing-and-sales/our-insights/building-brands-in-emerging-markets

Molino, C. D., Exarchos, P., & Ize, F. (2015, September 1). *Achieving customer-management excellence in emerging markets.* McKinsey & Company. https://www.mckinsey.com/industries/consumer-packaged-goods/our-insights/achieving-customer-management-excellence-in-emerging-markets#

Newlands, M. (2014). 4 tips for building a company that attracts the best investors. *Entrepreneur.* https://www.entrepreneur.com/article/235943

North, D. (2005). *Understanding the process of economic change.* Princeton University Press.

O'Cass, A., & Carlson, J. (2019). Introduction to the special issue–retailing and consumer Services in Emerging Markets. *Journal of Retailing and Consumer Services, 46,* 130–132.

OCED. (2020). *Business insights on emerging markets.* OECD. https://www.oecd.org/dev/EMnet-Business-Insights-2020.pdf

Oshri, I., Kotlarsky, J., & Willcocks, L. P. (2015). *The handbook of global outsourcing and offshoring: The definitive guide to strategy and operations* (3rd ed.). Palgrave Macmillan.

Pacek, N., & Thorniley, D. (2007). *Emerging markets: Lessons for business success and the outlook for different markets.* John Wiley & Sons.

Palmatier, R. W., Moorman, C., & Lee, J. (2019). *Handbook on customer centricity: Strategies for building a customer-centric organization.* Edward Elgar Publishing.

Pandey, N. (2019, May 3). *To counter Jio, Bharti Airtel launches loyalty programme for prepaid users.* mint. https://www.livemint.com/industry/telecom/airtel-relaunches-airtel-thanks-program-with-silver-gold-and-platinum-tiers-1556779439691.html

Patrawala, S. S. (2019, March 27). *Is China's facial recognition powered airport kiosks an attempt to invade privacy via an easy flight experience?* Packt Hub. https://hub.packtpub.com/chinas-facial-recognition-powered-airport-kiosks-an-attempt-to-invade-privacy/

Paul, J. (2019). Marketing in emerging markets: A review, theoretical synthesis and extension. *International Journal of Emerging Markets.*

Rafaeli, A., Ziklik, L., & Doucet, L. (2008). The impact of call center employees' customer orientation behaviors on service quality. *Journal of Service Research, 10*(3), 239–255.

Rao-Nicholson, R., Khan, Z., & Marinova, S. (2018). Balancing social and political strategies in emerging markets: Evidence from India. *Business Ethics: A European Review, 28*(1), 56–70.

Roy, S. K., Sekhon, H., & Nguyen, B. (2019). Service research in emerging markets: Business as usual? *Journal of Service Theory and Practice, 29*(5/6), 537–538.

Sarma, S. (2018). *Cultural nuances in changing consumer behavior: Lessons for cultural positioning. In global observations of the influence of culture on consumer buying behavior* (pp. 279–293). IGI Global.

Scott, W. R. (1995). *Institutions and organizations.* Sage.

Shah, D., Rust, R. T., Parasuraman, A., Staelin, R., & Day, G. S. (2006). The path to customer centricity. *Journal of Service Research, 9*(2), 113–124.

Sharma, R. (2021, April 11). *Technology will save emerging markets from sluggish growth.* Financial Times. https://www.ft.com/content/2356928b-d909-4a1d-b108-7b60983e3d22

Sheth, J., Jain, V., & Ambika, A. (2020). Repositioning the customer support services: The next frontier of competitive advantage. *European Journal of Marketing.*

Sheth, J. N. (2011). Impact of emerging markets on marketing: Rethinking existing perspectives and practices. *Journal of Marketing, 75*(4), 166–182.

Simons, R. (2014). Choosing the right customer. *Harvard Business Review, 92*(3), 48–55.

Singh, M. (2014). Good customer service makes the difference. *The Journal of Internet Banking and Commerce, 19*(2), 1–11.

Sinha, M., & Sheth, J. (2017). Growing the pie in emerging markets: Marketing strategies for increasing the ratio of non-users to users. *Journal of Business Research, 86*, 217–224.

Sinha, M., & Sheth, J. (2018). Growing the pie in emerging markets: Marketing strategies for increasing the ratio of non-users to users. *Journal of Business Research, 86*, 217–224.

Sirich. (2020). *Forbes.* https://www.forbes.com/sites/forbescommunicationscouncil/2020/03/25/data-transparency-in-the-age-of-privacy-protection/?sh=5b0d842746b2

Sivarajah, U., Kamal, M. M., Irani, Z., & Weerakkody, V. (2017). Critical analysis of big data challenges and analytical methods. *Journal of Business Research, 70*, 263–228.

Smirnova, M. M., Rebiazina, V. A., & Frösén, J. (2018). Customer orientation as a multidimensional construct: Evidence from the Russian markets. *Journal of Business Research, 86*, 457–467.

Snow, D., & Yanovitch, T. (2009). *Unleashing excellence: The complete guide to ultimate customer service.* Wiley.

Titan annual report. (2019). https://www.titancompany.in/sites/default/files/Annual_Report_2019_20.pdf

Vargo, S. L., & Lusch, R. F. (2016). Institutions and axioms: An extension and update of service-dominant logic. *Journal of the Academy of Marketing Science, 44*(1), 5–23.

Ward, C. (2018, November 30). Social customer service a go-to channel in emerging markets. *MyCustomer.* https://www.mycustomer.com/service/channels/social-customer-service-a-go-to-channel-in-emerging-markets

Williams, T. (2011, March 10). *Challenging the rise of India and China.* Global Atlanta. https://www.globalatlanta.com/challenging-the-rise-of-india-and-china/

Zeithaml, V. A., Jaworski, B. J., Kohli, A. K., Tuli, K. R., Ulaga, W., & Zaltman, G. (2020). A theories-in-use approach to building marketing theory. *Journal of Marketing, 84*(1), 32–51.

Service Management for Sustainable Business Transformation

Bo Enquist and Samuel Petros Sebhatu

1 Introduction

A new reality for business and society has come both before and after the COVID-19 pandemic. The crisis has highlighted the urgent need to rethink the human ecosystem, the relationship between humanity and nature, and, more specifically, *the service ecosystem*. Before the pandemic, the economic and social service systems were accelerated based on the trends of globalization and technology embedded in a narrow way on acting for sustainability practices such as greenwashing (see Sebhatu et al., 2021). The pandemic has rewritten the playground and will have an enduring impact on the way organizations look and services are delivered. The COVID-19 impact, coupled with globalization and technology, drives the business societal transformation. A transformation that takes place in complex environments demands the engagement of different types of stakeholders from different organizations and domains. Service management is not only for micro and meso processes; it must also meet global challenges of complexity and wicked problems in this new landscape (Waddock et al., 2015).

In this book chapter, we will go back to the roots of service management from a humanity point of view (Berry, 1999) and with a societal aspect (Laczniak & Murphy, 2012). We will expand the domain of service

---

B. Enquist • S. P. Sebhatu (✉)
CTF, Service Research Centre, Karlstad University, Karlstad, Sweden
e-mail: Bo.Enquist@kau.se; Samuel.Sebhatu@kau.se

© The Author(s), under exclusive license to Springer Nature Switzerland AG 2022
B. Edvardsson, B. Tronvoll (eds.), *The Palgrave Handbook of Service Management*,
https://doi.org/10.1007/978-3-030-91828-6_22

411

management from a narrow perspective of a dyad based on service provider and customer interactions to meet a bigger context and, at the same time, expanding the concept of service management. The focus is on the business mission *to serve someone*, with the insight that business and ethics are intertwined and cannot be separated (Freeman, 1994), and that *management with a societal perspective* includes a leadership thinking (Normann, 2001), a stakeholder orientation (Laczniak & Murphy, 2012), and a sustainable business transformation action (Sebhatu et al., 2021) to meet this new landscape at the micro, meso, and macro levels.

Service management for sustainable business transformation requires a broader framework to handle value co-creation, innovation, and sustainability for business societal transformation. This is related to a more values-based business model (Edvardsson & Enquist, 2009) and a change of mindset (Normann, 2001) to meet economic, social, and environmental challenges (Sebhatu et al., 2021), and the imperative "value for whom?" by an awareness of who is making and who is taking in value distribution (Mazzucato, 2018).

2 Theoretical and Conceptual Framework

Service Management Development Periods

The following brief overview of the history of service management and service research provides background to this chapter, seeing service management from a humanity point of view, and follows the developing periods of newer service research on value-in-exchange, value co-creation, and resource integration.

Period 1970–2000

In the article "Transitioning from Service Management to Service-Dominant Logic" (Gummesson et al., 2010), the authors provide a short history of service management (SM). Here are the highlights of the period from that article.

* *1970s–1990s.* Service research puts service on the agenda, as opposed to goods and the one-sided focus on the manufacturing sector. SM with service marketing as the most active area, but also human resource management, operations management, quality management, and other disciplines. In the end of this period, service was considered a perspective for any offering.

Service Management for Sustainable Business Transformation   413

- *1980s–2010.* Relational approaches in marketing embracing both goods and services (business-to-consumer and business-to-business) marketing such as relationship marketing and CRM.
- *1990s–2010.* The internet, e-mail, and mobile communication offer a new infrastructure for commercial and social relationship (ibid., p. 12).

The marketing perspective as the most active area in SM had its own research in *Relationship Marketing* (RM). Christian Grönroos contributed with an early article entitled "From Marketing Mix to Relationship Marketing: Towards a Paradigm Shift in Marketing," where RM is about mutual exchange, fulfillment of promises and trust between several parties or actors (Grönroos, 1994a).

A book by American service management pioneer Leonard L. Berry, *Discovering the Soul of Service* (Berry, 1999), offered deep insights into the *Soul of Service* for a service business to sustaining long-term success. Berry studied 14 award-winning US-based labor-intensive service companies to see how those enterprises developed a deep service culture based on human values. The lessons he learned from those world-class service companies were summarized as: *values-driven leadership, strategic focus, executional excellence, control of destiny, trust-based relationships, investment in employee success, acting small, brand cultivation, and generosity* (ibid., pp. 233–246).

"Green service quality" in Gummesson (1994) was one of the earliest contributions within service research to suggest that an ecological perspective was important, and he labeled this perspective as "green service management" (see Enquist et al., 2007).

Period 2000–Present

Schneider and White (2004) expanded SM in the area of service quality to a more multi-factorial view by conceptualizing and measuring service quality from a marketing perspective, recognizing the presence of customer as central to service operations and emphasizing the importance of introducing service quality into human-resource management. They called for a broader perspective on service management, including the possibility of integrating service management with TQM.

According to Edvardsson et al. (2005a), "service" is better understood as a perspective than as an activity.

Grönroos further developed what he called *service logic*, where relationship marketing and service management meet in *value in exchange* and *value creation* process, where the customer's own value creation process is important. Service providers facilitate this process and make value propositions. An earlier article (Grönroos, 2008) asked, "Who Creates Value? and Who Co-creates?" He further developed this in "Critical Service Logic: Making Sense of Value Creation and Co-Creation" (Grönroos & Voima, 2013).

In the *Journal of Marketing*, Stephen Vargo and Bob Lusch wrote an article entitled "Evolving to a New Dominant Logic to Marketing" (Vargo & Lusch, 2004). The article started a new era of service research focusing on Service-Dominant logic (S-D logic). An extension and update of S-D logic came a decade later (see Vargo & Lusch, 2016) in an article that illustrated the narrative and process of S-D logic as a loop: *Actors—Resource Integration—Service Exchange—Institutional and Institutional Arrangements—Service Ecosystems.* The arrangement of the loop generates a *value co-creation* process.

Service ecosystem is central in the process of S-D logic. A service ecosystem is multilevel in nature and can be viewed on micro, meso, and macro levels (actor-to-actor, Lusch & Vargo, 2014) as well as from processual, institutional, and systemic perspectives (Koskela-Huotari, 2018).

The update of the S-D logic consists of 11 foundational premises (FP), five of which are suggested as axioms (Vargo & Lusch, 2016, p. 18).

A year later, based on these axiom/foundational premises, Vargo and Lusch suggested using S-D logic as a broader framework. One of those possibilities for extension is the study of macro marketing, including *ethics, economic, environmental, and social sustainability*, as well as *public policy* (Vargo & Lusch, 2017). Other suggested areas are *dynamic strategy development and implementation*; *market and economy*, respectively *complexity economics*; and *smart service systems by cognitive computing*, respectively *big data*, to capture actor-centric behavior in a service ecosystem.

In the article "From Relationship Marketing to Total Relationship Marketing and Beyond" (Gummesson, 2017a), the author reflected on *relationships, networks*, and *interaction* in marketing and identified three paradigm shifts in marketing.

- *Paradigm 1 (until the 1970s)*—dominated by American marketing management and the marketing mix ("4Ps")
- *Paradigm 2 (1970s–2000)*—service marketing and management focusing on differences to goods marketing
- *Paradigm 3 (2000s–present)*—an era of commonalities, interdependencies and a systemic, stakeholder-centric approach

Management and Leadership

In the early article "From Scientific Management to Service Management: A Management Perspective for the Age of Service Competition," Christian Grönroos (1994b) showed how mainstream management principles have their roots in the Industrial Revolution and scientific management. Service management wants to shift that focus and give priority to five facets (ibid., p. 6): *overall management perspective, customer focus, holistic approach, quality focus*, and *internal development and reinforcement*.

In his 2001 book, Richard Normann changed the focus from the distinction of service as opposed to manufacturing to what he called service logic, which is about *from production to utilization; from product to process, from transaction to relationship* (ibid., p. 98). He made a distinction between management and leadership: If "management" is the art of achieving efficiency within a more-or-less defined framework, "leadership" is the art of navigating an organization through structural change (ibid., p. 269). The book's subtitle—*When the Map Changes the Landscape*—addressed the idea that a strong vision for reframing the business can serve as the *new business mission*. It is also about mobilizing, managing, and using resources in a more proactive way that is not limited to the boundary of the company itself (Normann, 2001, p. 10).

Peter Pruzan gave management a more societal perspective via a contemporary shift in management perspective, from a paradigm of "control" to one of "values." He argued for a paradigm of *values-based management* (Pruzan, 1998). In a later article, he looked at the interrelationship among *values, virtues*, and *visions* to develop corporate consciousness. He argued that conscious organizations seem to be more reflective, purposeful, and values-oriented (Pruzan, 2001).

The idea of values-based management was further developed in *values-based service* (Edvardsson & Enquist, 2009). That book expanded the service framework, where the authors introduced the notion of values-based service for sustainable business by combining service logic with a values-based business model, supported by the real-world context of IKEA. The book contributes with five principles for a sustainable values-based service business (ibid., pp. 110–112).

Stakeholder Theory Tensions

In the article "Stakeholder Theory and Marketing: Moving from a Firm-Centric to a Societal Perspective," Laczniak and Murphy (2012) argued that there is an urgent need for new research that adopts a broader and more inclusive stakeholder orientation. That article contributed with what the authors called a hard form of stakeholder theory:

Hard-form stakeholder theory suggests that the purpose of business organizations is broader than simply customer satisfaction at the firm level or wealth maximization for company shareholders. (Ibid., p. 288)

They went on to say that the purpose of business goes beyond the micro firm level and instead collectively intended to help promote the greater common good of the stakeholder network and the creation of "value" is to be understood broadly and socially (ibid.).

Lusch and Webster (2011) advocated a stakeholder-unifying, co-creation philosophy for all of marketing.

Edward Freeman is one of the pioneers of stakeholder theory and became well known for expanding strategic management with stakeholder thinking in his classic work *Strategic management: A stakeholder approach* (Freeman, 1984). In a later article (Freeman, 1994), he offered the insight that business and ethics are intertwined and cannot be separated. In a later article, "Tension in Stakeholder Theory" (Freeman et al., 2020), he and other researchers combined *business ethics, stakeholder theory*, and *strategic management* and contributed with what they labeled *Value Creation Stakeholder Theory*, which is about insights for human behavior in the context of business. It is not about shareholder versus stakeholder, but more about a narrow/reductionist versus broad/holistic perspective on business. It is also about the difference between a value chain (linear and singularly focused on financial value) and a value network (which includes the importance of share purpose and values) (ibid., p. 217).

Value Co-creation for Whom?

As we have shown, value co-creation is a central message for SM and contemporary service research. What is missing in most of today's service research is the question of *value for whom?* The intention of this chapter is to expand service research to also include a broader sustainable stakeholder view, and societal perspective for sustainable business transformation. Mazzucato (2018) addressed distribution of value, making a distinction between who is taking and who is making. Her message is one of a more inclusive and collective creation of value: "If the goal is to produce growth that is more innovation-led (smart growth), more inclusive and more sustainable, we need a better understanding of value to steer us" (ibid.). In this chapter, we are developing a framework in which value co-creation will be more inclusive and not just firm-centric. Patrick Murphy and Gene Laczniak contributed with "Ethical Foundations for Exchange in Service Ecosystems" (Murphy & Laczniak,

Service Management for Sustainable Business Transformation 417

2019). Based on Vargo and Lusch's (2017) article regarding a more humane or ethical ethos of S-D logic; Murphy and Laczniak (2019) argue that research must be directed toward the societal, ethical, and normative aspects of the service ecosystems:

(1) The relational nature of S-D logic (key relational virtues *trust, commitment*, and *diligence*), facilitating virtues (*fairness, integrity, respect, empathy*), communication, and action virtue *transparency*.
(2) The importance of both value and values, where value has to do with economic contributions, while values pertain to the ethical dimension of exchange.
(3) Stakeholder importance of S-D logic and exchange in service ecosystems.

Broader Framework for Sustainable Service Business

As we mentioned in the introduction to this chapter, service management for sustainable business transformation requires a broader framework to handle value co-creation, innovation, and sustainability for business societal transformation. Edvardsson and Enquist (2009), described above, outlined a broader framework of business practice with the help of IKEA, where social and environmental issues were not handled as externalities, but as a proactive part of the business model. As part of the investigation for that book (ibid.), three articles were published in service journals. One article was about expanding service brand, "Values-Based Service Brands: Narratives from IKEA" (Edvardsson et al., 2006); another was on expanding service quality, "Values-Based Service Quality for Sustainable Business" (Enquist et al., 2007); and the third was "Co-creating Customer Value Through Hyperreality in the Pre-purchase Service Experience" (Edvardsson et al., 2005b).

In Fisk et al., a book chapter titled "The Important Role of Shared Values in a Sustainable Service Business" (Edvardsson et al., 2014), values-based thinking was further developed in service research based on the economic, social, and environmental perspectives handled interdependently from a holistic point of view as part of a more integrative business model. This development of values-based thinking is based on Edvardsson and Enquist (2009) and the doctoral thesis *Corporate Social Responsibility for Sustainable Service Dominant Logic* (Sebhatu, 2010). In Enquist et al. (2015), the values-based position was described as a transcendence phenomenon found in sustainable business practices in real contexts, with four values-based organizations—Patagonia, IKEA, Starbucks, and Mayo Clinic—being offered.

In the book *Business Transformation for a Sustainable Future*, Sebhatu et al. (2021) show that sustainability must be embedded in a wider framework, both theoretically and contextually, by business-societal practice in the broadest sense, which will co-create a new meaning for the interrelationship among *sustainability, innovation*, and *transformation* to meet the complex challenges facing business and society in the twenty-first century. The aim of that book is to understand how sustainable societal practices can contribute to a broader view of business transformation, and vice versa, in a globalized world. It is an edited book with contributions from many researchers from different disciplines with different angles of value creation. An important reference from the introduction chapter of the book to expand the concept of sustainability is Peter Kemp, who identified five dimensions of sustainability (Kemp, 2011): *ethical, social, scientific, economic*, and *legal*. For Kemp, the concept of sustainability begins in ethics and ends in law. The scientific dimension is distinct and more appropriately applied to the problem of climate change than the "softer" dimensions, which might be applied to environmental sustainability, as is more common in today's business practice. The social dimension points to another current business concept: corporate social responsibility (CSR).

A global transformation agenda that is already in place today is the UN's Agenda 2030,[1] with its widely known seventeen Sustainable Developmental Goals (SDGs), a plan of action for "people, planet, prosperity, peace, and partnership." Such a global code of conduct to guide for operating with a societal perspective is given the general term *Hyper norm* (Laczniak & Murphy, 2012). A contribution from the Club of Rome 50th Anniversary Report in 2018 is that the socioeconomic goals (SDGs 1–12) cannot be tackled using conventional growth policies if the environmental goals (SDGs 13–15) are to be achieved (von Weizsäcker & Wijkman, 2018, p. 38).

"A Challenge-Driven Business Ecosystem: Addressing Fossil-Free Transformation" (Enquist & Sebhatu, 2021a) is an example of an ecosystem as an inspiration of *sustainable service business transformation*. The chapter contributes with *a dynamic ecosystem in a business-societal perspective for challenge-driven transformative change* covering not just economic value, but also relating to an open business model and a change of mindset. This dynamic and multilevel ecosystem has an *actor-to-actor* nature, where the macro level also includes the biosphere and is more systemic in its character, the meso level is more institutional, and the micro level is more processual. The

---

[1] https://www.un.org/sustainabledevelopment/development-agenda/.

network of complexity—where service innovation, social innovation, and corporate social responsibility address global challenges, under the guidance of Agenda 2030, to tackle transformation, innovation, and sustainability issues—needs to move from a firm-centric to a societal perspective.

Another contribution of *sustainable service business transformation* is two different cases of two values-driven privately owned companies: Löfbergs (see Sebhatu & Enquist, 2019) and IKEA (see Enquist & Sebhatu, 2021b). Those enterprises have a strong reporting mechanism and clear transformation agenda, guided by the SDGs. These two business organizations have achieved different levels of maturity in terms of innovative services that co-create value, transformation, and integration of resources, and sustainability thinking has a more circular and societal meaning in an interrelationship with both innovation and transformation.

Concluding Framework of Service Management for the Sustainable Business Transformation

To develop a theoretical and conceptual framework for this chapter, five areas have been investigated. The different areas contribute with fragmented descriptions on different theories and concepts. We have developed a matrix to make the framework more structured. On the vertical axis of the matrix, thirteen key labels and concepts have been identified and noted. With regard to service management for sustainable business transformation, the findings on the horizontal axis have been divided into two parts: *service management and newer service research*; and *theory for sustainable service business transformation*. The references in the second part have their background in Part 1, but are more concerned about sustainable service business transformation to meet global challenges of complexity and wicked problems of today. The thirteen labels and concepts will be used in the next section in real contexts as a template for case studies of service management for sustainable transformation—the case of IKEA.

3 Service Management for Sustainable Business Transformation: The Case of IKEA

Research Methodology and Method

The method was carried out in a dialectic between theory and practice. Using multidisciplinary theory building and our conceptual framework, we seek to reinterpret the dialectic between theory and practice in an explorative manner via a critical reflexive methodology (Alvesson & Kärreman, 2007; Alvesson & Sköldberg, 2010) in a specific context. The context of this study is a proactive value-based company. We are searching for new meaning and a deeper understanding of business practice (Enquist et al., 2015; Gummesson, 2017b; Kristensson Uggla, 2010). We are also opening up the dialectic between theory and practice by means of our multidisciplinary theory and conceptual framework (Table 1), built in order to address a specific context based on thick descriptions of the case study (Enquist et al., 2015; Gummesson, 2017b). In the present chapter, our empirical setting consists of a values-driven privately owned company, IKEA, that has a clear transformation agenda. IKEA has achieved different levels of maturity. Consistent with the concept of grounded theory, our case was developed over a long period. The data were collected between 2012 and 2020 in combination with field data (Alvesson & Sköldberg, 2010), such as interviews, interview transcripts, observations, transformation lab (T-lab) discussions, and documents (such as steering documents, field narratives of positive and negative incidents, key performance figures, and annual reports). Our data access was unique (Gummesson, 2017b) in that we were independent of any industry funding, but in cooperation with the company. The collected materials were transcribed, thematized, and analyzed through a within- and cross-case analysis (Eisenhardt, 1989) based on the grounded theory (Glaser, 1992). The case is analyzed based on the description, understanding, and interpretation of the research material.

Sources: A furniture dealer's testament (Kamprad, 1976); People & Planet Positive: IKEA Sustainability Strategy (IKEA, 2018); IKEA Sustainability Report FY19 (IKEA SR, 2019); IKEA Sustainability Report FY20 (IKEA SR, 2020); Annual Summary and Sustainability Report FY19 (Ingka Group, 2019); Circular Economy and Values-Based Sustainability Business Practice: People & Planet Positive at IKEA (Enquist & Sebhatu, 2021b); Edvardsson and Enquist (2009).

IKEA can be described as a values-based company that is driven by a service logic and grounded in a strong culture and a set of core values. The values form the compass that guides IKEA co-workers in their day-to-day work, and the IKEA culture is what is formed when these values are put into practice. IKEA was founded in 1943 by entrepreneur Ingvar Kamprad in the county of Småland, a poor part of Sweden, and it underwent a long journey, involving trial and error, to become the world-leading global home furnishings enterprise and brand as we know it today.

Vision and mission: Crucial in understanding IKEA today is its vision, which is also its mission—"*to create a better everyday life for the many people.*"

Service Management for Sustainable Business Transformation 421

Table 1 Key labels and concepts of service management for sustainable business transformation framework

Key Labels and Concepts	Service Management and Newer Service Research	Theory for Sustainable Service Business Transformation
Vision and mission		Strong vision for reframing the business can serve as the new business mission (Normann, 2001)
Values and hypernorms	"Soul of service" is values-driven (Berry, 1999)	Shared values, virtues, and visions are to develop corporate consciousness (Pruzan, 2001); value has to do with economic contributions while values pertain to the ethical dimension (Murphy & Laczniak, 2019); global code of conducts with a societal perspective is called hypernorms (Laczniak & Murphy, 2012)
Strategy	Strategic focus and control of destiny (Berry, 1999) ; S-D logic 2025, Dynamic strategy development and implementation (Vargo & Lusch, 2017)	
Management and leadership	Executional excellence (management) and values-driven leadership (Berry, 1999); SM as an overall management perspective gives high priority to the external efficiency of the firm, how customers perceive the quality of the core products, and the total performance of a firm (Grönroos, 1994b)	"Management" for efficiency, "leadership" for navigating an organization through structural change (Normann, 2001) Values-based management (Pruzan, 1998); values-based leadership for living the values (Edvardsson & Enquist, 2009)
Service ecosystem	Actor-to-actor (Lusch & Vargo, 2014); processual, institutional, and systemic perspectives (Koskela-Huotari, 2018)	Actor-to-actor-to-nature (Sebhatu et al., 2021); "Ethical foundations for exchange in service ecosystems" (Murphy & Laczniak, 2019)

(*continued*)

Table 1 (continued)

Key Labels and Concepts	Service Management and Newer Service Research	Theory for Sustainable Service Business Transformation
Value-in-exchange and value co-creation	Trust-based relationships (Berry, 1999); who creates value? and who co-creates? (Grönroos, 2008); making sense of value creation and co-creation (Grönroos & Voima, 2013); service is the fundamental basis of exchange and value is co-created by multiple actors, always including the beneficiary (Vargo & Lusch, 2016)	Relational nature of exchange in service ecosystems from ethical perspective (Murphy & Laczniak, 2019); values-based service for sustainable business by combining service logic with a values-based business model (Edvardsson & Enquist, 2009)
Stakeholder orientation	Stakeholder-unifying perspective for marketing (Lusch & Webster, 2011); total relationship marketing and beyond. 2000s– is beginning of an era of commonalities, interdependencies and a systemic, stakeholder-centric approach (Gummesson, 2017a)	Stakeholder orientation (Laczniak & Murphy, 2012); combine business ethics, stakeholder theory and strategic management (Freeman et al., 2020);
Service experience		Values-based service experience for co-creating value (Edvardsson & Enquist, 2009)
Service brand and communication	Brand cultivating (Berry, 1999);	Values-based service brands (Edvardsson & Enquist, 2006); values-based service brand and communication for values resonance (Edvardsson & Enquist, 2009)
Resource integration	Investment in employee success, (Berry, 1999); SM in the area of human resource management and operations management (Gummesson et al., 2010); Resource integration (Vargo & Lusch, 2016)	Using resources inside and particularly outside the boundaries of the traditional corporation more effectively becomes a mandatory skill for management (Normann, 2001)

(*continued*)

Service Management for Sustainable Business Transformation 423

Table 1 (continued)

Key Labels and Concepts	Service Management and Newer Service Research	Theory for Sustainable Service Business Transformation
Sustainability and CSR	Green service management (Gummesson, 1994); S-D logic 2025, macro marketing, including ethics, economic, environmental and social sustainability, as well as public policy (Vargo & Lusch, 2017)	Corporate social responsibility (CSR) as a strategy for sustainable service business (Edvardsson & Enquist, 2009); corporate social responsibility for sustainable service dominant logic (Sebhatu, 2010); Rethink triple bottom line (Elkington, 2019); sustainability needs to be embedded in a wider framework, theoretically as well contextually, within business-societal practice (Sebhatu et al., 2021). Five dimensions of sustainability (Kemp, 2011): ethical, social, scientific, economic, and legal.
Service quality and QM	Service quality (Gummesson et al., 2010); Broader perspective on service management—including the possibility of integrating service quality management with TQM (Schneider & White, 2004)	Values-based service quality for sustainable business (Enquist et al., 2007)
Innovation and transformation	S-D logic 2025, smart service systems by cognitive computing respectively big data to capture actor-centric behavior in a service ecosystem (Vargo & Lusch, 2017)	Interrelationship between sustainability, innovation, and transformation (Sebhatu et al., 2021); sustainability thinking has a more circular and societal meaning in an interrelationship with both innovation and transformation (Enquist & Sebhatu, 2021b; Sebhatu & Enquist, 2019)

The vision-mission statement is a compass of a never-ending transforming and value-creating process of the IKEA value chain/network. The IKEA vision has been with the organization from the very beginning and still influencing everything they achieve. It also impacts or influences the development of their products, sharing their ideas, sourcing and use of the raw materials, and generally the way IKEA acts in the world. IKEA also cares for every little thing and footprint and the extent of their track. This, in general, helps IKEA to keep their feet on the ground and to become more accessible and inclusive.

Values and hypernorms: IKEA culture and values are embedded in its history and the Swedish heritage. IKEA is guided by eight values: *togetherness, caring for people and planet; cost-consciousness; simplicity; renew and improve; different with a meaning; give-and-take responsibility*; and *lead by example*. IKEA's values have their roots in the company's founder, how his vision and values were realized through trial and error to build a dynamic entrepreneurial business model outside the mainstream, and how his view of ownership is centered on cost-consciousness and financial independence. The strong culture of IKEA is based on shared values and meanings. *A furniture dealer's testament* from Kamprad in 1976 is still of great importance in stating these values and meanings to create a better everyday life for the majority of people. By living these values, IKEA has created a strong and unique culture that brings the IKEA business network all together.

IKEA represents a good example of a company guided and inspired by the hyper-norms of the UN Sustainable Development Goals (SDGs) to meet global challenges by adopting sustainability thinking; at the same time, it plays an important role in contributing to the SDG outcomes.

Strategy: The People & Planet Positive strategy was re-launched in 2018 and includes ambitions leading up to 2030. The commitments are set for 2030 in line with the UN SDGs (see Table 2). Balancing economic growth and positive social impact with environmental protection and regeneration is the statement accompanying the strategy outlining what sustainability means to IKEA. For IKEA, the balancing is about P&PP Strategy, which is structured on three focus areas based on material topics where the sustainability issues can make most impact and what the stakeholders' expectation is.

Management and leadership: Management and leadership are interlinked in the IKEA business. The organization structure is very decentralized and empowered by a Scandinavian management style and leadership is about living the values. IKEA's governance structure is built upon different foundations and subgroups kept together with the label IKEA as one business and act as one brand. The Inter IKEA Group consists of three core businesses: franchise, range, and supply. The core businesses work together with franchisees and suppliers to co-create an even better IKEA offer and franchise system. Inter IKEA Group aims to provide the best possible conditions for implementing and operating the IKEA Concept and to create a strong platform for growth. The idea of IKEA franchising is a system build that *encourages everyone to contribute and collaborate*. The Ingka Group is the largest IKEA franchise, covering 32 markets and 90 percent of the retail sales. Management and

Service Management for Sustainable Business Transformation 425

Table 2 Overview of IKEA's ambitions and commitments of the key focus areas for implementing Agenda 2030

High Material Focus	Key Challenges	IKEA Focus Area	IKEA Commitments
* Health and well-being * Life at home and work impact * Resource efficiency * Climate footprint	Unsustainable consumption	*Healthy and sustainable living*	* Inspiring and enabling people to live healthier, more sustainable lives * Promoting circular and sustainable consumption * Creating a movement in society around better everyday living
* Resource efficiency * Climate footprint * Material use * Sourcing * Production impact * Logistics impact * Operation impacts	Climate change	*Circular and climate positive*	* Transforming into a circular business * Becoming climate positive * Regenerating resources, protecting ecosystems, and improving biodiversity
* Human rights * Decent work * Social impact	Inequality	*Fair and equal*	* Providing and supporting decent and meaningful work across the value chain * Being an inclusive business * Promoting equality

Source: People & Planet Positive: IKEA Sustainability Strategy—IKEA (2018)

leadership are about implementing the business idea. Each part of the IKEA business sets goals, targets, and roadmaps to deliver on the strategy. This allows for locally tailored and relevant implementation and activities.

Service ecosystem: *IKEA's people & planet ecosystem* is kept together with the ambition of becoming people- and planet-positive and inspired and enabling many people to live a better everyday life within the boundaries of the planet by 2030. The IKEA ecosystem is defined and kept together by *one brand* IKEA and the IKEA Vision and Mission, IKEA Values and Hypernorms, IKEA Strategy, IKEA Stakeholders, IKEA Resource integration by IKEA value chain.

Value-in-exchange and value co-creation: Over the last decade, the IKEA vision—"to create a better everyday life for the many people"—has led to the company being more interactive and collaborative with its customers and other stakeholders: networking, co-producing, and co-creating for mutual gain. IKEA is bringing the IKEA business closer to its customers through a diverse strategy of city-center locations, traditional suburban stores, improved capabilities for online shopping, as well as home deliveries and services.

Stakeholder orientation: Driving and supporting change together with IKEA stakeholders are an essential part of reaching the IKEA sustainability goals. The IKEA stakeholder dialogues and engagements are:

217,000 *Co-workers* throughout the different IKEA businesses; *Communities* to learn and share ideas; nearly 1600 *Suppliers* for minimizing environmental footprint and improving working condition; engaging with *Customers* to understand their needs to living more healthy and sustainable lives; *Partners and collaborators* increasingly important in solving big, complex challenges that impact IKEA business.

The social dimension of sustainability has been further strengthened to create a more societal business based on stakeholder orientation.

Service experience: There is a major transformation within IKEA business, which has been ongoing since 2015 and involves efforts to come closer to customers. Ingka Group, the retail group, claims that it is in the midst of its biggest transformation change process yet, with strong movements in digital development, store transformations, city expansion, services, and sustainability initiatives, "bringing IKEA to more people in new ways." A key concept is service experience by storytelling at social media and different internet platforms, using the showrooms at IKEA stores as experience rooms for stakeholder engagement.

Service experience at IKEA can be seen as materialized of IKEA business idea: While the IKEA vision expresses why we exist, the IKEA business idea says how we realize the vision. We want "to offer a wide range of well-designed, functional home furnishing products at prices so low that as many people as possible will be able to afford them."[2] We love these words because they capture the very essence of the IKEA brand.

The business idea is also linked to the concept of "Democratic Design," which has developed since 1995. The original three-dimensional concept has been re-conceptualized and is now five-dimensional, the two dimensions of *sustainability* and *quality* being added to *function, form,* and *low price*. Democratic design has a key role to play in realizing the IKEA business idea.

Service brand and communication: One brand, many companies. The IKEA business is defined as the business performed by all entities operating under the IKEA brand. Brands are living expressions of what a company stands for. They communicate what its products or services can do for people. The IKEA brand and marketing communication for values resonance (as opposed to dissonance) express IKEA's vision, which is to create a better everyday life for the many people. The largest retail group, Ingka Group, with its ambition to

---

[2] Ikea.com—mission statement.

Service Management for Sustainable Business Transformation

bringing IKEA to more people in new ways, says that IKEA vison is more relevant than ever before. As a big brand with a big purpose, IKEA has a unique opportunity to really make a positive impact on people and planet and contribute to wider changes in society.

Resource integration: The IKEA value chain includes sourcing and extracting raw material, manufacturing and transporting products, stores, customer travel to stores, product use in customers' homes, and product end-of-life. There is an ongoing transformation of the business model: simultaneously physical and digital; a lower cost structure so that products can reach new markets outside Europe; and the drive to make the IKEA network more sustainable—all happening concurrently.

Sustainability and CSR: Sustainability is an integrated part of the IKEA business. The sustainability challenges in the short and long term are continually being identified, monitored, and tackled throughout the entire IKEA value chain/network.

The environmental issues IKEA has faced over the years have been transformed in numerous small steps, from being a reputational (and potentially existential) threat to an opportunity to address social and environmental issues in a proactive manner by virtue of the company's vision in which daily business can contribute to genuine long-term sustainability.

The SDGs have been used as one of the key inputs when People & Planet and the ambitions from 2030 were developed. A systematic follow-up to activities specifically related to each SDG is done on yearly basis. Many of the activities contribute to multiple SDG goals.

Service quality and QM: Meeting quality standards and continual quality improvement have been never-ending processes to improve IKEA business. There are three types of code of conduct at IKEA business: IKEA suppliers (IWAY), IKEA franchises (Conduct), and Inter IKEA Group co-workers (Inter IKEA Group Code of Conduct).

IWAY is the IKEA suppliers' code of conduct. It is a long-standing program that communicates and ensures the minimum requirements on environmental, social, and working conditions, together with IKEA suppliers. It sets clear expectations and is the basis for developing dialogue and shared values. The updated IWAY6 will be launched in the 2021 financial year with the ambitions of not only defining basic requirements, but also achieving continual improvements, above and minimum.

Experts on specific topics from Inter IKEA Group and franchisees meet in working groups to share best practices and build knowledge through the value chain.

Innovation and transformation: IKEA works on a long-term basis for positive change. IKEA is a learning organization. Living the values is crucial for IKEA, as is being bold when facing challenges by listening, learning, and sharing knowledge and ideas to co-create a better world. It is not only what to do that matters, but also how do it. The IKEA business set-up makes investments for the future in new technologies, innovative materials, and ways of generating clean energy, as well as in social development in the IKEA value chain. Major changes are taking place in IKEA values, which are becoming more innovative, circular/regenerative, and caring/responsible.

The interlink among innovation, transformation, quality improvement, and sustainability is part of IKEA's cultural DNA and is used for sustainable business transformation. The Inter IKEA CEO and head of sustainability expressed this as a collaborative process:

> *We can't achieve all the big changes we want to see alone. Working together, leading by example, and finding better ways to get things done are the IKEA ways of working. … By relying on our own culture of entrepreneurship, always moving forward and not waiting for perfection, we can, and must, all work together to achieve breakthrough improvements.*

4 Discussion and Ecosystem Model

This book chapter has contributed with a deeper understanding, from a theoretical and conceptual point of view as well from an IKEA business practice perspective, that transformative change for meeting business and societal challenges is not an ad-hoc change process. It is a vision- and goal-driven change process. It is a combination of references that goes back to the roots of service management (Berry, 1999; Grönroos, 1994a, 1994b; Gummesson, 1994; Schneider & White, 2004) and the newer service perspectives of service logic (Grönroos, 2008; Normann, 2001) and S-D logic (Vargo & Lusch, 2004, 2016, 2017), but also includes more societal and sustainability thinking that meets global challenges and a sustainable business practice (Laczniak & Murphy, 2012; Edvardsson & Enquist, 2009; Sebhatu, 2021).

The thirteen key labels and concepts from the framework and business practice of IKEA in this chapter can be interlinked and contribute with a model: *Service Management Ecosystem Model for Sustainable Business Transformation*. The design of the model has been inspired by the models of Edvardsson and Enquist (2009), Edvardsson et al. (2006), and Enquist et al. (2007), but expanded to an ecosystem model (see Fig. 1). The model is built up of the following parts:

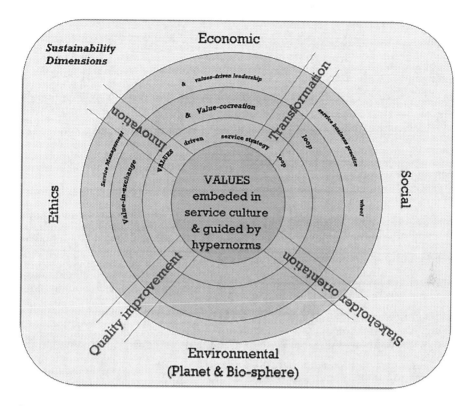

Fig. 1 Service management ecosystem model for sustainable business transformation

- The hub: *Values embedded in service culture and guided by hypernorms*

  Values (see Berry, 1999; Edvardsson & Enquist, 2009; Murphy & Laczniak, 2019; Pruzan, 2001). IKEA's eight values are embedded in a strong culture and guided by the UN SDGs.

- First loop: *Values-driven service strategy loop*

  Service strategy (Berry, 1999; Vargo & Lusch, 2017). IKEA the People & Planet Positive strategy

- The second loop: *Value-in-exchange and value-co-creation loop,* supported by *service brand and communication* as well as *service experience* to make/create value propositions.

References: Berry (1999); Grönroos (2008); Grönroos and Voima (2013); Vargo and Lusch (2016); Murphy and Laczniak (2019); Edvardsson and Enquist (2009); Normann (2001). Today, IKEA has a more interactive customer and stakeholder focus. IKEA is a big brand with a big purpose. A key concept is service experience by storytelling at social media and different internet platforms, using the showrooms at IKEA stores as experience rooms and stakeholder engagement.

* The wheel: *Service management and values-driven leadership service business practice wheel*

References: Berry (1999); Grönroos (1994b), Normann (2001), Edvardsson and Enquist (2009). IKEA management and leadership are interlinked in IKEA's business.

* Four drivers: *Transformation, innovation, quality improvement, stakeholder orientation*

References: Vargo and Lusch (2017), Sebhatu et al. (2021), Schneider and White (2004), Enquist et al. (2007), Lusch and Webster (2011), Laczniak and Murphy (2012). The links among innovation, transformation, quality improvement, and sustainability are part of IKEA's cultural DNA and used for sustainable business transformation. Driving and supporting change together with IKEA stakeholders is an essential part of reaching the IKEA sustainability goals.

* Sustainability dimensions: *Economic, social, environmental (planet + biosphere), ethical*

Sustainability: Gummesson (1994), Edvardsson and Enquist (2009), Sebhatu (2010), Sebhatu et al. (2021), Kemp (2011). All four dimensions are used in the transformation process at IKEA to become people- and planet-positive by 2030.

* Build up *service ecosystem* by *resource integration*

References: Vargo and Lusch (2014, p. 16); Koskela-Huotari (2018); Murphy and Laczniak (2019); Sebhatu et al. (2021); Normann (2001). IKEA's people & planet ecosystem is kept together with the ambition of becoming people- and planet-positive and inspired and enabling people to live a better everyday life within the boundaries of the planet 2030. There is an ongoing transformation of the internal and external resources: simultaneous physical and digital.

5 Concluding Implications and Future Research

Our concluding remark of this chapter is a need of future research on service management as a useful theory for business practice meeting the key challenges of today's business landscape for sustainable business transformation: *A service management framework for responsibility, resilience, and regenerative sustainable business transformation.*

By using IKEA business practice as an example, we can show that sustainability business transformation is more complex than what service management and the current service research can currently contribute.

Through its People & Planet Positive strategy 2030, IKEA has identified three key challenges—*unsustainable consumption, climate change*, and *inequality*—and tackled them via three focus areas for transformation: *healthy and sustainable living, circular and climate-positive*, and *fair and equal*. The IKEA sustainability development practice goes beyond green-, blue-, or SDG-washing and is more likely to be identified with sustainability thinking based on the three Rs (responsibility, resilience, and regeneration). In this chapter we have also highlighted that the service ecosystem of IKEA as a global actor must handle *systemic; institutional* and *processual;* and *macro* (including biosphere), *meso* and *micro* levels at the same time.

Studying service management for sustainability business transformation will generate empirical, theoretical, and methodological issues of complexity (see Gummesson, 2017b).

The contribution based on this chapter—investigating service *management for sustainable business transformation* to handle value co-creation, innovation, and sustainability for business transformation, not only from a firm-centric perspective, but also from a societal perspective—is almost complete. The main focus has been to highlight using the service management concept for moving from only being firm-centric to also including a broader sustainable stakeholder view, and societal perspective for business societal transformation, meeting those challenges of mobilizing, managing, and using resources in a more proactive way that is not limited to the boundary of the company itself. The theoretical and conceptual framework has ended up with thirteen key labels and concepts, which have also been used as a template of a case for service management for sustainable business transformation in a real context—the case of IKEA.

Learning from the contributions of this chapter and the ecosystem model (Fig. 22.1), we have drawn several managerial and societal implications with some recommendations for future research.

This chapter has a broad perspective with several managerial and societal implications. First the COVID-19 crisis has highlighted the urgent need to rethink the human ecosystem, the relationship between humanity and nature, and, more specifically, the service ecosystem. The chapter also argues that service management is not only for micro and meso processes, but must also meet global challenges of complexity and wicked problems in this new landscape, as a second implication. The third implication focuses on the business mission of serving people, with the insight that business and ethics are intertwined and cannot be separated, and that management with a societal perspective includes leadership thinking, stakeholder orientation, and a sustainable business transformation action. It is important for organizations to use resources inside and particularly outside the boundaries of the traditional corporation more effectively as it becomes a mandatory skill for management. The fourth implication is about "a strong vision" for reframing the business, which can serve as a new business mission aimed at searching a service business practice for developing a corporate consciousness. The strong vision is about moving from a narrow/reductionist perspective on business to a more broad/holistic one in a service ecosystem. Finally, in this chapter, we believe that sustainability thinking has a more circular and societal meaning in an interrelationship with both innovation and transformation.

Future research*:* The conclusion of this chapter is that service management for sustainable business transformation needs a broader framework to handle value co-creation, innovation, and sustainability for business societal transformation. Sebhatu et al. (2021) contributed with a deeper understanding about sustainability in business transformation for a sustainable future. Two discussions can be shared from that book:

* The "triple bottom line" (TBL) concept was introduced by John Elkington. Twenty-five years later he revisited the concept (Elkington, 2019) and concluded that the TBL has failed in its mission to bury the idea of the single bottom line. It was not intended merely as an accounting system, but rather as working toward a triple-helix of value creation, a genetic code for tomorrow's capitalism, spurring the regeneration of our economies, societies, and biosphere (ibid.). He rethinks the TBL for sustainable thinking with three Rs: **r**esponsibility, **r**esilience, **r**egeneration.

Service Management for Sustainable Business Transformation 433

* This is in line with the statement from the Club of Rome 50th Anniversary Report in 2018 that the socioeconomic goals (SDGs 1–12) cannot be tackled using conventional growth policies if the environmental goals (13–15) are to be achieved (von Weizsäcker & Wijkman, 2018).

References

Alvesson, M., & Kärreman, D. (2007). Constructing mystery: Empirical matters in theory development. *The Academy of Management Review, 32*(4), 1265–1281.

Alvesson, M., & Sköldberg, B. (2010). *Reflexive methodology: New vistas for qualitative research* (3rd ed.). Sage.

Berry, L. (1999). *Discovering the soul of service, the nine drivers of sustainable business success.* The Free Press.

Edvardsson, B., Gustafsson, A., & Roos, I. (2005a). Service portraits in service research: A critical review. *International Journal of Service Industry Management, 16*(1), 107–121.

Edvardsson, B., Enquist, B., & Johnston, B. (2005b). Co-creating customer value through hyperreality in the pre-purchase service experience. *Journal of Service Research, 8*(2), 149–161.

Edvardsson, B., Enquist, B., & Hay, M. (2006). Values-based service brands: Narratives from IKEA. *Managing Service Quality, 16*(3), 230–246.

Edvardsson, B., & Enquist, B. (2009). *Values-based service for sustainable business: Lessons from IKEA.* Routledge.

Edvardsson, B., Enquist, B., & Sebhatu, S. (2014). The important role of shared values in a sustainable service business. In R. P. Fisk, R. Russell-Bennett, & L. C. Harris (Eds.), *Serving customers: Global services marketing perspectives* (pp. 229–248). Tilde University Press.

Eisenhardt, K. M. (1989). Building theories from case study research. *Academy of Management Review, 14*(4), 532–550.

Elkington, J. (2019). 25 years ago, I coined the phrase "Triple Bottom Line." Here's why it's time to rethink it. *Harvard Business Review*, June 25.

Enquist, B., Edvardsson, B., & Sebhatu, S. P. (2007). Values-based service quality for sustainable business. *Managing Service Quality, 17*(4), 385–403.

Enquist, B., Sebhatu, S. P., & Johnson, M. (2015). Transcendence for business logics in value networks for sustainable service business. *Journal of Service Theory and Practice, 25*(2), 181–197.

Enquist, B., & Sebhatu, S. P. (2021a). A challenge-driven business ecosystem: Addressing Fossil-Free transformation. In S. P. Sebhatu, B. Enquist, & B. Edvardsson (Eds.), *Business transformation for a sustainable future.* PRME Book Series. Routledge.

Enquist, B., & Sebhatu, S. P. (2021b). The circular economy and values-based sustainability business practice: People & planet positive at IKEA. In S. P. Sebhatu,

B. Enquist, & B. Edvardsson (Eds.), *Business transformation for a sustainable future*. PRME Book Series, Routledge.

Freeman, E. (1984). *Strategic management: A stakeholder approach*. Pitman.

Freeman, R. E. (1994). The politics of stakeholder theory: Some future directions. *Business Ethics Quarterly, 4*(4), 409–421.

Freeman, E., Philips, R., & Sisodia, R. (2020). Tensions in Stakeholder Theory. *Business and Society, 59*(2), 213–231.

Glaser, B. (1992). *Basics of grounded theory analysis*. Sociology Press.

Grönroos, C. (1994a). From marketing mix to relationship marketing: Towards a paradigm shift in marketing. *Management Decision, 32*(2), 4–20.

Grönroos, C. (1994b). From scientific management to service management: A management perspective for the age of service competition. *International Journal of Service Industry Management, 5*(1), 5–20.

Grönroos, C. (2008). Service logic revisited: Who creates value? And who co-creates? *European Business Review, 20*(4), 298–314.

Grönroos, C., & Voima, P. (2013). Critical service logic: Making sense of value creation and co-creation. *Journal of the Academy of Marketing Science, 41*, 133–150.

Gummesson, E. (1994). Green service quality. In B. Edvardsson and E. E. Scheuing (Eds.), *Proceedings from QUIS 3, Quality in Services Symposium*, Karlstad, Sweden, June 1992, ISQA, New York, NY.

Gummesson, E., Lusch, R., & Vargo, S. (2010). Transitioning from service management to service-dominant logic. *International Journal and Quality and Service Sciences, 2*(1), 8–22.

Gummesson, E. (2017a). From relationship marketing to total relationship marketing and beyond. *Journal of Service Marketing, 31*(1), 16–19.

Gummesson, E. (2017b). *Case theory in business and management – Reinventing case study research*. SAGE.

IKEA. (2018). People & planet positive: IKEA sustainability strategy. Inter IKEA Systems BV. https://www.ikea.com/ms/ja_JP/pdf/people_planet_positive/IKEA_Sustainability_Strategy_People_Planet_Positive_v3.pdf

IKEA SR. (2019). IKEA sustainability report FY19. Inter IKEA Group. https://preview.thenewsmarket.com/Previews/IKEA/DocumentAssets/557393.pdf

IKEA SR. (2020). IKEA sustainability report FY20. Inter IKEA Group. https://about.ikea.com/en/sustainability/sustainability-report-fy20

Ingka Group. (2019). Annual summary & sustainability report FY19. INGKA Group. https://www.ingka.com/wp-content/uploads/2020/01/Ingka-Group-Annual-Summary-Sustainability-Report-FY19.pdf?

Kamprad, I. (1976). A furniture dealer's testament. Appendix in B. Torekull, *Leading by Design: The IKEA Story*. New York: Harper Business, 1999.

Kemp, P. (2011). *Citizen of the world: The cosmopolitan ideal for the twenty-first century*. Humanity Books/Prometheus Books.

Koskela-Huotari, K. (2018). *The Evolution of Markets: A Service Ecosystems Perspective*. Doctoral thesis, Karlstad Universities Studies, p. 6.

Kristensson Uggla, B. (2010). *Ricoeur, hermeneutics and globalization.* Continuum, Studies in Continental Philosophy. Continuum International Publishing Group.

Laczniak, G. R., & Murphy, P. E. (2012). Stakeholder theory and marketing: Moving from a firm-centric to societal perspective. *Journal of Public Policy & Marketing, 31*(2), 284–292.

Lusch, R., & Webster, F. E., Jr. (2011). A stakeholder-unifying, co-creation philosophy of marketing. *Journal of Macromarketing, 31*(2), 129–134.

Lusch, R., & Vargo, S. (2014). *Service dominant logic: Premises, perspectives, possibilities.* Cambridge University Press.

Mazzucato, M. (2018). *The value of everything: Making and taking in the global economy.* Penguin.

Murphy, P. E., & Laczniak, G. R. (2019). Ethical foundations for exchange in service ecosystems. In S. Vargo & R. Lusch (Eds.), *The Sage handbook of service-dominant logic.* Sage.

Normann, R. (2001). *Reframing business: When the map changes the landscape.* John Wiley & Sons.

Sebhatu, S. P. (2010). *Corporate Social Responsibility for Sustainable Service Dominant Logic.* Doctoral thesis, Karlstad Universities Studies, p. 10.

Sebhatu, S. P., & Enquist, B. (2019). Values-driven service innovation for transformational change. In P. Kristensson, P. Magnusson, & L. Witell (Eds.), *Service innovation for sustainable business: Stimulating, realizing and capturing the value from service innovation* (pp. 203–223). World Scientific.

Sebhatu, S. P., Enquist, B., & Edvardsson, B. (Eds.). (2021). *Business transformation for a sustainable future.* PRME Book Series, Routledge.

Pruzan, P. (1998). From control to values-based management and accountability. *Journal of Business Ethics, 17*, 1379–1394.

Pruzan, P. (2001). The question of organizational consciousness: Can organizations have values, virtues and visions? *Journal of Business Ethics, 29*, 271–284.

Schneider, B., & White, S. S. (2004). *Service quality: Research perspectives.* Sage Publications.

Vargo, S., & Lusch, B. (2004). Evolving to a new dominant logic to marketing. *Journal of Marketing, 68*(1), 1–17.

Vargo, S., & Lusch, B. (2016). Institutions and axioms: An extension and update of service-dominant logic. *Journal of the Academy Marketing Science, 44*, 5–23.

Vargo, S., & Lusch, B. (2017). Service-dominant logic 2025. *International Journal of Research in Marketing, 34*, 46–67.

Waddock, S., Meszoely, G. M., Waddell, S., & Dentoni, D. (2015). The complexity of wicked problems in large scale change. *Journal of Organizational Change Management, 28*(6), 993–1012.

von Weizsäcker, E., & Wijkman, A. (2018). *Come on! Capitalism, short-termism, population and the destruction of the planet: A report to the club of Rome 50th anniversary in 2018.* Springer Science + Business Media.

Transformative Service Research: Where We Are and Moving Forward at the Collective Level

Laurel Anderson and Ying Xue

Services are so pervasive that they, to a large extent, structure the world within which we live and are thus fundamental to well-being
—Anderson et al., 2019, working paper.

1 Overview of Transformative Service Research

Given the ubiquitousness of services, advocates of Transformative Service Research (TSR) (Anderson, 2010; Anderson et al., 2013, 2019; Rosenbaum et al., 2011) have championed the idea that service organizations and providers have a responsibility above and beyond traditional indicators of success such as profits, satisfaction, loyalty, and word of mouth. That responsibility is for wellbeing. Thus, TSR entails "service research that centers on creating uplifting changes and improvements in the wellbeing of ... individuals (consumers and employees), communities, and the ecosystem" (Anderson et al., 2013, p. 1204). In this chapter, we discuss the background of TSR, the growth

---

L. Anderson (✉)
W. P. Carey School of Business, Arizona State University, Tempe, AZ, USA
e-mail: Laurel.Anderson@asu.edu

Y. Xue
Arizona State University, Tempe, AZ, USA
e-mail: Yxue33@asu.edu

© The Author(s), under exclusive license to Springer Nature Switzerland AG 2022
B. Edvardsson, B. Tronvoll (eds.), *The Palgrave Handbook of Service Management*,
https://doi.org/10.1007/978-3-030-91828-6_23

of TSR, and themes evident in this growth; suggest what we believe is missing; and give an example of a current issue that exemplifies a direction that bears emphasis in TSR.

At a foundational level, TSR, with its emphasis on wellbeing, accounts for the interaction between consumer entities (individuals, collectives, and ecosystems) and service entities (employees/providers, processes, offerings, organizations, and industries), recognizing that these interactions are surrounded by macroenvironments that influence wellbeing outcomes. Public policy and cultural, technological, and economic environments have the most impact on these interactions (Anderson et al., 2013). Thus, TSR is focused on wellbeing outcomes such as access, equity, respect, decreased disparity, health, happiness, literacy, and sustainability. These outcomes include hedonic and eudemonic wellbeing, along with aspects of wellbeing that are more collective, societal, and ecological.

The resonance and growth of TSR have been gratifying to witness. The community of service researchers that has formed wants not only to better understand this connection between service and wellbeing but also to have an impact on wellbeing in a broad sense. Along with this growth in community have come increasingly more articles, special sessions at conferences, special journal issues, and research projects of a significant nature (ServCollab[1]). This is quite exciting to see. An indication of the resonance is found in the Service Research Priorities conducted every five years. TSR first appeared as a research priority in 2010 (Anderson, 2010). In 2015, "improving well-being through transformative service," in a process involving both academics and practitioners, was identified as the most important service research priority (Ostrom et al., 2015).

The first special issue dedicated to TSR was published in 2015 in the *Journal of Service Research*. As a reflection of the interest in wellbeing and services, this special issue received one of the highest number of submissions of any *JSR* special issue. This issue included a diversity of topics, paradigms, methods, and cultures. One novel theme arising from the special issue was that of the destruction of value. The destruction of value is sometimes unintentional, sometimes unknowingly destructive, and sometimes intended. This theme was exemplified by the award-winning paper in the issue by Per Skålén et al. (2015). These authors collected amazing data from the Arab Spring in Syria and analyzed this data through the theoretical lens of strategic action fields. They examined incumbents and challengers in services within that field. The regime, as incumbents, took away services to much of the population. In

---

[1] https://www.servcollab.org/

response, the population created new services under the constraints. So, destruction of value was an important part of the service interaction and (un) wellbeing. That study is a vivid, rather unusual example. To a greater extent, we see destruction of value in more routine aspects of life, such as chronic illness, in which people really do not want to be in the particular service; they would rather avoid participating in the service given the frequent negative aspects of the chronic facet. Thus, acknowledging negative aspects of services is important so that we can deal with them.

Special issues in TSR have now begun to delve deeper. A recent special issue at the *Journal of Service Research* focuses on a narrower, but still important, area: unintended consequences. Unintended consequences can cause harm but also might have a positive impact on wellbeing. This is one of the "gnarly issues" Anderson and Ostrom (2018) identified in their keynote address at the Frontiers in Service Conference. To further the understanding of TSR, we examine its evolution.

2   Transformative Service Research to Date

From 1993 to 2012, before the term "transformative service research" was widely established, wellbeing research was evident. In this 20-year span, Ostrom et al. (2014) found more than 100 articles examining the intersection of service and wellbeing in the top marketing and service journals. They identified seven themes in wellbeing service research of the time, including cocreation and wellbeing, employee wellbeing, vulnerable consumers, service access, service literacy, service design, and service systems. Among these themes, some are more challenging than others. For example, the examination of service systems is challenging because of the interconnectedness of the key stakeholders and the structural issues of the system.

Going forward, we conducted an analysis of TSR publications in the major journals in marketing and service research (*Journal of Service Research, Journal of Service Management*, and *Journal of Marketing*) from 2013 to 2020. We found more than 50 articles contributing to this wellbeing research. We are gratified by this strong momentum of TSR research and increased publications. We conducted a thematic analysis based on the research questions and focus of these articles to categorize the research. We find that some wellbeing themes identified previously have continued their growth, sometimes with a shift in emphasis. We also recognize new trends in TSR, some of which are driven internally by proactive service researchers and others that are propelled externally by frequently occurring crises, which require researchers to reexamine existing systems and put wellbeing at the center of the service outcomes. We begin by assessing those previous TSR themes that are continuing to grow.

Growth of TSR Themes

Cocreation and wellbeing. Given the centrality of value cocreation in service, the interaction between customers and employees and the context in which those interactions take place inevitably affect the wellbeing of both parties. Beyond 2013, this theme has continued to make a signification contribution to TSR. In cocreation research, while studies on wellbeing from the consumer perspective are steadily increasing (De Keyser & Lariviere, 2014; Guo et al., 2013; Mende et al., 2018; Spanjol et al., 2015; Sweeney et al., 2015; Tang et al., 2016; Van Doorn & Mende, 2014; Winterich & Nenkov, 2015), research has also begun putting more emphasis on employee wellbeing (Henkel et al., 2017; Sharma et al., 2016a; Sweeney et al., 2015; Troebs et al., 2020; Van Jaarsveld et al., 2019; Yue et al., 2020). Some recent TSR research has even gone beyond the usual customer–employee dyad and included other entities in the cocreation process. For example, Van Jaarsveld et al. (2019) integrate employees' supervisors into the examination of cocreation and find that supervisor interpersonal justice (e.g., being treated with dignity and respect) can mitigate the negative effect on employees' wellbeing caused by the demand of customer interpersonal injustice.

In addition, some research has skipped over customer–employee cocreation and turned to employee–organization cocreation. Sharma et al. (2016a) combine "internal marketing" with TSR and treat employees as internal customers of the firm. They show that "internal service quality" has a significant and positive impact on employees' wellbeing and, in turn, improves their performance toward the ultimate customer. This finding aligns with Sharma et al.'s (2016) finding that organizational culture can support and facilitate cocreation.

Vulnerable consumers and new inclusions. In parallel with transformative consumer research efforts is a growing discussion on vulnerable consumers in TSR. Poverty and the base of the pyramid are gaining attention from service researchers (Blocker & Barrios, 2015; Fisk et al., 2016; Gebauer & Reynoso, 2013; Martin & Hill, 2015; Schaefers et al., 2018). In this theme we observe more discussions in TSR of other groups of vulnerable consumers, including the elderly or children (Kabadayi et al., 2020; Odekerken-Schröder et al., 2020), the stigmatized (Yao et al., 2015), and racial and ethnic minorities

(Castillo-Lavergne & Destin, 2019; Bone et al., 2014). Arising from this focus on vulnerable consumers is research delving into the reasons inequality and disparity are so pronounced among these consumers. Studies into bias and restricted access are scrutinizing major causes of the inequality. For example, Bone et al. (2014) investigate the experience of ethnic minority consumers who seek access to financial services. They uncover systemic restricted choice, which in turn negatively affects minorities' self-constructs.

New Trends

Multidisciplinary approach in TSR. Often, the most profound and influential findings in TSR come from interdisciplinary research in service, and as such, we have called for a multidisciplinary approach in TSR (Anderson & Ostrom, 2015). Happily, we note that some recent service research studies are using multidisciplinary approaches in order to evaluate wellbeing problems from many different angles. For example, Leonard Berry has a long and prolific body of work in the medical and health fields. His recent article titled "When the Aims and the Ends of Health Care Misalign" (Berry et al., 2021) appears in the special issue of *Journal of Service Research* on TSR: Unintended Consequences and includes both marketing academics and health practitioners. Significant movement in addressing complex wellbeing problems can only be accomplished through a multidisciplinary effort. The insights from different perspectives ensure a more holistic view, which in turn makes successful solutions more likely to be achieved. With increased calls for the relevance and impact of business research such as from the Responsible Research in Business and Management network (RRBM), this more holistic perspective is critical.

Shifting from micro-level wellbeing to macro-level wellbeing. As mentioned, TSR is service research with a focus on "creating uplifting changes and improvements in the well-being of consumer entities: individuals (consumers, and employees), communities as well as ecosystems" (Anderson et al., 2013, p. 1204). However, research at the collective level has been rather sparse. In response to repeated calls (e.g., Anderson, 2010; Anderson & Ostrom, 2015; Anderson et al., 2013), we are encouraged to see that more recent research in TSR has gone beyond individual wellbeing and emphasized the wellbeing of collective entities, such as communities, society, and the natural environment. More service scholars are examining service design and innovation through a holistic lens of the service ecosystem and considering the wellbeing of various stakeholders across multiple levels (Leo et al., 2019; Patrício et al., 2017; Vink et al., 2020). Interestingly, service design research seems to be leading the way in this approach to macro-level aspects of wellbeing.

Bridging transformation in society. Service research focused on the societal level reveals that service can act as a "bridge" for change to more macro structures in society. In the context of a nonprofit service for the homeless group, Blocker and Barrios (2015) show that service design and practices can contest and transform dominant social structures and stimulate social actions. In the context of refugee crises, Alkire et al. (2020) suggest that bridging service design and social entrepreneurship under the TSR paradigm can create greater synergetic effects to advance multilevel wellbeing and social impact. In the case of the Arab Spring, Skålén et al. (2015) show that activists can cocreate value with information communication technology that is able to transform a social movement through service.

Transformation and organizations. We also find more TSR focus at the meso or firm level and the significant impact on consumers' and employees' wellbeing. For example, Mirabito and Berry (2015) posit that an organization's human resources strategy (e.g., workplace wellness program) can improve employees' productivity and wellbeing and, in turn, enhance their effectiveness in serving customers. In addition, service research using an institutional perspective addresses employees' adoption of or resistance to service design and innovation. Kurtmollaiev et al. (2018) contend that when organizations try to implement new service designs, they should consider how the organization-wide transformation might change employees' mindsets and routines. Employees' resistance to and action inertia toward certain service innovation can be due to misunderstanding or the discrepancy between organizational legacies (e.g., culture, working language) and practices of new service designs.

Sustainability of the natural environment. Although TSR on environmental sustainability is still in its infancy, some researchers have begun addressing this topic (e.g., Wunderlich et al., 2013). In the environmental arena of TSR, we observe two major streams related to this research focus: (1) how to reduce people's negative impact on the natural environment (e.g., reducing use of resources) (Baron et al., 2018) and (2) how to increase people's positive impact on the environment (e.g., making better use of existing resources) (Wunderlich et al., 2013). Guyader et al. (2019) conceptualize "green service" as transformational service geared toward improving the wellbeing of the natural ecosystem in order to "better the quality of life of present and future generations" (Anderson, 2010, p. 9). They combine TSR and resource integration theory and posit that green service can be constituted by homeopathic processes (e.g., reducing, recirculating, recycling) of mitigating the impact of consumption on environment heteropathic processes (e.g., redistributing, reframing, renewing) of re-creating natural resources.

Crises

In the past decade, a variety of market shocks occurring globally, including natural disasters, civil unrest, terrorism, and pandemics, have challenged the market space. The most recent and far-reaching crisis is the 2019 outbreak of COVID-19. Undoubtedly, when a crisis happens, service is often among the most wounded, shaped, and transformed business sectors. Motivated by the COVID-19 crisis, more scholars are delving into research with a focus on wellbeing rather than customer satisfaction. This trend is evidenced by the growing TSR-related articles published in service journals in 2020 and 2021.

Multidimensional wellbeing and crisis. A crisis such as the COVID-19 pandemic brings significant challenges to the wellbeing of both consumers and employees. To a large extent, this stems from the inseparable, high-contact, value cocreation nature of services. The multidimensional aspect of wellbeing is apparent and vivid. During the pandemic, multiple forms of contact—customer-to-customer, customer-to-employee, employee-to-employee, and customer/employee–physical servicescape—have led to serious illness and even death. Safety is at the center of service design and innovation. Above and beyond physical safety, however, multiple other dimensions of wellbeing are paramount in a pandemic, including emotional, informational, and financial safety (Berry et al., 2020). On the customer side, the drivers of psychological wellbeing in a "traditional" context may not be the same as in a crisis context. For example, eudaimonic needs become more pronounced during times of crisis, and service providers are more likely to foster wellbeing when they focus on meeting eudaimonic needs over the hedonic needs that are typically emphasized in traditional service encounters (Barnes et al., 2020). On the employee side, the wellbeing of many employees who still work on the frontlines is significantly challenged by more demands from customers, institutions, and regulators in a crisis (Voorhees et al., 2020). The subjective wellbeing of employees who do not interact with customers due to the remote service is significantly affected as well because of aspects such as job-loss stress and the difficulty in transferring their existing skills to the new work reality (Tuzovic & Kabadayi, 2020). This raises the following TSR questions: Will the impacts of the COVID-19 pandemic on the wellbeing of customers and employees continue after the crisis has passed? Which impacts will persist, and how long will they last?

New technology and crisis. Crises have a potential silver lining. The COVID-19 pandemic has sped up the deployment of new technology such as artificial intelligence (AI) and robotics in service design and delivery. Before the pandemic, the benefits of integrating AI and robotics into service were well known: increased convenience, time saving, aspects of more personalized experience, and enhanced consumer capabilities. During the COVID-19 crisis, however, some benefits of new technology are particularly evident. For example, vulnerable consumers such as older adults and children are particularly affected by social isolation caused by the pandemic. Companion robots have the potential to mitigate feelings of loneliness (Odekerken-Schröder et al., 2020) as entertainers, enablers, friends, and mentors to isolated elderly and children (Henkel et al., 2020b). However, with greater advances in and adoption of AI and robotics in service, consumers are also likely to experience negative outcomes. Will children transfer how they treat robots into the way they interact with real people? Will a companion robot make older adults even more isolated after the pandemic? This accelerated adoption of new technology caused by a crisis can have unintended consequences, many of which are still unknown and await investigation.

The need for increased separateness and decreased contact during the pandemic has also led to a wave of service adaptations (e.g., firms' efforts to improve safety) and service transformations (e.g., innovations that can offer safety and additional benefits that did not exist before). Service organizations, emboldened by the imperative to innovate and overcome the crisis, are increasingly introducing robots in frontline encounters. However, customers' perceptions of robots in service encounters and employees' acceptance of the new technology still need to be investigated. Mende et al. (2019) show that an anthropomorphic robot can elicit consumer discomfort (e.g., eeriness, perceived threat to human identity) and result in compensatory consumption. Augmenting or substituting human employees with robots can also cause job loss, which raises both ethical and wellbeing issues. McLeay et al. (2020) find that consumers' personal characteristics (i.e., openness to change and preference for ethical/responsible service provider) and cognitive evaluations (i.e., perceived innovativeness, perceived ethical/societal reputation, and perceived innovativeness–responsibility fit) can influence their trust in the ethics of a firm when it replaces employees with robots, thus affecting service employee wellbeing. Henkel et al. (2020a) demonstrate that augmenting service employees with an AI emotion recognition tool can improve employees' effectiveness in regulating customer emotions and thus create a heightened sense of goal attainment, which contributes to employee wellbeing. Multiple dimensions must be considered when putting technology and crisis under a TSR lens.

One dominant question for crisis and wellbeing research is, What aspects of the service, innovations, and experience continue after the crisis is resolved or managed?

From these trends, we ask what is missing in TSR research and what are important research directions to consider.

3 What Is Missing?

To address what is missing from TSR research and what might be fruitful research directions to pursue, we begin by considering Anderson and Ostrom's (2018) keynote address to attendees of the Frontiers in Service Conference. Anderson and Ostrom identify four gnarly issues in TSR that research needs to address: Who gets to define wellbeing? What are unintended wellbeing consequences of services? What wellbeing tradeoffs are there in services? and How can access and equity issues in services be addressed? The first and last issues are specific issues that correspond to previously mentioned calls for further research at the collective, macro, and societal levels. We concur with these calls and argue that, given the current global issues related to the COVID-19 pandemic, global unrest, fake news, and falsehoods in conjunction with diffused social media, this is an even more critical level to address.

Although we observe some movement in the direction of more collective levels of research, research (especially empirical research) that focuses on the macro level is scant, and thus further research is required. Two aspects of service are especially important to consider when conducting collective-level research. Services both seek to provide offerings that improve collective wellbeing but also are so ubiquitous that they create the world and structures within which people live. According to Anderson (2010, p. 10), "In considering these macro dimensions, services have the ability to uplift and transform communities. They also, often unwittingly, have the ability to marginalize, judge, and stigmatize citizens and communities and to compromise sustainability. Thus, service researchers have a responsibility to add this social level to their research agendas."

To support this call and illustrate possibilities for and implications of social-level directions in TSR, we consider a relevant and compelling concept. We suggest that the concept of mutuality is timely and intriguing and that research in this area would further the development and impact of TSR.

4 Mutuality: We Are All in This Together

The concept of mutuality is meant to capture the centrality of solidarity and social cohesion, and the motto, "We are all in this together" (Berezin & Lamont, 2016, p. 201), helps depict its essence. The concept of mutuality builds on community health and cultural sociology research, which argues that noticeably better health outcomes exist in societies that are more socially inclusive. Especially important in terms of many of the issues in today's world, social capital research has demonstrated that social cohesion and a strong sense of belonging and trust are positively correlated with better health (Berkman, 2000; Kawachi & Berkman, 2000). Mutuality is not only demonstrated in research but also adopted as a goal in the work of several organizations focused on wellbeing. For example, mutuality is one of the bases for the Robert Wood Johnson Foundation's (2021) Culture of Health strategic framework meant to promote better health across the spectrum of the social gradient, acknowledging that healthier communities encompass an "overall sense of connectedness that benefits all residents." And the Organisation for Economic Cooperation and Development (2011, p. 17) advocates for a cohesive society because it "works towards the wellbeing of all members, fights exclusion and marginalization, creates a sense of belonging, promotes trust, and offers its members the opportunity of upward mobility."

Given the importance of mutuality, as part of cultural and institutional factors that enable or constrain mutuality, the impact of services should be considered. What can and do services do that prohibit or encourage mutuality? What part can service play in bringing about community connectedness? Years ago, in his book *The Careless Society* (1995), John McKnight suggested that at times, services disrupt community and community connection by taking over and commercializing actions and practices that had previously been part of the community. For example, McKnight uses the professionalized services of a bereavement counselor to illustrate the substitution for a community that comes together to support someone in grief. The consequences of a lack of community connection on health are jarring especially during the COVID-19 pandemic, with isolation vividly demonstrating the impact. We review this example to flesh out issues arising from using the social lens of mutuality and to illustrate possible research questions.

5 Mutuality: Are We in This Pandemic Together?

On March 11, 2020, the World Health Organization declared COVID-19 a worldwide pandemic. The rapid onset, spatial extent, and complex consequences make this disease a once-in-a-century global disaster. Vaccines are one of the most important weapons to eradicate this infectious disease. To achieve herd immunity to COVID-19, the percentage of vaccinated people needs to reach a certain threshold. However, vaccine skepticism and hesitancy have been issues long before the coronavirus pandemic (History of Vaccines, 2020; Smith, 2017). MacDonald and SAGE Working Group on Vaccine Hesitancy (2015, p. 4163) define vaccine hesitancy as "delay in acceptance or refusal of vaccination despite availability of vaccination services." Surveys suggest that approximately 20%–22% of those in the United States would choose not to get vaccinated against the coronavirus, even if a vaccine is cheap and easily available (Hamel et al., 2021). Vaccine skepticism and resistance are major obstacles to combating the coronavirus in a timely manner through herd immunity (Wouters et al., 2021). The coronavirus pandemic requires a collective global response to eradicate or even dampen its devastation; thus, a sense of mutuality is critical. However, there seems to be hesitancy even among medical providers. Two studies of nurses' vaccination intention and vaccine hesitancy, one in Israel (Dror et al., 2020) and one in Hong Kong (Kwok et al., 2021), find that approximately one-third of the nurses are hesitant and do not intend to take the vaccine. Such vaccine hesitancy raises questions about how to gain mutuality.

As mentioned, research shows that societies that are more socially inclusive have demonstrably better health outcomes and that a strong sense of belonging, social cohesion, and trust are positively correlated with better health (Berkman, 2000; Kawachi & Berkman, 2000). We argue that mutuality could have an impact on the thorny issue of vaccine hesitancy and use this as an example while proposing research questions. Furthermore, we suggest two essential aspects to mutuality, without which it would be difficult to achieve consensus on whether "we are in this pandemic together": a robust infrastructure that reflects and promotes mutuality and shared values (in this case for public health).

The Foundation of Mutuality: A Robust and Connected Infrastructure

Vaccine hesitancy is complex and context specific, varying across time, place, and vaccine types, and it is the result of contextual influences arising from historical, sociocultural, environmental, health system/institutional, economic, and political factors (MacDonald & SAGE Working Group on Vaccine Hesitancy, 2015). Service structures and infrastructures are contextual affordances that can support or hinder mutuality. The societal value of safe and effective COVID-19 vaccines is enormous. A robust and connected health infrastructure during such a severe adverse event supports social cohesion and builds public trust that the system is able to consolidate and integrate resources quickly and efficiently for community wellbeing.

Israel and the Palestinian West Bank provide a vivid example that raises research questions relevant to mutuality and TSR. During the COVID-19 vaccine rollout phase, Israel set the example as the fastest country in the world to vaccinate its population. As Dr. Isaac Bogoch, an infectious disease physician and member of Ontario government's vaccine distribution task force, said: "I think it's remarkable watching how organized Israel is mobilizing vaccine rollout in a very expedited manner. And they should be recommended for it" (Gollom, 2021). In Israel, all citizens over the age of 18 years are required by law to register with one of the country's four health maintenance organizations in a highly digital system that coordinates with the Israeli government and local officials. Other countries that have performed well against COVID-19 are those "that in general have good public-health infrastructures—and we [in the United States] just don't," said Helene Gayle, the head of the Chicago Community Trust and a veteran of the CDC (Friedman, 2021).

Before the COVID-19 outbreak, Shahbari et al. (2020) conducted qualitative research among the minority Arab population living in Israel to examine the factors related to their high response rate to vaccinations despite expressions of hesitancy. Their results show that Israel's strong health service system has played a major role in its pre-pandemic vaccination deployment success, with nurses nurturing the trust of citizens from different ethnic and cultural backgrounds. This indicates that Israel's success is due to its strong health infrastructures, which were well established before the pandemic. However, during the initial period of the vaccine rollout, controversy arose as Israel, which occupies the West Bank and Gaza, denied that it had responsibility for some of those areas. The boundaries of mutuality were drawn.

This example raises many general research questions: How do services define the "we" or boundaries in mutuality? What types of service structures promote mutuality and can call on the public to act cohesively and efficiently? In what ways do service structures reflect and influence the cultures within which they are embedded? When does the professionalization of services take away from the sense and caring of the community?

However, a strong infrastructure does not guarantee mutuality. Shared values, here a sense of togetherness, move things forward. For example, a country can have a powerful public health infrastructure, but if its citizens do not prioritize public health as a shared value, they will not be willing to participate in activities that advance the public good.

The Core of Mutuality: Shared Values and a Sense of Community

Mutuality is built on shared cultural frameworks, identity, and values (Berezin & Lamont, 2016). The shared values regarding vaccine hesitance (or any issue) do not usually reflect just one thing; layers of issues and values, such as trust or distrust, likely exist. With regard to vaccine hesitancy, research has tried to understand the layered shared values among specific groups. For example, considering the historical analysis of vaccine refusal, Blum (2006) posits that vaccine resistance can be traced back to shared values in a community, such as how much power governments should exercise and the subscription to personal rights versus the collective good. Indeed, the Kaiser Family Foundation's COVID-19 Vaccine Monitor, an ongoing research project that follows public attitude and experiences with COVID-19 vaccinations in the United States, found that Republican men were among the most vaccine hesitant. By a 71% to 26% difference, this group thought that getting the COVID-19 vaccine was a "personal choice" versus "part of everyone's responsibility to protect the health of others" (Hamel et al., 2020). This strikes at the core of mutuality. Chen and Fu's (2019) research on vaccines reveals that negative history and past problems with vaccines can stiffen a community's resolve against vaccination. If people question the safety or effectiveness of a vaccine or the fairness of the system, persuading them to move beyond those negative associations can be difficult. For example, ethnic minority groups are less likely to get the COVID-19 vaccine because of the distrust caused by both historical and present-day injustice and inequality. As Giselle Corbie-Smith, a professor at the University of North Carolina and the director of the UNC Center for Health Equity Research, said: "For Black and

Brown people, this is a time of watchful waiting. It's a skepticism of a system that has consistently demonstrated that their health is not a priority" (Friedman, 2021).

Distrust is difficult to break, as it is deeply embedded in the mentality and shared values stemming from history. This raises the following TSR research questions: On what levels does mutuality based on shared values usually develop? How can mutuality be accomplished at a broader national or global level? What are the best ways to approach entrenched shared values and distrust to gain mutuality? Within service systems, what is more likely to engender and maintain trust despite changing macro environments?

This vaccine-hesitant example and the mutuality concept are meant to illustrate TSR issues and questions at a more collective level than what we usually see. We hope that this will encourage researchers to delve into this needed area of research.

The COVID-19 pandemic provides one example in which focus on the collective level is paramount. Other contexts and fields of research could also benefit from a stronger focus on the collective level in general and mutuality in particular. Sustainable consumption, data protection, biases, and the sharing economy are all examples that rely on mutuality and the recognition that we are in this together. As with vaccine hesitancy, it is apparent that in several of these cases, the larger the collective of concern, the more complex and challenging mutuality becomes. The social cohesion that Berezin and Lamont (2016) note fosters a sense of community and solidarity, but these factors are difficult to accomplish the larger the collective unit, presenting even greater challenges for transformative service efforts.

References

Alkire, L., Mooney, C., Gur, F. A., Kabadayi, S., Renko, M., & Vink, J. (2020). Transformative service research, service design, and social entrepreneurship an interdisciplinary framework advancing wellbeing and social impact. *Journal of Service Management, 31*(1), 24–50.

Anderson, L. (2010). Improving well-being through transformative service. In A. Ostrom, M. J. Bitner, & S. W. Brown, et al. (Eds.), *Moving Forward and Making a Difference: Research Priorities for the Science of Service. Journal of Service Research, 13*(1), 4–36.

Anderson, L., Mathras, D., Ostrom, A., & Bitner, M. (2019). *Surrounded by services: Alternative wellbeing lenses for examining the transformative effects of services on consumers.* Working Paper.

Anderson, L., & Ostrom, A. L. (2015). Transformative service research: Advancing our knowledge about service and well-being. *Journal of Service Research, 18*(3), 243–249.

Anderson, L., & Ostrom, A. L. (2018). *Hoping for hope: Tackling gnarly issues in transformative service research*. Keynote address at Frontiers in Service Conference, Austin, Texas (9/7/2018).

Anderson, L., Ostrom, A. L., Corus, C., Fisk, R. P., Gallan, A. S., Giraldo, M., ... Williams, J. D. (2013). Transformative service research: An agenda for the future. *Journal of Business Research, 66*(8), 1203–1210.

Barnes, D. C., Mesmer-Magnus, J., Scribner, L. L., Krallman, A., & Guidice, R. M. (2020). Customer delight during a crisis: Understanding delight through the lens of transformative service research. *Journal of Service Management, 32*(1), 129–141.

Baron, S., Patterson, A., Maull, R., & Warnaby, G. (2018). Feed people first: A service ecosystem perspective on innovative food waste reduction. *Journal of Service Research, 21*(1), 135–150.

Berezin, M., & Lamont, M. (2016). Mutuality, mobilization, and messaging for health promotion: Toward collective cultural change. *Social Science and Medicine, 165*, 201–205.

Berkman, L. F. (2000). Social support, social networks, social cohesion and health. *Social Work in Health Care, 31*(2), 3–14.

Berry, L., Danaher, T., Aksoy, L., & Keiningham, T. (2020). Service safety in the pandemic age. *Journal of Service Research, 23*(4), 391–395.

Berry, L. L., Attai, D. J., Scammon, D. L., & Awdish, R. L. A. (2021). When the aims and the ends of health care misalign. *Journal of Service Research.* https://doi.org/10.1177/1094670520975150

Blocker, C. P., & Barrios, A. (2015). The transformative value of a service experience. *Journal of Service Research, 18*(3), 265–283.

Blum, J. D. (2006). Balancing individual rights versus collective good in public health enforcement. *Medicine and Law, 25*(2), 273–281.

Bone, S. A., Christensen, G. L., & Williams, J. D. (2014). Rejected, shackled, and alone: The impact of systemic restricted choice on minority consumers' construction of self. *Journal of Consumer Research, 41*(2), 451–474.

Castillo-Lavergne, C. M., & Destin, M. (2019). How the intersections of ethnic and socioeconomic identities are associated with well-being during college. *Journal of Social Issues, 75*, 1116–1138.

Chen, X., & Fu, F. (2019). Imperfect vaccine and hysteresis. *Proceedings of the Royal Society B: Biological Sciences, 286*(1894), 20182406–20182406.

De Keyser, A., & Lariviere, B. (2014). Save like the joneses: How technical and functional service quality drive consumer happiness: Moderating influences of channel usage. *Journal of Service Management, 25*(1), 30–48.

Dror, A. A., Eisenbach, N., Taiber, S., Morozov, N., Mizrachi, M. M., Zigron, A., Srouji, S., & Sela, E. (2020). Vaccine hesitancy: The next challenge in the fight against COVID-19. *European Journal of Epidemiology, 35*, 775–779.

Fisk, R. P., Anderson, L., Bowen, D. E., Gruber, T., Ostrom, A., Patrício, L., Reynoso, J., & Sebastiani, R. (2016). Billions of impoverished people deserve to be better served: A call to action for the service research community. *Journal of Service Management, 27*(1), 43–55.

Friedman, U. (2021). One country has jumped ahead on vaccinations. https://www.theatlantic.com/ideas/archive/2021/01/why-israels-vaccine-success-might-be-hard-replicate/617780/

Gebauer, H., & Reynoso, J. (2013). An agenda for service research at the base of the pyramid. *Journal of Service Management, 24*(5), 482–501.

Gollom, M. (2021, January 2). *Why Israel is leading the world with COVID-19 vaccinations.* CBC. https://www.cbc.ca/news/world/israel-covid-vaccinations-1.5859396.

Guo, L., Arnould, E., Gruen, T., & Tang, C. (2013). Socializing to co-produce: Pathways to consumers' financial well-being. *Journal of Service Research, 16*(4), 549–563.

Guyader, H., Ottosson, M., Frankelius, P., & Witell, L. (2019). Identifying the resource integration processes of green service. *Journal of Service Management, 31*(4), 839–859.

Hamel, L., Kirzinger, A., Muñana, C., & Brodie, M. (2020). *KFF health tracking poll – December 2020: COVID-19 and Biden's health care agenda.* Kaiser Family Foundation. https://www.kff.org/coronavirus-covid-19/report/kff-health-tracking-poll-december-2020/

Hamel, L., Lopes, L., Kearney, A., & Brodie, M. (2021, March 15–22). *COVID-19 vaccine monitor (KFF health tracking poll).* Kaiser Family Foundation. https://www.kff.org/coronavirus-covid-19/poll-finding/kff-covid-19-vaccine-monitor-march-2021/

Henkel, A., Boegershausen, J., Rafaeli, A., & Lemmink, J. (2017). The social dimension of service interactions: Observer reactions to customer incivility. *Journal of Service Research, 20*(2), 120–134.

Henkel, A., Bromuri, S., Iren, D., & Urovi, V. (2020a). Half human, half machine – Augmenting service employees with AI for interpersonal emotion regulation. *Journal of Service Management, 31*(2), 247–265.

Henkel, A. P., Čaić, M., Blaurock, M., & Okan, M. (2020b). Robotic transformative service research: Deploying social robots for consumer well-being during COVID-19 and beyond. *Journal of Service Management, 31*(6), 1131–1148.

History of Vaccines. (2020). *History of anti-vaccination movement.* https://www.historyofvaccines.org/content/articles/history-anti-vaccination-movements.

Kabadayi, S., Hu, K., Lee, Y., Hanks, L., Walsman, M., & Dobrzykowski, D. (2020). Fostering older adult care experiences to maximize well-being outcomes: A conceptual framework. *Journal of Service Management, 31*(5), 953–977.

Kawachi, I., & Berkman, L. (2000). Social cohesion, social capital, and health. In L. F. Berkman & I. Kawachi (Eds.), *Social epidemiology* (pp. 174–190). Oxford University Press.

Kurtmollaiev, S., Fjuk, A., Pedersen, P. E., Clatworthy, S., & Kvale, K. (2018). Organizational transformation through service design: The institutional logics perspective. *Journal of Service Research, 21*(1), 59–74.

Kwok, K. O., Li, K. K., Wei, W. I., Tang, A., Wong, S., & Lee, S. S. (2021). Editor's choice: Influenza vaccine uptake, COVID-19 vaccination intention and vaccine hesitancy among nurses: A survey. *International Journal of Nursing Studies, 114*, 103854.

Leo, W. C., Laud, G., & Chou, G. Y. (2019). Service system well-being: Conceptualising a holistic concept. *Journal of Service Management, 30*(6), 766–792.

MacDonald, N. E., & SAGE Working Group on Vaccine Hesitancy. (2015). Vaccine hesitancy: Definition, scope and determinants. *Vaccine, 33*(34), 4161–4164.

Martin, K. D., & Hill, R. P. (2015). Saving and well-being at the base of the pyramid: Implications for transformative financial services delivery. *Journal of Service Research, 18*(3), 405–421.

McKnight, J. (1995). *The careless society: Community and its counterfeits.* Basic Books.

McLeay, F., Osburg, S., Yoganathan, V., Patterson, A., Brady, M., Hollebeek, L., & Sprott, D. (2020). Replaced by a robot: Service implications in the age of the machine. *Journal of Service Research, 24*(1), 104–121.

Mende, M., Scott, M. L., & Bolton, L. E. (2018). All that glitters is not gold: The penalty effect of conspicuous consumption in services and how it changes with customers and contexts. *Journal of Service Research, 21*(4), 405–420.

Mende, M., Scott, M. L., van Doorn, J., Grewal, D., & Shanks, I. (2019). Service robots rising: How humanoid robots influence service experiences and elicit compensatory consumer responses. *Journal of Marketing Research, 56*(4), 535–556.

Mirabito, A. M., & Berry, L. L. (2015). You say you want a revolution? Drawing on social movement theory to motivate transformative change. *Journal of Service Research, 18*(3), 336–350.

Odekerken-Schröder, G., Mele, C., Russo-Spena, T., Mahr, D., & Ruggiero, A. (2020). Mitigating loneliness with companion robots in the COVID-19 pandemic and beyond: An integrative framework and research agenda. *Journal of Service Management, 31*(6), 1149–1162.

Organisation for Economic Co-operation and Development. (2011). *Perspectives on global development 2012: Social cohesion in a shifting world.* OECD Publishing.

Ostrom, A., Mathras, D., & Anderson, L. (2014). Transformative service research: An emerging subfield focused on service and well-being. In R. Rust (Ed.), *Handbook on research in service marketing* (pp. 557–579). Edward Elgar Publishing Ltd.

Ostrom, A. L., Parasuraman, A., Bowen, D. E., Patrício, L., & Voss, C. A. (2015). Service research priorities in a rapidly changing context. *Journal of Service Research, 18*(2), 127–159. https://doi.org/10.1177/1094670515576315

Patrício, L., Gustafsson, A., & Fisk, R. (2017). Upframing service design and innovation for research impact. *Journal of Service Research, 21*(1), 3–16.

Robert Wood Johnson Foundation. (2021). *Creating healthier communities.* https://www.rwjf.org/en/cultureofhealth/taking-action/creating-healthier-communities.html

Rosenbaum, M., Corus, C., Ostrom, A., Anderson, L., Fisk, R., Gallan, A., ... Williams, J. (2011). Conceptualization and aspirations of transformative service research. *Journal of Research for Consumers, 19*, 1–6.

Schaefers, T., Moser, R., & Narayanamurthy, G. (2018). Access-based services for the base of the pyramid. *Journal of Service Research, 21*(4), 421–437.

Shahbari, A. E., Gesser-Edelsburg, A., & Mesch, G. S. (2020). Perceived trust in the health system among mothers and nurses and its relationship to the issue of vaccinations among the Arab population of Israel: A qualitative research study. *Vaccine, 38*(1), 29–38.

Sharma, P., Kong, T., & Kingshott, R. P. J. (2016a). Internal service quality as a driver of employee satisfaction, commitment and performance: Exploring the focal role of employee well-being. *Journal of Service Management, 27*(5), 773–797.

Sharma, S., Jodie, D., Tracey, S., & Gallan, S. (2016b). Cocreation culture in health care organizations. *Journal of Service Research, 19*(4), 438–457.

Skålén, P., Aal, K. A., & Edvardsson, B. (2015). Cocreating the Arab spring: Understanding transformation of service systems in contention. *Journal of Service Research, 18*(3), 250–264.

Smith, T. C. (2017). Vaccine rejection and hesitancy: A review and call to action. *Open forum. Infectious Diseases, 4*(3), ofx146–ofx146.

Spanjol, J., Cui, A. S., Nakata, C., Sharp, L. K., Crawford, S. Y., Xiao, Y., & Watson-Manheim, M. B. (2015). Co-production of prolonged, complex, and negative services: An examination of medication adherence in chronically ill individuals. *Journal of Service Research, 18*(3), 284–302.

Sweeney, J., Danaher, T., & McColl-Kennedy, J. (2015). Customer effort in value cocreation activities: Improving quality of life and behavioral intentions of health care customers. *Journal of Service Research, 18*(3), 318–335.

Tang, C., Guo, L., & Gopinath, M. (2016). A social-cognitive model of consumer well-being: A longitudinal exploration of the role of the service organization. *Journal of Service Research, 19*(3), 307–321.

Troebs, C. C., Wagner, T., & Herzog, W. (2020). Do customer discounts affect frontline employees? *Journal of Service Research.* https://doi.org/10.1177/1094670520933694

Tuzovic, S., & Kabadayi, S. (2020). The influence of social distancing on employee well-being: A conceptual framework and research agenda. *Journal of Service Management, 32*(2), 145–160.

Van Doorn, J., & Mende, M. (2014). Coproduction of transformative services as a pathway to improved consumer well-being: Findings from a longitudinal study on financial counseling. *Journal of Service Research, 18*(3), 351–368.

Van Jaarsveld, D. D., Walker, D., Restubog, S., Skarlicki, D., Chen, Y., & Frické, P. (2019). Unpacking the relationship between customer (in)justice and employee turnover outcomes: Can fair supervisor treatment reduce employees' emotional turmoil? *Journal of Service Research*. https://doi.org/10.1177/1094670519883949

Vink, J., Koskela-Huotari, K., Tronvoll, B., Edvardsson, B., & Wetter-Edman, K. (2020). Service ecosystem design: Propositions, process model, and future research agenda. Journal of Service Research. https://doi.org/https://doi.org/10.1177/1094670520952537.

Voorhees, C., Paul, F., & Sterling, B. (2020). Don't forget about the frontline employee during the COVID-19 pandemic: Preliminary insights and a research agenda on market shocks. *Journal of Service Research, 23*(4), 396–400.

Winterich, K. P., & Nenkov, G. Y. (2015). Save like the joneses: How service firms can utilize deliberation and informational influence to enhance consumer well-being. *Journal of Service Research, 18*(3), 384–404.

Wouters, O. J., Shadlen, K. C., Salcher-Konrad, M., Pollard, A. J., Larson, H. J., Teerawattananon, Y., & Jit, M. (2021). Challenges in ensuring global access to COVID-19 vaccines: Production, affordability, allocation, and deployment. *The Lancet, 397*(10278), 1023–1034.

Wunderlich, P., Kranz, J., Totzek, D., Veit, D., Picot, A., Huang, M. H., & Rust, R. T. (2013). The impact of endogenous motivations on adoption of IT-enabled services: The case of transformative services in the energy sector. *Journal of Service Research, 16*(3), 356–371.

Yao, T., Zheng, Q., & Fan, X. (2015). The impact of online social support on patients' quality of life and the moderating role of social exclusion. *Journal of Service Research, 18*(3), 369–383.

Yue, Y., Nguyen, H., Growth, M., Johnson, A., & Frenkel, S. (2020). When heroes and villains are victims: How different withdrawal strategies moderate the depleting effects of customer incivility on frontline employees. *Journal of Service Research*. https://doi.org/10.1177/1094670520967994

Service Design for Systemic Change in Legacy Organizations: A Bottom-Up Approach to Redesign

Ingo O. Karpen, Josina Vink, and Jakob Trischler

1 Introduction

Over the last 30 years service design has evolved to become a key approach to service innovation (Patrício et al., 2018). Through a variety of principles, processes and practices adopted from different design disciplines, service design helps, for example, visualize complex systems, bring challenges or ideas to life and make prototypes testable (Karpen et al., 2017). Further, its human-centered and participatory approach is useful for exploring user needs which are key to developing successful new service offerings and experiences (Trischler et al., 2018). Beyond a focus on innovating service processes and touchpoints, studies have also shown that service design can be used as a change driver in organizations (Kurtmollaiev et al., 2018; see also Buchanan, 2008) and service systems (Vink et al., 2019).

Amid a recent shift toward a more systemic perspective on service design, there is growing acknowledgment that a central requirement for realizing systemic change is to understand and change institutions, that is, changing entrenched and widely shared social structures such as norms, rules, roles and

---

I. O. Karpen (✉) • J. Trischler
CTF, Service Research Center, Karlstad University, Karlstad, Sweden
e-mail: Ingo.karpen@kau.se; Jakob.trischler@kau.se

J. Vink
Institute of Design, Oslo School of Architecture and Design, Oslo, Norway
e-mail: Josina.vink@aho.no

© The Author(s), under exclusive license to Springer Nature Switzerland AG 2022
B. Edvardsson, B. Tronvoll (eds.), *The Palgrave Handbook of Service Management*,
https://doi.org/10.1007/978-3-030-91828-6_24

beliefs that create mutual expectations (Vink et al., 2021). These institutions rely on people doing things together and are dependent on actors' individual interpretations and enactments (Hallett & Ventresca, 2006; Karpen & Kleinaltenkamp, 2018). Change by service design thus needs to be accompanied by addressing such conventions (institutions) that guide value co-creation activities in those systems, while proactively considering the role of individuals that constitute and enact the system. This chapter draws on a systemic understanding of service design in order to investigate its application for change in legacy organizations.

Change through service design may be relatively easy in small firms or start-ups, which are flexible and fast-moving in their mentality and structure, but what if systemic change is the aim in well-established and rigid organizations, such as legacy organizations? We define legacy organizations as *well-established, entrenched and highly regulated constellations of actors, resources and structures.* Legacy organizations are often connected through and enacted by historically grown, stable ways of interacting, sense-making or serving people. One problem linked to legacy organizations, such as hospitals, schools, government organizations and legal institutions, among others, is that they often function based on outdated or obsolete organizational characteristics, such as modus operandi and/or organizational purpose, which can result in established ways of working or mindsets that hinder innovation or adaptation and do not necessarily reflect state-of-the-art thinking (see, e.g., Oliveira et al., 2005; Wang et al., 2015). For example, the way society conceives of legacy organizations, such as courts or universities, might change over time, yet along with the entrenched ways of working there is often an internal lack or lag of collective reflection related to the organization's purpose in wake of its changing environment. However, legacy organizations and related service ecosystems play a critical role in ensuring well-being outcomes in society given the amount of customers they serve and responsibilities they carry. Legacy organizations are indeed central to the functioning of many business sectors and society at large, and when necessary, have the responsibility to innovate and potentially even reinvent themselves amid emerging contexts.

This chapter conceptually links theory on service design with legacy organizations to address the following research question: *How might service design be applied to realize change in legacy organizations?* We argue that service design is particularly useful to facilitate systemic change in legacy organizations through its strength of building an understanding and shaping of subjective meaning or attitudes at a micro level (e.g., among individuals), that in turn can catalyze collective action at meso (e.g., team or department) or macro level (e.g., an organization and its network). Often the needs and stressors of human beings fall secondary to the necessities of processes and procedures in legacy organizations. We propose that service design can help challenge the often fossilized structures and primacy of institutions in legacy organizations by addressing and leveraging individuals' perspectives and experiences. As such, we argue that service design offers a key contribution to service management in legacy organizations as there is often a need to shift from simply managing quality services toward reimagining the structures and purposes of these organizations. In so doing, service design has potential to change the microfoundation of a focal organization as an enabler and catalyst for broader systemic change.

In line with the above proposition, we argue that both the role of the designer as well as design approaches need to be carefully considered and defined in order to develop the microfoundations of systemic change in legacy organizations. In order to illustrate our arguments, we link our narrative to examples of service design applied in legacy organizations in two contexts, namely by way of change initiatives in the healthcare system in Norway and in the legal system in Australia. Examples from the first context reflect on service design work happening within the Center for Connected Care (C3), working with hospitals and municipalities in Norway, to support a systemic shift from centralized care in hospitals and clinics to decentralized care in homes and communities. The second example considers reform initiatives within the Australian legal sector, where systemic change toward better service provision reflected a key motivation. These examples and subsequent theorizing help demonstrate the important role service design can play in facilitating a bottom-up process of change in legacy organizations. While we provide concrete managerial tools, we also offer clearer understanding of theorizing change in legacy organizations, specifically how micro-foundational changes can inform meso- or macro-foundational change.

2 Legacy Organizations and Their Challenges for Design: Legacy Effects

Across countries, a significant amount of social, economic and innovative activity emerges in legacy organizations, providing service to the community. Building on our earlier definition, we view legacy organizations as those with a history (e.g., well-established and entrenched) whereby shared institutions or conventions (e.g., beliefs and practices) have been passed on to at least one or more staff generations and express an identification with the past (cf. Dacin et al., 2019). Due to their history and extended development, legacy organizations are typically highly regulated and set in their work and control mechanisms. Many legacy organizations, such as courts, banks and schools, among others, are framed by the historic design of the legislation that governs their existence. Thus, legacy organizations are simultaneously stable and tend to be only dynamic when necessary, given their orientation to maintain long-held traditions while facing the need to evolve with market conditions.

Fundamental beliefs or practices about how to do business or how to serve customers (e.g., citizens, patients and students) tend to live on in legacy organizations. For instance, courts may have developed certain procedures several staff generations ago, which might still be in place today. Similarly, hospitals, schools, universities or government departments might have institutionalized certain (cultural or work) practices that managed to survive social and technological challenges and changes. Even long-established businesses, such as wineries, breweries, distilleries, car manufacturers, restaurants, hotels, pharmacies, jewelers, banks, clothing manufacturers or retailers, often maintain elements of the past or might even leverage those very legacies in their marketing activities to enable nostalgic, mystic, romantic or otherwise symbolic experiences.

Maintaining legacies of the past such as specific meanings or practices, however, comes with benefits and challenges. On the one hand, legacy elements may offer symbolic value to customers, seeking to identify with aspects of the past. Similarly, legacies can offer stability and purpose to employees in otherwise often chaotic lives or work contexts, given that they can rely on traditions and find comfort in long-held and shared beliefs. On the other hand, legacies can hinder progress by clinging on to potentially outdated or even obsolete ways of doing business. For example, legacy organizations might continue using an outdated communication or case/client management system (e.g., data management in hospitals and courts). Likewise, hard-to-shake beliefs might infiltrate or act as resistance to future-oriented innovation efforts (Vink et al., 2019).

Legacy organizations are, thus, in danger of becoming self-reproductive systems that are ignorant to individual user needs and potentially "hostile to creativity" (e.g., Dougherty & Hardy, 1996, p. 1122). Researchers have previously pointed toward the dangers of such legacies in a design context. For instance, Junginger (2015) highlights that organizations might have become entrenched in their own ways of solving problems and innovating, creating challenges for designers seeking to facilitate organizational change. Further, there is recognition that when doing service design in contexts where actors are stuck in the status quo, there is a need to address head on the resistance of persistent mental models that are impeding innovation (Vink et al., 2019).

We will now elaborate in more detail why legacy organizations can be different to and challenging to work with for service designers relative to other types of organizations.

In many ways, facilitating change through design can be more difficult in legacy organizations given the extended period of time over which beliefs and practices have become institutionalized, and thus form part of the DNA of an organization. Specific ways of thinking and working can develop into and manifest in comprehensive bureaucracy, identity and power structures. Thus, legacies not only remain intrinsic to their carriers (e.g., in the mind of individual human beings) but can also become evident and live on in objects, symbols, structures, cultures or processes. Accordingly, traditions can remain vibrant even when individual staff leave the focal organization as the shared beliefs (e.g., identity) or practices (e.g., rituals) continue to be embedded in the organization. It can thus be difficult to overcome or remove existing legacy elements due to their common stickiness in the organization.

Barriers to change in legacy organizations can also manifest across well-established and often rigid and/or comprehensive hierarchies (O'Reilly & Binns, 2019). For instance, hospitals and courts typically run parallel hierarchies across medical/legal staff and administrative/support staff. The result can be opinions or roles that are perceived of or manifest in 'unequal worth', which can be problematic in co-design workshops, for example, where collaboration is central and all opinions equally relevant (Trischler et al., 2019). Similarly, such structures can be the foundation for political dynamics or tensions counterproductive to designerly change efforts. For instance, comprehensive or rigid hierarchies can create role-based feelings of entitlement, power plays or autocratic tendencies that risk jeopardizing collaborative efforts.

Dovey (2009, pp. 137–138) highlights that hierarchy in legacy organizations can even be baked into architecture and the design of spaces, when reflecting on three Australian court buildings: "In each of these buildings the hierarchical division between the judiciary and everyone else [e.g. support staff] extends well beyond the courtroom to encompass the ancillary spaces, where there are sharp distinctions of comfort, space, light and view. Many of the support staff and jury areas occupy window-less environments which they inhabit for lengthy periods. [...] There is a sense in which the commitment to principles of justice goes only so far. A broader principle that unhealthy environments are assigned on the basis of social hierarchy tends to prevail." However, there are also legal examples emerging such as 'community justice centers' whereby architecture and procedures successfully break with legal traditions and are designed to create empathetic spaces that make a difference in serving the individual users across stakeholder types (Halsey & de Vel-Palumbo, 2020).

Furthermore, many legacy organizations exist with substantive complexities that have grown over time. Government or government-affiliated institutions often have multiple divisions, which themselves might have multiple program lines and hierarchical structures. Similarly, legacy businesses might have developed a substantial breadth of customer service lines and actual services with comprehensive back-end structures. Often there are little synergies realized across these organizational units with differing priorities, and end-to-end user journey thinking was not necessarily a dominant paradigm at the founding of many legacy organizations. As such, systemic service design might encounter barriers in working with and overcoming organizational silos as well as group thinking. Various organizational teams or units might accordingly struggle to see the need for, or motivation to, collaborate.

Depending on the type and sector of the legacy organization, employees might have experienced prolonged periods of stress as many of these systems are not necessarily set up to cope with the emerging needs and demands, or might have compromised individual well-being in potentially unhealthy architectural environments. For example, hospital or court staff might have to overcompensate for a lack of outdated and/or limited resources, often leaving little time for proactive innovation or disruptive contributions. Rather, employees might have developed their own 'system hacks' over time to maneuver day-to-day pressures and demands, dearly holding on to such artificial constructs of comfort and safety. Any change initiative can thus be seen by them to represent a threat to their hacks that help them manage bureaucracy or hierarchy.

The above discussion highlights some of the challenges that designers need to work with and potentially overcome. Service design aims at greater well-being of various types of stakeholders involved, independent of their status or role in service actualization. Legacy organizations with rigid structures might otherwise accept compromising the long-term well-being of lower status members or the potential dominance of patriarchal structures in view of favoring higher status members or specific identities. At the same time, service design aims to facilitate smooth service processes across various units and individuals, connecting front- and back-end service elements. This can be tricky when existing spaces have been built with the legacy premise of status and exclusion. Legacy organizations are hence in danger of succumbing to "the pull of precedent", "historic templates" and "the weight of tradition", reinforcing existing practice (cf., Rowden & Jones, 2018, pp. 317–318). In the next section, we go one step further by illustrating how service design may be applied to facilitate change in legacy organizations.

3 Service Design Approaches in Legacy Organizations

Overview

As noted in the introduction of this chapter, we view the power of service design in understanding and shaping individual-level phenomena, such as subjective experiences, meanings and attitudes, which in turn can inform and inspire change in more collective and intersubjective phenomena, such as institutions (e.g., widely shared beliefs about what is right or wrong or behavioral expectations) that govern human behavior. This view builds on service ecosystem design as recently introduced by Vink et al. (2021), which involves the intentional shaping of institutions and their physical enactments to facilitate the emergence of desired value co-creation forms. It delineates how service design can be an approach to build the foundation for systemic change within service ecosystems, which we here apply to legacy organizations. Service ecosystem design, as such, brings a theoretical lens and can help to inform practical approaches to intentional change within service management. It stresses the importance of building people's awareness of the institutionalized ways of thinking and acting that are often taken for granted, especially in legacy organizations, and leveraging physical enactments to intentionally reform the invisible norms, rules, roles and beliefs that guide service exchange.

We here discuss how service design may enable change in legacy organizations. Specifically, in order to tackle the challenges faced by legacy organizations, service design practitioners have been developing and adapting their approaches to be appropriate for these often rather rigid, highly entrenched contexts. Below we describe three illustrative approaches of the many available ways for designing in collaboration with legacy organizations: Unpacking underlying assumptions, playful experimentation and visually supported dialogue. Each of these approaches is supported with empirical illustrations for contextualization, drawing on the experience of the authors. However, it is important to note that none of these examples are necessarily fitting for all contexts. While the approaches we present here are not an exhaustive list of those relevant for service design in legacy organizations, the selected approaches share a common feature that we argue is particularly important to realize change in legacy organizations: tapping into individual agency to catalyzing collective change. We illustrate the service design approaches by drawing from healthcare (Norway) and legal (Australia) service contexts. Both contexts represent archetypical legacy organizations (hospitals and courts) fitting the characteristics outlined above and both aimed to become more user-centric.

Unpacking Underlying Assumptions

Systemic change can be difficult to catalyze amid many rigid structures that reinforce the status quo and may keep the traditional systems stuck in place. In order to move from subconsciously reproducing highly institutionalized ways of thinking and acting, toward intentionally changing the system, actors need an awareness of the institutionalized patterns of behavior that they enact (Vink et al., 2021). Service design can help individuals and groups of actors to build this awareness by working with them to unpack the underlying assumptions of the systems that they operate within. By focusing on underlying assumptions and making them more explicit for actors, service design helps actors move from single-loop learning where they improve performance within the existing norms, toward double-loop learning where they can modify their assumptions and adapt the norms (Argyris & Schön, 1978). In so doing, service design challenges individual-level assumptions and interpretations of institutions that in turn can shape group-level beliefs and practices.

One example of unpacking underlying assumptions can be seen within service design work within the Norwegian healthcare system in Larvik municipality for a service called Helsehjelpen. Here service designers worked to build an understanding of the often unspoken statements that the actors connected with the service and believed to be true, through interviews and observations. One of the core assumptions is based on the highly institutionalized belief in Norway that the healthcare system should act as a social safety net "catching people when they fall down". By visualizing that assumption and crafting alternative underlying metaphors for the service (shown in Fig. 1), the designers were able to support individual and collective questioning and dialogue about some of the underlying assumptions in the system, supporting more intentional direction setting. This approach supported the development of an alternative collective direction for reimagining the service with a tour guide metaphor in mind, rather than the traditional safety net metaphor, creating common grounds for systemic change.

Service Design for Systemic Change in Legacy Organizations... 465

Who is Helsehjelpen?

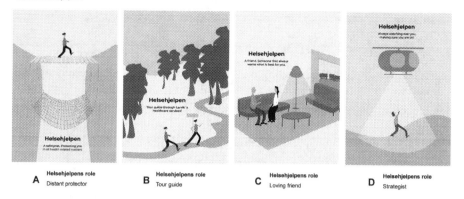

Fig. 1 Metaphors for Helsehjelpen (Designers: Maria Våge Traasdahl, Ameesha Timbadia and Greta Hohmann)

Working with the technique of uncovering assumptions in an Australian court context revealed equally relevant and potentially disadvantageous beliefs from a service management perspective. For example, some court staff might realize that they operate with an assumption that their court language and legal terms can be sufficiently understood by court users, while empirical research shows challenges in meaning making for many court users implicated by emotional and intellectual burdens. Similarly, judicial officers might acknowledge that they do not interpret their role as being service providers in court (i.e., serving the public), but rather assume that their role is simply and mainly to dispense the law. Accordingly, a judicial officer might state that their primary purpose is to make decisions about cases, to hear and determine cases. In stark contrast, another judicial officer might assume that their role is rather to do the most they can to achieve the best possible results for the people involved.

Whatever the individually held assumptions, these subsequently influence daily practices and collective action. Fundamental assumptions about core service and interaction elements can thus vary significantly and manifest across individual and collective levels, likely historically grown in the legal system, and can threaten the value and effectiveness of services provided. For instance, a non-understanding court user, especially when self-representing without professional legal support, who is blinded by the jargon used and procedures in the courtroom, might not necessarily flag their non-understanding or their non-readiness to engage as a user. This in turn can significantly compromise court hearings and outcomes (e.g., misinterpreting court decisions and possible conditions). Uncovering dominant assumptions

466 I. O. Karpen et al.

through service design can help individuals recognize potential dangers of unquestioned beliefs and facilitate a collective awareness and reflexive process around such assumptions. Moreover, uncovering individual yet problematic assumptions can help define a new agenda for the focal legacy organization; for example, developing concrete service orientation initiatives and goals, as well as updating the organization's purpose or philosophy to drive new behaviors. Service designers can subsequently use various visualization forms, such as assumption maps, to further facilitate dialogue in relevant teams. In combination, these efforts can help create micro- and meso-level change, ultimately with the potential to contribute to more systemic practice change.

Playful Experimentation

Amid legacy organizations, there is a need to deal with the stress that many individual and collective actors persistently face when attempting to catalyze systemic change within structures that are no longer fit for purpose. While the intentions of bureaucratic structures were originally to reduce stress, they have often paradoxically contributed to furthering anxiety for many actors involved (Menzies Lyth, 1988). Service design brings a playful approach to experimentation that can help rejuvenate individual staff amid the potential burnout they may experience when trapped in the system for too long. Playfulness can be a means to unleash creativity within such rigid systems, but it must be done mindfully so that it is not dismissed as not being relevant, or offending 'authorities', given these systems might have professional values and expectations that conflict with those of play. Exploratory prototyping (Floyd, 1984) can be a way to facilitate creative participation and support reflection on regular ways of working.

One example of such an approach done within a service design project in the Norwegian healthcare system was a series of eight tiny tests that were performed with a half a dozen healthcare staff to explore alternative ways of working for a short period of time (each experiment lasted approximately two hours). The aim of these experiments was to build an understanding of the possible consequences of doing things differently. One of these tests was a small experiment with three healthcare staff in a local municipality over one morning to test out dividing their roles differently within their service and reflecting on how that affected the time they spent. The designer created wristbands, signs and little diaries for staff to keep track of their reflections in the process. Based on this test one staff member said, "It's been really interesting to be conscious about what we do". There was a feeling that the process was fun and it helped them to see their everyday ways of working and some of the traps in that approach a little clearer. Another staff member reflected saying, "looking at our routines, we say every single day that we have to get better at taking five-minute breaks, at having lunch not in front of our computers, and it never happens because there's one million things happening at once". This example and the eight other tiny tests resulted in insight into the implications of possible changes and some new practices that healthcare staff continued with to improve their services (Fig. 2).

As part of legal sector projects, service designers brought together a range of different system members, such as judicial officers, administrative/registry staff, leadership staff and consultants. The aim was to play and experiment with a new key performance measurement system, to better understand what really matters in a court context and how to capture this. Many legal institutions in Australia have long been guided by public management/government-induced performance measures, which are historically very efficiency- and output-oriented. Such measures include, for example, the number of cases finalized per year versus newly initiated cases, leading to something labeled 'clearance rate' or cases finalized in a specified period as part of commonly reported 'case statistics'. However, this legacy performance measurement approach ignores quality of the service in the process and desired outcomes (against outputs) from various stakeholder perspectives, and might even incentivize non-service-oriented practices. Given the often

Fig. 2 Test called TogetherApart with healthcare staff. (Designer: Angel Lamar, Photo: Mette Landsverk)

government-required reporting along these measures, over time beliefs have developed at individual and collective level that these measures cannot be changed or even questioned, being conditioned by the 'tyranny of the past' and respective legislative frameworks.

To facilitate a mental break-free from such a stalemate position, designers engaged in experimentation with workshop participants. Specifically, to develop and play with new measures, participants were presented with 'what if' scenarios, whereby the focal legal institution was free to choose their own measures, creating boundaryless moments in an ideal measurement world. Facilitated by printed visuals that worked similar to coloring books (see, e.g., Fig. 3) and guided tasks, individuals and teams brought their ideas together to prototype a systemic approach of new 'measures that matter' and discuss why they matter from different stakeholder perspectives, which among other approaches informed strategic priorities and design initiatives. These new measures significantly surpass the conventional throughput/output measures of the court toward both more experience-oriented measures and outcome measures, considering external private and professional users (e.g., experiencing procedural justice, feeling safe and feeling heard), employees (e.g., feeling valued and feeling supported), government (e.g., feeling proud of contributions to collective safety and development) and societal outcomes (e.g., feeling confident about legal system and recidivism rates). While a court might be obliged to report based on (legislative) government standards, there is an opportunity to go beyond these fossilized approaches and focus on what matters to people, which this project sought to support.

Service design again was helpful in these instances across both contexts to enable individuals and subsequently collectives to free themselves from legacy boundaries and support the development of new directions and align toward new practices.

Visually Supported Dialogue

As mentioned previously, legacy organizations can be wrought with siloed and hierarchical complexity that is challenging to navigate and coordinate. Amid the subsystems that can have myopic mandates causing organizational divides (Kaufman et al., 2014), there is often a need to create alternative structures that support collaboration and communication to catalyze intentional systemic change. Service design can aid in such an effort through facilitating conversations with supportive visualizations between a wide variety of stakeholders (Ojasalo et al., 2015) who work across disciplines (Joly et al., 2019). By

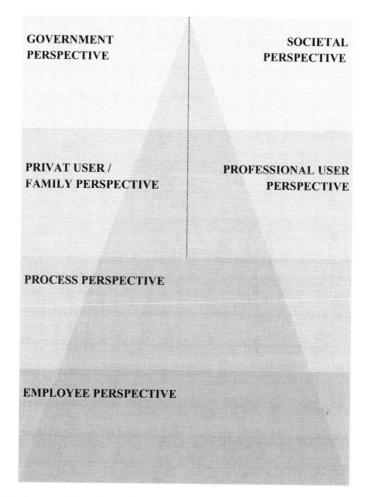

Fig. 3 Illustrative canvas to play with metrics that matter. (Illustration by Ingo Karpen)

strategically bringing actors together from across silos and levels of the organization to engage in reflective dialogue, there is an opportunity for actors to zoom out of their subsystems and explore the ways in which the subsystems of an organization interact and the result of the current structures and power dynamics.

One example of such a visually supported dialogue was done within a series of service design workshops within the Center for Connected Care (C3) in Norway. The workshops brought together actors from hospitals, municipalities, health technology companies and research institutions to explore how to build a more connected system across the current fragmentation. Together workshop participants were able to share their perspectives on the system and how it is working (and not working) today. With the support of interactive visual prompts, such as illustrated comics of real-life service situations, they unpacked the perspectives that unfold within different healthcare situations (see Fig. 4). With a visual map, they also reflected on the power dynamics between perspectives, together considering which perspectives were positioned as more central and powerful than others within these healthcare situations. Drawing on individual knowledge, this helped to develop some shared view among actors, while acknowledging many differences, and building a critical understanding of the consequences of current power dynamics in the system.

In another example in the legal sector, workshop participants were invited to build visual representations of their organizational structure and culture during service design workshops, shown in Figs. 5–7. The visualizations show, for instance, the constant pressure that people might experience and the competing interests, potentially making them feel like being puppets that despite tight control mechanisms can't live up to expectations. Moreover, the creative artifacts also point to embedded silo-thinking, which workshop participants highlighted to be detrimental for the desired systemic change. In a first step, these visualizations helped the design team to get a different 'feel' for the organization and (in)validate earlier findings around what it means to work at a

Fig. 4 Perspectives workshop. (Photo by Thiago Freitas)

Service Design for Systemic Change in Legacy Organizations... 471

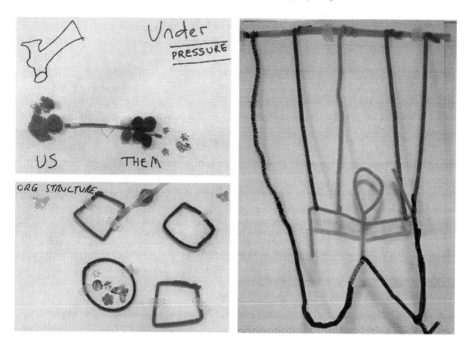

Figs. 5–7 Illustrative examples of staff creating visual representations of their organizational structure and culture. (Images by Ingo Karpen)

focal legacy organization. Importantly though, individuals could make their voice heard and express their perspectives on paper, even in creative ways and subsequent storytelling. This helped participants on the one hand to vent various emotions, while on the other hand it was a shared awareness-making process that collectively highlighted and motivated the need for change.

Many of the visualizations were self-explanatory (e.g., silo visualizations of organizational structure), while others triggered significant questioning among participants related to the symbolism used in certain visualizations. Workshop participants were intrigued to hear the individual explanations and stories, creating a compassionate, even therapeutic, atmosphere to support each other, but also to call for action with direct work implications.

Drawing on individual perceptions and lived realities, these types of collaborative activities can help recognize areas of relevance and urgency, and subsequently inform design initiatives. This could also be combined with visualization tasks picturing desired cultural or structural future states. Particularly from a psychological perspective, such a positive reframing can help substantiate the motivation for change and help participants remain positive after potentially confronting or exhausting discussions. In this example, we can also see the power of service design in transitioning both individual and collective levels. A micro-foundational understanding of organizational culture and structure was combined through shared sense-making into collective insights and implications. At the end of the day, a service ecosystem and its change significantly depends on the aggregated effects of the actions of its individual members.

Together these approaches show concrete ways that service design taps into individual agency to facilitate collective change. Through the approaches shared as well as many others, the service design process in the Norwegian healthcare context has led to collective awareness of the implications of the status quo and possible systemic shifts, shared aims across organizations, as well as efforts to work toward these collective aims, such through collaborative projects across organizations. In the Australian legal context, these and other service design approaches have helped to build the foundation for a long-term transition by engaging front-line staff and leadership, as well as facilitating mutual trust and support in the process.

4 Discussion

The persistent beliefs and practices, bureaucracy, hierarchy, fragmentation and stress often associated with legacy organizations can present serious barriers to innovation efforts. When confronted by the daunting challenges of catalyzing systemic change in legacy organizations, the practice of service design must continue to evolve. As illustrated in this chapter's examples, a systemic approach to service design can aid outdated legacy organizations in building bottom-up awareness of their taken-for-granted beliefs and practices, and support more experimental practices to help actors break free from the status quo. At the end of the day, a system is only as good as its individual members and the contributions these members can make to collective functioning. With this in mind, the strengths of service design are particularly relevant for uncovering individual-level phenomena (e.g., individuals' beliefs, attitudes and experiences) that build the microfoundation for collective-level phenomena (e.g., team or organizational beliefs, attitudes and experiences). Similarly, institutions, which are characterized by a sense of sharedness or degree of collective practice, require individual change in attitudes and/or practice (Karpen & Kleinaltenkamp, 2018), so that their collective enactment can change over time. Toward this end, the human-centered and collaborative nature of service design brings out important insights and implications across these levels of analysis. In doing so, service designers can help build individual and collective awareness for challenges of the status quo, while facilitating the motivation for change. Service designers can play a role in engaging stake-holders in actual change processes, for instance, by co-developing new practices or rituals in context that manifest across individual and collective levels. This may also include co-developing concrete goals or measures that help track the success of initiatives, as well as gamified approaches to achieving such defined goals.

Drawing from service design theory and reflecting on practical experiences of doing service design in legacy organizations, below we highlight three illustrative challenges to consider for service design to support change in legacy organizations: (1) evolving the role of the designer, (2) expanding the role of the staff and service users, and (3) shifting the role of service design methods and projects. In doing so, we zoom out from the focus on particular approaches presented earlier and instead explore how the overall practice of service design must continue to evolve to be effective in the context of legacy organizations, and supporting systemic change more broadly, deriving practical implications.

Evolving the Role of the Designer

In early literature, service designers were positioned as experts that should use service design tools to systematically plan, manage and control services (Shostack, 1982, 1984). However, since that time, the role of the service designer has evolved to often become a facilitator of co-design processes that engage staff and service users (see, e.g., Steen, 2013; Trischler et al., 2018). Working toward systemic change in legacy organizations supports an even further evolution toward becoming a strategic steward or custodian of ongoing designing within the overall systems of the organization, helping others build awareness of the entrenched beliefs and practices within the organization, and support them in intentionally altering them when they are no longer serving the organization and its constituents. In this way, service design shifts toward infrastructuring, which involves designing the scaffolding for others to continue doing the service design work (Bjögvinsson et al., 2012). This infrastructuring involves service designers working to develop the organizational capabilities, interactive practices and individual abilities needed for facilitating service design throughout the organization and scaling solutions (Karpen et al., 2017).

In addition, the positioning of service designers in relation to legacy organizations is often not straightforward. Service designers working with legacy organizations can be confronted with the 'radical's dilemma' where they need to navigate their own degree of embeddedness to strategically enable or drive the desired changes. "If they stand too much inside the system they risk losing their radical edge; if they stand too far outside they risk having little impact. It follows that the most crucial skill they need to learn is how to navigate the inherently unstable role of being both insiders and outsiders; campaigners and deliverers; visionaries and pragmatists" (Mulgan, 2014, p. 1). In this way, service designers must get comfortable in the in-between-space, neither fully external nor fully internal to prompt both radical and incremental change (Romm & Vink, 2019). Another recognition is that legacy organizations can be overly critical toward designers by applying the same mental models they apply to their own people. For example, in a hospital or court context the role of a designer's authority, credibility and legitimacy can be overemphasized. Accordingly, carrying specific titles (e.g., university degrees) as a designer can be an important 'must-have' to be perceived as sufficiently legitimate and 'worth collaborating with'.

Expanding the Role of Staff and Service Users

In early service design work staff and service users were less actively involved as direct contributors across the design process, which then advanced to a role of providing greater input (Edvardsson & Olsson, 1996). When it comes to systemic change in legacy organizations, it seems evermore important to meaningfully involve stakeholders, for instance, to balance day-to-day demands for staff with the need for change. Maintaining both individual and collective buy-in for major change initiatives will require them having a say in the process, not only in one-off workshops but by way of ongoing engagement in designerly work. Service designers can benefit in this case early on by identifying organizational champions that already do things differently in their locally adapted practice, and/or are willing to try out new things in 'safe' (e.g., well prepared and scenario-planned) experiments.

In this context, especially legacy organizations can benefit from dedicated 'test environments' where new approaches can be prototyped (see also Svensson & Hartmann, 2018). For example, an Australian legal organization declared one of its sites a 'court of innovation', whereby the local judicial officers and stakeholders were willing to continuously try out new practices before scaling them across the system. Another challenge in legacy organizations can be access to relevant people. For instance, taking doctors or judicial officers out of their day-to-day duties to participate in workshops cannot only have significant cost implications but also have major flow-on effects for patients or court users, whose procedures or hearings might have to be postponed, requiring ethical judgments of the service design team. Hence, service designers have a responsibility to make these initiatives count and not to waste resources or limit the possibility of threatening people's well-being, while needing to develop strong ethical standards informing such decisions. On the other hand, being exposed to positive co-design experiences can further reinforce stakeholders' desire for change and build capacity for effective participation (Trischler et al., 2019). Particularly early engagements and workshops are critical in hitting this mark to (re)encourage participation.

Finally, design work will require participants to often make themselves vulnerable, such as when sharing sensitive information about work situations (e.g., cultural-political issues or their ways of hacking the system to cope with challenges). Service designers thus need to constantly work on building and maintaining trust, as the required contribution of participants increases.

Shifting the Role of Service Design Methods and Projects

Conventionally, service design methods and approaches are more focused on new service development, particularly improving touchpoints and user experience journeys (e.g., Bitner et al., 2008). Often these types of improvement or innovation projects have a relatively narrow focus, rather than aiming to change a focal service system such as a legacy organization. For example, service designers might lead the redevelopment of a new customer onboarding process or a new complaint or return process. While these types of service design projects often involve both front-end and back-end changes, they are not necessarily systemic in that they challenge the functioning or foundational building blocks of an organization.

In the past, the notion of strategic design has been used in reference to such larger-scale projects, which often might start or target macro-level changes at the outset (Windahl et al., 2020; Calabretta et al., 2016). However, service design methods and tools can very well support larger-scale projects. To do so, service designers need to carefully reflect on how their methods and tools that might have been initially developed for micro-level contexts can be transformed to support meso- and macro-level initiatives at the same time. Given the likely significant timescale associated with change in legacy organizations, service designers might also seek to facilitate the building of competencies and practices within the client organization for an ongoing change or improvement process. Legacy organizations are prone to the risk of losing momentum on change initiatives given the many competing demands and complexities. Hence, service designers should ideally prepare the ground for continuous design-driven initiatives with increasing in-house support and leadership.

5   Concluding Remarks

In this chapter we draw on the recent developments in the service design field to illustrate how systemic change through service design might be catalyzed in legacy organizations. Through illustrative examples, which included service design projects conducted in a healthcare system and legal system, we showed that service design approaches can help to engage stakeholders, tap into their agency to design and give them a space to reflect, play, experiment and challenge themselves and others. In doing so, service design can help improve the readiness of stakeholders to either challenge existing practices or create and implement new practices. Without such readiness (see Danatzis et al., 2021), individual stakeholders might function as barriers to change within the system. Thereby, service designers themselves become stewards of change by enabling staff and users to drive initiatives further. Importantly, co-design in this context should not be seen in the narrow sense of idea generation only, but can be as broad as co-designing the purpose of an organization or system. In the context of legacy organizations, the deliberate work of service designers is put into perspective, especially in contrast to the longevity and scale of legacy organizations and the ongoing design work that sustains them.

We hope that this chapter encourages future research in advancing service design from a more systemic stance, acknowledging the role of microfoundations for meso- and macro-level change. In addition, this chapter helps to position service design as a necessary aspect of service management in legacy organizations, shifting the focus from effective execution of what is, to collectively reimagining what should or could be within future services. The service design approaches presented in this chapter are examples of how change initiatives in legacy organizations can be triggered or a foundation built. Yet, as all service design tools, these are often customized and need adjustment to the specific context to be meaningful. Further, this chapter focused on a specific approach to enabling change: tapping into agency at the individual level as a starting point for collective change. Yet, there might be other or complementary ways to achieve change in legacy organizations. For example, and as briefly mentioned in this chapter, service design can help uncover and diffuse 'system hacks' invented by service staff. Unpacking these hacks can give insights into legacy barriers and challenges, and how staff locally deal with and improvise around these. From a theoretical perspective, this connects service design back to practice-driven institutionalism, which seeks to understand individual-level, everyday work practices on the ground as foundation for collective-level, institutional change (Smets et al., 2017). Co-design may also be used to explore alternative rituals within organizations as a starting point for organizational change. For instance, based on uncovering outdated assumptions, individual actors might be willing to co-develop and try out new rituals that over time might become the foundation for new institution-alized practices. These examples showcase the versatility and potential of ser-vice design as well as the opportunities for future research especially in order to further develop systemic conceptualization of service design as introduced by Vink et al. (2021) within and beyond the context of legacy organizations.

Acknowledgments We would like to express our appreciation for all the participants and designers involved in the examples we have shared within this chapter. Josina Vink would also like to acknowledge funding from the Norwegian Research Council through the Center for Connected Care (C3). Finally, Ingo Karpen would like to thank Mark Madden for the inspiring discussions and feedback related to legal design in legacy organizations.

References

Argyris, C., & Schön, D. (1978). *Organizational learning: A theory of action perspective*. Addison Wesley Publishing.

Bitner, M. J., Ostrom, A. L., & Morgan, F. N. (2008). Service Blueprinting: A practical technique for service innovation. *California Management Review, 50*(3), 66–94.

Bjögvinsson, E., Ehn, P., & Hillgren, P. A. (2012). Design things and design thinking: Contemporary participatory design challenges. *Design issues, 28*(3), 101–116.

Buchanan, R. (2008). Introduction: Design and organizational change. *Design Issues, 24*(1), 2–9.

Calabretta, G., Gemser, G., & Karpen, I. O. (2016). *Strategic design: Eight essential practices every strategic designer must master*. BIS Publishers.

Dacin, M. T., Dacin, P. A., & Kent, D. (2019). Tradition in organizations: A custo-dianship framework. *Academy of Management Annals, 13*(1). https://doi.org/10.5465/annals.2016.0122

Danatzis, I., Karpen, I. O., & Kleinaltenkamp, M. (2021), Actor ecosystem readiness: Understanding the nature and role of human abilities and motivation in a service ecosystem. *Journal of Service Research*, online first. https://doi.org/10.1177/10946705211032275

Dougherty, D., & Hardy, C. (1996). Sustained product innovation in large, mature organizations: Overcoming innovation-to-organization problems. *Academy of Management Journal, 39*(5), 1120–1153.

Dovey, K. (2009). Open court: Transparency and legitimation in the courthouse. In K. Dovey (Ed.), *Becoming places: Urbanism/architecture/identity/power* (pp. 125–138). Routledge.

Edvardsson, B., & Olsson, J. (1996). Key concepts for new service development. *The Service Industries Journal, 16*(2), 140–164.

Floyd, C. (1984). A systematic look at prototyping. In R. Budde, K. Kuhlenkamp, L. Mathiassen, & H. Zullighoven (Eds.), *Approaches to prototyping*. Springer-Verlag.

Hallett, T., & Ventresca, M. J. (2006). Inhabited institutions: Social interactions and organizational forms in Gouldner's Patterns of Industrial Bureaucracy. *Theory and Society, 35*(2), 213–236.

Halsey, M., & de Vel-Palumbo, M. (2020). Courts as empathic spaces: Reflections on the Melbourne neighbourhood justice centre. *Griffith Law Review, 27*(2), 182–201.

Joly, M. P., Teixeira, J. G., Patrício, L., & Sangiorgi, D. (2019). Leveraging service design as a multidisciplinary approach to service innovation. *Journal of Service Management, 30*(6), 681–715.

Junginger, S. (2015). Organizational design legacies and service design. *The Design Journal, 18*(2), 209–226.

Karpen, I. O., Gemser, G., & Calabretta, G. (2017). A multilevel consideration of service design conditions: Towards a portfolio of organisational capabilities, interactive practices and individual abilities. *Journal of Service Theory and Practice, 27*(2), 384–407.

Karpen, I. O., & Kleinaltenkamp, M. (2018). Coordinating resource integration and value cocreation through institutional arrangements: A phenomenological perspective. In R. F. Lusch & S. L. Vargo (Eds.), *Handbook of service-dominant logic* (pp. 284–298). SAGE.

Kaufman, N. J., Castrucci, B. C., Pearsol, J., Leider, J. P., Sellers, K., Kaufman, I. R., … Jarris, P. E. (2014). Thinking beyond the silos: Emerging priorities in workforce development for state and local government public health agencies. *Journal of Public Health Management Practice, 20*(6), 557–565.

Kurtmollaiev, S., Fjuk, A., Pedersen, P. E., Clatworthy, S., & Kvale, K. (2018). Organizational transformation through service design: The institutional logics perspective. *Journal of Service Research, 21*(1), 59–74.

Menzies Lyth, I. (1988). *Containing anxiety in institutions: Selected essays* (Vol. 1). Free Association Books.

Mulgan, G. (2014). *The radical's dilemma: An overview of the practice and prospects of social and public labs*. Nesta. https://media.nesta.org.uk/documents/social_and_public_labs_-_and_the_radicals_dilemma.pdf

O'Reilly, C. A., & Binns, A. J. M. (2019). The three stages of disruptive innovation: Idea generation, incubation and scaling. *California Management Review, 61*(3), 49–71.

Ojasalo, K., Koskelo, M., & Nousiainen, A. K. (2015). Foresight and service design boosting dynamic capabilities in service innovation. In R. Agarwal, W. Selen, G. Roos, & R. Green (Eds.), *The handbook of service innovation* (pp. 193–212). Springer.

Oliveira, M. D., Magone, J. M., & Pereira, J. A. (2005). Nondecision making and inertia in Portuguese health policy. *Journal of Health Politics, Policy and Law, 30*(1–2), 211–230.

Patrício, L., Gustafsson, A., & Fisk, R. (2018). Upframing service design and innovation for research impact. *Journal of Service Research, 21*(1), 3–16.

Romm, J., & Vink, J. (2019). Investigating the "in-betweenness" of service design practitioners in healthcare. In M. A. Pfannstiel & C. Rasche (Eds.), *Service design and service thinking in healthcare and hospital management* (pp. 117–135). Springer.

Rowden, E., & Jones, D. (2018). Design, dignity and due process: The construction of the Coffs Harbour courthouse. *Law, Culture and the Humanities, 14*(2), 317–336.

Shostack, G. L. (1982). How to design a service. *European Journal of Marketing, 16*(1), 49–63.

Shostack, L. G. (1984). Designing services that deliver. *Harvard Business Review, 62*(1), 133–139.

Smets, M., Aristidou, A., & Whittington, R. (2017). Towards a practice-driven institutionalism. In R. Greenwood, C. Oliver, T. Lawrence, & R. Meyer (Eds.), *The Sage handbook of organizational institutionalism* (pp. 384–411). Sage.

Steen, M. (2013). Co-design as a process of joint inquiry and imagination. *Design Issues, 29*(2), 16–28.

Svensson, P. O., & Hartmann, R. K. (2018). Policies to promote user innovation: Makerspaces and clinician innovation in Swedish hospitals. *Research Policy, 47*(1), 277–288.

Trischler, J., Dietrich, T., & Rundle-Thiele, S. (2019). Co-design: From expert- to user-driven ideas in public service design. *Public Management Review, 21*(11), 1595–1619.

Trischler, J., Pervan, S. J., Kelly, S. J., & Scott, D. R. (2018). The value of codesign: The effect of customer involvement in service design teams. *Journal of Service Research, 21*(1), 75–100.

Vink, J., Edvardsson, B., Wetter-Edman, K., & Tronvoll, B. (2019). Reshaping mental models—Enabling innovation through service design. *Journal of Service Management, 30*(1), 75–104.

Vink, J., Koskela-Huotari, K., Tronvoll, B., Edvardsson, B., & Wetter-Edman, K. (2021). Service ecosystem design: Propositions, process model, and future research agenda. *Journal of Service Research, 24*(2), 168–186.

Wang, V., Lee, S. Y. D., & Maciejewski, M. L. (2015). Inertia in health care organizations: A case study of peritoneal dialysis services. *Health Care Management Review, 40*(3), 203–213.

Windahl, C., Karpen, I. O., & Wright, M. (2020). Strategic design: Orchestrating and leveraging market-shaping capabilities. *Journal of Business & Industrial Marketing, 35*(9), 1413–1424.

Part IV

Service Design and Innovation

Service Design: Innovation for Complex Systems

Birgit Mager and Nick de Leon

1 Service and the Circus—Witnessing the End of Service Management

As children, a service experience that we found enchanting was the circus! Exotic, magical, dreamlike fantasies were brought into the ring. As a service manager, one must be aware not only of the magic of such experiences, which can indeed be an inspiration for the designing of user experiences, but also that there is another connection worth considering.

Indeed, the term 'manager' originated in the circus, where it implied artful mastery of horses in the ring. The deep roots of management lie in the idea of a strong hand (manus = Latin: hand) that trains and manipulates in order to demonstrate an individual's own power, standing in the center of the circus ring, and to ensure his or her own success as the master of the performance. Even though the role and tasks of management have evolved significantly, the core idea of a central person who directs others and makes decisions drives the implementation of these decisions, and ensures and measures the success of these decisions remains unchanged. This is a concept that must be critically

---

B. Mager (✉)
Service Design Network gGmbH, Köln, Germany
e-mail: mager@service-design.de

N. de Leon
School of Design, Royal College of Art, London, UK
e-mail: nick.leon@rca.ac.uk

© The Author(s), under exclusive license to Springer Nature Switzerland AG 2022
B. Edvardsson, B. Tronvoll (eds.), *The Palgrave Handbook of Service Management*,
https://doi.org/10.1007/978-3-030-91828-6_25

reflected upon, because a service cannot be 'managed'. You may wonder how I arrive at such a statement.

First, let us consider how service innovation has evolved since the early 80s. Over the last 40 years, we have witnessed the emergence and adoption of business process engineering and optimization, beginning with concepts like total quality management (TQM) and, subsequently, the application of Kaizen, continuous improvement, and Lean, which were adopted from the manufacturing industry by the service sector in the 1990s and early 2000s (Powell, 1995). In those decades, organizations took on specialist TQM and then Lean practitioners to develop their own competences to optimize their business processes and engineer them to ensure that they are robust, repeatable, and deliver consistent outcomes. However, this approach considers the people involved in the delivery of the processes as 'objects' in a system along with other digital and process entities. Processes were engineered rather than designed and while customer satisfaction and net promoter score (NPS) are considered important indicators, they are too often set alongside many other key performance indicators (KPIs). This approach relies on compliance to set processes and the belief that almost all possible use cases and scenarios can be foreseen and designed for by the 'Circus Ringmaster'.

2 Complex Systems and Wicked Problems

We can consider services as complex ecosystems (Vink et al., 2021). It is commonly known that complex systems—with their characteristics of interconnectedness, mutual influence, and inherent dynamics—cannot be controlled. These complex systems are adaptive and their behavior may be emergent and non-intuitive in nature. Services may often appear as living entities that are developed and co-produced in the fabric of people, processes, structures, technologies, and the environment. Moreover, the nature of the problems and challenges encountered within these complex systems has also changed significantly.

With complex systems, we recognize that a deterministic approach is unlikely to be suitable to respond to small changes in sensitive parameters—we cannot envision all cases nor can all aspects of the experience be codified. In a highly globalized and interconnected world that is subject to economic turbulence, public health, and a climate emergency, there is a potent need for agility, flexibility, and empowerment of service managers in order to develop in them a greater capacity to innovate. Moreover, because innovation in services occurs closer to the 'edge' rather than in a centralized research and development (R&D) laboratory, it implies distributing service design capabilities and skillsets across the workforce while ensuring consistency in the application of practices, processes, tools, and resources for innovation led by service design.

Horst Rittel calls such problems within complex systems 'wicked problems' (Rittel, 1973). We will never be able to understand these problems conclusively in all respects because we always make decisions based on insufficient information. We cannot really test the solutions to these problems because many of the effects—whether desired or undesired—will be felt only after a certain time period. Moreover, we cannot undo the introduction of solutions to these types of problems. The idea of a strong hand standing at the center of the 'service ring'—controlling development, implementation, and delivery of such complex systems—can be questioned.

The same is true for the management of people—customers, users, and, above all, employees. They cannot be managed. If organizations and their so-called managers do not succeed in creating attractive ecosystems of growth and attractive employee journeys, as opposed to believing that they can control them, they will fail—fail in terms of attracting and nurturing the right people and in delivering valuable services and service experiences.

We are at an inflection point where management needs to be reimagined. If service management in the past was about optimizing processes, managing interfaces, developing and documenting service level agreements, demarcation, governance, and security—basically being in control and handling bureaucracy and administration—now and in the future, internal and external users are at the center of service management. Management consultants and solution architects can help an organization re-engineer its business processes, devise the organizational structure and the information technology (IT) systems required to deliver it, establish a governance model that includes key metrics, embody performance goals in service-level agreements, and establish a change management process that enables the processes to evolve over time. However, almost all these change management procedures may be cumbersome by design, particularly if the service has been outsourced in order to reduce operating costs and the cost of change for the provider of outsourced services. In this case, the role of service management may even be part of the outsourced responsibilities of the service provider. In a world of empowered customers and users—for example, the rapid changes needed to adapt to the pandemic—such an approach creates barriers to the very innovations required for an organization to thrive and may even threaten the organization's survival. Therefore, we need a new model of the 'service manager', one that has the capacity to facilitate and enable innovation and not be a potential barrier to it; one where 'managing' is redefined.

Fred Collopy and Richard Boland defined management as 'designing' (Collopy & Boland, 2004). Thus, we can say that service managers design customer relationships within complex technical, economic, and social systems. To understand the implications of this new understanding of (service) management, it is of course useful and necessary to examine the evolution of design and what design means today. Subsequently, we come back to the connection between service management and service design.

3   Continuous Design Evolution

Design is a process of creative work, but it is also the result of creative work; equally, it is an attitude. According to Victor Papanek, we are all designers simply because we are busy every day, from morning to night, shaping our environment in various ways (Papanek, 1995). However, from this general concept of design, one can differentiate the professional designer, who—through training and experience—systematically uses design as a force for innovation.

Over the last two decades, the importance of design and the value of design thinking (Brown, 2008) as a tool for innovation has been recognized by both businesses and governments. It has become a tool not only for product innovation but also for the development of business strategy (Martin, 2009) and service design (Sangiorgi, 2009; Kimbell, 2011). Further, design thinking has also led to service science and service design as a means of service innovation (Spohrer & Maglio, 2004) and organizational and management innovation (Gruber et al., 2015; Collopy & Boland, 2004); it has also been successful in the emergent field of design for policy (Bason, 2014). Designers have helped to translate technological innovation into user value, thereby creating compelling product and service experiences that leading firms have, in turn, successfully transformed into business value. Further, design has also been applied to public service innovation; the most notable example in this regard is the UK Government portal (Gov.UK), which is recognized by other national governments and by international design awards (Government Digital Service, 2015; Gruber et al., 2015; Mager, 2016). During this period, management scholars have, consequently, focused on design management and service design for innovation in both products and services and have studied the impact of these two aspects on business performance (e.g. Black & Baker, 1987; Bruce &

Service Design: Innovation for Complex Systems 487

Bessant, 2002; Chiva & Alegre, 2009; Gemser & Leenders, 2001; Hargadon & Sutton, 1997; Moultrie & Livesey, 2014).

Therefore, we can consider that design as a discipline is in a state of continuous evolution, accompanied by cultural and technological changes. Design has its roots in arts and crafts, which blossomed in the industrial revolution and acquired a holistic meaning in the field of brand development and design, as producer markets changed to consumer markets; design has found function in all facets of organizations—from visual identity to corporate identity, product and packaging design, interior design, and corporate fashion, among other aspects. As the world became digitized, web design, interface design, and user experience design came into being, the focus no longer being on the material shape of end devices but on the journey through user interfaces. Last but not least, service design provides a solution to the need for the systematic design of complex service systems. What is common in this diversity of design approaches? What are the most important attributes of design that have led to it making such an important contribution?

First, design is the ability to reframe—that is, to substantially question briefings, to turn them around, to reformulate them, and to arrive at new questions on the basis of intensive qualitative and quantitative research. The quality of and potential for innovative answers are based on the quality of the question. On the other hand, the ability to create and materialize future scenarios that do not yet exist is inherent to design—iteratively condensing ideas from a variety of possibilities, transforming them into concepts, and developing them from low-fidelity to high-fidelity prototypes.

Furthermore, design represents what is often called a T-shaped approach, an approach that is very broad and interdisciplinary on the one hand and demonstrates deep skills in mindset, process, and methodology on the other. This leads to cross-siloed, co-creative, and multidisciplinary ways of working, where designers help to make points of view and interests transparent through visualization and prototyping, involve different stakeholders, and develop a common language and perspective.

In the past, the 'human-centred' nature of design was considered one of its key characteristics and was repeatedly emphasized. Whether in economic issues, digital offerings, or physical products, design has placed people at the center. Indeed, for decades, this was a great step forward, because, in the dynamics of product and market development, people and their needs were too often simply overlooked. Even today, the focal point of design is to ensure that value is being created for humans; however, humans are only one aspect of the system.

488 B. Mager and N. de Leon

> **Box:** The End of the Human-centric Attitude
>
> Let us take a side-step: I propose that we have reached the end of this distinct focus on human-centeredness. Humans have seen themselves as the center of the world for far too long, dominating and exploiting other life forms. Today, we feel the consequences of this all too clearly. It is important to recognize that design has played no small role in this development. Climate change, environmental pollution, the destruction of species, forest dieback, forest fires are all consequences of a man-made, designed reality. Thinking of man as the exploiter, as the measure of all things has had its day. This must be radically reflected in design. We need an ecology- and system-oriented design: a design in which the rights of all life forms are taken into account; a design where nature and technology as stakeholders have a seat at the table and a voice in the space of our innovation projects. We can call this life-centered design (Mau, 2020).

4 Service Design—The Design of Invisible Products

What is service design? Since the mid-nineties, at a time when the tertiary sector—which had hitherto been badly neglected in science and research—was gaining importance in the economy, designers have been devoting themselves to the design of services, the design of invisible, immaterial products. Until the emergence of service design, organizations had no research and development budgets, let alone departments systematically dedicated to the design and innovation of services. Disciplines such as service marketing, service engineering, and service management emerged in parallel, and all of these have now established themselves as relevant fields of study and work in universities and organizations.

According to one definition, service design functions in concert with relevant stakeholders—often with users and employees at the center—to choreograph processes, technologies, and interactions in complex systems in order to create value for them. Service design uses a systematic and iterative process that continuously aims to bring service innovation through design to organizations in the public and private sectors. This process is presented in different versions, but basically, it is assumed that there is an exploration, a creation, a verification, and an implementation. The so-called Double Diamond, first published by the UK Design Council in 2005 (Fig. 1), is probably the most popular process model. However, in my opinion, it has certain failings: possible iterations between the phases are omitted, implementation is not necessarily seen as part of a complete design process, and there appears to be an

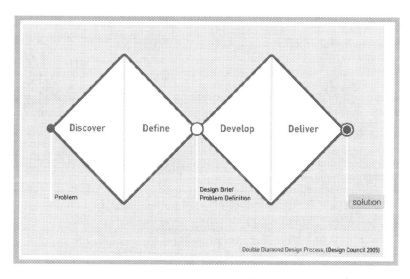

Fig. 1 Adapted from the Double Diamond, UK Design Council 2005

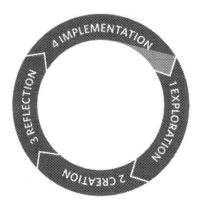

Fig. 2 Mager, B., 2004, unpublished

endpoint to service design. In reality, if service design is to actually contribute to substantial innovation and quality improvement of services, it must be a continuous process (Fig. 2); indeed, it must be an attitude embedded in culture.

Specific methods are connected with the phases, and a very good overview of these phases can be found in 'This is Service Design Doing' (Stickdorn et al., 2018). However, over and above systematically applying these methods, service design at its best brings about a cultural and organizational change, a change that aims at continuous innovation—both internally and in the user's world.

Until ten years ago, it was mostly external design agencies that practiced service design, but the landscape has undergone significant transformation. Management consultancies such as Accenture, PricewaterhouseCoopers (PwC), McKinsey, and Deloitte have bought service design agencies and established their own internal service design departments. Moreover, companies have built design teams in-house to focus on cultural transformation through service design (Mager & Moussavian, 2017). How does this affect service management?

5 Service Management and Design

Will service design replace service management? We cannot assume that it will. However, we can envision how service design could complement service management and be integrated as a permanent approach and attitude. What might this mean in concrete terms for the role of the future service manager?

Service managers are certainly not bureaucrats or simply administrators of processes, contracts, silos, and budgets; they are innovators both in terms of incremental and potentially radical innovation. They can identify opportunities for both improvements to service delivery and enhancements to the service experience as well as partner with service designers to identify new opportunities and create those enhancements, as well as adopt specific service design practices and processes in their discipline.

Therefore, we can envision the emergence of a new role, that of the 'designing service managers' (DSMs) who have the responsibility to continuously drive quality improvement and innovation within complex systems to meet the needs and expectations of internal and external users. When they do this using the highly collaborative service design approach, the consequence is continuous exploration within the system, with users, employees, and other stakeholders. This implies that employees and project teams must have sufficient time to develop innovations based on qualitative and quantitative research and be trained in service design methods and a service design mindset so that they can bring collective imagination as well as know-how to the new service innovation process. Moreover, there must be sufficient room for open-ended research questions, because these are more likely to lead to more radical insights and corresponding innovations. Work must be done across silos, and all departments that contribute to service development and delivery must be involved. Therefore, DSMs must ensure, in budgets and project planning, that appropriate time and financial resources are available as well as that intellectual capacity to deliver service innovation is developed.

The experience of firms such as Ernst and Young (EY), Accenture, and McKinsey has demonstrated the importance of service design in their portfolio of client services through the acquisition of service design agencies. In addition, these firms have created integrated teams to serve their clients and developed innovative new services by combining solution architects, service managers, and service designers into these integrated teams. They have trained their more traditional service development and delivery teams in service design and have appointed service managers with hybrid skills. These firms recognize that their clients not only need to transform their services to be customer-led with highly differentiated experiences, but that when their clients outsource services to them, they demand agility and even adaptive services. We call these living services—services that can adapt to new contexts of use and individual customers' or users' needs and do so with a degree of autonomy, using both machine learning and data analytics.

Further, sufficient space must be made available to work on potential scenarios for the future co-creatively with users, employees, and other stakeholders. Space here implies both time and physical space to translate ideas and concepts into prototypes and continuously test and develop these prototypes: space, in the temporal and physical dimensions, is required because innovation actually also needs a so-called surface on which it can spread. Digital surfaces have developed amazing potential, particularly during the coronavirus pandemic—but undoubtedly these will soon be supplemented again by materially tangible and graspable worlds. What is required is a working climate in which curiosity and critical questioning are desired and encouraged and errors are embraced as learning opportunities—flat hierarchies enable all actors to contribute.

Such framework conditions have presumably already developed as formative for service management in numerous companies today, possibly not always as explicitly and possibly not always with the corresponding support from the environment. Therefore, the question that arises is with regard to how an appropriate force field can be created within the company in which these methodical and cultural service design approaches can operate. Or, to put it another way, how stable resources can be developed that can work side by side with service management on continuous innovation.

6 Service Management and Service Design

All (wo-)men are designers. All that we do almost all the time is design, for design is basic to all human activity. The planning and patterning of any act toward a desired foreseeable end constitutes the design process. Any attempt

492   B. Mager and N. de Leon

to separate design, to make it "a thing" by itself works counter to the fact that design is the primary underlying matrix of life. (Papanek, 1995)

It is by no means new to think of human activities as 'design activities'. Nor is it entirely new to view managers as designers. However, there has been little systematic exploration in service management of what exactly this implies for roles and tasks and, particularly, attitudes.

The following six premises should provide an impetus for DSMs to reflect on and position themselves in the role.

Premise 1: Exploration is the key to success. This does not merely imply regularly examining the net promoter score (NPS) or other quantitative data. It implies in-depth qualitative and quantitative continuous exploration of user needs, user experiences, competitors, employee qualifications and motivation, technology analysis, and constant engagement with a changing societal value architecture that forms the basis for successful innovation. Today, innovations are no longer to be classified as special components but as everyday components of service management, and the pandemic has put this into sharper focus.

Premise 2: Successful innovation must break through boundaries. The experiences that users have with services know no departmental boundaries nor do they know any boundaries among the channels through which the services are provided. Thus, successfully designing service management implies working across the boundaries of organizational silos and delivery channels. The user journey must be considered and designed holistically in its functional and emotional dimensions, and interdisciplinary co-creative ways of working must be established by default.

Premise 3: The success of DSMs lies in the development of optimal alternatives. While management used to be about deciding among given alternatives, systematically implementing the selected alternative, and measuring success by quantitative metrics, today, a large part of the challenge is to develop optimal and innovative alternatives. Using interdisciplinary co-creative service design methods, alternative concepts are developed from a variety of ideas and then evaluated and translated into relevant business models. In an early phase of this development of alternatives, the boundaries must not be drawn too tightly. This is the space in which there is freedom to think the unthinkable, to wish for what is not yet feasible, and to dream about things that do not yet exist. The movement in a space of the divergent toward a focus on the convergent breaks the boundaries of the obvious.

Premise 4: Prototypical and iterative ways of working save time and money and yield better results. In the past, concepts were, far too often, developed at the draftsman's table and communicated in PowerPoint. Based on abstract criteria, evaluations were made on Excel sheets to finally arrive at decisions. The reality test then came at the very end and could be harrowing and potentially extraordinarily costly. In design-driven service management, prototypes are used throughout the service design process, tested in all versions—from low to high fidelity—with users and stakeholders, and iteratively refined. This saves time and money and leads to the best options.

Premise 5: Satisfied employees are directly correlated with satisfied users.

DSMs view service delivery as a performance—in both senses of the word. Keeping the stage in view also means considering employees as actors who are responsible for obtaining applause from users on this front stage. To do this, they must be secure in their role and be motivated and supported by props and backstage processes. Technologies are nothing but tools that serve people. The Internet of Things (IoT) and artificial intelligence (AI)— wonderful opportunities for individualized, proactive services—are not ends in themselves but merely props on the service stage. Service-level agreements must be translated into scripts, and service processes must be transformed into user and employee journey maps. Employee training is nothing more than a rehearsal on the service stage—a rehearsal in a play that is majorly shaped by employees. Companies like the Nationwide Building Society have intensified their focus on using service design to transform the employee workplace experience; they have recognized this as a precursor to great customer experience. In the battle for talent, a great employee experience enables a company to attract and retain top talent and get the most from their creative capacity, particularly in designing and delivering a superior customer experience.

Premise 6: Ethics and sustainability are integral components of sustainable services.

As mentioned at the outset, we are at the end of the human-centric design era and at the beginning of a time when we must integrate nature and the intelligent world of things as stakeholders into our design processes. System-centered service design goes hand-in-hand with system-centered DSMs. Moreover, when we refer to systems, we consider both hard and soft systems—both technological and management systems with socio-cultural and socio-political systems as well as nature-based systems. Together, we ensure that the relevant non-human actors are systematically included in the process—as nature or object personas—in nature journey maps, smart technology scenarios, and much more. Service design offers innovative methods to anchor the holistic, system-centered approach in projects and to continuously follow questions regarding diversity, inclusion, and other basic ethical principles. This is what we mean by life-centered design, an approach to innovation that considers people, the planet, the purpose, as well as the profit and economic sustainability of services.

7 Service Management Requires Service Design

Even though service design will become an integral part of the thinking and working methods of DSMs in the future, this does not replace cooperation with professional service designers—either as external or internal partners. After all, the tasks in design service management are so diverse and extensive that an in-depth adoption of the processes, methods, and the 'magic' of design cannot become a core component of the role. DSMs create the freedom needed, establish the partnerships required, and generate a fundamental understanding of how to design services within their department and organization. Training employees and defining procedures and methods form the skeleton; the flesh is then created through tangible projects in cooperation with internal and external service design resources.

Of course, this raises the question of whether to build up internal professional service design resources, as outlined in the Service Design Labs model, or whether and how to select and use external agencies and develop successful partnerships.

Our recommendation would be to build basic service design skills within the organization and distribute throughout it, with a special concentration on the service management function to enable the new role of DSMs. These distributed resources, with service design capabilities, would be complemented by an expert team of service design professionals who provide advice, guidance, and leadership for complex strategic innovations as well as in terms of the development, adoption, and management of the service design-led innovation model within an organization. Moreover, wherever appropriate, they would collaborate with external partners to guarantee having sufficient resources and gain an external perspective.

8 Conclusion

Service design has become an indispensable dimension in the design and delivery of services over the past 25 years. Service management has already sporadically integrated processes and methods that have originated in service design, but there are numerous opportunities for greater convergence and cooperation in terms of delivering value to all stakeholders. Service managers are redefining their roles, and DSMs will not stand in the 'service (circus) ring' but will be innovators at heart, closely collaborating with service designers.

References

Bason, M. C. (2014). *Design for policy*. Gower Publishing, Ltd..

Black, C. D., & Baker, M. J. (1987). Success through design. *Design Studies, 8*, 207–216.

Brown T (2008) Design thinking. Harvard Business Review 86:84–92, 141.

Bruce, M., & Bessant, J. (2002). *Design in business: Strategic innovation through design*. FT/Prentice Hall.

Chiva, R., & Alegre, J. (2009). Investment in design and firm performance: The mediating role of design management. *Journal of Product Innovation Management, 26*, 424–440.

Collopy, F., & Boland, R. (2004). *Managing as designing*. Stanford University Press.

Gemser, G., & Leenders, M. (2001). How integrating industrial design in the product development process impacts on company performance. *Journal of Product Innovation Management, 18*, 28–38.

Government Digital Service (2015) Government design principles. Retrieved January 9, 2015, from https://www.gov.uk/design-principles

Gruber, M., de Leon, N., George, G., & Thompson, P. (2015). Managing by design. *Academy of Management Journal, 58*(1), 1–7.

Hargadon, A., & Sutton, R. I. (1997). Technology brokering and innovation in a product development firm. *Administrative Science Quarterly, 42*, 716–749.

Kimbell, L. (2011). Designing for service as one way of designing services. *International Journal of Design, 5*(2), 41–52.

Mager B (2016) Service design impact report, public sector. Retrieved August 10, 2018, from https://www.service-design-network.org/books-and-reports/impact-report-public-sector

Mager B, Moussavian R (2017). *Design thinking in-house*. Köln International School of Design.

Martin, R. (2009). *The design of business: Why design thinking is the next competitive advantage*. Harvard Business Press.

Mau, B. (2020). *MC24*. London/New York.

Moultrie, J., & Livesey, F. (2014). Measuring design investment in firms: Conceptual foundations and exploratory UK survey. *Research Policy, 43*, 570–587.

Papanek, V. (1995). *The green imperative*. Thames & Hudson.

Powell, T. C. (1995). Total quality management as competitive advantage: A review and empirical study. *Strategic Management Journal, 16*(1), 15–37.

Rittel, H. (1973). Dilemmas in a general theory of planning. *Policy Science, 4*, 155–169. https://doi.org/10.1007/BF01405730

Sangiorgi D (2009) Building up a framework for service design research. Paper presented at the 8th European Academy of Design Conference, The Robert Gordon University, .

Spohrer, J., & Maglio, P. P. (2004). The emergence of service science: Toward systematic service innovations to accelerate co-creation of value. *Production and Operations Management, 17*(3), 238–246.

Stickdorn, M., Hormess, M., Lawrance, A., & Schneider, J. (2018). *This is service design doing*. O'Reilly.

UK Design Council. (2005). *Eleven lessons: Managing design in eleven global brands. A study of the design process*.

Vink, J., Koskela-Huotari, K., Tronvoll, B., Edvardsson, B., & Wetter-Edman, K. (2021). Service ecosystem design: Propositions, process model, and future research agenda. *Journal of Service Research, 24*(2), 168–186.

The Multiple Identities of Service Design in Organizations and Innovation Projects

Daniela Sangiorgi, Stefan Holmlid, and Lia Patricio

Design, as a field of knowledge and practice, has been around for well over a century for industrial purposes, with design professionals originally defined as someone "who is qualified by training, technical knowledge, experience and visual sensibility to determine the materials, mechanisms, shape, colour, surface finishes and decoration of objects which are reproduced in quantity by industrial processes" (ICSID); only recently, the use of *the* "designerly" ways of knowing, thinking, and acting, distinguished from the ones of science and art (Cross, 2001), is applied to the wide field of service.

Service design has for long played an important role in service management (Ostrom et al., 2015). Early approaches such as service blueprinting aimed to systematically define the service process to ensure that the service was delivered as promised and customer expectations were met in a more controlled

---

D. Sangiorgi (✉)
Department of Design, Politecnico di Milano, Milan, Italy
e-mail: daniela.sangiorgi@polimi.it

S. Holmlid
Department of Computer and Information Science, Linköpings Universitet,
Linköping, Sweden
e-mail: stefan.holmlid@liu.se

L. Patricio
Center of Industrial Engineering and Management, University of Porto,
Porto, Portugal
e-mail: lpatric@fe.up.pt

© The Author(s), under exclusive license to Springer Nature Switzerland AG 2022
B. Edvardsson, B. Tronvoll (eds.), *The Palgrave Handbook of Service Management*,
https://doi.org/10.1007/978-3-030-91828-6_26

service environment (Shostack, 1982, 1984). These early approaches, that captured certain aspects of service design, developed through the integration of service and design perspectives (Joly et al., 2019), to achieve a deeper understanding of human experiences for designing better customer journeys within dyadic service interactions (Sangiorgi, 2009). For the last couple of decades, service design has been established and developed alongside a set of disciplinary fields, among those service management and other service sciences, taking on a constructive and integrative approach, thus being formed as a professional practice in interaction with others. More recently, service design has evolved as an action-oriented, human-centered, collaborative approach to creating new service futures and transforming service systems (Sangiorgi, 2011; Rodrigues et al., 2020; Koskela-Huotari et al., 2021).

However, how designers develop and maintain their professional identities is poorly understood (Tracey & Hutchinson, 2016). A recent pilot study confirmed that there is a lack of occupational mandate for service designers in organizations (Blomkvist et al., 2020). This indicates that an integrated view of the developing roles and identities of service design is missing. This chapter makes a twofold contribution to this challenge. First, through a review of the conceptual lens of professional identity, it explores the multiple identities and roles of service design in the literature, especially in the most recent service design developments. Second, it extends this understanding through a qualitative study with key experts and practitioners in the service design arena, examining their multiple service design identities in their life trajectories; how they craft their service design roles in organizations; and delineating their identities in relation to existing and emergent service design scenarios. While identity is a useful theoretical construct to study the evolution of service design practice, our conclusions elaborate on the implications for service design and service management and their interactions.

1 Introduction

In general discourse, identity is often referred to either as a personal construct or as a social construct. The former adopts an individual's point of view and relies on the distinguishing aspects that persons highlight as defining themselves. The latter relies on the distinguishing aspects of a group, that makes a person belong to that group, often marked with a professional label (see e.g. Berger & Luckmann, 1966; Clifford, 1988).

In this chapter we are specifically interested in identity expressed by practitioners within a specific profession, often referred to as professional identity.

On the one hand, from the individual perspective, professional identity is described as someone's professional self-conception, based on attributes, beliefs, experiences, motives, and values (Ibarra, 1999; Schein, 1978). On the other hand, from a collective perspective, professional identity is described as being a member of a group, or having a specific role in professional contexts, interactively creating an identity that has meaning to the individual (Giddens, 1991; Weick, 1995; Burke & Stets, 1999).

Professional identity can be a topic of discussion within a profession, usually focusing on identity as being the professional competence, and what the respective practitioners should know (Kunrath et al., 2020; Gray, 2014). For some professions strict control mechanisms exist, such as in medical and some engineering professions. For others there are more loosely defined accreditation processes, and for yet others, the control mechanisms are peer-based, as in the specific case of the design and management disciplines.

Another way of understanding a professional identity is to focus on what the practitioners are doing in relationship to larger contexts and cultures (Svenningsson & Alvesson, 2003). The practice(s) individuals are part of become central to identity and identity development (Shove et al., 2012). These practices are constituted of materials, competence, and meanings that develop over time (Shove et al., 2012). The formation of practice, as well as the individual identities articulated within such a practice, is partly directed by individual human choice and aspiration, and partly driven by values and social structures (Giddens, 1984). This is multi-faceted, where a practice does not necessarily develop and grow inside organizational or other institutional boundaries, but in networks spanning across and beyond these (Brown & Duguid, 1998; Orr, 1996).

Literature on professional identity provides two perspectives that support the understanding of identities we wish to bring with the chapter. First, professional identity can be focused on the profession as a group and its context. The notion of communities of practice brings the concepts of movement from being a peripheral participant to becoming a core member of a community (Lave & Wenger, 1991; Wenger, 1996). The notion of collaborative communities brings the distinction between collaboration and coordination (Adler & Heckscher, 2006). Moreover, the practices develop over time, establish through networks and communities, develop through scaling and institutionalization, and transform or collapse (Shove et al., 2012), sometimes temporarily engaging in practice blending or forming hybrids (Holmlid, 2015; Lam, 2020).

Second, the professional identity can focus on the individual practitioner, where the organizational culture, specifically when design is valued (Gray,

500   D. Sangiorgi et al.

2014), can be an influencing factor, leading practitioners to adapt their use of language and concepts to the context (Liu & Hinds, 2012). This goes alongside the opportunities created that advance the individuals' self-conception (Dall'Alba, 2009). The trajectories formed are consistent with individuals being carriers of a practice, holding a current identity, and paving the way for careers for others to follow (Shove et al., 2012). The concept of being a core or legitimate peripheral participant is manifolded, for example, designers and managers often identify as being either outside the other practice or peripheral to it (Adams et al., 2011). It is also common that individuals need to act as if they were part of a practice, using an altered identity to be able to be part of certain contexts (Ibarra, 1999). Taking on new roles, or being part of new organizational contexts, are triggers for developing identity (Björklund et al., 2020; Watson, 2009), to renegotiate and articulate new meanings for the actions and self-conception (Linstead & Thomas, 2002). The individual perspective also opens up for conceptualizing "role identity", where role is understood "as the positions we take on in relation to others" (Caza et al., 2018); here roles can be considered as "mediators of identity work", where the daily micro evolutions of roles and role transitions in organizations stimulate the construction of identity over time (Järventie-Thesleff & Tienari, 2016).

Both perspectives of individual professional trajectories and the relationship with a larger organizational context and culture have been part of our reflection on the ongoing development of service design identities. The following section provides a journey on how service design communities of practice have been shaping and informing the debate on what service designers are and can do in service organizations. We then introduce our qualitative study based on interviews with design experts aiming to untangle and reveal the interconnections between individual and contextual pathways and discuss how they view the multiple identities service designers can take in service organizations, and the implications for a more design-awareness in service management.

2   The Singular and the Plural Identities in Service Design

Service design has been an articulated object of design research since the '90s, providing the basis for the gradual consolidation and recognition of a subfield of design theory and practice (Morello, 1991; Hollins & Hollins, 1991; Manzini, 1993; Erlhoff et al., 1997; Pacenti, 1998), being defined as a creative, human-centered, and iterative approach to service development, innovation, and transformation (Meroni & Sangiorgi, 2011). While there is no set methodology, service design practice includes working with users and stakeholders, engaging multidisciplinary teams, adopting aesthetic and visual competences and skills, and facilitating creative processes. Service design tools help to "understand experiences and contexts for further use and communication in the (service) innovation process" (Wetter-Edman, 2014, p. 81), while service design professionals are described as professional interpreters of people's experiences through narrative inquiry, ideation, and prototyping (Ibid).

Associated with the evolution of the service economy and the call for a greater social responsibility, service design has been developing in connection with service management by addressing the ongoing debate on the nature and characteristics of service as an object of design and the potential contribution to service innovation (Meroni & Sangiorgi, 2011; Kimbell, 2014; Blomkvist et al., 2016). In particular, the debate has been initially focused on legitimating this novel and emerging design practice within the academic and professional design and service management communities, creating and adjusting a dedicated vocabulary and set of methods in part deriving from service-related disciplines, such as service marketing, service research, and lately service science, and in part deriving from design practices such as interaction design, participatory design, product service system design, system design (Holmlid, 2007, 2009; Costa et al., 2018), or design for social innovation. The social construction of this developing professional identity has been reinforced with the emergence of the first service design studios (e.g. Livework and Engine), preliminary explorations of the contribution of Design in the public sector in particular in the UK (e.g. Cottam & Leadbeater, 2004; Parker & Heapy, 2006; Thomas, 2008), a network for professionals, an academic conference, and developing studies on design for sustainability and social innovation (Meroni, 2007; Jégou & Manzini, 2008; Thackara, 2007; Holmlid et al., 2021).

While the multiplicity of the service sector already revealed the diversity of service design applications and potential specializations, some key qualities have been defined in comparison to interaction and product design (Holmlid, 2007), and the notion of human-centered design, in its double meaning of centering any design process around the study and understanding of people, and of engaging users and other relevant actors in the co-design of the solution (Meroni & Sangiorgi, 2011). The consolidating set of practices around this evolving discipline and professional identity was therefore constructed around mainly user studies approaches (Kimbell & Seidel, 2008), in particular ethnographically inspired methods such as interviews and participant observation (Blomberg et al., 1993; Blomberg & Darrah, 2015; Segelström &

Holmlid, 2015); visualizations of user experiences via methods deriving mostly from interaction design, such as storyboards, use cases (Morelli & Tollestrup, 2007), personas, scenarios; and participatory design approaches (Holmlid, 2009), applied within the typical format of collaborative design workshops (Brandt, 2006; Holmlid et al., 2015).

The growing recognition and agreement on these core qualifications of service design practice has quickly become broader, when service design started to consider more systemic implications of the organizational settings (Sangiorgi, 2009; Junginger & Sangiorgi, 2009) or wider service delivery networks to enable improved service experiences (Morelli, 2006; Morelli & Tollestrup, 2007; Patrício et al., 2011), as well as considering the transformational potential of service design processes (Burns et al., 2006; Sangiorgi, 2011). This expansion was also motivated by the wider understanding of "service", not anymore considered as specific delivery outputs or offerings, but also as a mindset and organizational logic able to inform business development and innovation practices, centered on a different understanding of value (Kimbell, 2011; Wetter-Edman et al., 2014; Foglieni & Holmlid, 2017). Considering "value" as co-created in use with users, and not delivered as something embedded in service outputs (Vargo & Lusch, 2008; Grönroos, 2011), meant shifting the attention of organizations from their internal resources to the actual impact on service actors. Service design has therefore acknowledged this transformational meaning of service (singular), reflecting on the role design professionals could play in transforming service systems (Koskela-Huotari et al., 2021; Holmlid et al., 2017; Rodrigues, 2020), building human-centered design capabilities and promoting innovation mindsets in organizations (Bailey, 2012; Malmberg & Wetter-Edman, 2016; Malmberg, 2017; Karpen et al., 2017; Patrício et al., 2018).

This evolution has been testified by the ever-growing service design consultancy work dedicated to design education and training for client organizations, to inform and facilitate long-term and sustainable change toward people-centered and service-oriented innovation approaches and thinking (Sangiorgi et al., 2014). Studies on how to better develop design capabilities in both private and public organizations have therefore been developing in recent years (Kurtmollaiev et al., 2018; Aricò, 2018; Holmlid & Malmberg, 2018), together with the interest and exploration of different forms of organizational design-led innovation labs, valued as promising strategies to initiate and sustain organizational transformation (Carstensen & Bason, 2012; Mulgan, 2014, Junginger, 2015; Malmberg & Wetter-Edman, 2016) and transformation of broader service systems such as healthcare (Patrício et al., 2020; Malmberg et al., 2019).

Furthermore, this expanding transformational identity of service design has been accelerated by the recent and growing international recognition of Design Thinking, intended as a creative and people-centered approach to problem-solving, that has been promoted within the business and management literature (Boland & Collopy, 2004; Brown, 2009; Martin, 2009; Lockwood, 2010). In recent years, we have seen a growing number of multinational private companies, government departments, healthcare organizations, and business consultancies initiating design-led innovation units, with the ambition to support these wider transformational processes.

While the notion of Design Thinking has been very effective in the growing awareness and interest in the potential role of designers within multidisciplinary environments, and at different organizational positions, it has also been criticized for the tendency to generalize and simplify what designers do, think, and know (Kimbell & Street, 2009). To counteract the risk of flattening what designing means, some studies have started questioning the actual nature, foundations, and impact of design and design thinking, proposing instead a more situated, cultural, and embodied understanding of design practices (Kimbell, 2011; Laursen & Haase, 2019).

In parallel with the evolution within the design field, service design has developed as a multidisciplinary approach in the service research area, complementing the mindset, processes, and tools of design (Joly et al., 2019). While service marketing has contributed to designing for customer experiences with service blueprinting (Shostack, 1982), service operations have focused on designing service processes and the integration of frontstage and backstage operations (Sampson, 2012), and efforts have been made to integrate management and interaction perspectives for the design of technology-enabled services (Teixeira et al., 2017; Korper et al., 2020). This multidisciplinary evolution has led service design to expand beyond the design field and to strengthen its contribution to service management. First, service design professionals grounded in the design areas have increasingly incorporated these multiple contributions coming from the service management field (Joly et al., 2019). Second, service design has become an important component of service management practice. On the one hand, service managers look for design approaches to enhance the customer experience and develop innovative value co-creating solutions (Yu & Sangiorgi, 2018). On the other hand, service design has been increasingly acknowledged as an approach to change organizational mindsets and innovation practices (Sangiorgi et al., 2019).

This multidisciplinarity has also widened its spectrum as the understanding of service design evolved from the sole action of design experts to a broader collaborative effort where everybody designs. This implies the combination of expert design (played by experts that operate professionally as designers), with diffuse design (played by "not experts", with their designing capacity) (Manzini, 2015). This refocus from "designers" to "designing" means that service design is decentralized from designers as individual expert practitioners, to the collective of people engaged on a daily basis with service system and organizational change (Sangiorgi & Prendiville, 2017). Design experts can build upon the tools, competences, and mindset of service design practice to become part of this ongoing broader process that they support and facilitate (Manzini, 2015). Diffused design work requires collaboration and coordination with expert designers (Manzini, 2015), to make good use of the different capacities and competences (Holmlid & Malmberg, 2018). This also means that service design moves beyond discrete projects to become an ongoing process that is embedded in organizational practices (Junginger, 2009; Holmlid et al., 2017), such as by establishing closer designer-client relationships while facilitating organizational learning (Yu & Sangiorgi, 2018).

As a further consideration in this development, service design often transcends the boundaries of individual organizations, given the fundamental role value networks (Patrício et al., 2018) and wider service ecosystems play in the collaborative construction of service systems (Vink et al., 2020; Caic et al., 2019). Issues of sustainability of change and larger and long-term society transformation (Morelli & De Götzen, 2017; Malmberg et al., 2019; Fisk et al., 2020) are demanding a renovated effort to qualify service designers' role and identity, also when certain projects demand designers to better define their positionality, while acknowledging the multiverse nature of design views and practices (Akama et al., 2020).

This evolution of service design as both a sub-field of design and an approach adopted and practiced by multiple actors in organizations has led to multiple identities and roles of service design. While this ongoing evolution is a positive demonstration of the growing relevance of design in service management, service design has been defined more by the evolving context and multiple interacting design communities than by predefined and static roles and identities. As such, we recognize the utility to draw a line and consolidate certain professional and organizational identities service design is playing in organizations today, while defining the trajectories of newly developing ones. This exploratory study into the multiple identities of service design within service organizations and innovation projects is aligned with other developing international initiatives, such as "Transforming designers[1]" or the "Service

---

[1] https://www.transformingdesigners.com/.

Design Map²" that are similarly aiming to map what service design is doing today, as well as where it is developing. The next section will introduce our research methodology to then review the key insights we developed on this evolving practice.

3   Methodology

To advance our understanding of the evolving service design practice and identities, we adopt a twofold research approach. First, we draw on practice theory as a lens to examine literature on service design (Jaakkola, 2020), to advance and systematize our understanding of the multiple service design practices and identities. Aligned with a "practice turn" in organizational and management studies, we focus on "micro-level social activities, processes and practices" and we value the study of practice as a special concept that "allows researchers to engage in a direct dialogue with practitioners" (Golsorkhi et al., 2015). Second, we build upon a qualitative study based on in-depth interviews with service design experts and professionals to gain a deeper understanding of how these practices and identities come to life in organizations.

Following a theoretical sampling approach (Charmaz, 2014), we purposefully selected a rich and diversified set of service design experts. On the one hand, to ensure that the interviewees had enough experience to be able to characterize service design as a practice, we selected interviewees with at least five years of professional experience in the service design arena. On the other hand, the sample comprised service design experts with multiple backgrounds, professional experience, and sectors, as shown in Table 1.

Data collection involved semi-structured interviews, starting with background information and then reflecting upon the interviewees' journey toward service design, their service design practice, and role as service designers in both projects and embedding service design in organizational practices and logics. In the end, interviewees were invited to explore the future of service design. The nine interviews illustrate a diverse range of service designer profiles (see Table 1), with five grounded in design education, two coming from computer science, one with management education and one from cognitive science.

The interviews were recorded and transcribed. The transcription of all the interviews was analyzed and discussed by the research team, leading to a first structuring of the results into the broad categories of service design identities;

---

² https://www.servicedesignmap.polimi.it/.

Table 1 Sample design

	Current position	Current organization	Sector	Academic background	Professional experience
SD1	Chief of staff	National government, ministry	Public services and public administration	BSc in Informatics Engineering, MSc in Service Engineering and Management, PhD in Industrial Engineering and Management in service design	11 years of experience in service design and technology-enabled services and digital transformation
SD2	Head of design	Research laboratory for the development of new smart products and services	Energy	BSc in Communication Design, MSc in Strategy and Communication Design	12 years of international experience in marketing, communication, and service design in companies from different industries such as real estate, insurance, or telco.
SD3	Service design lead	National office of a large global consulting company	IT and Management Consultancy	BSc in Informatics Engineering, Master in Service Engineering and Management	6 years as service design lead, with a special focus on digital transformation in the financial services sector
SD4	Design lead	Network of specialized companies, supporting the adoption of new technology	Business consultancy	BSc in Graphic Design, Master in Product Service System Design	6 years working as a designer across university education, healthcare research, and consultancy settings
SD5	Service designer	Service design consultancy	Design consultancy	MeDes _ Master of European Design	6 years of experience as service designer working for public and third sector organizations, and currently in a service design consultancy.

The Multiple Identities of Service Design in Organizations...   507

SD6	Customer experience lead	Insurance company	Insurance	BSc in Interior Design; Master in Product Service System Design	8 years of experience as service designer in different companies, from telco, design consultancy, and insurance.
SD7	Strategy & Service Design Lead	Management Consulting	Business Consultancy	BSc in Industrial Design; Master in Product Service System Design	8 years of experience as service designer working initially in start-ups to then move to a business consultancy
SD8	Service designer	Insurance company	Financial, insurance	Management; Industrial Engineering	7 years of experience as service designer working as an entrepreneur, consultant, and in-house designer
SD9	User experience lead	Insurance company	Financial, insurance	Cognitive Science; BSc in Cognitive Science Design; Master and PhD in Design	7 years of experience, working as consultant and in-house designers

508   D. Sangiorgi et al.

crafting the service design role; embedding service design in the organization and the future of service design. These were then clustered, distinguishing reflections on service design individual identities from service design collective identities.

4   Service Design Identities in Practice

Building upon the examination of service design literature through the lens of practice theory and the qualitative study of service design experts and practitioners, we characterize the individual and collective identities of service design, as it can be seen in Table 2.

Table 2 Individual and collective service design identities

	Identity types	
Individual identity	Individual identity life trajectories (beyond individual organizations)	• Adopting and adapting SD approaches and tools to new projects and knowledge domains • Connect, dialogue, and integrate service design knowledge with other multidisciplinary areas, promoting hybridization • Advocate for the potential of service design across different departments and clients
	Service design role identity (role transitions and identity work in organizations)	• From service concepts to implementation and measurement • From enhancing the service experience to organizational transformation • From operational focus to playing a more strategic role and developing long-term visions • From performing to embedding service design in the organization
Collective identity	Collective identity in relation to service design community	Perception of service design today: • Human-centered and holistic approach to problem framing and innovation • Deep understanding of users and stakeholders' experiences and journeys • A systematized process and a set of research and visualization tools • Attitude and capability to facilitate collaborative innovation processes Perception of service design futures: • Specialized service design • Technical service design • Vertical service design • General service design • Service design leadership • Speculative service design

From the individual perspective, we characterize service design professional identity in terms of how these service design experts and practitioners craft their individual trajectories and their roles in organizations. Their relation to service design is partly affected by their background, even if the considerations on the changing identities of service design overlap, generating a common vision on a core identity that is then extended or reframed along their personal professional journey and experience in different organizations. From the collective perspective, we characterize how service designers describe themselves as being members of a community, and their perception of service design today and in the future.

Service Design Individual Identities

The individual perspective on service design identities refers to a professional self-conception, based on attributes, beliefs, experiences, motives, and values.

Individual Identity Life Trajectories

The evolution of service design identities is strongly dependent on the individual identity work done by the designers in their own professional journey and on their own ability to craft their role in organizations. All of the interviewees are guided by their own vision and ambition of what designers are and should do, even if this understanding is also shaped by their own experiences and the organizational contexts they encounter and interact with.

> *I would say as a designer, what is important for me is the cause I am using my skills for, rather than making money, and becoming senior in my career. (SD5)*

The crafting of the professional identity seems to be partly developing thanks to their ability to study, adopt and adapt service design approaches and tools to new projects and new knowledge domains; at the same time there seems to be a clear predisposition in the interviewees to connect, dialogue and integrate service design knowledge with other multidisciplinary areas, promoting a hybridization process, becoming themselves hybrid profiles, more flexible than before and open to address the oncoming tasks and challenges.

> *It was my most relevant experience because I felt lost but I think I became hybrid somehow. I don't feel like the same designer that I was when I joined this ecosystem. I'm still a designer, but a designer that: learned how to create new conversations among stakeholders, manage budget and plan like a pure project manager. (SD7)*

510   D. Sangiorgi et al.

Another ingredient that is very important in the process is multidisciplinarity. Yesterday I had a meeting with the minister with engineers and designers /…/, leading the methodology, consultants from [a consulting company], people from strategic management of government, lawyers of the other cabinet, and this multidisciplinarity brings a lot of value to the table that traditional engineering does not offer. This service design approach has been very important for the success of the projects I have been implementing throughout my career. (SD1)

This transformation of their role happens also when they manage to introduce and sell the potential of service design across different departments, clients and stages of design projects, aiming to expand the potential impact of design approaches, operating often as facilitators and dot connectors in innovation projects, going against siloed thinking.

the approach of service design really creates relationships with the client, we spend time clarifying the end to end journey, trying to help them, which pieces they need to put together, put the designer in front of basically every single stream of the conversation on the customer side /… / So you talk to the marketing, to the product, to the innovation, to the legal /… / You ended up becoming the strategic person for the company. (SD4)

Succeeding in this evolution, they often enter into high-level leadership positions, getting a seat around the decision-making tables, but also taking the necessary steps to build the relevant skills to better succeed in those roles (e.g. developing stakeholder management, project management, middle management or facilitator skills).

Service Design Role Identities

This initial and limited understanding of service design is then challenged as the interviewees grow professionally and as they actively expand the given boundaries of predefined roles, leading to some fundamental evolutions of their own interpretation of service design and of their role and identity in organizations. From the interviews, six main evolutions seem to be happening in practice.

Service design is becoming more integrated with measurement and data analytics practices, anticipating Key Performance Indicators (KPI) and expected impacts from the start of the innovation process and connecting the design work with large datasets analysis.

The Multiple Identities of Service Design in Organizations...

When I started to work in the hospital I understood that design could be used also for the testing part... How can I actually design so that I can test what I have done? We were designing demonstrators for technologies... /.../ I started to understand that the parts of research, design and test are really connected and there is the need of something that keeps everything together. (SD4)

How can larger datasets be part of what we do as service designers, to be able to connect what we learn from 20 customers to other larger patterns in society. (SD8)

<u>Service design is expanded toward implementation stages</u>, supporting organizational and technological development, introducing more technical expertise, but also more project management and stakeholder management skills.

what I really learned during the work experience, is that the implementation is the most important part actually /... / And so I learned more product management competences, because then you really have to collaborate with other people, and to really put hands on, and give the right direction, who is implementing to implement in the right way. (SD6)

We need to design the frontend, but also how this aligns with the backstage, the systems, otherwise we are just daydreaming. Daydreaming is very important, but you need to walk the talk, to ensure the experience you are designing can become a service that is integrated in the landscape of the organization. (SD3)

<u>Service design is given a fundamental role in organizational transformation</u>, leveraging service design to change the organizational mindset and practices, but also demonstrating the potential of working in a more collaborative manner, operating as "dot connectors", as designing services across multiple channels require more integrated processes.

When you work as a consultant, you can go back home to those that think the same as you do, but as in-house designer you cannot escape the organizational politics, if you want to be part of moving the organization into something new. (SD8)

The role of service design /.../ is not making small changes, it is all about asking where are we now, where do we need to be, and how can we make it happen, in a way that we look at the different actors and they can understand the purpose, and the transition is smooth, and how we can get there. /.../ So service design goes beyond the experience to the implications and the transformation you need to undertake in the organization. (SD3)

<u>Service design is becoming more strategic and entering the management and leadership roles</u>, connecting with strategic management and strategic

512   D. Sangiorgi et al.

design, linking the single product/service design with a wider strategic vision, and developing the needed leadership skills.

> *Now, design is a part of the strategy, an articulation of the business, what the future holds, how we want to position ourselves, and this is very much true for the [my organization], they put a service designer in the first layer of decision making. In the business decisions, I am one of them, and I think this is what will happen in big organizations. (SD2)*

<u>Service design is playing an important role in setting longer-term visions</u> for organizations and wider service systems, by adopting more speculative, scenarios building or foresight skills and approaches.

> */.../ for some things you need more time. /.../ the immediacy, and the need to improve, in a fire-fighting mode, is always happening /.../ I have been in some sessions on speculative design, and people are very eager to do that, but while there are tools for service design, we would like to have more tools for speculative design. (SD2)*

> *Service design has now been integrated into a group working with strategic development of where the company will be in 5–10 years, and what needs to be done today to make that possible. (SD9)*

Furthermore, the identity transformation is paralleled with the <u>effort and role played by designers to educate, train, and support the organization to learn about service design</u>, or design thinking, intended more as a mindset or a structured approach to innovation and transformation, that transcends the use of specific tools.

> *Now it has become standard practice to have design driven customer insight work done, there is no longer a need to fight for those resources. (SD9)*

This has been described as a very structured endeavor with internal Masters, hackathons, seminars, and design challenges, where a service design unit can support the organization in their transformational journey or as a more emergent process aiming to make the value of service design more explicit. Examples of initiatives are engaging personnel in design projects, formalizing the knowledge into training programs and playbooks, creating opportunities to develop a growing community of practitioners or "antennas" in the organizations, and/or increasing the size and role of design units within the organizations themselves.

The Multiple Identities of Service Design in Organizations... 513

We have deliberately been working to increase the capability of the organization to take care of the results of the service design work, by setting up processes with other roles where the goal is to take the learnings to next steps and levels. (SD8)

The company is aware and recognizes the importance of service design, more design thinking we call it, we have a MA in design thinking, which is twice a year for 20/30 people /.../ what they want to promote is a change in mindset. (SD6)

And we came up with a new organizational structure based on knowledge-based communities, and I was the facilitator of that area that was service design. When we started our service design community I actually had to write a definition of service design, and I run workshops about it, and we had 15 to 20 people in the room that would come to me in the end saying, this is very interesting /... / I have been doing this for the past 5 years... And this community has been growing also with our projects. (SD3)

Service Design Collective Identities

The collective perspective on service design identities refers to being a member of a group or community of practice, or having a specific role in professional contexts, interactively creating an identity that has meaning to the individual.

Service Design Today

There is a current agreement on service design as being a creative, human centered, and holistic approach to problem framing and innovation, based on a deep understanding of users and stakeholders' experiences and journeys, supported by a set of research, visualization and materialization methods and approaches, and qualified by the attitude and capability to facilitate collaborative innovation processes.

While this core identity clearly emerges from the interviews, there is a common reflection on how this understanding is not enough, in particular in contexts where there is a strong association between service design and the tools used as well as the connection of service design to only the initial stages of a design process. Three aspects stand out in the material.

The service design tools without an adequate mentality do not help, and it is fundamental to consider the service design approach as both a design and a service mindset.

we cannot focus on designing that single touchpoint, we need to understand the system and the service before /.../ You need to have a service mind. (SD4)

514 D. Sangiorgi et al.

The service design tools without a structured approach, that links back end with front end, and concept development with implementation, are described as inadequate. Effective service design requires a structured approach that builds upon the tools.

> I had an idea in the beginning, that I liked to understand customers and other stakeholders, to listen more than talking, but I did not have a clue on how to do it in a structured manner, and service design gave me that. And now it is helping me to consolidate the way I implement projects in my different roles. (SD1)

Tools are just a limited perception of what service design can actually do, limiting designers to stay at the user research stage.

> The understanding of service design at the company has mainly been that we work with customer insights, that it is mostly about interviewing customers. (SD8)

Service Design Futures

When asked to reflect on the future of service design both as their own individual practice and also more widely in terms of the overall field, six different scenarios have been emerging.

Specialized service design: this vision suggests the need for service designers to critically engage with fundamental issues affecting the future of humanity and the environment, going deeper into understanding the implications and therefore creating better approaches and expertise to address for example gender or ethical issues, environmental crisis, or technological revolution.

> I think service designers might need to specialize in specific subjects. We are often generalist, holistic, and crafters, but today's context is very complex and the elements that influence the context are new and wide. We might need to continue to be generalist, but also we need designers to specialize in technology, human behaviours, ethics, etc. (SD7)

Technical service design: this vision is a call for service designers to expand their knowledge and expertise beyond the user research and conceptual stage to address technical and managerial issues related to making things real, expanding their impact toward the implementation stages.

> There will be a set of designers that are disenchanted about all this designers' thing, it is more a technical job of getting things done that work, and implementing such things, not really caring about the part that is more aesthetic, that is another profession. (SD4)

Vertical service design: this scenario considers the tendency in certain large contexts to create divisions into service design roles, also in relation to UX and UI developing figures, to create further specialisms into multidisciplinary teams.

> *I can't tell if I work for a large organization I think I will need to decide whether to transition into becoming a user researcher or an interaction designer... Alternatively if I continue with small companies I can still be a service designer, because I can still be multidisciplinary because there are not enough people to do that. (SD5)*

General design: this vision recalls the need to erase design labels in the future, to avoid limiting designers' contribution, supporting more hybrid and developing roles, without predefining tasks and specialized expertise.

> *In the future I see that designers should drop all these categories, and go back to be designers. Of course you are stronger in something, but at least you know how to move in the journey of all the projects. (SD4)*

Service design leadership: this scenario builds on the growing strategic roles service designers are playing in organizations, and the need to create adequate training processes and expertise to further support these leadership roles, to bring designers at the decision tables.

> *Of course when you are going in the upper levels of an organization, usually in [insurance company] there are no designers in the higher positions because we are missing some competences that you need in that kind of position, so we probably need to train people that can be the chief, with more management competences mixed with the mindset and view of the designers... this kind of mix of competences can be useful to sit at the big level in order to have an impact in the organization. (SD6)*

Speculative service design: this vision considers the need for service design to embed and apply approaches and expertise coming from speculative and foresight approaches, to enhance the ability of service designers in the shaping of long-term scenarios for specific sectors or organizational development.

> *I have this love for design speculation. I think sometimes we need to take 3–4 days, I know it is hard, and then really craft the future, build design scenarios, and think how do we get there, because this will prepare us way better to make future decisions. (SD2)*

5   Discussion

This study has enabled a deeper understanding of how the development of multiple service design identities is an ongoing process—identity as becoming instead of being (Ashforth, 2000)—that results from service designers' self-reflection and aspirations, but also from the interaction with the organizational contexts and multiple communities of practice. These encounters result in a constant negotiation and co-creation of professional identities and the roles service designers can play in organizations (Svenningsson & Alvesson, 2003). The original imprint deriving from education is enriched, but also challenged when developing professionally, and the nature and contribution of service design changes, given the specific needs and opportunities of the organization. We consider the conceptualization of these individual journeys and the emerging multiple service design professional identities as a fundamental contribution for a better understanding, adopting and integrating service design in organizations, and to leverage service design contribution to service management.

In particular, while there is an acknowledgment that designers currently are moving toward strategic and leadership positions in organizations, the implications and the nature of this evolution for service design as a professional identity and the managerial implications have not been debated. Moreover, it is not fully recognized what can distinguish a service design profile from other designers' identities, at these different levels and in such roles in organizations.

Service design is considered in service management, as a fundamental enhancer of the customer experience, but it is also recognized as a lever to anchor and orient all organizational processes to an outside-in perspective (Andreassen et al., 2016). In certain contexts, service design has been considered as a central competence to achieve overarching transformation processes, such as for person-centered care (Freire & Sangiorgi, 2010; Malmberg et al., 2019). Also, service design has been seen as a key approach to service innovation (Patrício et al., 2018). Still, its role and professional identity seem to be anchored on specific stages in innovation and development processes, which can be a limitation to its potential transformational role (Holmlid et al., 2017). The interviews we conducted have illustrated the barriers but also the drivers—on both the organization and designers' side—for the transitions of this limited view of service design, toward other and more extended positions in organizations (see Table 3). Directly and indirectly, these form a set of implications for management, as well as for design.

The Multiple Identities of Service Design in Organizations...   517

Table 3 Evolving service design identities

Identity change	Role evolution	Barriers to change	Drivers to change
Service design & innovation	Extended role from exploratory & concept design to implementation within innovation processes	Limited awareness of service design as both a process and a mindset in organizations; Lack of a perception of service design added value compared to existing UX, UI, or management roles in organizations; limited experimentation and openness to change in designers.	Acknowledgment of service design's role in service innovation; development of technical knowledge; facilitation role across departments; adoption of a holistic approach; development of demonstration projects.
Service design & (first-line) management	From service design execution to managing design or innovation teams containing service design	Position, funding, and role of service design teams; possible friction with external design agencies; limited recognition across the organization; fear of losing a pure designer identity in designers.	Increasing the recruitment of designers; diversification of designers' roles; visibility of designers' contribution to innovation; developing middle management skills
Service design & strategic management	From service design lead to a strategic management position or a role in strategic management boards and units	Limited design awareness and culture of design as transversal skills and approach to innovation. Limited business skills and knowledge of designers.	Developing strategic management skills; increased inclusion of design in tactical decision-making; utilizing design lead roles; using user customer insight work as strategic decision material
Service design & transformation	From service design in single projects to contribution toward larger- and longer-term value change and transformation	Dominant traditional organizational culture; change adverse long-standing personnel and departments	Interpretation and use of service design approach as a transformational driver within long-term planning

(continued)

518   D. Sangiorgi et al.

Table 3 (continued)

Identity change	Role evolution	Barriers to change	Drivers to change
Service design & organizational development	From service design lead to organizational directing roles for future development	Lack of investment and dedicated support for service design leadership in organizations; limited business and leadership skills and knowledge in service designers	Systematic and long-term plan to instill design approaches and mindset in and across the organization
Critical and speculative service design	From short-term projects to critically exploring possible futures and long-term pathways	Short-term view; lack of an ecosystem perspective; limited specialized knowledge and critical attitude of service design	Find a balance between short-term projects for immediate outcomes; exploring, imagining, and testing new service futures

At a **tactical and innovation project level**, when service designers extend their role from performing operative tasks, such as user research and mapping customer journeys, to considering project management roles and technical knowledge to better support implementation processes along all the innovation journey, the original contribution service design is associated with service design's holistic perspective and collaborative mindset. This is considered as a distinguishing quality if compared with, for example, UX and UI designers, whose role and recognition have been growing in organizations, increasingly investing in digital transformation processes. Here the risk is perceived with managers not being able to clearly distinguish the added value of service designers, limiting their contributions to specific stages in the innovation process, or to the design of individual touchpoints; also a limitation is described when designers themselves constrain their contribution to given roles and tasks, instead of being available to experiment and expand their knowledge and skills, taking full advantage in particular of the opportunities digitalization might generate.

When service design becomes increasingly visible in organizations, and the number of recruited designers is growing, service designers might take a **(Service) Design Lead** role, taking on different responsibilities depending on the position, funding, and ownership of innovation projects of their teams. Depending on the organizational structure and history, this might clash with other units or with the pre-existing roles of external design agencies. Also, here designers need to further develop team and project management skills, that might be perceived as a loss of a traditional designer identity, and might require an active reconstruction of a designerly attitude to managerial roles. A fundamental lever to support this new identity and legitimacy of design, beyond simply recruiting designers, becomes therefore an active endeavor to make service design and service design projects more visible and accessible, promoting its approach in informal or more formal settings, to enhance its potential impact. This is in line with a classical definition of design management that combines tactical management of corporate design functions and activities, with the "strategic advocacy of design across the organization as a key differentiator and driver of organizational success" (Design Management Institute[3]).

Different it is when service design is legitimated to accompany specific transformational processes in organizations to address significant market changes or to achieve new competitive positions, starting from the articulation of new value propositions. Here service design identity is associated with **a transformational driver** for deeper organizational and cultural changes, supporting transformational programs, engaging with different departments in innovation projects or formal training plans (Kurtmollaiev et al., 2018). The barriers are here described as the resistance of long-standing personnel or departments, that might embody a more siloed and product-centric logic, that might clash with the implications of more customer-centric and digital logics. Integrating design capabilities in systematic and long-term programs for organizational learning becomes the main driver to implement this professional identity.

When service designers enter and are part of strategic management boards introducing a design perspective on key business decisions, the **strategic role of design** requires the integration of business and design competences. Here a service innovation perspective requires organizations to develop design capability on operative, tactical, and strategic levels, that go beyond siloed departmental logics; demanding "design management to be placed at a corporate level, that is not just at a departmental level or local level, but at a higher strategic level that serves to emphasize future direction" (Gloppen, 2011). The awareness of the potential impact of service design on strategic management and leadership is still very limited, and in some interviews remains more as an aspiration, to be achieved with further business training and organizational support. Few studies have been looking into the role of service design at a

---

[3] See: https://www.dmi.org/page/What_is_Design_Manag.

corporate strategic level, where "service design leadership takes on a user- and human-centered design perspective in leadership tasks and looks at new ways of mobilizing cross-functional talents, allocating resources and ensures necessary empowerment to manage the transition to a new future" (Gloppen et al., 2017, p. 231).

Besides a service design leadership role, the interviews have led us to a further reflection, that together with a strategic view, it has been emphasized both the capability to envision futures, through speculative design approaches, and also the need to critically advance specialized knowledge and novel approaches to better address **fundamental issues for service futures**, such as gender or ethical issues, environmental crisis, or technological revolution. We find these perspectives aligned with an understanding of strategic design intended as "the use of design-driven processes, principles and practices to intentionally innovate interdependent value-creating systems, advancing organizational and communal well-being" (Windahl et al., 2020, pp. 1415–1416). This perspective goes beyond the boundaries of individual organizations and business profit, to acknowledge the need to contribute to more sustainable futures, working at a meta and ecosystem level (Vink et al., 2020). The barriers here are the short-sighted perspective of organizations and the time pressure that might limit more strategic and transformational choices, as well as a limited specialization and critical attitude of service designers when approaching the contemporary societal implications of service innovation.

6   Conclusions

This study has developed a more articulated understanding of the key evolutions and trajectories of service design as a field that the academic community has been studying. It has also opened up further questions in relation to the identities and the real worklife and journeys professional service designers conduct in and across organizations and the implications this can have for service design and service management.

A first consideration concerns the professional development of service designers from more operational and tactical roles to more strategic and leadership positions, where service designers evolve and enrich their role by embedding other design, business, and management competences and skills. These evolutions and hybridization are at times described as an identity crisis, while other times they are represented as the necessary development of a more mature and fully acknowledged professional identity. This dual transformation of the individual designers and of the communities of practice in the organizational context has been mostly studied from the perspectives of designers facilitating organizational change and learning (Junginger & Sangiorgi, 2009), while "how design professionals negotiate themselves in and around organizations" (Björklund et al., 2020, p. 83) has not been investigated. Also, while there is a growing awareness of the need to adjust design interventions to the existing organizational design legacies (Junginger, 2012), this study has instead discussed how this adjustment can be a negotiation with and within organizations that can impact service designers' professional identity.

Furthermore, while there has been an interest in how service design ethos has been used to construct an occupational mandate, and differentiate from other traditional designers or management consultants (Fayard et al., 2017), this study points to the importance played by the individual ambition, values, and evolving interpretation of their own practice to the actual crafting of the future of service designers' professional identity and collectively of their own disciplinary field. With this chapter, we suggest how a reflection on these individual professional stories should play a fundamental role in the ongoing reflection on service design education, but also on the consolidated understanding of service design as a multidisciplinary practice and field (Joly et al., 2019). Few studies have explored the integration of competences and approaches within service design projects (e.g. Teixeira et al., 2017), but there is scope to further explore the quality and implications of the hybridization of service design practice in organizations and education. Specific skills such as project management, business, and leadership skills have been highlighted as developed on the ground or requiring dedicated training, while new emerging competences and expertise on contemporary challenges can open the way for new professional trajectories, where the term "service" might not be necessary anymore.

Service design has made a significant journey with service management over the years, moving from a stage in new service development to leveraging service innovation processes, changing organizational mindsets, and catalyzing service system transformation. This work suggests possible transversal and vertical trajectories when integrating design skills in organizations, as well as potential strategies to enable strategic capability development and impactful use of expert and diffused design capacities. Finally, this study has opened the ground for service design to further collaborate and leverage synergies with service management, by both integrating a service management perspective in service design approaches and embedding a design approach across the organization in an ongoing design process to assume a more transformative role.

References

Adams, R. S., Daly, S. R., Mann, L. M., & Dall'Alba, G. (2011). Being a professional: Three lenses into design thinking, acting, and being. *Design Studies, 32*(6), 588–607.

Adler, P. S., & Heckscher, C. (2006). Towards a collaborative community. In C. Heckscher & P. S. Adler (Eds.), *The firm as a collaborative community: Reconstructing trust in the knowledge economy*. Oxford University Press.

Akama, Y., Fennessy, L., Harrington, S., & Farago, A. (2020). *ServDes. 2020 Tensions, Paradoxes and Plurality Conference Proceedings*, 2–5 February 2021, Melbourne, Australia.

Andreassen, T. W., Kristensson, P., Lervik-Olsen, L., Parasuraman, A., McColl-Kennedy, J. R., Edvardsson, B., & Colurcio, M. (2016). Linking service design to value creation and service research. *Journal of Service Management, 27*(1), 21–29.

Aricò. (2018). *Service design as a transformative force: Introduction and adoption in an organizational context* (Doctoral dissertation). Delft University of Technology.

Ashforth, B. (2000). *Role transitions in organizational life: An identity-based perspective*. Routledge.

Bailey, S. G. (2012). Embedding service design: The long and the short of it. In *ServDes. 2012 Conference Proceedings Co-Creating Services* (pp. 31–41). Linköping University Electronic Press, Linköpings universitet.

Berger, P., & Luckmann, T. (1966). *The social construction of knowledge*. Doubleday.

Björklund, T. A., Keipi, T., & Maula, H. (2020). Crafters, explorers, innovators, and co-creators: Narratives in designers' identity work. *Design Studies, 68*, 82–112.

Blomberg, J., & Darrah, C. (2015). Towards an anthropology of services. *The Design Journal, 18*(2), 171–192.

Blomberg, J., Giacomi, J., Mosher, A., & Swenton-Wall, P. (1993). Ethnographic field methods and their relation to design. In D. Shuler & A. Namioka (Eds.), *Participatory design. Principles and practices*. LEA Publishers.

Blomkvist, J., Clatworthy, S., & Holmlid, S. (2016). Ways of seeing the design material of service. In *Service Design Geographies. The ServDes. 2016 Conference, Copenhagen 24–26 May 2016* (Vol. 125, pp. 1–13). Linköping University Electronic Press.

Blomkvist, J., Rodrigues, V., & Overkamp, T. (2020). Challenges facing service design practitioners: A pilot study. In *ServDes. 2020 Tensions, Paradoxes+ Plurality*. Linköping University Electronic Press.

Boland, R., & Collopy, F. (2004). *Managing as designing*. Bibliovault OAI Repository, the University of Chicago Press.

Brandt, E. (2006). Designing exploratory design games. A framework for participation in participatory design? *Proceedings of the Ninth Participatory Design Conference*, Trento, Italy.

Brown, J. S., & Duguid, P. (1998). Organizing knowledge. *California Management Review, 40*(3), 90–111.

Brown, T. (2009). *Change by design: How design thinking transforms organizations and inspires innovation.* Harper Business.

Burke, P. J., & Stets, J. E. (1999). Trust and commitment in an identity verification context. *Social Psychology Quarterly, 62*(4), 347–366.

Burns, C., Cottam, H., Vanstone, C., & Winhall, J. (2006). Transformation design. *RED Paper, 2.*

Caic, M., Holmlid, S., Mahrz, D., & Odekerken-Schroder, G. (2019). Beneficiaries' view of actor networks: Service resonance for pluralistic actor networks. *International Journal of Design, 13*(3), 69–88.

Carstensen, H. V., & Bason, C. (2012). Powering collaborative policy innovation: Can innovation labs help. *The Innovation Journal: The Public Sector Innovation Journal, 17*(1), 1–26.

Caza, B. B., Vough, H., & Puranik, H. (2018). Identity work in organizations and occupations: Definitions, theories, and pathways forward. *Journal of Organizational Behavior, 39*(June), 889–910. https://doi.org/10.1002/job.2318

Charmaz, K. (2014). *Constructing grounded theory* (2nd ed.). Sage.

Clifford, J. (1988). *The predicament of culture.* Harvard University Press.

Costa, N., Patrício, L., Morelli, N., & Magee, C. L. (2018). Bringing service design to manufacturing companies: Integrating PSS and service design approaches. *Design Studies, 55*(1), 112–114.

Cottam, H., & Leadbeater, C. (2004). *Open welfare: Designs on the public good.* Design Council.

Cross, N. (2001). Designerly ways of knowing: Design discipline versus design science. *Design Issues, 17*(3), 49–55.

Dall'Alba, G. (2009). Learning professional ways of being: Ambiguities of becoming. *Educational Philosophy and Theory, 41*(1), 34–45.

Erlhoff, M., Mager, B., & Manzini, E. (1997). *Dienstleistung braucht Design, Professioneller Produkt- und Markenauftritt für Serviceanbieter.* Hermann Luchterhand Verlag GmbH.

Fayard, A.-L., Stigliani, I., & Bechky, B. A. (2017). How nascent occupations construct a mandate: The case of service designers' ethos. *Administrative Science Quarterly, 62*(2), 270–303.

Fisk, R. P., Alkire (née Nasr), L., Anderson, L., Bowen, D. E., Gruber, T., Ostrom, A. L., & Patrício, L. (2020). Elevating the human experience (HX) through service research collaborations: Introducing ServCollab, *Journal of Service Management,* 31 (4), 615–635.

Foglieni, F., & Holmlid, S. (2017). Determining service value: Exploring the link between value creation and service evaluation. *Service Science, 9*(1), 74–90.

Freire, K., & Sangiorgi, D. (2010). Service design and healthcare innovation: From consumption to co-production to co-creation. In *Service Design and Service Innovation Conference* (pp. 39–50). Linköping Electronic Conference Proceedings.

Giddens, A. (1984). *The constitution of society: Outline of the theory of structuration*. University of California Press.

Giddens, A. (1991). *Modernity and self-identity: Self and society in the late modern age*. Stanford University Press.

Gloppen, J. (2011). The strategic use of service design for leaders in service organizations. *FORMakademisk, 4*(2), 3–25.

Gloppen, J., Fjuk, A., & Clatworthy, S. (2017). The role of service design leadership in creating added customer value. In M. Lüders, T. W. Andreassen, S. Clatworthy, & T. Hillestad (Eds.), *Innovating for trust* (pp. 230–244). Edward Elgar Publishing Limited.

Golsorkhi, D., Rouleau, L., Seidl, D., & Vaara, E. (2015). Introduction: What is strategy as practice? 1–30. https://doi.org/10.1017/CCO9781139681032.001

Gray, C. M. (2014). Evolution of design competence in UX practice. In *Proceedings of the SIGCHI Conference on human factors in computing systems* (pp. 1645–1654). ACM.

Grönroos, C. (2011). Value co-creation in service logic: A critical analysis. *Marketing Theory, 11*(3), 279–301.

Hollins, G., & Hollins, B. (1991). *Total design: Managing the design process in the service sector*. Pitman.

Holmlid, S. (2007). Interaction design and service design: Expanding a comparison of design disciplines. In *2nd Nordic Design Research Design Conference*, Stockholm.

Holmlid, S. (2009). Participative; co-operative; emancipatory: From participatory design to service design. In *Conference Proceedings ServDes. 2009; DeThinking Service; ReThinking Design; Oslo Norway 24–26 November 2009* (No. 059, pp. 105–118). Linköping University Electronic Press.

Holmlid, S. (2015). Composition and blending of practices. In D. Sangiorgi, A. Prendiville, J. Jung, & E. Yu (Eds.), *Design for service innovation & development: Final Report* (pp. 49–51). AHRC Project AH/L013657/1. Available at http://imagination.lancs.ac.uk/sites/default/files/outcome_downloads/desid_report_2015_web.pdf

Holmlid, S., Ekholm, D., & Dahlstedt, M. (2021). Practice occludes diffusion: Scaling sport-based social innovations. In *Social innovation in sport* (pp. 57–77). Palgrave Macmillan.

Holmlid, S., & Malmberg, L. (2018). Learning to design in public sector organisations: A critique towards effectiveness of design integration. In *ServDes2018. Service Design Proof of Concept, Proceedings of the ServDes. 2018 Conference, 18–20 June, Milano, Italy* (No. 150, pp. 37–48). Linköping University Electronic Press.

Holmlid, S., Mattelmäki, T., Visser, F. S., & Vaajakallio, K. (2015). Co-creative practices in service innovation. In *The handbook of service innovation* (pp. 545–574). Springer.

Holmlid, S., Wetter-Edman, K., & Edvardsson, B. (2017). Breaking free from NSD: Design and service beyond new service development. In D. Sangiorgi &

A. Prendiville (Eds.), *Designing for service: Key issues and new directions* (pp. 95–104). Bloomsbury Publishing.

Ibarra, H. (1999). Provisional selves: Experimenting with image and identity in professional adaptation. *Administrative Science Quarterly, 44*(4), 764–791.

Jaakkola, E. (2020). Designing conceptual articles: Four approaches. *Journal of the Academy of Marketing Science, 10*, 18–26.

Järventie-Thesleff, R., & Tienari, J. (2016). Roles as mediators in identity work. *Organization Studies, 37*(2), 237–265. https://doi.org/10.1177/0170840615604500

Jégou, F., & Manzini, E. (2008). *Collaborative services. Social innovation and design for sustainability*. Edizioni Polidesign.

Joly, M. P., Teixeira, J. G., Patrício, L., & Sangiorgi, D. (2019). Leveraging service design as a multidisciplinary approach to service innovation. *Journal of Service Management, 30*(6), 681–715.

Junginger, S. (2009). Design in the organization: Parts and wholes. *Design Research Journal, 2*(9), 23–29.

Junginger, S. (2012). Public innovation labs—A byway to public sector innovation? In J. Christensen & S. Junginger (Eds.), *Highways and byways to radical innovation* (1st ed.). University of Southern Denmark & Design School.

Junginger, S. (2015). Organizational Design Legacies and Service Design. *The Design Journal, 18*(2), 209–226, https://doi.org/10.2752/175630615X14212498964277

Junginger, S., & Sangiorgi, D. (2009). Service design and organisational change. Bridging the gap between rigour and relevance. *IASDR09 Conference*, 19–22 October, Seoul.

Karpen, I. O., Gemser, G., & Calabretta, G. (2017). A multilevel consideration of service design conditions. Towards a portfolio of organisational capabilities, interactive practices and individual abilities. *Journal of Service Theory and Practice, 27*(2), 384–407.

Kimbell, L. (2011). Designing for service as one way of designing services. *International Journal of Design, 5*(2), 41–52.

Kimbell, L. (2014). *The service innovation handbook: Action-oriented creative thinking toolkit for service organizations*. BIS Publishers.

Kimbell, L., & Seidel, V. P. (2008). Designing for services—Multidisciplinary perspectives. *Proceedings from the exploratory project on designing for services in science and technology-based enterprises.*

Kimbell, L., & Street, P. E. (2009, September). Beyond design thinking: Design-as-practice and designs-in-practice. In *CRESC Conference, Manchester* (pp. 1–15).

Korper, A. K., Patrício, L., Holmlid, S., & Witell, L. (2020). Service design as an innovation approach in technology startups: A longitudinal multiple case study. *Creativity and Innovation Management, 29*(2), 303–323.

Koskela-Huotari, K., Patrício, L., Zhang, J., Karpen, O., Sangiorgi, D., Anderson, L., & Bogicevic, V. (2021). Service system transformation through service design: Linking analytical dimensions and service design approaches. *Journal of Business Research, 136*, 343–355.

Kunrath, K., Cash, P., & Kleinsmann, M. (2020). Social-and self-perception of designers' professional identity. *Journal of Engineering Design, 31*(2), 100–126.

Kurtmollaiev, S., Fjuk, A., Pedersen, P. E., Clatworthy, S., & Kvale, K. (2018). Organizational transformation through service design: The institutional logics perspective. *Journal of Service Research, 21*(1), 59–74.

Lam, A. (2020). Hybrids, identity and knowledge boundaries: Creative artists between academic and practitioner communities. *Human Relations, 73*(6), 837–863.

Laursen, L. N., & Haase, L. M. (2019). The shortcomings of design thinking when compared to designerly thinking. *The Design Journal, 22*(6), 813–832.

Lave, J., & Wenger, E. (1991). *Situated learning: Legitimate peripheral participation.* Cambridge University Press.

Linstead, A., & Thomas, R. (2002). What do you want from me? A poststructuralist feminist reading of middle managers' identities. *Culture and Organization, 8*(1), 1–20.

Liu, L., & Hinds, P. (2012). The designer identity, identity evolution, and implications on design practice. In *Design thinking research* (pp. 185–196). Springer, Berlin, Heidelberg.

Lockwood, T. (2010). Design thinking in business: An interview with Gianfranco Zaccai. *Design Management Review, 21*(3), 16–24.

Malmberg, L. (2017). *Building design capability in the public sector: Expanding the horizons of development* (Doctoral dissertation). Linköping University.

Malmberg, L., Rodrigues, V., Lännerström, L., Wetter-Edman, K., Vink, J., & Holmlid, S. (2019). Service design as a transformational driver toward person-centered care in healthcare. In M. Pfannstiel & C. Rasche (Eds.), *Service design and service thinking in healthcare and hospital management.* Springer.

Malmberg, L., & Wetter-Edman, K. (2016). Design in public sector: Exploring antecedents of sustained design capability. In *20th DMI: Academic Design Management Conference-Inflection Point: Design Research Meets Design Practice, Boston, USA, July 22–29, 2016* (pp. 1286–1307). Design Management Institute.

Manzini, E. (1993). Il design dei servizi. La progettazione del prodotto-servizio. *Design Management, 4*, 7–12.

Manzini, E. (2015). *Design, when everybody designs: An introduction to design for social innovation.* The MIT Press.

Martin, R. (2009). *The design of business: Why design thinking is the next competitive advantage.* Harvard Business School Publishing. Rotman Design Works.

Meroni, A. (Ed.). (2007). *Creative communities. People inventing sustainable ways of living.* Edizioni Polidesign.

Meroni, A., & Sangiorgi, D. (Eds.). (2011). *Design for services.* Gower.

Morelli, N. (2006). Developing new product service systems (PSS): Methodologies and operational tools. *Journal of Cleaner Production, 14*(17), 1495–1501.

Morelli, N., & De Götzen, A. (2017). A multilevel approach for social transformations and its implications on service design education. *The Design Journal, 20*(Supp 1), S803–S813. https://doi.org/10.1080/14606925.2017.1353026

Morelli, N., & Tollestrup, C. (2007). *New representation techniques for designing in a systemic perspective*. Paper presented at the Nordic Design Research Conference, Stockholm, Sweden.

Morello, A. (1991). *Design e mercato dei prodotti e dei Servizi*. Document for the Doctorate Programme in Industrial Design. Milano: Politecnico di Milano.

Mulgan, G. (2014). *Design in public and social innovation: What works and what could work better*. Nesta.

Orr, J. E. (1996). *Talking about machines: An ethnography of a modern job*. Cornell University Press.

Ostrom, A. L., Parasuraman, A., Bowen, D. E., Patrício, L., & Voss, C. A. (2015). Service research priorities in a rapidly changing context. *Journal of Service Research, 18*(2), 127–159.

Pacenti, E. (1998). *Il progetto dell' interazione nei servizi. Un contributo al tema della progettazione dei servizi*. PhD thesis in industrial design, Politecnico di Milan.

Parker, S., & Heapy, J. (2006). *The journey to the interface. How public service design can connect users to reform*. Demos.

Patrício, L., De Pinho, N. F., Teixeira, J. G., & Fisk, R. P. (2018). Service design for value networks: Enabling value cocreation interactions in healthcare. *Service Science, 10*(1), 76–87.

Patrício, L., Fisk, R. P., Falcão e Cunha, J., & Constantine, L. (2011). Multilevel service design: From customer value constellation to service experience blueprint. *Journal of Service Research, 14*(2), 180–200.

Patrício, L., Gustafsson, A., & Fisk, R. P. (2018). Upframing service design and innovation for research impact. *Journal of Service Research, 21*(1), 3–16.

Patrício, L., Sangiorgi, D., Mahr, D., Čaić, M., Kalantari, S., & Sundar, S. (2020). Leveraging service design for healthcare transformation: Toward people-centered, integrated, and technology-enabled healthcare systems. *Journal of Service Management, 31*(5), 889–909.

Rodrigues, V. (2020). *Designing for resilience: Navigating change in service systems* (Vol. 2065). Linköping University Electronic Press.

Rodrigues, V., Holmlid, S., & Blomkvist, J. (2020). Patterns of disruption: Diagnosing response mechanisms in actor networks. In *ServDes. 2020 Tensions, Paradoxes+ Plurality*. Linköping University Electronic Press.

Sampson, S. (2012). Visualizing service operations. *Journal of Service Research, 15*, 182–198.

Sangiorgi, D. (2009). Building a framework for Service Design research. *EAD Conference 'Connexity'*, 1–3 April, Aberdeen.

Sangiorgi, D. (2011). Transformative services and transformation design. *International Journal of Design, 5*(2), 29–40.

Sangiorgi, D., Michelle, F., McAllister, S., Mulvale, G., Sneyd, M., Vink, J., & Warwick, L. (2019). Designing in highly contentious areas: Perspectives on a way forward for mental healthcare transformation. *Design Journal, 22*, 309–330.

Sangiorgi, D., & Prendiville, A. (Eds.). (2017). *Designing for service: Key issues and new directions*. Bloomsbury Publishing.

Sangiorgi, D., Prendiville, A., & Ricketts, A. (Eds.) (2014). Design for Service Innovation and Development. *AHRC funded research report*. Lancaster University, ISBN 978-1-86220-323-5.

Schein, E. H. (1978). *Career dynamics: Matching individual and organizational needs*. Addison-Wesley.

Segelström, F., & Holmlid, S. (2015). Ethnography by design: On goals and mediating artefacts. *Arts and Humanities in Higher Education, 14*(2), 134–149.

Shostack, G. L. (1982). How to design a service. *European Journal of Marketing, 16*(1), 49–63.

Shostack, G. L. (1984). Designing services that deliver. *Harvard Business Review, 62*(1), 133–139.

Shove, E., Pantzar, M., & Watson, M. (2012). *The dynamics of social practice: Everyday life and how it changes*. Sage.

Svenningsson, S., & Alvesson, M. (2003). Managing managerial identities: Organizational fragmentation, discourse and identity struggle. *Human Relations, 56*(10), 1163–1193.

Teixeira, J., Patrício, L., Huang, K.-H., Fisk, R. P., Nóbrega, L., & Constantine, L. (2017). The MINDS method: Integrating management and interaction design perspectives for service design. *Journal of Service Research, 20*(3), 240–258.

Thackara, J. (2007). *Wouldn't it be Great if ... London*: Dotto07, Design Council.

Thomas, E. (Ed.). (2008). *Innovation by design in public services*. Solace Foundation Imprint.

Tracey, M. W., & Hutchinson, A. (2016). Uncertainty, reflection, and designer identity development. *Design Studies, 42*, 86–109.

Vargo, S. L., & Lusch, R. F. (2008). Service-dominant logic: Continuing the evolution. *Journal of the Academy of Marketing Science, 36*(1), 1–10.

Vink, J., Koskela-Huotari, K., Tronvoll, B., Edvardsson, B., & Wetter-Edman, K. (2020). Service ecosystem design: Propositions, process model, and future research agenda. *Journal of Service Research*. https://doi.org/10.1177/1094670520952537

Watson, T. J. (2009). Entrepreneurial action, identity work and the use of multiple discursive resources. *International Small Business Journal, 7*(3), 251–274.

Weick, K. E. (1995). *Sensemaking in organizations* (Vol. 3). Sage.

Wenger, E. (1996). *Communities of practice: Learning, meaning and identity*. Cambridge University Press.

Wetter-Edman, K. (2014). *Design for service – a framework for articulating designers' contribution as interpreter of users' experience*. Doctoral dissertation, University of Gothenburg, Gothenburg.

Wetter-Edman, K., Sangiorgi, D., Edvardsson, B., Holmlid, S., Grönroos, C., & Mattelmäki, T. (2014). Design for value co-creation: Exploring synergies between design for service and service logic. *Service Science, 6*(2), 106–121.

Windahl, C., Karpen, I. O., & Wright, M. R. (2020). Strategic design: Orchestrating and leveraging market-shaping capabilities. *Journal of Business and Industrial Marketing, 35*(9), 1413–1424. https://doi.org/10.1108/JBIM-03-2019-0133

Yu, E., & Sangiorgi, D. (2018). Service Design as an approach to implement the value cocreation perspective in new service development. *Journal of Service Research, 21*(1), 40–58.

Tracing the Systems Turn in Service Design and Innovation: Convergence Toward Service System Transformation

Kaisa Koskela-Huotari and Josina Vink

1 Introduction

Service design and service innovation are both identified as service research priorities (Ostrom et al., 2015) and gaining increasing scholarly attention due to their significant role in creating new forms of value cocreation among various actors within service contexts (Patrício et al., 2018). While the service management literature initially discussed service design and innovation in an interchangeable manner under the umbrella term of new service development (see, e.g., Edvardsson & Olsson, 1996; Gummesson, 1994), the two have since been distinguished into their own discourses, and both have accumulated wide bodies of literature that are rather disconnected from one another. Service innovation is often seen as an outcome, such as a new process or service offering that creates value for one or more actors (Snyder et al., 2016). However, there is also a growing body of literature that views service innovation itself as a process (Gallouj & Weinstein, 1997; Toivonen & Tuominen,

---

K. Koskela-Huotari (✉)
Department of Marketing and Strategy, Stockholm School of Economics,
Stockholm, Sweden
e-mail: kaisa.koskela.huotari@hhs.se

J. Vink
Institute of Design, Oslo School of Architecture and Design, Oslo, Norway
e-mail: Josina.Vink@aho.no

© The Author(s), under exclusive license to Springer Nature Switzerland AG 2022
B. Edvardsson, B. Tronvoll (eds.), *The Palgrave Handbook of Service Management*,
https://doi.org/10.1007/978-3-030-91828-6_27

2009; Helkkula et al., 2018). Service design, on the other hand, is most often viewed as an approach to achieve desired outcomes, such as service innovations, that are characterized by creativity, human-centeredness, and iteration (see, e.g., Meroni & Sangiorgi, 2011; Patrício et al., 2018).

Over time, both discourses have been influenced by and studied within varying disciplinary settings. Service innovation, for example, is not only studied in service management, but rather it "represents a cross-road for various research interests from different academic disciplines that explore multiple dimensions, follow unique approaches, build varied conceptual and analytical frameworks, and adopt distinct perspectives" (Rubalcaba et al., 2012, p. 697). The same applies to service design research which reflects multiple perspectives and operates at the intersection of a number of disciplines including marketing, operations management, information systems, and design (Joly et al., 2019). For example, service design methods are often developed based on input from multiple disciplines, such as the MINDS method that integrates management and interaction design perspectives (Grenha Teixeira et al., 2017). As such, the two discourses have developed unique positioning and research traditions in relation to their core phenomena.

There have been several calls to examine how service innovation and service design discourses can be used to cross-fertilizing each other. Barrett et al. (2015), for example, urge scholars to consider "how service innovation theory informs and may be applied in the design of services, of service systems, and of service ecosystems." Also, Patrício and colleagues (2018, p. 5) note that a "deeper understanding is needed as to how service design and service innovation processes complement each other to create successful new services." In addition, there are calls within both discourses to develop more integrative and overarching frameworks that can guide scholars and practitioners (see, e.g., Gallouj & Savona, 2009; Rubalcaba et al., 2012; Sangiorgi, 2009; Wetter-Edman et al., 2014).

In the recent years, both service design and service innovation discourses have been progressively embracing systems thinking. In part, this development is connected with both literatures becoming more integrated with service-dominant (S-D) logic's service ecosystem perspective (see, e.g., Baron et al., 2018; Koskela-Huotari et al., 2016; Vink et al., 2021a). The ongoing "systems turn" in these literatures imply a more holistic, rather than reductionistic, understanding of both the outcomes of service design and innovation, and the processes bringing forth such outcomes. In this chapter, we argue that in addition to representing the direction to which both service innovation and service design research are moving, this "systems turn" is also causing the two discourses to convergence toward informing a common phenomenon of *service system transformation*. As such, systems thinking also represents an opportunity to reconcile the two discourses with one another and generate integrative frameworks.

The purpose of this chapter is to provide an overview of the ongoing "systems turn" in service design and service innovation discourses and show the convergence that is resulting from this development. More specifically, while tracing the "systems turn" in both literatures, we also gather the main insights of the emerging, intersectional understanding of how service system transformation, that is, transformation within service systems and systems of such systems—service ecosystems—unfolds (Koskela-Huotari et al., 2021). Although, this almost simultaneous "systems turn" has resulted in a lot of similarities within the insights that the two discourses have so far generated, there are also fruitful differences due to varying nature of the underlying assumptions, positioning of the researchers, framing of the core phenomenon, and interdisciplinary connections that the literatures have gathered while being separated. As such, both discourses provide complementing perspectives in understanding service system transformation that can help both academics and practitioners. They shed light, especially, on the nature and role of intentional design and innovation interventions, but also have begun to contextualize these intentional efforts to bring forth change as part of the broader systemic processes at play.

The remaining content of this chapter is structured as follows: first, we give an overview of the origins and early views, as well as the more recent systems turn in both the service design and service innovation literature. We, then, show how the two discourses are converging to inform a common phenomenon of service system transformation. We also elaborate why and how service design and service innovation can act as complementary perspectives in understanding how transformation within service systems unfolds and give an account of the main insights of the emerging, intersectional understanding of service system transformation before concluding the chapter.

Systems Turn in Service Design

Service design first emerged in academic literature in the early 1980s, became a discipline in the 1990s, established itself as a profession in around 2000, and has since become a maturing area of research (Sangiorgi & Prendiville, 2015). Within service research, service design has been recognized as a priority research area for over a decade as it applies across service contexts and it is critical for bringing service strategy and innovation to life (Ostrom et al.,

534   K. Koskela-Huotari and J. Vink

2010, 2015). To position the development of the "systems turn" in service design, this section begins by providing a brief overview of the early views of service design in academic literature on service management and then shows how the discourse changes by building a more systemic understanding of both the object of service design and the process of designing itself.

Service Design: Origins and Early Views

The earliest academic contributions to service design as a discipline introduced tools, including molecule modeling and service blueprinting, for marketers to more systematically design, manage, and modify services (Shostack, 1982). Amid these early developments, service designers as a unique profession were still relatively unheard of (Gummesson, 1989). The early views of service design focused on the design of service encounters (Bitner et al., 1990) with emphasis on the important role of the physical environment of services in influencing customer and employee behavior (Bitner, 1992).

In these discussions the understanding of service design was informed by a quality management perspective, where service design was understood as an early stage of new service development, a stage focused on creating the prerequisites for service (Edvardsson & Olsson, 1996; Edvardsson, 1997). The prerequisites of the service include the service concept—how the customer's needs are satisfied; the service system—the resources available to realize the service concept; and service process—the chain of activities to produce the service (Edvardsson & Olsson, 1996). The view of the service system in this early literature on service design focuses on the elements that are needed to deliver a service including the people, the equipment, and the physical environment (Berry et al., 1994). Such early views are underpinned by a goods-dominant logic, positioning service design as an early step in a linear new service development process that is clearly separated from implementation (Yu & Sangiorgi, 2014).

These early views of service design were echoed in the approaches that followed with many service scholars building on the service blueprint, such as by developing it to support the integrated design of multi-interface services (Patrício et al., 2008) and creating a user-friendly workshop guide to support the application of the blueprint in practice (Bitner et al., 2008). Other contributions to the evolving discourse of service design include the development of design principles to enable experience-centric services (Zomerdijk & Voss, 2010). Further method development for service design includes a toolkit to support cross-functional teams in designing touchpoints in new service development (Clatworthy, 2011). Reflecting on these early contributions to service design, scholars highlighted the service interface, including its tangible and intangible components, as the object of service design (Secomandi & Snelders, 2011).

Service Design: Systems Turn

While there was language highlighting the concept of "service systems" in early contributions to service design, this conceptualization was limited to recognition of the detailed components needed to enable a functioning service. Taking the understanding of the service system in service design further in the late 1990s, Tax and Stuart (1997) highlight challenges with integrating new services into existing service systems. These scholars develop a non-linear process model for managing service design that supports service system integration. By recognizing that "changes to any element of the existing system represent a "new" service, they account for the complexities and risks inherent in altering service systems" (Tax & Stuart, 1997; p. 127). This more integrative lens on service design is built on by Stuart (1998), who acknowledges that previous research on service design includes a "lack of recognition that the individual elements interrelate and interact to define a service system" (p. 472) and has "overlooked the considerable influence that the organizational culture and internal politics have on the new service design concept" (p. 474). In adjacent discussions of designing product service systems (PSS), there has been an understanding of the socially constructed nature of these systems that have "characteristics ... determined by the different cultural, social, economic and technological frames of the actors involved in their construction" (Morelli, 2002, p. 5).

In the years that followed, Patrício et al. (2011) proposed a new interdisciplinary method to explicitly support the integration of service offerings across system levels, called "multilevel service design" (MSD). Around this time, there was also an emergence of an alternative conceptualization of service design, often referred to as "design for service" (Kimbell, 2011; Meroni & Sangiorgi, 2011). This perspective, grounded in early service-dominant logic, recognized that designers could not completely control service (Meroni & Sangiorgi, 2011) but could build platforms to create the conditions for actors to shape value in use within a socio-material world (Kimbell, 2011). This view gave way toward a focus on co-design and the recognition that design is an ongoing process, where service design scholars "situate design as a continuous process and activity, and so ... use the term *designing* as a verb" (Akama &

Prendiville, 2013, p. 31). This conceptualization of service design starts to see design as an ongoing, circular process of discovery and actualization, which is inherently transformative for actors involved (ibid.). This understanding contributes to a more systemic understanding of design that recognizes the feedback loops that are part of the process, moving away from the linear reductionist model.

Building further on this conceptualization, Wetter-Edman et al. (2014) explicate how service design involves interpreting existing service systems and proposing new ones to support value cocreation by engaging actors in service system redesign. Here service system redesign is understood as a process of engaging actors in the negotiation of future service system configurations, including actors, resources, technology, and institutionalized norms and rules that guide actors' resource integration and value creation, to create the desired experiences.

Further developments saw a continued turn toward a systemic perspective on service design with growing recognition that designing never ends in organizations and that service design requires working with existing design legacies (Junginger, 2015). Also emphasizing the organizational context, Karpen et al. (2017) delineate the multi-level conditions for service design that include organizational-level service design capabilities, interactive service design practices, and individual-level service design abilities. This multi-level approach to systems, common in service design literature, is also built on in further method development that aids in addressing the complexity of technology-enabled services across multiple service interfaces (Grenha Teixeira et al., 2017).

Summarizing and advancing the systemic understanding of service design, Sangiorgi et al. (2017) highlight the service system as a fundamental unit for service design and bring forward diverse sociological paradigms on systems, including functionalist, interpretative, emancipatory, and postmodernism, to inform service design practices. Through this process, they highlight the increasing complexity of service systems with a focus on many-to-many interactions, interdependencies with expanding system boundaries, systems defined through participatory processes, and the need to account for emergence that arises through the self-organization of complex service systems. New method development within service design then brings forward an approach for designing services as enablers of many-to-many value cocreating interactions that works toward balanced centricity among actor networks (Patrício et al., 2018). Along this same vein, Čaić and colleagues (2019) develop a new service design method that aids in building an understanding of beneficiaries' perspective on how actor networks are configured and identify three different kinds of networks from beneficiaries' perspectives: hierarchical, focalized, and bundled.

More recently, there has been an increasing focus on the critical role of institutionalized social structures within the evolving systemic view on service design. In particular, Kurtmollaiev et al. (2018) show how the adoption of service design contributed to changing a multi-national telecom organization's institutional logics through the evolution of both the material and the symbolic aspects of the service system, showing the transformative potential of service design in reshaping service system structures. Furthermore, research on service design processes within the healthcare context demonstrates the possibility of service design to support the transformation of not just of aspects of institutionalized social structures that are perceived as external to actors, but also actor's own mental models—the assumptions and beliefs that guide their behavior and interpretation of their environment (Vink et al., 2019, see also Vink, 2019).

Bringing forward the conceptualization of service ecosystem design, Vink and colleagues (2021a, p. 169) view service design as "the intentional shaping of institutional arrangements and their physical enactments by actor collectives through reflexivity and reformation to facilitate the emergence of desired value cocreation forms." This systemic conceptualization of the process of service design stresses that service design is always an embedded process of shaping institutionalized social structures that result in emergent outcomes based on the interactions within and between both conflicting and aligned design and non-design processes (ibid., 2021a). This focus on multi-actor configurations governed by institutions has also been integrated into systemic approaches to service design focused on service user experiences within the public sector (Trischler & Westman Trischler, 2021).

In this way, service design discourse has taken a systemic turn from a narrower, reductionist focus on the touchpoints and interfaces toward a broader more integrative focus on designing for and within service systems, with a specific emphasis on the importance of reshaping institutionalized social structures that give shape to these systems. Next, we show how the service innovation literature has gone through a similar kind of development that has resulted in a more holistic understanding of the related outcomes and processes.

Systems Turn in Service Innovation

The recognition of service innovation—and the construction of its legitimacy as something distinct from product innovation—started very gradually in the late 1980s (Rajala et al., 2016). After the initial "denial phase," the literature on service innovation has grown slowly but steadily (Helkkula et al., 2018; Rajala et al., 2016; Toivonen & Tuominen, 2009) to the point where the topic is now considered as one of the main research priorities in the field of service research (Ostrom et al., 2015). This section first gives a brief overview of the origins and early views of service innovation discussion before turning its focus to the more recent systemic account of service innovation that is considered to be an "emerging" conceptual archetype within the literature (Helkkula et al., 2018).

Service Innovation: Origins and Early Views

The early works on service innovation, such as Barras's (1986) model of the "reverse innovation cycle" within service firms and Soete and Miozzo's (1989) taxonomy of different types of innovation characteristics of services, were important to carve out service innovation as its own distinct topic from the otherwise very product-focused innovation discussion. Within service management, increasing focus was placed on new service development (sometimes also called service design, see e.g., Edvardsson & Olsson, 1996; Gummesson, 1994) that can be seen as a precursor to the currently very vibrant service innovation discussion. Here, the special nature of service, such as the customer's role as a co-producer of service, were deemed important to consider in developing new services to the extent that any such efforts were seen as "a matter of creating conditions for producing added value for the customer" (Edvardsson & Olsson, 1996, p. 159).

Compared to these early "demarcation" views in which service innovation was portrayed as something completely different from product innovation due to the dominance of the latter, more and more of the recent work in service innovation represents that of a "synthesis" perspective (Coombs & Miles, 2000; Gallouj & Savona, 2009; Witell et al., 2016). Such studies use some kind of a transcending service-based view to understand the forms and types of innovation across industries and sectors (cf., Gallouj & Savona, 2009). Very often this is service-dominant (S-D) logic's conceptualization of service as a process of using one's resources for someone's benefit that drastically differs from the more traditional conceptualization of services as units of output (i.e., intangible products). S-D logic's tendency to zoom out its conceptualization of value cocreation into broader configurations of actors than just customer-service provider dyads has also very much led the service innovation discussion to see the emergence of the "systemic" conceptual archetype within the literature (Helkkula et al., 2018).

Service Innovation: Systems Turn

In an early example of an explicit systemic take on service innovation, Gallouj and Weinstein (1997) highlighted that one form of service innovation outcomes is recombinative innovations, in which clusters of innovations emerging from different service industries are combined in such a way as to constitute systems. Another early example of a systems view in service innovation literature relates to the discussion of the development and innovation of integrated solutions (Hakanen & Jaakkola, 2012; Windahl & Lakemond, 2006). The development of such solutions, defined as "bundles of products and/or services that meet customer specific needs and have higher potential for value creation than the individual parts would have alone," involves the collaboration between multiple actors, either within or between organizations (Hakanen & Jaakkola, 2012, p. 594).

This systemic view on the outcomes of service innovation was also complemented with a more systemic understanding of the process that leads to service innovation. In one of the earliest contributions of this nature, Toivonen and Tuominen (2009) show through extensive empirical observation that service innovations are rarely the results of a deliberate activity within service organizations. Rather "they emerge in the process of service provision on the basis of clients' needs, and are recognized as innovations only a *posterior*" (Toivonen & Tuominen, 2009, p. 887). As such, the innovation processes within service organizations take on also other forms than the traditional R&D model of innovation in which an idea emerges and is then developed further prior to any market application (ibid.). This insight is supported by Vargo et al. (2015), according to whom the systemic view of (service) innovation goes specifically against the stage-gate approach (i.e., basic research, applied research, development, production, and diffusion) of the linear model of innovation.

As discussed, the systems turn in service innovation is often coupled with S-D logic's processual conceptualization of service and the resulting realization of the interconnectedness of value cocreation. This led to scholars studying (service) innovation as "not just a new offering but rather improved customer value cocreation" (Rubalcaba et al., 2012, p. 697) and arguing that the product–service distinction should not constrain the understanding of innovation (Lusch & Nambisan, 2015). Lusch and Nambisan (2015) offered a broadened conceptualization of service innovation that is based on the meta-theoretical foundations of S-D logic. According to them (ibid., p. 161), service innovation is "the rebundling of diverse resources that create novel resources that are beneficial (i.e., value experiencing) to some actors in a given context; this almost always involves a network of actors, including the beneficiary (e.g., the customer)." Aligned with this, though not always explicitly using S-D logic, service innovation scholars have begun to highlight the cooperative nature and the participation of numerous actors beyond isolated firms within service innovation (Rajala et al., 2016; Rubalcaba et al., 2012). This also led several scholars to note that the proper unit of analysis for service innovation should not be the service offering but rather the service (eco)system (Edvardsson & Tronvoll, 2013; Lusch & Nambisan, 2015; Rubalcaba et al., 2012).

The theorization of service systems or service ecosystems in connection to service innovation led scholars to acknowledge the critical roles of social structures. Edvardsson and Tronvoll (2013, p. 20), for example, argued that service innovation can be viewed as "a phenomenon embedded in social structures and taking place within social systems, in which actors adopt certain social positions and roles to interact and recreate social structures." Echoing this view, Barrett and colleagues (2015) highlighted explicitly the role of institutions and institutional arrangements as the all-too-often under-recognized, if not ignored, elements of innovation. The introduction of institutions—actor-generated rules, norms, and beliefs—and institutional arrangements—sets of interrelated institutions—as the fifth axiom of S-D logic (Vargo & Lusch, 2016) paved the way to scholars to view service innovation "a process that unfolds through changes in the institutional arrangements that govern resource integration practices in service ecosystems" (Koskela-Huotari et al., 2016, p. 2964). In many studies, service innovation is seen as equal to institutional work, that is, actors' purposeful efforts to create, disrupt, and maintain institutions (Baron et al., 2018; Vargo et al., 2015; Koskela-Huotari et al., 2016). Research in this stream has also highlighted the importance of institutional complexity—the multiplicity of institutional arrangements confronting actors with conflicting prescriptions for action (Siltaloppi et al., 2016) and plasticity—the ability of systems to adapt, take, and retake (Chandler et al., 2019) as the prerequisites of service innovations within service ecosystems.

Embracing systems thinking further, recent works have begun to highlight service innovation as an emergent property (Akaka et al., 2019, see also Koskela-Huotari, 2018). This view is supported by Miles (2008) who argues that because services are performed for particular clients in a particular circumstance, service innovation should be examined as emergent, interactive, and dynamic. Recent work is also arguing that the diffusion and, especially the institutionalization process of a novel value cocreation solution should be considered a part of the innovation process, rather than something separate from it (Vargo et al., 2020). Such a systemic conception of service innovation also points to the importance of the positive or negative feedback loops that enable or restrict the institutionalization of novel value cocreation solutions (ibid.). As such, the service innovation literature is increasingly moving away from a narrower focus on innovation outputs and acknowledging the critical role of both the process and the (institutional) context of innovation outcomes. More specifically, the literature has broadened its unit of analysis to that of the service (eco)system and is using more and more systems terminology and concepts to explain service innovation.

Convergence Toward Informing Service System Transformation

As shown above, both service design and service innovation literatures are increasingly embracing systems thinking which, we argue, is resulting in an increasing convergence of the two discussions. This section shows how the identified "systems turn" has increased the level of abstraction in the conceptualizations of both service design and service innovation to the extent that they can be seen to inform a common phenomenon: *service system transformation*. The section also shows how the two discussions, due to their varying research traditions and informing theories and disciplines, can be seen as distinct, yet complementary "windows" into this common phenomenon. The section ends by giving an account of the main insights within the emerging, intersectional understanding of service system transformation.

Convergence Toward a Common Phenomenon

Figure 1 illustrates the development of the service design and service innovation discourses over time. Initially, service design and service innovation were terms used more or less interchangeably within the umbrella phenomenon of new service development (see, e.g., Edvardsson & Olsson, 1996; Gummesson, 1994). From these common origins, the two concepts grew increasingly apart and over time developed into their own discourses that have been influenced by and studied within varying disciplinary settings. While service design is especially informed by marketing, operations management, information systems, and design disciplines (Joly et al., 2019), the intellectual background of service innovation also includes economics, engineering, and other social sciences (Witell et al., 2016). As such, the two literatures have become to reflect different research traditions and are uniquely positioned in relation to the phenomena under study.

Recent years have, however, witnessed both service design and service innovation discourses undergo a "systems turn," meaning that they both embrace a more holistic, rather than reductionistic, understanding of the outcomes of service design and innovation and the processes bringing forth such outcomes. This development is partly connected with both literatures becoming more integrated with service-dominant (S-D) logic and service science (see, e.g., Edvardsson & Tronvoll, 2013; Koskela-Huotari et al., 2016; Patrício et al., 2011; Vink et al., 2021a), but also with other forms of input such as systemic design (e.g., Wildhagen & Stralberg, 2021). By tracing the nature of this "systems turn, we argue that in addition to representing the direction to which both service innovation and service design discourses are turning, this development is also causing them to converge toward informing a common phenomenon as the level of abstraction within the conceptualizations of the two discourses is increasing. This transcending and common phenomenon we identify to be service system transformation is defined as "the reconfiguring of actors, resources, resource-integration practices, and the corresponding

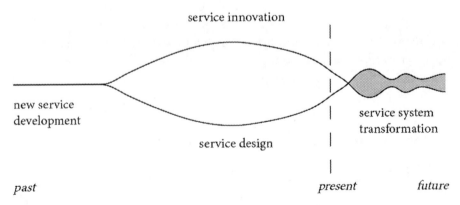

Fig. 1 Divergence and convergence of service design and service innovation discourses

institutional arrangements within or across service systems" (Koskela-Huotari et al., 2021, p. 344).

As a support for this argument, Table 1 includes illustrative examples of the systemic conceptualizations of service design and service innovation from the literature. These conceptualizations show how both discourses have begun to view their core phenomenon as something that occurs among value cocreating multi-actor configurations, where the actors within service systems seek to change the elements or practices involved in value cocreation (Kimbell, 2011; Edvardsson & Tronvoll, 2013; Lusch & Nambisan, 2015; Wetter-Edman

Table 1 Systemic conceptualizations of service design and service innovation

Systemic conceptualizations	
Service design	Service innovation
"...proposing and creating new kinds of value relation within a socio-material configuration involving diverse actors including people, technologies and artifacts" (Kimbell, 2011, p. 42)	"...changes in structure that stem from either a new configuration of resources or a new set of schemas and that result in new practices that are valuable to the actors in a specific context" (Edvardsson & Tronvoll, 2013, p. 24)
"...a continuous growth, movement and transformation of people, relationships and understandings" (Akama & Prendiville, 2013)	"...the rebundling of diverse resources that create novel resources that are beneficial (i.e., value experiencing) to some actors in a given context; this almost always involves a network of actors, including the beneficiary (e.g., the customer)" (Lusch & Nambisan, 2015, p. 161)"
"...explores service systems to understand them from the perspectives of actors, their value co-creation activities, experience and assessment of value-in-context in order to project/imagine and design new future service systems" (Wetter-Edman et al., 2014, p. 116)	"...the co-creation or collaborative recombination of practices that provide novel solutions for new or existing problems" (Vargo et al., 2015, p. 70)
"...a powerful transformative force that is capable of changing institutions" (Kurtmollaiev et al., 2018, p. 70)	"...a process that unfolds through changes in the institutional arrangements that govern resource integration practices in service ecosystems" (Koskela-Huotari et al., 2016, p. 2964)"
"...the intentional shaping of institutional arrangements and their physical enactments by actor collectives through reflexivity and reformation to facilitate the emergence of desired value cocreation forms" (Vink et al., 2021a, p. 169)	"...a process of changing value cocreation practices in service ecosystems that entails reconfiguring the institutional arrangements the actors are enacting" (Akaka et al., 2019, p. 652)

et al., 2014). The identification of these configurations as service systems or systems of such systems, that is, service ecosystems, has also led scholars to increasingly highlight the critical role of social structures, often discussed as institutional arrangements or institutional logics, as the object of change in both design and innovation efforts (Baron et al., 2018; Koskela-Huotari et al., 2016; Kurtmollaiev et al., 2018; Vargo et al., 2015; Vink et al., 2021a). Furthermore, it has also led scholars to realize the intentional and interventional nature of actors' efforts to shape social structures among the broader systemic and institutional processes at play within service systems (see, e.g., Vink et al., 2021a, Vargo et al., 2020). All in all, both discourses have converged to shed light on service system transformation, that is, how change within service systems and service ecosystems unfolds.

Complementary Nature as Perspectives

During their years apart (see Fig. 1), service design and service innovation discourses have been influenced by varying disciplinary inputs and, as such, grown to embrace different research assumptions and methods. Table 2 presents how the service design and service innovation discourses differ from one another in terms of their temporal and phenomenal positioning as well as in regard to the dominant research methods, levels of analysis, and research focuses. We argue that these differences are fruitful as they enable service design and service innovation to act as complementary "windows" into how service system transformation emerges and unfolds. They also illustrate the potential blind spots that each of the discourses may have regarding service system transformation as a phenomenon.

In regard to temporal positioning, service design research emphasizes potentiality as it is often aimed at understanding the shaping of desired future

Table 2. Perspective differences between service design and service innovation

	Service design	Service innovation
Temporal positioning	Prospective, working with potentiality	Retrospective, tracing path dependencies
Phenomenal positioning	Insider, part of the doing	Outsider, observing the doing and its outcomes
Dominant research methods	Action research, participatory methods	Case studies
Dominant level of analysis	Zoomed in	Zoomed out
Dominant research focuses	Methods, project perspective	Outcomes, impact

service systems (Wetter-Edman et al., 2014). On the other hand, service innovation as a form of inquiry mainly works with retrospective accounts of service systems transformation as usually there needs to be a change that is recognized as a service innovation before the research process begins (Baron et al., 2018; Koskela-Huotari et al., 2016). Thus, while service design will more likely offer prospective accounts of service system transformation, service innovation generates insights from a more retrospective perspective and traces its path dependencies.

In relation to phenomenal positioning, service design researchers are often situated as insiders to the service design process and part of the doing, recognizing that service design methods cannot be separated from people and that service system transformation starts with the people involved, thus privileging a first-hand perspective (Akama & Prendiville, 2013). Alternatively, the researchers studying service innovation tend to be positioned as observers analyzing the doing and its outcomes at a distance (Toivonen & Tuominen, 2009; Chandler et al., 2019). Hence, service design and service innovation discourses offer both "insider" and "outsider" insights into the phenomenon of service system transformation.

Informed by the disciplinary influences from design and information systems, the dominant research methods in service design are action-oriented research approaches, such as design science research and research through design, that work to catalyze the studied phenomena through the process of the research itself and generate practical knowledge (Patrício et al., 2019). On the contrary, research on service innovation tends to be primarily informed through case studies, using in-depth interviews, observations, and archival data to build theoretical knowledge (e.g., Chandler et al., 2019; Koskela-Huotari et al., 2016; Toivonen & Tuominen, 2009). The combination of service design and service innovation discourses, thus, brings forth multiple research methods with their own strengths that can offer valuable input into robust studies of service system transformation.

Through its approach, the dominant level of analysis in the literature on service design tends to relatively zoom in, focusing on practices and approaches for catalyzing service system transformation often employed by individuals and groups (e.g., Vink et al., 2019; Wetter-Edman et al., 2018). Literature on service innovation tends to focus mainly on a more zoomed-out level of analysis, attending to the transformation that the innovation efforts catalyze within and among organizations, industries, and markets (e.g., Koskela-Huotari et al., 2016; Rajala et al., 2016). In this way, the integration of insights and the use of both service design and service innovation in informing service systems transformation enables studying the phenomenon at several (analytical) levels of aggregation (e.g., micro, meso, and macro, cf., Vargo & Lusch, 2017).

In terms of the content of research that is in focus, service design discourse primarily concentrates on the development of new methods and the analysis of projects aiming at change (Patrício et al., 2011; Grenha Teixeira et al., 2017), whereas service innovation discourse tends to focus more on outcomes and the impact of such changes (Helkkula et al., 2018; Snyder et al., 2016). Due to these differences, service design and service innovation discourses can act as important, complementing perspectives in generating insights on service system transformation. The following section elaborates on the current state of this emerging, intersectional understanding.

The Emerging, Intersectional Understanding of Service System Transformation

The "systems turn" in service design and service innovation discourses has resulted both literatures to generate significant insights into how transformation in service systems emerges and unfolds. They do so, especially, by shedding light on the nature of the intentional design and innovation interventions, but also by contextualizing how these intentional efforts bring forth change as part of the broader systemic and institutional processes at play within service systems.

The "systems turn" in both service design and service innovation is characterized by scholars moving beyond attention to a temporary output toward a more holistic, processual understanding of service within the complex process of value cocreation (e.g., Kimbell, 2011; Edvardsson & Tronvoll, 2013). In doing so, these literatures both increasingly acknowledge the multi-actor nature of value cocreation, and the multi-actor nature of change that this implies (e.g., Patrício et al., 2018; Lusch & Nambisan, 2015). This has led to an extended understanding of the actors who are identified to be the "innovators" or the "designers" and an acknowledgment of the collective nature of innovation and design efforts (see, e.g., Vargo et al., 2015; Vink et al., 2021a). As such, this necessitates a broader, more inclusive study of multi-actor actions to understand service system transformation.

Within these literature streams, there is acknowledgment that institutionalized social structures are the core materials of all design and the source of both momentum and resistance in innovation efforts (e.g., Baron et al., 2018; Siltaloppi et al., 2016; Vink and Koskela-Huotari, 2021a). As such within service system transformation, these social structures are key leverage points for realizing intentional change. Both research streams also highlight the importance of institutionalized social structures in long-term change and their influence on people when designing and innovating (e.g., Koskela-Huotari et al., 2016; Kurtmollaiev et al., 2018). This is critical because it situates intentional efforts to catalyze service system transformation as being enabled and constrained by existing service systems and their structures, and necessitates deliberate strategies for actors to become reflexive or aware of prevailing social structures in order to intentionally shape them (Vink et al., 2021a). According to Vink and Koskela-Huotari (2021b), such reflexivity can be built with the help of service design methods by tapping into their affordances for different modes of reflexivity. Furthermore, recent research brings forward a critical understanding that people are part of the very systems they are trying to influence (Akama & Prendiville, 2013; Vink et al., 2019; Vink, Wetter-Edman, & Koskela-Huotari, 2021b). As such, service systems transformation cannot be understood as a process of change that is external to actors, but rather requires actors to change themselves, including their own patterns of thinking and acting.

Service design and service innovation can both be understood as intentional efforts by multiple actors to bring forth service system transformation. As previously mentioned, institutional work, the purposive shaping of institutionalized social structures, is recognized as a core process by which service system transformation can be intentionally catalyzed (Vargo et al., 2015; Vink et al., 2021a). However, in both research traditions, scholars recognize that the outcomes of design and innovation interventions are emergent and ever unfolding in and through the ongoing processes of self-adaptation of systems (Akama & Prendiville, 2013; Akaka et al., 2019). In particular, there is recognition that the outcomes of any deliberate efforts to catalyze service system transformation emerge through the dynamics catalyzed by both positive and negative feedback loops between a focal change effort and other conflicting and aligned intentional and unintentional actions (Vink et al., 2021a). This is critical for the understanding of service system transformation as it suggests that changes made in the system may have unintentional effect, and purposeful transformation demands an appreciation of the interplay between a complex constellation of actors and their actions.

These converging bodies of literature have started to identify important prerequisites of intentional service system transformation. In particular, institutional complexity, or conflicting prescriptions for actions from the multiplicity of institutionalized social structures, is needed for actors to even recognize the opportunity or need for change (Siltaloppi et al., 2016). Furthermore, reflexivity, an awareness of the multiplicity of social structures inhabited by oneself and others, is also needed, in order for actors to intentionally reshape these structures in service system (Vink & Koskela-Huotari, 2021b; Vink et al., 2021a). In addition, plasticity, the ability of service systems to adapt their form, is another prerequisite to such transformations (Chandler et al., 2019). Recognition of these prerequisites can aid scholars and practitioners in better understanding when, where, and why service system transformation is possible.

Through the integration of knowledge and research traditions from both service design and service innovation, a more holistic, robust, and nuanced understanding of strategic change efforts in service system can be developed. These common insights provide an important foundation for understanding the fundamental, transcendent phenomenon of service system transformation (Koskela-Huotari et al., 2021) which is at the core of both the theory and practice of service management.

2 Conclusion

In this chapter, we have shown how both service design and service innovation discourses are undergoing a "systems turn." We argue that this development is resulting in a convergence of the two research streams toward building an understanding of the transcending phenomenon of service system transformation. In other words, by highlighting their parallel integration of a systemic worldview and the emerging commonalities, we are bringing these two essential components of service management back together after nearly three decades of separation. We want to emphasize that our purpose here has not been to argue that service innovation and service design are (or are becoming) the same thing. Rather, we strongly believe that both discourses have their unique sets of strengths that through a careful reconciliation and integration can provide the basis for creating a very powerful framework of understanding how change within social systems can be initiated, fostered, institutionalized, and scaled. Importantly, both discourses also have their limitations and blind spots that the other discourse can help to reveal when scholars from both fields engage in a respectful dialogue and mutual process of learning. We hope that our chapter represents a stepping stone on this important journey.

References

Akaka, M. A., Koskela-Huotari, K., & Vargo, S. L. (2019). Further advancing service science with service-dominant logic: Service ecosystems, institutions, and their implications for innovation. In P. P. Maglio, C. A. Kieliszewski, J. C. Spohrer, K. Lyons, L. Patrício, & Y. Sawatani (Eds.), *Handbook of service science* (Vol. II, pp. 641–659). Springer International Publishing.

Akama, Y., & Prendiville, A. (2013). Embodying, enacting and entangling design: A phenomenological view to co-designing services. *Swedish Design Journal, 1*(13), 29–40.

Baron, S., Patterson, A., Maull, R., & Warnaby, G. (2018). Feed people first: A service ecosystem perspective on innovative food waste reduction. *Journal of Service Research, 21*(1), 135–150.

Barras, R. (1986). Towards a theory of innovation in services. *Research Policy, 15*(4), 161–173.

Barrett, M., Davidson, E., Prabhu, J., & Vargo, S. L. (2015). Service innovation in the digital age: Key contributions and future directions. *MIS Quarterly, 39*(1), 135–154.

Berry, L. L., Parasuraman, A., & Zeithaml, V. A. (1994). Improving service quality in America: Lessons learned. *Academy of Management Perspectives, 8*(2), 32–45.

Bitner, M. J. (1992). Servicescapes: The impact of physical surroundings on customers and employees. *Journal of Marketing, 56*(April), 57–71.

Bitner, M., Booms, B., & Tetreault, M. (1990). The service encounter: Diagnosing favorable and unfavorable incidents. *Journal of Marketing, 54*(1), 71–84.

Bitner, M. J., Ostrom, A. L., & Morgan, F. N. (2008). Service blueprinting: A practical technique for service innovation. *California Management Review, 50*(3), 66–94.

Čaić, M., Holmlid, S., Mahrz, D., & Odekerken-Schroder, G. (2019). Beneficiaries' view of actor networks: Service resonance for pluralistic actor networks. *International Journal of Design, 13*(3), 69–88.

Chandler, J. D., Danatzis, I., Wernicke, C., Akaka, M. A., & Reynolds, D. (2019). How does innovation emerge in a service ecosystem? *Journal of Service Research, 22*(1), 75–89.

Clatworthy, S. (2011). Service innovation through touch-points: Development of an innovation toolkit for the first stages of new service development. *International Journal of Design, 5*(2), 15–28.

Coombs, R., & Miles, I. (2000). Innovation, measurement and services: The new problematique. In J. S. Metcalfe & I. Miles (Eds.), *Innovation systems in the service economy - measurement and case study analysis* (pp. 85–103). Kluwer Academic Publishers.

Edvardsson, B. (1997). Quality in new service development: Key concepts and a frame of reference. *International Journal of Production Economics, 52*(1–2), 31–46.

Edvardsson, B., & Olsson, J. (1996). Key concepts for new service development. *Service Industries Journal, 16*(2), 140–164.

Edvardsson, B., & Tronvoll, B. (2013). A new conceptualization of service innovation grounded in SD logic and service systems. *International Journal of Quality and Service Sciences, 5*(1), 19–31.

Gallouj, F., & Savona, M. (2009). Innovation in services: A review of the debate and a research agenda. *Journal of Evolutionary Economics, 19*(2), 149.

Gallouj, F., & Weinstein, O. (1997). Innovation in services. *Research Policy, 26*(4–5), 537–556.

Grenha Teixeira, J., Patrício, L., Huang, K. H., Fisk, R. P., Nóbrega, L., & Constantine, L. (2017). The MINDS method: Integrating management and interaction design perspectives for service design. *Journal of Service Research, 20*(3), 240–258.

Gummesson, E. (1989). Nine lessons on service quality. *The TQM Magazine, 1*(2). https://doi.org/10.1108/EUM0000000002993

Gummesson, E. (1994). Service management: An evaluation and the future. *International Journal of Service Industry Management, 5*(1), 77–96.

Hakanen, T., & Jaakkola, E. (2012). Co-creating customer-focused solutions within business networks: A service perspective. *Journal of Service Management, 23*(4), 593–611.

Helkkula, A., Kowalkowski, C., & Tronvoll, B. (2018). Archetypes of service innovation: Implications for value cocreation. *Journal of Service Research, 21*(3), 284–301.

Joly, M. P., Teixeira, J. G., Patrício, L., & Sangiorgi, D. (2019). Leveraging service design as a multidisciplinary approach to service innovation. *Journal of Service Management, 30*(6), 681–715.

Junginger, S. (2015). Organizational design legacies and service design. *The Design Journal, 18*(2), 209–226.

Karpen, I. O., Gemser, G., & Calabretta, G. (2017). A multilevel consideration of service design conditions: Towards a portfolio of organisational capabilities, interactive practices and individual abilities. *Journal of Service Theory and Practice, 27*(2), 384–407.

Kimbell, L. (2011). Designing for service as one way of designing services. *International Journal of Design, 5*(2), 41–52.

Koskela-Huotari, K. (2018). *The evolution of markets—A service ecosystems perspective.* (PhD dissertation). Karlstad University, Karlstad University Press.

Koskela-Huotari, K., Edvardsson, B., Jonas, J. M., Sörhammar, D., & Witell, L. (2016). Innovation in service ecosystems—Breaking, making, and maintaining institutionalized rules of resource integration. *Journal of Business Research, 69*(8), 2964–2971.

Koskela-Huotari, K., Patrício, L., Zhang, J., Karpen, I. O., Sangiorgi, D., Anderson, L., & Bogicevic, V. (2021). Service system transformation through service design: Linking analytical dimensions and service design approaches. *Journal of Business Research, 136*, 343–355.

Kurtmollaiev, S., Fjuk, A., Pedersen, P. E., Clatworthy, S., & Kvale, K. (2018). Organizational transformation through service design: The institutional logics perspective. *Journal of Service Research, 21*(1), 59–74.

Lusch, R. F., & Nambisan, S. (2015). Service innovation: A service-dominant logic perspective. *MIS Quarterly, 39*(1), 155–175.

Meroni, A., & Sangiorgi, D. (2011). *Design for services.* Grower.

Miles, I. (2008). Patterns of innovation in service industries. *IBM Systems Journal, 47*(1), 115–128.

Morelli, N. (2002). Designing product/service systems: A methodological exploration. *Design Issues, 18*(3), 3–17.

Ostrom, A. L., Bitner, M. J., Brown, S. W., Burkhard, K. A., Goul, M., Smith-Daniels, V., Demirkan, H., & Rabinovich, E. (2010). Moving forward and making a difference: Research priorities for the science of service. *Journal of Service Research, 13*(1), 4–36.

Ostrom, A. L., Parasuraman, A., Bowen, D. E., Patrício, L., & Voss, C. A. (2015). Service research priorities in a rapidly changing context. *Journal of Service Research, 18*(2), 127–159.

Patrício, L., Fisk, R. P., & Falcão e Cunha, J. (2008). Designing multi-interface service experiences: The service experience blueprint. *Journal of Service Research, 10*(4), 318–334.

Patrício, L., Fisk, R. P., Falcão e Cunha, J, & Constantine, L. (2011). Multilevel service design: From customer value constellation to service experience blueprinting. *Journal of Service Research, 14*(2), 180–200.

Patrício, L., Gustafsson, A., & Fisk, R. (2018). Upframing service design and innovation for research impact. *Journal of Service Research, 21*(1), 3–16.

Patrício, L., Grenha Teixeira, J., & Vink, J. (2019). A service design approach to healthcare innovation: From decision-making to sense-making and institutional change. *AMS Review, 9*(1), 115–120.

Rajala, R., Gallouj, F., & Toivonen, M. (2016). Introduction to the special issue on multiactor value creation in service innovation: Collaborative value creation in service. *Service Science, 8*(3), iii–viii.

Rubalcaba, L., Michel, S., Sundbo, J., Brown, S. W., & Reynoso, J. (2012). Shaping, organizing, and rethinking service innovation: A multidimensional framework. *Journal of Service Management, 23*(5), 696–715.

Sangiorgi, D. (2009). Building up a framework for service design research. *Proceedings of the 8th European Academy of Design Conference*, Scotland, Aberdeen, 415–420.

Sangiorgi, D., & Prendiville, A. (2015). A theoretical framework for studying service design practices: First steps to a mature field. *Design Management Journal, 9*(1), 61–73.

Sangiorgi, D., Patrício, L., & Fisk, R. (2017). Designing for interdependence, participation and emergence in complex service systems. In D. Sangiorgi & A. Prendiville (Eds.), *Designing for service: Key issues and new directions, ebook* (pp. 72–86). Bloomsbury.

Secomandi, F., & Snelders, D. (2011). The object of service design. *Design Issues, 27*(3), 20–34.

Shostack, G. L. (1982). How to design a service. *European Journal of Marketing, 16*(1), 49–63.

Siltaloppi, J., Koskela-Huotari, K., & Vargo, S. L. (2016). Institutional complexity as a driver for innovation in service ecosystems. *Service Science, 8*(3), 333–343.

Snyder, H., Witell, L., Gustafsson, A., Fombelle, P., & Kristensson, P. (2016). Identifying categories of service innovation: A review and synthesis of the literature. *Journal of Business Research, 69*(7), 2401–2408.

Soete, L., & Miozzo, M. (1989). *Trade and development in services: A technological perspective* (Report No. 89–031). Maastricht Economic Research Institute on Innovation and Technology (MERIT), Limburg University.

Stuart, I. (1998). The influence of organizational culture and internal politics on new service design and introduction. *International Journal of Service Industry Management, 9*(5), 469–485.

Tax, S. S., & Stuart, I. (1997). Designing and implementing new services: The challenges of integrating service systems. *Journal of Retailing, 73*(1), 105–134.

Toivonen, M., & Tuominen, T. (2009). Emergence of innovations in services. *The Service Industries Journal, 29*(7), 887–902.

Trischler, J., & Westman Trischler, J. (2021). Design for experience—A public service design approach in the age of digitalization. *Public Management Review.* https://doi.org/10.1080/14719037.2021.1899272

Vargo, S. L., & Lusch, R. F. (2016). Institutions and axioms: An extension and update of service-dominant logic. *Journal of the Academy of Marketing Science, 44*(4), 5–23.

Vargo, S. L., & Lusch, R. F. (2017). Service-dominant logic 2025. *International Journal of Research in Marketing, 34*(1), 46–67.

Vargo, S. L., Wieland, H., & Akaka, M. A. (2015). Innovation through institutionalization: A service ecosystems perspective. *Industrial Marketing Management, 44*, 63–72.

Vargo, S. L., Akaka, M. A., & Wieland, H. (2020). Rethinking the process of diffusion in innovation: A service-ecosystems and institutional perspective. *Journal of Business Research, 16*, 526–534.

Vink, J. (2019). *In/visible—Conceptualizing service ecosystem design.* (PhD dissertation). Karlstad University, Karlstad University Press.

Vink, J., & Koskela-Huotari, K. (2021a). Social structures as service design materials. *International Journal of Design, 15*(3), 29–43.

Vink, J., & Koskela-Huotari, K. (2021b). Building reflexivity using service design methods. *Journal of Service Research.* https://doi.org/10.1177/10946705211035004

Vink, J., Edvardsson, B., Wetter-Edman, K., & Tronvoll, B. (2019). Reshaping mental models—Enabling innovation through service design. *Journal of Service Management, 30*(1), 75–104.

Vink, J., Koskela-Huotari, K., Tronvoll, B., Edvardsson, B., & Wetter-Edman, K. (2021a). Service ecosystem design: Propositions, process model, and future research agenda. *Journal of Service Research, 24*(2), 168–186.

Vink, J., Wetter-Edman, K., & Koskela-Huotari, K. (2021b). Designerly approaches to shaping social systems: The social structures approach. *She Ji: The Journal of Design, Economics, and Innovation, 7*(2), 242–261.

Wetter-Edman, K., Sangiorgi, D., Edvardsson, B., Holmlid, S., Grönroos, C., & Mattelmäki, T. (2014). Design for value co-creation: Exploring synergies between design for service and service logic. *Service Science, 6*(2), 106–121.

Wetter-Edman, K., Vink, J., & Blomkvist, J. (2018). Staging aesthetic disruption through design methods for service innovation. *Design studies, 55*(March), 5–26.

Wildhagen, B., & Stralberg, E. (2021). Combining service and systemic design in Norway's public sector: How StimuLab supports user-oriented experimentation and innovation. *Touchpoint—The Journal of Service Design, 12*(2), 36–39.

Windahl, C., & Lakemond, N. (2006). Developing integrated solutions: The importance of relationships within the network. *Industrial Marketing Management, 35*(7), 806–818.

Witell, L., Snyder, H., Gustafsson, A., Fombelle, P., & Kristensson, P. (2016). Defining service innovation: A review and synthesis. *Journal of Business Research, 69*(8), 2863–2872.

Yu, E., & Sangiorgi, D. (2014). Service design as an approach to new service development: Reflections and future studies. *The Proceedings of the Fourth Service Design and Innovation Conference*. Lancaster, United Kingdom, 194–204.

Zomerdijk, L. G., & Voss, C. A. (2010). Service design for experience-centric services. *Journal of Service Research, 13*(1), 67–82.

Service Innovation in Networks: Co-creating a Network Business Model

Kars Mennens, Dominik Mahr, Paul C. van Fenema, Tom Schiefer, and Adriana Saraceni

1   Introduction

Increasingly, studies in service innovation research stress the important role of networks in accessing resources for innovation (Raddats et al., 2019). In particular, digital opportunities demand firms to tap into resources beyond their own organization when innovating (Sjödin et al., 2020). Specifically for service innovation in B2B markets, cooperation is essential to leverage economic, social, and cognitive experiences that customers desire (Acharya et al., 2020).

K. Mennens (✉) • T. Schiefer • A. Saraceni
Department of Marketing & Supply Chain Management and Brightlands Institute of Supply Chain Innovation (BISCI), School of Business and Economics, Maastricht University, Maastricht, Netherlands
e-mail: k.mennens@maastrichtuniversity.nl; t.schiefer@maastrichtuniversity.nl; a.saraceni@maastrichtuniversity.nl

D. Mahr
Department of Marketing & Supply Chain Management and Service Science Factory (SSF), School of Business and Economics, Maastricht University, Maastricht, Netherlands
e-mail: d.mahr@maastrichtuniversity.nl

P. C. van Fenema
Department of Military Business Studies, Faculty of Military Sciences, Netherlands Defence Academy, Breda, Netherlands
e-mail: pc.v.fenema@mindef.nl

© The Author(s), under exclusive license to Springer Nature Switzerland AG 2022   **555**
B. Edvardsson, B. Tronvoll (eds.), *The Palgrave Handbook of Service Management*, https://doi.org/10.1007/978-3-030-91828-6_28

In line with Mustak (2014, p. 152), we denote this as network service innovation or "the process of innovating services through combining the ideas, knowledge, capabilities and technologies of more than two interconnected actors."

Service innovation requires the creation of joint value together with stakeholders (Vargo & Lusch, 2008). However, kick-starting such co-creation with stakeholders presents organizations with a daunting challenge: How to achieve early alignment among the stakeholders regarding the joint value proposition or resources dedicated (Larsson et al., 1998)? Even though researchers have pointed at obstacles (Thorgren et al., 2009) and made suggestions on how to overcome cognitive barriers or develop trust (Eisingerich et al., 2009; Skippari et al., 2017), there is a lack of research that explicates how organizations could achieve alignment as they develop network business models and value propositions (Payne & Frow, 2014). In this vein, service research increasingly calls for innovation studies that extend the level of analysis to the network level (Barile et al., 2016). In practice, many network collaborations fail (Bierly & Gallagher, 2007; Weigel & Hadwich, 2018). Often, the lack of a common vision of the value proposition, inequality of commercial returns, or the lack of trust within the network are causing these failures (Engelbracht et al., 2019). We therefore consider early-stage alignment on elements of the network business model a complex craft for practitioners: in order to materialize strategic motives for service cooperation, partners need to articulate and calibrate their interests on the organizational, dyadic (so between two organizations), and network level (Jocevski et al., 2020).

In this chapter, we contribute to filling the knowledge gap related to the process of achieving early-stage alignment for network service innovation. We assume an initial answer to the "why" of service-oriented network cooperation, that is, partners have been selected (Lumineau & Oliveira, 2018). Our focus is on shifting from this initial "why" toward the "how" of cooperation, bridging strategic views on network cooperation and service design. We take an action-based research approach to closely interact with practitioners involved in the complex craft of early-stage alignment for network service innovation. We propose a service design-based process that is supported by generative scripts for the organizational level, the interorganizational dyadic level, and multi-organizational network level. They provide practitioners with a methodology to achieve early-stage alignment on elements of the network business model such as the network value proposition. We showcase our methodology in an illustrative case study on data science within a maritime service logistics network. Data science combines classical disciplines such as statistics, data mining, databases, and distributed systems in an effort to make abundantly available data more valuable (van der Aalst, 2016), thereby providing opportunities for digital service innovation.

Our chapter offers three contributions to theory. First, we advance service research by developing a methodology for early-stage alignment of partners for network service innovation. Successful collaboration in a service network is a challenge, causing many networks to fail (Weigel & Hadwich, 2018). Our methodology allows organizations to create early alignment on essential elements of the network business model, such as the network value proposition, thereby preventing a potential lack of a common vision of value creation or merely superficial alignment. Second, our developed strategic process maps out the value constellation of the network partners which enable the development of specific, user-centered service concepts, hereby enriching service design research. Rather than viewing the value network as a spontaneous co-creation combination, we offer a systematic approach where network actors iteratively co-create shared value propositions. These constructs undergird future network innovation and prepare for new institutional arrangements (Kowalkowski & Witell, 2020). Third, we contribute to the literature on the multi-level nature of network business models. Recently, researchers have called for action-based research to deepen our understanding of these multiple levels (Jocevski et al., 2020). The generative scripts we developed delineate the elements that should be considered at each of the different levels of the network business model. Thereby, they equip practitioners and academics with a basic template to articulate the *who, what, how,* and *why* of network business models.

Upon presenting the theoretical background of service innovation networks in the next section, we introduce the empirical context and research methodology. Next, we present our findings, which lead to the theoretical and managerial implications and suggestions for further research.

2 Conceptual Background

In this section, we discuss the conceptual background against which we develop our methodology to achieve early-stage alignment for network service innovation. First, we consider extant literature on service innovation in networks. Second, we discuss the importance of the business model and value proposition in achieving early-stage alignment for network service innovation. Finally, we turn to service design literature to explain how a network business model and value proposition can be constructed.

Service Innovation in Networks

Service innovation refers to the creation of new value propositions by developing existing or creating new collaborative practices and/or resources, or else by integrating practices and resources in new ways (Liu et al., 2020; Skålén et al., 2015). Whereas traditionally service innovation research departed from a manufacturer-centric perspective, these efforts have evolved toward a multi-actor co-creation perspective (Grönroos, 2011). Organizations that develop new digital services often need to do so through network efforts (Barrett et al., 2015; Nylén & Holmström, 2015). Accessing that knowledge often requires collaboration with customers, suppliers, competitors, public sector agencies, universities, or other knowledge institutions (Laursen & Salter, 2006). External collaboration is essential in services contexts (Leiponen, 2005; Mina et al., 2014), because these innovations require joint actions across a network, rather than within any one organization (Lusch & Nambisan, 2015).

Network service innovation promises new business benefits, as explored in prior literature pertaining to servitization strategies (Lay, 2014), service business models (Ojasalo & Ojasalo, 2018), and operational strategies (Baines et al., 2009). To this end, identifying the right partners is a critical success factor for developing new value propositions (Liu et al., 2020). With these partners, dynamic interactions can lead to new network configurations, in which a (temporary) equilibrium results from the adoption of new resources, new practices, and a reallocation of roles across the network (Liu et al., 2020; van Fenema & Keers, 2018). However, we still lack a clear understanding of how network collaboration and organizational change are achieved (Kowalkowski et al., 2017; Vendrell-Herrero et al., 2017). Studying business models at the network level may provide the necessary insights into early-stage alignment for network service innovation and ensure preparation for service design. Network business models shed light on the orchestration of various involved actors, their resources, and the necessary activities aimed at developing such service innovations (Jocevski et al., 2020). As such, we argue that agreement on the business model reflects early-stage alignment and that it provides the overarching value narrative for service design in networks (Tax et al., 2013). In the next section, we discuss business models and value propositions from a network-level perspective.

Business Models and Value Propositions to Achieve Early-Stage Alignment

Business models articulate the logic that demonstrates how value is created and delivered (Teece, 2010). In turn, Schön (2012) argues that organizations reflect their business model, which details their value proposition, revenues, and costs (Osterwalder & Pigneur, 2010; Schön, 2012; Teece, 2018). In extant literature, researchers typically refer to these dimensions as pertaining to a specific company and take a firm-centric perspective on the concept. However, an increasing number of authors argue that the development of digital service innovations demands the design of a business model beyond the single firm perspective (Jocevski et al., 2020). Potential revenues and costs remain highly uncertain in such collaborative and exploratory innovation processes. Hence, the network value proposition should be the central element of the business model for network service innovation (Teece, 2018). A value proposition can be defined as "an encapsulation of a strategic management decision on what the company believes its customers value the most and what it is able to deliver that gives it competitive advantage" (Payne & Frow, 2014, p. 215).

As conceptualized at the network level (Bankvall et al., 2017), we define the network value proposition as strategic management decisions about what organizations believe establish a win-win situation for the network by creating the most value for each individual organization. This view is consistent with the service-dominant (S-D) logic, which stresses the need for multiple actors to participate and collaborate to offer value propositions (Vargo & Lusch, 2016). Therefore, a network value proposition consists of network- and organizational-level commitments and content elements that synchronize goals and risks. Establishing network configurations that provide resources and define interaction practices and roles is critical for developing new value propositions (Liu et al., 2020). In the following section, we turn to the literature on service design to explain how the network business model and value propositions can be constructed to achieve early-stage network alignment.

Designing the Network Business Model and Value Proposition

The development of new customer-centric value propositions and new service concepts are central to service design (Patrício et al., 2019), which increasingly shifts toward investigating the value constellations in networks of actors

(Patrício et al., 2020). Successful innovation in such service networks demands creating new, and altering existing rules between the actors as to how the resources are integrated (Koskela-Huotari et al., 2016), and considering activities at multiple network levels and their interdependencies in practice (Karpen et al., 2017). To complement this initial research, service design would benefit from taking a strategic perspective to understand under what institutional rules actors would commit to a shared value creation prior to the actual service concept development. The study should employ an action-oriented approach that involves network actors to co-create future resource constellations and to iteratively define equilibria between the various resource holders and beneficiaries (Čaić et al., 2019).

A recent literature review provides some guidelines on how to design the network business model by positioning it as a multi-level concept consisting of (1) an organizational-level that represents the value architecture of a particular organization (Keen & Williams, 2013), (2) a dyadic-level where the business model acts as the linking agent between two organizations (Mangematin & Baden-Fuller, 2015), and (3) the network-level which acts as a relational aggregator (Jocevski et al., 2020). Besides these levels, the network business model contains four dimensions: The *who, what, how,* and *why* (Jocevski et al., 2020). *Who* refers to the actors that are part of the network, their different roles, and the value exchange between them (Komulainen et al., 2006). Whereas *what* relates to the network value proposition (Palo & Tähtinen, 2013), *how* is about the specific activities that create network value (Andersson & Mattsson, 2015). Finally, *why* refers to the reasons underlying network service innovation collaboration, such as mutual dependency to achieve common strategic objectives (Iivari et al., 2016). These levels and dimensions of the network business model provide the basic structure for the generative scripts as presented in the results section. Developing and using these scripts constitute our methodology to relate strategic views on network cooperation and service design, and thereby achieve early-stage alignment. Our empirical approach is explained next.

3 Methodology

Empirical Setting

A service logistics network dedicated to the development and maintenance of maritime equipment for a Navy organization provides our study context. This network is appropriate for addressing our research objective for several reasons. First, the network comprises companies and subsidiaries of multinationals with a prolonged history of interactions, so they have built trust over time that contributes to their willingness to collaborate. The current network is part of a larger, open innovation consortium that engages in dialogue and has offered some initial commitment to service innovation collaboration and a shared servitization roadmap, though with limited network-level investments so far (Pikka et al., 2011). Interpersonal contacts across organizational boundaries tend to be intense within this network, but interorganizational relationships have been mostly transactional.

Second, the vessels maintained by the network have a very high value and a long asset lifecycle (several decades), but they get renewed and updated with new software and systems during maintenance. They also rely on complex technologies, requiring sophisticated, increasingly digitized services that complement the primary products. Thus, they constitute complex product-service systems (Zhang et al., 2017). Due to the longevity of the underlying assets, network service innovation processes persist for the long term and involve intense collaboration among network partners.

Third, in this maritime service logistics network, three organizations actively seek to develop digital service innovations collectively by leveraging their data science capabilities. The studied project in particular focuses on how data storage and quantitative business process analysis can result in service innovation (van der Aalst, 2016). Our study focuses on this particular project carried out by the three organizations. We refer to these as BuildCo, a global shipbuilding and maritime service company that acknowledges industry dynamics and thus has invested in digital product development and service capabilities; ShipCo, a Navy organization that operates the ships and maintains them in cooperation with industry actors; and ElecCo, an international system integrator, responsible for products and services.

Research Design and Data Analysis

The phenomenon of network service innovation remains largely unexplored, so we conducted a qualitative, nested case study with an action-based research approach. Qualitative case study research offers an effective way to gain new knowledge about a specific phenomenon (Eisenhardt, 1989) and make a conceptual contribution (Siggelkow, 2007). We implemented a nested case study approach (Thomas, 2011), so the results that emerge from the network and participating organizations are integrated and evaluated holistically across the multiple levels of analysis. Unlike a regular multiple case study, a nested version gains integrity from a wider case, such as the maritime service logistics network. The primary unit of analysis is the data science network of three organizations.

Action research provides inputs into ongoing dynamic processes through collaborative inquiry; researchers participate alongside practitioners as insiders who solve practical problems (Lindhult & Hazy, 2016). As such, the research question was defined in a collaborative effort between the researchers and practitioners (Nenonen et al., 2017). The data collection and interaction among the research team and practitioners took various forms over a multi-year timeframe. For example, interaction, knowledge sharing, and feedback took place during plenary meetings of the open innovation project at the consortium level. We provided status updates about the particular data science project and received additional feedback, while keeping control of the theorizing process (Nenonen et al., 2017). During interviews with members of the three companies, BuildCo, ShipCo, and ElecCo, informants filled in the scripts. Furthermore, the network validated the scripts and designed a service innovation concept during a four-hour face-to-face workshop that we led. During this workshop, we gathered the participants' outputs created during the workshop and engaged in extensive notetaking as well.

In line with Nenonen et al.'s (2017) suggestion, we employed an abductive approach, such that we went back and forth between theoretical insights from literature and empirical observations based on the interviews, workshops, scripts, and plenary sessions. Abduction covers the middle ground between induction and deduction, allowing for the interplay between conceptual and empirical domains (Nenonen et al., 2017). Specifically, we leveraged existing theory in developing the scripts and preparing the interviews and workshop, and employed textual analysis to our novel empirical observations emanating from the interactions with the practitioners.

4 Results

In this section, we present the results of this chapter in four steps. First, we offer an overview of our proposed early-stage alignment process. Second, we provide insight into how the generative scripts were designed and included as a key component in the early-stage alignment methodology. Third, we discuss the findings related to the generative scripts emanating from our illustrative case study. Finally, we conclude with a reflection on the main outcomes of the early-stage alignment process for network service innovation.

Early-Stage Alignment Process

Our methodology regarding how organizations can develop early alignment for network service innovation consists of four main iterative steps inspired by service design processes and principles (Mahr et al., 2013), and is depicted in Fig. 1.

First, in the *Define* phase, data is gathered about the network's needs (Liedtka, 2015). In our case, the overarching goal was set to achieve early-stage alignment on data-driven service innovation collaboration. Second, during the *Ideate* phase, individual and plenary sessions determine the network's perspective on what constitutes early alignment. This input provides the basis for the design of generative scripts that are created by the researchers, filled with content by the practitioners, and collectively validated in the third phase: *Develop*. During the fourth and final phase, *Evaluate*, the network assesses whether alignment is achieved and whether this provides a foundation for further network service innovation collaboration and iteration of the process.

Scripts and Network Service Innovation

The generative scripts are templates that provide a minimal structure for the development of new insights; they elicit practitioners' thoughts on early alignment regarding service innovations in networks (Boxenbaum & Rouleau, 2011; Okhuysen & Eisenhardt, 2002). The semi-structured nature of the generative scripts granted practitioners enough freedom to express their individual organization's perspective and expectations, while we as researchers remained in control of the overall research agenda. We developed three scripts, each focused on the different levels and aspects or considerations of business models and value propositions in networks (Jocevski et al., 2020):

(1) Network-level perspective on the goals, composition, resources, and functioning of the network;

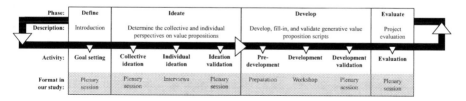

Fig. 1 Overview of the early-stage alignment process for network service innovation

564   K. Mennens et al.

(2) Organizational-level perspective to zoom in on the partner-specific roles, goals, resources, and challenges;
(3) Relationship-level perspective that sheds light on dyadic relationship dynamics across organizations.

The scripts are shown in Tables 1, 2, and 3 and include the data in light gray italics. The content of the scripts relates to generic network collaboration dimensions, in the context of service innovation, such as goal setting and instrumentality (i.e., how to achieve goals), which was informed by extant literature on business models and value propositions (e.g., Jocevski et al., 2020; Levina & Ross, 2003; Osterwalder & Pigneur, 2010; Payne & Frow, 2014; Rumble & Minto, 2017). Once we developed the scripts, they were provided to company representatives by the researchers during workshops and interviews. We invited them to reflect on their current practices and fill in the script forms. With this design effort, the researchers' knowledge base is combined with the environment. The practitioners' responses formed the basis for subsequent group discussions and ultimately generated the consensus constituting early-stage alignment. We combined both individual and collective sessions since such design efforts require individual creativity. All in all, achieving consensus represents a collaborative effort in which sharing information and ideas is essential (Prud'homme van Reine, 2017).

Findings from Illustrative Case Study

Within the wider maritime service logistics network, the initial suggestion was raised that BuildCo, ShipCo, and ElecCo could potentially collaborate on network service innovation. This was sparked by the recognition of greater digital service innovation opportunities, particularly stemming from data science, combined with the realization that innovations in this field could not be achieved by any firms individually or through traditional bilateral relationships (Sjödin et al., 2020). Innovation for digital services often requires multiple actors to collaborate (Tronvoll et al., 2020).

On the basis of the input gathered during the *Ideate* phase, we generated the scripts as depicted in Tables 1, 2, and 3 (text in gray italics indicates examples of the practitioners' responses). We distinguish network, partner, and relationship levels; these levels define the focus of our analyses for investigating early-stage alignment for network service innovation (Jocevski et al., 2020). We acknowledge that the achievement of network service innovation alignment implies a process that demands a continuing role by the associated

Service Innovation in Networks: Co-creating a Network Business... 565

Table 1 Network-level generative script (script 1 of 3)

Network-level generative script	
The network around the	*Data science case.*
Aims to serve	*ShipCo as a customer. The main goal of the network is to improve the performance of ShipCo's vessels at the lowest total cost of ownership. The underlying goals are to acquire knowledge by setting up a data infrastructure, share/ generate data, and integrate subsystems to provide added value to the network.*
By achieving	*Data-driven maintenance to increase vessel availability and standardization by harmonizing the interfaces of data sharing, while continuing the use of organization-specific systems.*
Through	*Data sharing to support AI-based predictive maintenance models. Possibly, but not necessarily, combine operational models in shared projects.*
Performed by	*Combining data from ShipCo, BuildCo, and ElecCo.*
The collaboration is supported informally by	*Contact between experts who meet in a combined data science pilot team.*
And formally by	*Defining the roles of each party in a strategic cooperation agreement, having signed a non-disclosure agreement, and setting up contracts.*
A win-win-win situation is created and maintained if	*There is improved maintenance for ShipCo and capability development for BuildCo and ElecCo to be used in external markets.*
In 5 years, the network will	*Achieve significant performance improvement through co-creation among the network partners, while finding a balance between an open platform to integrate and a closed structure to protect each company's data.*

actors, afforded for instance through resources provided (Vargo & Lusch, 2016).

The organizations in the network formulated a combined goal to be pursued collectively, in the form of a network value proposition, as well as a shared understanding of each organization's resource contributions. In terms of content, the emerging network value proposition combined (1) improved maintenance and performance of the Navy organization's assets at the lowest total cost of ownership, with (2) greater development of each supplier's capabilities to leverage in their respective markets.

To deliver this network value proposition, a network-level goal (Table 1) was established, namely, to develop new service innovations proactively within the network, enabled by data science.

566 K. Mennens et al.

Table 2 Organizational-level generative script (script 2 of 3)

Organizational-level generative script, ElecCo	
The network around the	*Data science case.*
Includes the partners	*ShipCo and BuildCo.*
That aims to achieve, within the network	*Increased performance at equal or lower costs. The underlying aims are to avoid unexpected technical failures and enable data-driven, condition-based maintenance, integrated and real-time awareness of the ship's condition, data correlations, and catering to limited crew size aboard the ships.*
And beyond the network	*Capability development to be leveraged in external markets, similar to BuildCo. There is a situation of coopetition with BuildCo with respect to sharing knowledge for external markets.*
And wants to avoid	*Unavailability of ships and unpredictable performance. Also, starting the cooperation without having the different roles of each company clearly defined, risking overlapping interests or unclear intellectual property protections.*
The partner involves	*Data analysts, participation in steering committee of data science pilot.*
Who contribute competences, knowledge, or expertise such as	*Predictive maintenance models.*
And resources or assets such as	*ElecCo's owned configuration data.*
While facing challenges such as	*Availability of data, including classified data, which other parties in the network may not want to share.*
The partner has its own network	*Around data science there is only the cooperation with ShipCo and BuildCo.*
And revenue model	*Co-create within the network to explore external market opportunities.*
The partner's role in the network is best described as	*Owner, operator, core maintainer.*

On the individual partner (organizational) level (Table 2), it resulted in anticipated opportunities and benefits, such as being able to satisfy the customer within the network, as well as other customers in the longer term. However, working toward the network-level goal also led to risks and challenges for each individual partner, such as worries about intellectual property or data protection.

Finally, on the relationship level (Table 3), the goal to achieve improved performance at the lowest total cost of ownership, through network service innovation, generated dyadic risks, such as worrying about being able to

Table 3 Relationship-level generative script (script 3 of 3)

Relationship-level generative script, ShipCo & ElecCo		
ShipCo → ElecCo *Open relationship.*	**Dyadic Expectations: Hopes**	**ElecCo → ShipCo** *Data and knowledge sharing with an open mind.*
Influenced by circumstances: Political decisions, bankruptcy, hostile clients.	**Risks: Worries**	*There may not be enough data sharing, and data usage may not be correct.*
Interaction *Information sharing in the form of sensor data, configuration data, and usage data. Sharing is starting to happen. In previous collaborations, data and information were not made available. Difficulties of sharing data include (1) not being paid for data to reduce costs in building phase, (2) protecting own data, (3) not actively having collected data before, and (4) sensitive data is not always allowed to be shared.*		
ShipCo → ElecCo –	**Flow of: Material**	**ElecCo → ShipCo** *Provision of sensors.*
ShipCo paid part of the installation costs for the engineering service.	**Financial**	–
Sensor data.	**Data**	*The tools ElecCo is using, as well as configuration data.*

manage interorganizational processes despite differences in organizational agility, but also potential benefits, such as integrating specific skills and expertise.

Reflection on Early-Stage Alignment for Network Service Innovation

During early-stage alignment, organizations lay the foundation for a service ecosystem in strategic value and design-delivery terms (Vink et al., 2020). The illustrative case study led to three main outcomes of the early-stage alignment process for network service innovation. The first outcome relates to the articulation of a combined goal to be pursued collectively (Shinkle et al., 2012), involving learning from each other and building mutual awareness. The second outcome is the anticipation and distribution of the capabilities and resources required for network service innovation (Karpen et al., 2017).

Lastly, the third outcome of the early-stage alignment process refers to the emotions and feelings that come to light, such as worries about future coordination efforts, data sharing, and IP. We learned that early-stage alignment concerns these three interrelated outcomes: a combined goal, feasibility, and processed emotions. Careful crafting of these outcomes influences the likelihood of successfully progressing through subsequent collaboration phases—including institutional arrangements and service design—required for network service innovation.

5 Discussion

Pursuing digital opportunities forces firms to bundle resources when innovating (Sjödin et al., 2020). Therefore, modern organizations increasingly aspire to engage in digital service innovation collectively, in networks (Raddats et al., 2019). This requires the exploration of more flexible, multidisciplinary collaboration between relevant stakeholders (Gray et al., 2011). However, often these collaborations fail due to the lack of a common vision for the network, unequal distribution of commercial returns, or the absence of trust. Better insight in early-stage alignment increases the chances of success. In this chapter, we develop and illustrate a methodology consisting of a four-stage iterative process and generative scripts. This methodology enables organizations to overcome these challenges and achieve early-stage alignment for network service innovation. In turn, such early-stage alignment should lead to a common goal, fair distribution of capabilities and resources, and processed emotions.

Theoretical Implications

Our chapter offers four contributions to theory. First, we advance service research by offering a methodology for establishing early-stage alignment for network service innovation. Successful network service innovation collaboration is a challenge, since it is difficult to establish a common vision for the network, develop trust, and ensure equal commercial returns (Engelbracht et al., 2019). By enabling early-stage alignment on essential elements of a network business model, in particular the network value proposition, our methodology enables networks to overcome the difficulties associated with network service innovation. Our process and generative scripts provide novel insights into the growing body of literature on achieving network service innovation. Second, we contribute to the contextual dimension of service design research by offering a strategic process that precedes the development of new service concepts involving multiple actors in a network. Our scripts facilitate the participation of various stakeholders in the iterative co-creation of a shared value proposition, alignment on institutional rules, and ensure commitment on resources integration. Moving from dyadic value propositions toward a network value proposition implies more complex resource constellations and balancing out several dyadic relationships within a service network until an equilibrium is found (Čaić et al., 2019). Third, we develop the body of literature related to the multi-level nature of network business models. Recently, researchers have conceptualized the network business model on multiple levels: single-firm, dyadic, and network. They have called for action-based research to deepen our understanding of this concept (Jocevski et al., 2020). The generative scripts we developed through our action-based approach delineate the elements that should be considered at each of the levels of the network business model. These scripts provide a basic template to investigate into the *who, what, how,* and *why* of network business models. Fourth, we advance scholarly literature pertaining to network value propositions. The value proposition is a key concept in services literature, since services are defined in terms of customer-determined benefit (Vargo & Lusch, 2008), and the value proposition articulates how customer value is created (Payne & Frow, 2014). Ballantyne et al. (2011) suggest that case study research and action research strategies can be leveraged to explore co-creational approaches to value proposition development. In turn, through action research, our process operationalizes the construction of the network value proposition, consisting of network-, organization-, and relationship-level commitments to achieve collective value creation.

Managerial and Societal Implications

This chapter grants managers an effective method for initiating service innovation collaboration in a network. They face the daunting task of forging new value linkages between their own organizations and potential partner organizations. Our method enables organizations to overcome some of the challenges related to early-stage network collaboration. For instance, collective validation of a network value proposition ensures that a common vision for the network is established. More specifically, we provide a strategic process and generative scripts that can be used to achieve early-stage alignment for network service innovation in the sense of developing clear ideas and ensuring the legitimacy of service innovation endeavors both within and between participating organizations. Moreover, in a more operational sense, managers can use the scripts to identify resources they might contribute, modes of interaction, and possible tensions or implementation challenges. With our method, service innovation managers can link their own organization's interests with their ambitions to cooperate in a network. Our chapter may offer benefits to wider society as well. Besides the pursuit of digital opportunities, grand challenges such as the energy transition and COVID-19 pandemic increasingly require innovation collaboration between various stakeholders (for instance, companies, knowledge institutes, and governmental organizations) with different interests. By facilitating early-stage alignment, our methodology can assist these parties in paving the way for collaborative service innovation to tackle these challenges.

Limitations and Further Research

The empirical context of our illustrative case study pertains to one network with three organizations that have a prolonged history of doing business together, targeting assets (vessels) with very long lifecycles. The customer has limited opportunities for selecting suppliers, and in structural terms, the network is relatively uncomplicated as it includes only three organizations. Therefore, the transferability of the insights to other contexts might be limited, such as those featuring many market entrants, no prior relationships, or more complex networks. In addition, we focused on the early alignment for a network service innovation project at strategic organizational and network levels. We call for further research to address more fine-grained practices and to elaborate institutional arrangements and service designs. This will involve interactions among members of different organizations at different levels, such as procurement and commercial managers, as well as engineers working in a joint data science team. The development process we propose might be extended to evaluate actual service design and development outcomes as well across multiple levels.

References

Acharya, C., Ojha, D., Patel, P. C., & Gokhale, R. (2020). Modular interconnected processes, fluid partnering, and innovation speed: A loosely coupled systems perspective on B2B service supply chain management. *Industrial Marketing Management, 89*, 209–219. https://doi.org/10.1016/j.indmarman.2019.05.007

Andersson, P., & Mattsson, L.-G. (2015). Service innovations enabled by the "internet of things". *IMP Journal, 9*(1), 85–106. https://doi.org/10.1108/imp-01-2015-0002

Baines, T., Lightfoot, H., Peppard, J., Johnson, M., Tiwari, A., Shehab, E., & Swink, M. (2009). Towards an operations strategy for product-centric servitization. *International Journal of Operations and Production Management, 29*(5), 494–519. https://doi.org/10.1108/01443570910953603

Ballantyne, D., Frow, P., Varey, R. J., & Payne, A. (2011). Value propositions as communication practice: Taking a wider view. *Industrial Marketing Management, 40*(2), 202–210. https://doi.org/10.1016/j.indmarman.2010.06.032

Bankvall, L., Dubois, A., & Lind, F. (2017). Conceptualizing business models in industrial networks. *Industrial Marketing Management, 60*, 196–203. https://doi.org/10.1016/j.indmarman.2016.04.006

Barile, S., Lusch, R., Reynoso, J., Saviano, M., & Spohrer, J. (2016). Systems, networks, and ecosystems in service research. *Journal of Service Management, 27*(4), 652–674. https://doi.org/10.1108/JOSM-09-2015-0268

Barrett, M., Davidson, E., Prabhu, J., & Vargo, S. L. (2015). Service innovation in the digital age: Key contributions and future directions. *MIS Quarterly: Management Information Systems, 39*(1), 135–154. https://doi.org/10.25300/MISQ/2015/39:1.03

Bierly, P. E., & Gallagher, S. (2007). Explaining alliance partner selection: Fit, trust and strategic expediency. *Long Range Planning, 40*(2), 134–153. https://doi.org/10.1016/j.lrp.2007.03.001

Boxenbaum, E., & Rouleau, L. (2011). New knowledge products as bricolage: Metaphors and scripts in organizational theory. *Academy of Management Review, 36*(2), 272–296. https://doi.org/10.5465/amr.2009.0213

Čaić, M., Mahr, D., & Oderkerken-Schröder, G. (2019). Value of social robots in services: social cognition perspective. *Journal of Services Marketing, 33*(4), 463–478. https://doi.org/10.1108/JSM-02-2018-0080

Eisenhardt, K. M. (1989). Building theories from case study research. *Academy of Management Review, 14*(4), 532–550. https://doi.org/10.5465/amr.1989.4308385

Eisingerich, A. B., Rubera, G., & Seifert, M. (2009). Managing service innovation and interorganizational relationships for firm performance: To commit or diversify? *Journal of Service Research, 11*(4), 344–356. https://doi.org/10.1177/1094670508329223

Engelbracht, W., Schoen, A., Shah, T., & Nevin, M. (2019). Strategic alliances An essential weapon in the growth arsenal. In *Deloitte & Touche LLP*.

Gray, D., Sundstrom, E., Tornatzky, L. G., & McGowen, L. (2011). When triple helix unravels: A multi-case analysis of failures in industry–University Cooperative Research Centres. *Industry and Higher Education, 25*(5), 333–345. https://doi.org/10.5367/ihe.2011.0057

Grönroos, C. (2011). Value co-creation in service logic: A critical analysis. *Marketing Theory, 11*(3), 279–301. https://doi.org/10.1177/1470593111408177

Iivari, M. M., Ahokangas, P., Komi, M., Tihinen, M., & Valtanen, K. (2016). Toward ecosystemic business models in the context of industrial internet. *In Toward Ecosystemic Business Models in the Context of Industrial Internet, 4*(2), 42–59. https://doi.org/10.5278/ojs.jbm.v4i2.1624

Jocevski, M., Arvidsson, N., & Ghezzi, A. (2020). Interconnected business models: Present debates and future agenda. *Journal of Business and Industrial Marketing, 35*(6), 1051–1067. https://doi.org/10.1108/JBIM-06-2019-0292

Karpen, I. O., Gemser, G., & Calabretta, G. (2017). A multilevel consideration of service design conditions: Towards a portfolio of organisational capabilities, interactive practices and individual abilities. *Journal of Service Theory and Practice, 27*(2), 384–407. https://doi.org/10.1108/JSTP-05-2015-0121

Keen, P., & Williams, R. (2013). Value architectures for digital business: Beyond the business model. *MIS Quarterly: Management Information Systems, 37*(2), 643–647. https://www.jstor.org/stable/43825929?casa_token=SSaGIOyf2w8AAAAA:fb6g4l43-9YuDY02MX01n9z_KnNFjl3vDWzRU5E3dLGuHPbi93ppn9fS1 EmOyJSv4JGUbfn3heiZIK3g81q_j9EKbn8I-O31sr9ZWxrglmYUI6kVgKc

Komulainen, H., Mainela, T., Sinisalo, J., Tähtinen, J., & Ulkuniemi, P. (2006). Business model scenarios in mobile advertising. *International Journal of Internet Marketing and Advertising, 3*(3), 254–270. https://doi.org/10.1504/IJIMA.2006.010739

Koskela-Huotari, K., Edvardsson, B., Jonas, J. M., Sörhammar, D., & Witell, L. (2016). Innovation in service ecosystems-Breaking, making, and maintaining institutionalized rules of resource integration. *Journal of Business Research, 69*(8), 2964–2971. https://doi.org/10.1016/j.jbusres.2016.02.029

Kowalkowski, C., Gebauer, H., Kamp, B., & Parry, G. (2017). Servitization and deservitization: Overview, concepts, and definitions. *Industrial Marketing Management, 60*, 4–10. https://doi.org/10.1016/j.indmarman.2016.12.007

Kowalkowski, C., & Witell, L. (2020). Typologies and frameworks in service innovation. In *The Routledge handbook of service research insights and ideas* (pp. 109–130). Routledge.

Larsson, R., Bengtsson, L., Henriksson, K., & Sparks, J. (1998). The interorganizational learning dilemma: Collective knowledge development in strategic alliances. *Organization Science, 9*(3), 285–305. https://doi.org/10.1287/orsc.9.3.285

Laursen, K., & Salter, A. (2006). Open for innovation: The role of openness in explaining innovation performance among U.K. manufacturing firms. *Strategic Management Journal, 27*(2), 131–150. https://doi.org/10.1002/smj.507

Lay, G. (2014). Servitization in industry. *Servitization in Industry, 9783319069*. https://doi.org/10.1007/978-3-319-06935-7

Leiponen, A. (2005). Organization of knowledge and innovation: The case of finnish business services. *Industry and Innovation, 12*(2), 185–203. https://doi.org/10.1080/13662710500087925

Levina, N., & Ross, J. W. (2003). From the vendor's perspective: Exploring the value proposition in information technology outsourcing. *MIS Quarterly: Management Information Systems, 27*(3), 331–364. https://doi.org/10.2307/30036537

Liedtka, J. (2015). Perspective: Linking design thinking with innovation outcomes through cognitive bias reduction. *Journal of Product Innovation Management, 32*(6), 925–938. https://doi.org/10.1111/jpim.12163

Lindhult, E., & Hazy, J. K. (2016). Complexity approach to joint value discovery in service innovation management. *International Journal of Complexity in Leadership and Management, 3*(1/2), 115. https://doi.org/10.1504/ijclm.2016.075046

Liu, H., Purvis, L., Mason, R., & Wells, P. (2020). Developing logistics value propositions: Drawing Insights from a distributed manufacturing solution. *Industrial Marketing Management.* https://doi.org/10.1016/j.indmarman.2020.03.011

Lumineau, F., & Oliveira, N. (2018). A pluralistic perspective to overcome major blind spots in research on interorganizational relationships. *Academy of Management Annals, 12*(1), 440–465. https://doi.org/10.5465/annals.2016.0033

Lusch, R. F., & Nambisan, S. (2015). Service innovation: A service-dominant logic perspective. *MIS Quarterly, 39*(1), 155–175.

Mahr, D., Kalogeras, N., & Odekerken-Schröder, G. (2013). A service science approach for improving healthy food experiences. *Journal of Service Management, 24*(4), 435–471. https://doi.org/10.1108/JOSM-04-2013-0089

Mangematin, V., & Baden-Fuller, C. (2015). Introduction: Business models and modelling business models. *Advances in Strategic Management, 33*, xi–xxii. https://doi.org/10.1108/S0742-3322201533

Mina, A., Bascavusoglu-Moreau, E., & Hughes, A. (2014). Open service innovation and the firm's search for external knowledge. *Research Policy, 43*(5), 853–866. https://doi.org/10.1016/j.respol.2013.07.004

Mustak, M. (2014). Service innovation in networks: A systematic review and implications for business-to-business service innovation research. *Journal of Business and Industrial Marketing, 29*(2), 151–163. https://doi.org/10.1108/JBIM-05-2013-0122

Nenonen, S., Brodie, R. J., Storbacka, K., & Peters, L. D. (2017). Theorizing with managers: How to achieve both academic rigor and practical relevance? *European Journal of Marketing, 51*(7–8), 1130–1152. https://doi.org/10.1108/EJM-03-2017-0171

Nylén, D., & Holmström, J. (2015). Digital innovation strategy: A framework for diagnosing and improving digital product and service innovation. *Business Horizons, 58*(1), 57–67. https://doi.org/10.1016/j.bushor.2014.09.001

Ojasalo, J., & Ojasalo, K. (2018). Service logic business model canvas. *Journal of Research in Marketing and Entrepreneurship, 20*(1), 70–98. https://doi.org/10.1108/JRME-06-2016-0015

Okhuysen, G. A., & Eisenhardt, K. M. (2002). Integrating knowledge in groups: How formal interventions enable flexibility. *Organization Science, 13*(4), 370. https://doi.org/10.1287/orsc.13.4.370.2947

Osterwalder, A., & Pigneur, Y. (2010). *Business model generation: A handbook for visionaries, game changers, and challengers.* https://doi.org/10.5367/ijei.2014.0149

Palo, T., & Tähtinen, J. (2013). Networked business model development for emerging technology-based services. *Industrial Marketing Management, 42*(5), 773–782. https://doi.org/10.1016/j.indmarman.2013.05.015

Patrício, L., Grenha Teixeira, J., & Vink, J. (2019). A service design approach to healthcare innovation: From decision-making to sense-making and institutional change. *AMS Review, 9*(1–2), 115–120. https://doi.org/10.1007/s13162-019-00138-8

Patrício, L., Sangiorgi, D., Mahr, D., Čaić, M., Kalantari, S., & Sundar, S. (2020). Leveraging service design for healthcare transformation: Toward people-centered, integrated, and technology-enabled healthcare systems. *Journal of Service Management, 31*(5), 889–909. https://doi.org/10.1108/JOSM-11-2019-0332

Payne, A., & Frow, P. (2014). Developing superior value propositions: A strategic marketing imperative. *Journal of Service Management, 25*(2), 213–227. https://doi.org/10.1108/JOSM-01-2014-0036

Pikka, V., Iskanius, P., & Page, T. (2011). The business enabling network – A tool for regional development. *International Journal of Innovation and Regional Development, 3*(3/4), 324. https://doi.org/10.1504/ijird.2011.040529

Prud'homme van Reine, P. (2017). The culture of design thinking for innovation. *Journal of Innovation Management, 5*(2), 56–80. https://doi.org/10.24840/2183-0606_005.002_0006

Raddats, C., Kowalkowski, C., Benedettini, O., Burton, J., & Gebauer, H. (2019). Servitization: A contemporary thematic review of four major research streams. *Industrial Marketing Management, 83*, 207–223. https://doi.org/10.1016/j.indmarman.2019.03.015

Rumble, R., & Minto, N. A. (2017). How to use analogies for creative business modelling. *Journal of Business Strategy, 38*(2), 76–82. https://doi.org/10.1108/JBS-09-2016-0091

Schön, O. (2012). Business model modularity – A way to gain strategic flexibility? *Controlling & Management, 56*(S2), 73–78. https://doi.org/10.1365/s12176-012-0388-4

Shinkle, G. A., Devinney, T., Elshaw, J., Folta, T., Gary, S., Kirkman, N., … Yetton, P. (2012). Organizational aspirations, reference points, and goals: Building on the past and aiming for the future. *Journal of Management, 38*(1), 415–455. https://doi.org/10.1177/0149206311419856

Siggelkow, N. (2007). Persuasion with case studies. *Academy of Management Journal, 50*(1), 20–24. https://doi.org/10.5465/AMJ.2007.24160882

Sjödin, D., Parida, V., Kohtamäki, M., & Wincent, J. (2020). An agile co-creation process for digital servitization: A micro-service innovation approach. *Journal of Business Research, 112*, 478–491. https://doi.org/10.1016/j.jbusres.2020.01.009

Skålén, P., Gummerus, J., von Koskull, C., & Magnusson, P. R. (2015). Exploring value propositions and service innovation: A service-dominant logic study. *Journal of the Academy of Marketing Science, 43*(2), 137–158. https://doi.org/10.1007/s11747-013-0365-2

Skippari, M., Laukkanen, M., & Salo, J. (2017). Cognitive barriers to collaborative innovation generation in supply chain relationships. *Industrial Marketing Management, 62*, 108–117. https://doi.org/10.1016/j.indmarman.2016.08.002

Tax, S. S., McCutcheon, D., & Wilkinson, I. F. (2013). The Service Delivery Network (SDN): A customer-centric perspective of the customer journey. *Journal of Service Research, 16*(4), 454–470. https://doi.org/10.1177/1094670513481108

Teece, D. J. (2010). Business models, business strategy and innovation. *Long Range Planning, 43*(2–3), 172–194. https://doi.org/10.1016/j.lrp.2009.07.003

Teece, D. J. (2018). Business models and dynamic capabilities. *Long Range Planning, 51*(1), 40–49. https://doi.org/10.1016/j.lrp.2017.06.007

Thomas, G. (2011). A typology for the case study in social science following a review of definition, discourse, and structure. *Qualitative Inquiry, 17*(6), 511–521. https://doi.org/10.1177/1077800411409884

Thorgren, S., Wincent, J., & Örtqvist, D. (2009). Designing interorganizational networks for innovation: An empirical examination of network configuration, formation and governance. *Journal of Engineering and Technology Management – JET-M, 26*(3), 148–166. https://doi.org/10.1016/j.jengtecman.2009.06.006

Tronvoll, B., Sklyar, A., Sörhammar, D., & Kowalkowski, C. (2020). Transformational shifts through digital servitization. *Industrial Marketing Management, 89*, 293–305. https://doi.org/10.1016/j.indmarman.2020.02.005

van der Aalst, W. (2016). Data science in action. *Process Mining*, 3–23. https://doi.org/10.1007/978-3-662-49851-4_1

van Fenema, P. C., & Keers, B. M. (2018). Interorganizational performance management: A co-evolutionary model. *International Journal of Management Reviews, 20*(3), 772–799. https://doi.org/10.1111/ijmr.12180

Vargo, S. L., & Lusch, R. F. (2008). Service-dominant logic: Continuing the evolution. *Journal of the Academy of Marketing Science, 36*(1), 1–10. https://doi.org/10.1007/s11747-007-0069-6

Vargo, S. L., & Lusch, R. F. (2016). Institutions and axioms: An extension and update of service-dominant logic. *Journal of the Academy of Marketing Science, 44*(1), 5–23. https://doi.org/10.1007/s11747-015-0456-3

Vendrell-Herrero, F., Bustinza, O. F., Parry, G., & Georgantzis, N. (2017). Servitization, digitization and supply chain interdependency. *Industrial Marketing Management, 60*, 69–81. https://doi.org/10.1016/j.indmarman.2016.06.013

Vink, J., Koskela-Huotari, K., Tronvoll, B., Edvardsson, B., & Wetter-Edman, K. (2020). Service ecosystem design: Propositions, process model, and future research agenda. *Journal of Service Research*, 1–19. https://doi.org/10.1177/1094670520952537

Weigel, S., & Hadwich, K. (2018). Success factors of service networks in the context of servitization – Development and verification of an impact model. *Industrial Marketing Management, 74*, 254–275. https://doi.org/10.1016/j.indmarman.2018.06.002

Zhang, Y., Ren, S., Liu, Y., & Si, S. (2017). A big data analytics architecture for cleaner manufacturing and maintenance processes of complex products. *Journal of Cleaner Production, 142*, 626–641. https://doi.org/10.1016/j.jclepro.2016.07.123

Beyond the Line of Visibility: Toward Sustainable Service Innovation

Lars Witell, Per Carlborg, and Hannah Snyder

Over the past few decades, developing service innovations has been the golden standard for many businesses and a must if a firm wants to create a competitive advantage. Creating and launching new services by connecting buyers and suppliers through platforms has become an appealing idea for many firms in their quest for increased customer value. This has enabled new business models to thrive and companies such as Uber, Airbnb, and Spotify to challenge existing markets. However, although many of these new types of service innovations are seen as success stories, the sustainability of these firms can be questioned. For example, despite being on the market for more than 15 years, Spotify has been struggling to make a profit on its core service (Musicbussinessworldwide, 2021). Others have struggled with legal issues when entering new markets. Firms such as Uber and Airbnb had repeatedly run into trouble with legislation when entering new markets and have been banned from operation in certain cities and countries (Reuters, 2021). Other

L. Witell (✉)
CTF, Service Research Center, Karlstad University, Karlstad, Sweden
e-mail: Lars.witell@kau.se

P. Carlborg
Örebro University School of Business, Örebro, Sweden
e-mail: per.carlborg@oru.se

H. Snyder
Department of Marketing, BI Norwegian Business School, Oslo, Norway

© The Author(s), under exclusive license to Springer Nature Switzerland AG 2022
B. Edvardsson, B. Tronvoll (eds.), *The Palgrave Handbook of Service Management*,
https://doi.org/10.1007/978-3-030-91828-6_29

firms have struggled with ethical issues such as workers' conditions and unfair competition.

So how can the current research in service innovation help in understanding and overcoming problems in relation to service innovation and sustainability? In fact, there is no lack of research in the area of service innovation. Actually, the case is quite the opposite. Over the past few decades, scholars have investigated what a service innovation is (Gallouj & Weinstein, 1997; Gustafsson et al., 2020), how to design and create new services (Parasuraman, 2010; Patrício et al., 2018), how to measure the return on service innovation efforts (Feng et al., 2020), and service innovation implementation and adoption (Cadwallader et al., 2010). These are all important questions; however, they focus on a narrow part of service innovation. In this chapter, we argue that researchers need to take a broader view of service innovation, ones that include sustainability dimensions beyond the line of visibility (i.e., factors that are not visible for customers (Bitner et al., 2008)) to aid in understanding and building knowledge of the current landscape of service innovation. If we do not do this, there is a chance that as researchers we will become irrelevant and outpaced by reality. To stay relevant, we need to understand the full picture of how modern firms operate, how service innovations can enhance sustainability, and how to tackle the current struggles and issues facing firms. In this chapter, we discuss the past and future of service innovation research, highlighting the factors beyond the line of visibility and presenting some potential avenues for advancing the research field.

1 The Past and Future of Service Innovation Research

A service innovation can be defined as a new process or offering that is put into practice and creates value for one or more stakeholders (Gustafsson et al., 2020). There is no lack of research on the topic of service innovation, ranging from what a service innovation is, to how to develop it, to how to measure it, and to how to implement it (Table 1).

Early on, both Barras (1986) and Miles (1993) concluded that new services play a vital role in the diffusion of new technologies and organizational structures; therefore, it is crucial to understand the nature, mechanisms, and role of services if we want to understand the new economy. There have been several attempts at theorizing and conceptualizing service innovation and synthesizing the research. For example, different research has examined what

Beyond the Line of Visibility: Toward Sustainable Service Innovation   579

Table 1 Summarizing the research on service innovation

Research area	Main questions	Type of articles	Example of references
Theorizing and conceptualizing	• What is a service innovation? • How can service innovation be defined? • What are the different categories/modes of service innovation? • How has the research on service innovations evolved? • What are the different perspectives on service innovation? • How is it different from product innovation?	Conceptual and literature reviews	Barras (1986) Carlborg et al. (2014) Coombs and Miles (2000) Gallouj and Weinstein (1997) Helkkula et al. (2018) Lusch and Nambisan (2015) Miles (1993) Skålén et al. (2015) Snyder et al. (2016) Witell et al. (2016)
Create and design	• How can service innovation be created? • What are the different stakeholders involved in creating service innovations? • What is the role of service design in service innovation? • How can customers be involved?	Conceptual and empirical articles	Alam (2002) Bitner et al. (2008) Edvardsson et al. (2010) Elg et al. (2012) Gustafsson et al. (2012) Holmlid et al. (2015) Magnusson et al. (2003)
Operationalization, measurement, and performance	• How can we operationalize service innovation? • How can we measure it? • What is the return on service innovation efforts? • What is the effect of service innovation on firm performance?	Empirical articles	Aas and Pedersen (2011) Agarwal and Selen (2011) Cainelli et al. (2006) Feng et al. (2020) Grawe et al. (2009) Lin (2013)
Implementing service innovation	• How can service innovation be implemented? • What are the enablers and barriers to be considered?	Conceptual and empirical articles	Cadwallader et al. (2010) Enz (2012) Frambach et al. (1998) Martin et al. (2016)

service innovation is (Gustafsson et al., 2020; Toivonen & Tuominen, 2009; Witell et al., 2016), the evolution of service innovation research (Carlborg et al., 2014), and the categories/modes of service innovation (Snyder et al., 2016). Researchers have also suggested alternative perspectives on service innovation, such as a service-dominant logic perspective (Lusch & Nambisan, 2015; Ordanini & Parasuraman, 2010), a Lancastrian perspective (Gallouj & Weinstein, 1997), and the role of institutions and organizational structure in service innovation (Chandler et al., 2019). Depending on the perspective, it has been argued that service innovation can be considered similar to product innovation, totally different than product innovation and, more recently, that service innovation and product innovation have some different features but that theories should be broad enough to encompass both (Carlborg et al., 2014; Coombs & Miles, 2000; Ordanini & Parasuraman, 2010).

In addition, plenty of research has focused on how to design and create service innovations. For example, Bitner et al. (2008) focused on "blueprinting" as a practical approach for addressing many of the challenges in service innovation, here with a particular focus on customer experience. Holmlid et al. (2015) suggested that to design successful service innovation, co-creative practices, where different people are brought together to share, make sense, and collaborate, are essential for rethinking current and exploring future possibilities. There have also been several articles advocating for the role of customers in service innovation (Magnusson et al., 2003; Witell et al., 2011). Other research has focused on how we operationalize and measure the return on service innovations (Aas & Pedersen, 2011; Feng et al., 2020). Finally, there has also been research on how to implement service innovations (Cadwallader et al., 2010).

Overall, this provides a substantial, but perhaps a bit scattered, knowledge base of service innovation. Instead, we need to look at what is being overlooked. Service research in general (Saviano et al., 2017) and service innovation in particular (Calabrese et al., 2018; Gallouj et al., 2018) have suggested that service innovations need to be sustainable. That is, service innovation should contribute to major societal challenges and sustainable development (Gallouj & Djellal, 2018). The problem is not the existing studies per se but what we are not studying. With the development of globalization and digitalization, service innovation has witnessed a veritable explosion in terms of users and the range of service possibilities. The core of service and of service innovation is the idea of co-production and value co-creation—now, this possibility has increased to be almost omnipresent; between users, user and platforms operators, and between providers and users. Hence, service innovation engages multiple actors and has the potential to increase sustainability in several ways: reduced ecological footprints (through more efficient services and reduced resource usage), reduced social inequality (through the connectivity it enables between actors), and reduced economic inequality through more inclusive services available for broader layers of organizations and people. However, despite turbulence and rapidly changing markets and struggles for companies, service innovation studies have still focused on a quite narrow part of the service innovation phenomenon. Research on service innovation has been unable to fully understand the dynamics of the underlying service system that is the foundation for (and monetizes) service provision. This creates a large invisible or hidden area that obstructs an overarching understanding of the phenomena—which is especially evident in the platform economy where activities of value creation and service valorization are more detached from each other.

2 Sustainability and Service Innovation

Addressing sustainability challenges from a service innovation standpoint can be seen in the light of early notions on sustainability principles (i.e., the basic terms that provide a ground for actions), which emphasize the three pillars of environmental, economic, and social principles (WCED, 1987). Arriving from a broad range of schools of thought, sustainability is vaguely defined. However, environmental performance is designated in terms of reducing resource usage and energy consumption. Economic principles are denominated by the terms such as environmental accounting, eco-efficiency, ethical investments, and transparency. Finally, social principles are guided by responsibility for social issues, human development, and equality (see, e.g., Glavič & Lukman, 2007). Sustainability has been argued to be a major driver for service innovation and typically targets one or several of these dimensions. For example, transport services offer new ways of organizing transportation that can contribute to sustainability through better and more efficient ways of connecting people. Thus, a transport service is not only a matter of mobility but can also address environmental challenges. Although some have argued for a "natural greenness" of services based on immateriality characteristics (Djellal & Gallouj, 2016), others have shown how services can create rebound effects and actually have a negative impact on the overall environmental footprint (Agrawal & Bellos, 2017). Specific literature streams and theoretical concepts have been introduced to address the three dimensions of sustainability. For example, green service innovation (Djellal & Gallouj, 2016) emphasizes environmental sustainability challenges; sustainable business model innovation (Geissdoerfer et al., 2018) focuses on economic sustainability challenges; and social innovation (van der Have & Rubalcaba, 2016) addresses social sustainability challenges. Even if these theoretical concepts show that service innovation researchers have started to approach sustainability challenges (e.g., reducing ecological footprint, reducing social inequality, etc.), the link between sustainability and service innovation is still underdeveloped. How service innovation contributes to overall increased sustainability through different forms of innovative activities is often hidden behind layers of invisibility. Often, the service innovation's focus on user value overshadows the other effects that appear in the larger network of actors who are engaged in the service ecosystem.

3   Service Innovation and the Line of Visibility

A key part of service innovation is developing value propositions that fit the prerequisites for customers so that they can co-create value. Figure 1 provides an illustration of how value creation and value capture take place, and how parts of the service system are hidden for the customer. Traditionally, the line of visibility separates the activities in the value creation process that are seen

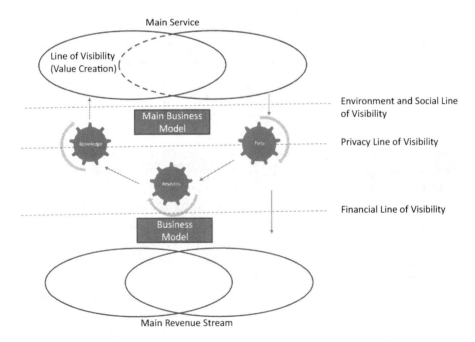

Fig. 29.1   The line of visibility

by the customer, from those that are invisible (Bitner et al., 2008). In one way, the line of visibility separates value co-creation from value facilitation (Grönroos, 2011) or hides the employee actions and the activities they perform when preparing to serve customers. Parasuraman and Grewal (2000) argued that if it improves the customer experience, it can be beneficial to move the line of visibility to show how frontline employees use new technology. If service providers are transparent consumers can better evaluate both what value is co-created and how it is co-created.

Discussing the sustainability of service innovation, we can ask the following: Does it matter what is behind the line of visibility? Do consumers actually care? This remains somewhat unanswered. Concerning the traditional line of visibility, Liu et al. (2015) argue that transparency matters for three reasons. First, allowing customers to see through value creation can be important to a service provider who wishes to minimize uncertainty related to its brand promise and the capabilities needed to provide service. Second, transparency matters because firms find it increasingly difficult to hide negative information when things go wrong or prevent negative news from spreading. Third, lack of transparency and knowledge within the company can create problems even for members of the same organization. For example, it is not uncommon that the people working with research and development are not fully aware of the innovation strategy or revenue streams. This lack of transparency and knowledge could also hinder innovation. Despite this, the full story about companies' innovations and innovation strategy is usually not that transparent. Research on service innovation has highlighted that service innovations are often not built on a single innovation but on bundles of new services. Gustafsson and Johnson (2006) viewed this as linked activities and that what is linked and how it is linked are the key to service innovation. They further argued that such bundles of innovations make the service difficult to copy and help in differentiating the brand. One could argue that, in the short run, having strong lines of visibility would make it harder for competitors to copy the service innovation and to not draw attention to more shady parts of the organizations' strategy. If a service innovation is a bundle of new services, then we would expect the line of visibility to hide an important factor for the success of the service innovation, such as the use of data or the hidden business model. Without this component, the service innovation will take longer for competitors to copy.

Transparency can be seen from either the perspective of the customer or the service provider, and Liu et al. (2015) describe these two perspectives as follows. From the service providers' perspective, transparency has been discussed in terms of the ability to be seen through or the degree of visibility and accessibility of information provided. From the customer's perspective,

584   L. Witell et al.

transparency has been discussed as a customer's subjective view of being provided the relevant information held by the service provider in an interaction. In addition, a third perspective could be transparency between members within the same organization. Researchers, though, have argued that transparency is equally important when performing research on service innovation. Even if we can understand why businesses want to keep certain aspects hidden, often we as researchers follow the same line of reasoning, and take the easy way out by studying only what is available to us. This makes the current research tradition a bit naïve, and perhaps service research fail to fully understand how service innovations happen, develop, and survive over time.

4   Introducing Additional Lines of Visibility to Guide Service Research

We suggest that to get better and more accurate knowledge, we need to broaden our analysis and consider more dimensions of service innovations. Extending the transparency from value creation to the different dimensions of sustainability and privacy suggests that service providers need to be transparent in multiple areas. The literature shows that service providers do not suffer but rather have much to gain from being transparent (Liu et al., 2015), even more so when a firm is perceived as not performing too well regarding the environmental or social dimension. However, many of the present service innovations are platform businesses, and these have grown considerably over the last decade. So far, the research on service innovation has focused mostly on value creation (for consumers) and what is in front of the line of visibility (Witell et al., 2016). Nevertheless, is the line of visibility the only border that is relevant for value creation? We argue that the service literature should consider additional lines of visibility that are relevant to designing and evaluating the sustainability of service innovations. These lines of visibility concern the environment, social issues, financial issues, and privacy and are illustrated in Fig. 1. We consider them a key ingredient to better understand what a service innovation is, what the effects are, and how they can be managed. A more detailed understanding includes previous neglected or hidden aspects so that the effects of a service innovation are evident not only when it comes to value creation for the consumer but also for the environment, society, financially, and in privacy matters. Putting our focus on these types of issues will aid in theory development and tackling managerial challenges.

Considering the triple bottom line, we argue that firms that are not transparent with their service innovations have introduced several lines of visibility to hide the effects of their service innovations both to the public, their customers, and even members of the organization. The environmental line of visibility hinders both consumers and researchers from seeing the direct and indirect effects on the environment that the service innovation causes. As an example, it is not evident what happens when a customer returns a product that was bought online. It can either have very positive social implications, such as being donated to a person in need, or it can have very negative environmental implications in that new clothes are being burned. The social line of visibility hinders consumers from seeing the social implications of the service innovation. As an example, it is not evident to customers under what working conditions a driver or delivery person performs their services. In addition, it is not always evident that someone working in the innovation department has full knowledge of other members of the organization's working conditions, specially not when the distance between different groups of employees is large (both with regard to knowledge and also geographical).

The financial line of visibility hinders consumers and researchers from seeing the full extent of the business model, that is, how the firm makes money from service provision. The privacy line of visibility hinders consumers and researchers from seeing exactly how the data provided by the customer are used. As an example, many apps provide value for customers without charging customers. Still, these service innovations are profitable for the service provider. In this case, both the financial line of visibility and the line of privacy hinder consumers from seeing how value creation takes place. Behind the line of privacy, the data provided from consumers are gathered, and the data when using the app are combined with data from using the smartphone. Behind the financial line visibility, the data gathered from consumers are sold to other firms that use these data to target their ads to consumers. All in all, the lack of transparency from companies and failure to take these factors into account lead to flawed research. We, therefore, advocate that researchers put more effort in including new dimensions and perspectives of service innovation into their research.

5 A Path Forward for Service Innovation Research

To provide theoretical guidance and aid in solving some of the challenges businesses, markets, and society are facing, we suggest three interesting areas that could inspire and advance research on service innovation (see Table 2). To address these research areas, new research designs and approaches may be needed. To reach beyond the line of visibility, a systems perspective is needed

586 L. Witell et al.

Table 2 Research agenda

Area	Potential research questions
Including factors beyond the line of visibility	• What are the dimensions of service innovation seen in the light of visibility?
	• What is a sustainable service innovation?
	• How can companies be sustainable over time by leveraging service innovations?
	• How do we determine the success of a new service? What are the dangers and advantages of a lack of transparency?
	• To what extent and in what areas should companies be transparent?
	• To what extent does transparency hinder or support the adoption of service innovations?
The interplay between the different service innovations	• How can we understand the differences between the main service innovation and the underlying/supporting service innovations?
	• How do different business models function together?
	• How can we understand the interplay between different actors involved in a specific service innovation?
	• How should businesses manage service innovation with multiple business models?
The balance between different types of value	• How can companies balance different types of value?
	• How should we measure the impact of service innovation?
	• What actors should companies focus on when designing their service innovation strategies?
	• What is the danger of focusing too much on user value?
	• How can we manage the long-term–short-term dilemma?

that expands the boundaries of the study object. There is also a need to follow study objects over time to uncover the relationship between service innovation and sustainability.

Including Factors Beyond the Line of Visibility

Although researchers have been very diligent in addressing the various aspects of service innovation that are easy to access and visible for consumers, the factors beyond the line of visibility have to a large extent been neglected. This is the case for many reasons: sometimes, the relevance of these factors to service innovation is hard to grasp, and other times, we do not have access to the information. However, as we have argued above, to truly understand the phenomena of service innovation and the struggles and challenges companies face, we need to understand these factors. For example, if we want to

Beyond the Line of Visibility: Toward Sustainable Service Innovation **587**

understand how service innovations can be sustainable, we cannot just look at one service innovation in isolation; we also need to see the system and structure that it is embedded in, and if not, we face the risk of drawing the wrong conclusion, hence building theory on inaccurate facts or noncomplete data. For example, company A is not really generating any revenue on their main service innovation but still manages to grow their business and expand. To understand these kinds of businesses, we probably need to take other less visible factors into account, such as complementing innovations/revenue streams, investment capital, market conditions, and legislation. Of course, this increases the complexity of the analysis but has the potential for us as researchers to answer important questions regarding the design and sustainability of service innovations while shedding light on less obvious service innovations, how companies can leverage service innovations, and what actually determines the success of new services. This also puts the focus on transparency. Understanding modern business challenges requires increased transparency of business models and markets. We should be aware that there will be some resistance from different actors when it comes to increased transparency; however, we believe that the degree of transparency is an important area that could potentially help companies gain sustainability over time.

The Interplay Between Different Service Innovations

In their studies of service innovations in businesses, researchers have focused on single service innovations. The assumption is that firms develop one service innovation, and its success is measured if it diffuses on the market or not. However, service innovations do not operate in a vacuum; sometimes, other services are needed or form an ecosystem that is a prerequisite for the service innovation to succeed. When it comes to business models, there is often a type of symbiosis between multiple business models, where one business model is based on attracting users and another is based on profiting from the data gathered from these users. However, existing research does not capture this interplay between service innovations. We could even question the results of some research addressing single service innovations. Depending on the research question, the results might be more or less valid. When innovating services, there is a need to understand how phasing out an obsolete service will influence existing services and what role the service innovation will have to adopt among existing services. An example would be a car manufacturer introducing a sharing service as an alternative revenue stream, such as what Volvo or BMW have done. In these cases, the effects on the existing business model are limited, but there will be other effects, such as increased use of

588 L. Witell et al.

vehicles. Instead of replacing owning a car with sharing a car, there is a risk that using a bicycle or public transportation will be replaced by sharing a car. In this case, the introduction of a new business model becomes an experiment for the car manufacturer, one that is not profitable and has negative environmental effects. More knowledge is needed to understand the introduction of new business models and service innovations and how they interact to build more sustainable businesses.

The Balance Between Different Types of Value: Economic, Social, and Environmental

Because value typically emerges in the context of institutions and among multiple actors, an asynchrony and narrow focus on user value (e.g., value in use) risks disfavoring the development of sustainable service innovation because of a lack of balanced value creation on a (eco)systemic level. To overcome such an idiosyncratic condition, sustainable service innovation must acknowledge multiple and simultaneous value creation on different levels, including in the economic, social, and environmental domains. By acknowledging value creation in all these dimensions (e.g., how a service innovation relates to social inequality, ecological footprints, and economic prosperity among actors), both researchers and practitioners can pioneer a more long-term and sustainable way to foster value creation. By neglecting or underestimating the effects of service innovations in one or several of the abovementioned dimensions, the fundamental long-term flaws of service innovation will be evident. This can be formulated as the long-term–short-term dilemma of service innovation: overemphasizing value in use (user value) creates a focus on short-term benefits but does not take into account its negative effects on the (eco)system, which typically will be uncovered gradually. In contrast, a sustainable long-term service innovation can have no or a negative effect on user value in the short run.

To encourage sustainable service innovation, one important component is to develop structured measurements to follow up the impact of a service innovation—not only focusing on user value, but also covering the broad range of actors and their related environmental and social effects. This is a key issue for practitioners in deploying a true engagement in sustainability challenges and for researchers in informing/illuminating sustainable service innovation. Here, the measurements should focus on how the values within the whole system are affected in the short and long run and how they include rebound effects (e.g., if a new car-sharing service transforms bikers and bus travelers into car travelers, the positive effects of increased user value might be overshadowed by the negative effects it gives rise to at the (eco)systemic level).

6 Conclusion

For service research to be managerially relevant and contribute to the sustainable development of society, there is a need to address the right questions and move beyond the line of visibility. This book chapter has introduced the need for transparency in service research. Instead of focusing solely on value creation for consumers, there is a need to focus on transparency and moving beyond the financial, environmental, social, and privacy lines of visibility. Because vacuousness can be dangerous when moving into the field of sustainability, we should try to explore what lies behind the line of visibility of service innovation. The service literature has addressed environmental and social issues in transformative service research (Anderson & Ostrom, 2015) and bottom of the pyramid research (Gebauer & Reynoso, 2013), and there are single research initiatives that focus on either the environmental, social, or financial effects. However, we argue that in addition to these initiatives, there is a need to use such ideas in traditional service research. By doing this, service innovation can better contribute to sustainable development—considering sustainability at a societal level—and not only for increasing market revenues.

Service research has a tradition of being customer-focused, and value creation is performed with or by the customer. There is a rising number of concerns regarding the implications of this assumption—several critical voices have been raised based on what happens behind the line of visibility in the platform economy, where both employees and consumers are exploited. By challenging the assumptions in service research, we have an opportunity to address these important societal issues and increase the relevance of research on service innovation.

References

Aas, T. H., & Pedersen, P. E. (2011). The impact of service innovation on firm-level financial performance. *Service Industries Journal, 31*(13), 2071–2090. https://doi.org/10.1080/02642069.2010.503883

Agarwal, R., & Selen, W. (2011). Multi-dimensional nature of service innovation: Operationalisation of the elevated service offerings construct in collaborative service organisations. *International Journal of Operations & Production Management, 31*(11), 1164–1192. https://doi.org/10.1108/01443571111178484

Agrawal, V. V., & Bellos, I. (2017). The potential of servicizing as a green business model. *Management Science, 63*(5), 1545–1562.

Alam, I. (2002). An exploratory investigation of user involvement in new service development. *Journal of the Academy of Marketing Science, 30*(3), 250–261.

Anderson, L., & Ostrom, A. L. (2015). Transformative service research: Advancing our knowledge about service and well-being. *Journal of Service Research, 18*(3), 243–249.

Barras, R. (1986). Towards a theory of innovation in services. *Research Policy, 15*(4), 161–173. https://doi.org/10.1016/0048-7333(86)90012-0

Bitner, M. J., Ostrom, A. L., & Morgan, F. N. (2008). Service blueprinting: A practical technique for service innovation. *California Management Review, 50*(3), 66.

Cadwallader, S., Jarvis, C. B., Bitner, M. J., & Ostrom, A. L. (2010). Frontline employee motivation to participate in service innovation implementation. *Journal of the Academy of Marketing Science, 38*(2), 219–239. https://doi.org/10.1007/s11747-009-0151-3

Cainelli, G., Evangelista, R., & Savona, M. (2006). Innovation and economic performance in services: A firm-level analysis. *Cambridge Journal of Economics, 30*(3), 435–458.

Calabrese, A., Castaldi, C., Forte, G., & Levialdi, N. G. (2018). Sustainability-oriented service innovation: An emerging research field. *Journal of Cleaner Production, 193*, 533–548.

Carlborg, P., Kindström, D., & Kowalkowski, C. (2014). The evolution of service innovation research: A critical review and synthesis. *The Service Industries Journal, 34*(5), 373–398. https://doi.org/10.1080/02642069.2013.780044

Chandler, J. D., Danatzis, I., Wernicke, C., Akaka, M. A., & Reynolds, D. (2019). How does innovation emerge in a service ecosystem?. *Journal of Service Research, 22*(1), 75–89.

Coombs, R., & Miles, I. (2000). Innovation, measurement and services: The new problematique. In J. S. Metcalfe & I. Miles (Eds.), *Innovation systems in the service economy* (pp. 85–103). Springer US. http://link.springer.com/chapter/10.1007/978-1-4615-4425-8_5

Djellal, F., & Gallouj, F. (2016). Service innovation for sustainability: Paths for greening through service innovation. In F. In Djellal & F. Gallouj (Eds.), *Service innovation* (pp. 187–215). Springer.

Edvardsson, B., Gustafsson, A., Kristensson, P., & Witell, L. (2010). Service innovation and customer co-development. In P. P. In Cheryl, A. Kieliszewski, & J. C. Spohrer (Eds.), *Handbook of service science* (pp. 561–577). Springer.

Elg, M., Engström, J., Witell, L. and Poksinska, B. (2012). Co-creation and learning in health-care service development. *Journal of Service Management, 23*(3), 328–343.

Enz, C. A. (2012). Strategies for the implementation of service innovations. *Cornell Hospitality Quarterly, 53*(3), 187–195. https://doi.org/10.1177/1938965512448176

Feng, C., Ma, R., & Jiang, L. (2020). The impact of service innovation on firm performance: A meta-analysis. *Journal of Service Management* (ahead-of-print). https://doi.org/10.1108/JOSM-03-2019-0089

Frambach, R. T., Barkema, H. G., Nooteboom, B., & Wedel, M. (1998). Adoption of a service innovation in the business market: An empirical test of supply-side variables. *Journal of Business Research, 41*(2), 161–174.

Gallouj, F., & Djellal, F. (Eds.). (2018). *A research agenda for service innovation.* Edward Elgar Publishing.

Gallouj, F., Rubalcaba, L., Toivonen, M., & Windrum, P. (2018). Understanding social innovation in services industries. *Industry and Innovation, 25*(6), 551–569.

Gallouj, F., & Weinstein, O. (1997). Innovation in services. *Research Policy, 26*(4–5), 537–556. https://doi.org/10.1016/S0048-7333(97)00030-9

Gebauer, H., & Reynoso, J. (2013). An agenda for service research at the base of the pyramid. *Journal of Service Management, 24*(5), 482–502.

Geissdoerfer, M., Vladimirova, D., & Evans, S. (2018). Sustainable business model innovation: A review. *Journal of Cleaner Production, 198*, 401–416. https://doi.org/10.1016/j.jclepro.2018.06.240

Glavič, P., & Lukman, R. (2007). Review of sustainability terms and their definitions. *Journal of Cleaner Production, 15*(18), 1875–1885.

Grawe, S. J., Chen, H., & Daugherty, P. J. (2009). The relationship between strategic orientation, service innovation, and performance. *International Journal of Physical Distribution & Logistics Management, 39*(4), 282–300. https://doi.org/10.1108/09600030910962249

Grönroos, C. (2011). Value co-creation in service logic: A critical analysis. *Marketing Theory, 11*(3), 279–301.

Gustafsson, A., & Johnson, M. (2006). *Competing in a service economy.* John Wiley & Sons.

Gustafsson, A., Kristensson, P., & Witell, L. (2012). Customer co-creation in service innovation: A matter of communication? *Journal of Service Management, 23*(3), 311–327. https://doi.org/10.1108/09564231211248426

Gustafsson, A., Snyder, H., & Witell, L. (2020). Service innovation: A new conceptualization and path forward. *Journal of Service Research.* https://doi.org/10.1177/1094670520908929

Helkkula, A., Kowalkowski, C., & Tronvoll, B. (2018). Archetypes of service innovation: implications for value cocreation. *Journal of Service Research, 21*(3), 284–301.

Holmlid, S., Mattelmäki, T., Visser, F. S., & Vaajakallio, K. (2015). Co-creative practices in service innovation. In R. Agarwal, W. Selen, G. Roos, & R. Green (Eds.), *The handbook of service innovation* (pp. 545–574). Springer. https://doi.org/10.1007/978-1-4471-6590-3_25

Lin, L. (2013). The impact of service innovation on firm performance. *The Service Industries Journal, 33*(15–16), 1599–1632. https://doi.org/10.1080/02642069.2011.638712

Liu, Y., Eisingerich, A. B., Auh, S., Merlo, O., & Chun, H. E. H. (2015). Service firm performance transparency: How, when, and why does it pay off? *Journal of Service Research, 18*(4), 451–467.

Lusch, R. F., & Nambisan, S. (2015). Service innovation: A service-dominant logic perspective. *MIS Quarterly, 39*(1), 155–176.

Magnusson, P. R., Matthing, J., & Kristensson, P. (2003). Managing user involvement in service innovation experiments with innovating end users. *Journal of Service Research, 6*(2), 111–124. https://doi.org/10.1177/1094670503257028

Martin, D., Gustafsson, A., & Choi, S. (2016). Service innovation, renewal, and adoption/rejection in dynamic global contexts. *Journal of Business Research, 69*(7), 2397–2400. https://doi.org/10.1016/j.jbusres.2016.01.008

Miles, I. (1993). Services in the new industrial economy. *Futures, 25*(6), 653–672. https://doi.org/10.1016/0016-3287(93)90106-4

Musicbussinesssworldwide. (2021). Retrieved March 14, 2021, from https://www.musicbusinessworldwide.com/loss-making-spotify-will-continue-to-focus-on-growth-over-profit-for-next-few-years/

Ordanini, A., & Parasuraman, A. (2010). Service innovation viewed through a service-dominant logic lens: A conceptual framework and empirical analysis. *Journal of Service Research, 14*(1), 3–23. https://doi.org/10.1177/1094670510385332

Parasuraman, A. (2010). Service productivity, quality and innovation: Implications for service-design practice and research. *International Journal of Quality and Service Sciences, 2*(3), 277–286. https://doi.org/10.1108/17566691011090026

Parasuraman, A., & Grewal, D. (2000). The impact of technology on the quality-value-loyalty chain: A research agenda. *Journal of the Academy of Marketing Science, 28*(1), 168–174.

Patrício, L., Gustafsson, A., & Fisk, R. (2018). Upframing service design and innovation for research impact. *Journal of Service Research, 21*(1), 3–16. https://doi.org/10.1177/1094670517746780

Reuters. (2021). Retrieved March 14, 2021, from https://www.reuters.com/article/us-uber-britain-factbox-idUSKBN1XZ25F

Saviano, M., Barile, S., Spohrer, J. C., & Caputo, F. (2017). A service research contribution to the global challenge of sustainability. *Journal of Service Theory and Practice, 27*(5), 951–976.

Skålén, P., Gummerus, J., Von Koskull, C., & Magnusson, P. R. (2015). Exploring value propositions and service innovation: a service-dominant logic study. *Journal of the Academy of Marketing Science, 43*(2), 137–158.

Snyder, H., Witell, L., Gustafsson, A., Fombelle, P., & Kristensson, P. (2016). Identifying categories of service innovation: A review and synthesis of the literature. *Journal of Business Research, 69*(7), 2401–2408. https://doi.org/10.1016/j.jbusres.2016.01.009

Toivonen, M., & Tuominen, T. (2009). Emergence of innovations in services. *The Service Industries Journal, 29*(7), 887–902. https://doi.org/10.1080/02642060902749492

Van der Have, R. P., & Rubalcaba, L. (2016). Social innovation research: An emerging area of innovation studies? *Research Policy, 45*(9), 1923–1935.

WCED, S. W. S. (1987). World commission on environment and development. *Our common future, 17*(1), 1–91.

Witell, L., Kristensson, P., Gustafsson, A., & Löfgren, M. (2011). Idea generation: Customer co-creation versus traditional market research techniques. *Journal of Service Management, 22*(2), 140–159. https://doi.org/10.1108/09564231111124190

Witell, L., Snyder, H., Gustafsson, A., Fombelle, P., & Kristensson, P. (2016). Defining service innovation: A review and synthesis. *Journal of Business Research, 69*(8), 2863–2872.

Managing Employee Empowerment and Engagement to Foster Service Innovation

Jon Sundbo and Lars Fuglsang

1 Introduction

This chapter will discuss employees' engagement in service innovation based on empirical research and a conceptual model. Employees, particularly front-line personnel, play a special and central role in service innovation. However, it is still not clear how service firms can manage employees' engagement in service innovation processes along different stages of the innovation process. Particularly, there is a need to explore how managers can both induce innovation activities top-down and support and direct bottom-up innovation activities of employees. This requires particular management capabilities. Empowering employees top-down to engage in innovation activities and encouraging them to take initiatives more independently as intrapreneurs bottom-up (Pinchot, 1985) is an obvious but challenging path for service firms. Further, this managerial endeavor and employees' independent intrapreneurial activities can also lead to difficulties and even losses for the firm. Management must find ways to use "restrained management" (Fuglsang & Sundbo, 2016), that is, while exercising control over the overall innovation process, they must also give others with direct knowledge and experience of services freedom to innovate, as it is difficult for managers to fully understand the practical context of innovation. The key issue of this chapter is therefore

---

J. Sundbo (✉) • L. Fuglsang
Roskilde University, Roskilde, Denmark
e-mail: sundbo@ruc.dk; fuglsang@ruc.dk

© The Author(s), under exclusive license to Springer Nature Switzerland AG 2022
B. Edvardsson, B. Tronvoll (eds.), *The Palgrave Handbook of Service Management*,
https://doi.org/10.1007/978-3-030-91828-6_30

595

596   J. Sundbo and L. Fuglsang

to explore how empowerment and engagement of employees can be balanced since neither passivity from the employees nor maximal intrapreneurship is optimal (Sundbo, 1996). It is assumed that engagement and innovation drives must be balanced to create optimal value for the service firm, while the innovation system must be reflexive to assess the market and economic effects of the innovation and employee engagement (Sundbo & Fuglsang, 2002).

The purpose of this chapter is thus to discuss the concept of balanced innovation management as related to different stages of the service innovation process based on a model and some case examples. We first describe what the literature reports about employees' role in innovation processes. Then, the model will be presented and illustrated using three case examples. Finally, we will conclude by drawing out the implications for management.

2   General Characteristics of Service Innovation Processes and Employees' Role

In this section, we describe the main specificities of service innovation processes. Generally, service innovation can be defined as the intertwined processes of developing new ideas and implementing these ideas in practice (Fuglsang, 2010). Innovations can be new to society, new to the market, and/ or new to the firm. Service innovations can represent radical as well as incremental new ideas. Different types of innovation are usually distinguished in the literature such as service innovation, service delivery innovation, organizational innovation, conceptual and systemic innovation (see e.g. Sundbo, 1997; Windrum, 2008; Barcet, 2010; Arundel, 2019). Innovation processes differ between services and manufacturing (Barcet, 2010; Rubalcaba et al., 2012; Snyder et al., 2016) since R&D departments and laboratories are very rare among service firms, and the few exceptions most often take the form of psychological and sociological experimental units (Gascó, 2017; Sundbo & Sørensen, 2014). Innovations in service firms are traditionally incremental (small), based on practical ideas developed from customer encounters, not very systematic, and driven by intrapreneurship (Fuglsang, 2010; Sundbo, 1997; Toivonen, 2010). Further, service innovations that normally integrate product and process renewal, which is a consequence of services according to the service theory (Grönroos, 2000), must be consumed in the moment of production and co-produced with the customer (Matthing et al., 2004). The delivery process and the service product cannot be separated. Service innovations are generally less radical and groundbreaking than manufacturing innovations. Conversely, they are very practice based and market based and often grounded in customers' concrete problems. The path from conceiving an idea to creating value for customers is, thus, shorter than that for developing and introducing goods.

Employees' innovative behavior is acknowledged as an approach that service companies can pursue to develop innovations. It encompasses management-led (corporate) activities for releasing and directing employees' innovative potential, and intrapreneurship activities defined as in-house entrepreneurship by independent, pro-active employees (Pinchot, 1985). Employees' innovative behavior in services can especially be described in relation to service encounters, bricolage activities, and intrapreneurship. Through their *encounters* with customers, a firm's employees, particularly frontline personnel, see the customers' problems, which often form the basis for successful service innovation, with a short journey from problem and need detection to realized innovations. Research has demonstrated that many employees in customer-encounter situations attempt to solve customers' problems using only the means at hand—which has been termed *bricolage* (Fuglsang, 2010; Fuglsang & Sørensen, 2011; Witell et al., 2017). Many employees have a drive to be *intrapreneurs* (Pinchot, 1985; Sundbo, 1997), which means that they act independent of management and strive to find new solutions and fight for their ideas within the organization.

Since employees' behavior in and after customer encounters is so important for service firms' innovation, management needs to empower employees (Bowen, 2016; Engen & Magnusson, 2015, 2018; Sundbo, 1999). Employees' intrapreneurship and bricolage cannot be planned from above, but management can empower employees to be innovative and give them freedom to independently solve customers' problems.

However, empowering employees, and the engagement of intrapreneurs and bricoleurs, also raise problems for management (Sundbo, 2010, 2013). Not all employees are entrepreneurial and overly strong attempts to empower employees and encourage them to be entrepreneurial can create anxiety and resistance in the organization. Management cannot control individual intrapreneurial and bricolage activities because employees develop these independently, often in collaboration with customers in concrete situations (Fuglsang, 2010). Employees' engagement in innovation activities can, with or without empowerment, lead to the firm's services developing in many different directions that not always are coherent. Employees can, for personal or institutional reasons (Hollebeek et al., 2018), also be so strongly engaged in and devote so much time to innovation activities that the total innovation effort in the firm leads to a loss, instead of profit (Sundbo, 1996, 2010, 2013).

3   Employee Involvement in Service Innovation

Employees' involvement concerns their concrete actions of innovations. Employees can be involved in many types of innovation activities, at several stages of the innovation process, from initial idea, through development, and ultimately to implementation. They can also take different roles in the innovation process (Engen & Magnusson, 2018; Sundbo, 1998), as further described in the next section. A fine-grained understanding of employees' involvement in innovation activities provides useful insight for strategic management toward developing an innovation culture (Fuglsang & Sørensen, 2011). We now delineate four modes of innovation drawn from research, with implications for various employee involvements. Specifically, they comprise employees directly engaged in innovation: (1) as integrated with work practice, (2) as a separate task, (3) as a separate function, and (4) as a networked activity:

First, employees may engage directly in innovation activities that are integrated with their everyday work practices (Brown & Duguid, 1991; Jensen et al., 2007). Various terms have been used in the literature for this phenomenon, such as "on the spot innovation" (Fuglsang & Sørensen, 2011), "ad hoc innovation" (Gallouj & Weinstein, 1997; Slåtten et al., 2011; Slåtten & Mehmetoglu, 2011), "tinkering" (Timmermans & Berg, 1997), or "bricolage activity" (Fuglsang, 2010). Employees solve problems on the spot and implement new ideas directly in situated work tasks. Examples include the service encounter where employees get ideas from their interaction with clients, and service repair work. In this mode, employees' involvement is part of a routinized work-innovation system. Through repetition and accumulation within the organization, on the spot and ad hoc innovations can be counted as innovation if they are repeated and when they lead to larger innovations over time. Often such innovations are situated activities, and hence create changes at the task level; over time, however, such innovations may become system-wide if picked up by other employees and by management.

Second, employees may become involved in innovation activities as a separate task. This refers to service firms organizing innovation activities as a separate and distinct task or activity (e.g. Gebauer et al., 2008, 2018) including NSD projects (e.g. Melton & Hartline, 2010, 2013). They may employ an "innovation manager" to facilitate the innovation process and ensure an outcome that fits the firm's strategy. Therefore, management leads this type of employee involvement and plays a role in selecting, developing, implementing, and stopping ideas. Employees are typically involved in idea-generation activities using their knowledge from the practical context of innovation. However, employees can also be involved in implementing selected ideas at the task level. In large corporations, idea generation can be handled through digital platforms, and managers can be involved in a comprehensive assessment of ideas.

Third, employees may be involved in service innovation as a separate function. Some service companies have R&D departments, or innovation labs (Sund et al., 2021; Sundbo & Sørensen, 2014), staffed with people whose main task is to develop new services. Thus, innovation is functionally differentiated as a separate function in the firm. These innovators have knowledge of the firm's resources and capabilities but also screen the market and conduct "skunk" work, as some distance from the organization can be important for generating radical new ideas. Sometimes, the development department can be a management team, while external actors may also be involved, such as technology providers, public authorities, or citizens. Other employees within the organization are involved in testing the ideas in practice.

Finally, employees may be involved in innovation activities through networking (Brown & Duguid, 2001; von Hippel, 1988). As members of practice communities, employees draw on colleagues to solve problems and can advocate new solutions through acts of intrapreneurship. Knowledge can often flow more freely within such a practice community than between different departments within a firm. For example, nurses, schoolteachers, taxi drivers, and service employees in banks are all members of practice communities. However, employees also have personal networks within or across firms that they can draw on to solve problems or get ideas for innovation that they promote through intrapreneurship.

These different modes of employee involvement vary along two dimensions that pose challenges for management. First, employees' degree of influence on innovation varies: it is higher in ad hoc innovation activities than in management-led idea generation. Second, the extension of innovation activities varies, with some activities concerning only changes to a specific work task and others concerning organization- or system-wide changes. Finally, the interaction of situated- and system-wide innovation activities must be carefully balanced to create value for the firm.

4 Proposed Models for Employee-Based Service Innovation

The issues of engaging and empowering employees in service organizations, together with balancing to avoid the risks of wasted resources and strategic diffuseness, have been the basis for models and general considerations in the literature. Here we summarize some of the most important models and considerations with the aim of presenting two general models, which will then be illustrated by case descriptions. The first model expresses innovation as a dual process in service firms; this process is a balance of empowerment and control. This model is seen from a system perspective. The second model expresses different roles that employees can have in service innovation processes. This second model is more seen from a micro social-psychological perspective.

One model integrates all factors related to balanced employee-based service innovation (Sundbo, 1996). It is formed as a dialectic system between engaged employees and responsible management. This model emphasizes all the encouragement and entrepreneurial mechanisms that determine employees' engagement in service innovation processes and the managerial system that guides this engagement. The managerial system contains two principal subsystems: an inducement system (Binswanger & Ruttan, 1978), which encourages employees to engage in innovation activities, and a control system, which ensures that these activities do not drain too many resources or split the firm's development in different directions. The model, which draws on empirical studies of service firms, is based on service innovation as a process with different steps from idea to fully implemented innovation; employees engage in different activities along the process. It can be drawn as follows (Fig. 1):

Employees' engagement in innovation processes can be driven by their own entrepreneurial spirit, encouragement from the managerial system, or coincidental customer encounters (Edvardsson et al., 2012; Matthing et al., 2004)—where employees use bricolage (Fuglsang, 2010; Witell et al., 2017). Management of the process is guided by the firm's strategy as a framework, managers' intuition and entrepreneurial "trial and error" drive, or an innovative culture developed in the firm. This management function can be

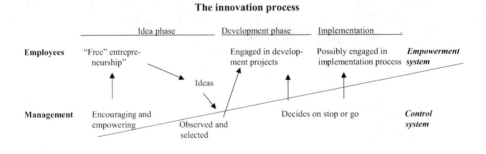

(drawn after Sundbo 1996 p. 407)

Fig. 1 The innovation process. (Drawn after Sundbo, 1996, p. 407)

performed by the top manager, middle managers, or a special innovation department (which is not the same as an R&D department in manufacturing). Who delivers empowerment and control can change along the innovation process, often with middle managers overseeing the first steps, the innovation department managing the middle stage, and top managers responsible for the final part.

One part of the innovation system is organizational learning (Senge, 1990). Different individuals in the organization, often a specific middle manager or an innovation department, attempt to learn how to empower employees in the most beneficial way (Sundbo, 1997). This learning is often seen within the framework of the firm's strategy or business model, a form of strategic reflexive learning (Sundbo & Fuglsang, 2002).

Others have approached engaging and empowering employees in service innovation processes by emphasizing the different roles they can have. "Role" is a social-psychological concept that characterizes the behavior in which people engage or is ascribed by the social group, including the workgroup or the wider organization (Goffman, 1959; Mead, 1934). Roles can be achieved: some people create their role through social struggling, such as intrapreneurship in organizations. Achieved roles do not necessarily lead to specific formal positions and sometimes lead to conflict with existing norms and habits. Roles can also be ascribed by the social group, and in service organizations by the manager. This may lead to a position of responsibility (e.g. innovation manager) or to new behavior that is positively sanctioned through feedback from management, which can be called empowerment. Defining different roles in innovation processes is also a way to model the empowered service innovation processes. Lessem (1987) identified seven roles that employees can take in innovation processes: (1) Adventurer, (2) Innovator, (3) Designer, (4) Leader, (5) Entrepreneur, (6) Change agent, and (7) Animateur. Sundbo (1998) subsequently identified five roles: (1) Idea provider, (2) Innovator, (3) Decision maker, (4) Developer, and (5) Sponsor or champion—a person who supports and encourages the idea providers and innovators (Pinchot, 1985; Burgelman, 1983). Wolcott and Lippitz (2007) suggested a model with four intrapreneurship roles for employees: (1) Enabler, (2) Opportunist, (3) Producer, and (4) Advocate. More recently, Bowen (2016) suggested that employees can take the following four roles: (1) Innovator, (2) Differentiator (equivalent to bricoleurs, getting ideas from customer encounters), (3) Enabler (encouraging customers to present innovation ideas), and (4) Coordinator. These works show that employees have different roles in different phases of the innovation process. Research demonstrates that employees' innovative efforts are most individual

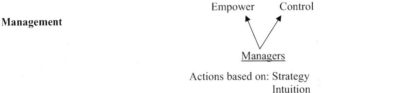

	Innovation phases:	Idea	Roles Development	Implementation
Employee engagement		*Idea provider* (present ideas) *Intrapreneur* (action) *Bricoleur* (customer problem solving, direct implementation)	*Developer* (project member, designer) *Coordinator* (leader, decision maker) *Sponsor* (support innovators)	*Producer* (production and delivery of the innovation) *Learner* (ensure organi- zational learning)

Management

Employees
Empower   Control
         \/
        Managers

Actions based on: Strategy
                  Intuition
                  Corporate culture
                  Top-entrepreneurship (managers act
                                        proactively)

Fig. 2 Model for empowerment and engagement of employees in service innovation processes

and detached from the organizational hierarchical structure in the first idea phase, then become more systematized and embedded in the organizational structure as the development proceeds toward implementation (Sundbo, 1997).

This suggests a general model for managing employee empowerment and engagement to foster service innovation (Fig. 2). The model has two levels, one describing the management side and emphasizing the balance of empowerment and control, and the other describing how employees engage based on roles and phases in the innovation process.

5 Cases

To illuminate the referred research results and the model, we present three cases containing the mechanisms described above. The cases represent different types of services and different forms of employee engagement and empowerment.

Small Bank—Laan & Spar

The small Danish bank Laan & Spar Bank introduced several programs to empower and engage employees to create innovations and organizational learning (Sundbo, 1999). The overall approach was to train employees with the aim of increasing engagement in developing the organization and its product portfolio. The bank wanted to enhance service quality and customer satisfaction, pursuant to the strategic goal of growth and increased customer loyalty. Management also wanted to develop new bank products and engage employees in innovation activities. The programs focused on employees' behavior. Employees were encouraged to listen to customers to get ideas for new services and delivery processes. The start of this empowerment development was, thus, a top-down management initiative based on new strategic goals; however, the aim was to empower employees to run the processes independently, generating ideas and initiating innovation processes and learning. By creating an entrepreneurial culture in the bank, management hoped to create a self-going innovation and development mechanism where employees themselves make innovations.

Several training programs were established and employees were encouraged to get ideas for innovations and fight to realize those ideas. The whole organization, including middle managers, was told to accept and encourage employee-based ideas and employees' actions for developing new services, better customer relations, and a more efficient and dynamic organization. Many employees presented ideas and many working groups were established to develop and implement the ideas. The HRM department was in charge of the training systems and organizational development, while the top manager made stop-go decisions in each group, thereby exercising control (see Fig. 2). In many cases the groups exercised self-control, for example, by rejecting ideas that proved unrealizable. This often happened when employees from other departments, such as marketing or a special product department, were involved: they brought new experiences into the process.

Employees were encouraged to play roles as idea providers and intrapreneurs (see Fig. 2). As the aim was to systematize organizational development and innovation, the bricoleur role was not encouraged. Each employee was instructed to tell the rest of the organization about their isolated solution for a single client, enabling this solution to be implemented throughout the organization. As employees were involved in the development groups, they also played the role of developers and, sometimes, coordinators. The sponsor role was superfluous as top management had empowered employees, leaving little resistance against new ideas. When ideas were implemented, some employees were assigned the role of producer through job positions in a new department or group dedicated to producing and delivering the new service or back-office function.

The empowering process was followed and results measured. After the programs had run for some years, they were assessed as successful initiatives. Many new ideas had been presented and some implemented. Customer satisfaction and organizational vitality had increased and employees had become more engaged in their work and the bank's problems and strategy.

However, this case also reveals some of the challenges of empowering employees. Some employees began to resist the intrapreneur role because it created an excessive workload—they had to undertake their normal tasks alongside engaging in intrapreneurial activities. What can be called the "extended barter" between employees and the firm (Sundbo, 1999) tipped too much toward the negative side. Some employees felt that the engagement and interesting development activities, which they assessed as positive, were outweighed by the family problems that their increased workload created. Further, the learning role did not function. As demonstrated in other cases (Sundbo, 1997), interest in storing the learning of all the innovation and empowering activities was limited in Laan & Spar, among both employees and managers.

Software Service—Ibistic

Ibistic is a small Norwegian firm, which also operates in Denmark and has an IT development department in Spain. It provides administrative business services, including invoice processing, travel accountancy, and purchase administration. The firm's services are IT-software based, but customers often interact with Ibistic employees. The market for such administrative services is very competitive and the services pretty standardized. Therefore, the firm is very dependent on customer care and its services are very price sensitive.

Ibistic wished to innovate and introduce new services to satisfy existing customers and attract new ones (Sørensen et al., 2013). The firm's innovation attempts were organized in two ways. Software innovations were handled by the Spanish development department, as the equivalent of a manufacturing R&D department. The other innovation route was based on customer needs and employees' interaction with customers, from whom 80% of innovations stemmed. This was not as well-organized as the software development department, but management encouraged employees to listen to customers and present ideas for innovation based on customer encounters. Further, many employees independently formed ideas from customer encounters, often based on bricolage or customers raising a problem, and they presented these ideas to managers and the whole organization.

Those who encounter customers are the salespersons, product line managers, and employees in the help desk function. They acted as bricoleurs or idea providers, but rarely as intrapreneurs due to limited available time for entrepreneurial and innovative activities. Their contribution generally did not extend beyond observing a customer need or generating an idea; there were no structured procedures for how to pass on ideas or customer needs to managers and others in the organization. Mostly, employees raised their ideas with product line managers, who had formal responsibility for innovation and acted as developers and coordinators.

This innovation system ensured that innovations were based on concrete customer needs, but they were only incremental improvements. There was also a schism between the frontline personnel (salespersons) and production line managers, who sometimes had different interpretations of customers' problems and which ideas to promote. Also, communication between them was sometimes very brief and superficial, which can lead to misunderstandings. However, if a product line manager identified a wider business perspective for a new idea, they could start a development process involving different categories of employees.

Elderly Care—Copenhagen Municipality

The third case is a home help service for the elderly in Copenhagen, Denmark. This public service was developed during the 1960s and 1970s to enable people to stay longer in their own home without dependency on relatives. Regulations and procedures prescribe how to ensure cost-effectiveness, compliance with due process of law, universalism, and fairness. A common "language" has been created that regulates the work in detail and divides it into certain tasks and packages. The work is done by a visitation officer acting in accordance with a detailed visitation scheme. Therefore, development and innovation of home-care services are usually seen as internally driven and top down. The dominant structure involves politicians and public managers making decisions on development, innovation, or reform of the service, which home-care organizations then apply in a manner relevant to their area. Home helpers thus implement new ideas through a management-led implementation process.

The case study shows, however, that this is too narrow a view on employees' involvement in innovation activities (Fuglsang, 2010; Fuglsang & Sørensen, 2011). Rather than merely being informed about changes and adapting them to their work tasks, employees played a much more active role. First, visitation officers and other staff in the municipal organization were involved in specific innovation tasks. Through regular small workshops, they provided ideas on how to widen and improve services, such as using idle resources to add services requested by elderly clients. For example, drivers could use their available time to transport the elderly to a shopping center. For an idea deemed relevant and usable by the management, managers could allocate a small amount of resources for testing the idea and checking whether it fits with other practices, tasks, and the overall obligations and strategy of the organization. Here, employees had the role of idea providers.

Another pattern of innovation identified in the case was bricolage. When visiting elderly clients, home helpers often encounter unforeseen events that have to be dealt with immediately. For example, finding that an elderly person is sick, the home helper could suggest serving lunch on the bed using the ironing board as a table; to avoid scaring a deaf client by suddenly appearing in the living room, the home helper could alert the client of their presence by stamping on the floor to create vibrations. Though small, these inventions are nevertheless deemed extremely important for service quality. The bricolage activities entailed using available resources accumulated over time to solve problems on the spot. They added up to larger innovations over time, as home helpers discussed their bricolage acts with colleagues over lunch, enabling wider adoption in the organization and thereby affecting the overall service offer. In this regard, employees acted as coordinators and sponsors.

These acts of bricolage can go on unnoticed by management. However, a more strategic and formalized approach to bricolage can be developed and supported by managers, who then function as sponsors. Thus, the researchers of this case (Fuglsang & Sørensen, 2011) intervened to explore how bricolage acts could be better integrated with organizational processes. Home helpers were asked to send ideas for bricolage to the researchers during a two-month period. Incoming ideas from management and employees were categorized as "easy to use," "usable but not immediately," and "difficult to use." This experiment demonstrated that it was possible to use bricolage in a more strategic and controlled way as a path to innovation.

Overall, this case shows that bricolage can emerge from service encounters within work tasks, based on employees' values, and be directly implemented into work tasks. Beyond this, bricolage acts can also be integrated into organizational processes through a more strategic approach. Research on bricolage activity in small firms (Baker & Nelsen, 2005) has similarly shown that brico-lage can be managed in two ways: as parallel bricolage and as strategic brico-lage. Parallel bricolage is a broad culture of bricolage encouraged by management, whereas strategic bricolage implies that certain bricolage acts are selected strategically to fit the organization and then further developed through management–employee collaboration. The first implies that employ-ees have control, whereas the second entails a more system-wide, management-led control system.

The cases illustrate the proposed models. The three cases' position in the two models is compared in Table 1.

The three cases can be seen on a scale from most to least active employee engagement in innovation activities. Laan & Spar clearly has the most active engagement and empowerment system, which was successful; however, this case also demonstrates that too much pressure on innovation engagement, in the long run, can dis-engage some employees. The elderly care case is an example of how strongly employees' intrapreneurship drive can break through a tight control system. The Ibistic case may more express a typical situation in service firms: there is some encouragement of employees' engagement in innovation activities and some engagement from employees, but the manage-ment does not really follow up and control and there are some organizational frictions.

6   Conclusion: Implications for Management

Empowering and engaging employees to foster service innovation is a com-plex process with many activities, roles, and control mechanisms but no stan-dard structure. Therefore, it makes demands on management, who must be aware of and have an active role in service innovation processes. The proposed model can be a tool for analyzing the situation in single firms and guiding the process. The management should emphasize the balance of control and empowerment that is expressed in the model Fig. 1. Too much control com-bined with too little empowerment might lead to little innovation as the elderly care case demonstrates. Too much empowerment and too little control of employees' engagement and well-being might lead employees to get tired in the entrepreneurship process such as the Laan & Spar case demonstrates. The Ibistic case is an example of a service firm that manages to engage the employ-ees in innovation processes, but the follow-up system with selection and development of the ideas could be better.

608 J. Sundbo and L. Fuglsang

Table 1 Comparison of the three cases

	Laan & Spar Bank	Ibistic	Elderly care
Empowerment and control system (Model Fig. 1)	Active empowerment programs. Light control, which includes little control with employees' well-being. Top management decision in the development phase.	General encouragement of employees' innovation effort. However, only little follow-up on this effort. No particular control system.	No empowerment of employees or encouragement of employees' innovation effort. Strong control system
Management actions (Model Fig. 2)	Creating empowering engagement, intrapreneurship, and learning programs to enhance customer satisfaction.	A mixture without clear connection: R&D department to develop technology, general encouragement of employee intrapreneurship.	Emphasizing standard procedures and "following the rules."
Employee roles (Model Fig. 2)	Employees took the role of intrapreneurs. Many of them took other roles such as developer, coordinator, and producer. Only the learner role did not function well.	Frontline employees mostly took roles in the idea phase. Other employees took over in the development and implementation phase. Communication between these two groups was not efficient.	Employees took the role of bricoleurs themselves. They did not enter other roles
Result: Innovation and entrepreneurship	Much innovation and entrepreneurship and many innovations, but several employees got tired of this and in the development phase felt a decrease in well-being.	Several incremental innovations	Some incremental innovations or service adaptions, based on frontline employees' co-created bricolage with customers.

The management should also emphasize the different roles that employees can play in the innovation process such as expressed in the model Fig. 2. Employees have different competencies and are different persons. How can that be utilized to create different roles thus the spectrum of roles mentioned in Fig. 2 can be covered? Laan & Spar bank is an example of an active attempt to let employees carry out their different personalities and competencies in different roles, which resulted in comprehensive innovation processes. Ibistic is an example of a service organization that not has managed to create a spectrum of engaging roles with the consequence that innovation is limited. The elderly care case is an example of management that neither has managed to create a spectrum of engaged roles, but the employees themselves have developed their own personal roles and started bricolage innovation processes.

Managers need to do the following that is expressed in Table 2:

Overall, managing employee empowerment and engagement to foster service innovation is a compound task for managers. It is organizationally underpinned by both practice-based innovation (i.e. innovations that transpire in and emerge from employees' everyday practices at the task level) and more structured innovation processes that sponsor and control employees'

Table 2 Recommendations for management to create an efficient employee-base innovation system

Understand the innovation process, the roles of employees, and their own roles.
Engage and empower employees in innovation processes. This means creating a general entrepreneurial culture and allocating freedom and time for each employee to participate in these processes
Discover employees' own initiatives and intrapreneurship. In particular, bricolage tends not to be observed by others in the organization but has the potential to considerably boost business because it is directly customer-oriented
When introducing their own innovation ideas and acting as top entrepreneurs (Sundbo, 1997), they should be aware of the advantage of involving employees, particularly the frontline personnel, in testing and implementing ideas. Frontline personnel encounter customers, so their knowledge about what customers might accept can be particularly valuable
Provide control and help to adjust the innovation process and employees' role behavior to avoid wasting resources and dividing business development in too many directions (which erodes the strategic line). Employees should be involved in these considerations because they have knowledge of the practical context of innovation and can, thus, contribute to strategic reflexivity (Sundbo & Fuglsang, 2002). The process of management can sometimes be collective
Secure organizational learning about innovation processes and engaging and empowering employees. Despite its importance, this is often forgotten because interest is low after concrete innovations have been implemented

innovation activity and idea generation to enable integration with organizational processes. As a compound activity, it may itself be weakly regulated and there is potential for sharing this task with employees.

References

Arundel, A., Bloch, C., & Ferguson, B. (2019). Advancing innovation in the public sector: Aligning innovation measurement with policy goals. *Research Policy, 48*(3), 789–798.

Baker, T., & Nelson, R. E. (2005). Creating something from nothing: Resource construction through entrepreneurial bricolage. *Administrative Science Quarterly, 50*(3), 329–366.

Barcet, A. (2010). Innovation in services: A new paradigm and innovation model. In F. Gallouj & F. Djellal (Eds.), *The handbook of innovation and services*. Edward Elgar.

Binswanger, H., & Ruttan, V. (1978). *Induced innovation*. John Hopkins University Press.

Bowen, D. E. (2016). The changing role of employees in service theory and practice: An interdisciplinary view. *Human Resource Management Review, 26*(1), 4–13.

Brown, J. S., & Duguid, P. (1991). Organizational learning and communities-of-practice: Toward a unified view of working, learning, and innovation. *Organization Science, 2*(1), 40–57.

Brown, J. S., & Duguid, P. (2001). Knowledge and organization: A social-practice perspective. *Organization Science, 12*(2), 198–213.

Burgelman, R. A. (1983). A process model of internal corporate venturing in the diversified major firm. *Administrative Science Quarterly, 28*(2), 223–244.

Edvardsson, B., Kristensson, P., Magnusson, P., & Sundstrom, E. (2012). Customer integration within service development – A review of methods and an analysis of insitu and exsitu contributions. *Technovation, 32*(7–8), 419–429.

Engen, M., & Magnusson, P. (2015). Exploring the role of front-line employees as innovators. *Service Industries Journal, 35*(6), 303–324.

Engen, M., & Magnusson, P. (2018). Casting for service innovation: The roles of frontline employees. *Creativity and Innovation Management, 27*(3), 255–269.

Fuglsang, L. (2010). Bricolage and invisible innovation in public service innovation. *Journal of Innovation Economics, 1*(5), 67–87.

Fuglsang, L., & Sørensen, F. (2011). The balance between bricolage and innovation: Management dilemmas in sustainable public innovation. *Service Industries Journal, 31*(4), 581–595.

Fuglsang, L. and Sundbo, J. (2016). Innovation in public service systems. In Toivonen, M. (Ed.), Service Innovation. Springer.

Gallouj, F., & Weinstein, O. (1997). Innovation in services. *Research Policy, 26*(4-5), 537–556.

Gascó, M. (2017). Living labs: Implementing open innovation in the public sector. *Government Information Quarterly, 34*(1), 90–98.

Gebauer, H., Krempl, R., Fleisch, E., & Friedli, T. (2008). Innovation of product-related services. *Managing Service Quality, 18*(4), 387–404.

Goffman, E. (1959). *The presentation of self in everyday life*. Doubleday.

Grönroos, C. (2000). *Service management and marketing: A customer relationship management approach*. Wiley.

Hollebeek, L. D., Andreassen, T. W., Smith, D. L. G., Gronquist, D., Karahasanovic, A., & Márquez, Á. (2018). Epilogue – Service innovation actor engagement: An integrative mode. *Journal of Services Marketing, 32*(1), 95–100.

Jensen, M. B., Johnson, B., Lorenz, E., & Lundvall, B. Å. (2007). Forms of knowledge and modes of innovation. *Research Policy, 36*(5), 680–693.

Lessem, R. (1987). *Intrapreneurship*. Wildwood House.

Matthing, J., Sanden, B., & Edvardsson, B. (2004). New service development: Learning from and with customers. *International Journal of Service Industry Management, 15*(5), 479–498.

Mead, G. H. (1934). *Mind, self and society*. University of Chicago Press.

Melton, H. L., & Hartline, M. D. (2010). Customer and frontline employee influence on new service development performance. *Journal of Service Research, 13*(4), 411–425.

Melton, H. L., & Hartline, M. D. (2013). Employee collaboration, learning orientation, and new service development performance. *Journal of Service Research, 16*(1), 67–81.

Pinchot, G. (1985). *Intrapreneuring*. Harper & Row.

Rubalcaba, L., Michel, S., Sundbo, J., Brown, S., & Reynoso, J. (2012). Shaping, organizing and rethinking service innovation: A multidimensional framework. *Journal of Service Management, 23*(5), 696–715.

Senge, P. (1990). *The fifth discipline. The art and practice of the learning organization*. Century Business.

Slåtten, T., & Mehmetoglu, M. (2011). What are the drivers for innovative behavior in frontline jobs? A study of the hospitality industry in Norway. *Journal of Human Resources in Hospitality & Tourism, 10*(3), 254–272.

Slåtten, T., Svensson, G., & Sværi, S. (2011). Empowering leadership and the influence of a humorous work climate on service employees' creativity and innovative behaviour in frontline service jobs. *International Journal of Quality and Service Sciences, 3*(3), 267–284.

Snyder, H., Witell, L., Gustafsson, A., Fombelle, P., & Kristensson, P. (2016). Identifying categories of service innovation: A review and synthesis of the literature. *Journal of Business Research, 69*(7), 2401–2408.

Sørensen, F., Sundbo, J., & Mattsson, J. (2013). Organisational conditions for service encounter-based innovation. *Research Policy, 42*(8), 1446–1456.

Sund, K. J., Bogers, M., & Sahramaa, M. (2021). Managing business model exploration in incumbent firms: A case study of innovation labs in European banks. *Journal of Business Research, 128*, 11–19.

Sundbo, J. (1996). The balancing of empowerment. A strategic resource based model of organizing innovation activities in service and low-tech firms. *Technovation, 16*(8), 397–446.

Sundbo, J. (1997). Management of innovation in services. *Service Industries Journal, 17*(3), 432–455.

Sundbo, J. (1998). *The organization of innovation in services*. Roskilde University Press.

Sundbo, J. (1999). Empowerment of employees in small and medium-sized service firms. *Employee Relations, 7*(1–2), 105–127.

Sundbo, J. (2010). The toilsome path of service innovation: The effects of the law of low human multi-task capability. In F. Gallouj & F. Djellal (Eds.), *The handbook of innovation and services*. Edward Elgar.

Sundbo, J. (2013). Blocking mechanisms in user and employee based service innovation. *Économies et Sociétés, Serie Économie et gestion des services, 14*(3–4), 479–506.

Sundbo, J., & Fuglsang, L. (Eds.). (2002). *Innovation as strategic reflexivity*. Routledge.

Sundbo, J., & Sørensen, F. (2014). The lab is back – Towards a new model of innovation in services. In C. Bilton & S. Cunningham (Eds.), *The handbook of management and creativity*. Edward Elgar.

Timmermans, S., & Berg, M. (1997). Standardization in action: Achieving local universality through medical protocols. *Social Studies of Science, 27*(2), 273–305.

Toivonen, M. (2010). Different types of innovation processes in services and their organisational implications. In F. Gallouj & F. Djellal (Eds.), *The handbook of innovation and services*. Edward Elgar.

Von Hippel, E. (2005). *Democratizing Innovation*. MIT Press.

Windrum, P. (2008). Innovation and entrepreneurship in public services. In P. Windrum & P. Koch (Eds.), *Innovation in public sector services. Entrepreneurship, creativity and management* (pp. 3–20). Edward Elgar.

Witell, L., Gebauer, H., Jaakkola, E., Hammedi, W., Patricio, L., & Perks, H. (2017). A bricolage perspective on service innovation. *Journal of Business Research, 79*, 290–298.

Wolcott, R. C., & Lippitz, M. J. (2007). The four models of corporate entrepreneurship. *Sloan Management Review*, October.

Understanding Key Market Challenges Through Service Innovation

Bo Edvardsson, Bård Tronvoll, and Lars Witell

1 Introduction

Service innovation is a key source of competitive advantage across firms and markets (Helkkula et al., 2018), and it has become critical to firm growth and profitability (Flint, 2006). Rubalcaba et al. (2012) argue that "innovation is not just a new offering but rather improved customer value cocreation" (p. 697). To succeed, firms face key market challenges both when designing and introducing new services into the market (Gustafsson et al., 2020). Therefore, service innovation can be used as a lens to understand how firms can overcome key market challenges to improve their performance. However, currently available theoretical frameworks for service innovation cannot explain how new solutions diffuse across markets, resulting in value creation for all engaged actors (e.g., customers, employees, firms).

This book chapter focuses on service innovation in relation to three key market challenges—novelty, diffusion and value capture. This focus is chosen, as firms need to offer new and value-creating solutions to the market, that is, provide *novelty* (Nijssen et al., 2006), as well as identify solutions that are

---

B. Edvardsson (✉) • L. Witell
CTF, Service Research Center, Karlstad University, Karlstad, Sweden

B. Tronvoll
CTF, Service Research Center, Karlstad University, Karlstad, Sweden

Inland Norway University of Applied Sciences, Elverum, Norway
e-mail: bo.edvardsson@kau.se; bard.tronvoll@inn.no; lars.witell@kau.se

© The Author(s), under exclusive license to Springer Nature Switzerland AG 2022
B. Edvardsson, B. Tronvoll (eds.), *The Palgrave Handbook of Service Management*,
https://doi.org/10.1007/978-3-030-91828-6_31

accepted and used by a growing number of customers, that is, promote *diffusion* (Rogers, 1965), while securing value created in the market place—*value capture* (Chesbrough et al., 2006). As these key market challenges do not exist in isolation, understanding their interdependency is vital, which necessitates service innovation frameworks that can explain how business actors find novel ways to create, diffuse and capture value. Recent theoretical frameworks have extended the business view to include service structures, social practices and processes enabling or inhibiting service innovations (see, e.g., Lusch & Nambisan, 2015). Some of these theoretical frameworks portray service innovation as an institutional change process (see, e.g., Vargo et al., 2015). Although many approaches have been suggested, none of the existing frameworks addresses the interdependencies among market challenges, novelty, diffusion and value capture. This gap in extant knowledge is also reflected in a recent literature review (Singh et al., 2020), and the growing recognition by service innovation scholars that existing research needs to be augmented in order to better understand service innovation performance (Gustafsson et al., 2020).

This book chapter provides an integrating framework on service innovation that can be applied to elucidate three key market challenges: *novelty, diffusion* and *value capture*. The remainder of the chapter is structured as follows. First, a review of pertinent service innovation literature is provided, focusing on the existing frameworks aimed specifically at service innovation. Next, we introduce a new framework denoted as *structuration of service innovation*, with the emphasis on the systemic and dynamic nature of service innovation, including social interactions among multiple collaborating actors. We subsequently use the newly proposed framework to explain novelty, diffusion and value capture from the perspective of engaged actors. The chapter closes with the key theoretical implications and managerial guidelines that can be derived from this work.

2 Service Innovation Frameworks

In order to develop an integrated framework on service innovation that is capable of explaining novelty, diffusion and value capture, we have reviewed the existing frameworks, which can broadly be classified under three categories (Kowalkowski & Witell, 2020): (1) the Lancasterian approach, (2) the dynamic capability approach and (3) the service-dominant (S-D) logic approach. These three approaches respectively emphasize different characteristics of service innovation, the types of resources needed to facilitate service innovation, and how actors, resources and institutional arrangements are integrated to foster service innovation. In what follows, these framework categories are discussed in terms of their ability to capture novelty, diffusion and

Table 1 An overview of the existing service innovation frameworks

Approach	The Lancasterian approach	The dynamic capability approach	The Service-dominant (S-D) logic approach	Structuration of service innovation
Description	The Lancasterian approach describes service innovation according to its characteristics	*The dynamic capability approach emphasizes the types of resources needed to facilitate service innovation*	*The service-dominant (S-D) logic approach emphasizes how actors, resources and institutional arrangements are integrated to foster service innovation*	Renewal of value creation conceptualized through agency, structure and states
Example of a service innovation / Definition	Any change affecting one or more terms of one or more vectors of characteristics	A service innovation is a new service experience or service solution that consists of one or several dimensions	Service innovation entails developing existing or new provision practices, representational practices, and organizational practices and/or the operand and operand resources that these integrate	The rebundling of resources with the aim of creating novelty, beneficial to the actors in a given context
Core concepts	Vectors of characteristics: offerings, technology and competencies Modes: radical, incremental, improvement, formalization, ad hoc and recombinative innovations	Dimensions: new service concept, new customer interaction, new value system/business partners, new revenue model, new organizational or technological service delivery system	Service ecosystem, resource integration, value co-creation, institutions	Agency, structure and states
Key market challenges addressed	Novelty and diffusion	Novelty, diffusion and value capture[a]	Novelty, diffusion and value capture[a]	Novelty, diffusion and value capture
Key references	Gallouj and Weinstein (1997), Windrum and Garcia-Goni (2008)	Den Hertog et al. (2010)	Skålén et al. (2015), Vargo et al. (2015)	Edvardsson et al. (2018)

[a]Although all market challenges are addressed in these approaches, they are not incorporated into a single framework

616   **B. Edvardsson et al.**

value capture (see Table 1). The key characteristics of these frameworks are subsequently compared to the structuration of service innovation framework.

The Lancasterian approach was first proposed by Gallouj and Weinstein (1997) to describe service innovation according to its characteristics, such as offerings, technology and competencies. According to Gallouj and Savona (2009), service innovation results from changes in any of these characteristics, allowing six innovation modes to emerge: radical, incremental, improvement, formalization, ad hoc and recombinative innovations. For service, recombinative innovation is a fundamental mode, as it captures the essence of innovation and requires exploration and mobilization of an extended set of resources and competencies (knowledge and skills) in the target market, in order to classify innovations based on their degree of novelty.

The dynamic capabilities approach emphasizes "the firm's ability to integrate, build, and reconfigure internal and external competencies to address rapidly changing environments" (Teece et al., 1997, p. 516). Guided by this premise, Den Hertog et al. (2010) proposed a conceptual framework with six dynamic service innovation capabilities: (1) signaling user needs and technological options, (2) conceptualizing, (3) (un)bundling, (4) co-producing and orchestrating, (5) scaling and stretching and (6) learning and adapting. These authors further argue that novelty ranges from new to the firm to new to the world. However, they do not elaborate on how this distinction shapes service innovation conceptualization.

In their service-dominant (S-D) logic approach, Vargo and Lusch (2016) applied a systemic lens to suggest that actors are resource integrators that co-create value guided by institutions in service ecosystems. Previously, Vargo et al. (2015, p. 69) posited that institutional theory needs to be extended by focusing on "the social practices and processes that drive value creation and, more specifically, innovation—the combinatorial evolution of new, useful knowledge." They further argued that institutionalization—the maintenance, disruption and change of institutions—is a central process for technology and market innovation. More recently, Edvardsson and Tronvoll (2013) explored how and why actors are reconfiguring resources and altering schemas [institutionalized arrangements] as a basis for innovation in service systems. Lusch and Nambisan (2015) described service innovation as a collaborative process in service ecosystems building on (1) service ecosystems, (2) service platforms and (3) resource integration, thus emphasizing the importance of the underlying mechanisms that shape and direct actors' roles and resource integration processes, for which agency is crucial.

To conclude, the three approaches presented above and summarized in Table 1 show that a wide range of frameworks is available to understand and explain the renewal of value creation through service innovation. However, none of these approaches captures all three market challenges (novelty, diffusion and value capture) and their interdependencies in one coherent framework.

3 Structuration of Service Innovation

The structuration of service innovation framework is an integrative framework for service innovation that can be adopted to better understand and explain the three key market challenges—novelty, diffusion and value capture. The framework draws on the existing models based on the service-dominant (S-D) logic approach and introduces structuration as an overarching concept to denote the central role of actors and their capacity to innovate. We argue that actors are both enabled and inhibited by social and business structures. As actors simultaneously affirm the societal structures and the system itself, there is a "duality of structure." In this context, "structure" refers to a virtual order of practices organized according to procedural rules that guide action and have no enduring material aspect. We view the service innovation process as grounded in states in which the initiating, realizing and outcome states are unfolding as a part of the recursive dynamic interplay between agency and structure.

Through their purposeful activities (agency), actors and their activities are focused on creating a practice that over time represents the system structures. Their actions are both enabled and inhibited by these self-generated social and business constructs, that is, the practices organized through procedural rules that guide action. Therefore, the service innovation process is grounded in initiating, realizing and outcome states unfolding in the recursive dynamics between agency and structure. To become an innovation, the initiating state must realize resource integration and value co-creation, resulting in a sufficient value for the engaged actors to become sustainable in a given market. To become a service innovation, that is, innovation that is viable in the target market, its value-in-context must match the engaged actors' ability to extract value.

The proposed structuration of service innovation framework (see Fig. 1) thus incorporates *agency* (the ability to act purposefully) as we argue that it is the basis for operating on and reconfiguring resources to foster service innovation within markets. According to the proposed framework, *structure* provides guidelines for enabling and inhibiting actors' use of resources in specific contexts with specific value creation outcomes in mind (Scott, 2008). On the

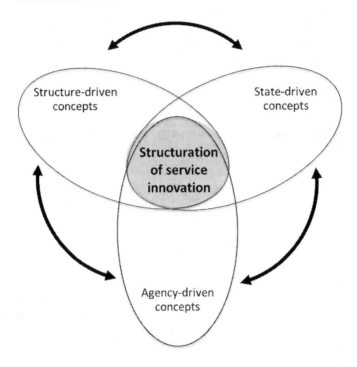

Fig. 1 Conceptualizing the structuration of service innovation

Table 2 Conceptualizing structuration of service innovation

Concept	Definition	Selected references
Structuration of service innovation	Renewal of value creation is conceptualized through agency, structure and states	Agency (Giddens, 1984; Giddens & Pierson, 1998) Structure (Giddens, 1984; Orlikowski, 2000) States (Kelly & Storey, 2000; Robertson, 1967)
Agency	Actors' use of resources expressed through innovative value propositions	Actors (Lusch & Nambisan, 2015) Resources (Kleinaltenkamp et al., 2012) Value proposition (Payne & Frow, 2014)
Structure	Institutionalized norms and rules enabling renewed, innovative value creation	Institutions and institutional arrangements (Kleinaltenkamp et al., 2012; Lusch & Nambisan, 2015)
State	The initiating, realizing and outcome phases from idea to creation of a market	Initiating (Perks & Riihela, 2004) Realizing (Methlie & Pedersen, 2007) Outcomes (Simmons & Fajans, 2007)

other hand, *state* emphasizes firms' coordinating roles in innovation processes, as the processes establish resources and help realize the potential of service innovations within markets (novelty, diffusion and value capture). Table 2 provides definitions of the key concepts captured by the structuration of service innovation framework.

Agency

Agency denotes actors' disposition and capacity to act purposefully and make free choices according to their individual and collective intentions. Actors (firms, employees, customers and partners) are invited to integrate and operate on available resources to co-create value for themselves and others, directed by a value proposition. As innovating actors have specific intentions and novel outcomes in mind, they give energy and direction to the service innovation process. Tronvoll (2017) argues that actors play a key role as the foundational resource for value co-creation in the service ecosystem. Consequently, actors can operate on or use relevant, available resource configurations within service ecosystems (Vargo & Lusch, 2008).

Service innovations entail creating new and attractive value propositions in a particular context for the engaged beneficiaries. According to Lusch and Nambisan (2015), value propositions can connect one actor with other interested actors in the service ecosystem in order to enhance their own and the service ecosystem's viability. Thus, a value proposition guides and directs service innovations and helps actors develop "more effective value propositions for participating in beneficiaries' resource-integrating, value-creating practices through service" (Lusch & Vargo, 2014, p. 87). In sum, innovative actors' intentions and agency guide service innovation processes and outcomes in service ecosystems.

IKEA's key service innovation builds on how value can be co-created in smarter ways, using customers' agency, including knowledge, skills and motivation, as reflected in the company's "solutions to real-life problems at home for the many" value proposition. As cost containment is needed to offer low prices and reach out to the many, IKEA designs and offers its products in flat packages, and customers who assemble the furniture co-create the solutions. The company's value proposition is communicated in various slogans enhancing the actors' focus, such as "We pack flat, you do the job, and together we make money" or "Democratic design," suggesting that good design, concerning both function and esthetics, is not just for those who can afford it but for everyone. This example illustrates a service innovation that builds on

620   B. Edvardsson et al.

integrating resources and actors in an existing institutional realm that lowers costs, which is crucial for product diffusion and value capture. Novelty and smart resource integration processes can explain the success of IKEA's service innovation efforts.

Structure

Structures are the coordinating social and business mechanisms that guide and shape actors, relationships and practices (Kjellberg & Helgesson, 2007). According to Vargo and Lusch (2016), structures form institutional arrangements expressed in "rules, norms, meanings, symbols, practices, and similar aides to collaboration" (p. 6) and "institutional arrangements facilitate coordination of activity in value co-creating service ecosystems" (p. 14). Institutions denote relatively independent rules, and interrelated sets of institutions produce institutional arrangements, which in turn shape how actors use resources by regulating (enabling or inhibiting) actors' resource integration and value co-creation efforts (Alderson, 1965). However, innovative actors challenge and change existing institutionalized norms, rules and habits, and thus the ways of co-creating value with and for engaged actors (Lusch & Vargo, 2014). Similarly, service innovation changes institutionalized norms and rules and establishes new ones while retaining those that are still useful (Koskela-Huotari et al., 2016).

In a digital world with the Internet as a "global institutionalized structure," new ways of integrating and using existing resources emerge. Service innovations are made possible by the smart use of mobile and social technologies and the creation of new norms and rules for multiple actors engaged in resource integration. For example, AirBnB changed the notion of hotel service by breaking the market rules for how accommodation is provided. The company's online resource platforms enable customers and other actors to connect and interact on their own terms. In a similar vein, Uber has also created a successful service ecosystem through collaboration with other brands and service systems already available in the markets of many countries. Uber Eats has scaled up very fast since the service was launched in 2014, fueled by the COVID-19 pandemic. While changes to institutional arrangements have enabled these innovations, some markets have been resistant to changes, especially those threaten the viability of existing services. Social and business structures provide a basis for explaining why and how novelty is achieved and innovation is diffused within markets, while allowing identification of factors that can inhibit or enable the value capture for engaged actors.

State

The process of innovation denotes the realization of novelty through actor engagement (Storbacka et al., 2016). The service innovation process is driven by innovative actors' ideas, their creativity, intentions and access to resources. In pertinent literature, the service innovation process is conceptualized as comprising of three states—initiating an innovation, realizing the innovation and capturing the outcomes—which implies market creation grounded in diffusion and value capture.

In the initiating state, useful ideas are generated and formulated, focusing on the novelty and how it can be co-created with and for engaged actors, including firms and their customers, partners and suppliers. This innovation phase mainly pertains to formulating a value proposition in relation to what already exists and what changes are needed in service ecosystems (Lusch & Vargo, 2014). In this state, the value proposition is formulated and tested, ensuring that it resonates with a sufficient number of actors. The aim of this evaluation is to receive sufficient support for the service innovation process to be realized, that is, determine that it would manifest in novelty, diffusion and value capture for engaged actors. The realizing state concerns value-in-context for the engaged actors as a result of service innovation. Thus, it includes value capture throughout the service innovation process, including the strategic, tactical and operational levels, as well as addressing any differences among actors.

In this context, "outcome" denotes novelty or renewed value-in-context for engaged market actors, as service innovations require creating a market through diffusion to ensure that they become sustainable (Vargo et al., 2015). Diffusion and market creation through service innovation that attracts customers constitute a complex social, technological and institutional process. We argue that service innovations emerge in the states of initiating, realizing and outcome creation within service ecosystems during the service innovation process.

The challenges actors face when managing the service innovation processes—that is, the initiating, realizing and outcome states—are not easy to handle. However, history has shown that these challenges do not halt entrepreneurial, creative actors' efforts. In 1943, Thomas Watson, the long-time chair of IBM, stated, "I think there is a world market for maybe five computers" and Albert Einstein in 1932 found "not the slightest indication that nuclear energy will ever be obtainable." Yet, innovators ignore such predictions, as exemplified by Henry Ford's recognition that "If I had asked people what they wanted, they would have said faster horses" and by the comment from one of the inventors of Post-It notes, Spencer Silver from 3M who said "If I had thought about it, I wouldn't have done the experiment." The literature is full of similar examples. The states in the innovation process suggested in the proposed framework help explain how actors initiate ideas resulting in novelty that can diffuse across markets and co-create value for engaged actors. Sometimes the initiation and realization states require the adoption of well-crafted ways of breaking established norms or rules, while sometimes it is necessary to adjust to rules that might not be possible to change.

4 Discussion

In this section, we discuss the interdependencies underpinning the structuration of service innovation before applying the newly proposed framework to explain key market challenges for businesses and other organizations in their service innovation efforts.

The Interdependencies Underpinning the Structuration of Service Innovation

The structuration of service innovation framework zooms out from the narrow perspective focusing on the creation of offerings, specific changes in resources or the introduction of new ways of using resources. Instead, the framework acknowledges the social and business resources and processes that connect actors, thereby fostering innovation. Furthermore, our framework resonates with the ideas put forth by Kleinaltenkamp et al. (2012), who emphasized the importance of innovative forms of collaboration involving multiple actors and the coordination of activities in service ecosystems. Consequently, as most existing service innovation frameworks are too narrow in scope, they cannot explain key market challenges underlying the service innovation phenomena. This issue is addressed by the newly proposed framework as it enables simultaneous zooming in on the interdependencies among novelty, diffusion and value capture from the perspective of multiple market actors, rather than focusing on the value capture linked to specific actors only.

Using the Framework to Explain Key Market Challenges

Different actors (and groups of actors) extract different value in line with their intentions and reasons for engaging in value co-creation activities, guided by the available institutional arrangements. Traditionally, novelty has been viewed through newness, ranging from new to the firm to new to the world, or has been classified as incremental or radical innovations (Snyder et al., 2016).

In our framework, *novelty* refers to changes in agency and/or structure manifested in the value proposition. It is designed throughout different states in the service innovation process and it is actor-defined and context-specific. Actors' agencies foster changes in resource integration and structures, resulting in enough strategic benefits for the engaged actors. New forms of strategic benefits are important for a novel value proposition to pass through the different states of the service innovation process and diffuse in the market.

Diffusion of service innovation starts in the outcome state of the service innovation process, and is influenced by the existing structures and institutional arrangements. As multiple actors constantly evaluate the diffusion process in different ways (Muniesa, 2011), they may either support the diffusion process or decide to step out of the system and even warn others to become engaged. Diffusion of service innovation has previously been captured through the criticized reverse product cycle (Barras, 1986), according to which, it starts via new technologies aimed at improving efficiency, followed by improvements in the quality of existing services and the introduction of new services.

Value capture is always rooted in existing and institutionalized market practices (Kjellberg & Helgesson, 2007) and form the basis for sustainability of service innovations. Value capture is not a challenge for individual actors only, but is rather a multi-actor challenge. Hence, to continue the collaboration, all engaged actors need to capture "enough" value in relation to their value proposition. Furthermore, the involved firms' business models often need to change to capture the value created by innovation.

5   Conclusions

We believe that the presented framework can contribute to the development of service research in emerging fields, such as green innovations, digital service innovations and new social services. This prompts us to ask: *What is the characterizing DNA in these innovative ecosystems?* Social innovation is a field that

Theoretical Implications

Recent approaches to service innovation have moved away from Lancasterian characteristics and dynamic capabilities in recognition of the need to gain a systemic understanding of innovation, drawing on service-dominant logic (Di Pietro et al., 2017). The introduction of the concepts of agency, structure and state through the structuration of service innovation enables researchers to zoom in on the interplay of different theoretical concepts to better understand service innovation. The new framework thus broadens the understanding of service innovation and transcends the business and social system divide (Edvardsson et al., 2011).

By introducing this framework, we highlight the duality and interdependencies of agency, structures and states of service innovation. We also recognize that structuration is crucial for conceptualizing service innovation within markets, as it enables or inhibits new and useful ways of co-creating value for businesses, public and government services, and nonprofit organizations, while improving social and private life. Institutional arrangements and work practices enable actors to use or inhibit them from using resources in a specific context with a specific value creation outcome in mind. The new framework addresses how and why actors innovate when reconfiguring resources and altering institutionalized arrangements and how they perform the process (Edvardsson & Tronvoll, 2013).

Managerial Implications

The first benefit of the proposed framework stems from conceiving novelty, diffusion and value capture as separate yet interdependent challenges which need to be addressed simultaneously to ensure the success of service innovation. Even though an entrepreneur develops a novel value proposition with the potential for value capture, it might not still diffuse in the market, as service innovation diffusion is strongly coupled to value capture for all engaged actors.

The second contribution of our framework is realized by adding the service innovation process to the existing frameworks. We argue that institutionalized arrangements need to be both broken, kept and maintained, and suggest that timing is crucial when different institutionalized arrangements are challenged and changed to enable the scaling up of innovations. For example, when moving toward electrical mobility, in what state should different actors, including governments and international standardization organizations, be involved? Moreover, what market structures and rules need to be challenged to enable a novel value proposition.

References

Alderson, W. (1965). *Dynamic Marketing Behavior*. Richard D. Irwin.

Barras, R. (1986). Towards a theory of innovation in services. *Research Policy, 15*(4), 161–173.

Chesbrough, H., Birkinshaw, J., & Teubal, M. (2006). Introduction to the research policy 20th anniversary special issue of the publication of "Profiting from Innovation" by David. *Research Policy, 35*(8), 1091–1099.

Den Hertog, P., van der Aa, W., & de Jong, M. W. (2010). Capabilities for managing service innovation: Towards a conceptual framework. *Journal of Service Management, 21*(4), 490–514.

Di Pietro, L., Edvardsson, B., Reynoso, J., Renzi, M. F., Toni, M., & Mugion, G. R. (2017). A scaling up framework for innovative service ecosystems: Lessons from Eataly and KidZania. *Journal of Service Management, 29*(1), 146–175.

Edvardsson, B., & Tronvoll, B. (2013). A new conceptualization of service innovation grounded in S-D logic and service systems. *International Journal of Quality and Service Sciences, 5*(1), 19–31.

Edvardsson, B., Tronvoll, B., & Gruber, T. (2011). Expanding understanding of service exchange and value co-creation: A social construction approach. *Journal of the Academy of Marketing Science, 39*(2), 327–339.

Edvardsson, B., Tronvoll, B., & Witell, L. (2018). An ecosystem perspective on service innovation. In F. Gallouj & F. Djellal (Eds.), *A research agenda for service innovation* (pp. 85–102). Edward Elgar Publishing.

Flint, D. J. (2006). Innovation, symbolic interaction and customer valuing: Thoughts stemming from a service-dominant logic of marketing. *Marketing Theory, 6*(3), 349–362.

Gallouj, F., & Savona, M. (2009). Innovation in services: A review of the debate and a research agenda. *Journal of Evolutionary Economics, 19*(2), 149–172.

Gallouj, F., & Weinstein, O. (1997). Innovation in services. *Research Policy, 26*(4–5), 537–556.

Giddens, A. (1984). *The constitution of society: Outline of the theory of structure.* University of California Press.

Giddens, A., & Pierson, C. (1998). *Conversations with Anthony Giddens: Making sense of modernity*. Stanford University Press.

Gustafsson, A., Snyder, H., & Witell, L. (2020). Service innovation: A new conceptualization and path forward. *Journal of Service Research, 23*(2), 1–5.

Helkkula, A., Kowalkowski, C., & Tronvoll, B. (2018). Archetypes of service innovation: Implications for value cocreation. *Journal of Service Research, 21*(3), 284–301.

Kelly, D., & Storey, C. (2000). New service development: Initiation strategies. *Library Consortium Management: An International Journal, 2*(5/6), 104–122.

Kjellberg, H., & Helgesson, C. F. (2007). On the nature of markets and their practices. *Marketing Theory, 7*(2), 137–162.

Kleinaltenkamp, M., Brodie, R. J., Frow, P., Hughes, T., Peters, L. D., & Woratschek, H. (2012). Resource integration. *Marketing Theory, 12*(2), 201–205.

Koskela-Huotari, K., Edvardsson, B., Jonas, J. M., Sörhammar, D., & Witell, L. (2016). Innovation in service ecosystems—Breaking, making, and maintaining institutionalized rules of resource integration. *Journal of Business Research, 69*(8), 2964–2971.

Kowalkowski, C., & Witell, L. (2020). Typologies and frameworks in service innovation. In E. Bridges & K. Frowler (Eds.), *The Routledge handbook of service research insights and ideas* (pp. 109–130). Routledge.

Lusch, R. F., & Nambisan, S. (2015). Service innovation: A service-dominant (S-D) logic perspective. *MIS Quarterly, 39*(1), 155–175.

Lusch, R. F., & Vargo, S. L. (2014). *Service-dominant logic: Premises, perspectives, possibilities*. Cambridge University Press.

Methlie, L. B., & Pedersen, P. (2007). Business model choices for value creation of mobile services. *Info, 9*(5), 70–85.

Muniesa, F. (2011). A flank movement in the understanding of valuation. *Sociological Review, 59*, 24–38.

Nijssen, E. J., Hillebrand, B., Vermeulen, P., & Kemp, R. (2006). Exploring product and service innovation similarities and differences. *International Journal of Research in Marketing, 23*(3), 241–251.

Orlikowski, W. J. (2000). Using technology and constituting structures: A practice lens for studying technology in organizations. *Organization Science, 11*(4), 404–428.

Payne, A., & Frow, P. (2014). Developing superior value propositions: A strategic marketing imperative. *Journal of Service Management, 25*(2), 213–227.

Perks, H., & Riihela, N. (2004). An exploration of inter-functional integration in the new service development process. *Service Industries Journal, 24*(6), 37–63.

Robertson, T. S. (1967). The process of innovation and the diffusion of innovation. *Journal of Marketing, 31*(1), 67–89.

Rogers, E. M. (1965). *Diffusion of innovations*. Free Press of Glencoe.

Rubalcaba, L., Michel, S., Sundbo, J., Brown, S. W., & Reynoso, J. (2012). Shaping, organizing, and rethinking service innovation: A multidimensional framework. *Journal of Service Management, 23*(5), 696–715.

Scott, W. R. (2008). *Institutions and organizations: Ideas and interests.* Sage Publications.

Simmons, R., & Fajans, P. M. L. (2007). *Scaling up health service delivery: From pilot innovations to policies and programmes.* World Health Organization.

Singh, S., Akbani, I., & Dhir, S. (2020). Service innovation implementation: A systematic review and research agenda. *The Service Industries Journal, 40*(7–8), 491–517.

Skålén, P., Gummerus, J., Koskull, C., Von, P., & Magnusson. (2015). Exploring value propositions and service innovation: A service-dominant logic study. *Journal of the Academy of Marketing Science, 43*(2), 137–158.

Snyder, H. L., Witell, A., Gustafsson, P., Fombelle, P., & Kristensson, P. (2016). Identifying categories of service innovation: A review and synthesis of the literature. *Journal of Business Research, 69*(7), 2401–2408.

Storbacka, K., Brodie, R. J., Böhmann, T., Maglio, P. P., & Nenonen, S. (2016). Actor engagement as a microfoundation for value co-creation. *Journal of Business Research, 69*(8), 3008–3017.

Teece, D., Pisano, G., & Shuen, A. (1997). Dynamic capabilities and strategic management. *Strategic Management Journal, 18*(7), 509–533.

Tronvoll, B. (2017). The actor: The key determinator in service ecosystems. *Systems, 5*(2), 38–51.

Vargo, S. L., & Lusch, R. F. (2008). Service-dominant logic: Continuing the evolution. *Journal of the Academy of Marketing Science, 36*(3), 1–10.

Vargo, S. L., & Lusch, R. F. (2016). Institutions and axioms: An extension and update of service-dominant logic. *Journal of the Academy of Marketing Science, 44*(1), 5–23.

Vargo, S. L., Wieland, H., & Akaka, M. A. (2015). Innovation through institutionalization: A service microsystems perspective. *Industrial Marketing Management, 44*(1), 63–72.

Customer-to-Customer Interactions in Service

Kristina Heinonen and Richard Nicholls

1 Introduction

A few weeks ago, I was travelling to London by train. I arrived at the railway station about 15 minutes before the scheduled departure time. Unfortunately, there was a long queue to the ticket counter. A few minutes later, when I was 2nd in the queue and very close to buying my ticket, the customer being served started asking questions about connections to Edinburgh. He could not make up his mind and it took up a lot of time. At last he bought a ticket and it was for travel on the next day! Other passengers, including me, were irritated and frustrated—especially as the counter had a big sign saying, 'Tickets only—no information given'. There was no time left to buy a ticket, and I had to board my train without a ticket and buy one from the conductor at extra cost.

Customers are constantly influenced not only by the activities of service organizations but also by the activities of other actors and resources in the service setting. Other customers present during the service are one such influence on the service. Usually referred to as customer-to-customer interaction (CCI),

---

K. Heinonen (✉)
Department of Marketing, Centre for Relationship Marketing and Service Management (CERS), Hanken School of Economics, Helsinki, Finland
e-mail: kristina.heinonen@hanken.fi

R. Nicholls
Customer Interactions Research Group (CIRG), Worcester Business School, University of Worcester, Worcester, UK
e-mail: r.nicholls@worc.ac.uk

© The Author(s), under exclusive license to Springer Nature Switzerland AG 2022
B. Edvardsson, B. Tronvoll (eds.), *The Palgrave Handbook of Service Management*,
https://doi.org/10.1007/978-3-030-91828-6_32

interactions among customers are a significant phenomenon and, indeed, in some service settings more significant than employee-to-customer interactions (Zhang et al., 2010; Colm et al., 2017). Furthermore, as technology and the sharing economy develops, there are more and more interactions between customers in various contexts. Many millions of customer-to-customer interactions take place each day, and some have a profound and lasting effect on value creation and the customer's overall perception of the service and its provider. While service organizations are usually not blamed for negative influence on customers by peer customers, they are typically held responsible for dealing with it (e.g. Baker & Kim, 2018) and will be blamed for failing to do so (e.g. Colm et al., 2017). Furthermore, CCI and the failure to manage it can impact employee satisfaction and retention (Nicholls & Gad Mohsen, 2019), making CCI a challenging phenomenon for organizations in general.

The interaction between the provider and the customer has traditionally been a way for managers to build customer loyalty and relationships, by managing the service environment, improving service quality and creating customer satisfaction (Barsky & Labagh, 1992; Bitner, 1992). This is not surprising since the nexus of the service has classically been on customer-provider relationships and service encounters: "The focal relationship is the one between a supplier or provider of goods or services and buyers and users of these goods or services" (Grönroos, 2004, p. 101). The classic notion of service was manifested in customers' perceptions of service encounters, that is, the "moment of interaction between the customer and the firm" (Bitner et al., 1990, p. 71). Nonetheless, the mainstream marketing literature has been largely silent on the effect of interactions among customers on the service experience (Brocato et al., 2012).

However, the seminal study by Martin and Pranter (1989) approached service from a different perspective and was one of the first to explicitly explore customer-to-customer interactions, suggesting that other customers in the service environment are also part of the service. Although service research has also acknowledged the influence of other aspects than customer-employee interactions on customers' service experience, such as servicescapes (e.g. Bitner, 1992), the notion of other customer influence has received considerably less attention in mainstream service research (Nicholls, 2010; Colm et al., 2017). This phenomenon is generally referred to as CCI and can be defined as the *customer-to-customer (C2C) interaction between out-groups, usually viewed as a stranger(s), in the same physical service setting, behaving and/or appearing in a way that influences the service of the focal customer(s).* These out-groups are different to in-groups, such as accompanying friends and family. CCI research has tended to focus on interpersonal interaction in the service environment. For instance, customers support each other in the service, for example, by providing "product/service related information that employees would normally be expected to supply" (Harris & Baron, 2004, p. 299). CCI links to other service roles customers take, such as self-service, participation and co-creation (Bateson, 1985; Bitner et al., 1997; Bendapudi & Leone, 2003; Dong & Sivakumar, 2017).

While CCI is classically construed as occurring onstage in a physical service setting, the growing infusion of technology in services in recent decades has resulted in more interaction opportunities and widespread connections between customers and other actors. Service delivery is increasingly outside the service provider's domain highlighting interactions and behavior that influence customers in their own domain, often through technology, when they live their everyday lives (Heinonen et al., 2010; Grönroos & Voima, 2013): "what customers do beyond the point of interaction with the service provider may be just as vital for enabling customer engagement as what happens during service encounters" (Heinonen & Strandvik, 2018, p. 148). Indeed, social value creation and customer-to-customer interactions represent alternative opportunities for customer value creation (Grönroos & Voima, 2013; Heinonen et al., 2018). The aim of this chapter is thus to explore interactions among customers—labeled customer-to-customer interactions (CCI)—in the service setting. We review scholarly contributions on CCI with the purpose to present an overview of how customers' perceptions of the service are influenced by the other customers present in the service. The focus is on conceptualizing the range of CCI, including key terms used for CCI as well as the main methods for studying CCI. The conceptualization of CCI is further used to direct attention to the managerial strategies for supporting CCI.

This chapter is structured into four sections. The first section provides a brief outline of the background of CCI and distinguishes it from customer-provider interactions. This is followed by a conceptualization of the main ways in which customer-to-customer interactions occur. This central section of the chapter digs deeper into the characteristics of CCI. The third section discusses the managerial approaches to CCI. And the fourth section concludes the chapter by putting forward an agenda for future research into CCI.

2 Customer Interactions as Service Encounters

Service Encounters as Interactions and Touchpoints Between the Customer and the Provider

Service encounters are one of the key phenomena in service research and the foundation of customers' service experiences. Service encounters denote interactions and touchpoints between the customer and the provider, typically a service employee, and essentially represent the service as experienced by the customer (Bitner et al., 1990). In other words, they involve all interactions that influence a customer's overall perception of the service. The interactions are different based on whether the customer goes to the service organization, the service organization comes to the customer, or whether the interaction occurs at arm's length (Lovelock, 1983). Service encounters were traditionally categorized in three types (Shostack, 1985): the direct personal encounter referred to direct human interaction, the indirect personal encounter verbal but no face-to-face interaction, and the remote encounter occurring without human interaction with the service provider, such as through mail or machine.

Today, it is widely acknowledged that customers' service experiences are formed not only in the actual service encounter, or moment of truth (Normann, 1984), but interactions also occur pre-service and post-service (c.f. Lemon & Verhoef, 2016). These interactions or touchpoints are individual contacts, either physical or virtual, between the firm and the customer at distinct points which customers encounter products, services, brands, places, people, processes, channels, technologies (Lemon & Verhoef, 2016; Buttle & Maklan, 2019). Service researchers often enumerate these points in terms such as service setting; service systems and technologies; frontline employees and other customers. A number of service/retailing frameworks attempt to capture the elements that customers interact with during their service experience (Bitner, 1992; Tombs & McColl-Kennedy, 2003; Turley & Chebat, 2002; Lemon & Verhoef, 2016).

An important aspect of most interaction frameworks is human interaction. Indeed, some service management researchers use the term *interaction* to refer specifically to human interaction, commonly investigating the interaction taking place between employees and customers (E2C). The scope of this research includes identifying component parts of E2C interaction (e.g. Price et al., 1995); employee value-added (e.g. Bettencourt & Gwinner, 1996); employee empathy, courtesy, reliability and responsiveness (e.g. Wieseke et al., 2012; Parasuraman et al., 1985), examining specific interaction contexts such as cross-cultural interaction (e.g. Sharma et al., 2015), exploring interactions with certain groups (e.g. Baker et al., 2007) and service recovery (e.g. Fernandes et al., 2018). However, it is largely assumed that the service interaction and customer-service relationship are the customer's key focus (Heinonen et al., 2010; McColl-Kennedy et al., 2015).

Yet, although service encounters strongly highlight customer-employee interactions, encounters include interactions with other actors as well. Customers also encounter other actors in the service setting, such as friends, peers and strangers; however, these interactions have received relatively less focus in research (Nicholls, 2010). To some extent service frameworks have taken 'other customers' into account (e.g. Eiglier & Langeard, 1977; Booms & Bitner, 1981; Gummesson, 1993; Tombs & McColl-Kennedy, 2003; and Baron & Harris, 2010), but given that the extent of C2C interaction often exceeds that of E2C interaction (e.g. Miao & Mattila, 2013), this inattention is surprising. While the C2C literature is relatively small compared to the E2C literature, it is no longer negligible (Colm et al., 2017).

Customer-to-Customer Interactions (CCI) in Service Settings

Researchers examining CCI have been strongly influenced by the meaning of interaction between customers conveyed in seminal service management contributions such as the servuction system (Eiglier & Langeard, 1977; Bateson, 1985). Despite early conceptual contributions (e.g. Eiglier & Langeard, 1977), Martin and Pranter's seminal article in 1989 is often recognized as the breakthrough point in research attention to onstage CCI within the service management community. It was followed by a period of 'crawling out' of CCI literature during the 1990s. In the twenty-first century, however, the amount of scientific literature identifying itself as addressing CCI has grown rapidly and, since around 2010, explosively. This section discusses some of the factors that have influenced this growth.

The interest in CCI has been influenced by wider, paradigmatic shifts in marketing. Significant changes in how marketing science is comprehended led to a re-conceptualization of how the customer's role is understood. The growth of interest in relationships in marketing, and influential frameworks such as the 30Rs (Gummesson, 1997), stimulated interest in relationships beyond the focal firm, and raised the profile of CCI. Indeed, the emergence of the term *C2C*, given the well-established usage of *B2B*, highlighted the conceptual relevance of CCI.[1] Customers are increasingly portrayed as having an active role in value creation (Grönroos, 2008). Consumption can be usefully understood in terms of value which is co-created by the provider and the consumer (Prahalad & Ramaswamy, 2004). The service-dominant logic perspective (Vargo & Lusch, 2004), with its portrayal of customers as operant resources, together with the customer-dominant logic highlighting the customer's domain of service (Heinonen et al., 2010), have provided an enhanced theoretical foundation to the research of CCI.

The growing interest in CCI over the last three decades is partly due to the realization that CCI is applicable to a wide range of service. The pervasiveness of CCI is evident in the fact C2C interactions outnumber interactions between customers and employees in some service settings (Nicholls, 2010). Early work emphasizes CCI's relevance to retailing and leisure settings (e.g. Harris et al., 1995; Grove & Fisk, 1997). As the number of empirical studies grew it became apparent that CCI is relevant in a diverse range of service, including education (e.g. Hoffman & Lee, 2014); tourism and hospitality (e.g. Huang & Hsu, 2010; Nicholls, 2011), leisure (e.g. Zhang et al., 2010; Kim et al., 2020), passenger transportation (e.g. Harris & Baron, 2004; Small & Harris, 2014), personal services (e.g. Moore et al., 2005) and membership organizations (e.g. Gruen et al., 2000). Other factors explaining the increasing relevance of CCI include the growth of self-service technologies, and the attendant reduction in employee presence (Kim & Yi, 2017), and the emergence of the sharing economy (Heinonen et al., 2018).

The amount of research on CCI is actually greater than is first apparent. This is because a wide range of terminology, other than 'CCI', has been used to refer to CCI or aspects of it (Table 1), and a wide range of research methods utilized to study CCI (Table 2). These methods, often qualitative and exploratory in nature, range from asking consumers to recall CCI, through the observation of CCI, to methods rooted in the physical sciences. The next section explores the conceptualizations of CCI with the main emphasis on physical service settings.

---

[1] While CCI and C2C interaction are often used interchangeably to refer to customer-to-customer interaction, in this chapter we use CCI.

Table 1 Key terms used for CCI

CCI term	Reference
General CCI	
Compatibility management	Martin and Pranter (1989)
Observable Oral Participation between customers (OOP2)	Harris et al. (1995)
Fellow customer	Martin (1995)
Unacquainted influence	McGrath and Otnes (1995)
Other customers	Grove and Fisk (1997)
Negative CCI	
Interclient conflict	Shamir (1980)
Other customer failure	Huang (2008)
Other customer service failures/other customer-generated service failures	Baker and Kim (2018)
Other customer caused service failures	Kim and Baker (2020)
CCI in service sub-sector	
Guest-to-guest interaction	Papathanassis (2012)
Tourist-to-tourist interaction	Huang and Hsu (2009)
Student-to-student interaction	Rowley (1996)

3 Conceptualizing the Range of Customer-to-Customer Interactions

Much research attention has been paid to exploring different types of CCI. Common phenomena of CCI types include the provision of information to other customers, the sharing of space with other customers and social exchange between customers (Heinonen et al., 2018). Most research that identifies itself as concerning CCI has focused on direct on-site CCI, and mainly in physical, rather than virtual, service settings. This section conceptualizes the scope of CCI.

C2C interactions are generally seen as *verbal and/or behavioral* (e.g. Grove & Fisk, 1997; Nicholls, 2010; Söderlund, 2011). While verbal C2C interaction (i.e. "one customer says something to another customer"—Söderlund, 2011, p. 176) normally meets the dictionary meaning of interaction (e.g. "mutual or reciprocal action or influence"—Merriam-Webster), the use of the term *interaction* in the CCI literature can extend beyond the dictionary meaning of the term. In other words, behavioral interaction such as physically assisting another customer can also be seen as interacting. 'Interaction' might also be considered as including interactions where both customers are directly and explicitly engaging with each other, as well as more implicit interactions where, for example, only one customer is aware they are having a relevant interaction (e.g. overhearing a long phone conversation on the train). Research

Table 2 The range of CCI research methods

Method	References (examples)
Recall of CCI	
Critical incident technique	Grove and Fisk (1997), Zhang et al. (2010) and Nicholls (2020)
Observable oral participation—OOP2 (a service setting exit interview technique that asks customers about C2C conversations)	Baron et al. (1996) and Harris et al. (1995)
In-depth interviews	Schmidt and Sapsford (1995) and Nicholls and Gad Mohsen (2019)
Introspection	Baron et al. (2007), Ekpo et al. (2015) and Lloyd-Parkes and Deacon (2021)
Questionnaires	Martin (1996) and Huang and Hsu (2010)
Observation	
Video observation	vom Lehn (2006)
Participant observation	Arnould and Price (1993), McGrath and Otnes (1995), Cheang (2002), Harris and Baron (2004) and Rihova et al. (2018)
Netnography	Ekpo et al. (2015) and Gursoy et al. (2017)
Experiments	
Field experiments	Schmitt et al. (1992), Levy (2015) and Schaefers et al. (2016)
Scenarios	Thakor et al. (2008), Huang (2010) and Miao (2014)
Methods based on physical sciences	
Biometric studies (e.g. analyzing saliva samples; micturition delay)	Evans and Wener (2007) and Middlemist et al. (1976)

has recognized the explicit and implicit aspects to CCI (e.g. Martin & Pranter, 1989; Nicholls, 2010; Tombs & McColl-Kennedy, 2010; Kim & Choi, 2016). Both *explicit and implicit interactions* may influence the focal customer's perceptions of a service. The conceptual framework (Fig. 1) provides an overview of CCI types based on these two dimensions: *behavior* representing verbally centered and physically centered interaction, as well as explicitness representing explicit and implicit interaction. Figure 1 is depicted for analytical reasons in a two-by-two matrix; although some CCI types may be located in multiple quadrants, the matrix is useful to provide an abstraction of the CCI typologies.

The lower-left corner (Quadrant A) of Fig. 1 labeled *physical interaction* accommodates CCI situations in which other customers influence the service experience primarily through their actions rather than verbally. It involves

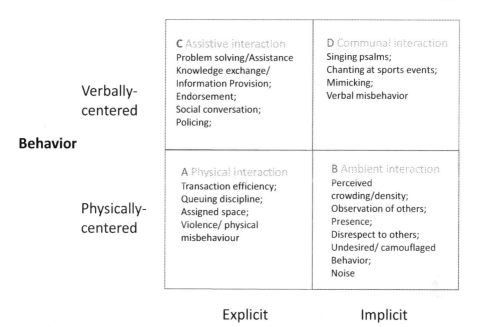

Fig. 1 Conceptual framework of CCI

explicit behavioral and bodily interactions between customers, such as pushing others or standing in the way. Research contributes several significant categories here. For example, transaction efficiency (Nicholls, 2020) concerns other customer behavior at the point of transaction that impacts the time of the focal customer (e.g. another customer being slow at the checkout). Queuing discipline (Grove & Fisk, 1997) relates to other customer behavior that is perceived as contravening queuing conventions (e.g. jumping the queue). Assigned space (Nicholls, 2020) concerns behavior by another customer that infringes space that has been allocated to the focal customer (e.g. a reserved train seat). Violence or physical misbehavior (Harris & Reynolds, 2004) covers a range of misbehaviors by other customers, sometimes extreme (e.g. hitting a customer), that impact the focal customer's experience. For a review of studies which include aspects of explicit behavioral C2C interaction see Heinonen et al. (2018) and Nicholls (2020).

Quadrant B in the lower-right of Fig. 1 also refers to behavioral interactions, but unlike Quadrant A, it is less explicit and more covert. This *ambient interaction* may involve looking at or overhearing others. Often these other customers simply form part of the overall service setting. Collectively they may create a certain ambiance that influences the focal customer's experience (e.g. Ekpo et al., 2015; Nicholls & Gad Mohsen, 2015). For example, Quadrant B accommodates mass communal behaviors such as spectators performing a Mexican Wave or a Viking Thunderclap at a sports stadium.[2] Similarly, the sheer numbers of other customers may contribute to a perception of crowding (Hui & Bateson, 1991). Observation of the behavior of other customers (Colm et al., 2017) can also provide useful informational cues about how to consume the service (e.g. do other customers order their drink at the bar or at the table?). Such learned behavior is typically picked up without the other customers realizing that they are being helpful and without verbal exchange, so is implicit C2C behavior and different in intent and gratitude to the verbal assistance that is found in Quadrant C. Observation can also bring about C2C comparison (and envy) of service levels received by others (e.g. Anaya et al., 2016; Ludwig et al., 2017) or awareness of another customer treating others with disrespect (e.g. Dorsey et al., 2016; Henkel et al., 2017). The appearance of another customer, which includes visual and olfactory aspects, although more specific than the general ambiance, is also a type of implicit CCI. The appearance of another customer might cause a customer to anticipate a certain sort of behavior or at least suggest a raised degree of unpredictability, for example, if hotel guests are swimming nude in the pool (Bitner et al., 1994). Appearance is a common aspect of undesired customers (e.g. Harris & Reynolds, 2004). Noise in the shared use space (Nicholls, 2020) impacts the service experience of a customer who also has the use of that space (e.g. another customer's mobile ringing during a movie).

Quadrant B also involves mere presence of another customer. Mere presence refers to C2C situations where another customer is simply present, and not explicitly interacting or seeking to interact, and this very presence influences the focal customer. Some service research is based on other customers merely being present and thus potentially influencing the focal customer's behavior and self-awareness. Examples include (1) others being present when buying an embarrassing product or revealing personal information (Nichols et al., 2015); (2) the presence of others making concentration on tasks more difficult (e.g. Luck & Benkenstein, 2015) and (3) experiencing the pressure of the noninteractive social presence of a queue behind (e.g. Dahm et al., 2018).

The upper-left corner of Fig. 1 (Quadrant C), labeled *assistive interaction*, is perhaps the most common type of CCI. This type involves conversations between customers, frequently goal-oriented for assistance or support or merely spending time while waiting. Information provision by another

---

[2] To the extent that such mass ambiance actions include verbal aspects, they might be considered to cross both quadrants B and D.

customer, including product endorsement, is one of the most common C2C types in retail (e.g. McGrath & Otnes, 1995; Baron et al., 1996). C2C assistance is widely reported in the literature (e.g. Grove & Fisk, 1997; Parker & Ward, 2000; Nicholls & Gad Mohsen, 2015; Tomazelli et al., 2017; Kim & Yi, 2017). Social conversations (cf. consumption-related conversations—Nicholls, 2020) between customers are common in travel and leisure contexts (e.g. Harris & Baron, 2004; Yin & Poon, 2016). Some explicit verbal C2C interaction takes place to police or protest in response to what is deemed inappropriate other customer behavior and is sometimes referred to as 'echo-CCI' (Nicholls, 2010).

Finally, Quadrant D in the upper-right corner of Fig. 1 depicts implicit verbal interaction. This type of CCI labeled *communal interaction* occurs commonly in large social gatherings such as sports events, concerts or group activities when other customers are singing, chanting or generally making noise, but it is not directed at specific customers. Such implicit verbal exchange can often be understood in terms of making a collective meaning, that is, sharing of rituals symbolic behavior, mimicking and in other ways acting symbolically (Gainer, 1995; Heinonen et al., 2018). Limited research attention has been paid to collective meaning making by CCI researchers, but it is present in brand communities (e.g. Schau et al., 2009), sports and entertainments events (e.g. Fairley & Tyler, 2012), or festivals (e.g. Rihova et al., 2018). This type of implicit verbal interaction also involves implicit verbal misbehavior, such as crying baby in a restaurant or other customers complaining or shouting to a service employee (Martin, 1996).

4 How Can CCI Be Managed?

Although, the "customer may be less easily controlled than employees (and the physical environment)" (Söderlund, 2011, p. 174), there are possibilities for influencing CCI (Martin, 2016; Nicholls, 2010). This position contrasts to the early days of service science when interactions between customers, while included within the 'participant' label of the 7P services marketing mix, were considered rarely to be within the control of the marketer (Booms & Bitner, 1981). In Table 3 we outline four key thematic strategies how managers can attempt to influence CCI. These strategies are aligned to the four quadrants in Fig. 1. *Contextual mediation* is concerned with managing explicit physically centered interaction (Quadrant A) and focuses on issues such as designing the environment to give customers adequate space, and creating and managing rules surrounding behavior. *Perceptual enhancement* concerns managing the more implicit aspects of physically centered interaction (Quadrant B), and includes the management of the collective impression that customers form of the density, flow and crowdedness of the service setting, and providing a sense of social predictability and orderliness. *Customer advocacy* concerns explicit verbally centered interaction (Quadrant C) and focuses on issues such as designing the environment to assist appropriate customers verbal exchange and supporting C2C good citizenship. *Social bonding* concerns the more implicit, collective aspects of verbally centered interaction (Quadrant D), and includes actions designed to generate collective verbal responses from audiences and other gatherings.

5 Going Forward: Avenues for Future CCI Research

The chapter has so far conceptualized and discussed the interaction occurring between customers, labeled customer-to-customer interactions, showing a broad range of CCI influencing the focal customer's perceptions of service. Based on this we develop implications for further research in C2C interactions and suggestions for broadening the conceptual understanding of C2C behavior.

A main avenue for future research is to explore the conceptual reach of C2C behavior. It is essential to explore how CCI relates to other theoretical constructs such as service experience, customer loyalty, and customer purchase behavior. Such research can advance the understanding of how other customers influence a focal customer's experiences and behavior. Moreover, to appreciate the full scope of CCI research it is important to recognize the existence of a body of literature that researches the same topics as the so-called CCI literature but which typically does not identify itself conceptually as researching CCI, for example research into topics such as crowding, mobility and third places. This literature, partly because it tends not to contain the typical terms used in systematic literature searches on CCI, is often overlooked by CCI researchers. Awareness of this literature questions existing assumptions about the extent of CCI-related research and the historical timeline of CCI research. It becomes clearer that research into CCI is far from 'minimal' and that it includes important contributions from before the field was formally identified and staked-out in Martin and Pranter's (1989) seminal paper.

Customer-to-Customer Interactions in Service 641

Table 3 Strategies for managing CCI

Topic	Strategy	Description	Example
Contextual mediation (Quadrant A) *Designing spatial and temporal convenience*	Sociofugal design	Designing the space to separate customers and give them their own 'bubble'	Own cubicle for customers in library
	Hygienic environment	Designing and maintaining the environment to minimize customer-to-customer hygiene issues	Frequent cleaning of gym equipment
	Behavior rules	Creating, communicating, monitoring and enforcing rules relating to the use of shared space and queuing	'No feet on seat' posters on trains
	Employee intervention	Training employees to spot misbehavior and to intervene effectively	Staff monitoring and controlling customers at a pool or ice rink
Perceptual enhancement (Quadrant B) *Influencing indirect behavior between customers*	Psychological management of queues	Organizational efforts to reduce the time perception of waiting and generally make waiting a more positive experience	Entertainers in theme park queues
	Density and space perception management	Designing customer flows and other customer visibility to reduce perceptions of crowding and to optimize actual and perceived density levels	Seating customers in restaurants to make it appear livelier
	Segmentation	Physical and sequential segmentation of customers in order to improve compatibility	Swimming pools with physical and/or time zones for serious swimmers and leisure swimmers
	Policing and surveillance	Patrolling the service setting to provide reassurance and ensure a suitable environment and to deter undesired behaviors	Security patrols at shopping malls

(continued)

Table 3 (continued)

Topic	Strategy	Description	Example
Customer advocacy (Quadrant C) *Catalyzing and mediating appropriate communication between customers*	Customer education	Training customers how to use the service and to interact appropriately with others	Directional signage
	Communication support	Facilitating customers' verbal interactions through relevant channels	Bulletin board or online discussion forum for sharing tips and resources
	Support citizenship	Encouraging and expressing gratitude to customers who have provided verbal assistance to other customers	Thanking a customer who has helped translate for a foreigner
	Sociopetal design	Designing the service setting to encourage verbal exchange between customers	Lounge area on a cruise ship
Social bonding (Quadrant D) *Fostering and stimulating indirect communication in groups*	Sociopetal design	Designing the service setting so that customers are more socially aware that they form a collective group	At a sports stadium a camera zooming in on supporters and showing them on a big screen
	Service cheer-leading	Designing the service setting to involve customers, often in the audience, to contribute to the atmosphere.	Performer encouraging the audience to join in the chorus of a song.
		Includes actions that enhance the bonding of a group by making it more removed from everyday life	Boat tour guide telling passengers to hold on tight as a big wave is approaching

Also many non-marketing disciplines contain studies that deal with CCI without identifying or labeling themselves as such. Within psychology, for example, relevant topics include the social psychology of queues (e.g. Schmitt et al., 1992); crowding (e.g. Hui & Bateson, 1991) and personal space and its intrusion (e.g. Evans & Wener, 2007). Sociologists have provided insights into how people interact with each other in urban and other environments (e.g. Gorman, 1979; Honkatukia & Svynarenko, 2018). Mobility researchers have studied issues like quiet carriage atmosphere (Hughes et al., 2017) on passenger trains. Some authors focus on a CCI-related concept but without making connections to CCI. For example, user noise in libraries; outdoor recreational conflict and third places. Many tourism and leisure studies, such as high-risk leisure consumption (e.g. Celsi et al., 1993), serious leisure (e.g. Kane & Zink, 2004), and tourist authenticity (e.g. MacLennan & Moore, 2011), contain significant undercurrents of CCI content that is not usually explicitly recognized as such. Embracing such studies can expand the granular understanding of CCI and carry several lessons for aspiring CCI researchers. Firstly, the CCI literature is far more extensive and older than most mainstream CCI writings suggest. Secondly, much relevant literature will be undetected in so-called systematic search that centers on self-identifying search terms such as 'customer-to-customer interaction', 'fellow customers', 'C2C'. Search strategies that draw on approaches such as manual searching and pearling are recommended. Thirdly, there are research methods available (e.g. Evans & Wener, 2007) beyond the usual ones employed in service management and marketing research. Indicating a need to extend the C2C research domain, Heinonen et al. (2018) developed an extensive list of further research questions around the theoretical and conceptual perspectives, the methods and the research contexts of C2C in the service research field.

There is therefore a pronounced need for future research to further identify and integrate research outside the mainstream service management area that is based on CCI. Certain disciplines, such as social psychology and urban sociology, are likely to be fertile grounds for such research. Likewise, certain industry-specific research, such as adventure tourism, cruises or festivals, is likely to reveal CCI-related research. Also, certain interdisciplinary research communities, such as mobility researchers, conduct research that is relevant to CCI.

Table 4 delineates key issues for future research. Within the scope of on-site interactions, there is potential for further conceptual research into issues such as *transtemporality* and *reciprocity* to help clarify what exactly constitutes a CCI. CCI can occur across time but in the same physical space and still influence another customer; for example, a previous customer at a gym may not have wiped down a piece of equipment after using it (Nicholls, 2005). Other literature also shows customers can be aware of the past presence of other customers. For example, consumer contamination concerns is detrimental to customer satisfaction when knowing products had previously been touched by other shoppers (Argo et al., 2006). The current COVID-19-related contamination issues, including concern over touching of service facility items by

644   K. Heinonen and R. Nicholls

Table 4 Key issues for future research

Theme	Future research questions
Transtemporality	Are customers aware of each other and their role in others' service experience?
	To what extent are customers perceptions of other customers influenced by their previous customer-to-customer experience?
Reciprocity	Who is assisting who?
	Are customers mutually benefiting each other?
	How do customers differentiate between other customer behaviors they deem to be (1) directed at them and (2) not directed at them?
	How does the perception of other customers vary according to whether the perceiving customer is alone or accompanied?
Digital CCI	How do CCI differ in a physical and digital context?
	In an e-learning context what is the influence of other customers' transaction efficiency, for example when a student takes an excessive amount of time to ask a question?
Non-verbal interaction	How are customers observing each other? Are customer mimicking each other?
	What is the relative influence of spoken CCI in comparison to non-verbal interaction?
Organizational perspective	What is the role of triadic interactions, that is between the FLE and customers A and B, for service experience?
	What strategies and tactics can be utilized by FLEs to handle CCI?
	What is the impact of replacing employee-based service with self-service on CCI?
	How can organizations train and support FLEs regarding CCI?
	How can organizations detect and record CCI?
	What are the consequences of CCI intervention on employee satisfaction?
	How can organizations support helpful CCI?
C2C influence	How is the term 'interaction' used in C2C research?
	In what ways is the term 'influence' broader than 'interaction'?
	To what extent is it useful, whether academically or managerially, to have a broader perspective on C2C?
	To what extent is WOM a pre-service experience phenomenon that reflects a *customer-to-potential-customer relationship* (Martin, 2016) rather than a customer-to-customer one?
	What is the influence of other customers on focal customer(s)?
	How are customers influencing each other's value creation?
	How is value created in different CCI?

previous users, are likely to increase research interest in transtemporal CCI. These examples indicate that while customers are not simultaneously in the service environment, they still influence each other through their actions.

The issue of CCI reciprocity is another area needing conceptual refinement. Colm et al. (2017, p. 5) conceptualize CCI as having bidirectional exchange (i.e. "both parties participate") or unidirectional exchange (i.e. "one party is passive and unaware of participation"). In some situations, the focal customer is aware of the behavior and/or appearance of another customer, but that other customer is not necessarily aware of her/his behavior and of its impact on others. For example, a customer may be unaware that they are blocking the view of another customer at the cinema.

Moreover, given the technology advancements, it is clear that more research is needed in online services and the occurrence of e-CCI[3] (Nicholls, 2005), or virtual C2C interaction (Gummesson, 2009). Although most on-site CCI studies are based in physical service settings, there are studies set in e-CCI contexts, such as online multiplayer games (Choi & Kim, 2020); virtual health communities (Mpinganjira, 2019); mega events (Kharouf et al., 2020) and retailing (Betzing et al., 2020). Further research needs to explore the role and interplay of physical and virtual CCI. Interaction, as seen in the light of current multi-interface service environments (c.f. Patrício et al., 2008), is much broader in scope than traditionally depicted in terms of physical encounters between two actors.

Another promising topic is non-verbal CCI. Research on CCI in physical settings has tended to place more emphasis on spoken interaction. Sometimes this has been related to the methodology employed focusing on C2C conversations as the raw data, for example the *Observable Oral Participation 2* (OOP2) research (Harris et al., 1995). It has, however, been suggested that non-verbal interactions between customers may be more common than verbal ones (Lin et al., 2020). Future research could specifically address this type of CCI. A wide range of non-verbal CCI contexts exists in physical service settings, such as communicating waiting; gaze avoidance, negotiating shared space; and body glossing. Likewise, research is needed into how interacting customers combine both verbal and non-verbal messages.

The organizational and employee perspective of CCI represents an important area for future research in CCI. Studies have examined themes such as service provider roles in managing CCI (Pranter & Martin, 1991); how FLEs view CCI (Nicholls & Gad Mohsen, 2019); the impact of perceived employee CCI service recovery effort on customer satisfaction (Huang, 2008) and the effectiveness of FLE apologies on recovering other customer failure

---

[3] The focus here is on e-CCI as interactions occurring between two or more customers during the delivery of an e-service rather than as online interaction or communication occurring between a customer and a potential customer (i.e. e-WOM, the online equivalent of traditional word-of-mouth).

(McQuilken et al., 2017). Likewise, broad approaches to managing CCI, such as segmentation, service design, employee training and customer education, have been proposed (Martin, 2016; Nicholls, 2010). Many research opportunities, however, remain. Such research suggestions are in line with the need "for CCI research to broaden its focus from studying CCI to studying the effective management of CCI" (Nicholls & Gad Mohsen, 2019, p. 812).

Given the different angles from which C2C has been investigated, together with the wide range of terminology and meaning, future research could usefully refocus conceptual understanding of C2C Interaction as C2C Influence. By developing a more integrated understanding of how various researchers have operationalized CCI phenomena, the field of C2C behavior may be able to both spread its roots and organize its knowledge in a more accessible way. In addition to the explicit and implicit outgroup interactions covered in Fig. 1, areas of C2C that could be included within the wider scope are issues about word-of-mouth or WOM (e.g. Libai et al., 2010; Rahman et al., 2015), interactions between owners of goods (e.g. McAlexander et al., 2002) and in-group interactions such as the influence of friends and family (e.g. Ward, 2006; Zhang et al., 2014). Therefore, a holistic understanding of C2C results in greater awareness of logical distinctions and nuances between areas of C2C research.

Such research would serve both to highlight the significance of C2C and to encourage researchers to be more aware of where their work fitted in terms of previous contributions. With the increased awareness among researchers of the role of CCI in value creation, the use of the term *CCI* continues to evolve. While the term *CCI* is probably the prevalent term used in the literature, it is applied with different meanings and this can cause confusion. Research indicates that customers are influencing each other's value creation either directly or indirectly, with important emotional, functional and social outcomes (Heinonen et al., 2018). More research is needed to understand how CCI "emerges, develops and builds toward value outcomes over time" (Heinonen et al., 2018, p. 725). The complexity and many nuances of CCI furthers the need to have an inclusive interpretation of the term *customer-to-customer interaction*. Indeed, the term *CCI* might more appropriately be understood as *Customer-to-customer Influence* rather than *Customer-to-customer Interaction*. The adoption of the term *C2C Influence* to refer to this field would also overcome the semantic difficulty that some C2C interactions are only perceived by one of the customers involved, and thus might not be called 'interaction' in the usual dictionary meaning of the word. The notion of C2C influence, including C2C value creation, is clearly an important avenue for future research.

In conclusion, CCI is a diverse and maturing area of research, and the advancements in technology has made interactions among customers easier and more prevalent. As a research field it is thus growing and intersects with important research areas such as customer experience, value creation, service failure and recovery as well as service design.

References

Anaya, G. J., Miao, L., Mattila, A. S., & Almanza, B. (2016). Consumer envy during service encounters. *Journal of Services Marketing, 30*(3), 359–372.

Argo, J. J., Dahl, D. W., & Morales, A. C. (2006). Consumer contamination: How consumers react to products touched by others. *Journal of Marketing, 70*(2), 81–94.

Arnould, E. J., & Price, L. L. (1993). River magic: Extraordinary experience and the extended service encounter. *Journal of Consumer Research, 20*(1), 24–45.

Baker, M., & Kim, K. (2018). Other customer service failure: Emotions, impacts, and attributions. *Journal of Hospitality and Tourism Research, 42*(7), 1067–1085.

Baker, S. M., Holland, J., & Kaufman-Scarborough, C. (2007). How consumers with disabilities perceive "welcome" in retail servicescapes: A critical incident study. *Journal of Services Marketing, 21*(3), 160–173.

Baron, S., & Harris, K. (2010). Toward an understanding of consumer perspectives on experiences. *Journal of Services Marketing, 24*(7), 518–531.

Baron, S., Harris, K., & Davies, B. J. (1996). Oral participation in retail service delivery: A comparison of the roles of contact personnel and customers. *European Journal of Marketing, 30*(9), 75–90.

Baron, S., Patterson, A., Harris, K., & Hodgson, J. (2007). Strangers in the night: Speeddating, CCI and service businesses. *Service Business, 1*(3), 211–232.

Barsky, J. D., & Labagh, R. (1992). A strategy for customer satisfaction. *Cornell Hotel and Restaurant Administration Quarterly, 33*(5), 32–40.

Bateson, J. E. (1985). Self-service consumer: An exploratory study. *Journal of Retailing, 61*(3), 49–76.

Bendapudi, N., & Leone, R. P. (2003). Psychological implications of customer participation in co-production. *Journal of Marketing, 67*(1), 14–28.

Bettencourt, L. A., & Gwinner, K. (1996). Customisation of the service experience: The role of the frontline employee. *International Journal of Service Industry Management, 7*(2), 2–20.

Betzing, J. H., Kurtz, M., & Becker, J. (2020). Customer participation in virtual communities for local high streets. *Journal of Retailing and Consumer Services, 54*, 102025.

Bitner, M. J. (1992). Servicescapes: The impact of physical surroundings on customers and employees. *Journal of Marketing, 56*(2), 57–71.

Bitner, M. J., Booms, B. H., & Mohr, L. A. (1994). Critical service encounters: The employee's viewpoint. *Journal of Marketing, 58*(4), 95–106.

Bitner, M. J., Booms, B. H., & Tetreault, M. S. (1990). The service encounter: Diagnosing favorable and unfavorable incidents. *Journal of Marketing, 54*(1), 71–84.

Bitner, M. J., Faranda, W. T., Hubbert, A. R., & Zeithaml, V. A. (1997). Customer contributions and roles in service delivery. *International Journal of Service Industry Management, 8*(3), 193–205.

Booms, B. H., & Bitner, M. J. (1981). Marketing strategies and organizational structures for service firms. In J. H. Donnelly & W. R. George (Eds.), *Marketing of services* (Proceedings series) (pp. 47–51). American Marketing Association.

Brocato, E. D., Voorhees, C. M., & Baker, J. (2012). Understanding the influence of cues from other customers in the service experience: A scale development and validation. *Journal of Retailing, 88*(3), 384–398.

Buttle, F., & Maklan, S. (2019). *Customer relationship management: Concepts and technologies*. Routledge.

Celsi, R. L., Rose, P. L., & Leigh, T. W. (1993). An exploration of high-risk leisure consumption through skydiving. *Journal of Consumer Research, 20*(1), 1–23.

Cheang, M. (2002). Older adults' frequent visits to a fast-food restaurant: Nonobligatory social interaction and the significance of play in a "third place". *Journal of Aging Studies, 16*(3), 303–321.

Choi, B., & Kim, H. S. (2020). Online customer-to-customer interactions, customer–firm affection, firm-loyalty and participation intention. *Asia Pacific Journal of Marketing and Logistics, 32*(8), 1717–1735.

Colm, L., Ordanini, A., & Parasuraman, A. (2017). When service customers do not consume in isolation: A typology of customer copresence influence modes (CCIMs). *Journal of Service Research, 20*(3), 223–239.

Dahm, M., Wentzel, D., Herzog, W., & Wiecek, A. (2018). Breathing down your neck!: The impact of queues on customers using a retail service. *Journal of Retailing, 94*(2), 217–230.

Dong, B., & Sivakumar, K. (2017). Customer participation in services: Domain, scope, and boundaries. *Journal of the Academy of Marketing Science, 45*(6), 944–965.

Dorsey, J. D., Ashley, C., & Oliver, J. D. (2016). Triggers and outcomes of customer-to-customer aisle rage. *Journal of Retailing and Consumer Services, 32*, 67–77.

Eiglier, P., & Langeard, E. (1977). Services as systems: Marketing implications. In P. Eiglier (Ed.), *Marketing consumer services: New insights* (pp. 83–103). Marketing Science.

Ekpo, A. E., Riley, B. K., Thomas, K. D., Yvaire, Z., Gerri, G. R. H., & Munoz, I. I. (2015). As worlds collide: The role of marketing management in customer-to-customer interactions. *Journal of Business Research, 68*, 119–126.

Evans, G. W., & Wener, R. E. (2007). Crowding and personal space invasion on the train: Please don't make me sit in the middle. *Journal of Environmental Psychology, 27*(1), 90–94.

Fairley, S., & Tyler, B. D. (2012). Bringing baseball to the big screen: Building sense of community outside of the ballpark. *Journal of Sport Management, 26*(3), 258–270.

Fernandes, T., Morgado, M., & Rodrigues, M. A. (2018). The role of employee emotional competence in service recovery encounters. *Journal of Services Marketing, 32*(7), 835–849.

Gainer, B. (1995). Ritual and relationships: Interpersonal influences on shared consumption. *Journal of Business Research, 32*(3), 253–260.

Gorman, B. (1979). Seven days, five countries. *Urban Life, 7*(4), 469–491.

Grönroos, C. (2004). The relationship marketing process: Communication, interaction, dialogue, value. *Journal of Business & Industrial Marketing, 19*(2), 99–113.

Grönroos, C. (2008). Service logic revisited: Who creates value? And who co-creates? *European Business Journal, 20*(4), 298–314.

Grönroos, C., & Voima, P. (2013). Critical service logic: Making sense of value creation and co-creation. *Journal of the Academy of Marketing Science, 41*(2), 133–150.

Grove, S. J., & Fisk, R. P. (1997). The impact of other customers on service experiences: A critical incident examination of 'getting along'. *Journal of Retailing, 73*(1), 63–85.

Gruen, T. W., Summers, J. O., & Acito, F. (2000). Relationship marketing activities, commitment, and membership behaviors in professional associations. *Journal of Marketing, 64*(3), 34–49.

Gummesson, E. (1993). *Quality Management in Service Organizations.* International Service Quality Association, St. John's University.

Gummesson, E. (1997). Relationship marketing as a paradigm shift: Some conclusions from the 30R approach. *Management Decision, 35*(4), 267–272.

Gummesson, E. (2009). *Marketing as networks: The birth of many-to-many marketing.* Publishing House Djursholm.

Gursoy, D., Cai, R., & Anaya, G. J. (2017). Developing a typology of disruptive customer behaviors: Influence of customer misbehavior on service experience of by-standing customers. *International Journal of Contemporary Hospitality Management, 29*(9), 2341–2360.

Harris, K., & Baron, S. (2004). Consumer-to-consumer conversations in service settings. *Journal of Service Research, 6*(3), 287–303.

Harris, K., Baron, S., & Ratcliffe, J. (1995). Customers as oral participants in a service setting. *Journal of Services Marketing, 9*(4), 64–76.

Harris, L. C., & Reynolds, K. L. (2004). Jaycustomer behavior: An exploration of types and motives in the hospitality industry. *Journal of Services Marketing, 18*(5), 339–357.

Heinonen, K., Jaakkola, E., & Neganova, I. (2018). Drivers, types and value outcomes of customer-to-customer interaction: An integrative review and research agenda. *Journal of Service Theory and Practice, 28*(6), 710–732.

Heinonen, K., & Strandvik, T. (2018). Reflections on customers' primary role in markets. *European Management Journal, 36*(1), 1–11.

Heinonen, K., Strandvik, T., Mickelsson, K. J., Edvardsson, B., Sundström, E., & Andersson, P. (2010). A customer-dominant logic of service. *Journal of Service Management, 21*(4), 531–548.

Henkel, A. P., Boegershausen, J., Rafaeli, A., & Lemmink, J. (2017). The social dimension of service interactions: Observer reactions to customer incivility. *Journal of Service Research, 20*(2), 120–134.

Hoffman, D. K., & Lee, S. H. (2014). A CIT investigation of disruptive student behaviors: The students' perspective. *Marketing Education Review, 24*(2), 115–126.

Honkatukia, P., & Svynarenko, A. (2018). Intergenerational encounters on the metro: Young people's perspectives on social control in the media city. *Emotion, Space and Society, 32*. https://doi.org/10.1016/j.emospa.2018.10.001

Huang, J., & Hsu, C. H. (2010). The impact of customer-to-customer interaction on cruise experience and vacation satisfaction. *Journal of Travel Research, 49*(1), 79–92.

Huang, J., & Hsu, C. H. C. (2009). Interaction among fellow cruise passengers: Diverse experiences and impacts. *Journal of Travel & Tourism Marketing, 26*(5–6), 547–567.

Huang, W. (2010). Other-customer failure: Effects of perceived employee effort and compensation on complainer and non-complainer service evaluations. *Journal of Service Management, 21*(2), 191–211.

Huang, W. H. (2008). The impact of other-customer failure on service satisfaction. *International Journal of Service Industry Management, 19*(4), 521–536.

Hughes, A., Mee, K., & Tyndall, A. (2017). 'Super simple stuff?': Crafting quiet in trains between Newcastle and Sydney. *Mobilities, 12*(5), 740–757.

Hui, M. K., & Bateson, J. E. G. (1991). Perceived control and the effects of crowding and consumer choice on the service experience. *Journal of Consumer Research, 18*(2), 174–184.

Kane, M. J., & Zink, R. (2004). Package adventure tours: Markers in serious leisure careers. *Leisure Studies, 23*(4), 329–345.

Kharouf, H., Biscaia, R., Garcia-Perez, A., & Hickman, E. (2020). Understanding online event experience: The importance of communication, engagement and interaction. *Journal of Business Research, 121*, 735–746.

Kim, H. S., & Choi, B. (2016). The effects of three customer-to-customer interaction quality types on customer experience quality and citizenship behavior in mass service settings. *Journal of Services Marketing, 30*(4), 384–397.

Kim, K., Byon, K. K., & Baek, W. (2020). Customer-to-customer value co-creation and co-destruction in sporting events. *The Service Industries Journal, 40*(9–10), 633–655.

Kim, S. Y., & Yi, Y. (2017). Embarrassed customers: The dark side of receiving help from others. *Journal of Service Management, 28*(4), 788–806.

Kim, Y. S., & Baker, M. A. (2020). Customers' reactions to other customer caused service failures: The effects of tie strength on customer loyalty. *Journal of Hospitality Marketing & Management, 29*(6), 682–701.

Lemon, K. N., & Verhoef, P. C. (2016). Understanding customer experience throughout the customer journey. *Journal of Marketing, 80*(6), 69–96.

Levy, S. E. (2015). An examination of customer-to-customer interactions: A field experiment approach. In *Marketing, technology and customer commitment in the new economy* (pp. 265–269). Springer.

Libai, B., Bolton, R., Bügel, M. S., De Ruyter, K., Götz, O., Risselada, H., & Stephen, A. T. (2010). Customer-to-customer interactions: Broadening the scope of word of mouth research. *Journal of Service Research, 13*(3), 267–282.

Lin, H., Zhang, M., & Gursoy, D. (2020). Impact of nonverbal customer-to-customer interactions on customer satisfaction and loyalty intentions. *International Journal of Contemporary Hospitality Management, 32*(5), 1967–1985.

Lloyd-Parkes, E., & Deacon, J. H. (2021). Exploring in-store shopping experiences and resultant purchasing influence: An autoethnographic approach. In K. Quartier, A. Petermans, T. C. Melewar, & C. Dennis (Eds.), *The value of Design in Retail and Branding* (pp. 147–157). Emerald Publishing Limited.

Lovelock, C. H. (1983). Classifying services to gain strategic marketing insights. *Journal of Marketing, 47*(3), 9–20.

Luck, M., & Benkenstein, M. (2015). Consumers between supermarket shelves: The influence of inter-personal distance on consumer behavior. *Journal of Retailing and Consumer Services, 26*, 104–114.

Ludwig, N. L., Barnes, D. C., & Gouthier, M. (2017). Observing delightful experiences of other customers: The double-edged sword of jealousy and joy. *Journal of Service Theory and Practice, 27*(1), 145–163.

MacLennan, J., & Moore, R. L. (2011). Conflicts between recreational subworlds: The case of Appalachian Trail long-distance hikers. *The Cyber Journal of Applied and Recreation Research, 13*(1), 1–17.

Martin, C. L. (1995). The customer compatibility scale: Measuring service customers' perceptions of fellow customers. *Journal of Consumer Studies & Home Economics, 19*(3), 299–311.

Martin, C. L. (1996). Consumer-to-consumer relationships: Satisfaction with other consumers' public behavior. *Journal of Consumer Affairs, 30*(1), 146–169.

Martin, C. L. (2016). Retrospective: Compatibility management: Customer-to-customer relationships in service environments. *Journal of Services Marketing, 30*(1), 11–15.

Martin, C. L., & Pranter, C. A. (1989). Compatibility management: Customer-to-customer relationships in service environments. *Journal of Services Marketing, 3*(3), 5–15.

McAlexander, J. H., Schouten, J. W., & Koenig, H. F. (2002). Building brand community. *Journal of Marketing, 66*(1), 38–54.

McColl-Kennedy, J. R., Cheung, L., & Ferrier, E. (2015). Co-creating service experience practices. *Journal of Service Management, 26*(2), 249–275.

McGrath, M. A., & Otnes, C. (1995). Unacquainted influencers: When strangers interact in the retail setting. *Journal of Business Research, 32*(3), 261–272.

McQuilken, L., Robertson, N., & Polonsky, M. (2017). Recovering from other-customer-caused failure: The effect on focal customer complaining. *Journal of Hospitality Marketing & Management, 26*(1), 83–104.

Miao, L. (2014). Emotion regulation at service encounters: Coping with the behavior of other customers. *Journal of Hospitality Marketing & Management, 23*(1), 49–76.

Miao, L., & Mattila, A. (2013). Psychological distance and other customers. *Journal of Hospitality & Tourism Research, 37*(1), 51–77.

Middlemist, R. D., Knowles, E. S., & Matter, C. F. (1976). Personal space invasions in the lavatory: Suggestive evidence for arousal. *Journal of Personality and Social Psychology, 33*(5), 541–546.

Moore, R., Moore, M. L., & Capella, M. (2005). The impact of customer-to-customer interaction in a high personal contact service setting. *Journal of Services Marketing, 19*(7), 482–491.

Mpinganjira, M. (2019). Willingness to reciprocate in virtual health communities: The role of social capital, gratitude and indebtedness. *Service Business, 13*, 269–287.

Nicholls, R. (2005). *Interactions between service customers*. PUE Publishing.

Nicholls, R. (2010). New directions for customer-to-customer interaction research. *Journal of Services Marketing, 24*(1), 87–97.

Nicholls, R. (2011). Customer-to-customer interaction (CCI): A cross-cultural perspective. *International Journal of Contemporary Hospitality Management, 23*(2), 209–223.

Nicholls, R. (2020). What goes on between customers? A cross-industry study of customer-to-customer interaction (CCI). *Journal of Service Theory and Practice, 30*(2), 123–147.

Nicholls, R., & Gad Mohsen, M. (2015). Other customer age: Exploring customer age-difference related CCI. *Journal of Services Marketing, 29*(4), 255–267.

Nicholls, R., & Gad Mohsen, M. (2019). Managing customer-to-customer interaction (CCI)—Insights from the frontline. *Journal of Services Marketing, 33*(7), 798–814.

Nichols, B. S., Raska, D., & Flint, D. J. (2015). Effects of consumer embarrassment on shopping basket size and value: A study of the millennial consumer. *Journal of Consumer Behaviour, 14*(1), 41–56.

Normann, R. (1984). *Service management*. Wiley.

Papathanassis, A. (2012). Guest-to-guest interaction on board cruise ships: Exploring social dynamics and the role of situational factors. *Tourism Management, 33*(5), 1148–1158.

Parasuraman, A., Zeithaml, V. A., & Berry, L. L. (1985). A conceptual model of service quality and its implications for future research. *Journal of Marketing, 49*(4), 41–50.

Parker, C., & Ward, P. (2000). An analysis of role adoptions and scripts during customer-to-customer encounters. *European Journal of Marketing., 34*(3/4), 341–358.

Patrício, L., Fisk, R. P., & Falcão e Cunha, J. (2008). Designing multi-interface service experiences: The service experience blueprint. *Journal of Service Research, 10*(4), 318–334.

Prahalad, C. K., & Ramaswamy, V. (2004). *The future of competition.* Harvard Business School Press.

Pranter, C. A., & Martin, C. L. (1991). Compatibility management: Roles in service performances. *Journal of Services Marketing, 5*(2), 43–53.

Price, L. L., Arnould, E. J., & Deibler, S. L. (1995). Consumers' emotional responses to service encounters. *International Journal of Service Industry Management, 6*(3), 34–63.

Rahman, K., Karpen, I. O., Reid, M., & Yuksel, U. (2015). Customer-to-customer interactions and word of mouth: Conceptual extensions and empirical investigations. *Journal of Strategic Marketing, 23*(4), 287–304.

Rihova, I., Buhalis, D., Gouthro, M. B., & Moital, M. (2018). Customer-to-customer co-creation practices in tourism: Lessons from customer-dominant logic. *Tourism Management, 67*, 362–375.

Rowley, J. E. (1996). Customer compatibility management: An alternative perspective on student-to-student support in higher education. *International Journal of Educational Management, 10*(4), 15–20.

Schaefers, T., Wittkowski, K., Benoit, S., & Ferraro, R. (2016). Contagious effects of customer misbehavior in access-based services. *Journal of Service Research, 19*(1), 3–21.

Schau, H. J., Muñiz, A. M., Jr., & Arnould, E. J. (2009). How brand community practices create value. *Journal of Marketing, 73*(5), 30–51.

Schmidt, R., & Sapsford, R. (1995). Issues of gender and servicescape: Marketing UK public houses to women. *International Journal of Retail & Distribution Management, 23*(3), 34–40.

Schmitt, B. H., Dube, L., & Leclerc, F. (1992). Intrusions into waiting lines: Does the queue constitute a social system? *Journal of Personality and Social Psychology, 63*(5), 806–815.

Shamir, B. (1980). Between service and servility: Role conflict in subordinate service roles. *Human Relations, 33*(10), 741–756.

Sharma, P., Tam, J. L., & Kim, N. (2015). Service role and outcome as moderators in intercultural service encounters. *Journal of Service Management, 26*(1), 137–155.

Shostack, G. L. (1985). Planning the service encounter. In J. A. Czepiel, M. R. Solomon, & C. F. Surprenant (Eds.), *The service encounter* (pp. 243–254). Lexington Books.

Small, J., & Harris, C. (2014). Crying babies on planes: Aeromobility and parenting. *Annals of Tourism Research, 48*, 27–41.

Söderlund, M. (2011). Other customers in the retail environment and their impact on the customer's evaluations of the retailer. *Journal of Retailing and Consumer Services, 18*(3), 174–182.

Thakor, M. V., Suri, R., & Saleh, K. (2008). Effects of service setting and other consumers' age on the service perceptions of young consumers. *Journal of Retailing, 84*(2), 137–149.

Tomazelli, J., Broilo, P. L., Espartel, L. B., & Basso, K. (2017). The effects of store environment elements on customer-to-customer interactions involving older shoppers. *Journal of Services Marketing, 31*(4/5), 339–350.

Tombs, A. G., & McColl-Kennedy, J. R. (2003). Social servicescape conceptual model. *Marketing Theory, 3*(4), 37–65.

Tombs, A. G., & McColl-Kennedy, J. R. (2010). Social and spatial influence of customers on other customers in the social-servicescape. *Australasian Marketing Journal, 18*(3), 120–131.

Turley, L. W., & Chebat, J. C. (2002). Linking retail strategy, atmospheric design and shopping behaviour. *Journal of Marketing Management, 18*(1–2), 125–144.

Vargo, S. L., & Lusch, R. F. (2004). Evolving to a new dominant logic of marketing. *Journal of Marketing, 68*(1), 1–17.

vom Lehn, D. (2006). Embodying experience: A video-based examination of visitors' conduct and interaction in museums. *European Journal of Marketing, 40*(11/12), 1340–1359.

Ward, C. (2006). He wants, she wants: Gender, category, and disagreement in spouse's joint decisions. *Advances in Consumer Research, 33*, 117–123.

Wieseke, J., Geigenmüller, A., & Kraus, F. (2012). On the role of empathy in customer-employee interactions. *Journal of Service Research, 15*(3), 316–331.

Yin, C. Y., & Poon, P. (2016). The impact of other group members on tourists' travel experiences. *International Journal of Contemporary Hospitality Management., 28*(3), 640–658.

Zhang, J., Beatty, S. E., & Mothersbaugh, D. (2010). A CIT investigation of other customers' influence in services. *Journal of Services Marketing, 24*(5), 389–399.

Zhang, X., Li, S., Burke, R. R., & Leykin, A. (2014). An examination of social influence on shopper behavior using video tracking data. *Journal of Marketing, 78*(5), 24–41.

Understanding and Managing Customer Experiences

Elina Jaakkola, Larissa Becker, and Ekaterina Panina

1 Importance of Customer Experience for Service Firms

Customer experience (CX) is viewed as a vital source of competitive advantage in today's markets (Homburg et al., 2015). The creation of a superior customer experience is key to attaining satisfied and loyal customers, and compelling CX can set a firm apart from its competitors (Grewal et al., 2009; Kandampully et al., 2018). Indeed, a McKinsey survey found that 90 percent of CEOs place customer experience among their top three priorities (Dias et al., 2016). Customer experience is now one of the key strategies that several industry leaders have adopted—including Marriott, Starbucks, Amazon, and Disney—and is highlighted as a research priority within academic service research (Ostrom et al., 2015).

The importance of CX first was acknowledged in hedonic consumption contexts, such as hospitality and entertainment, in which the essence of the service offering is the creation of "extraordinary" or "peak" experiences

---

E. Jaakkola (✉) • E. Panina
Turku School of Economics, University of Turku, Turku, Finland
e-mail: elina.jaakkola@utu.fi; Ekaterina.panina@utu.fi

L. Becker
Faculty of Management and Business, Tampere University, Tampere, Finland

Postgraduate Program of Management, IMED, Passo Fundo, Brazil
e-mail: larissa.brazbecker@tuni.fi

© The Author(s), under exclusive license to Springer Nature Switzerland AG 2022
B. Edvardsson, B. Tronvoll (eds.), *The Palgrave Handbook of Service Management*,
https://doi.org/10.1007/978-3-030-91828-6_33

655

656 E. Jaakkola et al.

(Arnould & Price, 1993; Holbrook & Hirschman, 1982). Today, firms and other organizations across contexts—such as health care (McColl-Kennedy et al., 2017), public service (Olsson et al., 2013), and business-to-business markets (Witell et al., 2020)—highlight CX's importance as a precursor of customer satisfaction. From the service management perspective, every step of the service delivery process is an experience-creating touchpoint in which the service environment's design and functionality and the customer's interaction with providers and other customers affect CX (Jaakkola et al., 2015).

This chapter offers a state-of-the-art overview of the current understanding of customer experience. The aim is to provide researchers and managers with a "big-picture" CX frame that clarifies what CX is, how it emerges, and how it can be managed in service contexts. More detailed and deeper insights on CX's various aspects then can be situated and understood within this overall frame. The chapter starts by outlining extant CX literature to help readers navigate through this rich, but fragmented, research domain. Subsequent sections discuss CX from two perspectives: first, how experiences emerge from the customer's perspective, and second, how service firms can seek to design and manage CX. The customer perspective on CX highlights what customers feel, think, and sense while in touch with different types of service elements during their journeys toward accomplishing smaller and larger goals in their everyday lives. The CX management perspective addresses service providers' activities while considering how they use these insights to design journeys intended to create particular experiences for their customers. Ultimately, the goal is to develop truly customer-centric service.

2 Definition and Research Background for Customer Experience

Despite the rapid increase in interest in CX, no consensus on the concept's actual meaning exists among scholars and managers alike. For service marketing and management, the CX concept's roots relate to customer perceptions and evaluations of service encounters and "moments of truth," as well as to service blueprinting, that is, the providers' attempt to understand and design service from the customer perspective (Bitner et al., 2008; McColl-Kennedy et al., 2015). However, CX is more than customer satisfaction or good process design: CX in the service context can be defined as *the customer's sensorial, affective, cognitive, relational, and behavioral responses and reactions to any direct or indirect contact with the service offering, across multiple touchpoints during the*

Understanding and Managing Customer Experiences 657

entire customer journey (cf. Becker & Jaakkola, 2020; McColl-Kennedy et al., 2015). In other words, CX is created not only by elements that the service provider can control—such as service interface, atmosphere, assortment, and price—but also by elements outside of their control, such as other customers' influence (McColl-Kennedy et al., 2015). In service settings, direct contact with the service offering often means personal interaction between customers and frontline service employees or customers visiting a physical or virtual service infrastructure. Indirect contact with the offering refers to instances in which the service as such is not present, but customers encounter it through, for example, word of mouth in social media forums (Jaakkola et al., 2015).

It should be noted that customer experiences are not just those special, memorable moments during which something extraordinary happens, as every service encounter creates an experience. Some encounters are designed to be experiential, aiming to create a strong customer response—for example, Disney World or a Michelin-starred restaurant, in which an important element of the service offering is the experiential stimuli's uniqueness. However, in many contexts, the offering itself is routine and mundane (Carù & Cova, 2003), triggering only a weak response in the customer. In such contexts, a positive experience for the customer might be a seamless, hassle-free process during which everything just works—sometimes a superior experience occurs when the customer hardly needs to pay any attention to the service process (cf. Becker & Jaakkola, 2020).

The confusion around what CX entails can be explained partly by the fragmentation of academic research on the concept. For example, systematic reviews have identified eight literature fields that study CX (Becker & Jaakkola, 2020) and three different research perspectives on experience (Helkkula, 2011). The scope and nature of customer experience as a research phenomenon are viewed quite differently across literature fields, making it difficult to grasp the phenomenon and approaches to its study as a whole. The literature fields can be divided roughly into clusters: those who view CX as a customer's reactions and responses to *managerial stimuli* and those who view experiences as responses to the customer's *overall consumption process*, beyond firm-customer interactions (Becker & Jaakkola, 2020). Table 1 provides a brief overview of the key literature fields that address CX.

Research that focuses on experiences as a response to managerial stimuli views CX mainly as an *outcome* of provider-customer interaction (cf. Helkkula, 2011). Typically, researchers' goal is to study how firms can design experience stimuli to improve customer experiences in different types of service contexts (Verhoef et al., 2009) or along the customer journey (Patrício et al., 2011).

658 E. Jaakkola et al.

Some studies have developed measures to capture brand experiences (Brakus et al., 2009) or the quality of experiences (Kuppelwieser & Klaus, 2020).

Research that focuses on experiences as responses to the consumption process adopts a *phenomenological* view of experience, emphasizing the individual, subjective, and contextual nature of consumer experiences (Becker & Jaakkola, 2020; Helkkula et al., 2012). These studies typically adopt a broad view of experience, addressing the entire consumption journey affected by many types of firms, customers, and other stakeholders, all of which can contribute to customer experience, but are not necessarily under the firm's control or even market-related (see, e.g., Akaka & Schau, 2019; Akaka et al., 2015).

Interestingly, service design research can be viewed as a bridge between these two perspectives. Service design adopts a *process* view in which the main focus is on the mapping and designing of well-functioning customer journeys. As such, service design inherently holds a managerial interest. Simultaneously, service design views customer journeys and CX from the perspective of consumers' lifeworlds, including different types of stakeholders in the service ecosystem, as well as contextual factors that affect the creation of meaning for consumers (Patrício et al., 2011; Teixeira et al., 2012)—a perspective that corresponds with the phenomenological perspective.

Despite apparent fragmentation, some common ground for CX research has been put forth to establish a shared core of the concept. Building on a systematic literature analysis by Becker and Jaakkola (2020), the key premises of customer experience are summarized in Box 1. The following sections discuss in more detail how customer experiences emerge and how service firms can influence these experiences. The former views CX as a response to the consumption process, while the latter views CX as a response to managerial stimuli.

Box 1 Key Premises of Customer Experience (Becker & Jaakkola, 2020)
- Customer experience comprises customers' non-deliberate, spontaneous responses and reactions to offering-related stimuli along the customer journey.
- Customer experience stimuli reside within and outside firm-controlled touch-points, affecting customer experience in a dynamic manner.
- Customer experience is subjective and context-specific because responses to offering-related stimuli and their evaluative outcomes depend on customer, situational, and sociocultural contingencies.
- Firms cannot create the customer experience, but they can monitor, design, and manage a range of stimuli that affect such experiences.

Table 1 Overview of the research background of customer experience (cf. Becker & Jaakkola, 2020)

	Literature field	Perspective on CX	Exemplary references
CX as responses to managerial stimuli; Outcome-based view	Services marketing	CX comprises a customer's assessment of or response to service encounter elements, for example, any direct or indirect contact with the servicescape, frontline employees, or other customers.	Bitner et al. (1990) Kwortnik and Thompson (2009) Kandampully et al. (2018)
	Retailing	CX comprises a customer's responses to retail mix elements, such as physical and online environments, merchandise, or advertising that should be integrated seamlessly.	Verhoef et al. (2009) Grewal et al. (2009) Barann et al. (2022)
	Online marketing	CX comprises a customer's psychological state and flow, perception, or subjective response that emerges during online interactions.	Novak et al. (2000) Rose et al. (2012)
	Branding	CX comprises a customer's responses to brand-related stimuli, such as brand design and communications.	Brakus et al. (2009) Kuehnl et al. (2019)
	Experiential marketing	CX is the main content of the offering; providers can stage a memorable experience.	Pine and Gilmore (1998) Hamilton and Wagner (2014)
Process view	Service design	CX emerges through all interactions that a customer has with a firm, its partners, and other customers during the customer journey that can be mapped and designed.	Patrício et al. (2008, 2011) Teixeira et al. (2012)
CX as responses to consumption process; Phenomenological view	Consumer research	CX emerges through an individual's consumption process and relates to sense of community, practice, symbolic meaning, and identity.	Holbrook and Hirschman (1982) Arnould and Price (1993) Akaka and Schau (2019)
	Service-dominant logic	Experiences emerge for different types of actors involved in resource integration, embedded in context, and connecting with value.	Vargo and Lusch (2008) Helkkula et al. (2012) Akaka et al. (2015)

3 How Does Customer Experience Emerge? A Customer-Centric Perspective

Imagine a person who wants to take her friend out for dinner on his birthday. She browses some restaurant websites and looks at review apps, such as TripAdvisor, to find a place that seems appealing. She calls the restaurant to make a reservation and feels frustrated by the long waiting time. Later, she calls a cab to go to the restaurant and chats with the friendly driver. The two friends wait a few minutes at the bar, feeling excited about the trendy atmosphere, before being directed to their table. While they are ordering, she gets distressed by other customers who are very loud and somewhat rude to their waiters. She and her friend toast to his birthday and have a meal that looks, smells, and tastes wonderful. She posts on social media about the restaurant, pays the bill by card effortlessly, then takes another cab home, feeling safe. At home, she gets a "high" from the likes and comments that her social media posts are receiving. She also leaves a review on the restaurant's Facebook page. Finally, she is pleased by a very warm "thank you" message from her friend, who compliments her excellent choice of restaurant.

The story above is a short illustration of a *customer journey*. As noted in the previous section, customer experiences emerge as responses and reactions to stimuli within and outside firm-controlled touchpoints that form the customer journey (see Box 1). To understand the emergence of CX, one needs to understand customer journeys.

A *customer journey* can be defined as the process that customers undergo to achieve particular purchase or service goals (Becker et al., 2020; Hamilton & Price, 2019). Customer journeys encompass direct and indirect interactions with a service offering before, during, and after the core service encounter (Voorhees et al., 2017). These direct and indirect interactions are called *touchpoints*, that is, the points at which the customer and service provider or its offering "touch" (McColl-Kennedy et al., 2019).

It is noteworthy that *the customer journey always is depicted from the customer's perspective* and, therefore, can offer a customer-centric view of the customer's process in accessing and using the service (Jaakkola & Terho, 2021; McColl-Kennedy et al., 2019). The customer journey encompasses not only encounters with a service provider, but *also touchpoints outside the service provider's control*, such as interactions with other consumers (cf. Baron & Harris, 2010). In the restaurant example, the customer interacted with a taxi company, other customers in the service environment, her friend, independent review apps, social media, and her social network. All these touchpoints were part of her customer journey and influenced her experience. Lemon and

Verhoef (2016) identified four types of touchpoints that customers can experience along their customer journey, presented below in the context of the aforementioned customer journey example (see Box 2).

> **Box 2 Different Types of Touchpoints That Comprise the Customer Journey (cf. Lemon & Verhoef, 2016)**
> - *Brand-owned touchpoints* are designed and managed by the service provider, such as a restaurant's service environment, the website, and the customer's interactions with employees.
> - *Partner-owned touchpoints* are designed jointly by the service provider and its partner(s), such as the customer using a credit card company's service to pay for the bill at a restaurant. The lines between brand-owned and partner-owned touchpoints are blurred from the customer's perspective.
> - *Customer-owned touchpoints* are customer actions that are part of the customer journey, but are not controlled by the service provider, such as the customer posting about her experience on social media.
> - *Social/external touchpoints* are other touchpoints external to the service provider that influence the customer experience, such as interacting with the review apps, taxi company, and other customers.

To sum up, it is critical to gain a broad perspective on the customer journey to capture customer experiences fully. In this chapter, we discuss two approaches for obtaining a broader, more customer-centric perspective on the customer journey: analyzing the customer's goals (Section "A Goal-Oriented Perspective on Customer Journeys for Comprehensive CX Insight") and contextual factors that can influence CX (Section "The Role of the Customer's Context in the Customer Experience").

A Goal-Oriented Perspective on Customer Journeys for Comprehensive CX Insight

Depicting a journey from the customer's perspective should offer a broad picture of the factors that influence CX. The service literature offers alternative frameworks that help service providers think about customer journeys through a customer-centric perspective (see Box 3). What is common in these frameworks is the attempt to identify the range of organizations and other actors (e.g., other customers) that play a role in fulfilling a particular customer need along a process of activities. In this chapter, we focus on the *goal-oriented perspective on customer journeys* (Becker et al., 2020).

The goal-oriented perspective suggests that *to obtain a truly customer-centric perspective on the customer journey, service providers should think about a*

662   E. Jaakkola et al.

> Box 3 Alternative Frameworks to Obtain a Customer-Centric Perspective on Customer Journeys
> - The *goal-oriented perspective on customer journeys* presents journeys as goal-oriented and hierarchical, with three levels: journeys toward higher-order goals; customer journeys; and touchpoints (Becker et al., 2020).
> - The *customer's value constellation (CVC)* entails all organizations that enable a customer to perform an activity. This framework also involves a hierarchical view of customer journeys in relation to activities (Patrício et al., 2011; Teixeira et al., 2012).
> - The *service delivery network (SDN)* entails all organizations responsible for providing an overall, connected service from a customer's perspective (Tax et al., 2013).
> - *Consumer experience modeling (CEM)* analyzes customer interactions with several actors within an experience domain, placing special emphasis on customer-to-customer interactions (Baron & Harris, 2010).

customer's goals. These goals can be organized into a hierarchy with higher-order and lower-order goals (Austin & Vancouver, 1996). For instance, if a person has a higher-order goal of living a healthier lifestyle, they need to set lower-order, more-concrete goals. These lower-order goals can relate to healthier eating, exercising, and relaxing. To achieve the goal of eating better, they need to set further goals, such as buying healthier food or consulting a nutritionist. Basically, lower-order goals are the means to achieve higher-order goals (Fig. 1).

Understanding the customer's goal hierarchy offers a means of situating the customer journey in its broader context. *Customers engage in customer journeys to achieve service or purchase goals.* Viewing goals as organized in a hierarchy suggests that these particular service or purchase goals are subordinate to higher-order goals, while simultaneously being superordinate to lower-order goals. To illustrate this, Fig. 2 depicts three levels of the customer journey: (1) the journey toward higher-order goals; (2) the customer journey; and (3) touchpoints.

The *journey toward higher-order goals* represents the process that customers undergo to achieve some important goals in their unique contexts (e.g., to have a successful career, to live a healthier lifestyle, to live a sober life). Consider the journey toward a healthier lifestyle: It involves customers' activities (e.g., going jogging every morning) and interactions with friends (e.g., going to the gym with a friend) and relatives (e.g., agreeing not to have unhealthy snacks at home). It also can involve interactions with several service providers, such as gyms, nutritionists, meditation apps, and self-help groups (e.g., Weight Watchers).

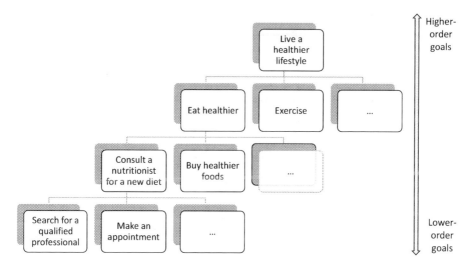

Fig. 1 Illustration of a consumer's goal hierarchy

The *customer journey* represents the processes that customers undergo to achieve a particular service or purchase goal that supports the higher-order goal. A customer who is trying to achieve a healthier lifestyle will engage in customer journeys with the previously mentioned services, such as gyms, nutritionists, or meditation apps. These customer journeys, in turn, can be divided into multiple touchpoints.

Touchpoints represent the moments of direct or indirect interaction with a service provider and its offerings to achieve even more concrete goals. For instance, a customer journey with a gym encompasses the customer researching the gym online, choosing a membership plan, interacting with the gym's frontline employees, using the gym's equipment, etc. Each of these touchpoints serves more concrete goals in the goal hierarchy. For instance, a customer might ask the gym employees for tips on how to increase resistance while training.

The goal-oriented framework can help service providers understand (i) the customer's ultimate, higher-order needs, (ii) the broader context in which the customer journey is embedded, and (iii) the range of actors that form external touchpoints along the journey and affect customer experiences. Failing to understand this broader context leads to a myopic view on why customers engage in customer journeys. The next section sheds light on the contextual factors that influence the customer experience.

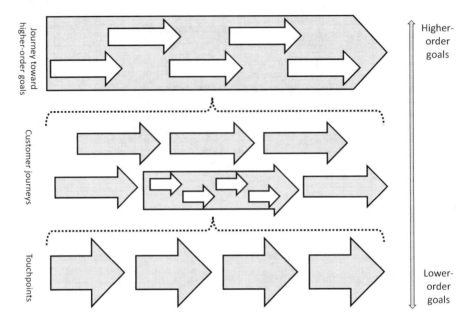

Fig. 2 A goal-oriented view of customer journeys (Becker et al., 2020)

The Role of the Customer's Context in the Customer Experience

Another important aspect to be considered to obtain a customer-centric perspective on the customer journey is the customer's context, as it plays an important role in customer experience emergence and evaluation (see Box 1). Customer experience emerges in the customer's specific and unique context (De Keyser et al., 2020; Lemon & Verhoef, 2016). In other words, contingencies related to customers themselves and their broader environments affect not only how customers respond to stimuli (i.e., the customer experience), but also whether their experiences are evaluated positively or negatively (Becker & Jaakkola, 2020). This is why customer experiences are individual and subjective: Even if a service provider offers exactly the same service to two customers, their customer experiences are not the same because they depend on several contextual factors.

Previous research has identified three groups of contingencies that affect the customer experience and how it is evaluated. First, *customer contingencies* refer to those related to customers themselves, such as a customer's characteristics (e.g., mood), resources (e.g., skills), past experiences, and motivation (Becker & Jaakkola, 2020; De Keyser et al., 2020; Verhoef et al., 2009). For example, a customer's level of tiredness likely would influence how the customer responds to a training session at the gym.

Second, *situational contingencies* refer to those related to the immediate context, or "interaction network," in which the customer journey is embedded, such as the type of service the customer interacts with, the presence of companions or other customers, and other firms that are part of a customer's journey (Baron & Harris, 2010; Becker & Jaakkola, 2020). In the gym example, training with a companion might make the training session more pleasant.

Finally, *sociocultural contingencies* refer to the broader system in which a customer is embedded, including, for instance, societal norms and rules, cultural aspects, and practices (Akaka et al., 2015; Becker & Jaakkola, 2020). For example, it is customary for customers to clean equipment after using it at the gym. If another customer breaks this norm, this likely affects the customer experience. However, if the customer is embedded in a cultural environment in which this is not the norm, failure to clean the equipment might not affect the customer experience to the same extent.

To sum up, customers' individual goals and varying stimuli within a range of touchpoints, many of which reside outside the service provider's sphere of influence, influence customer experience formation. Better understanding a customer's higher-order goals and their broader contexts will allow service providers to better manage the customer experience. The next section discusses how service providers can obtain this broad understanding and use it to design, monitor, and influence stimuli at various touchpoints throughout a customer journey.

4   CX Management in Service Firms

Researchers generally agree that positively evaluated customer experiences benefit service providers, in ways that include increased engagement and frequency of use, customer satisfaction, and customer loyalty and commitment (Mascarenhas et al., 2006; Srivastava & Kaul, 2016), leading to lower customer price sensitivity and positive word of mouth, among other effects (Zeithaml, 2000). This section homes in on the service firms' possibilities to manage customer experiences toward these desirable outcomes.

Customer experience management can be defined as *"the strategy to engineer the customer's experience in such a way as to create value for both the customer and the firm"* (Verhoef et al., 2009, p. 38). While CX in itself cannot be managed, firms can *affect customer experiences by monitoring, designing, and managing a range of stimuli* at and across different touchpoints that comprise the customer journey (see Box 1). Thus, customer experience management focuses on: (1) understanding CX along the broader customer journey; (2) designing, monitoring, and influencing stimuli at various touchpoints; and (3) fostering an organizational culture in which such an approach can thrive. The next sections will discuss these three key management activities.

Gaining an Understanding of Customer Experience

A central aspect of customer experience management is understanding customers' journeys toward higher-order goals and the firm's place there, as well as customers' experiences at touchpoints along their journeys with the firm. Firms can use tools such as *customer journey mapping* and *sentiment analysis*—as well as *customer effort score, net promoter score*, and other measurements—to evaluate the current situation, identify pain points (bottlenecks and other points at which the experience can be improved), and discover strategic opportunities (where the firm does especially well and what kind of customer experience is valued).

The goal-oriented framework for customer journeys (Fig. 2) can help service providers gain comprehensive insights on customer experiences and the stimuli that trigger them. By learning about customers' reactions to particular stimuli at brand-owned touchpoints, a physiotherapy center, for example, can focus on simplifying the online booking system or creating private seating areas in its vestibule. On the customer journey level, the center might consider ways to increase customers' confidence in doing recommended exercises at home by learning what other resources and services they use. Recognizing other actors in the customer journey can be an opportunity to collaborate and develop stronger partnerships and better offerings (cf. Baron & Harris, 2010). Finally, by tapping into higher-order goals, in which booking a massage session can be part of a regular self-care routine for one customer and a step toward severe injury recovery for another, a physiotherapy center can create customer personas for each typical journey.

Based on this current state analysis, firms can develop monitoring practices to track customer experience using qualitative and quantitative measures (McColl-Kennedy et al., 2019). Recently, technologically oriented firms have started to use AI and machine learning technologies to analyze vast amounts of qualitative data from multiple sources. Data can be gathered from customers and their communities, as well as from firms' own systems, employees, and partner networks (Chakravorti, 2011).

Designing the Controllable and Influencing the Uncontrollable

Designing touchpoints and journeys builds on an idea of the kind of customer experience the service provider wants their customers to have. Service providers might wish to differentiate from competition by aiming to provide the "best" customer experiences, and design touchpoints and journeys to ensure constant customer delight. In a more nuanced approach, the service provider chooses which dimensions of experience they want to emphasize, and creates differentiating "experience environments" along the customer journey (Prahalad & Ramaswamy, 2004). These intended experiences should then guide the touchpoint and journey design (Becker & Jaakkola, 2020).

From a service provider perspective, a touchpoint can be viewed as a "way to facilitate the service encounter and create interactions with customers" (Voorhees et al., 2017, p. 270). Dissecting the touchpoint further, it includes stimuli ranging from pre-determined cues (such as music and lighting) to uncontrollable factors (such as weather or other customers), an interface (a transmitter and a medium for stimuli), and an encounter (an actual moment of customer contact with the touchpoint) (Barann et al., 2022). Service literature provides a wealth of studies on service encounters in diverse forms, including interactions that occur face-to-face (e.g., Bitner et al., 1990), between humans and computers (HCI) (e.g., Patrício et al., 2008), and even between humans and service robots (e.g., Čaić et al., 2018). In addition to facilitating the attainment of service goals, touchpoints can become important sites of service recovery. Employees or systems' ability to alleviate the range of negative emotions originating in service failures and provide appropriate solutions can influence customer experience meaningfully (e.g., Smith & Bolton, 2002; Van Vaerenbergh et al., 2019).

Several useful tools can be applied to design service experiences across multiple encounters (see Box 4). Service blueprinting (Bitner et al., 2008) considers customer actions, visible employee actions, invisible employee actions, support processes, and physical evidence throughout a service process. Multilevel service design, in turn, represents the shift in service design thinking from studying single service encounters to service systems in which experiences are considered at the value constellation, service, and service encounter levels (Patrício et al., 2011).

In examining brand-owned touchpoints from the customer journey level, firms also should consider the potential variation or uniformity of experience across multiple touchpoints. Extant research generally recommends designing

668 E. Jaakkola et al.

> **Box 4 Different Approaches to CX Design**
> - The *experiential grid* encompasses strategic issues related to the depth, intensity, breadth, and linkage of intended experiences (Schmitt, 1999).
> - The *touchpoint as stimulus-interface-encounter* introduces a detailed conceptualization of a touchpoint, including pre-planned and unexpected elements (Barann et al., 2022). While developed in the omni-channel retail context, the conceptualization is rooted in the service science perspective.
> - The *service experience blueprint (SEB)* addresses interactions with technology and the multichannel nature of new services, focusing on designing multi-interface service experiences (Patrício et al., 2008).
> - The *multilevel service design (MSD)* is an approach to designing a service offering at multiple levels, that is, the service concept, service system, and service encounter (Patrício et al., 2011). The approach includes the design of value constellations, a systemic view of services, and multi-interface service encounters.

journeys in which touchpoints are united by a common theme, provide consistent stimuli, and adapt to customers' goals and contexts (Jaakkola & Terho, 2021; Homburg et al., 2015). Then again, many recreational services aim for unpredictable and exciting journeys to serve their adventurous customers, in which inconsistency and effort associated with moving along the journey keep customers excited (see Siebert et al., 2020). However, thrilling journeys are not reserved only for amusement parks. The more complex the service systems get, the more they are prone to mistakes and failures. Recently, Van Vaerenbergh et al. (2019) introduced the idea of service recovery journeys, which carry a level of emotional and cognitive involvement unusual for regular service journeys. Interestingly, for many low-involvement services, such as insurance or IT services, service failure provides a rare opportunity to facilitate extraordinary, memorable, and loyalty-inducing experiences.

As for touchpoints outside the firm's control, firms might want to consider stretching their influence within their partner networks and customer communities. However, there are limits to the degree of control that is still beneficial to the firm: Decisions must be made regarding how much the firm wants to associate with particular touchpoints or get involved in the customer's life. In any case, monitoring practices should be in place to keep firm's metaphoric finger on the pulse of customers' extended journeys to reveal new opportunities and points of influence.

Developing a Conducive Culture and Building Supportive Structures

While research on how to measure and influence customer experience has been growing exponentially over the past couple of decades, few studies have examined customer experience management from an internal perspective, as a holistic organization-wide management approach. This research branch emphasizes the development of a customer-centric orientation in organizational culture and processes (Lemon & Verhoef, 2016).

To support the design and management of touchpoints and journeys, ownership of these processes should be spread across organizational functions. Strategic customer experience management requires collaboration between functions responsible for strategic work, human resources, information technology, operations, partner and network management, and marketing and communications (Kandampully et al., 2018; Kwortnik & Thompson, 2009; Mosley, 2007). Thus, responsibility for the customer experience should not be locked within one function, and it is not enough to spread ownership across the organization. To manage contingencies and support reactive customer experience improvements, ownership should extend vertically through multiple hierarchy levels within the organization, including both top management commitment and each employee's customer-centric behaviors (Chakravorti, 2011; Mosley, 2007).

We should understand that culture both affects and is derived from behaviors (Ind & Bjerke, 2007), that is, certain cultural mindsets toward customer experiences (Homburg et al., 2015) can be achieved only if ruling systems and structures do not impede desirable, customer-centric behaviors. The processes and methods directed at building supportive structures and fostering a customer-centric culture represent the firm's capabilities to renew customer experiences continuously (Homburg et al., 2015). For example, designing customer-journey-oriented information systems has proven vital for breaking down organizational siloes and closing knowledge gaps, combined with reorganizing employees into cross-functional teams and "communities of practice" (Berry et al., 2006; Chakravorti, 2011; Kwortnik & Thompson, 2009). Taking a broader view of the consumer journey, a firm can consider integrating its systems and practices across its service network. In addition, designing appropriate incentives, performance measurements, and training programs with a customer experience strategy in mind encourages employees to experiment with and consciously drive customer experience improvements (Berry et al., 2006; Mosley, 2007; Chakravorti, 2011).

670 E. Jaakkola et al.

With the maturing of CX management practice, we now can see more and more recruitment of CX managers who are tasked with organizing participatory environments and improving internal communication, information systems, and measurement practices. CX managers are responsible for bringing customer insight to all functions, prioritizing, and giving direction to CX improvement efforts, as well as developing a culture in which each person within the organization can take ownership of their role in experience creation. Despite the title, the actual management of customer experience remains the whole organization's task, supporting the notion that only if seen as a firmwide endeavor and enhanced by knowledge management and cultural change practices can customer experience management take it upon itself to support customers on their journeys toward higher-order goals.

5   Conclusion

This chapter provided a state-of-the-art overview of customer experience as understood in the marketing and service research. Due to its increasingly pivotal role in service management, researchers and managers need to understand what customer experience is, how it emerges, and how it can be managed. While extant research on customer experience is fragmented across many different research domains, common ground exists on which CX research can be built (Becker & Jaakkola, 2020). Researchers studying customer experience should be aware of the various perspectives on the concept and navigate the fragmented research field by defining their positioning carefully, as well as the part of the broader CX phenomenon that their research can address.

This chapter discussed customer experiences and journeys from both the customer's and service provider's perspectives. First, we highlighted that for the customer, experiences emerge across various interactions with, for instance, service providers, products, apps, information sources, friends, and communities that they encounter in their lives when seeking to fulfill their needs and pursue their goals. Therefore, a customer journey with a particular service provider always is embedded in a complex web of other journeys. We posited that considering customers' higher- and lower-order goals is beneficial, as it can help service providers better understand their customers' profound needs, as well as the broader context and range of actors that shape customer experiences.

Second, we determined that while service providers cannot directly create and control customer experiences, they can seek to monitor, design, and

Understanding and Managing Customer Experiences   671

Table 2 Future research avenues on customer experience

Perspective	Potential research questions
Customer perspective on CX	• What are the dynamics of CX formation? • What are the different ways through which customer-to-customer interaction can affect CX? • How do touchpoints outside a service provider's control contribute to customers' perceived service failures? • Can positive CX lead to unwanted customer outcomes?
Organizational perspective on CX	• How do firms use different CX strategies for differentiation? • How can firms utilize personas developed on the basis of customers' higher-order goals for personalized journeys? • What role should the CX manager play in developing effective CX management practice? • How can firms engage customers in CX improvement?
Contextual perspective on CX	• What are the special features of CX and CX management in a particular context, such as professional or business-to-business services? • What are the service-type-related contingencies for CX formation? • When do customers appreciate unpredictable versus seamless customer journeys? • How does the nature of the touchpoint (online/digital vs. physical) affect customer responses to experience stimuli?
Methodological perspective on CX	• How can the broader consumer journey be mapped? • How can service providers identify customers' higher-order goals? • How can qualitative insights on different types of customer CX responses be captured in real time? • What is the unit of analysis for studying CX management as a firmwide approach?

manage the stimuli that give rise to customer experiences at different touchpoints. Thus, to manage customer experiences, organizations should develop methods to understand what customers feel, think, and sense along their broader consumer journeys; design stimuli that could trigger intended CX; and foster an experience- and customer-focused organizational culture. Ultimately, we emphasized that understanding customer experiences and journeys is a prerequisite for developing truly customer-oriented service businesses.

CX and CX management offer a fruitful arena for future research. This chapter has provided a big-picture perspective on the phenomenon, and students and researchers can dive more deeply into a particular aspect to learn more and develop novel insights. Table 2 suggests important research questions that can inspire future research.

References

Akaka, M. A., & Schau, H. J. (2019). Value creation in consumption journeys: Recursive reflexivity and practice continuity. *Journal of the Academy of Marketing Science, 47*(3), 499–515.

Akaka, M. A., Vargo, S. L., & Schau, H. J. (2015). The context of experience. *Journal of Service Management, 26*(2), 206–223.

Arnould, E. J., & Price, L. L. (1993). River magic: Extraordinary experience and the extended service encounter. *Journal of Consumer Research, 20*(1), 24–45.

Austin, J. T., & Vancouver, J. B. (1996). Goal constructs in psychology: Structure, process, and content. *Psychological Bulletin, 120*(3), 338–375.

Barann, B., Hermann, A., Heuchert, M., & Becker, J. (2022). Can't touch this? Conceptualizing the customer touchpoint in the context of omni-channel retailing. *Journal of Retailing and Consumer Services, 65*(March), 102269.

Baron, S., & Harris, K. (2010). Toward an understanding of consumer perspectives on experiences. *Journal of Services Marketing, 24*(7), 518–531.

Becker, L., & Jaakkola, E. (2020). Customer experience: Fundamental premises and implications for research. *Journal of the Academy of Marketing Science, 48*, 630–648.

Becker, L., Jaakkola, E., & Halinen, A. (2020). Toward a goal-oriented view of customer journeys. *Journal of Service Management, 31*(4), 767–790.

Berry, L. L., Wall, E. A., & Carbone, L. P. (2006). Service clues and customer assessment of the service experience: Lessons from marketing. *Academy of Management Perspectives, 20*(2), 43–57.

Bitner, M. J., Booms, B. H., & Tetreault, M. S. (1990). The service encounter: Diagnosing favorable and unfavorable incidents. *Journal of Marketing, 54*(1), 71.

Bitner, M. J., Ostrom, A. L., & Morgan, F. N. (2008). Service blueprinting: A practical technique for service innovation. *California Management Review, 50*(3), 66–94.

Brakus, J. J., Schmitt, B. H., & Zarantonello, L. (2009). Brand experience: What is it? How is it measured? Does it affect loyalty? *Journal of Marketing, 73*(3), 52–68.

Čaić, M., Odekerken-Schröder, G., & Mahr, D. (2018). Service robots: Value co-creation and co-destruction in elderly care networks. *Journal of Service Management, 29*(2), 178–205.

Carù, A., & Cova, B. (2003). Revisiting consumption experience: A more humble but complete view of the concept. *Marketing Theory, 3*(2), 267–286.

Chakravorti, S. (2011). Managing organizational culture change and knowledge to enhance customer experiences: Analysis and framework. *Journal of Strategic Marketing, 19*(2), 123–151.

De Keyser, A., Verleye, K., Lemon, K. N., Keiningham, T. L., & Klaus, P. (2020). Moving the customer experience field forward: Introducing the touchpoints, context, qualities (TCQ) nomenclature. *Journal of Service Research, 23*(4), 433–455.

Dias, J., Ionutiu, O., Lhuer, X., & van Ouwerkerk, J. (2016). *The four pillars of distinctive customer journeys*. Retrieved February, 2021, from www.mckinsey.com/

business-functions/digital-mckinsey/our-insights/the-four-pillars-of-distinctive-customer-journeys

Grewal, D., Levy, M., & Kumar, V. (2009). Customer experience management in retailing: An organizing framework. *Journal of Retailing, 85*(1), 1–14.

Hamilton, R., & Price, L. L. (2019). Consumer journeys: Developing consumer-based strategy. *Journal of the Academy of Marketing Science, 47*(2), 187–191.

Hamilton, K., & Wagner, B. A. (2014). Commercialized nostalgia: Staging consumer experiences in small businesses. *European Journal of Marketing, 48*(5/6), 813–832.

Helkkula, A. (2011). Characterizing the concept of service experience. *Journal of Service Management, 22*(3), 367–389.

Helkkula, A., Kelleher, C., & Pihlstrom, M. (2012). Characterizing value as an experience: Implications for researchers and managers. *Journal of Service Research, 15*(1), 59–75.

Holbrook, M. B., & Hirschman, E. C. (1982). The experiential aspects of consumption: Consumer fantasies, feelings, and fun. *Journal of Consumer Research, 9*(1), 132–140.

Homburg, C., Jozić, D., & Kuehnl, C. (2015). Customer experience management: Toward implementing an evolving marketing concept. *Journal of the Academy of Marketing Science, 45*(3), 377–401.

Ind, N., & Bjerke, R. (2007). The concept of participatory market orientation: An organization-wide approach to enhancing brand equity. *Journal of Brand Management, 15*(2), 135–145.

Jaakkola, E., & Terho, H. (2021). Service journey quality: Conceptualization, measurement, and customer outcomes. *Journal of Service Management, 32*(6), 1–27.

Jaakkola, E., Helkkula, A., & Aarikka-Stenroos, L. (2015). Service experience cocreation: Conceptualization, implications, and future research directions. *Journal of Service Management, 26*(2), 182–205.

Kandampully, J., Zhang, T., & Jaakkola, E. (2018). Customer experience management in hospitality: A literature synthesis, new understanding, and research agenda. *International Journal of Contemporary Hospitality Management, 30*(1), 21–56.

Kuehnl, C., Jozic, D., & Homburg, C. (2019). Effective customer journey design: Consumers' conception, measurement, and consequences. *Journal of the Academy of Marketing Science, 47*(3), 551–568.

Kuppelwieser, V. G., & Klaus, P. (2020). Measuring customer experience quality: The EXQ scale revisited. *Journal of Business Research, 126*, 624–633.

Kwortnik, R. J., & Thompson, G. M. (2009). Unifying service marketing and operations with service experience management. *Journal of Service Research, 11*(4), 389–406.

Lemon, K. N., & Verhoef, P. C. (2016). Understanding customer experience throughout the customer journey. *Journal of Marketing, 80*, 69–96.

Mascarenhas, O. A., Kesavan, R., & Bernacchi, M. (2006). Lasting customer loyalty: A total customer experience approach. *Journal of Consumer Marketing, 23*(7), 397–405.

McColl-Kennedy, J. R., Gustafsson, A., Jaakkola, E., Klaus, P., Radnor, Z. J., Perks, H., & Friman, M. (2015). Fresh perspectives on customer experience. *Journal of Services Marketing, 29*(6/7), 430–435.

McColl-Kennedy, J. R., Danaher, T. S., Gallan, A. S., Orsingher, C., Lervik-Olsen, L., & Verma, R. (2017). How do you feel today? Managing patient emotions during health care experiences to enhance well-being. *Journal of Business Research, 79*, 247–259.

McColl-Kennedy, J. R., Zaki, M., Lemon, K. N., Urmetzer, F., & Neely, A. (2019). Gaining customer experience insights that matter. *Journal of Service Research, 22*(1), 8–26.

Mosley, R. W. (2007). Customer experience, organizational culture, and the employer brand. *Journal of Brand Management, 15*(2), 123–134.

Novak, T. P., Hoffman, D. L., & Yiu-Fai, Y. (2000). Measuring the customer experience in online environments: A structural modeling approach. *Marketing Science, 19*(1), 22–42.

Olsson, L. E., Gärling, T., Ettema, D., Friman, M., & Fujii, S. (2013). Happiness and satisfaction with work commute. *Social Indicators Research, 111*(1), 255–263.

Ostrom, A. L., Parasuraman, A., Bowen, D. E., Patrício, L., & Voss, C. A. (2015). Service research priorities in a rapidly changing context. *Journal of Service Research, 18*(2), 127–159.

Patrício, L., Fisk, R. P., & e Cunha, J. F. (2008). Designing multi-interface service experiences: The service experience blueprint. *Journal of Service Research, 10*(4), 318–334.

Patrício, L., Fisk, R. P., e Cunha, J. F., & Constantine, L. (2011). Multilevel service design: From customer value constellation to service experience blueprinting. *Journal of Service Research, 14*(2), 180–200.

Pine, B. J., & Gilmore, J. H. (1998). Welcome to the experience economy. *Harvard Business Review, 76*, 97–105.

Prahalad, C. K., & Ramaswamy, V. (2004). Co-creation experiences: The next practice in value creation. *Journal of Interactive Marketing, 18*(3), 5–14.

Rose, S., Clark, M., Samouel, P., & Hair, N. (2012). Online customer experience in e-retailing: An empirical model of antecedents and outcomes. *Journal of Retailing, 88*, 308–322.

Schmitt, B. H. (1999). Experiential marketing. *Journal of Marketing Management, 15*(13), 53–67.

Siebert, A., Gopaldas, A., Lindridge, A., & Simões, C. (2020). Customer experience journeys: Loyalty loops versus involvement spirals. *Journal of Marketing, 84*(4), 45–66.

Smith, A. K., & Bolton, R. N. (2002). The effect of customers' emotional responses to service failures on their recovery effort evaluations and satisfaction judgments. *Journal of the Academy of Marketing Science, 30*(1), 5–23.

Srivastava, M., & Kaul, D. (2016). Exploring the link between customer experience-loyalty-consumer spending. *Journal of Retailing and Consumer Services, 31*, 277–286.

Tax, S. S., McCutcheon, D., & Wilkinson, I. F. (2013). The service delivery network (SDN): A customer-centric perspective of the customer journey. *Journal of Service Research, 16*(4), 454–470.

Teixeira, J., Patrício, L., Nunes, N. J., Nóbrega, L., Fisk, R. P., & Constantine, L. (2012). Customer experience modeling: From customer experience to service design. *Journal of Service Management, 23*(3), 362–276.

Van Vaerenbergh, Y., Varga, D., De Keyser, A., & Orsingher, C. (2019). The service recovery journey: Conceptualization, integration, and directions for future research. *Journal of Service Research, 22*(2), 103–119.

Vargo, S. L., & Lusch, R. F. (2008). Service-dominant logic: Continuing the evolution. *Journal of the Academy of Marketing Science, 36*, 1–10.

Verhoef, P. C., Lemon, K. N., Parasuraman, A., Roggeveen, A., Tsiros, M., & Schlesinger, L. A. (2009). Customer experience creation: Determinants, dynamics, and management strategies. *Journal of Retailing, 85*(1), 31–41.

Voorhees, C. M., Fombelle, P. W., Gregoire, Y., Bone, S., Gustafsson, A., Sousa, R., & Walkowiak, T. (2017). Service encounters, experiences, and the customer journey: Defining the field and a call to expand our lens. *Journal of Business Research, 79*, 269–280.

Witell, L., Kowalkowski, C., Perks, H., Raddats, C., Schwabe, M., Benedettini, O., & Burton, J. (2020). Characterizing customer experience management in business markets. *Journal of Business Research, 116*, 420–430.

Zeithaml, V. A. (2000). Service quality, profitability, and the economic worth of customers: What we know and what we need to learn. *Journal of the Academy of Marketing Science, 28*(1), 67–85.

How Customers' Resources Influence Their Co-creation Experience

Helena Alves and Cátia Jesus

1 Introduction

Consumer experience (CE) has been a focus of study in management, because creating memorable experiences for customers results in satisfaction, which is fundamental in achieving competitive advantage (McColl-Kennedy et al., 2015; Mosavi et al., 2018). Experiences emerge throughout dynamic experiences, formed, and reformed through interactive cultural and social processes (Akaka & Vargo, 2015), and consequently, each consumer's experience will be unique, based on a different combination of relations and resources as well as individual and shared knowledge (Vargo & Lusch, 2008, 2016). Each consumer's experience is influenced by their resources, although these can be complemented by others existing in the market (Gummesson & Mele, 2010).

According to service-dominant logic (SDL), no individual actor possesses all the resources necessary to co-create value (Lusch & Vargo, 2014). Rather, actors have access to and can operate on a wide range of resources to extract

H. Alves (✉)
Department of Management and Economics and NECE, University of Beira Interior, Covilhã, Portugal
e-mail: halves@ubi.pt

C. Jesus
Department of Management and Economics, University of Beira Interior, Covilhã, Portugal
e-mail: cjesus@ubi.pt

© The Author(s), under exclusive license to Springer Nature Switzerland AG 2022
B. Edvardsson, B. Tronvoll (eds.), *The Palgrave Handbook of Service Management*,
https://doi.org/10.1007/978-3-030-91828-6_34

value during service-for-service exchanges. Through resource integration, actors can co-create value for themselves but also create new potential resources that they might exchange with other actors (Lusch & Vargo, 2014). Value is co-created when an actor integrates and operates on own resources, such as knowledge, skills, and competences with other public, private, or market-faced resources in an effort to arrive at intended outcomes such as increased well-being for the focal actor and/or for other actors (Vargo & Lusch, 2004, 2008, 2011). Each actor's context, as well as their knowledge and skills, affects their ability to access and leverage resources, as well as their ability to indirectly access and leverage resources beyond the immediate context (Uzzi, 1997).

Albrecht et al. (2017) consider that resource integration (RI) provides a promising lens to explore how customers use service offers together with a variety of other resources in contexts of collective consumption, where various actors and consumers are also present, and how that creates value. However, creating value in these contexts is still little explored (Kelleher et al., 2019), highlighting the need for research in this field.

Research and narratives related to resource integration are conceptually rich, but predominantly theoretical. Among the few empirical studies, business-to-business research has shown the collective nature of RI in that context, emphasizing collaborative activities between organizations' managers, customers, and suppliers (Macdonald et al., 2016). Also standing out are empirical studies exploring the consumer's role in a business-to-consumer context (McColl-Kennedy et al., 2012) and studies focusing on customers as resource integrators (Baron & Warnaby, 2011). All the studies/approaches have enhanced understanding of the resources individuals integrate, but this matter is not yet clear in a dynamic context of events.[1] Therefore, the intention here is to study resource integration in an event context.

The research combines the theoretical groundings of consumer experience (CE) with its value co-creation processes, according to service-dominant logic (SDL), giving particular importance to resource integration by event consumers. The intention is to understand the operant physical, cultural, and social resources essential for the consumer's experience of global co-creation. The co-creation process will have repercussions in results of the experience—such as satisfaction and behavioural intentions—which will also be studied and analysed. The review of studies on consumption experience revealed this has

---

[1] Considering the typology of Getz and Page (2016), this research defined *"event context"* as festivals or cultural phenomena/celebrations. These celebrations are less dependent on premises, since they can take place in parks, streets, theatres, and other public or private places. In this typology, the authors identified and underlined as classic topics: myths, rituals, traditions, symbolism, ceremonies/celebrations, shows, host-guest interactions (and the role of the outsider), authenticities, pilgrimages, carnivals, commemorations, and there is some debate about their impacts and meanings.

been studied in relation to antecedents, consumers' personal factors, physical structure, service quality, collaborators, access, and trust (Bueno et al., 2019). However, so far, no study has determined the influence of the various types of resources on the results of service experience.

To fulfil this objective, the influence of consumer resources in the event context will be studied. Events, whether cultural, sporting, political, or of another nature, are characterized by the absence of controllability and risks they present for operation and marketing management, as they are held in different contexts (of time, space, or consumers) (Tum et al., 2006; Berridge, 2007; Bowdin et al., 2012). Their mobility and irregularity present challenges to event management and the co-creation of experiences, due to the uncertainty regarding the value propositions that can be offered and the expectations that can be created (Lugosi et al., 2020).

So far, the literature on service and experience co-creation has been based on the ability to manage consumption experiences, in spaces and times outside the organization's influence (Grönroos & Voima, 2013) and has therefore highlighted the need to develop propositions or strategies to manage or facilitate co-creation (Ellis et al., 2019). However, empirical evidence of what happens in consumption experiences in the event context is limited (Laing, 2018; Lugosi et al., 2020). Therefore, this research aims to study the resources most used by consumers in the context of cultural events, as well as the influence these have on the final result of the experience. To do so, two studies were carried out, one qualitative (Study 1), based on the Customer Journey Maps method, aiming to identify the resources used by consumers in the event context (first research objective); and another quantitative (Study 2), aiming to test the relationship between the resources of event consumers and the results of their co-creation experience (second research objective). The study hopes to contribute to the management of co-creation experiences in the context of cultural events. From a theoretical perspective, it intends to contribute to the literature on value co-creation, above all regarding integration of the consumer's operant resources, in an event context, and their effect on the results of the experience.

2 Theoretical Background

The Consumer Experience

For some authors, consumers' experience is their personal interpretation of the service process and their interaction/involvement during the various contacts with the service (Meyer & Schwager, 2007; Ding et al., 2010; Johnston

& Kong, 2011). Adhikari and Bhattacharya (2016) classify the consumer experience according to two visions: the prospective vision, which analyses CE as the expectation in relation to a sensory involvement with the product/service, and the reflective vision, which analyses CE during and after consumption of the experiential product/service or sensory interaction (Bos et al., 2015). Meyer and Schwager (2007) define consumer experience as the internal and subjective responses of consumers who have direct and indirect contact with organizations, which end up being a cumulative impact—both emotional and practical—of the customer's encounters and interactions with the organization (Stangl, 2014). In the same connection, Klaus and Maklan (2013) highlight it as the affective and cognitive assessment of direct and indirect encounters with the organization. This assessment results from the interaction between the consumer and the organization, being moulded by the characteristics of both and by the influence of the surrounding environment (Same & Larimo, 2012). For Gentile et al. (2007), the consumer experience is the result of a series of interactions between the consumer and the experience, which causes reactions. Therefore, Brakus et al. (2009) state that the experience derives from behavioural and affective constructions of assessment.

Many researchers concentrate on a more wide-ranging perspective, where holistically the consumer experience incorporates all the cognitive, sensory, social, emotional, and spiritual responses from the consumer's interaction with the organization (Schmitt, 1999, 2003; Gentile et al., 2007; Brakus et al., 2009; Verhoef et al., 2009; Lemke et al., 2011; Bolton et al., 2014; Keyser et al., 2015). For Walls et al. (2011), CE is also a multi-dimensional construction of a holistic nature, resulting from the interaction of internal factors, such as emotion and cognition, but also external factors, such as interactions, physical experiences, and situational factors. Therefore, when consumers consider or have a consumption experience, they are influenced by internal factors of a subjective situation, but also, be external factors produced by the organizations which will influence how consumers engage in the consumption experience. Here, Schmitt et al. (2015) defend the most wide-ranging view of the subject, suggesting that all service exchanges lead to consumer experience, irrespective or their form and nature.

Based on different epistemological and ontological origins, experience (of the customer, consumer, or service) has been characterized in the marketing and service literature in three ways: as a process, a result, or a phenomenon (Helkkula, 2011). Experience based on the process implies understanding of the different elements and phases that are interlinked with experiential learning (Edvardsson et al., 2005). Conception/management of the customer's experience requires the existence of various elements that function holistically to meet or exceed their expectations, that is, delivering value to the customer requires an inter-functional perspective (Bitner et al., 2008). Network approaches facilitate the inclusion of stakeholders in creating experiences (Binkhorst & Dekker, 2009).

Experiences have also been presented based on the results being considered as an antecedent/consequence of other constructions (Helkkula, 2011). This approach was used by many studies focusing on service management and marketing, seeking to understand how organizations could delineate and manage their experiences to create competitive advantage. Therefore, it became extremely important to identify the factors that affect experience (Doorn et al., 2010; Verhoef et al., 2009), as well as the creation of performance variables (Klaus & Maklan, 2012). Employees' behaviour and attitudes, the environment, inter-personal relations, and technical quality emerge as elements with an influence and direct impact on CE (Bharwani & Jauhari, 2013). This field of research has analysed how experiences are co-created within encounters and relations between the organization and its consumers, which means the parties can directly influence each other's experiences and value processes (Grönroos, 2008).

Finally, experiences can be based on a phenomenological perspective, highlighting service-dominant logic, service logic, and the theory of consumer culture. This phenomenological perspective is a very useful lens, since it intends to understand the consumer's value creation experience, rather than focusing on organizations' attempts to incorporate value in market offers or appropriating the values created by consumers (Kelleher & Peppard, 2011).

The discussion around service-dominant logic re-centred attention on the consumer experience, on the premise that the value is singular and phenomenologically determined by the consumer (Vargo & Lusch, 2008). Here, authors were concerned about summarizing and characterizing what had been identified as an evolutionary change in marketing: (a) the focus changed to the beneficial processes, that is, the service; (b) the conceptualization of value changed from the value of the exchange to the use of the value, and (c) value came to be understood as something that is co-created, rather than produced and delivered. The experience is considered as subjective and specific to the context (Vargo & Lusch, 2008; Mukhtar et al., 2012; Helkkula et al., 2012). Instead of the value being assessed objectively in monetary terms, it is assessed subjectively in the social context (Edvardsson et al., 2011). This scenario highlights consumers' active and pro-active role in creating value, which can influence individually and collectively where, when, and how value is created (Kelleher & Peppard, 2011; Grönroos, 2011). This approach is the one that recognizes best the co-creation experience in relation to actual encounters and services, considering direct and indirect interactions in forming value. As such, the experience is personal, relational, and social (Helkkula, 2011; Helkkula et al., 2012).

This research will be based on a phenomenological perspective, to understand the consumer's resources and their influence on the experience. According to Bueno et al. (2019), studies on customer experience have identified satisfaction and behavioural intentions as outcomes of experience, with these two variables being most commonly used in studies to measure the results of the customer experience. These two outcomes of experience will also be adopted in this research.

Customers' Resources and Experience

Becker and Jaakkola (2020) systematized studies on consumer experience from two perspectives: (1) the experience as a response to firms' stimuli, or (2) the response to consumption processes. These authors also systematized the fields of marketing that have focused most on the consumer experience, namely service marketing, studying the experience as the response to the service environment, service personnel, and core service; experiential marketing, where the consumer experience has been studied as the response to cues, thematic content, events, and brand-related advertising; or SDL, where the experience has been studied as the result of eco-systems.

According to this last perspective, SDL, experience is seen as "a subjective phenomenon emerging through responses to the holistic service process. Experiences are co-created among many actors involved in resource integration, embedded in context, and connected with value" (Becker & Jaakkola, 2020, p. 635), which underlines the fundamental role of resources. According to SDL, all actors try to increase the viability of their systems through the exchange and integration of resources, whether market, public or private (Lusch & Vargo, 2014). Therefore, a fundamental starting point is the actor's own resources.

According to Kleinaltenkamp (2015), the resources integrated by actors are all the tangible and intangible elements characteristic of the actor or which are accessible at the moment of making the decision to incorporate resources, being used by the actors to achieve intended objectives with recourse to integration processes. Altinay et al. (2016) emphasize the existence of operant resources—which act on other resources—and operand resources—which are tangible resources attributed or put into practice.

How Customers' Resources Influence Their Co-creation Experience   **683**

A resource effectively becomes a resource according to the context of its use: useless for some actors in certain contexts, or crucial, with great value, for other actors in other contexts (Frery et al., 2015). Resources can be defined as something that has the potential to be produced or used by actors, allowing, and promoting resource integration, as well as effort to co-create value (Edvardsson & Tronvoll, 2013; Bharwani & Jauhari, 2013; Yi & Gong, 2013; Tommasetti et al., 2015; Aal et al., 2016, Iyanna, 2016; Troisi et al., 2019; Zhang et al., 2019; Xiao et al., 2020; Halbusi et al., 2020; Becker & Jaakkola, 2020). In this respect, the authors distance themselves from the narrow view of resources, as only being linked to offers, and concentrate on facilitators of the service eco-system, including information, knowledge, values, skills, physical products, brands, natural resources, and experience rooms. Chandler and Vargo (2011), Kleinaltenkamp (2015) and Plé (2016) qualify resources as valuable since they are central to SDL and directly related to the actors.

Rodie and Kleine (2000) divide resources into mental, emotional, and physical. In turn, Hobfoll (2002) underlines that an individual's resources can include materials, conditions (social status), the self (self-esteem and self-efficacy), and social resources; also highlighting the existence of *"energies"* (time, money, and knowledge) as resources that do not have an intrinsic value but gain value in acquiring other resources. Then again, Arnould et al. (2006) classify operant resources in physical resources (physical and mental capacity such as energy, emotion, and strengths), social resources (family and commercial relations and brand, or consumer communities), and cultural resources (specialized aptitudes and knowledge, as well as life experiences, stories, and imagination).

3   Studies: Qualitative and Quantitative Approach

Study 1: Study of the Customer Journey Map at the Óbidos Christmas Town event (OCT)[2]

Since there is little empirical evidence on what resources are integrated by consumers in the event context, a first study of a qualitative nature was carried out, based on the Customer Journey Maps method, to understand and

---

[2] OCT is an event held annually in the town of Óbidos in Portugal. It takes place in December in the outdoor space of the castle, in an open field, in a scenario with its own characteristics. From year to year, the organization changes the theme of the event, but always involving many craft establishments, exhibitions, and medieval aspects of this enchanting town, even before entering the enclosure. The enjoyment of children and adults is ensured after entering the venue with many games, activities, amusements, shows, and entertainment everywhere.

684 H. Alves and C. Jesus

identify what types of resources are used by consumers in the event context (first research objective).

Methodology

The customer journey maps (CJM) are a visual, process-oriented method that conceptualizes and structures consumers' experiences (Nenonen et al., 2008). They are used to "reflect patterns of thought, processes, considerations, paths and experiences that individuals pass through in their daily lives" (Nenonen et al., 2008, p. 5), that is, they allow understanding of how customers behave, feel and what their motivations/attitudes are throughout the journey taken (Zomerdijk & Voss, 2010), considering consumers' mental models, the flow of interactions and touchpoints. Thus, consumer's journey is a systematic and schematic approach that, through several contact episodes, facilitates the understanding of the experience and processes (Hagen & Bron, 2014).

CJM method was chosen to understand, describe, and schematize in detail the experience, as well as resource integration and co-creation processes (CP) of consumers at the OCT event. Adopting an exploratory, interpretative, and descriptive approach, the aim was to: (1) describe the CE throughout the purchase stages; and (2) identify the resources integrated by consumers and understand how and when the co-creation process occurs in an event context.

Considering the exploratory character of this qualitative study, it was decided to hold 12 semi-structured interviews with consumers (the interview script can be provided by the authors) who had attended the eleventh OCT event, that is, the one held in 2016/2017. The participants agreed to the interviews being recorded on an audio file (WAV). This solution allowed the conversation to flow better, capturing details, and facilitated transcription, coding, and analysis of each interview held. The interviews were held between 20 January and 25 February 2017, each one lasting 40 minutes on average. The interviewees were 5 men and 7 women, all national/Portuguese tourists aged between 25 and 64. Seven were married and five were single, with a level of education between secondary school and a master's degree. Five had already visited the event previously, while seven were visiting for the first time. However, all the interviewees visited the event with someone (spouse, family, or friends). The data obtained were treated and analysed using NVIVO 11 PLUS software.

Results

The results of Study 1 will be presented briefly, and these will be the basis of Study 2. The results obtained demonstrate the existence of various processes of value co-creation and resource integration by consumers at the event. It was therefore possible to determine and understand what type of resources are integrated and in what circumstances, finding that during their experience consumers valorize, activate, and use all the operant (physical, social, and cultural) and operand resources (monetary and tangible goods). However, it is important to underline that their importance varied over the three phases of purchase. Table 1 presents the summary of the results obtained regarding resource integration and co-creation processes in the three stages of purchase. The Appendix 1 presents some excerpts from the interviews and additional observations.

Table 1 Resources and co-creation processes over the three phases of purchase

Phase	Stage	Resources	Co-creation processes
Pre-purchase	Awareness and discovery of the event	Social	Information sharing among actors through relations and communication are essential resources for the learning basis of the consumer's value co-creation and resource integration
	Consideration, comparison, and seeking/ gathering information	Cultural, physical, and operational	Information processing by the consumer allows assessment of the benefits and sacrifices of the CP
			Consumers' capacities, skills, and knowledge can reduce the uncertainty, increase control of the co-creation environment, and also master their role of co-creator and resource integrator
			They turn to operand resources to gain economic benefits, through discounts and vouchers
	Decision-making and online purchase	Cultural, physical, and operational	Consumers' involvement makes them co-producers, allowing a better match with their needs and demands. They obtain psychological benefits and confidence in their co-creation capacities
			They resort to their operand resources, through various electronic means, to achieve their objectives

(*continued*)

Table 1 (continued)

Phase	Stage	Resources	Co-creation processes
Purchase during the event	Arrival/decision and local purchase	Social commercial	The existence of relational aspects among actors means greater and better CP by the consumer
	Entry to the enclosure	Physical and social	The consumer's capacity to improve the social and emotional bonds with other actors is considered essential. This dimension translates into actions destined to establish or develop a social and emotional connection among actors during the interaction
	Use and choices during the event	Physical	Consumers' physical skills are contextualized within cultural models and transposed to the context
		Social	The relations and social contexts of the interactions are fundamental matters. Joint actions can understand and exploit similarities among actors, share mutual interests, adopt perspectives, or establish a personal bond that creates a mutual basis of understanding among actors; translating into an important CP that generates social and emotional value during interaction at the event
		Cultural	Consumers' experiences are dependent on the context and vary according to socio-cultural configurations. Consumers with greater cultural resources contribute more and better CP.
		Operand	Consumers resort mainly to their economic resources to be able to use products and services. The amount of these resources affects the consumer's exchange behaviour with organizations: the greater the resources the greater the CP behaviour

(*continued*)

Table 1 (continued)

Phase	Stage	Resources	Co-creation processes
Post-purchase	Feedback	Social	Information sharing by consumers (virtual and face-to-face) is essential for them to be able to convey details about their experience to other consumers, and to convey information to actors or collaborators about what displeased them most in the course of the experience
		Cultural	At the time of sharing the past experience and respective photographs on social networks and other virtual platforms
		Physical	Expend energy and efforts in sharing information (virtual and face-to-face) with other actors and in spreading opinions about the event
		Operand	They resort to their operand resources, through various electronic means, to achieve their objectives

Study 2: Relation Between Consumers' Resources and the Results of Their Experience

As previously mentioned, the researches related to resource integration are predominantly theoretical. Thus, this second study intends to fill this gap in the event context, proposing and testing a model that considers the consumer's resources and the results of their co-creation experience (second research objective).

Research Hypotheses

Various studies on consumer participation have demonstrated that customers have personal resources that they use actively in co-creating value (Iyanna, 2016; Xiao et al., 2020). Chan et al. (2010) discovered that consumer satisfaction is increased through that active participation, concluding that consumer participation allows the organization and the actors involved to create various categories of value together (such as economic values or relational values). In this connection, Franke and Schreier (2010) say that if the experience evolves as expected and ends up being successful, confirming expectations, participation in co-creation activities will increase the customer's satisfaction, also providing a sense of fulfilment. Similarly, Grissemann and Stokburger-Sauer

(2012) confirmed that the level of co-creation affects consumer satisfaction in relation to the service experience. The authors highlight that, in fact, as satisfaction results from the consumer's assessment of the experience, the assessment itself will also depend on the customer's contribution to the process. Therefore, when the final result of the co-created service is adjusted to the customer's needs, the effort in the process is perceived as positive and complements the subjective value linked to the experience (Franke & Schreier, 2010). Chan et al. (2010) also mention that value co-creation is necessary for participation to have an effect, since customers are willing to cooperate only if they anticipate benefits in creating the service offer. As such, a hypothesis is established, emphasizing the relation between consumers' physical resources and their satisfaction, expecting this to have a positive influence:

Hypothesis 1 Consumers' physical resources have a positive influence on their satisfaction

Generally, consumers' assessment of their inputs influences global satisfaction with the experience in the service organization (Grissemann & Stokburger-Sauer, 2012), but also the other possible contributions. Piller et al. (2011), Nysveen and Pedersen (2014) and Haro et al. (2014) highlight that consumers who participate in co-creation activities are more likely to engage in positive word-of-mouth strategies (word-of-mouth marketing), form stronger long-term relations with the organization and present higher levels of trust and loyalty. Consumer involvement in co-creation activities also influences consumers' behavioural responses, such as the intention to purchase and willingness to pay (Payne et al., 2008; Cermark et al., 2011; Grissemann & Stokburger-Sauer, 2012; Xia & Suri, 2014; Alarcón et al., 2017). Here, Laurent and Kapferer (1985) underline that customers with a higher level of involvement are more loyal, spend more money, and have more favourable behavioural intentions towards the organization. This led to formulating the hypothesis highlighting the relation between consumers' physical resources and their behavioural intentions, expecting this to be positive:

Hypothesis 2 Consumers' physical resources have a positive influence on their behavioural intentions

Considering the importance of intangible factors in consumption processes, it can be stated that value-co-creation derives mainly from consumers' mental attitudes towards their potential involvement in the service experience

(Tommasetti et al., 2015). McColl-Kennedy et al. (2012) reveal that individuals' cerebral activities represent the series of aptitudes and expectations held psychologically by consumers to cooperate with service providers. According to the study by Luszczynska et al. (2005), individuals with higher levels of self-efficacy choose to perform more challenging tasks and demonstrate their skills by exploring challenges in the surrounding environment. In this way, they establish new objectives and find it easier to face the challenges that emerge. This is also accompanied by feelings of pride/honour regarding the co-creation performance (Franke & Schreier, 2010). According to Luszczynska et al. (2005), the perception of self-efficacy reflects consumers' individual perception of their capacities to organize and implement specific actions leading to certain levels of results. Martínez and Martínez (2007) demonstrated that customer satisfaction is stimulated by cognitive and affective factors, highlighting the level of excitement as an even stronger influence on satisfaction. According to Grissemann and Stokburger-Sauer (2012), satisfaction with performance in the co-creation process is understood as customers' satisfaction with participation in the service creation. Following this line of thought, various studies have revealed the customer's clarity and capacity as factors helping consumers to participate constructively in processes of service creation and delivery, also affecting their experience of value co-creation and the results arising from the process (Chen et al., 2011; Grönroos & Ravald 2011; Hunt et al., 2012; Ranjan & Read, 2016). Therefore, a hypothesis was established, highlighting a positive relation between consumers' cultural resources and their satisfaction:

Hypothesis 3 Consumers' cultural resources have a positive influence on their satisfaction

As mentioned previously, various studies have shown that consumers' participation in organizational activities has a direct increase in their personal satisfaction and perceptions of quality (Czepiel, 1990). Similarly, future behaviour is determined by consumers' explanations of the results of their own behaviour (Martinko & Thomson, 1998). Applying this reasoning to the co-creation context, Grissemann and Stokburger-Sauer (2012) find that the value customers derive from the process, and consequently their future behaviour, is determined by their assessment of how much of the success of the process can be attributed to them. Therefore, when the co-created service meets customers' needs, the effort in the process is also perceived as positive and complements the subjective value attributed to the service, leading to consumers' positive behaviour in the future. This is because efforts made in the co-creation process are understood as a gratifying and pleasurable experience that is transferred to assessment of the product's value and future behaviour (Franke & Schreier, 2010). Xie et al. (2008) also demonstrated that positive thought can be considered an essential component of value continuation and co-creation processes, underlining consumers' expectations as something fundamental, since they are intrinsic to the psychological assets at the basis of the consumption process (Tommasetti et al., 2015). These arguments lead to the hypothesis that consumers' cultural resources have a positive influence on their behavioural intentions:

Hypothesis 4 Consumers' cultural resources have a positive influence on their behavioural intentions

According to Walter et al. (2010), due to the nature of the service, consumers are actively involved in creating meanings through interactions in the physical and social environment. Gummesson and Mele (2010) mention that consumers must provide various resources, which leads to obtaining greater value. Through sharing information with other actors, customers may be able to meet their specific needs. On the other hand, if consumers fail to convey precise information, the quality of value co-creation may be low. However, Yi and Gong (2013) consider this information-sharing as a key to successful value co-creation. Customers' assessment of their own information influences their assessment of general satisfaction with the service firm (Bendapudi & Leone, 2003). Therefore, if consumers feel that value creation partners' contribution is not distributed fairly, their satisfaction diminishes (Walter et al., 2010; Grissemann & Stokburger-Sauer, 2012). Consumer satisfaction can also be associated with citizenship behaviour (Chen & Chen, 2010; Grissemann & Stokburger-Sauer, 2012; Bharwani & Jauhari, 2013; Yi & Gong, 2013; Halbusi et al., 2020). According to Yi and Gong (2013), consumers should fulfil their duties, that is, they should be cooperative and accept indications the organization and actors involved can provide. Therefore, the more obvious consumers' responsible behaviour, the greater the likelihood of co-creation and their satisfaction with the process. Hedonic value, such as the wish to enjoy or the enjoyment derived, can also affect customer satisfaction, as it is a motivational force stimulating consumers to participate in co-production (Vargo et al., 2008; Yi & Gong, 2013; Halbusi et al., 2020), and if value co-creation occurs in a social environment, the more pleasant and positive it is, the greater the likelihood of becoming involved in the co-creation process (Lengnick-Hall et al., 2000; Yi & Gong, 2013), meaning added value and increased customer satisfaction (Halbusi et al., 2020). This suggests a hypothesis proposing a positive influence of consumers' social resources on their satisfaction:

Hypothesis 5 Consumers' social resources have a positive influence on their satisfaction

Based on social exchange theory, Grissemann and Stokburger-Sauer (2012) say that customers who receive benefits or a satisfactory service in a relational exchange will find it easier to respond in favour of the service providers, engaging in active and voluntary behaviour such as recommendations or other support actions. McColl-Kennedy et al. (2012) mention that a generally positive attitude by consumers concerning the relation with actors/suppliers will be more likely to achieve the desired results, together with customers' capacity to tolerate possible failings in the service and increased trust in the capacities and skills of the actors involved. Then again, Füller (2010) and Verleye (2015) highlight the need for good functioning of the mutual help system in communities and demonstrate that higher levels of connectivity have a positive effect on consumers' satisfaction and behavioural intention. Based on these arguments, the final hypothesis is proposed, that consumers' social resources have a positive influence on their behavioural intentions:

Hypothesis 6 Consumers' social resources have a positive influence on their behavioural intentions

Figure 1 presents the resulting conceptual model with the respective hypotheses.

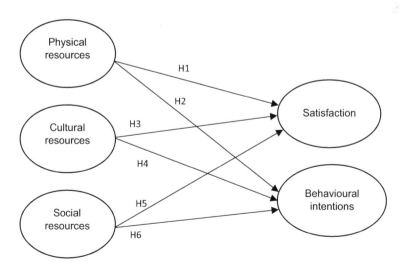

Fig. 1 Conceptual model

Methodology

The primary data for this study were obtained through a questionnaire elaborated and structured for the purpose. The variables studied were adapted clearly and objectively to this research and placed in the questionnaire in five separate parts: (1) information about the event visited; (2) co-creation experience and resource integration; (3) results of the experience; and (4) socio-demographic information. Table 2 shows the constructs analysed and their origin. The variables analysed in the model were measured through 7-point Likert-type scales.

To incorporate the first-order constructs and the respective indicators/variables, the literature review carried out and the results obtained in the qualitative study were considered. Therefore, the *physical resources* construct was sub-divided in two first-order constructs: (1) "*physical involvement*", adapting part of the "*physical engagement*" scale by Geus et al. (2016), and (2) "*affective/emotional involvement*" adapting part of the "*sense*" and "*feel*" scale by Tsaur et al. (2007) and the "*hedonic experience*" scale by Verleye (2015). The *cultural resources* construct was sub-divided in five first-order constructs: (1) "*searching for information*" and (2) "*consumer choices*" with the variables of the model being adapted, respectively, from the "*information seeking*" scale by Yi and Gong (2013) and part of the "*brand experience*" scale by Klaus et al. (2013); (3) "*consumer capacities*" were adapted from the "*skills*" scale by Merz et al. (2018) and the "*interaction*" scale by Ranjan and Read (2016), while the variables of the model related to (4) "*cognitive involvement*" were adapted from the "*knowledge*" scale by Ranjan and Read (2016), "*cognitive engagement*" by Geus et al. (2016) and "*knowledge*" by Merz et al. (2018). Finally, the variables of the model related to (5) "*consumer creativity*" were adapted from the "*think*" scale by Tsaur et al. (2007) and the "*creativity*" scale by Merz et al. (2018). The *social resources* construct was sub-divided in two first-order constructs: (1) "*consumer's responsible behaviour*" adapting to the event context the "*responsible behaviour*" scale by Yi and Gong (2013), and (2) "*consumer connectivity*" with adaptation of part of the "*other customers*" scale by Chang and Hong (2010) and joining part of the "*connectedness*" scale by Merz et al. (2018).

Concerning the results of the consumer's experience, for the *satisfaction* construct, the "*satisfaction*" scale by Schmitt (1999) and Tsaur et al. (2007) was adapted. The *behavioural intentions* construct was divided in three first-order constructs. In this way, the variables of the model related to (1) "*feedback*" were adapted from the "*feedback*" scale by Yi and Gong (2013) and the

How Customers' Resources Influence Their Co-creation Experience 693

Table 2 Constructs, scales, and main authors with ordinal scales

Second-order Constructs	First-order constructs (variables)	Main authors	Number of indicators (see Appendix 2)
CONSUMER'S CO-CREATION EXPERIENCE	Physical resources (CPR)	Physical involvement (PHY)	Geus et al. (2016)	4
		Affective/ emotional involvement (EMO)	Tsaur et al. (2007) (Schmitt) Verleye (2015)	8
	Cultural resources (CCR)	Searching for information (SEA)	Yi and Gong (2013)	3
		Consumer choices (CHO)	Klaus et al. (2013)	4
		Cognitive involvement (COG)	Merz et al. (2018) Geus et al. (2016) Ranjan and Read (2016)	6
		Consumer capacities (CAP)	Merz et al. (2018) Ranjan and Read (2016)	2
		Consumer creativity (CRE)	Tsaur et al. (2007) (Schmitt) Merz et al. (2018)	6
	Social resources (CSR)	Consumer connectivity (CON)	Chang and Hong (2010) Merz et al. (2018)	7
		Responsible behaviour (RES)	Yi and Gong (2013)	4
RESULTS	Satisfaction (SAT)	Satisfaction (SAT)	Tsaur et al. (2007)	5
	Behavioural intentions (CBI)	Feedback (FEE)	Yi and Gong (2013)	3
		Sharing (SHA)	Tsaur et al. (2007) (Schmitt)	2
		Loyalty (LOY)	Tsaur et al. (2007)	5

variables referring to (2) *"loyalty"* and (3) *"sharing"* were adapted from the *"behavioural intentions"* scale by Schmitt (1999) and Tsaur et al. (2007).

Before applying the questionnaire, a pre-test was performed with ten people, who responded and noted their own suggestions and observations. The sample of participants was accidental non-probability of the general population aged 18 or above. Based on participants' feedback, small alterations were made to the formulation and clarity of some questions, to help interpretation. The questionnaire was provided electronically through the SurveyMonkey platform. The link was announced on social networks, e-mails, and the databases of various Portuguese universities. The final sample is of 541 valid answers, distributed as follows: 58% from women and 42% from men; 47% are between 25 and 44 years old, 27.7% between 17 and 24, 24.2% between 45 and 64, and only 1.1% are over 65. 59.1% are single or divorced and 37% are married; 3.9% represent other situations.

Data analysis was based on assessing the structural equation model (SEM[3]), through SmartPLS 3.3. The model proposed demonstrates the existence of multi-dimensionality among its constructs, that is, presenting second-order constructs. As such, the two-step approach was used, moving on to assessment of the measurement and structural models. The first step involves adjusting the measurement model, and in the second step the structural model is adjusted (Marôco, 2010).

Results

Assessment of the Measurement Model: First Step

Since all the first-order constructs are determined and are reflective in the model (Fig. 2), it is necessary to examine and test the measurement model (Wright et al., 2012). The first step assesses: (1) individual reliability; (2) internal consistency; (3) convergent validity; and (4) discriminant validity (Hair et al., 2014).

To be able to analyse individual reliability, the simple correlations of each indicator with the respective construct are used, that is, the loadings of each indicator. According to Hair et al. (2014), loadings below 0.4 should be eliminated. Table 3 presents the simple correlation of the indicators and signals the

---

[3] The SEM model is a family of statistical models that attempts to explain relations between multiple variables (Hair et al., 2014). These relations are represented by parameters that indicate the magnitude of the effect that the independent variables have on dependent variables in a composite set of hypotheses regarding patterns of associations among the model's variables (Marôco, 2010).

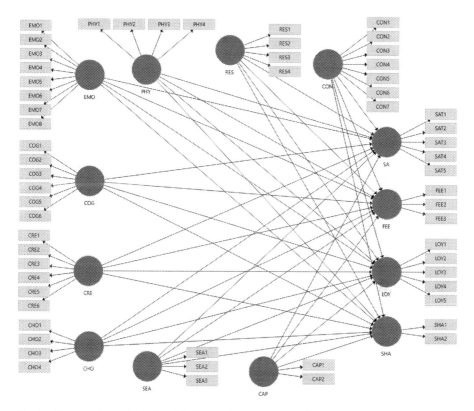

Fig. 2 Proposed model only with first-order constructs. (Source: Output SmartPLS 3.3)

need to eliminate ten indicators presenting loadings below the stipulated value: CHO2, CON4, CON5, CON6, CON7, CRE1, EMO3, EMO5, EMO8, and PHY2.

After eliminating those indicators, the model was run again, and together with the internal consistency and convergent validity analysis, it was necessary to eliminate three more indicators (CHO1, COG2, and EMO6), and to run the model once more. The cross loadings criterion showed the need to eliminate four more indicators (COG1, COG3, LOY5, and PHY4). Therefore, the final measurement model contains a total of 42 indicators.

The reliability analysis is concluded after confirming the respective internal consistency. Table 3 demonstrates that elimination of the indicators meant improved composite reliability of the constructs (CHO = 0.742; CON = 0.791; EMO = 0.804; and PHY = 0.890). This coefficient of composite internal consistency assesses whether the set of indicators of a latent construct is considered homogenous, this being confirmed by a value above 0.7 (Vinzi et al., 2010). Average Variance Extracted (AVE) measures the amount of variance a

Table 3 Indicators' simple correlations

Constructs	Items	Loadings	Initial composite reliability	Final composite reliability	Initial average variance extracted	Initial average variance extracted
CAP	CAP1	0.885	0.879	0.879	0.785	0.785
	CAP2	0.887				
CHO	CHO1	0.463	0.602	0.742	0.333	0.611
	CHO2	0.114				
	CHO3	0.514				
	CHO4	0.917				
COG	COG1	0.684	0.848	0.886	0.482	0.723
	COG2	0.649				
	COG3	0656				
	COG4	0.729				
	COH5	0.769				
	COG6	0.673				
CON	CON1	0.697	0.566	0.791	0.239	0.565
	CON2	0.566				
	CON3	0.065				
	CON4	0.055				
	CON5	0.182				
	CON6	0.178				
CRE	CRE1	0.150	0.922	0.959	0.689	0.823
	CRE 2	0.835				
	CRE 3	0.932				
	CRE 4	0.935				
	CRE 5	O.929				
	CRE 6	0.900				
EMO	EMO1	0.581	0.271	0.804	0.364	0.508
	EMO2	.0.813				
	EMO3	−0.488				
	EMO4	0.609				
	EMO5	0.510				
	EMO6	0.461				
	EMO7	0.596				
	EMO8	−0.689				
FEE	FEE1	0.821	0.860	0.860	0.671	0.671
	FEE2	0.791				
	FEE3	0.846				
LOY	LOY1	0.879	0.908	0.931	0.668	0.771
	LOY2	0.915				
	LOY3	0.843				
	LOY4	0.566				
PHY	PHY1	0.826	0.528	0.890	0.486	0.801
	PHY2	−0.591				
	PHY3	0.854				
	PHY4	0.428				

(continued)

Table 3 (continued)

Constructs	Items	Loadings	Initial composite reliability	Final composite reliability	Initial average variance extracted	Initial average variance extracted
RES	RES1	0.849	0.917	0.917	0.734	0.734
	RES2	0.871				
	RES3	0.867				
	RES4	0.841				
SAT	SAT1	0.882	0.946	0.946	0.780	0.780
	SAT2	0.948				
	SAT3	0.909				
	SAT4	0.812				
	SAT5	0.859				
SEA	SEA1	0.802	0.812	0.812	0.590	0.590
	SEA2	0.743				
	SE3	0.757				
SHA	SHA1	0.918	0.804	0.804	0.675	0.676
	SHA2	0.712				

construct is able to extract from its indicators, in relation to the variance associated with measurement errors. Values above 0.5 are considered reasonable, and thereby half the variance of the latent variable is explained through its indicators (Hair et al., 2011). The table confirms that elimination of the indicators led to improved convergent validity and that the various indicators converge/agree in representing the concept underlying the construct they are measuring (Chin, 2010). The last step concerns analysing discriminant validity. This analysis can check whether two latent constructs are measuring distinct concepts (Götz et al., 2010) and it is essential to analyse: (1) the Fornell-Larcker and (2) cross-loadings criterion. In the first criterion, the AVE of each latent construct must be greater that the variance of the other constructs of the model, that is, a comparison is made with the squared correlation of the latent constructs (Hair et al., 2011). As seen in Table 4, the square root of the AVE, appearing in bold in the diagonal in the table, is greater than the rest of the table to the left of the respective construct. Therefore, the correlations between the constructs are confirmed to be lower than the square root of the AVE.

According to the cross-loading criterion, the indicators associated with the latent construct must be above the indicators of the other constructs (Henseler et al., 2009). Table 5 demonstrates the discriminant validity of the model proposed. As the constructs do not present a greater contribution than that of the indicator itself, that is, the loading of each indicator is higher in its construct than any other (Chin & Dibbern, 2010), the model's indicators are found to be reliable.

Table 4 Discriminant validity of the constructs through the Fornell-Larcker criterion

	CAP	CHO	COG	CON	CRE	EMO	FEE	LOY	PHY	RES	SA	SEA	SHA
CAP	0.886												
CHO	0.209	0.781											
COG	0.654	0.186	0.850										
CON	0.381	0.238	0.364	0.752									
CRE	0.525	0.217	0.699	0.318	0.907								
EMO	0.244	0.229	0.370	0.195	0.590	0.713							
FEE	0.443	0.141	0.484	0.381	0.420	0.266	0.819						
LOY	0.263	0.314	0.416	0.277	0.518	0.627	0.423	0.878					
PHY	0.255	0.258	0.305	0.281	0.441	0.704	0.291	0.610	0.895				
RES	0.188	0.007	0.277	0.159	0.295	0.305	0.392	0.412	0.301	0.857			
SA	0.250	0.321	0.419	0.272	0.512	0.665	0.372	0.776	0.677	0.434	0.883		
SEA	0.437	0.181	0.410	0.250	0.401	0.259	0.291	0.224	0.231	0.201	0.234	0.768	
SHA	0.211	0.224	0.348	0.283	0.419	0.502	0.450	0.654	0.400	0.292	0.537	0.240	0.822

Source: Output SmartPLS 3.3

Table 5 Discriminant validity of the constructs through cross-loadings

	CAP	CHO	COG	CON	CRE	EMO	FEE	LOY	PHY	RES	SA	SEA	SHA
CAP1	0.884	0.210	0.587	0.318	0.444	0.214	0.369	0.252	0.235	0.130	0.229	0.380	0.191
CAP2	0.888	0.161	0.572	0.357	0.485	0.219	0.416	0.213	0.218	0.202	0.214	0.395	0.183
CHO3	0.037	0.519	0.021	0.146	0.043	0.039	0.017	0.060	0.076	0-0.027	0.092	0.149	0.098
CHO4	0.222	0.976	0.200	0.227	0.230	0.244	0.152	0.333	0.266	0.015	0.332	0.163	0.223
COG4	0.517	0.161	0.883	0.306	0.640	0.348	0.390	0.392	0.287	0.237	0.431	0.332	0.333
COG5	0.525	0.189	0.884	0.296	0.604	0.313	0.415	0.377	0.249	0.244	0.370	0.355	0.327
COG6	0.652	0.117	0.779	0.336	0.532	0.277	0.441	0.282	0.242	0.226	0.250	0.368	0.215
CON1	0.205	0.354	0.129	0.727	0.149	0.070	0.215	0.096	0.173	0.010	0.168	0.182	0.143
CON2	0.275	0.167	0.227	0.592	0.112	-0.062	0.238	0.002	0.016	-0.010	0.047	0.156	0.068
CON3	0.365	0.121	0.391	0.904	0.350	0.265	0.370	0.350	0.315	0.226	0.295	0.224	0.315
CRE2	0.437	0.160	0.609	0.224	0.837	0.525	0.309	0.461	0.379	0.320	0.445	0.354	0.357
CRE3	0.510	0.220	0.677	0.303	0.932	0.525	0.434	0.480	0.384	0.256	0.465	0.386	0.378
CRE4	0.520	0.218	0.657	0.331	0.934	0.545	0.436	0.490	0.423	0.258	0.473	0.375	0.415
CRE5	0.456	0.235	0.626	0.299	0.928	0.571	0.383	0.490	0.443	0.253	0.500	0.352	0.402
CRE6	0.452	0.139	0.597	0.276	0.900	0.510	0.330	0.423	0.365	0.256	0.433	0.348	0.343
EMO1	0.129	0.129	0.214	0.085	0.378	0.653	0.156	0.342	0.404	0.196	0.352	0.179	0.298
EMO2	0.231	0.290	0.326	0.247	0.50	0.824	0.267	0.638	0.714	0.269	0.705	0.224	0.452
EMO4	0.124	0.070	0.172	0.099	0.338	0.682	0.136	0.306	0.386	0.215	0.361	0.122	0.281
EMO7	0.181	0.082	0.310	0.057	0.442	0.682	0.157	0.391	0.388	0.175	0.347	0.199	0.359
FEE1	0.431	0.108	0.450	0.346	0.385	0.188	0.820	0.311	0.230	0.193	0.288	0.285	0.303
FEE2	0.260	0.062	0.360	0.261	0.351	0.284	0.790	0.425	0.255	0.429	0.329	0.182	0.470
FEE3	0.397	0.175	0.380	0.328	0.297	0.184	0.847	0.306	0.231	0.342	0.297	0.249	0.335
LOY1	0.263	0.245	0.401	0.285	0.477	0.575	0.436	0.903	0.578	0.457	0.743	0.217	0.634
LOY2	0.235	0.290	0.406	0.248	0.500	0.588	0.390	0.930	0.576	0.387	0.744	0.223	0.626
LOY3	0.245	0.300	0.321	0.260	0.382	0.472	0.351	0.828	0.461	0.319	0.603	0.177	0.520
LOY4	0.179	0.276	0.324	0.177	0.452	0.558	0.301	0.849	0.517	0.269	0.623	0.163	0.502
PHY1	0.188	0.168	0.229	0.249	0.342	0.576	0.232	0.487	0.875	0.269	0.556	0.155	0.317
PHY3	0.263	0.284	0.311	0.254	0.440	0.678	0.285	0.597	0.915	0.271	0.650	0.251	0.393

(*continued*)

Table 5 (continued)

	CAP	CHO	COG	CON	CRE	EMO	FEE	LOY	PHY	RES	SA	SEA	SHA
RES1	0.198	−0.020	0.260	0.128	0.261	0.282	0.308	0.362	0.289	0.849	0.389	0.179	0.226
RES2	0.203	0.014	0.279	0.210	0.308	0.319	0.371	0.372	0.277	0.871	0.417	0.215	0.264
RES3	0.125	0.026	0.223	0.083	0.223	0.211	0.323	0.351	0.231	0.867	0.370	0.161	0.258
RES4	0.111	0.005	0.180	0.118	0.211	0.227	0.338	0.324	0.234	0.841	0.304	0.125	0.251
SAT1	0.192	0.282	0.343	0.245	0.410	0.546	0.306	0.677	0.557	0.393	0.882	0.187	0.495
SAT2	0.218	0.310	0.372	0.243	0.479	0.630	0.331	0.760	0.657	0.411	0.948	0.213	0.489
SAT3	0.237	0.306	0.391	0.255	0.470	0.628	0.338	0.701	0.659	0.423	0.910	0.236	0.475
SAT4	0.209	0.219	0.367	0.252	0.415	0.528	0.345	0.597	0.521	0.365	0.813	0.157	0.422
SAT5	0.248	0.293	0.380	0.207	0.482	0.597	0.323	0.684	0.583	0.319	0.858	0.235	0.489
SEA1	0.368	0.114	0.337	0.168	0.318	0.227	0.222	0.177	0.192	0.166	0.170	0.802	0.153
SEA2	0.395	0.125	0.349	0.335	0.317	0.125	0.289	0.131	0.138	0.131	0.117	0.744	0.176
SEA3	0.253	0.174	0.264	0.085	0.289	0.241	0.167	0.204	0.200	0.164	0.244	0.756	0.220
SHA1	0.221	0.169	0.361	0.282	0.433	0.487	0.476	0.650	0.389	0.369	0.538	0.221	0.917
SHA2	0.102	0.223	0.176	0.161	0.215	0.313	0.209	0.378	0.245	0.032	0.303	0.172	0.715

Source: Output SmartPLS 3.3

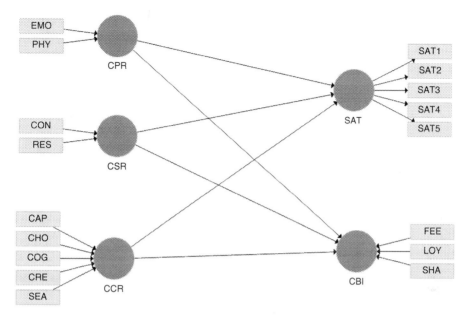

Fig. 3 Proposed model with reflective and formative constructs. (Source: Output SmartPLS 3.3)

Assessment of the Measurement Model: Second Step

At this stage, the model proposed has a different structure (Fig. 3) and it is necessary to assess it as a whole. Once again, the measurement model and the structural model are evaluated, underlining the fact that now the model combines reflective constructs (only SAT) and the second-order constructs are now formative (CPR, CSR, CCR, and CBI), calculated through the scores of the first-order dimensions. The measurement model results in two moments of assessment: reflective and formative.

Second Step: Reflective Constructs

The construct relating to SAT continues to function as a reflective construct, and so it is necessary to test the measurement model once again (Hair et al., 2011). Table 6 presents loadings above 0.70 for individual reliability, a very good internal consistency value considering the reference value (0.60–0.70 for exploratory studies) and a value above 0.50 for convergent validity; thereby complying with all the parameters of reference.

702   H. Alves and C. Jesus

Table 6 Assessment of individual reliability, internal consistency, and convergent validity

Construct	Items	Loadings	Composite reliability	Average variance extracted
SAT	SAT1	0.881	0.946	0.780
	SAT2	0.947		
	SAT3	0.909		
	SAT4	0.813		
	SAT5	0.859		

Adapted: Output SmartPLS 3.3

Table 7 Assessment of discriminant validity: Fornell-Larcker and cross-loadings

	CBI	CCR	CPR	CSR	SAT
SAT	0.758	0.566	0.727	0.479	0.883
CAP	–	–	–	–	0.250
CHO	–	–	–	–	0.321
COG	–	–	–	–	0.419
CON	–	–	–	–	0.272
CRE	–	–	–	–	0.512
EMO	–	–	–	–	0.665
FEE	–	–	–	–	0.372
LOY	–	–	–	–	0.776
PHY	–	–	–	–	0.677
RES	–	–	–	–	0.434
SAT1	–	–	–	–	0.881
SAT2	–	–	–	–	0.947
SAT3	–	–	–	–	0.909
SAT4	–	–	–	–	0.813
SAT5	–	–	–	–	0.859
SEA	–	–	–	–	0.234
SHA	–	–	–	–	0.537

Adapted: Output SmartPLS 3.3

To determine discriminant validity, the criterion of cross-loadings was used, finding they support validity through the reliability of the indicators. Table 7 also presents the square root of AVE on the diagonal of the correlation matrix through the Fornell-Larcker criterion. Here, the values on the diagonal are found to be above the correlations between other constructs and discriminant validity is confirmed.

Second Step: Formative Constructs

While criteria such as individual and composite reliability are commonly applied in assessing reflective measures, a perspective of reliability is unsuitable to evaluate formative measures (Diamantopoulos & Winklhofer, 2001).

How Customers' Resources Influence Their Co-creation Experience   703

Hair et al. (2011) also emphasize it is not possible to assess formative measures by empirical means, that is, through convergent and discriminant validity. They stress that traditional statistical assessment criteria for reflective scales cannot be transferred directly to formative indicators and propose three fundamental steps: (1) analyse the possibility of multicollinearity, (2) assess indicator weights, and (3) study the significance of the weights. Analysis of multicollinearity concerns the possibility of the information provided by an indicator being redundant due to high levels of multicollinearity, which can make indicators unstable and non-significant (Diamantopoulos & Winklhofer de 2001; Cenfetelli & Bassellier, 2009). As such, their analysis implies that the variance inflation factor (VIF) values should be under 5, otherwise this implies that 80% of the indicator's variance is explained by the other indicators related by the same construct (Hair et al., 2011). Table 8 confirms the absence of multicollinearity problems among the formative indicators, since the VIF values presented are below the stipulated values.

In order to assess the weights of each indicator and study their significance, Hair et al. (2011) recommend using the bootstrapping technique, with a minimum number of samples equal to 5000 and a number of cases equal to the relevant observations. The question raised is whether each indicator contributes to forming the variable according to its intended content, that is, aiming to determine whether the indicators are relevant. Table 9 demonstrates assessment of the weights of the formative indicators, thereby allowing understanding of the composition of each latent variable and each indicator's contribution to the construct. The table also allows confirmation of the T Statistic. Therefore, with a 90% level of confidence (for CAP and SHA) and 99% confidence for the others, it can be stated that all the formative indicators are statistically significant, except for SEA.

Assessment of the Structural Model

Assessment of the structural model should consider non-parametric criteria based on the variance to estimate the quality of the internal model (Henseler et al., 2009). The criteria are centred on: (1) determination coefficient (R^2) of the dependent constructs, (2) significance of the path (β) coefficient through the bootstrapping procedure, and (3) the Stone-Geisser test (Q2) which assesses the capacity of predictive relevance through the blindfolding procedure (Hair et al., 2011). Table 10 presents the effects of these criteria for the endogenous variables and the results of the structural model.

Table 8 Analysis of multicollinearity

	CAP	CHO	COG	CON	CRE	EMO	FEE	LOY	PHY	RES	SEA	SHA
VIF	10.887	10.070	20.531	10.026	20.052	10.984	10.301	10.813	10.984	10.026	10.316	10.865

Adapted: Output SmartPLS 3.3

How Customers' Resources Influence Their Co-creation Experience 705

Table 9 Weights and levels of significance of the formative indicators

Construct	Indicators	Outer weights	T Statistics[a]
CPR	EMO	0.545	8.653
	PHY	0.539	8.589
CCR	CAP	-0.135	1.840
	COG	0.320	3.162
	CRE	0.674	8.551
	CHO	0.349	6.577
	SEA	0.035	0.520
CSR	CON	0.488	7.161
	RES	0.798	16.047
CBI	FEE	0.291	4.593
	LOY	0.767	13.413
	SHA	0.101	1.729

Adapted: Output SmartPLS 3.3
[a]*Critical t-values for a two-tailed test*: 1.65 for a 10% level of significance, 1.96 for a 5% level of significance, and 2.58 for a 1% level of significance (Hair et al., 2011)

Table 10 Effects on the endogenous/dependent variables

Hypotheses	R^2	Q^2	β	T Statistics	Result
SAT	0.596	0.458	–	–	–
H1): CPR → SAT	–	–	0.551	13.943	**Supported**
H3): CCR → SAT	–	–	0.181	4.444	**Supported**
H5): CSR → SAT	–	–	0.193	4.874	**Supported**
CBI	0.571	–	–	–	–
H2): CPR → CBI	–	–	0.388	7.638	**Supported**
H4): CCR → CBI	–	–	0.279	6.295	**Supported**
H6): CSR → CBI	–	–	0.277	6.443	**Supported**

Adapted: Output SmartPLS 3.3

Hair et al. (2011) describe endogenous latent variables as substantial, moderate, or weak, when the determination coefficient presents 0.75, 0.5, and 0.25 respectively. In this specific case, the determination coefficient (R^2) describes all the endogenous variables as moderate, with it being important to note that both SAT and CBI are explained by the CPR, CCR, and CSR constructs in 60% and 57% respectively. Concerning the significance of the path coefficient (β), all the values presented are significant. The Stone-Geisser test (Q^2) is a procedure that is only applied to endogenous constructs with a reflective measurement model, that is, in this specific case it is only applied to SAT and as the value presented is above zero, the construct has predictive relevance. To finalize assessment of the structural model and obtain the results, it is necessary to analyse the significance of the path coefficient and the T Statistic. As mentioned above, all the weights present positive values, and with observation

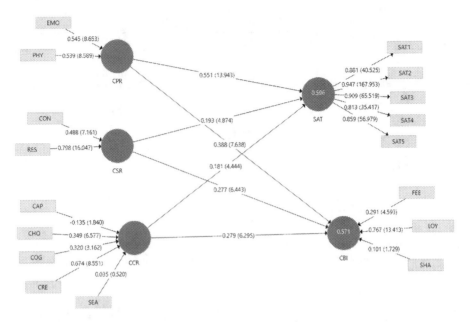

Fig. 4 Schematized summary of assessment of the proposed model. (Source: Output SmartPLS 3.3)

of the T Statistic it can be stated that with a 99% level of confidence, all the relations and hypotheses are statistically significant and corroborated. Figure 4 presents a schematized summary of the assessment of the proposed model.

4 Analysis and Discussion of the Model's Results

The results obtained reveal that consumers' physical resources (CPR) have a positive and significant influence on satisfaction ($\beta = 0.551$; t = 13.943) and on consumers' behavioural intentions ($\beta = 0.388$; t = 7.638), leading to confirmation of Hypotheses 1 and 2. Therefore, corroboration of Hypothesis 1 is consistent with the arguments of Chan et al. (2010), McColl-Kennedy et al. (2012), Grissemann and Stokburger-Sauer (2012), and Geus et al. (2016). Those studies agree that positive results, and naturally greater satisfaction, are obtained whenever the consumer engages more actively throughout the process. In the same line of thought, Franke and Schreier (2010) highlight that when the final result of the co-created service matches the consumer's needs, the effort in the process is perceived as positive and complements the subjective value linked to the service. Similarly, Hypothesis 2 is accepted, in accordance with the conclusions of Payne et al. (2008), Cermark et al. (2011) and Grissemann and

Stokburger-Sauer (2012) when stating that customers' involvement in co-creation activities influences their behavioural responses positively, for example, repurchase intention and willingness to pay more. It is therefore found that more active, participative consumers, that is, those who integrate most physical resources end up engaging in positive word-of-mouth strategies, share feedback, and develop stronger, long-term relations with the company.

The results obtained from the model also demonstrate a positive and significant effect of consumers' cultural resources (CCR) on their satisfaction ($\beta = 0.181$; $t = 4.444$) and on their behavioural intentions ($\beta = 0.279$; $t = 6.295$), meaning corroboration of Hypotheses 3 and 4, respectively. Confirmation of Hypothesis 3 is consistent with the arguments of Martínez and Martínez (2007), Chen et al. (2011), Grönroos and Ravald (2011), and Hunt et al. (2012), who highlight that customer satisfaction is stimulated positively by cognitive factors. Those studies revealed customers' knowledge, capacity and clarity as factors aiding constructive participation in service-creation processes, also affecting the results arising from the process; something that was also confirmed in this research. Similarly, Hypothesis 4 was confirmed and revealed a positive influence of cultural resource integration on the consumer's behavioural intentions. This agrees with the arguments of Franke and Schreier (2010) and Grissemann and Stokburger-Sauer (2012). Those authors found that the value customers derive from the process, and consequently their future behaviour, is determined by their evaluation of how much they are responsible for the success of the process. Therefore, consumers' cognitive and skilful participation is understood as a gratifying experience that will translate into favourable future behaviour.

As already mentioned, the results obtained demonstrate a significant and positive effect of social resources (CSR) on satisfaction ($\beta = 0.193$; $t = 4.874$), but also on consumers' behavioural intentions ($\beta = 0.277$; $t = 6.443$), which allows confirmation of Hypotheses 5 and 6, respectively. Corroboration of Hypothesis 5 is consistent with the studies by Walter et al. (2010), Gummesson and Mele (2010), and Halbusi et al. (2020). The authors highlight the importance of customers being actively involved in creating meanings through interactions in the social sphere, resulting in added value and increased satisfaction. The same situation occurs with those involved complying with their duties. Therefore, and in agreement with Yi and Gong (2013), the more obvious the responsible behaviour of those involved, the greater the resource integration and satisfaction with the process. The results emphasize the volatility of the social environment and the positive consequences in terms of satisfaction with the factors and the process itself. Finally, Hypothesis 6 was confirmed, showing a positive influence of social resource integration on consumers' behavioural intentions. This agrees with the arguments of Füller (2010), Grissemann and Stokburger-Sauer (2012), and Verleye (2015), who stress the need for good functioning of mutual help in communities, where higher levels of connectivity have a positive effect on customers' behavioural intention. Similarly, consumers who receive benefits arising from a relational exchange will find it easier to return the favour, engaging in spontaneous behaviour that can correspond to sharing, recommendations, feedback, or support actions.

5 Limitations and Future Lines of Research

This study has some limitations, among them the decision to use in-depth interviews in the qualitative study. Although this gave detailed understanding of the phenomenon, it did not allow real observation of the consumer's behaviour, or the event organizers' efforts to influence their customers' choices. Then in the empirical study, the fact of the context being cultural events and the responses being obtained online, mainly through social networks, e-mail, and university and polytechnic databases, can limit their generalization due to being more restricted to online communities. This agrees with the limitations presented regarding the adoption of a convenience approach. The questionnaire also required respondents' collaboration/perception regarding the last event they attended, but some of the answers may have been given based on an event with a positive or negative impact on their memory, and not necessarily the latest one.

Some of the limitations mentioned can be overcome or used as a starting point for future research. Therefore, some future lines of study are suggested. This research dealt with events of a cultural nature, but it would be useful to extend to other types of events (e.g.: business events, educational events, political events, entertainment events, or even private events) and determine the distinct behaviours of the relations and hypotheses of the proposed model. It would be especially interesting to determine the differences, if any, in terms of consumers' resource integration in the various typologies of events, as well as in the results of the experience. In addition, since consumers have different levels and access to resources depending on their cultural context (high-income contexts vs low-income contexts) it would be interesting to study how resources integration differ among these different contexts.

For better understanding of consumers' resource integration, it is considered crucial to identify unsatisfied demand, and so studies should be made in this area, with detailed analysis of the factors that do not contribute to the co-creation experience, as well as factors that restrict and inhibit consumers' resource integration. It would also be important to understand the impact on events' success and future. That is, instead of considering only the demand side of cultural events, the supply side could also be considered, in order to determine whether organizations understand the market and consequently make efforts to adapt to current trends. As such, it would be interesting to assess how the adoption of service-dominant logic and value co-creation with the various actors and institutions will impact on organizations' structure and process.

6 Conclusions

In the area of marketing and service, consumers' value co-creation, through their resource integration, is topical, developing, and found to be extremely important for the majority of event organizations. Here, and as defended by Kotler et al. (2011), the structure of value creation is different, and organizations need consumers' own commitment. This study focused on understanding the resources most used by the consumer at cultural events, and the influence of those resources on the results of the consumer's co-creation experience.

Resource integration emerges here as a key mechanism in value creation which is exclusive to each actor. Value is linked to the meaning of value-in-use and the consumer can apply, but also use, resources that contribute to creating benefits and values. The studies made confirmed that consumers have a great variety of complex operant resources (characterized in physical, cultural, and social resources). Each consumer is known to be unique, with their own psychographic factors, and all those factors influence the degree of development of the value co-creation process. However, the studies revealed that consumers activate and use all their resources during the event, albeit with different intensities.

As contributions to theory, Study 1 clarified, described, and projected the experience and resource integration of consumers at the event. The results obtained demonstrated, over the three phases of purchase, the existence of various processes of value co-creation, and resource integration among event consumers, and it was possible to determine the type of integrated resources and in what circumstances. Consumers were found to activate, and use all their operant (physical, social, and cultural) and operand (monetary resources and tangible goods) resources. However, it should be underlined that their importance varies over the three phases of purchase, at various touchpoints.

Study 1 led to obtaining more detailed conclusions about consumers' resource integration throughout their experience in a service eco-system, improving understanding of the nature and role of the resources consumers and actors integrate in a dynamic event context, resulting in value creation. The qualitative nature of this study also provided a complement and consolidation for the empirical approach of the study. Here, Study 2 proposed a model highlighting the influence and importance of resources in the final result of consumers' experience, with a wide-ranging approach and new measuring of the event consumer's co-creation experience.

The hypotheses formulated were all corroborated, finding that all resources (physical, cultural, and social) have a direct and positive influence on the results of the co-creation experience, specifically on event consumers' satisfaction and behavioural intentions. Overall, the proposed model was found to represent the data suitably, and to be an acceptable model to present resource integration in the process of the co-creation experience and the respective results in the actual experience. The model proposed is of an exploratory nature and the endogenous variables incorporated are considered moderate with variances of 60% for satisfaction and 57% for behavioural intentions.

This study contributes to research in the field of the co-creation experience in marketing, according to SDL, giving special importance to resource integration (physical, cultural, and social) by consumers in the context of a cultural event. This implies that consumers contribute and use their operant resources to act on the resources of the organization and associated actors at the cultural event, this being an essential and explanatory component of the results and value for the consumer. The creation of value for the consumer (both value-in-use and value-in-context) needs operant and operand resources from all the actors involved, corresponding to joint implementation and integration. However, and as argued by Arnould et al. (2006), consumers' operant resources are dynamic and flexible over time and context. Therefore, it is the very robustness of operant resources (physical, cultural, and social) that determines consumers' satisfaction and behavioural intentions.

From a practical-professional perspective, the study also makes pertinent contributions to event organizations and knowledge of event management, principally if these are based on the consumer and their role in the process. The study aims to draw attention to dynamic and systematic professional practices so that organizations can achieve the differentiation necessary nowadays. Constructing value propositions that consider the value-in-context view and the relations of all actors involved will increase an organization's proactiveness and its own power, leading to increased viability of its whole ecosystem and its results.

In a cultural event context, the inclusion of functions and processes that are not usual and traditional is a bonus. Therefore, event organizations concerned about projecting the service holistically, in a more complete and innovative way, will manage to hold on to their advantages. The results obtained also highlighted the relevance of event organizations becoming aware of the full extent of their consumers' experience (pre-purchase, purchase, and post-purchase). Therefore, they should strive to form the ideal conditions at all stages of the service, to create more easily a positive impression in the consumer, leading to positive results from the experience. Event organizations should be aware of the opportunities and limitations of their action and should never ignore the role and central involvement of consumers in the event context, as confirmed in the results obtained. To be able to achieve those advantages more easily, organizations should focus effectively on consumers and on the whole relevant eco-system.

Considering consumers as a key part, organizations should potentialize value co-creation and the integration of physical, social, and cultural resources by consumers. By understanding the importance and essence of consumers' operant resources, organizations will be able to re-adjust methods and allow improvements that contribute to substantial value co-creation practices. Knowledge and understanding of these practices are essential for organizations and the actors involved to be able to contribute value propositions that facilitate resource integration and mean positive results for the consumer. That is, today's event organizations cannot study and analyse only consumers' operand resources (such as their purchasing power). In particular, they need to understand the different types of operant resources the consumer can use in the exchange process, since those resources will allow firms to anticipate the values desired by consumers and help them to create value-in-use. Event organizations must know the importance of each component of the consumer's physical, cultural, and social resources in the value co-creation process, and initiate measures to improve consumers' operant resources, allowing interaction and resource integration to occur as efficiently as possible. Measures to improve consumers' operant resources at cultural events can include, for example: a dynamic, attractive, and interactive context of collective consumption where customers can immerse, interact, and share a space in the consumption act, involving different social resources, but also physical and individual resources. Event organizers should also provide detailed information/instructions about the event, in order to increase and activate the consumer's cultural resources more easily. In this connection, the organization should develop and take special care in communicating with the consumer (at all levels and using various channels), improving and activating operant resources as much as possible.

Summarizing, organizations must consider all actors, and particularly consumers, as co-creators, that is, they must take a positive attitude in all their actions to incorporate resources, and not as something negative or with uncalculated risks for the organization. Connecting this matter to the main role of the event organizer (i.e., providing in quantity the resources and elements most valued by consumers, so that on their side it is easier to engage in the process of resource integration), they will be able to strengthen relations, generate feelings of belonging and increase satisfaction and behavioural intentions in the long term; and consequently, achieve differentiation and retention of their advantages in relation to the competition.

Acknowledgements This research is financed by National Funds through the FCT—Foundation for Science and Technology in the scope of UIDB/04630/2020.

Appendix 1

Phase	Stage	Resources	Interview excerpts	
Pre-purchase	Awareness and discovery of the event	Social	*We were having coffee with friends when the OCT event came up in conversation. We had already participated for two years together, but immediately we decided that we wanted to relive the experience again*	The statement indicates relationship and communication as fundamental resources in consumer discovery and decision-making. In this sense, the sharing of information and positive experiences are seen as the basis for learning for and during the value CP, confirming that the incorporation of resources from friends and family is crucial in the process of consumers. Some interviewees also reported that they *had knowledge of the event through Facebook and social media*, demonstrating that the event organization's commitment to the customer creates emotional involvement and involves the consumer in a co-creation process
	Consideration, comparison, and seeking/gathering information	Cultural, physical, and operand	*We also considered going to Santa Maria da Feira to visit the Perlim event, but after searching the internet we ended up giving up on the idea* *I was aware of the discounts that were advertised on the event page and got tickets with a 30% discount. But then I still got in touch with the organization to clarify another doubt*	At this stage, the cultural and physical resources of consumers are highlighted because they depend on their abilities, skills, and knowledge, as well as the energy and will invested in the process. Respondents were concerned with obtaining up-to-date information, advantageous solutions, and opinions. In the search for information, they sought to clarify service requirements and satisfy other cognitive needs, directly with the organization of the event or with other customers (directly or indirectly). According to Yi and Gong (2013), the search for information is relevant for consumers for two reasons: (1) to reduce uncertainty, and thus be able to understand and control their environment/co-creation context and (2) master the role of value co-creators, and thus become more integrated in the value co-creation process

	Decision-making and online purchase	Cultural, physical, and operand	*I bought tickets for half price on Black Friday. Super simple and fast process, just log in with Facebook, indicate the preferred date, the amount, and pay*	At this stage, the cultural and physical resources of consumers gained more prominence. There're also the greatest dissimilarities between respondents. Only five interviewees demonstrated skills with technologies and purchased the tickets online. These interviewees look for more beneficial solutions and for that they get involved in the process. In this case, respondents reduced costs (in time and energy) and achieved economic rewards (lower prices) and gained psychological benefits of satisfaction and confidence in their ability to co-create value for themselves. The opposite scenario occurred with the remaining respondents who purchased tickets on the day and without any kind of discount. Regarding operational resources, it was verified the existence of economic resources, through discount coupons and vouchers that consumers were able to take advantage of. But also, the need for tangible goods/materials for customers to actively play the roles of co-creators, using computers, mobile phones, or other electronic devices
Purchase during the event	Arrival/ decision and local purchase	Social commercial	*I don't trust machines and technologies much, I like being in contact with people much more*	The interviewees who demonstrated skills and abilities with the technologies and bought tickets online quickly entered the event without any constraints, but the remaining interviewees revealed a special interest in contextual elements and employee-consumer interaction. As such, they use commercial social resources to fulfil their goals. The co-creation of value in a service context takes place in a social environment, as such it is necessary that consumers use social resources and, above all, that there are relational aspects such as courtesy, kindness, and respect between employees and consumers (Yi & Gong, 2013); since these interpersonal relationships are necessary for successful co-creation of value. If consumers are faced with a more pleasant and positive social environment, it is natural that they are more easily involved in a value co-creation process
	Entry to the enclosure	Physical and social	*The employees responsible for security and entry into the enclosure didn't provide any information and were not very pleasant*	The respondents mainly highlighted physical resources, in terms of their energy and emotions, but also social resources in terms of relationships with employees. Most interviewees said that *entry into the venue was relatively quick* especially for those who buy on online platforms. Allied to this factor, there is the service provided by employees, which seems not to have pleased all the interviewees. The interpretations of consumers about the behaviour of employees change their expectations and influence their co-creation experience. The organization's ability to improve social and emotional bonds with consumers and other value network partners is seen as fundamental, since this dimension translates into actions aimed at establishing or improving a social and emotional connection between employees and consumers during the service interaction. Joint actions can explore similarities between the two actors, share mutual interests, take perspectives, or establish a personal bond that creates a mutual basis of understanding between the actors, translating into an important PC that generates social and emotional value during the event

(*continued*)

(continued)

Phase	Stage	Resources	Interview excerpts	
	Use and choices during the event	Physical	*It was very fun…we all walked on the ice rink, and lost count of the falls and laughter given. It was also funny to slide on the buoy… penalty is the time that is expected for the time that the descent lasts* *Even activities for children are very common… I haven't seen any major differences over time… not to mention that they are very expensive There is magic and joy everywhere, and that they are magnified by all the scenarios and structures created. It's all thought out in detail, and it goes through for people. It's a very beautiful and welcoming event designed for pure fun*	Consumers use their energies and strengths to enjoy the event. In this sense, respondents who visited the event with friends, but also with family with young children were the most active and participative throughout the event and the various attractions/activities. The active participation of consumers is possible due to the attractions existing in the venue, but they emphasize the process elements, such as waiting times as influencing elements of their experience throughout the event. In these circumstances, consumers who are willing to take advantage of activities activate and employ greater physical resources (especially at the level of effort) than consumers who do not expect; physical and mental differences of consumers are visible Other two important influencing elements in the choices and decisions of consumers are: the novelty factor and price factor. Several studies have suggested that the dynamic effects of the consumer experience occur due to the consumer himself, because the consumer eventually changes over time after repeated experiences with a specific service or experience. While some customers develop relationships with brands that have lasting effects, others constantly require extraordinary experiences. Consumer emotions also emerge as a very important and constantly mentioned physical resource. Environmental stimuli influence the emotional state of consumers, stimulating their participation and influence the attitudes and preferences of consumers and their RI

Social	The first stop was for the typical group photo… we were approached by the photographers of the event, who happened to be very friendly, and we took advantage to leave our mark!!	These resources are popular with consumers, alerting to the importance of memories about the service, but mainly to the influence that the elements of employee-customer interaction have exerted on their purchasing decisions and experience. This situation also occurred throughout the event with the attendance of the various employees who, as a rule, were considered *professional and friendly*. Thus, the interpersonal nature of the interaction between employees and customers contributes to satisfaction in an event environment and for the development of consumer value CP
	[…] at least informed people right at the entrance that they have the possibility to leave and re-enter with the stamp, but no one gave that indication. […] I advise to pass the information to other clients	Some interviewees cooperated with the organization of the event for the benefit of others. Thus, the creation of value by customers is intended to share positive/negative experiences to influence decisions and purchasing behaviour of other actors. Consumer involvement in co-creation is related to the sharing of consumer experiences which provides a source of information for the organization to reorganize its portfolio and allows other consumers to integrate a cognitive process where they make judgements based on these experiences. Consumer-consumer interaction also played a crucial role in the experience and RI of the interviewees. Testimony demonstrates the influence of other consumers' resources on consumer decision and behaviour. Thus, the idea that consumers act on resources produced by the organization (conducted by the company itself or other customers) to realize, recover, or even create preferred cultural schemes (Arnould et al., 2006) does not always occur and in their absence, there is some dissatisfaction
	There was a spectacle that took place in the mythical house where the whole true story took place, but as my family does not like supernatural tales very much, I ended up not going	Continue

(*continued*)

Phase	Stage	Resources	Interview excerpts	
		Cultural	*I interacted with all […] they're very fun, friendly, and professional. They delight everyone.* *I felt I was living the tales of my childhood. We were approached by Puss in Boots and Tintin who had lost Milú. They were fantastic and instantly contributed to exceed the expectations of event. Excellent characterizations and interpretations!!*	The staging of experiences in which the organization builds contexts, and the client is part of them, that is, the consumer is involved, but the context is oriented by the organization, is especially related to this stage. In this sense, specialized animation, through characters and extras, is an element that contributes to the creation of the atmosphere and the experience of consumers. The consumers with higher cultural resources (at the level of knowledge, stories, and imagination) obtain greater satisfaction from the lived experience, that is, a person who does not know the characters and the story/narrative will not understand the context of the event and will not be able to contribute to resources and co-creation processes that are favourable
		Operand	*It would be great to pay for the entrance to the enclosure and then not pay anything else of the most captivating attractions for the children*	At this stage consumers mainly use their economic resources to be able to enjoy products and services that the event has at their disposal. It's important to highlight the link between the physical resources and the operational resources of the customers. This type of event requires analogy, since customer participation/involvement requires some sacrifices at the monetary level, and there is a proportionality relationship: the greater the participation, the greater the consumer's monetary sacrifices. It's also important to highlight that the amount of operational resources affects consumer exchange behaviours with organizations (Arnould et al., 2006).

| Post-purchase | Feedback | Social | *I will talk about the diversity of activities, but I will also have to mention how expensive it becomes… For people who have children this turns out to be a very significant factor that becomes even a financially penalizing aspect, the organization should review its pricing policy* | In this stage interviewees use and value social resources when sharing the experience lived in conversations with family and friends, in a word-of-mouth context, but also in the sharing of recommendations/improvements to the organization of the event. Sharing information by consumers is essential so that they can convey details of their experience to other consumers, as well as to be able to transmit information to actors or employees about what they have most displeased throughout the experience. These shares will shape and offer a service that meets the unique and specific needs of customers (Yi & Gong, 2013). |
| | | Cultural Physical Operand | *I've shared photos on Facebook… and so I can dedicate a post to the event on my travel blog* | Interviewees also valued cultural resources when sharing the experience experienced and their photos on social networks and virtual platforms, when you expose all your experience. In this stage interviewees also use and value their physical resources since they do not mind depositing energy and efforts in sharing information with other actors and dissemination of appreciations, which are generally favourable. Results demonstrate that the operand resources that the consumer has are important for the dissemination of the experience. As in pre-purchase, consumers use computers or other electronic devices to share information |

Appendix 2

Constructs	Concept	Author(s)	Item
Consumer Physical Resources (CPR)	Physical Involvement (PHY)	Geus et al. (2016)	I felt active and energetic throughout the event
			I was not involved physically in the event
			The efforts, strengths, and energies employed were worth
			I experienced things and situations that were unknown or new to me
	Emotional Involvement (EMO)	Tsaur et al. (2007) (Schmitt) Verleye (2015)	The event stimulated my senses (touch, sight, hearing, smell, and taste)
			The event was interesting and enjoyable
			The event did not please me sensorially
			The event made me react emotionally
			The event did not appeal to my feelings
			The event caused a certain mood in the consumer
			I felt a sense of adventure
			I felt bored at the event
Consumer Social Resources (CSR)	Consumer Connectivity (CON)	Merz et al. (2018) Chang and Hong (2010)	I am connected to other consumers of this event
			I belong to one or more brand communities that are related to this event
			I have socialized with the other consumers of the event
			I do not feel well when other consumers of the event behave inappropriately, for example, when they shout, laugh, or speak too loudly
			I do not like it when other customers at the event make me spend more time than I am supposed to buy or enjoy what I want
			I do not like when other customers interrupt my conversation with the event staff
			My emotion and experience at the event are negatively influenced when other consumers contribute to disorder or confusion
	Responsible Behaviour (RES)	Yi and Gong (2013)	During the event I followed the rules, orders, or directives of the employees and the organization of the event
			I performed all the tasks that are required by the organization of the event
			All my behaviours were adequate
			I fulfilled the responsibilities and laws stipulated by the society in which we live

How Customers' Resources Influence Their Co-creation Experience

Consumer Cultural Resources (CCR)			
Information Search (SEA)	Yi and Gong (2013)	I have asked other people for information about what the event had to offer
		I have paid attention to other people's opinions about the event
		I have searched for information about the event on the internet or media
Consumer Choices (CHO)	Klaus et al. (2013)	I always consider different event options to ensure I get the best offer
		I do not choose an event based on experience only. There are other important factors such as time spent, effort, and price
		What matters to me is that event provides the best experiences
		Although there are many events of this type, I will always prefer this one
Cognitive Involvement (COG)	Merz et al. (2018)	I consider myself informed about what the event has to offer
		I know this event very well
	Geus et al. (2016)	I consider myself an expert at this event
		When attending this event, I got new knowledge
	Ranjan and Read (2016)	The event made me reflect on a theme and share the subject with others
		I like to save some time and effort to share my ideas and suggestions with the event organizers to improve their processes, products, and services
Consumer Capacity (CAP)	Ranjan and Read (2016)	During the process I was able to express my specific needs and requirements
	Merz et al. (2018)	To get the maximum benefit from the process, I had to play a proactive role during the event (apply my skills, knowledge, time, and so on)
Consumer Creativity (CRE)	Tsaur et al. (2007) (Schmitt)	The event intrigued me
		The event stimulated my curiosity
		The event appealed to my creative thinking
	Merz et al. (2018)	When I attended the event, I felt creative
		When I attended the event, I felt imaginative
		When I attended the event, I felt curious
Satisfaction (SAT)	Tsaur et al. (2007)	The event met my expectations
		My satisfaction with the event was high
		My presence at the event made up for the effort and time spent
		The benefits and values I acquired at the event outweighed the price
		If an ideal event corresponded to 7, what number would you give to the one you mentioned?

(continued)

Constructs	Concept	Author(s)	Item
Behavioural Intentions (CBI)	Feedback (FEE)	Yi and Gong (2013)	If I have a useful idea on how to improve the service, I let the organization know
			When I receive a good service/experience, I comment with interested parties
			When I have a problem, I let the organization of the event know about it
	Sharing (SHA)	Tsaur et al. (2007) (Schmitt)	I will share (or I have already shared) the experiences of the event
			I will share (or have already shared) the photos of the event on social networks or other virtual platforms
	Loyalty (LOY)	Tsaur et al. (2007)	I have spoken or will speak positively about the event to others
			I have already recommended or intend to recommend the event
			I intend to participate again in the event
			I will encourage friends and family to participate
			I will consider the same event as the first choice when I recreate myself again

*

References

Aal, K., Pietro, L., Edvardsson, B., Renzi, M., & Mugion, R. (2016). Innovation in service ecosystems: An empirical study of the integration of values, brands, service systems and experience rooms. *Journal of Service Management, 27*(4), 619–651.

Adhikari, A., & Bhattacharya, S. (2016). Appraisal of literature on customer experience in tourism sector: Review and framework. *Current Issues in Tourism, 19*(4), 296–321.

Akaka, M., & Vargo, S. (2015). Extending the context of service: From encounters to ecosystems. *Journal of Services Marketing, 29*(6/7), 453–462.

Alarcón, R., Ruiz, S., & López, I. (2017). Sharing co-creation experiences contributes to consumer satisfaction. *Online Information Review, 41*(7), 969–984.

Albrecht, K., Walsh, G., & Beatty, E. (2017). Perceptions of group versus individual service failures and their effects on customer outcomes: The role of attributions and customer entitlement. *Journal of Service Research, 20*(2), 188–203.

Altinay, L., Sigala, M., & Waligo, V. (2016). Social value creation through tourism enterprise. *Tourism Management, 54*, 404–417.

Arnould, J., Price, L., & Malshe, A. (2006). Toward a cultural resource-based theory of the customer. In R. Lusch & S. Vargo (Eds.), *The Service-Dominant logic of marketing: Dialog, debate, and directions*. Routledge.

Baron, S., & Warnaby, G. (2011). Individual customers' use and integration of resources: Empirical findings and organizational implications in the context of value co-creation. *Industrial Marketing Management., 40*(2), 211–218.

Becker, L., & Jaakkola, E. (2020). Customer experience: Fundamental premises and implications for research. *Journal of the Academy of Marketing Science, 48*(4), 630–648.

Bendapudi, N., & Leone, R. (2003). Psychological implications of customer participation in. *Journal of Marketing, 67*, 14–28.

Berridge, G. (2007). *Events design and experience. Events management*. Routledge.

Bharwani, S., & Jauhari, V. (2013). An exploratory study of competencies required to co-create memorable customer experiences in the hospitality industry. *International Journal of Contemporary Hospitality Management, 25*(6), 823–843.

Binkhorst, E., & Dekker, T. (2009). Agenda for co-creation tourism experience research. *Journal of Hospitality Marketing & Management, 18*(2), 311–327.

Bitner, M., Ostrom, A., & Morgan, F. (2008). Service Blueprinting: A practical technique for service innovation. *California Management Review, 50*(3), 66–94.

Bolton, R., Gustafsson, A., McColl-Kennedy, J., Sirianni, N., & Tse, D. (2014). Small details that make big differences: A radical approach to consumption experience as a firm's differentiating strategy. *Journal of Service Management, 25*(2), 253–274.

Bos, L., McCabe, S., & Johnson, S. (2015). Learning never goes on holiday: An exploration of social tourism as a context for experiential learning. *Current Issues in Tourism, 18*(5), 859–875.

Bowdin, G., Allen, J., Harris, R., McDonnell, I., & O'Toole, W. (2012). *Events management*. Routledge.

Brakus, J., Schmitt, B., & Zarantello, L. (2009). Brand Experience: What is it? How is it measured? Does it affect loyalty? *Journal of Marketing, 73*(3), 52–68.

Bueno, V., Weber, B., Bomfim, L., & Kato, T. (2019). Measuring customer experience in service: A systematic review. *The Service Industries Journal, 39*(11–12), 779–798.

Cenfetelli, R., & Bassellier, G. (2009). Interpretation of formative measurement in information systems research. *MIS Quarterly, 33*(4), 689–707.

Cermark, P., File, M., & Prince, A. (2011). Customer participation in service specification and delivery. *Journal of Applied Business Research, 10*(2), 90–97.

Chan, K., Yim, C., & Lam, K. (2010). Is customer participation in value creation a double-edged sword? Evidence from professional financial services across cultures. *Journal of Marketing, 74*(3), 48–64.

Chandler, J., & Vargo, S. (2011). Contextualization and value-in-context: How context frames exchange. *Marketing Theory, 11*(1), 35–49.

Chang, T., & Hong, S. (2010). Conceptualizing and measuring experience quality: The customer's perspective. *The Service Industries Journal, 30*(14), 2401–2419.

Chen, C., & Chen, F. (2010). Experience quality, perceived value, satisfaction and behavioral intentions for heritage tourists. *Tourism Management, 31*(1), 29–35.

Chen, Y., Fay, S., & Wang, Q. (2011). The role of marketing in social media: How online consumer reviews evolve. *Journal of Interactive Marketing, 25*(2), 85–94.

Chin, W. (2010). How to write up and report PLS analyses. In V. Vinzi, W. Chin, J. Henseler, & H. Wang (Eds.), *Handbook of partial least squares: Concepts, methods and applications* (pp. 655–690). Springer.

Chin, W., & Dibbern, J. (2010). An introduction to a permutation based procedure for multi-group pls analysis: Results of tests of differences on simulated data and a cross cultural analysis of the sourcing of information system services between Germany and the USA. In V. Vinzi, W. Chin, J. Henseler, & H. Wang (Eds.), *Handbook of partial least squares* (pp. 171–193). Springer Handbooks of Computational Statistics.

Czepiel, J. (1990). Service encounters and service relationships: Implications for research. *Journal of Business Research, 20*(1), 13–21.

Diamantopoulos, A., & Winklhofer, H. (2001). Index construction with formative indicators: An alternative to scale development. *Journal of Marketing Research, 38*(2), 269–277.

Ding, D., Hu, P., Verma, R., & Wardell, D. (2010). The impact of service system design and flow experience on customer satisfaction in online financial services. *Journal of Service Research, 13*(1), 96–110.

Doorn, J., Lemon, K., Mittal, V., Nass, S., Pick, D., Pirner, P., & Verhoef, P. (2010). Customer engagement behavior: Theoretical foundations and research directions. *Journal of Service Research, 13*(3), 253–266.

Edvardsson, B., Gustafsson, A., & Roos, I. (2005). Service portraits in service research: A critical review. *International Journal of Service Industry Management, 16*(1), 107–121.

Edvardsson, B., & Tronvoll, B. (2013). A new conceptualization of service innovation grounded in SD logic and service systems. *International Journal of Quality and Service Sciences, 5*(1), 19–31.

Edvardsson, B., Tronvoll, B., & Gruber, T. (2011). Expanding understanding of service exchange and value co-creation: A social construction approach. *Journal of the Academy of Marketing Science, 39*(2), 327–339.

Ellis, D., Freeman, A., Jamal, T., & Jiang, J. (2019). A theory of structured experience. *Annals of Leisure Research, 22*(1), 97–118.

Franke, N., & Schreier, M. (2010). Why customer value mass-customized products: The importance of process effort and enjoyment. *Journal of Product Innovation Management, 27*(7), 1020–1031.

Frery, F., Lecocq, X., & Warnier, V. (2015). Competing with ordinary resources. *MIT Sloan Management Review, 56*(3), 69–77.

Füller, J. (2010). Refining virtual co-creation from a consumer perspective. *California Management Review, 52*(2), 98–123.

Gentile, C., Spiller, N., & Noci, G. (2007). How to sustain the customer experience: An overview of experience components that co-create value with the customer. *European Management Journal, 25*(5), 395–410.

Getz, D., & Page, S. (2016). Progress and prospects for event tourism research. *Tourism Management, 52*, 593–631.

Geus, S., Richards, G., & Toepoel, V. (2016). Event experience scale. *Scandinavian Journal of Hospitality and Tourism, 16*(3), 274–296.

Götz, O., Gobbers, K., & Krafft, M. (2010). Evaluation of structural equation models using the Partial Least Squares (PLS) approach. In V. Vinzi, W. Chin, J. Henseler, & H. Wang (Eds.), *Handbook of partial least squares* (pp. 450–461). Springer Handbooks of Statistics.

Grissemann, U., & Stokburger-Sauer, N. (2012). Customer co-creation of travel services: The role of company support and customer satisfaction with the co-creation performance. *Tourism Management, 33*(6), 1483–1492.

Grönroos, C. (2008). Service logic revisited: Who creates value? And who co-creates? *European Business Review, 20*(4), 298–314.

Grönroos, C. (2011). Value co-creation in service logic: A critical analysis. *Marketing Theory, 11*(3), 279–301.

Grönroos, C., & Ravald, A. (2011). Service as business logic: Implications for value creation and marketing. *Journal of Service Management, 22*(1), 5–22.

Grönroos, C., & Voima, P. (2013). Critical service logic: Making sense of value creation and co-creation. *Journal of the Academy of Marketing Science, 41*(2), 133–150.

Gummesson, E., & Mele, C. (2010). Marketing as value co-creation through network interaction and resource integration. *Journal of Business Market Management, 4*(4), 181–198.

Hagen, M., & Bron, P. (2014). Enhancing the experience of the train journey: Changing the focus from satisfaction to emotional experience of customers. *Transportation Research Procedia, 1*, 253–263.

Hair, J., Black, W., Babin, B., & Anderson, R. (2014). *Multivariate data analysis*. Pearson Education.

Hair, J., Ringle, C., & Sarstedt, M. (2011). PLS-SEM: Indeed a silver bullet. *Journal of Marketing Theory and Practice, 19*(2), 139–151.

Halbusi, H., Estevez, P., Eleen, T., Ramayah, T., & Uzir, M. (2020). The roles of the physical environment, social servicescape, co-created value, and customer satisfaction in determining tourists' citizenship behavior: Malaysian Cultural and Creative Industries. *Sustainability, 12*(3229), 1–23.

Haro, M., Ruiz, M., & Cañas, R. (2014). The effects of the value co-creation process on the consumer and the company. *Expert Journal of Marketing, 2*(2), 68–81.

Helkkula, A. (2011). Characterizing the concept of service experience. *Journal of Service Management, 22*(3), 367–389.

Helkkula, A., Kelleher, C., & Pihlström, M. (2012). Characterizing value as an experience: Implications for service researchers and managers. *Journal of Service Research, 15*(1), 59–75.

Henseler, J., Ringle, C., & Sinkovics, R. (2009). The use of partial least squares path modeling in international marketing. *Advances in International Marketing, 20*, 277–319.

Hobfoll, S. (2002). Social and psychological resources and adaptation. *Review of General Psychology, 6*(4), 307–324.

Hunt, D., Geiger, S., & Varca, P. (2012). Satisfaction in the context of customer co-production: A behavioral involvement perspective. *Journal of Consumer Behaviour, 11*(5), 347–356.

Iyanna, S. (2016). Insights into consumer resource integration and value co-creation process. *The Journal of Applied Business Research, 32*(3), 717–728.

Johnston, R., & Kong, X. (2011). The customer experience: A road-map for improvement. *Managing Service Quality, 21*(1), 5–24.

Kelleher, C., & Peppard, J. (2011). Consumer experience of value creation-a phenomenological perspective. In A. Bradshaw, C. Hackley, & P. Maclaran (Eds.), *ACR European advances in consumer* (pp. 325–332). Association for Consumer Research.

Kelleher, K., Wilson, H., Macdonald, K., & Peppard, J. (2019). The score is not the music: Integrating experience and practice perspectives on value co-creation in collective consumption contexts. *Journal of Service Research, 22*(2), 120–138.

Keyser, A., Lemon, K., Klaus, P., & Keiningham, T. (2015). *A framework for understanding and managing the customer experience*. Marketing Science Institute Working Paper Series, 15–121.

Klaus, P., Gorgoglione, M., Buonamassa, D., Panniello, U., & Nguyen, B. (2013). Are you providing the "right" customer experience? The case of Banca Popolare di Bari. *International Journal of Bank Marketing, 31*(7), 506–528.

Klaus, P., & Maklan, S. (2012). EXQ: A multiple-item scale for assessing service experience. *Journal of Service Management, 23*(1), 5–33.

Klaus, P., & Maklan, S. (2013). Towards a better measure of customer experience. *International Journal of Market Research, 55*(2), 227–246.

Kleinaltenkamp, M. (2015). Value creation and customer effort—the impact of customer value concepts. In J. Gummerus & C. Koskull (Eds.), *The Nordic school, service marketing and management for the future* (pp. 283–294). CERS, Hanken School of Economics.

Kotler, P., Kartajaya, H., & Setiwan, I. (2011). *Marketing 3.0—Do Produto e do Consumidor até ao Espírito Humano.* Actual Editora.

Laing, J. (2018). Festival and event tourism research: Current and future perspectives. *Tourism Management Perspectives, 25*, 165–168.

Laurent, G., & Kapferer, J. (1985). Measuring consumer involvement profiles. *Journal of Marketing Research, 22*(1), 41–53.

Lemke, F., Moira, C., & Hugh, W. (2011). Customer experience quality: An exploration in business and consumer contexts using repertory grid technique. *Journal of the Academy of Marketing Science, 39*(6), 846–869.

Lengnick-Hall, C., Claycomb, V., & Inks, L. (2000). From recipient to contributor: Examining customer roles and experienced outcomes. *European Journal of Marketing, 34*, 359–383.

Lugosi, P., Robinson, R., Walters, G., & Donaghy, S. (2020). Managing experience co-creation practices: Direct and indirect inducement in pop-up food tourism events. *Tourism Management Perspectives, 35*, 100702.

Lusch, R., & Vargo, S. (2014). *Service-dominant logic: Premises, perspectives, possibilities.* Cambridge University Press.

Luszczynska, A., Gutiérrez-Doña, B., & Schwarzer, R. (2005). General self-efficacy in various domains of human functioning. Evidence from five countries. *International Journal of Psychology, 40*(2), 80–89.

Macdonald, K., Kleinaltenkamp, M., & Wilson, N. (2016). How business customers judge solutions: Solution quality and value in use. *Journal of Marketing, 80*(3), 96–120.

Marôco, J. (2010). *Análise Estatística: Com utilização do SPSS.* Edições Sílabo.

Martínez, C., & Martínez, G. (2007). Consumer satisfaction with a periodic reoccurring sport event and the moderating effect of motivations. *Sport Marketing Quarterly, 16*, 70–81.

Martinko, M., & Thomson, N. (1998). A synthesis and extension of the Weiner and Kelley attribution models. *Basic & Applied Social Psychology, 20*(4), 271–284.

McColl-Kennedy, J., Gustafsson, A., Jaakkola, E., Klaus, P., Radnor, Z., Perks, H., & Friman, M. (2015). Fresh perspectives on customer experience. *Journal of Services Marketing, 29*(6/7), 430–435.

McColl-Kennedy, J., Vargo, S., Dagger, T., Sweeney, J., & Kasteren, Y. (2012). Health care customer value cocreation practice styles. *Journal of Service Research, 15*(4), 370–389.

Merz, M., Zarantonello, L., & Grappi, S. (2018). How valuable are your customers in the brand value co-creation process? The development of a Customer Co-Creation Value (CCCV) scale. *Journal of Business Research, 82*, 79–89.

Meyer, C., & Schwager, A. (2007). Understanding customer experience. *Harvard Business Review, 85*(2), 116–126.

Mosavi, S., Sangari, M., & Keramati, A. (2018). An integrative framework for customer switching behavior. *The Service Industries Journal, 38*(15–16), 1067–1094.

Mukhtar, M., Ismail, M., & Yahya, Y. (2012). A hierarchical classification of co-creation models and techniques to aid in product or service design. *Computers in Industry, 63*(4), 289–297.

Nenonen, S., Rasila, H., Junnonen, J., & Kärnä, S. (2008). Customer Journey—a method to investigate user experience. *European Facility Management Conference, Manchester, UK.*

Nysveen, H., & Pedersen, P. (2014). Influences of co-creation on brand experience: The role of brand engagement. *International Journal of Market Research, 56*(6), 807–832.

Payne, A., Storbacka, K., & Frow, P. (2008). Managing the co-creation of value. *Journal of the Academy of Marketing Science, 36*(1), 83–96.

Piller, F., Ihl, C., & Vossen, A. (2011). A typology of customer co-creation in the innovation process. New forms of collaborative production and innovation: Economic, social, legal and technical characteristics and conditions. *SSRN Electronic Journal, 4*, 1–26.

Plé, L. (2016). Studying customers' resource integration by service employees in interactional value co-creation. *Journal of Services Marketing, 30*(2), 152–164.

Ranjan, K., & Read, S. (2016). Value co-creation: Concept and measurement. *Journal of the Academy of Marketing Science, 44*, 290–315. https://doi.org/10.1007/s11747-014-0397-2

Rodie, A., & Kleine, S. (2000). Consumer participation in services production and delivery. In T. Swartz & D. Iacobucci (Eds.), *Handbook of services marketing and management* (pp. 111–125). Sage.

Same, S., & Larimo, J. (2012). Marketing theory: Experience marketing and experiential marketing. *7th International Scientific Conference "Business and Management 2012", Vilnius, Lithuania*, 480–487.

Schmitt, B. (1999). Experiential marketing. *Journal of Marketing Management, 15*(1), 53–67.

Schmitt, B. (2003). *Customer experience management: A revolutionary approach to connecting with your customers.* Wiley.

Schmitt, H., Brakus, J., & Zarantonello, L. (2015). From Experiential psychology to consumer experience. *Journal of Consumer Psychology, 25*, 166–171.

Stangl, B. (2014). The experience economy, co-creation and its implications for the tourism industry and research. *ISCONTOUR—International Student Conference in Tourism Research.*

Tommasetti, A., Troisi, O., & Vesci, M. (2015). Customer value co-creation: A conceptual measurement model in a Service Dominant Logic perspective. In E. Gummesson, C. Mele, & F. Polese (Eds.), *Service dominant logic, network and systems theory and service science: Integrating three perspectives for a New Service Agenda*. Proceedings of the 2015 Naples Forum on service—ISBN: 979-12-200-0486-2.

Troisi, O., Santovito, S., Carrubbo, L., & Sarno, D. (2019). Evaluating festival attributes adopting SD logic: The mediating role of visitor experience and visitor satisfaction. *Marketing Theory, 19*(1), 85–102.

Tsaur, S., Chiu, Y., & Wang, C. (2007). The visitor's behavioral consequences of experiential marketing. *Journal of Travel & Tourism Marketing, 21*(1), 47–64.

Tum, J., Norton, P., & Wright, J. N. (2006). *Management of event operations*. Oxford: Elsevier.

Uzzi, B. (1997). Social structure and competition in interfirm networks: The paradox of embeddedness. *Administrative Science Quarterly, 42*(1), 35–67.

Vargo, L., & Lusch, R. (2004). Evolving to a new dominant logic of marketing. *Journal of Marketing, 68*(1), 1–17.

Vargo, S., & Lusch, R. (2008). Service-dominant logic: Continuing the evolution. *Journal of the Academy Marketing Science, 36*(1), 1–10.

Vargo, S., & Lusch, R. (2011). It's all B2B…and beyond: Toward a systems perspective of the market. *Industrial Marketing Management, 40*(2), 181–187.

Vargo, S., & Lusch, R. (2016). Institutions and axioms: An extension and update of service-dominant logic. *Journal of the Academy of Marketing Science, 44*(1), 5–23.

Vargo, S., Maglio, P., & Akaka, M. (2008). On value and value co-creation: A service systems and service logic perspective. *European Management Journal., 26*(3), 145–152.

Verhoef, P., Lemon, K., Parasuraman, A., Roggeveen, A., Tsiros, M., & Schlesinger, L. (2009). Customer experience creation: Determinants, dynamics and management strategies. *Journal of Retailing, 85*(1), 31–41.

Verleye, K. (2015). The co-creation experience from the customer perspective: Its measurement and determinants. *Journal of Service Management, 26*(2), 321–342.

Vinzi, V., Trinchera, L., & Amato, S. (2010). PLS path modelling: From foundations to recent developments and open issues for model assessment and improvement. In V. Vinzi, W. Chin, J. Henseler, & H. Wang (Eds.), *Handbook of partial least squares: Concepts, methods and applications* (pp. 47–82). Springer.

Walls, A., Okumus, F., Wang, Y., & Kwun, D. (2011). An epistemological view of consumer experiences. *International Journal of Hospitality Management, 30*(1), 10–21.

Walter, U., Edvardsson, B., & Öström, A. (2010). Drivers of customers' service experiences: A study in the restaurant industry. *Managing Service Quality, 20*(3), 236–258.

Wright, R., Campbell, D., Thatcher, J., & Roberts, N. (2012). Operationalizing multidimensional constructs in structural equation modeling: Recommendations for is research. *Communications of the Association for Information Systems, 30*(23), 367–412.

Xia, L., & Suri, R. (2014). Trading effort for money: Consumers' cocreation motivation and the pricing of service options. *Journal of Service Research, 17*(2), 228–241.

Xiao, M., Ma, Q., & Li, M. (2020). The impact of customer resources on customer value in co-creation: The multiple mediating effects. *Journal of Contemporary Marketing Science, 3*, 33–56.

Xie, C., Bagozzi, R., & Troye, S. (2008). Trying to presume: Toward a theory of consumers as co-creators of value. *Journal of the Academy of Marketing Science, 36*(1), 109–122.

Yi, Y., & Gong, T. (2013). Customer value co-creation behavior: Scale development and validation. *Journal of Business Research, 66*, 1279–1284.

Zhang, C. X., Fong, L. H. N., & Li, S. (2019). Co-creation experience and place attachment: Festival evaluation. *International Journal of Hospitality Management, 81*, 193–204.

Zomerdijk, L., & Voss, C. (2010). NSD processes and practices in experiential services. *Journal of Product Innovation Management, 28*, 63–80.

Measuring and Managing Customer Experience (CX): What Works and What Doesn't

Janet R. McColl-Kennedy and Mohamed Zaki

Use new technology with purpose to make the experience feel more human—without creating frustrations for customers and while empowering employees.
—Clarke and Kinghorn (2018)

1 Introduction

Customer Experience (CX) is a central focus of service management literature viewing customer evaluations as an outcome of interactions between customers, employees, systems and processes in a service context (Bitner et al., 1997). Organizations have customers regardless of whether they are internal or external and regardless of being called guests, members, patients or clients. It is well established that facilitating a meaningful customer experience is essential to achieving competitive advantage (Bolton et al., 2014; Homburg et al., 2017; Verhoef et al., 2009), greater revenue and greater employee satisfaction (Rawson et al., 2013).

J. R. McColl-Kennedy (✉)
University of Queensland, Brisbane, QLD, Australia
e-mail: j.mccoll-kennedy@business.uq.edu.au

M. Zaki
Cambridge Service Alliance, University of Cambridge, Cambridge, UK
e-mail: mehyz2@cam.ac.uk

© The Author(s), under exclusive license to Springer Nature Switzerland AG 2022
B. Edvardsson, B. Tronvoll (eds.), *The Palgrave Handbook of Service Management*,
https://doi.org/10.1007/978-3-030-91828-6_35

It is not surprisingly therefore that facilitating and managing great customer experiences is among the top priorities of CEOs around the world (Dixon et al., 2010; Toman et al., 2013; Lemon & Verhoef, 2016). Forrester (2016) found improving customer experience to be *the* top priority for over 70% of businesses (Flavián et al., 2019). Some would even say that experience is everything in service management (Clarke & Kinghorn, 2018). Indeed, there is evidence to suggest that a significant number of customers are prepared to walk away after just one bad experience. Certainly competition is tough and customers can take their business elsewhere. So it is critical that organizations know what their customers value in the customer experience. Getting to know what customers want in their experience with an organization, as well as what they don't want is vital in service management. When customers feel they are getting an experience that they value, they are likely to be loyal, say positive things about the organization, even advocate and continue buying, often buying more, from that organization. In short, customers are looking for meaningful, authentic human experiences without the frustrations so often associated with interactions between humans and machines (Clarke & Kinghorn, 2018).

While some organizations think they know what their customers value and so they focus on designing the customer experience in terms of what they think is best for the organization, most firms are interested in better understanding what their customers think about their experiences and how the firm can turn customer experience from good to great. We know that small details can make big differences (Bolton et al., 2014). Many organizations spend vast amounts of money, sometimes millions of dollars, in an effort to get to know their customers better and understand what is important in the customer experience. But many firms are not very good at listening to their customers and this isn't from want of trying. Millions of dollars are spent on collecting information. Yet, organizations report that they are not satisfied with the answers they are receiving from their customers. It appears that the problem is not a lack of effort on the part of the organization, but rather that the tools that are widely in use still today are imprecise—not measuring what they are supposed to be measuring. Knowing what to measure, how to measure it, in order to gain rich insights that matter to customers through multiple data sources, and especially what to do with open-ended feedback has not been clear until now (Zaki et al., 2021).

2 Conceptualizations of Customer Experience (CX)

Before exploring a widely employed range of practical tools used to measure customer experience, we will first consider some key conceptualizations of customer experience. This next section provides an overview of a range of definitions of customer experience (CX) highlighting key elements. As shown in Table 1, several definitions have been offered on CX. Frow and Payne (2007) are one of the first to define customer experience as holistic, comprised of multiple touchpoints in a journey. This notion of a journey over time is echoed by Neslin et al. (2006) and McColl-Kennedy et al. (2019). There is general agreement among researchers that a customer's perception of his/her experience is holistic in nature, involving multiple internal and subjective responses

Table 1 Illustrative examples of conceptualizations of customer experience (CX)

Becker and Jaakkola (2020)	Customer experience is viewed as non-deliberate, spontaneous responses and reactions to particular stimuli provided by a firm
Holmlund et al. (2020)	A customer's response to interactions with an organization before, during or after purchase or consumption, across multiple channels, and across time
McColl-Kennedy et al. (2019)	Customer experience is viewed a journey, comprising value creation elements (resources, activities, context, interactions and customer role) and both customer discrete emotions and cognitive responses at touchpoints across the journey
Kranzbuhler et al. (2018)	CX is comprised of discrete touchpoints at which customers have cognitive, affective, behavioral, sensorial and social responses to the interaction resulting in a customer experience
Bolton et al. (2018)	CX encompasses customers' cognitive, emotional, social, sensory and value responses to the organization's offerings over time, including pre- and post-consumption
Homburg et al. (2017)	Customer experience is the evolvement of a person's sensorial, affective, cognitive, relational and behavioral responses to a firm or brand by living through a journey of touchpoints along pre-purchase, purchase, and post-purchase situations and continually judging this journey against response thresholds of co- occurring experiences in a person's related environment
Lemon and Verhoef (2016)	CX is comprised of the customer's cognitive, affective, emotional, social and sensory elements
Rawson et al. (2013)	A complete experience—on the way to purchase and after, that is comprised of multiple touchpoints in the journey
Frow and Payne (2007)	Holistic, comprised of multiple touchpoints in a journey

to interactions with an organization (Meyer & Schwager, 2007; Schmitt et al., 2015). Customers respond to a range of stimuli in the service environment and this is acknowledged by Lemon and Verhoef (2016) who highlight that CX is comprised of the customer's cognitive, affective, emotional, social and sensory elements. Voorhees et al. (2017) underscore that the customer experience takes place throughout many interactions, including multiple "moments of truth" that influence customer outcomes. This conceptualization is consistent with the view that customer experience is a process (Grönroos, 1998; Rawson et al., 2013), comprised of interactions and activities across multiple touchpoints. Homburg et al. (2017) define customer experience as the evolvement of a person's sensorial, affective, cognitive, relational, and behavioral responses to a firm or brand by living through a journey of touchpoints along pre-purchase, purchase, and post-purchase situations and continually judging this journey against response thresholds of co- occurring experiences in a person's related environment. McColl-Kennedy et al. (2019) elaborate on the interactions and activities, identifying key elements of the customer experience as comprising value creation elements (resources, activities, context, interactions and customer role) and both customer discrete emotions and cognitive responses at touchpoints across the journey. Becker and Jaakkola (2020) suggest that customer experience should be viewed as non-deliberate, spontaneous responses and reactions to particular stimuli provided by a firm. Indeed, Rawson et al. (2013) emphasize the importance of viewing the customer experience as a "complete experience" taking into account the experience on the way to purchase all the way through to after purchase.

3 Traditional CX Tools Are Too Blunt

Historically, organizations have used customer satisfaction metrics to measure customer experience. However, widely used customer satisfaction metrics often fail to reveal what customers *really* think and feel about the service experience. In the digital era, organizations need to take deep dives into the data if they are serious about understanding what their customers value to gain rich insights into what is wrong from their customers' perspectives, and importantly what needs to change in order to provide seamless, meaningful experiences (Zaki et al., 2021).

Among the most popular tools, used widely by organizations, are satisfaction and loyalty surveys, as well as Net Promoter Scores (NPS). These tools provide numeric scores. As such, they give the impression that they are precise, accurate measures. At best, they can be regarded as blunt instruments which tell us very little about what customers are really thinking, feeling and doing. At worst, they are misleading.

Net Promoter Score (NPS) provides the percentage of customers who would recommend a given organization to their friends and family. NPS was developed by Frederic Reichheld (2003) to measure loyalty. But it is reportedly the most commonly used customer experience metric because it is simple and easy to use (Morgan, 2019). Most firms still focus on one question "How likely are you to recommend this company to a friend or colleague?" on a scale of 1 to 10. It is overly simplistic and is really a measure of positive word of mouth rather than customer experience.

Customer satisfaction measures are relatively easy to administer and can be used to produce impressive-looking graphics and they are generally based on large quantities of data. But the sheer volume of data does not mean that the results ensure insights into what customers really value. Our research shows that relying on these scores alone can be misleading masking serious problems with the business. Not only is quantitative surveying more resource-intensive, customers are also finding filling out surveys increasingly intrusive and are becoming less inclined to participate (Morgan, 2019; Holmlund et al., 2020). Another critical weakness is that they cannot pick up customer emotions. By masking significant customer dissatisfaction, firms can lose customers without knowing *why* (Zaki et al., 2021).

Interestingly, organizations use many qualitative approaches, such as focus groups, interviews or by manually reading and analyzing open-ended comments from their customers as part of a survey. However, organizations typically do not delve deeply into the free text comments that customers provide in these qualitative approaches. This is because analyzing thousands and thousands of comments "by hand" is not only time-consuming and labor intensive, it is also difficult to categorize the comments into useful themes. Therefore, open-ended feedback that firms receive is often ignored (McColl-Kennedy et al., 2019). If used at all, organizations have traditionally grouped the open-ended free text comments into two broad, overly simplified categories (1) positives ("compliments") or (2) negatives ("complaints"). When this occurs, organizations lose a great deal of valuable information that potentially can offer insights into *why* customers think and feel the way they do. McColl-Kennedy et al. (2019) found that organizations can pick up on a third category labeled "suggestions" to listen to customers' ideas to improve the experience. These could be suggestions to improve processes such as ways to reduce wait times, improve communication between frontline employees and customers, communications internally within the organization, using mobile apps to provide information in real time to customers and enable them to provide feedback easily through their phone or tablet.

Another metric used to measure customer experience is the customer effort score (CES) (Morgan, 2019). CES measures how much work customers have to do through an interaction with the brand or organization. It is typically measured by asking customers "How much effort did you have to put in to resolve the issue?" on a scale from Very Low Effort to Very High Effort. This metric may help firms to determine customer friction points and find ways to create a more seamless experience.

The churn rate is another metric used by organizations (Ascarza & Hardie, 2013; Morgan, 2019). The churn rate tracks how many customers discontinued doing business with an organization over a particular period of time. The thinking behind this metric is that customers will not leave the organization if they're having a good experience. Churn rate is calculated by dividing the number of customers lost during the timeframe by the number of customers at the beginning of the timeframe. In essence the churn rate is the opposite of the retention rate.

4 Multiple Metrics Are Recommended

But it is in the open ended free text where customers can best articulate what they do not like (and like) about their customer experience. They can also elaborate on *why* this is the case, providing context which is very important for a full understanding. None of this can be obtained through simple numeric scores. While traditionally it has been time-consuming to classify and make sense of these comments, it is in the free text comments that customers express their true feelings (McColl-Kennedy et al., 2019), and these turn out to be a much more reliable predictor of their behavior than the boxes they have checked. In a similar vein, Becker and Jaakkola (2020) call for the development of new dynamic measurement approaches.

Many customers today use smart, real-time digital devices, including mobile apps which enable firms to collect more precise real-time data about their customers' journeys. In fact, an unprecedented volume of textual data generated from a wide range of sources and formats such as news items, industrial reports, online chatter, surveys, interviews, blogs, scripts and notes are available to organizations and it is expected that the number and complexity of these qualitative data documents will only increase in the future (Zaki & McColl-Kennedy, 2020). By 2025 the International Data Group predicts that there will be 163 ZB of data globally, with around 80% of business-relevant information originating from unstructured forms, primarily text (Techrepublic, 2017). Consequently, large amounts of data, including textual data such as actual comments from customers, from Twitter, Facebook, customer blogs, as well as the more traditional online and telephone surveys are generated at many touchpoints across the customer journey. Clearly, firms need to review and re-think the approach they are taking to measure customer experience.

5 New Digital Technologies Offer Useful Ways to Measure and Manage CX

Due to digital advances, organizations have access to a vast array of data about what customers think about the organization's products and services, much of which is in free text form (Zaki, 2019). For example, textual data such as verbatim comments from customers are now generated across the customer journey. User-generated content and free text feedback contain excellent sources to delve into the customer's views (Tirunillai & Tellis, 2014) providing insights into what customers really think about specific pain points throughout the customer journey. A recent study has indicated that AI and machine learning in the management toolkit has shown increasing implementation, with approximately a 10% increase in use year on year since 2018 (Moorman, 2021). It is expected that AI and machine learning use will increase by 20% in the next three years. Although AI has yet to be widely adopted by marketers and customer experience managers it offers great promise as it enables organizations to mine huge datasets and extract meaningful insights from customers about what they value and do not value in CX.

Text mining can be used to extract customer views from unstructured comments (Pang & Lee, 2008). For instance, Xiang et al. (2015) applied text mining to customer reviews to understand the relationship between customer experience and satisfaction. Culotta and Cutler (2016) used a social network mining model to analyze multiple Twitter datasets in order to investigate how strongly consumers associate with different brands.

Text mining and other emerging technologies such as AI offer potentially more effective ways to measure and manage customer experience (Zaki et al., 2021). An important learning from McColl-Kennedy et al. (2019) is the need to connect both qualitative data <u>and</u> quantitative data to enable organizations to gain rich insights. Through this approach the authors were able to identify seven root causes of problems for the customer for a complex B2B service highlighting distinct opportunities for improving the CX. In that specific setting root causes identified were: capability, communication, parts, price value, process adherence, quality and service capacity (McColl-Kennedy et al.,

2019). Their model enabled the identification of what was influencing and responsible for each root cause. For instance they found the "parts" root cause centered around parts being unavailable (*resources*), problems around *customer activities* picking up parts, issues with customers not being able to collect parts on weekends (*context*), shortcomings in *interactions* between the employees and customers regarding the ordering and delivery of spare parts and what the *role* of the customer was and what it should be.

6   Need to Think Multi-channels Across Physical, Social and Digital

Assessment at the various touchpoints contribute to the overall customer experience across the customer journey. At times these may be in one channel, such as face to face. At other times the channel may be virtual, such as online shopping. Prior work has demonstrated that customers may utilize different channels for different aspects of their customer journey.

For instance, some may purchase in one channel but seek post-purchase assistance in another (De Keyser et al., 2015; Verhoef et al., 2009).

Further, it is important to think not only about physical channels, consideration of digital increasingly needs to be incorporated in customer experience measures as well as new forms of social interactions. New technologies are changing the way organizations interact with their customers and transforming the customer experience (Lemon, 2016; Van Doorn et al., 2017). AI, robots and virtual reality are already playing a role in the customer experience. These new ways of engaging with customers will not completely replace face-to- face encounters but increasingly they will operate alongside them. Managers will need to understand customer experiences across the digital, physical and social realms, and design services and facilitate experiences accordingly.

As outlined by Bolton et al. (2018), organizations need to think about the customer experience in terms of all three realms—the physical, digital and social realms, and not in isolation but viewing them as connected. That is how customers view them. Edvardsson et al. (2010) also highlighted the importance of social, as well as interactions between customers and between customers and employees, and the role of technology, in addition to the physical elements of the servicescape. Bolton et al. (2018) argue that customer experience can be conceptualized within a three dimensional space—low to high digital density, low to high physical complexity and low to high social presence—yielding eight octants.

Digital technologies can be used to design optimal and seamless customer experiences (Flavián et al., 2019). Managers are encouraged to think more broadly about the advantages of using different channels, such as virtual reality (VR), augmented reality (AR) and mixed realities (MR) in order to provider richer experiences for their customers (Brynjolfsson et al., 2013; Verhoef et al., 2015).

7   A Robust Conceptual Framework Is Required

In order for these new technologies, such as AI to be useful, researchers and managers need to apply a conceptual framework as the technology does not automatically provide the deep insights required. Villarroel Ordenes et al. (2014) proposed a framework comprising three elements of the customer experience (1) activities; (2) resources and (3) context. They used a linguistics-based text mining approach to automate sentiment analysis of customer feedback in the context of carpark and transfer services at a UK airport. Their model captured customer activities and resources, company activities and resources, and customer sentiment (complaints and compliments) demonstrating how certain features of linguistics-based text mining, such as dictionaries and linguistic patterns, can be used to analyze textual customer feedback.

Baxendale et al. (2015) take an integrated view of customer experience, highlighting the importance of understanding multiple touchpoints, interactions at the touchpoints and modeling the valence of the customer's affective response at the respective touchpoints along the customer journey. Further, they develop and implement a new tool designed to collect real-time customer experience data for selected consumer goods.

McColl-Kennedy et al. (2019) building on and extending Villarroel Ordenes et al. (2014)'s work developed a CX framework that takes into account the customers' perspective as the starting point using both qualitative and quantitative data. McColl-Kennedy et al.'s (2019) CX framework directs machine learning to provide meaning from the unstructured customer data. It works by classifying the data according to the following components: (1) customer touchpoints, (2) value creation elements, (3) emotions and (4) cognitive responses. McColl-Kennedy et al. (2019) followed the six-step established approach of Chapman et al. (2000) and Hevner et al. (2004) and applied advanced text mining techniques to two years of customer feedback in a complex B2B heavy asset service setting and tested it on two additional datasets.

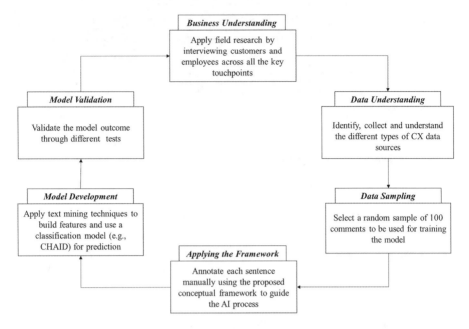

Fig. 1 Step-by-step guide for practitioners to apply AI to measure CX

In the next section a step-by-step guide for practitioners to apply and measure customer experience using AI, is summarized below and illustrated in Fig. 1.

8 Practical Guidelines for Practitioners

Step 1 is Business Understanding. Here the aim at this stage is to understand in depth the organization and its various services and products. It is recommended that field research be carried out, including for instance interviews with customers and frontline employees as well as managers. Shadowing employees across all the key touchpoints was undertaken by McColl-Kennedy et al. (2019) and is highly recommended as it enables observation of processes, practices and interactions to be observed first hand. For example, they interviewed 34 employees and 20 customers to understand the customer experience from the respective informants' perspectives.

Step 2 is the Data Understanding phase. This step involves building and testing of the customer experience analytic developed from interrogation of a dataset of longitudinal customer experience responses obtained from a survey administered by a third-party market research firm. McColl-Kennedy et al.

(2019) adapted and extended the linguistic text mining approach introduced by Villarroel Ordenes et al. (2014). In addition to obtaining the quantitative scores for customers' ratings of 12 questions (10-point scale from "Very Satisfied" to "Very Dissatisfied")—overall satisfaction, repurchase, referral, resource availability, responsiveness, communication, service completion duration, preparation, service quality, invoice timeliness and invoice accuracy, they analyzed responses to the free text question. They collected two years of survey data from a large B2B firm.

The third step is Data Sampling. Following established practice, McColl-Kennedy et al. (2019) used a random sample of 100 comments from the dataset in the training stage to provide rich text for data understanding and pattern development (Singh et al., 2011). These comments were divided into separate sentences. Two coders independently classified each comment following the conceptual framework. Macros and linguistic pattern rules were developed and applied to the conceptual framework. Resulting patterns were then mapped to the root causes. This is a very important stage as it enables an organization to understand the root causes and identify opportunities to improve CX by taking steps to address the problems.

The fourth step is Applying the Conceptual Framework. Here, for example, the coders manually annotated each sentence in terms of (1) touchpoints, (2) all value creation elements—resources, activities, context, interactions and customer's role, (3) discrete emotions and (4) cognitive responses. A judge was employed when disagreement was encountered. Using a fine-grained approach enables text mining algorithms to capture specialized vocabulary used by customers. This offers a better way to identify pain points that matter to customers than the general linguistics-based text mining applications (Villarroel Ordenes et al., 2014) that are expected to be too coarse to capture important details that matter to the specific customers (Bolton et al., 2014).

The fifth step is Model Development. To develop their text mining model, McColl-Kennedy et al. (2019) used text mining techniques such as Part of Speech (POS) to capture different forms of speech (e.g., verbs, nouns) and they developed patterns using macros and linguistic pattern rules applied to the conceptual framework. This step is essential to enable the text mining model to map automatically the customers' verbatim words to the four CX dimensions (touchpoints, value creation elements, emotions and cognitive responses). They evaluated and extended the dictionaries as appropriate. New concepts and patterns were developed and the researchers iterated back and forth and then mapped each element to root causes, enabling the firm to identify opportunities to improve the customer experience.

The sixth and final step is Model Validation. McColl-Kennedy et al. (2019) employed five different tests: (1) a manual linguistics validation; (2) a second dataset validation; (3) a second firm validation; (4) feedback from the customer experience team at the focal organization and (5) a CHAID analysis.

By using chi-square automatic interaction detection (CHAID) classification technique, McColl-Kennedy et al. (2019) were able to predict to what extent customers were satisfied with the customer experience and generate meaningful insights. For example, this technique enables a firm to identify critical touchpoints from the customer's perspective, including potentially new touchpoints previously unknown, to understand what really matters to the customer at each touchpoint, map each touchpoint to its root cause, that is, the specific firm action or strategy, and finally to take specific actions to improve the experience at each touchpoint, as well as the overall CX.

Their model is able to uncover customers who are at risk of leaving the firm, even customers who give high satisfaction scores (or NPS scores). Customers with high satisfaction scores normally would be viewed by an organization as "satisfied", or those with high NPS scores would be deemed "very likely to recommend", and therefore not identified by the firm as requiring attention. However, McColl-Kennedy et al. (2019) demonstrate that these customers are voicing their concerns in the free text comments and require follow-up by the organization to address their concerns. Relying solely on the numeric scores gives an incomplete picture of the true feelings of the respective customers.

Further, the text mining model enabled an entire "hidden" segment of supposedly highly satisfied customers to be identified. Analysis showed that 42% of customers who give scores of 9.5 and above (out of 10) actually complained. Customers who give scores between 7 and 9.4 (44%) complain too. Complaints from customers who gave satisfaction scores of 7 or greater were often ignored by organizations despite accounting for a significant portion of sales. Sales figures indicated that when these customers' concerns were not addressed sales went down markedly. For instance, one so called "satisfied" customer reduced purchases from over $200,000 to less than $2000. A key takeaway is that ignoring small details that can be identified through the text analytics model, can mean big losses for firms.

9   Conclusion

This chapter has highlighted the importance of using multiple metrics to measure and manage customer experience. New technologies, including AI and text mining, offer organizations today with an efficient way of delving deeply into what customers are really saying, thinking and feeling about their experience with the organization and how their experience could be improved, and importantly what things should be improved in the experience.

Attention was drawn to the need to develop a conceptual framework to guide the text mining such as that developed and tested by McColl-Kennedy et al. (2019) and a practical step-by-step guide for organizations to implement was provided. Technology per se does not fix customer experience problems but it can be an enabler of better customer experience provided the technology is guided by a sound conceptual framework. We encourage both researchers and practitioners to re-evaluate their approach and the measures they are currently using in their attempt to better measure and manage the customer experience. We also encourage researchers and practitioners to consider using the new AI technologies that can enable free text comments provided by customers, in real time across the range of channels and over multiple touchpoints, to be more easily analyzed. The bottom-line customer experience is a key differentiator in today's highly competitive world.

References

Ascarza, E., & Hardie, B. G. (2013). A joint model, or usage and churn in contractual settings. *Marketing Science, 32*(4), 570–590.

Baxendale, S., Macdonald, E. K., & Wilson, H. N. (2015). The impact of different touchpoints on brand consideration. *Journal of Retailing, 91*(2), 235–253.

Becker, L., & Jaakkola, E. (2020). Customer experience: Fundamental premises and implications for research. *Journal of the Academy of Marketing Science, 48*, 630–648.

Bitner, M. J., Faranda, W. T., Hubbert, A. R., & Zeithaml, V. A. (1997). Customer contributions and roles in service delivery. *International Journal of Service Industry Management, 8*(3), 193–205.

Bolton, R., McColl-Kennedy, J. R., Cheung, L., Gallan, A. S., Orsingher, C., Witell, L., & Zaki, M. (2018). Customer experience challenges: Bringing together digital, physical and social realms. *Journal of Service Management, 29*(5), 776–808.

Bolton, R. N., Gustafsson, A., McColl-Kennedy, J. R., Sirianni, N. J., & Tse, D. K. (2014). Small details that make big differences: A radical approach to consumption experience as a Firm's differentiating strategy. *Journal of Service Management, 25*(2), 253–274.

Brynjolfsson, E., Hu, Y. L., & Rahman, M. S. (2013). Competing in the age of omnichannel retailing. *MIT Sloan Management Review, 54*(4), 23–29.

Chapman, P., Clinton, J., Kerber, R., & Khabaza, T. (2000). CRISP-DM 1.0 step-by-step data mining guide. ftp://ftp.software.ibmcom/software/analytics/spss/support/Modeler/Documentation/14/UserM anual/CRISP-DM.pdf

Clarke, D., Kinghorn, R. (2018). *Experience is everything: here's how to get it right.* https://www.pwc.com/us/en/advisory-services/publications/consumer-intelligence- series/pwc-consumer-intelligence-series-customer-experience.pdf

Culotta, A., & Cutler, J. (2016). Mining brand perceptions from twitter social networks. *Marketing Science, 35*(3), 343–362.

De Keyser, A., Lemon, K. N., Klaus, P., & Keiningham, T. L. (2015). *A Framework for Understanding and Managing the Customer Experience.* Working Paper Series No. 15-121, Marketing Science Institute. www.msi.org/reports/a-framework-for-understandingand-managing-the-customer-experience/

Dixon, M., Freeman, K., & Toman, N. (2010). Stop trying to delight your customers. *Harvard Business Review, 88*, 116–122.

Edvardsson, B., Enquist, B., & Johnston, R. (2010). Design dimensions of experience rooms for service test drives: Case studies in several service contexts. *Managing Service Quality: An International Journal, 20*(4), 312–327.

Flavián, C., Ibáñez-Sánchez, S., & Orús, C. (2019). The impact of virtual, augmented and mixed reality technologies on the customer experience. *Journal of Business Research, 100*, 547–560.

Forrester. (2016). 72% of Businesses Name Improving Customer Experience their Top Priority. Retrieved January 14, 2018, from https://goo.gl/k55uNy

Frow, P., & Payne, A. (2007). Towards the 'perfect' customer experience. *Journal of Brand Management, 15*(2), 89–101.

Grönroos, C. (1998). Marketing services: The case of a missing product. *Journal of Business & Industrial Marketing, 13*, 322–338.

Hevner, A. R., March, S. T., Park, J., & Ram, S. (2004). Design science in information systems research. *MIS Quarterly, 28*(1), 75–105.

Holmlund, M., Van Vaerenbergh, Y., Ciuchita, R., Ravald, A., Sarantopoulos, P., Villarroel Ordenes, F., & Zaki, M. (2020). Customer experience Management in the age of big data analytics: A strategic framework. *Journal of Business Research, Feb*, 1–10.

Homburg, C., Jozić, D., & Kuehnl, C. (2017). Customer experience management: Toward implementing an evolving marketing concept. *Journal of the Academy of Marketing Science, 45*(3), 377–401.

Kranzbuhler, A., Kleijnen, M., Morgan, R. E., & Teerling, M. (2018). The multilevel nature of customer experience research: An integrative review and research agenda. *International Journal of Management Reviews, 20*(2), 433–456.

Lemon, K. N. (2016). The art of creating attractive consumer experiences at the right time: Skills marketers will need to survive and thrive. *GfK Marketing Intelligence Review, 8*(2), 44–49.

Lemon, K. N., & Verhoef, P. C. (2016). Understanding customer experience throughout the customer journey. *Journal of Marketing, 80*(6), 69–96.

McColl-Kennedy, J. R., Zaki, M., Lemon, K. N., Urmetzer, F., & Neely, A. (2019). Gaining customer experience insights that matter. *Journal of Service Research, 22*(1), 8–26.

Meyer, C., & Schwager, A. (2007). Understanding customer experience. *Harvard Business Review, 85*(2), 116–126.

Moorman, C. (2021, February 2021). *Top ten results from the CMO survey.* Retrieved March 30, 2021, from https://tinyurl.com/yx75qt3f

Morgan, B. (2019). *The 20 Best Customer Experience Metrics For Your Business.* Forbes. Retrieved March 31, 2020, from https://www.forbes.com/sites/blakemorgan/2019/07/29/the-20-best-customer-experience-metrics-for-your-business/?sh=6286e01058cc

Neslin, S. A., Gupta, S., Kamakura, W., Lu, J., & Mason, C. H. (2006). Defection detection: Measuring and understanding the predictive accuracy of customer churn models. *Journal of Marketing Research, 43*(2), 204–211.

Pang, B., & Lee, L. (2008). Opinion mining and sentiment analysis. *Foundations and Trends in Information Retrieval, 2*(1-2), 1–35.

Rawson, A., Duncan, E., & Jones, C. (2013). The truth about customer experience. *Harvard Business Review, 91*(9), 90–98.

Reichheld, F. (2003). One number you need to grow. *Harvard Business Review, 81*(12), 46–55.

Schmitt, B., Brakus, J. J., & Zarantonello, L. (2015). From experiential psychology to consumer experience. *Journal of Consumer Psychology, 25*(1), 166–171.

Singh, S. N., Hillme, S., & Wang, Z. (2011). Efficient methods for sampling responses from large-scale qualitative data. *Marketing Science, 30*(3), 532–549.

Techrepublic. (2017). Unstructured data: A cheat sheet. Retrieved August 9, 2019, from www.techrepublic.com/article/unstructureddata-the-smart-persons-guide

Tirunillai, S., & Tellis, G. J. (2014). Mining marketing meaning from online chatter: Strategic brand analysis of big data using latent Dirichlet allocation. *Journal of Marketing Research, 51*(4), 463–479.

Toman, N., Dixon, M., & DeLisi, R. (2013). *The effortless experience: Conquering the new battleground for customer loyalty.* Penguin.

Van Doorn, J., Mende, M., Noble, S. M., Hulland, J., Ostrom, A. L., Grewal, D., & Petersen, J. A. (2017). Domo Arigato Mr Roboto: Emergence of automated social presence in organizational frontlines and customers' service experiences. *Journal of Service Research, 20*(1), 43–58.

Verhoef, P. C., Kannan, P. K., & Inman, J. J. (2015). From multichannel to Omichannel Channel retailing: Introduction to the special issue on multi-channel retailing. *Journal of Retailing, 91*(2), 174–181.

Verhoef, P. C., Lemon, K. N., Parasuraman, A., Roggeveen, A., Tsiros, M., & Schlesinger, L. A. (2009). Customer experience creation: Determinants, dynamics and management strategies. *Journal of Retailing, 85*(1), 31–41.

Villarroel Ordenes, F., Theodoulidis, B., Burton, J., Gruber, T., & Zaki, M. (2014). Analyzing customer experience feedback using text mining: A linguistics-based approach. *Journal of Service Research, 17*(3), 278–295.

Voorhees, C. M., Fombelle, P. W., Gregoire, Y., Bone, S., Gustafsson, A., Sousa, R., & Walkowiak, T. (2017). Service encounters, experiences and the customer journey: Defining the field and a call to expand our lens. *Journal of Business Research, 79*(10), 269–280.

Xiang, Z., Zvi, S., John, H. G., & Muzaffer, U. (2015). What can big data and text analytics tell us about hotel guest experience and satisfaction?. *International Journal of Hospitality Management, 44*, 120–130.

Zaki, M. (2019). Digital transformation: Harnessing digital Technologies for the Next Generation of services. *Journal of Services Marketing, 33*(4), 429–435.

Zaki, M., & McColl-Kennedy, J. R. (2020). Text Mining Analysis Roadmap (TMAR) for Service Research. Special Issue on Qualitative Methods in Service Research, *Journal of Services Marketing, 34*(1), 30-47.

Zaki, M., McColl-Kennedy, J. R., & Neely, A. (2021). AI can help you hear what your customers are trying to tell you!. *Harvard Business Review*. https://hbr.org/2021/05/using-ai-to-track-how-customers-feel-in-real-time

Improving Service Quality Through Individuals' Satisfaction. Evidence from the Healthcare Sector

Roberta Guglielmetti Mugion, Maria Francesca Renzi, and Laura Di Pietro

Abbreviations

EFQM	European Foundation for Quality Management
IEGSI	Internal and External Global Satisfaction Index
OBNs	Objected Bayesian Networks
SB	Service Blueprint
SEC	Service Excellence Chain
SPC	Service Profit Chain

1 Introduction

Quality management thinking proposes a richness of theories, models, methods and tools on service quality, offering a holistic and systemic view to manage organizations, which focuses on total employee involvement and customer satisfaction to achieve continuous improvement (Dahlgaard et al., 2011) successfully.

R. Guglielmetti Mugion (✉) • M. F. Renzi • L. Di Pietro
Department of Business Studies, Roma Tre University, Rome, Italy
e-mail: roberta.guglielmettimugion@uniroma3.it;
mariafrancesca.renzi@uniroma3.it; laura.dipietro@uniroma3.it

© The Author(s), under exclusive license to Springer Nature Switzerland AG 2022
B. Edvardsson, B. Tronvoll (eds.), *The Palgrave Handbook of Service Management*,
https://doi.org/10.1007/978-3-030-91828-6_36

Undoubtedly, service quality dimensions (Parasuraman et al., 1985) present several differences in product service dimensions (Garvin, 1984). Due to its main characteristics (i.e. intangible nature, high customer involvement, interaction with staff, individuality, simultaneity of production and consumption and perishability), the service quality concept is more difficult to define. The service operations are characterized by the fact that some activities are realized with the customer's engagement, and some operations have both high- and low-visibility processes (Slack et al., 2010). Even visibility can affect the customers' perceptions of the delivered service quality. Service quality presents a strong subjective side challenging to control since the main actors of service operations are external. It can be measured by collecting customers' feedback and opinions matched with the objective side, namely internal performance indicators.

Some authors (George, 1977; Albrecht & Zemke, 1985) suggested that front-line employees are essential elements in the service delivery process. Indeed, the quality of service interaction contributes to ensuring customer satisfaction (Duffy & Ketchand, 1998) since employees represent the main point of contact between company and customer (Hartline et al., 2000; Rupp et al., 2007). Accordingly, they can catch customers' feedback and opinions (Lovelock & Wirtz, 2010; Nasr et al., 2014), especially on service quality at the decisive moment. Besides, the interaction between customers and employees significantly affects customer perceived value (Yi & Gong, 2012) and employees' well-being. Indeed, customer and employee outcomes are strongly correlated (Yoon & Suh, 2003; Nasr et al., 2015).

The role of employees and customer is widely discussed in the literature, and several contributions underline the positive association between employee satisfaction and customer satisfaction (Harter et al., 2002; Chi & Gursoy, 2009). Anyway, only a few contributions demonstrate this linkage through empirical case studies using quantitative techniques (Guglielmetti Mugion et al., 2020b; Raharjo et al., 2016; Musella et al., 2017).

Besides, a recent field of study, the transformative service research (TSR), has evidenced the propulsive role that operators and consumers can provide in social well-being. In particular, TSR studies the contribution that services can generate to raise individual and collective well-being (Ostrom et al., 2010; Anderson & Ostrom, 2015). As highlighted by Chen et al. (2020), subjective well-being depends on the co-creation process of multiple actors. As noticed by Jaakkola et al. (2015), "customers and workers can be considered key actors with their unique and subjective experiences informing the nature of the service experience" (Edgar et al., 2017, p. 86).

A careful analysis of the quality management theories was developed in the service field. As a result, it emerges that pivotal models (i.e. GAP model, Valdani and Busacca's model, Service Profit Chain [SPC], Service Excellence Chain [SEC]) and tools related to service quality (i.e. SERVQUAL, Service Blueprint [SB], Internal and External Global Satisfaction Index [IEGSI]) jointly consider the internal and external perspectives. Although it is not possible to find an explicit declaration in all these theoretical models, recognizing the synergy between employees and customer satisfaction emerged in the historical evolution of the service quality approaches. Specifically, the whole of these approaches can be valuable for the healthcare sector.

The healthcare sector is an operating context particularly suited to the empirical study of this innovative research. Care and assistance services for potential and intrinsic characteristics can be considered engines for a broader and more general transformation of modern society. It is worth emphasizing the relevance of the healthcare industry, which is also confirmed by the 2030 Agenda of the UN, which introduced the "Health and Wellness" Goal that is the commitment, among the 17 Sustainable Development Objectives, to initiate and implement concrete actions aimed at ensuring the health, well-being for all and all ages. There is a growing need to redefine a human-centred society capable of finding a new balance between economic progress and social well-being, thanks to implementing advanced technologies in different sectors and social activities. However, public and private healthcare providers should improve their performance's efficiency and effectiveness by acting on their flexibility and quality to achieve citizens' well-being and quality of life.

Quality management theories and practices are crucial to achieve better performances through the combination and efforts of healthcare professionals, patients, families, researchers to foster better patient outcomes and professional development (Ahmed et al., 2019). Furthermore, as clarified by the Institute for Healthcare Improvement (www.ihi.org), in the healthcare industry, there is a growing emphasis on the development of a patient-centric approach, based on a more proactive role of patients in the co-creation, as well as the need to create joy in the work of physicians and nurses, transforming burnout into the engagement. Kaartemo and Känsäkoski (2018) emphasize the need to investigate healthcare professionals' role in the value co-creation process. Moreover, there is limited evidence on the effect of quality improvement practices acting on patient-level and professional-level outcomes (Groene et al., 2010). Accordingly, understanding the antecedents of internal and external satisfaction and their relationship is vital in improving people's quality of life.

748 R. Guglielmetti Mugion et al.

Consequently, healthcare service quality is an operating context particularly suited to this innovative research empirical studies. Care and assistance services for potential and intrinsic characteristics are engines for a broader and more general modern society transformation. As a landmark, Donabedian (1988) suggested that "good structure (attributes of the settings and resources) increases the likelihood of good process (systems of activities to produce value), and good process increases the likelihood of good outcome (effects of health care on the health status of patients and populations)".

This chapter aims to define healthcare service quality in healthcare, concentrating on developing an integrated perspective between internal and external satisfaction. Our primary assumption is the critical linkage between personnel and customers' perceptions to optimize service quality.

It is valuable to clarify that the focus is on the healthcare field; hence, the internal customer refers to the provider of care, namely physicians, nurses and administrative staff operating in a healthcare organization, whereas the external customer is the consumer of care, namely patients, their families and society.

In the following sections of the chapter, the main approaches of quality management thinking concerning the linkage between internal and external customer satisfaction in the healthcare sector are proposed. In the historical evolution of the theory, it is possible to evidence an implicit or explicit recognition of this relationship's significance that seems to be growingly crucial in pursuing service quality improvement.

This chapter is organized as follows. First, the main theories and methods on service quality are described using a funnel-viewpoint (generic to specific). The focus is tracing through a historical evolution of the leading quality management approaches linking internal and external perspectives. Second, a brief overview of service quality dimensions in healthcare is presented. Then, three case studies are presented to show practical implications in the healthcare sector.

2 Theory and Methods for Measuring Service Quality Through the Lens of Internal and External Satisfaction

In this paragraph, theoretical background on the pivotal model of service quality is provided to shed lights on the valorization of the internal-external customer chain. Specifically, the following model is presented and discussed:

GAP model and its evolution, Valdani and Busacca's model, Service Blueprint, Service Profit Chain, Performance Excellence Models and Service Excellence Chain.

The GAP Model and Its Evolution

Parasuraman et al. (1991) theorized that the GAP model was theorized after a rigorous analysis based on a wide-ranging multi-sectoral study highlighting the leading factors that determined the evaluations' quality the services by customers. It is based on the expectation-confirmation theory (Oliver, 1980), and it illustrates how consumers assess quality.

The conceptual scheme of the GAP model proposed by the three authors is proposed below (see Fig. 1).

The GAP model is based on the assumption that the quality of service perceived by customers can be defined as the degree of deviation between customer expectations and their perceptions. Thus, the GAP between expected and perceived quality measures the degree of customer satisfaction concerning the service provided by the company and can, in turn, be broken down into five GAPs, which can, in turn, occur in the planning, design and delivery of the service.

The model foresaw the following five GAPs:

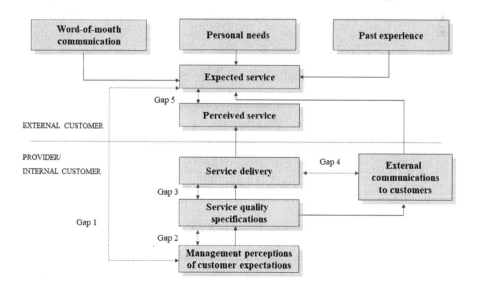

Fig. 1 GAP model. (Source: Parasuraman et al., 1991)

- GAP 1: the difference between customer expectations and how the management interprets them. This GAP is determined, in most cases, by the lack and inaccuracy of external and internal information (the former obtained, for example, from market research, the latter deriving from the analysis of complaints, inappropriate interpretation of data by managers, etc.).
- GAP 2: the difference between how managers have interpreted customer expectations and how they have been transformed into service design phase service specifications. In this case, the GAP can be associated with the difficulty of transforming generic characteristics into service standards.
- GAP 3: the difference between the service provided and the pre-established quality standards. This GAP can be determined by the reluctance and/or the inability of the contact staff to realize, during the service delivery phase, the designed specifications; it can be related to the insufficient capacity of the staff to give customer assistance, poor qualification of the team, lack of adequate training and inadequacy of internal systems for supporting contact personnel;
- GAP 4: the difference between the promised service, defined through external communication to customers and the delivered service.
- GAP 5: The consequence of the four GAPs presented is the leading cause of customer dissatisfaction.

In particular, GAP 1 and 2 evidence the vital role of the management is being aware of the customers' needs and planning the service design process. On the other hand, GAP 3 highlights the crucial role of human resources in service delivery and creates service quality based on pre-established standards. How this delivery is carried out certainly has a significant impact on customer satisfaction. Hence, the GAP model evidences the staff's crucial role in delivering service quality (GAP 3), implicitly assuming that it can influence customer satisfaction/dissatisfaction (GAP 5).

Based on the GAP model, the SERVQUAL survey is the most acknowledged tool for assessing service quality, comparing customer expectations with their delivered service experience.

It examines service quality using a Likert-scale questionnaire that measures the following dimension of service quality—previously defined: Tangibles, Reliability, Responsiveness, Assurance and Empathy (Parasuraman et al., 1991; Parasuraman et al., 2002).

The SERVQUAL scale consists of 44 questions based on the five components mentioned above and proposed in a questionnaire. The first 22-item group surveys customer expectations, whereas the second 22-item group deals with customer perceptions of the service consumption, using a Likert scale.

The SERVQUAL survey is created and used to investigate internal and external customer satisfaction, giving relevance to the staff satisfaction even if there is not, posed by the authors, an explicit linkage with the customer's satisfaction.

Numerous authors have contributed worldwide to adopt the GAP model and use the SERVQUAL tool during the last decade. Mauri et al. (2013) proposed an interesting systematic literature review of the GAP model from 1985 to 2013, emphasizing strengths and criticisms related to the GAP model and SERVQUAL instrument that emerged to be the most acknowledged and rigorous theoretical cornerstone.

Frost and Kumar (2000) proposed the "Internal Service Quality Model" as an adaptation of the original "GAP Model" developed by Parasuraman. The model evaluated the dimensions and their relationships that determine service quality among internal customers (front-line staff) and internal suppliers (support staff) within a large service organization. It included three of the original five GAPs: GAP 1, 3 and 5.

Large and König (2009) proposed a model of internal service quality to improve the internal customer orientation of purchasing departments, evidencing four distinct service GAPs: performance GAP from the internal customers' perspective, performance GAP from the purchasers' perspective, expectation GAP and perception GAP.

Bitner et al. (2010) proposed integrating technology as a vital enabler for effectiveness and productivity in delivering services in the original GAP model. They illustrate some interesting strategies associated with the GAPs, underlining the need to align human resources to excellent practices and be aware of their role in generating customer satisfaction.

Valdani and Busacca's Model

Afterwards, an evolution of the GAP model was proposed by the Italian authors Valdani and Busacca, which in 1992 elaborated an enlarged version. What emerges from this model is a link among management, human resources and customers. The model proposed by Valdani and Busacca (Valdani & Busacca 1992; Valdani 1992) stated that "If we assume the service quality as the ability of the company to satisfy customer's needs, the customer satisfaction analysis can be focused on verifying the consonance among the following issues: (1) the quality planned by the top management; (2) the quality desired by the consumer; (3) the quality objectives perceived by company personnel; (4) the quality delivered by the market; (5) the quality perceived by the consumer". This model analyses the differences between the management's planned quality and the desired and perceived quality by the customer, the staff and the market. The perceptions of management and staff for internal processes (such as planning, implementation and delivery) and the relationships between the various organizational levels are analysed about internal GAPs. On the one hand, the external GAPs study the customer perspective regarding expectations and perceptions concerning the company's offer and the manager and staff, always concerning the company's request.

This model presents eight GAPs, and it can be applied to both products and services (Fig. 2).

The first GAP highlighted by the model is the "symphony GAP" (GAP 1), verifying the alignment between the quality planned by the company management and consumer expectations. It is determined by the inadequacy of the analysis of evolutionary trends related to market behaviour and needs by the difficulty in giving answers to its customers to their changing needs and the difficulty of the customer's ability to promptly declare their expectations. The "value GAP" (GAP 2) represents the difference between the expected quality and the quality perceived by the customer. Finally, the "perception GAP" (GAP 3) represents the difference between the satisfaction theoretically obtainable from the customer's service/product and perceived. The organization ability to

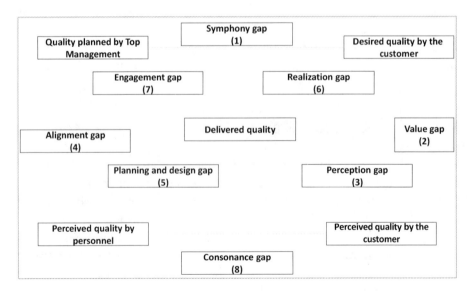

Fig. 2 Valdani and Busacca's model. (Source: Valdani & Busacca, 1992)

increase customer satisfaction is based on understanding the mental processes that govern the perception of the offer's quality and image characteristics.

The "alignment GAP" (GAP 4) represents the divergence between the quality planned by the top management and the quality standards perceived by the staff. The competitive success of a product/service depends on the organization's rate and the processes that lead to its conception and development. This GAP occurs if the management is not concerned with encouraging the participation of all the company's components by orienting them towards a unified vision on customer satisfaction problems. Management must implement effective internal communication, share the vision and values with the staff, and promptly disseminate company policies, strategies and objectives related to customer satisfaction.

The "planning and design GAP" (GAP 5) refers to the design process and represents the divergence between the company standards and the customer's actual needs. On the other hand, the "realization GAP" (GAP 6) represents the organization inability to ensure service/product compliance with the designed technical specifications. The "engagement GAP" (GAP 7) generally occurs in management-led change processes to spread the culture of customer satisfaction. It represents the deviation between planned standards and the level of delivered quality. The customer's needs can be met if all the company's components commit themselves consciously and achieve company objectives. Finally, the "consonance GAP" (GAP 8) represents the divergence between the quality standards perceived and declared by the staff and the customer's perceptions. This GAP has an impact on the credibility and corporate image.

What emerged from Valdani and Busacca's model is that they clearly express a connection between the personnel and the delivered service quality. The consonance GAP (GAP 8) represents the explicit connection between staff's and customers' satisfaction should be aligned to provide a good service/product quality level.

The Service Blueprint

The Service Blueprint (SB) is a helpful diagram able to visualize several service components, namely showing the customer journey backstage and on-stage activities (Shostack, 1982). As stated by Bitner et al. (2008), service providers generally use a service blueprint to visualize the dynamic service delivery process (Ryu et al., 2020). The map allowed highlighting the main activities of the service process delivery. It will enable the customer role in the workflow and even depicts the employees' viewpoint by highlighting the contact points between front office and back office.

The physical evidence and the adopted technologies in the process are illustrated in the diagram. Three lines are depicted: the line of interaction, the line of internal interaction and the visibility line.

The SB is a tool that proposes the utility to depict the front and back-end in the same diagram admitting that in the process management, it is fruitful to visualize the critical contact points between employees and customer together with the involved technologies and physical evidence.

The Service Profit Chain

The first theoretical model that directly expresses the importance of the relationship between internal and external customer satisfaction is the Service Profit Chain theory (SPC) (Heskett et al., 2008).

According to the SPC, employees' satisfaction indirectly affects customer satisfaction through employees' productivity and service value. The SPC model's core idea is that a direct relationship exists between profit, growth, customer loyalty, customer satisfaction, employee satisfaction, loyalty and productivity (Heskett et al., 1994, 2008). The linkages in the chain are proposed by Heskett et al. (2008) as follows: (1) profit and growth are stimulated primarily by customer loyalty; (2) loyalty is a direct result of customer satisfaction; (3) satisfaction is primarily influenced by the value of services provided to customers; (4) value is created by satisfied, loyal and productive employees; (5) employee satisfaction results primarily from high-quality support services and policies that enable employees to deliver results to customers. Finally, the authors have emphasized that organizational sub-units where employee perceptions positively allow achieving superior business performance (Gelade & Young, 2005) (Fig. 3).

Further studies based on the main assumptions of the SPC tried to demonstrate the connection between internal and external link by using quantitative techniques. In healthcare, Raharjo et al. (2015), contributed to show that there is a positive relationship between the level of satisfaction of the medical staffs and their patients.

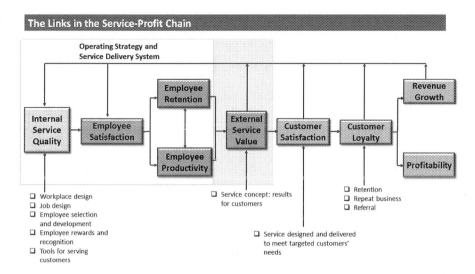

Fig. 3 The Service Profit Chain. (Source: Heskett et al., 1994)

Performance Excellence Models

Performance excellence models and the related awards (i.e. Malcolm Baldrige National Quality Award, Deming Award and European Foundation for Quality Management [EFQM], etc.) are consolidated frameworks that stimulate the competitiveness of private and public organizations among different cultures. They propose a holistic approach to organizations management for achieving sustainable success and performance excellence (Dahlgaard et al., 2011). These models recommend a holistic view to achieve excellence of performance in organizations.

In the structure of these frameworks, people and customers' role in terms of both enablers and achieved results are strongly valourized. For example, the Baldrige award model showed an interrelation among its seven categories that comprise the customer and workforce focus (Foster, 2017) (Fig. 4).

Specifically, the last version of the European Foundation for Quality Management (EFQM, 2019) is dedicated to organizations willing to achieve success by measuring their maturity level on the path to creating sustainable value. Engaging key stakeholders (such as people, customer, suppliers, etc.) is one of the main cornerstones proposed by the model for achieving sustainable value. According to the model, an outstanding organization provides results data for stakeholder perceptions and strategic and operational performance (Fig. 5).

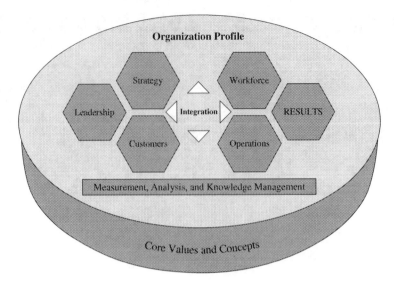

Fig. 4 Baldridge award framework. (Source: Foundation for the Malcolm Baldrige Award, 2015. Criteria for Performance Excellence, 2015)

Fig. 5 European Foundation for Quality Management framework. (Source: EFQM, 2019)

The Service Excellence Chain

An SPC evolution is the Service Excellence Chain (SEC) in the healthcare sector (Guglielmetti et al., 2020b). The model is focused on performance excellence that links organizational performance with employees' satisfaction and well-being and patients' satisfaction, jointly considering different approaches from the quality management theories—such as performance excellence models and the SPC. Moreover, the SEC proposed a quantitative tool for linking internal and external customer satisfaction with a unique index.

The SEC model was tested with structural equation models. It indicates that the organizational excellence perceptions affect the employees' satisfaction. The employees' perceptions of patients' satisfaction predict employee satisfaction and the level of well-being at work. On the other hand, the relation between patients experience and satisfaction affects the patients' loyalty. This concept is becoming even more important because patients' are growingly able to select where they take care of themselves. Loyalty is a mechanism that produces word of mouth that can affect the hospital image, contributing to building its attractiveness for both staff and patients (Fig. 6).

The Internal–External Global Satisfaction Index (IEGSI) is calculated as the linear combination of attribute evaluations with some weights (Musella et al., 2017). The index provides a numeric value of the patient satisfaction accounting for the employee satisfaction. Overall, it can predict organizational and service quality improvement.

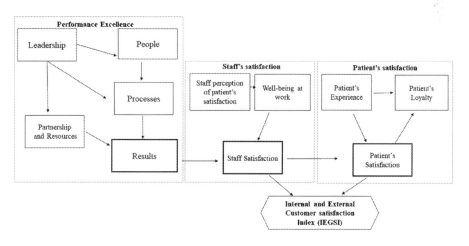

Fig. 6 Service excellence chain in healthcare. (Source: Guglielmetti et al., 2020)

Internal–External Global Satisfaction Index (IEGSI)
$IEGSI = mean(X_j) * mean(Y_j) * w_j$ X = patient satisfaction by unit/ward Y = employee satisfaction by unit/ward w = unit/ward relevance for managers (uniform in this case) j = 1, 2 unit/wards

Source: Guglielmetti et al., 2020

SEC and IEGSI contributed to connecting employees' and customers' satisfaction by using advanced statistical techniques. They promote the adoption of quality management thinking in the healthcare sector, conjointly measuring and monitoring employees' and patients' satisfaction, endorsing the awareness that this linkage is key to accomplishing service excellence.

From Theory to Practice

Our findings suggest that there is a growing interest in literature for the analysis of the relationship between customers and employees satisfaction, mainly in the healthcare context, even because the emergent frameworks (i.e. EFQM, 2019) propose to handle sustainable organizations with a holistic approach considering the stakeholders' perceptions.

The implementation of the above concepts is proposed in three case studies that demonstrate the concrete implications in the real healthcare context.

In each case study, some theoretical issues are proposed as follows:

Case study	Main goal	Context	Related theoretical issues
One	Defining and designing service quality dimensions Measuring internal and external satisfaction in an emergency unit	The emergency unit within a hospital	Valdani and Busacca's GAP Model (Valdani & Busacca, 1992) GAP Model (Parasuraman et al., 1985) Service Blueprint Qualitative survey tools
Two	Measuring employees' and customers' satisfaction in hospitals	Cardiology and maternity units within a hospital	Performance Excellence Models Employees' satisfaction survey Picker's Patient Experience (PPE; Jenkinson et al., 2002)
Three	Linking with index employees' and customers' satisfaction in hospitals	Cardiology and maternity units within a hospital	Service Excellence Chain IEGSI Index (Guglielmetti et al., 2020)

3 Case Studies on Patients' and Staff's Satisfaction in Healthcare

The following section analyses how measuring service quality in a hospital, highlighting that linking together employees' and customers' satisfaction is a crucial factor. It is not a simple task because the measurement process can be complex, and it can need the usage of advanced statistical techniques. Indeed, it is possible to develop surveys using qualitative and/or quantitative techniques for investigating employees' and customers' feedback. To collect reliable data, it is necessary to plan the surveys tool in a very rigorous model, obtaining hospital top management's engagement. Concerning the quantitative data, it is possible to link employees' and patients' satisfaction by applying advanced statistical techniques.

Case Study One: Defining and Designing Service Quality Dimensions in the Emergency Room

Hospitals are multifaceted organizations that are even more engaged in service quality delivery. Especially in the public area, they are worldwide characterized by budgetary pressure, cutbacks, recovery logic and waste reduction even though to the detriment of patients' dignity and service quality, having to face at the same time the growth of care requests at the public level due to the ageing phenomenon, the reduction of population incomes and the Covid-19 pandemic. Although efficiency and health expenditure seems to be related, there are opportunities for improvement without increasing health expenditure (Murray and Frenk, 1999). Inside a hospital, the more critical situation, in terms of performance efficiency, is evidenced within the Emergency Department, mainly characterized by overcrowding, staff and patients' dissatisfaction (Moskop et al., 2009). Hence, it is clear the need to improve the community and patients' well-being, in an inclusive and social perspective, implementing innovative solutions for simplifying the accessibility to the healthcare services and reducing waiting times, decreasing the level of stress for both patients and their families, optimizing the level of efficiency, effectiveness and flexibility. Some activities are completely "visible" to its customers in a hospital context, such as reception desks answering people's queries. These staffs operate in what is termed a front office. Other parts of the hospital have little, if any, customer "visibility", such as the surgery rooms. The medical staff perform vital but low-contact tasks in the back office (Slack et al., 2010).

760   R. Guglielmetti Mugion et al.

The emergency unit is, by its nature, one of the most critical areas within a hospital since it responds to a large variety of cases and represents the main point of access to emergency health services. A constant impossibility of planning activities characterizes their organization due to the continuous flow of the process and free access without reservation. The growing pressure for assistance and the consequent overcrowding of emergency rooms, the constant complaints related to waiting times and the scares attention to patients demonstrate how it is urgent to improve their delivered service quality.

Several actors are involved in the emergency unit operations, and the lack of coordination and communication can affect patients' and employees' satisfaction. It is vital to verify the consonance among the following issues: "(1) the quality planned by the hospital top management and by the emergency unit management; (2) the quality desired by the patient of the emergency room; (3) the quality objectives perceived by personnel operating in the emergency room; (4) the quality delivered by other hospitals; (5) the quality perceived by the patient" (Valdani & Busacca, 1992).

As suggested by the GAP model, the healthcare quality dimensions' definition can be adapted from the service theory (Parasuraman et al., 1985). The SB is also helpful in depicting the workflow of the process and identifying the level of visibility among the involved actors.

Table 1 Emergency department quality dimensions adapted by the GAP model

Service quality dimensions	Adaptation for the emergency unit
Tangible aspects	It is the physical comfort of the healthcare provider. It represents the hygiene conditions and adequateness of service facilities equipment and technologies, waiting rooms and spaces, exterior aspect/appearance of medical, nurses and administrative staff.
Service reliability	It is the ability of the healthcare provider to dependably and accurately perform the promised service. As a result, patients receive the most appropriate treatment, and it is carried out accurately.
Responsiveness	It is the willingness of the healthcare provider to be helpful and prompt in providing service. For example, the time between requiring treatment and receiving it is kept to the minimum and for the time for test results.
Assurance	It is the competence and courtesy of the healthcare provider staff. Competent, courteous, friendly and helpful medical, nurses and administrative staff represent it.
Empathy	It is tailored attention to the patient. It is represented by the customized relationship established by medical and nurse's staff with their patients, promptly consulting and informing patients and their families, taking care of their specific needs by disclosing a sympathetic side and giving them emotional support.

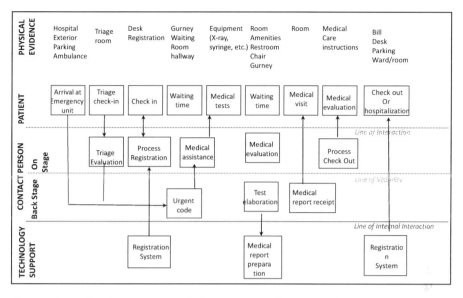

Fig. 7 The SB for the emergency delivery process of an Italian hospital. (Source: Own elaboration)

An analysis of the emergency department of an Italian hospital is proposed. Firstly, the service quality dimensions of the emergency service are identified as follows (Table 1).

Even if service design proposes addressing all these dimensions simultaneously (Foster, 2017), empathy represents one of the relevant dimensions for measuring patients' satisfaction (Jenkinson et al., 2002).

The emergency process is structured on the following main activities: reception and triage, waiting, medical assistance and post-emergency handling. The SB was mapped, and it shows several contact points between the front office (represented mainly by medical and nurses staff) and the customer/patients within an emergency room process (Fig. 7).

The hospital management declared that the emergency department has some problems such as handling a large number of patients—not always in dangerous conditions—overcrowding, long waiting times, and consequently system malfunctions, lack of updated information and general internal and external dissatisfaction.

A qualitative survey was developed involving patients and staff operating in the emergency department to identify the causes of dissatisfaction and plan some actions to improve the delivered service quality.

The tools used for data collection inside the emergency department were the following:

762   R. Guglielmetti Mugion et al.

Table 2 Qualitative surveys for measuring internal and external perceptions of an Italian emergency department

Qualitative survey type	Tool	Details	Numbers	Main results
Observation	Check-list	Details of the observation (date, time, area); patients details; Number of medical/ nurses staff; structure; waiting room for walking patients with soft triage; waiting room for family members	18 days Duration for each day: 3 hours	* Overcrowding * Scarce comfort of the waiting room * Poor personal communication of staff with patients * Lack of facilities in the waiting room * Poor hygiene conditions of hallways and waiting rooms
In-depth interview	Topic guide	Understanding the dynamics of the emergency unit, identify strength, weaknesses and improvement insights of their job and the emergency department	Four nurses, five physicians and a health executive	* Insufficient number of beds * Poor integration with other departments for post-emergency hospitalization * Inadequate logistics and layout of spaces * Non-optimal comfort of the environment * Lack of facilities for patients * Excessive bureaucratization of practices

* indirect observation, for analysing patients' viewpoint;
* in-depth interview for investigating healthcare professionals' perspectives (Table 2).

Quality Highlights Case One

First, it is essential to identify the context by analysing the service quality dimensions and mapping the service process delivery workflow, the involved actors and the interaction level. The comparison between the collected data from the two perspectives allows understanding that there is an alignment between staff and patients' perceptions of the emergency department's dissatisfaction.

Although the qualitative survey did not directly link employees' and patients' satisfaction, it provides valuable insights that allow identifying a coherence between the two perspectives.

Case Study Two: Measuring Employees' and Customers' Satisfaction in Hospitals[1]

This Italian hospital case describes how it is possible to measure employees' and patients' satisfaction by developing a quantitative survey and identifying potential opportunities to connect it. The hospital top management selects maternity and cardiology units as the survey object since they are strategic and need to improve their service quality level. This experience is the first empirical survey that contextually adopted the EFQM-based 4P model (Dahlgaard et al., 2011) and Picker's Patient Experience (PPE) Questionnaire (Jenkinson et al., 2002) to build the questionnaire structures. The former is devoted to collect employees' perception, and the latter aimed to investigate the level of patient satisfaction (Raharjo et al., 2016). Both questionnaires were simultaneously administered in the two hospital units; blocking the two wards within the same period allowed for a fairer comparison. The reason is the need to

Table 3 The questionnaire construct

Employees' questionnaire dimensions	Patients' questionnaire dimensions	Scaling
Leadership	Continuity and transition	7-point Likert scale
People	Coordination of care	7-point Likert scale
Partnership and resources	Emotional support	7-point Likert scale
Processes	Involvement of family and friend	7-point Likert scale
Product/service results	Information and education	7-point Likert scale
Overall employee satisfaction	Respect for patient preferences	7-point Likert scale
	Physical comfort (treatment)	7-point Likert scale
	Overall, patients' satisfaction	7-point Likert scale
	Patients' loyalty	7-point Likert scale

---

[1] Adapted by Raharjo, H., Guglielmetti Mugion, R., Di Pietro, L., & Toni, M. (2016). Do satisfied employees lead to satisfied patients? An empirical study in an Italian Hospital. *Total Quality Management & Business Excellence*.

collect perceptions related to some interactions between respondents. Matching the patients with the care providers requires additional data collection efforts but represents a crucial aspect because it is necessary to understand which medical/nurses team encountered a specific patient to depict the actual situation. In addition, Partial Least Square-Structural Equation Modelling (PLS-SEM) was used as a powerful statistical technique for identifying key drivers of employee and patient satisfaction and improvement priorities (Table 3).

An importance-performance matrix analysis (PLS-IPMA) was performed to relate the latent variable scores of overall satisfaction for the patients and the employees. The data were collected during the same period when the patients had some interactions with the employees. Note that the PLS-IPMA analysis converts the scale of 1 to 7 into 0 to 100. For details on the method, see Hair et al. (2014). According to the sample, it can be seen that the patients in the cardiology ward are more satisfied than those in the maternity ward (p-value = 0.011). However, there is insufficient evidence to say that the cardiology unit employees are more satisfied than those in the maternity unit (p-value = 0.327), although the mean and the median are higher than those of maternity. Note that this finding does not indicate that the two wards' employees have the same satisfaction level. The PLS-IPMA analysis also identifies key driver constructs or items for patient satisfaction and employee satisfaction. Using overall satisfaction as the target construct for both employees and patients, the plots for importance (total effects) and

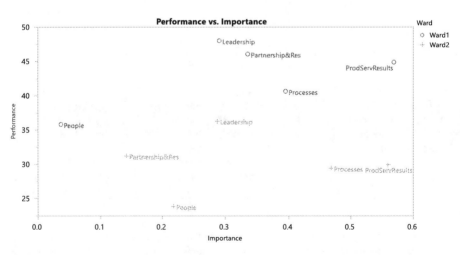

Fig. 8 IPMA for employee satisfaction model (Ward 1 = Maternity; Ward 2 = Cardiology)

Improving Service Quality Through Individuals' Satisfaction...

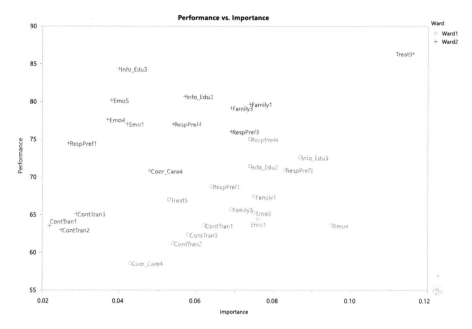

Fig. 9 IPMA for patient satisfaction model (Ward 1 = Maternity; Ward 2 = Cardiology)

performance (average latent scores) are shown in Figs. 8 and 9. Considering the number of indicators and constructs, we use constructs for the employee satisfaction model and indicators/items for the patient satisfaction model.

As shown in Fig. 8, Ward 1 generally has higher performance on all constructs. The construct "Products/Services results" is the most important predictor of employee satisfaction in both wards. The following crucial key driver is "Processes", which is higher in Ward 1 than in Ward 2. The importance of "Leadership" for employee satisfaction is relatively equal in both wards. Interestingly, among the role of "Partnership & Resources" and "People" in the two wards, "Partnership & Resources" is considerably more critical in the maternity ward than "People" for predicting employee satisfaction. In the cardiology ward, the reverse is true!

Another interesting observation is the emotional dimension of patient experience (Emo1, Emo4 and Emo5), which, to patient satisfaction, are much more important in the maternity ward (Ward 1) than in the cardiology unit (Ward 2).

766   R. Guglielmetti Mugion et al.

Table 4 The sample

Healthcare professionals sample	Patient sample
Total respondents: 73	Total respondents: 102
Maternity ward respondents: 41	Maternity ward respondents: 70
Cardiology ward respondents: 32	Cardiology ward respondents: 32

Table 5 The sample

Healthcare professionals' sample	Patient sample
Total respondents: 73	Total respondents: 314
Maternity ward respondents: 47	Maternity ward respondents: 157
Cardiology ward respondents: 26	Cardiology ward respondents: 157

Quality Highlights Case Two

The case revealed that the relationship between internal (employee) and external (patient) satisfaction is key. The PLS-SEM models provide helpful information for logically connecting the two viewpoints. Indeed, it emerged that a higher patient satisfaction level in one ward was associated with higher employee satisfaction in the same ward.

Case Study Three: Linking with Index Employees' and Customers' Satisfaction in Hospitals[2]

The third case is aimed at showing the more structured way to connect employees' and patients' satisfaction by adopting a quantitative index. Specifically, a quantitative survey was carried out in two wards in an Italian hospital located in the Sicily Region, namely maternity and cardiology units.

Concerning the patients' perspectives, it is the same Table 4, whereas, for the employee's perspective, the questionnaire structure is very similar to the one presented in Table 4. Still, it was optimized by adding a set of items for measuring the employees' satisfaction, well-being at work and employee perceptions related to patients' satisfaction. The surveys were administered face to face for each ward, interviewing at the same time both employees and patients. The observed sample is composed of 73 employees and 314 patients (Table 5).

As a result of the research, an overall index was realized to mathematically link internal and external satisfaction (see "The Service Excellence Chain" section). The IEGSI is modelled through Bayesian Networks (BN) and Object

---

[2] Adapted by Guglielmetti Mugion, R., Musella, F., Di Pietro, L., & Toni, M. (2020b). The "service excellence chain": An empirical investigation in the healthcare field. *The TQM Journal*.

Improving Service Quality Through Individuals' Satisfaction... 767

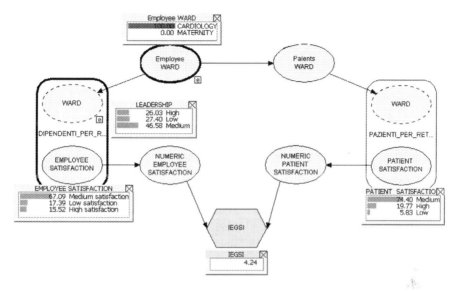

Fig. 10 IEGSI measure in the cardiology unit

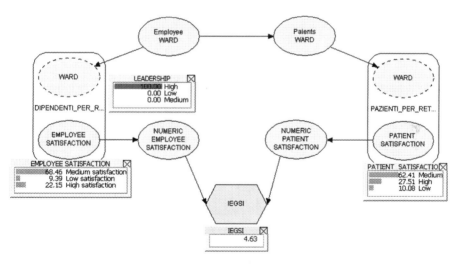

Fig. 11 OOBN scenario for IEGSI measure in the cardiology unit, acting on leadership

Oriented Bayesian Networks (OOBN). It provides an overall measure to predict organizational improvement, establishing the assumption that employees' engagement satisfaction and patients' satisfaction are directly connected.

Here following we show how we built the IEGSI index in the cardiology unit.

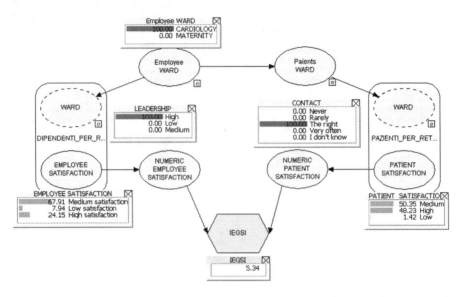

Fig. 12 OOBN scenario for IEGSI measure in the cardiology unit, acting both on leadership and patients' contact

Given a certain level of employee's satisfaction, the mean value of patient satisfaction accounting for internal satisfaction (IEGSI) is 4.24 (Fig. 10).

Thus, in the cardiology unit, the IEGSI is 4.24. Through the BN, it is possible to predict scenarios for improvement by acting on the available constructs. For example, if leadership is improved, the IEGSI increases from 4.24 to 4.63 (around 9%) (Fig. 11). Besides, by enhancing the patient contact until the level "adequate", the IEGSI increases to 5.34 (+16%) (Fig. 12).

Quality Highlights Case Three

Advanced statistical techniques support linking internal and external satisfaction through a unique, concise index, a terse and straightforward measure available for managers in the internal dashboard of Key Performance Indicators (KPIs). In addition, the simulation of scenarios for improvement can achieve performance effectiveness and efficiency by acting on available service quality dimensions and resources.

4 Summary

This chapter explained the relevance of measuring the linkage between internal and external satisfaction for pursuing service quality improvement. A synergic approach between employees' and patients' satisfaction is vital for companies and healthcare organizations for planning continuous improvement of delivered services.

Several models and tools highlighted the importance of customer focus and employee involvement in the quality management theories. An evolution of these approaches is retraced by emphasizing the employees-customers-satisfaction chain. The practical implications are described in three cases contextualized in healthcare hospitals and an emergency unit. This chapter contributes to research-based knowledge on healthcare service quality that is even more willing to enhance individuals' well-being, organizations and societies by pursuing a sustainable value.

References

Ahmed, E. S., Ahmad, M. N., & Othman, S. H. (2019). Business process improvement methods in healthcare: A comparative study. *International Journal of Health Care Quality Assurance, 32*(5), 887–908. https://doi.org/10.1108/IJHCQA-07-2017-0116

Albrecht, K., & Zemke, R. (1985). *Service America! Doing business in the new economy*. Dow Jones-Irwin.

Anderson, L., & Ostrom, A. L. (2015). Transformative service research: Advancing our knowledge about service and well-being. *Journal of Service Research, 18*(3), 243–249.

Bitner, M. J., Ostrom, A. L., & Morgan, F. N. (2008). Service blueprinting. A practical technique for service innovation. *California Management Review, 50*(3), 66–94.

Bitner, M. J., Zeithaml, V. A., & Gremler, D. D. (2010). Technology's impact on the GAPs model of service quality. In *Handbook of service science* (pp. 197–218).

Chen, T., Dodds, S., Finsterwalder, J., Witell, L., Cheung, L., Falter, M., Garry, T., Snyder, H., & McColl-Kennedy, J. R. (2020). Dynamics of well-being co-creation: A psychological ownership perspective. *Journal of Service Management*, ahead-of-print. https://doi.org/10.1108/JOSM-09-2019-0297

Chi, C. G., & Gursoy, D. (2009). Employee satisfaction, customer satisfaction, and financial performance: An empirical examination. *International Journal of Hospitality Management, 28*(2), 245–253.

Dahlgaard, J. J., Pettersen, J., & Dahlgaard-Park, S. M. (2011). Quality and lean health care: A system for assessing and improving the health of healthcare organizations. *Total Quality Management & Business Excellence, 22*(6), 673–689.

Donabedian, A. (1988). The quality of care: How can it be assessed? *JAMA, 260*(12), 1743–1748.

Duffy, J. A. M., & Ketchand, A. A. (1998). Examining the role of service quality in overall service satisfaction. *Journal of Managerial Issues*, 240–255.

Edgar, F., Geare, A., Saunders, D., Beacker, M., & Faanunu, I. (2017). A transformative service research agenda: A study of workers' well-being. *Service Industries Journal, 37*(1), 84–104. https://doi.org/10.1080/02642069.2017.1290797

EFQM. (2019). *Improving organizations.* www.efqm.org

Foster, S. T. (2017). *Managing quality. Integrating the supply chain.* Pearson.

Foundation for the Malcolm Baldrige Award. (2015). *Criteria for performance excellence, 2015.*

Frost, F. A., & Kumar, M. (2000). INTSERVQUAL – An internal adaptation of the GAP model in a large service organization. *Journal of Services Marketing, 14*(5), 358–377.

Garvin, D. (1984). What does 'product quality really mean?'. *Sloan Management Review*, 25–43.

Gelade, G. A., & Young, S. (2005). Test of a service profit chain model in the retail banking sector. *Journal of Occupational and Organizational Psychology, 78*(1), 1–22.

George, W. R. (1977). The retailing of services: A challenging future. *Journal of Retailing*, 85–98.

Groene, O., Klazinga, N., Wagner, C., Arah, O. A., Thompson, A., Bruneau, C., & Sũol, R. (2010). Investigating organizational quality improvement systems, patient empowerment, organizational culture, professional involvement and the quality of care in European hospitals: The "Deepening our Understanding of Quality Improvement in Europe (DUQuE)" project. *BMC Health Services Research, 10*, 1–10. https://doi.org/10.1186/1472-6963-10-281

Guglielmetti Mugion, R. G., Arcese, G., Toni, M., & Silvestri, L. (2020a). Life cycle management and sharing economy: methodological framework and application in sustainable mobility. In *Customer satisfaction and sustainability initiatives in the fourth industrial revolution* (pp. 152–166). IGI Global.

Guglielmetti Mugion, R., Musella, F., Di Pietro, L., & Toni, M. (2020b). The "service excellence chain": An empirical investigation in the healthcare field. *The TQM Journal.* https://doi.org/10.1108/TQM-11-2018-0181

Hair Jr, J. F., Sarstedt, M., Hopkins, L., & Kuppelwieser, V. G. (2014). Partial least squares structural equation modeling (PLS-SEM): An emerging tool in business research. *European Business Review.*

Harter, J. K., Schmidt, F. L., & Hayes, T. L. (2002). Business-unit-level relationship between employee satisfaction, employee engagement, and business outcomes: A meta-analysis. *Journal of Applied Psychology, 87*(2), 268.

Hartline, M. D., Maxham, J. G., III, & McKee, D. O. (2000). Corridors of influence in disseminating customer-oriented strategy to customer contact service employees. *Journal of Marketing, 64*(2), 35–50.

Sasser, W. E., Schlesinger, L. A., & Heskett, J. L. (1997). *Service profit chain.* Simon and Schuster.

Heskett, J. L. (2002). Beyond customer loyalty. *Managing Service Quality: An International Journal.*

Heskett, J. L., Jones, T. O., Loveman, G. W., Sasser, W. E., & Schlesinger, L. A. (1994). Putting the service-profit chain to work. *Harvard Business Review, 72*(2), 164–174.

Jaakkola, E., Helkkula, A. and Aarikka-Stenroos, "Service experience co-creation: conceptualization, implications, and future research directions", *Journal of Service Management, 26*(2), 182–205. https://doi.org/10.1108/JOSM-12-2014-0323.

Jenkinson, C., Coulter, A., & Bruster, S. (2002). The Picker Patient Experience Questionnaire: Development and validation using data from in-patient surveys in five countries. *International Journal for Quality in Healthcare, 14*(5), 353–358.

Kaartemo, V., & Känsäkoski, H. (2018). Information and knowledge processes in health care value co-creation and co-destruction. *SAGE Open, 8*(4). https://doi.org/10.1177/2158244018820482

Large, R. O., & König, T. (2009). A GAP model of purchasing's internal service quality: Concept, case study and internal survey. *Journal of Purchasing and Supply Management, 15*(1), 24–32.

Lovelock, C., & Wirtz, J. (2010). *Services marketing: People, technology, strategy* (7th ed.). Prentice-Hall Series in Marketing.

Mauri, A. G., Minazzi, R., & Muccio, S. (2013). A review of literature on the GAPs model on service quality: A 3-decades period: 1985–2013. *International Business Research, 6*(12), 134.

Moskop, J. C., Sklar, D. P., Geiderman, J. M., Schears, R. M., & Bookman, K. J. (2009). Emergency department crowding, part 1—Concept, causes, and moral consequences. *Annals of Emergency Medicine, 53*(5), 605–611.

Murray, C. J., & Frenk, J. (1999). *A WHO framework for health system performance assessment.* World Health Organization.

Musella, F., Guglielmetti Mugion, R., Raharjo, H., Di Pietro, L., & Toni, M. (2017). Reconciling internal and external satisfaction through probabilistic graphical models: An empirical Study. *International Journal of Quality and Service Sciences, 9*(3/4), 347–370.

Nasr, L., Burton, J., Gruber, T., & Kitshoff, J. (2014). Exploring the impact of customer feedback on the well-being of service entities: A TSR perspective. *Journal of Service Management, 25*(4), 531–555.

Nasr, L., Burton, J., & Gruber, T. (2015). When good news is bad news: The negative impact of positive customer feedback on front-line employee well-being. *Journal of Services Marketing, 29*(6–7), 599–612. https://doi.org/10.1108/JSM-01-2015-0052

Oliver, R. L. (1980). A cognitive model of the antecedents and consequences of satisfaction decision. *Journal of Marketing Research, 17*(11), 460–469.

Ostrom, A. L., Bitner, M. J., Brown, S. W., Burkhard, K. A., Goul, M., Smith-Daniels, V., & Rabinovich, E. (2010). Moving forward and making a difference: Research priorities for the science of service. *Journal of Service Research, 13*(1), 4–36.

Parasuraman, A., Zeithaml, V. A., & Berry, L. L. (1985). A conceptual model of service quality and its implications for future research. *Journal of Marketing, 49*(4), 41–50.

Parasuraman, A., Berry, L. L., & Zeithaml, V. A. (1991). Understanding customer expectations of service. *Sloan Management Review, 32*(3), 39–48.

Parasuraman, A., Berry, L., & Zeithaml, V. (2002). Refinement and reassessment of the SERVQUAL scale. *Journal of Retailing, 67*(4), 114–139.

Raharjo, H., Mugion, R. G., Eriksson, H., Gremyr, I., Di Pietro, L., & Renzi, M. F. (2015). Excellence models in the public sector. Relationships between enablers andresults. *International Journal of Quality and Service Sciences.*

Raharjo, H., Guglielmetti Mugion, R., Di Pietro, L., & Toni, M. (2016). Do satisfied employees lead to satisfied patients? An empirical study in an Italian hospital. *Total Quality Management & Business Excellence, 27*(7–8), 853–874.

Rupp, D., Holub, S., & Grandey, A. (2007). A cognitive-emotional theory of customer injustice and emotional labor: Implications for customer service, fairness theory, and the multifocal perspective. In D. DeCremer (Ed.), *Advances in the psychology of justice and effect, information age* (pp. 199–226).

Ryu, D. H., Lim, C., & Kim, K. J. (2020). Development of a service blueprint for the online-to-offline integration in service. *Journal of Retailing and Consumer Services, 54*, 101944.

Shostack, G. (1982). How to design a service. *European Journal of Marketing, 16*(1), 49–63.

Slack, N., Chambers, S., & Johnston, R. (2010). *Operations management.* Pearson Education.

Valdani, E. (1992). L'impresa Proattiva. Un nuovo modello di impresa per generare valore. *Economia & Management, N. 4.*

Valdani, E., & Busacca, B. (1992). Customer satisfaction: Una Nuova Sfida. *Economia & Management, N. 2.*

Yi, Y., & Gong, T. (2012). Customer value co-creation behavior: Scale development and validation. *Journal of Business Research, 66*(9), 1279–1284.

Yoon, M. H., & Suh, J. (2003). Organizational citizenship behaviors and service quality as external effectiveness of contact employees. *Journal of Business Research, 56.*

Service Productivities' Next Top-Models

Christiane Hipp and Silvia Gliem

1 Introduction

The pressure for service companies for productivity does not mainly arise from exogenous conditions like the market mechanism but endogenous ones. Elements of a culture for productivity and innovation such as the people working for the organisation, management and leadership culture (Aarons et al., 2011; Akin & Hopelain, 1986, pp. 21–27) are the leverage-points for productivity improvements and conditions service companies can influence setting impulses from within necessary to implement changes for the good of productivity improvements.

There are three actors in a service process. They form the service triad, which consists of service customers, the service company, and the employees working in the frontline of service provision (Carson et al., 1997, pp. 100–102). The so-called frontline employees or customer contact employees (Chebat & Kollias, 2000; Hartline et al., 2000) actively participate together in the production of the service (Gummesson, 1998, p. 8; Nerdinger & Pundt, 2018, p. 4; Wirtz & Ehret, 2017, p. 32). In these "moments of truth" (Bitner et al., 2000, p. 139), customer value co-creation or value co-production (Gummesson, 1998, p. 8; Vargo & Lusch, 2004, p. 11) takes place. During these phases of co-creation, things can go wrong. Hence, there are several

---

C. Hipp (✉) • S. Gliem
Brandenburg University of Technology Cottbus-Senftenberg, Cottbus, Germany
e-mail: christiane.hipp@b-tu.de; gliem@b-tu.de

© The Author(s), under exclusive license to Springer Nature Switzerland AG 2022

773

B. Edvardsson, B. Tronvoll (eds.), *The Palgrave Handbook of Service Management*,
https://doi.org/10.1007/978-3-030-91828-6_37

points in a service process where there can be co-destruction instead of co-creation (Echeverri & Skålén, 2011; Kashif & Zarkada, 2015; Plé & Chumpitaz Cáceres, 2010). For example, customers are not able to communicate their wishes correctly or forget to bring along an object or information needed for the service process. In such situations, it is the frontline employees' job to anticipate these can-go-wrong-things and, in any case, cushion and guide the customers along the steps of the service process to make it as productive as possible.

Research has recognised the relevance of frontline employees (Larivière et al., 2017; Rafaeli et al., 2017) in their function not only as service process facilitators but also as essential for customer retention (Ganesh, 2016; Hennig-Thurau, 2004; Singh, 2000), word-of-mouth (Collier et al., 2018; Lim et al., 2017; Verleye et al., 2016), service failure tolerance (Chebat & Kollias, 2000; Liao, 2007; Wenchao, 2009) and service recovery (Van Vaerenbergh & Orsingher, 2016), customer perceived quality (Dhar, 2015; Prentice, 2013), customer satisfaction (Jha et al., 2013; Rod et al., 2016), or interaction quality (Clemes et al., 2011; Ekinci & Dawes, 2009)—to name a few.

Needless to say, frontline employees are not the only leverage-point for service productivity improvement. Others, such as technology, described by Ostrom et al. (2015, p. 129) as "cross-cutting" research priority, or customer participation in service processes (Jo Bitner, Faranda, Hubbert, & Zeithaml, 1997; Kelley et al., 1990), are as well leverage-points for service productivity but will not be addressed in this context. This chapter aims to create a theoretical basis and therefore conducts a review of service productivity models that account for frontline employees. This examination of the service productivity models is relevant for an empirical analysis of frontline employee influencing factors that should follow in later research. The remainder of this chapter is structured as follows: Section 2 shows that service and service productivity are multi-layered concepts. Basic views on both concepts are discussed from which requirements for service productivity models are derived. Then, there is the review of the service productivity models. Starting with a description of the essential components of the model, model changes, additions, and further developments are discussed. The previously derived conclusions regarding service productivity models are integrated into the considerations. In the synopsis, the authors offer the reader a brief summary of the streams in service productivity research that arose from the review and were reflected in the models presented. They conclude with challenges for future model development and next steps in research.

Service Productivities' Next Top-Models   775

2 Definition of Fundamental Concepts: Service and Service Productivity

Many service definitions and classifications show that a service needs an object or person to conduct the service. This object or person is the so-called *external factor* (Hill, 1977, p. 337, 1999, p. 428). Lovelock (1983, p. 12) showed in his classification that the external factor is diverse and can be of a tangible and intangible nature. More interaction with the external factor "customer" goes together with a loss of control, and what is value co-creation can turn into value co-destruction (Chase, 1978, p. 138). With the rise of ICT, there took place a reduction in customer-provider interaction. At the same time, new ICT provided ways for service providers to interact with the customer, also reducing interactions with the customer (Bitner, 2001; Vuorinen et al., 1998). Therefore, the classification into low- and high-contact service is no longer sufficient. Instead, the classification into low-, high-, and contact-only-when-needed service better reflects the variability of service interactions in the different service industries.

The discussion above showed that the definition of what a service constitutes is ambiguous and subject to discussion. When diving deeper into a specific service class and a specific service industry, a detailed description of its peculiarities is recommended. However, at this point, service is defined in a broader sense. Service is defined as a process producing an observable change at the external factor (customers or customer's objects).

Closely related to the discussion about service definition is the definition of service productivity (Dobni et al., 2000, p. 92). Taking a look at service productivity research reveals that one possible reason for the missing consensual definition of service productivity might be missing "conceptual clarity" (Johnston & Jones, 2004; Lehmann & Kölling, 2010; Rutkauskas & Paulavičiene, 2005). Productivity embraces efficiency, efficacy, and performance, as well as utilisation, quality, and predictability (Johnston & Jones, 2004, p. 202; Lehmann & Kölling, 2010, p. 4). Alternatively, when reflecting upon productivity detached from a service point of view, it is the other way around. It is "the central core" and "purely a physical phenomenon" (Tangen, 2005, p. 43) that is wrapped by profitability and then by performance in the triple P-model (Tangen, 2005, p. 43; firstly published in Tangen, 2002; see Fig. 1).

Then, as indicated by Jääskeläinen (2009, p. 448, 2010, pp. 25–26), the analysis level differs. For example, Babin and Boles (1998, p. 82) defined productivity as part of individual job performance (micro-level). Many researchers adapted this definition, for example, Karatepe and his peers (Karatepe & Uludag, 2008; Karatepe, 2013; Karatepe & Aleshinloye, 2009; Karatepe et al., 2006, 2014; Karatepe & Kilic, 2007) as well as Hussain et al. (2003, p. 2), and Gibbs and Ashill (2013, p. 306). Dewettinck and Buyens (2006, p. 11) considered productivity as part of the supervisor-rated performance (micro-level) and economic performance (macro- or meso-level).

Besides different levels of analysis of productivity and its unclear character, there is still the traditional view of productivity as a concept representing an output-input relation (Vuorinen et al., 1998, p. 379). This concept evolved from the manufacturing industries. It does not give credit for the complexity of service and thus is not directly transferable to the service industry (Hill, 1999; Jääskeläinen, 2009; Johnston & Jones, 2004; Nordgren, 2009; Parasuraman, 2002, 2010; Sahay, 2005, p. 10; Vuorinen et al., 1998). Drucker (1991, p. 72) admitted that there is more than one way to increase productivity in manufacturing, but "In Knowledge and service work, working smarter is the only key. What is more, it is a more complex key, one that requires looking closely […]". Grönroos and Ojasalo (2004, p. 416) talk of "open systems." Accordingly, what productivity encompasses and what it means to improve it differs. Finally, one could translate this discussion into a requirement for service productivity models. Service productivity models shall combine knowledge from several disciplines, for example, operations management, human resource management, and service science. In other words, service productivity models should incorporate interdisciplinary learnings.

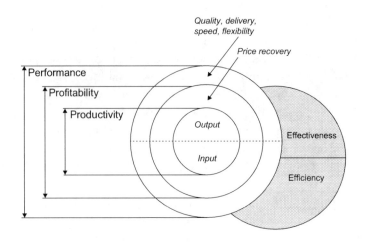

Fig. 1 The triple P-model (Tangen, 2005, Figure 2)

3 Service Productivities' Next Top-Models

To promote a clear arrangement of the models, the differentiation between different schools of thought applied in service quality research (e.g., Barnes, 2017; Ekinci et al., 1998; Gummesson & Grönroos, 2012) was adopted for service productivity models and extended by a German School. This classification of service productivity models into schools of thought was considered appropriate because of the increased transparency and visibility of previous research contributions.

Only those models are presented, which offer the possibility to account for frontline employees in some form. The fact that service productivity and service quality are to be researched jointly is also reflected in the research activities of the prominent representatives of the various schools of thought. Thus, some representatives' research activities are not limited to service productivity alone and include research in service quality.

Nordic School: Service Productivity Models of Grönroos, Gummesson, and Ojasalo

Various service productivity models belong to the Nordic School. Prominent representatives of the Nordic School are, amongst others, Grönroos, Ojasalo, and Gummesson. Grönroos (1990) early acknowledged that services have to be treated differently in marketing (and later productivity) than in the manufacturing industry. In his often-quoted service quality model, Grönroos (1984, pp. 36–37) elaborates on the gap between the expected and actual perceived quality by the customer. He points out that the image of the firm models this gap. A superior image of the firm increases customer expectations that, when not met, widens the gap between expected and perceived service quality (Grönroos, 1984, p. 40).

Gummesson (1991, p. 60) introduced the concept of part-time marketers. These can be customers or employees that do marketing—but not as their primary field of dedication. With this concept, Gummesson (1987, p. 17) assigned minor roles to marketing and sales departments of services firms and major relevance to other personnel, for example, the frontline employees (Gummesson, 1998, p. 8). He emphasises the necessity to see service marketing as a holistic and not as a unidirectional and isolated task (Gummesson, 1987, p. 17). Through his views on service marketing and associated research, he triggered the development of relationship marketing research. At the centre of his "total relationship marketing approach" (Gummesson & Grönroos,

2012, p. 486) are 30 relationships in four groups. One group targets special market relations, for example, between frontline employees and customers (Gummesson, 1996, p. 33). Moreover, he sees the service encounter as one source for service productivity (Gummesson, 1998, p. 8). He favours the assumption that frontline employees as one of the leading actors in service encounters are influential drivers of service productivity. Therefore, frontline employees encompass a significant research object.

Grönroos and Ojasalo (2004, p. 417) created a service productivity model beyond the traditional productivity concept established in the manufacturing industries. Rather than a ratio of input and output, they understand service productivity as a function of three interrelated efficiencies (internal efficiency, external efficiency, and capacity efficiency). Internal and external efficiencies "describe how efficiently a firm converts resources internally and how effectively it creates external interest in the conversion output" (Grönroos & Ojasalo, 2004, p. 416). They adopted the concepts of internal and external efficiency from Ekholm (1984 as cited in Grönroos & Ojasalo, 2004, p. 416).

Figure 2 displays the model showing an input- and an output-side. On the input side, there are two components: the service provider's inputs and the service customer's inputs. Personnel is listed as service provider input. Frontline employees form one group of personnel of service providers and, as such, are incorporated into the model. As indicated by the suspension points in the service provider input box, the list of service provider inputs is incomplete. It reveals the researchers' awareness that service productivity assessment may require different inputs and, depending on the service, more or fewer inputs.

The output side consists of four components: output quality, the service provider's image, customer perceived quality, and output quantity. The output quality is assumed to be directly related to the service providers' image and indirectly to customer perceived quality, making the service provider's image a mediator. The firm's image is a component of Grönroos' service quality model and consists of functional and technical quality. Technical quality points to the result of the service process, and functional quality denotes how the result of the service process is delivered to the customer (Grönroos, 1984, pp. 38–39). Thus, frontline employees are incorporated into the service provider inputs on the input and output sides. On the output side, functional quality embodies service delivery quality, which cannot do without frontline employees. In sum, generating "a certain level of perceived service quality with a given resource structure" (Grönroos & Ojasalo, 2004, p. 416) is the service organisation's ability to uphold external efficiency.

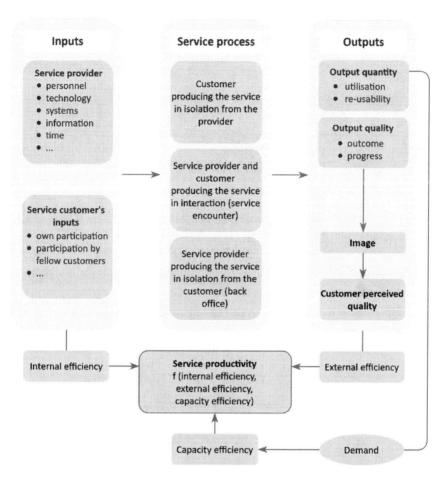

Fig. 2 Service productivity model of Grönroos and Ojasalo. (Source: Grönroos & Ojasalo, 2004, p. 418)

The internal and external efficiency profit from mutual learning (Grönroos & Ojasalo, 2004, 2015; Lasshof, 2006). In these "learning relationships" (Grönroos & Ojasalo, 2004, p. 419), service customers gain knowledge of how to participate in the service process efficiently and become more competent over time (Grönroos & Ojasalo, 2015, p. 300). Service providers get to know how to guide customers efficiently through the service process and become aware that different types of customers have different needs (Grönroos, 1999).

The third efficiency completing the service productivity function is the capacity efficiency that depicts the "management of demand" (Grönroos & Ojasalo, 2004, p. 417). Capacity efficiency has a direct relationship with the demand that, in turn, is directly related to output quantity. The output quantity is relevant for capacity efficiency. It serves to capture if the service can be utilised or re-utilised when not consumed (Grönroos & Ojasalo, 2004, p. 418).

The inputs and outputs are combined during the service process, consisting of three phases: two phases where either customer or provider act alone and the service encounter (cf. middle column in Fig. 2; Grönroos & Ojasalo, 2004, p. 417). Dependent on the service, one or two of these three phases dominate the other. For example, in low-contact service, the service encounter is rather short, whereas in high-contact service, the service encounter is of great importance. Additionally, for a contact-only-when-needed service, the service encounter might be of no importance at all when the service transaction proceeds without complications.

Although Grönroos' and Ojasalo's approach to define service productivity as a function of internal, external, and capacity efficiency is considered a novelty, there is still an input- and output-side as a clear link to traditional productivity concepts. It is open to discussion whether it is necessary to unplug service productivity models entirely from this component of traditional productivity concepts. Notwithstanding this argument, other researchers stuck to the "ratio aspect" of service productivity (e.g., Rutkauskas & Paulavičiene, 2005, p. 31; Vuorinen et al., 1998, p. 380), in which, for example, also front-line employees have their place.

North American School

Similarly to the Nordic School, the North American School initially focused on service quality research. In contrast to the Nordic School, the North American School developed service quality models ready to apply in practice (Ekinci et al., 1998, p. 63). The main contributors to the North American School are Parasuraman, Zeithaml, and Berry (1985) with the service gap model (1), Cronin and Taylor (1992) with the SERVPERF approach (2), Johnston and Jones (2004) with their service productivity model (3), and Parasuraman (2002, 2010) with his Dual-Perspective Framework of Service Productivity (4).

1. Service Gap Model by Parasuraman et al. (1985)

The service gap model by Parasuraman et al. (1985) can be considered highly influential in service research. The influence of this model is also shown by the vast amount of replication studies (replication studies conducted between 1988 and 2008 are reviewed by Ladhari (2009); newer studies are, for example, Ali and Raza (2015), Li et al. (2015), Roslan et al. (2015)). Also, the critical appraisal (Babakus & Boller, 1992; T. J. Brown et al., 1993; Buttle, 1996) resulted in the continuous development, modification, and improvement of the service gap model by Parasuraman and his colleagues (Parasuraman et al., 1993, 1994, 1991a, 1991b) as well as by other researchers (e.g., Babakus & Boller, 1992; Frost & Kumar, 2000; Lai et al., 2007; Luk & Layton, 2002; Murmann, 1999, p. 17) prove its relevance. Moreover, the publication and open discussion triggered the development of new models, for example, SERVPERF by Cronin and Taylor (1992) or the model of service quality of direct and indirect customer contact scenarios by Murmann (1999, p. 77).

The service gap model aims to improve customer perceived service quality (Parasuraman et al., 1985, pp. 46–48). By using qualitative research methods, five gaps were identified that target the difference between expectations and actual perceptions of different actors of the service triad (service customer, frontline employee, and service organisation) about different aspects of a service process (Parasuraman et al., 1985, pp. 43–45). As announced, the service gap model was subject to discussion (Babakus & Boller, 1992; Bitner et al., 2010; Buttle, 1996; Rosene, 2003), which nurtured the further development of the model (Parasuraman et al., 1991b) as well as the conceptualisation of new models such as the SERVPERF model.

2. SERVPERF Approach by Cronin and Taylor (1992)

Cronin and Taylor (1992, p. 59), who believe that service quality is a performance-based variable instead of the gap between expectation and perception of service (1992, pp. 56–57), developed the SERVPERF scale assessing service quality.

Therefore, they adopted the SERVQUAL scale and complemented it with items asking for the importance of the service quality dimensions and overall measures for customer assessed service quality, satisfaction, and purchase intentions (Cronin & Taylor, 1992, p. 60). The main difference between the service gap model and the SERVPERF approach is the perspective on service quality. Is it performance minus expectations or a broader comprehension of quality? SERVPERF maps service productivity by capturing the difference between customer expectations and perceived customer performance, the importance of the performance characteristics contained in the expectation and performance items, and three global indicators of overall service quality, overall satisfaction, and purchase intent (Cronin & Taylor, 1992, pp. 66–67).

As pointed out earlier, service productivity is an ambiguous concept, and one could interpret the performance component of SERVPERF as the incorporation of productivity. In other words, SERVPERF can be interpreted as a model of service productivity when considering performance as a productivity concept.

As the SERVQUAL instrument, SERVPERF was subject to discussions (Brady et al., 2002). The follow-up research contains SERVPERF scale applications, for example, in hospitality service (Unuvar et al., 2016) and educational service (Abdelkrim & Salim, 2015; Adedamola et al., 2016). However, the field is dominated by comparisons between the SERVQUAL and the SERVPERF scale: H. Lee et al. (2000); Adil et al. (2013); Mitra (2012); Aydin (2017); Machado et al. (2014).

3. Service Productivity Model by Johnston and Jones (2004)

In line with Parasuraman (2002, 2010), Johnston and Jones (2004, p. 202) point out that customer and provider sides must be considered when looking at service productivity. Thus, there are two productivities (cf. Fig. 3): operational productivity and customer productivity (Johnston & Jones, 2004, pp. 205–206).

Operational productivity is "a function of the ratio of operational outputs to inputs over a period, where inputs are materials, customers, staff, costs, etc. and outputs are customers, used resources, revenue, etc." (Johnston & Jones, 2004, p. 205). Customer productivity is "a function of the ratio of customer inputs, such as time effort and cost, to customer [outputs] such as [...] experience, outcome and value" (Johnston & Jones, 2004, p. 206).

Thus, managing service productivity means balancing both operational and customer productivity. Johnston and Jones (2004, pp. 207–211) consider five main issues for this task: the consideration of the productivity paradox (not denounced as such by Johnston & Jones, 2004, p. 207), the systematic and purposeful management of bottleneck situations, proactive co-creation on the part of the customer, and meaningful task and job design to, for example, compensate for the adverse effects on service customers' satisfaction expected to result from fluctuations in capacity (Johnston & Jones, 2004, pp. 210–211).

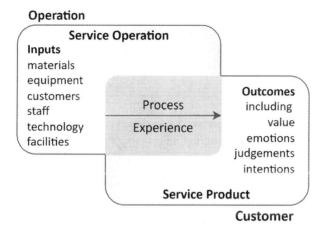

Fig. 3 Service productivity model by Johnston and Jones. (Source: Johnston et al., 2012, p. 7)

In their discussion of crucial issues for balancing operational and customer productivity, Johnston and Jones (2004, pp. 207–211) point to frontline employees' role in service encounters. For example, when talking about "bottlenecks" in service processes, frontline employees are the ones entertaining people queuing for attractions in theme parks (Johnston & Jones, 2004, p. 209). They approve the added value of frontline employees in banking service encounters in comparison to service executed by automats apart from ATMs (Johnston & Jones, 2004, p. 210) or the advantages of "multi-skilled employees" (Johnston & Jones, 2004, p. 211) in hospitality service.

4. Dual-Perspective Framework of Service Productivity (Parasuraman, 2002, 2010)

Parasuraman (2002, p. 8) proposes "a conceptual framework for understanding the interplay between service quality and productivity." In contrast to Grönroos' and Ojasalos' service productivity model, service quality is centred because of its importance for the overall evaluation of a service transaction/process. In line with other researchers, Parasuraman (2002, p. 7, 8, 2010, pp. 279–280) sees service productivity as a concept beyond the output-input relation present in the manufacturing industry. Figure 4 presents the dual-perspective framework and shows that, just as in Grönroos' and Ojasalos' model, he integrated the provider's and customer's perspectives and considered it compulsory to understand and leverage service productivity.

Both sides contribute inputs and achieve outputs due to a service transaction (Parasuraman, 2010, p. 279). Service firms contribute to each service process with several inputs. Apart from equipment and technology, there is labour personalised by management and frontline personnel (Parasuraman, 2002, p. 8).

The elements of the model are connected with three relationships that reflect known elements of service quality and productivity research, such as the co-creation processes between the service provider and service customer, the provision of resources for the service production on behalf of the service provider (Parasuraman, 2010, p. 280). The third relationship describes the positive influence of the service customers' satisfaction with the service on the service providers' outputs (Parasuraman, 2010, p. 281), for example, by positive word-of-mouth or increased customer loyalty. Thus, the service provider's ability to efficiently combine the inputs necessary for providing and delivering the service is a crucial part of service productivity (Parasuraman, 2002, p. 8, 2010, p. 281). It involves "labour," which is embodied, amongst others, by frontline employees.

German School

For the topic of service productivity, the German School of thought is newly introduced. Up to now, there was only a Nordic and a North American School of thought. One of the most prominent researchers is Corsten (1994), who

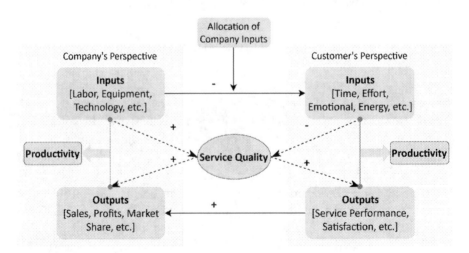

Fig. 4 Relationship between service quality and service productivity. (Source: Parasuraman, 2002, p. 8)

developed a service productivity model, which divides the service process into two phases, of which each has its productivity (1). Building on this, Lasshof (2006) created a model that focuses on improving labour division between the service provider and service customer (2). A very different approach, the Koblenz Service Productivity Model (3), concludes the chapter.

1. Service Productivity Model of Corsten (1994)

In addition to its importance in the context of German service productivity research, the model of Corsten (1994, p. 60) is relevant because it was developed especially for services in which interactions between frontline employees and service customers play an essential role. Therefore, Corsten's model is notable for this chapter centred on frontline employees as one of the key drivers for improving service productivity.

Corsten (1994, p. 1) depicted the service process in two phases: firstly, the pre-service encounter, and secondly, the service encounter. In the pre-service encounter phase, the service provider allocates all the resources necessary to serve the customer in the service encounter. During the service encounter, the allocated resources are used for serving the customer, and additional factors are combined into an output (Fig. 5).

Corsten's (1994, p. 61) comprehension of service productivity is similar to that of Grönroos and Ojasalo (2004, p. 417) and Johnston and Jones (2004, pp. 205–206). Service productivity is a composite of several productivities. First, the productivity of inputs deployed before the service encounter occurs (pre-service encounter productivity). Second, the service encounter's productivity consists of the external factor's inputs: the customer or a customer's object, further inputs supplied by the service provider, and service personnel (service encounter productivity).

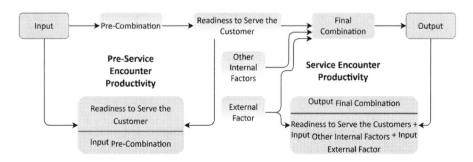

Fig. 5 Two-stage service productivity model. (Source: Corsten, 1994, p. 61)

786 C. Hipp and S. Gliem

Furthermore, Corsten (1994, pp. 46–47) included a capacity dimension and is convinced that quality is another component of service productivity (1994, p. 52). He disagrees with a solely quantitative perspective on productivity (1994, p. 50) as concluded by Grönroos and Ojasalo (2004, p. 421), who consider a financial perspective as the only one "to incorporate the quality variations caused by the heterogeneity of services and the effects on perceived quality by customer participation in the service process."

A decision on the extent to which service customers perform tasks within the service process depends strongly on the service context (see, for example, Jo Bitner et al., 1997, pp. 194–195) and the customer's willingness to participate in the service process as such generally (Corsten, 1994, pp. 67–68). Working on this question, Lasshof (2006) designed a service productivity model aiming at the efficient labour division between the service provider and service customer. It can be considered as a further development of Corsten's model and is explained hereafter.

2. Service Productivity Model of Lasshof (2006)

Lasshof (2006, pp. 119–125) addressed the labour division between service providers and service customers that Corsten had raised with his service productivity model. As stated, the transfer of tasks onto the customer is a leverage-point for service productivity but poses advantages and disadvantages (Corsten, 1994, p. 66). Therefore, Lasshof (2006, pp. 150–152) centres her service productivity model on the improvement of labour division between the service provider and service customer, in particular for service where the customer or a customer's object plays a crucial role (Lasshof, 2006, pp. 122–124, 220). Lasshof fills a research gap with her work, as the discussion about labour division has always been carried out on a theoretical level (Lasshof, 2006, pp. 150, 154–155).

The discussion about the optimal division of labour between service providers and service customers is centred on the overriding goal of guiding service customers within the service process so that the process runs smoothly and optimally. Besides, the customer's expertise in the service process plays a role (Lasshof, 2006, pp. 165–167): the higher the customers' know-how, the higher the productivity—up to a certain point. Then, increasing customer know-how decreases productivity, for example, a customer who is well-informed about a product, asks complicated and particular questions, and prolongs the service encounter (Lasshof, 2006, pp. 167–168). Therefore,

Lasshof's model serves best customers with little know-how (Lasshof, 2006, pp. 172, 220).

3. Koblenz Service Productivity Model (2012)

Kutsch et al. (2012, p. 15) developed a similar comprehension of service productivity as Vuorinen et al. (1998) and Rutkauskas and Paulavičiene (2005). They stick to the output-input ratio. The model measured the output and input factors regarding their degree of fulfilment and, multiplied by a weight, matching the specific service context. Thereby, the more critical factors share a more significant influence on the overall result than minor importance factors. The resulting ratio then informs about the service firm's productivity at one determined point in time (Kutsch et al., 2012).

In contrast to Corsten and Lasshof, Kutsch et al. (2012) do not see the service process as several phases. They measure fulfilment degrees of inputs and outputs and overall productivity multiple times during a service process. Thus, the model aims at the measurement of service productivity. In contrast, productivity management is seen as a subsequent step, for which it is especially helpful to determine the relationships between the different output and input factors (Kutsch et al., 2012).

The model was tested successfully in an IT services firm. The firm had to decide on the input and output factors and the weights for the factors (Kutsch et al., 2012). Allowing the firm to decide this for themselves is considered one drawback of this model because it can be hard to make and susceptible to subjective judgement. At the same time, this allows one to include frontline employees and the factors influencing them to match the specific service context.

Other Service Productivity Models

Apart from the service productivity models presented previously, there are service productivity models not assignable to any of the schools of thought.

In the last decade, several researchers (Balkan, 2011; Jääskeläinen, 2009; Pfannstiel, 2016; Supic et al., 2012) assessed service productivity following the objective matrix approach by Felix and Riggs (1983). "Productivity by objectives is a holistic approach to overcome the obstacles that inhibit productivity" (Felix & Riggs, 1983, p. 173). In other words, they propose productivity enhancement guided by objectives—objectives that have been selected

788   C. Hipp and S. Gliem

beforehand. Furthermore, productivity by objectives sees the inclusion of stakeholders influenced by these productivity enhancements as essential part of the productivity improvement process' success and sustainability (Felix & Riggs, 1983, p. 173).

The measurement and analysis of service productivity with data envelopment analysis (DEA) is an approach present in service research since the late 1980s (Avkiran, 2006; Emrouznejad & Cabanda, 2014). Initially published by Charnes et al. (1978), it is an approach originating in mathematics and "calculating the relative efficiency of objects on multiple criteria" (Weber, 1996, p. 29). Consequently, multiple inputs and outputs can be included (Sherman & Gold, 1985, pp. 300–301). When finding out which unit or subsidiary is the most productive, DEA provides information about the level of costs and resources needed to be reallocated to make a unit as productive as the most productive one. By this, calculations about the additional service provided with the resources at hand are included (Sherman & Zhu, 2006, pp. 50–51). To sum up, DEA is a tool for uncovering weak areas in a service firm and lead managers to take actions accordingly.

Researchers also used the balanced scorecard methodology that goes back to Kaplan and Norton (1992) to analyse service productivity or its surrogates. In the following, two examples are presented. Borchert et al. (2013, p. 170) developed the Service Navigator for small- and medium-sized service firms. It conceptually builds on an extensive comprehension of service productivity and the management model of St Gallen (Borchert et al., 2013). The Service Navigator draws on three levels of understanding service productivity. Firstly, there is the output-input ratio. Secondly, indicators representing the degree of fulfilment regarding customer demands, for example, customer satisfaction, customer perceived quality, or customer loyalty, extend the output-input ratio. Thirdly, indicators point to the internal efficiency established by Grönroos and Ojasalo in their service productivity model.

A second balanced scorecard method is the service scorecard by Gupta and Tyagi (2008). Influenced by other performance and quality assessment tools, for example, six sigma methodology, their service scorecard has an overall service performance index (SPIN) consisting of seven elements. The seven elements represent "the seven most important attributes of service businesses" (Tyagi & Gupta, 2013, p. 5), aggregating information about the performance on the operational, tactical, and strategical level of the firm (Tyagi & Gupta, 2013, p. 5). For every element, Tyagi and Gupta (2013, pp. 5–7, 10) propose concrete measures that have to be customised to the specific service context.

4 Synopsis

In the previous sections of this chapter, several service productivity models and approaches were presented. Apart from the Nordic School and North American School, the German School was added. Some models could not be assigned to any of these schools of thought.

The researchers could make one observation during the elaborations on the service productivity models. As soon as the research community granted that productivity paradigms and standards from the manufacturing industry could not be transferred to the service industry and service quality issues are related strongly to a service's productivity, it was clear that service productivity models always should incorporate the service customer's perspective. Thus, issues around service encounters, customer integration, and the roll-out of the service dominant-logic experienced much conceptual, qualitative, and quantitative research.

Moreover, researchers realised that the service industry's complexity necessitates productivity models mapping this complexity and, at the same time, balancing complexity and doability (Petz et al., 2019, p. 2020). Maybe this was the reason that all service productivity models see service productivity as a *composition* of either more than one *productivity* (matrix approaches, for example, Jääskeläinen (2009), Pfannstiel (2016), and Supic et al. (2012)), *efficiency* (Grönroos & Ojasalo, 2004), or the *difference between expected and perceived performance* (SERVPERF model by Cronin and Taylor (1992)).

In a way, the SERVPERF model and the matrix approach are very similar to each other. Both use a kind of target-performance comparison. SERVPERF does this via collecting data about the customer's expectation of the service and the customer perceived service performance. The matrix approach, especially the Bayreuth Productivity Analysis (Pfannstiel, 2016), collected data about the ideal manifestation of single productivities, the target, and the actual performance. Even the approaches that focus less on the holistic comprehension of service productivity and more on measuring and quantifying service productivity incorporate this complexity. This complexity is considered by assigning weights to inputs and outputs corresponding to their significance for the firm's productivity (e.g., Koblenz Service Productivity Model) and selecting inputs and outputs under the specific service context (e.g., DEA and Balanced Scorecard methods).

So, which conclusions are drawn in the light of examining the different service productivity models regarding the next step in research model building, which is the derivation of a theoretical framework?

As explained before, the reviewed service productivity models vary in their degree regarding their feasibility. Researchers chose a holistic approach, as, for example, Grönroos and Ojasalo and Parasuraman, or picked a particular problem within an already existent model and dealt with it, for example, Lasshof. Also, some contributions integrated several approaches or made the approaches doable for practitioners, for example, the Koblenz Service Productivity Model or Bayreuth Productivity Analysis.

Regarding the Grönroos-Ojasalo-service-productivity-model, there are several contributions from other researchers. For example, the service encounter was the focal point for the German School's two service productivity models. Corsten's service productivity model differentiated between pre-service-encounter-stage productivity and service encounter-stage productivity and added depth to this part of Grönroos' and Ojasalos' model. Lasshof focused on the service encounter and centred on the labour division between the service provider and the service customer. Furthermore, she recognised the significance of the service customer's know-how regarding the service process for productivity and thus complemented the customer input side. On the output side, the elements targeting the service customer's point of view could be enriched by the service gap model by Parasuraman, Zeithaml, and Berry or the SERVPERF model by Cronin and Taylor. The next challenging step will be to identify the most suitable model to operationalise and test real data. Refining one of the service productivity model components is something Grönroos and Ojasalo themselves state as a worthwhile research goal. They state that testing the "relative importance of the various components of the model [...]" (Grönroos & Ojasalo, 2004, p. 422) is a future task.

References

Aarons, G. A., Hurlburt, M., & McCue Horwitz, S. (2011). Advancing a conceptual model of evidence-based practice implementation in public service sectors. *Administration and Policy in Mental Health and Mental Health Services Research, 38*(1), 4–23. https://doi.org/10.1007/s10488-010-0327-7

Abdelkrim, Y., & Salim, B. A. (2015). Assessment of the service quality in the preparatory school of economics through Servperf model. *Romanian Economic and Business Review, 10*(4), 127–136.

Adedamola, O., Modupe, O., & Ayodele, A. (2016). Measuring students' perception of classroom quality in private universities in Ogun State, Nigeria using SERVPERF. *Mediterranean Journal of Social Sciences, 7*(2), 318–323. https://doi.org/10.5901/mjss.2016.v7n2p318

Adil, M., Ghaswyneh, O. F. M. A., & Albkour, A. M. (2013). SERVQUAL and SERVPERF: A review of measures in services marketing research. *Global Journal of Management and Business Research Marketing, 13*(6), 64–76. https://doi.org/10.1108/09604520610711909

Akin, G., & Hopelain, D. (1986). Finding the culture of productivity. *Organizational Dynamics, 14*(3), 19–32.

Ali, M., & Raza, S. A. (2015). Service quality perception and customer satisfaction in Islamic banks of Pakistan: The modified SERVQUAL model. *Total Quality Management and Business Excellence, 28*(5–6), 559–577. https://doi.org/10.1080/14783363.2015.1100517

Avkiran, N. K. (2006). *Data envelopment analysis.* N. K. Avkiran.

Aydin, B. (2017). Comparing Servqual and Servperf methods in measuring service quality: An implementation in a public hospital. In C. Cobanoglue, F. DeMicco, P. J. Moreo, & A. Morvillo (Eds.), *Global Conference on Service Management* (pp. 204–206). Volterra.

Babakus, E., & Boller, G. W. (1992). An empirical assessment of the SERVQUAL scale. *Journal of Business Research, 24*(3), 253–268. https://doi.org/10.1016/0148-2963(92)90022-4

Babin, B. J., & Boles, J. S. (1998). Employee behavior in a service environment: A model and test of potential differences between men and women. *Journal of Marketing, 2*(62), 77–91.

Balkan, D. (2011). Enterprise productivity measurement in services by OMAX (Objective Matrix) method and an application with Turkish emergency service. In *Reser Conference, Productivity of Services Next Gen–Beyond Output/Input* (pp. 1–13). RESER.

Barnes, J. (2017). *Measuring service quality in the low-cost airline industry.* University of Stirling.

Bitner, M. J. (2001). Service and technology: Opportunities and paradoxes. *Managing Service Quality: An International Journal, 11*(6), 375–379.

Bitner, M. J., Brown, S. W., & Meuter, M. L. (2000). Technology infusion in service encounters. *Journal of the Academy of Marketing Science, 28*(1), 138–149.

Bitner, M. J., Zeithaml, V. A., & Gremler, D. D. (2010). Technology's impact on the gaps model of service quality. In P. P. Maglio, C. Kieliszewski, & J. Spohrer (Eds.), *Handbook of service science* (pp. 197–218). Springer. https://doi.org/10.1007/978-1-4419-1628-0

Borchert, M., Koch, E., Strina, G., Klinkhammer, S., Hamburger, J., & Heinen, E. (2013). Der Service Navigator als Instrument des Produktivitätsmanagements in KMU-Dienstleistungsunternehmen. In O. Thomas & M. Nüttgens (Eds.), *Dienstleistungsmodellierung 2012* (pp. 169–191). Springer Gabler. https://doi.org/10.1007/978-3-658-00863-5

Brady, M. K., Cronin, J. J., & Brand, R. R. (2002). Performance-only measurement of service quality: A replication and extension. *Journal of Business Research, 55*(1), 17–31. https://doi.org/10.1016/S0148-2963(00)00171-5

Brown, T. J., Churchill, G. A., Jr., & Peter, J. P. (1993). Research note: Improving the measurement of service quality. *Journal of Retailing, 69*(1), 127–139.

Buttle, F. A. (1996). SERVQUAL: Review, critique, research agenda. *European Journal of Marketing, 30*(1), 8–32. https://doi.org/10.1108/03090569610105762

Carson, P. R., Carson, K. D., Knouse, S. B., & Roe, C. W. (1997). Balance theory applied to service quality: A focus on the organisation, provider, and consumer triad. *Journal of Business and Psychology, 12*(2), 99–120. https://doi.org/10.1023/a:1025061816323

Charnes, A., Cooper, W. W., & Rhodes, E. (1978). Measuring the efficiency of decision making units. *European Journal of Operational Research, 2*(6), 429–444.

Chase, R. B. (1978). Where does the customer fit in a service operation? *Harvard Business Review, 56*(6), 137–142.

Chebat, J.-C., & Kollias, P. (2000). The impact of empowerment on customer contact employees' roles in service organisations. *Journal of Service Research, 3*(1), 66–81. https://doi.org/10.1177/109467050031005

Clemes, M. D., Gan, C., & Ren, M. (2011). Synthesising the effects of service quality, value, and customer satisfaction on behavioral intentions in the motel industry. *Journal of Hospitality & Tourism Research, 35*(4), 530–568. https://doi.org/10.1177/1096348010382239

Collier, J. E., Barnes, D. C., Abney, A. K., & Pelletier, M. J. (2018). Idiosyncratic service experiences: When customers desire the extraordinary in a service encounter. *Journal of Business Research, 84*(2017, Feb.), 150–161. https://doi.org/10.1016/j.jbusres.2017.11.016

Corsten, H. (1994). Produktivitätsmanagement bilateraler personenbezogener Dienstleistungen. *Schriften Zur Unternehmensführung, 52*, 43–78. https://doi.org/10.1007/978-3-663-05878-6

Cronin, J. J., & Taylor, S. A. (1992). Measuring service quality: A reexamination and extension. *Journal of Marketing, 56*(3), 55. https://doi.org/10.2307/1252296

Dewettinck, K., & Buyens, D. (2006). *Linking job motivating potential to frontline employee attitudes and performance: Testing the mediating role of psychological empowerment* (Vlerick Leuven Gent Working Paper Serien 2006 No. 26). Ghent.

Dhar, R. L. (2015). Service quality and the training of employees: The mediating role of organisational commitment. *Tourism Management, 46*, 419–430. https://doi.org/10.1016/j.tourman.2014.08.001

Dobni, D., Brent Ritchie, J. R., & Zerbe, W. (2000). Organisational values: The inside view of service productivity. *Journal of Business Research, 47*(2), 91–107. https://doi.org/10.1016/S0148-2963(98)00058-7

Drucker, P. F. (1991, November–December). The new productivity challenge. *Harvard Business Review*, 69–79.

Echeverri, P., & Skålén, P. (2011). Co-creation and co-destruction: A practice-theory based study of interactive value formation. *Marketing Theory, 11*(3), 351–373. https://doi.org/10.1177/1470593111408181

Ekinci, Y., & Dawes, P. L. (2009). Consumer perceptions of frontline service employee personality traits, interaction quality, and consumer satisfaction. *Service Industries Journal, 29*(4), 503–521. https://doi.org/10.1080/02642060802283113

Ekinci, Y., Riley, M., & Fife-Schaw, C. (1998). Which school of thought? The dimensions of resort hotel quality. *International Journal of Contemporary Hospitality Management, 10*(2), 63–67. https://doi.org/10.1108/09596119810207200

Emrouznejad, A., & Cabanda, E. (2014). Managing service productivity using data envelopment analysis. *International Series in Operations Research and Management Science, 215*(June), 1–17. https://doi.org/10.1007/978-3-662-43437-6_1

Felix, G. H., & Riggs, J. L. (1983). Productivity measurement by objectives. *Global Business and Organizational Excellence, 2*(4), 386–393.

Frost, F. A., & Kumar, M. (2000). INTSERVQUAL: An internal adaptation of the GAP model in a large service organisation. *Journal of Services Marketing, 14*(5), 358–377. https://doi.org/10.1108/08876040010340991

Ganesh, A. (2016). Understanding the relationship between employee motivation and customer retention. *XIMB Journal of Management, 13*(I), 101–114.

Gibbs, T., & Ashill, N. J. (2013). The effects of high performance work practices on job outcomes. *International Journal of Bank Marketing, 31*(4), 305–326. https://doi.org/10.1108/IJBM-10-2012-0096

Grönroos, C. (1984). A service quality model and its marketing implications. *European Journal of Marketing, 18*(4), 36–44.

Grönroos, C. (1990). Relationship marketing approach to the marketing function in service contexts: The marketing and organisational behavior influence. *Journal of Business Research, 20*(1), 3–12.

Grönroos, C. (1999). Internationalisation strategies for services: A retrospective. *Journal of Services Marketing, 13*(4/5), 290–297. https://doi.org/10.1108/JSM-11-2015-0354

Grönroos, C., & Ojasalo, K. (2004). Service productivity: Towards a conceptualisation of the transformation of inputs into economic results in services. *Journal of Business Research, 57*(4), 414–423. https://doi.org/10.1016/S0148-2963(02)00275-8

Grönroos, C., & Ojasalo, K. (2015). Service productivity as mutual learning. *International Journal of Quality and Service Sciences, 7*. https://doi.org/10.1108/IJQSS-03-2015S0035

Gummesson, E. (1987). The new marketing: Developing long-term interactive relationships. *Long Range Planning, 20*(4), 10–20. https://doi.org/10.1016/0024-6301(87)90151-8

Gummesson, E. (1991). Marketing-orientation revisited: The crucial role of the part-time marketer. *European Journal of Marketing, 25*(2), 60–75. https://doi.org/10.1108/VINE-10-2013-0063

Gummesson, E. (1996). Relationship marketing and imaginary organisations: A synthesis. *European Journal of Marketing, 30*(2), 31–44. https://doi.org/10.1108/03090569610106635

Gummesson, E. (1998). Productivity, quality and relationship marketing in service operations. *International Journal of Contemporary Hospitality Management, 10*(1), 4–15. https://doi.org/10.1108/09596119810199282

Gummesson, E., & Grönroos, C. (2012). The emergence of the new service marketing: Nordic School perspectives. *Journal of Service Management, 23*(4), 479–497. https://doi.org/10.1108/09564231211260387

Gupta, P., & Tyagi, R. (2008). *A complete and balanced service scorecard: Creating value through sustained performance improvement.* Pearson.

Hartline, M. D., Maxham, J. G., & McKee, D. O. (2000). Corridors of influence in the dissemination of customer-oriented strategy to customer contact service employees. *Journal of Marketing, 64*(2), 35–50. https://doi.org/10.1509/jmkg.64.2.35.18001

Hennig-Thurau, T. (2004). Customer orientation of service employees. *International Journal of Service Industry Management, 15*(5), 460–478. https://doi.org/10.1108/09564230410564939

Hill, P. (1977). On goods and services. *Review of Income and Wealth, 23*(4), 315–338.

Hill, P. (1999). Tangibles, intangibles and services: A new taxonomy for the classification of output. *The Canadian Journal of Economics, 32*(2), 426–446. https://doi.org/10.2307/2175876

Hussain, K., Khan, A., & Bavдk, A. (2003). The effect of job performance on frontline employee job satisfaction and quitting intent: The case of hotels in Turkish Republic of Northern Cyprus. *EMU Journal of Tourism Research, 4*(1), 1–6.

Jääskeläinen, A. (2009). Identifying a suitable approach for measuring and managing public service productivity. *Proceedings of the European Conference on Intellectual Capital,* June, 271–278.

Jääskeläinen, A. (2010). *Productivity measurement and management in large public service organisations.* Tampere University of Technology.

Jha, S., Deitz, G. D., Babakus, E., & Yavas, U. (2013). The role of corporate image for quality in the formation of attitudinal service loyalty. *Journal of Service Research, 16*(2), 155–170. https://doi.org/10.1177/1094670512466441

Jo Bitner, M., Faranda, W. T., Hubbert, A. R., & Zeithaml, V. A. (1997). Customer contributions and roles in service delivery. *International Journal of Service Industry Management, 8*(3), 193–205. https://doi.org/10.1108/09564239710185398

Johnston, R., Clark, G., & Shulver, M. (2012). *Service operations management* (4th ed.). Pearson.

Johnston, R., & Jones, P. (2004). Service productivity: Towards understanding the relationship between operational and customer productivity. *International Journal of Productivity and Performance Management, 53*(3), 201–213. https://doi.org/10.1016/S0148-2963(02)00275-8

Kaplan, R. S., & Norton, D. P. (1992). The balanced scorecard: Measures that drive performance. *Harvard Business Review, 70*(Jan.–Feb.), 71–79.

Karatepe, O. M. (2013). High-performance work practices and hotel employee performance: The mediation of work engagement. *International Journal of Hospitality Management, 32*(1), 132–140. https://doi.org/10.1016/j.ijhm.2012.05.003

Karatepe, O. M., & Aleshinloye, K. D. (2009). Emotional dissonance and emotional exhaustion among hotel employees in Nigeria. *International Journal of Hospitality Management, 28*(3), 349–358. https://doi.org/10.1016/j.ijhm.2008.12.002

Karatepe, O. M., Beirami, E., Bouzari, M., & Safavi, H. P. (2014). Does work engagement mediate the effects of challenge stressors on job outcomes? Evidence from the hotel industry. *International Journal of Hospitality Management, 36*, 14–22. https://doi.org/10.1016/j.ijhm.2013.08.003

Karatepe, O. M., & Kilic, H. (2007). Relationships of supervisor support and conflicts in the work-family interface with the selected job outcomes of frontline employees. *Tourism Management, 28*(1), 238–252. https://doi.org/10.1016/j.tourman.2005.12.019

Karatepe, O. M., & Uludag, O. (2008). Role stress, burnout and their effects on frontline hotel employees' job performance: Evidence from Northern Cyprus. *International Journal of Tourism Research, 10*(2016, Apr.), 111–126. https://doi.org/10.1002/jtr.645

Karatepe, O. M., Uludag, O., Menevis, I., Hadzimehmedagic, L., & Baddar, L. (2006). The effects of selected individual characteristics on frontline employee performance and job satisfaction. *Tourism Management, 27*(4), 547–560. https://doi.org/10.1016/j.tourman.2005.02.009

Kashif, M., & Zarkada, A. (2015). Value co-destruction between customers and frontline employees. *International Journal of Bank Marketing, 33*(6), 672–691. https://doi.org/10.1108/IJBM-09-2014-0121

Kelley, S. W., Donnelly, J. H. J., & Skinner, S. J. (1990). Customer participation in service production and delivery. *Journal of Retailing, 66*(3), 315–335.

Kutsch, H., Bertram, M., & Kortzfleisch, H. von. (2012). *Entwicklung eines Dienstleistungsproduktivitätsmodells (DLPMM) am Beispiel von Arbeitsberichte aus dem Fachbereich Informatik* (Arbeitsberichte aus dem Fachbereich Informatik No. 8). Koblenz.

Ladhari, R. (2009). A review of twenty years of SERVQUAL research. *International Journal of Quality and Service Sciences, 1*(2), 172–198. https://doi.org/10.1108/17566690910971445

Lai, F., Hutchinson, J., Li, D., & Bai, C. (2007). An empirical assessment and application of SERVQUAL in mainland China's mobile communications industry. *International Journal of Quality & Reliability Management, 24*(3), 244–262. https://doi.org/10.1108/02656710710730852

Larivière, B., Bowen, D. E., Andreassen, T. W., Kunz, W., Sirianni, N. J., Voss, C., … De Keyser, A. (2017). "Service Encounter 2.0": An investigation into the roles of technology, employees and customers. *Journal of Business Research, 79*, 238–246. https://doi.org/10.1016/j.jbusres.2017.03.008

Lasshof, B. (2006). *Produktivität von Dienstleistungen: Mitwirkung und Einfluss des Kunden*. Fernuniversität Hagen.

Lee, H., Lee, Y., & Yoo, D. (2000). The determinants of perceived service quality and its relationship with satisfaction. *Journal of Services Marketing, 14*(3), 217–273.

Lehmann, C., & Kölling, M. (2010). The productivity of services: A systematic literature review and research directions. *Proceedings of the XX. International RESER Conference*, 1–23.

Li, M., Lowrie, D. B., Huang, C. Y., Lu, X. C., Zhu, Y. C., Wu, X. H., et al. (2015). Evaluating patients' perception of service quality at hospitals in nine Chinese cities by use of the ServQual scale. *Asian Pacific Journal of Tropical Biomedicine, 5*(6), 497–504. https://doi.org/10.1016/j.apjtb.2015.02.003

Liao, H. (2007). Do it right this time: The role of employee service recovery performance in customer-perceived justice and customer loyalty after service failures. *Journal of Applied Psychology, 92*(2), 475–489. https://doi.org/10.1037/0021-9010.92.2.475

Lim, E. A. C., Lee, Y. H., & Foo, M.-D. (2017). Frontline employees' nonverbal cues in service encounters: A double-edged sword. *Journal of the Academy of Marketing Science, 45*(5), 657–676. https://doi.org/10.1007/s11747-016-0479-4

Lovelock, C. H. (1983). Classifying services to gain strategic marketing insights. *Journal of Marketing, 47*(3), 9–20. https://doi.org/10.2307/1251193

Luk, S. T. K., & Layton, R. (2002). Perception gaps in customer expectations: Managers versus service providers and customers. *The Service Industries Journal, 22*(2), 109–128. https://doi.org/10.1080/714005073

Machado, M. A., Ribeiro, A., & Basto, M. (2014). An empirical assessment of customer satisfaction and quality of service: Comparing Servqual and Servperf. *Revista Gestão Industrial*, 264–283.

Mitra, S. (2012). A review of service quality research in India. *Journal of IMS Kolkata, 4*, 54–66.

Murmann, B. (1999). *Qualität mehrstufiger Dienstleistungsinteraktionen*. Gabler.

Nerdinger, B. F. W., & Pundt, A. (2018). Leadership of service employees—A narrative review. *Journal of Service Management Research, 40*(1), 3–15.

Nordgren, L. (2009). Value creation in health care services—Developing service productivity. *The International Journal of Public Sector Management, 22*(90), 114–127. https://doi.org/10.1108/09513550910934529

Ostrom, A. L., Parasuraman, A., Bowen, D. E., Patrício, L., & Voss, C. A. (2015). Service research priorities in a rapidly changing context. *Journal of Service Research, 18*(2), 127–159. https://doi.org/10.1177/1094670515576315

Parasuraman, A. (2002). Service quality and productivity: A synergistic perspective. *Managing Service Quality: An International Journal, 12*(1), 6–9. https://doi.org/10.1108/09604520210415344

Parasuraman, A. (2010). Service productivity, quality and innovation. *International Journal of Quality and Service Sciences, 2*(3), 277–286. https://doi.org/10.1108/17566691011090026

Parasuraman, A., Berry, L. L., & Zeithaml, V. A. (1991a). Perceived service quality as a customer-based performance measure: An empirical examination of organisational barriers using an extended service quality model. *Human Resource Management, 30*(3), 335–364. https://doi.org/10.1002/hrm.3930300304

Parasuraman, A., Berry, L. L., & Zeithaml, V. A. (1991b). Refinement and reassessment of the SERVQUAL scale. *Journal of Retailing, 67*(4), 420–450.

Parasuraman, A., Berry, L. L., & Zeithaml, V. A. (1993). More on improving service quality measurement. *Journal of Retailing, 69*(1), 140–147. https://doi.org/10.1016/S0022-4359(05)80007-7

Parasuraman, A., Zeithaml, V. A., & Berry, L. L. (1985). A conceptual model of service quality and its implications for future research. *Journal of Marketing, 49*(4), 41–50. https://doi.org/10.1177/002224298504900403

Parasuraman, A., Zeithaml, V. A., & Berry, L. L. (1994). Alternative scales for measuring service quality: A comparative assessment based on psychometric and diagnostic criteria. *Journal of Retailing, 70*(3), 201.

Petz, A., Duckwitz, S., Schmalz, C., Meyer, S., & Schlick, C. M. (2019). Development of a model for the comprehensive analysis and evaluation of service productivity. *International Scholarly and Scientific Research & Innovation, 6*(10), 2019–2024.

Pfannstiel, M. A. (2016). Bayreuth productivity analysis—A method for ascertaining and improving the holistic service productivity of acute care hospitals. *International Journal of Health Planning and Management, 31*(1), 65–86. https://doi.org/10.1002/hpm.2250

Plé, L., & Chumpitaz Cáceres, R. (2010). Not always co-creation: Introducing interactional co-destruction of value in service-dominant logic. *Journal of Services Marketing, 24*(6), 430–437. https://doi.org/10.1108/08876041011072546

Prentice, C. (2013). Service quality perceptions and customer loyalty in casinos. *International Journal of Contemporary Hospitality Management, 25*(1), 49–64. https://doi.org/10.1108/09596111311290219

Rafaeli, A., Altman, D., Gremler, D. D., Huang, M. H., Grewal, D., Iyer, B., Parasuraman, A., & de Ruyter, K. (2017). The future of frontline research: Invited commentaries. *Journal of Service Research, 20*(1), 91–99. https://doi.org/10.1177/1094670516679275

Rod, M., Ashill, N. J., & Gibbs, T. (2016). Customer perceptions of frontline employee service delivery: A study of Russian bank customer satisfaction and behavioural intentions. *Journal of Retailing and Consumer Services, 30*, 212–221.

Rosene, F. (2003). Complacency and service quality: An overlooked condition in the GAP Model. *Journal of Retailing and Consumer Services, 10*(1), 51–55. https://doi.org/10.1016/S0969-6989(02)00055-3

Roslan, N. A. A., Wahab, E., & Abdullah, N. H. (2015). Service quality: A case study of logistics sector in Iskandar Malaysia using SERVQUAL model. *Procedia—Social and Behavioral Sciences, 172*, 457–462. https://doi.org/10.1016/j.sbspro.2015.01.380

Rutkauskas, J., & Paulavičiene, E. (2005). Concept of productivity in service sector. *Engineering Economics, 3*(43), 29–34.

Sahay, B. S. (2005). Multi-factor productivity measurement model for service organisation. *International Journal of Productivity and Performance Management, 54*(1), 7–22. https://doi.org/10.1108/17410400510571419

Sherman, H. D., & Gold, F. (1985). Bank branch operating efficiency: Evaluation with data envelopment analysis. *Journal of Banking and Finance, 9*, 297–315.

Sherman, H. D., & Zhu, J. (2006). *Service productivity management: Improving service performance using Data Envelopment Analysis (DEA)*. Springer.

Singh, J. (2000). Performance productivity and quality of frontline employees in service organisations. *Journal of Marketing, 64*(Apr.), 15–34. https://doi.org/10.1007/s13398-014-0173-7.2

Supic, Z. T., Marinkovic, S., Vukasinovic, Z., Spasovski, D., & Jaksic, M. L. (2012). Designing productivity indicators in healthcare department: A case of pediatric orthopedics. *HealthMED, 6*(2), 659–671. http://dspace.balikesir.edu.tr/xmlui/bitstream/handle/20.500.12462/8816/zeker%C4%B1ya-goktas.pdf?sequence=1&isAllowed=y#page=324

Tangen, S. (2002). *A theoretical foundation for productivity measurement and improvement of automatic assembly systems*. KTH Royal Institute of Technology Stockholm.

Tangen, S. (2005). Demystifying productivity and performance. *International Journal of Productivity and Performance Management, 54*(1), 34–46. https://doi.org/10.1108/17410400510571437

Tyagi, R., & Gupta, P. (2013). Gauging performance in the service industry. *Journal of Business Strategy, 34*(3), 4–15. https://doi.org/10.1108/JBS-10-2012-0059

Unuvar, S., Kaya, M., Faculty, T., & Campus, A. K. (2016). Measuring service quality by Servperf method: A research on hospitality enterprises. *Australian Academy of Accounting and Finance Review, 2*(4), 354–362.

Van Vaerenbergh, Y., & Orsingher, C. (2016). Service recovery: An integrative framework and research agenda. *Academy of Management Perspectives, 30*(3), 328–346. https://doi.org/10.5465/amp.2014.0143

Vargo, S. L., & Lusch, R. F. (2004). Evolving to a new dominant logic for marketing. *Journal of Marketing, 68*(1), 1–17. http://web.b.ebscohost.com/ehost/pdfviewer/pdfviewer?vid=2&sid=72c0ef80-d796-4289-9bb8-8d172ef44817%40sessionmgr102

Verleye, K., Gemmel, P., & Rangarajan, D. (2016). Engaged customers as job resources or demands for frontline employees? *Journal of Service Theory and Practice, 26*(3), 363–383.

Vuorinen, I., Järvinen, R., & Lehtinen, U. (1998). Content and measurement of productivity in the service sector. *International Journal, 9*(4), 377–396. https://doi.org/10.1108/09564239810228876

Weber, C. A. (1996). A data envelopment analysis approach to measuring vendor performance. *Supply Chain Management: An International Journal, 1*(1), 28–39. https://doi.org/10.1108/13598549610155242

Wenchao, W. (2009). A research on service failure and culture's impact on service recovery effectiveness. *Management and Service Science, 2009. MASS '09. International Conference On.* https://doi.org/10.1109/ICMSS.2009.5303167

Wirtz, J., & Ehret, M. (2017). Capturing value in the service economy. *Journal of Service Management Research, 1*(1), 22–38.

Effective Service Operations Management: Aligning Priorities in Healthcare Operations with Customer Preferences

Lu Kong, Hessam Sadatsafavi, and Rohit Verma

1 Introduction

One of the fundamental issues service operations management aims to solve is to develop strategies to allocate limited resources. To accomplish this, the priorities of tasks need to be identified. Similar to what are recognized as "competitive priorities" in operations strategy (namely cost, quality, delivery, and flexibility) (Boyer & Verma, 2009), the healthcare system has goals that compete for resources, including but not limited to maximization of population health, reduction of inequities in health, and financial protection against the costs of ill health. Quality is in the eye of the beholder, and this is especially true when it refers to the quality of healthcare services. This chapter presents a study in which healthcare customers' perspectives are used as an anchor to explore the healthcare system's priority. The priorities of tasks in the

---

L. Kong (✉)
University of South Florida, Tampa, FL, USA
e-mail: kongl@usf.edu

H. Sadatsafavi
Sentara Clinical and Business Intelligence Division, Norfolk, VA, USA
e-mail: hxsadats@sentara.com

R. Verma
VinUniversity, Hanoi, Vietnam

Cornell University, Ithaca, NY, USA
e-mail: rohit.v@vinuni.edu.vn

© The Author(s), under exclusive license to Springer Nature Switzerland AG 2022
B. Edvardsson, B. Tronvoll (eds.), *The Palgrave Handbook of Service Management*,
https://doi.org/10.1007/978-3-030-91828-6_38

802   L. Kong et al.

healthcare system also reveal the priorities in healthcare operations management (HOM) research. More attention from academic scholars shall be focused on the healthcare tasks and topics with high priorities.

This chapter will focus on answering the following three relevant questions: (1) What are the most concerning issues in the healthcare system from its customers' perspective? (2) What factors account for these perceptions? (3) Is there alignment between healthcare task priorities and healthcare operations research?

A multi-year study shows that, in general, customers are most concerned about (1) cost of care, (2) access to care and coverage, and (3) quality and efficiency. Those customer concerns are found to be associated with health policies, sociodemographic characteristics, and living conditions. We then compare customers' pressing concerns and themes of published healthcare research within operations management discipline, and respectfully make suggestions for potential future healthcare operations research directions.

2   Background

The recent outbreak of the COVID-19 pandemic has drawn considerable attention to how each nation's healthcare system operates with limited resources. Since resource allocation is one of the fundamental issues operations management aims to solve, an operations strategy perspective can be useful in assessing healthcare priorities, which then contribute to resource allocation. This chapter discusses a study using data from the U.S. to explore healthcare priorities from its customers' perspectives. More importantly, we discuss the implications generated for healthcare stakeholders and healthcare operations researchers.

Healthcare is one of the biggest industries in the U.S. in terms of its economic value. With the recent rapid growth rate, the healthcare industry's share of GDP is projected to be 19.7% by 2026.[1] In contrast, the GDP percentage for developed counties that are known for their sound healthcare systems is around 10% (Germany, 11.3%; Canada, 10.4%; and Japan, 10.7%). Despite its size, the U.S. healthcare system faces many issues, such as higher health costs but no better care quality, and high uninsured number (27.6 million in 2016[2]). As is the case of healthcare systems in many countries, policies and plans on how to allocate limited resources have to be established to achieve the optimal solutions, and priorities on healthcare have to be set properly at multiple levels, from overall strategy to specific budgeting for individual patients.

---

[1] CMS National Health Expenditure Projections 2017–2026.

[2] https://www.kff.org/uninsured/fact-sheet/key-facts-about-the-uninsured-population/

An operations strategy perspective can used to assess potential priority mismatches. Just as in all operations systems, healthcare system has goals that compete for limited resources, such as maximizing population health, reducing inequities in health, and protecting against the costs of ill health. To set health priorities to achieve an optimal set of solutions, policy makers have to make strategic decisions such as setting budgets for healthcare expenditures (in contrast to other spending areas such as education), emphasizing primary care versus tertiary care, deciding which diseases to alleviate, allocating resources among different population groups, and setting budget limits for individual patients. Multiple stakeholders are involved in this process. Normally, these stakeholders include government officials, healthcare professionals, public and lay representatives, and government commissions. Usually, macro-level decisions, such as national healthcare budgets, are usually made by politicians, whereas care providers and other healthcare professionals are responsible for micro-level decisions, such as the level of intervention in individual patient care.

However, policy decisions may not be based on rational processes, causing the limited resources are not used to the optimal extent. The major reason is due to the nature and complexity of the decision process, the decisions are mostly ad hoc and based on historical or political patterns rather than on current realities. For example, although research shows that strong primary care is associated with improved population health (Kringos et al., 2013) and that investing in primary care is more effective than paying for tertiary care (MOH Republic of Ghana Ministry of Health, 1998), the U.S. continues to invest in specialty care and new technologies, leading to a shortage of primary care providers and rising costs of care. Unable to apply a holistic view and neglecting many factors that influence the process, policy makers are not doing particularly well and need assistance in making those decisions (Baltussen & Niessen, 2006; McDaniels et al., 1999; Bazerman & Moore, 2013).

To make better choices, politicians, healthcare professionals, and healthcare researchers need to better understand the major issues of the healthcare system and concerns from various perspectives. Of crucial importance among these perspectives is that of the public, for the following reasons: due to the public funds applied to the healthcare system, citizens are important stakeholders of the system, involving the public in policy making promotes the principles of democracy; encouraging public insights in making decisions that affect individuals' lives can, in turn, improve public confidence in the healthcare system (Traulsen & Almarsdóttir, 2005); and the public provides a perspective about the values and priorities of the community that could improve the quality of priority decisions (Ham, 1993).

804 L. Kong et al.

During the recent decade, we have seen a gradual increase in the quantity of healthcare operations management research. Additionally, the trend has also shifted from the analysis of single healthcare delivery organizations to a broader perspective of a healthcare ecosystem which includes multiple entities. One reason for this trend is that healthcare system stakeholders include more than just care providers and patients. Entities such as government, policy makers, and pharmaceutical companies also play important roles. As a result, the trend encourages operations management researchers to think about the interactions among entities while setting future research priorities (Dai & Tayur, 2019).

From an operations management perspective, we conduct this study to identify consumers' perceptions of healthcare priorities with a goal of contributing to healthcare resource allocation. Comparing our findings with a thorough healthcare operations management literature review from several top operations management journals over the past decade, we explore the alignments between issues in healthcare consumers' perception and the topics addressed by our fellow researchers. Based on our results, we respectfully suggest future research opportunities in healthcare operations management.

3 A Systematic Literature Review in HOM

Although many problems in healthcare operations management are not analytically different from those in other industries, healthcare and health services have distinctive characteristics. For example, one essential attribute of healthcare is people's quality of life. However, quality of life is difficult to measure, and it is awkward to quantify this with a dollar value. Also, the healthcare system involves shared decision processes among a variety of decision makers, including physicians, nurses, patients, and administrators, and it entails complex reimbursement and payment mechanisms (Pierskalla & Brailer, 1994). Thus, we use the taxonomy framework Dai et al. (2018), Dai and Tayur (2019) proposed in their handbook and HOM review paper, rather than the traditional operations management topics to categorize the sampled HOM articles. In this framework, the sampled HOM articles are grouped into three levels by the scope of issues they are dealing with: macro, meso, and micro. With this framework, seven operations management journals such as *Production and Operations Management, Management Science, Manufacturing & Service Operations Management, Decision Analysis, Journal of Operations Management, Decision Sciences,* and *Operations Research* are reviewed. And 205 articles published from 2007 to 2017 are included in this review.

We categorize all sampled articles into 21 thrusts, as shown in Fig. 1. Among all thrusts, the most studied are organization design (21.5%), design of delivery (17.6%), ambulatory care (15.1%), and resource allocation (10.7%). Barely 10% of all the articles we sampled (9.8%) touched upon macro-level topics, which deal with the broad strategic directions or overarching policies, the general role of different entities, and the design and structure

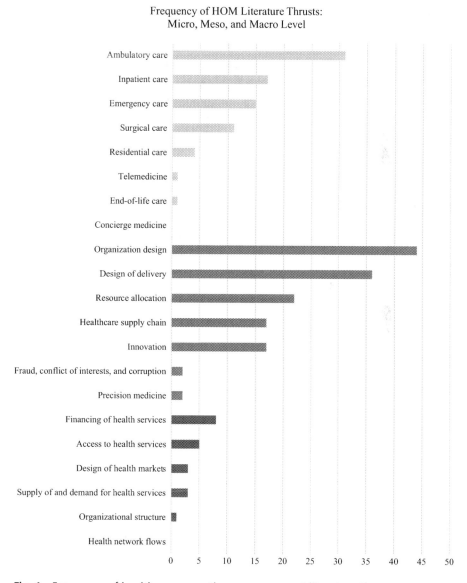

Fig. 1 Frequency of healthcare operations management literature thrusts

of the national healthcare system. Among those articles, more than half are focused on the financing of health service (3.9%) and access to health services (2.4%). None talk about health network flow topics, such as the consolidation of hospitals and payers.

The majority (68.3%) of sampled articles explore meso-level thrusts in HOM. These deal with the problems that extend beyond specific operations problems within an organization, but are not as broad as the design of general health markets. Among those papers, many studied organization design (21.5%)—for instance, hospital design and service flow design—and many explored designs of delivery (10.7%), such as referral strategies, infection prevention, and treatment management. A fair number of papers studied resource allocation (10.7%), the healthcare supply chain (8.3%), and health innovations (8.3%), such as studies on electronic medical records systems.

Thirty-nine percent of sampled articles studied micro-level thrusts, that is, specific problems in a single organization, such as ambulatory care (15.1%), inpatient care (8.3%), emergency care (7.3%), and surgical care (5.4%). Only a couple of papers focused on residential care, telemedicine, and end-of-life care (in total 3%), and none studied concierge medicine. Many papers falling into the micro scope studied scheduling, staffing, and capacity planning. Among all specific operations issues, scheduling is the more thoroughly studied. Some 52 papers out of 205 focus on the scheduling issue of patients or care providers.

4 Public Involvement in Healthcare Priority Setting

Needless to say, the public is an important stakeholder in the healthcare system. As decision makers are increasingly pressured to engage the public in the priority setting processes, many researchers have explored the involvement of the public in healthcare priority setting: the methods, the scope of public engagement, and the results.

In their review, Mitton et al. (2009) sampled 175 empirical articles and found that the majority (58%) of studies used the "middle level interactive" methods to collect public opinions. Those methods include poll and survey, referendum, consultation document, interactive websites, focus group, and study circle. About a quarter (24%) of researchers used "low level interactive" methods to gather information from the public. Those methods include traditional publicity, public hearing, and hotline. Finally, a small portion of studies involved the public with "high level interactive" methods, which include but are not limited to consensus conference, deliberative poll, and town voting meetings (Rowe & Frewer, 2005).

In practice, the public tends to focus on the location of health service provision along with non-medical aspects. The majority of studies on public involvement in health priorities engage the public in the macro-level issues, which deal with the broad system design and functions. Only a small number of studies engage the public in meso- and micro-level issues, which deal with problems related to more specific services, programs, and populations.

Despite the increasing number of studies in this area, the results are not as satisfactory. In general, research points out that at this stage, public involvement in healthcare priority setting is relatively informal and operates on an ad hoc basis, rather than a formal approach. Little research has provided evidence having produced practical guidance for policy making.

5 External Factors Affecting Consumers' Perceptions on Healthcare

Many external factors, such as government healthcare policies and general economic status, may affect people's perception of healthcare systems. This chapter focuses on government policies when examining the external impact, due to the necessity of government supervision and legislation in healthcare. Researchers have studied the consistency between public opinion and government policy and the potential rationale for such policy (Monroe, 1998; Burstein, 1998), and have argued that sociologists should review the importance of public policy when analyzing public perception.

As indicated above, government policies have great impact on the entire healthcare system, including care providers, healthcare organizations, insurance companies, and pharmaceutical companies, not to mention the ultimate consumers of healthcare—patients. Research predicts that policy interventions, if appropriate, could significantly improve population health (Mehta et al., 2017). Even non-health-related social policies, such as receiving government housing assistance and unemployment benefits, can unexpectedly affect consumers' health status.

Particularly in the U.S., the Patient Protection and Affordable Care Act (ACA), enacted on March 2010, introduced major changes in overarching government health policies that affect the healthcare system and population welfare. The ACA's main goals of making affordable health insurance available to more people, expanding the Medicaid program to cover more people, and improving quality of care while lowering the costs were believed to be the U.S. healthcare system's most significant regulatory overhaul since the passage of Medicare and Medicaid in 1965.

6   Effects of Sociodemographic and Other Internal Factors on Consumer Perceptions

In addition to external factors, personal characteristics and experiences can also influence people's perceptions on healthcare. Firstly, personal characteristics contribute to people's health status. In their 2018 National Vital Statistic Reports, the Center for Disease Control and Prevention (CDC) listed ten leading causes of death in the U.S. This list, which is led by heart disease, cancer, and accidents, gives only the primary pathophysiological conditions identified at the time of death rather than their root causes (McGinnis & Foege, 1993). Each of the conditions results from a combination of internal causes, such as genetic predispositions, and external factors, such as behavioral. For example, heart disease is well known to be related to tobacco use, elevated serum cholesterol levels, hypertension, obesity, and inadequate physical activity. Some argue that healthcare (or the lack thereof) only contributes to 10% of premature deaths, while behavioral patterns contribute to about 40%, followed by genetic predisposition (30%), social circumstances (15%), and environmental exposure (5%) (Schroeder, 2007). The World Health Organization defined social determinants of health as the "conditions in which people are born, grow, live, work, and age." Per the request of the WHO Regional Office for Europe, a group of scholars at University College London summarized the pure evidence on the social determinants of health. They listed the social gradient, stress, early life, social exclusion, work, unemployment, social support, addiction, food, and transport as ten social determinants of health (Wilkinson & Marmot, 2003).

The link between socioeconomic and health status is also well established: people with higher socioeconomic status, which is "a composite construct of income, total wealth education, emplacement, and residential neighborhood (Schroeder, 2007)," are healthier than those with lower socioeconomic status, in terms of age of death and number of disability, and this is true through all social classes (Minkler et al., 2006; Isaacs & Schroeder, 2004; and Marmot, 2001). One study found that the difference in life expectancy between the richest 1% and poorest 1% of U.S. individuals (age 40–76) is 14.6 years

(Chetty et al., 2016). A possible explanation for this dichotomy is that people with lower socioeconomic states might be more likely to engage in unhealthy behaviors.

Chetty et al. (2016) also found that the location of one's home affects a person's health status, especially for the poor, and this variation is significantly correlated with health behaviors such as smoking. In their report, Heiman and Artiga (2015) summarized health-related neighborhood and physical environmental factors such as housing, transportation, safety, parks, playgrounds, walkability, and geographic factors.

7 A Multi-year Study on Public Perceptions of Healthcare

A multi-year study with the time span of 2016 through 2018 was conducted to answer the three questions we identified in the introduction section. An annual survey targeting New York State adult residents who are age 18 and over was collected. Eight-hundred valid interviews were conducted each year. Table 1 shows some of the questions designed for and used in this study.

As stated above, health customers' social-demographic characteristics and living environment have the potential to affect their healthcare perceptions and concerns. Thus, we also include secondary data achieved from variety of public sources. As shown in Table 2, all archival data are at the county level, describing the counties' characteristics, including physical living environment, socioeconomic facets, and healthcare facts.

The survey question that was used as dependent variable in our later analysis was in the form of open-ended question: "In your opinion, what is the MOST important problem in U.S. healthcare that needs to be urgently addressed?" Thus, qualitative analysis is necessary: similar concepts need to be clustered into categories. We read through all answers, identify frequent topics, determine categories, assign categories to each response, and conduct frequency analysis on the topics.

Using three separated binary logistic Generalized estimating equation regression models, we explore the external and internal factors that are associated with the probability healthcare customers believe certain specific healthcare issues should be given the highest priority in U.S. healthcare system.

Table 3 shows all major categories extracted from the open-ended question and a brief description of each category, along with some example responses assigned to each category.

Table 1 List of interview questions and response choices used in our study

Construct	Interview question	Response choices
Most urgent healthcare issue	In your opinion, what is the MOST important problem in U.S. healthcare that needs to be urgently addressed?	Open-ended
Rating of last visit experience	How would you rate the overall level of customer service experience during your most recent visit to the healthcare facility?	– Very poor – Somewhat poor – Average – Somewhat positive – Very positive
Employment status	Last week, did you do any work for either pay or profit? Include any job from which you were on vacation, temporarily absent, or on layoff	– Yes – No – Retired – Disabled – Unable to work
Social ideology	When it comes to social issues, do you usually think of yourself as	– Extremely liberal – Liberal – Slightly liberal – Moderate or middle of the road – Slightly Conservative – Conservative – Extremely Conservative
Political party	Generally speaking, when it comes to political parties in the U.S., how would you best describe yourself?	– Strong Democrat – Not very strong Democrat – Independent, close to Democrat – Independent, close to neither – Independent, close to Republican – Not very strong Republican – Strong Republican
Marital status	Are you married, divorced, separated, widowed, or single?	– Married – Divorced – Separated – Widowed – Single
Age	What year were you born?	– Age was calculated from the year of birth
Gender	Recorded by the interviewer	– Male – Female

(*continued*)

Effective Service Operations Management: Aligning Priorities... 811

Table 1 (continued)

Construct	Interview question	Response choices
Education level	What is the last grade or class that you completed in school?	– None, or grades 1–8 – High school incomplete (grades 9–11) – High school graduate (grade 12 or GED certificate) – Technical, trade, or vocational school after high school – Some college, no four-year degree (including Associate degree) – College graduate (BS, BA, or other four-year degree) – Post-graduate training or professional schooling after college
Household income before taxes	Two questions covered income. The first question asked interviewees what was their total household income in 2015 from all sources, before taxes. Follow-up questions asked interviewees instead of a specific number, indicate if their total household income was under or over $50,000, and then use a scale to indicate their income level. Best responses obtained from these questions were used to code income	

Frequency percentage of major categories was calculated and summarized in Fig. 2.

The conclusions from the qualitative analysis are as follows. First of all, the high cost of care is the issue of greatest concern for healthcare customers during the three years of the study. These costs include the expense of care in general, of medication and of insurance. Other issues of high concern are access to care, quality of service, and low efficiency. Among all respondents, only a small portion (2.8%) believes that there is no problem in U.S. healthcare that needs urgent attention.

At a closer look, among all respondents referring access as their highest priority healthcare concern, 65.7% believe the essence of the problem is the lack

Table 2 Archival data: variables, sources, and descriptive analysis

Variables	Description and source	Unit	Min	Max	Mean	SD
Population density/1000	Population density per square mile of land area by county, data of 2010. Source: http://www.census.gov	Count	0.02	69.47	15.78	23.22
Percent poverty	Poverty estimates by county, data of 2015. Source: http://www.census.gov	Percentage	6.00	30.30	15.71	5.50
Percent uninsured	Percent without health insurance coverage by county, data of 2015. Source: http://www.census.gov	Percentage	4.90	20.20	8.88	2.83
Weighted average TPS quality score	TPS (Total Performance Score) weighted by total number of staffed beds by each county. Archived 03/03/2018. Source: https://www.ahd.com	Score, range 0–100	21.04	64.00	33.71	6.57
Sum of total beds	Number of total staffed beds by county. Archived 03/03/2018. Source: https://www.ahd.com	Count	67.00	6150	2858.55	2199.15
Length of life	Calculated score by county, data of 2017. The lower the better health ranking. Source: http://www.countyhealthrankings.org/	Score	-1.07	1.21	-0.27	0.54
Health behaviors	Calculated score by county, data of 2017. The lower the better health ranking. Source: http://www.countyhealthrankings.org/	Score	-0.52	0.40	-0.10	0.22
Clinical care	Calculated score by county, data of 2017. The lower the better health ranking. Source: http://www.countyhealthrankings.org/	Score	-0.24	0.29	-0.02	0.14
Physical environment	Calculated score by county, data of 2017. The lower the better health ranking. Source: http://www.countyhealthrankings.org/	Score	-0.07	0.08	0.01	0.04
Monthly premium	Monthly premiums for second lowest cost silver plans (SLCSP), by county—individual. Data of 2016, 2017, and 2018. Source: https://nystateofhealth.ny.gov/	USD	353.19	618.25	460.29	66.51
Price-adjusted Medicare reimbursement per enrollee	The amount of price-adjusted Medicare reimbursements per enrollee by county. Data of 2016, 2017, and 2018. Source: http://www.countyhealthrankings.org	USD	6796.00	11980.00	9435.29	1109.39
Average cost of drugs	The average of three prices from the most common pharmacy of the particular region. Six of top ten prescribed drugs in the U.S. were used for price comparison. Data of 2010. Source: https://apps.health.ny.gov/pdpw/SearchDrugs/Home.action; https://www.medicinenet.com/top_drugs_prescribed_in_the_us/views.htm	USD	80.00	340.00	125.76	33.32

Effective Service Operations Management: Aligning Priorities...   813

Table 3 List of topics (categories) of perceived customer healthcare issues

Category	Category description	Example responses
High costs of care	Includes concerns with costs of healthcare, such as costs in general, costs of medication, and costs of insurance	"Cost. We shouldn't have to spend this much money to keep ourselves healthy"
Lack of access to care	Comments concern coverage and access to healthcare of entire population and certain sub-population groups	"Affordable healthcare for all"; "Insurance for the poor"; "We need to provide more universal healthcare"
Low quality and inefficiency	Concerns regarding wait time, scheduling, resource waste, communication, clinical competency, hospital quality, and healing environment	"You should not have to wait for your appointment"; "I think the quality of the healthcare needs to be improved"
Unmet health issues	Comments regarding treatment for specific diseases, special care for certain population groups, drug issues, and preventive care	"The health of the elderly"; "Maybe preventative care through healthier living"; "Heroin epidemic"
Insurance policy and coverage	Comments related to health insurance policies such as coverage of certain items, coverage of visiting certain physicians and hospitals	"Deductibles, high premiums, and the level of coverage"; "The price or the fact that only certain insurances are only accepted in certain places"
Negative comments of Affordable Care Act	Comments that express negative opinions about Affordable Care Act and mandatory insurance	"Obamacare needs to be removed"; "The conflict between taking care of people who can't buy healthcare because of their situation and the people who are forced to buy healthcare because of regulations when it's not right for their situation"
Positive comments of Affordable Care Act	Comments that express negative opinions about Affordable Care Act or worry about repealing Affordable Care Act without a functional plan	"Obamacare, needs to be reformed a little bit. Good for communities though"; "Preventing the appeal of the Affordable Care Act"; "We need the Affordable Care Act to remain. We need people to be covered"

(continued)

814   L. Kong et al.

Table 3 (continued)

Category	Category description	Example responses
System deficiency	Comments concern healthcare system abuse, the role and power of insurance and pharmaceutical companies, immigrants occupying resources	"Insurance companies, and their whole behavior towards healthcare"; "I think the most urgent problem is that people are using the emergency room as their regular doctor"
Barriers to physical access	Physical access to healthcare, such as transportation, need reference, and introduction to a specialist, or not enough time with physician	"Transportation and accessibility"; "Inability to access the best doctors hard to change different doctors when you have been seen one. Cannot switch very easily"
Negative comments of government role	Comments about government policies, regulations, laws, and being too involved in the healthcare system	"Getting the government out of it is the biggest issue"; "Being able to sell insurance nation-wide instead of being limited to states"
Positive comments of government role	Comments that demand more government involvement, more laws, regulations, and so on	"The health insurance as a whole it needs regulation"
No problem	Respondents that do not have any issues with the current healthcare system	"No problems with healthcare"; "I am being taken care of very well"
Others	Other issues than stated above with frequency lower than 5	"Racism"; "The middle class"; "There should be more employment"

of availability of coverage of the population. Another 28.5% state that the problem is a lack of a single payer system or universal healthcare. When the respondents list quality and efficiency as their top concerns, 46.4% are worried about efficiency of the system and communication among stakeholders, 31.8% believe the quality of care and service needs urgent improvement, 14.2% question the competency of healthcare providers, and others believe the hospital and healing environment needs to be improved. Among all respondents who list unmet health issues as the most urgent healthcare concern, 43.9% want to prioritize developing a cure and treatment for specialized diseases such as cancer, 20.0% believe preventive care should be given a high priority, 15.8% appeal for better senior care, and 20.3% believe drug issues, such as over-prescription and legalization of marijuana, should be top priorities.

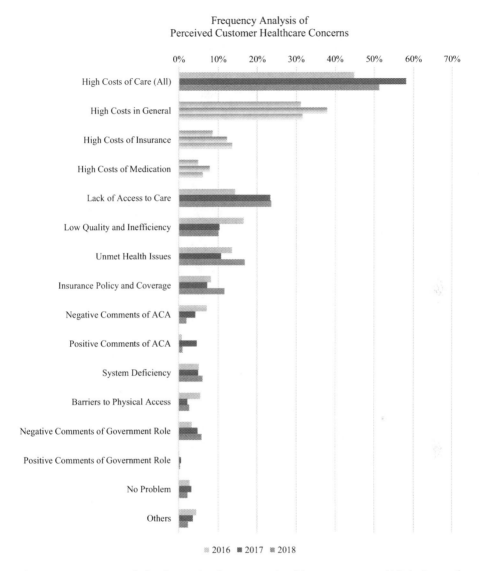

Fig. 2 Frequency analysis of perceived customer healthcare concerns. *High Costs of Care (All) includes: High Costs in General, High Costs of Insurance, and High Costs of Medication

Change in frequency by year is also directly observable. In 2016, the top three healthcare priorities among the respondents were costs of care, quality and efficiency, and access to care. In 2017, more respondents worried about costs of care and access, and fewer about quality and efficiency and unmet health issues. The year 2018 saw an increase in the number of respondents who worried that costs of insurance continue to increase. However, that year's respondents focused less attention on general costs of care and costs of medication. More tension rises on the availability and costs of insurance policies and coverage, and on unmet health issues, especially treatments for specialized diseases. Negative comments regarding government involvement increased over the three years, and negative comments on the ACA decreased.

We further explore what external and internal factors may affect the most concerned healthcare issues.

Cost of Care

Our result shows that year, gender, employment status, self-reported personal future financial status, household income, social ideology, and education level are statistically significant in explaining cost of care as the most important healthcare issue. Respondents in 2017 are 17.2% more likely to be concerned with costs than in 2016; male respondents are 17.9% more likely than females to be concerned with costs; the unemployed are most likely to worry about costs of care, while the people who are not able to work are least likely to worry; respondents who feel unconfident about their future financial status are 38.5% more likely to be concerned with cost of care than those who feel confident; liberals are 38.5% more likely than Conservatives to worry about costs of care; and the relationship line between education level and probability of worrying about costs goes down and up, with people who are college graduated least likely to be concerned with costs. Counterintuitively, as income level increases, the probability of worrying about costs increases as well.

On the county level, population density, uninsured percentage, length of life, and average costs of drugs are negatively associated with the probability of worrying about costs, whereas clinical care quality is positively associated.

Access of Care

Result shows that year, number of children in household, household income, political party, social ideology, and education level are statistically significant in explaining the probability of healthcare customers perceiving lack of access as the most important healthcare issue.

In years 2017 and 2018, respondents are 58.3% more likely to worry about access to care and coverage than in 2016; Democrats and liberals are more likely to be concerned with access to care than conservative Republicans; and college graduates are most likely to worry about access to care than those with less education. Number of children in household is negatively associated with the probability of believing access should be given the highest priority among all healthcare issues, whereas household income is positively associated.

On the county level, average monthly insurance premium is positively associated with the probability of perceiving lack of access as the most important healthcare issue.

Quality and Efficiency of Care

Controlling for the repeated measures and all other sociodemographic characteristics, result shows that year, gender, most recent hospital visit experience, social ideology, the part of the state in which one lives, and education level are statistically significant in explaining whether healthcare customers believe that the quality of care and lack of efficiency are the most important issues in healthcare. Respondents were 66.7% more likely to be concerned with quality and efficiency in 2016 than in 2017 and 2018; female respondents are more concerned with this issue; people who are more conservative are more likely to be concerned with quality and efficiency; people who live in downstate New York are more likely to worry about quality and efficiency than those who live in upstate; and people who had a better experience during their most recent hospital visit are less likely to worry about the quality and efficiency.

On the county level, poverty level is positively related to the probability of being concerned with quality of care and low efficiency, and clinical care quality is negatively related.

8   Conclusions and Discussions

The above-stated results provide empirical evidence for the "Iron Triangle of Health Care." This concept was first introduced in 1994 by William Kissick (1994), the father of Medicare, describing three issues which are the primary concerns of all healthcare systems: cost, access, and quality. Those three issues compete for resources, and it was believed that when one of the three changes, the other two will be affected. Over the years, government policy makers have attempted to solve this complicated problem set, for example, by improving quality of care without increasing cost. The "Iron Triangle of Health Care" issues happen to be what worries customers the most. This finding provides confirmatory information for healthcare industry stakeholders who have been devoted to addressing those issues.

Cost of care, access to care and coverage for all, and quality of care and system efficiency are perceived by healthcare customers as the healthcare issues that need to be most urgently addressed. This information, above all, tells us what customers want in healthcare: they want it to be affordable, they want access to insurance coverage, and they want reliable care. As a consequence, resources should be allocated accordingly. Along with rising costs, the concept "value of care" has become increasingly popular. In the healthcare context where the information asymmetry level is high, the issues of who should be the one to decide how much to spend on a case and where should the point be to stop treatment from the value point of view are ethically difficult to determine. Yet operations management theories on the decision-making process, for both providers and patients, may shed some light. The uninsured rate has always been lower in the U.S. than in some other developed countries such as Germany and Japan. While it is the government's responsibility to decide whether a single payer system should be adopted, the operations management field could expand the insurance coverage rate under the current system by methods such as modeling the insurance companies' product price system and patients' decision process of choosing an insurance product. Regarding quality of care, the recent "patient-centered care" concept emphasizes the role of patients and their participation in co-creating high quality care. Under this concept, the quality of non-clinical aspects of care, such as emotional wellbeing, is considered as important as the clinical aspect of care, including physical wellbeing. In this regard, the operations management field could build upon service operation theories and infuse service excellence into healthcare settings.

In facing resource allocation issues, those that are not important to customers are as crucial as those that are. Few respondents in our survey commented on the physical access to health service, such as lack of transportation or being too far away from any healthcare facility. Also, only several people mentioned any concern over the quality of the hospitals, in terms of safety and cleanness. As a developed country, basic infrastructures such as healthcare facilities and transportation networks are well developed. Thus, further investments in those areas may not achieve marginal utility as high as would be true in other areas.

We discover that the alignments and mismatches between current HOM research streams and customers' perceived issues are mixed. That is, fair alignments exist in some areas, as many papers are studying what customers are frequently worried about. Meanwhile, mismatches also exist when concerns that worry customers are not being addressed by research or when research focuses on issues that are not frequently brought up by customers.

Effective Service Operations Management: Aligning Priorities... 819

Looking more deeply into alignment issues, we note that customers' most frequently mentioned concern is cost of care, but not many healthcare operations management (HOM) research articles directly address the cost issue. That said, many research studies questions that help contain or even reduce the cost of care. For example, at the micro level we find HOM papers that examined issues on ambulatory care (Cayirli et al., 2008; Liu & Ziya, 2014; and Liu, 2016), inpatient care (Lemay et al., 2017), and emergency care (Batt & Terwiesch, 2015) focused on scheduling and queuing of both patients and care providers, with a goal of reducing idle time and improving efficiency, thus decreasing costs in the long run. Quality remains an operations problem, and many customers brought up their concerns with quality of care and service. Likewise, many research papers are indeed trying to solve this matter, with studies that include quality of clinical care (Kong et al., 2020; Anderson et al., 2014), quality of service in healthcare settings (Zheng et al., 2018; Theokary & Ren, 2011), and the combination and tradeoff between the two (Senot et al., 2015).

The most noticeable mismatch in the HOM literature is access to care and coverage. This was the second most frequently mentioned healthcare issue of customers, but it was not explored often in HOM literature. To be clear, access does not mean the physical access to healthcare services, such as "need a referral" or "need transportation to facility," or "waitlist is too long." Instead, this issue involves peoples' access to insurance coverage at a macro level, such as "universal healthcare" or "everyone should be covered for healthcare." This requires macro-level decision making, and some may argue that it is more political than operational. However, when viewed as allocating healthcare resources to different population and locations on a national level, access is one of the original issues that operations management has tried to address ever since World War II. Many research opportunities emerge from here, such as exploring how insurance companies could provide affordable coverage to broader population groups while still making a reasonable profit, or modeling the decision process of how customers choose whether to purchase insurance, and, if so, what kind of insurance to have. Another issue that appears more frequently in this study than in previous research is unmet health issues. Here, operations management could at least contribute to the expansion of preventive care and improve the quality of senior care. Research directions such as identifying the optimal locations of preventive care clinics to improve coverage of the local communities, the decision process to use for offering preventive care services, the insurance policies to cover preventive care, and the application of healthcare operations methods to senior care facilities could be beneficial.

9 Implications

The study presented in this chapter has several implications for healthcare stakeholders, including healthcare insurers, providers, and policy makers, in terms of where to allocate more resources and where not to. For example, when non-healthcare companies move into healthcare area, such as Amazon. com, Berkshire Hathaway, and JPMorgan, they may want to contain the costs for customers and broaden the access to coverage before rushing to new incentives. Healthcare policy makers could draw upon our findings and encourage more value-based healthcare programs and policies to contain customer costs and increase value. Also, the findings regarding personal characteristics could help companies design and market their products to better align with customer segments.

This study also provides implications for service operations management, especially healthcare operations management researchers. For example, more research is needed in solving insurance coverage issues, such as developing affordable insurance products and customer decision process in shopping for insurance products. Also, operations management researchers can contribute to the exploration of unmet health issues, such as efficiently expand of preventive care, and improve the quality of senior care.

References

Anderson, D., Gao, G., & Golden, B. (2014). Life is all about timing: An examination of differences in treatment quality for trauma patients based on hospital arrival time. *Production and Operations Management, 23*(12), 2178–2190.

Baltussen, R., & Niessen, L. (2006). Priority setting of health interventions: The need for multi-criteria decision analysis. *Cost effectiveness and resource allocation, 4*(1), 14.

Batt, R. J., & Terwiesch, C. (2015). Waiting patiently: An empirical study of queue abandonment in an emergency department. *Management Science, 61*(1), 39–59.

Bazerman, M., & Moore, D. A. (2013). *Judgment in managerial decision making.* John Wiley & Sons.

Boyer, K., & Verma, R. (2009). *Operations and supply chain management for the 21st century.* Cengage Learning.

Burstein, P. (1998). Bringing the public back in: Should sociologists consider the impact of public opinion on public policy? *Social Forces, 77*(1), 27–62.

Cayirli, T., Veral, E., & Rosen, H. (2008). Assessment of patient classification in appointment system design. *Production and Operations Management, 17*(3), 338–353.

Chetty, R., Stepner, M., Abraham, S., Lin, S., Scuderi, B., Turner, N., Bergeron, A., & Cutler, D. (2016). The association between income and life expectancy in the United States, 2001–2014. *JAMA, 315*(16), 1750–1766.

Dai, T., & Tayur, S. (Eds.). (2018). *Handbook of healthcare analytics: Theoretical minimum for conducting 21st century research on healthcare operations.* John Wiley & Sons.

Dai, T., & Tayur, S. R. (2019, Forthcoming). Healthcare operations management: A snapshot of emerging research. *Manufacturing & Service Operations Management.*

Ham, C. (1993). Priority setting in the NHS: Reports from six districts. *BMJ, 307*(6901), 435–438.

Heiman, H. J., & Artiga, S. (2015). Beyond health care: The role of social determinants in promoting health and health equity. *Health, 20*(10), 1–10.

Isaacs, S. L., & Schroeder, S. A. (2004). Class—The ignored determinant of the nation's health. *The New England journal of medicine.*

Kissick, W. L. (1994). *Medicine's dilemmas: Infinite needs versus finite resources.* Yale University Press.

Kong, L., Hu, K., & Verma, R. (2020, May 20). *Service chains' operational strategies: Standardization or customization? Evidence from the nursing home industry.* Evidence from the Nursing Home Industry (SSRN).

Kringos, D. S., Boerma, W., van der Zee, J., & Groenewegen, P. (2013). Europe's strong primary care systems are linked to better population health but also to higher health spending. *Health Affairs, 32*(4), 686–694.

Lemay, B., Cohn, A., Epelman, M., & Gorga, S. (2017). New methods for resolving conflicting requests with examples from medical residency scheduling. *Production and Operations Management, 26*(9), 1778–1793.

Liu, N. (2016). Optimal choice for appointment scheduling window under patient no-show behavior. *Production and Operations Management, 25*(1), 128–142.

Liu, N., & Ziya, S. (2014). Panel size and overbooking decisions for appointment-based services under patient no-shows. *Production and Operations Management, 23*(12), 2209–2223.

Marmot, M. (2001). Inequalities in health. *New England Journal of Medicine, 345*(2), 134–135.

McDaniels, T. L., Gregory, R. S., & Fields, D. (1999). Democratizing risk management: Successful public involvement in local water management decisions. *Risk Analysis, 19*(3), 497–510.

McGinnis, J. M., & Foege, W. H. (1993). Actual causes of death in the United States. *JAMA, 270*(18), 2207–2212.

Mehta, N. K., Patel, S. A., Ali, M. K., & Venkat Narayan, K. M. (2017). Preventing disability: The influence of modifiable risk factors on state and national disability prevalence. *Health Affairs, 36*(4), 626–635.

Minkler, M., Fuller-Thomson, E., & Guralnik, J. M. (2006). Gradient of disability across the socioeconomic spectrum in the United States. *New England Journal of Medicine, 355*(7), 695–703.

Mitton, C., Smith, N., Peacock, S., Evoy, B., & Abelson, J. (2009). Public participation in health care priority setting: A scoping review. *Health Policy, 91*(3), 219–228.

MOH Republic of Ghana Ministry of Health. (1998). *Health sector five year programs of work: 1997–2001*. Ministry of Health.

Monroe, A. D. (1998). Public opinion and public policy, 1980–1993. *Public Opinion Quarterly, 62*(1).

Pierskalla, W. P., & Brailer, D. J. (1994). Applications of operations research in health care delivery. *Handbooks in Operations Research and Management Science, 6,* 469–505.

Rowe, G., & Frewer, L. J. (2005). A typology of public engagement mechanisms. *Science, Technology, & Human Values, 30*(2), 251–290.

Schroeder, S. A. (2007). We can do better—Improving the health of the American people. *New England Journal of Medicine, 357*(12), 1221–1228.

Senot, C., Chandrasekaran, A., Ward, P. T., Tucker, A. L., & Moffatt-Bruce, S. D. (2015). The impact of combining conformance and experiential quality on hospitals' readmissions and cost performance. *Management Science, 62*(3), 829–848.

Theokary, C., & Ren, J. Z. (2011). An empirical study of the relations between hospital volume, teaching status, and service quality. *Production and Operations Management, 20*(3), 303–318.

Traulsen, J. M., & Almarsdóttir, A. B. (2005). Pharmaceutical policy and the lay public. *Pharmacy World and Science, 27*(4), 273–277.

Wilkinson, R. G., & Marmot, M. (Eds.). (2003). *Social determinants of health: The solid facts*. World Health Organization.

Zheng, S., Tucker, A. L., Ren, Z. J., Heineke, J., McLaughlin, A., & Podell, A. L. (2018). The impact of internal service quality on preventable adverse events in hospitals. *Production and Operations Management, 27*(12), 2201–2212.

Service Failure and Complaints Management: An Overview

Chiara Orsingher, Arne De Keyser, Dorottya Varga, and Yves Van Vaerenbergh

1 Introduction

Service failures occur on a regular basis. To appreciate their occurrence, it is sufficient to recall one's own experience. Just remember how many times a meal was delivered too late, a call center employee responded rudely, or a failed product was not replaced at no costs. Even easier to remember is the array of negative emotions that typically followed a service failure and the desire to restore the initial situation to obtain what the service organization should have delivered in the first place. Service failures require organizations to manage the sequence of events that follow the service failure by organizing

---

C. Orsingher (✉)
Department of Management, University of Bologna, Bologna, Italy
e-mail: chiara.orsingher@unibo.it

A. De Keyser
Department of Marketing, EDHEC Business School, Lille, France
e-mail: arne.dekeyser@edhec.edu

D. Varga
imec-SMIT, Vrije Universiteit Brussel, Brussel, Belgium
e-mail: dorottya.varga@vub.be

Y. Van Vaerenbergh
Department of Marketing, KU Leuven, Leuven, Belgium
e-mail: yves.vanvaerenbergh@kuleuven.be

© The Author(s), under exclusive license to Springer Nature Switzerland AG 2022
B. Edvardsson, B. Tronvoll (eds.), *The Palgrave Handbook of Service Management*,
https://doi.org/10.1007/978-3-030-91828-6_39

a set of appropriate responses aimed at restoring the regular service experience. In this chapter, we build on the notion of the service recovery journey (SRJ, Van Vaerenbergh et al., 2019) to illustrate the sequence of customer and organizational responses toward service failures. The SRJ conceptualizes service failure and recovery in the form of a series of events underlying the recovery process and consists of pre-recovery, recovery, and post-recovery phases, which collectively shape the service recovery experience.

Figure 1 illustrates the structure of this chapter, which sequentially shows customer and organizational responses toward the failure and recovery

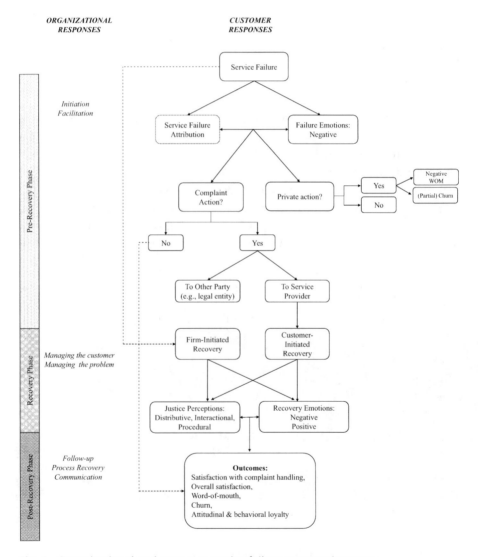

Fig. 1 Organizational and customer service failure-recovery journey

journey. We first define service failure. Then, we describe customer emotional and cognitive reactions to failures, and the organizational responses that follow before the recovery process. Then, we portray the array of organizational responses that organizations can adopt to recover the failure, and customer emotional and cognitive reactions to these. Finally, we delineate the organizational actions at the end of the recovery journey. We conclude this chapter by providing several clues on how service organizations should set up an effective and sustainable service recovery system.

2 What Is a Service Failure?

Service failures are defined in various ways, including service performances that fall below customers' expectations (Hess, 2008; Hoffman & Bateson, 1997), mistakes that lead to customer dissatisfaction (Bitner et al., 1990), or customer norm deviance (Fullerton & Punj, 2004) that leads to dysfunctional behavior (Kjeldgaard et al., 2021; Fisk et al., 2010). From a customer journey perspective, service failures represent temporary or permanent interruptions of the customer's regular service experience (Van Vaerenbergh et al., 2019). For example, a wrong dish served at a restaurant temporarily impedes a customer from sharing the social act of dining together with friends; a canceled flight permanently impedes a customer to be on time and participate in the wedding ceremony of a friend.

Generally speaking, service failures can be classified around two dimensions: failure type and failure magnitude. Failure type refers to whether the failure concerns the outcome of the service experience, that is, what customers actually receive from the service, or the process, that is, how the service is delivered (Bitner et al., 1990; Gronroos, 1988). Outcome failures occur when the service organization does not accomplish the basic service need (e.g., delivery of a wrong meal). Process failures occur when the delivery of the core service is flawed or defective in some way (e.g., a receptionist treats a customer rudely during check-in) (Smith et al., 1999).

Service failure magnitude or severity of the failure refers to a customer's perceived intensity of a service problem (Craighead et al., 2004) or the magnitude of loss experienced by customers from a failure (Smith et al., 1999). Customer losses from failures can be tangible, entailing the loss of monetary or product/service value, or intangible, representing losses in, among others, psychic energy, convenience, time, and shared social experiences (Craighead et al., 2004; Hart et al., 1990).

3   Customer Responses Following a Service Failure

Service failures may trigger a wide array of emotional reactions. Cognitive appraisal theory (CAT) explains the mechanism through which the intensity, valence, and type of emotion arise (Lazarus, 1966, 1991). According to CAT, emotions are mental states that result from the cognitive appraisal of a situation (Bagozzi et al., 1999; Smith & Bolton, 2002). A key part of this appraisal relates to how goal-congruent events are (Johnson & Stewart, 2005). Goal-congruent events trigger positive emotions, and goal-incongruent events trigger negative emotions (Johnson & Stewart, 2005). As a service failure represents a goal-incongruent event, it typically generates negative customer emotions. What emotion is felt depends on further appraisal dimensions (Ortony et al., 1988), of which causal attribution is particularly relevant in the context of service failure.

Attribution theory describes the process through which customers make causal explanations for service failures. Customers do so because they have a need to understand, control, and predict their environment (Weiner, 2000). For example, a customer that is obliged to spend several hours at the airport because a flight is delayed likely engages in an active search for the causes of this service failure: Is the failure caused by bad weather, a mechanical breakdown, poor management, or air traffic control problems (Van Vaerenbergh et al., 2014)? Engaging in an attributional process allows customers to understand the environment and to manage their emotions more effectively.

Customers tend to attribute the causes of service failures along two core dimensions. The first dimension is the stability attribution, which entails causes that are temporary or erratic versus permanent or constant over time (Folkes, 1984). For example, an employee that accidentally spills a drink over the customer might be construed as an unstable cause, whereas an employee that does not make an effort to remember the name of a loyal customer might be construed as a stable cause. The second dimension is the controllability attribution, which entails customers' beliefs that the service organization could have prevented the failure (Choi & Mattila, 2008). A flight crew arriving late at the airport is an example of a controllable cause, whereas bad weather conditions are not. Van Vaerenbergh et al.'s (2014) meta-analysis shows that stability and controllability attribution affect customer negative emotions. Yet, controllability attributions have a stronger effect on negative emotions than stability attributions. This result suggests that customers who believe that the outcome of the service could have been different had the organization acted in a reliable manner experience strong negative emotions and evaluations (Van Vaerenbergh et al., 2014). Conversely, since customers are less accurate in determining a service failure's degree of persistence, they are more uncertain about their stability attributions and tend to react less emotionally.

In sum, the service failure and the attributional process lead customers to experience negative emotions such as anger, frustration, and regret. The strength of these emotional reactions depends on the service failure severity and attributions. This process, in turn, leads customers to decide on whether and how they wish to act on these experienced emotions. We can distinguish between three different reactions to service failures: remaining silent, taking private action, or complaining.

The majority of customers prefer to remain silent if the problem is not severe enough, they are under time pressure, they have an introverted nature, they don't expect a solution to come from complaining, they perceive complaining to be too effortful, they don't know who is to blame, and/or they fear to damage their future interactions with the organization (e.g., Sands et al., 2020; Bitner et al., 2000; Choi & Mattila, 2008; DeWitt & Brady, 2003). However, both the academic and business literature highlight the risk of having silent dissatisfied customers. Silent customers make it harder for the organization to identify a failure, understand the causes of the service failure, and recover from it. Other customers may take private action, such as talking negatively about a service organization to others (e.g., online forums or blogs) and/or (partially) taking their business elsewhere. Finally, some customers will decide to complain either to the service organization or to a third party (e.g., take legal action) while some others may take both private actions and complain simultaneously.

In the remainder of this chapter, we will focus on customers who complain to the service organization. These customers initiate an interaction with the service organization and explicitly request the service organization to recover from the failure (i.e., customer-initiated recovery journey). In some situations, service organizations may also reach out to customers who have not complained directly to them (or who are unaware of a failure) and start a firm-initiated recovery journey.

4   Organizational Responses Following a Service Failure

To consider organizational response options following a failure, we need to distinguish between a pre-recovery and recovery phase. Response options can be classified as relating to compensation, favorable employee behavior, and organizational procedures.

The Pre-recovery Phase

The pre-recovery phase covers the time between initial awareness of a service failure and the first interaction between the customer and the organization (Van Vaerenbergh et al., 2019). Failure reporting is critical in this phase, as it provides organizations with an opportunity to restore the damage in a subsequent phase. The literature identifies two potential organizational procedures as response options: initiation and facilitation (Van Vaerenbergh et al., 2019). Initiation refers to the proactive behavior of the organization toward the service failure. In some instances, the organization can initiate the failure even before the customer notices it. For example, credit card services can detect fraudulent transactions on a customer's account, deactivate the card immediately, and issue a new one. Facilitation refers to how easy organizations make it for the customer to express their dissatisfaction (Davidow, 2003). As complaining requires customers to make an effort, facilitating the expression of their dissatisfaction is a first step to prevent customers from engaging in damaging private actions like negative word-of-mouth and switching to the competition.

The Recovery Phase

The recovery phase starts after initial contact is established with the customer and stops when a satisfactory recovery occurs or when the customer gives up his or her quest to receive an appropriate response from the organization. During this time frame, the organization should rectify or compensate for the original failure. The recovery phase is central to the customer's service recovery journey. Organizations need to be mindful of adequately treating the customer (i.e., managing the customer) and offering a solution to the customer's problem (i.e., managing the problem; Zeithaml et al., 2017).

Managing the Customer

Response options in this stage pertain to all three types of organizational responses: apology as a compensation option; excuse, justification, referential account, credibility feedback; courtesy, empathy, and willingness to listen as favorable employee behavior options; and recovery time as an organizational procedure option.

One of the most precise recommendations in recovery research is that organizations should apologize for service failures. An apology refers to the public expression of remorse through which the organization acknowledges the complainant's distress (Davidow, 2003) and can be considered as a psychological reward for the customer's "social loss" (Gelbrich & Roschk, 2011). An empathetic and sincere apology provides an emotional benefit that can offset the lack of attention customers feel after experiencing a failure (Roschk & Gelbrich, 2014). Although apologizing for the failure should be the first step in the recovery phase, an apology alone is oftentimes insufficient to satisfy and retain customers. Other response options should always accompany an apology.

Many customers also seek to understand why the failure occurred and expect organizations to account for the problem by providing an explanation (Davidow, 2003). Four types of explanations can be distinguished: excuse, justification, referential account, and credibility feedback. An excuse refers to shifting the organization's responsibility for the failure onto external causes or circumstances (Wang et al., 2009). Justification refers to accepting full responsibility but rationalizing the failure by pointing to the fulfillment of a superordinate goal (Shaw et al., 2003). Referential account refers to an attempt to minimize the failure's importance by invoking downward comparison, for example, with those who are worse off (Bradley & Sparks, 2012). Credibility feedback refers to informing customers about what the organization is currently doing or planning to do to prevent the same failure from occurring in the future (Davidow, 2003). Excuses typically result in greater customer satisfaction but only if they are perceived as clear, detailed, and credible. Other research shows that justifications could be more effective than excuses or referential accounts. If customers perceive the justification to be fair, they will attribute less responsibility to the organization, and thus, they will be more satisfied (Wang et al., 2009). Similarly, credibility feedback is an important indicator of the organization's trustworthiness, thus positively influencing customers' satisfaction.

In terms of other favorable employee behavior, employees' courtesy, empathy, and willingness to listen are critical interpersonal skills to effectively manage customers' emotional reactions. Courtesy refers to behavior that demonstrates politeness and respect (Liao, 2007), empathy refers to the provision of caring, individual attention (Tax et al., 1998), and willingness to listen refers to the employee's commitment to carefully listen to the customer's description of the unsatisfactory event (Nguyen & McColl-Kennedy, 2003). The amount and quality of information obtained in this phase may help organizations identify the cause of the problem and develop an effective solution. Research almost unanimously shows that favorable employee behaviors improve customer outcomes (Liao, 2007).

Finally, recovery time is a critical response option for managing both customers and their problems. Recovery time is the amount of time that elapses between the customers' initial complaint and the organization's handling of that complaint (Hogreve et al., 2017). The provision of a quick, initial response to the customer's complaint is an important step in the "managing the customer" stage as a quick response attenuates customer anger and regret (Chebat & Slusarczyk, 2005), but only if the organization provides a proper resolution for the failure in the "managing the problem" stage.

Managing the Problem

Response options in this stage include immediate or delayed monetary compensation, new/replacement goods, and new/reperformed services as compensation options; effort as a favorable employee behavior; and recovery time, customer participation, flexibility, and employee empowerment as organizational procedure options.

Compensation can be conceptualized as a resource that rewards customers for their loss due to the organization's failure and can be classified by the timing (i.e., immediate and delayed) and nature of compensation (new/exchanged goods and new/reperformed services). Delayed monetary compensation and immediate monetary compensation refer to a quantifiable amount of money provided in the future (e.g., voucher, store credit) or the present (e.g., discount, money back), respectively. New/replacement goods and new/reperformed services refer to the exchange of an object or activity that was initially deemed unsatisfactory. Research shows that a bad product (service) should be replaced (reperformed), and a monetary loss should be matched with immediate monetary compensation (Roschk & Gelbrich, 2014). An additional aspect to consider is the amount of compensation to offer. Gelbrich et al.

(2015) show that the level of optimal compensation differs according to customers' choice of handling the failure: acceptance versus rejection (e.g., a customer decides whether or not to stay at the pre-booked hotel even though the air-conditioning is not working). In the case of service acceptance, compensation between 0% and 20% exerted the highest customer satisfaction. In the case of service rejection, compensation between 70% and 80% was associated with the highest return in satisfaction, while satisfaction was much lower for both lower levels of compensation or even overcompensation.

In terms of favorable employee behavior, employee effort has an important role in managing customers' problems. Customers prefer to interact with employees who invest a significant amount of energy in finding the most appropriate solution (Mostafa et al., 2014).

Looking at organizational procedures, recovery time is again critical in this stage of the recovery phase. The faster the organization offers a resolution for the problem, the more favorable the customer outcomes (Larivière & Dirk Van den Poel, 2005). However, speed per se is not always beneficial. Organizations should not strive to provide the fastest response possible but should rather set the right expectations. For example, organizations can clearly indicate the timeframe of responding to customer complaints in their procedures. Customers tend to accept that organizations need time to develop a solution to their problem. Negative consequences arise only if the time taken by the organization is perceived as too long. For example, research suggests that customers' recovery time zone of tolerance is shorter using social media (i.e., expecting an answer within 1–6 hours) than other channels such as phone or email (i.e., expecting an answer within 6–12 hours; Istanbulluoglu, 2017).

Customer participation refers to explicitly involving the customer in the recovery process. Such participation gives customers a feeling of control over the recovery journey, which makes them less likely to demand additional monetary compensation (Roggeveen et al., 2012). Customers also appreciate flexibility in the problem resolution stage. Flexibility can range from treating all customers on an equal basis according to organizational procedures to provide a response that is customized to the situation and the complainant's wishes (Sparks & McColl-Kennedy, 2001). On the one hand, treating customers equally guarantees fairness across customers but may not effectively resolve each customer's problem. On the other hand, customization better addresses individuals' needs but might lead customers to perceive that they are being treated less favorably than others. Organizations facing these situations might benefit from offering customers a choice, as long as this choice is part of the organizations' procedures and available to many customers. Finally,

832   C. Orsingher et al.

employee empowerment refers to delegating decision authority concerning the organizational responses to customer complaints to frontline employees. Frontline employees usually know the initial problem and can respond most adequately in a timely manner. Employee empowerment grants employees the authority to customize their response to customers' needs leading to favorable customer outcomes (Boshoff & Leong, 1998).

5   Customer Responses Following the Organizational Recovery Efforts

Customers' Cognitive, Emotional, and Behavioral Reactions

Customers' cognitive, emotional, and behavioral reactions provide the litmus test of organizational efforts to recover from service failures. Customers typically evaluate the service organization's responses through the lens of fairness: has the organization handled the complaining customer fairly? Researchers typically drew upon justice theory as framework for predicting customer reactions to the organization's recovery efforts. This theory is rooted in social psychology and concerns individuals' evaluations of the fairness of exchanges and reactions to conflict situations (Orsingher et al., 2010).

Researchers conceptualized justice as a multidimensional construct, consisting of distributive, procedural, and interactional justice. Distributive justice centers on the perceived fairness of the redress offered to the customer to resolve the complaint (Orsingher et al., 2010). Customers who believe the organization's compensation restores the initial service or offsets the inconvenience caused by the failure display high perceptions of distributive justice. Procedural justice represents customer evaluations of the fairness of the policies, procedures, and criteria organizations use to handle the recovery journey. An easy, quick, and flexible complaint process (Tax et al., 1998; Smith et al., 1999) driven by clear, readable, and customer-oriented procedures (Severt, 2002) build customer perceptions of procedural justice. Finally, interactional justice captures the quality of the interpersonal treatment customers receive during the recovery process (Orsingher et al., 2010; Colquitt et al., 2001). Interactional justice includes customers' evaluation of the empathy, politeness, effort, and honesty of the employees handling the complaining customer.

Across an abundant body of research, justice dimensions have shown to affect customer satisfaction with complaint handling and customer overall

Service Failure and Complaints Management: An Overview 833

satisfaction with the organization, albeit with different strengths. Two meta-analyses reveal the relative strengths of justice dimensions on satisfaction with complaint handling and overall satisfaction. Distributive justice typically has the largest impact on satisfaction with complaint handling, followed by interactional justice, whereas procedural justice has a non-significant effect (Gelbrich & Roschk, 2011; Orsingher et al., 2010). Thus, customers evaluate organizational efforts mostly on the compensation offered and the interpersonal relationship with the employees managing the customer, whereas procedures remain in the background (Gelbrich & Roschk, 2011; Orsingher et al., 2010). Interestingly, the situation is different for overall satisfaction. Distributive justice does not play a prominent role; rather, interactional justice exerts a slightly stronger effect than distributive justice, and the effect of procedural justice is weak but significant.

These findings show that all three justice dimensions are important in a service failure and recovery context. They affect differently the level of satisfaction that customers feel immediately after the complaint is handled and the overall evaluation of the organization. Namely, the fairness of the redress drives mainly satisfaction with complaint handling but less overall satisfaction. The fairness of the interpersonal treatment is relevant in immediate evaluations but even more in the overall evaluation. The fairness of the procedures does not significantly impact the immediate satisfaction but becomes more relevant for overall satisfaction. This observation suggests that the evaluation of the organizational complaint handling procedures shapes the evaluation of the organization as a whole, beyond the specific failure event. The different nature of the two satisfaction constructs is also reflected in the way they subsequently affect customer outcomes: satisfaction with complaint handling is more strongly related to positive word-of-mouth, whereas overall satisfaction is more strongly related to customer loyalty (Gelbrich & Roschk, 2011; Orsingher et al., 2010).

Customers not only react cognitively to recovery efforts, but they also react emotionally. When a satisfactory recovery happens, customers display an array of positive emotions such as relief, happiness, pleasure, and gratitude (Su et al., 2021). Positive emotions are correlated to important customer outcomes such as satisfaction with recovery and overall satisfaction (Valentini et al., 2020), exit behavior (Chebat & Slusarczyk, 2005), next-buy decisions (Larivière & Dirk Van den Poel, 2005), and (reduced) customer churn (Knox & Van Oest, 2014). Although the vast majority of studies focuses on the negative outcomes of a service failure, research shows that a well-executed recovery triggers positive emotional reactions. Interestingly, the strength of the relationship between positive emotions and customer outcomes is—in

834   C. Orsingher et al.

absolute terms—stronger than the one with negative outcomes (Valentini et al., 2020). In other words, the positive emotions that stem from a good recovery are more strongly related to positive outcomes than are the negative outcomes that stem from the service failure.

These findings mirror the ones observed when comparing customer satisfaction levels between complaining customers who have received a good recovery with customers who have undergone a regular service experience. The phenomenon, called the service recovery paradox, has been conceptually defined as a situation in which a customer's post-failure satisfaction exceeds pre-failure satisfaction (De Matos et al., 2007). The paradox has been ascribed to a deviation of the service experience from the regular service script, which produces an increased sensitivity in the customer regarding the failure and the redress process. As a consequence, satisfaction with the recovery process becomes more salient than satisfaction with the initial attributes in influencing the final evaluation (de Matos et al., 2007; Magnini et al., 2007). An alternative explanation comes from a psychological phenomenon called the contrast effect, according to which a positive event (e.g., a good service recovery) appears more positive when preceded by a negative one (i.e., a service failure) than not (Olsen & Pracejus, 2004).

Meta-analytic findings have concluded that satisfaction increases after a high service recovery effort suggesting the existence of the service recovery paradox (de Matos et al., 2007). However, the effect is non-significant on repurchase intentions, word-of-mouth, and corporate image. Presumably, when evaluating satisfaction with complaint handling, customers are influenced by the redress and the recovery process they have received. Still, when evaluating their likelihood of repurchasing from the same organization, customers think that their original desired outcome was not accomplished in the service experience. Therefore, it is not worth repurchasing from this organization (de Matos et al., 2007).

Boundary Conditions of Customer Reactions to Service Recovery

The literature on service recovery has been enriched by several studies aimed at understanding the boundary conditions of the effects of organizational efforts on customer outcomes. Some of those have focused on how the type and way of redress offered affect customer outcomes. For example, compensation in the form of a banknote or banknote-like coupon fosters customer tipping and cross-buying behavior more than an intangible credit entry. A compensation accompanied by a handwritten note from the service employee affects satisfaction with complaint handling, customer tipping and cross-buying more than an impersonal, typewritten note from the organization (Roschk & Gelbrich, 2014).

Other studies have investigated how the customer relationship with the organization affects customers' perceptions of the recovery process. For example, customer perceptions of the strength of their relationships with the organization affects the way high compensation is perceived: high relationship quality customers respond to high compensation levels with higher levels of satisfaction with complaint handling and overall satisfaction than low relationship quality customers (Gelbrich et al., 2015). In the online public complaining context, however, research shows that customers tend to hold a grudge, especially after a series of failures. Over time, strong-relationship customers' feelings of revenge toward the organization decrease more slowly, and their need to stop any interaction with the organization increases more rapidly than that of weak-relationship customers (Grégoire et al., 2009). When behavioral outcome variables are observed, findings report that satisfaction with complaint handling positively affects purchase volume, yet this relationship becomes less strong when customers' level of affective commitment toward the organization increases (Evanschitzky et al., 2011). Similarly, as the relationship gets longer, the positive effect of successful service recovery on customers' change in cross-buying decreases (Béal et al., 2019). All in all, this suggests that loyal customers become less sensitive to the organizations' recovery actions.

Double Deviation

Customers are not always satisfied with organizations' responses to their complaints and experience negative emotions after recovery. The 2020 Customer Rage Survey shows that no less than 58% of respondents felt that they received nothing in return for their complaint efforts. The lack of appropriate response to a service failure is often referred to as "double deviation" (Bitner et al., 1990). The consequences of double deviation can be quite severe. Surachartkumtonkun et al. (2015) show that while a service failure mainly triggers low-level negative emotions such as frustration or annoyance, a failed service recovery leads to customer rage. Customers feel betrayed and feel as if they can no longer trust the organization (Basso & Pizzutti, 2016; Grégoire & Fisher, 2006). In the worst-case scenario, a double deviation might lead a customer to leave the organization, take revenge by spreading offline and online negative word-of-mouth or by engaging in verbal and physical aggression toward frontline employees (e.g., Joireman et al., 2013; Surachartkumtonkun et al., 2015). In the best-case scenario, customers who experience a double deviation might consider starting a second service recovery journey. Research shows that organizations face a difficult time recovering from a failed recovery. Johnston and Fern (1999), for example, show that customers expect much more from the organization when recovering a failed recovery compared to recovering a service failure—that is, better, faster, and more extensive recovery.

Later studies supported this perspective and showed that offering an apology, compensation, and an explanation for why the initial service recovery failed might reduce customers' desire to take revenge for a service failure (Joireman et al., 2013). Offering an apology and promising that the failure will not happen again in the future are particularly effective at restoring trust among the customer (Basso & Pizzutti, 2016). Customers consider an apology following a double deviation as a sign of integrity, while they consider a promise as a sign of competence. A follow-up study by Pacheco et al. (2019) shows that the effectiveness of offering an apology and a promise depends upon the timing at which these trust recovery tactics are offered. An apology was most effective when offered immediately or shortly after the failed recovery while promising that the failure would not happen again was more effective when offered at a later time after the double deviation.

6 Organizational Responses Following the Recovery Efforts

The post-recovery phase follows the end of the recovery phase, during which customers reflect and evaluate their experiences in the previous two phases. Research identifies two organizational procedures that serve as response options: follow-up and process recovery communication. Follow-up refers to procedures aimed at checking whether the problem was resolved to the customer's satisfaction and is typically appreciated by customers but only if the problem was initially resolved in an effective manner (Mostafa et al., 2014). Process recovery communication informs customers about the steps the organization has taken to prevent a recurring failure and tends to enhance customers' satisfaction, repurchase intentions and word-of-mouth intentions (Van Vaerenbergh et al., 2012), and, for major failures, even influences

Service Failure and Complaints Management: An Overview 837

organization-level stock returns (Rasoulian et al., 2017). Van Vaerenbergh et al. (2012) show that, overall, customers perceive a process recovery communication as an organizational action that is fair and as an investment in the customer relationship. Process recovery communication appears particularly effective in case of complaining customers who received unsatisfactory complaint handling and non-complaining customers who have experienced service failure. Research also suggests that a process recovery communication significantly affects customer satisfaction shortly after the service failure, yet these effects do not last over time (Fang et al., 2013).

Hence, the two post-recovery response options serve different purposes. Follow-up processes should be initiated if customers were satisfied in the recovery phase, while process recovery communication is recommended for customers who leave that phase dissatisfied.

Table 1 summarizes the organizational responses directed at customers throughout the service recovery journey.

Table 1 Summary of the organizational responses throughout the service recovery journey

Phase type of response	Pre-recovery	Recovery	Post-recovery
Compensation		• Immediate monetary compensation • Delayed monetary compensation • New/exchanged goods • New/reperformed service	
Employee behavior		• Apology • Excuse • Justification • Referential account • Credibility feedback • Courtesy • Effort • Empathy • Willingness to listen	
Organizational procedures	• Facilitation • Initiation	• Customer participation • Employee empowerment • Flexibility • Recovery time	• Follow-up • Process recovery communication

7 Organizing the Service Recovery System

As shown in the previous sections, service failures are critical moments of truth that need to be managed well by the organization. We not only need to consider how an organization can respond to individual service failures, as was discussed in the previous sections of this chapter. We also need to consider what service organizations need to do to deal with service failures systematically. Smith et al. (2009) identified the structural dimensions of a service recovery system—accessibility, formality, decentralization, comprehensiveness, influence, human intensity, and system intensity—which allow organizations to translate service recovery into their operations more sustainably and consistently. Table 2 provides a summary of the key organization actions that with each structural dimension.

Investments in (aspects of) service recovery systems have been linked to several indicators of organizational performance. Johnston (2001) and Johnston and Michel (2008) reported positive associations between a complaint management system and organizational performance because of higher levels of customer satisfaction and retention, higher employee satisfaction and retention levels, and higher levels of organizational efficiency attributed to process improvements. Multilevel studies, collecting data among organizations, employees, and customers simultaneously, also provide evidence for the positive benefits of investing in a service recovery system. De Jong and De Ruyter (2004) show that aspects of a service recovery system (i.e., empowerment, formality, and human intensity) are significant antecedents of employees' recovery performance, which in turn influences loyalty intentions and share of wallet. A more recent study, capturing all proposed dimensions of the service recovery system, shows that a service recovery system positively affects frontline employees' service recovery performance and customer satisfaction, which in turn spill over to customer loyalty (Kamath et al., 2020).

Hence, managers not only need a good understanding of what needs to be done when recovering a service failure but also need a good understanding of how they can implement service recovery within the organization sustainably with the seven dimensions of the service recovery system, as proposed by Smith et al. (2009), forming an excellent starting point.

Service Failure and Complaints Management: An Overview   839

Table 2 Dimensions of a sustainable service recovery system

Structural dimension	Organizational actions
Accessibility (i.e., how the organization captures the voice of the customer when a service failure occurs)	• Making it easy for customers to report service failures by opening multiple channels where customers can report service failures (e.g., phone, face-to-face, and social media) • Motivate frontline employees to stimulate complaints • Invest in systems that allow for the proactive detection of service failures
Formality (i.e., the degree to which a recovery system is driven by explicit rules, procedures, and norms)	• Develop a formal documentation of the service recovery process that contains a formal set of rules and procedures on how to deal with service failures • Document how frontline employees register and forward information about service failures, how frontline employees need to interact with dissatisfied customers, and how the organization might replace a good, reperform a service, or offer a monetary or non-monetary compensation • Make sure these guidelines are known, followed, and respected by everyone within the organization • Review these procedures on a regular basis
Decentralization (i.e., the locus of authority or devolution of responsibilities for handling the recovery activities)	• Make service recovery the responsibility of the entire organization, not just the "customer service" department • Allow branches and individual employees to recover service failures themselves without asking approval from a "centralized" department • Empower employees to address service failures as soon as possible, without redirecting the customer to another employee or another channel
Comprehensiveness (i.e., the degree to which organizations develop a good understanding of the range of solutions that are practical, possible, fair, and understood by customers)	• Perform a detailed investigation into the causes of failures for a specific customer • Develop a range of solutions for service failures that are most appropriate from the perspective of the customer • Identify an exhaustive list of potential responses to service failures and indicate which response is most appropriate given a particular situation • In line with the decentralization dimension, keep the set of potential responses flexible so that frontline employees can tailor the service recovery to the particular situation

(continued)

840   C. Orsingher et al.

Table 2 (continued)

Structural dimension	Organizational actions
Influence (i.e., the degree to which customers are involved in the service recovery process)	• Involve customers in the service recovery procedures by explicitly asking for input on how the service failure should be addressed. This input can concern both the service recovery process and solution • In line with the comprehensiveness dimension, keep the organizational system sufficiently flexible in order to deviate from standard processes and solutions
Human intensity (i.e., the set and the magnitude of resources committed to recovery in the form of employee training and evaluation)	• Develop human resource practices specifically for service recovery, for example, by offering training, rewarding frontline employees for effective service recovery, developing employee recovery performance evaluations, and testing candidate's service recovery knowledge and skills during selection and assessment, among others • Develop a culture where frontline employees are receptive toward customer complaints about service failures
System intensity (i.e., the degree to which an organization dedicates resources to altering and improving current operations)	• Develop systems that allow the organization to capture and store data about service failures • Systematically analyze service failures to identify the root cause of failures and improve those processes that cause the failure to occur (i.e., "process recovery") • Close the loop by communicating these improvements back to the complaining customer

Note: *Recommendations based on* Contiero et al. (2016), Homburg and Fürst (2005, 2007), Smith et al. (2009), Santos-Vijande et al. (2013), *and* Van Vaerenbergh and Orsingher (2016)

8   Conclusion

This chapter provided an overview of the key findings of service failure and recovery literature, organized along a journey perspective. To be successful in managing service failures and resulting customer complaints, service organizations need to understand the different phases of the service recovery journey and implement appropriate response options in the pre-recovery phase by initiating and facilitating the recovery process, in the recovery phase by activating the three dimensions of compensation, favorable employee behavior, and organization procedures, and in the post-recovery phase by providing feedback and reassurance to customers. In doing so, an initially negative experience eventually might translate into positive customers' outcomes like satisfaction, repurchase behavior, and word-of-mouth. While far from easy, dealing with service failures and complaints may represent a profit center and is vital for long-term success, making that it needs to be implemented in an appropriate and sustainable manner within any service organization.

References

Bagozzi, R. P., Gopinath, M., & Nyer, P. U. (1999). The role of emotions in marketing. *Journal of the Academy of Marketing Science, 27*(2), 184–206. https://doi.org/10.1177/0092070399272005

Basso, K., & Pizzutti, C. (2016). Trust recovery following a double deviation. *Journal of Service Research, 19*(2), 209–223. https://doi.org/10.1177/1094670515625455

Béal, M., Sabadie, W., & Grégoire, Y. (2019). The effects of relationship length on customer profitability after a service recovery. *Marketing Letters, 30*(3), 293–305. https://doi.org/10.1007/s11002-019-09505-8

Bitner, M. J., Booms, B. H., & Tetreault, M. S. (1990). The service encounter: Diagnosing favorable and unfavorable incidents. *Journal of Marketing, 54*(1), 71–84. https://doi.org/10.1177/002224299005400105

Bitner, M. J., Brown, S. W., & Meuter, M. L. (2000). Technology infusion in service encounters. *Journal of the Academy of Marketing Science, 28*(1), 138–149. https://doi.org/10.1177/0092070300281013

Boshoff, C., & Leong, J. (1998). Empowerment, attribution and apologising as dimensions of service recovery: An experimental study. *International Journal of Service Industry Management, 9*(1), 24–47. https://doi.org/10.1108/09564239810199932

Bradley, G., & Sparks, B. (2012). Explanations: If, when, and how they aid service recovery. *Journal of Services Marketing, 26*(1), 41–51. https://doi.org/10.1108/08876041211199715

Chebat, J. C., & Slusarczyk, W. (2005). How emotions mediate the effects of perceived justice on loyalty in service recovery situations: An empirical study. *Journal of Business Research, 58*(5), 664–673. https://doi.org/10.1016/j.jbusres.2003.09.005

Choi, S., & Mattila, A. S. (2008). Perceived controllability and service expectations: Influences on customer reactions following service failure. *Journal of Business Research, 61*(1), 24–30. https://doi.org/10.1016/j.jbusres.2006.05.006

Colquitt, J. A., Conlon, D. E., Wesson, M. J., Porter, C. O., & Ng, K. Y. (2001). Justice at the millennium: A meta-analytic review of 25 years of organizational justice research. *Journal of Applied Psychology, 86*(3), 425. https://doi.org/10.1037/a0031757

Contiero, E., Ponsignon, F., Smart, P. A., & Vinelli, A. (2016). Contingencies and characteristics of service recovery system design: Insights from retail banking.

International Journal of Operations & Production Management. https://doi.org/10.1108/IJOPM-06-2015-0325

Craighead, C. W., Karwan, K. R., & Miller, J. L. (2004). The effects of severity of failure and customer loyalty on service recovery strategies. *Production and Operations Management,* *13*(4), 307–321. https://doi.org/10.1111/j.1937-5956.2004.tb00220.x

Davidow, M. (2003). Organizational responses to customer complaints: What works and what Doesn't. *Journal of Service Research,* *5*(3), 225–250. https://doi.org/10.1177/1094670502238917

De Matos, C. A., Henrique, J. L., Rossi, A. V., & C. (2007). Service recovery paradox: A meta-analysis. *Journal of Service Research,* *10*(1), 60–77. https://doi.org/10.1177/1094670507303012

DeWitt, T., & Brady, M. K. (2003). Rethinking service recovery strategies: The effect of rapport on consumer responses to service failure. *Journal of Service Research,* *6*(2), 193–207. https://doi.org/10.1177/1094670503257048

Evanschitzky, H., Brock, C., & Blut, M. (2011). Will you tolerate this? The impact of affective commitment on complaint intention and postrecovery behavior. *Journal of Service Research,* *14*(4), 410–425. https://doi.org/10.1177/1094670511423956

Fang, Z., Luo, X., & Jiang, M. (2013). Quantifying the dynamic effects of service recovery on customer satisfaction: Evidence from Chinese mobile phone markets. *Journal of Service Research,* *16*(3), 341–355. https://doi.org/10.1177/10946705 12445504

Fisk, R., Grove, S., Harris, L. C., Keeffe, D. A., Daunt, K. L., Russell-Bennett, R., & Wirtz, J. (2010). Customers behaving badly: A state-of-the-art review, research agenda and implications for practitioners. *Journal of Services Marketing,* *24*(6), 417–429. https://doi.org/10.1108/08876041011072537

Folkes, V. S. (1984). Consumer reactions to product failure: An attributional approach. *Journal of Consumer Research,* *10*(4), 398–409. https://doi.org/10.1086/208978

Fullerton, R. A., & Punj, G. (2004). Repercussions of promoting an ideology of consumption: Consumer misbehavior. *Journal of Business Research,* *57*(11), 1239–1249. https://doi.org/10.1016/S0148-2963(02)00455-1

Gelbrich, K., Gäthke, J., & Grégoire, Y. (2015). How much compensation should a firm offer for a flawed service? An examination of the nonlinear effects of compensation on satisfaction. *Journal of Service Research,* *18*(1), 107–123. https://doi.org/10.1177/1094670514543149

Gelbrich, K., & Roschk, H. (2011). A meta-analysis of organizational complaint handling and customer responses. *Journal of Service Research,* *14*(1), 24–43. https://doi.org/10.1177/1094670510387914

Grégoire, Y., & Fisher, R. J. (2006). The effects of relationship quality on customer retaliation. *Marketing Letters,* *17*(1), 31–46. https://doi.org/10.1007/s11002-006-3796-4

Grégoire, Y., Tripp, T. M., & Legoux, R. (2009). When customer love turns into lasting hate: The effects of relationship strength and time on customer revenge and avoidance. *Journal of Marketing, 73*(6), 18–32. https://doi.org/10.1509/jmkg.73.6.18

Gronroos, C. (1988). Service quality: The six criteria of good perceived service. *Review of Business, 9*(3), 10.

Hart, C. W. L., Heskett, J. L., & Sasser, W. E., Jr. (1990). The profitable art of service recovery. *Harvard Business Review, 68*(4), 148–156.

Hess, R. L. (2008). The impact of firm reputation and failure severity on customers' responses to service failures. *Journal of Services Marketing, 22*(5), 385–398. https://doi.org/10.1108/08876040810889157

Hoffman, K., & Bateson, J. (1997). *Essentials of services marketing.* The Dryden Press.

Hogreve, J., Bilstein, N., & Mandl, L. (2017). Unveiling the recovery time zone of tolerance: When time matters in service recovery. *Journal of the Academy of Marketing Science, 45*(6), 866–883. https://doi.org/10.1007/s11747-017-0544-7

Homburg, C., & Fürst, A. (2005). How organizational complaint handling drives customer loyalty: An analysis of the mechanistic and the organic approach. *Journal of Marketing, 69*(3), 95–114. https://doi.org/10.1509/jmkg.69.3.95.66367

Homburg, C., & Fürst, A. (2007). See no evil, hear no evil, speak no evil: A study of defensive organizational behavior towards customer complaints. *Journal of the Academy of Marketing Science, 35*(4), 523–536. https://doi.org/10.1007/s11747-006-0009-x

Istanbulluoglu, D. (2017). Complaint handling on social media: The impact of multiple response times on consumer satisfaction. *Computers in Human Behavior, 74*, 72–82. https://doi.org/10.1016/j.chb.2017.04.016

Johnson, A. R., & Stewart, D. W. (2005). Reappraisal of the role of emotion in consumer behavior. In N. K. Malhotra (Ed.), *Review of marketing research* (pp. 3–33). ME Sharpe.

Johnston, R. (2001). Linking complaint management to profit. *International Journal of Service Industry Management, 12*(1), 60–69. https://doi.org/10.1108/09564230110382772

Johnston, R., & Fern, A. (1999). Service recovery strategies for single and double deviation scenarios. *Service Industries Journal, 19*(2), 69–82.

Johnston, R., & Michel, S. (2008). Three outcomes of service recovery: Customer recovery, process recovery and employee recovery. *International Journal of Operations & Production Management, 28*(1), 79–99.

Joireman, J., Grégoire, Y., Devezer, B., & Tripp, T. M. (2013). When do customers offer firms a "second chance" following a double deviation? The impact of inferred firm motives on customer revenge and reconciliation. *Journal of Retailing, 89*(3), 315–337. https://doi.org/10.1016/j.jretai.2013.03.002

Jong, A. D., & De Ruyter, K. (2004). Adaptive versus proactive behavior in service recovery: The role of self-managing teams. *Decision Sciences, 35*(3), 457–491. https://doi.org/10.1111/j.0011-7315.2004.02513.x

Kamath, P. R., Pai, Y. P., & Prabhu, N. K. (2020). Determinants of recovery satisfaction and service loyalty: The differing effects of service recovery system and service recovery performance. *Journal of Service Theory and Practice.* https://doi.org/10.1108/JSTP-12-2019-0251

Kjeldgaard, D., Nøjgaard, M., Hartmann, B. J., Bode, M., Lindberg, F., Mossberg, L., & Östberg, J. (2021). Failure: Perspectives and prospects in marketing and consumption theory. *Marketing Theory.* https://doi.org/10.1177/14705931219 92539

Knox, G., & Van Oest, R. (2014). Customer complaints and recovery effectiveness: A customer base approach. *Journal of Marketing, 78*(5), 42–57. https://doi.org/10.1509/jm.12.0317

Larivière, B., & Dirk Van den Poel, D. (2005). Investigating the post-complaint period by means of survival analysis. *Expert Systems with Applications, 29*(3), 667–677. https://doi.org/10.1016/j.eswa.2005.04.035

Lazarus, R. S. (1966). *Psychological stress and the coping process.* McGraw Hill.

Lazarus, R. S. (1991). Progress on a cognitive-motivational-relational theory of emotion. *American Psychologist, 46*(8), 819. https://doi.org/10.1037/0003-066X.46.8.819

Liao, H. (2007). Doing it right this time: The role of employee service recovery performance in customer-perceived justice and customer loyalty after service failures. *Journal of Applied Psychology, 92*(2), 475–489. https://doi.org/10.1037/0021-9010.92.2.475

Magnini, V. P., Ford, J. B., Markowski, E. P., & Honeycutt, E. D. (2007). The service recovery paradox: Justifiable theory or smoldering myth? *Journal of Services Marketing.* https://doi.org/10.1108/08876040710746561

Mostafa, R., Lages, C. R., & Sääksjärvi, M. (2014). The CURE scale: A multidimensional measure of service recovery strategy. *Journal of Services Marketing.* https://doi.org/10.1108/JSM-09-2012-0166

Nguyen, D. T., & McColl-Kennedy, J. (2003). Diffusing customer anger in service recovery: A conceptual framework. *Australasian Marketing Journal, 11*(2), 46–55. https://doi.org/10.1016/S1441-3582(03)70128-1

Olsen, G. D., & Pracejus, J. W. (2004). Integration of positive and negative affective stimuli. *Journal of Consumer Psychology, 14*(4), 374–384. https://doi.org/10.1207/s15327663jcp1404_7

Orsingher, C., Valentini, S., & De Angelis, M. (2010). A meta-analysis of satisfaction with complaint handling in services. *Journal of the Academy of Marketing Science, 38*(2), 169–186. https://doi.org/10.1007/s11747-009-0155-z

Ortony, A., Clore, G. L., & Collins, A. (1988). *The cognitive structure of emotions.* Cambridge University Press.

Pacheco, N. A., Pizzutti, C., Basso, K., & Van Vaerenbergh, Y. (2019). Trust recovery tactics after double deviation: Better sooner than later? *Journal of Service Management.* https://doi.org/10.1108/JOSM-02-2017-0056

Rasoulian, S., Grégoire, Y., Legoux, R., & Sénécal, S. (2017). Service crisis recovery and firm performance: Insights from information breach announcements. *Journal of the Academy of Marketing Science, 45*(6), 789–806. https://doi.org/10.1007/s11747-017-0543-8

Roggeveen, A. L., Tsiros, M., & Grewal, D. (2012). Understanding the co-creation effect: When does collaborating with customers provide a lift to service recovery? *Journal of the Academy of Marketing Science, 40*(6), 771–790. https://doi.org/10.1007/s11747-011-0274-1

Roschk, H., & Gelbrich, K. (2014). Identifying appropriate compensation types for service failures: A meta-analytic and experimental analysis. *Journal of Service Research, 17*(2), 195–211. https://doi.org/10.1177/1094670513507486

Sands, S., Campbell, C., Shedd, L., Ferraro, C., & Mavrommatis, A. (2020). How small service failures drive customer defection: Introducing the concept of micro-failures. *Business Horizons, 63*(4), 573–584. https://doi.org/10.1016/j.bushor.2020.03.014

Santos-Vijande, M. L., del Río-Lanza, A. B., Suárez-Álvarez, L., & Díaz-Martín, A. M. (2013). The brand management system and service firm competitiveness. *Journal of Business Research, 66*(2), 148–157. https://doi.org/10.1016/j.jbusres.2012.07.007

Severt, D. E. (2002). *The customer's path to loyalty: A partial test of the relationships of prior experience, justice, and customer satisfaction.* Doctoral dissertation, Virginia Tech.

Shaw, J. C., Wild, E., & Colquitt, J. A. (2003). To justify or excuse? A meta-analytic review of the effects of explanations. *Journal of Applied Psychology, 88*(3), 444–458. https://doi.org/10.1037/0021-9010.88.3.444

Smith, A. K., & Bolton, R. N. (2002). The effect of customers' emotional responses to service failures on their recovery effort evaluations and satisfaction judgments. *Journal of the academy of marketing science, 30*(1), 5–23.

Smith, A. K., Bolton, R. N., & Wagner, J. (1999). A model of customer satisfaction with service encounters involving failure and recovery. *Journal of Marketing Research, 36*(3), 356–372. https://doi.org/10.1177/002224379903600305

Smith, J. S., Karwan, K. R., & Markland, R. E. (2009). An empirical examination of the structural dimensions of the service recovery system. *Decision Sciences, 40*(1), 165–186. https://doi.org/10.1111/j.1540-5915.2008.00220.x

Sparks, B. A., & McColl-Kennedy, J. R. (2001). Justice strategy options for increased customer satisfaction in a service recovery setting. *Journal of Business Research, 54*(3), 209–218. https://doi.org/10.1016/S0148-2963(00)00120-X

Su, L., Raju, S., & Laczniak, R. N. (2021). The roles of gratitude and guilt on customer satisfaction in perceptions of service failure and recovery. *Journal of Service Science and Management, 14*(1), 12–33. https://doi.org/10.4236/jssm.2021.141002

Surachartkumtonkun, J., McColl-Kennedy, J. R., & Patterson, P. G. (2015). Unpacking customer rage elicitation: A dynamic model. *Journal of Service Research, 18*(2), 177–192. https://doi.org/10.1177/1094670514556275

Tax, S. S., Brown, S. W., & Chandrashekaran, M. (1998). Customer evaluations of service complaint experiences: Implications for relationship marketing. *Journal of Marketing, 62*(1), 60–76. https://doi.org/10.1177/002224299806200205

Valentini, S., Orsingher, C., & Polyakova, A. (2020). Customers' emotions in service failure and recovery: a meta-analysis. *Marketing letters, 31*(2), 199–216.

Van Vaerenbergh, Y., Larivière, B., & Vermeir, I. (2012). The impact of process recovery communication on customer satisfaction, repurchase intentions, and word-of-mouth intentions. *Journal of Service Research, 15*(3), 262–279. https://doi.org/10.1177/1094670512442786

Van Vaerenbergh, Y., & Orsingher, C. (2016). Service recovery: An integrative framework and research agenda. *Academy of Management Perspectives, 30*(3), 328–346. https://doi.org/10.5465/amp.2014.0143

Van Vaerenbergh, Y., Orsingher, C., Vermeir, I., & Larivière, B. (2014). A meta-analysis of relationships linking service failure attributions to customer outcomes. *Journal of Service Research, 17*(4), 381–398. https://doi.org/10.1177/1094670514538321

Van Vaerenbergh, Y., Varga, D., De Keyser, A., & Orsingher, C. (2019). The service recovery journey: Conceptualization, integration, and directions for future research. *Journal of Service Research, 22*(2), 103–119. https://doi.org/10.1177/1094670518819852

Wang, C.-Y., Mattila, A. S., & Bartlett, A. (2009). An examination of explanation typology on perceived informational fairness in the context of air travel. *Journal of Travel & Tourism Marketing, 26*(8), 795–805.

Weiner, B. (2000). Attributional thoughts about consumer behavior. *Journal of Consumer Research, 27*, 382–387. https://doi.org/10.1080/10548400903356194

Zeithaml, V. A., Bitner, M. J., & Gremler, D. D. (2017). *Services marketing* (7th ed.). McGraw Hill.

Part V

Service Interaction, Quality and Operation

Expanding the Scope of Service Recovery

Bård Tronvoll

Retaining customers is vital for all firms (Kumar et al., 2015), especially when a service failure has happened. After a service failure, the firm should initiate recovery efforts to undo the harm the customer has experienced. Therefore, service recovery is vital for the firm because it may be the "last defense" against customer defections. Previous research has found that service recovery, depending on the perceived quality of the attempt, can positively impact the relationship between customers and service providers (Kim et al., 2012) and prompt the expected purchase utilities, quality perceptions (Smith & Bolton, 2002; Tax et al., 1998), trigger the customers' emotional state (Tronvoll, 2011), and encourage favorable word of mouth (Rust & Chung, 2006), satisfaction and loyalty (Maxham, 2001; McCollough & Gremler, 2004).

Service provision occurs in complex, human-based systems involving multiple actors, and the more actors involved, the greater the potential for errors, mistakes, or service failures. This suggests that service recovery is a critical topic for all service ecosystems. Despite its significance in determining customer experience and firm performance, service recovery is often limited to operationally oriented customer care and complaint management departments. This practice narrows the understanding of service recovery as a

---

B. Tronvoll (✉)

CTF, Service Research Center, Karlstad University, Karlstad, Sweden

Inland Norway University of Applied Sciences, Elverum, Norway
e-mail: bard.tronvoll@inn.no

© The Author(s), under exclusive license to Springer Nature Switzerland AG 2022
B. Edvardsson, B. Tronvoll (eds.), *The Palgrave Handbook of Service Management*,
https://doi.org/10.1007/978-3-030-91828-6_40

response to customer-initiated dialogue and does not participate in the strategic planning processes of the firm (Stone, 2011). As businesses have become more complex and integrated, it has also grown to require a new conception of service recovery, transcending traditional dyadic customer–firm relations to encompass the broader service ecosystem as a strategic issue.

The origin of service recovery is rooted in customer recovery by representing a business function responsible for responding to customer complaints to maintain the customer's favorable experience. Beyond the customer, service recovery has been portrayed as an intraorganizational issue, focusing on procedural and employee recovery (e.g., Bowen & Johnston, 1999; Johnston & Michel, 2008; Sparks & McColl-Kennedy, 1998). The focus on procedural considerations is necessary to secure proper service provision and adapts in personalized ways through connections to employees and how employees are debriefed after confronting angry customers. However, service recovery needs to expand beyond organizational boundaries, such that it also includes an interorganizational issue requiring the integration of partners throughout the broader service ecosystem. Therefore, this chapter proposes a broader systemic scope, expanding service recovery to include the concept of network recovery.

To be competitive, the firm must include the broader service ecosystem and focus on attracting and maintaining customers. In doing so, service recovery becomes an essential antecedent for the viability of the service ecosystems. In creating a favorable service experience for all actors, the service ecosystem actors are forming a partnership or network in close dialogue to enhance their service recovery efforts. A consequence of the extended scope is that service recovery is not limited to a customer strategy but rather must be integrated with the firm's overall business strategy. Håkansson (1987, p. 10) emphasizes that a firm's external relationships "are one of the most valuable resources that a firm possesses" and therefore demand careful attention. As firms evolve from mainly self-contained, hierarchical bureaucracies to complex service ecosystems (Lusch et al., 2010), the ecosystem provides quick access to resources and know-how that the firm cannot create internally (Håkansson & Snehota, 1995). Managing both intra- and interorganizational relationships, including service recovery efforts among the service ecosystem actors, becomes important. Network recovery is understood as the efforts made by the focal firm's failed attempt to cocreate value as part of the ecosystem value proposition.

Even as service recovery research efforts expand, scholars still call for more rigorous, comprehensive model-building efforts (Parasuraman, 2006; Zhu et al., 2004). Scholars argue that extant service recovery research is limited in the number of service recovery and complaint management issues it addresses (Rust & Chung, 2006). In line with this call for more rigorous conceptualizations of service recovery efforts, this chapter frames quadric service recovery components pertaining to the customer, employee, procedure, and network, forming cornerstones of recovery efforts, each adaptively connected to the others. Accordingly, this chapter expands the concept of service recovery to include service ecosystem activities and thus network recovery. It details the different focus areas of service recovery, emphasizing network recovery, thereby expanding service recovery literature beyond customer, employee, and procedural topics.

The rest of this book chapter details, first, different service recovery components linked within a proposed service recovery framework; second, a description of service ecosystems, network recovery, and network characteristics, including structures, relationships, and network dynamics. Finally, this chapter concludes with three propositions framing service recovery.

1 Types of Service Recovery Components

Service recovery can be defined in various ways, such as the action a firm takes to respond to a service failure (Grönroos, 1990) or, in more detail, a "process that identifies service failure, effectively resolves customer problems, classifies their root causes and yields data that can be integrated with other measures of performance to assess and improve the service system" (Tax & Brown, 2000, p. 272). In turn, previous research categorizes three service recovery components related to customer, procedural, and employee recoveries (Johnston & Michel, 2008);

* *Customer recovery*: Customer recovery efforts arise when the firm recognizes an unfavorable experience as an indicator of conflict between the customer and the service firm (Homburg & Fürst, 2005; Tax et al., 1998). Four activities likely are necessary to recover customers (e.g., Bowen & Johnston, 1999): (a) *response*, or the acknowledgment that a problem has occurred, which might feature an apology, empathy, speedy recovery, and management involvement; (b) *information* in the form of some explanation for the unfavorable experience, listening to the customer's view of a solution, agreeing on a solution, providing assurance it will not happen again, and apologizing; (c) *action*, which is a correction of the unfavorable experience, to undo the harm done or ensure customers that the firm will look into procedures to prevent it from happening in the future, along with follow-up actions to confirm; and (d) *compensation*, which might take a token, equivalent, refund, or "big gesture" forms. When customers experience

poor recovery processes, they feel disappointed with the process and/or outcome, such that the recovery worsens the situation; more than half of all service recovery efforts appear to make the problem worse (Kelley et al., 1993). This double or even triple deviation (Bitner et al., 1990; Edvardsson et al., 2011b) reinforces customer recovery difficulty.

* *Procedural recovery*: Procedural recovery pertains to rules and guidelines about how customers should be treated during the service recovery process. The ability to gather feedback and complaints from customers, employees, or other actors and then turn them into real improvements is missing from many firms (Gross et al., 2007). Tax et al. (1998) identify five vital elements for the procedural component: process control, decision control, accessibility, timing or speed, and flexibility. That is, a fair process provides the complainer with some control over the disposition, is easy to access and flexible, and concludes in a convenient and timely fashion. Spreng and Mackoy (1996) argue that the prime purpose of service recovery is to drive improvements throughout the organization; improvements to recovery procedures can lead to cost reductions, for example, by removing inefficient and ineffective processes and reducing the number of failures. It might be more important for the service firm to emphasize procedural recovery, rather than a single customer recovery, to expand the recovery focus from a single transaction to management operations. Procedural recovery also influences the single customer transaction because, for many customers, the problem is not the unfavorable experience itself but rather their sense that the system might not change, such that the problem is likely to happen again (Johnston & Clark, 2005). Through process recovery, the firm improves its service provision and signals to customers that it has taken the incident seriously.
* *Employee recovery*: Employee recovery refers to the firm's ability to help and recover employees who have been exhausted by meeting customers' demands and following rigid rules or regulations. Although the customer is central in the recovery process, the firm and its employees also are necessary to facilitate such efforts. Regardless of this effect, frontline employees are vital to service recovery operations because they deal with complaining customers. Employees may find themselves sandwiched between understandable customer grievances and unchangeable organizational policies and procedures, which gives rise to high levels of stress (Johnston & Michel, 2008). Bowen and Johnston (1999) suggest internal service recovery, or employee recovery, is important to the overall recovery process, such that the organization must support employees in their difficult task of dealing with complaining customers. Johnston and Clark (2005, p. 398) offer a

more detailed description of the problem: "some organisations just let their staff soak up the pressure resulting from their inadequate service systems leading not only to dissatisfied and disillusioned customers but also stressed and negatively disposed staff who feel powerless to help or sort out the problems." Negative feedback, such as complaining customers, can reduce employee performance (Becker & Klimoski, 1989) and commitment (Pearce & Porter, 1986), create role stress, and ultimately harm overall job satisfaction and organizational commitment (Singh et al., 1996).

Service recovery has expanded from a single recovery component (customer recovery) to include procedural and employee components. However, the recovery components used are related to a customer and intraorganizational approach. To emphasize the wider scope of service recovery, Roggeveen, Tsiros, and Grewal (2012, p. 772) used the concept of co-recovery to propose that value cocreation depends on the joint efforts of the customer and the service firm, conceptualized as a process in which "the customer shapes or personalizes the content of the service recovery through joint collaboration with the service provider." Xu et al. (2014) further develop this understanding and define service recovery as a process that refers to actions and interactions carried out by the involved actors when integrating resources to cocreate a solution after a service failure. Arsenovic et al. (2019) continue this line of arguments arguing for a collaborative recovery understood as a process in which multiple actors (including the customer) interact and integrate resources through organized activities to recover a failed situation and achieve a favorable recovery experience.

This broader understanding of service recovery call for a service ecosystem view, emphasizing the collaboration among multiple actors when integrating and deploying resources to cocreate value for themselves and others. The service ecosystem, defined as a "relatively self-contained, self-adjusting system of resource-integrating actors connected by shared institutional arrangements and mutual value creation through service exchange" (Vargo & Lusch, 2016, pp. 10–11), highlights the collaborative and multi-actor nature of service provision. The firms collaborating within the service ecosystem offering a value proposition to the end customer is here call *network partners*. The service ecosystem lens also emphasizes the importance of institutional arrangements— "the rule of the game" (North, 2005) consisting of rules, norms, meanings, and symbols—in guiding the relationship between the network partners by defining appropriate behavior as well as by enabling and constraining business and social action (Vargo & Lusch, 2016). Thus, the fourth component of service recovery must recognize that firms are embedded in a service

854   B. Tronvoll

ecosystem and part of a complex network mechanism. The rest of this chapter elaborates on the network aspects of service recovery. By expanding the scope, the service recovery field will gain a stronger position.

2   The System as a Focus Area

Organizations with complementary strategies, resources, and capabilities join forces to meet customers' needs in a manner that benefits all the network partners in the service ecosystem. To deal with competition, service provision gets organized, whether directly or indirectly, as a network of firms, even if the customer never recognizes or reflects on the different network partners involved. For example, a tourist interacts with several network partners during the cocreation of a holiday—the tour operator assembles different events, a travel agent sells and invoices the tour, the airline provides transportation, a hotel accommodates the traveler, and a historical site operator shows the tourist about the destination, and so on. All these firms cocreate value, together with the tourist, in different phases of the holiday to achieve a favorable overall experience; however, the tourist likely views the experience as an integrated service provision without noticing or reflecting on the different network partners involved.

Thus, a network is a composite of many partners, tied together through patterns of relationships (Iacobucci & Hopkins, 1992); and held together by "the trinity of competencies, relationships and information" (Lusch et al., 2010, p. 21). A business relationship can be understood as a process in which two or more partners "form strong and extensive social, economic, service and technical ties over time, with the intent of lowering total costs and/or increasing value, thereby achieving mutual benefit" (Anderson & Narus, 1991, p. 96). A central function of a network is to create value with customers by connecting them to others in the network in a synchronous manner (Stabell & Fjeldstad, 1998). To execute this mediation, firms often depend on partner organizations that operate within the service ecosystem. These service ecosystems, in turn, add value by collaborating with and coordinating among the members (Woolfall, 2006). Thus, dependence on other network partners has important implications for how the firms compete and manage service recovery processes. Because competing as a network limits the decision-making autonomy of each firm (Moeller, 2010), service recovery by network firms requires that they become cognizant of the developments of their common recovery strategy and practices.

Actors, among firms and customers, are resource integrators during their value cocreation processes (Vargo & Lusch, 2004), and through resource integration, actors and the service ecosystems transform specialized competencies into value propositions with market potential (Vargo & Lusch, 2008). To accomplish this task, firms must recognize and act on value cocreation in the context of service ecosystems (systems of systems) (Lusch et al., 2010). Consequently, value cannot be distributed or created by a single firm; it is facilitated by all engaged actors. As Lusch et al. (2010) posit, firms evolve from self-contained, hierarchical bureaucracies into complex networks of relationships, with resource providers of all kinds. In turn, they seek to focus on distinctive competencies as sources of competitive advantage and rely on strategic partners to develop adaptive, collaborative advantages that provide distinctive competencies as components of the market offering (Lusch & Webster, 2011).

In combination, the three existing recovery components (customer recovery experienced in the service encounter, procedural and employees recoveries experienced in the service operation) and the network recovery (the core of service management) constitute the service recovery diamond; see Fig. 1.

These four components affect the focal firm's ability to recover value in the process with an intermediate or final customer. As part of the overall service

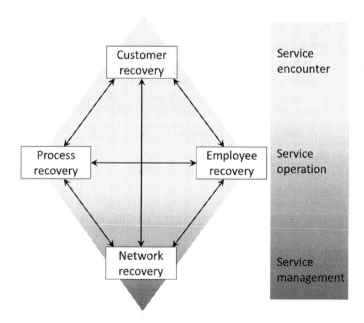

Fig. 1 The service recovery diamond

recovery efforts, network recovery is essential because the firm interacts with other firms through its network relations, and this critical strategic issue confronts management through interorganizational relationships. By expanding service recovery efforts to include network partners, service recovery extends from only being consumer-oriented to integrate a strategic and business-oriented view.

3 Network Recovery

In any service ecosystem, inhibiting factors will always block the development of relationships; relationships are not self-run (Walter, 1998). One important issue relates to the cost of maintaining relationships, in that firms must invest money, resources, and time to make them work. The ability to manage business networks is rare, and an estimated 60% of partnerships fail (Spekman et al., 2000). These difficulties are due to various influences, including a lack of consideration of network partners during service failures. Interactions with network partners to form a common recovery platform represent a lengthy investment.

A complex service ecosystem increases the probability of a service failure, and series of seemingly unrelated or minor negative incidents, over time and across different network partners, can escalate into an unfavorable service experience for all actors. It is mainly a challenge when customers carry their unfavorable experiences over to the next stage of the value cocreation process, especially if the subsequent network partner is unaware of previous unfavorable service experiences and offers no recovery efforts. If these problems persist, and the problem-causing network partner never recommends recovery activities, the network could lose its competitiveness and ability to retain and attract customers; in the worst case, customers exit the service ecosystem, threatening its existence. Continuing with the holiday example, a tourist might experience a service failure with the hotel, resulting in an unfavorable service experience; the network partners should work to increase its competitiveness by having the hotel alert the next partner in line, such as the airline, so that it could issue the apology and compensate the tourist in some way on the flight home. Then the network can convince the tourist all its members are professional in their efforts to cocreate favorable recovery experiences. If the hotel's service failures are repetitive, though, tourists will continue having bad experiences, which endangers the competitiveness and the viability of the entire service ecosystem.

Thus, network recovery is defined as *the activities a firm performs with other network partners to recover and sustain its position and the viability of the service ecosystem.* Consequently, network recovery can include both recovery efforts directed toward the other network partners or those toward their customers. The proposed description of service recovery from a service ecosystem perspective features three intertwined characteristics that clarify the network recovery component: network structure, network relationships, and network dynamics. Network structure refers to the network memberships (the firms involved offering value proposition to the end customer), including the composition of the network—the identities, status, resources, access, and the overall configuration within the network. Network relationships and institutions entail a set of institutionalized rules and norms that govern appropriate behavior within the network and give insight into how it works. Network dynamics refer to how the changes among the network partners evolve.

Network structure: A firm's recovery activities aim to retain existing customers and attract new ones to the service ecosystem through service excellence. In both situations, network partners attempt to optimize their intra- and interorganizational infrastructure to become competitive and provide a more favorable service experience. Among other tactics, network firms might select new or exclude poorly performing partners. Research into network formation considers partner selection and network configuration critical to their success because these choices affect overall performance (Moeller, 2010). In a fragmented network, the network splits into two or more unconnected subgroups, with few interactions or communication, which can complicate a common recovery strategy (Wey et al., 2008). A resourceful, dominant network partner with robust procedural recovery processes exerts substantial power over smaller firms and may constrain intraorganizational relationships and recovery activities. Similarly, the non-membership or exit of a major partner (Oliver & Ebers, 1998) can cause negative effects to flow through the network and even lead to excluding some marginal partners in the network. Therefore, the choices of network partners restrict and enlarge the opportunity set of future relationships and service recovery efforts available to the network (Gulati, 1995).

Network relationships constitute cooperative arrangements among organizations, providing mutual benefits through trust and transaction-specific investments (Jarillo, 1988). The relationships arise in an atmosphere marked by power dependence between the firms, a state of conflict or cooperation, overall relationship closeness, and firms' mutual expectations (Håkansson, 1982). The network relationship rests on the basic constructs of trust (e.g., Doney & Cannon, 1997), commitment (e.g., Gundlach et al., 1995), and adaptation (e.g., Hailén et al., 1991), such that the relationships are founded and framed within the norms and rules valid within the social context of the network (Edvardsson et al., 2011b).

Sobrero and Schrader (1998) differentiate two aspects of network governance: (i) A contractual governance refers to the mutual exchange of rights between network partners to govern the combination of resources and create a favorable recovery experience. (ii) Procedural governance refers to the mutual exchange of information to combine resources in a recovery process. Contractual and procedural governance determine how coordination can occur, representing vehicles for mutual benefit within the network. The governance and nature of the relationships among various firms in the network influence the extent to which networks recovery is constrained. The choice of recovery governance mode for a network relationship depends on the strength, properties of the resources exchanged the history of the relationship and the nature and density of other linkages that the network might embed. Firms can realize performance benefits if their partners repeatedly adapt the network configuration.

Network dynamics; Service ecosystems evolve, driven by, for example, the partners' shared activities, interactions, and affiliations. Changes might result from network structures and relationships, though the main drivers relate to knowledge sharing and network learning (Dyer & Nobeoka, 2000). Thus, most dynamics within networks can be understood by examining the degree of interdependence among network partners and their ability to share knowledge and influence other partners in the network. The extent of interdependency among partners often relates to the distribution of competence across the network to perform service recovery efforts toward customers, employees, and network partners.

A firm's competencies, knowledge sharing, and recovery learning provide the basis for network dynamics. To coordinate service recovery activities, network partners must actively promote knowledge sharing and establish a recovery learning atmosphere. When networks grow more complex, learning, agility, and adaptability become even more critical to survival and growth (Achrol & Kotler, 1999). When recovery competence is shared, learning gets perpetuated and institutionalized (Shrivastava, 1983), and organizational learning entails "the process within the organization by which knowledge about action-outcome relationships and the effects of the environment on these relationships is developed" (Duncan & Weiss, 1978, p. 84). Service recovery learning represents a process for capturing implicit knowledge generated in ongoing recovery interactions by involved partners. When different partners interact to improvise solutions or recover a customer, their actions often entail new knowledge and an evolving service recovery understanding, such as about customers' needs and willingness to participate in the service recovery process, procedural issues, the strain on employees, or ways to interact with network partners. If such knowledge gets captured, internalized by partners, and formalized in practices, it becomes part of the recovery learning exchange and may provide a unique source of competitive advantage.

4 Conceptualizing and Extending the View of Service Recovery

A service recovery process usually is initiated by a customer indicating an unfavorable service experience; such complaint behavior should become the spark for recovery activities throughout the organization and by network partners. Whatever recovery activity the firm chooses in response to complaining customers; it can affect its relationship with other network partners. This influence becomes especially obvious if the firm performs poorly or engages in no recovery activities at all. When different partners in a network cocreate the service provision together, it usually requires a common customer recovery strategy, which demands a coordinated, integrated service recovery strategy across all network partners.

Competitive advantage depends on how well the network partners can adjust to one another and learn about and adapt to significant environment discontinuities. Service recovery adaption by all network partners refers to modifying a strategy or resources to enhance complementarity (Pillai, 2006), requiring a communication process to encourage adaption in attitudes and knowledge (Johanson & Mattsson, 1987). As a result of the interaction, a common reference to service recovery develops through shared knowledge and learning and emerges as a common system or language to refer to constraining rules and standardized processes and procedures. From this basis, three premises follow to help define service recovery and, subsequently, network recovery.

Proposition #1
Service recovery is an essential strategic issue confronting all business levels with intra- and interorganizatorial relationships.

Service ecosystems increasingly influence strategic choices because an unfavorable service experience of the end customer resulting in negative word of mouth, prompting weak customer loyalty, affects the service ecosystem viability and network partners' competitiveness. The ability to manage service recovery efforts thus becomes critical to sustaining competitiveness and achieving strategic goals. A review of service recovery components reveals that service recovery mostly has been treated at encounter (customer recovery) and operational (procedural and employee recovery) levels. However, it also has evolved to become more than just a damage-control mechanism. Service recovery is part of the firm's strategic planning and ensures that the offering and network cooperation improve continuously. Tax and Brown (1998) suggest that recovering customers should be the cornerstone of any customer strategy. If network recovery is a central service recovery effort and a service management issue, service recovery strategies must be determined at the top management level. Service recovery transcends a customer strategy and becomes part of the overall business strategy.

The aspects communicated and promised to customers and markets are part of the business strategy. Thus Vargo and Lusch (2008) assert that the firm can only offer value propositions; similarly, Ballantyne et al. (2011) reformulate value propositions based on reciprocity. Reciprocal value propositions can be used to initiate and guide recovery activities between network partners and become part of a platform for communicative interaction. That is, reciprocal value propositions provide the basis for communicating recovery efforts and constitute practices with the potential to integrate recovery activities, relationship development, and knowledge renewal. Reciprocal recovery propositions must be developed by network partners, through knowledge sharing manifested as customer complaints. Network partners take interchangeable initiating and participating roles in this process. Coherent communication to customers about willingness to perform recovery efforts also is a necessity.

The four components of service recovery reveal how important and integrated the recovery process has become in the firm's overall business strategy. Johnston and Clark (2001) suggest dividing firm concerns into encounter-related, operations-related, and business-related issues, which mimic different levels. All concerns and hierarchical levels in the firm should focus on service recovery, but they consider different service recovery components. The front-line employee's primary focus is to give customers a favorable service experience by facilitating value cocreation; their core domain in the service recovery process is encounter-related (customer) recovery. Middle management instead focuses on creating service routines and processes to ensure favorable service provision outcomes and prevent customer disappointment. In the case of a failure, middle management must enforce recovery procedures and take care of employees whom customers have badgered. Thus, middle management's core domain is operational (procedural and employee) recoveries. Instead, top management takes overall responsibility for service recovery efforts, with special responsibility for business-related concerns and network partners (network recovery).

Proposition #2
Service recovery efforts constitute customer, procedural, employees, and network recovery components.

The transition of service recovery from a single effort to an intertwined set of recovery efforts reflects a changing view of service problems and a sense of broader responsibility for solving these problems when they emerge. The field of service recovery started with a narrow, transactional focus on a single customer before it expanded to adopt a proactive stance and feature more dynamism concerning the surrounding environment or context. In line with this expansion, network recovery entails quadric components in the service recovery diamond and expands the scope of service recovery. By including network recovery, the scope of service recovery expands to encompass all aspects of the firm's presence and contribute to the viability of the service ecosystem.

As part of the integrated recovery process, knowledge sharing and acquisition is a desirable byproduct of collaboration (Child, 2001). The type of learning generated depends on the partners' purpose, involvement, and needs, which also determines the level and scope of knowledge that can be transferred among network partners. The types of learning can be categorized as technical, systemic, or strategic (Wegner & Antonello, 2012), which reflect hierarchical encounter, operational, and business levels, and thus customer, procedural, employee, and network recovery components respectively. The strategic level refers to the construction and sharing of meanings by managers; it involves reflective processes that generate new insights and promote strategic proactiveness.

A firm's attempt to cocreate value with customers can be undermined by another network partner; to be effective, network partners must have complementarity, goal compatibility, and high commitment to network success (Othman & Sheehan, 2011). Service ecosystems and network partners are heterogeneous and complex, so the creation of recovery efforts in terms of both knowledge and procedural advantages is shaped and constrained by the characteristics of the external environment within which the firm operates. In particular, network partners should agree on a common way to handle recovery performance issues through common rules and adapt to knowledge sharing among partners.

Proposition #3

Network structures, relationships, and dynamics are intertwined and influence the efforts to fulfill the network partners' responsibility for service ecosystem viability.

Network recovery depends on many circumstances related to the conditions of the focal firm, the network itself, and the service ecosystem. The firm has two broad management strategies for enhancing its network recovery efforts: it can identify partners that "fit its needs exactly" (Ouchi, 1979, p. 840) or design a network that promotes desired behaviors in service recovery components. In practice, as implied by governance typologies (e.g., Wathne & Heide, 2000), the former strategy can be implemented through network characteristics, such as selecting partners and socialization efforts, whereas the latter strategy tends to be based on relationship knowledge, sharing, and learning.

According to Wilkinson (2008, p. 96), choosing a firm for cooperation or being selected is only the start of a business relationship. As firms interact over time, they learn about each other and alter their behaviors, attitudes, and beliefs. Without relationships, no firm can operate; that is, relationships are the basis of the business. Moreover, business relationships enable firms to stay competitive when they conduct necessary recovery efforts. They also allow a firm to access the skills and resources of its network partners. Therefore, "a relationship is a type of organization that takes on a life of its own to some extent; it is a living thing that is continually being and becoming" (Ford et al., 2011, p. 1).

5   Conclusion

In complex service ecosystems, service recovery becomes vital for the competitiveness and survival of the firm, its network partners, and the viability of the service ecosystem. Service recovery literature highlights three types of recovery components: customer, procedural, and employee. This chapter expands the scope to argue for a fourth recovery component, namely, network recovery. The introduction of network recovery moves service recovery beyond its traditional customer context to include business-to-business settings and strengthens that service recovery is a strategic issue. Network recovery can be portrayed according to network characteristics, such as network structure, network relationships, and network dynamics. The proposed description of varied service recovery components thus emphasizes both network recovery and a service recovery strategy. The four service recovery components constitute the service recovery diamond associated with the service encounter, service operation, and service management levels, making service recovery a business strategy issue.

References

Achrol, R. S., & Kotler, P. (1999). Marketing in the network economy. *Journal of Marketing, 63*(4), 146–163. http://search.ebscohost.com/login.aspx?direct=true &AuthType=ip,url,uid,cookie&db=buh&AN=2444283&loginpage=Login. asp&site=ehost-live&scope=site

Anderson, J. C., & Narus, J. A. (1991). Partnering as a focused market strategy. *California Management Review, 33*(3), 95–113. http://search.ebscohost.com/ login.aspx?direct=true&db=buh&AN=4760977&site=ehost-live

Arsenovic, J., Edvardsson, B., & Tronvoll, B. (2019). Moving toward collaborative service recovery: A multiactor orientation. *Service Science, 11*(3), 201–212. https:// doi.org/10.1287/serv.2019.0241

Ballantyne, D., Frow, P., Varey, R. J., & Payne, A. (2011). Value propositions as communication practice: Taking a wider view. *Industrial Marketing Management, 40*(2), 202–210. https://doi.org/10.1016/j.indmarman.2010.06.032

Becker, T. E., & Klimoski, R. J. (1989). A field study of the relationships between the organizational feedback environment and performance. *Personnel Psychology, 42*(2), 343–358. http://search.ebscohost.com/login.aspx?direct=true&AuthType= ip,url,uid,cookie&db=buh&AN=6258877&loginpage=Login.asp&site=ehost-live&scope=site

Bitner, M. J., Booms, B. H., & Tetreault, M. S. (1990). The service encounter: Diagnosing Favorable and Unfavorable incidents. *Journal of Marketing, 54*(1), 71–84.

Bowen, D. E., & Johnston, R. (1999). Internal service recovery: Developing a new construct. *International Journal of Service Industry Management, 10*(2), 118. http:// search.ebscohost.com/login.aspx?direct=true&AuthType=ip,url,uid,cookie&db= buh&AN=4038058&loginpage=Login.asp&site=ehost-live&scope=site

Child, J. (2001). Learning through strategic alliances. In M. Dierkes, A. B. Antal, J. Child, & I. Nonaka (Eds.), *The handbook of organizational learning and knowledge* (pp. 657–680). Oxford University Press.

Doney, P. M., & Cannon, J. P. (1997). An examination of the nature of trust in buyer-seller relationships. *Journal of Marketing, 61*(2), 35. http://search.ebscohost.com/login.aspx?direct=true&db=buh&AN=9705011685&site=ehost-live

Duncan, R. B., & Weiss, A. (1978). Organizational learning: Implications for organization design. In B. M. Staw (Ed.), *Research in organizational behavior*. JAI Press.

Dyer, J. H., & Nobeoka, K. (2000). Creating and managing a high-performance knowledge-sharing network: The Toyota case. *Strategic Management Journal,*

21(3), 345. http://search.ebscohost.com/login.aspx?direct=true&db=buh&AN=2975709&site=ehost-live

Edvardsson, B., Tronvoll, B., & Gruber, T. (2011a). Expanding understanding of service exchange and value co creation. *Journal of the Academy of Marketing Science, 39*(2), 327–339.

Edvardsson, B., Tronvoll, B., & Höykinpuro, R. (2011b). Complex service recovery processes: How to avoid triple deviation. *Managing Service Quality, 21*(4), 331–349. https://proxy.hihm.no/ebsco/{targetURLRemainder}

Ford, D. I., Gadde, L.-E., Håkansson, H., & Snehota, I. (2011). *The business marketing course: Managing in complex networks* (3rd ed.). Wiley.

Grönroos, C. (1990). *Service management and marketing*. Lexington Books.

Gross, G., Caruso, B., & Conlin, R. (2007). *A look in the Mirror: The VOC scorecard*. McGraw-Hill.

Gulati, R. (1995). Does familiarity breed trust? The implications of repeated ties for contractual choice in alliances. *Academy of Management Journal, 38*(1), 85–112. https://doi.org/10.2307/256729

Gundlach, G. T., Achrol, R. S., & Mentzer, J. T. (1995). The structure of commitment in exchange. *Journal of Marketing, 59*(1), 78–92.

Hailén, L., Johanson, J., & Seyed-Mohamed, N. (1991). Interfirm adaptation in business relationships. *Journal of Marketing, 55*(2), 29–37. http://search.ebscohost.com/login.aspx?direct=true&db=buh&AN=9105272298&site=ehost-live

Håkansson, H. (1982). *International marketing and purchasing of industrial goods : An interaction approach*. Wiley.

Håkansson, H. (1987). *Industrial technological development: A network approach*. Croom Helm.

Håkansson, H., & Snehota, I. (1995). *Developing relationships in business networks*. Routledge.

Homburg, C., & Fürst, A. (2005). How organizational complaint handling drives customer loyalty: An analysis of the mechanistic and the organic approach. *Journal of Marketing, 69*(3).

Iacobucci, D., & Hopkins, N. (1992). Modeling dyadic interactions and networks in marketing. *Journal of Marketing Research, 29*(1), 5–17. http://search.ebscohost.com/login.aspx?direct=true&AuthType=ip,url,uid,cookie&db=buh&AN=9602205286&loginpage=Login.asp&site=ehost-live&scope=site

Jarillo, J. C. (1988). On Strategic Networks. *Strategic Management Journal, 9*(1), 31–41. http://search.ebscohost.com/login.aspx?direct=true&db=bth&AN=12492895&site=ehost-live

Johanson, J., & Mattsson, L.-G. (1987). Interorganizational relations in industrial systems: A network approach compared with the transaction-cost approach. *International Studies of Management & Organization, 17*(1), 34–48. http://search.ebscohost.com/login.aspx?direct=true&AuthType=ip,url,uid,cookie&db=buh&AN=5814839&loginpage=Login.asp&site=ehost-live&scope=site

Johnston, R., & Clark, G. (2001). *Service operations management*. Financial Times Prentice Hall.

Johnston, R., & Clark, G. (2005). *Service operations management* (2nd ed.). Financial Times/Prentice Hall.

Johnston, R., & Michel, S. (2008). Three outcomes of service recovery. *International Journal of Operations & Production Management, 28*(1), 79–99. Retrieved from http://search.ebscohost.com/login.aspx?direct=true&AuthType=ip,url,uid,cookie&db=buh&AN=31171522&loginpage=Login.asp&site=ehost-live&scope=site

Kelley, S. W., Hoffman, K. D., & Davis, M. A. (1993). A typology of retail failures and recoveries. *Journal of Retailing, 69*(4), 429–452.

Kim, T., Jung-Eun Yoo, J., & Lee, G. (2012). Post-recovery customer relationships and customer partnerships in a restaurant setting. *International Journal of Contemporary Hospitality Management, 24*(3), 381–401. https://doi.org/10.1108/09596111211217879

Kumar, V., Bhagwat, Y., & Xi, Z. (2015). Regaining "lost" customers: The predictive power of first-lifetime behavior, the reason for defection, and the nature of the win-Back offer. *Journal of Marketing, 79*(4), 34–55. https://doi.org/10.1509/jm.14.0107

Lusch, R. F., Vargo, S. L., & Tanniru, M. (2010). Service, value networks and learning. *Journal of the Academy of Marketing Science, 38*(1), 19–31. https://doi.org/10.1007/s11747-008-0131-z

Lusch, R. F., & Webster, F. E. (2011). A stakeholder-unifying, cocreation philosophy for marketing. *Journal of Macromarketing, 31*(2), 129–134. https://doi.org/10.1177/0276146710397369

Maxham, J. G. I. (2001). Service recovery's influence on consumer satisfaction, positive word-of-mouth, and purchase intentions. *Journal of Business Research, 54*(1), 11–24.

McCollough, M. A., & Gremler, D. D. (2004). A conceptual model and empirical examination of the effect of service guarantees on post-purchase consumption evaluations. *Managing Service Quality, 14*(1), 58–74. http://search.ebscohost.com/login.aspx?direct=true&AuthType=ip,url,uid,cookie&db=buh&AN=12151575&loginpage=Login.asp&site=ehost-live&scope=site

Moeller, K. (2010). Partner selection, partner behavior, and business network performance: An empirical study on German business networks. *Journal of Accounting & Organizational Change, 6*(1), 27–51.

North, D. C. (2005). *Understanding the process of economic change*. Princeton University Press.

Oliver, A. L., & Ebers, M. (1998). Networking network studies: An analysis of conceptual configurations in the study of inter-organizational relationships. *Organization Studies (Walter de Gruyter GmbH & Co. KG.), 19*(4), 549–583. http://search.ebscohost.com/login.aspx?direct=true&db=buh&AN=1185040&site=ehost-live

Othman, R., & Sheehan, N. T. (2011). Value creation logics and resource management: A review. *Journal of Strategy and Management, 4*(1), 5–24.

Ouchi, W. G. (1979). A conceptual framework for the design of organizational control mechanisms. *Management Science, 25*(9), 833–848. http://search.ebscohost.com/login.aspx?direct=true&db=bth&AN=7348000&site=ehost-live

Parasuraman, A. (2006). Modeling opportunities in service recovery and customer-managed interactions. *Marketing Science, 25*(6), 590–593. http://search.ebscohost.com/login.aspx?direct=true&AuthType=ip,url,uid,cookie&db=buh&AN=23934012&loginpage=Login.asp&site=ehost-live&scope=site

Pearce, J. L., & Porter, L. W. (1986). Employee responses to formal performance appraisal feedback. *Journal of Applied Psychology, 71*(2), 211–218. http://search.ebscohost.com/login.aspx?direct=true&AuthType=ip,url,uid,cookie&db=buh&AN=6239387&loginpage=Login.asp&site=ehost-live&scope=site

Pillai, K. G. (2006). Networks and competitive advantage: A synthesis and extension. *Journal of Strategic Marketing, 14*(2), 129–145. https://doi.org/10.1080/09652540600659756

Roggeveen, A. L., Tsiros, M., & Grewal, D. (2012). Understanding the cocreation effect: When does collaborating with customers provide a lift to service recovery? *Journal of the Academy of Marketing Science, 40*(6), 771–790. https://doi.org/10.1007/s11747-011-0274-1

Rust, R. T., & Chung, T. S. (2006). Marketing models of service and relationships. *Marketing Science, 25*(6), 560–580. http://search.ebscohost.com/login.aspx?direct=true&AuthType=ip,url,uid,cookie&db=buh&AN=23934008&loginpage=Login.asp&site=ehost-live&scope=site

Shrivastava, P. (1983). A typology of organizational learning systems. *Journal of Management Studies, 20*(1), 7–28. http://search.ebscohost.com/login.aspx?direct=true&AuthType=ip,url,uid,cookie&db=buh&AN=4553288&loginpage=Login.asp&site=ehost-live&scope=site

Singh, J., Verbeke, W., & Rhoads, G. K. (1996). Do organizational practices matter in role stress processes? A study of direct and moderating. *Journal of Marketing, 60*(3), 69. http://search.ebscohost.com/login.aspx?direct=true&AuthType=ip,url,uid,cookie&db=buh&AN=9607293485&loginpage=Login.asp&site=ehost-live&scope=site

Smith, A. K., & Bolton, R. N. (2002). The effect of customers' emotional responses to service failures on their recovery effort evaluations and satisfaction judgments. *Journal of the Academy of Marketing Science, 30*(1), 5–23.

Sobrero, M., & Schrader, S. (1998). Structuring inter-firm relationships: A meta-analytic approach. *Organization Studies (Walter de Gruyter GmbH & Co. KG.), 19*(4), 585–615. http://search.ebscohost.com/login.aspx?direct=true&db=buh&AN=1185041&site=ehost-live

Sparks, B. A., & McColl-Kennedy, J. R. (1998). The application of procedural justice principles to service recovery attempts: Outcomes for customer satisfaction.

Advances in Consumer Research, 25(1), 156–161. http://search.ebscohost.com/login.aspx?direct=true&db=buh&AN=83386422&site=ehost-live

Spekman, R. E., Isabella, L. A., & MacAvoy, T. C. (2000). *Alliance competence: Maximizing the value of your partnerships.* Wiley.

Spreng, R. A., & Mackoy, R. D. (1996). An empirical examination of a model of perceived service quality and satisfaction. *Journal of Retailing, 72*(2), 201–215.

Stabell, C. B., & Fjeldstad, Ø. D. (1998). Configuring value for competitive advantage: On chains, shops, and networks. *Strategic Management Journal, 19*(5), 413. https://proxy.hihm.no/ebsco/{targetURLRemainder}

Stone, M. (2011). Literature review on complaints management. *Journal of Database Marketing & Customer Strategy Management, 18*(2), 108–122. https://doi.org/10.1057/dbm.2011.16

Tax, S. S., & Brown, S. W. (1998). Recovery and learning from service failure. *Sloan Management Review, 40*(1), 75–88.

Tax, S. S., & Brown, S. W. (2000). Service recovery: Research insights and practices. In T. Schwartz & D. Iacobucci (Eds.), *Handbook of services marketing and management.* Sage Publications.

Tax, S. S., Brown, S. W., & Chandrashekaran, M. (1998). Customer evaluations of service complaint experiences: Implications for relationship marketing. *Journal of Marketing, 62*(2), 60–76.

Tronvoll, B. (2011). Negative emotions and their effect on customer complaint behaviour. *Journal of Service Management, 22*(1), 111–134.

Vargo, S. L., & Lusch, R. F. (2004). Evolving to a new dominant logic for marketing. *Journal of Marketing, 68*(1), 1–17.

Vargo, S. L., & Lusch, R. F. (2008). Service-dominant logic: Continuing the evolution. *Journal of the Academy of Marketing Science, 36*(1), 1–10.

Vargo, S. L., & Lusch, R. F. (2016). Institutions and axioms: An extension and update of service-dominant logic. *Journal of the Academy of Marketing Science, 44*(1), 5–23. https://doi.org/10.1007/s11747-015-0456-3

Walter, A. (1998). *Der Beziehungspromotor. Ein personaler Gestaltungsansatz fur erfolgreiches Relationship Marketing.* Gabler.

Wathne, K. H., & Heide, J. B. (2000). Opportunism in interfirm relationships: Forms, outcomes, and solutions. *Journal of Marketing, 64*(4), 36–51. http://search.ebscohost.com/login.aspx?direct=true&db=bth&AN=3789053&site=ehost-live

Wegner, D., & Antonello, C. S. (2012). Inter-organizational learning: A study of small-firm networks in southern Brazil. *African Journal of Business Management, 6*(1), 129–139.

Wey, T., Blumstein, D. T., Shen, W., & Jordán, F. (2008). Social network analysis of animal behaviour: A promising tool for the study of sociality. *Animal Behaviour, 75*(2), 333–344. https://doi.org/10.1016/j.anbehav.2007.06.020

Wilkinson, I. (2008). *Business relating business: Managing organisational relations and networks.* Edward Elgar.

Woolfall, D. (2006). A game and network perspective on m-business partnerships. *Business Process Management Journal, 12*(3), 265–280. http://search.ebscohost.com/login.aspx?direct=true&db=bth&AN=21302701&site=ehost-live

Xu, Y., Edvardsson, B., & Tronvoll, B. (2014). Recovering service failure through resource integration. *The Service Industries Journal, 34*(16), 1253–1271. https://doi.org/10.1080/02642069.2014.942652

Zhu, Z., Sivakumar, K., & Parasuraman, A. (2004). A mathematical model of service failure and recovery strategies. *Decision Sciences, 35*(3), 493–525. https://doi.org/10.1111/j.0011-7315.2004.02597.x

Technology in Service

Anastasia Nanni and Andrea Ordanini

1 Technology in Service Systems

Service System

One of the most widespread and accepted perspectives to evaluate and analyze a service is the systemic one, which considers the service as the result of a series of interactions among different actors, processes, and resources (Maglio & Spohrer, 2008). Various authors adopted the service system perspective. For instance, Cardoso et al. (2012) state that a service system consists of elements such as people, facilities, and tools that are organized in structure and perform a behavior (i.e., a business process) in order to achieve a goal (i.e., value creation). Along the same line, the Service-Dominant logic argues that in order to create value, all the actors involved in the service engage in interdependent and reciprocally beneficial service exchanges (Lusch & Vargo, 2014). Whatever the perspective, in a service system the interacting elements of the service depend on one another in determining the overall effectiveness. In this chapter, we focus on the technology as one of the key elements of a service system

---

A. Nanni (✉)
Bocconi University, Milan, Italy
e-mail: anastasia.nanni@unibocconi.it

A. Ordanini
BNP Paribas Chair in Marketing & Service Analytics, Bocconi University, Milan, Italy
e-mail: andrea.ordanini@unibocconi.it

© The Author(s), under exclusive license to Springer Nature Switzerland AG 2022
B. Edvardsson, B. Tronvoll (eds.), *The Palgrave Handbook of Service Management*,
https://doi.org/10.1007/978-3-030-91828-6_41

and discuss its role in the set of interactions that characterize the different elements of such a system.

Let's start with an example to introduce how technology shapes the service system's way of working. Consider a customer who contacts an interior designer to design her new kitchen: the customer and the designer interact to find a service outcome that is the most functional for the customer. The customer explains her needs; the designer uses her skills and professionalism to design the kitchen. The interaction and the shared understanding of these two actors, however, is not the only factor that contributes to the success of the service. In order to create a project, the designer will use a software that should (i) allow her to create a composition that is closest to the appearance that the kitchen will have once built, (ii) give the possibility to customize the kitchen features (e.g., different materials and colors), (iii) be easy to use so that the designer can propose a set of alternatives to the customer on time, and (iv) be easy to read so that the customer is able to evaluate the alternatives proposed and suggest some adaptations. This example shows how technology (i.e., the software) plays a key role in the service offering and shapes attitudes and behaviors of the service actors involved: the interior designer interacts with the software to create the composition, and the customer interacts with the software to evaluate the proposed alternatives. All the elements of the systems (customer, interior design, and software) depend on each other to deliver an effective service and should be aligned to ensure a proper outcome. A simple software may facilitate customer interaction but could limit the alternatives that the designer can offer, while a sophisticated software gives more opportunities to the designer but can frustrate the customer interaction: in short, the skills of the actors should be aligned with the features of the technology to ensure success.

The remainder of the chapter will adopt this systemic perspective and discuss the fundamental issue of alignment between technology and the other elements of the service system, an issue that characterize almost all the services offerings nowadays.

Pyramid Model: The Central Role of Technology

The elements that compose a service system (e.g., people, technology, and processes) can be structured in different ways on the basis of the type of service and their level of interaction. Services marketing literature has discussed the elements that were in common to most service systems for long time, proposing different frameworks. One of the most relevant and parsimonious frameworks is the so-called Pyramid model (Parasuraman & Grewal, 2000), which posits that technology, firm, employee, and customers are the fundamental dimensions of a service. This framework emphasizes the linkages between technology and the other dimensions as a key factor to make service effective and improve customer experience (Fig. 1). Similarly, the importance of technology is highlighted by the service innovation definitional framework proposed by Gallouj and Weinstein (1997), which highlights firm, customer, and technology as interconnected elements of any service offering.

Recalling our previous example of the new kitchen project, the role of software (i.e., technology) is central since it is the means through which the actors of the system deliver the service: the interior design and her collaborators (i.e., the firm and the employees in the pyramid model) uses the technology (the software) to create the project and the customer uses it to evaluate the proposed alternatives.

Another example concerning a different service can be useful to understand the central role of technology in the service system. A customer who wants to buy a flight ticket can use different ways: (i) online, (ii) at the airport in the self-service kiosks, and (iii) at the airline's dedicated corner. In the first case (i.e., online), the customer can use either the company website or third-party platform (e.g., Sky scanner). In both cases, in order to deliver an effective service, the website should be easy to use and updated on the availability of seats, and it should allow the customer to pay for the ticket. Moreover, the website should be able to record the customer's reservation and transmit the information to the company's server so that, once the customer arrives at the airport, the ticket is validated by an employee who already has all the information about the reservation. In the second case (airline's self-service kiosk), it is

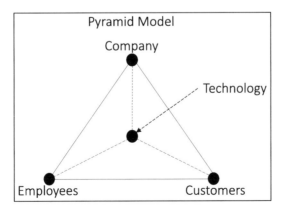

Fig. 1 The pyramid model (Parasuraman & Grewal, 2000)

872   A. Nanni and A. Ordanini

essential that there are enough self-service kiosks to allow the customer to easily access the service. Moreover, as in the online case, the kiosk should allow the customer to make her reservation quickly and easily and transmit the information to the company's server so that the employee can finalize and validate the sale of the ticket. In the third case, the customer decides to buy the ticket in the corner of the airline company, where there is an employee ready to serve him. Unlike the first two cases in which the customer interacts mainly with technology (low contact service), in this case, the customer interacts mainly with the employee (high contact service) (Sampson & Froehle, 2006). For the service to be effective, the employee should be friendly and able to understand the customer, provide all the necessary information, check the availability of seats, register the customer's reservation, and print the ticket. In order to do so, the employee uses a computer that allows her to have access to all the information and procedures necessary to provide the service. In all the service modes we have seen in this example, even in the one in which the interaction between people (customer and employee) is substantial, technology plays a central role in connecting and transmitting information between *firm* (airline company), *employee*, and *customer*, ultimately determining the success of the service.

2   From Service System to Smart Service System

In the previous paragraph, we explained that technology plays an important role in service systems. Nowadays it might seem obvious that, with the advent of the Internet, technology has become an essential part of almost all services. Services marketing scholars began to explore the effects of integrating technology into services since the 1950s, and the related literature that followed can be grouped into four stages, according to the type of technologies that has been investigated: (i) Vending automation (1950–1970), (ii) Process automation (computers) (1970–2000), (iii) Self-Service Technologies (2000–2005), (iv) Digital Services (2005–2015), and (v) Artificial Intelligence (2015–) (Fig. 2).

Vending Automation (1950–1970). Vending automation is the first type of technology studied in services marketing literature. In this stream, the authors focus on the effects of vending machines in service settings. Still (1952) investigates how automatic vending machines affect the sales of cigarettes underlining the shift from personal selling (employee serving the customers) to machine selling (customers interact with the vending machines). Still (1952) observes that in the store using vending machines, the sales decreases by 50%. The author concludes that customers, in that period, prefer personal selling for three main reasons: the vending machines go very quickly out of customers' favorite brands, customers have to exert extra effort to exchange coins of the wrong denominations for coins that work in the machine, and surprisingly, customers spend more time and, consequently, are more bothered to purchase cigarettes from a machine than from the cashier in person. Ten years later, in 1961, Andreasen and Ferber (1962) collected data over 10-week period about the sales through vending machines (with bread, butter, eggs, cigarettes, and cold beverages) in a chain of grocery stores. Results show that the sales through vending machines are far below the level than what the management of the chain expected. In order to have more information, the author interviews the customers who use the vending machines and concludes that since customers are intrigued by the vending machines and the opportunity to buy in such a narrow area with an increase of new customers, the low level of sales is likely due to the lack of advertising by the company. The results of these two studies may seem surprising nowadays. While in the 50s and 60s vending machines had recently entered the market, over the years the sector has grown, and the machines have evolved (e.g., allowing payment by credit cards or apps) and are now used daily by most of the population. Currently, vending machines are quite widespread (15 million worldwide) with a revenue of around $23 billion in 2018 (Globe Newswire, 2020).

Process automation—Computers (1970–2000). The first big technology revolution in service organizations was brought by the advent of computers, which aimed at automating various internal processes that were traditionally

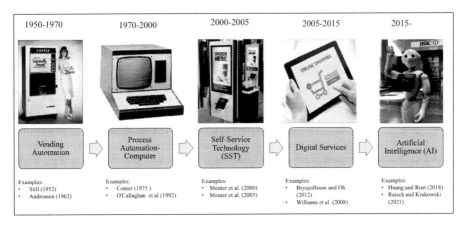

Fig. 2 Evolution of technology in Services Marketing Literature

executed by the workforce. Companies started using computers during the 1960s, but only at the beginning of the 1970s, software houses worldwide were able to satisfy the exploding demand for application programs for managerial use (Heinz Nixdorf Museums Forum, 2021). Quinn et al. (1987) discuss how service companies started to use technology, in particular computers, to make the back-office (vs. the front office) processes more efficient. Hence, scholars in services marketing investigated the role of computer-based technology mainly as enhancer/facilitator of employees' productivity. Comer (1975) discusses the implementation of three software (CALLPLAN, SCHEDULE, and ALLOCATE) designed to assist sales managers in planning calls (to customers), estimating the value of such calls, and determining the effects of alternative call allocation strategies. The author concludes that the use of this software can increase sales managers' productivity; however, he suggests companies proceed with a gradual, carefully prepared implementation of this type of software given the high monetary costs involved.

O'Callaghan et al. (1992) investigate through a questionnaire the adoption of electronic data interchange (EDI) by insurance carriers to their independent agent communities. Authors find that EDI has three advantages: faster transmission, greater accuracy, and more complete information about the transactions.

Nowadays, all companies use personal computers to assist employees in carrying out their daily work. The spread of Covid-19 and the increase in work from home have led to an intensification in the use of computers even in jobs where it was previously limited. This trend is evident, for instance, in the education sector, where more than 1.2 billion children in 186 countries started using online learning because of school closures due to the pandemic (World Economic Forum, 2020). In 2019, global investments for education technology were $18.66 billion; however, this data is projected to reach $350 billion by 2025 (World Economic Forum, 2020).

Self-Service Technologies (2000–2005). While the previous process automation phase focused on the effect of technology "inside" the service organization, another stream of service marketing literature then focused on the effect of technology in the customer encounters. In this sense, a great deal of attention was placed on the role of Self-Service Technologies (SSTs). Compared to computers, SSTs operate mainly in front office: specifically, they allow customers to co-produce a service independently from the direct interaction with service employees (e.g., ATMs, automated checkout) (Meuter et al., 2000). Meuter et al. (2000) identify, through an incident study, some possible causes of satisfaction (e.g., easy to use; saved time) and dissatisfaction (e.g., technology failure and process failure) of customers about SSTs. An important part of the extant literature on SSTs focuses on factors influencing customers' use of the technology. Meuter et al. (2005) argue that innovation characteristics (e.g., compatibility, relative advantage, perceived risk) and individual differences (e.g., inertia, technology anxiety, need for interaction) are the factors influencing the probability that a customer uses the SSTs instead of personal selling.

Digital Services (2005–2015). The advent of the Internet at the onset of the twenty-first century has further reshaped how many services are delivered. The Internet has allowed the birth of a set of brand-new services, called digital services (e.g., Wikipedia, Tripadvisor.com). Brynjolfsson and Oh (2012) estimated, also considering the time spent on consumption, that the increase in consumer surplus created by free digital services amounted to $100 billion per year in the United States.

Williams et al. (2008) propose a taxonomy of digital services that has two main dimensions: a set of fundamental design objectives (e.g., service delivery and service maturity) and a set of fundamental service provider objectives (e.g., business, interaction). Based on the analysis of 12 leading digital companies (e.g., Amazon, eBay, Expedia) the authors conclude that malleability/adaptability and pricing are two key factors for digital service success.

Internet has totally revolutionized the world of services, permanently changing the structure of entire industries. For example, in music industry the advent of the internet has caused a radical change in the nature of its production and consumption, shifting from a product-centric (vinyl and compact discs) to a service-centric (streaming) structure. Digital music services such as iTunes and Spotify allow millions of people all over the world to enjoy a massive variety and quantity of music in a way that has never before been possible. Some data can help to understand the extent of the digital transformation in the music industry: in 2000 revenues from CD sales were $13.36 billion (Music Business Research, 2015), while in 2020, they were 129 million accounting for less than 4% of music industry revenues (RIAA, 2021). In contrast, in 2020 revenues from digital music (streaming and download) amounted to $5.15 billion, 93% of total music industry revenues (RIAA, 2021).

Also retailing industry has been deeply influenced by the digital revolution. Internet gave companies the opportunity to have direct contact with customers (e.g., e-commerce), drastically reducing the number of intermediaries. This context facilitated the emergence of digital third-party platforms such as Amazon and Ebay that allow companies to sell their products online to customers. Over the years, Amazon has expanded the range of services offered entering in food delivery (Amazon Pantry) and publishing (e-book and Amazon Kindle) industries. In 2000, the leading retailer in US was Walmart with net sales of $916 million (CNNMoney, 2000), while in 2019, that position was held by Amazon with net sales of $280.5 billion (Statista, 2021).

Artificial Intelligence (2015–). Artificial Intelligence (AI) is considered one of the most impactful technology trajectories for the next years, with breakthrough effects that are mostly expected in the area of service activities. John McCarthy, recognized as the father of AI, defined AI as "the science and engineering of making intelligent machines" (McCarthy, 2007; Ostrom et al., 2019). Huang and Rust (2018) proposed a "taxonomy" of AI technologies based on the extent to which the intelligence embedded in the solution is able to mimic and perform a range of human behaviors and emotions. This categorization includes four major types of AI: mechanical, analytical, intuitive, and empathetic.

* *Mechanical Intelligence* is a solution able to perform mechanical routines. This technology automatically performs repeated tasks such as searching information in big datasets (e.g., Google search algorithm)
* *Analytical Intelligence* is able to solve more complex problems and its capabilities include information-processing, logical reasoning, and mathematical skills. These abilities allow this technology to perform systematic data-intensive tasks (e.g., AlphaZero)
* *Intuitive Intelligence* is able to think creatively, adapting its modus operandi to novel problems and situations (e.g., Siri, Alexa).
* *Empathetic Intelligence* is the AI with the highest level of humanization and, contrary to the others, has the ability to recognize, understand, and respond properly to emotions mimicking human behaviors (e.g., Replika).

These four types of AI represent a true breakthrough innovation, with a wide range of applications across many services. Indeed, the potential impact of AI in a service context is expected to be pervasive, intricate, and multi-faceted, ultimately transforming traditional service systems in the so-called *Smart* Service Systems (Lim & Maglio, 2019).[1] An example of the shift toward smart service systems can be found in the automotive industry. Some manufacturers (e.g., Volvo) use AI to collect data from sold cars in order to provide useful information to assist drivers on safety, navigation, tire pressure monitoring, and vehicle fleet management (Lim & Maglio, 2019). Smart service systems essentially leverage on knowledge integration, since AI is able to

---

[1] We adopted Lim and Maglio definition of Smart Service Systems that refers specifically to the integration of AI in the service system. We acknowledge that there are other definitions of Smart Service Systems related to the integration of Smart Products (i.e., Internet of Things-IoT) in services (e.g., Beverungen et al., 2019).

collect and elaborate a large amount of data. The capacity of AI to collect and transfer data allows the elements of a smart service system to be more interconnected, dynamic, and proactive (Lim & Maglio, 2019).

Initial academic efforts investigating the effects of AI integration in smart service systems posit that organizations will greatly benefit from using AI either for process automation or for human skills augmentation (Daugherty & Wilson, 2018). However, it is not yet clear how companies can exploit the potential of AI. Raisch and Krakowski (2021) recently suggest that companies should use AI for both automation and augmentation because focusing on either one or the other can harm firm long-term performance: in fact, automation alone can lead to the loss of human skills while augmentation alone can lead to a loss of efficiency.

Given the pervasive expected effect of AI in the near future, and the still unclear consequences of its integration in service systems, the remainder of the chapter will focus on the multi-faceted role of AI in service systems.

3 Contingent Effects of Technology: Configurational Approach

The expected revolutionary effects of AI in service raise an essential question: how to exploit the potential of the various AI solutions (i.e., *mechanical, analytical, intuitive,* and *empathetic*) to improve customers' service experience avoiding their pitfalls? To address this question, we resort to a theoretical framework that is in line with the systemic nature of the service offerings and the complex interactions brought by AI solutions in such offerings: the configuration set theory (Doty et al., 1993).

According to configuration set theory, there is not a unique solution or a universal answer to integrate AI in a service offering, but the final outcome depends on how AI solutions align with the other elements of the smart service systems: firm, employees, and customers. In a nutshell, configuration set theory posits that the effectiveness of a specific element is attributed to the fit among all the contextual, structural, and strategic elements that operate in the system. According to Drazin and Van de Ven (1985), "fit" is the internal consistency of multiple elements and structural characteristics of the system that, ultimately, affect the performance of the overall service. The importance of fit between attributes implies that different elements in a given context are not intrinsically and individually relevant, but they depend on how they are aligned (Venkatraman, 1989). The same perspective is adopted also by information system literature. In particular, the Fit-Appropriation Model (FAM) proposes that the performance of a team (group of work) is influenced by the "fit" between task they have to perform, the technology they use, and the way the team appropriates of the technology, meaning the way they use and approach the technology in relation to the task (Fuller & Dennis, 2009). In service systems, employees and consumers are the actors who work together for the same objective (i.e., a positive service outcome) using the technology that should be in fit with the other elements of the system. Some examples may help to understand how configuration logic helps understanding the potential consequences of AI solutions integration into service systems.

Consider one hotel that has been in the market for a long time with a very loyal customer base, which decides to substitute some of their frontline employees with a robot capable to give information about hotel services which customers can book autonomously. Using the pyramid model, we can identify the following elements of the service systems with their specific features: (1) the hotel is in the market for a long time, and it has its well-established identity and routines (*firm*); (2) the empathetic AI (*technology*) is able to understand and mimic human emotions; (3) the technology is meant to substitute the *employees*; (4) the *customers* who are loyal to the hotel. In this case, even if the AI is able to perform social behavior, it could have a detrimental effect on the service experience since the customers could have developed a rapport with the employees and may not be confident to interact with a machine (Giebelhausen et al., 2014). Consider now the same scenario but with an analytical AI solution, which provides customers with suggestions based on their preferences while in presence of an employee. Here, the technology could have a positive effect on service experience since customers may feel safer using new technology with the assistance of an employee (Reinders et al., 2008). Further, consider the original scenario, but with a hotel that is a newcomer in the market. The presence of an extremely sophisticated technology could improve customer service experience since it is a key element of innovativeness and could attract customers interested in a technology intensive experience. Finally, the effect of the AI technologies may be still different if we move to a more standardized service context: consider a postal office that has replaced one of its employees with a robot that is able to collect mails and paying bills. Maybe in this case an intuitive technology will improve customer experience more than an empathetic one because the scope of the customer is to spend the shortest amount of time in the postal office. As shown in the examples above, each of the elements in the service system, individually, exhibits complex trade-offs on service experience, but some aligned combinations could be beneficial to service experience, while other misaligned sets could be detrimental.

Figure 3 visually represents the idea that the effectiveness of AI integration does not depend on each individual element of the smart service system (technology, firm, employee, and customers), but on their level of alignment and fit. In the next section, we will discuss some concrete empirical cases to highlight the configurational nature of AI solutions in service systems, intentionally providing cases of alignment as well as misalignment between AI and the other elements of the service system.

4 Empirical Cases

Fit Between Service System's Elements: Recommendation Algorithm in Streaming Platforms

The first case of AI integration in service systems we present reflects a successful alignment case and concerns recommendation algorithms in streaming platforms. Streaming platforms use machine learning to customize the content to be offered to their customers (Analytical Intelligence). For instance, Netflix uses around 107 algorithms which estimate the likelihood that a particular customer will watch a specific title based on customers' viewing history

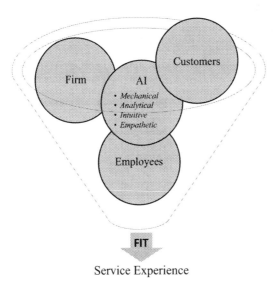

Fig. 3 Configurational approach

and ratings, the titles watched by similar customers (i.e., people who watched the same titles), and information about the title (i.e., genre, actors, release year). Moreover, the AI solutions collect from each customer the time of the day they watch, on which device, and how long they watch. All the collected data are used to create a personalized homepage. The AI not only chooses which titles to include in the rows of customers' homepage, but it also ranks each title within the row and the rows themselves (e.g., Continue Watching, Trending Now, Comedies). AI personalizes the so-called artworks or thumbnails. The artworks highlight a scene from the title or an actor in the movie. Different artworks for each new movie or TV series are assigned to different customers, based on the taste communities (e.g., customers who like a particular actor are most likely to click on an artwork that shows the actor).

The recommendation system is a successful example of AI integration in service, as Netflix accounts for $1 billion a year in value from customer retention (Business Insider, 2016).

In this case, the elements of the service system are the firm (Netflix resources), the customers, and the AI (Recommendation system, Analytical Intelligence). Consumers of the streaming platform have specific needs: they use the service to entertain themselves and relax. Without the personalized recommendation system, finding titles in a very extensive catalog (more than 15,400 titles) would take too long and the probability that customers choose titles they do not like and leave the platform is very high. The recommendation system reduces customers' frustration (the searching time is 60–90 seconds) and helps the firm not only to retain customers but also to collect data about customers' habits and run A/B tests to continuously improve the service offering (The Netflix Tech Blog, 2017). Here a powerful and sophisticated technology allows the supplier to extend the breadth and depth of its offering, but the intuitive and seamless customer interface allows consumers to gain a valuable consumption experience: a perfect case of configurational fit.

From Fit to Misfit Among Service System's Dimensions: Shelf-Scanning Robots in Supermarkets

In 2017, Walmart started introducing shelf-scanning robots in some of its stores (initially 50 stores). The robots are six-foot tall mini self-driving cars with a periscope attachment on top that uses computer vision to see like a human does. The introduction of robots was intended to reduce labor costs while managing inventory more effectively and thus reducing waste and increasing sales. During the last 3 years, Walmart increased the number of stores using shelf-scanning robots, given the encouraging results of the first rollouts.

Until 2020, the elements of the service system were in fit: the firm (Walmart) wants to improve efficiency in inventory management, the AI is able to check and report if there are out-of-stock products or if the products are misplaced, employees are busy serving customers and are not able to check the products of every single aisle, and customers who want to find on the shelves the items that they want to buy. Walmart stores are large, and it's hard for employees to keep track of individual items. The robots help reducing out-of-stock items, keeping more products available when customers want to buy them. The service systems worked, even with some difficulties: for instance, some employees feel they are pushed to work like robots themselves or some customers feel uncomfortable in presence of the robots (The Washington Post, 2019).

In 2020, due to the Covid-19 pandemic, some actors of the service system changed their behaviors. In particular, many customers who used to shop in person, during the pandemic, started to shop online or pick up orders. As more shoppers shifted to online delivery, more employees walked the aisles of the store frequently to collect online orders and spotted inventory problems (The Wall Street Journal, 2020). The change in customers' and, consequently, in employees' behavior made the role of robots redundant, because now employees can perform the same task in a more effective way (The Wall Street Journal, 2020). For this reason, Walmart decided to remove the robots from its stores after three years of experimentation. This example is informative, as it reveals how configurational fit cannot be taken for granted and should always be checked: an exogenous shock can make even a sophisticated and well-working technology redundant, and not in fit anymore with the other elements of the service system.

Partial Fit Between Service Dimensions: Machine Learning in Banking Ticketing System

A global bank operating in more than 60 countries planned to reshape its main business processes through the integration of AI. The renovation process started with the integration of an AI solution (Analytical Intelligence) in the internal system of ticketing to support employees. Before the integration of the AI solution, the ticketing support process was entirely handled by human resources. When an employee needs any kind of support regarding a banking procedure, specifically about mortgage granting, she opens a ticket using an internal platform in which she explains what the problem is. Once the ticket is opened, the ticket is then sent to a centralized back-office task force of employees, for resolution.

The proposed AI solution recognizes and analyzes the content of the ticket and automatically provides the most appropriate response given the level of accumulated knowledge together with a level of confidence for the proposed solution. When the AI self-estimates that the level of confidence of its proposed solution is above 90%, the response is directly sent back to the branch employee who raised the request; otherwise, the response suggested by the AI is sent to the back-office employees that are free to consider, integrate, or discard the suggestion before sending back the feedback to the branch employee. In this case, the dimensions of the service system are the *firm* that wants to improve productivity and quality, the *employees* who open the tickets to solve a problem, and the AI *technology* that automatically responds to employees' tickets and *customers* who are searching for a banking service.

Despite some positive effects of the integration of AI, after one year of implementation some trade-offs emerged: AI generates a positive efficiency effect on the time to handle the ticket but a negative one on the satisfaction of the branch employees involved in the process. AI also produces positive spillovers on customer satisfaction but mostly on the efficiency of the process at the encounter and makes branches more prudent/selective in granting mortgages. Hence, there is a partial fit between the elements of the system, as the AI is able to satisfy both the firm's need to increase productivity by reducing ticket processing times and the consumers' need for quick and precise answers. Yet, regarding the employees, they are searching for timely and accurate responses: while AI is able to respond much faster than a human, the content of the responses provided by the AI is not able to fully satisfy the employees' needs. Looking at the textual content of the solutions provided by AI, they leave less option to the branch employees, meaning that analytical intelligence provides the most straightforward solution to the problem while humans are more inclined to propose multiple ways to solve the problem.

In this case, the bank did not poorly design the service system, but the configurational logic that characterizes service system's way of working suggests the proposed AI may require some adjustments, such as collecting more data to train the AI or redefine the algorithm to better meet the employees' need for more accuracy.

5 Conclusions

In this chapter, we have discussed the role of technology in service systems. We started by reviewing the concept of the service system and the theoretical framework proposed by Parasuraman and Grewal (2000), the Pyramid Model, which posits that technology, firm, employees, and customers are the fundamental interconnected dimensions of service. The model emphasizes the linkages between technology and the other dimensions as an essential factor to make service effective and improve customer experience (Sect. 1). We then sketched how service marketing literature discussed the role of technology in service systems over the years, identifying five main stages: (i) vending automation (1950–1970), (ii) process automation—computers (1970–2000), (iii) customer automation—self-service technologies (2000–2005), (iv) digital services (2005–2015), and (v) artificial intelligence (2015–) (Fig. 2). Compared to the other technologies, AI represents a breakthrough innovation, with a wide range of applications in services. The impact of AI is expected to be pervasive and intricate, transforming the service system in *Smart* Service System. Smart Service Systems are interconnected, dynamic, and proactive due to the presence of AI (Lim & Maglio, 2019) (Sect. 2). However, the expected revolutionary effects of AI in service carry significant uncertainties about the exploitation of such technology (i.e., *how* to make AI valuable). By adopting a configurational approach, we propose how the effectiveness of a smart service system depends on how AI solutions align with the other elements of the system: firm, employee, and customers (Sect. 3). Along this line, in Sect. 4, we present three empirical cases with different levels of configurational fit: recommendation algorithm in streaming platforms (good fit between AI and other service dimensions), shelf-scanning robots in supermarket (from fit to misfit between AI and service dimensions), and machine learning in banking ticketing system (partial fit between AI and service dimensions).

References

Andreasen, A. R., & Ferber, R. (1962). Automated grocery shopping. *Journal of Marketing, 26*(4), 64–66.

Beverungen, D., Müller, O., Matzner, M., Mendling, J., & Vom Brocke, J. (2019). Conceptualizing smart service systems. *Electronic Markets, 29*(1), 7–18.

Brynjolfsson, E., & Oh, J. (2012). The attention economy: Measuring the value of free digital services on the internet. In *ICIS*. Association for Information Systems.

Business Insider. (2016, June 14). Why Netflix thinks its personalized recommendation engine is worth $1 billion per year. [Web log post]. Retrieved February 20, 2021, from https://www.businessinsider.com/netflix-recommendation-engine-worth-1-billion-per-year-2016-6?IR=T

Cardoso, J., Pedrinaci, C., Leidig, T., Rupino, P., & Leenheer, P. (2012). D open semantic service networks. In *The international symposium on services science (ISSS 2012)* (pp. 1–15). Leipzig.

CNNMoney. (2000, May 9). Retailers post healthy 1Q. Retrieved February 20, 2021, from https://money.cnn.com/2000/05/09/companies/retail_earnings/

Comer, J. M. (1975). The computer, personal selling, and sales management. *Journal of Marketing, 39*(3), 27–33.

Daugherty, P., & Wilson, H. J. (2018). *Human 1 machine: Reimagining work in the age of AI*. Harvard Business Review Press.

Doty, D. H., Glick, W. H., & Huber, G. P. (1993). Fit, equifinality, and organizational effectiveness: A test of two configurational theories. *Academy of Management Journal, 36*(6), 1196–1250.

Drazin, R., & Van de Ven, A. H. (1985). Alternative forms of fit in contingency theory. *Administrative Science Quarterly*, 514–539.

Fuller, R. M., & Dennis, A. R. (2009). Does fit matter? The impact of task-technology fit and appropriation on team performance in repeated tasks. *Information Systems Research, 20*(1), 2–17.

Gallouj, F., & Weinstein, O. (1997). Innovation in services. *Research Policy, 26*(4–5), 537–556.

Giebelhausen, M., Robinson, S. G., Sirianni, N. J., & Brady, M. K. (2014). Touch versus tech: When technology functions as a barrier or a benefit to service encounters. *Journal of Marketing, 78*(4), 113–124.

Globe Newswire. (2020, March 25). Global connected vending machines market report (2019 to 2024), 4th ed. Retrieved February 20, 2021, from https://www.globenewswire.com/news-release/2020/03/25/2006076/0/en/Global-Connected-Vending-Machines-Market-Report-2019-to-2024-4th-Edition.html#:~:text=There%20are%20about%2015%20million,are%20now%20considering%20adding%20connectivity

Heinz Nixdorf Museums Forum. (2021). Computers in business and professions—1970 to 1980. Retrieved February 20, 2021, from https://www.hnf.de/en/permanent-exhibition/exhibition-areas/computers-in-business-and-professions-1970-to-1980.html

Huang, M. H., & Rust, R. T. (2018). Artificial intelligence in service. *Journal of Service Research, 21*(2), 155–172.

Lim, C., & Maglio, P. P. (2019). Clarifying the concept of smart service system. *Handbook of Service Science, Volume II*, 349–376.

Lusch, R. F., & Vargo, S. L. (2014). *Service-dominant logic: Premises, perspectives, possibilities*. Cambridge University Press.

Maglio, P. P., & Spohrer, J. (2008). Fundamentals of service science. *Journal of the Academy of Marketing Science, 36*(1), 18–20.

McCarthy, J. (2007, November 12). What is artificial intelligence? [Web log post]. Retrieved February 20, 2021, from http://www-formal.stanford.edu/jmc/

Meuter, M. L., Bitner, M. J., Ostrom, A. L., & Brown, S. W. (2005). Choosing among alternative service delivery modes: An investigation of customer trial of self-service technologies. *Journal of Marketing, 69*(2), 61–83.

Meuter, M. L., Ostrom, A. L., Roundtree, R. I., & Bitner, M. J. (2000). Self-service technologies: Understanding customer satisfaction with technology-based service encounters. *Journal of Marketing, 64*(3), 50–64.

Music Business Research. (2015, March 26). The recorded music market in the US, 2000–2014. Retrieved February 20, 2021, from https://musicbusinessresearch.wordpress.com/2015/03/26/the-recorded-music-market-in-the-us-2000-2014/

O'Callaghan, R., Kaufmann, P. J., & Konsynski, B. R. (1992). Adoption correlates and share effects of electronic data interchange systems in marketing channels. *Journal of Marketing, 56*(2), 45–56.

Ostrom, A. L., Fotheringham, D., & Bitner, M. J. (2019). Customer acceptance of AI in service encounters: understanding antecedents and consequences. In *Handbook of Service Science, Volume II* (pp. 77–103). Springer.

Parasuraman, A., & Grewal, D. (2000). The impact of technology on the quality-value-loyalty chain: A research agenda. *Journal of the Academy of Marketing Science, 28*(1), 168–174.

Quinn, J. B., Baruch, J. J., & Paquette, P. C. (1987). Technology in services. *Scientific American, 257*(6), 50–59.

Raisch, S., & Krakowski, S. (2021). Artificial intelligence and management: The automation–augmentation paradox. *Academy of Management Review, 46*(1), 192–210.

Reinders, M. J., Dabholkar, P. A., & Frambach, R. T. (2008). Consequences of forcing consumers to use technology-based self-service. *Journal of Service Research, 11*(2), 107–123.

RIAA. (2021). Mid-Year Music Industry Revenue Report | RIAA. Retrieved February 20, 2021, from https://www.riaa.com/reports/2020-mid-year-music-industry-revenue-report-riaa/

Sampson, S. E., & Froehle, C. M. (2006). Foundations and implications of a proposed unified services theory. *Production and Operations Management, 15*(2), 329–343.

Statista. (2021, January). Spotify's monthly active users 2015–2020. Retrieved February 20, 2021, from https://www.statista.com/statistics/367739/spotify-global-mau/

Still, R. R. (1952). The effect of an automatic vending machine installation on cigarette sales. *Journal of Marketing, 17*(1), 61–63.

The Netflix Tech Blog. (2017, November 29). Innovating faster on personalization algorithms at Netflix Using Interleaving [Web log post]. Retrieved February 20,

2021, from https://netflixtechblog.com/interleaving-in-online-experiments-at-netflix-a04ee392ec55

The Wall Street Journal. (2020, November 2). Walmart Scraps Plan to have robots scan shelves. Retrieved February 20, 2021, from https://www.wsj.com/articles/walmart-shelves-plan-to-have-robots-scan-shelves-11604345341

The Washington Post. (2019, June 6). As Walmart turns to robots, it's the human workers who feel like machines. Retrieved February 20, 2021, from https://www.washingtonpost.com/technology/2019/06/06/walmart-turns-robots-its-human-workers-who-feel-like-machines/?noredirect=on

Venkatraman, N. (1989). The concept of fit in strategy research: Toward verbal and statistical correspondence. *Academy of Management Review, 14*(3), 423–444.

Williams, K., Chatterjee, S., & Rossi, M. (2008). Design of emerging digital services: A taxonomy. *European Journal of Information Systems, 17*(5), 505–517.

World Economic Forum. (2020, April 29). The COVID-19 pandemic has changed education forever. This is how. Retrieved February 20, 2021, from https://www.weforum.org/agenda/2020/04/coronavirus-education-global-covid19-online-digital-learning/

Smart Technologies in Service Provision and Experience

Cristina Mele, Tiziana Russo Spena, and Valtteri Kaartemo

1 Introduction

Digital and cognitive technologies have evolved rapidly in the last 20 years. The spread of the Internet, smart phones, and intelligent objects has contributed to an exponential increase in connectivity. The growing number of connected smart devices configures complex systems in which objects and people interact and communicate through the exchange of data and access to a multiplicity of information. The adoption of novel technologies (e.g., artificial intelligence [AI], chatbots, wearables, augmented reality, blockchain) promises to transform people's lives and society through higher levels of connectedness, greater computational processing, and more complex decision-making

C. Mele (✉) • T. R. Spena
Department of Economics, Management and Institutions,
University of Naples Federico II, Naples, Italy
e-mail: cristina.mele@unina.it; tiziana.russospena@unina.it

V. Kaartemo
Turku School of Economics, University of Turku, Turku, Finland
e-mail: valtteri.kaartemo@utu.fi

© The Author(s), under exclusive license to Springer Nature Switzerland AG 2022
B. Edvardsson, B. Tronvoll (eds.), *The Palgrave Handbook of Service Management*,
https://doi.org/10.1007/978-3-030-91828-6_42

involving extraordinary volumes of data (Huang & Rust, 2018). Such features make it possible to define technologies as smart; although the term "SMART" often refers to "self-monitoring, analysis, and reporting technology", in a more general view, technology is referred to as "smart" when it is able to perform tasks and accomplish objectives that traditionally required human intelligence and capabilities. The concept of smartness is in its infancy in business studies: for example, in the context of AI and the Internet of Things/Everything (Langley et al., 2021), where smart objects can use input data to sense, reason, and perform actions to reach a certain goal. Extant studies refer to (1) a device's set of capabilities, including adaptability, reactivity, multifunctionality, ability to cooperate, and human-like interaction (Rijsdijk & Hultink, 2009); or (2) a service system's ability to increase the frequency and intensity of value co-creation (Lim & Maglio, 2018).

However, the concept of smartness has not been explained in depth. We offer an understanding of smartness in service provision as it relates to the use of smart technologies that either take over human actors' tasks (automation) or improve human actors' agency (augmentation) in the service process. In addition, we argue that smartness relates to the impact of technology on service experience and value co-creation (Heller et al., 2021).

This chapter indeed focuses on smart service technologies and how technologies' smartness can make both service provision and service experience smarter. We will show that smart service provision deploys intelligent automation and augmentation to foster systems of insight. These processes initiate systems of engagement and enable smart service experiences wherein both hedonic and utilitarian value are co-created.

2 Smart Service Technology and Smart Services

Smart services have been defined as services delivered to or via smart technologies (Wünderlich et al., 2015). For example, augmented reality offers new ways to provide and experience services by engaging users in an immersive value co-creation context. Furthermore, medical analysis and treatment benefit from bracelets with sensors that gather and analyse data, which facilitates novel ways of sharing, learning, controlling, adapting, and acting. Smart services are not industry-specific; rather, they potentially extend to all industries, including energy, healthcare, transportation, the domestic sphere, and education. The implementation of smart services relates to critical outcomes in the resource integration process, including cost and time saving, greater speed and control, reduced service supply costs and waiting times for service delivery, and higher perceived levels of personalization. One case could be the use of a chatbot to interact with customers, have a conversation with them, give information, and discover customer needs by automating and scaling. Recently, research has focused on the impact of smart technologies on both service providers and customers. From this research, we identify four main trends.

First, scholars have discussed the impact of smart service technologies on service provision. Most research on AI and robotics in value co-creation has focused on how these technologies support service providers (Kaartemo & Helkkula, 2018). Scholars are also interested in how to transform service provision, affect service strategies, and divide tasks between human and non-human agents (Huang & Rust, 2018; Mele et al., 2020b). Lam et al. (2017) explained how the ability to handle a greater volume of data, as well as provide faster analysis and use versatile data, may improve service quality and reduce service costs. Automation and machine learning raise many questions about augmented intelligence enabling higher-skilled professionals to provide enhanced service compared to the lower-cost labour force.

Second, another research stream considers how customers perceive the use of smart services on the frontline (De Keyser et al., 2019; Marinova et al., 2017). Service researchers have considered how service quality and experience are impacted by robotic automation, machine learning, or deep-learning technologies (Xiao & Kumar, 2021). For instance, scholars are interested in understanding the service quality (Choi et al., 2020) and responsibility perceptions (Jörling et al., 2019) of human–robot interaction in various contexts. Mende et al. (2019) ran seven experiments that revealed how customers behave differently with frontline service robots compared with frontline humans. Interestingly, people are more willing to buy status goods and eat more when served by a humanoid service robot. However, it is worth noting that people may act differently depending on the type of smart technology (humanoid vs self-service robot) or the degree of automated social presence (McLeay et al., 2021). Third, a wider set of studies on robot anthropomorphism (van Pinxteren et al., 2019) concentrates on the attribution of human characteristics, motivations, intentions, and emotions to non-human agents.

Fourth, recent studies have led to increasing empirical evidence on the impact of smart technology on service provision and experience. However, this evidence remains fragmented. Thus, it is not clear how the smartness of service technology impacts service practices. Below, we develop new frames for conceptualizing smart service provision and smart service experiences.

890   C. Mele et al.

3   Smartness of Service Technology for Service Practices

Service literature addresses how novel technologies promise broader applications for augmented human–machine interactions (Huang & Rust, 2018; Wirtz et al., 2018), with specific focus on how to transform data into usable intelligence by incorporating digitally empowered systems (e.g., devices, new tools) that offer new opportunities to integrate resources and enable value creation and innovation.

Mele et al. (2020a) propose the concept of smart nudging to refer "to the uses of cognitive technologies to affect people's behaviour predictably, without limiting their options or altering their economic incentives" (p. 950). According to the authors, several choice architectures and nudges affect value co-creation by (1) widening resource accessibility, (2) extending engagement, or (3) augmenting human actors' agency. Cognitive technologies are unlikely to engender smart outcomes by themselves; instead, they enable designs of conditions and contexts that promote smart behaviours by amplifying capacities for self-understanding, control, and action.

Given such emerging opportunities, there is a need to frame how different service technologies and their smartness affect service practices. No studies have explicitly addressed the smartness of technologies in relation to service practices. We argue that the full potential of the smartness of novel technologies to affect service practices lies in the provision of smart-technology-enabled value propositions (i.e., smart service provision) and the experience of smart-technology-enabled solutions (i.e., smart service experience). Table 1 synthesizes the features of the smart technologies.

Smart Service Provision

Service provision concerns the deployment and offer of value propositions (i.e., different combinations of resources) to potential beneficiaries as input for their value-creation processes (Vargo & Lusch, 2008). Smart features that utilize new technologies are transforming service provision. Smart service provision is an emerging concept referring to connected objects able to sense their condition and context, a provision which "thus allows for real-time data collection, continuous communication and interactive feedback" (Wünderlich et al., 2015, p. 443). In other words, smart service provision enables interactive feedback, connectivity, and responsiveness (Huang & Rust, 2018; Larivière et al., 2017). For example, in retailing, smart apps use integration,

Smart Technologies in Service Provision and Experience   891

Table 1 Definition and features of smart technologies

Technologies	Definition	Main features	Main references
Blockchain	Distributed digital ledger programmed to collect and certify data and information, which are recorded in an immutable way in a public register	Transparency, trust, safety, simplification, traceability, reliability, automation	Angelis and Ribeiro da Silva (2019), Chen (2018), Pilkington (2016)
Chatbots and intelligent conversational systems	Computer programs that interact with users using natural language	Conversational capability, automatic response, emotional intelligence, autonomous reasoning, trained ability	Kumar et al. (2016), Luo et al. (2019), van Pinxteren et al. (2020)
Smart wearables	Smart objects or processes designed to generate data and communicate in an automatic way	Status diagnoses, interactions, data processing, connection	Gao et al. (2015), Park (2020)
Service robots	System-based autonomous and adaptable interfaces that interact, communicate, and deliver service to customers	Autonomous decision capability, learning ability, adaptation, ability to initiate tasks	Huang and Rust (2021), McLeay et al. (2021), Wirtz et al. (2018, 2021)
Social robots	Autonomous systems that can understand social cues through facial- and voice-recognition technology and interact with users in a human-like manner	Human-like capabilities, communicating via natural language, reading and expressing emotions, social ability	Čaić et al. (2019), Wirtz et al. (2018)
Virtual or augmented reality	Intelligent image-recognition technology based on the ability to correlate a series of data with a particular image, superimposing the data in a contextual manner on the frame	Immersion, mix of physical and digital elements, widening of perceptions	Farah et al. (2019), Tredinnick (2018)

with location-based searches to provide personalized recommendations for purchasing products integrated or, in healthcare, a smart device can help to improve the quality of treatment by transferring patient data to physicians. To understand how the smartness of service provision is deployed, we consider the concepts of automation and augmentation. The former concerns routine or regular tasks, and the latter non-routine or irregular tasks (Rouse & Spohrer, 2018). Automation implies that machines take over human tasks—for example, smart thermostats that allow users to schedule, monitor, and remotely control home temperatures—while augmentation means that humans collaborate closely with machines to perform a task (Raisch & Krakowski, 2021), such as a wearable outfit that can control the wearer's temperature, track their movements, and provide real-time insights to act on.

Intelligent Automation

Intelligent automation combines technologies, tools, and methods to execute activities automatically and on behalf of knowledge workers. It is achieved "by mimicking the capabilities that knowledge workers use in the performing of work activities, i.e., language, vision, executing, thinking, learning" (Bornet et al., 2021, p. 1), with benefits of increased speed, reduced cost, enhanced quality, and improved process resilience and reliability.

With the rapid development of robot technology, more robots have been introduced and applied, particularly in frontline services or in homes (Wirtz et al., 2018). Service robots take over many routine tasks with a range of potential benefits to organizations, including increased effectiveness, productivity gains, enhanced reliability, improved compliance, and stronger security (Huang & Rust, 2018; Lu et al., 2021) They are capable of autonomous decision-making based on the data they collect via various sensors and other sources (internet- and cloud-based systems), and they adapt to the different operative situations or frontline contexts (Huang & Rust, 2021; McLeay et al., 2021). Household, hospitality, and tourism businesses provide many examples of robots successfully employed to deliver service tasks of varying complexity (see iRobot Roomba illustration).

> **iRobot Roomba** is a robotic vacuum cleaner equipped with a sensor and intelligent system. As a result, it has autonomous navigation, can be controlled via mobile phone, and can fulfil multipurpose tasks. Increasingly, it is becoming part of domestic life, taking on some of the burden of dull, dirty, and dangerous jobs

New technologies allow prompt and smooth service interactions (Castellano et al., 2018). For example, chatbots are always available to foster information exchange and transfer in a fast, easy, and timely way (see Unicorn Bay Bot illustration). Human–chatbot interactions provide information to consumers, while firms obtain information on consumers by tracking what they do and analysing the questions they ask (Luo et al., 2019; van Pinxteren et al., 2020). The ability to access information from a wider knowledge base by using connected systems such as messaging or social platforms (e.g., Facebook) provides chatbots with computational capacities (Wilson-Nash et al., 2020) that go beyond repetitive behaviours. They can get closer to customers' real needs and habits and can anticipate future interactions and executions. In retail, intelligent agents can look for opportunities to exceed customers' expectations by identifying cross-/up-selling opportunities that resonate with customers (Luo et al., 2019; Pantano & Pizzi, 2020).

Unicorn Bay

> **Unicorn Bay Bot** for Telegram helps users when they need information about the stock market and have no time to search for it online. This chatbot has information about all stock exchanges (and updates every 15 minutes)

In a different setting, blockchain technologies promise to affect service organizations and processes beyond simply creating new currencies (Chen, 2018). Researchers have discussed the numerous distinctive features of blockchain (e.g., disintermediation, security) and their ability to make processes smoother and more reliable (see Dedit Education illustration). Blockchain provides automatic recording of information in an unchangeable way between different users who exchange "assets". The consensus mechanism is based on this innate immutability (Pilkington, 2016). Service process operations are moving towards more coordinated and automated networks while being redesigned to reduce the need for intermediaries, thus assuring more security and speed in information transmission. Smart contracts and tokens facilitate, execute, and enforce asset exchanges between multiple parties (Angelis & Ribeiro da Silva, 2019; Chen, 2018).

> **Dedit Education** is a platform that allows schools and universities to notarize their students' certificates in a secure and reliable way. The fingerprint that is inserted in the blockchain is generated for each file. The entity signs the transaction with a private key to give the original authorship of the certificate, facilitating a posteriori verification of authenticity by third parties. The student, universities, and companies can easily verify that the document is authentic and unmodified. The institution has its public key on its website. The diploma's hash value—which uniquely identifies the contents of the file—is saved in the blockchain

Intelligent Augmentation

New technologies enable wider access to resources (information, data, relations, interactions) otherwise unavailable to human beings, thereby augmenting actors' knowledge and capabilities (Mele et al., 2020a). Intelligent augmentation enables new opportunities for human intelligence, knowledge, and capabilities. It provides adaptive aids for determining how humans can perform tasks: such intelligent analysis assesses the availability of necessary knowledge and skills and determines the required training interventions (Rouse & Spohrer, 2018).

The possible applications of internet connection have radically changed due to smart objects (e.g., smart glasses, smart watch, smart shirts, smart lens, and smart bangles) (see Google glasses illustration). Specifically, wearables enable continuous data exchange and deliver actionable information to help actors understand information in ways that reveal new insights and enable their decision-making (Park, 2020). Wearables support actors with ongoing feedback, alerts, and recommendations appropriate to each actor's choice and use contexts. A main application of this technology is in the healthcare ecosystem (Wang & Hajli, 2017). Notable examples are wearables that monitor parameters of wellness, such as sleep and calories, and medical devices for elderly or vulnerable people or those with chronic diseases (Gao et al., 2015).

Smart Technologies in Service Provision and Experience 895

Google glasses are glasses with an integrated camera. Their lenses act as screens that show different types of information. They provide surgeons with additional information and visual guidance during surgical procedures

These tools assist doctors and professionals in capturing health data whenever required, thus increasing their work efficiency.

Apart from routine automated tasks, service robots can perform tasks that require high cognitive and analytical skills by analysing large volumes of data, integrating internal and external information, and recognizing patterns and relating them to customer profiles (Mele et al., 2020a; Wirtz et al., 2021). For example, service robots in healthcare can help doctors analyse large quantities of data in a cost- and time-efficient way by identifying possible diagnoses, proposing the best solutions, and making recommendations (Wirtz et al., 2021). Recent developments demonstrate that robots are increasingly capable of more sophisticated physical and cognitive activities, including detecting worsening dementia, identifying hazards such as spills on a shop floor, and offering wealth-management advice. In a different context, social assistive robots are powerful tools that provide services to fragile or elderly people (Čaić et al., 2019; Odekerken-Schröder et al., 2020; van Doorn et al., 2017) (see MARIO project illustration).

The MARIO project addresses the difficult challenges of loneliness, isolation, and dementia in older people through innovations and multifaceted inventions offered by service robots. MARIO is based on the robot Kompaï R&D, by Robosoft, which can assist the elderly and people with disabilities by speaking, understanding language, and moving independently

Smart Service Experience

Service experience refers to "a customer's individual and subjective response to any direct or indirect contact with the provider" (Jaakkola et al., 2015, p. 12). Such an experience can be physical or digital, lived, observed, or imagined, and can relate to a single event, set of events, or process (Helkkula, 2011). As a subjective response, it is always context-specific and is co-created when actors engage with the service offering (Patrício et al., 2011) and integrate resources with other actors (Vargo & Lusch, 2008). The service experience relates not only to the shopping or consumption phase but to the whole customer journey by enacting the customer's cognitive, emotional, and behavioural responses (Verhoef et al., 2009).

Recent contributions have addressed the role of intelligent technology in making experiences smart for customers (Hoyer et al., 2020). Kabadayi et al. (2019) argue that "the advancements in smart technologies hold key potential to enhance their experiences overall by transforming conventional service experiences into smart service experiences" (p. 334). In other words, a technology-mediated experience is one where a service is delivered through smart devices with the possibility of real-time interactions alongside capacities of autonomy, visibility, accessibility, monitoring, sensing, and communication (Gonçalves et al., 2020). Conversely, perceived risk and privacy and safety concerns can worsen the experience.

To understand how experience with smart services arises, we consider utilitarian and hedonic value. Utilitarian value concerns task compilations and is extrinsic: the experience helps a customer to achieve a specific objective (Hong et al., 2017). Hedonic value relates to fun and enjoyment (Ryu et al., 2010) and is intrinsic: the experience is enjoyed for its own sake (Hong et al., 2017).

Utilitarian Value

Digital and cognitive technologies efficiently foster the acquisition of products, services, or information, reflecting a more task-oriented, cognitive shopping outcome (Babin et al., 1994). Utilitarian value is provided via fulfilment of functional needs. This dimension includes items such as more information, convenience, quick service, decision effectiveness, goal orientation, and money saved.

Studies on wearable devices advocate their greater potential for self-awareness or self-control interaction capabilities deployed through remote control systems, as well as their data-processing capabilities (Gao et al., 2015). Studies regarding healthcare have addressed how smart wearables (devices, clothes, etc.) provide actors with actionable insights so that they can establish commitment and consistency, thereby enhancing the decision-making process (see FIT medical sensing t-shirt illustration). By focusing on pertinent information, these solutions widen opportunities for actors, thus reducing their sense of risk and cognitive efforts, and personalizing treatment (Wang & Hajli, 2017).

FIT T-shirt The is capable of monitoring vital signs—including electrocardiography, body temperature, and movement—using complex signal-processing technology, ultra-low-power electronics, and low-power wireless microcontrollers

Trust-enabling technologies and a security-first mindset are key to utilitarian value (Angelis & Ribeiro da Silva, 2019). Blockchain ensures trusted transactions, data security, and transparent auditability, which help create informed and engaged actors. Blockchain is founded on a chain of custody, ensuring complete traceability (past and present) of the various operators' actions and behaviours. The validated blocks of transactions, linked to a time chain, act as a decentralized and immutable network that facilitates information exchange so that all participants have access to a transparent and shared database. As contracts and documentation are managed digitally, actors experience enhanced trust and security (see Authentico illustration).

Authentico has created, through blockchain technologies, an innovative system to protect consumers by supporting the fight against the foreign imitation of Italian agri-food products. The blockchain used by Authentico is Quadrans, a public blockchain that allows the notarization of relevant documents to verify a product's authenticity. The blockchain document-notarization system supports the company in certifying quality documentation to be shared with the consumer.

Hedonic Value

People often use novel technologies for fun, playfulness, joy, and excitement (Ryu et al., 2010). These hedonic dimensions of value refer to social, emotional, and epistemic aspects of service experience. Hedonic behaviour is guided by affective motivations, such as entertainment and emotions, and by socially satisfying interactions.

By learning from previous conversations and using their learning to continuously adapt their actions (Wilson-Nash et al., 2020), chatbot technologies influence decision-making by using emotional associations, social effects, and behavioural signals (Murray & Häubl, 2009) (see Woebot illustration). Social robots can detect emotional states such as happiness or sadness, read mood, intuit customer needs, and respond in contextually and emotionally appropriate ways. In healthcare socially assistive robotics play the role of trainers that monitor the progress of the medical treatment given, so that it can be modified if necessary. Some robots, typically toy robots, can activate and maintain social interaction and assume facial expressions and gestural movements, even imitating the expressions and movements of the user. Furthermore, playing with pet robots facilitates personal attachment and can be therapeutic for lonely elderly people or those suffering from dementia. Living with a pet robot keeps elderly people in better psychological condition, wards off depression, and contributes to general well-being (McGlynn et al., 2017) (see Paro illustration).

Woebot is a digital assistant with which users can interact either by typing text or by sending images of their faces, voice messages, or videos. The system recognizes the user's emotions and transmits the results to the conversation service, which can then record the emotional peaks. Through the dialogues, users' psychological problems are monitored and analysed. Subsequently, the service generates natural language to suggest solutions that improve the user's mood, adopting emergency measures where necessary

Paro is a pet seal, 55 centimetres long and weighing just over 2.5 kilos. It can move its eyes, head, and fins, and it has numerous sensors that make it sensitive to light and touch all over its body, including its whiskers. Among its characteristics, it can recognize the medical patient's voice and learn information, such as the patient's personal and behavioural habits

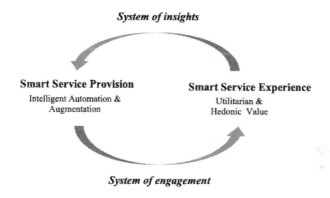

Fig. 1 Smart service practices

Virtual and augmented realities modify the service context to offer a novel experience by increasing opportunities for enjoyment, fantasy, and happiness (Farah et al., 2019; Tredinnick, 2018). The virtual solutions exploit the "wow" factor capable of capturing attention through surprise and virtual magic. The immersive and fantasy experience overcomes time and spatial constraints, requires emotional involvement and mental efforts (Bridges & Florsheim, 2008), and guarantees the augmented experience. The addition of detailed information helps to improve the user's perception by offering support (in case of need) or suggestions (in case of choice) (Farah et al., 2019). For example, IKEA, the Swedish furniture multinational, has found an effective way to meet customer needs (see IKEA Place illustration). Additionally, in fashion retail, virtual dressing rooms enable customers to try on various clothes and accessories and to take pictures and share them on social media. Similarly, in the beauty sector, virtual make-up try-on allows customers to virtually try nail polish, lipstick, or eye shadow and to see the results in a "magic mirror". Make-up artists can suggest looks to the client for make-up tests.

IKEA Place app uses augmented reality technology to facilitate both online and in-store shopping. By using the camera, customers can view products from the IKEA catalogue in 3D as if they were standing in front of them. By scanning the free floor, choosing an item, moving, rotating, and placing it, customers can, with just a few clicks, buy the product and share it on social networks with their friends.

4 A Virtuous Cycle Between Systems of Insights and Systems of Engagement

The wider adoption of smart technologies allows companies to implement an architecture based on the systems of insights and the systems of engagement through which smart service provision enhances smart service experience (Fig. 1). The systems of insight and the systems of engagement are not stand-alone; there is a dynamic interplay between them. Smart technologies (i.e., AI, chatbot, wearables, etc.) support providers in capturing insights that offer a richer engagement to improve the customer experience. Such a close connection with customers, allowing yet more data to be collected, reinforces the systems of insight.

Through technologies, smart service provision can sense a customer's condition and his/her surroundings, thereby enabling continuous interactive feedback to fulfil customers' needs at specific times and/or in specific contexts. Moreover, the "always on" connection and maintenance of smart products allow service providers to establish and cultivate close ties with their customers (Gonçalves et al., 2020), enabling the use of customer behaviour data that will translate to better information about customer needs (Wünderlich et al., 2015). In this way, systems of insight work to spur intelligent automation and augmentation actions. The systems of insight provide rich and updated knowledge about customers through the collection and analysis of data and social feeds (social media, service interactions, web clickstream data, and geospatial and time information). Providers can predict actors' behaviours and preferences, identify needs and correlations, and determine the design of automated actions. In addition, by leveraging behaviour-driven insights, the providers can apply advanced analytics to operational contexts at the point at which they generate customer interaction data, support actors in making better decisions based on massive data and multiple interactive responses, and augment actors' capabilities (Huang & Rust, 2021; Mele et al., 2020a).

By prompting intelligent automation and augmentation, systems of insight foster systems of engagement for a smart service experience. From wearables to social robots, technologies can both capture and leverage data insights to provide the elements of connected experiences where the consumer not only experiences the product or brand, but also becomes part of the complete experience (Kabadayi et al., 2019). Utilitarian and hedonic values are the levers of the systems of engagement, which involve engaging customers on the basis of their specific task-oriented or emotional needs and providing the contextual conditions to improve experience. The systems of engagement allow interactions that lead customers towards goal attainment and the desired experience (Gonçalves et al., 2020).

In summary, the smartness of service technology and service provision relates to the development of systems of insight that foster systems of engagement to improve the smart service experience and generate further insights.

5 Conclusions

In this chapter, we have conceptualized smart service provision and smart service experience. Smart service provision relates to the use of smart technologies in service delivery. Rather than arguing that there is a clear division between "smart" and "unintelligent" technologies, we maintain that technologies enable different levels of intelligent automation and augmentation along a continuum. Intelligent automation refers to processes that enable automated actions in regular tasks, including automated social presence. Intelligent augmentation refers to technology's support in non-routine or irregular tasks, such as adaptive aiding. Smart service provision deploys intelligent automation and augmentation to foster systems of insight. Both intelligent automation and intelligent augmentation can support systems of engagement that promise to enact a smart service experience with utilitarian and hedonic value.

Several new questions arise for scholars and practitioners. For instance, we need more empirical research to understand how the addition of intelligent automation and augmentation influences the smart service experience. It is important to understand when service providers benefit more from intelligent automation and when from increasing intelligent augmentation. This would help companies design and implement new strategies for service provision in different industries. Moreover, we need more empirical research on how smart technologies mediate service experiences, and the perception of utilitarian and hedonic value. Specifically, studies could deepen understanding of the effective contribution of smart technologies to providers and in customers' decision-making processes. Could there be such a thing as too much feedback, too much granularity, and too quick a response time coming from a huge amount of data? How can providers and customers balance the physical context, online world, and traditional and smart technologies? We encourage future research to tackle the role of smart services from both sides of the coin: provision and experience.

References

Angelis, A., & Ribeiro da Silva, E. (2019). Blockchain adoption: A value driver perspective. *Business Horizons, 62*(3), 307–314.

Babin, B. J., Darden, W. R., & Griffin, M. (1994). Work and/or fun: Measuring hedonic and utilitarian shopping value. *Journal of Consumer Research, 20*(4), 644–656.

Bornet, P., Barkin, I., & Wirtz J. (2021). *Intelligent automation: Learn how to harness artificial intelligence to boost business and make our world more human.* https://intelligentautomationbook.com

Bridges, E., & Florsheim, R. (2008). Hedonic and utilitarian shopping goals: The online experience. *Journal of Business Research, 61*(4), 309–314.

Čaić, M., Mahr, D., & Odekerken-Schröder, G. (2019). Value of social robots in services: Social cognition perspective. *Journal of Services Marketing, 33*(4), 463–478.

Castellano, S., Khelladi, I., Charlemagne, J., & Susini, J. P. (2018). Uncovering the role of virtual agents in co-creation contexts. *Management Decision, 56*(6), 1232–1246.

Chen, Y. (2018). Blockchain tokens and the potential democratization of entrepreneurship and innovation. *Business Horizons, 61*(4), 567–575.

Choi, Y., Choi, M., Oh, M., & Kim, S. (2020). Service robots in hotels: Understanding the service quality perceptions of human-robot interaction. *Journal of Hospitality Marketing & Management, 29*(6), 613–635.

De Keyser, A., Köcher, S., Alkire, L., Verbeeck, C., & Kandampully, J. (2019). Frontline service technology infusion: Conceptual archetypes and future research directions. *Journal of Service Management, 30*(1), 156–183.

Farah, M. F., Ramadan, Z. B., & Harb, D. H. (2019). The examination of virtual reality at the intersection of consumer experience, shopping journey and physical retailing. *Journal of Retailing and Consumer Services, 48*, 136–143.

Gao, Y., Li, H., & Luo, Y. (2015). An empirical study of wearable technology acceptance in healthcare. *Industrial Management & Data Systems, 115*(9), 1704–1723.

Gonçalves, L., Patrício, L., Grenha Teixeira, J., & Wünderlich, N. V. (2020). Understanding the customer experience with smart services. *Journal of Service Management, 31*(4), 723–744.

Helkkula, A. (2011). Characterising the concept of service experience. *Journal of Service Management, 22*(3), 367–389.

Heller, J., Chylinski, M., de Ruyter, K., Keeling, D. I., Hilken, T., & Mahr, D. (2021). Tangible service automation: Decomposing the technology-enabled engagement process for augmented reality. *Journal of Service Research, 24*(1), 84–103.

Hong, J. C., Lin, P. H., & Hsieh, P. C. (2017). The effect of consumer innovativeness on perceived value and continuance intention to use smartwatch. *Computers in Human Behavior, 67,* 264–272.

Hoyer, W. D., Kroschke, M., Schmitt, B., Kraume, K., & Shankar, V. (2020). Transforming the customer experience through new technologies. *Journal of Interactive Marketing, 51,* 57–71.

Huang, M. H., & Rust, R. T. (2018). Artificial intelligence in service. *Journal of Service Research, 21*(2), 155–172.

Huang, M. H., & Rust, R. T. (2021). Engaged to a robot? The role of AI in service. *Journal of Service Research, 24*(1), 30–41.

Jaakkola, E., Helkkula, A., & Aarikka-Stenroos, L. (2015). Understanding and advancing service experience co-creation. *Journal of Service Management, 26*(2), 182–205.

Jörling, M., Böhm, R., & Paluch, S. (2019). Service robots: Drivers of perceived responsibility for service outcomes. *Journal of Service Research, 22*(4), 404–420.

Kaartemo, V., & Helkkula, A. (2018). A systematic review of artificial intelligence and robots in value co-creation: Current status and future research avenues. *Journal of Creating Value, 4*(2), 211–228.

Kabadayi, S., Ali, F., Choi, H., Joosten, H., & Lu, C. (2019). Smart service experience in hospitality and tourism services. *Journal of Service Management, 30*(3), 326–348.

Kumar, V., Dixit, A., Javalgi, R. R. G., & Dass, M. (2016). Research framework, strategies, and applications of intelligent agent technologies (IATs) in marketing. *Journal of the Academy of Marketing Science, 44*(1), 24–45.

Lam, S. K., Sleep, S., Hennig-Thurau, T., Sridhar, S., & Saboo, A. R. (2017). Leveraging frontline employees' small data and firm-level big data in frontline management: An absorptive capacity perspective. *Journal of Service Research, 20*(1), 12–28.

Langley, D. J., van Doorn, J., Ng, I. C., Stieglitz, S., Lazovik, A., & Boonstra, A. (2021). The internet of everything: Smart things and their impact on business models. *Journal of Business Research, 122,* 853–863.

Larivière, B., Bowen, D., Andreassen, T. W., Kunz, W., Sirianni, N. J., Voss, C., ... De Keyser, A. (2017). "Service encounter 2.0": An investigation into the roles of technology, employees and customers. *Journal of Business Research, 79*, 238–246.

Lim, C., & Maglio, P. P. (2018). Data-driven understanding of smart service systems through text mining. *Service Science, 10*(2), 154–180.

Lu, V. N., Wirtz, J., Kunz, W. H., Paluch, S., Gruber, T., Martins, A., & Patterson, P. G. (2021). Service robots, customers and service employees: What can we learn from the academic literature and where are the gaps? *Journal of Service Theory and Practice, 30*(3), 361–391.

Luo, X., Tong, S., Fang, Z., & Qu, Z. (2019). Frontiers: Machines vs. humans: The impact of artificial intelligence chatbot disclosure on customer purchases. *Marketing Science, 38*(6), 937–947.

Marinova, D., de Ruyter, K., Huang, M. H., Meuter, M. L., & Challagalla, G. (2017). Getting smart: Learning from technology-empowered frontline interactions. *Journal of Service Research, 20*(1), 29–42.

McGlynn, S. A., Kemple, S., Mitzner, T. L., King, C. H. A., & Rogers, W. A. (2017). Understanding the potential of PARO for healthy older adults. *International Journal of Human-Computer Studies, 100*, 33–47.

McLeay, F., Osburg, V. S., Yoganathan, V., & Patterson, A. (2021). Replaced by a robot: Service implications in the age of the machine. *Journal of Service Research, 24*(1), 104–121.

Mele, C., Russo-Spena, T., Kaartemo, V., & Marzullo, M. L. (2020a). Smart nudging: How cognitive technologies enable choice architectures for value co-creation. *Journal of Business Research, 31*(6), 1149–1162.

Mele, C., Spena, T. R., Tregua, M., Laddaga, C., Ranieri, A., Ruggiero, A., & Gargiulo, R. (2020b). Understanding robot acceptance/rejection: The SAR model. In *2020 29th IEEE international conference on robot and human interactive communication (RO-MAN)* (pp. 470–475). IEEE.

Mende, M., Scott, M. L., van Doorn, J., Grewal, D., & Shanks, I. (2019). Service robots rising: How humanoid robots influence service experiences and elicit compensatory consumer responses. *Journal of Marketing Research, 56*(4), 535–556.

Murray, K. B., & Häubl, G. (2009). Personalization without interrogation: Towards more effective interactions between consumers and feature-based recommendation agents. *Journal of Interactive Marketing, 23*(2), 138–146.

Odekerken-Schröder, G., Mele, C., Russo-Spena, T., Mahr, D., & Ruggiero, A. (2020). Mitigating loneliness with companion robots in the COVID-19 pandemic and beyond. *An integrative framework and research agenda, 31*(6), 1149–1162.

Pantano, E., & Pizzi, G. (2020). Forecasting artificial intelligence on online customer assistance: Evidence from chatbot patents analysis. *Journal of Retailing and Consumer Services, 55*. https://doi.org/10.1016/j.jretconser.2020.102096

Park, E. (2020). User acceptance of smart wearable devices: An expectation-confirmation model approach. *Telematics and Informatics, 47.* https://doi.org/10.1016/j.tele.2019.101318

Patrício, L., Fisk, R. P., & Falcão e Cunha, J., & Constantine, L. (2011). Multilevel service design: From customer value constellation to service experience blueprinting. *Journal of Service Research, 14*(2), 180–200.

Pilkington, M. (2016). Blockchain technology: Principles and applications. In F. X. Olleros & M. Zhegu (Eds.), *Research handbook on digital Transformations* (pp. 225–253). Edward Elgar Publishing.

Raisch, S., & Krakowski, S. (2021). Artificial intelligence and management: The automation–augmentation paradox. *Academy of Management Review, 46*(1), 192–210.

Rijsdijk, S. A., & Hultink, E. J. (2009). How today's consumers perceive tomorrow's smart products. *Journal of Product Innovation Management, 26*(1), 24–42.

Rouse, W. B., & Spohrer, J. C. (2018). Automating versus augmenting intelligence. *Journal of Enterprise Transformation, 8*(1–2), 1–21.

Ryu, K., Han, H., & Jang, S. S. (2010). Relationships among hedonic and utilitarian values, satisfaction and behavioral intentions in the fast-casual restaurant industry. *International Journal of Contemporary Hospitality Management, 22*(3), 416–432.

Tredinnick, L. (2018). Virtual realities in the business world. *Business Information Review, 35*(1), 39–42.

van Doorn, J., Mende, M., Noble, S. M., Hulland, J., Ostrom, A. L., Grewal, D., & Petersen, J. A. (2017). Domo arigato Mr. Roboto: Emergence of automated social presence in organizational frontlines and customers' service experiences. *Journal of Service Research, 20*(1), 43–58.

van Pinxteren, M. M., Pluymaekers, M., & Lemmink, J. G. (2020). Human-like communication in conversational agents: A literature review and research agenda. *Journal of Service Management, 31*(2), 203–225.

van Pinxteren, M. M., Wetzels, R. W., Rüger, J., Pluymaekers, M., & Wetzels, M. (2019). Trust in humanoid robots: Implications for services marketing. *Journal of Services Marketing, 33*(4), 507–518.

Vargo, S. L., & Lusch, R. F. (2008). Service-dominant logic: Continuing the evolution. *Journal of the Academy of Marketing Science, 36*(1), 1–10.

Verhoef, P., Lemon, K. N., Parasuraman, A., Roggeveen, A., Tsiros, M., & Schlesinger, L. A. (2009). Customer experience creation: Determinants, dynamics and management strategies. *Journal of Retailing, 85*, 31–41.

Wang, Y., & Hajli, N. (2017). Exploring the path to big data analytics success in healthcare. *Journal of Business Research, 70*, 287–299.

Wilson-Nash, C., Goode, A., & Currie, A. (2020). Introducing the socialbot: A novel touchpoint along the young adult customer journey. *European Journal of Marketing, 54*(10), 2621–2643.

Wirtz, J., Kunz, W., & Paluch, S. (2021). The service revolution, intelligent automation and service robots. *European Business Review, 38*–44.

Wirtz, J., Patterson, P. G., Kunz, W. H., Gruber, T., Lu, V. N., Paluch, S., & Martins, A. (2018). Brave new world: Service robots in the frontline. *Journal of Service Management, 29*(5), 907–931.

Wünderlich, N. V., Heinonen, K., Ostrom, A. L., Patricio, L., Sousa, R., Voss, C., & Lemmink, J. G. (2015). Futurizing smart service: Implications for service researchers and managers. *Journal of Services Marketing, 29*(6/7), 442–447.

Xiao, L., & Kumar, V. (2021). Robotics for customer service: A useful complement or an ultimate substitute? *Journal of Service Research, 24*(1), 9–29.

Rapport-Building Opportunities and Challenges in Technology-Infused Service Encounters

Sijun Wang and Dwayne D. Gremler

The advancement of service technologies in general, and service robots in particular, has presented new opportunities for organizations to connect—and stay connected—with their customers (Bolton et al., 2018; Huang & Rust, 2020; Keyser et al., 2019; Kumar et al., 2019). As more service robots (e.g., Pepper by SoftBank Robotics, AIBO by Sony, and Facebook Messenger Bots) find their way into service encounters, understanding if and how rapport might be cultivated between customers and service robots becomes an important issue in these technology-infused service encounters (i.e., "service encounter 2.0") (Larivière et al., 2017). To lay a foundation for service researchers to explore the opportunities and challenges of cultivating customer rapport through service robots (CRR), in this chapter we first review the *customer-employee rapport (CER)* literature and the *virtual rapport* literature. We then elaborate on the distinct nature of CRR as well as the opportunities and potential challenges of CRR. Moreover, we propose a few societal

---

S. Wang
Marketing at the College of Business, Loyola Marymount University,
Los Angeles, CA, USA
e-mail: sijun.wang@lmu.edu

D. D. Gremler (✉)
Department of Marketing, Schmidthorst College of Business, Bowling Green State University, Bowling Green, OH, USA
e-mail: gremler@bgsu.edu

© The Author(s), under exclusive license to Springer Nature Switzerland AG 2022
B. Edvardsson, B. Tronvoll (eds.), *The Palgrave Handbook of Service Management*,
https://doi.org/10.1007/978-3-030-91828-6_43

implications as service firms adopt more service robots to build CRR in technology-infused service encounters.

1 Technological Advancements in Service Delivery

Recent technological advancements have empowered service employees and service organizations to interact with customers autonomously, intelligently, adaptively, and cost-efficiently (Bolton et al., 2018; Keyser et al., 2019; Kumar et al., 2019). Technological developments in service contexts, especially in the domain of artificial intelligence (AI), have led scholars to develop research propositions, identify theoretical frameworks, and conduct empirical studies on the opportunities and challenges brought by this new wave of service technological advancements (cf. Blut et al., 2021; Huang & Rust, 2018; Kumar et al., 2019). Powered by the dramatic improvement of AI technology, *service robots*—defined as "system-based autonomous and adaptable interfaces that interact, communicate, and deliver service to an organization's customers" (Wirtz et al., 2018, p. 909)—have been placed in the spotlight both in business practices (e.g., Guzman & Pathania, 2016) and in research investigations (cf. Blut et al., 2021). Indeed, techniques such as machine learning and deep learning have improved the perceived intelligence level of service robots in understanding customer needs, solving customer problems, and learning from every customer interaction, thus creating a wave of adoption of service robots in recent years (Guzman & Pathania, 2016; Kumar et al., 2019).

Service robots can take on various forms, from software agents (e.g., apps powered by AI) to embodied conversation robots (e.g., lifelike robots capable of carrying on conversation with humans). Meanwhile, service robots are capable of both assisting customers (e.g., providing information) (Keyser et al., 2019) and influencing customers' purchase decisions (Kidd, 2008; Lucas et al., 2018). The *functional efficacy* of service robots (i.e., service robots' ability to perform a service task to a satisfactory or expected degree) has been repeatedly confirmed. For example, a European telecommunications company reported that its chatbot conversations resolved 82% of customers' common queries; this rate reached 88% when combined with live intervention by a contact employee (Guzman & Pathania, 2016). Luo et al. (2019) find voice chatbots to be as effective as experienced employees and four times more effective than inexperienced employees in persuading customers to purchase financial services.

More importantly, advancements in robotic engineering have also greatly improved the *social efficacy* (i.e., the ability to create satisfactory social experiences for human participants) of service robots, including their ability to create a sense of social presence (i.e., a "degree of salience of the other person in the interaction"; Short et al., 1976, p. 65) and the feeling of being with a "real" person, through a wide array of design cues (e.g., Adam et al., 2020; Blut et al., 2021; van Doorn et al., 2017; Wirtz et al., 2018). For example, *non-verbal anthropomorphical design cues* such as physical appearance (including hair and gender), facial expressions, nodding, smiling, and hand gestures have been found to improve people's perceptions of service robots' intelligence, warmth, empathy, and sociability (Blut et al., 2021; Gratch et al., 2007; Larivière et al., 2017; van Doorn et al., 2017; Wilson et al., 2017). Researchers have further found that rapport between humans and service robots can be formed via *verbal anthropomorphical design cues*, including exhibiting empathy through making small talk, self-disclosing, thanking, and adopting ice-breakers in the human-robot interactions (Araujo, 2018; Cassell & Bickmore, 2003; Lucas et al., 2018). In addition, technological developments in speech recognition, kinetic interface (where the movement of people is captured and used as input for interaction with computing systems), and detection of emotional cues have allowed smart service robots such as Pepper to more precisely detect customer emotions and mood. Smart service robots can be now trained to adopt appropriate strategies to create emotional attachments with customers much as service employees would in a typical, face-to-face service encounter (e.g., Accenture, 2018; Adam et al., 2020). Therefore, service robots, powered by advances in AI technology, appear to possess sufficient social efficacy to cultivate rapport in commercial settings.

As the technological advancements of robotic engineering, especially service robots, facilitate the replacement of human service employees with AI (Huang & Rust, 2018), service firms' traditional reliance on frontline employees to build rapport with customers (CER) will be challenged. Meanwhile, such advancements may provide new opportunities for firms to enhance the customer's experience through the cultivation of customer-robot rapport (CRR) as well. Therefore, it is important for managers and employees in service organizations to understand the very nature of CRR and the how CRR might be cultivated. Fortunately, the rich CER literature that has emerged over the past two decades has identified a variety of rapport-building strategies and best practices (e.g., small talk, humor, pacing, and mimicking) (e.g., Gilliam et al., 2014; Gremler & Gwinner, 2000, 2008; Jacob et al., 2011). We suggest service researchers can lean on the CER literature to enrich our understanding of CRR.

2 CER in Service Settings

Customer-employee rapport (CER) represents a unique aspect of customer-employee relationships, focusing on the harmonious nature of interactions (Gremler & Gwinner, 2000). Formally, rapport has been defined as "a customer's perception of having an enjoyable interaction with a service provider employee, characterized by a personal connection between the two interactants" (Gremler & Gwinner, 2000, p. 92). The two dimensions of CER, "personal connection" and "enjoyable interaction," reflect the affective and evaluative aspects of customer-employee interactions.

Antecedents and Outcomes of CER. Previous studies have discovered a variety of employee characteristics influence their motivations and abilities to develop rapport with customers, including customer orientation (e.g., Hennig-Thurau, 2004), selling orientation (e.g., Tsaur & Ku, 2019), expertise (e.g., Giebelhausen et al., 2014), and emotional competence (e.g., Tsaur & Ku, 2019), as well as rapport-building behaviors such as connecting behavior (e.g., Gremler & Gwinner, 2008) and deep acting (e.g., Medler-Liraz, 2016). CER has been found to lead to various positive outcomes such as customer satisfaction, customer loyalty, and customer compliance (e.g., Delcourt et al., 2013; Gremler & Gwinner, 2000; Tsaur & Ku, 2019).

Whether and how these antecedents and outcomes of CER are applicable and hold true to CRR in commercial settings remains unknown. Given that most service management readers are likely more familiar with CER, which is based on human-to-human interactions, than with virtual rapport, which is based on human-robot interactions, the following sections will elaborate on how humans' experiences with virtual rapport can be enhanced by a set of robotic design cues (e.g., non-verbal anthropomorphic design cues and verbal anthropomorphic design cues) and human factors (e.g., gender and personality).

Virtual Rapport. Recent research from various fields has examined how humans react to robots and has included a focus on the rapport-building process as a key robotic design element. Borrowing the concept of (human) rapport developed in social psychology (Tickle-Degnen & Rosenthal, 1990), robotic engineers have coined the term *virtual rapport* (Weiss et al., 2010; Gratch et al., 2007; Lucas et al., 2018) to capture humans' emotional and cognitive assessment of their experience with robots. Virtual rapport has been conceptualized as encompassing humans' assessments of their sense of connection with a robot (i.e., emotional rapport), their sense of mutual understanding with a robot (i.e., cognitive rapport), and their reported occurrence of a robot's verbal and non-verbal behavior to elicit harmonious feelings for humans (i.e., behavioral rapport) (Gratch et al., 2007; Gris, 2013). Note that the focus of virtual rapport has been on the intelligence of a robot and the sense of connection humans may have with the robot, not on the *enjoyable interactions* that might occur between human and robots. More importantly, virtual rapport is generally studied in the non-commercial settings such as robot-human companionships and robot-assisted coaching. In contrast to virtual rapport, CER particularly emphasizes enjoyable interactions and mutual understanding aspects of human-to-human encounters in the commercial settings (cf. Gremler & Gwinner, 2000).

Most studies on virtual rapport have been conducted in non-commercial settings; customer-robot rapport (i.e., CRR) in commercial settings has received little research attention. It is important to make a distinction between CRR in commercial settings and virtual rapport in non-commercial settings because interactions between customers and robots in commercial settings tend to be more defined in the task scope (e.g., answering customer inquiries), shorter in duration, and require simpler human inputs than most human-robot interactions in the non-commercial settings. For example, Sony's AI robots interact with humans over a long period of time with much broader end goals (e.g., forming an intimate relationship with a lonely senior) in a more complex environment (e.g., senior care facilities) (cf. Sharkey & Sharkey, 2012). The rapport-building mechanisms in such non-commercial settings most likely differ from those in typical commercial settings, due to the differences of task scope, duration of the interactions, and interactive contexts in non-commercial versus commercial settings. The limited studies on CRR found in the service literature to date have primarily focused on customers' personal connections with service robots without addressing other facets of CRR (e.g., Qiu et al., 2020).

Definition of CRR. Given the preceding discussion, we define customer-robot rapport (CRR) as *a customer's perception of having a sense of an intelligent, enjoyable, and social presence with a service robot, characterized by a personal connection with the robot.* Our definition denotes the additional roles of perceived intelligence and social presence in the cognitive component of CRR in addition to the two dimensions of CER—"personal connection" and "enjoyable interaction" (Gremler & Gwinner, 2000). In other words, this conceptualization of CRR encompasses four facets, namely intelligence, social presence, enjoyable interaction, and personal connection.

Besides the personal connection and enjoyable interaction dimensions, research in both service marketing literature and robotic engineering literature has confirmed the criticality of perceived intelligence and social presence when customers form a rapport with robots (e.g., Blut et al., 2021; Qiu et al., 2020). For example, Qiu et al. (2020) find customer perceptions of robot intelligence are positively associated with customer-robot rapport. Similarly, Blut et al.'s (2021) recent meta-analysis on anthropomorphism finds that a customer's sense of social presence in the interactions with a service robot fully mediates the role of anthropomorphic design cues and CRR. Therefore, the definition we have offered—which includes four components, namely intelligence, social presence, enjoyable interaction, and personal connection—guides our discussion.

3   Antecedents of Virtual Rapport

Previous research on virtual rapport could shield some light on future research on CRR in the service literature. Most studies of virtual rapport build their models on the well-established social response theory (Nass & Moon, 2000), which states that human-computer interactions are fundamentally social. In particular, according to the computers-are-social-actors (CASA) paradigm, a person may perceive a sense of social presence through interacting with a computer system in general (Nass & Moon, 2000) and with a service robot in particular (e.g., Weiss et al., 2010; Qiu & Benbasat, 2009). Various anthropomorphic cues have been found to be able to facilitate a sense of social presence, which leads humans to automatically and unconsciously react to robots in the same way they do toward other humans (e.g., Gratch et al., 2007; Qiu et al., 2020; Seo et al., 2018; Wilson et al., 2017). The following section will review findings related to robotic design cues and customer factors and their roles in building virtual rapport.

Robotic Design Cues. Virtual rapport has been found to be positively associated with various *non-verbal anthropormorphic design cues* of robots, including hand gestures (e.g., Wilson et al., 2017), behavioral realism (e.g., von der Putten et al., 2010), displays of positive listening behaviors such as nodding and smiling (Gratch et al., 2007), and gender (Gris, 2013; Kramer et al., 2016). Similarly, virtual rapport is enhanced through *verbal anthropormorphic design cues* that incorporate human-to-human social relational techniques—such as engaging in small talk with humans, self-disclosing, utilizing expert jargon, making ice-breaking jokes, sharing backstories, and engaging humans with other social dialogue (Cassell & Bickmore, 2003; Lucas et al., 2018). Furthermore, *higher-level, complex relational strategies* have also been found to empower robots to build virtual rapport with people. For example, the capacity of empathetic interactional tactics can be designed to build a social companionship with children (e.g., Leite et al., 2012, 2014). The important roles of various design cues that have been found to drive virtual rapport should encourage service firms to incorporate these design cues to enhance CRR in commercial settings (cf. Lee et al., 2012).

Human Factors. In addition to the importance of previously mentioned design features of robots in building virtual rapport, previous studies report that human traits, sociodemographics, and contextual factors also play important roles in the rapport-building process. For example, Kramer et al. (2016) find embodied robots of the opposite gender significantly enhance virtual rapport and subsequent student performance and effort. Further, people who score high in extraversion and agreeableness report a significantly greater level of rapport with robots than those who are more introverted and less agreeable (Seo et al., 2018). Blut et al.'s (2021) review on anthropomorphism also suggests customer traits and predispositions (e.g., computer anxiety) and sociodemographics (e.g., gender) moderate their reactions to anthropomorphic cues of robots. However, the impact of humans' traits and personalities on the rapport with a robot are far from being conclusive. For instance, Brixey and Novick (2017) report no support for the similarity effects, that is, no difference in virtual rapport when the similarity levels between humans and robots' extraversion (vs. introversion) vary. Overall, the virtual rapport literature seems to have limited discussion on human factors that influence virtual rapport and has inconclusive findings so far. Thus, more research is needed to help service firms understand how customer (user) factors impact the CRR building process.

4   Outcomes of Virtual Rapport

Virtual rapport between students and teaching robots has been found to significantly enhance student performance and effort (Kramer et al., 2016). Similarly, robotic dogs (e.g., Sony's AI Robot) and real dogs have been found to equally benefit elderly consumers through the development of rapport and building emotional connections with them (Sharkey & Sharkey, 2012). Additionally, Gratch et al. (2007) show that robots can be highly capable of creating the experience of virtual rapport *comparable* to a face-to-face condition. These studies seem to suggest similar, positive outcomes of virtual rapport as those of rapport experienced in human-to-human interactions (e.g., CER).

5   Opportunities of CRR

Based on the CER literature and the virtual rapport literature, the following sections will identify a set of opportunities and challenges for service firms to cultivate CRR through service robots. In terms of opportunities, the design features and characteristics of service robots would seem to provide at least four ways for service robots to develop rapport that are superior to what could be done by employees (i.e., CER). First, service robots are better positioned to develop CRR with a larger number of customers simultaneously and in a more cost-efficient manner than human service providers. This advantage of CRR exists because service robots are more connected and embedded with other internal and external information systems than employees, allowing service robots to possess more knowledge about each customer's transactional, behavioral, and attitudinal information. Such knowledge depth allows for highly customized and personalized services on a larger scale than a typical employee could deliver (Kumar et al., 2019). In addition, service robots can also solve several customer problems during one encounter rather than bouncing a customer back and forth between different human employees. This advantage can make customer experiences more personalized and enjoyable, thus leading to a higher level of CRR across a larger number of customers.

Second, AI-based delivery of services and information-sharing enables service robots to maintain a consistent level of CRR across customers and across encounters with the same customer. Human employees' innate constraints in maintaining emotional, cognitive, and psychological stability are the very reason why many CER studies have focused on customer-contact employees' varying motivations, abilities, and other personality differences such as agreeability (e.g., Giebelhausen et al., 2014). Service robots, on the other hand, are largely free of inconsistency attributable to human mistakes or poor memory and are thus more likely to deliver a more consistent rapport experience with customers. More importantly, even if a firm deploys different types of service robots, maintaining a consistent CRR level across various service robots is more achievable than maintaining a consistent level of CER across different frontline employees and across different service encounters (even with the same employee). Therefore, CRR has the potential to be more consistent across different encounters than CER.

Third, service robots' ability to extensively learn about customers' preferences/habits and adjust service deliveries could continuously enhance CRR. Previous research has confirmed service robots' capacity to improve their service performance based on learning from external stimuli, including customer feedback on past experiences and environmental situations (e.g., Sharkey & Sharkey, 2012). Such learning not only improves service robots' ability to serve customers better, it can also motivate customers to engage in nurturing behaviors toward service robots. For example, customers have been found to give their time, energy, and financial resources to enhance their emotional relationship with robots (Garrity et al., 1989; Lastovicka & Sirianni, 2011). Therefore, we posit that service robots can continuously enhance the level of CRR through their learning capacity.

Finally, service robots have a greater potential to build CRR with variant customer profiles than customer-contact employees. Service robots hold the promise of being quite versatile because their interaction styles can be adjusted in real-time through automatic self-monitoring. For instance, robotic engineers have reported that empathetic interaction capacity can be designed, and social dialogues can be adjusted, based on the humans' reactions (e.g., Leite et al., 2012, 2014; Lucas et al., 2018). Robots can be trained to be culturally intelligent and multilingual when interacting with customers from different cultural backgrounds and speaking different languages; such training can be done at a relatively reasonable cost (e.g., Lucas et al., 2018) compared to training frontline employees up to the same level (if it is even possible). In addition, service robots can record/monitor the rapport-building process in real-time when interacting with customers; such CRR-based interactions can be automatically analyzed (Cerekovic et al., 2017). Therefore, such automatic, real-time analyses can provide immediate feedback to robots for real-time adjustments toward more CRR-inducive verbal and non-verbal behavior.

6 Challenges of CRR

Service robots also have limitations in their ability to cultivate CRR. First, the limited intuitive and empathetic skills of service robots to date may stifle their ability to build CRR when confronted with sensitive and emotionally laden customer issues. Observations of customer-chatbot interactions suggest that when customers are emotionally irritated, the limited emotional capability of service robots can jeopardize the CRR building process (Accenture, 2018). Unless some dramatic technical advancement occurs in service robot/AI development, the mood-reading capabilities and the "softer" emotional skills will likely pose challenges in service robots' attempts to build CRR in service encounters in the foreseeable future (Huang & Rust, 2018, 2020).

Second, customers' initial acceptance of being served by robots may hinder the development of CRR. People's overall acceptance of computer systems and robots can vary (Nomura & Kanda, 2016), and a significant portion of customers may be hesitant to fully trust service robots. For example, Luo et al. (2019) report that revealing a chatbot's identity (as a robot, rather than a salesperson) leads to a substantial decrease in length of chat sessions and purchase rate due to concerns about the chatbot's intelligence and empathy; however, when the chatbot's identity is concealed comparable sales outcomes to those interacting with a human salesperson are reported. This result suggests that customer attitudes toward and trust in service robots might impose a barrier for CRR formation.

Third, a high initial cost of developing and training service robots may make CRR an unfeasible and/or unreasonable surrogate for CER in service settings. AI is largely based on deep learning and machine learning techniques; therefore, a large number of encounters may be needed for a service robot to be fully developed and trained to cultivate CRR. Some service encounters may be either too complex or occur too infrequently to sufficiently train a service robot to develop rapport. Even if there is a high occurrence of routine service encounters, developing a truly interactive, intelligent, and sociable service robot could require high financial investments by service organizations. Therefore, not all service organizations can harvest the potential benefits of CRR when designing service encounters.

Finally, customer expectations from CRR can be fluid, thus posing challenges for service firms to maintain CRR. As the service quality literature suggests, customer expectations can spiral up because of best practices in an industry as well as in other industries (Nomura & Kanda, 2016). As service technologies advance, customers will likely expect greater functional and social efficacy of service robots. Thus, service firms will need to make sufficient investments to keep up with customer demands for CRR because customer expectations of service robots' performance will likely increase over time.

7 Cultivating Rapport with Both CRR and CER

Now that we have addressed the opportunities and challenges for service firms to enhance their customers' experiences via CRR, we posit that CER and CRR can be both substitutive and complementary to each other, depending upon the varying characteristics of service encounters. Little is known regarding when and how service robots should be deployed—either independently or jointly with employees—to build strong rapport with customers. As shown in Fig. 1, we speculate that the variability of customer demands (i.e., the lack of consistency of what customers request and how customers present their requests in a typical service encounter) and complexity of service delivery (i.e., to what extent a typical service task can be completed without a complicated process) should dictate how to deploy service robots or human employees in a particular service encounter to achieve the optimal customer rapport experiences.

First, for service encounters with relatively low variability, service robots may be a better choice to build rapport with customers. AI's obvious advantage over human brains in recording a large number of past transactions and discovering patterns from the vast amount of data can empower service robots to continuously improve their ability to serve all customers. The low variability of customer requests allows service robots to "learn" from the repeated service encounters and find the best way to serve a large number of customers at negligible marginal cost. Therefore, service robots should be utilized to build CRR to achieve consistent CRR at a lower cost when the variability of customer demands is low. For example, 1-800-Flowers uses Facebook Messenger (a service robot in the form of chatbot) to help customers order flowers, make gift suggestions, and deliver updates on shipping without obvious human employee presence (www.1800flowers.com). This company benefits from CRR because the service chatbot is designed for a well-defined scope of tasks, thus leading to a desirable customer experience with negligible marginal cost.

On the other hand, when customers are involved in services high in variability and low in complexity, we suggest human employees rather than service robots should be deployed to build rapport with customers. The high

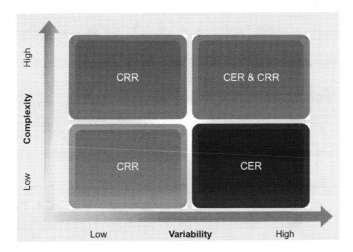

Fig. 1 Rapport building with service robots/employees

variability of customer demands makes the initial cost and barriers of developing and training service robots either too high or not feasible. Additionally, the low complexity of service delivery does not pose challenges to human employees' limit of cognitive capacity and their ability to gather, analyze, and evaluate complex information from internal and external sources in real time. Therefore, the benefits of CRR may not be enough to warrant the high costs and barriers of building a service robot for the task.

Finally, when service encounters are high in variability and high in complexity, we suggest deploying robot-employee teams to build strong rapport with customers. Such teams could complement each other in handling the two major challenges simultaneously; human employees could handle the variability challenges while service robots could fulfill the information demand and cognitive requirements in delivering complex services. The complementary benefits of employing both service robots and contact employees could lead to more "in-sync" experiences among customers when service firms deploy both service robots and contact employees than deploying either one of them independently. For example, Amazon's Style Check (a service robot in the form of software) is designed to suggest an outfit that fits the weather and consumers' fashion senses (www.amazon.com). On the one hand, this robot-enhanced experience benefits from the trained machine learning models using historical data and knowledge bases of fashion experts to reduce the complexity of decision rules and cognitive demands of human fashion advisors (e.g., "remember" previous feedbacks). On the other hand, human eyes are still needed to intervene when the AI-based models show low confidence or different models disagree to address unusual variability of customer demands. Obviously, more empirical studies are needed to validate the proposed scheme of deploying service employee and/or service robots to build optimal customer rapport with service employees, service robots, or both.

8 Negative Social Impacts of CRR

As our understanding of service robots and their impact on customer experience in general, and rapport in particular, is still in its infancy stage, we cannot draw definitive conclusions about how service robots will change the business landscape nor how (or if) they will provide economic and social benefits to customers. However, it is critical for the service discipline to anticipate and evaluate the potential impacts of deploying robots to serve customers on our society at large. The next two paragraphs focus on the potential negative social impacts of CRR.

First, service organizations could lose their ability to identify subtle customer needs if they rely solely on CRR. Even though service robots are becoming more capable of detecting human emotions and forming empathy with humans, a large portion of subtle customer reactions might not be registered, or be processed by, service robots. The long-term success of service organizations relies on the deep understanding of consumer needs. According to media richness theory (Daft & Lengel, 1986), face-to-face human interactions are more effective for communicating equivocal issues that contain uncertain or ambiguous information (e.g., customers' motivations to reject a solution) than are other non-human entities such as service robots. Additionally, deployment of service robots may alienate a significant portion of customers who prefer high-touch service be delivered by human providers. Therefore, service firms should pay special attention to such a loss of understanding subtle customer needs when solely deploying service robots to build CRR. Service firms are encouraged to uncover subtle customer needs through alternative methods such as in-depth interviews, focus groups, and ethnographic methods to enhance customers' rapport experiences.

Furthermore, as technology advancements allow service robots to build strong CRR with customers, some customers may change their social interaction choices. As customers begin to rely more on service robots than contact employees for their rapport experience, they may cut out human interactions, leading to social isolation, loneliness, and decreased physical and psychological well-being (cf. Lastovicka & Anderson, 2014). In addition, the cultivation of rapport with a robot might even change peoples' ability to interact with other humans. For example, Hill et al. (2015) report that people interacting with chatbots for a long period of time tend to use less rich vocabulary and greater profanity. Furthermore, given that people tend to feel service robots would not judge and have no emotions, antisocial behavior such as aggression and violent behavior could occur more frequently in service encounters with robots compared to those with human employees. Therefore, the long-term, unintended social impacts of CRR should be incorporated into the consideration of a service firm's deployment of service robots.

In sum, we believe that service robots have tremendous potential to develop rapport with customers. It is up to service employees, service organizations, and policy makers to be prepared to maximize their potential benefits and mitigate their potential costs and any negative impact.

References

1800flowers. (n.d.). Retrieved June 12, 2021, from https://www.1800flowers.com.

Accenture. (2018). Teaching machines to read our feelings. *The Wall Street Journal.*

Adam, M., Wessel, M., & Benlian, A. (2020). AI-based chatbots in customer service and their effects on user compliance. *Electronic Markets.*

Amazon. (n.d.). Retrieved June 12, 2021, from https://www.amazon.com/Washii-Style-Check/dp/B01LPS96B4.

Araujo, T. (2018). Living up to the chatbot hype: The influence of anthropomorphic design cues and communicative agency framing on conversational agent and company perceptions. *Computers in Human Behavior, 85,* 183–189.

Blut, M., Wang, C., Wunderlich, N. V., & Brock, C. (2021). Understanding anthropomorphism in service provision: A meta-analysis of physical robots, chatbots, and other AI. *Journal of the Academy of Marketing Science, 49,* 632–658.

Bolton, R. N., McColl-Kennedy, J. R., Cheung, L., Gallean, A. S., Orsingher, C., Witell, L., & Zaki, M. (2018). Customer experience challenges: Bringing together digital, physical and social realms. *Journal of Service Management, 29*(5), 71–84.

Brixey, J., & Novick, D. (2017). Building rapport with extraverted and introverted agents. Paper presented at the International Workshop on Spoken Dialogue Systems (IWSDS).

Cassell, J., & Bickmore, T. (2003). Negotiated collusion: Modeling social language and its relationship effects in intelligent agents. *User Modeling and User-Adapted Interaction, 13*(1), 89–132.

Cerekovic, A., Aran, O., & Gatica-Perez, D. (2017). Rapport with virtual agents: What do human social cues and personality explain? *IEEE Transactions on Affective Computing, 8*(3), 382–395.

Daft, R. L., & Lengel, R. H. (1986). Organizational information requirements, media richness and structural design. *Management Science, 32*(5), 554–571.

Delcourt, C., Gremler, D. D., van Riel, A. C. R., & van Birgelen, M. (2013). Effects of perceived employee emotional competence on customer satisfaction and loyalty: The mediating role of rapport. *Journal of Service Management, 24*(1), 5–24.

Garrity, T. F., Stallones, L., Marx, M. B., & Johnson, T. P. (1989). Pet ownership and attachment as supportive factors in the health of the elderly. *Anthrozoos, 3*(1), 35–44.

Giebelhausen, M., Robinson, S. G., Sirianni, N. J., & Brady, M. K. (2014). Touch versus tech: When technology functions as a barrier or a benefit to service encounters. *Journal of Marketing, 78*(July), 113–124.

Gilliam, D. A., Flaherty, K. E., & Rayburn, S. W. (2014). The dimensions of storytelling by retail salespeople. *The International Review of Retail, Distribution and Consumer Research, 24*(2), 231–241.

Gratch, J., Wang, N., Gerten, J., Fast, E., & Duffy, R. (2007). Creating rapport with virtual agents. In C. Pelachaud, J. C. Martin, G. Andre, G. Chollet, K. Karpouzis, & D. Pele (Eds.), *IVA 2007* (Vol. LNAI 4722, pp. 125–138). Springer Verlag.

Gremler, D. D., & Gwinner, K. P. (2000). Customer-Employee Rapport in Service Relationships. *Journal of Service Research, 3*(1), 82–104.

Gremler, D. D., & Gwinner, K. P. (2008). Rapport-building behaviors used by retail employees. *Journal of Retailing, 84*(3), 308–324.

Gris, I. (2013, December). Adaptive virtual rapport for embodied conversational agents. Paper presented at the Proceedings of the 15th ACM on International Conference on Multimodal Interaction.

Guzmán, I., & Pathania, A. (2016). Chatbots in customer service. Tech. rep. Accenture, accessed on March 10, 2022. https://bit.ly/Accenture-Chatbots-Customer-Service.

Hennig-Thurau, T. (2004). Customer orientation of service employees: Its impact on customer satisfaction, commitment, and retention. *International Journal of Service Industry Management, 15*(5), 460–478.

Hill, J., Ford, W. R., & Gerreras, I. G. (2015). Real conversations with artificial intelligence: A comparsion between human-human online conversations and human-chatbot conversations. *Computers in Human Behavior, 49*, 245–250.

Huang, M. H., & Rust, R. T. (2018). Artificial intelligence in service. *Journal of Service Research, 21*(2), 155–172.

Huang, M. H., & Rust, R. T. (2020). Engaged to a robot? The role of AI in service. *Journal of Service Research, 24*, 30–41.

Jacob, C., Gueguen, N., Martin, A., & Boulbry, G. (2011). Retail salespeople's mimicry of customers: Effects on consumer behavior. *Journal of Retailing and Consumer Services, 18*(5), 381–388.

Keyser, A. D., Kocher, S., Alkire, L., Verbeeck, C., & Kandampully, J. (2019). Frontline service technology infusion: Conceptual archetypes and future research directions. *Journal of Service Management, 30*(1), 156–183.

Kidd, C. D. (2008). Designing for long-term human-robot interaction and application to weight loss. (Doctor of Philosophy in Media Arts and Sciences). Massachusetts Institute of Technology.

Kramer, N. C., Karacora, B., Lucas, G. M., Dehghani, M., Ruther, G., & Gratch, J. (2016). Closing the gender gap in STEM with friendly male instructors? On the effects of rapport behavior and gender of a virtual agent in an instructional interaction. *Computers & Education, 99*, 1–13.

Kumar, V., Rajan, B., Venkatesan, R., & Lecinski, J. (2019). Understanding the role of artificial intelligence in personalized engagement marketing. *California Management Review, 61*(4), 135–155.

Larivière, B., Bowen, D., Andreassen, W., Kunz, W. H., Sirianni, N. J., Voss, C., & Keyser, A. D. (2017). 'Service encounter 2.0': An investigation into the roles of technology, employees and customers. *Journal of Business Research, 79*, 238–246.

Lastovicka, J. L., & Anderson, L. (2014). Loneliness, material possession love, and consumers' physical well-being. In Tatzel, M. (ed.), *Consumption and Well-Being in the Material World*. Springer, Dordrecht, 63–72.

Lastovicka, J. L., & Sirianni, N. J. (2011). Truly, madly, deeply: Consumers in the throes of material possession love. *Journal of Consumer Research, 38*(2), 323–342.

Lee, M. K., Forlizzi, J., Kiesler, S., Rybski, P., Antanitis, J., & Savetsila, S. (2012, March 5–8). Personalization in HRI: A longitudinal field experiment. Paper presented at the HRI'12, Boston, Massachusetts, USA.

Leite, I., Castellano, G., Pereira, A., Martinho, C., & Paiva, A. (2012). Modeling empathic behavior in a robotic game companion for children: An ethnographic study in real-world settings. Paper presented at the Seventh Annual ACM/IEEE International Conference on Human-Robot Interaction (HRI'12), New York, NY, USA.

Leite, I., Castellano, G., Pereira, A., Martinho, C., & Paiva, A. (2014). Empathic robots for long-term interaction. *International Journal of Social Robotics, 6*(3), 329–341.

Lucas, G. M., Boberg, J., Traum, D. R., Artstein, R., Gratch, J., Gainer, A., Johnson, E., Leuski, A., & Nakano, M. (2018). Culture, errors, and rapport-building dialogue in social agents. Proceedings of the 18th international conference on intelligent virtual agents.

Luo, X., Tong, S., Fang, Z., & Qu, Z. (2019). Frontiers: machines vs. humans: The impact of artificial intelligence chatbot disclosure on customer purchases. *Marketing Science, 38*(6), 937–947.

Medler-Liraz, H. (2016). The role of service relationships in employees' and customers' emotional behavior, and customer-related outcomes. *Journal of Services Marketing, 30*(4), 437–448.

Nass, C., & Moon, Y. (2000). Machines and mindlessness: Social responses to computers. *Journal of Social Issues, 56*, 81–103.

Nomura, T., & Kanda, T. (2016). Rapport-expectation with a robot scale. *International Journal of Social Robotics, 8*, 21–30.

Qiu, H., Li, M., Shu, B., & Bai, B. (2020). Enhancing hospitality experience with service robots. *Journal of Hospitality Marketing and Management, 29*(3), 247–268.

Qiu, L., & Benbasat, I. (2009). Evaluating anthropomorphic product recommendation agents. *Journal of Management Information Systems, 25*(4), 145–182.

Seo, S. H., Griffin, K., Young, J. E., Bunt, A., Prentice, S., & Loureiro-Rodriguez, V. (2018). Investigating people's rapport building and hindering behaviors when working with a collaborative robot. *International Journal of Social Robotics, 10*(12), 147–161.

Sharkey, A., & Sharkey, N. (2012). Granny and the robots: Ethical issues in robot care for the elderly. *Ethics and Information Technology, 14*(1), 27–40.

Short, J., Williams, E., & Christie, B. (1976). *The social psychology of telecommunications*. Wiley.

Tickle-Degnen, L., & Rosenthal, R. (1990). The nature of rapport and its nonverbal correlates. *Psychology Inquiry, 1*(4), 285–293.

Tsaur, S.-H., & Ku, P.-S. (2019). The effect of tour leaders' emotional intelligence on tourists' consequences. *Journal of Travel Research, 58*(1), 63–76.

van Doorn, J., Mende, M., Noble, S. M., Hullan, J., Ostrom, A. L., & Dhruv, G. (2017). Domo Arigato Mr. Roboto: Emergence of Automated Social Presence in Organizational Frontlines and Customers' Service Experiences. *Journal of Service Research, 20*(1), 43–58.

von der Putten, A. M., Kramer, N. C., Gratch, J., & Kang, S.-H. (2010). 'It doesn't matter what you are!' Explaining social effects of agents and avatars. *Computers in Human Behavior, 26*, 1641–1650.

Weiss, A., Igelsbock, J., Tscheligi, M., Bauer, A., Kuhnlenz, K., et al. (2010). Robots asking for directions-the willingness of passer-by to support robots. Paper presented at the HRI'10: Proceedings of the 5th ACM/IEEE International Conference on Human Robot Interaction.

Wilson, J. R., Lee, N. Y., Saechao, A., Hersheenson, S., Scheutz, M., & Tickle-Degnen, L. (2017). Hand gestures and verbal acknowledgements improve human-robot rapport. In *ICSR 2017* (pp. 334–344). LNAI 10652: Springer International Publishing AG.

Wirtz, J., Patterson, P. G., Kunz, W. H., Gruber, T., Lu, V. N., Paluch, S., & Martins, A. (2018). Brave new world: Service robots in the frontline. *Journal of Service Management, 29*(50), 907–931.

Part VI

Service Technology

Artificial Intelligence and Decision-Making: Human–Machine Interactions for Successful Value Co-creation

Francesco Polese, Sergio Barile, and Debora Sarno

1 Introduction

Hiring and bail decisions, credit risk predictions, and self-driving vehicles are examples of artificial intelligence (AI) oriented toward human decision-making (DM) (Shrestha et al., 2019). Those solutions are developing at a rapid pace, changing how value is co-created. However, humans and their resources still play a central role in understanding emotions and building trust with customers or in providing industry-specific and experience-based knowledge and communication skills (Paschen et al., 2021). In synthesis, the effectiveness of

---

F. Polese (✉)
Department of Management & Innovation Systems, University of Salerno, Fisciano, Italy
e-mail: fpolese@unisa.it

S. Barile
Department of Management, Sapienza University of Rome, Rome, Italy
e-mail: sergio.barile@uniroma1.it

D. Sarno
Department of Management and Quantitative Studies, University of Naples Parthenope, Naples, Italy
e-mail: debora.sarno@uniparthenope.it

© The Author(s), under exclusive license to Springer Nature Switzerland AG 2022
B. Edvardsson, B. Tronvoll (eds.), *The Palgrave Handbook of Service Management*,
https://doi.org/10.1007/978-3-030-91828-6_44

AI solutions[1] is dependent on human involvement (Jarrahi, 2018) since "computers plus humans do better than either one alone" (Campbell, 2016).

Furthermore, although managers involved in DM are ultimately responsible for decision outcomes, AI solutions could also be ineffective (leading to value co-destruction, Grundner & Neuhofer, 2021) due to emergent consequences (Maglio & Lim, 2018; Polese et al., 2021) and biases, a lack of fairness and transparency (Ashraf et al., 2018), suboptimal data collection, or other issues (Storbacka, 2019; Bock et al., 2020). One source of ineffectiveness could be the assessment of outcomes at an analytic level other than the (micro)level of human–machine interactions. This is the case for AI-supported decisions that maximize company profit in the short run but, over time, contribute to the dissolution of the ecosystem in which it operates, with implications for the company as well.

Since the "singularity"[2] has not yet come, humans are involved in interactions with machines when using machine outputs for DM, in providing learning inputs as machines work and, upstream, during the AI design and development phase. Indeed, humans mostly accept AI as an augmentation/ decision support tool rather than an automated tool to replace themselves (Davenport & Kirby, 2016; Duan et al., 2019). Thus, the main human purpose of using AI is intelligence augmentation (IA) through AI designed with the intention of augmenting human contributions (Jarrahi, 2018), although AI itself can also be augmented (Barile et al., 2018b, 2020).

Given that human–machine interactions—particularly in DM—are inevitable, potentially beneficial, and highly valued, the following questions then arise: "What should be taken into account for effective human–machine interaction in the field of DM? What should be the target for measuring such effectiveness?".

We assume a service ecosystem perspective[3] based on the service-dominant (S-D) logic (Vargo & Lusch, 2016) to transform these questions into concep-

---

[1] In this chapter, AI solutions refer to software/hardware systems provided by AI, lately also referred as "machines".

[2] Kurzweil (2005) foresees that when the singularity occurs, "there will be no clear distinction between human and machine".

[3] Under the service ecosystem perspective, service—in other words, the application of resources for the benefit of a part—is what an AI solution can provide. Moreover, overcoming a dyadic machine-to-developer/user orientation, S-D logic shows that service is exchanged for service in a service ecosystem, meaning that two or more parties interact to exchange service by integrating available resources (as data, knowledge, technologies, etc.), as is the case when humans and AI solutions interact. Furthermore, in order to identify the context in which the effectiveness of AI solution-based DM can be measured, we can

tually investigable ones at a general and holistic level. Through these lenses, both humans and machines can be considered actors,[4] and we can restate the previous research questions as follows: "What elements should be taken into account for successful value-co-creation through human–machine interactions in DM?"

Unfortunately, although some studies highlight that human–machine interactions foster new possibilities for value co-creation (Russo-Spena et al., 2019) and adopt S-D logic (Paschen et al., 2021), research on human–machine interaction in value co-creation processes is still in its infancy (Paschen et al., 2021) and only weak connections have been established with DM, value perception, and service ecosystem viability (Kaartemo & Helkkula, 2018).

AI studies oriented toward DM, in turn, offer an opportunity to understand how to improve both individual and group choices, influencing customer-related marketing phenomena and the behavior and DM of marketing managers (Vargo & Lusch, 2017). Furthermore, given that organizations can be viewed as networks of decisions to be orchestrated (Shrestha et al., 2019) to assure successful value co-creation (Polese, 2018), there is a specific call to understand how to design organizations to enable successful interactions between humans and AI solutions (Jordan, 2018).

In synthesis, the research question above is important and still unanswered. Thus, we examine DM enabled by human–machine interactions in an attempt to uncover the main processes, characteristics, constraints, and outcomes involved. To do so, we synthetize recent literature on AI and DM. Furthermore, by integrating the S-D logic perspective with the viable systems approach (vSa), we provide a framework that relates the knowledge process, knowledge endowment, context, and viability.

---

leverage the fact that according to S-D logic, the exchange of service occurs to co-create value, which is an increase in the viability of the service ecosystem. Indeed, a systems perspective is fundamental to developing a realistic understanding of how technology can shape value co-creation (Vargo et al., 2017). The service ecosystem, in particular, is characterized by actors, resources, and institutional arrangements structuring actors' behavior. In addition, to avoid overlooking each actor's view on the value that is co-created in interactions, S-D logic highlights that value is always uniquely and phenomenologically perceived by the beneficiary, although it is also always co-created, multidimensional, and emergent (Vargo & Lusch, 2017).

[4] S-D logic originally considered an actor as any human or collection of humans that can integrate resources to mutually exchange service (Lusch & Vargo, 2014). More recently, advances in cognitive computing and autonomous technologies have occasioned the acknowledgment that beyond humans, actors may include machines and technologies (Lusch et al., 2016).

930 F. Polese et al.

The remainder of the chapter is structured as follows: in the next section, insights are provided on AI and its use in DM; in the third section, a new framework is proposed to answer the research question ; and the closing section presents conclusions.

2 AI and DM

AI: Main Descriptive Elements

Although AI[5] was introduced in the 1950s, its current development and exploitation are due to recent advancements in the speed of data processing, cloud computing, and big data technologies (Duan et al., 2019). There is no agreed definition of AI; one of the very first characterized AI as "making a machine behave in ways that would be called intelligent if a human were so behaving" (McCarthy et al., 1955). More recently, AI has been considered to encompass "information technologies that act rationally based on the information they have ... to achieve the best outcome or, in case on uncertainty, the best expected outcome" (Paschen et al., 2021).

AI involves at least four types of technologies[6] (machine learning, speech recognition, natural language processing, and image recognition) and should show the following characteristics (Davenport & Kirby, 2016): the ability to handle a variety of data types and learn, transparency, multiple means of control to facilitate augmentation, flexibility to incorporate updates and modifications, robust reporting capabilities, and state-of-the-art IT hygiene.

---

[5] General characterizations of AI deal with narrow, general (or strong), and super AI. The first is related to the ability to accomplish a narrow set of goals, such as playing chess (Tegmark, 2017); general AI supports the "ability to accomplish any goal, including learning" (Tegmark, 2017, p. 39) across multiple domains; and artificial superintelligence refers to a science-fiction scenario in which machines can match or exceed human intellect. Since the last one seems "logically possible and utterly implausible" (Floridi, 2016), this work is oriented toward narrow and general AI, although it does not neglect the possibility that super AI will become a reality in the future.

[6] A more detailed organization of AI building blocks that extends the focus to the related processes distinguishes the following (Paschen et al., 2019): inputs (such as structured and/or unstructured data); processes (in terms of preprocesses such as natural language understanding and/or computer vision and main processes); the knowledge base (data storage); and outputs (information, in terms of natural language generation, image generation, and robotics). The main processes include problem-solving, which means selecting a solution that best achieves a goal, reasoning (deductive or inductive), and machine learning, which is not based on predefined rules and leverages the other two processes in order to (automatically or with human support) acquire new or modify existing knowledge, achieving desired outcomes more effectively. For example, based on medical research papers, medical records, and doctors' notes, Watson learned to identify cancer patterns. In our view, problem-solving, reasoning, and machine learning can be systematized and connected based on vSa, which posits these elements as part of the same process and not limited to a particular problem but instead dependent on the decision-maker.

Gartner has introduced a list of types of intelligences owned by individuals and needed for DM, including linguistic, logical-mathematical, spatial, interpersonal (the ability to recognize and understand other people's moods, desires, motivations, and intentions), and creative intelligence. Some of these intelligences can be connected to AI. A more general analysis of types of AI intelligence (the ability to learn from experience and adapt to the environment) has been carried out by Huang and Rust (2018), who suggest four types of intelligence involved in performing service tasks: *mechanical* (as in the case of the social robot Pepper, who is equipped with facial recognition capabilities); *analytical* (based on data, like, e.g., Toyota's in-car diagnostic system for technicians); *intuitive* (based on understanding, as in the case of Watson on "Jeopardy!"); and *empathetic* (based on experience, like Replika, who replaces psychiatrists in providing psychological comfort), possibly showing an automated social presence (van Doorn et al., 2017). We believe that AI should be able to show all of these types of intelligence to support DM in human–machine interactions. Indeed, as described later, the effectiveness of the decision may depend on the problem statement, which in turn depends on how the problem is understood by the decision-maker.

Other classifications have been oriented to investigate the autonomy of AI in DM. In particular, four levels of intelligence have been identified (Davenport & Kirby, 2016): *support for humans*; *repetitive task automation* (as in the case of insurance underwriting or financial trading applications); *context awareness and learning* (as in the case of driving recommendations based on data from the field/user); and *self-awareness* (similar to general/super AI).

As shown later, at least the first three levels of intelligence should be available to a machine interacting with humans, since the support that can be provided should always be contextualized.

Human–Machine Collaboration for DM

DM is currently one of the most diffuse applications of AI and has become particularly important in organizations, as it is directly related to their performance. As mentioned, numerous studies have agreed on the need to exploit AI through collaborations with humans to "augment and enhance each other's capabilities" (Miller, 2018, p. 2). The roles that humans can play in interacting with AI are expert, creator, conductor, and reviewer: the first two, when jointly performed, give rise to a feedback loop between parts and a continuous improvement in AI through machine learning (Paschen et al., 2021).

Shrestha et al. (2019) compared AI and human DM across five dimensions characterizing problems[7] to develop a typology of the human–machine interaction process: *full human-to-AI delegation* (as in dynamic flight pricing); *AI-to-human sequential DM* (as in healthcare monitoring); *human-to-AI sequential DM* (as in sports analytics); and *aggregated human–AI DM* (top management teams, boards), in which collective decision-making occurs through aggregation of the decision preferences of participants. This description of the diverse roles played by AI in DM reveals that there are always limitations to effective interaction between humans and machines. However, when collaboration is synchronous, it seems more effective.

Jarrahi (2018) highlights the complementarity of humans and AI solutions in DM processes: AI solutions can analyze decisions based on probability and an analytic approach but are not able to manage novel problems where intuition and holistic approaches are needed. He has developed this complementarity thesis based on three dimensions characterizing problems: *complexity* (intended as related to the number of variables involved in a problem); *equivocality* (the presence of simultaneous but divergent interpretations of a decision domain, which can derive from the conflicting interests of stakeholders); and *uncertainty* (a lack of information about alternatives and their consequences). Unfortunately, this interesting study does not allow us to assess the effectiveness of the decisions made nor does it describe how AI should be designed to effectively operate with specific decision-makers.

Finally, Vincent (2021) elaborates on collaboration between AI and humans based on human intuition, proposing two sequential approaches. The distinction between the two depends on the number of alternatives to be evaluated: the confirmatory method is appropriate to cases with few decision alternatives, while the exploratory method can be used in cases with many decision alternatives.

This distinction seems insufficient if the complexity of the alternatives is included in the analysis or the alternatives are not obvious enough to be identified at the start of the decision-making process.

3 Human–Machine Interactions for DM: An S-D Logic/vSa Framework

Understanding value co-creation processes in human–machine interactions can allow improvements to AI design/development/adoption projects and human training to ensure that DM can be both effective and trustworthy.

---

[7] Specificity of the decision space, interpretability of DM process and outcome, size of the alternative set, speed, and replicability of outcomes.

Indeed, although collaboration is fundamental (see above on the complementarity thesis), it may not be successful for humans (as when AI does not perform/performs the task wrong/badly), for AI (as when AI does not learn/learns incorrectly from human interaction), or for the ecosystem in which they interact (as when a process does not increase the ecosystem's overall viability).

The diverse studies of AI summarized and commented on earlier take into account the characteristics of the decisions to be made and the different processes that humans and AI should work on. However, these classifications lack an integrated consideration of (i) the knowledge process involved in making a decision, (ii) the characteristics of the decision-maker(s), (iii) the context, and (iv) the outcomes of the interaction.

The system perspective is the *fil rouge* among elements (i)–(iv). Indeed, systems are the fundamental unit of study for service and value co-creation. During the last two decades, the viable systems approach (vSa; Barile et al., 2012; Golinelli, 2010) has been developed to re-explore the contribution of systems thinking to management; help explain DM in service systems (Badinelli et al., 2012); and integrate S-D logic, service networks, and service systems (Barile et al., 2016).

To answer the research question presented in the introduction, we develop an integrated vSa/S-D logic framework organized into the four elements (i)–(iv), as reported in Fig. 1 and discussed later.

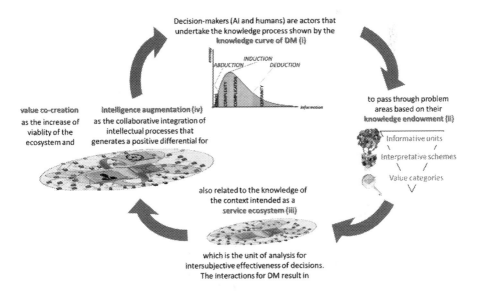

Fig. 1 The vSa/S-D logic framework for human–machine interactions for DM

(i) Knowledge Process in Decision-Making: The Knowledge Curve

Based on vSa, in this chapter, we use the knowledge curve (or 4Cs curve), which is able to capture the process of DM and knowledge acquisition (Barile & Saviano, 2018).

It is widely accepted that problems can be classified based on complexity (Barile et al., 2018a). However, a problem may appear immediately easy to solve to a decision-maker, or it could initially put the decision-maker in a problem area characterized by chaos. Thus, the curve (element (i) of Fig. 1) shows four problem areas (chaos, complexity, complication, and certainty—the four Cs) describing how the problem appears to the decision-maker. One of the axes of the diagram is clearly information, since data are fundamental to decision-making. Now more than ever, it has to be highlighted that data should be checked for veracity (e.g., preventing machine learning based on fake news from the web, as in the case of AI stating that Obama is Muslim, or on past decisions biased against a certain group). Furthermore, the decision-maker (a human, a machine, or a human collaborating with a machine) applies its knowledge endowment to make the decision by acquiring, synthetizing, and/or exploiting information. In other words, the decision-maker tries to reduce the problem entropy (the other axis of the diagram) by embedding information in known/ad hoc constructs/schemes. To show this, the curve depicts three special points related to the decision-maker's abilities needed to move from one problem area to another. In particular, the figure portrays diverse DM approaches and related abilities needed by the decision-makers that depend on its knowledge endowment with respect to the problem: deduction alone, that is, applying available schemes to solve a problem; induction and deduction, involving testing newly identified schemes to solve a problem before applying them; and abduction, induction, and deduction, that is, having a eureka moment to exit a chaotic problem area before starting to hypothesize new schemes.

The knowledge endowment curve completes and relates the classification of the main AI processes developed by Paschen et al. (2019). The process that the decision-maker goes through shows that contrary to what is argued by Vincent (2021), the alternatives cannot always be identified from the beginning. Thus, more flexible collaboration among AI and humans should be pursued.

The inclusion of the knowledge process in the framework reinforces the concept that acquiring data to cope with an issue may not be enough and highlights the diverse abilities that decision-makers (collaborating with each other) should have to reduce complexity in the knowledge process.

(ii) Characteristics of the Decision-Maker(s): The Knowledge Endowment

From the 4Cs curve, it follows that a decision cannot be classified as just complex, complicated, or easy to solve by a decision-maker because its related feasibility, effectiveness, and efficiency depend on the decision-maker's own knowledge endowment. Thus, all the intelligence types listed by Huang and Rust (2018) could be needed to make a decision because the problem statement and the capability to make the decision depend on the specific decision-maker. This also implies that the complexity of a decision cannot be objectified. Indeed, vSa adopts a constructivist approach to knowledge and DM processes (von Glasersfeld, 1984) that also echoes the German *Weltanschauung*, the worldview of the observer. In detail, inheriting the concept of requisite variety introduced by Ashby (1968), vSa forged a model of the knowledge endowment (or information variety) of any actor, characterized by three dimensions (Barile et al., 2013):

* informative units, the units of data retained by the actor;
* interpretation schemes or the cognitive schemes according to which the information is elaborated and understood by the actor;
* value categories, the basic values and strong beliefs of the actor.

Thus, according to this model, the knowledge of an actor is more than the sum of the informative units available. Matching the knowledge endowment with the 4Cs curve results in the interpretation of informative units being dependent on the cognitive schemes available or developed by the decision-maker to understand the problem, while value categories can direct the usage of the interpretation schemes and the consequent decision.

In the field of AI development, it is recognized that AI solutions show a knowledge endowment influenced by their developers, but they also evolve through machine learning based on human decisions, with the possible biases that characterize humans. Furthermore, self-reinforcement of previous decision pathways can also occur, as in the case of prediction of patrol hot zones that, due to patterns, show more crime and appear to be hotter zones than others, while other unsupervised areas have actually become hotter.

The inclusion of the knowledge endowment in the framework highlights the concept that every problem can be viewed and managed differently by decision-makers. Collaboration among humans and machines should then

936   F. Polese et al.

consider the characteristics of the specific actors with respect to the problem. Learning new schemes may not be enough: in a chaotic situation, value categories drive choices.

(iii) Context: The Service Ecosystem

From the previous framework elements, a question arises about the specific characteristics of the knowledge endowment of AI and humans in collaborations. For these to be successful, the knowledge endowment (and, particularly, the value categories) should be aligned with the context in which the decision is to be made. In vSa terms, the resolution pathway should be consonant with the value system (Barile, 2009).

Based on S-D logic, context can be described as networks of actors (provided by resources) and the institutional arrangements governing them. The context is where actors integrate resources and exchange service for value co-creation. It is interesting that a service ecosystem is a scalable concept, and multiple levels of analysis can be adopted, from the micro to the macro level (Chandler & Vargo, 2011), to observe actors sharing diverse institutional arrangements. Thus, the context and the related relevant level of analysis should be identified and known by decision-makers, who otherwise cannot make decisions aligned with the beliefs, norms, rules, and practices of the specific context of reference. Indeed, the problem (and decision) stakeholders are not just the problem owners (and possible supporters as problem analysts or solvers) but also problem users—who execute decisions—and problem customers—the beneficiaries or victims of the consequences of a decision. Among problem customers, "which ones should be included in the analysis gives rise to critical boundary judgments" (Daellenbach & McNickle, 2005, p. 57). Thus, the service ecosystem perspective promoted by S-D logic can enable the identification of the relevant context for a decision and, implicitly, the unit of analysis of value co-creation. As an example of elements characterizing the context, there are ethical guidelines published by European authorities against racial discrimination in the usage of AI. Such guidelines and the common values shared among European citizens relate to knowledge of the context and were triggered by racial disparities that emerged in the usage of an AI solution to make legal decisions based on the prediction of recidivism.[8]

---

[8] It was demonstrated that although race was not included in the set of decision parameters, black defendants were more likely to be incorrectly judged than white defendants because race was correlated with other data.

Moreover, Siltaloppi et al. (2016) state that institutions consist of formalized rules (laws) and of "more informal norms, including social expectations, values and moral codes that define appropriate behaviour ... including cognitive frames and schemes that encapsulate the assumptions and beliefs fundamental to making life comprehensible" (p. 335). This conceptualization shows that S-D logic can complement vSa to provide a formal and complete understanding of the characteristics of actors (and groups of actors). In DM terms, knowledge of the context is the element that helps the decision-maker build constraints and objective functions to model the problem, incorporating the logics of common understanding among service ecosystem actors in an attempt to satisfy their expectations and needs. Given the classification of levels of intelligence and autonomy of AI in DM by Davenport and Kirby (2016), effective DM should always include at least the first three levels since the support provided by AI to humans should always be contextualized.

According to vSa, consonant actors have a similar knowledge endowment (Barile et al., 2013), which implies a similar way of thinking and acting according to institutional arrangements. Related to these concepts, problem classifications may also diverge based on values and interests. Jackson and Keys (1984) highlight that divergence can be classed as unitary (shared common worldviews), pluralistic (shared common core, compatible worldviews that are the basis of compromises; Daellenbach & McNickle, 2005), and conflicting/coercive (irreconcilable values and worldviews that make compromise hard if not impossible). From consonance, intersubjectivity can be derived, "position[ing] [actor] sense-making not as scientifically clinical, nor as individually perceived, but interactively co-created" (Read & Sarasvathy, 2012, p. 227). Similarly, Ackoff (1974) recognizes intersubjectivity as "the social product of the open interaction of a wide variety of individual subjectivities", something on which a consensus can be built. Thus, consonance and the related intersubjectivity "offer a means to prioritize information inputs and a means to make judgement" (Read & Sarasvathy, 2012, p. 227).

The inclusion of context in the framework highlights that decisions are not effective or efficient in general; rather, this assessment depends on the alignment (consonance) of the decision-makers with the specific context of actors and institutional arrangements. A lack of consonance among decision-makers may bring irreconcilable worldviews and the impossibility of converging on a shared decision; a lack of consonance between decision-makers and the context may bring about decisions not effective for the context. Moreover, the level of analysis of the context should be set in considering its main dimensions.

(iv) Outcomes of the Interaction: Value Co-creation (and Intelligence Augmentation)

The fourth element of the framework—the value co-created due to interactions—depends on the previous three. When actors, on the basis of their resources and knowledge endowment, integrate resources and exchange service according to their understanding of the problem to be dealt with and knowledge of the context, they co-create value by making decisions. However, according to vSa, they must interact while sharing synergic purposes to derive successful value co-creation[9] (Polese, 2018) for themselves and eventually also viable for the whole ecosystem, thus showing systemic resonance (Wieland et al., 2012). This kind of viable form of value co-creation does not end with engagement but extends through the service ecosystem, invigorating it. Furthermore, it can in turn reinforce the viability of the participating actors in their search, as individuals, for viable conditions. In other words, decision-makers seeking to increase their viability try to adapt to their environment to engage other value propositions (they look for consonant conditions). To do so, they should be understandable to other actors in the context to make their decisions acceptable and trustworthy (Schneider & Leyer, 2019). Then, the higher the consonance of decision-makers with the macro level of the service ecosystem, the greater is the viability of the ecosystem in the long run. Thus, value co-creation derived from human–machine interaction should be assessed with a view to the context of reference provided by the problem owner but also evaluated in the wider service ecosystem. This focus on the macro level can provide guidance to understand the impact of decisions on the viability of the ecosystem and incorporate this understanding into the problem statement to assess the effectiveness of decisions.

Finally, in the particular field of human–machine interaction at the micro-level analysis of the context, augmentation of human abilities with AI should be considered. Specifically, recent literature from vSa highlights the need to further shift from the concept of artificial intelligence (AI) to that of intelligence augmentation (IA) in complex decision-making (Barile et al., 2018b; Bassano et al., 2020), focusing on the so-called homo digitalis and IA in systems. According to this new and still unexplored perspective, intelligence, as value, is not just a characteristic of an actor but a systemic outcome due to multiple-actor interactions. In other words, human–machine interactions do

---

[9] Viability is the system's primary purpose (Barile et al., 2012) and it depends on the system's "ability to adapt to a changing environment by identifying a role to play in each context … [and] then satisfying the expectations of other viable systems such as suppliers, customers, and other stakeholders" (Barile et al., 2016, p. 656).

not result in a mere amplification of human cognitive abilities but in a collaborative integration of intellectual processes that generate a positive differential, IA. IA can allow service ecosystems to evolve from an intelligent to a wise configuration, in which the rational component (the prerogative of AI) integrates with the emotional component (the prerogative of human intelligence).[10] This field of IA—and prodromal human–machine interactions—should be further studied in different contexts to derive insights for both users and developers, who still require many indications (Green & Viljoen, 2020).

The inclusion of value co-creation (and the focus on IA) in the framework highlights that the effectiveness of DM should be assessed at different levels of service ecosystems. Furthermore, the higher the contextual level taken into account by humans and machines to make the decision, the greater is the increase in the viability of the service ecosystem and thus the viability of the actors in the long run. IA is an interesting outcome of interactions that give rise to reflections on the knowledge endowment of both humans and machines to increase service ecosystem viability.

4   Conclusion

In this chapter, we have delineated how to better understand AI interactions with humans by combining S-D logic and vSa, outlining a framework to identify what should be taken into account for successful value co-creation from these interactions in the field of DM. In particular, through the four elements of the framework, we provide insights into service management theory and practices. First, we state the importance of the knowledge endowment of decision-makers to pass through problem areas and make the decision (element (ii) in the framework). This highlights that the understanding of problems, decision pathways, and final choices depend on decision-makers, with their information units, interpretation schemes, and values. This element can be particularly critical in human–machine interactions, given that the decision is made by a group of (at least two) actors who should be able to complement each other to properly contribute to the decision. Researchers should provide guidelines to make (AI) group choices. Furthermore, it must be coupled with the knowledge process undertaken to make a decision, which highlights the DM requirements to evolve over the decision pathway (element (i)). Information is not enough to make decisions, and actors must be able to

---

[10] Intelligence is the subjective ability to increase efficiency (the power to do) and wisdom is the ability to increase effectiveness (the effectiveness of doing) (Ackoff, 1989).

collaborate to elaborate them and move from chaos to certainty through abduction, deduction, and induction. Thus, for AI, this observation implies particular attention to the design of both working algorithms and interactional pathways with humans. On the human side, it has implications for recruiting and/or selecting the best personnel to work with, building organizational structures to facilitate interactions of multiple human decision-makers, and designing and selecting AI solutions based on actors' abilities to support interactions with AI and improve their experience.

Furthermore, we highlighted (element (iii)) the role of context (the service ecosystem), including shared institutional arrangements, in making decisions. This underlines the need for both designers and managers able to grasp the context and incorporate this knowledge during interactions, particularly when it is not available to the human side. In these cases, for sustainability purposes, the institutional arrangements of the service ecosystems should be made clear to human actors before they make decisions. Actor consonance with the context is the prerequisite for the intersubjective effectiveness of decisions. Indeed, this means that key values, beliefs, norms, and so on are shared not just by the actors involved in DM but also with the multiple other stakeholders of the context; similarly, the derived decisions should be positively evaluated by the wider network of actors.

Finally, since future DM will be fundamentally based on human–machine interactions, from a theoretical point of view, we reinforce the importance of a deeper understanding of it, both in terms of viability of service ecosystems and in terms of intelligence augmentation. Indeed, we have shown that the latter is clearly related to the former (element (iv)) and thus requires wise design and management not just to make effective decisions but also to make service ecosystems more viable. To this end, design and management should be oriented toward improving IA.

In conclusion, our framework can lay the groundwork for new conceptualizations of AI (more oriented toward collaboration with humans) and new orientations for humans to be selected, trained, and organized for AI-enabled DM in a specific context to increase the sustainability of our future course of actions.

References

Ackoff, R. L. (1974). The systems revolution. *Long-Range Planning, 7*, 2–20.
Ackoff, R. L. (1989). From data to wisdom. *Journal of Applied Systems Analysis, 16*, 3–9.
Ashby, R. W. (1968). Principles of self-organizing system. In W. Buckley (Ed.), *Systems research for behavioral science* (pp. 116–117). Aldine Transaction.

Ashraf, A., Vermeulen, J., Wang, D., Lim, B. Y., & Kankanhalli, M. (2018). Trends and Trajectories for Explainable. Accountable and Intelligible Systems: An HCI Research Agenda. In Proceedings of the 2018 CHI conference on Human Factors in Computing Systems, Association for Computing Machinery. .

Badinelli, R., Barile, S., Ng, I., Polese, F., Saviano, M., & Di Nauta, P. (2012). Viable service systems and decision making in service management. *Journal of Service Management, 23*(4), 498–526.

Barile, S. (2009). The dynamic of information varieties in the processes of decision making. In Proceedings of the 13th World Multi-Conference on Systemics, Cybernetics and Informatics, .

Barile, S., Lusch, R. F., Reynoso, J., Saviano, M., & Spohrer, J. (2016). Systems, networks, and ecosystems in service research. *Journal of Service Management, 27*(4), 652–674.

Barile, S., Pels, J., Polese, F., & Saviano, M. (2012). An introduction to the viable systems approach and its contribution to marketing. *Journal of Business Market Management, 5*(2), 54–78.

Barile, S., Piciocchi, P., Bassano, C., Spohrer, J., & Pietronudo, M. C. (2018b). Re-defining the role of artificial intelligence (AI) in wiser service systems. In T. Z. Ahram (Ed.), *AHFE 2018, AISC, 787* (pp. 159–170). Springer International Publishing AG.

Barile, S., Polese, F., Calabrese, M., Carrubbo, L., & Iandolo, F. (2013). A theoretical framework for measuring value creation based on the viable systems approach (vSa). In S. Barile (Ed.), *Contributions to theoretical and practical advances in management, a viable systems approach (vSa)*. Aracne.

Barile, S., Polese, F., Pels, J., & Sarno, D. (2018a). Complexity and governance. In A. Farazmand (Ed.), *Global encyclopedia of public administration, public policy, and governance*. Springer.

Barile, S., & Saviano, S. (2018). Complexity and sustainability in management: Insights from a systems perspective. In S. Barile, M. Pellicano, & F. Polese (Eds.), *Social dynamics in a systems perspective* (pp. 39–63). New Economic Windows, Springer.

Barile, S., Bassano, C., Lettieri, M., Piciocchi P., & Saviano, M. (2020). Intelligence Augmentation (IA) in Complex Decision Making: a New View of the VSA concept of Relevance. In J.C., Spohrer, & C., Leitner (Ed.s) AHFE 2020, AISC, 1208, 1–8. Springer Nature AG.

Bassano, C., Barile, S., Saviano, M., Cosimato, S., & Pietronudo, M. C. (2020). AI technologies & value co-creation in a luxury context. Proceedings of the 53rd Hawaii International Conference on Systems Sciences, 1618–1627.

Bock, D. E., Wolter, J. S., & Ferrell, O. C. (2020). Artificial intelligence: Disrupting what we know about services. *Journal of Services Marketing, 34*(3), 317–334.

Campbell, M. (2016, October 24). 20 years later, humans still no match for computers on the chessboard. NPR. Retrieved from https://www.npr.org/sections/alltech

considered/2016/10/24/499162905/20-years-later-humans-still-no-match-for-computers-on-the-chessboard

Chandler, J. D., & Vargo, S. L. (2011). Contextualization: Network intersections, value-in-context, and the co-creation of markets. *Marketing Theory, 11*(1), 35–49.

Daellenbach, H. G., & McNickle, D. C. (2005). *Management science: Decision making through systems thinking*. Palgrave.

Davenport, T. H., & Kirby, J. (2016). Just how smart are smart machines? *MIT Sloan Management Review, 57*(3), 21–25.

Duan, Y., Edwards, J. S., & Dwivedi, Y. K. (2019). Artificial intelligence for decision making in the era of big data—Evolution, challenges and research agenda. *International Journal of Information Management, 48*, 63–71.

Floridi, L. (2016). Should we be afraid of AI? Aeon. https://aeon.co/essays/true-ai-is-both-logically-possible-and-utterly-implausible

Golinelli, G. M. (2010). *Viable systems approach (VSA). Governing business dynamics*. Cedam.

Green, B., & Viljoen, S. (2020). Algorithm realism: Expanding the boundaries of algorithmic thought. Proceedings of the 2020 Conference on Fairness, Accountability, and Transparency, 19–31.

Grundner, L., & Neuhofer, B. (2021). The bright and dark sides of artificial intelligence: A futures perspective on tourist destination experiences. *Journal of Destination Marketing & Management, 19*, 100511.

Huang, M.-H., & Rust, R. T. (2018). Artificial Intelligence in service. *Journal of Service Research, 21*(2), 155–172.

Jackson, M. C., & Keys, P. (1984). Towards a system of systems methodologies. *The Journal of the Operational Research Society, 35*(6), 473–486.

Jarrahi, M. H. (2018). Artificial intelligence and the future of work: Human-AI symbiosis in organizational decision making. *Business Horizons, 61*(4), 577–586.

Jordan, M. (2018, April 19). Artificial intelligence—The revolution hasn't happened yet. Medium, https://medium.com/@mijordan3/artificial-intelligence-the-revolution-hasnt-happened-yet-5e1d5812e1e7

Kaartemo, V., & Helkkula, A. (2018). A systematic review of artificial intelligence and robots in value co-creation: Current status and future research avenues. *Journal of Creating Value, 4*(2), 211–228.

Kurzweil, R. (2005). *The singularity is near: When humans transcend biology*. Viking Press.

Lusch, R. F., & Vargo, S. L. (2014). Service-Dominant Logic: Premises, Perspectives, Possibilities. New York: Cambridge University Press.

Lusch, R. F., Vargo, S. L., & Gustafsson, A. (2016). Fostering a trans-disciplinary perspective on service ecosystems. *Journal of Business Research, 69*, 2957–2963.

Maglio, P., & Lim, C. (2018). Service-dominant logic, service science and the role of robots as actors. In S. L. Vargo & R. F. Lusch (Eds.), *The SAGE handbook of service-dominant logic*. Sage.

McCarthy, J. Minsky, M. L., Rochester, N., & Shannon, C. E. (1955). A proposal for the Dartmouth summer research project on Artificial Intelligence. http://www-formal.stanford.edu/jmc/history/dartmouth/dartmouth.html

Miller, S. (2018). AI: Augmentation, more so than automation. *Asian Management Insights, 5*(1), 1–20.

Paschen, J., Kietzmann, J., & Kietzmann, T. C. (2019). Artificial intelligence (AI) and its implications for market knowledge in B2B marketing. *Journal of Business and Industrial Marketing, 34*(7), 1410–1419.

Paschen, J., Paschen, U., Pala E. et al. (2021). Artificial intelligence (AI) and value co-creation in B2B sales: Activities, actors and resources. *Australasian Marketing Journal.*

Polese, F. (2018). Successful value co-creation exchanges: A VSA contribution. In S. Barile, M. Pellicano, & F. Polese (Eds.), *Social dynamics in a systems perspective* (pp. 19–37). New Economic Windows, Springer.

Polese, F., Frow, P., Nenonen, S., Payne, A., & Sarno, D. (2021). Emergence and phase transitions of service-ecosystems. *Journal of Business Research, 127*, 25–34.

Read, S., & Sarasvathy, S. D. (2012). Co-creating a course ahead from the intersection of service-dominant logic and effectuation. *Marketing Theory, 12*(2), 225–229.

Russo-Spena, T., Mele, C., & Marzullo, M. (2019). Practising value innovation through artificial intelligence: The IBM Watson case. *Journal of Creating Value, 5*(1), 11–24.

Schneider, S., & Leyer, M. (2019). Me or information technology? Adoption of artificial intelligence in the delegation of personal strategic decisions. *Managerial and Decision Economics, 40*, 223–231.

Shrestha, Y. R., Ben-Menahem, S. M., & von Krogh, G. (2019). Organizational decision-making structures in the age of artificial intelligence. *California Management Review., 61*(4), 66–83.

Siltaloppi, J., Koskela-Huotari, K., & Vargo, S. L. (2016). Institutional complexity as a driver for innovation in service ecosystems. *Service Science, 8*(3), 333–343.

Storbacka, K. (2019). Extending service-dominant logic—Outside marketing and inside managerial practice. In S. L. Vargo & R. F. Lusch (Eds.), *The SAGE handbook of service-dominant logic* (pp. 639–654). Sage.

Tegmark, M. (2017). *Life 3.0: Being human in the age of artificial intelligence.* Alfred A. Knopf.

van Doorn, J., et al. (2017). Domo Arigato Mr. Roboto: Emergence of automated social presence in organizational frontlines and customers' service experiences. *Journal of Service Research, 20*(1), 43–58.

Vargo, S. L., Koskela-Huotari, K., Edvardsson, B., Baron, S., Reynoso, J., & Colurcio, M. (2017). A systems perspective on markets—Toward a research agenda. *Journal of Business Research, 79*, 260–268.

Vargo, S. L., & Lusch, R. F. (2016). Institutions and axioms: An extension and update of service-dominant logic. *Journal of the Academy of Marketing Science, 44*(1), 5–23.

Vargo, S. L., & Lusch, R. F. (2017). Service-dominant logic 2025. *International Journal of Research in Marketing, 34*(1), 46–67.

Vincent, V. U. (2021). Integrating intuition and artificial intelligence in organizational decision-making. *Business Horizons, 64*(4), 425–438.

von Glasersfeld, E. (1984). An introduction to radical constructivism. In P. Watzlawick (Ed.), *The invented reality* (pp. 17–40). Norton.

Wieland, H., Polese, F., Vargo, S. L., & Lusch, R. F. (2012). Toward a service (eco) systems perspective on value creation. *International Journal of Service Science, Management Engineering, and Technology, 3*(3), 12–25.

Managing Artificial Intelligence Systems for Value Co-creation: The Case of Conversational Agents and Natural Language Assistants

Tom Lewandowski, Christian Grotherr, and Tilo Böhmann

1 Introduction: AI in Service

In recent years, digitalization has spurred service innovation in manifold ways (Barrett et al., 2015; Chandler et al., 2019). Key drivers of this innovation are technological advances such as augmented reality (AR), machine-2-machine interactions, and artificial intelligence (AI) (Lusch & Nambisan, 2015). Particularly, AI has had a lasting impact in many domains and organizations (Wang et al., 2020), as, for example, enhancing and automating technology in service encounters (Ostrom et al., 2019). The use of AI provides a new perspective to service contexts, essentially to "*provide value in service environments through flexible adaptation enabled by sensing, reasoning, conceptual learning, decision-making and actions*" (Bock et al., 2020, p. 317). The ongoing advancements in AI in the next few years will virtually transform all service sectors. They could even lead to AI-based systems becoming the most prevalent actors in service interaction (Xiao & Kumar, 2019). As a result, entirely new scenarios for value co-creation are conceivable (Bock et al., 2020).

Conversational agents (CAs) are one specific and prominent case of AI in service. CAs are automated, scalable, cost-effective service systems delivering services to actors through textual or auditory means (Bock et al., 2020), which

---

T. Lewandowski • C. Grotherr • T. Böhmann (✉)
Department of Informatics, Universität Hamburg, Hamburg, Germany
e-mail: Tom.Lewandowski@uni-hamburg.de; Christian.Grotherr@uni-hamburg.de;
Tilo.Boehmann@uni-hamburg.de

© The Author(s), under exclusive license to Springer Nature Switzerland AG 2022
B. Edvardsson, B. Tronvoll (eds.), *The Palgrave Handbook of Service Management*,
https://doi.org/10.1007/978-3-030-91828-6_45

enable new forms of service interaction and value co-creation scenarios. AI-based CAs can transform service encounters from human-centric to technology-dominant (Castillo et al., 2020). CAs influence conventional service offerings and enable individual and convenient interaction forms (Klaus & Zaichkowsky, 2020). From a service employees' perspective, CAs bear the potential to automate, augment, and assist service interactions in, for example, human-centered tasks by identifying new solution strategies, providing decision-making support, or problem-solving. In this regard, CAs possess significant potentials since service and interaction workers are exposed to occupational stress due to constantly increasing requests combined with the massive rise of information load (Semmann et al., 2018). From a customers' perspective, CAs also occur as a novel actor in the foreground in various customer support settings, which promote a new form of speed and personalize customer relationships. Consequently, CAs can appear as service actors between the provider and the customer, allowing novel value co-creation scenarios.

Despite the aforementioned potentials, increasing practical interest, and high popularity of CAs in various domains of research in recent years, many contributions investigate CAs solely from a technical perspective, for example, how to improve the natural language processing (NLP) component, or from a specific conceptual point of view, for example, how to design a concrete dialog flow often prototyped in a pre-service encounter stage, such as in lab and greenfield environments (Lu et al., 2020). However, as soon as they are instantiated in concrete service settings (e.g., as intelligent technology in the background or as a self-service platform in the frontline), they could often not meet expectations and already disappeared (Gnewuch et al., 2017). Thus, although a growing number of companies are adopting AI-based CAs in service settings, academics lag in studying its implications for service science (Bock et al., 2020; Lu et al., 2020).

Consequently, AI-based systems play a crucial role in digital-enabled service innovations; however, they cannot be discussed separately from the context such as the organization and environment. The service-dominant (SD)-logic perspective emphasizes the importance of analyzing actors such as customers, employees, and CAs within value co-creation processes. Following this view, CAs can be understood as socio-technical actors and active co-creators which implies a shift in designing such solutions beyond technological requirements.

The chapter aims to broaden CA design's perspective beyond its currently technological dominant perspective by applying a service systems perspective. Our insights are based on the nascent literature on CAs and on insights gained through a design science research (DSR) project on the implementation of CAs in real-life service settings. The research project seeks to develop and pilot novel interaction processes between customers, employees, and CAs (Semmann et al., 2018).

We structure our insights using Grotherr et al. (2018) multilevel framework for service system design. This framework builds on the tiered understanding of value co-creation and actor engagement posited by Storbacka et al. (2016) that links micro-level engagement activities to macro-level phenomena such as value co-creation and the associated institutional arrangements. We apply the Grotherr et al. (2018) framework as a comprehensive perspective to address technological design, work/service design, and institutional design in the context of CAs. This multilevel lens on service system design integrates DSR on CAs with service research.

2 Research Background

AI-Based Systems

The advances in information technologies (IT) as an enabler and contributor within a highly dynamic environment are key characteristics in service innovation (Barrett et al., 2015). One innovative IT field that has evolved from a technological trend to a ubiquitous phenomenon in the service landscape is AI-based systems. Although AI started to dominate our daily lives and academic interest has grown considerably, there is neither in science nor in practice a consistent definition of the term. Further, compared to traditional information systems (IS), the impact of AI systems in enterprise settings and for service systems is insufficiently studied (Bock et al., 2020; Wang et al., 2020). Typically, service researchers understand AI as a generic concept for a set of technologies capable of mimicking human behavior and learning how to solve tasks usually performed by human intelligence (Castillo et al., 2020). AI systems are often described as algorithms that operate not rule-based but, similar to the human brain, use cognitive or conversational functions and interact with a large amount of data. Nowadays, AI-based systems diffuse various application domains and contribute to multiple innovations (Wang et al., 2020). Service AI's field comprises configurations of technologies to provide value in internal and external service environments through flexible capabilities that cover perception and sensing, learning and acting (Bock et al., 2020). AI technologies include biometrics (e.g., computer vision), robotics, machine, and deep learning, as well as NLP.

AI-Based Conversational Agents

Conversational agents are one specific and prominent case of AI in service, describing intelligent, automated, and intangible systems delivering services to actors through natural language (Bock et al., 2020). Although the technical possibilities are not comparable with the current potentials in AI and data processing, the idea of communicating with computers has already existed for several years. Weizenbaum (1966) has previously taken initial steps toward an NLP component or, respectively, text-interface between humans and computers with *ELIZA*, a system generating responses to text inputs simulating a psychotherapist in a therapy session. Since then, various CAs with increasing capabilities and intelligence were developed (Brandtzaeg & Følstad, 2017), which will continue to rise in the upcoming years in service settings. At present, CAs exist in domains like customer service, marketing, entertainment, and education and have become significant in private households as well as in professional workplace contexts (Feng & Buxmann, 2020; Gnewuch et al., 2018). CAs promote a new form of flexibility, quality, speed, and personal ways to accomplish work tasks, access content, and services (Wilson & Daugherty, 2018). A transformation toward convenient, automated, multilingual, globally available, 24/7 support channels are already conceivable today (Følstad et al., 2018; Gnewuch et al., 2017).

As a result of their emerging interest in IS and service research, numerous designations, taxonomies, and concepts have been formulated over the years. In service literature, CAs are also known under synonyms such as service robots (e.g., Lu et al., 2020; Wirtz et al., 2021), chatbots (e.g., Castillo et al., 2020), virtual assistants (e.g., Bock et al., 2020), or voice bots (e.g., Klaus & Zaichkowsky, 2020). The subdivision is often made based on two dimensions ("Primary Mode of Communication," Gnewuch et al., 2017): The first class comprises *text-based CAs*, commonly known under synonyms such as chatbots or chatterbots (e.g., *ELIZA* or *Cleverbot*), while the second class embraces *speech-based CAs* as virtual or smart assistants (e.g., *Amazon Alexa* or *Apple's Siri*). However, the main concepts have remained principally the same due to a similar underlying architecture, and in many academic publications, no distinction is made (Meyer von Wolff et al., 2019). Conversational agents can be defined as *"system-based autonomous and adaptable interfaces that interact, communicate, and deliver service to an organization's customers"* (Wirtz et al., 2018, p. 909). The service interface is built on NLP technologies, including intelligent communication and a built-in machine learning component, allowing the user to communicate via human languages. In this context, the CAs become the dominant interaction partner and a new actor in the co-creation of value by representing the visible and customer-facing interface of large and integrated service systems (Wirtz et al., 2018). Thereby, they integrate *"multiple data sources (like databases or applications) to automate tasks or assist users [e.g., internal employees or external customers] in their (work) activities"* (Meyer von Wolff et al., 2019, p. 96). For example, instead of consulting a support hotline, an employee can submit the support request via natural language to a CA directly, which serves as an instantaneous assistant actor by scanning diverse knowledge and data sources in the background and providing answers to requests.

Managing these systems comes with novel challenges that are different to traditional IT systems used in service organizations. CAs have distinct characteristics that differentiate them from traditional IS as well as from other AI-based technologies for service provisioning:

First, CAs are *social actors*. These AI-based systems influence conventional service offerings and enable new individual and convenient socio-technical interactions (Klaus & Zaichkowsky, 2020). Often, they undertake a social position in the service delivery process in terms of being consulted as *"user's friend and helper,"* providing quick and accurate solutions to customer requests via natural language (Bock et al., 2020). Developers often design chatbots very humanlike. They were endowed with social features, provided with names, avatars, and communicative behaviors to attract users' attention and simulate a natural conversation (McTear et al., 2016). CAs learn from previous collaborations and increasingly make their own decisions augmented by a user-centric and intelligent component, extending service landscapes (Seeber et al., 2020; Stoeckli et al., 2019). Compared to conventional service provision in customer service settings, which consisted of a dyadic interaction between a customer and a service provider (representing the "face" of the organization), CAs will progressively represent the prevailing *customer-facing part of an extensive and integrated service system* (Ostrom et al., 2019; Wirtz et al., 2018). Therefore, CAs will transform all service sectors and need a new viewpoint on service management practices (Ostrom et al., 2019).

Second, CAs can be classified as *unfinished and learning IS*. CAs have few skills at the outset and can only engage in light-weight and simple initial tasks tended to be low in their cognitive and emotional complexity (Wirtz et al., 2021), while expectations among managers, employees, and customers are extremely high. However, AI-based CAs can be continuously trained and enhanced whereby they obtain access to increased amounts of data and are connected to diverse sources and systems in the IT and service landscape (Castillo et al., 2020; Xiao & Kumar, 2019). CAs benefit from a scaling effect.

Progressively, allowing them to make more recommendations, decisions, and actions with little or no human intervention (Xiao & Kumar, 2019). However, until this state can be achieved, a new understanding and engagement of all service-involved actors are needed. CAs learning process depends on the commitment of the individual service actors (customer and client-side) since the CA will only improve when used. Compared to conventional IS, which are mainly instituted to support service delivery, CAs come to the forefront as an actor in a field of tension: On the one hand, ambition is needed to take part in a continuous improvement process (Stieglitz et al., 2018), and on the other hand, customers are skeptical about CAs use (due to, e.g., initially limited capabilities) and service employees can develop negative attitudes toward CAs (e.g., due to loss of autonomy or job insecurity). Since customers hold nearly similar expectations considering the service provision, for example, regarding the service levels (Castillo et al., 2020), one question is how to manage CAs' limitations directly from the beginning. CA-caused service failures could decrease service quality, resulting in customer resource loss ("value co-destruction" instead of collaboratively and interactively value co-creation). Literature calls for research on how to manage these *new social and unfinished form of IS* to hinder "*failed chatbots*" and, in this context, how to engage and develop employees and customers "*to play their enabler, innovator, coordinator, and facilitator roles in modern service encounters*" (Lu et al., 2020, p. 380).

Particularly these findings on the challenges and risks of implementing CAs in service settings highlight the need to approach the design of CAs from a broader socio-technical perspective. Therefore, we will present a framework of these management challenges and derive research implications on managing AI systems in service organizations for value co-creation in the next section.

3 Designing and Managing Conversational Agents in Service Systems: A Multilevel Framework

Multilevel Design Framework for Service Systems

To achieve a more comprehensive understanding of the design challenges for CAs in service settings, we make use of Grotherr et al.'s multilevel framework for service systems design (Grotherr et al., 2018). This framework bridges the gap between abstract value co-creation and observable actor engagement with design elements on multiple levels. With this framework, we seek to contribute to transdisciplinary research discourse for the design of digital service systems by providing a foundational work for the emergence of next-level design theory for CAs.

Over the last few years, there have been significant shifts in digital-enabled business models and service systems. First, there is a movement away from a traditional perspective on services as single entities toward seeing value creation as a co-creative endeavor of multiple actors, resources, and systems of services. Second, opportunities can be found in the study of service systems, which are (1) technology-enabled, (2) actor-centered, and (3) shaped by *institutions*. Nonetheless, organizations are challenged to design competitive service systems in a dynamic market. On the one hand, customer demands are dynamic, and due to the rapid growth of technological advancements, new digital innovations emerge. On the other hand, there is also a need to take *institutions* and their shaping and transforming role into account (Vargo et al., 2015). In other words, developing service systems implies two central aspects which must be reflected by elaborating existing design approaches: (1) to cope with volatile environments and (2) to take a perspective on the design of service systems reflecting socio-technical artifacts as well as *institutions*.

In this regard, service systems become meaningful when actors engage, mobilize their resources, and integrate them for value co-creation. To understand unexpected resource constraints or lack of cooperation, a value-in-context mindset is essential (Chandler & Vargo, 2011). However, the observability and measurability of the value co-creation process in service system design appear highly challenging (Storbacka et al., 2016). One solution approach that has gained acceptance in service research in recent years is the focus on actor engagement as a microfoundation that is observable, measurable, and thus manageable. Actor engagement takes place on the *engagement platform* on the micro-level. These engagement practices represent actors' disposition to engage, lead to engagement activities, and are characterized by observable engagement properties (temporal, relational, and informational) (Storbacka et al., 2016).

In this context, Grotherr et al. (2018) proposed a *multilevel design framework for service systems* that can facilitate a service system's analysis and design of components for actor engagement on the macro-meso-micro-level. Contemporary service design theories are built on stability assumptions, such as defining a priori problem. These traditional approaches lack consideration of dynamics and do not provide realistic means for understanding human actions in their environment. The shift from *plan-oriented process models* toward *path-dependent design systems* builds a substantial basis for exploring and exploiting digital, actor-centered service systems. Moreover, by applying a *multilevel perspective, institutions, technology, actors,* and *resources* are captured in the design process. This approach emphasizes the design of individuals' interaction facilitated with technological advancements on micro-level and broad adjustment of prevalent *institutions* on macro-level.

On the one hand, the framework helps drill down from an abstract perspective of value co-creation and guides value propositions to observable actor engagement. On the other hand, to aggregate the observational results and drill up to implications for the service systems design (Grotherr et al., 2018). On the other hand, to cope with various design interventions' complexity, the *multilevel design framework for service systems* consists of two intertwined design cycles: (1) *institutional design* and (2) *engagement design*. The *engagement design* comprises interactional and socio-technical components, which facilitate actor engagement on the micro- and meso-level. The *institutional design* refers to reflections made on the meso-level, which have implications to value propositions and the service systems' institutional environment (see Fig. 1).

Within a service (eco-)system, an *engagement platform* facilitates the interaction between actors on the meso-level (Breidbach et al., 2014). They are intermediaries that enable organizations to co-create value with the customer by bringing actors and their resources together (e.g., Storbacka et al., 2016). Consequently, *engagement platforms* enable the process of resource mobilization and integration. Within our research project, the *engagement platform*

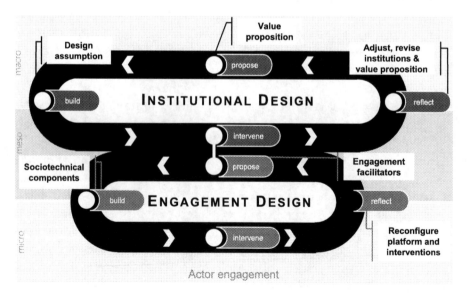

Fig. 1 Multilevel design framework for service systems. (Based on Grotherr et al., 2018)

exemplifies the AI-based CA and required design activities will be applied following the *engagement and institutional design* of the *multilevel design framework* (see Fig. 1).

Engagement Design with Conversational Agents

Conversational Agents as a New Engagement Platform that Differentiates from Former Customer (Self-) Services

CAs represent a novel type of platform for customer service. Compared to traditional customer service systems, where service exchange occurs between the customer and actors on the provider side via telephone or e-mail, CAs appear as a new automated and convenient customer channel and central platform (Espig et al., 2019; Gnewuch et al., 2017). Customers benefit from integrating information from different data sources to highly structured knowledge to deliver answers to service requests (Meyer von Wolff et al., 2019). However, CAs do not merely appear as another passive and intermediary (engagement) platform that intelligently integrates data and thus represents another information channel of an extensive and integrated service system. Instead, a CA outlines an active social actor that solves customer problems naturally, dialog-based, and intuitive (Gnewuch et al., 2017). CAs can offer customers a stable, homogeneous service at a low cost, which in the best case has no biases but can also map emotions and offer individual problem solutions (Wirtz et al., 2021).

Thus, they engage in resource integration by establishing relationships in different interaction scenarios. In the near future, CAs will *"increasingly fulfill the role of service employees and substitute tasks historically performed by human service personnel"* (Gnewuch et al., 2017, p. 4), leading to new co-creation scenarios on the engagement level. Conversational agents address and solve one of the core challenges of former customer service settings, in which it was virtually impossible to offer a more efficient and cost-effective service without at the same time compromising on the quality (e.g., personalization, individualization, and capabilities) (Gnewuch et al., 2017). In addition to existing self-service technologies (SSTs) for customer service (e.g., websites, portals [FAQs], or apps), CAs will be available to customers as an even more natural and constantly accessible technology-based channel and actor to perform various internal and external customer service forms. Compared to conventional self-service technologies (SSTs), they allow customers individual and flexible interactions and customer journeys (Wirtz et al., 2021).

954   T. Lewandowski et al.

Within our research project, different types of CAs are used as a central entry point and platform for IT, business, and product support, available for internal and external customers via various channels (e.g., enterprise messengers, internal self-service platforms, and request trackers). In addition to offering external product support (e.g., regarding questions about ordering and deliveries as well as complaint management), CAs are used for internal customers to answer different service requests, such as requests for information (e.g., regarding the configuration and use of software), incidents (e.g., password resets), change requests (e.g., request for a new e-mail address), and service catalog items (e.g., setting up new accounts for employees).

CAs as Novel Social Actors Require New Design Approaches and Knowledge

Since CAs represent a new type of *learning and social actor*, new design knowledge and approaches are needed to instantiate them in service settings. CAs affect customers' benevolence toward the provider by providing engaging, positively valanced advisory experiences for customers and leveraging the relationship-building potential with simulated one-to-one advisory interaction leading to a positive perception of service (Hildebrand & Bergner, 2020). However, although an initial version of a CA can be quickly developed and provisioned, and therefore numerous agents have been instantiated in service settings in recent years, most of them could not meet expectations (Gnewuch et al., 2017). For both customers and providers, initial expectations are too high and CAs are insufficiently designed and aligned to existing service settings. This can lead to service failures and subsequently to customers' confusion and dissatisfaction or, in the worst case, even to value co-destruction, thus negatively impacting the customer relationship and the company's image (Castillo et al., 2020). Consequently, CAs require *engagement design* and software development knowledge, which go far beyond traditional IS and service design approaches, as highlighted in the following.

Challenges Regarding the Engagement Design for CAs

The most crucial aspect of creating a good customer acceptance is to enable actors to deal with CAs seamlessly and efficiently for resource integration (Wirtz et al., 2018). The aspects described are reflected in the *engagement design*, which captures the ongoing design, development, and enhancement of socio-technical components such as engagement platforms. This encompasses the activities necessary to enable the CAs' evolution from its initial value proposition into *Technical Design, Interaction Design,* and *Service Design* activities in the CA context.

Technical Design: First, Technical Design is essential, as many CAs fail to understand customer inputs due to inadequate NLP capabilities. As CAs are *unfinished learning IS* new approaches, considering the dynamics are obligatory, need to be tested, evaluated, and reflected on the micro-level. The technical design sets the basis for adequate service, including the NLP component's design, which anchors the foundation for understanding customers and enabling resource integration and value co-creation. Once an organization has decided to embrace a CA as service channel and actor, technology selection becomes a key consideration (Schuetzler et al., 2021). In this context, machine learning CAs have become prevalent in recent years, possessing a growing number of capabilities and handling increasingly complex dialogs. According to Schuetzler et al. (2021) the vast majority of CAs in use today are supervised machine learning to accomplish their task. They use various sample messages to train the machine learning algorithm to distinguish different intents and allow it to properly understand the intent of a new message (Schuetzler et al., 2021). However, there exist numerous CA frameworks, technologies, bot builders, and configuration possibilities (e.g., Google DialogFlow, RASA.ai or the Microsoft Bot framework, Abdellatif et al., 2020; Sousa et al., 2019) that need to be thoroughly examined for their capabilities, customizability, and integration before being instantiated.

Building upon this, training is vital since (1) CAs possess limited abilities initially and (2) service environments constantly change. In comparison to conventional IS, AI-based systems need ongoing development and improvement of technical aspects (e.g., "NLP algorithms"), including, for example, supervised coaching and testing, to train their capabilities and stay current with changing tastes and technology in service systems (Xiao & Kumar, 2019). Actors' ambition is needed to understand that CAs possess limited skills initially and take part in a continuous learning and improvement process, expanding CA development *from traditional development* as a project setting *to a lifecycle environment, in which new functions (intents and entities) are continuously proposed, build (trained), reflected, and improved.*

Interaction Design: Second, Interaction Design is an essential prerequisite for socio-technical artifacts. CAs occur as new *social actors* in the front line, exhibit humanlike characteristics, interact with customers, and solve problems. Because CAs will increasingly accomplish more tasks as their capabilities evolve, many customers will build relationships with them. A customer conversation (e.g., complaint conversation) is characterized by, for example, small talk between the customer and the service employee, where employees can react and respond to the customer's emotions (e.g., frustration). As the customer conversation is progressively performed by the CAs, which learn from the collaboration and increasingly make their own decisions, the IS and service literature recommends a cooperative and anthropomorphic interaction design to foster actor engagement (e.g., Gnewuch et al., 2017; Hildebrand & Bergner, 2020; Van Pinxteren et al., 2020). In this context, organizations need to decide how they want customers to perceive CAs, which can be controlled by selecting various forms of social and anthropomorphic cues (Schuetzler et al., 2021).

For example, Schuetzler et al. (2021) distinguish between three types of implicit cues and signal types that can facilitate a humanlike interaction of a conversational agent: First, *identity cues* can be integrated into CAs' design to provide a pleasing humanlike visual appearance, for example, through selecting a human name, avatars, and self-references (such as "I like") in the dialog with the customer (Schuetzler et al., 2021). Second, *nonverbal cues* represent another opportunity to make the conversation design more natural and realistic, using typing delays, typing dots, or emoticons (Schuetzler et al., 2021). Third, *verbal cues* can be adopted to provide a natural dialog leading to satisfaction, trust, and emotional closeness (Schuetzler et al., 2021). *Verbal cues* include simulations of characteristics of natural dialogs, such as vast vocabulary and variability in the language.

In sum, a good speech comprehension and dialog design, as well as a comfortable and natural customer experience, can lead to a competitive advantage against competing providers. However, in the context of creating humanlike CAs, it is also necessary to evaluate which range and types of social cues and empathic design options are adopted, and it depends not only on, for example, the service type, the company goals, and external image, but also on the capabilities of the CA and the customers. In this regard, different socio-technical design options for the engagement platform must be proposed, implemented, and continuously reflected, evaluated, and improved.

Service Design: Third, Service Design is appropriate to enable actor engagement. Customer service is a highly standardized practice in traditional customer support service systems, with predefined processes, roles, and task responsibilities, including resource acquisition and handoffs. Customers are often guided clearly, step by step through a predetermined process. As the CA now performs simple tasks, the CA must be integrated smoothly into the simultaneous service process operation. The most challenging aspect denotes that the systems are in learning progress. Although the picture is often drawn that CAs will completely replace service employees and change entire service landscapes to meet better a firm's strategic goals, for example, profit through automation, different transition stages and handover routines will exist due to limited skills (e.g., Poser et al., 2021; Wintersberger et al., 2020). The transition stages include diverse augmentation and relief scenarios, where the CAs take over "lower" (easier for AI) tasks initially, starting with more knowledge retrieval and analytical tasks, before moving up to higher intelligence tasks (e.g., needing intuition and empathy) (Huang & Rust, 2018).

Furthermore, in this scenario, customers lose their opportunity to receive "human service," of that not all types of customers are ready. As a consequence, value is not only created in dyadic relations of a customer and a CA but amongst different configurations and combinations of actors such as employees, customers, and CAs integrating different resources knowledge and solving problems. Therefore, besides the classic human-CA interaction, in which the CA occurs as a central interface in a service context, hybrid intermediate designs are emerging (e.g., "humans-to-(human & machine) actor combinations," Storbacka et al., 2016).

One specific constellation examined in the research project involves the "*Hybrid Service Recovery Strategy*" (Poser et al., 2021). Since CAs have limited abilities at the outset and perform only simple and repetitive tasks (e.g., pre-assessing or easy manageable requests), dealing with the situation when the CA's abilities are exceeded is crucial for the live-support process to prevent service failures and dissatisfied or even loss of customers (Wintersberger et al., 2020). For example, at the beginning of the CA introduction, problems may arise due to the natural language understanding (NLU) or dialog management component's limited capabilities, leading to a situation where input is misinterpreted, the dialog process is hindered (intent or entity detection), or information retrieval or task execution is prevented (Poser et al., 2021). Further, few functions/tasks (intents and entities) are implemented and trained, causing users to reach the limits of the technology after only a few interactions. Therefore, some authors propose to indicate to the user the range of functions a CA possesses (e.g., Schuetzler et al., 2021), which is, however, difficult to display due to the compact language-based interface.

Instead of value co-creation, this results in value co-destruction, as customer queries can be misinterpreted, resulting in incorrect responses or no responses at all (Poser et al., 2021). To remedy this deficiency, procedures and processes should be determined when a "handoff event" (human intervention) occurs (Wintersberger et al., 2020). Our research project found the introduction and design of seamless handovers to be a crucial and challenging design aspect for *user engagement*. A CA that fails to respond to even first user

958 T. Lewandowski et al.

queries and further fails to uphold the service leads to user frustration, rapidly becomes a bad image, and is no longer used. Users then revert quickly to conventional service channels and their engagement is complex to re-achieve.

In order to enable efficient handovers of inappropriately (false positive) answered or unanswered requests, the CA must be designed to gather information around the request beforehand and be able to identify and transfer the information (relevant set of information extracted from the conversation in a workable format) to the right entity in order to ensure further processing (Poser et al., 2021). In the context of our research project, we investigated different types of handover implementations in CAs in real-life service settings. Two fallback strategies to ensure service continuity and recovery embrace asynchronous and synchronous handovers. An example of an asynchronous handover is creating a ticket by the CA when its capabilities are exceeded. In this case, the CA identifies, collects, and analyzes all necessary information from the chat interactions and generates and routes a ticket to a human assistant (e.g., Poser et al., 2021). An even more fluid handover scenario depicts synchronous handovers, where the CA is linked to a live chat. In this case, the service employee takes over the interaction and can access the chat history to solve the request as fast as possible (e.g., Schuetzler et al., 2021; Wintersberger et al., 2020).

Institutional Design

Intervention into Actors' Environment for Capturing Prevailing Institutions

It is relevant to consider that *CA management goes far beyond the engagement design*. From a service systems perspective, CAs are service systems embedded and connected with other service systems. These systems define the boundaries and context, such as institutional arrangements, organizational structures, and principles that facilitate the exchange and integration of resources (Lusch & Nambisan, 2015). *Institutions* are defined as "*humanly devised rules, norms, and beliefs that enable and constrain action and make social life at least somewhat predictable and meaningful*" (Vargo & Lusch, 2016, p. 11). Institutional arrangements are "*interrelated sets of institutions that together constitute a relatively coherent assemblage that facilitates [the] coordination of activity in value-co creating service ecosystems*" (Vargo & Lusch, 2016, p. 18). Thus, actors' disposition to engage (positive, negative, ambivalent) is therefore determined by social norms and shared beliefs (Li et al., 2018).

Consequently, CAs necessitate being *improved outside of labs within real-world environments*. Much research investigates CAs solely from a purely technical or interactional perspective in lab and greenfield environments. However, as soon as they are instantiated in concrete service settings, they often could not deliver their value proposition to customers (Castillo et al., 2020). Moreover, CAs certainly possess the potential *"to replace human workers in many service functions, but when it comes to customer service that involves intensive interactions with customers, it's never a purely technical issue"* (Xiao & Kumar, 2019, p. 22). In this regard, service systems design becomes meaningful to observe value co-creation in brownfield environments; however, it arises with several design challenges.

Although several service innovation approaches exist, service systems' redesign is usually more complicated than starting from scratch (Helkkula et al., 2018). First, as resources are scarce (Murphy, 2007), service systems designers have to start with what actors and resources are available (resource mobilization). Second, actors relate to single objects such as the CA platform and the overall context, such as social context and institutional logic. This may lead to several implicit (norms, values, roles) and explicit (laws, compliance) dualisms for actors and impact resource integration and mobilization. For instance, actors engage simultaneously in various service systems with multiple institutional arrangements, leading to role conflicts, as it is *"often not possible, feasible, or necessary for an actor to accept all value propositions"* (Chandler & Lusch, 2015, p. 6). This can lead to actor disengagement and, in the worst case, to negative engagement properties, which intend to affect negatively other actors or resources, leading to value co-destruction (Echeverri & Skålén, 2011). Therefore, service systems designers have to engage in institutional context to understand the values and norms of multiple, overlapping service systems which affect actors' needs and motivations and subsequent organizational mechanisms that enable a state of institutional arrangement and logic, which are considered in the *institutional design* (see Fig. 1).

Challenges Regarding the Institutional Design for CAs

In the CA context, *institutional design* encompasses the activities necessary to address two challenges that have to be captured in the service systems design process: (1) resource mobilization and integration remain challenging as resources in existing environments are challenging to control, and (2) actor engagement can vary regarding time and contribution. To enable CAs' *institutional design* diverse activities and areas need to be designed and managed to facilitate *engagement design* from macro-level and thus value co-creation. These elements include in forms of (1) data governance, (2) privacy and security, as well as (3) ethics and monitoring.

Data Governance: *Data availability and quality* play an essential role and require organizational attention and consent. The CA represents a novel kind of interface toward the customer, representing the "face" of the company and the company's knowledge in contexts of, for example, product counseling or problem-solving management. However, although companies possess vast amounts of data from the existing service environment, for example, in terms of internal databases and (legacy) systems (e.g., ticket systems), it is often not to be deprecated to acquire data. Further, the data often correspond to poor quality and necessitate to be adjusted in order to transform them into dialog-capable datasets to train the NLP component for the specific use cases. The additional effort to train and maintain NLP components distinguishes CA management from traditional IT systems used in service organizations. The engagement on the micro-level depends on the ongoing retrieval of *NLP-ready data sets* in the context of model and dialog training and knowledge expansion of the CA. The design needs preparation as part of the *institutional design* in terms of data acquisition, constant intervention, and reflection of the use cases to acquire new data sets, transpose them "dialogue-ready," and transfer them to "real knowledge," presented in the conversation with the customer. Adjustment due to constantly changing service environments and technology in service systems is needed (Xiao & Kumar, 2019).

Privacy and Security: *Institutions* on the macro-level comprise regulatory requirements, such as laws and rules, and other requirements imposed on the company by external influences. In the case of CAs, the main concerns that can arise are (1) (data) privacy concerns, along with (2) security concerns that may harm their use on both the customer and the employee side. According to the service literature, CAs need a new form of governance to deal with potential regulations early and accommodate customers with clear data protection policies (Bock et al., 2020). First, since CAs often elicit a negative attitude, through examples from private context, such as Amazon Alexa as "always listening and recording data leeches," it is also essential to create *system transparency and explain how learning CAs work* in combination with *clear data protection guidelines* toward employees and customers. The research contributions show that the lack of transparency regarding data protection negatively influences service customers' acceptance and willingness to use personalized AI services (Ostrom et al., 2019).

Ethics and Monitoring: *"Most organizations are governed by ethical values, codes and compliance. The same should be required by AI"* (Bock et al., 2020). Beyond the benefits of implementing CAs for customers and employees, CAs also entail risk areas for a company's reputation. Hence, governance is needed to ensure a significant consideration of AI-based service systems' *ethical design* (Bock et al., 2020). Since CAs can sense, process, and record the world around them, learn, and thus can misbehave (e.g., like Microsoft Tay) or biases conversations, it requires ethics standards and monitoring that uncover the risks associated with AI (Wirtz et al., 2018). Besides, as CAs are in a permanently changing and training process, there is a need to handle changes and errors in collaboration and accountability structures (e.g., mainly when they affect the direct customer conversation).

Employee Readiness and Engagement as Knowledge Integrators

As part of the *institutional design*, general CA acceptance must be created to build trustful expectations toward the service employees. In the beginning, service employees often possess adverse or skeptical attitudes regarding the cooperation with the CA, due to different reasons (e.g., loss of autonomy, job insecurity, or privacy and security concerns), which could lead to non-endorsement and therefore to service failures (Lu et al., 2020). For this reason, employees need to be picked up and trained early. Instead of letting negative attitudes take hold, the CA should be motivated as a new social actor, relieving overworked employees of tasks and leads to enhanced productivity and job satisfaction (Lu et al., 2020). Furthermore, the CA introduction requires new forms of collaboration.

In addition, management needs to foster new collaborative development and improvement approaches where employees, the CA, and developers continuously interact. Compared to a traditional IS, CAs as *unfinished and learning IS* exhibit the distinction that they inherit limited capabilities at the beginning of the roll-out. This leads to a new situation for the employees, as they can not only be specified as software users but also as *knowledge integrators*. Relying on the circumstance that service employees possess most of the knowledge related to service operations, for example, to solve customer requests or giving product advice, they should be intensively involved in the development and design process. The case of CAs demonstrates that service systems cannot generate value by themselves. They need to engage others to offer value propositions.

962   T. Lewandowski et al.

Shaping Value Propositions and Business Models Through
AI-Based Systems

Finally, CAs' introduction in the service frontline transforms interaction touchpoints with the customer and, thus, entire customer journeys and the value proposition leading toward *AI-shaped business models*, requiring new management approaches and *market competitive service designs*. Business models bridge technological and market innovations, and emphasize a service systems-centric approach to *"how firms do business"* (Peters et al., 2016, p. 140). In this context, CAs change the value co creation process and value proposition by (1) representing a new customer channel and (2) establishing new forms of customer relationships (e.g., changing the way how the customer perceives the provider/company/brand positioning) leading to new forms of revenue streams and reduced costs in the long term. In addition to the service system's design at the micro-meso-macro-level, it is essential to consider, analyze, and classify the business model to adapt it to current conditions continually.

4   Conclusion

Numerous companies already implement AI-based systems (Wang et al., 2020) as enhancing, augmenting, or automating technology in service encounters (Ostrom et al., 2019). AI-based systems can be both an outcome and a facilitator for value co-creation and service innovation. The multilevel perspective on designing such AI systems as exemplified by CAs provides a more comprehensive view of the design challenges for such technologies in service contexts. The case of CAs shows that service systems design needs to facilitate learning cycles on the individual micro-level and on the institutional macro-level to succeed in increasingly dynamic environments. To realize value, changes in actors' practices and *institutions* have to be integrated with each other. Moreover, changes in one service system's *institutions* must be integrated and aligned with other *institutions* into a broader service ecosystem context (Vargo & Lusch, 2015). This perspective is particularly valuable for the transformation of extant service systems with AI. The multilevel framework highlights the interdependencies of (re-)designing technologies, work processes, service interactions, as well as institutional arrangements framing for achieving a beneficial design and use of AI. We contribute to research on AI in service science and guide practitioners in designing service innovations in the context of CAs.

References

Abdellatif, A., Costa, D., Badran, K., Abdalkareem, R., & Shihab, E. (2020). *Challenges in chatbot development: A study of stack overflow posts.* Paper presented at the Proceedings of the 17th International Conference on Mining Software Repositories.

Barrett, M., Davidson, E., Prabhu, J., & Vargo, S. L. (2015). Service innovation in the digital age: Key contributions and future directions. *MIS Quarterly, 39*(1), 135–154.

Bock, D. E., Wolter, J. S., & Ferrell, O. C. (2020). Artificial intelligence: Disrupting what we know about services. *Journal of Services Marketing, 34*(3), 317–334.

Brandtzaeg, P. B., & Følstad, A. (2017). *Why people use chatbots.* Paper presented at the International Conference on Internet Science (INSCI), Cham.

Breidbach, C., Brodie, R., & Hollebeek, L. (2014). Beyond virtuality: From engagement platforms to engagement ecosystems. *Managing Service Quality, 24*(6), 592–611.

Castillo, D., Canhoto, A. I., & Said, E. (2020). The dark side of AI-powered service interactions: Exploring the process of co-destruction from the customer perspective. *The Service Industries Journal,* 1–26.

Chandler, J. D., & Lusch, R. F. (2015). Service systems: A broadened framework and research agenda on value propositions, engagement, and service experience. *Journal of Service Research, 18*(1), 6–22.

Chandler, J. D., & Vargo, S. L. (2011). Contextualization and value-in-context: How context frames exchange. *Marketing Theory, 11*(1), 35–49.

Chandler, J. D., Danatzis, I., Wernicke, C., Akaka, M. A., & Reynolds, D. (2019). How does innovation emerge in a service ecosystem? *Journal of Service Research, 22*(1), 75–89.

Echeverri, P., & Skålén, P. (2011). Co-creation and co-destruction: A practice-theory based study of interactive value formation. *Marketing Theory, 11*(3), 351–373.

Espig, A., Klimpel, N., Rödenbeck, F., & Auth, G. (2019). *Bewertung des Kundennutzens von Chatbots für den Einsatz im Servicedesk.* Paper presented at the International Conference on Wirtschaftsinformatik (WI), Siegen, Germany.

Feng, S., & Buxmann, P. (2020). *My virtual colleague: A state-of-the-art analysis of conversational agents for the workplace.* Paper presented at the Hawaii International Conference on System Sciences (HICSS), Hawaii.

Følstad, A., Nordheim, C. B., & Bjørkli, C. A. (2018). *What makes users trust a chatbot for customer service? An exploratory interview study.* Paper presented at the International Conference on Internet Science (INSCI).

Gnewuch, U., Morana, S., & Maedche, A. (2017). *Towards designing cooperative and social conversational agents for customer service.* Paper presented at the International Conference on Information Systems (ICIS), Seoul, South Korea.

Gnewuch, U., Morana, S., Adam, M., & Maedche, A. (2018). *Faster is not always better: Understanding the effect of dynamic response delays in human-chatbot interaction.* Paper presented at the European Conference on Information Systems (ECIS), Portsmouth, United Kingdom.

Grotherr, C., Semmann, M., & Böhmann, T. (2018). *Using microfoundations of value co-creation to guide service systems design – A multilevel design framework.* Paper presented at the International Conference on Information Systems (ICIS), San Francisco, California, USA.

Helkkula, A., Kowalkowski, C., & Tronvoll, B. (2018). Archetypes of service innovation: Implications for value cocreation. *Journal of Service Research, 21*(3), 284–301.

Hildebrand, C., & Bergner, A. (2020). Conversational robo advisors as surrogates of trust: Onboarding experience, firm perception, and consumer financial decision making. *Journal of the Academy of Marketing Science,* 1–18.

Huang, M.-H., & Rust, R. T. (2018). Artificial intelligence in service. *Journal of Service Research, 21*(2), 155–172.

Klaus, P., & Zaichkowsky, J. (2020). AI voice bots: A services marketing research agenda. *Journal of Services Marketing, 34*(3), 389–398.

Li, L. P., Juric, B., & Brodie, R. J. (2018). Actor engagement valence: Conceptual foundations, propositions and research directions. *Journal of Service Management, 29*(3), 491–516.

Lu, V. N., Wirtz, J., Kunz, W. H., Paluch, S., Gruber, T., Martins, A., & Patterson, P. G. (2020). Service robots, customers and service employees: What can we learn from the academic literature and where are the gaps? *Journal of Service Theory and Practice, 30*(3).

Lusch, R. F., & Nambisan, S. (2015). Service innovation: A service-dominant logic perspective. *MIS Quarterly, 39*(1), 155–175.

McTear, M. F., Callejas, Z., & Griol, D. (2016). *The conversational interface* (Vol. 6). Springer.

Meyer von Wolff, R., Hobert, S., & Schumann, M. (2019). *How may I help you?– State of the art and open research questions for chatbots at the digital workplace.* Paper presented at the Hawaii International Conference on System Sciences (HICSS), Hawaii.

Murphy, P. (2007). 'You are wasting my time': Why limits on connectivity are essential for economies of creativity. *University of Auckland Business Review, 9*(2), 16.

Ostrom, A. L., Fotheringham, D., & Bitner, M. J. (2019). Customer acceptance of AI in service encounters: Understanding antecedents and consequences. In *Handbook of service science, volume II* (pp. 77–103). Springer.

Peters, C., Maglio, P., Badinelli, R., Harmon, R. R., Maull, R., Spohrer, J. C., … Demirkan, H. (2016). Emerging digital frontiers for service innovation. *Communications of the Association for Information Systems: CAIS, 1*(39).

Poser, M., Singh, S., & Bittner, E. (2021). *Hybrid service recovery: Design for seamless inquiry handovers between conversational agents and human service agents.* Paper presented at the Hawaii International Conference on System Sciences (HICSS).

Schuetzler, R. M., Grimes, G. M., Giboney, J. S., & Rosser, H. K. (2021). Deciding whether and how to deploy chatbots. *MIS Quarterly Executive, 20*(1), 4.

Seeber, I., Waizenegger, L., Seidel, S., Morana, S., Benbasat, I., & Lowry, P. B. (2020). Collaborating with technology-based autonomous agents. *Internet Research, 30*(1).

Semmann, M., Grotherr, C., Vogel, P., Bittner, E., Biemann, C., & Böhmann, T. (2018). *Intelligent Collaboration of Humans and Language-Based Assistants (INSTANT)*. Paper presented at the International Conference on Information Systems (ICIS), San Francisco, USA.

Sousa, D. N., Brito, M. A., & Argainha, C. (2019). *Virtual customer service: Building your chatbot*. Paper presented at the Proceedings of the 3rd International Conference on Business and Information Management.

Stieglitz, S., Brachten, F., & Kissmer, T. (2018). *Defining bots in an enterprise context*. Paper presented at the International Conference on Information Systems (ICIS), San Francisco, USA.

Stoeckli, E., Dremel, C., Uebernickel, F., & Brenner, W. (2019). How affordances of chatbots cross the chasm between social and traditional enterprise systems. *Electronic Markets, 30*, 1–35.

Storbacka, K., Brodie, R. J., Böhmann, T., Maglio, P. P., & Nenonen, S. (2016). Actor engagement as a microfoundation for value co-creation. *Journal of Business Research, 69*(8), 3008–3017.

Van Pinxteren, M. M. E., Pluymaekers, M., & Lemmink, J. G. A. M. (2020). Human-like communication in conversational agents: A literature review and research agenda. *Journal of Service Management, 31*(2), 203–225.

Vargo, & Lusch. (2015). Institutions and axioms: An extension and update of service-dominant logic. *Journal of the Academy of Marketing Science, 44*(1), 5–23.

Vargo, & Lusch. (2016). Institutions and axioms: An extension and update of service-dominant logic. *Journal of the Academy of Marketing Science, 44*(1), 5–23.

Vargo, Wieland, H., & Akaka, M. A. (2015). Innovation through institutionalization: A service ecosystems perspective. *Industrial Marketing Management, 44*, 63–72.

Wang, L., Huang, N., Hong, Y., Liu, L., Guo, X., & Chen, G. (2020). *Effects of voice-based AI in customer service: Evidence from a natural experiment*. Paper presented at the International Conference on Information Systems (ICIS).

Weizenbaum, J. (1966). ELIZA – A computer program for the study of natural language communication between man and machine. *Communications of the ACM, 9*(1), 36–45.

Wilson, J. H. D., & Daugherty, P. R. (2018). Collaborative Intelligence: Humans and AI are joining forces. *Harvard Business Review.* Retrieved from https://hbr.org/2018/07/collaborative-intelligence-humans-and-ai-are-joining-forces

Wintersberger, P., Klotz, T., & Riener, A. (2020). *Tell me more: Transparency and time-fillers to optimize chatbots' waiting time experience*. Paper presented at the Proceedings of the 11th Nordic Conference on Human-Computer Interaction: Shaping Experiences, Shaping Society.

Wirtz, J., Patterson Paul, G., Kunz Werner, H., Gruber, T., Lu Vinh, N., Paluch, S., & Martins, A. (2018). Brave new world: Service robots in the frontline. *Journal of Service Management, 29*(5), 907–931.

Wirtz, J., Kunz, W., & Paluch, S. (2021). The service revolution, intelligent automation and service robots. *European Business Review.*

Xiao, L., & Kumar, V. (2019). Robotics for customer service: A useful complement or an ultimate substitute? *Journal of Service Research, 24*(1), 9–29.

Servitization and Digitalization as "Siamese Twins": Concepts and Research Priorities

Gerhard Satzger, Carina Benz, Tilo Böhmann, and Angela Roth

1 Introduction

Service management has gained increasing attention over time—in lockstep with the increasing importance of services. This *"servitization"* as a transformation toward value creation via services (Vandermerwe & Rada, 1988; Baines et al., 2017; Raddats et al., 2019) is observable both for economies in total and for enterprises individually: First, *national service sectors* account for the majority of national gross income—70% for the OECD on average, even

---

G. Satzger (✉) • C. Benz
Karlsruhe Service Research Institute (KSRI), Karlsruhe Institute of Technology (KIT), Karlsruhe, Germany

Institute of Information Systems and Marketing (IISM), Karlsruhe Institute of Technology (KIT), Karlsruhe, Germany
e-mail: gerhard.satzger@kit.edu; carina.benz@kit.edu

T. Böhmann
Department of Informatics, Universität Hamburg, Hamburg, Germany
e-mail: tilo.boehmann@uni-hamburg.de

A. Roth
Institute of Information Systems, Friedrich-Alexander Universität Erlangen-Nürnberg, Erlangen, Germany
e-mail: angela.roth@fau.de

© The Author(s), under exclusive license to Springer Nature Switzerland AG 2022
B. Edvardsson, B. Tronvoll (eds.), *The Palgrave Handbook of Service Management*,
https://doi.org/10.1007/978-3-030-91828-6_46

968   G. Satzger et al.

up to 77% for individual countries like the US. At the same time, this also reflects the importance of service employment.[1] Second, even *within individual companies*, business models change from focusing on products toward services as their key value propositions (Neely, 2009; Kowalkowski et al., 2017), as various industrial companies pursue innovation via service-led offerings (Parida et al., 2015). Drivers are not only changing user behavior and needs as, for example, in the sharing economy (Wirtz et al., 2019), but also the need and potential of providers to more deeply tap into the customer's application of their products which often times promises a higher degree of customization and customer integration, a higher level of differentiation, and, ultimately, higher financial margins (Martín-Peña et al., 2019). A famous and often-cited example is Rolls Royce's "Power by the Hour" model (Smith, 2013) in which aircraft engines are no longer sold but provided as a service—and which, interestingly enough, are also subject to a risk-sharing mechanism, as remuneration is based on effective service usage. Similarly, printer manufacturer Xerox has turned into a printing service provider (Mont, 2002), IT hardware and software company IBM has transformed into an IT service firm (Jetter et al., 2009), car manufacturers are adopting car sharing service business models (Zhang et al., 2021), and machinery providers offer "equipment as a service" (Stojkovski et al., 2021).

At the same time, we observe a true obsession in digital transformation. This partial or complete change of a business model (as the "the way to make money") is based on *digitalization* (Schüritz & Satzger, 2016): It exploits the opportunities that are provided by the digital representation of objects or processes (the result of a "digitization" process) and results in changes to products or services as a value proposition, to work and tasks of individuals, and to organizations as a whole. A typical example is Netflix having revolutionized the process of video rental—among others using digital means to stream movies and to individualize movie recommendations (Gomez-Uribe & Hunt, 2016). An economically particularly appealing option are digital services that can be "delivered" across a digital network. Many of them have already fundamentally changed even our personal lives—be it Google search, Booking.com hotel reservations, or Spotify music services. From an economic perspective, these services are particularly powerful as their ubiquity and the lack of a physical distribution need almost "automatically" create global markets and international competition. Whereas so far in Western economies globalization has often been negatively connoted with labor transferring over to

---

[1] While the service sector in OECD countries accounts for 70% of GDP, it employs 73% of the working population (https://data.worldbank.org/indicator/SL.SRV.EMPL.ZS, accessed Mar 5, 2021).

low-cost countries ("near-" or "offshoring"), it now could be seen in the light of huge market opportunities to tap surging global markets: While in 2014 the GDP of the G7 countries still surpassed the E7 one, this ratio will have dramatically changed by 2050 when E7 markets will be 50% larger[2] (Hawksworth & Chan, 2015, p. 8). For innovation, growth, and competitiveness of Western economies, it will be crucial what share of this market growth can be captured by their exports, among others in digital services.

This chapter will conceptually look at the "natural" links between the two trends—based upon two novel concepts of looking at and defining services. We first analyze an output-oriented or *value proposition*-based view on services. For each of the three dimensions defining a product-service continuum of value propositions, we discuss the impact of digitalization. Second, we will take a view on service that is centered around *value creation* and the associated resources, processes, and involved parties, that is, the service system—a perspective that over the last years has been propagated by the "Service Dominant Logic" literature (Vargo & Lusch, 2004). Both views will provide evidence that "building a digitalization capability goes hand in hand with adopting a servitization strategy" (Parida et al., 2015, p. 41). Finally, we sketch the results of a literature- and interview-based study to identify promising future research areas for value creation and innovation at the intersection of services and digital technology (Böhmann et al., 2021).

2 Value Proposition View: Digitalization as Driver of Service Systems

For decades, service management has dealt with mastering the intricacies of a fuzzy object of investigation—and researchers have for years indulged in endless debates on definitions. These efforts should serve to identify the specifics of service businesses, but also try to delineate academic sub-disciplines like Service Marketing or Service Operations. Many attempts have been made to separate products from services as different value propositions or outputs that are offered in the market—from service as "anything sold in trade that cannot be dropped on your foot" (Quinn, 1992, p. 4) to definitions that focus on the change of a condition of another entity (Hill, 1977), and to the popular IHIP criteria: intangibility, heterogeneity, inseparability, and perishability

---

[2] This projection is based on market sizes compared at market exchange rates. Measured at purchase power parity, E7 markets in 2050 are expected to even be twice the size of the G7 ones (Hawksworth & Chan, 2015, p. 8).

970   G. Satzger et al.

(Edvardsson et al., 2005): While all of them help to focus on particular challenges of "service" businesses, the distinctions are proxies at best and cannot fully represent the value exchange observable in practice (Moeller, 2010): A typical car repair would involve products like spare parts, but also perishable capacity of the garage or intangible know-how of the mechanic. As a consequence, a broad stream of literature has emerged that focuses on composing value propositions of products and services within hybrid products or product-service-systems[3] (Berkovich et al., 2011; Cavalieri & Pezzotta, 2012), sometimes built in a modular form (Wang et al., 2011).

A probably more realistic view emerged about two decades ago and received surprisingly little reception in the academic community—removing the assumption of dichotomous value propositions of products and services: Authors like Engelhardt et al. (1993) or Meffert et al. (2018) postulate a continuum of value propositions that has "pure products" or "pure services" only as extreme poles of a multi-dimensional continuum. Figure 1 identifies different dimensions that help to constitute such a continuum.

- *Intangibility* signifies the degree to which the value proposition is not represented by tangible elements: So, consulting advice could completely be rendered as oral advice—however, in reality it still may comprise tangible elements as written reports, presentation material, or other documents.
- *Integration of the customer* denotes the degree of customer involvement throughout the value creation process. Thus, for a standardized screw as a product, customer integration may be limited to the specification of the intended value proposition. A custom-made machine, though, may entail intense and continuous interaction with the customer to elicit requirements, co-design solutions, test, and implement products. In fact, this integration can further be segregated into two separate dimensions: *Interactivity* measures the degree of communication between provider and customer, while *individuality* characterizes the degree that the value proposition is tailored to the particular customer's needs: While a group language course may be highly interactive (but very standardized across different customer groups), a custom-made suit may involve only minimal interaction (communication of personal measures), but does result in a highly individualized solution.

---

[3] It may be noted that product-service systems denote *systems of value propositions* while service systems as introduced in the subsequent section will denote *systems of value creation partners and associated resources.*

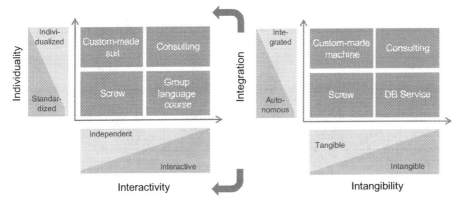

Fig. 1 Product-service dimensions and examples, based on Meffert et al. (2018, p. 18)

In essence, in our view this expanded perspective on services results in a *"III" continuum of value propositions* opposed to an IHIP paradigm trying to establish dichotomous classes of products and services. This continuum is depicted in Fig. 2 and also explains what service management should help to deal with: To manage organizations' capabilities to create and purposefully exploit intangibility, individualization, and interaction in value propositions.

With this continuum of value propositions as our base, we can now interpret servitization as the move of individual value propositions toward the upper right back corner of Fig. 2—for an economy or an individual enterprise (as described in Sect. 1). This should not only help us to understand services (and unify various historical service definitions) but also to relate digitalization to servitization processes:

- Digitalization will boost the share of a value proposition that is *intangible*—in particular driven by data, information, and knowledge being an increasingly important factor for competitive value propositions. An example would be data- and analytics-based services that can entirely be delivered across a network and may be offered "stand alone" or added to other existing offerings (Schüritz et al., 2017): So, most direct banking services are offered in completely digital form and physical assets are complemented by digital monitoring or predictive maintenance services.
- At the same time, digitalization will massively drive the options to *individualize* offers. First, this might be based on insights obtained on potential customers. Digitally obtainable, massively scalable information on customer usage will help to understand personal preferences of users—as illus-

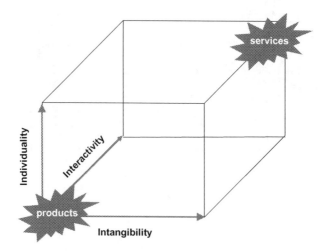

Fig. 2 "III" value proposition continuum

trated by the Netflix example earlier: Systematically observed customer choices enable AI-based recommendations for most likely favored movie selections. Second, digital means will also help to develop, test, and deploy individualized solutions, in particular for digitally rendered value propositions: Providers may use online A/B testing to evaluate new value propositions; DevOps concepts enable quick adaption and deployment of solutions—even different, individualized versions to different customers. Both, better understanding of customers and higher adaptability of solutions, will boost the options to pursue customer intimacy strategies (Wiersema & Treacy, 1993; Habryn et al., 2010).

- Finally, digitalization enhances *interactivity*—as is evident from simply reaching a broad set of customers in digital services. The advent of (digital) ecosystems and platforms in the B2C and B2B space is a testimony of the potential (Hein et al., 2020; Wirtz et al., 2019); intermediation platforms like Uber or eBay have only been able to dominate such ecosystems based on their ability to digitalize the interaction between providers and customers. In addition to reaching more (potential) customers, also the intensity of customer interaction, for example, the frequency of contacts via service apps, may increase. Data from the interaction itself may be captured and used, for example, for the anticipation of customer satisfaction (Baier et al., 2021) or the recognition of psychological states (Rafaeli et al., 2019).

3 Value Creation View: Digitalization as Driver of Service Systems

While many traditional service definitions rely on the type of value proposition (*"value in exchange"*), other delineations focus on processes or resource views reflecting a multi-perspective view on the service phenomenon (Fromm & Cardoso, 2015). The influential works of Vargo and Lusch (2004, 2008) propagating a "service-dominant logic" took this view even further focusing on *"value in use"* concepts and the co-creation of value by integrating resources across a service system. In particular, they abstracted value creation from the form that value is exchanged in, as this is only "masking" actual value creation (Akaka & Vargo, 2014). Consequently (in unison with the discussion in the previous section), the focus on value propositions (a "goods-dominant logic") and in particular a dichotomous split of value propositions should not distract from the underlying value creation activity—as in this perspective "everything is a service". We may note the very different use of the term "service" that certainly contributed to the controversial debate about the seminal works laying out a service-dominant logic perspective (Grönroos & Voima, 2013; Schueritz et al., 2019).

This system view, depicted in Fig. 3, should fundamentally change particular provider-focused approaches and elevate service design considerations to an overarching system level (Barile et al., 2016; Wolff & Satzger, 2018). The postulated discipline of service science intends "to advance our ability to design, improve, and scale service systems for business and societal purposes (e.g., efficiency, effectiveness, and sustainability)" (Maglio & Spohrer, 2008, p. 20).

In our value proposition-based "III" framework above, we could tie digitalization effects to the individual dimensions. Similarly, under the value creation lens, we can link digitalization effects to elements and links of a service system:

* Digitalization will *make more intangible resources available* in the service system: Data as well as the information and knowledge based upon them will form valuable resources that can be exploited by the partners in the system. A typical example is data generated from the sensorization of industrial and other assets in the "Internet of Things" (Martin et al., 2021): As an example, operational data from assets across many different partners may be used to develop digital twins or predictive maintenance concepts benefitting all partners. Similarly, data contributed by individuals in social

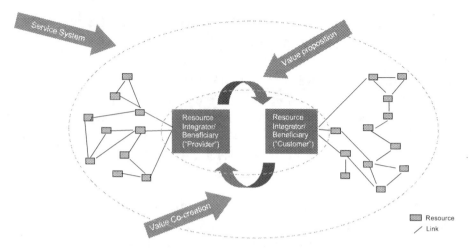

Fig. 3 Scheme of a service system

networks may add a valuable resource to understand needs and perceptions within the system (Kühl et al., 2016).
- Digitalization will also drive the ability to *find, select, connect, and engage* partners and resources in a service system (Sklyar et al., 2019), including catalyzing network architectures, network performance, or security mechanisms. The current hype around Distributed Ledger Technologies (DLT) and smart contracts being executed on them is an impressive example of how service systems are formed, run, and maintained in an open and transparent way (Rossi et al., 2019; Seebacher et al., 2021). Similarly, digital platforms (de Reuver et al., 2018; Hein et al., 2020) like Uber or eBay are connecting partners for more effective service systems.
- Digitalization enables to mimic and complement human cognitive abilities by capturing, digesting, and learning from data—represented in Artificial Intelligence applications (Kühl et al., 2019). These technological advancements increasingly turn assets or machines into intelligent agents that become *additional relevant actors* themselves within a service system (Storbacka et al., 2016; Huang & Rust, 2018).

Not surprisingly, the purposeful design of service systems is also reflected in the information systems (IS) community, where the call is for Service System Engineering that "takes the service system as the basic unit of analysis" and seeks to generate "evidence-based design knowledge on service systems that enhance collaborative and contextualized value creation" (Böhmann et al.,

Servitization and Digitalization as "Siamese Twins": Concepts... 975

2014, p. 74). This includes developing new service architectures, to enhance interaction, and to mobilize resources.

In this section, we have discussed the mutually enforcing relationship between servitization and digitalization under two different value creation perspectives. Under a value proposition lens, digitalization manifests in servitization along the dimensions of intangibility, individuality, and interactivity; under a value co-creation lens, digitalization builds and amplifies service systems by adding resources, actors, and connectivity. Thus, digitalization drives servitization, and servitization draws on digitalization; both are inseparable from each other—like Siamese twins.

In the following, we want to translate this into a concrete call to action in order to exploit the potential of both transformations for innovation and value creation (Sklyar et al., 2019).

4 Research Agenda: "High-Tech Meets High-Touch"

The conviction that servitization and digitalization are advancing in lockstep immediately triggers the question: What research topics will be key for enterprises and economies to drive innovation and stay competitive? To that end, we recently completed a comprehensive study initiated and funded by the German Ministry of Education and Research (Böhmann et al., 2021). We sketch our methodology, the identified trends, and resulting research fields in the following.

Methodology

The analysis undertaken was put into place to identify global trends in value creation as well as resulting key areas for innovation. The project team took a two-step approach to collect qualitative and quantitative input to then evaluate and triangulate. First, academic articles in journals and conferences have been screened using topic modeling as an unsupervised machine learning approach (Nikolenko et al., 2017). Our article corpus consisted of more than 571,000 articles listed in the academic database Scopus, with the term "service" to appear in either title, keywords, or abstract. Applying Latent Dirichlet Allocation (LDA) as specific algorithm for topic modeling (Blei et al., 2003), 80 topic clusters as displayed in Fig. 4 were identified and collaboratively labeled based on their term frequency.

These topic clusters have been interpreted and analyzed in terms of development over time and geographical coverage.[4] An example for results is shown in Fig. 5: We observe technology-savvy topics to be tremendously gaining importance over the last years. This trend is especially driven by high growth rates of topics like *cloud services, Internet of Things, data science,* or *cloud services*. Moreover, geographic coverage changes: While up to 2007, researchers based in the US were leading in terms of publication output, Asian countries have recently been catching up.

Second, we interviewed 24 leading academics and innovation-oriented practitioners between June 2019 and July 2020 on their perspectives on value creation and innovation. The results were qualitatively analyzed and summarized in a preliminary report. Feedback was collected from additional academics and practitioners in two iterations in the second half of 2020, leading to adaptations of the report in its final version.

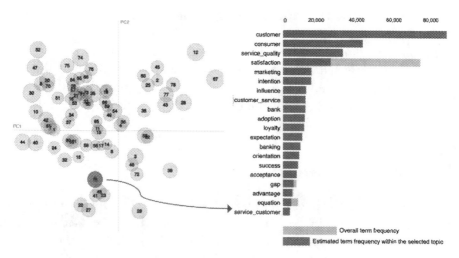

Fig. 4 Intertopic distance map (left) and term frequency for an exemplary topic "service quality" (right)

---

[4] It may be noted that—as typical for topic modeling—the clusters do not necessarily indicate coherent entities but are labeled based on their key terms as "labeling focuses on showing not the original words of a topic but rather a clearer label more akin to what a human summary of the data would provide" (Boyd-Graber et al., 2017, p. 40). These labels can provide a first orientation and form a starting base for additional research into those clusters.

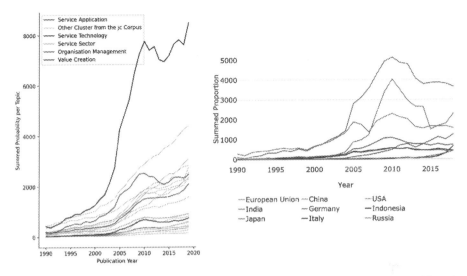

Fig. 5 Example for topic modeling results: Growth of selected topic clusters (left) and geographical development of total service publication output (right)

Identified Trends

Our observations from literature and expert interviews revealed four significant developments/trends (shown in Fig. 6) that affect and will shape successful value creation in the future.

Focus on value-in-use: While in the past providers have focused on "value-in-exchange" (very much in the sense of a goods-dominant logic), we observe an increasing emphasis on the value that customers actually experience ("value-in-use"). Digitalization offers ample opportunities to support this: First, as discussed above, digitalization enables the *individualization* of offerings, and, thus, higher value being generated by an individualized solution opposed to a standard one: For example, robo-advisory solutions automate the individualization of investment strategies based on customer profiling (Jung et al., 2018). Second, *remuneration* is increasingly *tied to value-in-use*, thus reflecting customer value and aligning incentives of providers and customers: Trumpf, a world market leader in laser cutting machines, recently announced an "Equipment as a Service (EaaS)" offering that will see them run their machines on customer premises and get reimbursed based on the parts produced—directly reflecting the value-in-use of the customer, with insurer Munich Re cooperating to help finance and insure risk (Stojkovski et al., 2021). Third, at the same time, *customer preferences* change and customers increasingly value characteristics like sustainability, carbon neutrality,

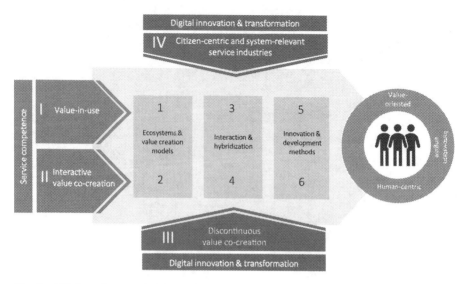

Fig. 6 "High-tech meets high-touch", based on Böhmann et al. (2021, p. 4)

"fair" production, digital sovereignty, data privacy, nutritional health, and so on. Providers need to reflect these emerging new values in shaping the customer experience: Digitalization may help to track, document, and communicate characteristics of solutions, for example, in supporting food source transparency via blockchain-based tracing across the whole food value chain (Yiannas, 2018).

Interactive value co-creation: As stated above, interaction opportunities drive servitization. We increasingly observe the possibility to *capture customer usage data* and to interconnect with the customer in real time, thus enabling new types of services: For example, insurance telematic tariffs can now be based on customer driving behavior captured alongside (physical) car usage—resulting in an individualized invoice based on customer value-in-use (see above). Similar opportunities also open up in the digital service space: Netflix recommendations—enabled by continuously collecting usage data and applying machine learning models—help the user to individually choose from a standard offering of several thousand movies. In fact, 80% of Netflix hours viewed are based on these recommendations (Gomez-Uribe & Hunt, 2016). Similarly, supporting customers in their service usage by interaction with *cognitive assistance* may form another type of collaborative value creation (Maedche et al., 2019)—from already "standard" conversational agents like Alexa to more fancy examples like CIMON (Crew Interactive Mobile Companion) supporting ISS astronaut Alexander Gerst in space (Schmitz et al., 2020).

Discontinuous value co-creation: New value creation processes are breaking with existing convictions or "rules". First, while we are used to discrete product (or service) lifecycles, digital services can typically be changed fast and delivered in real time from the cloud. In fact, development, experimentation, and deployment all merge: Google may explore new features of a service (potentially even applying A/B testing), select, and deploy promising features and retract them if not successful—all in real time and with immediate effect for all customers targeted. Second, we usually think in proportionally scaling value creation along a value chain or a service system. This assumption does not hold, though, for value generation, where part of it can be "softwaretized" and, thus, scales digitally without scaling physical resources at the same time. This enables organizations to focus on those "key components" of value generation and, thus, dominate the system: In October 2020, Deutsche Bahn, the leading German railroad operator, has abandoned their (traditionally scaling) bus systems, as competitor FlixMobility has just focused on the (digital) customer interface—"outsourcing" any scalability challenge to individual transport companies. In analogy to Uber in private transportation, or Airbnb in the accommodation space, the enterprise controls the value creation system via a digitalizable part of the system—without owning and running physical resources with all their scalability issues.

Focus on citizen-centric and system-relevant services: While the above-mentioned trends focus on service concepts, this fourth one targets particular domains. Acknowledging that in most Western economies more than 60% of employees perform work in services sectors, the digitalization impact on services has an overarching impact on employees and served customers. Not only has the Corona pandemic painfully illustrated the potential, but also the limited progress that digitalization has made so far in sectors like education, public services, health care, or retail: So, digitalization in healthcare administration could free up valuable time and resources for direct care with patients, improving efficiency, customer satisfaction, and, ultimately, effectiveness. Also, there is an increasing level of concern that global platform providers like Amazon, Uber, or Netflix are challenging national "service sovereignty" and often do not meet social responsibility, data privacy, fairness, or openness expectations.

Actionable Research Fields

From the four trends above, the study team extracted six distinct fields of research[5] that need to be tackled to advance value creation at the intersection of servitization and digitalization (summarized in Fig. 7). Ultimately, service thinking and digitalization options as laid out in Sects. 2 and 3 will significantly impact and shape future value creation—as "high-tech meets high-touch".

Understanding and designing for new dimensions of quality: As observed in the first trend above, customers increasingly apply novel criteria to judge the quality of services. We expect benefits from a deeper understanding of those criteria as well as from adapting or newly creating methods and tools to address these criteria during value creation. Research efforts should strive to translate changes in societal attitudes and values into measurable and communicable outcomes of value creation—this includes awareness for fair trade, decarbonization, or sustainability (e.g., addressed in energy consumption measures or reflected in upcoming ESG reporting (Mervelskemper & Streit, 2017)). In the digital space, additional quality criteria may apply, for example, data privacy (reflected in EU GDPR rules establishing worldwide benchmarks) or ethical application of Artificial Intelligence—as manifested in the Guidelines for Trustworthy AI issued by the EU Commission (2019). As a consequence, research needs to be devoted to ensure that such quality criteria can be met and be made transparent to the users or the public. An example

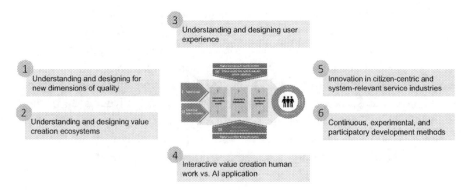

Fig. 7 Research agenda "high-tech meets high-touch", based on Böhmann et al. (2021, p. 11)

---

[5] The original source grouped the six research fields further into ecosystems & value creation models, interaction & hybridization, and innovation & development methods. It additionally emphasized the lenses under which those were extracted: value-orientation, innovation-orientation, and human-centricity.

are digital services delivered via the leading global digital platforms like Google or Facebook that are often quoted to violate such quality considerations as data privacy, equitable remuneration for data provision, or fairness (e.g., via biasing search results). New approaches are necessary that systematically integrate such new quality requirements into the design of value creation processes and/or the resulting products and services. Examples include fairness certifications for platforms (as for example fair.digital) or approaches to establish a user governance for data, as, for example, the "HAT (Hub of All Things)" project (Ng et al., 2014), to ensure digital sovereignty.

Understanding and designing value creation ecosystems: Value creation increasingly happens in the (digitally supported) dynamic collaboration of interconnected partners, typically called a service system or an ecosystem (Barile et al., 2016). Often this notion is associated with *digital platform* ecosystems dominated by well-known big players, but also materializes in any case where companies join complementary features to form a common value proposition, as in the Trumpf "EaaS" example above—implemented by a machine manufacturer and an insurance. Resulting research challenges address the understanding of mechanisms and the purposeful design of such ecosystems (Vink et al., 2021).

First, understanding of ecosystems implies insights into how a *decentralized ecosystem* may function, including questions of governance or intellectual property. New approaches like Distributed Ledger Technologies provide new means for disintermediated value creation in networks (Seebacher et al., 2021); Open Source approaches benefit from openly sharing data (Enders et al., 2020). This includes an understanding of roles in ecosystems that are more complex than in traditional dyadic relationships, for example, the customer as a "prosumer" (Chandler & Chen, 2015). Second, new *data-driven ecosystems* emerge based on "big data" (Fromm & Bloehdorn, 2014) availability, among others driven by sensorization of industrial assets, that is, the emergence of the Internet of Things. The systematic exploitation of data in analytics-based services (Hunke et al., 2020), or specifically in "smart services" (Beverungen et al., 2019; Maleshkova et al., 2020), will lead to "datatization as the next frontier of servitization" (Schüritz et al., 2017). Research needs to support the innovation of services and business models, posing particular challenges for distributed data sourcing in ecosystems, for example, tackled by federated or transfer learning approaches (Yang et al., 2019; Hirt et al., 2020). Third, the alignment of interests of ecosystem partners to ensure a joint focus on value-in-use as well as the fair distribution of jointly generated value (Conte et al., 2011) are subject of future research. Fourth, individual potential ecosystem partners need to be supported in decisions upon joining ecosystems and selecting particular roles, that is, in managing "embedded-ness" (Sklyar et al., 2019). Similarly, understanding underlying social structures (Edvardsson et al., 2011) and motivating and nudging partners to actively engage in ecosystems (Benz et al., 2020) seem promising future research topics.

Understanding and designing user experience: Value creation, even performed within larger and more complex ecosystems, needs to center on the customer experience and value-in-use. Digitalization may help to still scale delivery, while being able to individualize the value proposition and adapt it over time. This includes research questions like how ecosystems can be orchestrated for a unified and human-centric customer experience, how digital means can be used to capture customer experience and satisfaction (Baier et al., 2021), how digital traces can enrich the understanding of psychological states (Rafaeli et al., 2019), or how digital technology may sense and respond to emotions (Huang et al., 2019; Bromuri et al., 2021).

Interactive value creation between human work and Artificial Intelligence: Traditional interaction focused on dyadic relationships between providers and customers. Digitalization does catalyze this in many ways, for example, by supporting virtual or remote collaboration. However, it also adds digital technology, in particular AI-based applications or intelligent agents (Kühl et al., 2019), as a third actor in this relationship as an active source for value generation (Huang & Rust, 2018). From digital or cognitive assistants up to humanoid service robots (Wirtz et al., 2018), AI-based applications offer new opportunities to support value creation, for example, by individualizing customer interaction, by making it available in real time, or by providing deeper expertise (Hashimoto, 2020). The collaboration of humans and AI has to purposefully be designed and adapted to particular contexts. Examples are the distribution of work between humans and AI (Jarrahi, 2018; Vössing, 2020), tailoring of AI support to individuals (Feine et al., 2019), adoption issues of AI (Belanche et al., 2019; Nam et al., 2020; Fernandes & Oliveira, 2021), or the determination and provision of appropriate human skill levels (Manyika et al., 2017). Consequences on human work, employment, and customer experience need to be understood.

Innovation and resilience in system-relevant service sectors: Within the service sector, we observe domains affecting a huge number of users/consumers, for example, services that are consumed by almost any individual, like public services for citizens (government services, education, health care, or media and entertainment)—often accompanied by a correspondingly large share of employees involved in rendering these services. Not only does this create a high leverage for any innovation in value creation, but at the same

Servitization and Digitalization as "Siamese Twins": Concepts...

time it poses additional challenges: The current pandemic has painfully demonstrated that the system does lack resilience in system-relevant sectors; almost monopolistic digital platforms dominate service provision in some spaces; and innovation speed, for example, in e-government is low in many countries. Thus, a primary focus on those sectors should be an adequate target for future research.

Continuous, experimental, and participatory development methods: As stated above, traditional product lifecycles will lose importance, as digitalization will drive continuous innovation merging design, experimentation, and deployment phases. This needs to be supported by experimental and agile methods for creating new value propositions. At the same time, it calls for collaborative spaces in the real world where providers and users interact to explore and test new products and services. Examples are design thinking-based, human-centric approaches (Przybilla et al., 2021), or "living labs" (Dell'Era & Landoni, 2014).

5   Conclusion

Finally, we summarize that digitalization and servitization can be seen as "Siamese twins" in a way that both trends are inseparable and reinforce each other. This can conceptually be argued under both value proposition- and value creation-based paradigms. The purposeful design and application of digital technologies to service contexts is as important as the exploitation of digitalization via new service offerings and business models.

Our literature- and interview-based analysis on "high-tech meets high-touch" has revealed which trends indicate a set of research priorities that will be key to shape value creation in the future, to drive innovation, and to secure the competitiveness of enterprises, industries, and economies as a whole. Both service and information systems research will be able to significantly contribute to this—becoming decisive competitive factors.

References

Akaka, M. A., & Vargo, S. L. (2014). Technology as an operant resource in service (eco)systems. *Information Systems and E-Business Management, 12*(3), 367–384.

Baier, L., Kühl, N., Schüritz, R., & Satzger, G. (2021). Will the customers be happy? Identifying unsatisfied customers from service encounter data. *Journal of Service Management, 32*(2), 265–288.

Baines, T., Ziaee Bigdeli, A., Bustinza, O. F., Shi, V. G., Baldwin, J., & Ridgway, K. (2017). Servitization: Revisiting the state-of-the-art and research priorities. *International Journal of Operations & Production Management, 37*(2), 256–278.

Barile, S., Lusch, R., Reynoso, J., Saviano, M., & Spohrer, J. (2016). Systems, networks, and ecosystems in service research. *Journal of Service Management, 27*(4), 652–674.

Belanche, D., Casaló, L. V., & Flavián, C. (2019). Artificial Intelligence in FinTech: Understanding robo-advisors adoption among customers. *Industrial Management & Data Systems, 119*(7), 1411–1430.

Benz, C., Zierau, N., & Satzger, G. (2020). Not all tasks are alike: Exploring the effect of task representation on user engagement in crowd-based idea evaluation. *Proceedings of the 27th European Conference on Information Systems,* 1–17.

Berkovich, M., Leimeister, J. M., & Krcmar, H. (2011). Requirements engineering for product service systems. *Business & Information Systems Engineering, 3*(6), 369–380.

Beverungen, D., Müller, O., Matzner, M., Mendling, J., & vom Brocke, J. (2019). Conceptualizing smart service systems. *Electronic Markets, 29*(1), 7–18.

Blei, D. M., Ng, A. Y., & Jordan, M. I. (2003). Latent dirichlet allocation. *Journal of Machine Learning Research, 3*(1), 993–1022.

Böhmann, T., Leimeister, J. M., & Möslein, K. (2014). Service systems engineering. *Business & Information Systems Engineering, 6*(2), 73–79.

Böhmann, T., Roth, A., Satzger, G., Grotherr, C., Schymanietz, M., Wolff, C., Benz, C., Falk, S., Frank, J., Ganz, W., Hipp, C., Leimeister, J. M., & Stich, V. (2021). *High-Tech meets High-Touch: Die Dienstleistungswende als Chance für die Wertschöpfung und Beschäftigung der Zukunft.* Retrieved May 18, 2021, from https://dfdf.informatik.uni-hamburg.de/das-df2/positionen/

Boyd-Graber, J. L., Hu, Y., & Mimno, D. (2017). Applications of topic models. *Information Retrieval, 11*(2–3), 143–296.

Bromuri, S., Henkel, A. P., Iren, D., & Urovi, V. (2021). Using AI to predict service agent stress from emotion patterns in service interactions. *Journal of Service Management, 32*(4), 81–611.

Cavalieri, S., & Pezzotta, G. (2012). Product–service systems engineering: State of the art and research challenges. *Computers in Industry, 63*(4), 278–288.

Chandler, J., & Chen, S. (2015). Prosumer motivations in service experiences. *Journal of Service Theory and Practice, 25*(2), 220–239.

Conte, T., Blau, B., Satzger, G., van Dinther, C., & Weinhardt, C. (2011). Rewarding participation in service value networks – An approach to incentivize the joint provisioning of complex e-services. *E-Service Journal, 7*(2), 2–27.

de Reuver, M., Sørensen, C., & Basole, R. C. (2018). The digital platform: A research agenda. *Journal of Information Technology, 33*(2), 124–135.

Dell'Era, C., & Landoni, P. (2014). Living lab: A methodology between user-centred design and participatory design. *Creativity and Innovation Management, 23*(2), 137–154.

Edvardsson, B., Gustafsson, A., & Roos, I. (2005). Service portraits in service research: A critical review. *International Journal of Service Industry Management, 16*(1), 107–121.

Edvardsson, B., Tronvoll, B., & Gruber, T. (2011). Expanding understanding of service exchange and value co-creation: A social construction approach. *Journal of the Academy of Marketing Science, 39*(2), 327–339.

Enders, T., Wolff, C., & Satzger, G. (2020). Knowing what to share: Selective revealing in open data. *Proceedings of the 27th European Conference on Information Systems.*

Engelhardt, W. H., Kleinaltenkamp, M., & Reckenfelderbäumer, M. (1993). Leistungsbündel als Absatzobjekte. *Zeitschrift für betriebswirtschaftliche Forschung, 45*(5), 395–426.

EU Commission. (2019). *Ethics guidelines for trustworthy AI.*

Feine, J., Gnewuch, U., Morana, S., & Maedche, A. (2019). A taxonomy of social cues for conversational agents. *International Journal of Human-Computer Studies, 132*, 138–161.

Fernandes, T., & Oliveira, E. (2021). Understanding consumers' acceptance of automated technologies in service encounters: Drivers of digital voice assistants adoption. *Journal of Business Research, 122*, 180–191.

Fromm, H., & Bloehdorn, S. (2014). Big Data—Technologies and potential. In G. Schuh, V. Stich, G. Gudergan, & A. Walter (Eds.), *Enterprise-integration* (pp. 107–124). Springer.

Fromm, H., & Cardoso, J. (2015). Foundations. In J. Cardoso, H. Fromm, S. Nickel, G. Satzger, R. Studer, & C. Weinhardt (Eds.), *Fundamentals of service systems* (pp. 1–32). Springer.

Gomez-Uribe, C. A., & Hunt, N. (2016). The Netflix recommender system. *ACM Transactions on Management Information Systems, 6*(4), 1–19.

Grönroos, C., & Voima, P. (2013). Critical service logic: Making sense of value creation and co-creation. *Journal of the Academy of Marketing Science, 41*(2), 133–150.

Habryn, F., Blau, B., Satzger, G., & Kölmel, B. (2010). Towards measuring customer intimacy in B2B services. In J.-H. Morin, J. Ralyté, & M. Snene (Eds.), *Exploring service science. Proceedings of the First International Conference (IESS)* (pp. 1–14). Springer.

Hashimoto, D. A. (2020). *Artificial intelligence in surgery: An AI primer for surgical practice.* McGraw Hill.

Hawksworth, J., & Chan, D. (2015). *The world in 2050 will the shift in global economic power continue?*

Hein, A., Schreieck, M., Riasanow, T., Setzke, D. S., Wiesche, M., Böhm, M., & Krcmar, H. (2020). Digital platform ecosystems. *Electronic Markets, 30*(1), 87–98.

Hill, T. P. (1977). On goods and services. *Review of Income and Wealth, 23*(4), 315–338.

Hirt, R., Kuhl, N., Peker, Y., & Satzger, G. (2020). How to learn from others: Transfer machine learning with additive regression models to improve sales forecasting. *Proceedings of the 22nd IEEE Conference on Business Informatics (CBI), 1*, 20–29.

Huang, M.-H., & Rust, R. T. (2018). Artificial intelligence in service. *Journal of Service Research, 21*(2), 155–172.

Huang, M.-H., Rust, R., & Maksimovic, V. (2019). The feeling economy: Managing in the next generation of Artificial Intelligence (AI). *California Management Review, 61*(4), 43–65.

Hunke, F., Seebacher, S., Schüritz, R., & Satzger, G. (2020). Pathways from data to value: Identifying strategic archetypes of analytics-based services. *15th International Conference on Wirtschaftsinformatik*, 1035–1050.

Jarrahi, M. H. (2018). Artificial intelligence and the future of work: Human-AI symbiosis in organizational decision making. *Business Horizons, 61*(4), 577–586.

Jetter, M., Satzger, G., & Neus, A. (2009). Technological innovation and its impact on business model, organization and corporate culture – IBM's transformation into a globally integrated, service-oriented enterprise. *Business & Information Systems Engineering, 1*(1), 37–45.

Jung, D., Dorner, V., Glaser, F., & Morana, S. (2018). Robo-advisory. *Business & Information Systems Engineering, 60*(1), 81–86.

Kowalkowski, C., Gebauer, H., Kamp, B., & Parry, G. (2017). Servitization and deservitization: Overview, concepts, and definitions. *Industrial Marketing Management, 60*, 4–10.

Kühl, N., Scheurenbrand, J., & Satzger, G. (2016). Needmining: Identifying micro blog data containing customer needs. *Proceedings of the 24th European Conference on Information Systems*.

Kühl, N., Goutier, M., Hirt, R., & Satzger, G. (2019). Machine learning in Artificial Intelligence: Towards a common understanding. *Proceedings of the 52nd Hawaii International Conference on System Sciences, 6*, 5236–5245.

Maedche, A., Legner, C., Benlian, A., Berger, B., Gimpel, H., Hess, T., Hinz, O., Morana, S., & Söllner, M. (2019). AI-based digital assistants. *Business & Information Systems Engineering, 61*(4), 535–544.

Maglio, P. P., & Spohrer, J. (2008). Fundamentals of service science. *Journal of the Academy of Marketing Science, 36*(1), 18–20.

Maleshkova, M., Kühl, N., & Jussen, P. (Eds.). (2020). *Smart service management*. Springer.

Manyika, J., Lund, S., Chui, M., Bughin, J., Woetzel, J., Batra, P., Ko, R., & Sangvhi, S. (2017). *What the future of work will mean for jobs, skills, and wages*. McKinsey Report.

Martin, D., Kühl, N., & Satzger, G. (2021). Virtual sensors. *Business & Information Systems Engineering, 63*, 315–323.

Martín-Peña, M. L., Sánchez-López, J. M., & Díaz-Garrido, E. (2019). Servitization and digitalization in manufacturing: The influence on firm performance. *Journal of Business and Industrial Marketing, 35*(3), 564–574.

Meffert, H., Bruhn, M., & Hadwich, K. (2018). *Dienstleistungsmarketing Methoden, Grundlagen – Konzepte* (9th ed.). Springer Gabler.

Mervelskemper, L., & Streit, D. (2017). Enhancing market valuation of ESG performance: Is integrated reporting keeping its promise? *Business Strategy and the Environment, 26*(4), 536–549.

Moeller, S. (2010). Characteristics of services – a new approach uncovers their value. *Journal of Services Marketing, 24*(5), 359–368.

Mont, O. (2002). Drivers and barriers for shifting towards more service-oriented businesses: Analysis of the PSS field and contributions from Sweden. *The Journal of Sustainable Product Design, 2*(3/4), 89–103.

Nam, K., Dutt, C. S., Chathoth, P., Daghfous, A., & Khan, M. S. (2020). The adoption of artificial intelligence and robotics in the hotel industry: Prospects and challenges. *Electronic Markets*, 1–22.

Neely, A. (2009). Exploring the financial consequences of the servitization of manufacturing. *Operations Management Research, 1*(2), 103–118.

Ng, I., Pogrebna, G., & Ma, X. (2014). Smart home, smart things and smart me in the smart city: The hub-of-all-things resource integration and enabling tool (HARRIET). *IET Conference on Future Intelligent Cities.*

Nikolenko, S. I., Koltcov, S., & Koltsova, O. (2017). Topic modelling for qualitative studies. *Journal of Information Science, 43*(1), 88–102.

Parida, V., Sjödin, D. R., Lenka, S., & Wincent, J. (2015). Developing global service innovation capabilities: How global manufacturers address the challenges of market heterogeneity. *Research-Technology Management, 58*(5), 35–44.

Przybilla, L., Klinker, K., Lang, M., Schreieck, M., Wiesche, M., & Krcmar, H. (2021). Design thinking in digital innovation projects—Exploring the effects of intangibility. *IEEE Transactions on Engineering Management*, 1–15.

Quinn, J. B. (1992). *Intelligent enterprise: A knowledge and service based paradigm for industry.* The Free Press.

Raddats, C., Kowalkowski, C., Benedettini, O., Burton, J., & Gebauer, H. (2019). Servitization: A contemporary thematic review of four major research streams. *Industrial Marketing Management, 83*, 207–223.

Rafaeli, A., Ashtar, S., & Altman, D. (2019). Digital traces: New data, resources, and tools for psychological-science research. *Current Directions in Psychological Science, 28*(6), 560–566.

Rossi, M., Mueller-Bloch, C., Thatcher, J. B., & Beck, R. (2019). Blockchain research in information systems: Current trends and an inclusive future research agenda. *Journal of the Association for Information Systems, 20*(9), 1388–1403.

Schmitz, H.-C., Kurth, F., Wilkinghoff, K., Müllerschkowski, U., Karrasch, C., & Schmid, V. (2020). Towards robust speech interfaces for the ISS. *Proceedings of the 25th International Conference on Intelligent User Interfaces Companion*, 110–111.

Schueritz, R., Farell, K., Satzger, G., & Wixom, B. H. (2019). Designing for value co-creation — How provider and customer shape joint spheres that impact real value creation in data-driven services. *Proceedings of the 40th International Conference on Information Systems (ICIS).*

Schüritz, R., & Satzger, G. (2016). Patterns of data-infused business model innovation. *Proceedings of the IEEE Conference on Business Informatics (CBI)*, 133–142.

Schüritz, R. M., Seebacher, S., Satzger, G., Schwarz, L., & Schwarz, L. (2017). Datatization as the next frontier of servitization – Understanding the challenges for transforming organizations. *Proceedings of the International Conference on Information Systems (ICIS)*.

Seebacher, S., Schüritz, R., & Satzger, G. (2021). Towards an understanding of technology fit and appropriation in business networks: Evidence from blockchain implementations. *Information Systems and E-Business Management, 19*, 183–204.

Sklyar, A., Kowalkowski, C., Tronvoll, B., & Sörhammar, D. (2019). Organizing for digital servitization: A service ecosystem perspective. *Journal of Business Research, 104*, 450–460.

Smith, D. J. (2013). Power-by-the-hour: The role of technology in reshaping business strategy at Rolls-Royce. *Technology Analysis & Strategic Management, 25*(8), 987–1007.

Stojkovski, I., Achleitner, A., & Lange, T. (2021). *Equipment as a service: The transition towards usage-based business models*. Retrieved May 18, 2021, from https://papers.ssrn.com/sol3/papers.cfm?abstract_id=3763004

Storbacka, K., Brodie, R. J., Böhmann, T., Maglio, P. P., & Nenonen, S. (2016). Actor engagement as a microfoundation for value co-creation. *Journal of Business Research, 69*(8), 3008–3017.

Vandermerwe, S., & Rada, J. (1988). Servitization of business: Adding value by adding services. *European Management Journal, 6*(4), 314–324.

Vargo, S. L., & Lusch, R. F. (2004). Evolving to a new dominant logic for marketing. *Journal of Marketing, 68*(1), 1–17.

Vargo, S. L., & Lusch, R. F. (2008). Service-dominant logic: Continuing the evolution. *Journal of the Academy of Marketing Science, 36*, 1–10.

Vink, J., Koskela-Huotari, K., Tronvoll, B., Edvardsson, B., & Wetter-Edman, K. (2021). Service ecosystem design: Propositions, process model, and future research agenda. *Journal of Service Research, 24*(2), 168–186.

Vössing, M. (2020). *Designing human-computer collaboration: Transparency and automation for intelligence augmentation*. Dissertation KIT.

Wang, P. P., Ming, X. G., Li, D., Kong, F. B., Wang, L., & Wu, Z. Y. (2011). Modular development of product service systems. *Concurrent Engineering, 19*(1), 85–96.

Wiersema, F., & Treacy, M. (1993). Customer intimacy and other value disciplines. *Harvard Business Review, 71*(1), 84–93.

Wirtz, J., Patterson, P. G., Kunz, W. H., Gruber, T., Lu, V. N., Paluch, S., Martins, A., & Lu, N. (2018). Brave new world: Service robots in the frontline. *Journal of Service Management, 29*(5), 907–931.

Wirtz, J., So, K. K. F., Mody, M. A., Liu, S. Q., & Chun, H. E. H. (2019). Platforms in the peer-to-peer sharing economy. *Journal of Service Management, 30*(4), 452–483.

Wolff, C., & Satzger, G. (2018). System-oriented service delivery: The application of service system engineering to service delivery. *Proceedings of the European Conference on Information Systems (ECIS)*.

Yang, Q., Liu, Y., Chen, T., & Tong, Y. (2019). Federated machine learning. *ACM Transactions on Intelligent Systems and Technology, 10*(2), 1–19.

Yiannas, F. (2018). A new era of food transparency powered by blockchain. *Innovations: Technology, Governance, Globalization, 12*(1–2), 46–56.

Zhang, Y., Huang, M., Tian, L., Jin, D., & Cai, G. (2021). Build or join a sharing platform? The choice of manufacturer's sharing mode. *International Journal of Production Economics, 231*.

Toward a New Service Reality: Human–Robot Collaboration at the Service Frontline

Werner H. Kunz, Stefanie Paluch, and Jochen Wirtz

1 Introduction

Since their inception, robots have inspired authors, directors, and thinkers worldwide. But only recently, we see robots moving into people's everyday lives in the wake of rapidly developing computer technologies and robots.

Note: This chapter draws on the following publications: Jochen Wirtz, Paul Patterson, Werner Kunz, Thorsten Gruber, Vinh Nhat Lu, Stefanie Paluch, and Antje Martins (2018), "Brave New World: Service Robots in the Frontline," *Journal of Service Management*, Vol. 29, No. 5, pp. 907–931, https://doi.org/10.1108/JOSM-04-2018-0119; Jochen Wirtz (2020), "Organizational Ambidexterity: Cost-Effective Service Excellence, Service Robots, and Artificial Intelligence," *Organizational Dynamics*, Vol. 49, No. 3, pp. 1–9, https://doi.org/10.1016/j.orgdyn.2019.04.005; Jochen Wirtz, Werner Kunz and Stefanie Paluch (2022), "The Service Revolution, Intelligent Automat and Service Robots," The European Business Review, January-February, pp. 38–44., and Lu, Vinh Nhat, Jochen Wirtz, Werner Kunz, Stefanie Paluch, Thorsten Gruber, Antje Martins, and Paul Patterson (2020), "Service Robots, Customers, and Service Employees: What Can We Learn from the Academic Literature and Where are the Gaps?" *Journal of Service Theory and Practice,* Vol. 30 No. 3, pp. 361–391

W. H. Kunz (✉)
Department of Marketing, University of Massachusetts Boston, Boston, MA, USA
e-mail: werner.kunz@umb.edu

S. Paluch
School of Business and Economics, RWTH Aachen University, Aachen, Germany
e-mail: paluch@time.rwth-aachen.de

J. Wirtz
NUS Business School, National University of Singapore, Kent Ridge, Singapore
e-mail: jochen@nus.edu.sg

© The Author(s), under exclusive license to Springer Nature Switzerland AG 2022
B. Edvardsson, B. Tronvoll (eds.), *The Palgrave Handbook of Service Management*,
https://doi.org/10.1007/978-3-030-91828-6_47

One of the first business fields is services industries (e.g., hotels, restaurants, retail). Technologies rapidly become smarter and more powerful, while at the same time they get smaller, lighter, and cheaper. These technologies include hardware such as that related to physical robots, drones, and autonomous vehicles and their components (e.g., processors, sensors, cameras, chips), wearable technologies, and code or software such as analytics, speech processing, image processing, biometrics, virtual reality, augmented reality, cloud technologies, mobile technologies, geo-tagging, low-code platforms, robotic process automation (RPA), and machine learning (Bornet et al., 2021; Wirtz et al., 2018, 2022; Wirtz, 2020). Together, these technologies will transform virtually all service sectors (Kunz et al., 2019). Service robots and artificial intelligence (AI), combined with these technologies, will lead to rapid innovation that can dramatically improve the customer experience, service quality, and productivity all at the same time (Wirtz & Zeithaml, 2018).

We are now at a turning point, where humanoid robots (e.g., Pepper and Nao) and voice-based virtual assistants (e.g., Siri and Alexa) enter our daily lives. Due to the rapid advancements of robot technologies combined with artificial intelligence (AI), Big Data analytics, cameras, sensor, and speech recognition, so-called service robots are on the rise (Wirtz et al., 2018). They are capable of performing tasks autonomously without any human involvement (Joerling et al., 2019), bringing warmth and competence to the service delivery (Yoganathan et al., 2021), executing tasks by following their service-script and with prior knowledge (Huang & Rust, 2018), and are said to be an important source of innovation (Rust & Huang, 2014). In this chapter, we mainly focus on the organizational frontline, the point where the service is delivered to the customer, using the following definition: "Service robots are system-based autonomous and adaptable interfaces that interact, communicate and provide service to an organization's customers" (Wirtz et al., 2018, p. 909). Service robots are typically embedded in larger (virtual) networks that provide access to internal and external data. Autonomous robots can recognize and learn from their environments and make their own decisions without human intervention. With the help of cameras and sensors, robots can identify customers through facial or voice recognition and provide services according to the customer's profile, which they can access through the interconnectedness of the systems.

Robot- and AI-delivered service offers unprecedented economies of scale and scope as the bulk of the costs are incurred in their development. Physical robots cost a fraction of adding headcount, and virtual robots can be deployed at negligible incremental costs. Likewise, virtual service robots (e.g., chatbots and virtual agents) can be scaled at close to zero incremental costs. Such dramatic salability does not only apply to virtual service robots such as chatbots but also to 'visible' ones such as holograms. For example, an airport could install a hologram-based humanoid service robot every 50 meters to assist passengers and deal with common questions (e.g., provide arrival and departure information, directions to check-in counters for a particular airline, airport hotel) in all common languages. These holograms only require low-cost hardware (i.e., a camera, microphone, speaker, and projector) and do not need to take up floor space (travelers could push their baggage carts through a hologram when it gets crowded) (Wirtz et al., 2021a).

Already, many firms show eager interest in experimenting with service robots. For example, hotels are introducing humanoid robots in their lobbies to welcome guests, provide information, and entertain guests. The Mandarin Oriental Hotel in Las Vegas has introduced Pepper as their newest humanoid staff member. Pepper resides in the lobby, where she welcomes guests and helps them with directions. Her job is to provide information to hotel guests entertainingly and innovatively (Walsh, 2018). In Japan, the Henna Hotel is the first robot-staffed hotel, where guests can check in with an android woman, a robot, or a dinosaur robot. Luggage is delivered to the room by a porter robot, and the concierge robot Tully switches the light on and off for the guest (Kikuchi, 2018).

At airports, robots scan boarding passes and help passengers to find the right departure gate. Self-moving check-in kiosk robots detect busy areas and autonomously help passengers reduce waiting times (Paluch et al., 2020). At the airport, robots are used in the form of passenger guidance, maintenance, or security. At Amsterdam Airport Schiphol, the robot Spencer scans KLM passengers' boarding passes and helps them find the right departure gate. Kate, a self-moving check-in kiosk robot, works at Kansai Airport in Japan and detects busy areas, autonomously going there and helping passengers reduce waiting times. At Incheon Airport in South Korea, cleaning robots vacuum the airport and in Shenzhen's Bao'an International Airport, Anbot, a security robot, patrols the departure hall for suspicious behavior (Read, 2017).

The outbreak of COVID-19 has increased the demand for medical service robots that take over the medical care of contagious patients. For example, the social robot Ari interacts with COVID-19 patients to help them overcome their isolation. Other robots make sure that patients get their medicine, and they can monitor vital signs remotely. Additionally, autonomous robots disinfect hospitals and make sure patients and visitors follow the regulations and maintain social distancing (Schoepfer & Etemad-Sajadi, 2020).

Further, societal changes such as an increasing elderly population and declining workforce infuse robots in somewhat unexpected contexts, such as nursing care, which typically requires a more personal touch and individual attention. In Tokyo's Shin-tomi nursing home, robots help caretakers lift people and perform exercises with groups of elderly residents and initiate engaging conversations (Foster, 2018).

The above examples demonstrate that service industries are changing, and more businesses are considering reorganizing their organizational frontline service (Kunz & Walsh, 2020). Studies suggest that by 2025, 85% of customer interactions will occur without a human agent (Schneider, 2017). The market size for service robots is projected to reach USD 41.5 billion by 2027 (Fortune Business Insights, 2020).

Such robots in hotels, airports, and restaurants, as well as chatbots and delivery bots, are only the beginning of the service revolution. This means that similar to the shift that started during the Industrial Revolution from craftsmen to mass production, an accelerated shift in the service sector toward robot- and AI-delivered services can be expected. The exciting prospect is that many services, including healthcare and education, are likely to become available at much lower prices and better quality, leading to a dramatic increase in our standard of living.

In this chapter we want to illustrate the new service reality induced by innovative technology. We highlight the difference between older automated self-service technologies and service robots. Further, we analyze the difference between human service employees and service robots and show avenues for collaboration and specialization in the Service Robot Deployment Model. Finally, we close with managerial implications for the service frontline in the new service reality with robots.

2 Self-Service Technologies Versus Service Robots

Service robots have been defined as "system-based autonomous and adaptable interfaces that interact, communicate and deliver service to an organization's customers." (Wirtz et al., 2018). These abilities differentiate service robots from traditional self-service technologies (SSTs). We are familiar with the context of ticketing machines, websites, and apps (Yoganathan et al., 2021). As shown in Exhibit 1, service robots can deal with unstructured interactions and guide customers through their service journey. For example, a ticketing robot will not let customers get stuck as it can ask clarifying questions (e.g., "Is your return trip today?" "Can you travel off-peak?") and can even recover

Exhibit 1 Contrasting service robots with traditional self-service technologies

Service aspect	Self-service technologies (SSTs)	Service robots
Customer service scripts and roles	• Customers have to learn the service script and role and follow them closely	• Customers do not need to learn a particular role and script beyond what they would do when interacting with a frontline employee
	• Deviations from the script tend to lead to service failure and termination of the unsuccessful transactions	• Flexible customer journeys, interaction, and scripts are supported
	• Need to be self-explanatory and intuitive as customers have to control and navigate the interaction	• Can guide the customer through the service process very much like a service employee would
Customer error tolerance	• Generally, do not function when customers make errors or use the SST incorrectly	• Are customer error-tolerant
	• Are generally not effective in recovering customer errors; customers typically have to start the transaction again, or a service employee needs to take over	• Can recover customer errors and guide the customer to conclude a successful service transaction
Service recovery capability	• The service process tends to break down when there is a service failure; recovery is unlikely within the technology	• Are 'trained' to recover common service failures • Can recover the service by offering alternative solutions very much like a service employee would

Adapted from Jochen Wirtz, Paul Patterson, Werner Kunz, Thorsten Gruber, Vinh Nhat Lu, Stefanie Paluch, and Antje Martins (2018), "Brave New World: Service Robots in the Frontline," Journal of Service Management, Vol. 29, No. 5, p. 909, https://doi.org/10.1108/JOSM-04-2018-0119

customer errors (e.g., a wrong button pressed, incorrect information entered, or a rejected credit card). For most standard services, customers will interact with service robots much like service employees do (e.g., "I need a same-day return ticket and can I use Apple Pay?").

3 Human Service Employees Versus Service Robots

A key element of every service company is the employees that deliver the service to the customer. Thus, a comparison between technology is worthwhile, but a deeper understanding of the strengths and weaknesses of human service employees compared to robots is critical.

Emotional Touch vs. Customized Tech

It is common in service industries to say the frontline employee is the face of the company. The service is determined by the frontline personnel's skills, training, emotions, personality, and attitude. Depending on the company strategy, the human touch can be the key differentiating factor for service excellence. Personal service entails genuine emotions from one human being to another. In contrast, robots are not able to feel and express real emotions. This is important as the service management literature distinguishes between deep acting (employee displays true emotions) and surface acting (employee displays superficial, fake emotional response) (e.g., Wirtz & Jerger, 2017). A robot's emotional display is likely to be "fake" and displayed, and not authentic and truly felt. Consumers are likely to know this, perceive it, and respond accordingly. Thus, customers are unlikely to respond to robot-displayed emotions as they would to "heart-felt" and authentic emotions from human frontline employees (Wirtz et al., 2018).

Individual Person vs. System-Based Approach

Another distinction is that human employees are individuals with their personalities, skills, perceptions, biases, and services, showing heterogeneity over time and across individual employees. Education of the frontline personnel is needed, and employees need to know the processes to do a good job. People need to learn the routines, memorize all relevant information, and get used to the computer assistant system to access more information. This process takes time and is not seamless. Robots, on the other hand, are system-based approaches. They can be connected to a knowledge database and use all available information from customer relationship management (CRM) systems and the Internet to provide their service.

High Incremental Cost vs. Low Incremental Cost

Finally, human employees are not scalable. Every person adds significant costs to the company. In contrast, robots entail enormous economies of scale. Thus, much of the costs build up during the research and development. Physical robots have incremental costs, even though they are at a fraction of adding headcount. In comparison, virtual robots are likely to be deployed at negligible incremental costs (Wirtz et al., 2018). Other significant differences are summarized in Exhibit 2.

Toward a New Service Reality: Human–Robot Collaboration...

Exhibit 2 Contrasting frontline employees with service robots

Dimension	Service employees	Service robots
Employee/robot training and learning	⁎ Act as individuals, individual learning ⁎ Need training ⁎ Limited memory and access	⁎ Act as part of systems, are connected, system learning ⁎ Upgradable, system-wide ⁎ Virtually endless memory and access
Customer experience	⁎ Heterogeneous output ⁎ Customization and personalization depend on employee skill and effort ⁎ Unintended biases ⁎ Have genuine emotions ⁎ Can engage in deep acting ⁎ Can engage in out-of-box thinking and creative problem solving	⁎ Homogenous output ⁎ Customization and personalization can be delivered to scale with consistent quality and performance ⁎ Potentially no biases ⁎ Can mimic emotions ⁎ Can engage in surface acting ⁎ Limited out-of-box thinking, have rule-bound limits
Firm strategy	⁎ Service employees can be a source of competitive advantage ⁎ High incremental cost ⁎ Low economies of scale and scope ⁎ Differentiation on service can be based on better hiring, selection, training, motivation, and organization of service employees	⁎ Just the deployment of service robots is unlikely to be a source of competitive advantage in the eye of the customer (very much like ATMs are sold to banks) ⁎ Low incremental cost ⁎ High economies of scale and scope ⁎ Economies of scale and scope and related network and service platform effects will become important sources of competitive advantage

Adapted from Jochen Wirtz, Paul Patterson, Werner Kunz, Thorsten Gruber, Vinh Nhat Lu, Stefanie Paluch, and Antje Martins (2018), "Brave New World: Service Robots in the Frontline," Journal of Service Management, Vol. 29, No. 5, p. 909, https://doi.org/10.1108/JOSM-04-2018-0119

4 The Service Robot Deployment Model

Given these distinctive aspects of human employees and service robots, companies need to decide which tasks human employees will take care of and which are handled by robots in the future.

Tasks can be organized based on their need in doing cognitive and analytical work or emotional or social work. Depending on the combination of these two dimensions, Wirtz et al. (2018) proposed the Service Robot Deployment Model, where they predict which tasks will be done by humans, by robots, or in human–robot collaboration in the future (see Exhibit 3).

Exhibit 3 The Service Robot Deployment Model. (Adapted from Jochen Wirtz, Paul Patterson, Werner Kunz, Thorsten Gruber, Vinh Nhat Lu, Stefanie Paluch, and Antje Martins (2018), "Brave New World: Service Robots in the Frontline," Journal of Service Management, Vol. 29, No. 5, pp. 907–931, https://doi.org/10.1108/JOSM-04-2018-0119)

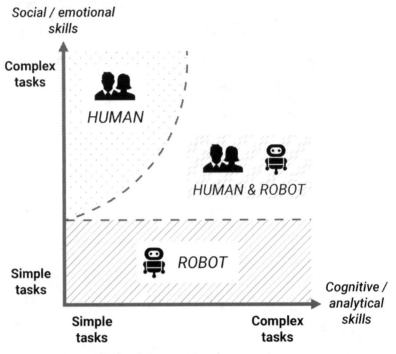

Given the system-based approach and the decreasing costs of computer calculations (i.e., Moore's law), robots have a clear advantage against human employees regarding cognitive and analytical work. On the other hand, human employees can provide the emotional touch of a service that is hard for robots to simulate. Therefore, when it comes to jobs with high cognitive/analytical tasks and low emotional/social work, robots will mainly provide these services, while when it comes to jobs with low cognitive/analytical tasks and high emotional/social work human employees are essential.

Some jobs in services might only need low cognitive/analytical work and little emotional/social work. Wirtz et al. (2018) assume that robots will be able to mimic simple emotional/social tasks in the future. Hence, they are a more cost-efficient solution than human employees. On the other hand, jobs that require high cognitive/analytical work and emotional/social work are likely to be delivered by humans supported by robots—robots will outperform humans on cognitive tasks, while humans will provide the emotional tasks of the job (Larivière et al., 2017).

Service Robot Infusion for Different Service Tasks

The persistent problem is that customers perceive service robots to have less competence than human service employees (Paluch et al., 2020). If companies are now considering the increased use of service robots, they must also make sure that service quality does not suffer. Customers may misunderstand the step and see it as a cost-saving measure, not interacting with the provider in different ways. We are currently still in the phase in which robots must prove themselves from the customer's perspective. In this phase, companies and managers can do a lot right and a lot wrong.

First, we need to understand the different service types. Therefore, we build on the matrix from Wirtz et al. (2018) and Paluch et al. (2020), in which service tasks are classified based on the level of cognitive/analytical skills and social/emotional skills. The underlying assumption is that robots benefit from artificial intelligence and can therefore better handle complex decision-making situations in which cognitive/analytical skills are highly demanded. Humans, however, can show real emotions since they can intuitively react to certain situations and are therefore better at displaying social/emotional skills.

Service Robots Take Over Routine and Repetitive Tasks

Initial deployments of service robots focused on simple and repetitive tasks that tended to be low in cognitive and emotional complexity. For example, physical robots in hotels deliver room service and bring baggage to guest rooms. However, text- and voice-based conversational agents increasingly handle routine customer interactions. Even when interacting with a human service employee, that employee may well be supported by AI, and calls are prescreened, preprocessed, and then escalated to the human agent because of their complexity. The outcome is that customer contact staff do not have to deal with high volumes of trivial customer requests but instead can spend their time on higher-value and higher-level tasks. For example, a chatbot for the NUS MBA Program handled 20,000 unique conversations per month right after launch and answered all the routine questions the admission team had to deal with previously (e.g., Do I need a GMAT? When are the fees payable? When is the application deadline?). As a result, the admission team can now focus on top-quality candidates and the more tricky and complex discussions.

In the *first scenario*, where cognitive-analytical skills and social/emotional skills are low, service robots can perfectly take over tasks, such as vacuuming the floor, mowing the lawn, patrolling airports, or delivering luggage to guest rooms to customers. In these service contexts, customers' expectations regarding emotions or any form of active, reciprocal interaction are low. The most important thing is that the job is done efficiently and effectively, so the robot's advantages outweigh human benefits, especially in terms of availability and delivering continuous service quality. This category of service jobs might not be among the most popular, and in times of labor shortages, we recommend these tasks be assigned to robots first. In some instances, it might be helpful to have human supervisors who can support service robots to ensure the reliability of the service.

Service Robots Outperform Humans with High Cognitive Skills

In addition to routine tasks, services that require high cognitive and analytical skills will be delivered effectively by service robots (e.g., financial services). For example, service robots can analyze large volumes of data, integrate internal and external information, recognize patterns, and relate these to customer profiles (Kunz et al., 2017). Then, within minutes, these robots can propose best-fitting solutions and make recommendations.

In the *second scenario*, where cognitive/analytical skills are high and social/emotional skills remain low, we expect the demand for service robots to increase. In professional service industries, such as insurance and accounting, or in legal contexts, significant amounts of information need to be analyzed quickly, and customers require reliable results and objective recommendations without much sentimentality. These analytical jobs can be better done by robots. A great advantage from the customer's perspective is the equal treatment by robots because robots' decision-making is solely based on available information, so customer discrimination is almost impossible. Companies should prioritize security and privacy concerns and communicate data usage transparency, especially when robots work with sensitive customer information (Wirtz et al., 2021a). It is also recommended to inform customers about changes in the frontline organization or the technology used to deliver the services because a well-informed customer can appreciate changes.

Emotional Skills Are a Human Asset that Is Difficult to Copy

It is difficult for robots to deal with emotions that go beyond a pleasant surface demeanor. Especially complex and emotionally demanding tasks are still better handled by service employees as they can bring genuine emotions such as excitement and joy or empathy and compassion to the service encounter. For example, in complaint and service recovery situations, humans can respond better to the individual context and show understanding.

In the *third scenario*, tasks require high social/emotional skills and less cognitive/analytical expertise. Human service employees have superior skills to perform tasks in hotels, restaurants, airlines, retail, or entertainment industries in which the personal experience is central for customers. These services are characterized by high interaction between the service employee and customer, and service quality is often measured based on the service counterpart's behavior. Considering our examples at the beginning of the chapter, hotels, restaurants, and airports are areas where service robots are preferably used, even though human service employees have better skills to deliver these services. Companies that have introduced service robots to deliver personal services (e.g., hairdressers, yoga teachers, or shopping assistants) should respect customers' different interaction preferences. Based on our analysis, we found two types of customers. Type 1 customers belong to the group that prefers human interaction and is reluctant to interact with service robots. Type 2 customers like the idea of avoiding personal interactions in service settings and are happy to give orders or push a touchscreen to receive their service. To maintain strong/good/positive service quality perceptions, managers should try to satisfy both customer segments by offering human and artificial alternatives and choosing according to their preferences.

Interestingly, service robots are already able to create a social presence with customers, so the customer has the feeling that somebody is taking care of them, even it is a robot (van Doorn et al., 2017). Companies can also offer their services as a two-tier model. Service robots will take over the initial contact, and for issues that require greater communication skills or psychological comfort, the service employee can take care of the situation. This approach seems suitable for complaint handling or service recovery situations that require experiential and contextual interactions and individualized treatment. In general, it is advisable not to leave the customer entirely alone with robots and to keep people available as a backup for troubleshooting or intervention in emergencies.

Service Robot and Human Employees Form Hybrid Teams in the Future

Human–robot teams will increasingly deliver tasks that require high cognitive and high emotional skills. For example, in a healthcare context, service robots will do the analytical work (e.g., analyze symptoms and compare them with databases to identify possible diagnoses), and humans will make the final recommendations and decisions and take over the social and emotional tasks (e.g., advising and persuading patients). For example, a traveler returns from Singapore to Munich with dengue fever; the symptoms only show up a week after returning. General practitioners in Germany may never see a dengue fever patient in their professional life and may not be effective in diagnosing it. On the other hand, a service robot compares patient data and symptoms and provides a 'hit list' of possible diseases with a fit index. The general practitioner can then work down the list and discuss with the patient (e.g., "Have you been in the tropics in the last two weeks?") and then identify the most likely diagnosis and test for it.

In the *fourth scenario*, cognitive/analytical skills and social/emotional skills are high, such as counseling, nursing, education, or medical services. In the future, these services can be delivered by hybrid teams (human service employees and service robots) to increase the outcome quality and, in general, to provide more accurate services. The newly formed teams provide innovative (business) opportunities and are proof that service robots are not only designed to replace or substitute human employees but to support joint decision-making (Jarrahi, 2018). In these hybrid teams, task responsibilities are distributed between service robots that process information and the service employee, who enriches the interaction with the customer with social and emotional competencies. There are already some examples of how hybrid human–robot teams work together at the frontline of services. For example, in the medical context, machines can carry out tasks that were previously performed by employees (skin cancer detection (Esteva et al., 2017), and human doctors can take care of the patient and discuss treatment options. As this example shows, robots do not necessarily replace human resources. Still, tasks and responsibilities are redefined and reassigned within the organization, so it is a matter of redistribution rather than substitution.

5 Implications for Managing Service in the Frontline

The digital revolution of the service sector will have enormous implications for business. The new capabilities induced by AI, intelligent automation, speech and image processing, biometrics, virtual and augmented reality, mobile technologies, robotic process automation (RPA), and machine learning are limitless. This new service reality brings up new pressing issues for service organizations to tackle. Some of these issues are described in the following sections (Exhibit 4).

The Service Industry Is at an Inflection Point

The service sector is at an inflection point concerning productivity gains and service industrialization, similar to the Industrial Revolution in manufacturing that started in the eighteenth century. For companies, this disruption and the continually evolving technology creates a growth opportunity in which new service offerings can be introduced or adapted, and business

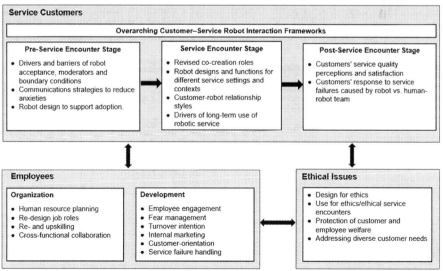

Exhibit 4 Future research directions in robotic service encounters. (Note: Adapted from Lu, Vinh Nhat, Jochen Wirtz, Werner Kunz, Stefanie Paluch, Thorsten Gruber, Antje Martins, and Paul Patterson (2020), "Service Robots, Customers, and Service Employees: What Can We Learn from the Academic Literature and Where are the Gaps?" Journal of Service Theory and Practice, Vol. 30 No. 3, pp. 361–391)

models can be reconsidered (Rust & Huang, 2014). Traditional service companies should use this artificial intelligence infusion to revive their image, brand, marketing, and positioning, to stay competitive in the long term (Huang & Rust, 2018).

Reconstruction of the Organizational Frontline

With service robots' implementation, organizations will inevitably be transformed and dramatically reorganized. This requires strong leadership and support, employee willingness, and ability to change. Employees will be assigned to new tasks and responsibilities and will need to develop the necessary skills (including RPA, programming, and technology troubleshooting). This means that the skills and competencies of human service representatives might change in the future, and the job market requirements can be affected by this shift. Thus, employees will focus in the future more on tasks that are still handled better by humans. This includes especially socio-emotional tasks (e.g., building rapport, creating a welcoming atmosphere), but might also include high-level cognitive analytical tasks despite the advantage of robots in this area. An example of this might be a cancer diagnosis. If a service task consists of a lot of responsibility, the customer might prefer a human being instead of a robot to make a last judgment call (Wirtz et al., 2018). The company itself must be ready for change, so the AI spirit can be experienced at all levels of the service company and not only at the customer frontline.

More Human–Robot Collaboration in the Future

We do not think that robots will completely substitute human service employees now or in the future. In fact, we strongly disapprove of this assumption for the service industry. As stated above, humans might be substituted by robots for some standardized tasks (e.g., routine tasks), but we do not want to generalize that to all kinds of service contexts. Instead, we predict that hybrid human–robot teams and collaboration will be the preferred service delivery model for the future (Wirtz et al., 2018). These hybrid teams will realize productivity and service quality gains for the company by combining the advantages of AI and human service representatives.

AI as Opportunity for Cost-Effective Service Excellence

We predict that hybrid human–robot teams and collaboration will be the future service model for many more complex service contexts. These hybrid teams will realize productivity and service quality gains for the company by combining the advantages of AI and human employees. Robots' enormous knowledge and data are an undeniable advantage for creating customized services (Bornet et al., 2021). Therefore, organizations should focus on implementing, managing, and fine-tuning the deployment of robot-employee-customer co-creation teams to deliver an unprecedented quality of interaction for their customers.

Service robots are not the answer to everything but might be an excellent way to increase customer service quality. The unlimited knowledge and immediate access to customer profiles are undeniable advantages that customize service offerings even further. Customers receive individual service or product recommendations based on their past purchase behavior and could save valuable time interacting with service robots. Another beneficial aspect is reduced waiting time for customers since they can immediately approach a service robot. When issues get more complex or require individual attention or recovery, employees can join the encounter and support the problem-solving process with emotional or social skills. These new ways of interacting could contribute to a better overall service experience.

Mitigate Potential Risks of Robot Deployment

Finally, organizations also need to mitigate potential misconceptions, prejudice, and anxieties related to customer-facing service robots, such as algorithm aversion, perceived loss of the human touch, and consumer privacy. This requires organizations to embrace corporate digital responsibility and develop a set of shared values, norms, and actionable guidelines on the responsible use of technology along the full cycle (Wirtz et al., 2021). For example, related to data, this includes their capturing (e.g., using biometrics or social media accounts), their use (e.g., to build variables such as a healthiness index or financial score), decision-making (e.g., approve loans and set interest rates), and their retirement (e.g., when is information on a bounced payment deleted from the firm's database).

We still believe that human service employees are primarily responsible for building trusting relationships with customers. Their empathic and benevolent behavior as well as genuine emotions are underlying foundations for trust and cannot be copied by robots at the moment. Again, service robots can assist employees with information and customized recommendations based on the customer profiles they access during the interaction. We expect that in the near future, it will be normal for service robots to be connected with CRM databases and use the information during customer interaction. As soon as service robots recognize customers through their sensors and cameras, they can retrieve customer profiles, address them by name, and help them with their requests.

In summary, service robots and AI will transform our service sector and bring unprecedented improvements to the customer experience, service quality, and productivity, all at the same time. That is, the service revolution has the potential to dramatically increase our standard of living as much as the Industrial Revolution did for manufactured goods. Only this time, services such as financial, logistics, healthcare, and education are being industrialized.

More research is needed to better understand how to implement service robots, the effect on the customer, and the employee who works side by side with the robot. Lu et al. (2020) gave a good overview of the service robot literature and worked out various areas where we need more research. We look forward to going on this academic journey together with our research field.

References

Bornet, P., Barkin, I., & Wirtz, J. (2021). *Intelligent automation—Learn how to harness artificial intelligence to boost business & make our world more human*. https://intelligentautomationbook.com

Esteva, A., Kuprel, B., Novoa, R. A., Ko, J., Swetter, S. M., Blau, H. M., & Thrun, S. (2017). Dermatologist-Level Classification of Skin Cancer with Deep Neural Networks. *Nature, 542*(2), 115–118.

Fortune Business Insights. (2020). *Service Robotics Market Size Report and Industry Forecast*. Retrieved February, 2021, from https://www.fortunebusinessinsights.com/industryreports/service-robotics-market-101805

Foster, M. (2018). *Aging Japan: Robots may have role in future of elder care*. Retrieved February, 2021, from https://www.reuters.com/article/us-japan-ageing-robots-wideimage/aging-japan-robots-may-have-role-in-future-of-elder-care-idUSKBN1H33AB

Huang, M. H., & Rust, R. T. (2018). Artificial intelligence in service. *Journal of Service Research, 21*(2), 155–172.

Jarrahi, M. H. (2018). Artificial intelligence and the future of work: Human-AI symbiosis in organizational decision making. Business Horizons, 61(4), 577–586.r.

Joerling, M., Boehm, R., & Paluch, S. (2019). Service robots: Drivers of perceived responsibility for service outcomes. *Journal of Service Research*. https://doi.org/10.1177/1094670519842334

Kikuchi, T. (2018). *Robot staff make Japan's Henn na Hotels quirky and efficient.* Retrieved February, 2021, from https://asia.nikkei.com/Business/Robot-staff-make-Japan-s-Henn-na-Hotels-quirky-and-efficient

Kunz, W., Aksoy, L., Bart, Y., Heinonen, K., Kabadayi, S., Ordenes, F. V., Sigala, M., Diaz, D., & Theodoulidis, B. (2017). Customer engagement in a big data world. *Journal of Services Marketing, 31*(2), 161–171.

Kunz, W., Heinonen, K., & Lemmink, J. (2019). Future service technologies—Is service research on track with business reality? *Journal of Services Marketing, 33*(4), 479–487.

Kunz, W., & Walsh, G. (2020). After the revolution—New opportunities for service research in a digital world. *Journal of Service Management, 31*(3).

Larivière, B., Bowen, D., Andreassen, T. W., Kunz, W., Sirianni, N. J., Voss, C., … De Keyser, A. (2017). "Service encounter 2.0": An investigation into the roles of technology, employees and customers. *Journal of Business Research, 79*, 238–246.

Lu, V. N., Wirtz, J., Kunz, W., Paluch, S., Gruber, T., Msartins, A., & Patterson, P. (2020). Service robots, customers, and service employees: What can we learn from the academic literature and where are the gaps? *Journal of Service Theory and Practice, 30*(3), 361–391.

Paluch, S., Wirtz, J. and Kunz, W. H. (2020). Service robots and the future of service. In M. Bruhn, M. Kirchgeorg, & C. Burmann (Eds.), *Marketing Weiterdenken—Zukunftspfade für eine marktorientierte Unternehmensführung* (pp. 423–435, 2nd ed.). Springer Gabler-Verlag. https://doi.org/10.1007/978-3-658-31563-4.

Read, B. (2017). *The rise of the airport robots.* Retrieved February, 2021, https://www.aerosociety.com/news/rise-of-the-airport-robots/

Rust, R. T., & Huang, M.-H. (2014). The service revolution and the transformation of marketing science. *Marketing Science, 33*(2), 206–221.

Schneider, C. (2017). *10 reasons why AI-powered, automated customer service is the future.* Retrieved February, 2021, from www.ibm.com/blogs/watson/2017/10/10-reasons-ai-powered-automated-customerservice-future/

Schoepfer, T., & Etemad-Sajadi, R. (2020). *The clever use of robots during COVID-19.* Retrieved February, 2021, from https://hospitalityinsights.ehl.edu/robots-during-covid-19

van Doorn, J., Mende, M., Noble, S. M., Hulland, J., Ostrom, A. L., Grewal, D., & Petersen, J. A. (2017). Domo Arigato Mr. Roboto: Emergence of automated social presence in organizational frontlines and customers' service experiences. *Journal of Service Research, 20*(1), 43–58.

Walsh, N. (2018). Next time you order room service, it may come by a robot. *The New York Times.* Retrieved February, 2021, from https://www.nytimes.com/2018/01/29/travel/the-next-time-you-order-room-service-it-may-come-by-robot.html

Wirtz, J., Hartley, N., Kunz, W., Tarbit, J., & Ford, J. (2021c, March 17). Corporate digital responsibility at the dawn of the digital service revolution. SSRN. https://ssrn.com/abstract=3806235 or https://doi.org/10.2139/ssrn.3806235

Wirtz, J., & Jerger, C. (2017). Managing service employees: Literature review, expert opinions, and research directions. *Service Industries Journal, 36*(15–16), 757–788.

Wirtz, J., Patterson, P. G., Kunz, W. H., Gruber, T., Lu, V. N., Paluch, S., & Martins, A. (2018). Brave new world: Service robots in the frontline. *Journal of Service Management, 29*(5), 907–931.

Wirtz, J. (2020). Organizational ambidexterity: Cost-effective service excellence, service robots, and artificial intelligence. *Organizational Dynamics, 49*(3). https://doi.org/10.1016/j.orgdyn.2019.04.005

Wirtz, J., Kunz, W., & Paluch, S. (2021b). The service revolution, intelligent automation and service robots. *European Business Review.*

Wirtz, J., Paluch, S., & Kunz, W. (2021a). Case study: Service robots in the frontline—How will Aarion Bank's customers respond? In J. Wirtz & C. Lovelock (Eds.), *Services marketing: People, technology, strategy* (9th ed.). World Scientific.

Wirtz, J., Paluch, S., & Kunz, W. (2022). Service Robots in the Frontline: How Will Aarion Bank's Customers Respond? In J. Wirtz, & C. Lovelock (Eds.), *Services Marketing: People, Technology, Strategy* (pp. 566-570, 9th ed.). New Jersey: World Scientific.

Wirtz, J., & Zeithaml, V. (2018). Cost-Effective Service Excellence. *Journal of The Academy of Marketing Science, 46*(1), 59–80.

Yoganathan, V., Osburg, V.-S., & Kunz, W. H. (2021). Waldemar Toporowski (2021): Check-in at the Robo-desk: Effects of automated social presence on social cognition and service implications. *Tourism Management, 85*, 104309.

Index[1]

A

Agility, 318, 319, 321, 322, 324, 325, 327, 329–330
Ambidexterity, 216, 219
Artificial Intelligence (AI), 735–738, 740, 741, 872, 876, 876n1, 877–883, 927–940, 992, 994, 999, 1003–1006
design, 928, 932
system, 945–962

B

Balanced innovation, 596
Behavior change, 303–312
Bricolage, 597, 598, 600, 605–607, 609
Business models, 555–570, 577, 581, 583, 585, 587, 588

C

Change of Era, 71–82
Chatbots, 948–950

Circular economy, 188–189
Co-creation, 303–312, 335, 338–340, 348, 349
Collective, 437–450
Competitive advantage, 129, 131–134, 140–142, 144
Complaint handling, 832–835, 837
Complex system, 483–495
Configuration, 877, 878
Consumer experience (CE), 658, 662, 677–682, 684
Contingent work, 228–232
Contract innovation, 247–259
Contracts, 247–256, 258, 259
Conversational agents, 945–962
Coordination, 53, 59–66
costs, 53, 59, 60
Cultural events, 679, 708–711
Culture, 353–355, 357–366
Customer-centric ecosystem, 395, 397
Customer-centricity, 395, 400, 401, 403, 404
Customer-centric models, 395

---

[1] Note: Page numbers followed by 'n' refer to notes.

© The Author(s), under exclusive license to Springer Nature Switzerland AG 2022
B. Edvardsson, B. Tronvoll (eds.), *The Palgrave Handbook of Service Management*,
https://doi.org/10.1007/978-3-030-91828-6

1009

1010 Index

Customer experience (CX), 129–145,
    224, 226, 232–235, 655–671,
    729–741, 827, 836, 837
  conceptual framework, 737–739, 741
  management, 665, 666, 669, 670
  metrics, 733
Customer journey, 657, 658, 660–667,
    669, 670
Customer participation, 236
Customer recovery, 850–853, 855,
    859, 860
Customer-robot rapport, 909, 911, 912
Customer services, 393–396, 398–404,
    948, 949, 953, 956, 959
Customer solutions, 174, 179, 192
customer success management (CSM),
    186, 190, 191
Customer-to-customer
    interaction, 629–647

D

Data science, 556, 561, 562, 564,
    565, 570
Decision-making, 927–940
Design capability, 502, 519
Diffusion, 613, 614, 617, 619–624
Digitalization, 188, 967–983
Dynamics, 151–165

E

Ecosystem, 202, 204, 211, 218, 220,
    411, 414, 416–418, 425, 428–432
  change, 472
Emergence, 372, 375–376,
    380–382, 386
Emerging markets, 393–406
Employee experience (EX), 129–145
Employee recovery, 850–852, 860
Employees' satisfaction, 754, 757, 758,
    760, 764–766, 768
Empowerment, 595–610
Era of Change, 73–76

Ethics, 412, 414, 416, 418, 432
Exclusivity, 263–274

F

Frontline employees, 773, 774, 777,
    778, 780, 781, 783–785, 787

G

Guanxi, 354, 361, 362

H

Healthcare operations, 801–820
Health policy, 802, 807
Hedonism, 264–267
Humanization of service, 224–228
Human-machine interaction, 927–940
Hybridization, 509, 520, 521

I

IKEA, 415, 417–432
Inclusive service, 87, 97, 99–100
Industry 4.0, 96–97
Information and Communication
    Technologies (ICT), 249, 251, 259
Information technologies, 53, 54, 59
Innovation
  management, 596
  roles, 601
Institutionalized social structures,
    537, 546, 547
Integrated framework, 614
Intelligence augmentation, 928, 938–940
Interactions, 629–647
Intrapreneurship, 596, 597, 599,
    601, 607

K

Knowledge endowment, 929, 934–936,
    938, 939

Index 1011

L

Lead, 318, 319, 324–326, 329
Leader, 318, 319, 321, 322, 323, 326, 329–331
Leadership style, 353, 354, 357, 360, 361, 363, 364
Luxury experiences, 265, 266, 270, 273
Luxury services, 263–274

M

Managerial theorizing, 155
Market challenges, 613–625
Mental model, 151–153, 155, 157–161, 163–165
Microfoundation, 459, 472, 476
Mindset, 487, 490
Motivation, 320, 324, 329
Multi-level framework, 947, 950–962

N

Narrative, 335, 337–338, 349
Network recovery, 850, 851, 855–862
Networks, 555–570
Nonownership value, 247–259
Novelty, 613, 614, 616, 617, 619–624

O

Operation strategy, 801–803
Organizational communication, 335–350

P

Paternalistic leadership, 354, 357, 361, 363–364
Patients' satisfaction, 757–759, 761, 763–769
Peer-providers, 107–110, 112–120
Platforms, 577, 580, 581, 584, 589
Procedural recovery, 852, 857

Product service systems, 211
Professional identity, 498, 499, 501, 509, 516, 519–521
Public perceptions, 807, 809–816

R

Reciprocal effects, 133, 143–144
Reflection, 151, 159–161, 163–165
Resilience, 318–321, 323–325, 327–330
Resources, 109–110, 114, 118–120, 122
Resources integration, 678, 682–685, 687, 692, 707–711

S

Self-leadership, 317–331
Self-service technology, 994–995
Service-dominant logic, 85–101, 372
Service recovery, 849–863
    journey, 824, 828, 836, 837, 840
    system, 825, 838–840
Services, 53–67
    capitalism, 248
    design, 483–495, 497–521
    designer, 498, 500, 504, 505, 509, 511, 512, 514–516, 518–521
    design methods, 93, 457–477, 531–548, 556–560, 563, 568, 570
    ecosystem, 250, 251, 257, 277–297, 371–387
    ecosystem design, 90, 92
    encounter, 630–635
    experiences, 263–274
    failure, 823–841
    frontline, 991–1006
    industries, 54–55
    infrastructures, 254
    infusion, 173–176
    innovation, 304, 311, 457, 531–548, 555–570, 577–589, 613–625

1012 Index

Services (*cont.*)
management, 71–82,
107–122, 411–433
productivity models, 773–790
profit chain, 353–357, 367
quality, 745–769
research, 531, 533, 538
revolution, 994, 1006
robots, 907–909, 911, 912,
914–919, 992–1006
strategy, 151–165, 170, 180
systems, 869–883, 969–975,
979, 981
system transformation, 531–548
Servitization, 169–193,
201–220, 967–983
SERVPERF, 780–782, 789, 790
SERVQUAL, 781, 782
Sharing economy, 107–122
Smart service ecosystems, 99
Smart service experience, 888–890,
896, 900, 901
Smart service provision, 888–892,
900, 901
Smart technology, 887–902
Socially responsible business, 371–387
Stakeholders, 411, 412, 414–417,
424–426, 430–432
Stories, 335, 338–341, 343, 346–349
Strategic mindsets, 129–145
Sustainability, 411, 412, 414,
417–419, 424, 426–428,
430–432, 577, 578,
580–584, 586–589
Systems of engagement, 888, 900–901

Systems of insights, 888, 900–901
Systems thinking, 532, 533, 541

T

Technology, 869–883
Technology-infused service
encounters, 907–919
Text mining, 735, 737, 739–741
Transformation, 304, 311, 411–433
Transformative resource integration,
292, 293, 297
Transformative Service Research (TSR),
278, 297, 437–450, 746
Transition, 202, 211–220
Transparency, 581, 583–585, 587, 589

V

Value
capture, 613, 614, 616,
617, 619–624
co-creation, 278–281, 283, 289–297,
372–375, 379, 380, 386, 678,
679, 685, 688–690, 709, 711
creation, 967, 969, 970, 973–983
postures, 371–387
proposition, 556–560, 563–565,
568, 569
Viable systems approach, 929, 933
Virtual Rapport, 907, 910–914

W

Wellbeing, 437–446, 448

Printed in the United States
by Baker & Taylor Publisher Services